"A very important guide. Gives a very clear, very factual picture. I must admit that I carry and use the book like a bible and refer to it often. Thank you *Billboard* and thank you Joel."

Hy Lit
Program Director
WSNI RADIO, Philadelphia

"For a number of years I have used a review of music from a specific year as a specialty on my radio show. In those years I've been nicknamed 'The Professor' for my history lessons on music. One of my choice sources for information has been Joel Whitburn's books. Thanks."

Scott Muni
WNEW-FM, New York

"There's nothing else like it — only Joel Whitburn could accurately track 7,269 records of the rock era. *The Billboard Book of Top 40 Hits* is worth its weight in solid gold!"

Arnie "Woo Woo" Ginsburg
WXKS-FM, Boston

"Don't stay home without it!"

Bruce Bradley
WYNY-FM, New York

"Hit records have changed the way we dress, dance, talk, and even perceive ourselves. They make us happy, sad, or just help us to pass the time. Music *is* the message, and with this book Joel has given us a firm platform to catalog those messages and memories."

Jack Armstrong
KFRC, San Francisco

"A valuable reference for oldies but goodies — we wouldn't leave home without it!"

Art Laboe
Los Angeles radio personality
President, Original Sound
Record Co., Hollywood

"Very informative — takes the guesswork out of pop music."

Joe Niagara
WPEN, Philadelphia

"*The Billboard Book of Top 40 Hits* is an invaluable aid to anyone interested in pop music."

Dick Biondi
WNMB-FM, North Myrtle Beach
South Carolina

THE Billboard BOOK OF TOP 40 HITS

JOEL WHITBURN

BILLBOARD BOOKS
An imprint of Watson-Guptill Publications/New York

Photo captions by Dave DiMartino, Rob Hoerburger, and Drew Wheeler
Picture Sleeves selected from Joel Whitburn's personal collection
Photography by Malcolm Hjerstedt of Munroe Studios, Inc.
Chart typesetting by TGA Communications, Inc.
Senior Editor: Tad Lathrop
Edited by Fred Weiler
Book and cover design by Bob Fillie
Graphic production by Stan Redfern

First published 1989 by Billboard Publications, Inc.
1515 Broadway, New York, NY 10036.

ISBN 8230-7527-3

Library of Congress Cataloging in Publication Data

Whitburn, Joel.
The Billboard book of top 40 hits / Joel Whitburn. — 4th ed.
p. cm.
ISBN 0-8230-7527-3
1. Popular music—United States—Discography. 2. Popular music—United States—Statistics. I. Billboard. II. Title. III. Title: Billboard book of top forty hits. IV. Title: Top 40 hits.
ML156.4.P6W44 1989
016.78164'026'6—dc20 89-9706
CIP
MN

Distributed in the United Kingdom by Guinness Publishing Ltd.,
33 London Road, Enfield, Middlesex, England EN2 6DJ.

ISBN 0-85112-389-9

Manufactured in the United States of America

First printing, 1989

2 3 4 5 6 7 8 9/94 93 92 91 90

Dedicated to
the fond recollections
conjured up by
the titles and artists
within this book.

The author wishes to give thanks to
the staff of Record Research:

Bill Hathaway
Kim Whitburn
Brent Olynick
Fran Whitburn
Kim Gaarder
Joanne Wagner
Janet Ko
Oscar Vidotto
Brian Niese
Phil Summers
Ruth Whitburn
Joyce Riehl

CONTENTS

AUTHOR'S NOTE

I know that falling snow is inaudible, but I can hear the snowflakes softly spiralling downward when I think of the first few bars of Foreigner's "Waiting For A Girl Like You." Suddenly, I'm immersed in the serenity of a frozen Wisconsin lake on a mild winter's day at dusk. I may be a thousand miles from that place, but it's vivid in my mind.

Actually, I'm not really listening to the record. My eyes are glancing at Foreigner's chart history while my brain quickly registers the title and calls up an experience along with it. This is not a conscious effort, it's an added bonus of chart researching.

Looking at the history of the *Billboard* charts is a lot like looking at a personal photo album. You recall the names and faces on each page, but memory fleshes out the two-dimensional images. Each page relates to an episode of life.

The story a songwriter tells may have absolutely no relation to the images a listener attaches to the song. Timing, melody, mood, and circumstance all influence the marriage of a memory to a hit. Just as no two people share all of the same experiences, no two have an identical list of treasured hits.

The charts demonstrate our nation's collective tastes. Record buyers and radio listeners choose the songs that will be part of the soundtrack to their lives. Every special request and trip to the record store increases the likelihood that a song will score on *Billboard*'s Hot 100 and claim a space in memory's picture book.

How did I connect *snow* with the Foreigner hit? "Waiting For A Girl Like You" peaked at the #2 position for 10 weeks beginning in November of 1981 and ending in January of 1982. During that snowy Christmas season, the hit spent the longest time of any record to remain at the #2 position without peaking at #1.

The radio in the background snaps me out of my winter reverie and transports me to a summer day in 1961. The saxophone of "Quarter To Three" is loud and invigorating on my car radio. It's the second week that Gary U.S. Bonds is at the top of the charts and I'm headed back to the lake for a Fourth Of July celebration.....

JOEL WHITBURN

ELVIS
ALBUM SEVEN BY RICK
HOLD THAT TIGER!
TOMMY ROE
LITTLE TOWN FLIRT
In Dreams
THE CRYSTALS
UPTOWN
JOHNNY NASH
TORTURE

JOEL WHITBURN: THE WORLD'S LEADING RECORD HOLDER

If Joel Whitburn ever invites you over to listen to records, plan on spending several months.

That's about how long it would take to spin through all of the 50,000 or so singles in Joel's collection—back to back with *no* breaks. (Take a few turns through Joel's 30,000+ albums, and you can figure on adding years to your listening time.)

Along the way, you'll hear every hit that ever made the Hot 100. It's quite an earful—but that's what it takes to compile books such as *The Billboard Book of Top 40 Hits* and the many other volumes published by Joel's Record Research firm.

It's been over two decades since Joel first painstakingly jotted a few weekly chart statistics on 3" x 5" file cards simply to keep tabs on his expanding personal record collection. As this labor of love has grown from a hobby into a business, "the world's foremost chart researcher" has published over 30 books detailing the history and development of charted music from 1890 to the present.

Today, with the help of computers, Joel and his team of researchers dissect *Billboard*'s charts in increasingly greater depth, packing each new Record Research volume with even more data and statistics. The radio and music industries worldwide, along with countless collectors, musicologists, and other music enthusiasts, rely regularly on Joel's books for accurate, detailed chart information.

Joel's vast music library—one of the largest privately held record collections in the world—completely fills a specially built, environmentally controlled underground vault adjacent to his Menomonee Falls, Wisconsin home. When not researching the charts, sports fan and outdoor enthusiast Joel enjoys relaxing with wife Fran and daughter Kim at his vacation home in northern Wisconsin—and, of course, browsing through record shops for a few more singles to "round out" his collection.

RESEARCHING THE CHARTS

From 1955 to 1958, before the introduction of the Hot 100, there were a number of pop charts published by *Billboard*, which were consulted by various members of the music trade. It wasn't until the introduction of the Hot 100 chart that the music industry settled down to consulting simply one chart as the definitive source for popular record chart data.

Here are the four pop charts that were researched for this book prior to the debut of the Hot 100 on August 4, 1958:

Chart Title	Dates Terminated	Chart Size
Most Played in Juke Boxes	June 17, 1957	20
Most Played by Jockeys	July 28, 1958	20-25
Top 100	July 28, 1958 (debuted on 11/12/55)	100
Best Sellers in Stores	Oct. 13, 1958 (continued for 11 weeks after Hot 100 debuted)	25-50

A chart-by-chart breakdown of the highest position a record attained on any of the above 1955-1958 Billboard Pop charts is listed below the title. However, if a record hit only the Top 100 or Hot 100, no chart information is shown below that title. Keep in mind, records that peaked at positions 51-100 could only have charted on the Top 100 or Hot 100.

pre If a record enters a newly published chart well after the record's peak chart performance, the word **pre** is shown after the position—meaning that the highest position would have been higher had the chart been published earlier.

end If a record had not yet peaked on a chart that was terminated, the word **end** is shown after the position—meaning that its highest position would have been higher had the chart continued.

The record's *date* of chart entry is taken from whichever chart it first appeared on. The date shown is *Billboard*'s actual issue date, and is not taken from the "week ending" dates as shown on the various charts when they were originally published. The issue and week ending dates were different until January 13, 1962, when *Billboard* began using one date system for both the issue and the charts inside.

The record's *highest position* (**POS**) is taken from the chart on which it achieved its highest ranking.

The record's *weeks charted* (**WKS**) and weeks at positions No. 1 or No. 2 are taken from the chart on which it achieved its highest total.

PEAK POSITION CHANGES

The following list consists of titles that show a different peak position than the one shown in our previous *Top 40 Hits* edition. All titles listed below are from double-sided hit records. From 1955-1958 *Billboard* ranked double-sided hits together at one position on both the Best Seller and Juke Box charts. They began this practice again in late 1969 and it continues through today. With this method of listing sides together, the side shown first can flip-flop from week to week, which accounts for the peak position changes below.

Previously, for double-sided hits, we determined the A-side based on overall chart performance, and gave full credit for all weekly positions to that side, even though it may have occasionally been shown as the B-side. Based on our new methodology, whenever a title is shown as the A-side, regardless of whether it's for one week or many weeks, those positions attained while listed as the A-side are used when determining its overall peak position. An example is Ricky Nelson's double-sided hit "A Teenager's Romance/I'm Walking." "I'm Walking" was shown as the A-side for the first 5 weeks climbing up to position #4 and then by the sixth week "A Teenager's Romance" was shown as the A-side at position #2, and stayed as the top side for the remaining 10 weeks charted. Thus "A Teenager's Romance" peaked at #2 and "I'm Walking" peaked at #4.

1955-1958

Prev. Pos.	New Pos.	
18	16	Paul Anka...Let The Bells Keep Ringing
25	30	Harry Belafonte...Island In The Sun
48	25	Harry Belafonte...Cocoanut Woman
20	10	Pat Boone...Chains Of Love
20	14	Pat Boone...There's A Gold Mine In The Sky
11	4	Pat Boone...It's Too Soon To Know
21	23	Pat Boone...For My Good Fortune
31	21	Pat Boone...Gee, But It's Lonely
21	13	Nat King Cole...Forgive My Heart
39	27	Sam Cooke...You Were Made For Me
20	12	Sammy Davis, Jr....Love Me Or Leave Me
21	19	Fats Domino...My Blue Heaven
6	8	Fats Domino...Valley Of Tears
22	6	Fats Domino...It's You I Love
48	32	Fats Domino...I Want You To Know
16	17	Four Lads...The Bus Stop Song
20	16	Four Lads...A House With Love In It
24	22	Four Lads...My Little Angel
17	18	Bill Haley...Mambo Rock
26	17	Bill Haley...Birth Of The Boogie
41	23	Bill Haley...Rock-A-Beatin' Boogie
20	15	Jim Lowe...Talkin' To The Blues
12	14	Jaye P. Morgan...Pepper-Hot Baby
40	12	Jaye P. Morgan...If You Don't Want My Love
17	4	Ricky Nelson...I'm Walking
18	12	Ricky Nelson...My Bucket's Got A Hole In It
23	13	Platters...It Isn't Right
31	20	Platters...One In A Million
23	16	Platters...He's Mine
25	11	Jack Scott...Leroy

1969-1988

1	3	Beatles...Something
–	14	Creedence Clearwater Revival...Fortunate Son
–	2	John Denver...Calypso
–	38	Tom Jones...Resurrection Shuffle
39	17	Paul McCartney & Wings...Sally-G
–	25	Donny Osmond...Young Love

THE ARTISTS

HOW TO USE THIS SECTION

This section lists, alphabetically by artist name, every single (45 RPM) record release to make the Top 40 on *Billboard*'s pop charts from January 1, 1955 through December 24, 1988.

Each artist's charted hits are listed in chronological order. A sequential number is shown in front of each song title to indicate that artist's number of Top 40 hits. All Top 10 hits are highlighted in dark type.

Columnar headings show the following data:

DATE: Date record debuted in the Top 40

POS: Record's highest charted position (highlighted in bold type)

WKS: Total weeks charted in the Top 40

LABEL & NO.: Original record label and number

Other data and symbols:

(1) A number in parentheses next to the peak position of records which peaked at No. 1 or No. 2 indicates the total weeks the record held that position
† Indicates record peaked in the year after it first charted
● RIAA certified gold record (million seller)
▲ RIAA certified platinum record (two million seller)

The Record Industry Association of America began certifying gold records in 1958 and platinum records in 1976. Prior to these dates, there are most certainly some hits that would have qualified for these certifications. Also, certain record labels have never requested RIAA certification for records that would have qualified for these awards. As of January 1, 1989, RIAA reduced its certification requirements for singles to 500,000 units for Gold and one million units for Platinum.

Letter(s) in brackets after titles indicate:
[I] instrumental
[N] novelty
[C] comedy
[S] spoken word
[F] foreign language
[X] Christmas
[R] reissue or remake of a previously charted single

This symbol is shown when dividing a double-sided hit. Complete chart data is listed for each side except in cases where both sides of a record were shown as a single listing on the charts. For the B-side of these records, only the weeks it charted as a "tag-along" are listed. See "Peak Position Changes" page for the complete methodology of listing double-sided hits.

Directly under nearly every artist name are brief notes about the artist or group that may be of special interest.

Directly under some song titles are brief notes that may be of special interest, such as a record that may have first charted on the Hot 100 at an earlier date, but did not reach the Top 40, or one that may feature a famous singer providing background vocals. If the song is featured in a Broadway musical or film, the title of the show is given under the record title. You will note the occasional use of POS in both title and artist trivia, which simply stands for "position."

Many artist listings have been reorganized in this edition so that an artist's complete chart history is at your fingertips. For example, a song by a duo, such as Paul McCartney & Michael Jackson, is now listed under both McCartney and Jackson. The precise duo name is shown in bold type below the song title. Also, a few artists that were previously separated are now combined, such as Dion and Dion & The Belmonts.

exact date of first chart appearance

peak chart position

total number of weeks on the charts

total number of weeks at #1 or #2

RIAA gold (●) or platinum (▲) single

+ a single which reached its chart position in the year following the year of its first chart appearance

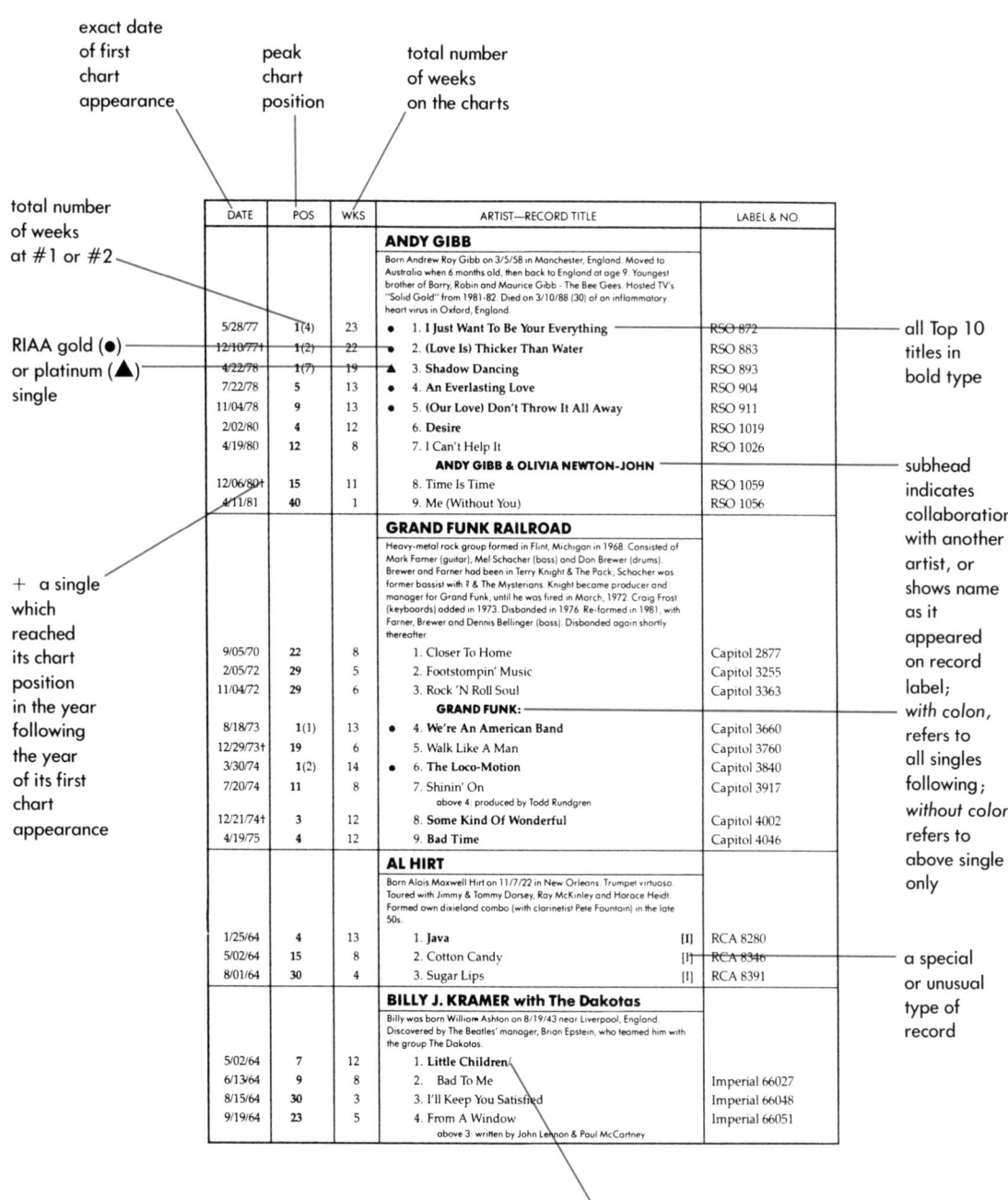

DATE	POS	WKS	ARTIST—RECORD TITLE	LABEL & NO.
			ANDY GIBB	
			Born Andrew Roy Gibb on 3/5/58 in Manchester, England. Moved to Australia when 6 months old, then back to England at age 9. Youngest brother of Barry, Robin and Maurice Gibb - The Bee Gees. Hosted TV's "Solid Gold" from 1981-82. Died on 3/10/88 (30) of an inflammatory heart virus in Oxford, England.	
5/28/77	1(4)	23	● 1. **I Just Want To Be Your Everything**	RSO 872
12/10/77+	1(2)	22	● 2. **(Love Is) Thicker Than Water**	RSO 883
4/22/78	1(7)	19	▲ 3. **Shadow Dancing**	RSO 893
7/22/78	**5**	13	● 4. **An Everlasting Love**	RSO 904
11/04/78	**9**	13	● 5. **(Our Love) Don't Throw It All Away**	RSO 911
2/02/80	**4**	12	6. **Desire**	RSO 1019
4/19/80	**12**	8	7. I Can't Help It	RSO 1026
			ANDY GIBB & OLIVIA NEWTON-JOHN	
12/06/80+	**15**	11	8. Time Is Time	RSO 1059
4/11/81	**40**	1	9. Me (Without You)	RSO 1056
			GRAND FUNK RAILROAD	
			Heavy-metal rock group formed in Flint, Michigan in 1968. Consisted of Mark Farner (guitar), Mel Schacher (bass) and Don Brewer (drums). Brewer and Farner had been in Terry Knight & The Pack; Schacher was former bassist with ? & The Mysterians. Knight became producer and manager for Grand Funk, until he was fired in March, 1972. Craig Frost (keyboards) added in 1973. Disbanded in 1976. Re-formed in 1981, with Farner, Brewer and Dennis Bellinger (bass). Disbanded again shortly thereafter.	
9/05/70	**22**	8	1. Closer To Home	Capitol 2877
2/05/72	**29**	5	2. Footstompin' Music	Capitol 3255
11/04/72	**29**	6	3. Rock 'N Roll Soul	Capitol 3363
			GRAND FUNK:	
8/18/73	1(1)	13	● 4. **We're An American Band**	Capitol 3660
12/29/73+	**19**	6	5. Walk Like A Man	Capitol 3760
3/30/74	1(2)	14	● 6. **The Loco-Motion**	Capitol 3840
7/20/74	**11**	8	7. Shinin' On	Capitol 3917
			above 4: produced by Todd Rundgren	
12/21/74+	**3**	12	8. **Some Kind Of Wonderful**	Capitol 4002
4/19/75	**4**	12	9. **Bad Time**	Capitol 4046
			AL HIRT	
			Born Alois Maxwell Hirt on 11/7/22 in New Orleans. Trumpet virtuoso. Toured with Jimmy & Tommy Dorsey, Ray McKinley and Horace Heidt. Formed own dixieland combo (with clarinetist Pete Fountain) in the late 50s.	
1/25/64	**4**	13	1. **Java** [I]	RCA 8280
5/02/64	**15**	8	2. Cotton Candy [I]	RCA 8346
8/01/64	**30**	4	3. Sugar Lips [I]	RCA 8391
			BILLY J. KRAMER with The Dakotas	
			Billy was born William Ashton on 8/19/43 near Liverpool, England. Discovered by The Beatles' manager, Brian Epstein, who teamed him with the group The Dakotas.	
5/02/64	**7**	12	1. **Little Children**/	
6/13/64	**9**	8	2. Bad To Me	Imperial 66027
8/15/64	**30**	3	3. I'll Keep You Satisfied	Imperial 66048
9/19/64	**23**	5	4. From A Window	Imperial 66051
			above 3: written by John Lennon & Paul McCartney	

all Top 10 titles in bold type

subhead indicates collaboration with another artist, or shows name as it appeared on record label; *with colon,* refers to all singles following; *without colon,* refers to above single only

a special or unusual type of record

/ a single with both sides charting; flip side follows

DATE	POS	WKS	ARTIST—RECORD TITLE	LABEL & NO.
			A	
			ABBA	
			Pop quartet formed in Stockholm, Sweden in 1970. Consisted of Frida Lyngstad and Agnetha Faltskog (vocals), Bjorn Ulvaeus (guitar) and Benny Andersson (keyboards). Benny and Bjorn recorded together in 1966. Bjorn and Agnetha married in 1971, divorced in 1978. Benny and Frida married in 1978, divorced in 1981. Disbanded in the early 80s.	
6/22/74	**6**	12	1. **Waterloo**	Atlantic 3035
10/12/74	**27**	4	2. Honey, Honey	Atlantic 3209
10/11/75	**15**	8	3. SOS	Atlantic 3265
3/27/76	**15**	8	4. I Do, I Do, I Do, I Do, I Do	Atlantic 3310
6/19/76	**32**	4	5. Mamma Mia	Atlantic 3315
9/25/76	**13**	11	6. Fernando	Atlantic 3346
1/22/77	**1**(1)	15	● 7. **Dancing Queen**	Atlantic 3372
6/04/77	**14**	10	8. Knowing Me, Knowing You	Atlantic 3387
1/28/78	**12**	9	9. The Name Of The Game	Atlantic 3449
5/06/78	**3**	14	● 10. **Take A Chance On Me**	Atlantic 3457
6/09/79	**19**	10	11. Does Your Mother Know	Atlantic 3574
12/08/79†	**29**	6	12. Chiquitita	Atlantic 3629
12/27/80†	**8**	16	13. **The Winner Takes It All**	Atlantic 3776
2/06/82	**27**	8	14. When All Is Said And Done all of the above: written and produced by Benny & Bjorn	Atlantic 3889
			GREGORY ABBOTT	
			Soul singer/songwriter from New York. At age 8, member of St. Patrick's Cathedral Choir. Psychology major at Boston University and Stanford; taught English at Berkeley.	
11/08/86†	**1**(1)	16	1. **Shake You Down**	Columbia 06191
			ABC	
			New-wave rock group from Sheffield, England. Formed as Vice Versa with Stephen Singleton and Mark White. Lead singer Martin Fry joined in 1980, group renamed ABC.	
10/30/82†	**18**	13	1. The Look Of Love (Part One)	Mercury 76168
2/26/83	**25**	8	2. Poison Arrow	Mercury 810340
9/28/85	**9**	11	3. **Be Near Me**	Mercury 880626
2/15/86	**20**	7	4. (How To Be A) Millionaire	Mercury 884382
8/01/87	**5**	12	5. **When Smokey Sings** a tribute to Smokey Robinson	Mercury 888604
			PAULA ABDUL	
			Los Angeles singer/choreographer. In 1987, named "Choreographer of the Year" by MTV. Choreographed Janet Jackson videos and "The Tracy Ullman Show."	
12/24/88†	**1**(3)	16	● 1. **Straight Up**	Virgin 99256

DATE	POS	WKS	ARTIST—RECORD TITLE	LABEL & NO.
			AC/DC	
			Hard-rock band formed in Sydney, Australia in 1974. Consisted of brothers Angus and Malcolm Young (guitars), Bon Scott (lead singer), Phil Rudd (drums) and Mark Evans (bass). Cliff Williams replaced Evans in 1977. Bon Scott died on 2/19/80 from alcohol abuse and was replaced by Brian Johnson. Simon Wright replaced Rudd in 1985. Angus and Malcolm are the younger brothers of George Young of The Easybeats.	
10/25/80	35	3	1. You Shook Me All Night Long	Atlantic 3761
2/07/81	37	5	2. Back In Black	Atlantic 3787
			ACE	
			Pub-rock quintet from Sheffield, England led by vocalist Paul Carrack. Disbanded in late 1976. Carrack joined Squeeze in 1981, then Mike & The Mechanics in 1985.	
4/05/75	3	11	1. **How Long**	Anchor 21000
			JOHNNY ACE	
			R&B vocalist/pianist/organist/composer, born John Marshall Alexander, Jr. on 6/9/29 in Memphis. Shot and killed himself playing Russian Roulette backstage at the City Auditorium in Houston on 12/24/54.	
2/19/55	17	9	1. Pledging My Love Best Seller #17 / Juke Box #17 / Jockey #19 with Johnny Board's Orchestra	Duke 136
			BARBARA ACKLIN	
			R&B singer/songwriter, born on 2/28/44 in Chicago. Cousin to Monk Higgins, who produced her first sessions for Special Agent in 1966 (as Barbara Allen).	
8/10/68	15	8	1. Love Makes A Woman	Brunswick 55379
			THE AD LIBS	
			Newark, New Jersey quintet: Mary Ann Thomas (lead singer), Hugh Harris, Danny Austin, Norman Donegan and Dave Watt.	
2/06/65	8	7	1. **The Boy From New York City**	Blue Cat 102
			BRYAN ADAMS	
			Born on 11/5/59 in Kingston, Ontario. Rock singer/songwriter/guitarist based in Vancouver, Canada.	
4/16/83	10	11	1. **Straight From The Heart**	A&M 2536
6/25/83	15	8	2. Cuts Like A Knife	A&M 2553
10/01/83	24	6	3. This Time	A&M 2574
11/24/84†	6	12	4. **Run To You**	A&M 2686
2/23/85	11	10	5. Somebody	A&M 2701
4/27/85	1(2)	14	6. **Heaven**	A&M 2729
7/13/85	5	12	7. **Summer Of '69**	A&M 2739
9/28/85	13	9	8. One Night Love Affair	A&M 2770
12/07/85†	15	9	9. It's Only Love **BRYAN ADAMS/TINA TURNER**	A&M 2791
4/11/87	6	10	10. **Heat Of The Night**	A&M 2921
7/04/87	26	6	11. Hearts On Fire	A&M 2948
9/12/87	32	5	12. Victim Of Love	A&M 2964
			JOHNNY ADAMS	
			Soul singer, born Lathan John Adams on 1/5/32 in New Orleans. Nicknamed "The Tan Canary." First recorded on the Ric label in 1959.	
7/26/69	28	4	1. Reconsider Me	SSS Int'l. 770

DATE	POS	WKS	ARTIST—RECORD TITLE	LABEL & NO.
			"CANNONBALL" ADDERLEY	
			Born Julian Edwin Adderley on 9/15/28 in Tampa. Nickname derived from "Cannibal" - in tribute to his love for food. Alto saxophonist/leader of jazz combo featuring brother Nat Adderley (cornet) and Joe Zawinul (piano; left in 1971 to form Weather Report; replaced by George Duke). Died of a stroke on 8/8/75 in Gary, Indiana.	
1/28/67	**11**	8	1. Mercy, Mercy, Mercy [I]	Capitol 5798
			THE ADDRISI BROTHERS	
			Pop singing/songwriting duo: Dick & Don Addrisi. Don died of cancer on 11/13/84 (45).	
2/26/72	**25**	7	1. We've Got To Get It On Again	Columbia 45521
5/14/77	**20**	8	2. Slow Dancin' Don't Turn Me On	Buddah 566
			AEROSMITH	
			Hard-rock band formed in Sunapee, New Hampshire in 1970. Consisted of Steven Tyler (lead singer), Joe Perry and Brad Whitford (guitars), Tom Hamilton (bass) and Joey Kramer (drums). Perry left for own Joe Perry Project in 1979. Whitford left in 1980. Original band reunited in April of 1984.	
7/12/75	**36**	3	1. Sweet Emotion	Columbia 10155
2/14/76	**6**	11	2. **Dream On** **[R]** originally charted in 1973 (POS 59)	Columbia 10278
6/26/76	**21**	10	3. Last Child	Columbia 10359
12/18/76†	**10**	11	4. **Walk This Way** revived in 1986 (with Tyler & Perry) as a "rap" hit by Run-D.M.C.	Columbia 10449
5/07/77	**38**	2	5. Back In The Saddle	Columbia 10516
9/02/78	**23**	7	6. Come Together	Columbia 10802
11/14/87	**14**	10	7. Dude (Looks Like A Lady)	Geffen 28240
2/27/88	**3**	15	8. **Angel**	Geffen 28249
7/09/88	**17**	8	9. Rag Doll	Geffen 27915
			THE AFTERNOON DELIGHTS	
			Female studio quartet from Boston.	
9/12/81	**33**	5	1. General Hospi-Tale [N] parody of TV's "General Hospital"	MCA 51148
			AFTER THE FIRE	
			English band led by Andy Piercy.	
3/05/83	**5**	14	1. **Der Kommissar** Kommissar: a Russian government official	Epic 03559
			A-HA	
			Trio formed in Oslo, Norway: Morten Harket (vocals), Pal Waaktaar (guitar, keyboards) and Mags Furuholem (keyboards).	
8/24/85	**1**(1)	15	1. **Take On Me**	Warner 29011
1/11/86	**20**	8	2. The Sun Always Shines On T.V.	Warner 28846
			AIR SUPPLY	
			Melbourne, Australia duo: Russ Hitchcock (b: 6/15/49) & Graham Russell (b: 6/1/50).	
3/08/80	**3**	17	1. **Lost In Love**	Arista 0479
7/19/80	**2**(4)	17	● 2. **All Out Of Love**	Arista 0520
11/15/80†	**5**	17	3. **Every Woman In The World**	Arista 0564
5/23/81	**1**(1)	14	● 4. **The One That You Love**	Arista 0604

DATE	POS	WKS	ARTIST—RECORD TITLE	LABEL & NO.
10/03/81	5	15	5. **Here I Am (Just When I Thought I Was Over You)**	Arista 0626
1/09/82	5	15	6. **Sweet Dreams**	Arista 0655
6/26/82	5	13	7. **Even The Nights Are Better**	Arista 0692
10/23/82	38	2	8. Young Love	Arista 1005
12/25/82†	38	5	9. Two Less Lonely People In The World	Arista 1004
8/13/83	2(3)	17	• 10. **Making Love Out Of Nothing At All**	Arista 9056
6/08/85	19	10	11. Just As I Am	Arista 9353
			JEWEL AKENS	
			Black vocalist/producer, born in Texas in 1940.	
2/06/65	3	12	1. **The Birds And The Bees**	Era 3141
			AL B. SURE!	
			Singer born Al Brown in Boston; raised in Mt. Vernon, New York.	
5/14/88	7	13	1. **Nite And Day**	Warner 28192
			ALABAMA	
			Country quartet from Fort Payne, Alabama: Randy Owen (vocals, guitar), Jeff Cook keyboards, fiddle), Teddy Gentry (bass, vocals) and Mark Herndon (drums, vocals). Randy, Jeff and Teddy are cousins.	
7/25/81	20	8	1. Feels So Right	RCA 12236
1/16/82	15	10	2. Love In The First Degree	RCA 12288
6/05/82	18	8	3. Take Me Down	RCA 13210
6/04/83	38	3	4. The Closer You Get all of above titles hit #1 on Billboard's Country charts	RCA 13524
			MORRIS ALBERT	
			Brazilian singer/songwriter born Morris Albert Kaisermann.	
8/23/75	6	16	• 1. **Feelings**	RCA 10279
			ARTHUR ALEXANDER	
			Born on 5/10/40 in Florence, Alabama. Teamed with Rick Hall in studio work at Muscle Shoals. First recorded for Judd in 1960.	
3/31/62	24	6	1. You Better Move On	Dot 16309
			ALIVE & KICKING	
			5-man, 1-woman pop/rock group, produced by Tommy James.	
7/04/70	7	10	1. **Tighter, Tighter**	Roulette 7078
			DAVIE ALLAN & THE ARROWS	
			Davie began as a session guitarist for Mike Curb in Los Angeles.	
9/09/67	37	3	1. Blue's Theme [I] from the film "The Wild Angels"	Tower 295
			DEBORAH ALLEN	
			Born Deborah Lynn Thurmond on 9/30/53 in Memphis. Country singer/songwriter.	
12/24/83†	26	7	1. Baby I Lied	RCA 13600
			DONNA ALLEN	
			Soul singer born in Key West and raised in Tampa. Former cheerleader with the Tampa Bay Buccaneers.	
3/28/87	21	9	1. Serious	21 Records 99497

DATE	POS	WKS	ARTIST—RECORD TITLE	LABEL & NO.
			REX ALLEN	
			Born on 12/31/24 in Wilcox, Arizona. Singer/guitarist/actor. Starred in 35 western films in the 50s. Narrator for over 80 Disney films during the 60s and 70s.	
10/06/62	17	4	1. Don't Go Near The Indians	Mercury 71997
			STEVE ALLEN with GEORGE CATES	
			Born on 12/26/21 in New York City. Comedian/actor/composer/author. Original star of TV's "Tonight Show," 1954. Played title role in 1956 film "The Benny Goodman Story."	
12/03/55	35	2	1. Autumn Leaves [I]	Coral 61485
			GENE ALLISON	
			R&B singer born on 8/29/34 in Nashville. First recorded for Calvert in 1956.	
3/10/58	36	1	1. You Can Make It If You Try Best Seller #36 / Top 100 #37	Vee-Jay 256
			THE ALLMAN BROTHERS BAND	
			Southern-rock band formed in Macon, Georgia in 1968. Consisted of brothers Duane (lead guitar) and Gregg Allman (keyboards), Dickey Betts (guitar), Berry Oakley (bass), and the drum duo of Jai Johnny Johanson and Butch Trucks. Duane and Gregg known earlier as Allman Joys and Hour Glass. Duane was the top session guitarist at Muscle Shoals studio. He was killed in a motorcycle crash on 10/29/71 at the age of 24. On 11/11/72, Oakley was killed in another cycle accident. He was replaced by Lamar Williams. Chuck Leavell (keyboards) added in 1972. After much turmoil, band regrouped in 1978 with a new lineup led by Gregg Allman and Dickey Betts.	
9/08/73	2(1)	13	1. **Ramblin Man**	Capricorn 0027
4/07/79	29	5	2. Crazy Love	Capricorn 0320
9/19/81	39	2	3. Straight From The Heart	Arista 0618
			GREGG ALLMAN	
			Keyboardist/vocalist, born on 12/8/47 in Nashville; raised in Daytona Beach, Florida. In 1965, Greg and brother Duane formed the Allman Joys which evolved into the Allman Brothers Band by 1969. Greg and Dickey Betts led band after Duane's death in October of 1971. Greg went solo in 1973. Married briefly to Cher in 1975.	
1/19/74	19	8	1. Midnight Rider	Capricorn 0035
			HERB ALPERT & THE TIJUANA BRASS	
			Herb was born on 3/31/35 in Los Angeles. Producer/composer/trumpeter/bandleader. Played trumpet since age 8. A&R for Keen Records, produced first Jan & Dean session, wrote "Wonderful World" hit for Sam Cooke. Formed A&M Records with Jerry Moss in 1962. Used studio musicians until early 1965, then formed own band.	
			THE TIJUANA BRASS featuring HERB ALPERT:	
11/10/62	6	11	1. **The Lonely Bull** [I] crowd noises dubbed in from bullring in Tijuana, Mexico	A&M 703
			HERB ALPERT & THE TIJUANA BRASS:	
10/16/65	7	13	2. **Taste Of Honey** [I]	A&M 775
1/22/66	11	7	3. Zorba The Greek/ [I] from the film of the same title	
2/05/66	38	2	4. Tijuana Taxi [I]	A&M 787
4/09/66	24	5	5. What Now My Love/ [I]	
4/09/66	27	4	6. Spanish Flea [I] theme song from TV's "The Dating Game"	A&M 792
7/09/66	18	6	7. The Work Song [I]	A&M 805

DATE	POS	WKS	ARTIST—RECORD TITLE	LABEL & NO.
7/09/66	**18**	6	7. The Work Song [I]	A&M 805
9/17/66	**28**	4	8. Flamingo [I]	A&M 813
12/03/66	**19**	6	9. Mame from the Broadway show "Mame"	A&M 823
4/01/67	**37**	2	10. Wade In The Water [I]	A&M 840
4/29/67	**27**	6	11. Casino Royale [I] from the film of the same title	A&M 850
7/22/67	**32**	3	12. The Happening [I]	A&M 860
9/30/67	**35**	3	13. A Banda [I]	A&M 870
			HERB ALPERT:	
5/25/68	**1**(4)	12	• 14. **This Guy's In Love With You**	A&M 929
8/25/79	**1**(2)	15	• 15. **Rise** **[I]**	A&M 2151
12/22/79†	**30**	6	16. Rotation [I]	A&M 2202
7/31/82	**37**	4	17. Route 101 [I]	A&M 2422
5/02/87	**5**	12	18. **Diamonds** lead & background vocals: Janet Jackson & Lisa Keith	A&M 2929
8/29/87	**35**	3	19. Making Love In The Rain vocal: Lisa Keith	A&M 2949
			THE AMAZING RHYTHM ACES	
			Memphis country-rock sextet: Russell Smith (lead vocals, guitar), Barry "Byrd" Burton (guitar, dobro), Billy Earhart III (keyboards), Jeff Davis (bass) and Butch McDade (drums). Disbanded in 1980.	
7/26/75	**14**	9	1. Third Rate Romance	ABC 12078
			THE AMBOY DUKES	
			Detroit rock group led by Ted Nugent.	
7/27/68	**16**	7	1. Journey To The Center Of The Mind	Mainstream 684
			AMBROSIA	
			Los Angeles-based pop group: David Pack and Joe Puerta (lead singers), Burleigh Drummond and Christopher North. North left in 1977.	
7/19/75	**17**	8	1. Holdin' On To Yesterday	20th Century 2207
4/02/77	**39**	2	2. Magical Mystery Tour from the film "All This & World War II"	20th Century 2327
9/30/78	**3**	14	3. **How Much I Feel**	Warner 8640
4/19/80	**3**	14	4. **Biggest Part Of Me**	Warner 49225
8/02/80	**13**	10	5. You're The Only Woman (You & I)	Warner 49508
			AMERICA	
			Trio formed in London, England in 1969. Consisted of Dan Peek, Gerry Beckley and Dewey Bunnell. All played guitars. Met at US Air Force base. With group Daze in 1970. Moved to U.S. in February, 1972. Won the 1972 Best New Artist Grammy Award. Peek left in 1976.	
3/04/72	**1**(3)	12	• 1. **A Horse With No Name**	Warner 7555
5/27/72	**9**	9	2. **I Need You**	Warner 7580
11/04/72	**8**	9	3. **Ventura Highway**	Warner 7641
2/24/73	**35**	2	4. Don't Cross The River	Warner 7670
9/21/74	**4**	11	5. **Tin Man**	Warner 7839
1/18/75	**5**	10	6. **Lonely People**	Warner 8048
4/26/75	**1**(1)	12	7. **Sister Golden Hair**	Warner 8086
8/16/75	**20**	7	8. Daisy Jane	Warner 8118

DATE	POS	WKS	ARTIST—RECORD TITLE	LABEL & NO.
6/12/76	**23**	6	9. Today's The Day above 5: produced by George Martin (Beatles' producer)	Warner 8212
8/21/82	**8**	15	10. **You Can Do Magic**	Capitol 5142
7/16/83	**33**	6	11. The Border	Capitol 5236
			THE AMERICAN BREED Integrated rock quartet from Cicero, Illinois led by Gary Loizzo.	
7/08/67	**24**	4	1. Step Out Of Your Mind	Acta 804
12/16/67†	**5**	12	● 2. **Bend Me, Shape Me**	Acta 811
3/16/68	**39**	3	3. Green Light	Acta 821
			THE AMES BROTHERS Vocal group from Malden, Massachusettes, formed in the late 40s. Family name Urick. Consisted of Ed (b: 7/9/27), Gene (b: 2/13/25), Joe (b: 5/3/24) and Vic (b: 5/20/26, d: 1/23/78). Own TV series in 1955. Ed acted on Broadway and TV.	
11/20/54†	**3**	15	1. **The Naughty Lady Of Shady Lane** Best Seller #3 / Jockey #3 / Juke Box #3	RCA 5897
9/24/55	**11**	11	2. My Bonnie Lassie Best Seller #11 / Top 100 #11 / Jockey #14 / Juke Box #16	RCA 6208
3/24/56	**35**	3	3. Forever Darling from the film of the same title	RCA 6400
5/19/56	**11**	20	4. It Only Hurts For A Little While Juke Box #11 / Top 100 # 15 / Jockey #15 / Best Seller #16	RCA 6481
7/22/57	**5**	16	5. **Tammy** Jockey #5 / Best Seller #24 / Top 100 #29 from the film "Tammy and The Bachelor"	RCA 6930
10/07/57	**5**	14	6. **Melodie D'Amour** Jockey #5 / Best Seller #12 / Top 100 #12	RCA 7046
3/31/58	**23**	2	7. A Very Precious Love Jockey #23 / Top 100 #65 from the film "Marjorie Morningstar"	RCA 7167
9/29/58	**17**	10	8. Pussy Cat Hot 100 #17 / Best Seller #20 end	RCA 7315
1/19/59	**37**	4	9. Red River Rose all of above (except #5): orchestra directed by Hugo Winterhalter	RCA 7413
2/22/60	**38**	2	10. China Doll	RCA 7655
			ED AMES One of The Ames Brothers. Played an Indian on the "Daniel Boone" TV series.	
2/11/67	**8**	10	1. **My Cup Runneth Over** from the musical "I Do, I Do"	RCA 9002
12/30/67†	**19**	4	2. Who Will Answer?	RCA 9400
			BILL ANDERSON Born James William Anderson on 11/1/37 in Columbia, South Carolina. Country singer/ songwriter/actor. Host of Nashville Network's TV game show "Fandango."	
5/11/63	**8**	11	1. **Still**	Decca 31458

DATE	POS	WKS	ARTIST—RECORD TITLE	LABEL & NO.
			CARL ANDERSON - see GLORIA LORING	
			LYNN ANDERSON	
			Born on 9/26/47 in Grand Forks, North Dakota; raised in Sacramento. Country singer; daughter of Liz Anderson.	
12/19/70†	**3**	14	● 1. **Rose Garden**	Columbia 45252
			LEE ANDREWS & THE HEARTS	
			Born Arthur Lee Andrew Thompson in North Carolina; moved to Philadelphia at age 2. Formed R&B vocal group, The Hearts, in 1953.	
12/09/57	**20**	10	1. Tear Drops Best Seller #20 / Top 100 #20 / Jockey #21	Chess 1675
6/16/58	**33**	1	2. Try The Impossible Best Seller #33 / Top 100 #33	United Art. 123
			THE ANGELS	
			Female pop trio from Orange, New Jersey, formed as the Starlets with sisters Phyllis "Jiggs" & Barbara Allbut, and Linda Jansen (lead singer). Jansen was replaced by Peggy Santiglia in 1962. Disbanded in 1967.	
12/04/61†	**14**	7	1. 'Til	Caprice 107
4/07/62	**38**	1	2. Cry Baby Cry	Caprice 112
8/10/63	**1**(3)	12	3. **My Boyfriend's Back**	Smash 1834
11/09/63	**25**	5	4. I Adore Him	Smash 1854
			THE ANIMALS	
			Formed in Newcastle, England in 1958 as the Alan Price Combo. Consisted of Eric Burdon (vocals), Alan Price (keyboards), Bryan "Chas" Chandler (bass), Hilton Valentine (guitar) and John Steel (drums). Price left in May of 1965, replaced by Dave Rowberry. Steel left in 1966, replaced by Barry Jenkins. Group disbanded in July, 1968. After a period with War, Burdon and the other originals reunited, 1983.	
8/15/64	**1**(3)	10	1. **The House Of The Rising Sun**	MGM 13264
10/17/64	**19**	6	2. I'm Crying	MGM 13274
3/06/65	**15**	6	3. Don't Let Me Be Misunderstood	MGM 13311
5/29/65	**32**	4	4. Bring It On Home To Me	MGM 13339
9/04/65	**13**	8	5. We Gotta Get Out Of This Place	MGM 13382
12/04/65†	**23**	8	6. It's My Life	MGM 13414
4/02/66	**34**	1	7. Inside-Looking Out	MGM 13468
6/04/66	**12**	8	8. Don't Bring Me Down	MGM 13514
			ERIC BURDON & THE ANIMALS:	
10/01/66	**10**	7	9. **See See Rider** #14 hit for Ma Rainey in 1925	MGM 13582
12/31/66	**29**	4	10. Help Me Girl	MGM 13636
4/22/67	**15**	6	11. When I Was Young	MGM 13721
8/19/67	**9**	8	12. **San Franciscan Nights**	MGM 13769
12/30/67†	**15**	6	13. Monterey	MGM 13868
6/22/68	**14**	10	14. Sky Pilot (Part One)	MGM 13939
			ANIMOTION	
			Techno-pop quintet led by Astrid Plane and Bill Wadhams. 4 of 5 members replaced in 1988, including Plane and Wadhams. New vocalists are Paul Engemann (formerly of Device) and Cynthia Rhodes (appeared in the films "Staying Alive" and "Dirty Dancing"; married Richard Marx on 1/8/89).	
3/02/85	**6**	14	1. **Obsession**	Mercury 880266

DATE	POS	WKS	ARTIST—RECORD TITLE	LABEL & NO.
7/27/85	**39**	1	2. Let Him Go	Mercury 880737
			PAUL ANKA Born on 7/30/41 in Ottawa, Canada. Performer since age 12. Father financed first recording, "I Confess" (RPM 472), in 1956. Wrote "My Way" for Frank Sinatra, "She's A Lady" for Tom Jones. Also wrote theme for TV's "Tonight Show." Own variety show in 1973. Long-time popular entertainer in Las Vegas.	
7/29/57	**1**(1)	18	1. **Diana** Best Seller #1 / Top 100 #2 / Jockey #2	ABC-Para. 9831
2/03/58	**7**	11	2. **You Are My Destiny** Top 100 #7 / Best Seller #9 / Jockey #9	ABC-Para. 9880
4/28/58	**15**	10	3. Crazy Love/ Best Seller #15 / Top 100 #19	
4/28/58	**16**	10	4. Let The Bells Keep Ringing Best Seller #16 / Jockey #18 / Top 100 #30	ABC-Para. 9907
12/15/58†	**29**	5	5. The Teen Commandments [S] **PAUL ANKA-GEORGE HAMILTON IV-JOHNNY NASH** inspirational talk from above 3 ABC-Paramount artists	ABC-Para. 9974
1/05/59	**15**	13	6. (All Of A Sudden) My Heart Sings	ABC-Para. 9987
4/20/59	**33**	3	7. I Miss You So	ABC-Para. 10011
6/08/59	**1**(4)	14	8. **Lonely Boy** from the film "Girl's Town"	ABC-Para. 10022
9/14/59	**2**(3)	14	9. **Put Your Head On My Shoulder** all of above: arranged and conducted by Don Costa	ABC-Para. 10040
11/30/59	**4**	12	10. **It's Time To Cry**	ABC-Para. 10064
3/07/60	**2**(2)	11	11. **Puppy Love**	ABC-Para. 10082
6/06/60	**8**	9	12. **My Home Town**	ABC-Para. 10106
8/22/60	**23**	6	13. Hello Young Lovers/	
9/12/60	**40**	1	14. I Love You In The Same Old Way	ABC-Para. 10132
10/10/60	**11**	7	15. Summer's Gone	ABC-Para. 10147
2/06/61	**16**	5	16. The Story Of My Love	ABC-Para. 10168
3/27/61	**13**	8	17. Tonight My Love, Tonight	ABC-Para. 10194
6/12/61	**10**	7	18. **Dance On Little Girl**	ABC-Para. 10220
9/11/61	**35**	1	19. Kissin' On The Phone	ABC-Para. 10239
3/17/62	**12**	9	20. Love Me Warm And Tender	RCA 7977
6/16/62	**13**	7	21. A Steel Guitar And A Glass Of Wine	RCA 8030
11/24/62	**19**	5	22. Eso Beso (That Kiss!)	RCA 8097
2/09/63	**26**	4	23. Love (Makes The World Go 'Round)	RCA 8115
5/25/63	**39**	1	24. Remember Diana	RCA 8170
2/01/69	**27**	6	25. Goodnight My Love	RCA 9648
7/27/74	**1**(3)	11	• 26. **(You're) Having My Baby**	United Art. 454
11/30/74†	**7**	11	27. **One Man Woman/One Woman Man**	United Art. 569
4/05/75	**8**	10	28. **I Don't Like To Sleep Alone**	United Art. 615
8/16/75	**15**	8	29. (I Believe) There's Nothing Stronger Than Our Love 26-27 & 29: backing vocals by Odia Coates	United Art. 685
11/29/75†	**7**	12	30. **Times Of Your Life**	United Art. 737
5/01/76	**33**	3	31. Anytime (I'll Be There)	United Art. 789
11/18/78	**35**	3	32. This Is Love	RCA 11395

DATE	POS	WKS	ARTIST—RECORD TITLE	LABEL & NO.
			ANN-MARGRET	
			Born Ann-Margret Olsson on 4/28/41 in Stockholm, Sweden. Moved to Wilmette, Illinois in 1946. Actress in many films and TV specials.	
8/21/61	**17**	6	1. I Just Don't Understand	RCA 7894
			ANNETTE	
			Born Annette Funicello on 10/22/42 in Utica, New York. Became a Mouseketeer in 1955. Backing group: The Afterbeats. In several teen films in the early 60s. Co-sarred with Frankie Avalon in the 1987 film "Back To The Beach."	
2/02/59	**7**	9	1. **Tall Paul**	Disneyland 118
12/14/59†	**20**	10	2. First Name Initial	Vista 349
3/07/60	**10**	8	3. **O Dio Mio**	Vista 354
6/20/60	**36**	3	4. Train Of Love	Vista 359
9/05/60	**11**	9	5. Pineapple Princess	Vista 362
			ADAM ANT	
			Born Stuart Goddard on 11/3/54 in London, England. Formed Adam & The Ants in 1976. Appeared in the film "Slam Dance" in 1987.	
12/11/82†	**12**	14	1. Goody Two Shoes	Epic 03367
			RAY ANTHONY	
			Born Raymond Antonini on 1/20/22 in Bentleyville, Pennsylvania; raised in Cleveland. Trumpeter/bandleader. Joined Al Donahue in 1939, then with Glenn Miller and Jimmy Dorsey from 1940-42. Led US Army band. Own band in 1946. Own TV series in the 50s.	
1/22/55	**19**	4	1. Melody Of Love	Capitol 3018
			FRANK SINATRA & RAY ANTHONY	
			Jockey #19	
1/19/59	**8**	13	2. **Peter Gunn** **[I]**	Capitol 4041
			title song from the hit TV series	
			SUSAN ANTON - see FRED KNOBLOCK	
			APOLLO 100	
			English studio band featuring Tom Parker.	
1/22/72	**6**	10	1. **Joy** **[I]**	Mega 0050
			adaptation of Bach's "Jesu, Joy of Man's Desiring"	
			THE APPLEJACKS	
			Dave Appell, leader of studio band from Philadelphia.	
10/06/58	**16**	9	1. Mexican Hat Rock [I]	Cameo 149
			Hot 100 #16 / Best Seller #29 end	
1/12/59	**38**	3	2. Rocka-Conga	Cameo 155
			APRIL WINE	
			Rock quintet from Montreal, Canada led by Myles Goodwyn.	
4/29/72	**32**	5	1. You Could Have Been A Lady	Big Tree 133
4/14/79	**34**	4	2. Roller	Capitol 4660
3/14/81	**21**	7	3. Just Between You And Me	Capitol 4975
			THE AQUATONES	
			Group formed in Valley Stream, Long Island, New York in 1957. Consisted of Lynn Nixon, Larry Vannata (lead singers); David Goddard and Eugene McCarthy.	
5/05/58	**21**	8	1. You	Fargo 1001
			Top 100 #21 / Best Seller #24	

DATE	POS	WKS	ARTIST—RECORD TITLE	LABEL & NO.
			THE ARBORS	
			Formed at the University of Michigan in Ann Arbor by two pairs of brothers: Edward & Fred Farran, and Scott & Tom Herrick.	
4/05/69	**20**	3	1. The Letter	Date 1638
			ARCADIA	
			English group features Duran Duran's Simon LeBon, Nick Rhodes and Roger Taylor. LeBon and Rhodes remain with Duran Duran.	
11/02/85	**6**	12	1. **Election Day** narration: Grace Jones	Capitol 5501
3/01/86	**33**	3	2. Goodbye Is Forever	Capitol 5542
			THE ARCHIES	
			Studio group created by Don Kirshner; based on the Saturday morning cartoon television series. Ron Dante was lead vocalist. All tunes written and produced by Jeff Barry.	
11/02/68	**22**	8	1. Bang-Shang-A-Lang	Calendar 1006
8/16/69	**1**(4)	18	● 2. **Sugar, Sugar**	Calendar 1008
12/20/69†	**10**	10	● 3. **Jingle Jangle**	Kirshner 5002
3/28/70	**40**	2	4. Who's Your Baby?	Kirshner 5003
			TONI ARDEN	
			Vocalist from New York City. Real name: Antoinette Aroizzone. Sang with Al Trace in 1945 and Joe Reichman in 1946.	
6/02/58	**13**	11	1. Padre Jockey #13 / Top 100 #18 / Best Seller #19	Decca 30628
			ARGENT	
			British rock quartet, consisted of ex-Zombies member Rod Argent (vocals, keyboards), John Verity (guitar), Jim Rodford (bass) and Robert Henrit (drums).	
7/08/72	**5**	11	1. **Hold Your Head Up**	Epic 10852
			RUSSELL ARMS	
			One of the regulars on TV's "Your Hit Parade."	
2/02/57	**22**	8	1. Cinco Robles (Five Oaks) Best Seller #22 / Top 100 #23 / Jockey #23 with Pete King and orchestra	Era 1026
			LOUIS ARMSTRONG	
			Trumpeter/vocalist, born Daniel Louis Armstrong in New Orleans, on 8/4/01 (not 7/4/1900, as Armstrong claimed). Nickname: Satchmo. Joined Joe "King" Oliver in Chicago in 1922. By 1929, had become the most widely-known black musician. Influenced dozens of singers and trumpet players, both black and white. Numerous appearances on radio, TV and in films. Died on 7/6/71 in New York.	
2/25/56	**20**	7	1. Mack The Knife (A Theme From The Threepenny Opera) **LOUIS ARMSTRONG & THE ALL STARS**	Columbia 40587
12/15/56	**29**	1	2. Blueberry Hill recorded in 1949 with Gordon Jenkins' orchestra	Decca 30091
2/29/64	**1**(1)	19	3. **Hello, Dolly!** **LOUIS ARMSTRONG & THE ALL STARS** title song from the Broadway musical	Kapp 573
3/19/88	**32**	3	4. What A Wonderful World [R] from the film "Good Morning, Vietnam"; originally "Bubbled Under" at POS 116 on 7/6/68 (ABC 10982)	A&M 3010

DATE	POS	WKS	ARTIST—RECORD TITLE	LABEL & NO.
			EDDY ARNOLD	
			Born on 5/15/18 near Henderson, Tennessee. Became popular on Nashville's "Grand Ole Opry" as a singer with Pee Wee King (1940-43). Nicknamed "The Tennessee Plowboy" on all RCA recordings through 1954. Country music's most prolific recording artist from 1945-55.	
12/01/56	**22**	1	1. I Wouldn't Know Where To Begin Jockey #22 / Top 100 #64	RCA 6699
11/13/65	**6**	10	2. **Make The World Go Away**	RCA 8679
3/12/66	**36**	5	3. I Want To Go With You	RCA 8749
6/18/66	**40**	1	4. The Last Word In Lonesome Is Me all of Eddy's hits were produced by Chet Atkins	RCA 8818
			THE ARROWS - see DAVIE ALLAN	
			THE ART OF NOISE	
			British techno-pop trio: Anne Dudley, J.J. Jeczalik and Gary Langan.	
9/20/86	**34**	4	1. Paranoimia with Max Headroom (a British "computer-generated" celebrity)	China 43002
12/24/88†	**31**	6	2. Kiss **THE ART OF NOISE featuring TOM JONES**	China 871038
			ARTISTS UNITED AGAINST APARTHEID	
			Benefit group of 49 superstar artists formed in protest of the South African government; proceeds for political prisoners in South Africa.	
12/07/85	**38**	3	1. Sun City	Manhattan 50017
			ASHFORD & SIMPSON	
			Husband-and-wife R&B vocal/songwriting duo: Nickolas Ashford (b: 5/4/42, Fairfield, SC) and Valerie Simpson (b: 8/26/46, New York City). Team wrote for Chuck Jackson and Maxine Brown. Joined staff at Motown and wrote and produced for many of the label's top stars. Valerie recorded solo in 1972.	
10/13/79	**36**	2	1. Found A Cure	Warner 8870
1/05/85	**12**	11	2. Solid	Capitol 5397
			ASHTON, GARDNER & DYKE	
			British pop trio: Tony Ashton, Kim Gardner and Roy Dyke.	
8/07/71	**40**	1	1. Resurrection Shuffle	Capitol 3060
			ASIA	
			English rock supergroup comprised of Steve Howe (Yes), Carl Palmer (Emerson, Lake & Palmer), Geoff Downes (Buggles, Yes) and John Wetton (King Crimson, Uriah Heep, Roxy Music). Howe replaced by Mandy Meyer (Krokus) in 1985.	
5/01/82	**4**	12	1. **Heat Of The Moment**	Geffen 50040
8/14/82	**17**	8	2. Only Time Will Tell	Geffen 29970
8/06/83	**10**	11	3. **Don't Cry**	Geffen 29571
11/12/83	**34**	5	4. The Smile Has Left Your Eyes	Geffen 29475
			THE ASSEMBLED MULTITUDE	
			Philadelphia-based studio group arranged and conducted by Tom Sellers.	
8/01/70	**16**	7	1. Overture From Tommy (A Rock Opera) [I]	Atlantic 2737

DATE	POS	WKS	ARTIST—RECORD TITLE	LABEL & NO.
			THE ASSOCIATION	
			Group formed in Los Angeles in 1965. Consisted of Terry Kirkman (plays 23 wind, reed and percussion instruments), Jules Alexander (guitar), Brian Cole (bass), Jim Yester (guitar), Ted Buechel Jr. (drums) and Russ Giguere (percussion). Larry Ramos joined in early 1968. Richard Thompson (keyboards) replaced Giguere in 1970. Cole died on 8/2/73 of a drug overdose. Thompson replaced by Rick Ulsky in 1974. Re-grouped with original surviving members on 9/26/80.	
6/25/66	7	8	1. **Along Comes Mary**	Valiant 741
9/03/66	1(3)	12	• 2. **Cherish**	Valiant 747
12/17/66	35	3	3. Pandora's Golden Heebie Jeebies	Valiant 755
6/03/67	1(4)	13	• 4. **Windy**	Warner 7041
9/09/67	2(2)	11	• 5. **Never My Love**	Warner 7074
2/10/68	10	8	6. **Everything That Touches You**	Warner 7163
6/22/68	39	2	7. Time For Livin'	Warner 7195
			RICK ASTLEY	
			Pop singer/guitarist born and raised in Manchester, England.	
1/23/88	1(2)	14	• 1. **Never Gonna Give You Up**	RCA 5347
4/30/88	1(1)	12	2. **Together Forever**	RCA 8319
8/06/88	10	10	3. **It Would Take A Strong Strong Man**	RCA 8663
			ATLANTA RHYTHM SECTION	
			Group formed of musicians from Studio One, Doraville, Georgia in 1971. Consisted of Rodney Justo (vocals), Barry Bailey, Paul Goddard, J.R. Cobb (guitars), Dean Daughtry (keyboards) and Robert Nix (drums). Cobb, Daughtry and band manager Buddy Buie had been with the Classics IV, others had been with Roy Orbison. Justo left after first album, replaced by Ronnie Hammond.	
11/09/74	35	2	1. Doraville	Polydor 14248
2/26/77	7	14	2. **So In To You**	Polydor 14373
3/25/78	7	12	3. **Imaginary Lover**	Polydor 14459
7/08/78	14	7	4. I'm Not Gonna Let It Bother Me Tonight	Polydor 14484
6/16/79	19	9	5. Do It Or Die	Polydor 14568
9/08/79	17	8	6. Spooky	Polydor 2001
10/10/81	29	4	7. Alien	Columbia 02471
			ATLANTIC STARR	
			Originally an 8-man, 1-woman soul band formed in 1976 in White Plains, New York. Lead singers: brothers Wayne & David Lewis, and Sharon Bryant. Barbara Weathers replaced Bryant in 1984. Porsha Martin replaced Weathers in 1989.	
5/15/82	38	3	1. Circles	A&M 2392
1/25/86	3	14	2. **Secret Lovers**	A&M 2788
4/25/87	1(1)	14	3. **Always**	Warner 28455
			JAN AUGUST - see RICHARD HAYMAN	
			PATTI AUSTIN with JAMES INGRAM	
			Patti was born on 8/10/48 in New York City. Back-up work in New York. God-daughter of Quincy Jones. Made Harlem's Apollo Theatre debut at age 4. In 1988 film "Tucker."	
12/04/82†	1(2)	18	• 1. **Baby, Come To Me**	Qwest 50036

DATE	POS	WKS	ARTIST—RECORD TITLE	LABEL & NO.
			SIL AUSTIN	
			Born Sylvester Austin in 1929 in Donellon, Florida. R&B tenor saxophonist. Played with the Tiny Bradshaw Band before forming own group.	
11/24/56	**17**	7	1. Slow Walk [I]	Mercury 70963
			Juke Box #17 / Top 100 #19 / Best Seller #20	
			AUTOGRAPH	
			Los Angeles-based rock quintet led by vocalist Steve Plunkett.	
2/23/85	**29**	5	1. Turn Up The Radio	RCA 13953
			FRANKIE AVALON	
			Born Francis Avallone on 9/18/39 in Philadelphia. Teen idol managed by Bob Marcucci. Worked in bands in Atlantic City, New Jersey in 1953. Radio and TV with Paul Whiteman, mid-50s. Singer/trumpet player with Rocco & His Saints in 1957. Co-starred in many films with Annette. In films "Disc Jockey Jamboree" (1957), "Guns Of The Timberland" (1960), "The Carpetbaggers" (1962) and "Back To The Beach" (1987).	
1/27/58	**7**	11	1. **Dede Dinah**	Chancellor 1011
			Top 100 #7 / Best Seller #9 / Jockey #24	
7/28/58	**9**	12	2. **Ginger Bread**	Chancellor 1021
			Hot 100 #9 / Best Seller #11	
11/17/58	**15**	10	3. I'll Wait For You	Chancellor 1026
2/23/59	**1**(5)	14	4. **Venus**	Chancellor 1031
6/01/59	**8**	10	5. **Bobby Sox To Stockings/**	
6/15/59	**10**	9	6. A Boy Without A Girl	Chancellor 1036
9/14/59	**7**	11	7. **Just Ask Your Heart**	Chancellor 1040
12/07/59	**1**(1)	12	8. **Why/**	
1/04/60	**39**	1	9. Swingin' On A Rainbow	Chancellor 1045
3/28/60	**22**	6	10. Don't Throw Away All Those Teardrops	Chancellor 1048
8/01/60	**32**	4	11. Where Are You	Chancellor 1052
			all of above: arranged and conducted by Peter De Angelis	
10/17/60	**26**	7	12. Togetherness	Chancellor 1056
5/05/62	**26**	4	13. You Are Mine	Chancellor 1107
			THE AVANT-GARDE	
10/26/68	**40**	1	1. Naturally Stoned	Columbia 44590
			written by game-show host Chuck Woolery	
			AVERAGE WHITE BAND	
			Vocal/instrumental group formed in Scotland in 1972. Consisted of Alan Gorrie (vocal, bass), Hamish Stuart (vocal, guitar), Onnie McIntyre (vocal, guitar), Malcolm Duncan (saxophone), Roger Ball (keyboards, saxophone) and Robbie McIntosh (drums). McIntosh died of drug poisoning in 1974, replaced by Steve Ferrone.	
			AWB:	
12/21/74†	**1**(1)	13	● 1. **Pick Up The Pieces** [I]	Atlantic 3229
4/26/75	**10**	12	2. **Cut The Cake**	Atlantic 3261
9/27/75	**39**	2	3. If I Ever Lose This Heaven	Atlantic 3285
12/20/75	**33**	3	4. School Boy Crush	Atlantic 3304
			AVERAGE WHITE BAND:	
10/16/76	**40**	1	5. Queen Of My Soul	Atlantic 3354

DATE	POS	WKS	ARTIST—RECORD TITLE	LABEL & NO.
			B	
			THE BABYS	
			John Waite, lead singer of British foursome.	
10/29/77	**13**	11	1. Isn't It Time	Chrysalis 2173
2/03/79	**13**	10	2. Every Time I Think Of You	Chrysalis 2279
3/08/80	**33**	3	3. Back On My Feet Again	Chrysalis 2398
			THE BACHELORS	
			Trio from Dublin, Ireland: brothers Declan & Con Cluskey with John Stokes.	
5/16/64	**10**	8	1. **Diane**	London 9639
8/01/64	**33**	2	2. I Believe	London 9672
1/30/65	**27**	4	3. No Arms Can Ever Hold You	London 9724
7/03/65	**15**	7	4. Marie	London 9762
11/06/65	**32**	3	5. Chapel In The Moonlight	London 9793
5/14/66	**38**	2	6. Love Me With All Of Your Heart	London 9828
			BACHMAN-TURNER OVERDRIVE	
			Hard-rock group formed in Vancouver, Canada in 1972. Randy Bachman (vocals, guitar), Tim Bachman (guitar), C. Fred Turner (vocals, bass) and Robbie Bachman (drums). Originally known as Brave Belt. Randy had been in The Guess Who and recorded solo. Tim Bachman left in 1973, replaced by Blair Thornton. Randy Bachman left in 1977. Randy and Tim regrouped with C.F. Turner in 1984.	
3/23/74	**23**	9	1. Let It Ride	Mercury 73457
6/29/74	**12**	10	2. Takin' Care Of Business	Mercury 73487
10/05/74	**1**(1)	12	• 3. **You Ain't Seen Nothing Yet**	Mercury 73622
2/01/75	**14**	7	4. Roll On Down The Highway	Mercury 73656
6/07/75	**21**	7	5. Hey You	Mercury 73683
2/28/76	**33**	3	6. Take It Like A Man	Mercury 73766
			JIM BACKUS & Friend	
			Jim played Thurston Howell III on TV's "Gilligan's Island." Also famous as the voice of Mr. Magoo in the cartoon series. Label misspelled last name as Bakus.	
7/21/58	**40**	2	1. Delicious! [N] Best Seller #40 / Top 100 #42	Jubilee 5330
			BAD COMPANY	
			British: Paul Rodgers (vocals), Mick Ralphs (guitar), Simon Kirke (drums) and Boz Burrell (bass). Paul and Simon from Free; Mick from Mott The Hoople; and Boz from King Crimson. In 1988, Rodgers and Burrell replaced by vocalist Brian Howe.	
8/31/74	**5**	11	1. **Can't Get Enough**	Swan Song 70015
2/08/75	**19**	6	2. Movin' On	Swan Song 70101
5/31/75	**36**	2	3. Good Lovin' Gone Bad	Swan Song 70103
7/26/75	**10**	11	4. **Feel Like Makin' Love**	Swan Song 70106
4/24/76	**20**	7	5. Young Blood	Swan Song 70108
4/14/79	**13**	12	6. Rock 'N' Roll Fantasy	Swan Song 70119

DATE	POS	WKS	ARTIST—RECORD TITLE	LABEL & NO.
			BADFINGER	
			British quartet originally known as The Iveys; leader Pete Ham committed suicide on 4/23/75 (27). Keyboardist Tom Evans left in 1977 (commmitted suicide in 1983). Yes keyboardist Tony Kaye was a member from 1978-82.	
3/07/70	**7**	11	1. **Come And Get It**	Apple 1815
			written by Paul McCartney; from the film "The Magic Christian"	
11/21/70	**8**	9	2. **No Matter What**	Apple 1822
12/18/71†	**4**	12	● 3. **Day After Day**	Apple 1841
			produced by George Harrison	
4/08/72	**14**	7	4. Baby Blue	Apple 1844
			produced by Todd Rundgren	
			JOAN BAEZ	
			Folk song stylist born in New York City on 1/9/41. Became a political activist while attending Boston University in the late 50s.	
8/28/71	**3**	13	● 1. **The Night They Drove Old Dixie Down**	Vanguard 35138
			written by Robbie Robertson (leader of The Band)	
11/08/75	**35**	2	2. Diamonds And Rust	A&M 1737
			PHILIP BAILEY with PHIL COLLINS	
			Philip was born on 5/8/51 in Denver. Percussionist/co-lead vocalist with Earth, Wind & Fire.	
12/08/84†	**2(2)**	16	● 1. **Easy Lover**	Columbia 04679
			ANITA BAKER	
			Soul singer born in Memphis on 12/20/57. Female lead singer of Chapter 8 (1976-84).	
9/13/86	**8**	11	1. **Sweet Love**	Elektra 69557
2/07/87	**37**	2	2. Caught Up In The Rapture	Elektra 69511
10/22/88	**3**	15	3. **Giving You The Best That I Got**	Elektra 69371
			GEORGE BAKER SELECTION	
			Dutch pop group led by Johannes (George Baker) Bouwens (b: 12/9/44).	
4/11/70	**21**	10	1. Little Green Bag	Colossus 112
1/10/76	**26**	5	2. Paloma Blanca	Warner 8115
			LaVERN BAKER	
			Born Delores Williams on 11/11/29 in Chicago. Recorded as "Little Miss Share Cropper" and "Bea Baker." After working with the Todd Rhodes Orchestra, 1952-53, toured Europe, solo. Returned to work for Atlantic Records and became one of the most popular female R&B singers in the early rock era. Backing group: The Gliders.	
1/15/55	**14**	11	1. Tweedlee Dee	Atlantic 1047
10/13/56	**22**	2	2. I Can't Love You Enough	Atlantic 1104
			Jockey #22 / Top 100 #48	
12/29/56†	**17**	14	3. Jim Dandy	Atlantic 1116
12/28/58†	**6**	15	4. **I Cried A Tear**	Atlantic 2007
6/01/59	**33**	2	5. I Waited Too Long	Atlantic 2021
5/01/61	**37**	3	6. Saved	Atlantic 2099
1/05/63	**34**	3	7. See See Rider	Atlantic 2167
			BALANCE	
			New York City rock trio led by Peppy Castro (founder of the Blues Magoos).	
8/15/81	**22**	9	1. Breaking Away	Portrait 02177

DATE	POS	WKS	ARTIST—RECORD TITLE	LABEL & NO.
			MARTY BALIN	
			Born on 1/30/43 in Cincinnati. Co-founder of Jefferson Airplane/Jefferson Starship/KBC.	
6/13/81	**8**	13	1. **Hearts**	EMI America 8084
10/10/81	**27**	5	2. Atlanta Lady (Something About Your Love)	EMI America 8093
			KENNY BALL & His Jazzmen	
			English dixieland jazz band formed in 1958.	
2/17/62	**2**(1)	12	1. **Midnight In Moscow** [I] original Russian title: "Padmeskoveeye Vietchera"	Kapp 442
			HANK BALLARD & THE MIDNIGHTERS	
			R&B vocal group from Detroit, formed in 1952 as The Royals: Henry Booth, Charles Sutton, Lawson Smith and Sonny Woods. In late 1953, Henry "Hank" Ballard (b: 11/18/36, Detroit) replaced Smith and became lead singer. Name changed to Midnighters in 1954. Had the original recording of "The Twist," written by Ballard, who is still active as a solo artist. After group disbanded in 1965, re-formed with Frank Stadford, Walter Miller and Wesley Hargrove. Worked in the James Brown Revue.	
7/18/60	**7**	13	1. **Finger Poppin' Time**	King 5341
8/29/60	**28**	6	2. The Twist [R] flip of Hank's first Hot 100 hit "Teardrops On Your Letter" (1959)	King 5171
10/17/60	**6**	11	3. **Let's Go, Let's Go, Let's Go**	King 5400
1/16/61	**23**	4	4. The Hoochi Coochi Coo	King 5430
3/20/61	**39**	1	5. Let's Go Again (Where We Went Last Night)	King 5459
5/01/61	**33**	3	6. The Continental Walk	King 5491
7/17/61	**26**	4	7. The Switch-A-Roo	King 5510
			THE BALLOON FARM	
			New York flower-pop quintet.	
3/16/68	**37**	4	1. A Question Of Temperature	Laurie 3405
			BALTIMORA	
			Baltimora is Jimmy McShane from Northern Ireland.	
1/11/86	**13**	10	1. Tarzan Boy	Manhattan 50018
			BANANARAMA	
			Female trio from London: Sarah Dallin, Keren Woodward and Siobhan Fahey. Got group name by combining the name of the cartoon show "The Banana Splits" with the Roxy Music song "Pyjamarama." Fahey married Dave Stewart (Eurythmics) on 8/1/87; left group in early 1988, replaced by Jacqui O'Sullivan.	
8/11/84	**9**	11	1. **Cruel Summer**	London 810127
7/19/86	**1**(1)	12	2. **Venus**	London 886056
8/15/87	**4**	12	3. **I Heard A Rumour**	London 886165
			THE BAND	
			Formed in Woodstock, New York in 1967: Robbie Robertson (guitar), Levon Helm (drums), Rick Danko (bass), Richard Manuel and Garth Hudson (keyboards). All from Canada (except Helm from Arkansas) and all were with Ronnie Hawkins' Hawks. Recorded extensively with Bob Dylan. Disbanded on Thanksgiving Day in 1976. Manuel committed suicide on 3/4/86 (42).	
11/29/69†	**25**	7	1. Up On Cripple Creek	Capitol 2635
10/14/72	**34**	6	2. Don't Do It	Capitol 3433

DATE	POS	WKS	ARTIST—RECORD TITLE	LABEL & NO.
			BAND AID	
			A benefit recording to assist famine relief in Ethiopia. All-star group organized by Bob Geldof of The Boomtown Rats.	
1/05/85	**13**	4	● 1. Do They Know It's Christmas? [X]	Columbia 04749
			with Paul Young, Boy George & Jon Moss (Culture Club), George Michael (Wham!), Sting, Phil Collins, Duran Duran, Bananarama, Spandau Ballet, Paul Weller (Style Council), Boomtown Rats, and members of Kool & The Gang, U2, Ultravox, Status Quo and Heaven 17	
			BANGLES	
			Female rock quartet formed in Los Angeles in January, 1981. Consists of sisters Vicki (lead guitar) & Debbi Peterson (drums), Michael Steele (bass) and Susanna Hoffs (guitar). Originally named The Bangs. Steele was previously in The Runaways. Hoffs starred in the 1987 film "The Allnighter."	
2/22/86	**2**(1)	14	1. **Manic Monday**	Columbia 05757
			written by Prince under the pseudonym "Christopher"	
6/14/86	**29**	10	2. If She Knew What She Wants	Columbia 05886
11/01/86	**1**(4)	15	3. **Walk Like An Egyptian**	Columbia 06257
3/14/87	**11**	9	4. Walking Down Your Street	Columbia 06674
12/05/87†	**2**(1)	14	5. **Hazy Shade Of Winter**	Def Jam 07630
			from the film "Less Than Zero"; written by Paul Simon	
11/12/88†	**5**	12	6. **In Your Room**	Columbia 08090
			DARRELL BANKS	
			Born Darrell Eubanks in 1938 in Buffalo. Soul singer. Killed by a gunshot wound in Detroit, in March of 1970.	
9/10/66	**27**	4	1. Open The Door To Your Heart	Revilot 201
			BAR-KAYS	
			R&B vocal/instrumental combo: Jimmy King (guitar), Ronnie Caldwell (organ), James Alexander (bass), Carl Cunningham (drums), Phalon Jones (saxophone) and Ben Cauley (trumpet). Formed by Al Jackson, drummer with Booker T & The MG's. The plane crash that killed Otis Redding (12/10/67) also claimed the lives of all the Bar-Kays except Alexander (not on the plane) & Cauley (survived the crash). Alexander re-formed the band. Appeared in the film "Wattstax"; much session work at Stax.	
7/01/67	**17**	9	1. Soul Finger [I]	Volt 148
12/04/76†	**23**	8	2. Shake Your Rump To The Funk	Mercury 73833
			CHRIS BARBER'S JAZZ BAND	
			Trombonist/leader Barber was born on 4/17/30 in Welwyn Garden City, England. Prolific and popular dixieland-styled band formed in 1949. Lineup on hit song included Barber (trombone), Monty Sunshine (clarinet), Dick Bishop (guitar), Dick Smith (bass) and Ron Bowden (drums).	
2/02/59	**5**	10	1. **Petite Fleur (Little Flower)** **[I]**	Laurie 3022
			written in 1952 by jazz great Sidney Bechet	
			KEITH BARBOUR	
			Singer/songwriter; formerly with The New Christy Minstrels. Married to TV actress Deidre Hall ("Our House" and "Days of Our Lives"), 1971-78.	
11/01/69	**40**	2	1. Echo Park	Epic 10486
			THE BARBUSTERS - see JOAN JETT	
			EDDIE BARCLAY	
			Head of the French recording company Compagnie Phonographique Francaise.	
7/16/55	**18**	1	1. The Bandit (O'Cangaceiro) [I]	Tico 249
			Juke Box #18	

DATE	POS	WKS	ARTIST—RECORD TITLE	LABEL & NO.
			BARDEUX	
			Los Angeles dance duo of female vocalists: Acacia (Stacy Smith) and Jazz.	
5/28/88	**36**	3	1. When We Kiss	Synthicd. 75018
			BOBBY BARE	
			Born on 4/7/35 in Ironton, Ohio. Country singer/songwriter/guitarist. First recorded for Capitol in 1956. Own TV series in the mid-80s.	
12/28/58†	**2(1)**	13	1. **The All American Boy** **[N]**	Fraternity 835
			written by Bill Parsons, but Bobby Bare is the real vocalist on this song (label error listed Parsons as the artist); upon its release, Bare was in the Army, so Parsons toured with the hit, lip-synching to the record	
8/18/62	**23**	7	2. Shame On Me	RCA 8032
6/29/63	**16**	9	3. Detroit City	RCA 8183
10/26/63	**10**	7	4. **500 Miles Away From Home**	RCA 8238
3/07/64	**33**	2	5. Miller's Cave	RCA 8294
			H.B. BARNUM	
			Born on 7/15/36 in Houston. Member of The Dyna-Sores.	
2/06/61	**35**	1	1. Lost Love [I]	Eldo 111
			RAY BARRETTO	
			Percussionist born in Brooklyn in 1939. With Tito Puente and Herbie Mann before forming his own group.	
5/11/63	**17**	7	1. El Watusi [F-N]	Tico 419
			BARRY & THE TAMERLANES	
			Pop trio led by Barry DeVorzon.	
11/16/63	**21**	5	1. I Wonder What She's Doing Tonight	Valiant 6034
			JOE BARRY	
			Singer/guitarist born Joe Barrios in Cut Off, Louisiana.	
5/29/61	**24**	5	1. I'm A Fool To Care	Smash 1702
			LEN BARRY	
			Born Leonard Borisoff on 12/6/42 in Philadelphia. In group The Dovells, 1957-63.	
10/23/65	**2(1)**	10	1. **1-2-3**	Decca 31827
1/22/66	**27**	5	2. Like A Baby	Decca 31889
4/09/66	**26**	5	3. Somewhere	Decca 31923
			CHRIS BARTLEY	
			Soul singer/guitarist born on 4/17/49 in New York City. Sang with the Soulful Inspirations and own group, the Mindbenders, in the mid-60s.	
8/19/67	**32**	2	1. The Sweetest Thing This Side Of Heaven	Vando 101
			BASIA	
			Polish-born, Britain-based, female pop-jazz singer/composer Basia Trzetrzelewska (pronounced: Basha Tshetshelevska). Former vocalist of the group Matt Bianco.	
9/24/88	**26**	7	1. Time And Tide	Epic 07730

DATE	POS	WKS	ARTIST—RECORD TITLE	LABEL & NO.
			COUNT BASIE	
			Born William Basie on 8/21/04 in Red Bank, New Jersey; died on 4/26/84. Jazz pianist/organist/band leader. Learned music and piano from mother, organ from Fats Waller. First recorded with own band in 1937 for Decca. Appeared in many films and toured into the 70s.	
2/04/56	**28**	3	1. April In Paris [I] written in 1932	Clef 89162
			TONI BASIL	
			Los Angeles vocalist/dancer/choreographer/actress/video director. Worked on the TV shows "Shindig" and "Hullabaloo." In the film "Easy Rider."	
10/09/82	**1**(1)	18	▲ 1. **Mickey**	Chrysalis 2638
			FONTELLA BASS	
			Born on 7/3/40 in St. Louis. Soul vocalist/pianist/organist. Mother was a member of Clara Ward Gospel Troupe. Sang in church choirs; with Oliver Sain Band, St. Louis; with Little Milton blues show to 1964. Married to trumpet player Lester Bowie.	
3/27/65	**33**	3	1. Don't Mess Up A Good Thing **FONTELLA BASS & BOBBY McCLURE**	Checker 1097
10/23/65	**4**	10	2. **Rescue Me**	Checker 1120
1/29/66	**37**	1	3. Recovery	Checker 1131
			SHIRLEY BASSEY	
			Born on 1/8/37 in Cardiff, Wales. Soul songstress.	
2/27/65	**8**	8	1. **Goldfinger** from the James Bond film of the same title	United Art. 790
			LES BAXTER	
			Born 3/14/22 in Mexia, Texas. Orchestra leader/arranger. Began as a conductor on radio shows in the 30s. Member of Mel Torme's vocal group, the Mel-Tones. Musical arranger for Capitol Records (Nat King Cole, Margaret Whiting and others), in 50s.	
4/09/55	**1**(2)	21	1. **Unchained Melody** Jockey #1 / Best Seller #2 / Juke Box #3 from the film "Unchained"	Capitol 3055
8/13/55	**5**	12	2. **Wake The Town And Tell The People** Jockey #5 / Juke Box #8 / Best Seller #10 / Top 100 #24 pre vocal: The Notables	Capitol 3120
2/18/56	**1**(6)	20	3. **The Poor People Of Paris** **[I]** Top 100 #1(6) / Jockey #1(6) / Best Seller #1(4) / Juke Box #1(3)	Capitol 3336
			BAY CITY ROLLERS	
			Formed in 1967 in Edinburgh, Scotland as the Saxons. Original members: brothers Alan & Derek Longmuir, Les McKeoun (lead singer), Eric Faulkner and Stuart "Woody" Wood.	
11/08/75†	**1**(1)	12	● 1. **Saturday Night**	Arista 0149
2/14/76	**9**	11	2. **Money Honey**	Arista 0170
5/22/76	**28**	4	3. Rock And Roll Love Letter	Arista 0185
9/18/76	**12**	12	4. I Only Want To Be With You	Arista 0205
6/25/77	**10**	12	5. **You Made Me Believe In Magic**	Arista 0256
11/19/77†	**24**	9	6. The Way I Feel Tonight	Arista 0272
			BAZUKA	
			Instrumental studio group assembled by soul producer Tony Camillo.	
6/07/75	**10**	11	1. **Dynomite - Part I** **[I]**	A&M 1666

Gregory Abbott got off Wall Street just in time: the former stock analyst's "Shake You Down" hit No. 1 on the Hot 100 in 1987, the same year that the stock market went bust.

AC/DC was the first nouveau-metal (i.e. post-Zeppelin) band to land a No. 1 album: *For Those About To Rock . . . We Salute You* (1981). The group is still looking for its first top-10 single.

Bryan Adams was a disco star long before he was a working-class hero. In 1979, he had a club hit with "Let Me Take You Dancing," featuring a Chipmunks-like lead vocal—thanks to a remix, done without Adams' consent, that sped up his voice.

Aerosmith's remake of the Shangri-Las' "Remember (Walking in the Sand)," featuring an uncredited back-up vocal from lead Shangri-La Mary Weiss, peaked at No. 67. Almost a decade later, Run-DMC's remake of Aerosmith's "Walk This Way," with *credited* guitar and vocals from Aerosmith's Joe Perry and Steve Tyler, peaked at No. 10. That's what giving those their due can do.

Herb Alpert and the Tijuana Brass had only two top-10 singles, but the ten albums they released between 1965 and 1968 spent 451 weeks in the Top 40. Alpert later went on to become the only artist to hit No. 1 as a singer ("This Guy's In Love With You," 1968) and instrumentalist ("Rise," 1979).

Animotion looked like a one-shot group when its "Obsession" peaked at No. 6 in 1985. Then they regrouped under new lead singer and *Dirty Dancing* actress Cynthia Rhodes, and returned to the top 20 in 1989 with "Room To Move."

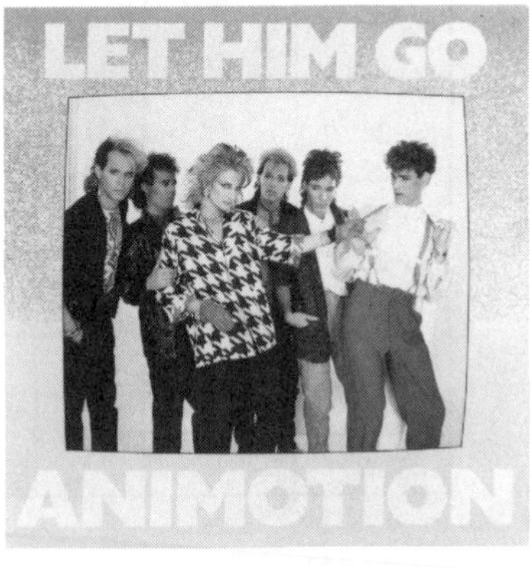

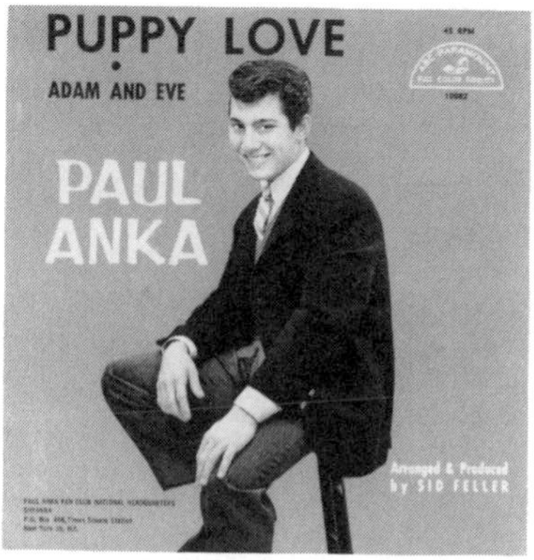

Paul Anka had three No. 1 singles: "Diana," "Lonely Boy," and "(You're) Having My Baby." But it's another of his compositions that's probably been the most-heard: the theme from "The Tonight Show starring Johnny Carson."

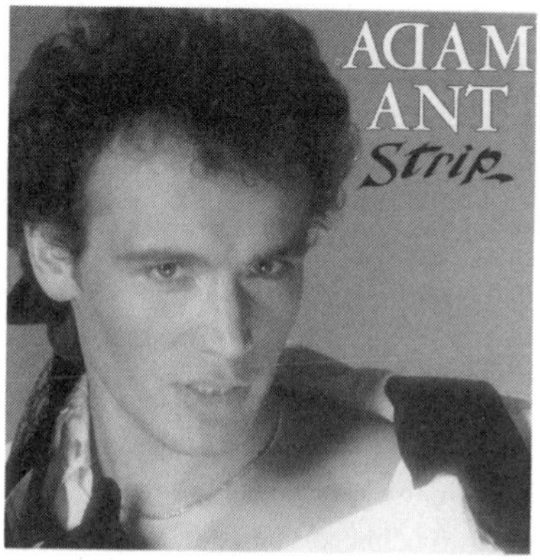

Adam Ant was one of the brightest stars of the British Explosion in the early 80's, and one of the quickest to burn out. His "Goody Two Shoes" hit No. 12 in January, 1983, and he never returned to the Top 40.

Ashford and Simpson are one of several married teams to write a No. 1 single—Diana Ross' "Ain't No Mountain High Enough" (September, 1970). They're still together today, as expressed in the biggest hit of their own: "Solid" (No. 12, 1985).

Rick Astley has a lot in common with Elvis Presley. Their first chart singles ("Never Gonna Give You Up" and "Heartbreak Hotel," respectively) both hit No. 1. Both songs were recorded for RCA, and both singers were 21 at the time. But Rick is English and Elvis was American—the similarity had to end somewhere.

Patti Austin has always been a singer of taste and foresight. She has charted with singles produced by Quincy Jones, Narada Michael Walden, and Jimmy Jam and Terry Lewis—all of whom went on to win Producer-of-the-Year Grammies.

DATE	POS	WKS	ARTIST—RECORD TITLE	LABEL & NO.
			BAY CITY ROLLERS	
			Formed in 1967 in Edinburgh, Scotland as the Saxons. Original members: brothers Alan & Derek Longmuir, Les McKeoun (lead singer), Eric Faulkner and Stuart "Woody" Wood.	
11/08/75†	**1**(1)	12	● 1. **Saturday Night**	Arista 0149
2/14/76	**9**	11	2. **Money Honey**	Arista 0170
5/22/76	**28**	4	3. Rock And Roll Love Letter	Arista 0185
9/18/76	**12**	12	4. I Only Want To Be With You	Arista 0205
6/25/77	**10**	12	5. **You Made Me Believe In Magic**	Arista 0256
11/19/77†	**24**	9	6. The Way I Feel Tonight	Arista 0272
			BAZUKA	
			Instrumental studio group assembled by soul producer Tony Camillo.	
6/07/75	**10**	11	1. **Dynomite - Part I** **[I]**	A&M 1666
			B. BUMBLE & THE STINGERS	
			Los Angeles session musicians: Ernie Freeman (piano), Plas Johnson, Rene Hall, Earl Palmer and Al Hassan.	
4/24/61	**21**	5	1. Bumble Boogie [I] adaptation of Rimsky-Korsakov's "Flight Of The Bumble Bee"	Rendezvous 140
3/31/62	**23**	7	2. Nut Rocker [I] adapted from Tchaikovsky's "The Nutcracker"	Rendezvous 166
			THE BEACH BOYS	
			Group formed in Hawthorne, California in 1961. Consisted of brothers Brian (keyboards, bass), Carl (guitar), and Dennis Wilson (drums); their cousin Mike Love (lead vocals, saxophone), and Al Jardine (guitar). Known in high school as Kenny & The Cadets, Carl & The Passions, then The Pendletones. First recorded for X/Candix in 1961. Jardine was replaced by David Marks from March, 1962 to March, 1963. Brian replaced by Bruce Johnston for personal appearances since April, 1965. Dennis Wilson drowned on 12/28/83 (39). Brian active again in 1987. Group was inducted into the Rock And Roll Hall Of Fame in 1988. Also see Fat Boys.	
9/15/62	**14**	10	1. Surfin' Safari	Capitol 4777
4/13/63	**3**	13	2. **Surfin' U.S.A./**	
5/25/63	**23**	8	3. Shut Down	Capitol 4932
8/17/63	**7**	11	4. **Surfer Girl/**	
9/07/63	**15**	7	5. Little Deuce Coupe	Capitol 5009
11/23/63	**6**	8	6. **Be True To Your School/** featuring cheerleading by The Honeys, and the march "On Wisconsin"	
11/30/63	**23**	6	7. In My Room	Capitol 5069
2/22/64	**5**	9	8. **Fun, Fun, Fun**	Capitol 5118
6/06/64	**1**(2)	13	● 9. **I Get Around/**	
6/27/64	**24**	6	10. Don't Worry Baby	Capitol 5174
9/19/64	**9**	8	11. **When I Grow Up (To Be A Man)**	Capitol 5245
11/21/64	**8**	8	12. **Dance, Dance, Dance**	Capitol 5306
3/13/65	**12**	7	13. Do You Wanna Dance?	Capitol 5372
5/01/65	**1**(2)	11	14. **Help Me, Rhonda**	Capitol 5395
8/07/65	**3**	9	15. **California Girls**	Capitol 5464
12/11/65†	**20**	5	16. The Little Girl I Once Knew	Capitol 5540
1/15/66	**2**(2)	9	17. **Barbara Ann** lead vocal: Dean Torrence (of Jan & Dean)	Capitol 5561

DATE	POS	WKS	ARTIST—RECORD TITLE	LABEL & NO.
4/09/66	3	10	18. **Sloop John B**	Capitol 5602
			originally a folk song originating from the West Indies in 1927	
8/20/66	8	7	19. **Wouldn't It Be Nice/**	
9/17/66	39	2	20. God Only Knows	Capitol 5706
10/29/66	1(1)	12	● 21. **Good Vibrations**	Capitol 5676
8/12/67	12	5	22. Heroes And Villains	Brother 1001
11/18/67	31	4	23. Wild Honey	Capitol 2028
1/13/68	19	6	24. Darlin'	Capitol 2068
8/17/68	20	7	25. Do It Again	Capitol 2239
4/05/69	24	6	26. I Can Hear Music	Capitol 2432
9/28/74	36	1	27. Surfin' U.S.A. [R]	Capitol 3924
			song now legally credited as Chuck Berry's "Sweet Little Sixteen"	
6/19/76	5	13	28. **Rock And Roll Music**	Brother 1354
9/18/76	29	4	29. It's O.K.	Brother 1368
6/09/79	40	1	30. Good Timin'	Caribou 9029
8/15/81	12	11	31. The Beach Boys Medley	Capitol 5030
			Good Vibrations/Help Me Rhonda/I Get Around/Shut Down/Surfin' Safari/Barbara Ann/Surfin' USA/Fun, Fun, Fun	
12/19/81†	18	8	32. Come Go With Me	Caribou 02633
6/08/85	26	7	33. Getcha Back	Caribou 04913
9/24/88	1(1)	15	▲ 34. **Kokomo**	Elektra 69385
			from the film "Cocktail"	
			BEASTIE BOYS	
			New York white rap trio formed in 1981, consisting of King Ad-Rock (Adam Horovitz - son of playwright Israel Horovitz), MCA (Adam Yauch) and Mike D (Michael Diamond).	
1/24/87	7	10	1. **(You Gotta) Fight For Your Right (To Party!)**	Def Jam 06595
			THE BEATLES	
			The world's #1 rock group was formed in Liverpool, England in the late 1950s. Known in early forms as the Quarrymen, Johnny & the Moondogs, The Rainbows, and the Silver Beatles. Named The Beatles in 1960. Originally consisted of John Lennon, Paul McCartney, George Harrison (guitars), Stu Sutcliffe (bass) and Pete Best (drums). Sutcliffe left in April, 1961 (died on 4/10/62); McCartney moved to bass. Best replaced by Ringo Starr in August, 1962. Group managed by Brian Epstein (died on 8/27/67) and produced by George Martin. First US tour in February, 1964. Won the 1964 Best New Artist Grammy Award. Own Apple label in 1968. Disbanded on 4/17/70. Inducted into the Rock And Roll Hall Of Fame in 1988.	
1/25/64	1(7)	14	● 1. **I Want To Hold Your Hand/**	
1/25/64	14	8	2. I Saw Her Standing There	Capitol 5112
2/01/64	1(2)	14	3. **She Loves You**	Swan 4152
2/22/64	3	10	4. **Please Please Me**	Vee-Jay 581
3/07/64	26	2	5. My Bonnie	MGM 13213
			THE BEATLES with TONY SHERIDAN	
3/21/64	2(4)	9	6. **Twist And Shout**	Tollie 9001
3/28/64	1(5)	9	● 7. **Can't Buy Me Love**	Capitol 5150
4/11/64	2(1)	9	8. **Do You Want To Know A Secret/**	
4/25/64	35	3	9. Thank You Girl	Vee-Jay 587

DATE	POS	WKS	ARTIST—RECORD TITLE	LABEL & NO.
5/02/64	**1**(1)	11	10. **Love Me Do/**	
5/16/64	**10**	7	11. P.S. I Love You	Tollie 9008
7/18/64	**1**(2)	12	● 12. **A Hard Day's Night**	Capitol 5222
8/01/64	**19**	7	13. Ain't She Sweet	Atco 6308
8/08/64	**12**	7	14. And I Love Her	Capitol 5235
8/15/64	**25**	5	15. I'll Cry Instead	Capitol 5234
			12, 14 & 15: from the film "A Hard Day's Night"	
9/19/64	**17**	5	16. Matchbox/	
9/26/64	**25**	4	17. Slow Down	Capitol 5255
12/05/64	**1**(3)	11	● 18. **I Feel Fine/**	
12/12/64	**4**	8	19. She's A Woman	Capitol 5327
2/27/65	**1**(2)	9	● 20. **Eight Days A Week/**	
3/20/65	**39**	1	21. I Don't Want To Spoil The Party	Capitol 5371
5/01/65	**1**(1)	9	22. **Ticket To Ride**	Capitol 5407
8/14/65	**1**(3)	12	● 23. **Help!**	Capitol 5476
			above 2: from film "Help" (originally "Eight Arms To Hold You")	
10/02/65	**1**(4)	9	● 24. **Yesterday**	Capitol 5498
			more than 2500 recorded versions of this song; the first 5 million performance song (25,000 hours of US radio and TV play)	
12/18/65†	**1**(3)	11	● 25. **We Can Work It Out/**	
12/25/65†	**5**	8	26. Day Tripper	Capitol 5555
3/05/66	**3**	9	● 27. **Nowhere Man**	Capitol 5587
6/11/66	**1**(2)	10	● 28. **Paperback Writer/**	
6/25/66	**23**	5	29. Rain	Capitol 5651
8/27/66	**2**(1)	8	● 30. **Yellow Submarine/**	
			title song from the Beatles' animated film	
9/10/66	**11**	6	31. Eleanor Rigby	Capitol 5715
3/04/67	**1**(1)	9	● 32. **Penny Lane/**	
3/11/67	**8**	7	33. Strawberry Fields Forever	Capitol 5810
7/29/67	**1**(1)	9	● 34. **All You Need Is Love/**	
8/12/67	**34**	2	35. Baby You're A Rich Man	Capitol 5964
12/09/67	**1**(3)	10	● 36. **Hello Goodbye**	Capitol 2056
3/23/68	**4**	10	● 37. **Lady Madonna**	Capitol 2138
9/14/68	**1**(9)	19	● 38. **Hey Jude/**	
9/14/68	**12**	11	39. Revolution	Apple 2276
5/10/69	**1**(5)	12	● 40. **Get Back/**	
5/10/69	**35**	3	41. Don't Let Me Down	Apple 2490
			above 2: with Billy Preston, organ	
6/21/69	**8**	8	● 42. **The Ballad Of John And Yoko**	Apple 2531
10/18/69	**1**(1)	16	● 43. **Come Together/**	
10/18/69	**3**	16	● 44. Something	Apple 2654
3/21/70	**1**(2)	13	● 45. **Let It Be**	Apple 2764
5/23/70	**1**(2)	10	46. **The Long And Winding Road**	Apple 2832
			above 2: from the film "Let It Be"	
6/19/76	**7**	11	47. **Got To Get You Into My Life**	Capitol 4274
			from the 1966 album "Revolver"	

DATE	POS	WKS	ARTIST—RECORD TITLE	LABEL & NO.
4/10/82	**12**	8	48. The Beatles' Movie Medley Magical Mystery Tour/All You Need Is Love/You've Got To Hide Your Love Away/I Should Have Known Better/A Hard Day's Night/Ticket To Ride/Get Back	Capitol 5107
8/30/86	**23**	7	49. Twist And Shout [R] revived through inclusion in films "Ferris Bueller's Day Off" and "Back To School"	Capitol 5624
			THE BEAU BRUMMELS	
			Formed in 1964 in San Francisco. Led by Sal Valentino (vocals) and Ron Elliott (guitar).	
1/30/65	**15**	8	1. Laugh, Laugh	Autumn 8
5/08/65	**8**	9	2. **Just A Little**	Autumn 10
8/28/65	**38**	1	3. You Tell Me Why	Autumn 16
			JEFF BECK - see DONOVAN	
			BOB BECKHAM	
			Stratford, Oklahoma pop-country singer. Moved to Nashville in 1959.	
10/12/59	**32**	10	1. Just As Much As Ever	Decca 30861
2/29/60	**36**	1	2. Crazy Arms	Decca 31029
			BEE GEES	
			Trio of brothers from Manchester, England: Barry (b: 9/1/47) and twins Robin and Maurice Gibb (b: 12/22/49). First performed December, 1955. To Australia in 1958, performed as the Gibbs, later as BG's, finally the Bee Gees. First recorded for Leedon/Festival in 1963. Returned to England in February, 1967, with guitarist Vince Melouney and drummer Colin Peterson. Toured Europe and USA in 1968. Melouney left in December, 1968, Robin left for solo career in 1969. When Peterson left in August of 1969, Barry and Maurice went solo. After 8 months, brothers reunited. Composed soundtracks of "Saturday Night Fever" and "Staying Alive"; in film "Sgt. Pepper's Lonely Hearts Club Band." Group was named for Barry Gibb, Bill Goode (a friend), and Bill Gates (a DJ).	
6/10/67	**14**	5	1. New York Mining Disaster 1941 (Have You Seen My Wife, Mr. Jones)	Atco 6487
7/29/67	**17**	7	2. To Love Somebody	Atco 6503
10/21/67	**16**	5	3. Holiday	Atco 6521
11/25/67	**11**	6	4. (The Lights Went Out In) Massachusetts	Atco 6532
2/10/68	**15**	8	5. Words	Atco 6548
9/07/68	**8**	10	6. **I've Gotta Get A Message To You**	Atco 6603
1/04/69	**6**	9	7. **I Started A Joke**	Atco 6639
4/12/69	**37**	3	8. First Of May	Atco 6657
12/26/70†	**3**	10	● 9. **Lonely Days**	Atco 6795
7/03/71	**1**(4)	14	● 10. **How Can You Mend A Broken Heart**	Atco 6824
2/05/72	**16**	7	11. My World	Atco 6871
8/26/72	**16**	7	12. Run To Me	Atco 6896
12/02/72	**34**	4	13. Alive	Atco 6909
6/28/75	**1**(2)	12	● 14. **Jive Talkin'**	RSO 510
10/18/75	**7**	13	15. **Nights On Broadway**	RSO 515
1/17/76	**12**	12	16. Fanny (Be Tender With My Love)	RSO 519
7/17/76	**1**(1)	12	● 17. **You Should Be Dancing**	RSO 853
10/02/76	**3**	16	● 18. **Love So Right**	RSO 859
1/29/77	**12**	9	19. Boogie Child	RSO 867

DATE	POS	WKS	ARTIST—RECORD TITLE	LABEL & NO.
8/13/77	**26**	5	20. Edge Of The Universe	RSO 880
10/08/77	1(3)	26	● 21. **How Deep Is Your Love**	RSO 882
12/24/77†	1(4)	22	▲ 22. **Stayin' Alive**	RSO 885
2/11/78	1(8)	18	▲ 23. **Night Fever** above 3: from the film "Saturday Night Fever"	RSO 889
11/18/78†	1(2)	17	▲ 24. **Too Much Heaven**	RSO 913
2/10/79	1(2)	13	▲ 25. **Tragedy**	RSO 918
4/21/79	1(1)	13	● 26. **Love You Inside Out**	RSO 925
10/10/81	**30**	4	27. He's A Liar	RSO 1066
5/28/83	**24**	6	28. The Woman In You from the film "Staying Alive"	RSO 813173
			THE BEGINNING OF THE END	
			Bahamas quartet consisting of brothers Raphael "Ray" (organ), Liroy "Roy" (guitar), Frank "Bud" Munnings (drums) and Fred Henfield (bass).	
6/05/71	**15**	10	1. Funky Nassau-Part I	Alston 4595
			HARRY BELAFONTE	
			Born Harold George Belafonte, Jr. on 3/1/27 in Harlem. Actor in American Negro Theater, Drama Workshop, mid-40s. Started career as a "straight pop" singer. Recorded for Jubilee Records in 1949, shortly afterward began specializing in folk music. Rode the crest of the calypso craze to worldwide stardom. Starred in 8 films from 1953-74. Replaced Danny Kaye in 1987 as UNICEF goodwill ambassador.	
11/24/56†	**14**	16	1. Jamaica Farewell Jockey #14 / Best Seller #17 / Top 100 #17 / Juke Box #17	RCA 6663
12/29/56	**12**	3	2. Mary's Boy Child [X] Best Seller #12 / Jockey #12 / Top 100 #15	RCA 6735
1/12/57	**5**	17	3. **Banana Boat (Day-O)** Best Seller #5 / Top 100 #5 / Jockey #5 / Juke Box #5	RCA 6771
3/23/57	**11**	10	4. Mama Look At Bubu Best Seller #11 / Top 100 #13 / Jockey #14 / Juke Box #18	RCA 6830
7/08/57	**25**	3	5. Cocoanut Woman/ Best Seller #25 / Top 100 #48	
7/08/57	**30**	3	6. Island In The Sun Best Seller #30 / Top 100 #42 from the film (starring Belafonte) of the same title	RCA 6885
			BELL & JAMES	
			Duo of Leroy Bell and Casey James. Began as songwriting team for Bell's uncle, producer Thom Bell.	
3/10/79	**15**	8	● 1. Livin' It Up (Friday Night)	A&M 2069
			THE BELL NOTES	
			Quintet from Long Island, New York: Carl Bonura (sax), Ray Ceroni (guitar), Lenny Giamblavo (bass), Peter Kane (piano) and John Casey (drums).	
2/09/59	**6**	11	1. **I've Had It**	Time 1004
			ARCHIE BELL & THE DRELLS	
			Archie was born on 9/1/44 in Henderson, Texas. Lead singer of the Drells, R&B vocal group from Leo Smith Junior High School in Houston. First recorded for Ovid in 1967. Recorded "Tighten Up" with group consisting of Bell, Huey "Billy" Butler, Joe Cross and James Wise. Bell was in US Army at time of hit. Later recordings consisted of Bell, Wise, Lee Bell and Willie Parnell. Still active in seaboard "beach music" scene.	
4/13/68	1(2)	13	● 1. **Tighten Up**	Atlantic 2478

DATE	POS	WKS	ARTIST—RECORD TITLE	LABEL & NO.
8/03/68	**9**	8	2. **I Can't Stop Dancing**	Atlantic 2534
1/04/69	**21**	8	3. There's Gonna Be A Showdown	Atlantic 2583
			BENNY BELL	
			Jewish risque songwriter from New York City.	
4/19/75	**30**	4	1. Shaving Cream [N] vocal: Paul Wynn; originally released in 1946	Vanguard 35183
			MADELINE BELL	
			In cast of "Black Nativity," toured England in the mid-60s; remained there. Formed group Blue Mink, 1969-73; commercial jingle singer since then.	
3/09/68	**26**	5	1. I'm Gonna Make You Love Me	Philips 40517
			VINCENT BELL	
			Veteran studio guitarist. Leader of the Ramrods. Also see Ferrante & Teicher.	
4/25/70	**31**	5	1. Airport Love Theme [I] from the film "Airport"	Decca 32659
			WILLIAM BELL	
			Born William Yarborough on 7/16/39 in Memphis. R&B singer.	
3/12/77	**10**	9	● 1. **Tryin' To Love Two**	Mercury 73839
			THE BELLAMY BROTHERS	
			Country duo from Darby, Florida: brothers Howard (b: 2/2/46; guitar) and David Bellamy (b: 9/16/50; guitar, keyboards). Made their professional debut in 1958. David wrote "Spiders And Snakes" hit for Jim Stafford. Moved to Los Angeles in 1973.	
3/06/76	**1**(1)	12	1. **Let Your Love Flow**	Warner 8169
7/14/79	**39**	2	2. If I Said You Have A Beautiful Body Would You Hold It Against Me	Warner 8790
			THE BELLS	
			Canadian quintet; lead singers Jacki Ralph and Cliff Edwards.	
3/27/71	**7**	11	● 1. **Stay Awhile**	Polydor 15023
			TONY BELLUS	
			Born on 4/17/36 in Chicago. Pop singer/accordionist.	
6/29/59	**25**	11	1. Robbin' The Cradle	NRC 023
			THE BELMONTS	
			Angelo D'Aleo, Fred Milano and Carlo Mastrangelo. Sang with Dion from 1957-60. Named after Belmont Avenue in New York.	
6/19/61	**18**	6	1. Tell Me Why	Sabrina 500
8/25/62	**28**	8	2. Come On Little Angel	Sabina 505
			JESSE BELVIN	
			Born Jessie Lorenzo Belvin on 12/15/32 in San Antonio, Texas. Jesse and his wife were killed in an auto accident on 2/6/60. Recorded with Marvin Phillips as "Jesse & Marvin." A pivotal figure in the development of the R&B sound on the West Coast. Also see The Shields.	
4/13/59	**31**	9	1. Guess Who written by Jesse's wife, Jo Anne Belvin	RCA 7469

DATE	POS	WKS	ARTIST—RECORD TITLE	LABEL & NO.
			PAT BENATAR	
			Born Patricia Andrzejewski, in Lindenhurst, Long Island, New York, in 1952. Married her producer/guitarist, Neil Geraldo, in 1982. In 1989, acted in an "ABC Afterschool Special."	
2/09/80	**23**	10	1. Heartbreaker	Chrysalis 2395
5/17/80	**27**	6	2. We Live For Love	Chrysalis 2419
10/18/80	**9**	15	● 3. **Hit Me With Your Best Shot**	Chrysalis 2464
1/31/81	**18**	10	4. Treat Me Right	Chrysalis 2487
8/01/81	**17**	9	5. Fire And Ice	Chrysalis 2529
10/31/81	**38**	2	6. Promises In The Dark	Chrysalis 2555
11/06/82	**13**	10	7. Shadows Of The Night	Chrysalis 2647
3/05/83	**20**	7	8. Little Too Late	Chrysalis 03536
5/21/83	**39**	3	9. Looking For A Stranger	Chrysalis 42688
10/15/83	**5**	14	● 10. **Love Is A Battlefield**	Chrysalis 42732
11/03/84†	**5**	14	11. **We Belong**	Chrysalis 42826
2/09/85	**36**	3	12. Ooh Ooh Song	Chrysalis 42843
7/27/85	**10**	11	13. **Invincible** theme from the film "Legend of Billie Jean"	Chrysalis 42877
12/14/85†	**28**	7	14. Sex As A Weapon	Chrysalis 42927
7/30/88	**19**	8	15. All Fired Up	Chrysalis 43268
			BOYD BENNETT & His Rockets	
			Born in Muscle Shoals, Alabama on 12/7/24. Attended high school in Tennessee and formed first band there. Later became a disc jockey in Kentucky.	
7/09/55	**5**	17	1. **Seventeen** Best Seller #5 / Juke Box #8 / Jockey #9 / Top 100 #28 pre	King 1470
11/12/55	**39**	1	2. My Boy - Flat Top above 2: vocals by Big Moe	King 1494
			JOE BENNETT & THE SPARKLETONES	
			Teenage band from Spartanburg, South Carolina. Consisted of Joe Bennett (vocals, guitar), Howard Childress (guitar), Wayne Arthur (bass) and Irving Denton (drums).	
9/23/57	**17**	9	1. Black Slacks Top 100 #17 / Best Seller #18 / Jockey #21	ABC-Para. 9837
			TONY BENNETT	
			Born Anthony Dominick Benedetto on 8/13/26 in Queens, New York. Jazz/ballad vocalist. Worked local clubs while in high school, sang in US Army bands. Audition record of "Boulevard Of Broken Dreams" earned a Columbia contract in 1950.	
5/05/56	**16**	11	1. Can You Find It In Your Heart Best Seller #16 / Juke Box #18 / Top 100 #19 / Jockey #20	Columbia 40667
8/18/56	**11**	7	2. From The Candy Store On The Corner To The Chapel On The Hill/ female vocal: Lois Winter Jockey #11 / Top 100 #33	
10/06/56	**38**	2	3. Happiness Street (Corner Sunshine Square)	Columbia 40726
11/17/56	**18**	4	4. The Autumn Waltz Jockey #18 / Top 100 #41	Columbia 40770
8/12/57	**9**	14	5. **In The Middle Of An Island** Best Seller #9 / Top 100 #9 / Jockey #13	Columbia 40965

DATE	POS	WKS	ARTIST—RECORD TITLE	LABEL & NO.
11/18/57	**22**	1	6. Ca, C'est L'amour Jockey #22 / Top 100 #96 from the film "Les Girls"	Columbia 41032
6/30/58	**23**	1	7. Young And Warm And Wonderful Jockey #23 / Best Seller #42 / Top 100 #57	Columbia 41172
9/22/58	**20**	8	8. Firefly Hot 100 #20 / Best Seller #45 end	Columbia 41237
9/29/62	**19**	10	9. I Left My Heart In San Francisco	Columbia 42332
2/16/63	**14**	10	10. I Wanna Be Around	Columbia 42634
6/01/63	**18**	6	11. The Good Life	Columbia 42779
10/31/64	**33**	6	12. Who Can I Turn To (When Nobody Needs Me) from the musical "The Roar Of The Greasepaint"	Columbia 43141
3/20/65	**34**	4	13. If I Ruled The World from the musical "Pickwick"	Columbia 43220
			GEORGE BENSON	
			Born on 3/22/43 in Pittsburgh. R&B-jazz guitarist. Played guitar from age 8. Played in Brother Jack McDuff's trio in 1963. House musician at CTI Records to early 70s. Influenced heavily by Wes Montgomery.	
7/17/76	**10**	11	1. **This Masquerade**	Warner 8209
9/03/77	**24**	7	2. The Greatest Love Of All from the film "The Greatest"; #1 hit for Whitney Houston in 1986	Arista 0251
4/22/78	**7**	10	3. **On Broadway**	Warner 8542
3/24/79	**18**	8	4. Love Ballad	Warner 8759
8/02/80	**4**	14	5. **Give Me The Night**	Warner 49505
11/21/81†	**5**	16	6. **Turn Your Love Around**	Warner 49846
8/27/83	**30**	6	7. Lady Love Me (One More Time)	Warner 29563
			BROOK BENTON	
			Born Benjamin Franklin Peay on 9/19/31 in Camden, South Carolina. R&B singer/ songwriter. In the Camden Jubilee Singers. To New York in 1948, joined Bill Langford's Langfordaires. With Jerusalem Stars in 1951. First recorded under own name for Okeh in 1953. Wrote "Looking Back," "A Lover's Question," "The Stroll," "It's Just A Matter Of Time," "Endlessly," "Thank You Baby," and many other hits. Died on 4/9/88 (56) of complications from spinal meningitis.	
2/09/59	**3**	14	1. **It's Just A Matter Of Time**	Mercury 71394
5/04/59	**12**	9	2. Endlessly/	
6/08/59	**38**	1	3. So Close	Mercury 71443
8/03/59	**16**	9	4. Thank You Pretty Baby	Mercury 71478
10/26/59	**6**	13	5. **So Many Ways**	Mercury 71512
2/08/60	**5**	12	6. **Baby (You've Got What It Takes)** **DINAH WASHINGTON & BROOK BENTON**	Mercury 71565
5/09/60	**37**	1	7. The Ties That Bind	Mercury 71566
6/06/60	**7**	10	8. **A Rockin' Good Way (To Mess Around And Fall In Love)** **DINAH WASHINGTON & BROOK BENTON**	Mercury 71629
8/22/60	**7**	13	9. **Kiddio/**	
8/29/60	**16**	10	10. The Same One	Mercury 71652
11/21/60	**24**	7	11. Fools Rush In	Mercury 71722
2/27/61	**11**	9	12. Think Twice/	
3/20/61	**28**	1	13. For My Baby	Mercury 71774

DATE	POS	WKS	ARTIST—RECORD TITLE	LABEL & NO.
6/05/61	**2**(3)	12	14. **The Boll Weevil Song** [N]	Mercury 71820
9/04/61	**20**	4	15. Frankie And Johnny	Mercury 71859
12/18/61†	**15**	5	16. Revenge	Mercury 71903
1/27/62	**19**	5	17. Shadrack written in 1931 as "Shadrack Meshack, Abednigo"	Mercury 71912
9/15/62	**13**	6	18. Lie To Me	Mercury 72024
12/08/62†	**3**	10	19. **Hotel Happiness**	Mercury 72055
4/06/63	**28**	4	20. I Got What I Wanted	Mercury 72099
7/13/63	**22**	4	21. My True Confession	Mercury 72135
10/05/63	**32**	5	22. Two Tickets To Paradise	Mercury 72177
2/15/64	**35**	3	23. Going Going Gone	Mercury 72230
1/31/70	**4**	12	• 24. **Rainy Night In Georgia**	Cotillion 44057
			BERLIN	
			Los Angeles electro-pop trio: Terri Nunn (vocals), John Crawford (bass) & Rob Brill (drums). Group went from a 6-piece band to a trio in 1985. Nunn left in 1987.	
4/07/84	**23**	8	1. No More Words	Geffen 29360
7/19/86	**1**(1)	13	2. **Take My Breath Away** love theme from the film "Top Gun"	Columbia 05903
			ROD BERNARD	
			Born on 8/12/40 in Opelousas, Louisiana. R&B singer/guitarist. On local radio since age 10. DJ for KSLO in 1957. First recorded for Carl in 1957.	
3/23/59	**20**	9	1. This Should Go On Forever	Argo 5327
			ELMER BERNSTEIN	
			Born on 4/4/22 in New York City. Composer/conductor for over 60 movie soundtracks.	
4/07/56	**16**	9	1. Main Title From "The Man With The Golden Arm" [I] Best Seller #16 / Top 100 #32 from the movie of the same title; featuring Shelly Manne, drums	Decca 29869
			CHUCK BERRY	
			Born Charles Edward Anderson Berry on 10/18/26 in San Jose, California. Grew up in St. Louis. Muddy Waters introduced Chuck to Leonard Chess (Chess Records) in Chicago. First recording, "Maybellene," was an instant success. Appeared in the film "Rock, Rock, Rock" in 1956, and several others. Inducted into the Rock And Roll Hall of Fame in 1986. Film documentary/concert tribute to Chuck, "Hail! Hail! Rock 'N' Roll," released in 1987. Regarded by many as rock's most influential artist.	
8/20/55	**5**	11	1. **Maybellene** Best Seller #5 / Juke Box #6 / Jockey #13 / Top 100 #42 pre	Chess 1604
6/30/56	**29**	1	2. Roll Over Beethoven	Chess 1626
4/20/57	**3**	15	3. **School Day** Best Seller #3 / Top 100 #5 / Jockey #6 / Juke Box #7	Chess 1653
11/11/57	**8**	13	4. **Rock & Roll Music** Top 100 #8 / Best Seller #9	Chess 1671
2/24/58	**2**(3)	11	5. **Sweet Little Sixteen** Best Seller #2 / Top 100 #2 / Jockey #5	Chess 1683
5/05/58	**8**	11	6. **Johnny B. Goode** Top 100 #8 / Best Seller #9 / Jockey #16	Chess 1691
9/15/58	**18**	5	7. Carol Hot 100 #18 / Best Seller #29	Chess 1700

DATE	POS	WKS	ARTIST—RECORD TITLE	LABEL & NO.
4/20/59	**32**	7	8. Almost Grown	Chess 1722
7/13/59	**37**	1	9. Back In The U.S.A.	Chess 1729
4/04/64	**23**	5	10. Nadine (Is It You?)	Chess 1883
6/13/64	**10**	7	11. **No Particular Place To Go**	Chess 1898
8/22/64	**14**	5	12. You Never Can Tell	Chess 1906
9/09/72	**1**(2)	12	● 13. **My Ding-A-Ling** **[N]**	Chess 2131
1/06/73	**27**	7	14. Reelin' & Rockin'	Chess 2136
			above 2: recorded live in Manchester, England; "Reelin'" was originally the flip side of "Sweet Little Sixteen"	
			BIG BOPPER	
			Born Jiles Perry Richardson on 10/24/30 in Sabine Pass, Texas. Disc jockey at KTRM in Beaumont, Texas. Wrote "Running Bear" for Johnny Preston. Died with Buddy Holly and Ritchie Valens in a plane crash in Iowa on 2/3/59 at the age of 28.	
8/04/58	**6**	22	1. **Chantilly Lace** **[N]**	Mercury 71343
			Hot 100 #6 / Best Seller #13 end	
12/22/58	**38**	1	2. Big Bopper's Wedding [N]	Mercury 71375
			BIG BROTHER & THE HOLDING COMPANY	
			Formed in San Francisco in 1965. Janis Joplin joined as lead singer in 1966. Sensation at the Monterey Pop Festival in 1967. Disbanded in 1972.	
9/28/68	**12**	8	1. Piece Of My Heart	Columbia 44626
			BIG COUNTRY	
			Rock quartet formed in Dunfermline, Scotland: Stuart Adamson (vocals, guitar), Bruce Watson (guitar), Tony Butler (bass) and Mark Brzezicki (drums).	
11/12/83	**17**	9	1. In A Big Country	Mercury 814467
			MR. ACKER BILK	
			Clarinetist/composer, born Bernard Stanley Bilk on 1/28/29 in Somerset, England.	
4/07/62	**1**(1)	15	● 1. **Stranger On The Shore** **[I]**	Atco 6217
			from the film "The Wonderful World Of The Brothers Grimm"	
			BILLY & LILLIE	
			Vocal duo of Billy Ford (b: 3/9/25, Bloomfield, New Jersey) and Lillie Bryant (b: 2/14/40, Newburg, New York). Backing group: Billy Ford & The Thunderbirds.	
1/13/58	**9**	10	1. **La Dee Dah**	Swan 4002
			Top 100 #9 / Best Seller #10 / Jockey #23	
1/05/59	**14**	8	2. Lucky Ladybug	Swan 4020
			BILLY & THE BEATERS - see BILLY VERA	
			BILLY JOE & THE CHECKMATES	
			Billy Joe Hunter.	
2/17/62	**10**	7	1. **Percolator (Twist)** **[I]**	Dore 620
			ELVIN BISHOP	
			Born on 10/21/42 in Tulsa, Oklahoma. Lead guitarist with Paul Butterfield's Blues Band (1965-68).	
4/03/76	**3**	12	● 1. **Fooled Around And Fell In Love**	Capricorn 0252
			lead vocal: Mickey Thomas (of Jefferson Starship)	

DATE	POS	WKS	ARTIST—RECORD TITLE		LABEL & NO.
			STEPHEN BISHOP		
			Pop-rock singer/songwriter from San Diego.		
1/22/77	**22**	7	1. Save It For A Rainy Day guitar solo: Eric Clapton; background vocals: Chaka Khan		ABC 12232
7/23/77	**11**	15	2. On And On		ABC 12260
10/28/78	**32**	5	3. Everybody Needs Love		ABC 12406
4/02/83	**25**	8	4. It Might Be You theme from the film "Tootsie"		Warner 29791
			THE BLACKBYRDS		
			Soul group founded in 1973 by jazz studies professor Donald Byrd while teaching at Howard University in Washington, DC.		
3/15/75	**6**	12	1. **Walking In Rhythm**		Fantasy 736
4/17/76	**19**	6	2. Happy Music		Fantasy 762
			BLACKFOOT		
8/04/79	**26**	6	1. Highway Song		Atco 7104
12/22/79	**38**	4	2. Train, Train		Atco 7207
			BLACK OAK ARKANSAS		
			Southern rock sextet led by Jim "Dandy" Mangrum.		
1/26/74	**25**	6	1. Jim Dandy female singer: Ruby Starr		Atco 6948
			BILL BLACK'S COMBO		
			Bill was born on 9/17/26 in Memphis; died of a brain tumor on 10/21/65. Bass guitarist. Session work in Memphis; backed Elvis Presley (with Scotty Moore, guitar; D.J. Fontana, drums) on most of his early records. Formed own band in 1959.		
12/21/59†	**17**	8	1. Smokie - Part 2	[I]	Hi 2018
3/21/60	**9**	11	2. **White Silver Sands**	**[I]**	Hi 2021
7/04/60	**18**	8	3. Josephine	[I]	Hi 2022
10/03/60	**11**	9	4. Don't Be Cruel Bill played bass on Elvis Presley's original hit	[I]	Hi 2026
12/12/60	**16**	7	5. Blue Tango	[I]	Hi 2027
3/06/61	**20**	4	6. Hearts Of Stone	[I]	Hi 2028
6/26/61	**25**	4	7. Ole Buttermilk Sky	[I]	Hi 2036
1/20/62	**26**	4	8. Twist-Her	[I]	Hi 2042
			CILLA BLACK		
			Born Priscilla White on 5/27/43 in Liverpool, England.		
7/25/64	**26**	4	1. You're My World		Capitol 5196
			JEANNE BLACK		
			Born on 10/25/37 in Mount Baldy, California. Appearances on local TV show, "Hometown Jamboree." Discovered by Cliffie Stone.		
5/02/60	**4**	10	1. **He'll Have To Stay** answer song to Jim Reeves' "He'll Have To Go"		Capitol 4368
			JACK BLANCHARD & MISTY MORGAN		
			Husband-and-wife country duo, both born in Buffalo. Jack, born on 5/8/42, plays saxophone and keyboards; Misty, born on 5/23/45, plays keyboards. Met and married while working in Florida.		
3/28/70	**23**	8	1. Tennessee Bird Walk	[N]	Wayside 010

DATE	POS	WKS	ARTIST—RECORD TITLE	LABEL & NO.
			BILLY BLAND	
			Born on 4/5/32 in Wilmington, North Carolina. R&B singer; formed group, the Four Bees, in 1954. First recorded solo for Old Town in 1955.	
3/28/60	**7**	13	1. **Let The Little Girl Dance**	Old Town 1076
			BOBBY BLAND	
			Born Robert Calvin Bland on 1/27/30 in Rosemark, Tennesse. Nicknamed "Blue." Sang in gospel group The Miniatures in Memphis, late 40s. Member of the Beale Streeters which included Johnny Ace, B.B. King, Rosco Gordon, Earl Forest and Willie Nix in 1949. Driver and valet for B.B. King; appeared in the Johnny Ace Revue, early 50s. First recorded in 1952, for the Modern label. Frequent tours with B.B. King into the 80s.	
1/20/62	**28**	3	1. Turn On Your Love Light	Duke 344
2/02/63	**22**	7	2. Call On Me/	
2/09/63	**33**	5	3. That's The Way Love Is	Duke 360
3/28/64	**20**	6	4. Ain't Nothing You Can Do	Duke 375
			MARCIE BLANE	
			Born on 5/21/44 in Brooklyn, New York.	
11/10/62	**3**	13	1. **Bobby's Girl**	Seville 120
			ARCHIE BLEYER	
			Born on 6/12/09 in Corona, New York; died on 3/20/89. Arranger/music director for Arthur Godfrey's TV show; founder of Cadence Records.	
12/04/54†	**17**	6	1. The Naughty Lady Of Shady Lane Jockey #17 / Juke Box #20 / Best Seller #26	Cadence 1254
			BLONDIE	
			New York City techno-pop sextet formed in 1975. Consisted of Debbie Harry (lead singer), Chris Stein, Frank Infante, Jimmy Destri, Gary Valentine and Clem Burke. Stein and Harry were married. Harry had been in the folk-rock group Wind In The Willows; did solo work from 1980; in several films. Disbanded in 1983.	
3/17/79	**1**(1)	14	● 1. **Heart Of Glass**	Chrysalis 2295
6/30/79	**24**	7	2. One Way Or Another	Chrysalis 2336
11/03/79	**27**	6	3. Dreaming	Chrysalis 2379
3/08/80	**1**(6)	19	● 4. **Call Me** from the film "American Gigolo"	Chrysalis 2414
6/21/80	**39**	3	5. Atomic	Chrysalis 2410
11/29/80†	**1**(1)	17	● 6. **The Tide Is High**	Chrysalis 2465
2/14/81	**1**(2)	14	● 7. **Rapture**	Chrysalis 2485
6/26/82	**37**	3	8. Island Of Lost Souls all of above: produced by Mike Chapman (except 5: Giorgio Moroder)	Chrysalis 2603
			BLOODROCK	
			Rock group from Fort Worth, Texas; Jim Rutledge, lead vocals.	
2/27/71	**36**	2	1. D.O.A.	Capitol 3009
			BLOODSTONE	
			Soul group from Kansas City, Missouri. Formed as the Sinceres; consisted of Charles McCormick, Willis Draffen, Charles Love, Henry Williams and Roger Durham (d: 1973).	
6/09/73	**10**	12	● 1. **Natural High**	London 1046
4/06/74	**34**	4	2. Outside Woman	London 1052

DATE	POS	WKS	ARTIST—RECORD TITLE	LABEL & NO.
			BLOOD, SWEAT & TEARS	
			Pop-jazz group formed by Al Kooper in 1968. Nucleus consisted of Kooper (keyboards), Steve Katz (guitar), Bobby Colomby (drums) and Jim Fielder (bass). Kooper replaced by lead singer David Clayton-Thomas in 1969. Clayton-Thomas replaced by Jerry Fisher in 1972. Katz left in 1973. Clayton-Thomas rejoined in 1974.	
3/15/69	**2**(3)	11	● 1. **You've Made Me So Very Happy**	Columbia 44776
6/07/69	**2**(3)	12	● 2. **Spinning Wheel**	Columbia 44871
10/25/69	**2**(1)	12	● 3. **And When I Die**	Columbia 45008
8/15/70	**14**	6	4. Hi-De-Ho	Columbia 45204
10/10/70	**29**	6	5. Lucretia Mac Evil	Columbia 45235
8/14/71	**32**	5	6. Go Down Gamblin'	Columbia 45427
			BOBBY BLOOM	
			Singer/songwriter; died from an accidental shooting on 2/28/74.	
10/17/70	**8**	11	1. **Montego Bay**	L&R/MGM 157
			THE BLOW MONKEYS	
			British quartet fronted by Dr. Robert (Robert Howard). Includes: Mick Anker, Neville Henry and Tony Kiley.	
6/14/86	**14**	10	1. Digging Your Scene	RCA 14325
			THE BLUE-BELLES - see PATTI LaBELLE & THE BLUE BELLES	
			BLUE CHEER	
			San Francisco hard-rock group led by Dickie Peterson (vocals, bass).	
3/23/68	**14**	10	1. Summertime Blues	Philips 40516
			BLUE HAZE	
			English.	
12/23/72†	**27**	7	1. Smoke Gets In Your Eyes #1 hit for Paul Whiteman in 1934	A&M 1357
			THE BLUE JAYS	
			R&B group from Los Angeles. Leon Peels, lead singer.	
9/04/61	**31**	4	1. Lover's Island	Milestone 2008
			BLUE MAGIC	
			Soul vocal group from Philadelphia. Consisted of Theodore Mills (lead vocals), Vernon Sawyer, Wendell Sawyer, Keith Beaton and Richard Pratt.	
6/08/74	**8**	15	● 1. **Sideshow**	Atco 6961
11/23/74	**36**	2	2. Three Ring Circus	Atco 7004
			BLUE OYSTER CULT	
			New York hard-rock quintet led by Donald "Buck Dharma" Roeser (lead guitar) and Eric Bloom (lead vocal).	
9/04/76	**12**	14	1. (Don't Fear) The Reaper	Columbia 10384
10/03/81	**40**	3	2. Burnin' For You	Columbia 02415

DATE	POS	WKS	ARTIST—RECORD TITLE	LABEL & NO.
			THE BLUE RIDGE RANGERS - see JOHN FOGERTY	
			BLUE STARS	
			4-man, 4-woman pop-jazz group from Paris, led by former American big band vocalist, Blossom Dearie.	
2/04/56	**16**	7	1. Lullaby Of Birdland [F]	Mercury 70742
			Jockey #16 / Best Seller #20 / Top 100 #20	
			arranged by Michel Legrand; composed by George Shearing	
			BLUE SWEDE	
			Swedish pop sextet; Bjorn Skiffs, lead singer.	
3/02/74	**1**(1)	14	● 1. **Hooked On A Feeling**	EMI 3627
9/07/74	**7**	8	2. **Never My Love**	EMI 3938
			BLUES BROTHERS	
			Jake (John Belushi; b: 1/24/49, Chicago) and Elwood Blues (Dan Aykroyd; b: 7/1/52, Ottawa, Ontario); originally created for TV's "Saturday Night Live." Belushi died of a drug overdose on 3/5/82 (33).	
1/06/79	**14**	9	1. Soul Man	Atlantic 3545
3/31/79	**37**	3	2. Rubber Biscuit [N]	Atlantic 3564
6/21/80	**18**	8	3. Gimme Some Lovin'	Atlantic 3666
			from the soundtrack "The Blues Brothers"	
1/31/81	**39**	2	4. Who's Making Love	Atlantic 3785
			BLUES IMAGE	
			Tampa, Florida rock quintet led by Mike Pinera.	
5/23/70	**4**	12	● 1. **Ride Captain Ride**	Atco 6746
			BLUES MAGOOS	
			Bronx, New York psychedelic rock quintet led by Peppy Castro. Originally known as the Bloos Magoos. Castro later became lead singer of Balance.	
1/07/67	**5**	10	1. **(We Ain't Got) Nothin' Yet**	Mercury 72622
			BOB B. SOXX & THE BLUE JEANS	
			Bobby Sheen with Darlene Love and Fanita James (both formerly with The Blossoms). Love and James later replaced by Gloria Jones and Carolyn Willis.	
12/08/62†	**8**	9	1. **Zip-A-Dee Doo-Dah**	Philles 107
3/23/63	**38**	3	2. Why Do Lovers Break Each Other's Heart?	Philles 110
			THE BOBBETTES	
			Female doo-wop quintet (ages 11-13 in '57) from New York City. Consisted of sisters Emma and Janice Pought, Laura Webb, Helen Gathers and Reather Dixon. Originally called the Harlem Queens.	
8/12/57	**6**	14	1. **Mr. Lee**	Atlantic 1144
			Top 100 #6 / Jockey #6 / Best Seller #7	
			song inspired by group's 5th grade teacher	
			MICHAEL BOLTON	
			From New Haven, Connecticut. Lead singer of Blackjack in the late 70s.	
11/07/87	**19**	10	1. That's What Love Is All About	Columbia 7322
2/13/88	**11**	10	2. (Sittin' On) The Dock Of The Bay	Columbia 07680

DATE	POS	WKS	ARTIST—RECORD TITLE	LABEL & NO.
			BON JOVI	
			New Jersey hard-rock quintet consisting of Jon Bon Jovi (actual spelling: Bongiovi; lead vocals), Richie Sambora (guitar), Dave Bryan (keyboards), Alec John Such (bass) and Tico Torres (drums).	
4/21/84	**39**	1	1. Runaway	Mercury 818309
10/11/86	**1**(1)	14	2. **You Give Love A Bad Name**	Mercury 884953
1/10/87	**1**(4)	13	3. **Livin' On A Prayer**	Mercury 888184
4/25/87	**7**	12	4. **Wanted Dead Or Alive**	Mercury 888467
10/01/88	**1**(2)	12	5. **Bad Medicine**	Mercury 870657
12/17/88†	**3**	13	6. **Born To Be My Baby**	Mercury 872156
			JOHNNY BOND	
			Born Cyrus Whitfield Bond on 6/1/15 in Enville, Oklahoma. Died of a heart attack on 6/12/78 (63). Country singer/actor; worked on radio from age 19. Appeared with Jimmy Wakely in 1937 and joined Gene Autry's Melody Ranch in 1940. Appeared in over 50 movies.	
8/22/60	**26**	7	1. Hot Rod Lincoln [N]	Republic 2005
			GARY U.S. BONDS	
			Singer/songwriter, born Gary Anderson on 6/6/39 in Jacksonville, Florida. To Norfolk, Virginia in the mid-50s. Signed to Legrand by Frank Guida. Wrote "Friend Don't Take Her," hit for Johnny Paycheck in 1972.	
10/31/60	**6**	11	1. **New Orleans** **U.S. BONDS**	Legrand 1003
6/05/61	**1**(2)	12	2. **Quarter To Three** **U.S. BONDS** music taken from "A Night With Daddy G" (Church Street Five)	Legrand 1008
7/31/61	**5**	9	3. **School Is Out**	Legrand 1009
11/06/61	**28**	2	4. School Is In	Legrand 1012
1/13/62	**9**	11	5. **Dear Lady Twist**	Legrand 1015
4/07/62	**9**	9	6. **Twist, Twist Senora**	Legrand 1018
7/07/62	**27**	4	7. Seven Day Weekend from the film "It's Trad-Dad"	Legrand 1019
5/02/81	**11**	13	8. This Little Girl	EMI America 8079
7/10/82	**21**	9	9. Out Of Work above 2: produced by Bruce Springsteen and Miami Steve Van Zandt	EMI America 8117
			BONEY M	
			Vocal group created in Germany by producer/composer Frank Farian.	
7/22/78	**30**	6	1. Rivers Of Babylon	Sire 1027
			BONNIE LOU	
			Born Bonnie Lou Kath on 10/27/24 in Bloomington, Illinois. Worked on radio KMBC-Kansas City and WLW-Cincinnati. On Midwestern Hayride for over 20 years.	
11/26/55	**14**	3	1. Daddy-O Juke Box #14 / Best Seller #25 / Top 100 #28	King 4835
			BONNIE SISTERS	
			Pat, Jean and Sylvia from New York City.	
2/25/56	**18**	3	1. Cry Baby Best Seller #18 / Top 100 #35	Rainbow 328

DATE	POS	WKS	ARTIST—RECORD TITLE	LABEL & NO.
			KARLA BONOFF	
			Singer/songwriter; born on 12/27/52 in Los Angeles.	
6/05/82	**19**	12	1. Personally	Columbia 02805
			BOOKER T. & THE MG's	
			Band formed by session men from Stax Records, Memphis, in 1962. Consisted of Booker T. Jones (b: 11/12/44, Memphis), keyboards; Steve Cropper (b: 10/21/42, Ozark Mountains, MO.), guitar; Donald "Duck" Dunn (b: 11/24/41, Memphis), bass; and Al Jackson, Jr. (b: 11/27/34, Memphis; murdered in 1975), drums. MG stands for Memphis Group. Jones was in a band with classmate Maurice White of Earth, Wind & Fire. Cropper and Dunn had been in the Mar-Keys. Much session work, recordings included horns by Andrew Love, Wayne Jackson and Joe Arnold, plus Isaac Hayes, piano. Jones received music degree from Indiana University, and married Priscilla Coolidge, sister of Rita. Produced for Rita Coolidge, Earl Klugh and Bill Withers. Produced Willie Nelson's "Stardust" album. Cropper and Dunn joined the Blues Brothers. Group disbanded in 1968, and reorganized for a short time in 1973.	
9/01/62	**3**	12	● 1. **Green Onions** **[I]**	Stax 127
5/20/67	**37**	3	2. Hip Hug-Her [I]	Stax 211
9/02/67	**21**	7	3. Groovin' [I]	Stax 224
8/03/68	**17**	7	4. Soul-Limbo [I]	Stax 0001
12/28/68†	**9**	11	5. **Hang 'Em High** **[I]** from the film of the same title	Stax 0013
4/05/69	**6**	10	6. **Time Is Tight** **[I]** from the soundtrack "Uptight"	Stax 0028
7/05/69	**37**	3	7. Mrs. Robinson [I] from the movie "The Graduate"	Stax 0037
			DANIEL BOONE	
			English singer/songwriter. Real name: Peter Lee Stirling.	
8/05/72	**15**	11	1. Beautiful Sunday	Mercury 73281
			DEBBY BOONE	
			Pat Boone's daughter. Born on 9/22/56 in Hackensack, New Jersey. Won the 1977 Best New Artist Grammy Award.	
9/17/77	**1**(10)	21	▲ 1. **You Light Up My Life** theme from the movie of the same title	Warner 8455
			PAT BOONE	
			Born Charles Eugene Boone on 6/1/34 in Jacksonville, Florida. To Nashville in the early 50s, attended Lipscomb College. Direct descendant of Daniel Boone. Won Ted Mack's Amateur Hour, Arthur Godfrey's Talent Scouts, in 1954. First recorded for Republic Records in 1954. Married Red Foley's daughter, Shirley, in 1954. Appeared in 15 films. Toured with wife and daughters Cherry, Linda Lee, Deborah Ann and Laura Gene in the mid-60s. Trademark: white buck shoes.	
4/02/55	**16**	12	1. Two Hearts Best Seller #16 / Juke Box #16	Dot 15338
7/09/55	**1**(2)	20	2. **Ain't That A Shame** Juke Box #1 / Best Seller #2 / Jockey #2 / Top 100 #21 pre	Dot 15377
10/29/55	**7**	10	3. **At My Front Door (Crazy Little Mama)/** Top 100 #7 / Juke Box #7 / Best Seller #8 / Jockey #10	
11/19/55	**26**	5	4. No Other Arms (No Arms Can Ever Hold You)	Dot 15422
12/24/55†	**19**	5	5. Gee Whittakers! Juke Box #19 / Top 100 #27	Dot 15435
2/04/56	**4**	18	6. **I'll Be Home/** Jockey #4 / Juke Box #4 / Top 100 #5 / Best Seller #6	

DATE	POS	WKS	ARTIST—RECORD TITLE	LABEL & NO.
2/04/56	**12**	10	7. Tutti' Frutti Top 100 #12 / Juke Box #13 / Best Seller #15 / Jockey #15	Dot 15443
4/28/56	**8**	9	8. **Long Tall Sally** Juke Box #8 / Top 100 #18 / Best Seller #23 / Jockey #23	Dot 15457
6/09/56	**1**(4)	19	9. **I Almost Lost My Mind** Juke Box #1(4) / Top 100 #1(2) / Best Seller #2 / Jockey #2	Dot 15472
9/22/56	**5**	17	10. **Friendly Persuasion (Thee I Love)/** Jockey #5 / Top 100 #8 / Juke Box #8 / Best Seller #9 from the Gary Cooper film "Friendly Persuasion"	
9/29/56	**10**	7	11. Chains Of Love Juke Box #10 / Best Seller #15 / Top 100 #20	Dot 15490
12/22/56†	**1**(1)	19	12. **Don't Forbid Me/** Top 100 #1(1) / Juke Box #1(1) / Jockey #2 / Best Seller #3	
1/26/57	**37**	2	13. Anastasia from the Ingrid Bergman film "Anastasia"	Dot 15521
3/23/57	**5**	13	14. **Why Baby Why/** Best Seller #5 / Top 100 #6 / Jockey #7 / Juke Box #7	
3/23/57	**27**	5	15. I'm Waiting Just For You	Dot 15545
5/13/57	**1**(7)	24	16. **Love Letters In The Sand/** Jockey #1(7) / Best Seller #1(5) / Top 100 #1(5) / Juke Box #2 end	
5/20/57	**14**	13	17. Bernardine Jockey #14 / Top 100 #23 above 2: from the film "Bernardine"	Dot 15570
8/12/57	**6**	14	18. **Remember You're Mine/** Jockey #6 / Best Seller #10 / Top 100 #20	
8/19/57	**14**	11	19. There's A Gold Mine In The Sky Best Seller #14 / Jockey #20 / Top 100 #28	Dot 15602
10/28/57	**1**(6)	19	20. **April Love** Jockey #1(6) / Best Seller #1(2) / Top 100 #1(1) from the film of the same title starring Pat Boone & Shirley Jones	Dot 15660
2/17/58	**4**	15	21. **A Wonderful Time Up There/** Best Seller #4 / Jockey #7 / Top 100 #10	
2/17/58	**4**	15	22. It's Too Soon To Know Best Seller #4 / Jockey #11 / Top 100 #13	Dot 15690
5/12/58	**5**	12	23. **Sugar Moon** Jockey #5 / Best Seller #10 / Top 100 #11	Dot 15750
7/14/58	**7**	10	24. **If Dreams Came True/** Jockey #7 / Best Seller #11 / Hot 100 #12	
8/04/58	**39**	1	25. That's How Much I Love You	Dot 15785
9/22/58	**23**	4	26. For My Good Fortune/ Hot 100 #23 / Best Seller #29	
10/06/58	**21**	2	27. Gee, But It's Lonely Best Seller #21 / Hot 100 #31	Dot 15825
11/17/58	**34**	5	28. I'll Remember Tonight from the film "Mardi Gras"	Dot 15840
1/26/59	**21**	8	29. With The Wind And The Rain In Your Hair	Dot 15888
4/06/59	**23**	7	30. For A Penny	Dot 15914
6/29/59	**17**	6	31. Twixt Twelve And Twenty	Dot 15955
9/28/59	**29**	4	32. Fools Hall Of Fame	Dot 15982
3/07/60	**18**	7	33. (Welcome) New Lovers	Dot 16048
5/22/61	**1**(1)	12	34. **Moody River**	Dot 16209

DATE	POS	WKS	ARTIST—RECORD TITLE	LABEL & NO.
9/04/61	**19**	5	35. Big Cold Wind	Dot 16244
12/25/61†	**35**	3	36. Johnny Will	Dot 16284
2/24/62	**32**	3	37. I'll See You In My Dreams	Dot 16312
6/30/62	**6**	10	38. **Speedy Gonzales** [N]	Dot 16368
			BOSTON	
			Rock group from Boston, spearheaded by Tom Scholz (guitars and keyboards) and Brad Delp (lead vocals). Originally a quintet, group also included Barry Goudreau (guitar), Fran Sheehan (bass) and Sib Hashian (drums). After an absence from the charts for 7 years ('79-'86), Boston returned as basically a duo: Scholz & Delp.	
10/16/76	**5**	14	1. **More Than A Feeling**	Epic 50266
2/12/77	**22**	6	2. Long Time	Epic 50329
6/18/77	**38**	2	3. Peace Of Mind	Epic 50381
8/26/78	**4**	10	4. **Don't Look Back**	Epic 50590
12/23/78†	**31**	5	5. A Man I'll Never Be	Epic 50638
10/04/86	**1**(2)	12	6. **Amanda**	MCA 52756
12/27/86†	**9**	10	7. **We're Ready**	MCA 52985
3/28/87	**20**	5	8. Can'tcha Say (You Believe In Me)/Still In Love	MCA 53029
			PERRY BOTKIN, JR. - see BARRY DeVORZON	
			BOURGEOIS TAGG	
			West Coast rock quintet led by Brent Bourgeois and Larry Tagg.	
12/05/87	**38**	2	1. I Don't Mind At All produced by Todd Rundgren	Island 99409
			JIMMY BOWEN with The Rhythm Orchids	
			Born on 11/30/37 in Santa Rita, New Mexico. Formed The Rhythm Orchids at West Texas State University with Buddy Knox, Don Lanier and Dave "Dicky Doo" Alldred. Jimmy became a producer and top record executive on the West Coast. In 1977, moved to Nashville. In 1984, became president of MCA Records in Nashville (renamed Universal Records in 1988).	
3/09/57	**14**	12	1. I'm Stickin' With You Top 100 #14 / Juke Box #15 / Best Seller #16 / Jockey #20 originally on Triple-D label (flip: "Party Doll" by Buddy Knox)	Roulette 4001
			DAVID BOWIE	
			Born David Robert Jones on 1/8/47 in London. First recorded as David Jones & the King Bees, Lower Third, Manish Boys in 1963. Brought highly theatrical values to rock through work with Lindsay Kemp Mime Troupe. Periods of reclusiveness heightened his appeal. Films "The Man Who Fell To Earth," 1976; "Just A Gigolo," 1978; "The Hunger," "Merry Christmas Mr. Lawrence," 1983; "Labyrinth" and "Absolute Beginners," 1986. In Broadway play "The Elephant Man," 1980.	
2/24/73	**15**	10	1. Space Oddity	RCA 0876
4/19/75	**28**	4	2. Young Americans	RCA 10152
8/02/75	**1**(2)	14	• 3. **Fame**	RCA 10320
1/10/76	**10**	16	4. **Golden Years**	RCA 10441
12/05/81†	**29**	8	5. Under Pressure **QUEEN & DAVID BOWIE**	Elektra 47235
4/09/83	**1**(1)	14	• 6. **Let's Dance**	EMI America 8158
7/09/83	**10**	11	7. **China Girl**	EMI America 8165
10/01/83	**14**	9	8. Modern Love	EMI America 8177

DATE	POS	WKS	ARTIST—RECORD TITLE	LABEL & NO.
9/29/84	**8**	10	9. **Blue Jean**	EMI America 8231
3/09/85	**32**	4	10. This Is Not America	EMI America 8251
			DAVID BOWIE/PAT METHENY GROUP (Pat is a jazz guitarist)	
			theme from the film "The Falcon And The Snowman"	
9/07/85	**7**	9	11. **Dancing In The Street**	EMI America 8288
			MICK JAGGER/DAVID BOWIE	
			from the Live-Aid concert	
4/25/87	**21**	7	12. Day-In Day-Out	EMI America 8380
9/05/87	**27**	5	13. Never Let Me Down	EMI America 43031
			THE BOX TOPS	
			Pop-rock group formed in Memphis in 1966. Included Alex Chilton (b: 12/28/50, Memphis; lead singer, guitar, bass, harmonica), Bill Cunningham (b: 1/23/50, Memphis; keyboards) and Gary Talley (b: 8/17/47, Memphis; guitar, bass). Reorganized after first hit to include Tom Boggs, drums; and Rick Allen, organ. Group disbanded in 1970. Chilton later formed the precursor new-wave pop band Big Star.	
8/26/67	**1**(4)	13	● 1. **The Letter**	Mala 565
12/02/67	**24**	5	2. Neon Rainbow	Mala 580
3/16/68	**2**(2)	12	● 3. **Cry Like A Baby**	Mala 593
6/08/68	**26**	6	4. Choo Choo Train	Mala 12005
10/12/68	**37**	1	5. I Met Her In Church	Mala 12017
2/08/69	**28**	9	6. Sweet Cream Ladies, Forward March	Mala 12035
8/23/69	**18**	7	7. Soul Deep	Mala 12040
			BOY GEORGE	
			Born George O'Dowd on 6/14/61. Former lead singer of Culture Club.	
2/20/88	**40**	1	1. Live My Life	Virgin 99390
			from the film "Hiding Out"	
			BOY MEETS GIRL	
			Seattle songwriting/recording duo: Shannon Rubicam and George Merrill. Wrote Whitney Houston's hits "How Will I Know" and "I Wanna Dance With Somebody." Married in 1988.	
5/25/85	**39**	1	1. Oh Girl	A&M 2713
10/15/88	**5**	16	2. **Waiting For A Star To Fall**	RCA 8691
			TOMMY BOYCE & BOBBY HART	
			Top pop songwriting duo and production team. Toured and recorded with The Monkees' Davy Jones and Mickey Dolenz in 1975.	
8/05/67	**39**	2	1. Out & About	A&M 858
1/20/68	**8**	9	2. **I Wonder What She's Doing Tonite**	A&M 893
8/03/68	**27**	6	3. Alice Long (You're Still My Favorite Girlfriend)	A&M 948
			BOYS CLUB	
			Duo formed in Minneapolis: Joe Pasquale and Gene Hunt (real name: Eugene Wolfgramm, formerly of family group, The Jets).	
11/19/88†	**8**	12	1. **I Remember Holding You**	MCA 53430
			BOYS DON'T CRY	
			British quintet; Nick Richards, lead singer.	
5/17/86	**12**	9	1. I Wanna Be A Cowboy	Profile 5084

DATE	POS	WKS	ARTIST—RECORD TITLE	LABEL & NO.
			JAN BRADLEY	
			Born on 7/6/43 in Byhalia, Mississippi; raised in Robbins, Illinois. Soul singer. First recorded for Formal in 1961. Became a social worker in 1976.	
2/02/63	**14**	9	1. Mama Didn't Lie	Chess 1845
			OWEN BRADLEY Quintet	
			Born on 10/10/15 in Westmoreland, Tennessee. Bandleader/record producer.	
7/29/57	**18**	4	1. White Silver Sands Jockey #18 / Top 100 #68 vocal by the Anita Kerr Quartet	Decca 30363
			LAURA BRANIGAN	
			Born on 7/3/57; raised in upstate New York. Pop singer. Has done some acting work.	
9/04/82	**2**(3)	22	• 1. **Gloria**	Atlantic 4048
4/02/83	**7**	13	2. **Solitaire**	Atlantic 89868
8/13/83	**12**	12	3. How Am I Supposed To Live Without You	Atlantic 89805
5/05/84	**4**	15	4. **Self Control**	Atlantic 89676
8/25/84	**20**	8	5. The Lucky One from the TV program "An Uncommon Love"	Atlantic 89636
9/07/85	**40**	2	6. Spanish Eddie	Atlantic 89531
11/28/87†	**26**	9	7. Power Of Love	Atlantic 89191
			BRASS CONSTRUCTION	
			Formed as Dynamic Soul by Randy Muller in Brooklyn in 1968. Randy produces the band Skyy.	
5/08/76	**14**	9	1. Movin' [I]	United Art. 775
			THE BRASS RING	
			New York studio band headed by Phil Bodner (producer/arranger/sax/clarinet).	
4/16/66	**32**	4	1. The Phoenix Love Theme [I] from the film "The Flight Of The Phoenix"	Dunhill 4023
3/04/67	**36**	2	2. The Dis-Advantages Of You [I] melody taken from a Benson & Hedges cigarette jingle	Dunhill 4065
			BOB BRAUN	
			Born Robert Earl Brown on 4/20/29 in Ludlow, Kentucky. Hosted TV show in Cincinnati.	
8/18/62	**26**	4	1. Till Death Do Us Part [S]	Decca 31355
			BREAD	
			Formed in Los Angeles in 1969. Consisted of leader David Gates (vocals, guitar, keyboards), James Griffin (guitar), Robb Royer (guitar) and Jim Gordon (drums). Originally called Pleasure Faire. Griffin and Royer co-wrote award-winning "For All We Know" with Fred Karlin in 1969. Mike Botts replaced Gordon after first album. Royer replaced by Larry Knechtel in 1971. Disbanded in 1973, reunited briefly in 1976. All songs written, produced and arranged by David Gates.	
7/11/70	**1**(1)	13	• 1. **Make It With You**	Elektra 45686
10/10/70	**10**	9	2. **It Don't Matter To Me**	Elektra 45701
1/30/71	**28**	4	3. Let Your Love Go	Elektra 45711
4/03/71	**4**	11	4. **If**	Elektra 45720
8/14/71	**37**	2	5. Mother Freedom	Elektra 45740
11/06/71	**3**	10	• 6. **Baby I'm-A Want You**	Elektra 45751

Frankie Avalon had all of his eight top-20 singles in the 50s, but he is perhaps best remembered for his mid-60s *Beach Party* film series with Annette Funicello. Their 1987 screen reunion, *Back to the Beach*, wiped out at the box office, but it did produce a mild tidal wave of a hit single—the Fat Boys and Beach Boys' remake of "Wipe Out" (No. 12, 1987).

Bad Company's first hit, "Can't Get Enough (Of Your Love)," rode the top 20 the same time as Barry White's "Can't Get Enough Of Your Love, Babe." There was little confusion between the two.

Philip Bailey shared lead vocals with Maurice White on seven top-10 hits as a member of Earth, Wind, & Fire. Bailey's only major hit on his own has been "Easy Lover," on which he shared lead vocals with his producer, Phil Collins.

Anita Baker's award-winning *Rapture* spent more than three years on the LP chart but just missed the top 10 (No. 11, January, 1987). Her follow-up, *Giving You The Best That I Got*, made it in its *second* week, on the way to a four-week run at No. 1.

Bananarama's "Cruel Summer," "Venus," and "I Heard A Rumour" all peaked in the top 10 in the month of September, but the group probably weren't the "September Girls" that archrivals the Bangles sang about on their No. 2 album, *Different Light*.

The Bangles' "Walk Like An Egyptian" topped the Hot 100 for four weeks in 1986, a feat bettered by only one female group—the Emotions, who held on to No. 1 for five weeks in 1977 with "Best Of My Love."

The Bar-kays lost four of their six members in the same 1967 plane crash that killed Otis Redding, but they regrouped under survivors James Alexander and Ben Cauley and backed Isaac Hayes on the No. 1 "Theme From Shaft" (1971).

The Bay City Rollers *didn't* turn into the "next Beatles," as "Rollermania" lasted only 17 weeks—the chart run of their first hit, "Saturday Night," which hit No. 1 in 1976.

The Beach Boys' "I Get Around" hit No. 1 on July 4, 1964, but wasn't certified a million-seller for another 17 1/2 *years*. Their 1988 comeback, "Kokomo," was certified a million-seller four *weeks* after hitting No. 1. That's probably the first time a group gained speed with age.

The Beastie Boys proved that rap music knows no boundary of color when their *Licensed To Ill* became the first rap album to hit No. 1 (February, 1987).

The Beatles scored No. 1 singles on an unprecedented four different labels—Capitol, Swan, Tollie, and Apple—and just missed a fifth when their Vee-Jay release, "Do You Want To Know A Secret," stopped at No. 2.

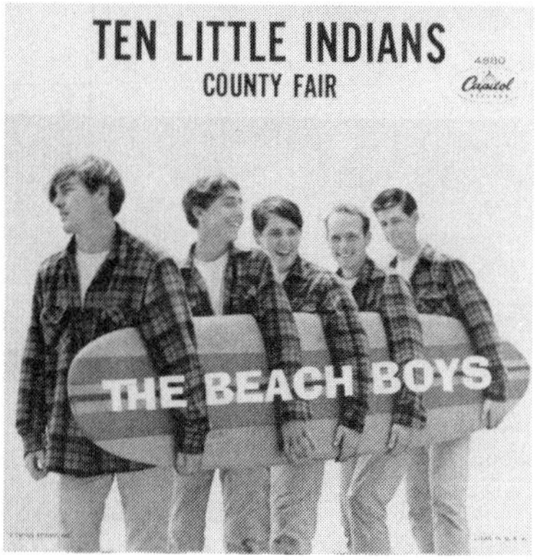

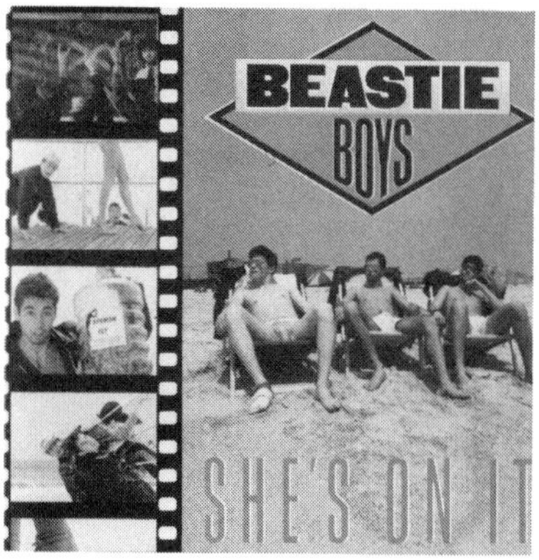

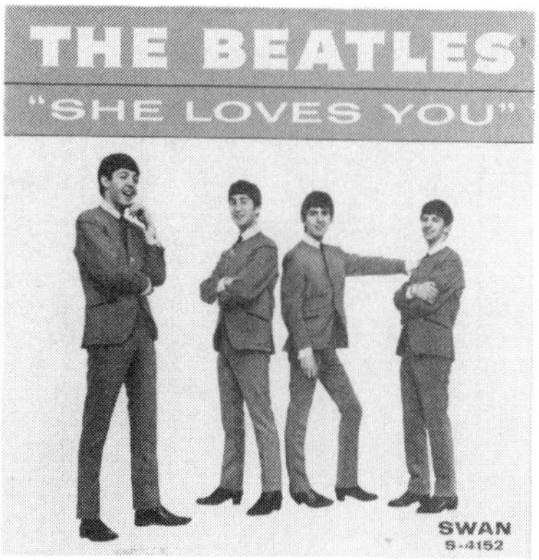

DATE	POS	WKS	ARTIST—RECORD TITLE	LABEL & NO.
2/05/72	**5**	11	7. **Everything I Own**	Elektra 45765
5/06/72	**15**	8	8. Diary	Elektra 45784
8/05/72	**11**	9	9. The Guitar Man	Elektra 45803
11/18/72	**15**	8	10. Sweet Surrender	Elektra 45818
2/17/73	**15**	8	11. Aubrey	Elektra 45832
12/04/76†	**9**	13	12. **Lost Without Your Love**	Elektra 45365
			BREAKFAST CLUB	
			New York-based dance/pop quartet. Madonna with group for a short time in the early 80s. Member Steve Bray co-produced Madonna's "True Blue" album.	
4/11/87	**7**	11	1. **Right On Track**	MCA 52954
			BREATHE	
			Band from suburban London: David Glasper (vocals), Ian "Spike" Spice, Marcus Lillington and Michael Delahunty (who left in 1988).	
6/11/88	**2(2)**	16	1. **Hands To Heaven**	A&M 2991
10/01/88	**3**	16	2. **How Can I Fall?**	A&M 1224
			BEVERLY BREMERS	
			Chicago-born actress/singer.	
1/22/72	**15**	10	1. Don't Say You Don't Remember	Scepter 12315
7/22/72	**40**	2	2. We're Free	Scepter 12348
			BRENDA & THE TABULATIONS	
			R&B group from Philadelphia, formed in 1966, with Brenda Payton, Jerry Jones, Eddie Jackson and Maurice Coates. Bernard Murphy was added in 1969. Reorganized in 1970 with vocalists Brenda Payton, Pat Mercer and Deborah Martin.	
3/25/67	**20**	6	1. Dry Your Eyes	Dionn 500
5/01/71	**23**	9	2. Right On The Tip Of My Tongue	Top & Bottom 407
			WALTER BRENNAN	
			Beloved character actor born on 7/25/1894 in Lynn, Massachusetts. Died on 9/21/74. First film role in 1924. Played Grandpa on "The Real McCoys" TV series.	
5/30/60	**30**	3	1. Dutchman's Gold [S] with Billy Vaughn & his orchestra	Dot 16066
4/21/62	**5**	9	2. **Old Rivers** **[S]**	Liberty 55436
12/01/62	**38**	1	3. Mama Sang A Song [S]	Liberty 55508
			BREWER & SHIPLEY	
			Folk-rock duo formed in Los Angeles: Mike Brewer and Tom Shipley.	
3/13/71	**10**	10	1. **One Toke Over The Line**	Kama Sutra 516
			TERESA BREWER	
			Born Theresa Breuer on 5/7/31 in Toledo, Ohio. Debuted on Major Bowes Amateur Hour at age 5, toured with show until age 12. Appeared on Pick & Pat radio show. First recorded for London in 1949. In the film "Those Red Heads From Seattle" in 1953.	
12/18/54†	**6**	12	1. **Let Me Go, Lover!** Juke Box #6 / Jockey #7 / Best Seller #8 with the Lancers (male vocal group)	Coral 61315
3/19/55	**17**	3	2. Pledging My Love Jockey #17 / Juke Box #18 / Best Seller #30	Coral 61362

DATE	POS	WKS	ARTIST—RECORD TITLE	LABEL & NO.
6/04/55	**20**	1	3. Silver Dollar Juke Box #20 above 3: orchestra directed by Jack Pleis	Coral 61394
7/30/55	**15**	4	4. The Banjo's Back In Town Juke Box #15	Coral 61448
3/03/56	**5**	17	5. **A Tear Fell/** Juke Box #5 / Top 100 #7 / Best Seller #9 / Jockey #9	
3/10/56	**17**	10	6. Bo Weevil Top 100 #17 / Jockey #20	Coral 61590
6/16/56	**7**	16	7. **A Sweet Old Fashioned Girl** Juke Box #7 / Top 100 #9 / Jockey #11 / Best Seller #12	Coral 61636
11/17/56	**21**	8	8. Mutual Admiration Society Top 100 #21 / Best Seller #24 / Jockey #24 from the musical "Happy Hunting"	Coral 61737
4/27/57	**13**	9	9. Empty Arms Juke Box #13 / Top 100 #18 / Jockey #19 / Best Seller #23	Coral 61805
11/11/57	**8**	11	10. **You Send Me** Jockey #8 / Best Seller #27 / Top 100 #31	Coral 61898
10/20/58	**38**	1	11. The Hula Hoop Song	Coral 62033
4/06/59	**40**	1	12. Heavenly Lover	Coral 62084
9/12/60	**31**	6	13. Anymore 4-13: orchestra directed by Dick Jacobs	Coral 62219
			BRICK Disco/jazz group formed in Atlanta in 1972. Consisted of Jimmy Brown (vocals), Ray Ransom, Donald Nevins, Reggie Hargis and Eddie Irons. Session work in the early 70s.	
11/20/76†	**3**	15	1. **Dazz**	Bang 727
10/01/77	**18**	10	2. Dusic	Bang 734
			ALICIA BRIDGES Atlanta-based disco singer/songwriter; originally from Lawndale, North Carolina.	
9/09/78	**5**	19	● 1. **I Love The Nightlife (Disco 'Round)**	Polydor 14483
			LILLIAN BRIGGS Pop singer discovered by Alan Freed in New York City.	
9/17/55	**18**	3	1. I Want You To Be My Baby Jockey #18 / Juke Box #19 / Best Seller #23 / Top 100 #53 pre	Epic 9115
			BRIGHTER SIDE OF DARKNESS R&B group formed at Calumet High School, Chicago in 1971; featuring 12-year-old lead singer Darryl Lamont, Ralph Eskridge, Randolph Murph and Larry Washington.	
1/06/73	**16**	8	● 1. Love Jones	20th Century 2002
			MARTIN BRILEY British session musician/songwriter. Moved to New York City in 1977.	
7/16/83	**36**	3	1. The Salt In My Tears	Mercury 812165
			JOHNNY BRISTOL Soul vocalist/composer/producer from Morgantown, North Carolina. Teamed with Jackie Beaver, recorded as Johnny & Jackie for Tri-Phi, 1961. Teamed with Harvey Fuqua as Motown producers until 1973. Production work for CBS.	
7/20/74	**8**	13	1. **Hang On In There Baby**	MGM 14715

DATE	POS	WKS	ARTIST—RECORD TITLE	LABEL & NO.
			HERMAN BROOD	
			Leader of rock band from the Netherlands.	
9/01/79	**35**	3	1. Saturdaynight	Ariola 7754
			BROOKLYN BRIDGE	
			Formed in Long Island, New York; Johnny Maestro (of The Crests), lead singer.	
1/04/69	**3**	10	● 1. **Worst That Could Happen**	Buddah 75
			DONNIE BROOKS	
			Born John Faircloth in Dallas; raised in Ventura, California. Early recording names: Johnny Faire, Dick Bush and Johnny Jordan.	
7/11/60	**7**	15	1. **Mission Bell**	Era 3018
12/26/60	**31**	3	2. Doll House	Era 3028
			THE BROTHERHOOD OF MAN	
			British studio group assembled by producer Tony Hiller.	
5/23/70	**13**	10	1. United We Stand	Deram 85059
6/19/76	**27**	4	2. Save Your Kisses For Me	Pye 71066
			THE BROTHERS FOUR	
			Folk-pop quartet: Dick Foley, Bob Flick, John Paine and Mike Kirkland. Formed while fraternity brothers at the University of Washington.	
3/21/60	**2**(4)	15	1. **Greenfields**	Columbia 41571
4/24/61	**32**	3	2. Frogg [N] new version of tune written back in 1580 as "Frog Went A Courtin'"	Columbia 41958
			THE BROTHERS JOHNSON	
			Los Angeles R&B duo of brothers George (b: 5/17/53) and Louis Johnson (b: 4/13/55). Played since age 7. Own band, the Johnson Three + 1, with brother Tommy and cousin Alex Weir. With Billy Preston's band to 1975.	
5/22/76	**3**	12	● 1. **I'll Be Good To You**	A&M 1806
9/18/76	**30**	6	2. Get The Funk Out Ma Face	A&M 1851
7/30/77	**5**	13	● 3. **Strawberry Letter 23**	A&M 1949
4/12/80	**7**	13	4. **Stomp!**	A&M 2216
			AL BROWN'S TUNETOPPERS	
			Born in Fairmont, West Virginia in 1930. Tunetoppers formed in 1953.	
5/02/60	**23**	5	1. The Madison dance calls: Cookie Brown	Amy 804
			THE CRAZY WORLD OF ARTHUR BROWN	
			Arthur was born on 6/24/44 in Whitby, England. Band included Carl Palmer of Emerson, Lake & Palmer.	
9/21/68	**2**(1)	11	● 1. **Fire**	Atlantic 2556
			BOBBY BROWN	
			Born on 2/5/69 in Boston. Former member of the teen R&B-pop group New Edition.	
8/20/88	**8**	14	● 1. **Don't Be Cruel**	MCA 53327
11/12/88†	**1**(1)	15	● 2. **My Prerogative**	MCA 53383

DATE	POS	WKS	ARTIST—RECORD TITLE	LABEL & NO.
			BOOTS BROWN & HIS BLOCKBUSTERS	
			Boots was born Milton "Shorty" Rogers on 4/14/24 in Lee, Massachusetts. Great jazz trumpeter/arranger/composer/bandleader.	
9/15/58	**23**	3	1. Cerveza [I] Best Seller #23 / Hot 100 #62	RCA 7269
			BUSTER BROWN	
			R&B vocalist/harmonica player, born on 8/15/11 in Cordele, Georgia. Died on 1/31/76.	
3/28/60	**38**	3	1. Fannie Mae	Fire 1008
			CHUCK BROWN & THE SOUL SEARCHERS	
			Washington, DC-based 9-member group.	
3/17/79	**34**	5	● 1. Bustin' Loose, Part 1	Source 40967
			JAMES BROWN	
			Born on 5/3/28 in Macon, Georgia. Raised in Augusta. Formed own vocal group, the Famous Flames. Cut a demo record of own composition "Please Please Please," in November of 1955, at radio station WIBB in Macon. Signed to King/Federal Records in January, 1956 and re-recorded the song. Cameo appearances in films "The Blues Brothers" and "Rocky IV." One of the originators of "Soul" music, billed as "The Godfather Of Soul." His backing group, The JB's, featured various personnel, including: Nat Kendrick, Bootsy Collins, Maceo Parker and Fred Wesley. Inducted into the Rock And Roll Hall Of Fame in 1986. On 12/15/88, received a 6-year prison sentence for leading police in an interstate car chase.	
5/30/60	**33**	2	1. Think	Federal 12370
4/03/61	**40**	2	2. Bewildered	King 5442
5/19/62	**35**	4	3. Night Train [I]	King 5614
5/18/63	**18**	7	4. Prisoner Of Love	King 5739
2/15/64	**23**	7	5. Oh Baby Don't You Weep (Part 1)	King 5842
9/12/64	**24**	5	6. Out Of Sight	Smash 1919
8/07/65	**8**	9	7. **Papa's Got A Brand New Bag (Part I)**	King 5999
11/20/65	**3**	10	8. **I Got You (I Feel Good)**	King 6015
5/07/66	**8**	8	9. **It's A Man's Man's Man's World**	King 6035
1/28/67	**29**	4	10. Bring It Up	King 6071
8/12/67	**7**	8	11. **Cold Sweat (Part 1)**	King 6110
11/25/67	**40**	1	12. Get It Together (Part 1)	King 6122
12/30/67†	**28**	5	13. I Can't Stand Myself (When You Touch Me)/	
2/17/68	**36**	4	14. There Was A Time	King 6144
3/23/68	**6**	10	15. **I Got The Feelin'**	King 6155
6/01/68	**14**	7	16. Licking Stick - Licking Stick (Part 1) all of above on King labeled as: James Brown & The Famous Flames	King 6166
9/14/68	**10**	10	17. **Say It Loud - I'm Black And I'm Proud (Part 1)**	King 6187
12/07/68	**31**	2	18. Goodbye My Love	King 6198
2/08/69	**15**	7	19. Give It Up Or Turnit A Loose	King 6213
4/19/69	**20**	6	20. I Don't Want Nobody To Give Me Nothing (Open Up The Door, I'll Get It Myself)	King 6224
6/21/69	**11**	10	21. Mother Popcorn (You Got To Have A Mother For Me) (Part 1)	King 6245
6/28/69	**30**	5	22. The Popcorn [I]	King 6240
9/27/69	**37**	2	23. World (Part 1)	King 6258

DATE	POS	WKS	ARTIST—RECORD TITLE	LABEL & NO.
11/01/69	**21**	5	24. Let A Man Come In And Do The Popcorn (Part One)	King 6255
12/13/69†	**24**	8	25. Ain't It Funky Now (Part 1) [I]	King 6280
1/24/70	**40**	2	26. Let A Man Come In And Do The Popcorn (Part Two)	King 6275
2/28/70	**32**	6	27. It's A New Day (Part 1)	King 6292
5/23/70	**32**	2	28. Brother Rapp (Part 1)	King 6310
8/01/70	**15**	7	29. Get Up (I Feel Like Being A) Sex Machine (Part 1)	King 6318
10/17/70	**13**	8	30. Super Bad (Part 1 & Part 2)	King 6329
1/16/71	**34**	5	31. Get Up, Get Into It, Get Involved (Part 1)	King 6347
3/13/71	**29**	6	32. Soul Power (Part 1)	King 6368
6/26/71	**35**	3	33. Escape-ism (Part 1) [S]	People 2500
7/17/71	**15**	9	34. Hot Pants (She Got To Use What She Got, To Get What She Wants) (Part 1)	People 2501
9/11/71	**22**	6	35. Make It Funky (Part 1)	Polydor 14088
12/04/71	**35**	3	36. I'm A Greedy Man (Part I)	Polydor 14100
2/26/72	**27**	4	37. Talking Loud And Saying Nothing (Part I)	Polydor 14109
4/01/72	**40**	2	38. King Heroin [S]	Polydor 14116
9/09/72	**18**	8	• 39. Get On The Good Foot (Part 1)	Polydor 14139
2/10/73	**27**	4	40. I Got Ants In My Pants (and i want to dance) (Part 1)	Polydor 14162
4/13/74	**26**	9	• 41. The Payback (Part 1)	Polydor 14223
8/03/74	**29**	4	42. My Thang	Polydor 14244
9/21/74	**31**	3	43. Papa Don't Take No Mess (Part I)	Polydor 14255
1/11/86	**4**	11	44. **Living In America** from the film "Rocky IV"; produced by Dan Hartman	Scotti Br. 05682
			MAXINE BROWN	
			Born in Kingstree, South Carolina. With gospel groups Manhattans and Royaltones in New York City in the late 50s.	
1/30/61	**19**	6	1. All In My Mind	Nomar 103
4/24/61	**25**	5	2. Funny	Nomar 106
12/05/64†	**24**	7	3. Oh No Not My Baby	Wand 162
			NAPPY BROWN	
			Born Napoleon Brown on 10/12/29 in Charlotte, North Carolina. R&B-gospel singer.	
4/30/55	**25**	4	1. Don't Be Angry Best Seller #25	Savoy 1155
			PETER BROWN	
			Soul vocalist/keyboardist/producer, born on 7/11/53 in Blue Island, Illinois. Attended the Art Institute of Chicago.	
10/08/77	**18**	8	1. Do Ya Wanna Get Funky With Me	Drive 6258
5/06/78	**8**	14	2. **Dance With Me** background vocal: Betty Wright	Drive 6269
			POLLY BROWN	
			English; lead singer of the British groups Pickettywitch and Sweet Dreams.	
2/08/75	**16**	7	1. Up In A Puff Of Smoke	GTO 1002

DATE	POS	WKS	ARTIST—RECORD TITLE	LABEL & NO.
			ROY BROWN	
			Vocalist/pianist, born on 9/10/25 in New Orleans. One of the originators of the New Orleans R&B sound. Wrote "Good Rocking Tonight." Died on 5/25/81 in Los Angeles.	
7/01/57	**29**	1	1. Let The Four Winds Blow Best Seller #29 / Top 100 #38	Imperial 5439
			RUTH BROWN	
			Born on 1/30/28 in Portsmouth, Virginia as Ruth Weston. In late 1946, sang for one month with Lucky Millinder's band, then fired. Later heard by Duke Ellington, who alerted Herb Abramson of the then-new Atlantic Records, who signed her to a contract. Became Atlantic Records' top selling artist of the 1950s. Married for a time to Willis Jackson. In later years, had acting roles in the TV shows "Hello, Larry" and "Checking In," plus several Broadway and Las Vegas musicals. Appeared in the films "Under The Rainbow" (1981) and "Hairspray" (1988). Starred in the 1988 musical "Black And Blue."	
3/02/57	**25**	5	1. Lucky Lips Best Seller #25 / Jockey #25 / Top 100 #26	Atlantic 1125
10/13/58	**24**	2	2. This Little Girl's Gone Rockin' sax solo: King Curtis	Atlantic 1197
			SHIRLEY BROWN	
			Born on 1/6/47 in West Memphis, Arkansas; raised in East St. Louis. Soul vocalist; worked with Albert King.	
11/23/74	**22**	6	1. Woman To Woman	Truth 3206
			JACKSON BROWNE	
			Born on 10/9/48 in Heidelberg, Germany. Vocalist/guitarist/pianist/composer. To Los Angeles in 1951. With Tim Buckley and Nico in 1967 in New York City. Returned to Los Angeles, concentrated on songwriting. His songs were recorded by Linda Ronstadt, Tom Rush, Joe Cocker, The Byrds, Johnny Rivers, Bonnie Raitt, and many others. Worked with the Eagles; produced Warren Zevon's first album. Wife Phyllis committed suicide on 3/25/76. Activist against nuclear power.	
4/08/72	**8**	9	1. **Doctor My Eyes**	Asylum 11004
2/19/77	**23**	6	2. Here Come Those Tears Again	Asylum 45379
3/04/78	**11**	12	3. Running On Empty	Asylum 45460
7/08/78	**20**	7	4. Stay/	
		7	5. The Load-Out	Asylum 45485
7/26/80	**19**	10	6. Boulevard	Asylum 47003
10/18/80	**22**	5	7. That Girl Could Sing	Asylum 47036
8/21/82	**7**	12	8. **Somebody's Baby** from the soundtrack "Fast Times At Ridgemont High"	Asylum 69982
7/16/83	**13**	12	9. Lawyers In Love	Asylum 69826
10/22/83	**25**	7	10. Tender Is The Night	Asylum 69791
11/23/85†	**18**	12	11. You're A Friend Of Mine **CLARENCE CLEMONS & JACKSON BROWNE** includes vocals by actress Daryl Hannah (Browne's girlfriend)	Columbia 05660
3/29/86	**30**	5	12. For America	Asylum 69566
			THE BROWNS	
			Family trio: Jim Ed Brown (b: 4/1/34, Sparkman, AR) and his sisters Maxine (b: 4/27/32, Sampti, LA) and Bonnie (b: 7/31/37, Sparkman, AR).	
8/03/59	**1**(4)	14	1. **The Three Bells**	RCA 7555
11/23/59	**13**	9	2. Scarlet Ribbons (For Her Hair)	RCA 7614
3/28/60	**5**	12	3. **The Old Lamplighter**	RCA 7700

DATE	POS	WKS	ARTIST—RECORD TITLE	LABEL & NO.
			BROWNSVILLE STATION	
			Rock trio from Ann Arbor, Michigan: Cub Koda, Michael Lutz and Henry Weck. Cub writes a column for the record collector's magazine, Goldmine.	
12/08/73†	**3**	13	● 1. **Smokin' In The Boy's Room**	Big Tree 16011
10/05/74	**31**	3	2. Kings Of The Party	Big Tree 16001
			DAVE BRUBECK QUARTET	
			David was born David Warren on 12/6/20 in Concord, California. Besides Brubeck (piano), quartet consists of Paul Desmond (alto sax), Joe Morello (drums) and Eugene Wright (bass). One of America's all-time most popular jazz groups on college campuses.	
9/25/61	**25**	7	1. Take Five [I]	Columbia 41479
			ANITA BRYANT	
			Born on 3/25/40 in Barnsdale, Oklahoma. As Miss Oklahoma, she was second runner-up to Miss America in 1958.	
7/27/59	**30**	7	1. Till There Was You from the Broadway musical "The Music Man"	Carlton 512
5/02/60	**5**	12	2. **Paper Roses**	Carlton 528
8/08/60	**10**	9	3. **In My Little Corner Of The World**	Carlton 530
12/26/60†	**18**	6	4. Wonderland By Night	Carlton 537
			RAY BRYANT COMBO	
			Born Raphael Bryant on 12/24/31 in Philadelphia. R&B-jazz pianist/bandleader.	
5/09/60	**30**	4	1. The Madison Time - Part I [S-I] dance calls: Eddie Morrison (died on 2/28/87 in Chicago)	Columbia 41628
			PEABO BRYSON	
			Born Robert Peabo Bryson on 4/13/51 in Greenville, South Carolina. R&B singer/ producer. First solo recording for Bang in 1970.	
9/03/83	**16**	15	1. Tonight, I Celebrate My Love **PEABO BRYSON/ROBERTA FLACK**	Capitol 5242
6/30/84	**10**	13	2. **If Ever You're In My Arms Again**	Elektra 69728
			B.T. EXPRESS	
			Brooklyn, New York disco septet. B.T. stands for Brothers Trucking.	
10/05/74	**2**(2)	14	● 1. **Do It ('Til You're Satisfied)**	Roadshow 12395
2/08/75	**4**	11	● 2. **Express** **[I]**	Roadshow 7001
9/06/75	**40**	2	3. Give It What You Got/	
9/13/75	**31**	4	4. Peace Pipe	Roadshow 7003
			THE BUBBLE PUPPY	
			Psychedelic rock band from Austin, Texas. Later recorded as Demian.	
3/15/69	**14**	7	1. Hot Smoke & Sasafrass	Int. Artists 128
			BUCHANAN & GOODMAN	
			Bill Buchanan and Richard "Dickie" Goodman conceived the idea of a radio show being interrupted by reports of flying saucers in 1956. Segments of popular records were taped and spliced into the dialogue. The record was heard by Alan Freed and he played it on his WINS-New York radio show. A national hit resulted and the "break-in" record was born. Buchanan left the music business in 1959, but Goodman remains active. Also see Dickie Goodman.	
8/11/56	**3**	10	1. **The Flying Saucer (Parts 1 & 2)** **[N]** Best Seller #3 / Top 100 #7 / Jockey #9 / Juke Box #9	Luniverse 101

DATE	POS	WKS	ARTIST—RECORD TITLE	LABEL & NO.
7/29/57	**18**	8	2. Flying Saucer The 2nd [N] Best Seller #18 / Top 100 #19	Luniverse 105
12/30/57	**32**	2	3. Santa & The Satellite (Parts I & II) [X-N] Top 100 #32 / Best Seller #36 naration: disc jockey Paul Sherman	Luniverse 107
			BUCHANAN BROTHERS	
			Producers Terry Cashman, Gene Pistilli and Tommy West.	
5/31/69	**22**	7	1. Medicine Man (Part I)	Event 3302
			LINDSEY BUCKINGHAM	
			Born on 10/3/47 in California. Guitarist/vocalist. Lindsey, along with Stevie Nicks, joined Fleetwood Mac in 1975. Lindsey left Fleetwood Mac in 1987.	
11/07/81†	**9**	14	1. **Trouble**	Asylum 47223
8/25/84	**23**	9	2. Go Insane	Elektra 69714
			THE BUCKINGHAMS	
			Chicago rock quintet: Dennis Tufano (lead singer), Carl Giammarese, Nick Fortune, Jon Paulos and Dennis Miccoli. Martin Grebb replaced Miccoli in 1967. Paulos died on 3/26/80 (32).	
1/21/67	**1**(2)	10	1. **Kind Of A Drag**	U.S.A. 860
4/08/67	**6**	10	2. **Don't You Care**	Columbia 44053
7/01/67	**5**	10	3. **Mercy, Mercy, Mercy**	Columbia 44182
9/30/67	**12**	7	4. Hey Baby (They're Playing Our Song)	Columbia 44254
12/23/67†	**11**	10	5. Susan	Columbia 44378
			BUCKNER & GARCIA	
			Atlanta-based duo: Jerry Buckner and Gary Garcia.	
1/30/82	**9**	14	● 1. **Pac-Man Fever** **[N]** inspired by the all-time #1 video game "Pac-Man"	Columbia 02673
			THE BUFFALO SPRINGFIELD	
			Superstar group formed in Los Angeles in 1966: Stephen Stills, Neil Young, Richie Furay, Dewey Martin and Bruce Palmer (replaced by Jim Messina after first 2 albums). Disbanded in 1968.	
2/18/67	**7**	11	1. **For What It's Worth (Stop, Hey What's That Sound)**	Atco 6459
			JIMMY BUFFETT	
			Born on 12/25/46 in Mobile, Alabama. Has BS degree in history and journalism from University of Southern Mississippi. After working in New Orleans, moved to Nashville in 1969. Settled in Key West in 1971.	
6/29/74	**30**	5	1. Come Monday	Dunhill 4385
5/07/77	**8**	15	2. **Margaritaville**	ABC 12254
10/22/77	**37**	3	3. Changes In Latitudes, Changes In Attitudes	ABC 12305
5/27/78	**32**	4	4. Cheeseburger In Paradise [N]	ABC 12358
10/20/79	**35**	3	5. Fins	MCA 41109
			THE BUGGLES	
			English duo: Geoff Downes and Trevor Horne (both joined group Yes in 1980). Downes became a member of Asia in 1981.	
12/15/79	**40**	1	1. Video Killed The Radio Star the premiere video on MTV's first show (8/1/81)	Island 49114
			BULL & THE MATADORS	
11/16/68	**39**	1	1. The Funky Judge	Toddlin' Town 108

DATE	POS	WKS	ARTIST—RECORD TITLE	LABEL & NO.
			BULLET	
12/25/71†	**28**	5	1. White Lies, Blue Eyes	Big Tree 123
			THE BUOYS	
			Rock quintet from northeastern Pennsylvania led by vocalist Bill Kelly.	
4/17/71	**17**	8	1. Timothy written by Rupert Holmes	Scepter 12275
			ERIC BURDON & WAR	
			Eric was born on 5/11/41 in Newcastle-On-Tyne, England. After leaving The Animals, Eric teamed up with the funk band War for 2 albums.	
7/11/70	**3**	13	● 1. **Spill The Wine**	MGM 14118
			SOLOMON BURKE	
			Born in 1936 in Philadelphia. Preached and broadcast from own church, "Solomon's Temple," in Philadelphia from 1945-55 as the "Wonder Boy Preacher." Church was founded for him by his grandmother. First recorded for Apollo in 1954. Left music to attend mortuary school, returned in 1960.	
11/13/61	**24**	7	1. Just Out Of Reach (Of My Two Open Arms)	Atlantic 2114
5/25/63	**37**	2	2. If You Need Me	Atlantic 2185
5/23/64	**33**	4	3. Goodbye Baby (Baby Goodbye)	Atlantic 2226
4/03/65	**22**	5	4. Got To Get You Off My Mind	Atlantic 2276
7/03/65	**28**	5	5. Tonight's The Night	Atlantic 2288
			DORSEY BURNETTE	
			Born on 12/28/32 in Memphis; died of a heart attack on 8/19/79 in Canoga Park, California. Older brother of Johnny Burnette, father of Billy Burnette.	
2/22/60	**23**	9	1. (There Was A) Tall Oak Tree	Era 3012
			JOHNNY BURNETTE	
			Born on 3/25/34 in Memphis; died on 8/1/64 in a boating accident on Clear Lake in California. Johnny, brother Dorsey and Paul Burlison formed the Johnny Burnette Rock 'N Roll Trio, 1953-57.	
8/15/60	**11**	11	1. Dreamin'	Liberty 55258
11/21/60	**8**	11	2. **You're Sixteen**	Liberty 55285
2/20/61	**17**	6	3. Little Boy Sad	Liberty 55298
11/06/61	**18**	4	4. God, Country And My Baby	Liberty 55379
			ROCKY BURNETTE	
			Born on 6/12/53 in Memphis. Son of Johnny Burnette.	
6/07/80	**8**	12	1. **Tired Of Toein' The Line**	EMI America 8043
			LOU BUSCH	
			Born on 7/18/10 in Louisville. Died on 9/19/79. Also recorded as Joe "Fingers" Carr.	
3/24/56	**35**	2	1. 11th Hour Melody	Capitol 3349
6/16/56	**19**	10	2. Portuguese Washerwomen [I] shown as: **JOE "FINGERS" CARR** Jockey #19 / Best Seller #25 / Top 100 #25	Capitol 3418
			KATE BUSH	
			Born on 7/30/58 in Plumstead, England.	
11/09/85	**30**	4	1. Running Up That Hill	EMI America 8285

DATE	POS	WKS	ARTIST—RECORD TITLE	LABEL & NO.
			THE BUSTERS	
9/28/63	**25**	5	1. Bust Out [I]	Arlen 735
			JERRY BUTLER	
			Born on 12/8/39 in Sunflower, Mississippi. Older brother of Billy Butler. Sang in the Northern Jubilee Gospel Singers, with Curtis Mayfield. Later with the Quails. In 1957, Butler and Mayfield joined the Roosters with Sam Gooden and brothers Arthur & Richard Brooks. Changed name to The Impressions in 1957. Left for solo career in autumn of 1958. Teamed again with writer Mayfield for a string of hits from 1960-66.	
6/16/58	**11**	9	1. For Your Precious Love **JERRY BUTLER & THE IMPRESSIONS** Best Seller #11 / Top 100 #11 / Jockey #25	Abner/Falcon 1013
11/07/60	**7**	13	2. **He Will Break Your Heart**	Vee-Jay 354
4/03/61	**27**	4	3. Find Another Girl	Vee-Jay 375
8/07/61	**25**	4	4. I'm A Telling You	Vee-Jay 390
10/30/61	**11**	11	5. Moon River from the film "Breakfast At Tiffany's"	Vee-Jay 405
8/18/62	**20**	4	6. Make It Easy On Yourself	Vee-Jay 451
12/28/63†	**31**	5	7. Need To Belong	Vee-Jay 567
9/19/64	**5**	11	8. **Let It Be Me** **BETTY EVERETT & JERRY BUTLER**	Vee-Jay 613
11/25/67	**38**	2	9. Mr. Dream Merchant	Mercury 72721
6/08/68	**20**	9	10. Never Give You Up	Mercury 72798
10/05/68	**16**	8	11. Hey, Western Union Man	Mercury 72850
1/18/69	**39**	2	12. Are You Happy	Mercury 72876
3/08/69	**4**	12	● 13. **Only The Strong Survive**	Mercury 72898
6/21/69	**24**	7	14. Moody Woman	Mercury 72929
9/06/69	**20**	9	15. What's The Use Of Breaking Up	Mercury 72960
2/05/72	**21**	10	● 16. Ain't Understanding Mellow **JERRY BUTLER & BRENDA LEE EAGER**	Mercury 73255
			JONATHAN BUTLER	
			Born in Capetown, South Africa. Soul singer/guitarist/songwriter.	
8/15/87	**27**	5	1. Lies	Jive 1038
			CHARLIE BYRD - see STAN GETZ	
			THE BYRDS	
			Folk-rock group formed in Los Angeles in 1964. Consisted of James "Roger" McGuinn, (12-string guitar), David Crosby (guitar), Gene Clark (percussion), Chris Hillman (bass) and Mike Clarke (drums). McGuinn, who changed his name to Roger in 1968, had been with Bobby Darin and The Chad Mitchell Trio. Clark had been with The New Christy Minstrels. All except Clarke had folk music background. Professional debut in March of 1965. First recorded as the Beefeaters for Elektra in 1965. Also recorded as the Jet Set. Clark left after "Eight Miles High." Crosby left in 1968 to form Crosby, Stills & Nash. Reformed in 1968 with McGuinn, Hillman, Kevin Kelly (drums) and Gram Parsons (guitar). Hillman and Parsons left to form the Flying Burrito Brothers. McGuinn again re-formed with Clarence White (guitar), John York (bass) and Gene Parsons (drums). Reunions with original members in 1973 and 1979. McGuinn, Clark and Hillman later recorded as a trio.	
6/05/65	**1**(1)	10	1. **Mr. Tambourine Man**	Columbia 43271
8/21/65	**40**	1	2. All I Really Want To Do	Columbia 43332

DATE	POS	WKS	ARTIST—RECORD TITLE	LABEL & NO.
11/06/65	**1**(3)	11	3. **Turn! Turn! Turn!** lyrics adapted by Pete Seeger from the Book of Ecclesiastes	Columbia 43424
4/30/66	**14**	6	4. Eight Miles High	Columbia 43578
10/22/66	**36**	2	5. Mr. Spaceman	Columbia 43766
2/18/67	**29**	3	6. So You Want To Be A Rock 'N' Roll Star	Columbia 43987
4/29/67	**30**	3	7. My Back Pages	Columbia 44054
			EDD BYRNES & CONNIE STEVENS	
			Byrnes: born Eddie Breitenberger on 7/30/33 in New York City. Best known as Kookie on the TV series "77 Sunset Strip."	
4/27/59	**4**	11	1. **Kookie, Kookie (Lend Me Your Comb)** **[N]**	Warner 5047
			C	
			THE CADETS	
			Los Angeles R&B quintet: Aaron Collins (lead singer), Ted Taylor, William "Dub" Jones (bass man for The Coasters), Willie Davis and Lloyd McCraw. Also recorded as The Jacks.	
7/21/56	**15**	7	1. Stranded In The Jungle [N] Best Seller #15 / Jockey #16 / Juke Box #16 / Top 100 #18	Modern 994
			THE CADILLACS	
			R&B vocal group formed at P.S. 139 in Harlem in 1953. Originally called the Carnations. The Cadillacs were the first R&B vocal group to extensively use choreography in their stage routines.	
2/04/56	**17**	5	1. Speedoo Best Seller #17 / Top 100 #30 song named after nickname of group's lead singer, Earl Carroll	Josie 785
1/12/59	**28**	3	2. Peek-A-Boo	Josie 846
			JOHN CAFFERTY & THE BEAVER BROWN BAND	
			Rock sextet from Rhode Island. Wrote and recorded the music for the soundtrack "Eddie & The Cruisers."	
9/15/84	**7**	11	1. **On The Dark Side** **[R]** originally charted on 10/8/83 (POS 64)	Scotti Br. 04594
12/08/84†	**31**	7	2. Tender Years [R] originally charted on 1/28/84 (POS 78) above 2: from the film "Eddie & The Cruisers"	Scotti Br. 04682
6/01/85	**22**	8	3. Tough All Over	Scotti Br. 04891
8/31/85	**18**	8	4. C-I-T-Y	Scotti Br. 05452
			TANE CAIN	
			Wife of Journey's Jonathan Cain.	
9/18/82	**37**	3	1. Holdin' On	RCA 13287
			AL CAIOLA	
			Born on 9/7/20 in Jersey City, New Jersey. Guitarist/composer/bandleader. First recorded for Savoy in 1955. Prolific studio work.	
1/16/61	**35**	4	1. The Magnificent Seven [I] from the film of the same title	United Art. 261

DATE	POS	WKS	ARTIST—RECORD TITLE	LABEL & NO.
5/01/61	**19**	5	2. Bonanza [I] theme from the TV series of the same title	United Art. 302
			BOBBY CALDWELL	
			Vocalist/composer/multi-instrumentalist, born on 8/15/51 in New York City. Wrote tracks for "New Mickey Mouse Club" TV show and commercials. With Johnny Winter in the early 1970s.	
2/03/79	**9**	12	1. **What You Won't Do For Love**	Clouds 11
			J.J. CALE	
			Born John J. Cale on 12/5/38 in Oklahoma City. Singer/songwriter/guitarist.	
3/11/72	**22**	8	1. Crazy Mama	Shelter 7314
			CAMEO	
			New York City soul-funk group, formed in 1974 as The New York City Players by Larry "Mr. B" Blackmon (drums) and Gregory "Straps" Johnson (keyboards). Vocals by Wayne Cooper and Tomi "Tee" Jenkins. Lineup since 1985: Blackmon, Jenkins and Nathan Leftenant.	
10/04/86	**6**	14	1. **Word Up**	Atl. Art. 884933
2/14/87	**21**	7	2. Candy	Atl. Art. 888193
			GLEN CAMPBELL	
			Born on 4/22/36 near Delight, Arkansas. Vocalist/guitarist/composer. With his uncle Dick Bills' band, 1954-58. To Los Angeles; recorded with The Champs in 1960; became prolific studio musician; with The Beach Boys, 1965. Own TV show, "The Glen Campbell Goodtime Hour," 1968-72. In films "True Grit," "Norwood" and "Strange Homecoming."	
11/25/67	**26**	7	1. By The Time I Get To Phoenix	Capitol 2015
5/25/68	**36**	2	2. I Wanna Live	Capitol 2146
8/03/68	**32**	3	3. Dreams Of The Everyday Housewife	Capitol 2224
11/02/68	**39**	1	4. Gentle On My Mind [R] originally charted in 1967 (POS 62)	Capitol 5939
11/16/68†	**3**	13	● 5. **Wichita Lineman**	Capitol 2302
3/08/69	**36**	1	6. Let It Be Me	Capitol 2387
			GLEN CAMPBELL & BOBBIE GENTRY	
3/15/69	**4**	10	● 7. **Galveston**	Capitol 2428
5/17/69	**26**	5	8. Where's The Playground Susie	Capitol 2494
8/23/69	**35**	2	9. True Grit from the John Wayne movie of the same title	Capitol 2573
11/01/69	**23**	7	10. Try A Little Kindness	Capitol 2659
1/31/70	**19**	7	11. Honey Come Back	Capitol 2718
3/14/70	**27**	6	12. All I Have To Do Is Dream	Capitol 2745
			BOBBIE GENTRY & GLEN CAMPBELL	
5/09/70	**40**	2	13. Oh Happy Day	Capitol 2787
9/26/70	**10**	9	14. **It's Only Make Believe**	Capitol 2905
3/27/71	**31**	4	15. Dream Baby (How Long Must I Dream) 1-15: produced, arranged and conducted by Al de Lory	Capitol 3062
6/21/75	**1**(2)	18	● 16. **Rhinestone Cowboy**	Capitol 4095
11/22/75†	**11**	11	17. Country Boy (You Got Your Feet In L.A.)	Capitol 4155
4/17/76	**27**	5	18. Don't Pull Your Love/Then You Can Tell Me Goodbye	Capitol 4245
3/05/77	**1**(1)	15	● 19. **Southern Nights**	Capitol 4376
8/13/77	**39**	2	20. Sunflower	Capitol 4445

DATE	POS	WKS	ARTIST—RECORD TITLE	LABEL & NO.
12/09/78	**38**	2	21. Can You Fool	Capitol 4584
			JO ANN CAMPBELL	
			Born on 7/20/38 in Jacksonville, Florida. First recorded for El Dorado in 1957. In the films "Johnny Melody," "Go Johnny Go" and "Hey, Let's Twist." Married Troy Seals in the early 60s; recorded together as Jo Ann & Troy in 1964.	
9/08/62	**38**	3	1. (I'm The Girl On) Wolverton Mountain	Cameo 223
			CANNED HEAT	
			Blues-rock band formed in Los Angeles in 1966. Consisted of Bob "The Bear" Hite (vocals, harmonica), Alan "Blind Owl" Wilson (guitar, harmonica, vocals), Henry Vestine (guitar), Larry Taylor (bass) and Frank Cook (drums). Cook replaced by Fito de la Parra in 1968. Vestine replaced by Harvey Mandel in 1969. Wilson died of a drug overdose on 9/3/70 (27). Hite died of a drug-related heart attack on 4/6/81 (36).	
9/07/68	**16**	7	1. On The Road Again	Liberty 56038
12/21/68†	**11**	9	2. Going Up The Country	Liberty 56077
11/07/70	**26**	6	3. Let's Work Together	Liberty 56151
			CANNIBAL & THE HEADHUNTERS	
			Four Mexican-American youths based in Los Angeles; led by Frankie "Cannibal" Garcia.	
4/17/65	**30**	6	1. Land Of 1000 Dances	Rampart 642
			ACE CANNON	
			Born on 5/5/34 in Grenada, Mississippi. Saxophonist since age 10. Worked with Bill Black's Combo (Hi Records' studio band).	
1/27/62	**17**	10	1. Tuff [I]	Hi 2040
5/19/62	**36**	1	2. Blues (Stay Away From Me) [I]	Hi 2051
			FREDDY CANNON	
			Born Frederick Picariello on 12/4/40 in Lynn, Massachusetts. Local work with own band, Freddy Karmon & The Hurricanes. Nickname "Boom Boom" came from big bass drum sound on his records. Band arrangements by Frank Slay on all Swan recordings. Also see Danny & The Juniors.	
5/25/59	**6**	10	1. **Tallahassee Lassie** song written by Freddy's mother	Swan 4031
12/07/59†	**3**	11	2. **Way Down Yonder In New Orleans** jazz song written in 1922	Swan 4043
3/07/60	**34**	3	3. Chattanooga Shoe Shine Boy	Swan 4050
5/30/60	**28**	4	4. Jump Over	Swan 4053
9/04/61	**35**	1	5. Transistor Sister	Swan 4078
5/26/62	**3**	12	6. **Palisades Park** written by Chuck ("Gong Show") Barris	Swan 4106
2/15/64	**16**	6	7. Abigail Beecher	Warner 5409
8/28/65	**13**	6	8. Action from the TV show "Where The Action Is"	Warner 5645
			JIM CAPALDI	
			Born on 8/24/44 in Evesham, England. Drummer with Traffic, 1967-74.	
5/28/83	**28**	5	1. That's Love	Atlantic 89849

DATE	POS	WKS	ARTIST—RECORD TITLE	LABEL & NO.
			THE CAPITOLS	
			R&B vocal trio from Detroit. Consisted of lead singer Sam George (murdered on 3/17/82 [39]), "Donald Norman" Storball and "Richard Mitchell" McDougall.	
5/21/66	**7**	11	1. **Cool Jerk**	Karen 1524
			THE CAPRIS	
			Italian vocal group from Queens, New York, formed in 1958. Consisted of Nick Santamaria (lead), Vinny Narcardo (baritone), Mike Mincelli (1st tenor), Frank Reina (2nd tenor) and John Cassese (bass). Group disbanded in 1959, re-formed when song "There's A Moon Out Tonight" was reissued on Lost Nite and became a hit in 1961.	
1/23/61	**3**	10	1. **There's A Moon Out Tonight**	Old Town 1094
			CAPTAIN & TENNILLE	
			The Captain: Daryl Dragon (b: 8/27/42, Los Angeles); and Toni Tennille (b: 5/8/43, Montgomery, AL). Husband and wife. Dragon is the son of notable conductor Carmen Dragon. Keyboardist with The Beach Boys, nicknamed the "Captain" by Mike Love. Duo had own TV show on ABC from 1976-77.	
5/24/75	**1**(4)	16	● 1. **Love Will Keep Us Together**	A&M 1672
10/04/75	**4**	14	● 2. **The Way I Want To Touch You**	A&M 1725
2/07/76	**3**	13	● 3. **Lonely Night (Angel Face)**	A&M 1782
5/08/76	**4**	12	● 4. **Shop Around**	A&M 1817
10/09/76	**4**	15	● 5. **Muskrat Love**	A&M 1870
4/02/77	**13**	8	6. Can't Stop Dancin'	A&M 1912
9/09/78	**10**	14	7. **You Never Done It Like That**	A&M 2063
1/27/79	**40**	1	8. You Need A Woman Tonight	A&M 2106
11/10/79†	**1**(1)	22	● 9. **Do That To Me One More Time**	Casablanca 2215
			IRENE CARA	
			Vocalist/actress/dancer/pianist, born on 3/18/59 in New York City. Professional debut at age 7. Won Obie Award for "The Me Nobody Knows" in 1970. Much TV work, including "Electric Company"; in films "Fame," "DC Cab" and "The Cotton Club."	
7/26/80	**4**	12	1. **Fame**	RSO 1034
9/27/80	**19**	9	2. Out Here On My Own above 2: from the film "Fame"	RSO 1048
4/16/83	**1**(6)	20	● 3. **Flashdance...What A Feeling** from the film "Flashdance"	Casablanca 811440
11/05/83	**13**	10	4. Why Me?	Geffen 29464
1/28/84	**37**	3	5. The Dream (Hold On To Your Dream) from the film "D.C. Cab"	Geffen 29396
4/14/84	**8**	11	6. **Breakdance**	Geffen 29328
			THE CARAVELLES	
			English duo: Andrea Simpson & Lois Wilkinson.	
11/23/63	**3**	10	1. **You Don't Have To Be A Baby To Cry**	Smash 1852
			THE CAREFREES	
			British group.	
4/11/64	**39**	1	1. We Love You Beatles [N]	London Int. 10614

DATE	POS	WKS	ARTIST—RECORD TITLE	LABEL & NO.
			TONY CAREY	
			Born on 10/16/53; raised in America. Settled in Germany in 1978. Ex-keyboardist with Rainbow; leader of the Planet P Project.	
3/31/84	**22**	8	1. A Fine Fine Day	MCA 52343
7/14/84	**33**	2	2. The First Day Of Summer	MCA 52388
			HENSON CARGILL	
			Born on 2/5/41 in Oklahoma City. Country singer.	
1/20/68	**25**	7	1. Skip A Rope	Monument 1041
			BELINDA CARLISLE	
			Born on 8/16/58 in Hollywood. Lead singer of the Go-Go's, 1978-84. Married to Morgan Mason, son of late actor James Mason.	
6/21/86	**3**	14	1. **Mad About You**	I.R.S. 52815
10/10/87	**1**(1)	15	2. **Heaven Is A Place On Earth**	MCA 53181
1/23/88	**2**(1)	13	3. **I Get Weak**	MCA 53242
5/07/88	**7**	10	4. **Circle In The Sand**	MCA 53308
			CARL CARLTON	
			Soul singer, born in 1952 in Detroit. Singing since age 9. First recorded for Lando in 1964.	
10/12/74	**6**	10	1. **Everlasting Love**	Back Beat 27001
9/26/81	**22**	7	● 2. She's A Bad Mama Jama (She's Built, She's Stacked)	20th Century 2488
			ERIC CARMEN	
			Born on 8/11/49 in Cleveland. Classical training at Cleveland Institute of Music from early years to mid-teens. Lead singer of the Raspberries from 1970-74.	
1/17/76	**2**(3)	14	● 1. **All By Myself**	Arista 0165
5/22/76	**11**	10	2. Never Gonna Fall In Love Again	Arista 0184
9/18/76	**34**	3	3. Sunrise	Arista 0200
9/24/77	**23**	8	4. She Did It	Arista 0266
10/28/78	**19**	7	5. Change Of Heart	Arista 0354
2/09/85	**35**	4	6. I Wanna Hear It From Your Lips	Geffen 29118
12/12/87†	**4**	16	7. **Hungry Eyes** from the film "Dirty Dancing"	RCA 5315
6/18/88	**3**	13	8. **Make Me Lose Control** all of above (except #7): written by Carmen	Arista 9686
			KIM CARNES	
			Born on 7/20/45 in Los Angeles. Vocalist/pianist/composer. Member of The New Christy Minstrels with husband/co-writer Dave Ellingson and Kenny Rogers, late 1960s. Wrote and performed commercials. Also see Randy Meisner.	
8/05/78	**36**	3	1. You're A Part Of Me **GENE COTTON with KIM CARNES**	Ariola 7704
4/12/80	**4**	14	2. **Don't Fall In Love With A Dreamer** **KENNY ROGERS with KIM CARNES**	United Art. 1345
6/14/80	**10**	15	3. **More Love**	EMI America 8045
4/11/81	**1**(9)	20	● 4. **Bette Davis Eyes** co-written by Jackie DeShannon	EMI America 8077
8/29/81	**28**	6	5. Draw Of The Cards	EMI America 8087
9/11/82	**29**	6	6. Voyeur	EMI America 8127

DATE	POS	WKS	ARTIST—RECORD TITLE	LABEL & NO.
12/25/82†	**36**	4	7. Does It Make You Remember	EMI America 8147
11/26/83	**40**	2	8. Invisible Hands	EMI America 8181
10/13/84	**15**	9	9. What About Me? **KENNY ROGERS with KIM CARNES & JAMES INGRAM**	RCA 13899
6/01/85	**15**	9	10. Crazy In The Night (Barking At Airplanes)	EMI America 8267
			RENATO CAROSONE	
			Male vocalist from Italy.	
5/12/58	**18**	9	1. Torero [F] Jockey #18 / Top 100 #19 / Best Sellers #20	Capitol 71080
			CARPENTERS	
			Richard Carpenter (b: 10/15/46) and sister Karen (b: 3/2/50; d: 2/4/83 of heart failure due to anorexia [32]). From New Haven, Connecticut. Richard played piano from age 9. To Downey, California in 1963. Karen played drums in group with Richard and bass player Wes Jacobs in 1965. The trio recorded for RCA in 1966. After a period with the band Spectrum, the Carpenters recorded as a duo for A&M in 1969. Won the 1970 Best New Artist Grammy Award. Hosts of the TV variety show "Make Your Own Kind Of Music" in 1971.	
6/27/70	**1(4)**	15	● 1. **(They Long To Be) Close To You**	A&M 1183
10/03/70	**2(4)**	14	● 2. **We've Only Just Begun**	A&M 1217
2/13/71	**3**	12	● 3. **For All We Know** from the film "Lovers & Other Strangers"	A&M 1243
5/22/71	**2(2)**	11	● 4. **Rainy Days And Mondays**	A&M 1260
9/11/71	**2(2)**	12	● 5. **Superstar**	A&M 1289
1/22/72	**2(2)**	11	● 6. **Hurting Each Other**	A&M 1322
5/13/72	**12**	8	7. It's Going To Take Some Time	A&M 1351
7/22/72	**7**	9	8. **Goodbye To Love**	A&M 1367
3/10/73	**3**	11	● 9. **Sing**	A&M 1413
6/16/73	**2(1)**	12	● 10. **Yesterday Once More**	A&M 1446
10/20/73	**1(2)**	16	● 11. **Top Of The World**	A&M 1468
4/27/74	**11**	9	12. I Won't Last A Day Without You	A&M 1521
12/07/74†	**1(1)**	12	● 13. **Please Mr. Postman**	A&M 1646
4/12/75	**4**	9	14. **Only Yesterday**	A&M 1677
8/16/75	**17**	7	15. Solitaire	A&M 1721
3/13/76	**12**	8	16. There's A Kind Of Hush (All Over The World)	A&M 1800
7/04/76	**25**	5	17. I Need To Be In Love	A&M 1828
6/18/77	**35**	3	18. All You Get From Love Is A Love Song	A&M 1940
11/05/77	**32**	4	19. Calling Occupants Of Interplanetary Craft	A&M 1978
7/04/81	**16**	8	20. Touch Me When We're Dancing	A&M 2344
			CATHY CARR	
			Songstress from the Bronx, New York; born on 6/28/36.	
4/07/56	**2(1)**	18	1. **Ivory Tower** Juke Box #2 / Top 100 #6 / Best Seller #7 / Jockey #9	Fraternity 734

DATE	POS	WKS	ARTIST—RECORD TITLE	LABEL & NO.
			JOE "FINGERS" CARR - see LOU BUSCH	
			VALERIE CARR	
			Black vocalist from the U.S.	
6/09/58	**19**	2	1. When The Boys Talk About The Girls Jockey #19 / Top 100 #84	Roulette 4066
			VIKKI CARR	
			Born Florencia Martinez Cardona on 7/19/41 in El Paso, Texas. A regular on the Ray Anthony musical variety TV show in 1962.	
9/30/67	**3**	11	1. **It Must Be Him**	Liberty 55986
1/27/68	**34**	1	2. The Lesson	Liberty 56012
6/28/69	**35**	4	3. With Pen In Hand	Liberty 56092
			PAUL CARRACK	
			Born on 4/22/51 in Sheffield, England. Lead singer of Ace (1973-76), Squeeze (1981) and Mike + The Mechanics (since 1985).	
10/30/82	**37**	2	1. I Need You	Epic 03146
12/19/87†	**9**	13	2. **Don't Shed A Tear**	Chrysalis 43164
4/23/88	**28**	5	3. One Good Reason	Chrysalis 43204
			KEITH CARRADINE	
			Leading actor since 1971. Son of John Carradine; half brother of David Carradine.	
6/12/76	**17**	12	1. I'm Easy from the movie "Nashville" (which Keith appeared in)	ABC 12117
			DAVID CARROLL	
			Born Nook Schrier on 10/15/13 in Chicago. Arranger/conductor since 1951 for many top Mercury artists.	
1/08/55	**8**	17	1. **Melody Of Love** [I] Jockey #8 / Best Seller #9 / Juke Box #12	Mercury 70516
12/17/55	**20**	1	2. It's Almost Tomorrow Jockey #20 / Top 100 #34 vocal: Jack Halloran Singers	Mercury 70717
			THE CARS	
			Rock group formed in Boston in 1976. Consisted of Ric Ocasek (lead vocals, guitar), Elliot Easton (guitar), Greg Hawkes (keyboards), Benjamin Orr (bass, vocals) and David Robinson (drums; formerly with the Modern Lovers). Ocasek, Orr and Hawkes had been in trio in the early 70s. Group named by Robinson, got start at the Rat Club in Boston. All songs written by Ocasek. Disbanded in 1988.	
8/12/78	**27**	7	1. Just What I Needed	Elektra 45491
12/09/78	**35**	5	2. My Best Friend's Girl	Elektra 45537
7/28/79	**14**	9	3. Let's Go	Elektra 46063
10/11/80	**37**	3	4. Touch And Go	Elektra 47039
12/12/81†	**4**	17	5. **Shake It Up**	Elektra 47250
3/24/84	**7**	11	6. **You Might Think**	Elektra 69744
5/26/84	**12**	11	7. Magic	Elektra 69724
8/11/84	**3**	14	8. **Drive**	Elektra 69706
11/10/84	**20**	10	9. Hello Again	Elektra 69681
3/09/85	**33**	5	10. Why Can't I Have You	Elektra 69657
11/16/85†	**7**	12	11. **Tonight She Comes**	Elektra 69589
3/08/86	**32**	4	12. I'm Not The One	Elektra 69569

DATE	POS	WKS	ARTIST—RECORD TITLE	LABEL & NO.
9/12/87	**17**	9	13. You Are The Girl	Elektra 69446
			KIT CARSON	
			Real name: Liza Morrow.	
12/31/55†	**11**	11	1. Band Of Gold	Capitol 3283
			Jockey #11 / Top 100 #17	
			MINDY CARSON	
			Born on 7/16/27 in New York City. Sang with Paul Whiteman in the 40s.	
8/27/55	**13**	8	1. Wake The Town And Tell The People	Columbia 40537
			Jockey #13 / Juke Box #13 / Best Seller #20 / Top 100 #33 pre	
1/05/57	**34**	2	2. Since I Met You Baby	Columbia 40789
			CARLENE CARTER - see ROBERT ELLIS ORRALL	
			CLARENCE CARTER	
			Born in 1936 in Montgomery, Alabama. R&B vocalist/guitarist. Blind since age 1; self-taught on guitar at age 11. Teamed with vocalist/pianist Calvin Scott as Clarence & Calvin, recorded for Fairlane in the early 60s. Carter went solo in 1966. Married for a time to Candi Staton.	
8/17/68	**6**	11	● 1. **Slip Away**	Atlantic 2508
11/30/68†	**13**	11	● 2. Too Weak To Fight	Atlantic 2569
3/29/69	**31**	5	3. Snatching It Back	Atlantic 2605
8/01/70	**4**	12	● 4. **Patches**	Atlantic 2748
			JUNE CARTER - see JOHNNY CASH	
			MEL CARTER	
			Born on 4/22/43 in Cincinnati. Soul vocalist/actor. Sang on local radio from age 4; with Lionel Hampton on stage show at age 9. With Paul Gayten, Jimmy Scott bands. Joined Raspberry Singers gospel group in the early 50s. Own gospel group, The Carvetts, in the mid-50s. Named Top Gospel Tenor in 1957. With Gospel Pearls in the early 60s. First recorded for Mercury in 1959. Has appeared as actor on TV's "Quincy," "Sanford And Son," "Marcus Welby, MD" and "Magnum P.I."	
7/24/65	**8**	11	1. **Hold Me, Thrill Me, Kiss Me**	Imperial 66113
11/27/65	**38**	2	2. (All Of A Sudden) My Heart Sings	Imperial 66138
5/21/66	**32**	2	3. Band Of Gold	Imperial 66165
			THE CASCADES	
			Group from San Diego consisting of John Gummoe, Eddie Snyder, David Stevens, David Wilson and David Zabo.	
1/26/63	**3**	13	1. **Rhythm Of The Rain**	Valiant 6026
			written by John Gummoe	
			ALVIN CASH & THE CRAWLERS	
			Born on 2/15/39 in St. Louis. Singer/dancer. Formed song/dance troupe, The Crawlers, in 1960, with brothers Robert, Arthur and George (ages 8-10). They never sang on any of Alvin's hits. Alvin moved to Chicago in 1963. First recorded for Mar-V-Lus in 1964. Cut "Twine Time" with backing band the Nightlighters from Louisville, who changed their name to the Registers.	
1/30/65	**14**	7	1. Twine Time [I]	Mar-V-Lus 6002

DATE	POS	WKS	ARTIST—RECORD TITLE	LABEL & NO.
			JOHNNY CASH	
			Born on 2/26/32 in Kingsland, Arkansas. To Dyess, Arkansas at age 3. Brother Roy had the Dixie Rhythm Ramblers band in late 40s. In US Air Force, 1950-54. Formed trio with Luther Perkins (guitar) and Marshall Grant (bass) in 1955. First recorded for Sun in 1955. On "Louisiana Hayride" and "Grand Ole Opry" shows in 1957. Own TV show for ABC from 1969-71. Worked with June Carter from 1961, married her in March of 1968. Daughter Rosanne Cash and stepdaughter Carlene Carter currently enjoying successful singing careers.	
10/20/56	**17**	11	1. I Walk The Line Best Seller #17 / Juke Box #17 / Top 100 #19 / Jockey #25	Sun 241
2/10/58	**14**	13	2. Ballad Of A Teenage Queen Jockey #14 / Best Seller #16 / Top 100 #16	Sun 283
6/09/58	**11**	13	3. Guess Things Happen That Way Best Seller #11 / Top 100 #11 / Jockey #18	Sun 295
9/01/58	**24**	6	4. The Ways Of A Woman In Love Hot 100 #24 / Best Seller #26	Sun 302
11/10/58	**38**	1	5. All Over Again	Columbia 41251
2/02/59	**32**	6	6. Don't Take Your Guns To Town	Columbia 41313
6/22/63	**17**	10	7. Ring Of Fire	Columbia 42788
3/14/64	**35**	3	8. Understand Your Man	Columbia 42964
6/29/68	**32**	6	9. Folsom Prison Blues original version released in 1956 on Sun 232	Columbia 44513
8/02/69	**2**(3)	11	● 10. **A Boy Named Sue** **[N]** recorded live at San Quentin prison	Columbia 44944
2/21/70	**36**	2	11. If I Were A Carpenter **JOHNNY CASH & JUNE CARTER**	Columbia 45064
4/25/70	**19**	6	12. What Is Truth	Columbia 45134
5/15/76	**29**	3	13. One Piece At A Time [N] **JOHNNY CASH & THE TENNESSEE THREE**	Columbia 10321
			ROSANNE CASH	
			Born on 5/24/55 in Memphis, daughter of Johnny Cash and Vivian Liberto. Raised by her mother in California, then moved to Nashville after high school graduation. Worked in the Johnny Cash Road Show. Married Rodney Crowell in 1979.	
6/13/81	**22**	7	1. Seven Year Ache	Columbia 11426
			CASHMAN & WEST	
			Duo of record producers Dennis "Terry Cashman" Minogue (b: 7/5/41) and Thomas "Tommy West" Picardo, Jr. (b: 8/17/42) Also see Buchanan Brothers.	
10/21/72	**27**	7	1. American City Suite Sweet City Song/All Around The Town/A Friend Is Dying	Dunhill 4324
			THE CASINOS	
			9-man group from Cincinnati formed by Gene Hughes (lead singer).	
1/28/67	**6**	10	1. **Then You Can Tell Me Goodbye**	Fraternity 977
			DAVID CASSIDY	
			Born on 4/12/50 in New York City. Son of actor Jack Cassidy and actress Evelyn Ward. Played Keith and was lead singer for TV's "The Partridge Family."	
11/13/71	**9**	11	● 1. **Cherish**	Bell 45150
3/25/72	**37**	2	2. Could It Be Forever	Bell 45187
6/10/72	**25**	5	3. How Can I Be Sure	Bell 45220

DATE	POS	WKS	ARTIST—RECORD TITLE	LABEL & NO.
10/14/72	**38**	2	4. Rock Me Baby	Bell 45260
			SHAUN CASSIDY	
			Born on 9/27/59 in Los Angeles. Son of actor Jack Cassidy and actress Shirley Jones. Played Joe Hardy on TV's "The Hardy Boys." Shaun & David Cassidy are half brothers. Cast member of TV's soap series "General Hospital" in 1987.	
6/04/77	**1(1)**	12	● 1. **Da Doo Ron Ron**	Warner 8365
8/20/77	**3**	15	● 2. **That's Rock 'N' Roll**	Warner 8423
11/26/77†	**7**	12	● 3. **Hey Deanie**	Warner 8488
4/22/78	**31**	5	4. Do You Believe In Magic	Warner 8533
			THE CASTAWAYS	
			Quintet formed at the University of Minnesota in 1965.	
9/18/65	**12**	9	1. Liar, Liar	Soma 1433
			THE CASTELLS	
			Santa Rosa, California quartet: Bob Ussery, Tom Hicks, Joe Kelly and Chuck Girard.	
7/03/61	**20**	7	1. Sacred	Era 3048
5/26/62	**21**	5	2. So This Is Love	Era 3073
			BOOMER CASTLEMAN	
			Owen "Boomer" Clarke of The Lewis & Clarke Expedition. Originally from Farmers Branch, Texas.	
5/31/75	**33**	3	1. Judy Mae	Mums 6038
			THE JIMMY CASTOR BUNCH	
			Jimmy was born on 6/2/43 in New York City. R&B singer/saxophonist/composer/arranger. Formed the Jimmy Castor Bunch in 1972, with Gerry Thomas (keyboards), Doug Gibson (bass), Harry Jensen (guitar), Lenny Fridie, Jr. (congas) & Bobby Manigault (drums).	
2/04/67	**31**	3	1. Hey, Leroy, Your Mama's Callin' You [I] shown only as: **JIMMY CASTOR**	Smash 2069
5/27/72	**6**	10	● 2. **Troglodyte (Cave Man)** **[N]**	RCA 1029
3/22/75	**16**	8	3. The Bertha Butt Boogie (Part 1) [N]	Atlantic 3232
			CAT MOTHER & the ALL NIGHT NEWS BOYS	
			New York rock quintet produced by Jimi Hendrix.	
7/12/69	**21**	6	1. Good Old Rock 'N Roll Sweet Little Sixteen/Long Tall Sally/Chantilly Lace/Whole Lotta Shakin' Goin On/Blue Suede Shoes/Party Doll	Polydor 14002
			CATE BROS.	
			Duo of twins Ernie (vocals/piano) and Earl (guitar), born on 12/26/42 in Fayetteville, Arkansas. Produced by Steve Cropper.	
4/17/76	**24**	8	1. Union Man	Asylum 45294
			GEORGE CATES	
			Born on 10/19/11 in New York City. Arranger for Bing Crosby, Teresa Brewer, The Andrews Sisters and others. Musical director of the Lawrence Welk TV Show for 25 years. Also see Steve Allen.	
4/21/56	**4**	19	1. **Moonglow And Theme From "Picnic"** **[I]** Top 100 #4 / Jockey #4 / Best Seller #5 / Juke Box #7 featuring The Stan Wrightsman Quartet; from the film "Picnic"	Coral 61618

The Bee Gees started as a quintet but had dwindled down to brothers Barry, Robin, and Maurice Gibb by the time the group racked up the first of nine No. 1 singles, "How Can You Mend a Broken Heart" (1971). Their "You Win Again" failed in the US but was the biggest hit in Europe for all of 1987.

Harry Belafonte was the second-biggest act of 1956, after Elvis. He had three top-three, million-selling albums: *Mark Twain And Other Favorites, Belafonte*, and *Calypso*. In 1985, he was instrumental in organizing USA for Africa's "We Are the World."

George Benson's "This Masquerade" was the first Grammy-winning Record of the Year of the 70s not to hit No. 1, but its peak position of No. 10 is stratospheric compared with that of the 1987 winner, Paul Simon's "Graceland," which topped out at No. 81.

Blackfoot began as another Jacksonville-based Southern-rock band (similar to the Allman Brothers and Lynyrd Skynyrd) with albums like *Flyin' High* (1976). They later anticipated the future and turned toward heavy metal with the 1981 LP *Marauder*.

Bloodstone's classic American soul harmonies were, ironically, first successful in Britain, but their "Natural High," as beatific a song as ever made the top 10, finally broke the group in the US in 1973. They were mainstays on the soul charts throughout the 70s.

The Blues Magoos' "We Ain't Got Nothin' Yet" was an explosive (read: loud) pre-punk classic (No. 5, 1967). They later drifted toward soft and Southern rock before disbanding in the early 70s.

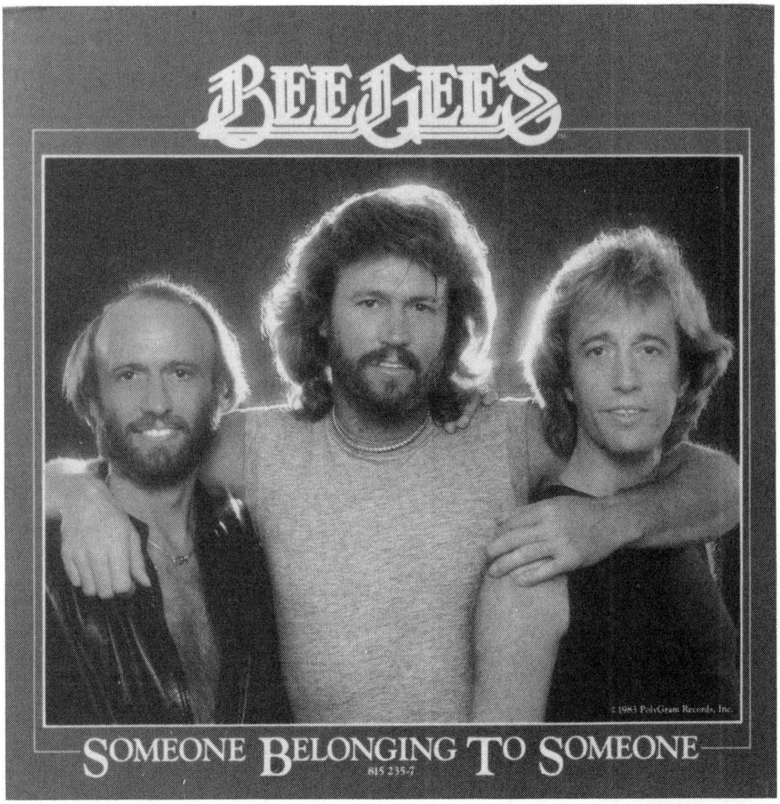

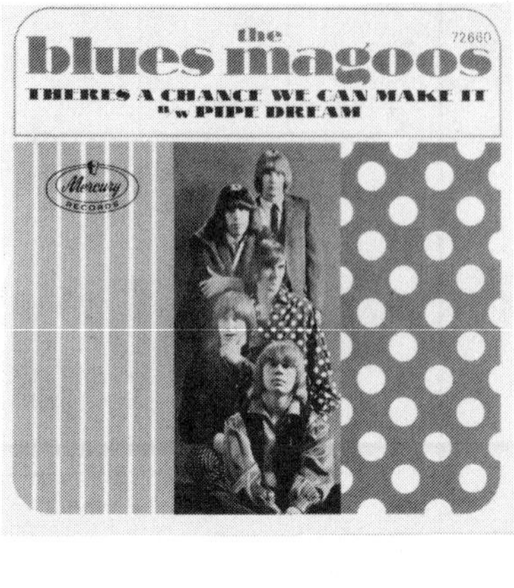

Bon Jovi has been called the "poor man's Van Halen," but their fans can't be *that* poor. Nine million of them bought the group's No. 1 LP *Slippery When Wet*, and another five million bought the No. 1 follow-up, *New Jersey*.

Pat Boone made a habit of recording "well-scrubbed" versions of top R & B hits like "Ain't That A Shame," the first of his five No. 1 singles.

David Bowie's two No. 1 singles were collaborations with partners of more famous teams. "Let's Dance" was co-produced by Nile Rodgers, who wrote and produced many hits with bassist Bernard Edwards. "Fame" was co-written with John Lennon. His famous partner was named Paul.

Laura Branigan's "Gloria" stalled at No. 2 behind Toni Basil's "Mickey," marking only the third time "name songs" occupied the top two. Paul Anka's "Diana" and Debbie Reynolds' "Tammy" held them down in 1957, the Four Seasons' "Sherry" and Tommy Roe's "Sheila" in 1962. What's in a name, anyway?

Bobby Brown got to the top the old-fashioned way: his *Don't Be Cruel* LP hit No. 1 without getting higher than No. 10 on the Compact Disk chart.

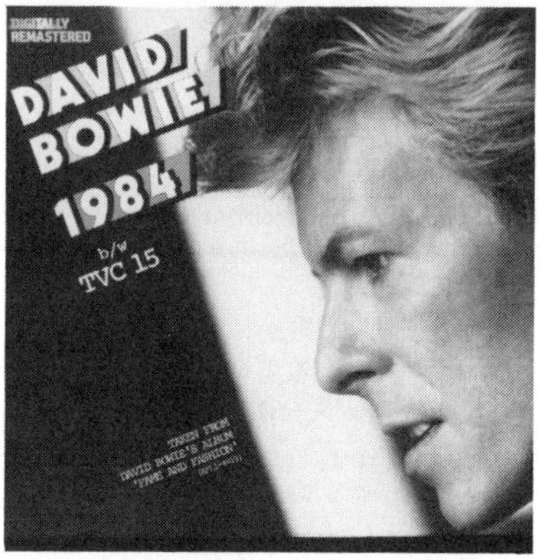

DATE	POS	WKS	ARTIST—RECORD TITLE	LABEL & NO.
			CATHY JEAN & THE ROOMMATES	
			Cathy was born on 9/8/45 in Brooklyn. Roommates: male teen-age vocal quartet from Queens, New York.	
3/06/61	**12**	10	1. Please Love Me Forever	Valmor 007
			FELIX CAVALIERE	
			Born on 11/29/43 in Pelham, New York. Lead singer of The Rascals after a stint with Joey Dee & The Starlighters.	
4/12/80	**36**	3	1. Only A Lonely Heart Sees	Epic 50829
			C COMPANY Featuring TERRY NELSON	
5/01/71	**37**	3	● 1. Battle Hymn Of Lt. Calley [S] Calley: U.S. Army officer court-martialled for the massacre of civilians at My Lai, Vietnam	Plantation 73
			CELEBRATION featuring MIKE LOVE	
			Mike is The Beach Boys' lead singer.	
6/03/78	**28**	4	1. Almost Summer from the film of the same title	MCA 40891
			CERRONE	
			Composer/producer/drummer, born Jean-Marc Cerrone in France in 1952.	
3/26/77	**36**	3	1. Love In 'C' Minor - Pt. I [I]	Cotillion 44215
			PETER CETERA	
			Born on 9/13/44 in Chicago. Lead singer and bass guitarist of Chicago for their first 17 albums.	
6/21/86	**1**(2)	14	1. **Glory Of Love** theme from the film "The Karate Kid Part II"	Full Moon 28662
10/11/86	**1**(1)	15	2. **The Next Time I Fall** **PETER CETERA with AMY GRANT**	Full Moon 28597
8/06/88	**4**	13	3. **One Good Woman**	Full Moon 27824
			CHAD & JEREMY	
			Folk-rock duo formed in the early 60s: Chad Stuart (b: 12/10/43, England) & Jeremy Clyde (b: 3/22/44, England). Broke up in 1967. Re-formed briefly in 1982.	
6/13/64	**21**	6	1. Yesterday's Gone	World Art. 1021
9/19/64	**7**	9	2. **A Summer Song**	World Art. 1027
12/12/64†	**15**	8	3. Willow Weep For Me	World Art. 1034
3/13/65	**23**	5	4. If I Loved You from the musical "Carousel"	World Art. 1041
5/29/65	**17**	6	5. Before And After	Columbia 43277
8/28/65	**35**	3	6. I Don't Wanna Lose You Baby	Columbia 43339
8/13/66	**30**	2	7. Distant Shores	Columbia 43682
			CHAIRMEN OF THE BOARD	
			Soul vocal group formed in Detroit in 1969. Consisted of General Norman Johnson, Danny Woods, Harrison Kennedy and Eddie Curtis. First recorded for Invictus in 1969. Johnson was leader of The Showmen from 1961-67; wrote "Patches," hit for Clarence Carter. Johnson went solo in 1976.	
2/07/70	**3**	12	● 1. **Give Me Just A Little More Time**	Invictus 9074
6/06/70	**38**	2	2. (You've Got Me) Dangling On A String	Invictus 9078
9/12/70	**38**	2	3. Everything's Tuesday	Invictus 9079
12/12/70†	**13**	9	4. Pay To The Piper	Invictus 9081

DATE	POS	WKS	ARTIST—RECORD TITLE	LABEL & NO.
			THE CHAKACHAS	
			Belgian sextet led by Gaston Boogaerts.	
2/19/72	**8**	10	● 1. **Jungle Fever** [I]	Polydor 15030
			RICHARD CHAMBERLAIN	
			Born on 3/31/35. Leading actor in films, theatre and television. Played lead role in TV's "Dr. Kildare," 1961-66.	
6/23/62	**10**	10	1. **Theme From Dr. Kildare (Three Stars Will Shine Tonight)**	MGM 13075
10/27/62	**21**	5	2. Love Me Tender	MGM 13097
3/09/63	**14**	7	3. All I Have To Do Is Dream	MGM 13121
			THE CHAMBERS BROTHERS	
			Four Mississippi-born brothers: George (bass), Willie (guitar), Lester (harmonica) and Joe (guitar). Formed as a gospel group in Los Angeles in 1954. Drummer Brian Keenan added in 1965.	
9/14/68	**11**	9	1. Time Has Come Today	Columbia 44414
12/21/68	**37**	2	2. I Can't Turn You Loose	Columbia 44679
			CHAMPAIGN	
			Interracial sextet from Champaign, Illinois; Pauli Carman and Rena Jones, lead singers.	
3/28/81	**12**	13	1. How 'Bout Us	Columbia 11433
5/14/83	**23**	9	2. Try Again	Columbia 03563
			THE CHAMPS	
			Instrumental combo from Los Angeles. Originally consisted of studio musicians Dave Burgess (rhythm guitar), Buddy Bruce (lead guitar), Danny Flores (sax; later changed name to Chuck Rio), Cliff Hils (bass) and Gene Alden (drums). Shortly after "Tequila" became a hit, Bruce and Hils were replaced by Dale Norris and Joe Burnas. 8 months after recording "Tequila," Flores and Alden left and were replaced by Jimmy Seals (sax) and Dash Crofts (drums). Other personnel changes followed and in 1960 guitarist Glen Campbell spent some time in the group.	
3/03/58	**1**(5)	16	1. **Tequila** [I] Best Seller #1(5) / Top 100 #1(5) / Jockey #1(2)	Challenge 1016
6/02/58	**30**	5	2. El Rancho Rock [I] Top 100 #30 / Best Seller #31	Challenge 59007
2/08/60	**30**	5	3. Too Much Tequila [I]	Challenge 59063
7/14/62	**40**	1	4. Limbo Rock [I]	Challenge 9131
			GENE CHANDLER	
			R&B singer/producer, born Eugene Dixon on 7/6/37 in Chicago. Formed the Gaytones at Englewood High School in 1955. Joined The Dukays vocal group in 1957. US Army, Germany, 1957-60. Rejoined The Dukays in 1960. First recorded for Nat in 1961. Changed name to "Gene Chandler" to avoid contract conflicts, then left group. Own label, Mr. Chand, in 1969.	
1/27/62	**1**(3)	11	1. **Duke Of Earl**	Vee-Jay 416
8/01/64	**19**	7	2. Just Be True	Constellation 130
11/14/64	**39**	1	3. Bless Our Love	Constellation 136
1/16/65	**40**	1	4. What Now	Constellation 141
5/22/65	**18**	6	5. Nothing Can Stop Me	Constellation 149
8/08/70	**12**	11	● 6. Groovy Situation	Mercury 73083

DATE	POS	WKS	ARTIST—RECORD TITLE	LABEL & NO.
			CHANGE	
			European/American studio group formed by Italian producer Jacques Fred Petrus.	
7/19/80	**40**	1	1. A Lover's Holiday	RFC 49208
			BRUCE CHANNEL	
			Born on 11/28/40 in Jacksonville, Texas. Appeared on "Louisiana Hayride" in 1958. First recorded for LeCam in 1962.	
2/10/62	1(3)	12	1. **Hey! Baby** harmonica player: Delbert McClinton	Smash 1731
			CHANSON	
			Studio disco band. Lead vocals by James Jamerson Jr. and David Williams.	
12/16/78†	**21**	9	1. Don't Hold Back	Ariola 7717
			CHANTAY'S	
			Teenage surf-rock quintet from Santa Ana, California: Bob Spickard (lead guitar), Brian Carman (rhythm guitar), Rob Marshall (piano), Warren Waters (bass) and Bob Welch (drums). First recorded for Downey in 1962. Disbanded in 1966.	
4/06/63	**4**	11	1. **Pipeline** **[I]**	Dot 16440
			THE CHANTELS	
			Vocal group from the Bronx. Formed in high school, with lead Arlene Smith, Sonia Goring, Rene Minus, Jackie Landry and Lois Harris. Group name taken from that of a rival school, St. Francis de Chantelle. Auditioned for Richard Barrett, who became their manager and obtained a contract with Gone/End Records.	
1/27/58	**15**	12	1. Maybe Top 100 #15 / Best Seller #16	End 1005
4/07/58	**39**	3	2. Every Night (I Pray) Best Seller #39 / Top 100 #40	End 1015
9/11/61	**14**	8	3. Look In My Eyes	Carlton 555
12/11/61	**29**	3	4. Well, I Told You	Carlton 564
			HARRY CHAPIN	
			Folk-rock storyteller. Born on 12/7/42 in New York City. Died in an auto accident on 7/16/81.	
4/22/72	**24**	9	1. Taxi	Elektra 45770
3/16/74	**36**	2	2. W-O-L-D	Elektra 45874
11/02/74	1(1)	12	● 3. **Cat's In The Cradle**	Elektra 45203
11/22/80	**23**	7	4. Sequel sequel to his 1972 hit "Taxi"	Boardwalk 5700
			TRACY CHAPMAN	
			Boston-based singer/songwriter born in Cleveland. Graduated from Tufts University in 1986 with an anthropology degree. Won the 1988 Best New Artist Grammy Award.	
7/16/88	**6**	12	1. **Fast Car**	Elektra 69412
			CHARLENE	
			Born Charlene D'Angelo on 6/1/50 in Hollywood.	
3/27/82	**3**	14	1. **I've Never Been To Me** **[R]** originally charted in 1977 (POS 97)	Motown 1611

DATE	POS	WKS	ARTIST—RECORD TITLE	LABEL & NO.
			JIMMY CHARLES	
			Born in 1942 in Paterson, New Jersey. R&B singer. Won Apollo Amateur Contest in 1958.	
9/05/60	**5**	11	1. **A Million To One** vocal backing: The Revelletts	Promo 1002
			RAY CHARLES	
			Born Ray Charles Robinson on 9/23/30 in Albany, Georgia. To Greenville, Florida while still an infant. Partially blind at age 5, completely blind at 7 (glaucoma). Studied classical piano and clarinet at State School for Deaf and Blind Children, St. Augustine, Florida, 1937-45. With local Florida bands, moved to Seattle in 1948. Formed the McSon Trio (also known as the Maxim Trio and the Maxine Trio) with G.D. McGhee (guitar) and Milton Garred (bass). First recordings were very much in the King Cole Trio style. Formed own band in 1954. Inducted into the Rock And Roll Hall Of Fame in 1986. Extremely popular performer with many TV and film appearances.	
11/25/57	**34**	1	1. Swanee River Rock (Talkin' 'Bout That River) Best Seller #34 / Top 100 #42	Atlantic 1154
7/20/59	**6**	11	2. **What'd I Say (Part I)**	Atlantic 2031
12/14/59	**40**	1	3. I'm Movin' On	Atlantic 2043
8/08/60	**40**	1	4. Sticks And Stones	ABC-Para. 10118
10/10/60	**1**(1)	10	5. **Georgia On My Mind** #10 hit for Frankie Trumbauer in 1931	ABC-Para. 10135
12/12/60	**28**	5	6. Ruby	ABC-Para. 10164
3/27/61	**8**	9	7. **One Mint Julep** [I]	Impulse 200
9/18/61	**1**(2)	11	8. **Hit The Road Jack**	ABC-Para. 10244
12/04/61†	**9**	10	9. **Unchain My Heart**	ABC-Para. 10266
4/21/62	**20**	4	10. Hide 'Nor Hair	ABC-Para. 10314
5/19/62	**1**(5)	14	● 11. **I Can't Stop Loving You**	ABC-Para. 10330
8/04/62	**2**(1)	9	12. **You Don't Know Me**	ABC-Para. 10345
12/01/62	**7**	9	13. **You Are My Sunshine/**	
12/08/62	**29**	5	14. Your Cheating Heart	ABC-Para. 10375
3/16/63	**20**	4	15. Don't Set Me Free	ABC-Para. 10405
4/27/63	**8**	8	16. **Take These Chains From My Heart**	ABC-Para. 10435
7/06/63	**21**	5	17. No One/	
7/06/63	**29**	4	18. Without Love (There Is Nothing)	ABC-Para. 10453
9/14/63	**4**	11	19. **Busted**	ABC-Para. 10481
12/21/63†	**20**	7	20. That Lucky Old Sun	ABC-Para. 10509
3/21/64	**38**	2	21. My Heart Cries For You/	
3/21/64	**39**	1	22. Baby, Don't You Cry	ABC-Para. 10530
1/15/66	**6**	9	23. **Crying Time**	ABC-Para. 10739
4/16/66	**19**	5	24. Together Again	ABC-Para. 10785
6/25/66	**31**	4	25. Let's Go Get Stoned	ABC/TRC 10808
10/01/66	**32**	2	26. I Chose To Sing The Blues	ABC/TRC 10840
6/10/67	**15**	9	27. Here We Go Again	ABC/TRC 10938
9/23/67	**33**	3	28. In The Heat Of The Night from the Sidney Poitier film of the same title	ABC/TRC 10970
12/02/67	**25**	3	29. Yesterday	ABC/TRC 11009
7/20/68	**35**	3	30. Eleanor Rigby	ABC/TRC 11090
4/17/71	**36**	4	31. Don't Change On Me	ABC/TRC 11291

DATE	POS	WKS	ARTIST—RECORD TITLE	LABEL & NO.
5/15/71	**36**	2	32. Booty Butt [I] **THE RAY CHARLES ORCHESTRA**	Tangerine 1015
			THE RAY CHARLES SINGERS	
			Ray was born on 9/13/18 in Chicago. Arranger and conductor for many TV shows including the "Perry Como Show," "Glen Campbell Show" and "Sha-Na-Na."	
5/02/64	**3**	12	1. **Love Me With All Your Heart (Cuando Calienta El Sol)**	Command 4046
7/25/64	**29**	4	2. Al-Di-La	Command 4049
12/19/64†	**32**	5	3. One More Time	Command 4057
			SONNY CHARLES	
			Former lead singer of The Checkmates, Ltd., an integrated quintet from Ft. Wayne, Indiana. Consisted of Sonny, Bobby Stevens, Harvey Trees, Bill Van Buskirk and Marvin Smith.	
5/31/69	**13**	10	1. Black Pearl **SONNY CHARLES & THE CHECKMATES, LTD.**	A&M 1053
1/22/83	**40**	2	2. Put It In A Magazine	Highrise 2001
			CHARLIE	
			British rock quintet led by Terry Thomas.	
8/06/83	**38**	2	1. It's Inevitable	Mirage 99862
			THE CHARMS	
			R&B vocal group from Cincinnati consisting of Otis Williams, Richard Parker, Donald Peak, Joe Penn and Rolland Bradley. Group first recorded for Rockin' in 1953. Otis later moved into the field of country music.	
11/27/54†	**15**	15	1. Hearts Of Stone Best Seller #15 / Juke Box #15 / Jockey #20	DeLuxe 6062
1/15/55	**26**	3	2. Ling, Ting, Tong Best Seller #26	DeLuxe 6076
			OTIS WILLIAMS & HIS CHARMS:	
4/14/56	**11**	15	3. Ivory Tower Jockey #11 / Top 100 #12 / Best Seller #13 / Juke Box #19	DeLuxe 6093
			THE CHARTBUSTERS	
			Washington, D.C. rock quartet.	
8/15/64	**33**	3	1. She's The One	Mutual 502
			CHASE	
			Jazz-rock band organized by trumpeter Bill Chase (formerly with Woody Herman and Stan Kenton). Bill Chase and 3 other members were killed in a plane crash on 8/9/74.	
6/26/71	**24**	8	1. Get It On	Epic 10738
			CHEAP TRICK	
			Rock quartet from Rockford, Illinois consisting of Rick Nielsen (guitar), Bun E. Carlos (real name: Brad Carlson; drums), Robin Zander (vocals) and Tom Petersson (bass; replaced by Jon Brant in 1980). Founded by Nielsen and Petersson, former members of Nazz. Peterson returned in 1988 (replaced Brant).	
5/26/79	**7**	13	● 1. **I Want You To Want Me**	Epic 50680
9/15/79	**35**	3	2. Ain't That A Shame	Epic 50743
10/27/79	**26**	5	3. Dream Police	Epic 50774
1/19/80	**32**	3	4. Voices	Epic 50814
5/21/88	**1**(2)	14	5. **The Flame**	Epic 07745

DATE	POS	WKS	ARTIST—RECORD TITLE	LABEL & NO.
8/20/88	**4**	12	6. **Don't Be Cruel**	Epic 07965
12/17/88	**33**	5	7. Ghost Town	Epic 08097
			CHUBBY CHECKER	
			Born Ernest Evans on 10/3/41 in Philadelphia. Did impersonations of famous singers. First recorded for Parkway in 1959. Cover version of Hank Ballard's "The Twist" started worldwide dance craze.	
6/15/59	**38**	2	1. The Class [N] imitations of Fats Domino, The Coasters, Elvis, and The Chipmunks	Parkway 804
8/08/60	**1**(1)	15	2. **The Twist**	Parkway 811
10/31/60	**14**	9	3. The Hucklebuck written in 1949; #5 hit for Tommy Dorsey; #10 for Frank Sinatra	Parkway 813
1/30/61	**1**(3)	14	4. **Pony Time**	Parkway 818
5/01/61	**24**	4	5. Dance The Mess Around	Parkway 822
7/03/61	**8**	15	6. **Let's Twist Again**	Parkway 824
10/02/61	**7**	11	7. **The Fly**	Parkway 830
11/20/61†	**1**(2)	18	8. **The Twist** **[R]** except for Bing Crosby's "White Christmas," "The Twist" is the only song in chart history to return to the #1 position after an absence of 1 year or more	Parkway 811
12/25/61	**21**	3	9. Jingle Bell Rock [X] **BOBBY RYDELL/CHUBBY CHECKER**	Cameo 205
3/10/62	**3**	12	10. **Slow Twistin'** female vocal: Dee Dee Sharp	Parkway 835
7/07/62	**12**	7	11. Dancin' Party	Parkway 842
9/29/62	**2**(2)	17	12. **Limbo Rock/**	
9/29/62	**10**	9	13. Popeye The Hitchhiker	Parkway 849
2/23/63	**20**	8	14. Let's Limbo Some More/	
3/23/63	**15**	7	15. Twenty Miles	Parkway 862
6/01/63	**12**	7	16. Birdland	Parkway 873
8/03/63	**25**	5	17. Twist It Up	Parkway 879
11/23/63	**12**	9	18. Loddy Lo/	
1/11/64	**17**	8	19. Hooka Tooka	Parkway 890
4/04/64	**23**	5	20. Hey, Bobba Needle	Parkway 907
7/11/64	**40**	1	21. Lazy Elsie Molly	Parkway 920
5/22/65	**40**	1	22. Let's Do The Freddie	Parkway 949
7/09/88	**16**	8	23. The Twist [R] **THE FAT BOYS with CHUBBY CHECKER**	Tin Pan 887571
			THE CHECKMATES, LTD - see SONNY CHARLES	
			CHEECH & CHONG	
			Comedians Richard "Cheech" Marin (b: Watts, California) and Thomas Chong (b: 5/24/40, Edmonton, Alberta, Canada). Starred in movies since 1980. Chong was the guitarist of Bobby Taylor's Vancouvers.	
9/29/73	**15**	7	1. Basketball Jones Featuring Tyrone Shoelaces [N]	Ode 66038
12/29/73†	**24**	5	2. Sister Mary Elephant (Shudd-Up!) [C]	Ode 66041
8/31/74	**9**	8	3. **Earache My Eye Featuring Alice Bowie** **[C]**	Ode 66102

DATE	POS	WKS	ARTIST—RECORD TITLE	LABEL & NO.
			THE CHEERS	
			Trio from Los Angeles consisting of actor Bert Convy, Gil Garfield and Sue Allen.	
9/24/55	**6**	11	1. **Black Denim Trousers** Best Seller #6 / Jockey #6 / Top 100 #13 / Juke Box #20 orchestra & chorus directed by Les Baxter	Capitol 3219
			CHER	
			Born Cherilyn LaPierre on 5/20/46 in El Centro, California. Worked as back-up singer for Phil Spector. Recorded with Sonny Bono as "Caesar & Cleo" in 1963. Recorded as "Bonnie Jo Mason" and "Cherilyn" in 1964. Married Bono in 1963, divorced in 1974. Married for a short time to Gregg Allman. Own TV series with Bono from 1971-77. Acclaimed film actress (won Best Actress Oscar in 1987 for "Moonstruck").	
8/07/65	**15**	6	1. All I Really Want To Do	Imperial 66114
11/06/65	**25**	3	2. Where Do You Go	Imperial 66136
3/26/66	**2**(1)	9	3. **Bang Bang (My Baby Shot Me Down)**	Imperial 66160
8/20/66	**32**	3	4. Alfie from the film of the same title	Imperial 66192
11/18/67	**9**	9	5. **You Better Sit Down Kids** all of above: produced by Sonny Bono	Imperial 66261
10/02/71	**1**(2)	14	• 6. **Gypsys, Tramps & Thieves**	Kapp 2146
2/12/72	**7**	10	7. **The Way Of Love**	Kapp 2158
6/03/72	**22**	6	8. Living In A House Divided	Kapp 2171
9/01/73	**1**(2)	14	• 9. **Half-Breed**	MCA 40102
2/02/74	**1**(1)	12	• 10. **Dark Lady**	MCA 40161
6/15/74	**27**	4	11. Train Of Thought	MCA 40245
3/17/79	**8**	11	• 12. **Take Me Home**	Casablanca 965
1/16/88	**10**	12	13. **I Found Someone**	Geffen 28191
4/30/88	**14**	9	14. We All Sleep Alone	Geffen 27986
			CHERI	
			Canadian duo: Rosalind Milligan Hunt and Lyn Cullerier.	
6/05/82	**39**	2	1. Murphy's Law [N] composed by Rosalind's mother, Geraldine Hunt	Venture 149
			CHERRELLE - see ALEXANDER O'NEAL	
			DON CHERRY	
			Born on 1/11/24 in Wichita Falls, Texas. Studied voice after service in mid-40s. Vocalist with Jan Garber band in late 40s. Accomplished professional golfer.	
12/10/55†	**4**	18	1. **Band Of Gold** Jockey #4 / Best Seller #5 / Top 100 #5 / Juke Box #5	Columbia 40597
4/14/56	**29**	6	2. Wild Cherry	Columbia 40665
8/11/56	**22**	6	3. Ghost Town Jockey #22 / Top 100 #26	Columbia 40705
			THE CHI-LITES	
			R&B vocal group from Chicago. Consisted of Eugene Record (lead vocals), Robert "Squirrel" Lester (tenor), Marshall Thompson (baritone) and Creadel "Red" Jones (bass). First recorded as the Hi-Lites on Daran in 1963. Record went solo in 1976.	
5/08/71	**26**	6	1. (For God's Sake) Give More Power To The People	Brunswick 55450
10/30/71	**3**	13	2. **Have You Seen Her**	Brunswick 55462

DATE	POS	WKS	ARTIST—RECORD TITLE	LABEL & NO.
4/15/72	**1**(1)	14	3. **Oh Girl**	Brunswick 55471
3/24/73	**33**	5	4. A Letter To Myself	Brunswick 55491
9/01/73	**30**	5	5. Stoned Out Of My Mind	Brunswick 55500
			CHIC	
			Disco group formed in New York City by producers Bernard Edwards (bass) and Nile Rodgers (guitar). Vocalists were Norma Jean Wright (replaced by Alfa Anderson) and Luci Martin; and Tony Thompson on drums. Wright began solo career in 1978; recorded as Norma Jean. Edwards recorded with the studio group Roundtree in 1978. Rodgers joined the Honeydrippers in 1984. Thompson joined the Power Station in 1985 and Edwards became their producer.	
12/10/77†	**6**	17	● 1. **Dance, Dance, Dance (Yowsah, Yowsah, Yowsah)**	Atlantic 3435
6/17/78	**38**	1	2. Everybody Dance	Atlantic 3469
11/18/78	**1**(6)	19	▲ 3. **Le Freak**	Atlantic 3519
3/10/79	**7**	12	● 4. **I Want Your Love**	Atlantic 3557
7/07/79	**1**(1)	14	● 5. **Good Times**	Atlantic 3584
			CHICAGO	
			Jazz-oriented rock group formed in Chicago in 1967. Consisted of Robert Lamm (keyboards), James Pankow (trombone), Lee Loughnane (trumpet), Terry Kath (guitar; d: 1/23/78 playing Russian roulette [31]), Walt Parazaider (reeds), Peter Cetera (bass) and Danny Seraphine (drums). Originally called The Big Thing, later Chicago Transit Authority. To Los Angeles in late 60s. Kath replaced by Donnie Dacus (left in 1979). Bill Champlin (keyboards) joined in 1982. Cetera left in 1985, replaced by Jason Scheff.	
4/25/70	**9**	11	1. **Make Me Smile**	Columbia 45127
8/01/70	**4**	11	2. **25 Or 6 To 4**	Columbia 45194
11/21/70†	**7**	11	3. **Does Anybody Really Know What Time It Is?**	Columbia 45264
3/06/71	**20**	6	4. Free	Columbia 45331
5/29/71	**35**	4	5. Lowdown	Columbia 45370
7/10/71	**7**	11	6. **Beginnings/**	
		11	7. Colour My World	Columbia 45417
10/30/71	**24**	6	8. Questions 67 And 68 [R] originally charted in 1969 (POS 71)	Columbia 45467
8/12/72	**3**	10	● 9. **Saturday In The Park**	Columbia 45657
11/18/72	**24**	6	10. Dialogue (Part I & II)	Columbia 45717
7/07/73	**10**	12	11. **Feelin' Stronger Every Day**	Columbia 45880
10/20/73	**4**	14	● 12. **Just You 'N' Me**	Columbia 45933
4/06/74	**9**	12	13. **(I've Been) Searchin' So Long**	Columbia 46020
7/13/74	**6**	8	14. **Call On Me**	Columbia 46062
10/26/74	**11**	10	15. Wishing You Were Here backing vocals by 3 of The Beach Boys	Columbia 10049
3/08/75	**13**	7	16. Harry Truman	Columbia 10092
5/10/75	**5**	7	17. **Old Days**	Columbia 10131
7/17/76	**32**	4	18. Another Rainy Day In New York City	Columbia 10360
8/21/76	**1**(2)	17	● 19. **If You Leave Me Now**	Columbia 10390
10/15/77	**4**	12	20. **Baby, What A Big Surprise** all of above: produced by James Wilkin Guercio	Columbia 10620
10/28/78	**14**	8	21. Alive Again	Columbia 10845
1/13/79	**14**	9	22. No Tell Lover	Columbia 10879

DATE	POS	WKS	ARTIST—RECORD TITLE	LABEL & NO.
6/26/82	1(2)	18	● 23. **Hard To Say I'm Sorry** from the film "Summer Lovers"	Full Moon 29979
10/23/82	22	8	24. Love Me Tomorrow	Full Moon 29911
5/12/84	16	10	25. Stay The Night	Full Moon 29306
8/25/84	3	15	26. **Hard Habit To Break**	Full Moon 29214
12/01/84†	3	14	27. **You're The Inspiration**	Full Moon 29126
3/09/85	14	10	28. Along Comes A Woman	Full Moon 29082
12/27/86†	3	13	29. **Will You Still Love Me?**	Full Moon 28512
4/25/87	17	8	30. If She Would Have Been Faithful...	Warner 28424
7/02/88	3	13	31. **I Don't Wanna Live Without Your Love**	Reprise 27855
10/15/88	1(2)	16	● 32. **Look Away**	Reprise 27766
			THE CHICAGO LOOP	
11/26/66	37	3	1. (When She Needs Good Lovin') She Comes To Me	DynoVoice 226
			THE CHIFFONS	
			Black vocal group from the Bronx. Formed while high school classmates; worked as back-up singers in 1960. Consisted of Judy Craig, Barbara Lee, Patricia Bennett and Sylvia Peterson. First recorded for Big Deal in 1960. Also recorded as The Four Pennies on the Rust label.	
3/09/63	1(4)	12	1. **He's So Fine**	Laurie 3152
6/08/63	5	9	2. **One Fine Day**	Laurie 3179
10/19/63	40	1	3. A Love So Fine	Laurie 3195
1/04/64	36	1	4. I Have A Boyfriend	Laurie 3212
5/28/66	10	7	5. **Sweet Talkin' Guy**	Laurie 3340
			CHILLIWACK	
			Canadian rock group led by Bill Henderson.	
10/31/81	22	11	1. My Girl (Gone, Gone, Gone)	Millennium 11813
2/27/82	33	3	2. I Believe	Millennium 13102
			THE CHIMES	
			Brooklyn-based vocal quintet led by Leonard Cocco.	
1/16/61	11	6	1. Once In Awhile	Tag 444
5/15/61	38	1	2. I'm In The Mood For Love	Tag 445
			THE CHIPMUNKS	
			Characters created by Ross Bagdasarian ("David Seville"). Named Alvin, Simon and Theodore after Liberty executives Alvin Bennett, Simon Waronker & Theodore Keep. Bagdasarian died on 1/16/72 (52); his son resurrected the act in 1980.	
12/08/58	1(4)	11	1. **The Chipmunk Song** [X-N]	Liberty 55168
			DAVID SEVILLE & THE CHIPMUNKS:	
2/23/59	3	9	2. **Alvin's Harmonica** [N]	Liberty 55179
7/13/59	16	6	3. Ragtime Cowboy Joe [N]	Liberty 55200
3/07/60	33	2	4. Alvin's Orchestra [N]	Liberty 55233
12/26/60	21	1	5. Rudolph The Red Nosed Reindeer [X-N]	Liberty 55289
1/06/62†	39	1	6. The Chipmunk Song [X-R]	Liberty 55250
3/31/62	40	1	7. The Alvin Twist [N]	Liberty 55424
12/29/62	40	1	8. The Chipmunk Song [X-R]	Liberty 55250

DATE	POS	WKS	ARTIST—RECORD TITLE	LABEL & NO.
			THE CHORDETTES	
			Female vocal group from Sheboygan, Wisconsin; formed in 1946. Consisted of Janet Buschman (nee Ertel; bass), her sister-in-law Carol Buschman (baritone), Lynn Evans (lead singer; replaced Dorothy Schwartz - nee Hummitzsch, 1953) and Margie Needham (tenor; replaced Jinny Lockard, 1953). With Arthur Godfrey from 1949-53. Ertel married Cadence owner Archie Bleyer in 1954; she died of cancer on 11/22/88.	
3/10/56	**14**	9	1. Eddie My Love Jockey #14 / Best Seller #17 / Top 100 #18	Cadence 1284
6/02/56	**5**	17	2. **Born To Be With You** Top 100 #5 / Jockey #5 / Juke Box #5 / Best Seller #7	Cadence 1291
10/13/56	**16**	10	3. Lay Down Your Arms Top 100 #16 / Juke Box #16 / Best Seller #18 / Jockey #20	Cadence 1299
9/16/57	**8**	8	4. **Just Between You And Me** Jockey #8 / Best Seller #15 / Top 100 #19	Cadence 1330
3/10/58	**2**(2)	12	5. **Lollipop** Best Seller #2 / Top 100 #2 / Jockey #2	Cadence 1345
5/26/58	**17**	7	6. Zorro Top 100 #17 / Best Seller #18 / Jockey #22	Cadence 1349
3/30/59	**27**	4	7. No Other Arms, No Other Lips	Cadence 1361
7/03/61	**13**	8	8. Never On Sunday	Cadence 1402
			CHRIS CHRISTIAN	
			Guitarist/songwriter/producer. With trio Cotton, Lloyd & Christian.	
11/14/81	**37**	3	1. I Want You, I Need You	Boardwalk 126
			CHRISTIE	
			English trio: Jeff Christie, Vic Elms and Mike Blakey.	
10/24/70	**23**	8	1. Yellow River	Epic 10626
			LOU CHRISTIE	
			Born Lugee Sacco on 2/19/43 in Glen Willard, Pennsylvania. Joined vocal group, the Classics, first recorded for Starr in 1960. Started long association with songwriter Twyla Herbert. Recorded as "Lugee & The Lions" for Robbee in 1961.	
2/16/63	**24**	6	1. The Gypsy Cried	Roulette 4457
4/27/63	**6**	10	2. **Two Faces Have I**	Roulette 4481
1/22/66	**1**(1)	10	• 3. **Lightnin' Strikes**	MGM 13412
4/23/66	**16**	4	4. Rhapsody In The Rain	MGM 13473
9/13/69	**10**	9	5. **I'm Gonna Make You Mine**	Buddah 116
			GAVIN CHRISTOPHER	
			Chicago-born soul singer/composer/producer.	
7/12/86	**22**	7	1. One Step Closer To You	Manhattan 50028
			THE CHURCH	
			Australian folk-rock quartet led by Steven Kilby (vocals). Includes: Peter Koppes, Marty Wilson-Piper and Richard Ploog.	
5/28/88	**24**	5	1. Under The Milky Way	Arista 9673
			EUGENE CHURCH & THE FELLOWS	
			Los Angeles native. Born on 1/23/38. Recorded with Jesse Belvin as The Cliques.	
2/23/59	**36**	2	1. Pretty Girls Everywhere featuring backing vocals by Bobby Day	Class 235

DATE	POS	WKS	ARTIST—RECORD TITLE	LABEL & NO.
			CINDERELLA	
			Pennsylvania-based heavy-metal band, consisting of Tom Keifer (lead singer, guitar, piano), Jeff LaBar (guitar), Eric Brittingham (bass) and Fred Coury (drums).	
1/17/87	**13**	8	1. Nobody's Fool	Mercury 884851
10/01/88	**12**	11	2. Don't Know What You Got (Till It's Gone)	Mercury 870644
			CITY BOY	
			British rock sextet; Lol Mason, lead singer.	
9/09/78	**27**	6	1. 5.7.0.5.	Mercury 73999
			C.J. & CO.	
			Detroit group, assembled by Dennis Coffey, which included Cornelius Brown Jr., Curtis Durden, Joni Tolbert, Connie Durden and Charles Clark.	
7/09/77	**36**	2	1. Devil's Gun	Westbound 55400
			JIMMY CLANTON	
			Born on 9/2/40 in Baton Rouge, Louisiana. Played in local bands, discovered by Ace Records while making a demo at Cosimo's studio in New Orleans. Recorded with famous New Orleans session men, including Huey "Piano" Smith, Earl King (guitar) and Lee Allen (tenor sax). Toured with Dick Clark's Caravan Of Stars, appeared in films and on TV. Disc jockey in Lancaster, Pennsylvania from 1972-76.	
7/21/58	**4**	15	1. **Just A Dream** Hot 100 #4 / Best Seller #4	Ace 546
11/17/58	**25**	5	2. A Letter To An Angel/	
12/01/58	**38**	2	3. A Part Of Me	Ace 551
8/17/59	**33**	6	4. My Own True Love melody is "Tara's Theme" from "Gone With The Wind"	Ace 567
12/21/59†	**5**	11	5. **Go, Jimmy, Go**	Ace 575
5/30/60	**22**	6	6. Another Sleepless Night	Ace 585
9/01/62	**7**	10	7. **Venus In Blue Jeans** above 2: written by Neil Sedaka	Ace 8001
			ERIC CLAPTON	
			Prolific rock-blues guitarist/vocalist; born on 3/30/45 in Ripley, England. With The Roosters in 1963, The Yardbirds, 1963-65, and John Mayall's Bluesbreakers, 1965-66. Formed Cream with Jack Bruce and Ginger Baker in 1966. Formed Blind Faith in 1968; worked with John Lennon's Plastic Ono Band, and Delaney & Bonnie. Formed Derek & The Dominos in 1970. After 2 years of reclusion (1971-72), Clapton performed his comeback concert at London's Rainbow Theatre in January, 1973. Began actively recording and touring again in 1974.	
11/14/70	**18**	8	1. After Midnight	Atco 6784
8/03/74	**1**(1)	10	• 2. **I Shot The Sheriff**	RSO 409
11/23/74	**26**	5	3. Willie And The Hand Jive	RSO 503
11/13/76	**24**	6	4. Hello Old Friend	RSO 861
2/04/78	**3**	17	• 5. **Lay Down Sally**	RSO 886
6/10/78	**16**	7	6. Wonderful Tonight	RSO 895
			ERIC CLAPTON & HIS BAND:	
11/25/78†	**9**	11	7. **Promises/**	
3/24/79	**40**	2	8. Watch Out For Lucy	RSO 910
7/26/80	**30**	5	9. Tulsa Time/	
		5	10. Cocaine	RSO 1039
3/14/81	**10**	12	11. **I Can't Stand It**	RSO 1060

DATE	POS	WKS	ARTIST—RECORD TITLE	LABEL & NO.
			ERIC CLAPTON:	
2/19/83	**18**	10	12. I've Got A Rock N' Roll Heart	Duck 29780
3/30/85	**26**	6	13. Forever Man	Duck 29081
			CLAUDINE CLARK	
			Born on 4/26/41 in Macon, Georgia. Moved to Philadelphia when very young. First recorded for Herald in 1958. Also recorded for Swan as "Joy Dawn."	
7/21/62	**5**	10	1. **Party Lights**	Chancellor 1113
			THE DAVE CLARK FIVE	
			Rock group formed in Tottenham, England in 1960. Consisted of Dave Clark (drums), Mike Smith (lead vocals, keyboards), Lenny Davidson (guitar), Dennis Payton (sax) and Rick Huxley (bass). First recorded for Ember/Pye in 1962. On the Ed Sullivan Show in March of 1964. In the film "Having A Wild Weekend" in 1965. Disbanded in 1973. Clark had been a stuntman in films; formed group to raise money for his soccer team, the Tottenham Hotspurs. Clark wrote the new London stage musical "Time."	
3/07/64	**6**	11	1. **Glad All Over**	Epic 9656
4/11/64	**4**	10	2. **Bits And Pieces**	Epic 9671
5/09/64	**11**	9	3. Do You Love Me	Epic 9678
6/20/64	**4**	9	4. **Can't You See That She's Mine**	Epic 9692
8/08/64	**3**	9	5. **Because**	Epic 9704
10/17/64	**15**	6	6. Everybody Knows (I Still Love You)	Epic 9722
12/05/64†	**14**	9	7. Any Way You Want It	Epic 9739
2/27/65	**14**	6	8. Come Home	Epic 9763
5/08/65	**23**	5	9. Reelin' And Rockin'	Epic 9786
7/10/65	**7**	8	10. **I Like It Like That**	Epic 9811
9/04/65	**4**	9	11. **Catch Us If You Can** from the film "Having A Wild Weekend"	Epic 9833
11/20/65	**1**(1)	11	12. **Over And Over**	Epic 9863
2/19/66	**18**	5	13. At The Scene	Epic 9882
4/23/66	**12**	5	14. Try Too Hard	Epic 10004
7/02/66	**28**	4	15. Please Tell Me Why	Epic 10031
4/15/67	**7**	7	16. **You Got What It Takes**	Epic 10144
7/01/67	**35**	2	17. You Must Have Been A Beautiful Baby	Epic 10179
			DEE CLARK	
			Born Delecta Clark on 11/7/38 in Blythsville, Arkansas. To Chicago in 1941. In Hambone Kids with Sammy McGrier and Ronny Strong, first recorded for Okeh in 1952. Joined R&B vocal group, the Goldentones, 1953. Group became the Kool Gents; billed as The Delegates for Vee-Jay recording, 1956. First solo recording for Falcon, 1957.	
1/12/59	**21**	6	1. Nobody But You	Abner 1019
5/25/59	**18**	9	2. Just Keep It Up	Abner 1026
9/14/59	**20**	9	3. Hey Little Girl	Abner 1029
1/04/60	**33**	5	4. How About That	Abner 1032
3/06/61	**34**	4	5. Your Friends	Vee-Jay 372
5/22/61	**2**(1)	12	6. **Raindrops**	Vee-Jay 383

DATE	POS	WKS	ARTIST—RECORD TITLE	LABEL & NO.
			PETULA CLARK	
			Born on 11/15/32 in Epsom, England. On radio at age 9; own show "Pet's Parlour" at age 11. TV series in England in 1950. First US record release for Coral in 1951. Appeared in over 20 British films, 1944-57; revived her film career in late 60s, starring in "Finian's Rainbow" and "Goodbye Mr. Chips."	
1/02/65	1(2)	13	● 1. **Downtown**	Warner 5494
4/03/65	**3**	9	2. **I Know A Place**	Warner 5612
7/31/65	**22**	5	3. You'd Better Come Home	Warner 5643
10/30/65	**21**	4	4. Round Every Corner	Warner 5661
1/15/66	1(2)	10	5. **My Love**	Warner 5684
4/02/66	**11**	7	6. A Sign Of The Times	Warner 5802
7/30/66	**9**	7	7. **I Couldn't Live Without Your Love**	Warner 5835
10/29/66	**21**	6	8. Who Am I	Warner 5863
12/31/66†	**16**	7	9. Color My World all of above: written and produced by Tony Hatch	Warner 5882
3/18/67	**3**	9	10. **This Is My Song** from the Charlie Chaplin film "A Countess From Hong Kong"	Warner 7002
6/17/67	**5**	7	11. **Don't Sleep In The Subway**	Warner 7049
9/16/67	**26**	4	12. The Cat In The Window (The Bird In The Sky)	Warner 7073
12/30/67	**31**	2	13. The Other Man's Grass Is Always Greener	Warner 7097
3/02/68	**15**	9	14. Kiss Me Goodbye	Warner 7170
8/24/68	**37**	1	15. Don't Give Up	Warner 7216
			ROY CLARK	
			Born on 4/15/33 in Meaherrin, Virginia. Superb guitar, banjo and fiddle player. With the TV series "Hee Haw" from the first show in 1969.	
7/12/69	**19**	6	1. Yesterday, When I Was Young	Dot 17246
			SANFORD CLARK	
			Born in 1935 in Tulsa, Oklahoma. Moved to Phoenix in his teens. Enlisted in US Air Force in 1960. Recorded again in mid-60s.	
8/11/56	**7**	15	1. **The Fool** Best Seller #7 / Juke Box #7 / Top 100 #9 / Jockey #16 featuring Al Casey, guitar	Dot 15481
			STANLEY CLARKE/GEORGE DUKE	
			Clarke: premier jazz-rock bassist, born on 6/30/51 in Philadelphia. Duke: prominent jazz-rock keyboardist, born on 1/12/46 in San Rafael, California.	
6/13/81	**19**	9	1. Sweet Baby	Epic 01052
			TONY CLARKE	
			Soul singer/songwriter, born in New York City; raised in Detroit. Acted in film "They Call Me Mr. Tibbs." Died in Detroit in 1970.	
5/08/65	**31**	2	1. The Entertainer	Chess 1924
			THE CLASH	
			Eclectic new-wave rock group formed in London in 1976. Consisted of Joe Strummer (vocals, lyricist), Mick Jones (guitar), Paul Simonon (bass) and Topper Headon (drums). Headon left in May, 1983; replaced by Peter Howard. Jones left band in 1984 to form Big Audio Dynamite. Political activists, they wrote songs protesting racism and oppression. Strummer disbanded The Clash in early 1986. Strummer appeared in the 1987 film "Straight To Hell."	
4/26/80	**23**	7	1. Train In Vain (Stand By Me)	Epic 50851

DATE	POS	WKS	ARTIST—RECORD TITLE	LABEL & NO.
11/13/82†	**8**	15	2. **Rock The Casbah**	Epic 03245
			THE CLASSICS	
			White vocal quartet from Brooklyn, formed in 1958. Consisted of Emil Stucchio (lead), Johnny Gambale, Tony Victor and Jamie Troy.	
7/20/63	**20**	5	1. Till Then #8 pop hit for the Mills Brothers in 1944	Musicnote 1116
			CLASSICS IV	
			Quintet formed in Jacksonville, Florida. Consisted of Dennis Yost (lead vocals), J.R. Cobb (lead guitar), Wally Eaton (rhythm guitar), Joe Wilson (bass; replaced by Dean Daughtry) and Kim Venable (drums). Cobb, Daughtry and producer Buddy Buie joined the Atlanta Rhythm Section in 1974.	
1/13/68	**3**	12	1. **Spooky**	Imperial 66259
			CLASSICS IV featuring DENNIS YOST:	
11/16/68	**5**	12	● 2. **Stormy**	Imperial 66328
2/22/69	**2(1)**	10	3. **Traces**	Imperial 66352
5/31/69	**19**	7	4. Everyday With You Girl	Imperial 66378
			DENNIS YOST & THE CLASSICS IV:	
12/09/72	**39**	3	5. What Am I Crying For?	MGM South 7002
			JUDY CLAY - see BILLY VERA	
			TOM CLAY	
			Disc jockey.	
7/24/71	**8**	7	1. **What The World Needs Now Is Love/Abraham, Martin And John** [S] vocal accompaniment by The Blackberries	Mowest 5002
			THE CLEFTONES	
			Doo-wop group from Queens, New York, formed at Jamaica High School in 1955. Consisted of Herbie Cox (lead), Charlie James (first tenor), Berman Patterson (second tenor), William McClain (baritone) and Warren Corbin (bass). Originally called the Silvertones.	
6/19/61	**18**	4	1. Heart And Soul	Gee 1064
			CLARENCE CLEMONS & JACKSON BROWNE	
			Clemons: saxophonist in Bruce Springsteen's E Street Band, born on 1/11/42 in Norfolk, Virginia.	
11/23/85†	**18**	12	1. You're A Friend Of Mine includes vocals by actress Daryl Hannah (Browne's girlfriend)	Columbia 05660
			JIMMY CLIFF	
			Jamaican reggae singer/composer. Real name: James Chambers. Starred in films "The Harder They Come" (1975) and "Club Paradise" (1986).	
12/27/69†	**25**	7	1. Wonderful World, Beautiful People	A&M 1146
			BUZZ CLIFFORD	
			Born Reese Francis Clifford III on 10/8/42 in Berwyn, Illinois.	
1/30/61	**6**	10	1. **Baby Sittin' Boogie** [N] babies' voices are by the children (boy & girl) of the producer	Columbia 41876
			MIKE CLIFFORD	
			Born on 11/6/43 in Los Angeles.	
10/13/62	**12**	8	1. Close To Cathy	United Art. 489

DATE	POS	WKS	ARTIST—RECORD TITLE	LABEL & NO.
			CLIMAX	
			Los Angeles-based quintet. Sonny Geraci, lead singer (formerly with The Outsiders).	
1/22/72	**3**	12	● 1. **Precious And Few** originally released on Carousel 30055	Rocky Road 30055
			CLIMAX BLUES BAND	
			Blues-rock quintet formed in Stafford, England; led by Colin Cooper & Peter Haycock.	
3/26/77	**3**	14	1. **Couldn't Get It Right**	Sire 736
4/04/81	**12**	17	2. I Love You	Warner 49669
			CLIMIE FISHER	
			U.K.-based duo: Simon Climie (vocals) and Rob Fisher (keyboards). Fisher was a member of Naked Eyes. Chrysalis songwriter Climie wrote Pat Benatar's "Invincible."	
7/02/88	**23**	6	1. Love Changes (Everything)	Capitol 44137
			PATSY CLINE	
			Born Virginia Hensley on 9/8/32 in Winchester, Virginia; killed in a plane crash with Cowboy Copas and Hawkshaw Hawkins on 3/5/63. Elected to Country Music Hall of Fame in 1973. Jessica Lange played Patsy in 1985 biographical film "Sweet Dreams."	
3/02/57	**12**	11	1. Walkin' After Midnight Juke Box #12 / Top 100 #17 / Best Seller #21 / Jockey #22	Decca 30221
7/24/61	**12**	10	2. I Fall To Pieces	Decca 31205
11/06/61	**9**	7	3. **Crazy**	Decca 31317
2/24/62	**14**	8	4. She's Got You	Decca 31354
			THE CLIQUE	
			Pop-rock quintet from Texas.	
9/27/69	**22**	7	1. Sugar On Sunday	White Whale 323
			ROSEMARY CLOONEY	
			Born on 5/23/28 in Maysville, Kentucky. One of the most popular singers of the 50s, Rosemary and sister Betty sang with the Tony Pastor band in late 40s before her solo career was launched. Rosemary was featured in "White Christmas" and several other 50s movies; after a period of personal difficulties, she re-emerged in the late 70s as a successful jazz and ballad singer.	
3/17/56	**20**	1	1. Memories Of You **BENNY GOODMAN TRIO with ROSEMARY CLOONEY** Juke Box #20 / Top 100 #52 from the film "The Benny Goodman Story"	Columbia 40616
4/13/57	**10**	9	2. **Mangos** Jockey #10 / Best Seller #23 / Top 100 #25	Columbia 40835
			THE CLOVERS	
			R&B group from Washington, DC. By 1949, personnel lineup was John "Buddy" Bailey (lead), Matthew McQuater, Harold Lucas, Harold Winely and Bill Harris. Bailey entered the Army in 1952, replaced by Billy Mitchell. Upon Bailey's return, Mitchell stayed in the group. Group had 13 consecutive top 10 R&B hits from 1951-54.	
7/28/56	**30**	3	1. Love, Love, Love	Atlantic 1094
11/02/59	**23**	5	2. Love Potion No. 9	United Art. 180

DATE	POS	WKS	ARTIST—RECORD TITLE	LABEL & NO.
			CLUB NOUVEAU	
			Sacramento-based dance/disco group formed and fronted by Jay King (producer/owner of King Jay Records). Early lineup: vocalists Valerie Watson and Samuelle Prater, with Denzil Foster and Thomas McElroy. Prater, Foster and McElroy left in 1988; replaced by David Agent and Kevin Irving.	
2/21/87	**1**(2)	12	● 1. **Lean On Me** King Jay/Warner 7" sold 600,000 units; Tommy Boy 12" sold 400,000	Warner 28430
7/18/87	**39**	1	2. Why You Treat Me So Bad	Warner 28360
			THE COASTERS	
			R&B group formed in Los Angeles in late 1955 from elements of the Robins. Originally consisted of Carl Gardner (ex-Robins; lead), Leon Hughes (tenor), Billy Guy (baritone lead), Bobby Nunn (ex-Robins; bass) and Adolph Jacobs (guitar). Noted for serio-comic recordings, primarily of Leiber & Stoller songs. Will "Dub" Jones (ex-Cadets) replaced Nunn in late 1958 and is heard on "Charlie Brown" and "Along Came Jones." Earl "Speedo" Carroll (ex-Cadillacs) joined group in 1961. Bobby Nunn died of a heart attack on 11/5/86 (61). Today there are two or three "Coasters" groups still working, some of which contain one or two original members. Inducted into the Rock And Roll Hall Of Fame in 1987.	
5/20/57	**3**	22	1. **Searchin'**/ Best Seller #3 / Top 100 #5 / Jockey #6 / Juke Box #10 end	
5/20/57	**8**	11	2. Young Blood Top 100 #8 / Jockey #10 / Juke Box #12 / Best Seller #14	Atco 6087
6/09/58	**1**(1)	15	3. **Yakety Yak** Top 100 #1 / Best Seller #2 / Jockey #2	Atco 6116
2/09/59	**2**(3)	12	4. **Charlie Brown** **[N]**	Atco 6132
6/01/59	**9**	8	5. **Along Came Jones** **[N]**	Atco 6141
9/07/59	**7**	11	6. **Poison Ivy**/	
9/21/59	**38**	1	7. I'm A Hog For You	Atco 6146
1/25/60	**36**	1	8. Run Red Run all of above: written & produced by Jerry Leiber & Mike Stoller	Atco 6153
2/27/61	**37**	2	9. Wait A Minute	Atco 6186
5/29/61	**23**	6	10. Little Egypt (Ying-Yang) [N]	Atco 6192
			ODIA COATES - see PAUL ANKA	
			EDDIE COCHRAN	
			Vocalist/guitarist, born Edward Ray Cochrane on 10/3/38 in Oklahoma City, Oklahoma; raised in Alberta Lea, Minnesota. Moved to Bell Gardens, California in 1953. Teamed with Hank Cochran (no relation) as the Cochran Brothers; first recorded as Country act for Ekko Records in 1954. Appeared in films "The Girl Can't Help It" and "Untamed Youth." Killed in a car accident near Bath, England on 4/17/60 (21). Accident also injured Gene Vincent. Inducted into the Rock And Roll Hall Of Fame in 1987.	
3/30/57	**18**	8	1. Sittin' In The Balcony Top 100 #18 / Jockey #18 / Juke Box #20 / Best Seller #22	Liberty 55056
8/25/58	**8**	12	2. **Summertime Blues** Hot 100 #8 / Best Seller #13 end	Liberty 55144
1/05/59	**35**	1	3. C'mon Everybody	Liberty 55166
			COCK ROBIN	
			Los Angeles pop quartet - vocals: Peter Kingsbery & Anna LaCazio. Reduced to duo of Kingsbery and LaCazio in 1987.	
8/17/85	**35**	3	1. When Your Heart Is Weak	Columbia 04875

DATE	POS	WKS	ARTIST—RECORD TITLE	LABEL & NO.
			BRUCE COCKBURN	
			Cockburn (pronounced CO-burn) was born on 5/27/45 in Canada. Singer/songwriter.	
5/03/80	**21**	9	1. Wondering Where The Lions Are	Millennium 11786
			JOE COCKER	
			Born John Robert Cocker on 5/20/44 in Sheffield, England. Own skiffle band, the Cavaliers, late 50s, later reorganized as Vance Arnold & The Avengers. Assembled the Grease Band in the mid-60s. First US tour, Woodstock Festival, in August of 1969. Successful tour with 43-piece revue, Mad Dogs And Englishmen, in 1970. Notable spastic stage antics were based on Ray Charles' movements at the piano.	
1/10/70	**30**	7	1. She Came In Through The Bathroom Window	A&M 1147
5/09/70	**7**	9	2. **The Letter** with Leon Russell & The Shelter People	A&M 1174
10/24/70	**11**	7	3. Cry Me A River recorded live at Fillmore East, New York on 3/27/70	A&M 1200
6/19/71	**22**	6	4. High Time We Went	A&M 1258
1/29/72	**33**	5	5. Feeling Alright [R] originally charted in 1969 (POS 69)	A&M 1063
10/07/72	**27**	5	6. Midnight Rider 4 & 6: with The Chris Stainton Band	A&M 1370
2/15/75	**5**	10	7. **You Are So Beautiful**	A&M 1641
10/02/82	**1**(3)	15	▲ 8. **Up Where We Belong** **JOE COCKER & JENNIFER WARNES** love theme from the film "An Officer & A Gentleman"	Island 99996
			DENNIS COFFEY & The Detroit Guitar Band	
			Detroit native Coffey was a session guitarist for The Temptations, The Jackson 5 and others. Coffey later formed C.J. & Co.	
11/13/71†	**6**	15	● 1. **Scorpio** **[I]**	Sussex 226
3/11/72	**18**	8	2. Taurus [I]	Sussex 233
			COZY COLE	
			Born William Randolph Cole on 10/17/09 in East Orange, New Jersey. Died of cancer on 1/29/81. Lead drummer for many swing bands, including Benny Carter, Willie Bryant, Cab Calloway and Louis Armstrong. Professional debut in 1928.	
9/29/58	**3**	14	1. **Topsy II/** **[I]** Hot 100 #3 / Best Seller #10 end	
10/27/58	**27**	3	2. Topsy I [I] Hot 100 #27 / Best Seller #45	Love 5004
12/28/58	**36**	1	3. Turvy II [I]	Love 5014

DATE	POS	WKS	ARTIST—RECORD TITLE	LABEL & NO.
			NAT KING COLE	
			Born Nathaniel Adams Coles on 3/17/17 in Montgomery, Alabama. Died of lung cancer on 2/15/65 in Santa Monica, California. Raised in Chicago. Own band, the Royal Dukes, at age 17. First recorded in 1936 in band led by brother Eddie. Toured with "Shuffle Along" musical revue, resided in Los Angeles. Formed King Cole Trio in 1939: Nat (piano), Oscar Moore (guitar; later joined brother's group, Johnny Moore's Three Blazers) and Wesley Prince (bass; replaced several years later by Johnny Miller). Long series of top-selling records led to his solo career in 1950. In films "St. Louis Blues," "Cat Ballou," and many other film and TV appearances. Stopped performing in 1964 due to ill health. Daughter Natalie is also a recording star.	
3/05/55	7	16	1. **Darling Je Vous Aime Beaucoup/** Jockey #7 / Best Seller #10 / Juke Box #14	
3/05/55	23	13	2. The Sand And The Sea Best Seller #23	Capitol 3027
5/07/55	2(1)	20	3. **A Blossom Fell/** Best Seller #2 / Juke Box #2 / Jockey #3	
5/21/55	8	10	4. If I May **NAT "KING" COLE & THE FOUR KNIGHTS** Jockey #8	Capitol 3095
7/16/55	24	2	5. My One Sin Best Seller #24	Capitol 3136
10/22/55	13	8	6. Someone You Love/ Best Seller #13 / Jockey #19 / Top 100 #21	
10/22/55	13	8	7. Forgive My Heart Best Seller #13 / Top 100 #21	Capitol 3234
3/03/56	18	3	8. Ask Me Jockey #18 / Top 100 #25	Capitol 3328
4/21/56	21	6	9. Too Young To Go Steady Jockey #21 / Top 100 #31 from the musical "Strip For Action"	Capitol 3390
7/21/56	16	12	10. That's All There Is To That **NAT "KING" COLE & THE FOUR KNIGHTS** Juke Box #16 / Best Seller #17 / Top 100 #18 / Jockey #18	Capitol 3456
11/03/56	11	10	11. Night Lights/ Jockey #11 / Top 100 #16 / Best Seller #17	
11/10/56	25	2	12. To The Ends Of The Earth Best Seller #25 / Jockey #25 / Top 100 #39	Capitol 3551
2/23/57	18	5	13. Ballerina Jockey #18 / Top 100 #36 all of above: orchestra conducted by Nelson Riddle	Capitol 3619
7/01/57	6	18	14. **Send For Me/** Best Seller #6 / Top 100 #7 / Jockey #9	
8/05/57	21	1	15. My Personal Possession **NAT "KING" COLE & THE FOUR KNIGHTS** Jockey #21 / Top 100 #63	Capitol 3737
10/21/57	30	4	16. With You On My Mind Best Seller #30 / Top 100 #33	Capitol 3782
2/24/58	33	3	17. Angel Smile Best Seller #33 / Top 100 #35	Capitol 3860
4/14/58	5	16	18. **Looking Back** Best Seller #5 / Top 100 #5 / Jockey #9	Capitol 3939
7/28/58	38	2	19. Come Closer To Me Best Seller #38 / Top 100 #41	Capitol 4004

DATE	POS	WKS	ARTIST—RECORD TITLE	LABEL & NO.
2/15/60	**30**	3	20. Time And The River	Capitol 4325
8/18/62	**2**(2)	13	21. **Ramblin' Rose**	Capitol 4804
12/01/62	**13**	8	22. Dear Lonely Hearts	Capitol 4870
5/25/63	**6**	9	23. **Those Lazy-Hazy-Crazy Days Of Summer**	Capitol 4965
9/28/63	**12**	9	24. That Sunday, That Summer	Capitol 5027
5/16/64	**22**	6	25. I Don't Want To Be Hurt Anymore	Capitol 5155
10/24/64	**34**	4	26. I Don't Want To See Tomorrow	Capitol 5261
			NATALIE COLE	
			Born on 2/6/50 in Los Angeles. Daughter of Nat "King" Cole. Professional debut at age 11. Married her producer, Marvin Yancey, Jr. Won the 1975 Best New Artist Grammy Award.	
10/04/75	**6**	11	1. **This Will Be**	Capitol 4109
2/28/76	**32**	5	2. Inseparable	Capitol 4193
6/26/76	**25**	7	3. Sophisticated Lady (She's A Different Lady)	Capitol 4259
2/26/77	**5**	14	● 4. **I've Got Love On My Mind**	Capitol 4360
2/11/78	**10**	15	● 5. **Our Love**	Capitol 4509
8/09/80	**21**	9	6. Someone That I Used To Love	Capitol 4869
8/22/87	**13**	10	7. Jump Start	Manhattan 50073
12/19/87†	**13**	11	8. I Live For Your Love	Manhattan 50094
3/19/88	**5**	12	9. **Pink Cadillac** written and recorded by Bruce Springsteen (flip of his 1984 hit "Dancing In The Dark")	EMI-Man. 50117
			DAVE & ANSIL COLLINS	
			Jamaican duo.	
7/03/71	**22**	8	1. Double Barrel	Big Tree 115
			DOROTHY COLLINS	
			Born Marjorie Chandler on 11/18/26 in Windsor, Ontario; star of TV's "Your Hit Parade." Married orchestra leader Raymond Scott.	
12/03/55	**16**	2	1. My Boy - Flat Top Juke Box #16 / Top 100 #22	Coral 61510
2/11/56	**17**	2	2. Seven Days Juke Box #17 / Top 100 #25	Coral 61562
			JUDY COLLINS	
			Contemporary folksinger born on 5/1/39 in Seattle; raised in Denver.	
11/23/68	**8**	9	1. **Both Sides Now**	Elektra 45639
1/09/71	**15**	11	2. Amazing Grace song attributed to hymn writer Rev. John Newton, 1779; recorded at St. Paul's Chapel, Columbia University	Elektra 45709
3/17/73	**32**	5	3. Cook With Honey	Elektra 45831
7/26/75	**36**	3	4. Send In The Clowns from the Broadway musical "A Little Night Music"	Elektra 45253
10/15/77	**19**	8	5. Send In The Clowns [R]	Elektra 45253
			PHIL COLLINS	
			Born on 1/30/51 in London. Vocalist/drummer/composer. Stage actor as a young child. With group Flaming Youth. Joined Genesis in 1970, became lead singer in 1975. Also with jazz-rock group Brand X. First solo album, 1981. Starred in 1988 film "Buster."	
4/11/81	**19**	9	1. I Missed Again	Atlantic 3790
7/11/81	**19**	8	2. In The Air Tonight	Atlantic 3824

DATE	POS	WKS	ARTIST—RECORD TITLE	LABEL & NO.
11/27/82†	**10**	16	3. **You Can't Hurry Love**	Atlantic 89933
3/26/83	**39**	3	4. I Don't Care Anymore	Atlantic 89877
3/10/84	**1**(3)	16	● 5. **Against All Odds (Take A Look At Me Now)** title song from the film "Against All Odds"	Atlantic 89700
12/08/84†	**2**(2)	16	● 6. **Easy Lover** **PHILIP BAILEY with PHIL COLLINS**	Columbia 04679
2/23/85	**1**(2)	12	7. **One More Night**	Atlantic 89588
5/11/85	**1**(1)	14	8. **Sussudio**	Atlantic 89560
7/27/85	**4**	13	9. **Don't Lose My Number**	Atlantic 89536
10/12/85	**1**(1)	16	10. **Separate Lives** **PHIL COLLINS & MARILYN MARTIN** love theme from the film "White Nights"	Atlantic 89498
3/29/86	**7**	11	11. **Take Me Home**	Atlantic 89472
9/17/88	**1**(2)	13	● 12. **Groovy Kind Of Love**	Atlantic 89017
11/26/88†	**1**(2)	13	13. **Two Hearts** above 2 from the film "Buster"	Atlantic 88980
			JESSI COLTER	
			Born Miriam Johnson on 5/25/47 in Phoenix. Country singer/songwriter. Worked with Duane Eddy from 1961, married to him from 1962-68. Married Waylon Jennings in 1969.	
4/26/75	**4**	14	1. **I'm Not Lisa**	Capitol 4009
			CHI COLTRANE	
			Born on 11/16/48 in Racine, Wisconsin. Moved to Chicago in the late 60s.	
9/30/72	**17**	9	1. Thunder And Lightning	Columbia 45640
			COMMANDER CODY & HIS LOST PLANET AIRMEN	
			Group formed while Cody (George Frayne) attended the University of Michigan. Band moved to San Francisco in 1968.	
4/15/72	**9**	11	1. **Hot Rod Lincoln** **[N]**	Paramount 0146
			COMMODORES	
			Formed in Tuskegee, Alabama in 1970. Consisted of Lionel Richie (vocals, saxophone), William King (trumpet), Thomas McClary (guitar), Milan Williams (keyboards), Ronald LaPread (bass) and Walter "Clyde" Orange (drums). First recorded for Motown in 1972. In film "Thank God It's Friday." Richie began solo work in 1981.	
7/06/74	**22**	6	1. Machine Gun [I]	Motown 1307
6/28/75	**19**	7	2. Slippery When Wet	Motown 1338
2/14/76	**5**	14	3. **Sweet Love**	Motown 1381
10/09/76	**7**	11	4. **Just To Be Close To You**	Motown 1402
2/19/77	**39**	1	5. Fancy Dancer	Motown 1408
6/25/77	**4**	13	6. **Easy**	Motown 1418
9/17/77	**5**	11	7. **Brick House**	Motown 1425
1/14/78	**24**	7	8. Too Hot Ta Trot	Motown 1432
7/08/78	**1**(2)	16	9. **Three Times A Lady**	Motown 1443
11/04/78	**38**	2	10. Flying High	Motown 1452
8/18/79	**4**	12	11. **Sail On**	Motown 1466
10/13/79	**1**(1)	15	12. **Still**	Motown 1474
1/26/80	**25**	6	13. Wonderland	Motown 1479

James Brown's biggest pop hit, "I Got You" (No. 3, 1965), was almost as popular more than twenty years later: it inspired Eric B. and Rakim's rap classic "I Feel Soul," was featured in the movie *Good Morning, Vietnam*, and was the first song the astronauts of the space shuttle *Discovery* heard their first morning in space.

Peabo Bryson hit the top 10 once on his own ("If Ever You're In My Arms Again," 1984), but he's better known for his duets with Natalie Cole, Melissa Manchester, and Roberta Flack.

The Buckinghams' "Kind of A Drag" hit No. 1 in good company. It was sandwiched among No. 1 singles by the Monkees, Rolling Stones, Supremes, and Beatles.

Jimmy Buffett has made practically an entire career out of one hit: the semi-autobiographical ode to a beachcomber, "Margaritaville" (No. 8, 1977).

Johnny Burnette's "product" lived on long after his tragic death at age 30 in 1964. His son Rocky hit the top 10 in 1980 with "Tired Of Toein' The Line," his son Billy co-wrote "Dream You," a cut on Roy Orbison's acclaimed *Mystery Girl*, and Ringo Starr took a cover of his "You're Sixteen" to No. 1 in 1974.

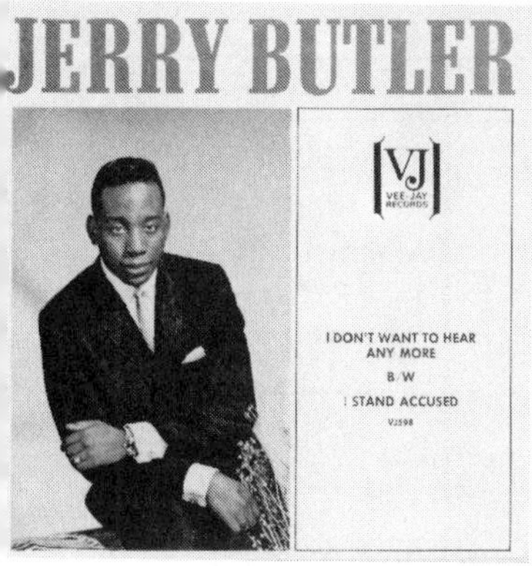

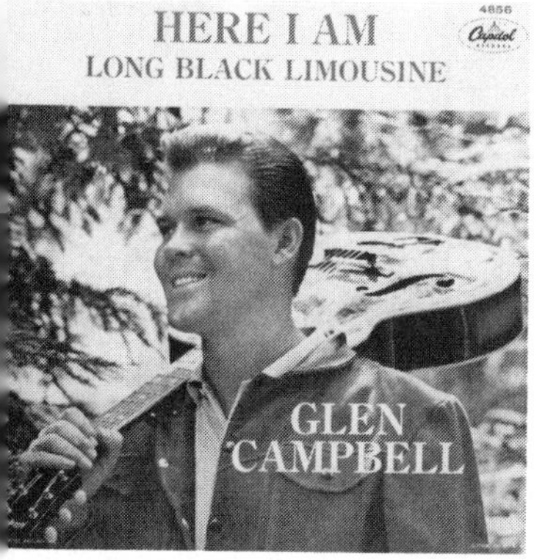

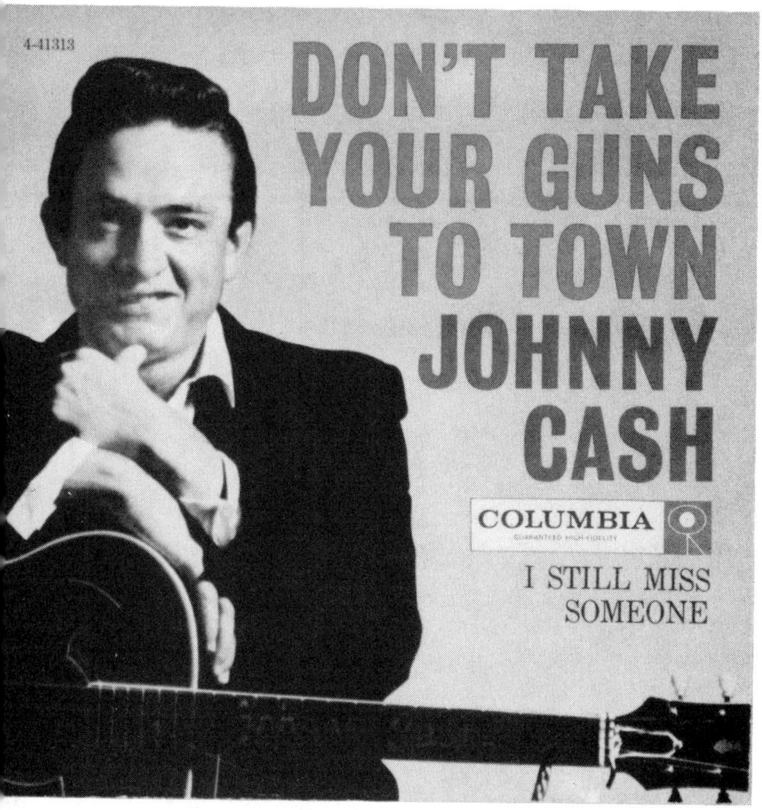

Jerry Butler's biggest solo hit, "Only The Strong Survive" (No. 4, 1969), proved an appropriate anthem for his later career, politics.

The Byrds' "Mr. Tambourine Man" was the first No. 1 rock single for Columbia Records. After that, the label never had a non-rock No. 1. Better late than never.

Glen Campbell proved that there's life after prime time: his popular TV show was canceled in 1972, but his two biggest singles were yet to come, the No. 1 "Rhinestone Cowboy" (1975) and "Southern Nights" (1977).

Kim Carnes' top-10 solo singles were both written by 60s legends: Smokey Robinson ("More Love," 1980) and Jackie DeShannon ("Bette Davis Eyes," 1981).

Johnny Cash paid mock tribute to a parent on his biggest pop hit, "A Boy Named Sue" (No. 2, 1969), but his own daughter was more serious when she took her father's composition "Tennessee Flat Top Box" to the top of the country chart in 1988.

Peter Cetera's 21st and 31st chart singles as the lead singer of Chicago reached No. 1 ("If You Leave Me Now" and "Hard To Say I'm Sorry"). On his own, he made it with his first try: "Glory Of Love," in 1986.

DATE	POS	WKS	ARTIST—RECORD TITLE	LABEL & NO.
7/12/80	**20**	11	14. Old-Fashion Love	Motown 1489
7/11/81	**8**	15	15. **Lady (You Bring Me Up)**	Motown 1514
10/10/81	**4**	15	16. **Oh No** Lionel Richie's last song as lead singer	Motown 1527
3/02/85	**3**	13	17. **Nightshift** a tribute to Marvin Gaye and Jackie Wilson	Motown 1773
			THE COMMUNARDS	
			British duo consisting of Bronski Beat vocalist Jimmy Sommerville and multi-instrumentalist Richard Coles.	
3/07/87	**40**	1	1. Don't Leave Me This Way backing vocal: Sara Jane Morris	MCA 52928
			PERRY COMO	
			Born Pierino Como on 5/18/12 in Canonsburg, Pennsylvania. Owned barbershop in hometown. With Freddy Carlone band in 1933; with Ted Weems, 1936-1942. In the films "Something For The Boys," "Doll Face," "If I'm Lucky" and "Words And Music," 1944-48. Own "Supper Club" radio series to late 1940s. Television shows (15 minutes) from 1948-55. Host of hourly TV shows from 1955-63.	
2/05/55	**2**(3)	14	1. **Ko Ko Mo (I Love You So)** Jockey #2 / Best Seller #4 / Juke Box #5	RCA 5994
6/11/55	**12**	5	2. Chee Chee-OO-Chee (Sang The Little Bird)/ Jockey #12 / Juke Box #14 / Best Seller #24	
6/25/55	**18**	1	3. Two Lost Souls above 2: **PERRY COMO & JAYE P. MORGAN** Jockey #18 from the Broadway musical "Damn Yankees"	RCA 6137
8/13/55	**5**	14	4. **Tina Marie/** Jockey #5 / Best Seller #6 / Juke Box #8 / Top 100 #12 pre	
8/20/55	**20**	1	5. Fooled Jockey #20	RCA 6192
11/19/55†	**11**	11	6. All At Once You Love Her Jockey #11 / Top 100 #24 from the Broadway musical "Pipe Dream"	RCA 6294
3/10/56	**1**(1)	20	7. **Hot Diggity (Dog Ziggity Boom)/** Jockey #1 / Best Seller #2 / Top 100 #2 / Juke Box #2	
3/10/56	**10**	10	8. Juke Box Baby Top 100 #10 / Jockey #11	RCA 6427
6/16/56	**4**	14	9. **More/** Best Seller #4 / Juke Box #6 / Jockey #8 / Top 100 #9	
6/23/56	**8**	12	10. Glendora Jockey #8 / Top 100 #14	RCA 6554
8/25/56	**18**	3	11. Somebody Up There Likes Me Juke Box #18 / Jockey #22 / Top 100 #26 from the film of the same title	RCA 6590
3/02/57	**1**(2)	19	12. **Round And Round** Jockey #1(2) / Best Seller #1(1) / Top 100 #1(1) / Juke Box #3	RCA 6815
5/27/57	**13**	7	13. The Girl With The Golden Braids Jockey #13 / Top 100 #15 / Best Seller #26	RCA 6904
10/14/57	**12**	14	14. Just Born (To Be Your Baby)/ Best Seller #12 / Jockey #13 / Top 100 #19	
10/21/57	**18**	8	15. Ivy Rose Jockey #18 / Top 100 #32	RCA 7050
1/13/58	**1**(1)	16	● 16. **Catch A Falling Star/** Jockey #1 / Best Seller #3 / Top 100 #9	

DATE	POS	WKS	ARTIST—RECORD TITLE	LABEL & NO.
1/20/58	**4**	12	17. Magic Moments Jockey #4 / Top 100 #27 / Best Seller #42	RCA 7128
4/21/58	**6**	11	18. **Kewpie Doll/** Jockey #6 / Best Seller #12 / Top 100 #12	
5/05/58	**19**	1	19. Dance Only With Me Jockey #19 from the Broadway musical "Say Darling"	RCA 7202
8/04/58	**28**	6	20. Moon Talk Best Seller #28 / Hot 100 #29	RCA 7274
11/17/58	**33**	2	21. Love Makes The World Go 'Round	RCA 7353
3/23/59	**29**	3	22. Tomboy	RCA 7464
2/22/60	**22**	6	23. Delaware [N]	RCA 7670
4/28/62	**23**	6	24. Caterina	RCA 8004
7/20/63	**39**	1	25. (I Love You) Don't You Forget It 1-2, 4, 6-12, 14-25: backing vocals by The Ray Charles Singers; all of above: orchestra conducted by Mitchell Ayres	RCA 8186
5/01/65	**25**	6	26. Dream On Little Dreamer backing vocals: The Anita Kerr Quartet	RCA 8533
5/31/69	**38**	1	27. Seattle from the TV series "Here Come The Brides"	RCA 9722
12/05/70†	**10**	13	28. **It's Impossible**	RCA 0387
5/19/73	**29**	8	29. And I Love You So	RCA 0906
			COMPANY B Miami-based dance/disco trio: Lori L, Lezlee Livrano and Susan Johnson.	
5/09/87	**21**	8	1. Fascinated	Atlantic 89294
			CON FUNK SHUN Soul band formed as Project Soul in Vallejo, California in 1968 by high school classmates Mike Cooper (lead vocals, guitar) and Louis McCall (drums). Moved to Memphis in 1972, changed name to Con Funk Shun. Cooper went solo in 1986.	
1/21/78	**23**	6	1. Ffun	Mercury 73959
2/28/81	**40**	1	2. Too Tight	Mercury 76089
			ARTHUR CONLEY Soul singer, born on 1/4/46 in Atlanta. Discovered by Otis Redding in 1965. First recorded for NRC as Arthur & The Corvets.	
4/01/67	**2(1)**	11	● 1. **Sweet Soul Music** originally written by Sam Cooke as "Yeah Man"	Atco 6463
7/01/67	**31**	3	2. Shake, Rattle & Roll	Atco 6494
4/06/68	**14**	9	3. Funky Street	Atco 6563
			RAY CONNIFF & THE SINGERS Born on 11/6/16 in Attleboro, Massachusetts. Trombonist-arranger with Bunny Berigan, Bob Crosby, Harry James, Vaughn Monroe, and Artie Shaw bands; later conductor- arranger on many hit albums in the 50s and 60s.	
7/09/66	**9**	9	1. **Somewhere, My Love** Lara's Theme from the film "Dr. Zhivago"	Columbia 43626
			CHRIS CONNOR Born on 11/8/27 in Kansas City, Missouri. Female jazz-styled singer; with Stan Kenton from 1952-53.	
2/16/57	**34**	3	1. I Miss You So	Atlantic 1105

DATE	POS	WKS	ARTIST—RECORD TITLE	LABEL & NO.
			NORMAN CONNORS	
			Born on 3/1/48 in Philadelphia. Jazz drummer with Archie Shepp, John Coltrane, Pharoah Sanders and others. Own group on Buddah in 1972.	
10/02/76	**27**	10	1. You Are My Starship vocal: Michael Henderson	Buddah 542
			BILL CONTI	
			Providence, Rhode Island native. Composer/conductor for the first 3 "Rocky" films.	
5/07/77	**1**(1)	13	● 1. **Gonna Fly Now** **[I]** theme from the film "Rocky"	United Art. 940
			THE CONTOURS	
			R&B vocal group formed in Detroit: Billy Gordon, Billy Hoggs, Joe Billingslea, Sylvester Potts, Huey Davis (guitar) and Hubert Johnson (d: 7/11/81). Dennis Edwards, a member in 1967, joined The Temptations in 1968.	
9/22/62	**3**	11	1. **Do You Love Me**	Gordy 7005
7/02/88	**11**	8	2. Do You Love Me [R] featured in the film "Dirty Dancing"	Motown Yest. 448
			SAM COOKE	
			Born on 1/22/35 in Chicago. Died from a gunshot wound on 12/11/64 (29) in Los Angeles. Son of a Baptist minister, sang in choir from age 6. His nephew is singer R.B. Greaves. Sam joined gospel group, the Highway Q.C.'s. Lead singer of the Soul Stirrers from 1950-56. First recorded secular songs in 1956 as "Dale Cook" on Specialty. String of hits on Keen label led to contract with RCA. Shot by female motel manager under mysterious circumstances. Inducted into the Rock And Roll Hall Of Fame in 1986. Revered as the definitive soul singer.	
10/28/57	**1**(3)	17	1. **You Send Me** Top 100 #1(3) / Best Seller #1(2) / Jockey #1(1) written by Sam's brother, Charles "L.C." Cooke	Keen 34013
12/23/57†	**18**	10	2. I'll Come Running Back To You Best Seller #18 / Top 100 #22	Specialty 619
1/06/58	**17**	7	3. (I Love You) For Sentimental Reasons Best Seller #17 / Top #43	Keen 4002
3/24/58	**26**	5	4. Lonely Island/ Best Seller #26 / Top 100 #39	
3/31/58	**27**	1	5. You Were Made For Me Best Seller #27 / Top 100 #39	Keen 4009
9/08/58	**22**	6	6. Win Your Love For Me Best Seller #22 / Hot 100 #33	Keen 2006
12/15/58	**26**	7	7. Love You Most Of All	Keen 2008
3/30/59	**31**	5	8. Everybody Likes To Cha Cha Cha	Keen 2018
7/06/59	**28**	4	9. Only Sixteen	Keen 2022
5/23/60	**12**	11	10. Wonderful World	Keen 2112
8/29/60	**2**(2)	13	11. **Chain Gang**	RCA 7783
12/19/60	**29**	4	12. Sad Mood	RCA 7816
3/20/61	**31**	4	13. That's It-I Quit-I'm Movin' On	RCA 7853
6/26/61	**17**	9	14. Cupid	RCA 7883
2/17/62	**9**	13	15. **Twistin' The Night Away**	RCA 7983
6/16/62	**17**	9	16. Having A Party/	
8/04/62	**13**	5	17. Bring It On Home To Me backing vocal: Lou Rawls	RCA 8036
10/20/62	**12**	8	18. Nothing Can Change This Love	RCA 8088

DATE	POS	WKS	ARTIST—RECORD TITLE	LABEL & NO.
2/02/63	13	8	19. Send Me Some Lovin'	RCA 8129
5/04/63	10	9	20. **Another Saturday Night**	RCA 8164
8/17/63	14	7	21. Frankie And Johnny	RCA 8215
11/09/63	11	8	22. Little Red Rooster	RCA 8247
2/15/64	11	7	23. Good News	RCA 8299
6/27/64	11	7	24. Good Times/	
7/04/64	35	4	25. Tennessee Waltz Hugo & Luigi produced all of above RCA recordings	RCA 8368
10/24/64	31	4	26. Cousin Of Mine	RCA 8426
1/16/65	7	9	27. **Shake/**	
2/13/65	31	4	28. A Change Is Gonna Come	RCA 8486
8/28/65	32	3	29. Sugar Dumpling	RCA 8631
			THE COOKIES	
			R&B vocal trio from New York with varying membership. Back-up work for Neil Sedaka, Carole King, and Little Eva. One member, Ethel "Earl-Jean" McCrea, later went solo.	
12/01/62	17	8	1. Chains	Dimension 1002
3/23/63	7	9	2. **Don't Say Nothin' Bad (About My Baby)**	Dimension 1008
1/18/64	33	4	3. Girls Grow Up Faster Than Boys	Dimension 1020
			EDDIE COOLEY & The Dimples	
			Eddie wrote "Fever" (hit for Little Willie John, Peggy Lee and The McCoys).	
11/24/56	20	8	1. Priscilla Best Seller #20 / Juke Box #20 / Top 100 #26	Royal Roost 621
			RITA COOLIDGE	
			Born on 5/1/44 in Nashville. Had her own group, R.C. And The Moonpies, at Florida State University. Moved to Los Angeles in the late 60s. Did back-up work for Delaney & Bonnie, Leon Russell, Joe Cocker and Eric Clapton. With Kris Kristofferson from 1971, married to him from 1973-80. Known as "The Delta Lady," for whom Leon Russell wrote the song of the same name.	
6/11/77	2(1)	17	• 1. **(Your Love Has Lifted Me) Higher And Higher**	A&M 1922
10/15/77	7	13	• 2. **We're All Alone**	A&M 1965
2/04/78	20	7	3. The Way You Do The Things You Do	A&M 2004
7/29/78	25	6	4. You	A&M 2058
1/05/80	38	2	5. I'd Rather Leave While I'm In Love	A&M 2199
8/06/83	36	4	6. All Time High from the James Bond film "Octopussy"	A&M 2551
			ALICE COOPER	
			Born Vincent Furnier on 2/4/48 in Detroit. Formed rock group in Phoenix in 1965; changed name to Alice Cooper in 1966. To Los Angeles in 1968, then to Detroit in 1969. Alice is known primarily for his bizarre stage antics. Appeared in the 1987 film "Prince Of Darkness."	
3/20/71	21	8	1. Eighteen	Warner 7449
6/24/72	7	10	2. **School's Out**	Warner 7596
10/21/72	26	6	3. Elected	Warner 7631
3/10/73	35	3	4. Hello Hurray	Warner 7673
5/12/73	25	8	5. No More Mr. Nice Guy	Warner 7691
5/03/75	12	11	6. Only Women	Atlantic 3254
10/30/76†	12	14	• 7. I Never Cry	Warner 8228

DATE	POS	WKS	ARTIST—RECORD TITLE	LABEL & NO.
6/11/77	**9**	13	8. **You And Me**	Warner 8349
11/11/78	**12**	11	9. How You Gonna See Me Now	Warner 8695
7/05/80	**40**	1	10. Clones (We're All)	Warner 49204
			LES COOPER & The Soul Rockers	
			Born on 3/15/31 in Norfolk, Virginia. Pianist/singer/arranger/leader.	
11/17/62†	**22**	11	1. Wiggle Wobble [I] tenor sax solo: Joe Grier (former lead singer of The Charts)	Everlast 5019
			KEN COPELAND	
4/20/57	**12**	8	1. Pledge Of Love Jockey #12 / Top 100 #17 / Best Seller #23	Imperial 5432
			JILL COREY	
			Born Norma Jean Speranza on 9/30/35.	
2/02/57	**21**	5	1. I Love My Baby (My Baby Loves Me) Jockey #21 / Top 100 #28	Columbia 40794
8/05/57	**11**	9	2. Love Me To Pieces Best Seller #11 / Jockey #11 / Top 100 #18 from the CBS TV show "Studio One, Summer Theatre"	Columbia 40955
			CORNELIUS BROTHERS & SISTER ROSE	
			Family group from Dania, Florida. Consisted of Edward, Carter and Rose. Billie Jo was added in 1973. All 15 Cornelius children play instruments or sing. Carter currently lives in Broward County, Florida, as Gideon Israel, the leader of a Muslim religious sect.	
5/15/71	**3**	13	● 1. **Treat Her Like A Lady**	United Art. 50721
6/17/72	**2**(2)	11	● 2. **Too Late To Turn Back Now**	United Art. 50910
9/23/72	**23**	7	3. Don't Ever Be Lonely (A Poor Little Fool Like Me)	United Art. 50954
2/03/73	**37**	2	4. I'm Never Gonna Be Alone Anymore	United Art. 50996
			DON CORNELL	
			Popular singer/guitarist who worked from late 30s with many bands, but achieved greatest success with Sammy Kaye ("It Isn't Fair") from 1946-50.	
5/14/55	**14**	6	1. Most Of All Jockey #14 / Best Seller #20	Coral 61393
9/10/55	**7**	13	2. **The Bible Tells Me So/** Best Seller #7 / Juke Box #8 / Jockey #18 / Top 100 #31 pre	
11/05/55	**26**	3	3. Love Is A Many-Splendored Thing from the film of the same title	Coral 61467
11/12/55	**25**	1	4. Young Abe Lincoln	Coral 61521
			THE CORSAIRS	
			R&B vocal quartet from La Grange, North Carolina consisting of brothers Jay "Bird" (lead singer), James and Moses Uzzell and cousin George Wooten.	
1/27/62	**12**	10	1. Smoky Places	Tuff 1808
			DAVE "BABY" CORTEZ	
			Born David Cortez Clowney on 8/13/38 in Detroit. Black keyboardist/composer. Played organ and sang with vocal group The Pearls from 1955-57. Frequent session work in New York. First recorded (as David Clowney) for Ember in 1956.	
3/30/59	**1**(1)	14	1. **The Happy Organ** [I]	Clock 1009
8/11/62	**10**	9	2. **Rinky Dink** [I]	Chess 1829

DATE	POS	WKS	ARTIST—RECORD TITLE	LABEL & NO.
			BILL COSBY	
			Born on 7/12/38 in Philadelphia. Top comedian of records, nightclubs, film and TV. His first 7 comedy albums were all million sellers. Played Alexander Scott on TV series "I Spy." Star of the highly-rated NBC-TV series "The Cosby Show."	
9/16/67	**4**	8	1. **Little Ole Man (Uptight-Everything's Alright) [N]**	Warner 7072
			DON COSTA	
			Born on 6/10/25 in Boston; died on 1/19/83 (57). Arranger for Vaughn Monroe, Frank Sinatra, Vic Damone, The Ames Brothers and many more. A&R director of ABC-Paramount Records, then for United Artists Records.	
6/27/60	**27**	4	1. Theme From "The Unforgiven" (The Need For Love) [I]	United Art. 221
8/29/60	**19**	14	2. Never On Sunday [I] from the film of the same title	United Art. 234
			ELVIS COSTELLO	
			Born Declan McManus in Liverpool, England on 8/25/55. Changed name to Elvis Costello in 1976. Formed backing band The Attractions in 1977. Leading eclectic rock singer for a decade. Appeared in the 1987 film "Straight to Hell."	
10/15/83	**36**	2	1. Everyday I Write The Book	Columbia 04045
			GENE COTTON	
			Born in Columbus, Ohio. Attended Ohio State University. Recording since 1972.	
1/22/77	**33**	3	1. You've Got Me Runnin'	ABC 12227
3/04/78	**23**	7	2. Before My Heart Finds Out	Ariola 7675
8/05/78	**36**	3	3. You're A Part Of Me **GENE COTTON with KIM CARNES**	Ariola 7704
11/11/78	**40**	2	4. Like A Sunday In Salem (The Amos & Andy Song)	Ariola 7723
			JOHN COUGAR - see MELLENCAMP	
			COUNT FIVE	
			5 teenagers from San Jose, California; Kenn Ellner, lead singer. Disbanded in 1968.	
9/24/66	**5**	9	1. **Psychotic Reaction**	Double Shot 104
			DON COVAY	
			Born in March, 1938 in Orangeburg, South Carolina. R&B singer/songwriter. Member of the Rainbows in 1955. Recorded as "Pretty Boy" with Little Richard's band for Atlantic in 1957. Formed group, The Goodtimers, in 1960.	
10/03/64	**35**	5	1. Mercy, Mercy **DON COVAY & THE GOODTIMERS**	Rosemart 801
8/11/73	**29**	5	2. I Was Checkin' Out She Was Checkin' In	Mercury 73385
			COVEN	
			Pop quintet featuring the voice of Jinx Dawson.	
10/30/71	**26**	6	1. One Tin Soldier (The Legend of Billy Jack) from the Tom Laughlin movie "Billy Jack"	Warner 7509
			THE COVER GIRLS	
			New York City-based black female dance trio: Louise "Angel" Sabater, Sunshine Wright and Caroline Jackson.	
1/30/88	**27**	8	1. Because Of You	Fever 1914

DATE	POS	WKS	ARTIST—RECORD TITLE	LABEL & NO.
5/21/88	**40**	1	2. Promise Me	Fever 1917
			THE COWBOY CHURCH SUNDAY SCHOOL	
			Lead vocal by a female adult singer - at 45 rpm, it sounds like a child's voice.	
1/01/55	**8**	21	1. **Open Up Your Heart (And Let The Sunshine In)** **[N]** Best Seller #8 / Jockey #18 / Juke Box #19	Decca 29367
			THE COWSILLS	
			Family pop group from Newport, Rhode Island. Consisted of five brothers, their little sister and mother (d: 1/31/85 [56]).	
10/21/67	**2**(2)	12	● 1. **The Rain, The Park & Other Things**	MGM 13810
2/03/68	**21**	6	2. We Can Fly	MGM 13886
6/22/68	**10**	9	3. **Indian Lake**	MGM 13944
3/29/69	**2**(2)	13	● 4. **Hair** from the rock musical "Hair"	MGM 14026
			CRABBY APPLETON	
			West Coast rock quintet led by Michael Fennelly.	
6/27/70	**36**	5	1. Go Back	Elektra 45687
			BILLY "CRASH" CRADDOCK	
			Country-rock singer, born on 6/16/39 in Greensboro, North Carolina. First recorded for Colonial in 1957. Nickname "Crash" came from his stock car racing hobby.	
7/27/74	**16**	9	1. Rub It In	ABC 12013
12/28/74†	**33**	2	2. Ruby, Baby	ABC 12036
			FLOYD CRAMER	
			Nashville's top session pianist. Born on 10/27/33 in Shreveport, Louisiana; raised in Huttig, Arkansas. Played piano from age 5. Moved to Nashville in 1955. Toured with Elvis Presley, Johnny Cash, Perry Como and Chet Atkins.	
10/31/60	**2**(4)	15	1. **Last Date** **[I]**	RCA 7775
3/13/61	**4**	11	2. **On The Rebound** **[I]**	RCA 7840
6/26/61	**8**	8	3. **San Antonio Rose** **[I]** written by Bob Wills in 1938	RCA 7893
2/24/62	**36**	2	4. Chattanooga Choo Choo [I] #1 hit for Glenn Miller in 1941	RCA 7978
			LES CRANE	
			TV talk-show host from San Francisco.	
10/23/71	**8**	10	1. **Desiderata** **[S]** originally a piece of prose, written in 1906 by Max Ehrmann	Warner 7520
			JOHNNY CRAWFORD	
			Born on 3/26/46 in Los Angeles. One of the original Mouseketeers. Played Chuck Connor's son (Mark McCain) in the TV series "The Rifleman," 1958-63.	
6/02/62	**8**	9	1. **Cindy's Birthday**	Del-Fi 4178
8/25/62	**14**	6	2. Your Nose Is Gonna Grow	Del-Fi 4181
11/24/62	**12**	7	3. Rumors	Del-Fi 4188
1/26/63	**29**	4	4. Proud	Del-Fi 4193

DATE	POS	WKS	ARTIST—RECORD TITLE	LABEL & NO.
			RANDY CRAWFORD - see THE CRUSADERS	
			THE ROBERT CRAY BAND	
			Born in Columbus, Georgia. Blues guitarist/vocalist. Played bass in fictional band, Otis Day & The Knights, in the film "Animal House." Band formed in 1974 as backing tour band for Albert Collins. 1988 lineup: Richard Cousins, Peter Boe & David Olson.	
3/21/87	**22**	6	1. Smoking Gun	Mercury 888343
			CRAZY ELEPHANT	
			Bubblegum studio concoction of producers Jerry Kasenetz and Jeff Katz. Ex-Cadillac member Robert Spencer on lead vocals. Touring group formed later.	
4/05/69	**12**	8	1. Gimme Gimme Good Lovin'	Bell 763
			CRAZY OTTO	
			German pianist Fritz Schulz-Reichel. Also see Johnny Maddox.	
2/26/55	**19**	5	1. Glad Rag Doll/ [I] Best Seller #19	
2/26/55	**21**	3	2. Smiles [I] Best Seller #21	Decca 29403
			CREAM	
			British supergroup: Eric Clapton (guitar), Ginger Baker (drums) & Jack Bruce (bass).	
2/24/68	**5**	12	● 1. **Sunshine Of Your Love**	Atco 6544
10/19/68	**6**	9	2. **White Room**	Atco 6617
2/08/69	**28**	6	3. Crossroads	Atco 6646
			CREEDENCE CLEARWATER REVIVAL	
			Rock group formed while members attended high school at El Cerrito, California. Consisted of John Fogerty (vocals, guitar), brother Tom Fogerty (guitar), Stu Cook (keyboards, bass) and Doug Clifford (drums). First recorded as the Blue Velvets for the Orchestra label in 1959. Recorded as the Golliwogs for Fantasy in 1964. Tom Fogerty left for a solo career in 1971 and group disbanded in October, 1972.	
9/28/68	**11**	9	1. Suzie Q. (Part One)	Fantasy 616
2/08/69	**2**(3)	12	● 2. **Proud Mary**	Fantasy 619
5/17/69	**2**(1)	12	● 3. **Bad Moon Rising**	Fantasy 622
8/09/69	**2**(1)	11	4. **Green River/**	
8/09/69	**30**	7	5. Commotion	Fantasy 625
11/08/69	**3**	13	● 6. **Down On The Corner/**	
11/08/69	**14**	13	7. Fortunate Son	Fantasy 634
2/07/70	**2**(2)	9	● 8. **Travelin' Band/**	
		9	9. Who'll Stop The Rain	Fantasy 637
5/02/70	**4**	10	● 10. **Up Around The Bend**	Fantasy 641
8/15/70	**2**(1)	12	● 11. **Lookin' Out My Back Door**	Fantasy 645
2/06/71	**8**	9	● 12. **Have You Ever Seen The Rain** 2-12: written, produced & arranged by John Fogerty	Fantasy 655
7/24/71	**6**	8	13. **Sweet Hitch-Hiker**	Fantasy 665
5/20/72	**25**	5	14. Someday Never Comes	Fantasy 676

DATE	POS	WKS	ARTIST—RECORD TITLE	LABEL & NO.
			MARSHALL CRENSHAW	
			Singer/songwriter/guitarist from Detroit. Played John Lennon in the road show of "Beatlemania" in 1976. Appeared in film "Peggy Sue Got Married" and portrayed Buddy Holly in the 1987 film "La Bamba."	
8/14/82	**36**	4	1. Someday, Someway	Warner 29974
			THE CRESCENDOS	
			Vocal quartet from Nashville; Dale Ward, lead singer.	
1/20/58	**5**	14	1. **Oh Julie** Top 100 #5 / Best Seller #6 / Jockey #7	Nasco 6005
			THE CRESTS	
			New York City vocal group formed in 1955. Consisted of lead singer Johnny Mastrangelo (Maestro; shown as Mastro on all The Crests' hits), Harold Torres, Talmadge Gough, J.T. Carter and Patricia Van Dross. Van Dross left group in 1958. Mastrangelo left for solo work as Johnny Maestro in 1960, replaced by James Ancrum. Maestro later formed Brooklyn Bridge.	
12/22/58†	**2**(2)	14	1. **16 Candles**	Coed 506
4/13/59	**28**	7	2. Six Nights A Week	Coed 509
9/14/59	**22**	9	3. The Angels Listened In	Coed 515
4/04/60	**14**	8	4. Step By Step	Coed 525
7/18/60	**20**	8	5. Trouble In Paradise	Coed 531
			THE CREW-CUTS	
			Vocal group from Toronto, Canada, formed in 1952. Consisted of John Perkins (lead), his brother Ray Perkins (bass), Pat Barrett (tenor) and Rudi Maugeri (baritone). All had sung in church. First called the Canadaires, changed name in 1954. Maugeri did vocal arrangements for the group. Disbanded in 1963.	
1/29/55	**3**	13	1. **Earth Angel/** Jockey #3 / Juke Box #8 / Best Seller #8	
1/29/55	**6**	14	2. Ko Ko Mo (I Love You So) Juke Box #6 / Best Seller #10 / Jockey #11	Mercury 70529
4/30/55	**14**	8	3. Don't Be Angry Best Seller #14 / Jockey #14 / Juke Box #19	Mercury 70597
6/25/55	**16**	7	4. A Story Untold Best Seller #16	Mercury 70634
8/27/55	**10**	8	5. **Gum Drop** Best Seller #10 / Jockey #14 / Juke Box #20 / Top 100 #80 pre	Mercury 70668
12/17/55†	**11**	15	6. Angels In The Sky/ Best Seller #11 / Top 100 #13 / Juke Box #13 / Jockey #16	
1/07/56	**31**	8	7. Mostly Martha	Mercury 70741
2/18/56	**18**	5	8. Seven Days Jockey #18 / Top 100 #20	Mercury 70782
1/26/57	**17**	3	9. Young Love Jockey #17 / Juke Box #17 / Top 100 #24 all of above: orchestra conducted by David Carroll	Mercury 71022
			THE BOB CREWE GENERATION	
			Crewe was born on 11/12/37 in Newark, New Jersey. Wrote many hits beginning with "Silhouettes" in 1957. One of the top producers of the 60s, including work with The 4 Seasons. Head of several labels, music publishing and production companies. Assembled The Bob Crewe Generation, an aggregation of studio musicians.	
1/21/67	**15**	7	1. Music To Watch Girls By [I] tune used in a Diet Pepsi commercial	DynoVoice 229

DATE	POS	WKS	ARTIST—RECORD TITLE	LABEL & NO.
			THE CRICKETS - see BUDDY HOLLY	
			THE CRITTERS	
			New Jersey quintet led by Don Ciccone, who later joined The 4 Seasons.	
9/03/66	**17**	8	1. Mr. Dieingly Sad	Kapp 769
8/05/67	**39**	3	2. Don't Let The Rain Fall Down On Me	Kapp 838
			JIM CROCE	
			Born on 1/10/43 in Philadelphia; killed in plane crash on 9/20/73 in Natchitoches, Louisiana. Vocalist/guitarist/composer. Recorded with wife Ingrid for Capitol in 1968. Lead guitarist on his hits, Maury Muehleisen, was killed in the same crash.	
7/22/72	**8**	10	1. **You Don't Mess Around With Jim**	ABC 11328
11/04/72	**17**	8	2. Operator (That's Not The Way It Feels)	ABC 11335
3/17/73	**37**	3	3. One Less Set Of Footsteps	ABC 11346
6/02/73	**1**(2)	16	● 4. **Bad, Bad Leroy Brown**	ABC 11359
10/13/73	**10**	13	5. **I Got A Name** from the film "The Last American Hero"	ABC 11389
12/01/73	**1**(2)	12	● 6. **Time In A Bottle**	ABC 11405
3/16/74	**9**	11	7. **I'll Have To Say I Love You In A Song**	ABC 11424
6/29/74	**32**	6	8. Workin' At The Car Wash Blues	ABC 11447
			BING CROSBY	
			The most popular entertainer of the 20th century's first 50 years. Harry Lillis Crosby was born on 5/2/01 (or 04) in Tacoma, Washington. He and singing partner Al Rinker were hired in 1926 by Paul Whiteman; with Harry Barris they became the Rhythm Boys and gained an increasing following. The trio split from Whiteman in 1930, and Bing sang briefly with Gus Arnheim's band. It was his early-1931 smash with Arnheim, "I Surrender, Dear," which earned Bing a CBS radio contract, and launched an unsurpassed solo career. Over the next three decades the resonant Crosby baritone and breezy persona sold more than 300 million records and was featured in over 50 movies (won Academy Award for "Going My Way," 1944). Bing died of a heart attack on 10/14/77 on a golf course near Madrid, Spain.	
12/31/55	**7**	2	1. **White Christmas** **[X-R]** Jockey #7 / Top 100 #18 with the Ken Darby Singers and Scott Trotter's Orchestra; originally hit #1 in December, 1942; made pop charts for 20 Christmas seasons; the best-selling record of all time	Decca 23778
10/06/56	**3**	22	2. **True Love** **BING CROSBY & GRACE KELLY** (died in an auto accident, 9/14/82-52) Jockey #3 / Top 100 #4 / Best Seller #5 / Juke Box #6	Capitol 3507
10/21/57	**25**	1	3. Around The World Best Seller #25 / Top 100 #54 from the Michael Todd film "Around The World In Eighty Days"; flip side is Victor Young's instrumental version	Decca 30262
12/23/57	**34**	2	4. White Christmas [X-R] Top 100 #34 / Best Seller #36	Decca 23778
12/19/60	**26**	2	5. White Christmas [X-R]	Decca 23778
12/18/61	**12**	3	6. White Christmas [X-R]	Decca 23778
12/29/62	**38**	1	7. White Christmas [X-R]	Decca 23778

DATE	POS	WKS	ARTIST—RECORD TITLE	LABEL & NO.
			DAVID CROSBY - see GRAHAM NASH	
			CROSBY, STILLS & NASH	
			Trio from Laurel Canyon, California, formed in 1968. Consisted of David Crosby (b: 8/14/41, Los Angeles; guitar), Stephen Stills (b: 1/3/45, Dallas; guitar, keyboards, bass) and Graham Nash (b: 1942, Lancashire, England; guitar). Crosby had been in the Byrds, Stills had been in Buffalo Springfield, and Nash was with The Hollies. Won the 1969 Best New Artist Grammy Award.	
8/02/69	**28**	6	1. Marrakesh Express	Atlantic 2652
10/25/69	**21**	9	2. Suite: Judy Blue Eyes written by Stephen Stills for Judy Collins	Atlantic 2676
			CROSBY, STILLS, NASH & YOUNG:	
4/04/70	**11**	10	3. Woodstock written by Joni Mitchell about festival in New York, August, 1969	Atlantic 2723
6/20/70	**16**	9	4. Teach Your Children	Atlantic 2735
7/11/70	**14**	7	5. Ohio written by Young after 4 students killed at Kent State Univ.	Atlantic 2740
10/10/70	**30**	6	6. Our House	Atlantic 2760
			CROSBY, STILLS & NASH:	
7/02/77	**7**	12	7. **Just A Song Before I Go**	Atlantic 3401
7/03/82	**9**	12	8. **Wasted On The Way**	Atlantic 4058
10/09/82	**18**	9	9. Southern Cross	Atlantic 89969
			CROSS COUNTRY	
			Jay Siegel, Mitch and Phil Margo; all formerly with The Tokens.	
9/22/73	**30**	4	1. In The Midnight Hour	Atco 6934
			CHRISTOPHER CROSS	
			Born Christopher Geppert on 5/3/51 in San Antonio, Texas. Formed own group with Rob Meurer (keyboards), Andy Salmon (bass) and Tommy Taylor (drums) in 1973. Won the 1980 Best New Artist Grammy Award.	
3/01/80	**2**(4)	17	1. **Ride Like The Wind** backing vocals: Michael McDonald	Warner 49184
7/05/80	**1**(1)	13	2. **Sailing**	Warner 49507
10/25/80	**15**	12	3. Never Be The Same	Warner 49580
4/25/81	**20**	7	4. Say You'll Be Mine	Warner 49705
8/29/81	**1**(3)	17	● 5. **Arthur's Theme (Best That You Can Do)** from the Dudley Moore movie "Arthur"	Warner 49787
1/22/83	**12**	13	6. All Right	Warner 29843
5/21/83	**33**	5	7. No Time For Talk	Warner 29662
12/24/83†	**9**	11	8. **Think Of Laura** popularized through play on TV's "General Hospital"; all of above: produced by Michael Omartian	Warner 29658
			CROW	
			Rock-blues quintet from Minneapolis - Dave Wagner, lead singer.	
11/29/69†	**19**	10	1. Evil Woman Don't Play Your Games With Me	Amaret 112
			CROWDED HOUSE	
			New Zealand/Australian trio founded by former Split Enz members Neil Finn (vocals, guitar, piano) and Paul Hester (drums) with Nick Seymour (bass).	
2/21/87	**2**(1)	15	1. **Don't Dream It's Over**	Capitol 5614

DATE	POS	WKS	ARTIST—RECORD TITLE	LABEL & NO.
5/30/87	**7**	11	2. **Something So Strong**	Capitol 5695
			RODNEY CROWELL	
			Born on 8/7/50 in Houston. Country songwriter/guitarist. Rosanne Cash's husband.	
6/28/80	**37**	2	1. Ashes By Now	Warner 49224
			THE CRUSADERS	
			Instrumental jazz-oriented group formed in Houston. 1979 lineup: Joe Sample (keyboards), Wilton Felder (reeds) and Nesbert "Stix" Hooper (drums).	
10/27/79	**36**	3	1. Street Life vocal: Randy Crawford	MCA 41054
			THE CRYSTALS	
			Female vocal group from Brooklyn. Consisted of Barbara Alston, Lala Brooks, Dee Dee Kennibrew, Mary Thomas and Patricia Wright. Discovered by producer Phil Spector.	
12/11/61†	**20**	7	1. There's No Other (Like My Baby)	Philles 100
4/28/62	**13**	8	2. Uptown	Philles 102
10/06/62	**1**(2)	12	3. **He's A Rebel** written by Gene Pitney	Philles 106
1/19/63	**11**	8	4. He's Sure The Boy I Love above 2 are actually Darlene Love (lead) & The Blossoms	Philles 109
5/11/63	**3**	10	5. **Da Doo Ron Ron (When He Walked Me Home)**	Philles 112
8/31/63	**6**	9	6. **Then He Kissed Me**	Philles 115
			THE CUFF LINKS	
			Group is actually the overdubbed voices of Ron Dante (The Archies).	
10/04/69	**9**	9	1. **Tracy**	Decca 32533
			CULTURE CLUB	
			Formed in London in 1981. Consisted of George "Boy George" O'Dowd (b: 6/14/61; vocals), Roy Hay (guitar, keyboards), Mikey Craig (bass) and Jon Moss (drums). Designer Sue Clowes originated distinctive costuming for the group. Won the 1983 Best New Artist Grammy Award.	
1/15/83	**2**(3)	18	1. **Do You Really Want To Hurt Me**	Epic/Virgin 03368
4/30/83	**2**(2)	13	2. **Time (Clock Of The Heart)**	Epic/Virgin 03796
7/16/83	**9**	12	3. **I'll Tumble 4 Ya**	Epic/Virgin 03912
10/29/83	**10**	12	4. **Church Of The Poison Mind**	Epic/Virgin 04144
12/10/83†	**1**(3)	16	● 5. **Karma Chameleon**	Epic/Virgin 04221
3/03/84	**5**	12	6. **Miss Me Blind** backing vocal: Jermaine Stewart	Epic/Virgin 04388
5/19/84	**13**	8	7. It's A Miracle	Epic/Virgin 04457
10/20/84	**17**	7	8. The War Song	Epic/Virgin 04638
1/12/85	**33**	5	9. Mistake No. 3	Epic/Virgin 04727
4/19/86	**12**	10	10. Move Away	Epic/Virgin 05847
			BURTON CUMMINGS	
			Born on 12/31/47 in Winnipeg, Canada. Lead singer of The Guess Who.	
11/06/76†	**10**	15	● 1. **Stand Tall**	Portrait 70001
10/24/81	**37**	2	2. You Saved My Soul	Alfa 7008

DATE	POS	WKS	ARTIST—RECORD TITLE	LABEL & NO.
			THE MIKE CURB CONGREGATION	
			Mike was born on 12/24/44 in Savannah, Georgia. Pop music mogul and politician. President of MGM Records, 1969-73. Elected lieutenant governor of California in 1978. Currently head of own company, Curb Records.	
2/27/71	**34**	4	1. Burning Bridges from the film "Kelly's Heroes"	MGM 14151
			THE CURE	
			British techno-rock quintet led by Robert Smith (vocals, guitar, keyboards) and Laurence Tolhurst (keyboards).	
1/09/87†	**40**	1	1. Just Like Heaven	Elektra 69443
			CUTTING CREW	
			British rock fivesome; Nick Van Eede, lead singer.	
3/21/87	**1**(2)	13	1. **(I Just) Died In Your Arms**	Virgin 99481
7/18/87	**38**	2	2. One For The Mockingbird	Virgin 99464
10/03/87	**9**	11	3. **I've Been In Love Before**	Virgin 99425
			CYMARRON	
			Pop trio: Richard Mainegra, Rick Yancey and Sherrill Parks.	
7/17/71	**17**	7	1. Rings	Entrance 7500
			JOHNNY CYMBAL	
			Scottish-born singer/songwriter/producer. Also recorded as Derek.	
3/16/63	**16**	8	1. Mr. Bass Man [N] bass singer: Ronnie Bright	Kapp 503
			THE CYRKLE	
			Pop group formed while attending Lafayette College in Easton, Pennsylvania. Signed to Columbia Records and managed by The Beatles' Brian Epstein.	
6/04/66	**2**(1)	11	1. **Red Rubber Ball** written by Paul Simon and Bruce Woodley (of The Seekers)	Columbia 43589
8/27/66	**16**	5	2. Turn-Down Day	Columbia 43729
			D	
			DADDY DEWDROP	
			Cleveland singer; real name: Richard Monda.	
4/10/71	**9**	11	1. **Chick-A-Boom (Don't Ya Jes' Love It)** **[N]**	Sunflower 105
			THE DADDY-O's	
			Produced by guitarist Billy Mure.	
6/23/58	**39**	3	1. Got A Match? [I] Best Seller #39 / Top 100 #40	Cabot 122
			DALE & GRACE	
			Vocal duo: Dale Houston (of Ferriday, LA) and Grace Brossard (of Prairieville, LA).	
10/26/63	**1**(2)	12	1. **I'm Leaving It Up To You**	Montel 921
2/08/64	**8**	7	2. **Stop And Think It Over**	Montel 922

DATE	POS	WKS	ARTIST—RECORD TITLE	LABEL & NO.
			ALAN DALE	
			Born Aldo Sigismondi on 7/9/26 in Brooklyn. Baritone singer formerly with Carmen Cavallaro; hosted his own TV show in 1951.	
4/30/55	**14**	7	1. Cherry Pink (And Apple Blossom White) Juke Box #14 / Jockey #19 / Best Seller #27 from the film "Underwater!"	Coral 61373
7/02/55	**10**	7	2. **Sweet And Gentle** Jockey #10 / Best Seller #12 / Juke Box #14	Coral 61435
			ROGER DALTREY	
			Born on 3/1/44 in London, England. Formed band, the Detours, who later became The Who. Roger was The Who's lead singer, and starred in the films "Tommy," "Lisztomania" and "McVicar."	
10/25/80	**20**	8	1. Without Your Love	Polydor 2121
			LIZ DAMON'S ORIENT EXPRESS	
			3-woman, 6-man vocal/instrumental group from Hawaii.	
1/30/71	**33**	3	1. 1900 Yesterday	White Whale 368
			VIC DAMONE	
			Born Vito Farinola on 6/12/28 in Brooklyn. Vic is among the most popular of postwar ballad singers; he also appeared in several movies and hosted a TV series (1956-57).	
6/02/56	**4**	16	1. **On The Street Where You Live** Jockey #4 / Best Seller #8 / Top 100 #8 / Juke Box #13 from the Broadway musical "My Fair Lady"	Columbia 40654
9/30/57	**16**	4	2. An Affair To Remember (Our Love Affair) Jockey #16 / Top 100 #35 from the Cary Grant movie "An Affair To Remember"	Columbia 40945
5/22/65	**30**	4	3. You Were Only Fooling (While I Was Falling In Love)	Warner 5616
			VIC DANA	
			Born on 8/26/42 in Buffalo, New York.	
4/25/64	**27**	5	1. Shangri-La	Dolton 92
3/06/65	**10**	8	2. **Red Roses For A Blue Lady**	Dolton 304
6/04/66	**30**	4	3. I Love You Drops	Dolton 319
			DANCER, PRANCER & NERVOUS	
12/28/59	**34**	1	1. The Happy Reindeer [X-N]	Capitol 4300
			THE CHARLIE DANIELS BAND	
			Formed in Nashville in 1971. Consisted of Charlie Daniels (b: 10/28/36, Wilmington, NC; vocals, guitar, fiddle), Tom Crain (guitar), Taz DiGregorio (keyboards), Charles Hayward (bass) and James W. Marshall (drums). Daniels was with the Jaguars from 1958-67. Went solo in 1968 and worked as a session musician in Nashville. Played on Bob Dylan's "Nashville Skyline" hit LP. In the film "Urban Cowboy."	
7/21/73	**9**	9	1. **Uneasy Rider** **[N]**	Kama Sutra 576
3/15/75	**29**	3	2. The South's Gonna Do It	Kama Sutra 598
7/21/79	**3**	12	● 3. **The Devil Went Down To Georgia**	Epic 50700
6/28/80	**11**	8	4. In America	Epic 50888
9/27/80	**31**	4	5. The Legend Of Wooley Swamp	Epic 50921
4/17/82	**22**	8	6. Still In Saigon	Epic 02828

DATE	POS	WKS	ARTIST—RECORD TITLE	LABEL & NO.
			THE DANLEERS	
			R&B quintet from Brooklyn; Jimmy Weston, lead singer. Group was named after their manager, Danny Webb, who wrote "One Summer Night."	
6/30/58	**7**	10	1. **One Summer Night** Jockey #7 / Best Seller #14 / Top 100 #16 originally released on AMP-3 label as by The Dandleers	Mercury 71322
			DANNY & THE JUNIORS	
			Formed while at high school in Philadelphia in 1955 as the Juvenairs, with Danny Rapp (b: 5/10/41; lead), David White (first tenor), Frank Maffei (second tenor) and Joe Terranova (baritone). White later joined The Spokesmen. Danny Rapp committed suicide on 4/8/83 (41).	
12/09/57†	**1**(7)	18	1. **At The Hop** Top 100 #1(7) / Best Seller #1(5) / Jockey #1(3) song originally written as "Do The Bop"	ABC-Para. 9871
3/10/58	**19**	7	2. Rock And Roll Is Here To Stay Best Seller #19 / Top 100 #19	ABC-Para. 9888
7/21/58	**39**	1	3. Dottie Best Seller #39 / Top 100 #41	ABC-Para. 9926
10/10/60	**27**	3	4. Twistin' U.S.A.	Swan 4060
			DANNY WILSON	
			Trio from Dundee, Scotland: brothers Gary (lead vocals, guitar) and Kit Clark (keyboards, percussion), and Ged Grimes (bass guitar). Group takes its name from a mid-1950s Frank Sinatra film.	
8/01/87	**23**	8	1. Mary's Prayer	Virgin 99465
			DANTE & The EVERGREENS	
			Dante Drowty (b: 9/8/41), lead singer of pop quartet from Los Angeles.	
6/13/60	**15**	8	1. Alley-Oop [N]	Madison 130
			TERENCE TRENT D'ARBY	
			England-based, soul-pop singer, born on 3/15/62 in New York City. Last name originally spelled Darby. Was a member of the US Army boxing team.	
2/27/88	**1**(1)	15	1. **Wishing Well**	Columbia 07675
6/18/88	**4**	13	2. **Sign Your Name**	Columbia 07911
10/08/88	**30**	5	3. Dance Litte Sister (Part One)	Columbia 08023
			BOBBY DARIN	
			Vocalist/pianist/guitarist/drummer, born Walden Robert Cassotto on 5/14/36 in the Bronx. Died of heart failure on 12/20/73 (37) in Los Angeles. First recorded in 1956 with "The Jaybirds" (Decca). First appeared on TV, in March, 1956, on the Tommy Dorsey Show. Won the 1959 Best New Artist Grammy Award. Married to actress Sandra Dee, 1960-67. Nominated for an Oscar for his performance in the film "Captain Newman, MD," 1963. Formed own record company, Direction, in 1968.	
6/30/58	**3**	13	1. **Splish Splash** Hot 100 #3 / Best Seller #4 / Jockey #5 end	Atco 6117
8/11/58	**24**	5	2. Early In The Morning **THE RINKY-DINKS** Hot 100 #24 / Best Seller #24 originally issued on Brunswick as by the Ding Dongs (to conceal Darin's identity who was under contract at Atco), Atco took over the master and issued it as by The Rinky-Dinks	Atco 6121
10/27/58	**9**	14	3. **Queen Of The Hop**	Atco 6127
2/23/59	**38**	2	4. Plain Jane	Atco 6133

DATE	POS	WKS	ARTIST—RECORD TITLE	LABEL & NO.
5/04/59	**2**(1)	13	5. **Dream Lover**	Atco 6140
9/07/59	**1**(9)	22	6. **Mack The Knife** written in 1928 as "Moritat" or "Theme From The Threepenny Opera"	Atco 6147
1/25/60	**6**	11	7. **Beyond The Sea**	Atco 6158
4/04/60	**21**	6	8. Clementine written in 1884 as "Oh, My Darling Clementine"	Atco 6161
6/20/60	**19**	5	9. Won't You Come Home Bill Bailey #1 hit for Arthur Collins in 1902	Atco 6167
10/17/60	**20**	8	10. Artificial Flowers from the musical "Tenderloin"	Atco 6179
2/20/61	**14**	7	11. Lazy River #19 hit for Hoagy Carmichael in 1932	Atco 6188
7/10/61	**40**	1	12. Nature Boy	Atco 6196
9/11/61	**5**	9	13. **You Must Have Been A Beautiful Baby** #1 hit for Bing Crosby in 1938	Atco 6206
1/13/62	**15**	8	14. Irresistible You/	
1/20/62	**30**	5	15. Multiplication from film "Come September" co-starring Bobby Darin & Sandra Dee	Atco 6214
4/14/62	**24**	5	16. What'd I Say (Part 1)	Atco 6221
7/21/62	**3**	9	17. **Things**	Atco 6229
10/27/62	**32**	3	18. If A Man Answers from the film of the same title (again with Darin & Dee)	Capitol 4837
2/02/63	**3**	12	19. **You're The Reason I'm Living**	Capitol 4897
5/25/63	**10**	7	20. **18 Yellow Roses**	Capitol 4970
10/08/66	**8**	9	21. **If I Were A Carpenter**	Atlantic 2350
2/11/67	**32**	3	22. Lovin' You	Atlantic 2376
			JAMES DARREN	
			Born James William Ercolani on 10/3/36 in Philadelphia. Singer and actor, studied acting in New York City. Moved to Hollywood in 1955. In films "Rumble On The Docks," "The Brothers Rico," "Operation Mad Ball," "Gunman's Walk," "Guns Of Navarone," "Because They're Young" and "Let No Man Write My Epitaph." Played the part of Moondoggie, Gidget's boyfriend, in "Gidget," "Gidget Goes Hawaiian" and "Gidget Goes To Rome." In "The Time Tunnel" TV series from 1966-67.	
11/06/61	**3**	12	1. **Goodbye Cruel World**	Colpix 609
2/17/62	**6**	8	2. **Her Royal Majesty**	Colpix 622
5/05/62	**11**	7	3. Conscience	Colpix 630
8/04/62	**39**	1	4. Mary's Little Lamb	Colpix 644
2/18/67	**35**	2	5. All from the film "Run For Your Wife"	Warner 5874
			THE DARTELLS	
			Oxnard, California band consisting of Dick Burns, Corky Wilkie, Rich Peil, Doug Phillips, Randy Ray and Gary Peeler. First recorded for Arlen in 1963.	
4/27/63	**11**	9	1. Hot Pastrami	Dot 16453
			DAVID & DAVID	
			Los Angeles duo: David Baerwald and David Ricketts.	
11/15/86	**37**	3	1. Welcome To The Boomtown	A&M 2857

DATE	POS	WKS	ARTIST—RECORD TITLE	LABEL & NO.
			DAVID & JONATHAN	
			Songwriting/producing/vocal duo from Bristol, England: David Roger Greenaway and Jonathan Roger Cook.	
1/29/66	**18**	5	1. Michelle written by Lennon/McCartney; produced by George Martin	Capitol 5563
			MAC DAVIS	
			Born on 1/21/42 in Lubbock, Texas. Vocalist/guitarist/composer. Worked as a regional rep for Vee-Jay and Liberty Records. Wrote "In The Ghetto," "Don't Cry Daddy," hits for Elvis Presley. Host of his own musical variety TV series from 1974-76. Appearances in several films, including "North Dallas Forty" in 1979.	
8/05/72	**1**(3)	13	● 1. **Baby Don't Get Hooked On Me**	Columbia 45618
5/25/74	**11**	14	2. One Hell Of A Woman	Columbia 46004
9/07/74	**9**	10	3. **Stop And Smell The Roses**	Columbia 10018
12/21/74†	**15**	8	4. Rock N' Roll (I Gave You The Best Years Of My Life)	Columbia 10070
			PAUL DAVIS	
			Born on 4/21/48 in Meridian, Mississippi. Singer/songwriter/producer.	
12/07/74†	**23**	8	1. Ride 'Em Cowboy	Bang 712
9/11/76	**35**	3	2. Superstar	Bang 726
10/29/77†	**7**	25	3. **I Go Crazy**	Bang 733
10/07/78	**17**	13	4. Sweet Life	Bang 738
4/12/80	**23**	6	5. Do Right	Bang 4808
11/28/81†	**11**	13	6. Cool Night	Arista 0645
3/20/82	**6**	13	7. **'65 Love Affair**	Arista 0661
8/28/82	**40**	2	8. Love Or Let Me Be Lonely	Arista 0697
			SAMMY DAVIS, JR.	
			Born on 12/8/25 in New York City. Vocalist/dancer/actor of Broadway, film and TV. With family dance act, the Will Mastin Trio, in the early 40s.	
5/28/55	**12**	12	1. Love Me Or Leave Me/ Best Seller #12 / Jockey #20 from the film of the same title	
6/04/55	**9**	11	2. Something's Gotta Give Best Seller #9 / Juke Box #16 / Jockey #20 from the film "Daddy Long Legs"	Decca 29484
7/02/55	**13**	6	3. That Old Black Magic Jockey #13 / Best Seller #16 / Juke Box #18	Decca 29541
10/06/62	**17**	10	4. What Kind Of Fool Am I from the musical "Stop The World-I Want To Get Off"	Reprise 20048
2/01/64	**17**	9	5. The Shelter Of Your Arms	Reprise 20216
6/24/67	**37**	4	6. Don't Blame The Children [S]	Reprise 0566
1/18/69	**11**	11	7. I've Gotta Be Me from the Broadway musical "Golden Rainbow"	Reprise 0779
4/15/72	**1**(3)	16	● 8. **The Candy Man** from the film "Willy Wonka And The Chocolate Factory"	MGM 14320
			SKEETER DAVIS	
			Country singer, born Mary Penick on 12/30/31 in Dry Ridge, Kentucky. Recorded with friend Betty Davis as the Davis Sisters, until Betty was killed in a car accident on 8/2/53. Formerly married to TV's "Nashville Now" host, Ralph Emery.	
9/05/60	**39**	1	1. (I Can't Help You) I'm Falling Too	RCA 7767

DATE	POS	WKS	ARTIST—RECORD TITLE	LABEL & NO.
1/16/61	**26**	2	2. My Last Date (With You)	RCA 7825
2/16/63	**2**(1)	13	3. **The End Of The World**	RCA 8098
9/21/63	**7**	11	4. **I Can't Stay Mad At You**	RCA 8219
			THE SPENCER DAVIS GROUP	
			R&B-styled rock group formed in Birmingham, England in 1963: Spencer Davis (vocals, rhythm guitar), Steve Winwood (lead vocals, lead guitar, keyboards), brother Muff Winwood (bass) and Pete York (drums). Steve Winwood left in 1967 to form the group Traffic; later, a successful solo artist. Muff became senior director of A&R at CBS U.K.	
1/28/67	**7**	9	1. **Gimme Some Lovin'**	United Art. 50108
4/08/67	**10**	7	2. **I'm A Man**	United Art. 50144
			TYRONE DAVIS	
			Soul singer, born on 5/4/38 in Greenville, Mississippi; raised in Saginaw, Michigan. To Chicago in 1959. Worked as valet/chauffeur for Freddie King until 1962. Working local clubs when discovered by Harold Burrage. First recorded for Four Brothers in 1965 as "Tyrone The Wonder Boy." His younger sister, Jean Davis, was a member of Facts Of Life.	
1/04/69	**5**	11	● 1. **Can I Change My Mind**	Dakar 602
4/12/69	**34**	2	2. Is It Something You've Got	Dakar 605
4/04/70	**3**	11	● 3. **Turn Back The Hands Of Time**	Dakar 616
8/25/73	**32**	3	4. There It Is	Dakar 4523
10/30/76	**38**	4	5. Give It Up (Turn It Loose)	Columbia 10388
			DAWN	
			Vocal trio formed in New York City: Tony Orlando (b: 4/3/44, New York City), Telma Hopkins (b: 10/28/48, Louisville) and Joyce Vincent (b: 12/14/46, Detroit). Orlando had recorded solo from 1961-63; Hopkins and Vincent had been back-up singers. Orlando was manager for April-Blackwood Music at the time of their first hit. Own TV show from 1974-76. Hopkins in TV series "Bosom Buddies" and "Gimme A Break." All of their hits produced by Hank Medress (The Tokens) and Dave Appell.	
8/29/70	**3**	13	● 1. **Candida**	Bell 903
12/05/70†	**1**(3)	16	● 2. **Knock Three Times**	Bell 938
4/10/71	**25**	5	3. I Play And Sing	Bell 970
7/10/71	**33**	6	4. Summer Sand	Bell 45107
			DAWN featuring TONY ORLANDO:	
11/13/71	**39**	1	5. What Are You Doing Sunday	Bell 45141
3/17/73	**1**(4)	17	● 6. **Tie A Yellow Ribbon Round The Ole Oak Tree**	Bell 45318
7/28/73	**3**	13	● 7. **Say, Has Anybody Seen My Sweet Gypsy Rose**	Bell 45374
			TONY ORLANDO & DAWN:	
12/01/73	**27**	7	8. Who's In The Strawberry Patch With Sally	Bell 45424
9/07/74	**7**	9	9. **Steppin' Out (Gonna Boogie Tonight)**	Bell 45601
1/11/75	**11**	8	10. Look In My Eyes Pretty Woman	Bell 45620
3/29/75	**1**(3)	10	● 11. **He Don't Love You (Like I Love You)**	Elektra 45240
7/12/75	**14**	6	12. Mornin' Beautiful	Elektra 45260
9/20/75	**34**	3	13. You're All I Need To Get By	Elektra 45275
2/21/76	**22**	6	14. Cupid	Elektra 45302

DATE	POS	WKS	ARTIST—RECORD TITLE	LABEL & NO.
			BOBBY DAY	
			Born Robert Byrd on 7/1/32 in Ft. Worth, Texas. R&B singer. To Watts, Los Angeles in 1948. Formed the Hollywood Flames in 1950. Wrote "Little Bitty Pretty One."	
8/04/58	**2**(2)	19	1. **Rock-in Robin** Hot 100 #2 / Best Seller #4 end	Class 229
			DORIS DAY	
			Born Doris Kappelhoff on 4/3/22 in Cincinnati. Doris sang briefly with Bob Crosby in 1940 and shortly thereafter became a major star with the Les Brown band ("Sentimental Journey"). Her great solo recording success was soon transcended by Hollywood as Doris became the #1 box office star of the late 50s and early 60s; her 1968-73 TV series was also popular.	
7/23/55	**13**	9	1. I'll Never Stop Loving You Jockey #13 / Best Seller #15 / Top 100 #93 pre from the film "Love Me Or Leave Me"	Columbia 40505
7/07/56	**2**(3)	22	2. **Whatever Will Be, Will Be (Que Sera, Sera)** Top 100 #2 / Jockey #2 / Best Seller #3 / Juke Box #3 from the film "The Man Who Knew Too Much"	Columbia 40704
7/21/58	**6**	12	3. **Everybody Loves A Lover** Jockey #6 end / Hot 100 #14 / Best Seller #17	Columbia 41195
			MORRIS DAY	
			Leader of Minneapolis funk group, The Time (formerly Prince's backing band). Born in Springfield, Illinois; raised in Minneapolis. Acted in the 1984 film "Purple Rain."	
3/26/88	**23**	6	1. Fishnet	Warner 28201
			TAYLOR DAYNE	
			Real name: Leslie Wonderman. Female dance singer from Long Island.	
11/14/87†	**7**	15	● 1. **Tell It To My Heart**	Arista 9612
3/12/88	**7**	11	2. **Prove Your Love**	Arista 9676
7/23/88	**3**	16	● 3. **I'll Always Love You**	Arista 9700
11/26/88†	**2**(1)	13	4. **Don't Rush Me**	Arista 9722
			DAZZ BAND	
			Cleveland ultrafunk band, formerly Kinsman Dazz. "Dazz" means "danceable jazz."	
5/15/82	**5**	16	1. **Let It Whip**	Motown 1609
			DEAD OR ALIVE	
			British pop-rock quartet; Pete Burns, lead singer.	
6/29/85	**11**	11	1. You Spin Me Round (Like A Record)	Epic 04894
1/31/87	**15**	9	2. Brand New Lover	Epic 06374
			BILL DEAL & THE RHONDELS	
			8-man New York City brassy-rock band.	
3/15/69	**39**	1	1. May I	Heritage 803
5/31/69	**35**	3	2. I've Been Hurt	Heritage 812
9/13/69	**23**	5	3. What Kind Of Fool Do You Think I Am	Heritage 817
			DEAN & JEAN	
			Welton Young and Brenda Lee Jones from Dayton, Ohio.	
12/14/63†	**35**	2	1. Tra La La La Suzy	Rust 5067
3/21/64	**32**	3	2. Hey Jean, Hey Dean	Rust 5075

DATE	POS	WKS	ARTIST—RECORD TITLE		LABEL & NO.
			JIMMY DEAN		
			Born Seth Ward on 8/10/28 in Plainview, Texas. Vocalist/piano/guitar/composer. With Tennessee Haymakers in Washington, DC, 1948. Own Texas Wildcats in 1952. Recorded for Four Star in 1952. Own CBS-TV series, 1957-58; ABC-TV series, 1963-66.		
1/06/58†	**32**	1	1. Little Sandy Sleighfoot Top 100 #32 / Best Seller #37	[X-N]	Columbia 41025
10/09/61	**1**(5)	13	● 2. **Big Bad John**		Columbia 42175
1/20/62	**24**	3	3. Dear Ivan	[S]	Columbia 42259
2/10/62	**22**	5	4. The Cajun Queen/	[S]	
2/10/62	**26**	5	5. To A Sleeping Beauty background music: "Memories"	[S]	Columbia 42282
4/14/62	**8**	9	6. **P.T. 109** an account of John F. Kennedy's heroism after his torpedo boat was destroyed in 1943		Columbia 42338
10/06/62	**29**	5	7. Little Black Book		Columbia 42529
5/22/76	**35**	2	● 8. I.O.U. Jimmy Dean's ode of thanks to his mother	[S]	Casino 052
			DeBARGE		
			Family group from Grand Rapids, Michigan. Consisted of lead vocalist Eldra (keyboards), Mark (trumpet, saxophone), James (keyboards), Randy (bass) and Bunny DeBarge (vocals). Brothers Bobby and Tommy were in Switch.		
3/26/83	**31**	6	1. I Like It		Gordy 1645
5/28/83	**17**	10	2. All This Love		Gordy 1660
11/26/83†	**18**	11	3. Time Will Reveal		Gordy 1705
3/09/85	**3**	14	4. **Rhythm Of The Night** from the Berry Gordy film "The Last Dragon"		Gordy 1770
6/22/85	**6**	12	5. **Who's Holding Donna Now**		Gordy 1793
			CHICO DeBARGE		
			DeBarge sibling, but not a member of the group DeBarge.		
12/27/86†	**21**	11	1. Talk To Me		Motown 1858
			EL DeBARGE		
			Eldra DeBarge (b: 6/4/61), lead singer of family group DeBarge.		
5/17/86	**3**	13	1. **Who's Johnny** theme from the film "Short Circuit"		Gordy 1842
			CHRIS DeBURGH		
			Pop-rock singer, born Christopher John Davidson on 10/15/50 in Ireland.		
6/11/83	**34**	4	1. Don't Pay The Ferryman		A&M 2511
4/04/87	**3**	14	2. **The Lady In Red**		A&M 2848
			THE DeCASTRO SISTERS		
			Peggy, Babette and Cherie; raised on their father's sugar plantation in Cuba.		
5/07/55	**17**	4	1. Boom Boom Boomerang Juke Box #17 / Best Seller #24 bass voice: Thurl Ravenscroft		Abbott 3003

Jimmy Charles' lone top-10 hit, "A Million To One," contained the line "We'll forgive them, because we love them," which made the song a surprise hit with teenagers, considering that line referred to parents.

Ray Charles is perhaps the most versatile performer of his generation. A formative influence on soul music and rock 'n' roll, he issued the classic LP *Modern Sounds In Country And Western Music* (No. 1, 1962) and was also a mainstay on the jazz charts. His most recent chart appearance was in a duet with Billy Joel on "Baby Grand."

Cheap Trick went nine years between its first and second top-10 hits, "I Want You To Want Me" (1979) and "The Flame" (1988). Incredibly, the group was still on the same label, Epic. That's called true faith.

Chubby Checker must have looked positively anorexic next to the Fat Boys when they cut a remake of "The Twist," which hit the top 20 in 1988. Checker had previously taken the song to No. 1 *twice* by himself, in 1960 and 1962.

Cher staged a major comeback in 1971 with the No. 1 "Gypsies, Tramps And Thieves," from the gold album *Cher*. In 1988, she staged another comeback with the No. 10 "I Found Someone," from the gold album *Cher*. Should she slump in the 90s, she knows what to do.

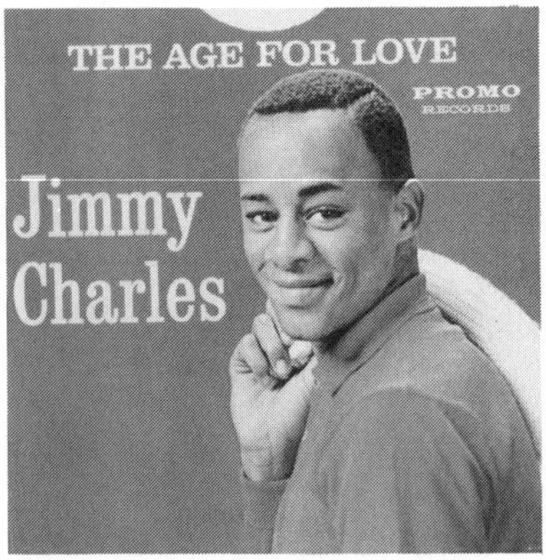

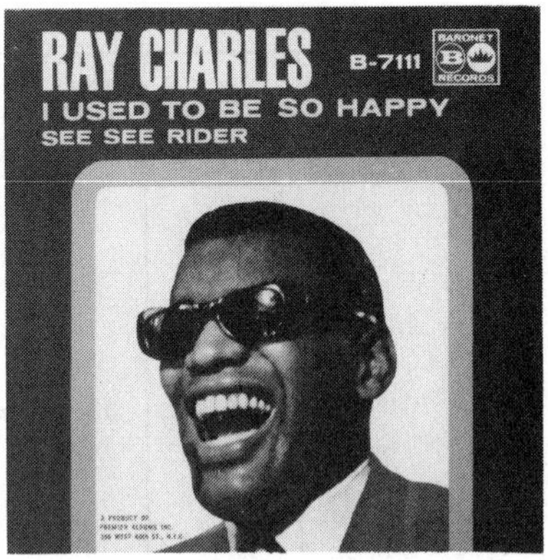

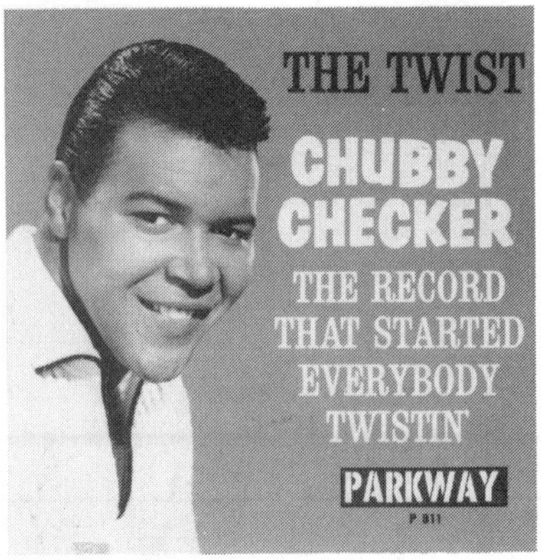

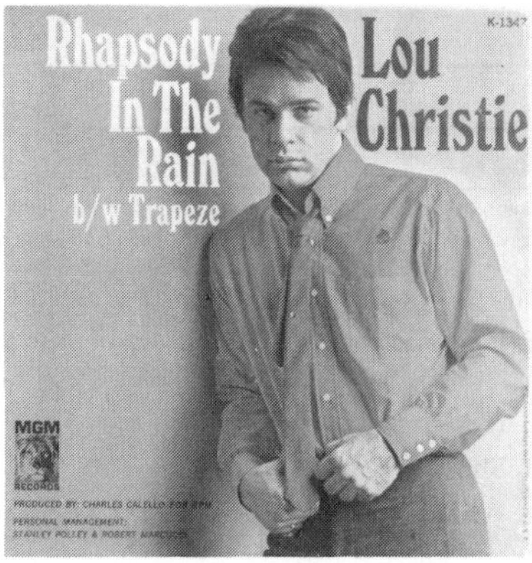

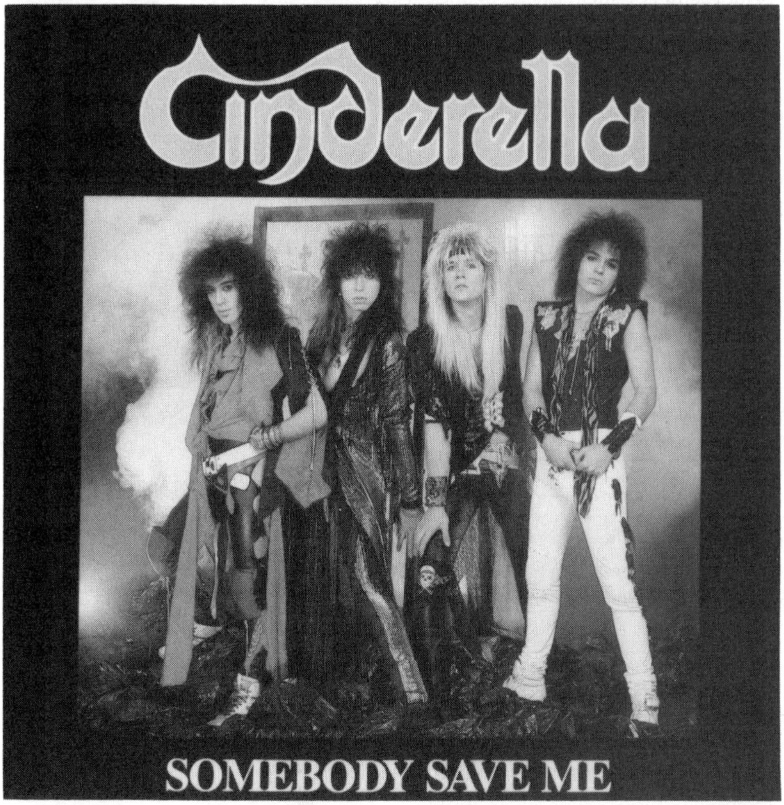

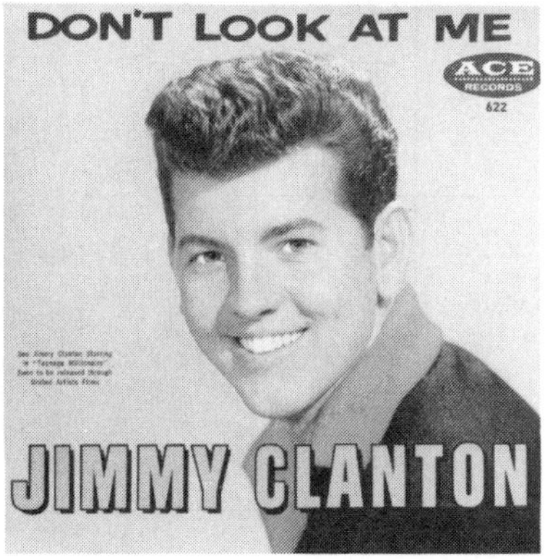

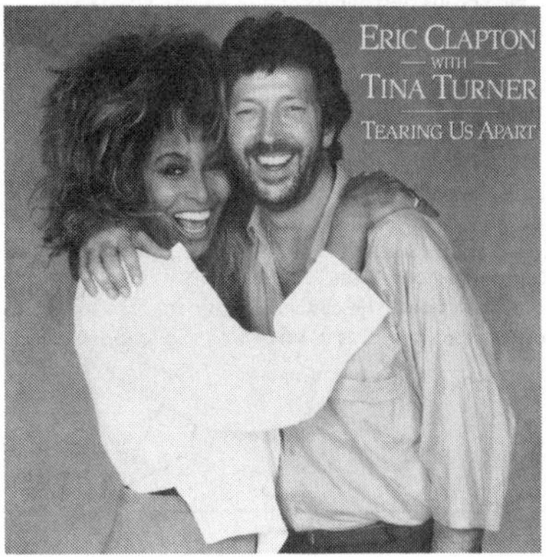

The Chordettes were a major link between the pop groups of the pre-rock era and the tougher rock groups of the early 60s. Their first hit, "Mr. Sandman," shared the top 20 with songs by the McGuire Sisters and Fontane Sisters, while their last, "Never On Sunday," shared the top 20 with songs by the Chantels and Ike and Tina Turner.

Lou Christie's "Rhapsody In The Rain" was banned by many radio stations for "explicit" lyrics about making love to the beating of windshield wipers. It still got to No. 16, though, paving the way for songs like "Little Red Corvette."

Cinderella hails from Pennsylvania, a state that was once a leading "heavy-metal" manufacturer—but then again, Perry Como and Bobby Vinton also come from there.

Jimmy Clanton was New Orleans' *other* big star of the early rock era. He had seven Top-40 hits between 1958 and 1962, all before he was 22.

Eric Clapton and Tina Turner seemed a match made in rock heaven; he is the leading blues-rock guitarist of his generation, and she is rock's most-honored female singer. "Tearin' Us Apart," however, didn't tear up the charts.

DATE	POS	WKS	ARTIST—RECORD TITLE	LABEL & NO.
			JOEY DEE & THE STARLITERS	
			Born Joseph DiNicola on 6/11/40 in Passaic, New Jersey. In September, 1960, Joey & The Starlighters became the house band at the Peppermint Lounge, New York City. After 1964, group included 3 members who later formed The Young Rascals, plus guitarist Jimi Hendrix.	
12/04/61†	**1**(3)	14	1. **Peppermint Twist - Part I** inspired by New York City's Peppermint Lounge club	Roulette 4401
3/03/62	**20**	4	2. Hey, Let's Twist	Roulette 4408
3/31/62	**6**	9	3. **Shout - Part I**	Roulette 4416
9/15/62	**18**	6	4. What Kind Of Love Is This from the film "Two Tickets To Paris"	Roulette 4438
6/01/63	**36**	1	5. Hot Pastrami With Mashed Potatoes - Part I	Roulette 4488
			JOHNNY DEE - see JOHN D. LOUDERMILK	
			KIKI DEE	
			Born Pauline Matthews on 3/6/47 in Yorkshire, England.	
10/19/74	**12**	10	1. I've Got The Music In Me **THE KIKI DEE BAND**	Rocket 40293
7/17/76	**1**(4)	15	● 2. **Don't Go Breaking My Heart** **ELTON JOHN & KIKI DEE**	Rocket 40585
			LENNY DEE	
			Organist.	
2/12/55	**19**	15	1. Plantation Boogie [I] Juke Box #19 / Best Seller #23	Decca 29360
			TOMMY DEE with Carol Kay & the Teen-Aires	
			Born Thomas Donaldson on 7/15/36 in Vicker, Virginia. Disc jockey; worked at KFXM-San Bernadino at time of hit - written on the air; first recorded by Eddie Cochran. Currently a producer/promoter/record company executive in Nashville.	
4/13/59	**11**	8	1. Three Stars [S] a tribute to Buddy Holly, Ritchie Valens and The Big Bopper	Crest 1057
			THE DEELE	
			R&B funk sextet from Cincinnati, led by Darnell "Dee" Bristol.	
4/02/88	**10**	12	1. **Two Occasions**	Solar 70015
			DEEP PURPLE	
			British hard-rock band. Original lineup: Ritchie Blackmore (guitar), Rod Evans (vocals), Jon Lord (keyboards), Ian Paice (drums) and Nicky Simper (bass). Evans and Simper left in 1969, replaced by Ian Gillan and Roger Glover. Numerous personnel changes from late 1973 on. Blackmore/Gillan/Lord/Paice reunited in 1984.	
8/24/68	**4**	9	1. **Hush**	Tetragramm. 1503
12/07/68	**38**	3	2. Kentucky Woman	Tetragramm. 1508
6/16/73	**4**	12	● 3. **Smoke On The Water**	Warner 7710
			RICK DEES & HIS CAST OF IDIOTS	
			Born Rigdon Osmond Dees III in Memphis, 1950. Disc jockey working at WMPS-Memphis when he conceived idea for "Disco Duck." Currently one of America's top radio DJs. Host of TV's "Solid Gold" since 1984.	
9/04/76	**1**(1)	16	▲ 1. **Disco Duck (Part 1)** **[N]**	RSO 857

DATE	POS	WKS	ARTIST—RECORD TITLE	LABEL & NO.
			DEF LEPPARD	
			Heavy-metal quintet formed in Sheffield, England in 1977: Joe Elliott (lead singer), Pete Willis & Steve Clark (lead guitars), Rick Savage (bass) and Rick Allen (drums; lost his left arm in an auto accident on New Year's Eve in 1984). Phil Collen replaced Pete Willis in late 1982.	
4/16/83	**12**	9	1. Photograph	Mercury 811215
7/09/83	**16**	9	2. Rock Of Ages	Mercury 812604
10/08/83	**28**	5	3. Foolin'	Mercury 814178
11/21/87	**19**	9	4. Animal	Mercury 888832
2/13/88	**10**	10	5. **Hysteria**	Mercury 870004
5/21/88	**2**(1)	15	6. **Pour Some Sugar On Me**	Mercury 870298
8/20/88	**1**(1)	13	7. **Love Bites**	Mercury 870402
12/03/88†	**3**	12	8. **Armageddon It**	Mercury 870692
			THE DeFRANCO FAMILY featuring TONY DeFRANCO	
			5-member family from Ontario, Canada: Tony (age 13), Merlina (16), Nino (17), Marisa (18) and Benny (19).	
9/29/73	**3**	14	● 1. **Heartbeat - It's A Lovebeat**	20th Century 2030
1/26/74	**32**	4	2. Abra-Ca-Dabra	20th Century 2070
5/25/74	**18**	6	3. Save The Last Dance For Me	20th Century 2088
			DeJOHN SISTERS	
			Julie and Dux DeGiovanni from Chester, Pennsylvania.	
12/25/54†	**6**	13	1. **(My Baby Don't Love Me) No More** Jockey #6 / Best Seller #8 / Juke Box #11	Epic 9085
			DESMOND DEKKER & THE ACES	
			Born Desmond Dacris on 7/16/41 in Kingston, Jamaica. Reggae's first successful artist.	
6/07/69	**9**	7	1. **Israelites**	Uni 55129
			DELANEY & BONNIE & FRIENDS	
			Delaney Bramlett (b: 7/1/39, Acton, IL) & wife Bonnie Lynn Bramlett (b: 11/8/44, Pontotoc County, MS) & Friends - backing artists who included at various times Leon Russell, Rita Coolidge, Dave Mason, Eric Clapton, Duane Allman and many others. Delaney & Bonnie dissolved their marriage and group in 1972.	
6/26/71	**13**	10	1. Never Ending Song Of Love	Atco 6804
			DELANEY & BONNIE:	
10/09/71	**20**	7	2. Only You Know And I Know	Atco 6838
			THE DELEGATES	
			A Dickey Goodman-type recording, featuring disc jockey Bob DeCarlo.	
11/04/72	**8**	6	1. **Convention '72** [N] featuring bits of some of the top pop hits of 1972	Mainstream 5525
			THE DELFONICS	
			Soul group from Philadelphia. Formed in 1965 as the Four Gents. Consisted of William and Wilbert Hart, Ritchie Daniels, and Randy Cain. First recorded for Moon Shot, 1967. Daniels left for the service in 1968, group continued as a trio. Cain was replaced by Major Harris in 1971. Harris went solo in 1974.	
2/24/68	**4**	12	1. **La - La - Means I Love You**	Philly Groove 150
10/05/68	**35**	4	2. Break Your Promise	Philly Groove 152

DATE	POS	WKS	ARTIST—RECORD TITLE	LABEL & NO.
1/25/69	**35**	1	3. Ready Or Not Here I Come (Can't Hide From Love)	Philly Groove 154
10/04/69	**40**	2	4. You Got Yours And I'll Get Mine	Philly Groove 157
2/07/70	**10**	10	● 5. **Didn't I (Blow Your Mind This Time)**	Philly Groove 161
7/25/70	**40**	1	6. Trying To Make A Fool Of Me	Philly Groove 162
			THE DELL-VIKINGS	
			Racially integrated R&B/rock group formed at the Air Force Serviceman's Club in Pittsburgh, 1955. Consisted of Norman Wright, Corinthian "Kripp" Johnson, Donald "Gus" Backus, David Lerchey and Clarence Quick. Gus & David are white, others black. First recorded for Fee Bee and Luniverse labels, then Dot. After discharge from the Air Force, Kripp formed new Dell-Vikings for the Dot label with Chuck Jackson, who went on to a successful solo career. Gus and the other members formed new Del Vikings group for Mercury in 1957.	
3/02/57	**4**	22	1. **Come Go With Me** Best Seller #4 / Top 100 #5 / Jockey #6 / Juke Box #6	Dot 15538
7/15/57	**9**	13	2. **Whispering Bells** Top 100 #9 / Best Seller #10 / Jockey #19	Dot 15592
7/15/57	**12**	1	3. Cool Shake **DEL VIKINGS** Jockey #12 / Top 100 #46	Mercury 71132
			THE DELLS	
			R&B vocal group formed at Thornton Township High School in Harvey, Illinois: Johnny Funches (lead), Marvin Junior (tenor), Verne Allison (tenor), Mickey McGill (baritone) and Chuck Barksdale (bass). First recorded as the El-Rays for Chess in 1953. Group remained intact into the 80s, with exception of Funches, who was replaced by Johnny Carter (ex-Flamingos) in 1960.	
2/17/68	**20**	7	1. There Is	Cadet 5590
7/20/68	**10**	10	2. **Stay In My Corner** original version on Vee-Jay hit POS 23 on the R&B charts in 1965	Cadet 5612
11/02/68	**18**	5	3. Always Together	Cadet 5621
2/08/69	**38**	2	4. Does Anybody Know I'm Here	Cadet 5631
6/21/69	**22**	6	5. I Can Sing A Rainbow/Love Is Blue	Cadet 5641
8/23/69	**10**	10	6. **Oh, What A Night** original version on Vee-Jay hit POS 4 on the R&B charts in 1956	Cadet 5649
9/18/71	**30**	6	7. The Love We Had (Stays On My Mind)	Cadet 5683
6/23/73	**34**	2	● 8. Give Your Baby A Standing Ovation	Cadet 5696
			THE DEMENSIONS	
			Vocal group from the Bronx, New York: Phil Del Giudice (lead), Lenny Dell, Howard Margolin and Marisa Martelli.	
8/08/60	**16**	9	1. Over The Rainbow first sung by Judy Garland in the movie "The Wizard Of Oz"	Mohawk 116
			THE EXOTIC SOUNDS OF MARTIN DENNY	
			Born on 4/10/11 in New York City. Composer/arranger/pianist. Originated the "Exotic Sounds" in Hawaii, featuring Julius Wechter (Baja Marimba Band) on vibes and marimba.	
4/27/59	**4**	13	1. **Quiet Village** **[I]** written by Les Baxter	Liberty 55162
11/16/59	**28**	2	2. The Enchanted Sea [I]	Liberty 55212

DATE	POS	WKS	ARTIST—RECORD TITLE	LABEL & NO.
			JOHN DENVER	
			Born John Henry Deutschendorf on 12/31/43 in Roswell, New Mexico. To Los Angeles in 1964. With the Chad Mitchell Trio from 1965-68. Wrote "Leaving On A Jet Plane." Starred in the film "Oh, God" in 1978.	
6/26/71	**2**(1)	14	● 1. **Take Me Home, Country Roads** backing vocals by Fat City (Bill Danoff & Taffy Nivert)	RCA 0445
1/06/73	**9**	12	2. **Rocky Mountain High**	RCA 0829
2/16/74	**1**(1)	13	● 3. **Sunshine On My Shoulders**	RCA 0213
6/15/74	**1**(2)	11	● 4. **Annie's Song** written by Denver for his wife Ann Martell (married 1967-83)	RCA 0295
10/05/74	**5**	10	● 5. **Back Home Again**	RCA 10065
1/11/75	**13**	8	6. Sweet Surrender	RCA 10148
4/05/75	**1**(1)	15	● 7. **Thank God I'm A Country Boy** above 2 recorded live at Universal City Amphitheater, California	RCA 10239
8/30/75	**1**(1)	13	● 8. **I'm Sorry/**	
10/11/75	**2**(4)	7	9. Calypso dedicated to Jacques Cousteau and those who served on his ship	RCA 10353
12/13/75†	**13**	9	10. Fly Away backing vocals by Olivia Newton-John	RCA 10517
3/20/76	**29**	4	11. Looking For Space	RCA 10586
10/02/76	**36**	2	12. Like A Sad Song	RCA 10774
4/30/77	**32**	3	13. My Sweet Lady also the flip side of "Thank God I'm A Country Boy"; all of above: produced by Milton Okun	RCA 10911
9/05/81	**36**	4	14. Some Days Are Diamonds (Some Days Are Stone)	RCA 12246
4/24/82	**31**	5	15. Shanghai Breezes	RCA 13071
			DEODATO	
			Born Eumir Deodato Almeida on 6/21/42 in Rio de Janeiro, Brazil. Keyboardist/ composer/arranger. Kool & The Gang's producer from 1979-82.	
2/17/73	**2**(1)	10	1. **Also Sprach Zarathustra** [I] theme from the film "2001: A Space Odyssey"; written by classical composer Richard Strauss in 1896	CTI 12
			DEPECHE MODE	
			All-synthesized band formed in Basildon, England consisting of David Gahan (vocals), Martin Gore, Vince Clarke and Andy Fletcher. Clarke left in 1982 (formed Yaz, then Erasure), replaced by Alan Wilder. Group name is French for "fast fashion."	
6/22/85	**13**	10	1. People Are People	Sire 29221
			DEREK	
			Derek is singer Johnny Cymbal.	
11/23/68†	**11**	11	1. Cinnamon	Bang 558

DATE	POS	WKS	ARTIST—RECORD TITLE	LABEL & NO.
			DEREK & THE DOMINOS	
			A gathering of alumni from Delaney & Bonnie & Friends. Featuring Eric Clapton (Derek), Bobby Whitlock, Jim Gordon and Carl Radle (died on 5/30/80).	
6/17/72	**10**	10	1. **Layla** **[R]**	Atco 6809
			Layla: nickname of George Harrison's wife; featuring Duane Allman, lead guitar; long version (7 minutes) of their 1971 hit (POS 51)	
			RICK DERRINGER	
			Born Richard Zehringer on 8/5/47 in Celina, Ohio. Lead singer/guitarist of The McCoys. Performed on and produced sessions for both Edgar & Johnny Winter's bands.	
3/02/74	**23**	6	1. Rock And Roll, Hoochie Koo	Blue Sky 2751
			TERI DeSARIO with K.C.	
			DeSario is a singer from Miami and K.C. is the leader of KC & The Sunshine Band.	
12/22/79†	**2**(2)	16	● 1. **Yes, I'm Ready**	Casablanca 2227
			JACKIE DeSHANNON	
			Born Sharon Myers on 8/21/44 in Hazel, Kentucky. Vocalist/composer. On radio at age 6. First recorded (as Sherry Lee Myers) for Glenn in 1959. To Los Angeles in 1960. Attained prominence as a prolific songwriter (over 600 to date). Co-writer of mega-pop hit "Bette Davis Eyes." Toured with The Beatles for 26 concerts in 1964.	
6/19/65	**7**	9	1. **What The World Needs Now Is Love**	Imperial 66110
7/26/69	**4**	10	● 2. **Put A Little Love In Your Heart**	Imperial 66385
12/06/69	**40**	1	3. Love Will Find A Way	Imperial 66419
			JOHNNY DESMOND	
			Born Giovanni Desimons on 11/14/20 in Detroit; died on 9/6/85. Sang with Bob Crosby, Gene Krupa, and Glenn Miller's military band. Featured on the "Breakfast Club" radio show throughout the 50s.	
3/26/55	**6**	11	1. **Play Me Hearts And Flowers (I Wanna Cry)**	Coral 61379
			Jockey #6 / Juke Box #11 / Best Seller #16	
8/13/55	**3**	16	2. **The Yellow Rose Of Texas**	Coral 61476
			Jockey #3 / Juke Box #4 / Best Seller #6 / Top 100 #16 pre	
12/03/55	**17**	1	3. Sixteen Tons	Coral 61529
			Jockey #17 / Top 100 #50	
			THE DETERGENTS	
			Trio from New York: Ron Dante (Archies/Cuff Links), Tommy Wynn and Danny Jordan.	
12/19/64†	**19**	6	1. Leader Of The Laundromat [N]	Roulette 4590
			parody of The Shangri-Las' "Leader Of The Pack"	
			DETROIT EMERALDS	
			Group formed in Little Rock, Arkansas by the Tilmon brothers: Abrim (d: 1982, heart attack), Ivory, Cleophus and Raymond. In 1970, group reduced to trio of: Abrim, Ivory and friend James Mitchell.	
2/19/72	**36**	4	1. You Want It, You Got It	Westbound 192
7/29/72	**24**	7	2. Baby Let Me Take You (In My Arms)	Westbound 203
			WILLIAM DeVAUGHN	
			R&B vocalist/songwriter/guitarist from Washington, DC. Worked for the federal government. Backed on hits by the MFSB band.	
5/18/74	**4**	10	● 1. **Be Thankful For What You Got**	Roxbury 0236

DATE	POS	WKS	ARTIST—RECORD TITLE	LABEL & NO.
			DEVICE	
			Los Angeles-based pop-rock trio: Paul Engemann (lead singer), Holly Knight (keyboards, bass) and Gene Black (guitar). Engemann joined Animotion in 1988.	
8/02/86	**35**	4	1. Hanging On A Heart Attack	Chrysalis 42996
			DEVO	
			Robotic rock group formed in Akron, Ohio, consisting of brothers Mark and Bob Mothersbaugh, brothers Jerry and Bob Casale, and Alan Myers. David Kendrick replaced Myers by 1988. Mark and Jerry met while both were art students at Kent State.	
10/04/80	**14**	15	● 1. Whip It	Warner 49550
			BARRY DeVORZON & PERRY BOTKIN, JR.	
			Songwriting/producing/arranging duo. Also see Barry & The Tamerlanes.	
10/02/76	**8**	16	● 1. **Nadia's Theme (The Young And The Restless) [I]** originally written as "Cotton's Dream" for the film "Bless The Beasts & Children"; then used as the theme song for TV's "The Young and The Restless," and finally as the music for Olympic gymnast Nadia Comaneci of Romania	A&M 1856
			THE DEVOTIONS	
			Quintet from New York City.	
4/04/64	**36**	1	1. Rip Van Winkle [N]	Roulette 4541
			DEXYS MIDNIGHT RUNNERS	
			Kevin Rowland, leader of 8-piece Birmingham, England band.	
2/26/83	**1**(1)	14	1. **Come On Eileen**	Mercury 76189
			CLIFF DeYOUNG	
			Cliff has acted in several made-for-TV movies (including "Sunshine").	
2/16/74	**17**	8	1. My Sweet Lady written by John Denver; from the TV soundtrack "Sunshine"	MCA 40156
			DENNIS DeYOUNG	
			Born on 2/18/47 in Chicago. Lead singer/keyboardist of Styx.	
9/22/84	**10**	12	1. **Desert Moon**	A&M 2666
			LEO DIAMOND	
			Born on 6/29/15 in New York City. Died in Los Angeles on 9/15/66. Arranger/lead harmonica player for the Borrah Minevitch Harmonica Rascals, 1930-46.	
2/19/55	**30**	1	1. Melody Of Love [I] Best Seller #30	RCA 5973
			NEIL DIAMOND	
			Born on 1/24/41 in Brooklyn. Vocalist/guitarist/composer. With Roadrunners folk group, 1954-56. Worked as song-plugger/staff writer in New York City. Wrote for The Monkees TV show. First recorded for Duel in 1961. Wrote score for film "Jonathan Livingston Seagull"; starred in and composed the music for "The Jazz Singer."	
9/10/66	**6**	9	1. **Cherry, Cherry**	Bang 528
11/26/66	**16**	6	2. I Got The Feelin' (Oh No No)	Bang 536
2/11/67	**18**	5	3. You Got To Me	Bang 540
4/29/67	**10**	8	4. **Girl, You'll Be A Woman Soon**	Bang 542
8/05/67	**13**	7	5. I Thank The Lord For The Night Time	Bang 547
10/28/67	**22**	6	6. Kentucky Woman	Bang 551
3/29/69	**22**	7	7. Brother Love's Travelling Salvation Show	Uni 55109

DATE	POS	WKS	ARTIST—RECORD TITLE	LABEL & NO.
7/12/69	**4**	12	● 8. **Sweet Caroline (Good Times Never Seemed So Good)**	Uni 55136
11/15/69	**6**	12	● 9. **Holly Holy**	Uni 55175
3/21/70	**24**	8	10. Shilo	Bang 575
5/16/70	**30**	4	11. Soolaimon (African Trilogy II)	Uni 55224
8/15/70	**21**	7	12. Solitary Man [R] re-entry of Neil's first hit (POS 55, 1966)	Bang 578
8/29/70	**1**(1)	14	● 13. **Cracklin' Rosie**	Uni 55250
11/21/70	**20**	9	14. He Ain't Heavy...He's My Brother	Uni 55264
12/05/70	**36**	5	15. Do It	Bang 580
4/03/71	**4**	8	16. **I Am...I Said**	Uni 55278
11/27/71	**14**	7	17. Stones	Uni 55310
5/13/72	**1**(1)	12	● 18. **Song Sung Blue**	Uni 55326
9/02/72	**11**	7	19. Play Me	Uni 55346
11/25/72	**17**	8	20. Walk On Water	Uni 55352
4/21/73	**31**	4	21. Cherry Cherry [R] live version of Neil's 1966 hit (from "Hot August Night" LP)	MCA 40017
11/24/73	**34**	3	22. Be from the film "Jonathan Livingston Seagull"	Columbia 45942
10/19/74	**5**	10	23. **Longfellow Serenade**	Columbia 10043
3/01/75	**34**	2	24. I've Been This Way Before	Columbia 10084
6/26/76	**11**	8	25. If You Know What I Mean	Columbia 10366
12/24/77†	**16**	9	26. Desiree	Columbia 10657
11/04/78	**1**(2)	15	● 27. **You Don't Bring Me Flowers** **BARBRA STREISAND & NEIL DIAMOND**	Columbia 10840
2/17/79	**20**	6	28. Forever In Blue Jeans	Columbia 10897
1/19/80	**17**	10	29. September Morn'	Columbia 11175
11/01/80†	**2**(3)	17	30. **Love On The Rocks**	Capitol 4939
1/31/81	**6**	12	31. **Hello Again**	Capitol 4960
5/02/81	**8**	13	32. **America** above 3: from the film "The Jazz Singer"	Capitol 4994
11/14/81†	**11**	12	33. Yesterday's Songs	Columbia 02604
3/06/82	**27**	5	34. On The Way To The Sky	Columbia 02712
6/19/82	**35**	4	35. Be Mine Tonight	Columbia 02928
10/02/82	**5**	11	36. **Heartlight** inspired by the film "E.T."	Columbia 03219
2/19/83	**35**	4	37. I'm Alive all of above (except #14): composed by Diamond	Columbia 03503

THE DIAMONDS

Vocal group from Ontario, Canada. Formed in 1953; consisted of Dave Somerville (lead), Ted Kowalski (tenor), Phil Leavitt (baritone) and Bill Reed (bass). Recorded for Coral in 1955; debuted on Mercury in January, 1956. Michael Douglas replaced Levitt in early 1958. Reed and Kowalski replaced in 1959 by Evan Fisher and John Felton (killed in a plane crash in 1982). Dave teamed with Four Preps' co-founder, Bruce Belland, as a duo from 1962-69.

DATE	POS	WKS	ARTIST—RECORD TITLE	LABEL & NO.
3/17/56	**12**	11	1. Why Do Fools Fall In Love Jockey #12 / Top 100 #16 / Best Seller #18 / Juke Box #19	Mercury 70790
5/12/56	**14**	11	2. The Church Bells May Ring Best Seller #14 / Juke Box #15 / Jockey #17 / Top 100 #20	Mercury 70835

DATE	POS	WKS	ARTIST—RECORD TITLE	LABEL & NO.
7/28/56	**30**	2	3. Love, Love, Love	Mercury 70889
9/29/56	**34**	1	4. Soft Summer Breeze/	
9/29/56	**35**	2	5. Ka-Ding-Dong	Mercury 70934
3/16/57	**2**(8)	21	6. **Little Darlin'** Best Seller #2 / Top 100 #2 / Jockey #2 / Juke Box #2 original version by Maurice Williams' group, The Gladiolas	Mercury 71060
7/15/57	**13**	2	7. Words Of Love Jockey #13 / Top 100 #76 written by Buddy Holly	Mercury 71128
9/30/57	**16**	1	8. Zip Zip Jockey #16 / Top 100 # 45	Mercury 71165
11/04/57	**10**	8	9. **Silhouettes** Jockey #10 / Top 100 #60	Mercury 71197
1/06/58	**4**	14	10. **The Stroll** Jockey #4 / Top 100 #5 / Best Seller #7 all of above: orchestra arrangements by David Carroll	Mercury 71242
5/19/58	**37**	1	11. High Sign Best Seller #37 / Top 100 #38	Mercury 71291
7/28/58	**16**	1	12. Kathy-O Jockey #16 end / Best Seller #41 / Hot 100 #45 ballad from the Patty McCormack movie of the same title	Mercury 71330
11/17/58	**29**	6	13. Walking Along	Mercury 71366
2/09/59	**18**	10	14. She Say (Oom Dooby Doom)	Mercury 71404
8/07/61	**22**	4	15. One Summer Night	Mercury 71831
			MANU DIBANGO Jazz-R&B saxophonist, born in 1934 in Cameroon, Africa.	
7/21/73	**35**	3	1. Soul Makossa [I]	Atlantic 2971
			DICK & DEEDEE Dick St. John Gosting and Deedee Sperling. Formed duo while students in high school at Santa Monica, California.	
8/28/61	**2**(2)	10	1. **The Mountain's High**	Liberty 55350
5/12/62	**22**	5	2. Tell Me	Liberty 55412
4/06/63	**17**	6	3. Young And In Love	Warner 5342
12/21/63†	**27**	4	4. Turn Around	Warner 5396
12/12/64†	**13**	10	5. Thou Shalt Not Steal	Warner 5482
			"LITTLE" JIMMY DICKENS Born on 12/19/25 in Bolt, West Virginia. Country singer who stands only 4'11" tall.	
11/13/65	**15**	5	1. May The Bird Of Paradise Fly Up Your Nose [N]	Columbia 43388
			DICKY DOO & THE DON'TS Vocal group from Philadelphia, consisting of Gerry "Jerry Grant" Granahan (lead), Harvey Davis (baritone), Ray Gangi (tenor), Al Ways (bass) and Dave "Dicky Doo" Alldred (ex-drummer of the Rhythm Orchids).	
2/17/58	**28**	6	1. Click-Clack Top 100 #28 / Best Seller #29	Swan 4001
5/12/58	**40**	1	2. Nee Nee Na Na Na Na Nu Nu [I] Top 100 #40 / Best Seller #42	Swan 4006

DATE	POS	WKS	ARTIST—RECORD TITLE	LABEL & NO.
			BO DIDDLEY	
			Unique and influential R&B-rock & roll guitarist/vocalist. Born Otha Ellas Bates McDaniel on 12/30/28 in McComb, Mississippi. Adopted as an infant by his mother's cousin, Mrs. Gussie McDaniel. Moved to Chicago at age 5. Began recording in 1955 with the Chess/Checker label. Name "bo diddley" is a one-stringed African guitar. His first record was a 2-sided #1 hit on the R&B charts, "Bo Diddley"/"I'm A Man." Inducted into the Rock And Roll Hall Of Fame in 1987.	
10/05/59	**20**	7	1. Say Man [N]	Checker 931
			DIESEL	
			Rock quartet from Holland.	
10/17/81	**25**	6	1. Sausalito Summernight	Regency 7339
			MARK DINNING	
			Born on 8/17/33 in Drury, Oklahoma. Died of a heart attack on 3/22/86. Brother of the Dinning Sisters vocal trio. First recorded for MGM in 1957.	
1/04/60	**1**(2)	14	1. **Teen Angel** written by Mark's sister, Jeannie	MGM 12845
			DINO, DESI & BILLY	
			Dino: Dean Martin's son, Dean Martin, Jr.; Desi: Lucille Ball and Desi Arnaz's son, Desiderio Arnaz IV; & Billy: a schoolmate from Beverly Hills, William Hinsche. Dino was killed on 3/21/87 (35) when his Air National Guard jet crashed.	
7/24/65	**17**	7	1. I'm A Fool	Reprise 0367
10/16/65	**25**	5	2. Not The Lovin' Kind	Reprise 0401
			KENNY DINO	
			Born on 2/12/42 in New York City.	
12/04/61	**24**	6	1. Your Ma Said You Cried In Your Sleep Last Night	Musicor 1013
			PAUL DINO	
			Born on 3/2/39 in Philadelphia.	
4/10/61	**38**	1	1. Ginnie Bell	Promo 2180
			DION	
			Born Dion DiMucci on 7/18/39 in the Bronx. Formed vocal group, Dion & The Belmonts, in the Bronx in 1958. Consisted of Dion (lead), Angelo D'Aleo (b: 2/3/40; first tenor), Freddie Milano (b: 8/22/39; second tenor) and Carlo Mastrangelo (b: 10/5/38; bass). Named for Belmont Avenue in the Bronx. Angelo was in the Navy in 1959 and missed some recording and picture sessions. Dion went solo in 1960. Moved to Miami in 1968. Brief reunion with the Belmonts in 1967 and 1972, periodically since then. Currently records contemporary Christian songs. Inducted into the Rock And Roll Hall Of Fame in 1989.	
			DION & THE BELMONTS:	
5/26/58	**22**	10	1. I Wonder Why Top 100 #22 / Best Seller #24	Laurie 3013
9/15/58	**19**	8	2. No One Knows Best Seller #19 end / Hot 100 #24 #1 hit for Hal Kemp & His Orchestra in 1937	Laurie 3015
1/05/59	**40**	1	3. Don't Pity Me	Laurie 3021
4/27/59	**5**	13	4. **A Teenager In Love**	Laurie 3027
1/11/60	**3**	11	5. **Where Or When** #1 hit for Hal Kemp & His Orchestra in 1937	Laurie 3044
5/16/60	**30**	2	6. When You Wish Upon A Star from the film "Pinocchio"; #1 hit for Glenn Miller in 1940	Laurie 3052

DATE	POS	WKS	ARTIST—RECORD TITLE	LABEL & NO.
8/15/60	**38**	1	7. In The Still Of The Night the Cole Porter classic; #3 hit for Tommy Dorsey in 1937	Laurie 3059
			DION:	
11/14/60	**12**	11	8. Lonely Teenager	Laurie 3070
10/02/61	**1**(2)	12	9. **Runaround Sue**	Laurie 3110
12/18/61†	**2**(1)	13	10. **The Wanderer/**	
12/18/61	**36**	1	11. The Majestic	Laurie 3115
5/05/62	**3**	9	12. **Lovers Who Wander**	Laurie 3123
7/21/62	**8**	8	13. **Little Diane**	Laurie 3134
11/24/62	**10**	9	14. **Love Came To Me**	Laurie 3145
1/26/63	**2**(3)	11	15. **Ruby Baby**	Columbia 42662
3/30/63	**21**	6	16. Sandy	Laurie 3153
5/04/63	**21**	6	17. This Little Girl	Columbia 42776
7/27/63	**31**	3	18. Be Careful Of Stones That You Throw	Columbia 42810
9/28/63	**6**	8	19. **Donna The Prima Donna**	Columbia 42852
11/23/63	**6**	9	20. **Drip Drop** above 2 shown as: **DION DiMUCCI**	Columbia 42917
11/02/68	**4**	12	● 21. **Abraham, Martin And John** a tribute to Lincoln, King and Kennedy	Laurie 3464
			DIRE STRAITS	
			Rock group formed in London by Mark Knopfler (lead vocals, lead guitar, songwriter, producer) and his brother David Knopfler (guitar), with John Illsley (bass) and Pick Withers (drums). David left in late 1979, replaced by Hal Lindes (who left in 1985). Added keyboardist Alan Clark in 1982. Terry Williams replaced drummer Pick Withers in 1983.	
2/17/79	**4**	12	1. **Sultans Of Swing**	Warner 8736
8/10/85	**1**(3)	13	2. **Money For Nothing** written by Sting and Mark Knopfler	Warner 28950
11/16/85†	**7**	15	3. **Walk Of Life**	Warner 28878
3/22/86	**19**	7	4. So Far Away	Warner 28789
			SENATOR EVERETT McKINLEY DIRKSEN	
			U.S. senator from Illinois, 1950-69. Born in Pekin, Illinois in 1896; died on 9/7/69 (73).	
1/07/67	**29**	3	1. Gallant Men [S]	Capitol 5805
			THE DIRT BAND - see THE NITTY GRITTY DIRT BAND	
			DISCO TEX & THE SEX-O-LETTES	
			Disco studio group assembled by producer Bob Crewe. Featuring lead voice Sir Monti Rock III (real name: Joseph Montanez, Jr.), owner of a chain of hairdressing salons.	
12/28/74†	**10**	9	1. **Get Dancin'**	Chelsea 3004
5/17/75	**23**	5	2. I Wanna Dance Wit' Choo (Doo Dat Dance), Part 1	Chelsea 3015
			THE DIXIEBELLES	
			Black female trio from Memphis: Shirley Thomas, Mary Hunt, Mildred Pratcher.	
10/26/63	**9**	8	1. **(Down At) Papa Joe's**	Sound Stage 2507
2/08/64	**15**	5	2. Southtown, U.S.A. above 2: featuring Jerry Smith (of Cornbread & Jerry), piano	Sound Stage 2517

DATE	POS	WKS	ARTIST—RECORD TITLE	LABEL & NO.
			THE DIXIE CUPS	
			Black female trio from New Orleans: Barbara Ann Hawkins, her sister Rosa Lee Hawkins, and Joan Marie Johnson. Discovered by singer/producer Joe Jones.	
5/16/64	**1**(3)	11	1. **Chapel Of Love**	Red Bird 001
8/01/64	**12**	7	2. People Say	Red Bird 006
11/21/64	**39**	1	3. You Should Have Seen The Way He Looked At Me	Red Bird 012
5/01/65	**20**	5	4. Iko Iko	Red Bird 024
			D.J. JAZZY JEFF & THE FRESH PRINCE	
			Philadelphia rap duo: disc jockey Jeff Townes with rapper Will Smith.	
6/18/88	**12**	10	● 1. Parents Just Don't Understand	Jive 1099
8/20/88	**15**	9	2. A Nightmare On My Street	Jive 1124
			CARL DOBKINS, JR.	
			Born Carl Edward Dobkins on 1/13/41 in Cincinnati. "Junior" added to last name when Carl started singing at age 16. First recorded for Fraternity, 1958. Left music, mid-60s.	
6/01/59	**3**	16	1. **My Heart Is An Open Book**	Decca 30803
1/18/60	**25**	8	2. Lucky Devil	Decca 31020
			DR. BUZZARD'S ORIGINAL "SAVANNAH" BAND	
			New York City Thirties-styled disco group formed by brothers Stony and "August Darnell" Browder, with Cory Daye, lead singer. Darnell left in 1980 to form Kid Creole & The Coconuts.	
12/11/76†	**27**	8	1. Whispering/Cherchez La Femme/Se Si Bon	RCA 10827
			DR. HOOK	
			Group formed in New Jersey in 1968. Fronted by Ray Sawyer (Dr. Hook - because of eye patch) and Dennis Locorriere. Appeared in and performed the music for the film "Who Is Harry Kellerman And Why Is He Saying Those Terrible Things About Me?" starring Dustin Hoffman.	
			DR. HOOK & THE MEDICINE SHOW:	
5/06/72	**5**	10	● 1. **Sylvia's Mother**	Columbia 45562
2/03/73	**6**	11	● 2. **The Cover Of "Rolling Stone"** [N]	Columbia 45732
			DR. HOOK:	
2/07/76	**6**	14	● 3. **Only Sixteen**	Capitol 4171
7/31/76	**11**	14	4. A Little Bit More	Capitol 4280
10/14/78†	**6**	16	● 5. **Sharing The Night Together**	Capitol 4621
6/02/79	**6**	16	● 6. **When You're In Love With A Beautiful Woman**	Capitol 4705
11/03/79†	**12**	14	7. Better Love Next Time	Capitol 4785
3/15/80	**5**	15	● 8. **Sexy Eyes**	Capitol 4831
11/29/80	**34**	6	9. Girls Can Get It	Casablanca 2314
3/27/82	**25**	6	10. Baby Makes Her Blue Jeans Talk	Casablanca 2347
			DR. JOHN	
			Born Malcolm "Mac" Rebennack on 11/21/40 in New Orleans. Pioneer "swamp rock"- styled instrumentalist.	
5/12/73	**9**	13	1. **Right Place Wrong Time**	Atco 6914

DATE	POS	WKS	ARTIST—RECORD TITLE	LABEL & NO.
			BILL DOGGETT	
			Born on 2/16/16 in Philadelphia. Leading jazz-R&B organist and pianist. Formed own band in 1938, recorded with the Jimmy Mundy Band in 1939. With the Ink Spots, Illinois Jacquet, Lucky Millinder, Louis Jordan, Ella Fitzgerald, Louis Armstrong, Coleman Hawkins and many others. Formed own combo in 1952. Still active into the 80s with a touring combo.	
8/25/56	**2**(3)	22	1. **Honky Tonk (Parts 1 & 2)** **[I]** Best Seller #2 / Top 100 #2 / Juke Box #2 / Jockey #6 sax player: Clifford Scott	King 4950
12/15/56†	**26**	5	2. Slow Walk [I]	King 5000
12/02/57	**35**	1	3. Soft [I] Best Seller #35 / Top 100 #51	King 5080
			THOMAS DOLBY	
			Born Thomas Morgan Dolby Robertson of British parentage on 10/14/58 in Cairo, Egypt. Master of computer-generated music and self-directed videos. Keyboardist of Bruce Woolley & The Camera Club, and the Lene Lovich band (1979-80). Began solo career in 1981. Film "Howard The Duck" featured Dolby's music under moniker "Dolby's Cube." Married to actress Kathleen Beller (Kirby Colby on TV's "Dynasty").	
3/19/83	**5**	15	1. **She Blinded Me With Science**	Capitol 5204
			FATS DOMINO	
			Born Antoine Domino on 2/26/28 in New Orleans. Classic New Orleans R&B piano-playing vocalist; heavily influenced by Fats Waller and Albert Ammons. Joined the Dave Bartholomew Band, mid-40s. Signed to Imperial record label in 1949. His first recording "The Fat Man" reportedly was a million-seller. Heard on many sessions cut by other R&B artists, including Lloyd Price and Joe Turner. In films "Shake, Rattle And Roll," "Jamboree," "The Big Beat" and "The Girl Can't Help It." Teamed with co-writer Dave Bartholomew on the majority of his hits. Lives in New Orleans with wife Rosemary and 8 children. Frequently appears in Las Vegas. Inducted into the Rock And Roll Hall Of Fame in 1986. One of the most popular & influential R&B stars.	
7/16/55	**10**	13	1. **Ain't That A Shame** Juke Box #10 / Best Seller #16 / Top 100 #86 pre label shows title as "Ain't It A Shame"	Imperial 5348
4/07/56	**35**	1	2. Bo Weevil	Imperial 5375
5/05/56	**3**	18	3. **I'm In Love Again/** Juke Box #3 / Best Seller #4 / Top 100 # 5 / Jockey #6	
5/05/56	**19**	13	4. My Blue Heaven Juke Box #19 / Top 100 #21 #1 hit for both Gene Austin and Paul Whiteman in 1927	Imperial 5386
7/28/56	**14**	8	5. When My Dreamboat Comes Home Juke Box #14 / Best Seller #21 / Top 100 #22 #3 hit for Guy Lombardo in 1937	Imperial 5396
10/13/56†	**2**(3)	21	6. **Blueberry Hill** Juke Box #2 / Best Seller #3 / Top 100 #4 / Jockey #7 #1 hit for Glenn Miller in 1940	Imperial 5407
1/12/57	**5**	12	7. **Blue Monday** Juke Box #5 / Best Seller #9 / Top 100 #9 / Jockey #9 from the film "The Girl Can't Help It"	Imperial 5417
3/09/57	**4**	14	8. **I'm Walkin'** Jockey #4 / Best Seller #5 / Top 100 #5 / Juke Box #5	Imperial 5428
5/27/57	**8**	13	9. **Valley Of Tears/** Best Seller #8 / Top 100 #13 / Jockey #13	
6/24/57	**6**	6	10. It's You I Love Best Seller #6 / Top 100 #22	Imperial 5442

DATE	POS	WKS	ARTIST—RECORD TITLE	LABEL & NO.
8/26/57	**29**	2	11. When I See You Best Seller #29 / Top 100 #36	Imperial 5454
10/21/57	**23**	6	12. Wait And See Best Seller #23 / Top 100 #27 from the film "Jamboree"	Imperial 5467
12/23/57†	**26**	9	13. The Big Beat/ Best Seller #26 / Top 100 #36 from the film of the same title	
12/30/57†	**32**	8	14. I Want You To Know Best Seller #32 / Top 100 #48	Imperial 5477
5/05/58	**22**	7	15. Sick And Tired Best Seller #22 / Top 100 #30	Imperial 5515
12/01/58†	**6**	12	16. **Whole Lotta Loving**	Imperial 5553
5/25/59	**16**	7	17. I'm Ready	Imperial 5585
8/10/59	**8**	10	18. **I Want To Walk You Home/**	
8/10/59	**17**	9	19. I'm Gonna Be A Wheel Some Day	Imperial 5606
11/09/59	**8**	10	20. **Be My Guest/**	
11/09/59	**33**	2	21. I've Been Around	Imperial 5629
2/15/60	**25**	5	22. Country Boy	Imperial 5645
7/04/60	**6**	11	23. **Walking To New Orleans/**	
7/18/60	**21**	7	24. Don't Come Knockin'	Imperial 5675
9/12/60	**15**	9	25. Three Nights A Week	Imperial 5687
11/14/60	**14**	11	26. My Girl Josephine/	
12/05/60	**38**	3	27. Natural Born Lover	Imperial 5704
2/06/61	**22**	6	28. What A Price/	
2/13/61	**33**	4	29. Ain't That Just Like A Woman #17 hit for Louis Jordan in 1946	Imperial 5723
4/03/61	**32**	2	30. Fell In Love On Monday/	
4/17/61	**32**	2	31. Shu Rah	Imperial 5734
6/19/61	**23**	5	32. It Keeps Rainin'	Imperial 5753
7/31/61	**15**	6	33. Let The Four Winds Blow	Imperial 5764
10/23/61	**22**	4	34. What A Party	Imperial 5779
12/25/61†	**30**	3	35. Jambalaya (On The Bayou) written and popularized (POS 1) by Hank Williams in 1952	Imperial 5796
3/17/62	**22**	5	36. You Win Again written and charted (Country) by Hank Williams in 1952 (POS 10)	Imperial 5816
10/26/63	**35**	2	37. Red Sails In The Sunset #1 hit for both Bing Crosby and Guy Lombardo in 1935	ABC-Para. 10484
			DON & JUAN	
			Black vocal duo from New York City: Roland Trone (d: 1983) and Claude Johnson of The Genies.	
2/24/62	**7**	9	1. **What's Your Name**	Big Top 3079
			BO DONALDSON & THE HEYWOODS	
			Cincinnati, Ohio septet. Regulars on Dick Clark's "Action '73" TV show.	
5/11/74	**1**(2)	12	● 1. **Billy, Don't Be A Hero**	ABC 11435
8/24/74	**15**	7	2. Who Do You Think You Are	ABC 12006
12/14/74	**39**	1	3. The Heartbreak Kid	ABC 12039

DATE	POS	WKS	ARTIST—RECORD TITLE	LABEL & NO.
			LONNIE DONEGAN & His Skiffle Group	
			Born Anthony Donegan on 4/29/31 in Glasgow, Scotland. Britain's "King of Skiffle." Member of Chris Barber's Jazz Band in 1954.	
3/31/56	**8**	11	1. **Rock Island Line** Best Seller #8 / Top 100 #10 / Jockey #10 / Juke Box #13	London 1650
8/14/61	**5**	9	2. **Does Your Chewing Gum Lose Its Flavor (On The Bedpost Over Night)** **[N]** #9 hit in 1924 for Ernest Hare & Billy Jones as "Does The Spearmint Lose Its Flavor On The Bedpost Overnight?"; first released by Lonnie in Britain in 1958	Dot 15911
			RAL DONNER	
			Born on 2/10/43 in Chicago. Narrator and Elvis' voice in the film "This Is Elvis." Died of cancer on 4/6/84 (41).	
5/01/61	**19**	8	1. Girl Of My Best Friend recorded by Elvis in 1960 on his "Elvis Is Back!" LP	Gone 5102
7/24/61	**4**	9	2. **You Don't Know What You've Got (Until You Lose It)**	Gone 5108
11/13/61	**39**	1	3. Please Don't Go	Gone 5114
2/03/62	**18**	4	4. She's Everything (I Wanted You To Be)	Gone 5121
			DONNIE & THE DREAMERS	
			Donnie is Louis Burgio. Italian-American vocal quartet from New York City.	
6/12/61	**35**	3	1. Count Every Star #4 hit for Ray Anthony's band in 1950	Whale 500
			DONOVAN	
			Born Donovan Phillip Leitch on 2/10/46 near Glasgow, Scotland. Singer/songwriter/ guitarist. To London at age 10. Worked Newport Folk Festival in 1965. Wrote score for film "If It's Tuesday This Must Be Belgium." In films "The Pied Piper Of Hamlin" (1972) and "Brother Sun, Sister Moon" (1973). In retirement from 1974-81.	
6/12/65	**23**	5	1. Catch The Wind	Hickory 1309
8/13/66	**1**(1)	10	2. **Sunshine Superman**	Epic 10045
11/19/66	**2**(3)	10	● 3. **Mellow Yellow** whispering vocals: Paul McCartney	Epic 10098
2/25/67	**19**	5	4. Epistle To Dippy	Epic 10127
8/26/67	**11**	6	5. There Is A Mountain	Epic 10212
12/09/67	**23**	5	6. Wear Your Love Like Heaven	Epic 10253
3/30/68	**26**	5	7. Jennifer Juniper	Epic 10300
6/29/68	**5**	10	8. **Hurdy Gurdy Man**	Epic 10345
10/19/68	**33**	4	9. Lalena	Epic 10393
3/01/69	**35**	2	10. To Susan On The West Coast Waiting/	
4/26/69	**7**	10	11. Atlantis	Epic 10434
8/30/69	**36**	2	12. Goo Goo Barabajagal (Love Is Hot) with the Jeff Beck Group; all of above: written by Donovan	Epic 10510

DATE	POS	WKS	ARTIST—RECORD TITLE	LABEL & NO.
			THE DOOBIE BROTHERS	
			Rock/R&B-styled group formed in San Jose, California in 1970: Pat Simmons (vocals, guitar), Tom Johnston (lead vocals, guitar, keyboards), John Hartman (percussion) and Dave Shogren (bass). First recorded for Warner in 1971. Many personnel changes. Michael McDonald (lead vocals, keyboards) joined in 1975. Johnston left in 1978. Tom Johnston wrote majority of hits from 1972-75; Michael McDonald from 1976-83. Disbanded in 1983. Re-formed in early 1988 with Johnston, Simmons, Hartman, Porter, Hossack and Bobby LaKind (percussion).	
9/23/72	**11**	10	1. Listen To The Music	Warner 7619
2/17/73	**35**	2	2. Jesus Is Just Alright	Warner 7661
5/26/73	**8**	11	3. **Long Train Runnin'**	Warner 7698
9/15/73	**15**	8	4. China Grove	Warner 7728
6/01/74	**32**	2	5. Another Park, Another Sunday	Warner 7795
1/11/75	**1**(1)	12	● 6. **Black Water** originally the flip side of Warner 7795	Warner 8062
5/17/75	**11**	9	7. Take Me In Your Arms (Rock Me)	Warner 8092
8/30/75	**40**	1	8. Sweet Maxine	Warner 8126
5/15/76	**13**	8	9. Takin' It To The Streets	Warner 8196
1/22/77	**37**	2	10. It Keeps You Runnin'	Warner 8282
2/10/79	**1**(1)	14	● 11. **What A Fool Believes**	Warner 8725
5/19/79	**14**	9	12. Minute By Minute	Warner 8828
9/15/79	**25**	6	13. Dependin' On You	Warner 49029
9/06/80	**5**	11	14. **Real Love**	Warner 49503
12/06/80†	**24**	7	15. One Step Closer all of above: produced by Ted Templeman	Warner 49622
			THE DOORS	
			Rock group formed in Los Angeles in 1965. Consisted of Jim Morrison (b: 12/8/43, Melbourne, FL; d: 7/3/71, Paris, France; lead singer), Ray Manzarek (keyboards), Robby Krieger (guitar) and John Densmore (drums). Controversial onstage performances by Morrison caused several arrests and cancellations. Morrison left group on 12/12/70. In film "A Feast Of Friends." Group disbanded in 1973.	
6/24/67	**1**(3)	14	● 1. **Light My Fire**	Elektra 45615
10/07/67	**12**	7	2. People Are Strange	Elektra 45621
12/30/67†	**25**	4	3. Love Me Two Times	Elektra 45624
5/04/68	**39**	3	4. The Unknown Soldier	Elektra 45628
7/13/68	**1**(2)	11	● 5. **Hello, I Love You**	Elektra 45635
1/04/69	**3**	12	● 6. **Touch Me**	Elektra 45646
4/24/71	**11**	9	7. Love Her Madly	Elektra 45726
7/24/71	**14**	9	8. Riders On The Storm	Elektra 45738
			CHARLIE DORE	
			British female vocalist.	
3/22/80	**13**	10	1. Pilot Of The Airwaves	Island 49166
			HAROLD DORMAN	
			Born on 12/23/26 in Sledge, Mississippi. To Memphis in 1955; recorded for Sun in 1957. Suffered two strokes in 1984.	
4/18/60	**21**	9	1. Mountain Of Love	Rita 1003

DATE	POS	WKS	ARTIST—RECORD TITLE	LABEL & NO.
			JIMMY DORSEY	
			Jimmy was born on 2/29/04 in Shenandoah, Pennsylvania. Died of cancer on 6/12/57. Great alto sax and clarinet soloist/bandleader beginning in 1935.	
4/13/57	**2**(4)	26	1. **So Rare** Top 100 #2 / Jockey #2 / Best Seller #3 / Juke Box #6 end featuring Jimmy on sax; recorded in New York on 11/11/56; #1 hit for Guy Lombardo in 1937	Fraternity 755
9/09/57	**21**	2	2. June Night Jockey #21 / Best Seller #27 / Top 100 #39 featuring Dick Stabile, sax; #2 hit for Ted Lewis & His Band in 1924	Fraternity 777
			LEE DORSEY	
			Born Irving Lee Dorsey on 12/24/24 in New Orleans. Moved to Portland, Oregon at age 10. Prizefighter in early 50s as "Kid Chocolate." Major hits produced by Allen Toussaint & Marshall Sehorn. Lee died of emphysema in New Orleans on 12/1/86.	
9/25/61	**7**	10	1. **Ya Ya**	Fury 1053
1/20/62	**27**	5	2. Do-Re-Mi	Fury 1056
7/31/65	**28**	4	3. Ride Your Pony	Amy 927
8/13/66	**8**	9	4. **Working In The Coal Mine**	Amy 958
11/19/66	**23**	5	5. Holy Cow	Amy 965
			THE TOMMY DORSEY ORCHESTRA	
			Tommy was born on 11/19/05 in Mahanoy Plane, Pennsylvania; choked to death on 11/26/56. Great trombonist and bandleader beginning in 1935. Tommy and brother Jimmy recorded together as the Dorsey Brothers Orchestra from 1928-35, reunited, 1953-56. Hosted musical variety TV show from 1954-56. Warren Covington fronted band after Tommy's death.	
9/15/58	**7**	14	1. **Tea For Two Cha Cha** [I] Hot 100 #7 / Best Seller #8 end classic tune, originally a #1 hit for Marion Harris in 1925	Decca 30704
			DOUBLE	
			German pop quartet led by Kurt Maloo & Felix Haug. Both were in jazz trio Ping Pong.	
8/09/86	**16**	9	1. The Captain Of Her Heart	A&M 2838
			CARL DOUGLAS	
			Born in Jamaica, West Indies. Studied engineering in the US and in England.	
11/09/74	**1**(2)	12	● 1. **Kung Fu Fighting**	20th Century 2140
			CAROL DOUGLAS	
			Born on 4/7/48 in Brooklyn. Worked on commercials. Member of The Chantels vocal group in the early 70s. Went solo in 1974.	
12/21/74†	**11**	11	1. Doctor's Orders	Midland I. 10113
			MIKE DOUGLAS	
			Real name: Michael Dowd. Long-time syndicated TV talk show host. Singer with Kay Kyser's band, 1945-50 (vocalist on Kyser's #1 hit "Ole Buttermilk Sky" in 1946).	
1/08/66	**6**	7	1. **The Men In My Little Girl's Life**	Epic 9876

DATE	POS	WKS	ARTIST—RECORD TITLE	LABEL & NO.
			RONNIE DOVE	
			Born on 9/7/40 in Herndon, Virginia; discovered while singing in Baltimore. Nearly all of Ronnie's hits were produced by Phil Kahl (V.P. of Diamond Records).	
9/26/64	**40**	1	1. Say You	Diamond 167
11/14/64	**14**	7	2. Right Or Wrong	Diamond 173
4/10/65	**14**	7	3. One Kiss For Old Times' Sake	Diamond 179
6/26/65	**16**	6	4. A Little Bit Of Heaven	Diamond 184
9/18/65	**21**	5	5. I'll Make All Your Dreams Come True	Diamond 188
11/27/65	**25**	4	6. Kiss Away	Diamond 191
2/05/66	**18**	7	7. When Liking Turns To Loving	Diamond 195
5/07/66	**20**	5	8. Let's Start All Over Again	Diamond 198
7/09/66	**27**	4	9. Happy Summer Days	Diamond 205
9/24/66	**22**	5	10. I Really Don't Want To Know	Diamond 208
12/10/66	**18**	6	11. Cry	Diamond 214
			THE DOVELLS	
			Vocal group formed at Overbrook High School in Philadelphia; originally called the Brooktones. Consisted of Leonard Borisoff ("Len Barry"), Arnie Silver, Jerry Gross ("Jerry Summers"), Mike Freda ("Mike Dennis") and Jim Meeley ("Danny Brooks"). Brooks left in 1962; Barry left in late 1963. Group continued as a trio. Recorded as The Magistrates for MGM in 1968.	
9/18/61	**2**(2)	14	1. **Bristol Stomp** Bristol: town near Philadelphia	Parkway 827
3/03/62	**37**	2	2. Do The New Continental	Parkway 833
6/23/62	**27**	5	3. Bristol Twistin' Annie	Parkway 838
9/15/62	**25**	7	4. Hully Gully Baby	Parkway 845
5/11/63	**3**	11	5. **You Can't Sit Down**	Parkway 867
			JOE DOWELL	
			Born on 1/23/40 in Bloomington, Indiana. Signed to Mercury's Smash label by Shelby Singleton, Jr. in Nashville.	
7/17/61	**1**(1)	12	1. **Wooden Heart** based on the German folk song "Muss I Denn," originally sung by Elvis Presley in the film "G.I. Blues"	Smash 1708
7/28/62	**23**	4	2. Little Red Rented Rowboat	Smash 1759
			LAMONT DOZIER	
			Born on 6/16/41 in Detroit. R&B singer/songwriter/producer. Recorded as "Lamont Anthony" for Anna in 1961. With brothers Brian and Eddie Holland in highly successful songwriting/production team for Motown. Trio left Motown in 1968 and formed own Invictus/Hot Wax label.	
2/16/74	**15**	9	1. Trying To Hold On To My Woman	ABC 11407
7/06/74	**26**	6	2. Fish Ain't Bitin'	ABC 11438
			CHARLIE DRAKE	
			Born on 6/19/25 in London, England.	
2/17/62	**21**	6	1. My Boomerang Won't Come Back [N]	United Art. 398
			PETE DRAKE & His Talking Steel Guitar	
			Pete was born on 10/8/32 in Atlanta. Nashville's top steel guitar sessionman. Died on 7/29/88 (55).	
4/11/64	**25**	5	1. Forever	Smash 1867

DATE	POS	WKS	ARTIST—RECORD TITLE	LABEL & NO.
			THE DRAMATICS	
			Soul group from Detroit. First recorded for Wingate as the Dynamics, 1966. Members in 1971: Ron Banks (lead singer), William Howard, Larry Demps, Willie Ford and Elbert Wilkins. Howard and Wilkins replaced by L.J. Reynolds and Lenny Mayes in 1973. Reynolds, formerly of Chocolate Syrup, began solo career in 1981.	
7/31/71	**9**	11	1. **Whatcha See Is Whatcha Get**	Volt 4058
3/04/72	**5**	11	2. **In The Rain**	Volt 4075
			RUSTY DRAPER	
			Born Farrell H. Draper in Kirksville, Missouri. Began career at the age of 12, singing and playing guitar over the radio in Tulsa, Oklahoma.	
8/20/55	**18**	4	1. Seventeen Best Seller #18 / Top 100 #88 pre	Mercury 70651
10/01/55	**3**	16	2. **The Shifting, Whispering Sands** Juke Box #3 / Best Seller #6 / Top 100 #7 / Jockey #14	Mercury 70696
12/31/55†	**11**	12	3. Are You Satisfied? Best Seller #11 / Juke Box #11 / Top 100 #12	Mercury 70757
9/22/56	**20**	8	4. In The Middle Of The House [N] Top 100 #20 / Jockey #24	Mercury 70921
5/27/57	**6**	12	5. **Freight Train** Jockey #6 / Top 100 #11 / Best Seller #17	Mercury 71102
			THE DREAM ACADEMY	
			English trio: Nick Laird-Clowes (guitar, vocals), Gilbert Gabriel (keyboards) and Kate St. John (vocals, oboe, saxophone).	
1/11/86	**7**	11	1. **Life In A Northern Town**	Warner 28841
5/31/86	**36**	3	2. The Love Parade	Reprise 28750
			THE DREAMLOVERS	
			Black vocal quintet formed while in high school in Philadelphia. Back-up vocal group for Chubby Checker's "The Twist."	
8/28/61	**10**	6	1. **When We Get Married**	Heritage 102
			THE DREAM WEAVERS	
			Wade Buff, lead singer of trio (other 2 members are female) from Miami, Florida.	
11/12/55†	**7**	21	1. **It's Almost Tomorrow** Juke Box #7 / Best Seller #8 / Top 100 #8 / Jockey #10	Decca 29683
5/19/56	**33**	1	2. A Little Love Can Go A Long, Long Way from the Goodyear TV Playhouse Production "Joey"	Decca 29905
			THE DRIFTERS	
			Vocal group formed to showcase lead singer Clyde McPhatter on Atlantic in 1953. Included Gerhart and Andrew Thrasher, Bill Pinkney and McPhatter (who went solo in 1955). Group continued with various lead singers until 1958. In 1958, manager George Treadwell disbanded the group and brought in The Five Crowns and renamed them The Drifters. The majority of The Drifters' pop hits were sung by 3 different lead singers: Ben E. King, 1959-60; Rudy Lewis, 1961-63; and Johnny Moore, 1957, and 1963-66. Rudy died of a heart attack in summer of 1964. Many personnel changes throughout career and several groups have used the name in later years. Inducted into the Rock And Roll Hall Of Fame in 1988.	
6/29/59	**2**(1)	14	1. **There Goes My Baby**	Atlantic 2025
11/02/59	**15**	9	2. Dance With Me/	
11/23/59	**33**	5	3. (If You Cry) True Love, True Love Johnny Lee Williams, lead singer	Atlantic 2040
3/14/60	**16**	6	4. This Magic Moment	Atlantic 2050

DATE	POS	WKS	ARTIST—RECORD TITLE	LABEL & NO.
9/19/60	1(3)	14	5. **Save The Last Dance For Me**	Atlantic 2071
12/31/60†	17	7	6. I Count The Tears all of above (except #3): Ben E. King, lead singer	Atlantic 2087
4/10/61	32	6	7. Some Kind Of Wonderful	Atlantic 2096
6/26/61	14	8	8. Please Stay	Atlantic 2105
9/25/61	16	9	9. Sweets For My Sweet	Atlantic 2117
3/24/62	28	4	10. When My Little Girl Is Smiling	Atlantic 2134
12/29/62†	5	11	11. **Up On The Roof**	Atlantic 2162
4/06/63	9	8	12. **On Broadway** above 6: Rudy Lewis, lead singer	Atlantic 2182
10/05/63	25	5	13. I'll Take You Home	Atlantic 2201
7/11/64	4	12	14. **Under The Boardwalk**	Atlantic 2237
10/10/64	33	5	15. I've Got Sand In My Shoes	Atlantic 2253
11/28/64	18	7	16. Saturday Night At The Movies above 4: Johnny Moore, lead singer	Atlantic 2260
			ROY DRUSKY	
			Born on 6/22/30 in Atlanta. Country singer/guitarist; leader of his band, The Loners. In films "The Golden Guitar" and "Forty-Acre Feud."	
6/26/61	35	1	1. Three Hearts In A Tangle	Decca 31193
			DUALS	
			Black instrumental duo from Los Angeles: Henry Bellinger and Johnny Lageman.	
10/02/61	25	6	1. Stick Shift [I]	Sue 745
			THE DUBS	
			R&B quintet; Richard Blandon, lead singer.	
11/18/57	23	8	1. Could This Be Magic Best Seller #23 / Top 100 #24	Gone 5011
			DAVE DUDLEY	
			Born on 5/3/28 in Spencer, Wisconsin. Country singer/guitarist/songwriter.	
7/20/63	32	4	1. Six Days On The Road	Golden Wing 3020
			GEORGE DUKE - see STANLEY CLARKE	
			PATTY DUKE	
			Full name: Anna Maria Patricia Duke Astin. Actress; married to actor John Astin. Won an Oscar for her performance in the film "The Miracle Worker," 1962. Starred in TV series "The Patty Duke Show," 1963-65, "It Takes Two," 1982-83, and "Hail To The Chief," 1985.	
7/17/65	8	8	1. **Don't Just Stand There**	United Art. 875
10/30/65	22	4	2. Say Something Funny	United Art. 915
			DAVID DUNDAS	
			London-based singer/songwriter/actor.	
11/27/76†	17	13	1. Jeans On originally a jingle in England for Brutus Jeans	Chrysalis 2094
			ROBBIE DUPREE	
			Singer/songwriter, born Robert Dupuis in Brooklyn, in 1947.	
5/03/80	6	15	1. **Steal Away**	Elektra 46621
8/09/80	15	12	2. Hot Rod Hearts	Elektra 47005

DATE	POS	WKS	ARTIST—RECORD TITLE	LABEL & NO.
			THE DUPREES	
			Italian-American vocal quintet from Jersey City: Joseph ("Joey Vann") Canzano, lead singer; Mike Arnone, Tom Bialablow, John Salvato and Joe Santollo. Joey Vann died on 2/28/84 (40).	
8/25/62	**7**	9	1. **You Belong To Me** #1 hit for Jo Stafford in 1952	Coed 569
11/10/62	**13**	6	2. My Own True Love Tara's Theme from "Gone With The Wind"	Coed 571
9/14/63	**37**	3	3. Why Don't You Believe Me #1 hit for Joni James in 1952	Coed 584
11/30/63	**18**	6	4. Have You Heard #4 hit for Joni James in 1953	Coed 585
			DURAN DURAN	
			Romantic-styled band formed in Birmingham, England in 1980. Consisted of Simon LeBon (b: 10/27/58; vocals), Andy Taylor (b: 2/16/61; guitar), Nick Rhodes (b: 6/8/62; keyboards), John Taylor (b: 6/20/60; bass) and Roger Taylor (b: 4/26/60; drums). None of the Taylors are related. Group named after a villain in the Jane Fonda film "Barbarella." In 1984, Andy & Roger left group. In 1985, Andy & John recorded with the supergroup The Power Station; Simon, Nick & Roger recorded as Arcadia. Lineup since 1986: Simon, Nick & John; changed spelling of name to Duranduran in 1988.	
1/22/83	**3**	16	1. **Hungry Like The Wolf**	Harvest 5195
4/09/83	**14**	9	2. Rio	Capitol 5215
6/18/83	**4**	12	3. **Is There Something I Should Know**	Capitol 5233
11/19/83	**3**	12	4. **Union Of The Snake**	Capitol 5290
1/28/84	**10**	10	5. **New Moon On Monday**	Capitol 5309
4/28/84	**1**(2)	15	6. **The Reflex**	Capitol 5345
11/03/84	**2**(4)	14	7. **The Wild Boys**	Capitol 5417
2/16/85	**16**	8	8. Save A Prayer	Capitol 5438
5/25/85	**1**(2)	13	9. **A View To A Kill** from the James Bond film of the same title	Capitol 5475
11/15/86†	**2**(1)	13	10. **Notorious**	Capitol 5648
3/14/87	**39**	1	11. Skin Trade	Capitol 5670
			DURANDURAN:	
10/22/88	**4**	13	12. **I Don't Want Your Love**	Capitol 44237
			DYKE & THE BLAZERS	
			Band led by Arlester "Dyke" Christian (b: 1943, Brooklyn). With O'Jays' backing band, the Blazers, in the mid-60s. Dyke was shot to death in 1971.	
7/05/69	**35**	3	1. We Got More Soul	Original Sound 86
11/01/69	**36**	1	2. Let A Woman Be A Woman - Let A Man Be A Man	Original Sound 89

Dee Clark took over Little Richard's band when Richard found God (the first time). He later got up to No. 2 on his own with "Raindrops" (1961).

Patsy Cline had only four top-20 hits, but is generally considered the all-time queen of modern country music. The film biography of her life, *Sweet Dreams*, led to a million-selling soundtrack and a million-selling compilation of her hits.

Club Nouveau's 1987 remake of "Lean On Me" hit No. 1 *and* won songwriter Bill Withers the Grammy for best R & B song of the year, something Withers couldn't even do himself. Though he also took the song to No. 1 in 1972, the R & B Grammy that year went to "Papa Was A Rolling Stone."

Joe Cocker became famous for his wild and raving excesses onstage in the early 70s, but his biggest hits have been tortured ballads: "You Are So Beautiful" (No. 5, 1975) and (with Jennifer Warnes) "Up Where We Belong (No. 1, 1982).

Nat "King" Cole recorded on one label, Capitol, through his entire career. The 22-year-span has been topped by one artist, Perry Como, who has recorded for RCA (and only RCA) for more than 45 years.

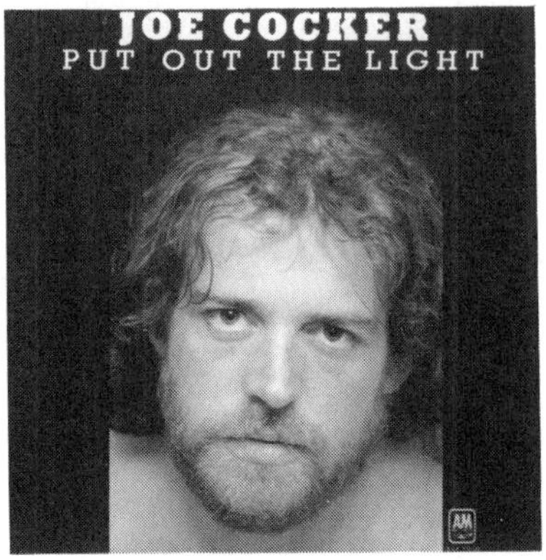

Natalie Cole had her first hit in 1975, but never had back-to-back top-20 singles until 1987–88, when she had three in a row make the top 15: "Jump Start," "I Live For Your Love," and a remake of Bruce Springsteen's "Pink Cadillac."

Phil Collins was a child actor, so it's no surprise that four of his six No. 1 singles came from movies: "Against All Odds" (title theme), "Separate Lives" (with Marilyn Martin, from *White Nights*), and "Groovy Kind of Love" and "Two Hearts" (from *Buster*).

Sam Cooke's catalogue is one of the most active in the history of pop. All five of his top ten singles later charted by other artists, and three other songs went on to bigger heights in the cover versions: "Only Sixteen" (No. 28 by Cooke, No. 6 by Dr. Hook), "Wonderful World" (No. 12 by Cooke, No. 4 by Herman's Hermits), and "Cupid" (No. 17 by Cooke, No. 4 by the Spinners).

The Cover Girls' "Promise Me" exemplified the dance-pop that kept independent labels thriving in the late 80s.

The Cowsills were the real-life inspiration for TV's Partridge Family, but while the Cowsills got to No. 2 twice ("The Rain, The Park, And Other Things," "Hair"), the Partridge Family made it all the way to No. 1, with "I Think I Love You."

Creedence Clearwater Revival had five No. 2 singles but never a No. 1. Even the Creedence sound-alike "Long Cool Woman In A Black Dress," by the Hollies, stopped at No. 2.

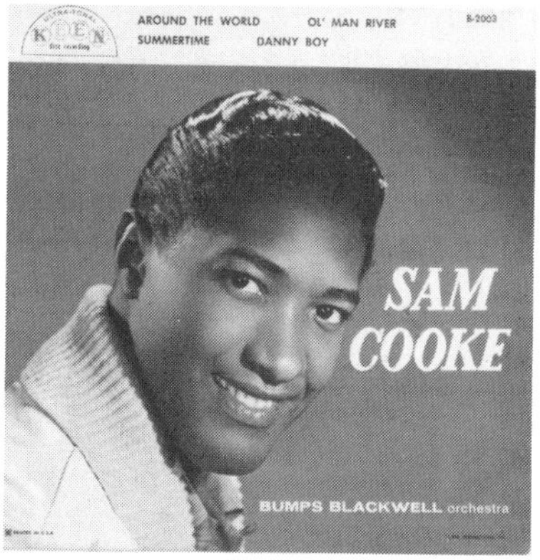

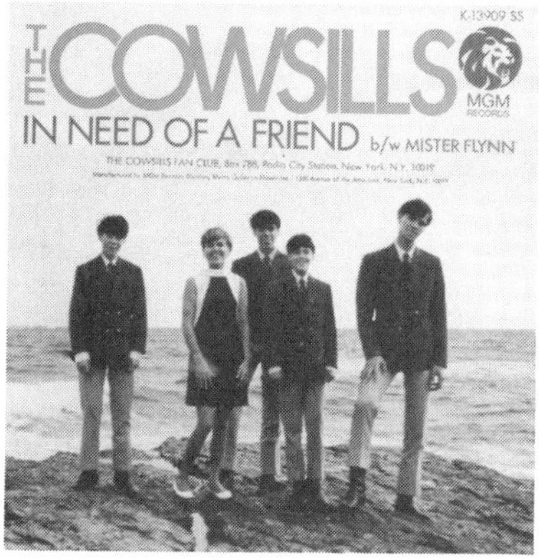

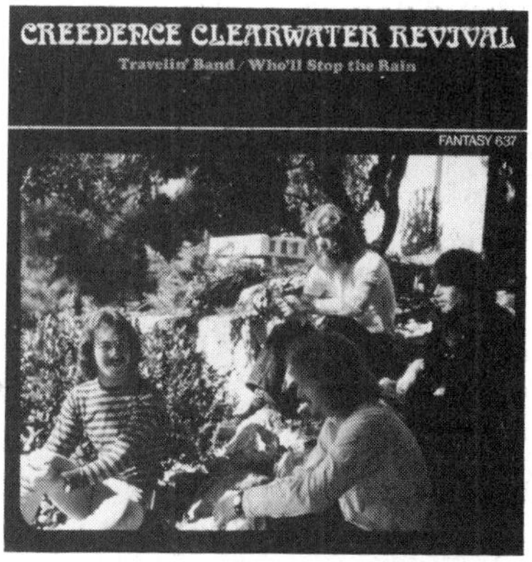

DATE	POS	WKS	ARTIST—RECORD TITLE	LABEL & NO.
			BOB DYLAN	
			Born Robert Allen Zimmerman on 5/24/41 in Duluth, Minnesota. Singer/songwriter/ guitarist/harmonica player. Took stage name from poet Dylan Thomas. To New York City in December, 1960. Worked Greenwich Village folk clubs. Signed to Columbia Records in October, 1961. Innovator of folk-rock style, 1965. Motorcycle crash on 7/29/66 led to short retirement. Films "Don't Look Back" (1965), "Eat The Document" (1969) and "Pat Garrett And Billy The Kid" (1973). Toured with Rolling Thunder Revue in 1976. Made film "Renaldo And Clara" (1978). Became a born-again Christian in 1979, songs reflecting his new faith. Co-starred with Fiona in the 1987 film "Hearts Of Fire." Inducted into the Rock And Roll Hall Of Fame in 1988. Member of the 1988 supergroup Traveling Wilburys.	
5/15/65	**39**	1	1. Subterranean Homesick Blues	Columbia 43242
8/14/65	**2**(2)	9	2. **Like A Rolling Stone**	Columbia 43346
10/09/65	**7**	7	3. **Positively 4th Street**	Columbia 43389
4/23/66	**2**(1)	9	4. **Rainy Day Women #12 & 35**	Columbia 43592
7/16/66	**20**	4	5. I Want You	Columbia 43683
10/01/66	**33**	3	6. Just Like A Woman	Columbia 43792
8/02/69	**7**	11	7. **Lay Lady Lay**	Columbia 44926
12/25/71†	**33**	4	8. George Jackson	Columbia 45516
9/29/73	**12**	11	9. Knockin' On Heaven's Door	Columbia 45913
3/29/75	**31**	3	10. Tangled Up In Blue	Columbia 10106
1/03/76	**33**	3	11. Hurricane (Part I) dedicated to boxer Rubin Carter, a convicted murderer	Columbia 10245
10/06/79	**24**	6	12. Gotta Serve Somebody all of above: written by Dylan	Columbia 11072
			RONNIE DYSON	
			Soul singer, born on 6/5/50 in Washington, DC; raised in Brooklyn. Lead part in the Broadway musical "Hair." In the film "Putney Swope."	
7/25/70	**8**	9	1. **(If You Let Me Make Love To You Then) Why Can't I Touch You?** from the Off-Broadway musical "Salvation"	Columbia 45110
4/07/73	**28**	4	2. One Man Band (Plays All Alone)	Columbia 45776

DATE	POS	WKS	ARTIST—RECORD TITLE	LABEL & NO.
			# E	
			EAGLES	
			Formed in Los Angeles in 1971. Consisted of Glenn Frey (vocals, guitar), Bernie Leadon (guitar), Randy Meisner (bass) and Don Henley (drums). Meisner had founded Poco; Leadon had been in the Flying Burrito Brothers; and Frey and Henley were with Linda Ronstadt. Debut album recorded in England in 1972. Don Felder (guitar) added in 1975. Leadon replaced by Joe Walsh in 1975; and Meisner replaced by Timothy B. Schmit in 1977. Disbanded in 1982.	
6/24/72	**12**	8	1. Take It Easy	Asylum 11005
9/30/72	**9**	10	2. **Witchy Woman**	Asylum 11008
2/03/73	**22**	6	3. Peaceful Easy Feeling	Asylum 11013
6/22/74	**32**	3	4. Already Gone	Asylum 11036
12/28/74†	**1**(1)	14	5. **Best Of My Love**	Asylum 45218
6/14/75	**1**(1)	14	6. **One Of These Nights**	Asylum 45257
9/27/75	**2**(2)	11	7. **Lyin' Eyes**	Asylum 45279
1/17/76	**4**	14	8. **Take It To The Limit**	Asylum 45293
12/25/76†	**1**(1)	13	● 9. **New Kid In Town**	Asylum 45373
3/12/77	**1**(1)	15	● 10. **Hotel California**	Asylum 45386
5/28/77	**11**	8	11. Life In The Fast Lane	Asylum 45403
12/23/78	**18**	5	12. Please Come Home For Christmas [X]	Asylum 45555
10/13/79	**1**(1)	13	● 13. **Heartache Tonight**	Asylum 46545
12/08/79†	**8**	12	14. **The Long Run**	Asylum 46569
3/01/80	**8**	12	15. **I Can't Tell You Why**	Asylum 46608
1/10/81	**21**	7	16. Seven Bridges Road	Asylum 47100
			EARL-JEAN	
			Earl-Jean McCrea of The Cookies.	
8/08/64	**38**	1	1. I'm Into Somethin' Good	Colpix 729
			THE EARLS	
			White doo-wop quartet from the Bronx: Larry Chance (lead), Bob Del Din, Eddie Harder and Jack Wray.	
1/12/63	**24**	4	1. Remember Then	Old Town 1130
			EARTH, WIND & FIRE	
			R&B group formed in Los Angeles in 1969, by Chicago-bred Maurice White (b: 12/19/41, Memphis; lead vocals, percussion, kalimba, songwriter, producer). Co-lead singer Philip Bailey joined in 1972. White had been a session drummer for Chess Records and with the Ramsey Lewis Trio, 1966-1969. Group generally contained 8-10 members, with frequent personnel shuffling. In films "Sgt. Pepper's Lonely Hearts Club Band" and "That's The Way Of The World." Group members Philip Bailey, Wade Flemons, Ronnie Laws and Maurice White had solo hits.	
4/27/74	**29**	7	1. Mighty Mighty	Columbia 46007
10/12/74	**33**	2	2. Devotion	Columbia 10026
3/22/75	**1**(1)	14	● 3. **Shining Star**	Columbia 10090
7/26/75	**12**	11	4. That's The Way Of The World	Columbia 10172
12/13/75†	**5**	12	● 5. **Sing A Song**	Columbia 10251
4/24/76	**39**	2	6. Can't Hide Love	Columbia 10309

DATE	POS	WKS	ARTIST—RECORD TITLE	LABEL & NO.
8/14/76	**12**	12	● 7. Getaway	Columbia 10373
12/11/76†	**21**	10	8. Saturday Nite	Columbia 10439
11/26/77†	**13**	13	9. Serpentine Fire	Columbia 10625
4/01/78	**32**	5	10. Fantasy	Columbia 10688
8/05/78	**9**	9	● 11. **Got To Get You Into My Life**	Columbia 10796
12/16/78†	**8**	11	● 12. **September**	ARC 10854
5/26/79	**6**	12	● 13. **Boogie Wonderland**	ARC 10956
			EARTH, WIND & FIRE with THE EMOTIONS	
7/28/79	**2**(2)	13	● 14. **After The Love Has Gone**	ARC 11033
10/31/81	**3**	16	● 15. **Let's Groove**	ARC 02536
2/12/83	**17**	10	16. Fall In Love With Me	Columbia 03375
			SHEENA EASTON	
			Born on 4/27/59 in Glasgow, Scotland. Vocalist/actress. Portrayed singer in the 1980 BBC-TV documentary "The Big Time." Sang the opening credits for the James Bond film "For Your Eyes Only." Won the 1981 Best New Artist Grammy Award. Appeared in 5 episodes of TV's "Miami Vice."	
2/28/81	**1**(2)	15	● 1. **Morning Train (Nine To Five)**	EMI America 8071
6/06/81	**18**	9	2. Modern Girl	EMI America 8080
8/22/81	**4**	14	3. **For Your Eyes Only** from the film of the same title	Liberty 1418
12/19/81†	**15**	12	4. You Could Have Been With Me	EMI America 8101
5/08/82	**30**	6	5. When He Shines	EMI America 8113
1/29/83	**6**	15	6. **We've Got Tonight**	Liberty 1492
			KENNY ROGERS & SHEENA EASTON	
9/10/83	**9**	14	7. **Telefone (Long Distance Love Affair)**	EMI America 8172
2/11/84	**25**	6	8. Almost Over You	EMI America 8186
9/22/84	**7**	15	9. **Strut**	EMI America 8227
1/19/85	**9**	9	10. **Sugar Walls** written and produced by Prince (as Alexander Nevermind)	EMI America 8253
11/30/85	**29**	4	11. Do It For Love	EMI America 8295
12/24/88†	**2**(1)	14	12. **The Lover In Me**	MCA 53416
			THE EASYBEATS	
			Rock quintet formed in Australia in 1965. All members were natives of England and returned there in 1966. Members George Young and Harry Vanda later formed Flash & The Pan. George is the older brother of AC/DC's Angus and Malcolm Young.	
4/22/67	**16**	8	1. Friday On My Mind	United Art. 50106
			THE EASY RIDERS - see TERRY GILKYSON	
			THE ECHOES	
			Brooklyn trio: Tommy Duffy, Harry Doyle and Tom Morrissey.	
3/27/61	**12**	9	1. Baby Blue	Seg-way 103

DATE	POS	WKS	ARTIST—RECORD TITLE	LABEL & NO.
			DUANE EDDY	
			Born on 4/26/38 in Corning, New York. Began playing guitar at age 5. At age 13, moved to Tucson, then to Coolidge, Arizona. To Phoenix in 1955, and then began long association with producer, songwriter Lee Hazlewood. Eddy's backing band, The Rebels, included 3 top sessionmen, Larry Knechtel on piano and Jim Horn and Steve Douglas on sax. Films "Because They're Young," "A Thunder Of Drums," "The Wild Westerners," "The Savage Seven" and "Kona Coast." Married to Jesse Colter, 1962-68. Duane originated the "twangy" guitar sound and is the all-time #1 rock and roll instrumentalist. Currently resides in Nashville.	
7/07/58	**6**	12	1. **Rebel-'Rouser** **[I]** Best Seller #6 / Top 100 #6 / Jockey #14 end handclaps and rebel yells by The Rivingtons	Jamie 1104
9/15/58	**27**	5	2. Ramrod [I] Best Seller #27 / Hot 100 #28	Jamie 1109
11/17/58	**15**	9	3. Cannonball [I]	Jamie 1111
2/02/59	**23**	8	4. The Lonely One [I]	Jamie 1117
4/20/59	**30**	2	5. "Yep!" [I]	Jamie 1122
6/29/59	**9**	11	6. **Forty Miles Of Bad Road** **[I]**	Jamie 1126
10/26/59	**37**	3	7. Some Kind-A Earthquake [I]	Jamie 1130
1/11/60	**26**	5	8. Bonnie Came Back [I] traditional Scottish tune "My Bonnie Lies Over The Ocean"	Jamie 1144
6/06/60	**4**	12	9. **Because They're Young** **[I]** from the film of the same title	Jamie 1156
10/31/60	**27**	4	10. Peter Gunn [I] new version with The Art Of Noise charted in 1986	Jamie 1168
1/16/61	**18**	7	11. "Pepe" [I] from the film of the same title	Jamie 1175
4/17/61	**39**	1	12. Theme From Dixie [I] classic Civil War song, written in 1860 by black composer Daniel Emmett; vocals: the Anita Kerr Singers & The Jordanaires	Jamie 1183
8/11/62	**33**	3	13. The Ballad Of Paladin [I] theme from the TV series "Have Gun-Will Travel"	RCA 8047
11/03/62	**12**	10	14. (Dance With The) Guitar Man	RCA 8087
2/23/63	**28**	5	15. Boss Guitar above 2: female vocal backing by The Rebelettes (The Blossoms)	RCA 8131
			EDISON LIGHTHOUSE	
			British pop quintet featuring lead singer Tony Burrows.	
2/28/70	**5**	12	● 1. **Love Grows (Where My Rosemary Goes)**	Bell 858
			DAVE EDMUNDS	
			Born on 4/15/44 in Cardiff, Wales. Singer/songwriter/guitarist/producer. Formed Love Sculpture in 1967. Formed rockabilly band Rockpile in 1976. Produced for Shakin' Stevens, Brinsley Schwarz, Stray Cats and others.	
1/16/71	**4**	9	1. **I Hear You Knocking** #2 R&B hit for Smiley Lewis; #2 pop hit for Gale Storm (both 1955)	MAM 3601
7/30/83	**39**	1	2. Slipping Away	Columbia 03877

DATE	POS	WKS	ARTIST—RECORD TITLE	LABEL & NO.
			THE EDSELS	
			R&B quintet from Youngstown, Ohio; George Jones, Jr. (lead), Marshall Sewell (bass).	
6/05/61	**21**	5	1. Rama Lama Ding Dong released on the Dub label in 1958 as "Lama Rama Ding Dong"	Twin 700
			EDWARD BEAR	
			Trio from Toronto, Canada; Larry Evoy, lead singer. Took name from a character in the beloved children's classic "Winnie The Pooh."	
1/27/73	**3**	12	● 1. **Last Song**	Capitol 3452
5/26/73	**37**	2	2. Close Your Eyes	Capitol 3581
			BOBBY EDWARDS	
			Real name: Robert Moncrief. Country singer from Anniston, Alabama.	
10/16/61	**11**	9	1. You're The Reason backing vocals: The Four Young Men	Crest 1075
			JONATHAN EDWARDS	
			Born on 7/28/46 in Minnesota. Formed bluegrass band, Sugar Creek, in 1965.	
12/04/71†	**4**	12	● 1. **Sunshine**	Capricorn 8021
			TOMMY EDWARDS	
			Born on 2/17/22 in Richmond, Virginia; died on 10/23/69. R&B singer/pianist/ songwriter. Performing since age 9. First recorded for Top in 1949.	
8/25/58	**1**(6)	19	1. **It's All In The Game** **[R]** Hot 100 #1(6) / Best Seller #1(3) end written by U.S. Vice President Charles Dawes in 1912 as "Melody In A Major"; Tommy's original version charted in 1951 (POS 18)	MGM 12688
11/17/58	**15**	9	2. Love Is All We Need	MGM 12722
3/02/59	**11**	8	3. Please Mr. Sun/ [R] Tommy's original version charted in 1952 (POS 22)	
3/23/59	**27**	4	4. The Morning Side Of The Mountain [R] Tommy's original version charted in 1951 (POS 24)	MGM 12757
6/08/59	**26**	4	5. My Melancholy Baby #9 hit for Walter Van Brunt in 1915	MGM 12794
6/06/60	**18**	7	6. I Really Don't Want To Know #11 hit for Les Paul & Mary Ford in 1954	MGM 12890
			WALTER EGAN	
			Born on 7/12/48 in Jamaica, New York.	
7/01/78	**8**	13	● 1. **Magnet And Steel**	Columbia 10719
			THE 8TH DAY	
			Group from Detroit, assembled by producers Holland-Dozier-Holland in 1966.	
6/05/71	**11**	10	● 1. She's Not Just Another Woman	Invictus 9087
10/16/71	**28**	6	2. You've Got To Crawl (Before You Walk)	Invictus 9098
			EL CHICANO	
			Mexican-American band, formed in Los Angeles as the VIP's in 1965. Included Jerry Salas (lead vocals), Mickey Lespron, Robert Espinosa, Fred Sanchez and Andre Baeza.	
5/02/70	**28**	5	1. Viva Tirado - Part I [I]	Kapp 2085

DATE	POS	WKS	ARTIST—RECORD TITLE	LABEL & NO.
12/22/73	**40**	1	2. Tell Her She's Lovely	MCA 40104
			THE EL DORADOS	
			Chicago R&B quintet featuring Pirkle Lee Moses, lead singer.	
10/15/55	**17**	6	1. At My Front Door Best Seller #17 / Top 100 #35	Vee-Jay 147
			DONNIE ELBERT	
			Vocalist/multi-instrumentalist, born on 5/25/36 in New Orleans. First recorded for DeLuxe in 1957. A&R director for Polygram Records, Canada, in the mid-80s.	
11/20/71	**15**	8	1. Where Did Our Love Go	All Platinum 2330
2/12/72	**22**	6	2. I Can't Help Myself (Sugar Pie, Honey Bunch)	Avco 4587
			THE ELECTRIC INDIAN	
			Instrumental group assembled from top Philadelphia studio musicians. Some members later joined MFSB.	
8/23/69	**16**	8	1. Keem-O-Sabe [I]	United Art. 50563
			ELECTRIC LIGHT ORCHESTRA	
			Group formed in Birmingham, England in 1971, by Roy Wood, Bev Bevans and Jeff Lynne of The Move. Wood left after their first album, leaving Lynne as the group's leader. Much personnel shuffling from then on. From a group size of 8 in 1971, the 1986 ELO consisted of 3 members: Lynne (vocals, guitar, keyboards), Bevan (drums) and Richard Tandy (keyboards). Lynne is a member of the 1988 supergroup Traveling Wilburys.	
1/25/75	**9**	10	1. **Can't Get It Out Of My Head**	United Art. 573
12/13/75†	**10**	12	2. **Evil Woman**	United Art. 729
4/10/76	**14**	9	3. Strange Magic	United Art. 770
11/13/76†	**13**	14	4. Livin' Thing	United Art. 888
3/05/77	**24**	6	5. Do Ya #93 hit for The Move (forerunner of ELO) in 1972	United Art. 939
7/09/77	**7**	16	● 6. **Telephone Line**	United Art. 1000
12/10/77†	**13**	10	7. Turn To Stone	Jet 1099
3/11/78	**17**	12	8. Sweet Talkin' Woman	Jet 1145
7/29/78	**35**	3	9. Mr. Blue Sky	Jet 5050
6/02/79	**8**	11	10. **Shine A Little Love**	Jet 5057
8/11/79	**4**	11	● 11. **Don't Bring Me Down**	Jet 5060
11/17/79	**37**	2	12. Confusion	Jet 5064
1/26/80	**39**	2	13. Last Train To London	Jet 5067
6/14/80	**16**	8	● 14. I'm Alive	MCA 41246
8/16/80	**13**	9	15. All Over The World	MCA 41289
8/30/80	**8**	10	16. **Xanadu** **OLIVIA NEWTON-JOHN/ELECTRIC LIGHT ORCHESTRA** above 3: from the film "Xanadu"	MCA 41285
8/08/81	**10**	13	17. **Hold On Tight**	Jet 02408
11/28/81	**38**	2	18. Twilight	Jet 02559
7/09/83	**19**	9	19. Rock 'N' Roll Is King above 3 shown only as: **ELO**	Jet 03964
3/01/86	**18**	7	20. Calling America all of above: written (except #1) and produced by Jeff Lynne	CBS Assoc. 05766

DATE	POS	WKS	ARTIST—RECORD TITLE	LABEL & NO.
			THE ELECTRIC PRUNES	
			Seattle psychedelic rock quintet; James Lowe, lead singer.	
1/21/67	**11**	8	1. I Had Too Much To Dream (Last Night)	Reprise 0532
4/22/67	**27**	5	2. Get Me To The World On Time	Reprise 0564
			THE ELEGANTS	
			White vocal group formed in Staten Island, New York in 1957: Vito Picone (lead singer), Arthur Venosa, Frank Tardogno, Carmen Romano and James Mochella. All were veterans of other groups.	
7/28/58	**1**(1)	16	1. **Little Star** Hot 100 #1 / Best Seller #2	Apt 25005
			LARRY ELGART & His Manhattan Swing Orchestra	
			Larry was born on 3/20/22 in New London, Connecticut. Alto saxman in brother Les' band and his own band.	
7/03/82	**31**	5	1. Hooked On Swing [I] In The Mood/Cherokee/American Patrol/Sing, Sing, Sing/Don't Be That Way/Little Brown Jug/Opus #1/Zing Went The Strings Of My Heart/String Of Pearls	RCA 13219
			JIMMY ELLEDGE	
			Born on 1/8/43 in Nashville. Discovered by Chet Atkins.	
12/25/61†	**22**	7	1. Funny How Time Slips Away written by Willie Nelson; produced by Chet Atkins	RCA 7946
			YVONNE ELLIMAN	
			Born on 12/29/51 in Honolulu. Portrayed Mary Magdalene in the rock opera "Jesus Christ, Superstar." Joined with Eric Clapton during his 1974 comeback tour.	
5/22/71	**28**	6	1. I Don't Know How To Love Him from the rock opera "Jesus Christ Superstar"	Decca 32785
11/06/76	**14**	12	2. Love Me	RSO 858
4/16/77	**15**	9	3. Hello Stranger	RSO 871
2/25/78	**1**(1)	16	● 4. **If I Can't Have You** from the film "Saturday Night Fever"	RSO 884
12/01/79	**34**	3	5. Love Pains	RSO 1007
			SHIRLEY ELLIS	
			Born in 1941 in the Bronx. Soul singer/songwriter. Was in the group The Metronomes.	
12/07/63†	**8**	10	1. **The Nitty Gritty**	Congress 202
1/09/65	**3**	10	2. **The Name Game**	Congress 230
4/03/65	**8**	7	3. **The Clapping Song (Clap Pat Clap Slap)**	Congress 234
			EMERSON, LAKE & PALMER	
			English classical-oriented rock trio formed in 1969. Consisted of Keith Emerson (with The Nice; keyboards), Greg Lake (King Crimson; vocals, bass, guitars) and Carl Palmer (Atomic Rooster; drums). Group split up in 1979, with Palmer joining supergroup Asia. Emerson & Lake regrouped in 1986 with new drummer Cozy Powell. Palmer returned in 1987, replacing Powell.	
10/21/72	**39**	2	1. From The Beginning	Cotillion 44158

DATE	POS	WKS	ARTIST—RECORD TITLE	LABEL & NO.
			THE EMOTIONS	
			Black female trio from Chicago, consisting of sisters Wanda (lead), Sheila and Jeanette Hutchinson. First worked as child gospel group called the Heavenly Sunbeams. Left gospel, became The Emotions in 1968. Jeanette replaced by cousin Theresa Davis in 1970, and later by sister Pamela; returned to group in 1978.	
7/19/69	**39**	1	1. So I Can Love You	Volt 4010
7/02/77	**1**(5)	17	● 2. **Best Of My Love**	Columbia 10544
5/26/79	**6**	12	● 3. **Boogie Wonderland**	ARC 10956
			EARTH, WIND & FIRE with THE EMOTIONS	
			ENCHANTMENT	
			Soul quintet from Detroit, formed in 1966 while in high school. Did soundtrack for the film "Deliver Us From Evil."	
3/05/77	**25**	5	1. Gloria	United Art. 912
3/11/78	**33**	4	2. It's You That I Need	Roadshow 1124
			ENGLAND DAN & JOHN FORD COLEY	
			Pop duo from Austin, Texas: Dan Seals (b: 2/8/50) and Coley (b: 10/13/51). Dan (brother of Jim Seals of Seals & Crofts) is currently a hot country artist.	
7/10/76	**2**(2)	17	● 1. **I'd Really Love To See You Tonight**	Big Tree 16069
10/30/76	**10**	12	2. **Nights Are Forever Without You**	Big Tree 16079
6/18/77	**21**	8	3. It's Sad To Belong	Big Tree 16088
11/05/77	**23**	6	4. Gone Too Far	Big Tree 16102
3/11/78	**9**	8	5. **We'll Never Have To Say Goodbye Again**	Big Tree 16110
4/07/79	**10**	10	6. **Love Is The Answer**	Big Tree 16131
			THE ENGLISH CONGREGATION	
			British group; Brian Keith, lead vocals.	
2/19/72	**29**	5	1. Softly Whispering I Love You	Atco 6865
			PRESTON EPPS	
			Bongo player from Oakland. Discovered by Original Sound owner, Art Laboe.	
6/01/59	**14**	9	1. Bongo Rock [I]	Original Sound 4
			THE EQUALS	
			Integrated British/Jamaican quintet led by Eddy Grant (guitar) and Derv Gordon (vocals).	
9/28/68	**32**	6	1. Baby, Come Back	RCA 9583
			ERASURE	
			British techno-soul duo of composer/producer/multi-instrumentalist Vince Clark and lyricist/vocalist Andy Bell. Clark was a member of Depeche Mode and Yaz.	
9/10/88	**12**	11	1. Chains Of Love	Sire 27844
			ERNIE - see JIM HENSON	
			ERUPTION	
			Jamaican techno-funk quintet featuring male vocalist Precious Wilson.	
6/10/78	**18**	6	1. I Can't Stand The Rain	Ariola 7686

DATE	POS	WKS	ARTIST—RECORD TITLE	LABEL & NO.
			THE ESCAPE CLUB	
			London-based rock quartet formed in 1983: Trevor Steel (vocals), John Holliday, Johnnie Christie and Milan Zekavica.	
9/17/88	**1**(1)	16	• 1. **Wild, Wild West**	Atlantic 89048
			THE ESQUIRES	
			Soul quintet from Milwaukee, formed at North Division High School in 1957 by Gilbert (lead singer), Alvis, and Betty Moorer (left in 1965). Joined by Sam Pace in 1961, Shawn Taylor in 1965, and Millard Edwards in 1967.	
9/16/67	**11**	10	1. Get On Up	Bunky 7750
12/16/67	**22**	5	2. And Get Away	Bunky 7752
			THE ESSEX	
			R&B quintet formed by members of the US Marine Corps at Camp LeJeune, North Carolina in 1962. Consisted of Anita Humes (lead), Walter Vickers, Rodney Taylor, Billie Hill and Rudolph Johnson.	
6/22/63	**1**(2)	10	1. **Easier Said Than Done**	Roulette 4494
9/14/63	**12**	6	2. A Walkin' Miracle	Roulette 4515
			DAVID ESSEX	
			Born David Cook on 7/23/47 in London, England. Portrayed Christ in the London production of "Godspell." Star of British films since 1970.	
1/12/74	**5**	14	• 1. **Rock On**	Columbia 45940
			GLORIA ESTEFAN - see MIAMI SOUND MACHINE	
			E.U.	
			E.U.: Experience Unlimited. 8-member male group from Washington, DC.	
5/14/88	**35**	4	1. Da'Butt from the film "School Daze"	EMI-Man. 50115
			EUROPE	
			Swedish rock quintet: Joey Tempest (vocals), Kee Marcello, John Leven, Mic Michaeli and Ian Haugland.	
2/21/87	**8**	9	1. **The Final Countdown** featured in the film "Rocky IV"	Epic 06416
6/06/87	**30**	4	2. Rock The Night	Epic 07091
8/22/87	**3**	12	3. **Carrie**	Epic 07282
9/24/88	**31**	4	4. Superstitious	Epic 07979
			EURYTHMICS	
			Synth/pop duo: Annie Lennox (b: 12/25/54, Scotland; vocals, keyboards, flute, composer) and David Stewart (b: 9/9/52, England; keyboards, guitar, synthesizer, composer). Both had been in the Tourists from 1977-80. First album recorded in Cologne, Germany, with drummer Clem Burke, formerly of Blondie. Stewart married Siobhan Fahey of Bananarama on 8/1/87. Lennox appeared in TV film "The Room."	
6/18/83	**1**(1)	17	• 1. **Sweet Dreams (Are Made of This)**	RCA 13533
10/15/83	**23**	6	2. Love Is A Stranger	RCA 13618
2/04/84	**4**	14	3. **Here Comes The Rain Again**	RCA 13725
5/19/84	**21**	7	4. Who's That Girl?	RCA 13800
8/11/84	**29**	5	5. Right By Your Side	RCA 13695
5/11/85	**5**	13	6. **Would I Lie To You?**	RCA 14078
8/17/85	**22**	7	7. There Must Be An Angel (Playing With My Heart)	RCA 14160

DATE	POS	WKS	ARTIST—RECORD TITLE	LABEL & NO.
11/02/85	18	8	8. Sisters Are Doin' It For Themselves	RCA 14214
			EURYTHMICS & ARETHA FRANKLIN	
8/30/86	14	9	9. Missionary Man	RCA 14414
			PAUL EVANS	
			Born on 3/5/38 in New York City. First recorded for RCA in 1957. Wrote hits "When" for the Kalin Twins, "Roses Are Red (My Love)" for Bobby Vinton, "I Gotta Know" and "The Next Step Is Love" for Elvis Presley. Wrote the score for the Broadway show "Loot" and film "Live Young." Writes and sings many commercial jingles.	
10/05/59	9	11	1. **Seven Little Girls Sitting In The Back Seat** with the Curls (female backing duo: Sue Singleton & Sue Terry)	Guaranteed 200
2/15/60	16	7	2. Midnite Special	Guaranteed 205
5/30/60	10	8	3. **Happy-Go-Lucky-Me**	Guaranteed 208
			BETTY EVERETT	
			Born on 11/23/39 in Greenwood, Mississippi. Vocalist/pianist. Performed in gospel choirs. To Chicago in the late 50s. First recorded for Cobra in 1958. Toured England in the mid-60s.	
3/21/64	6	10	1. **The Shoop Shoop Song (It's In His Kiss)**	Vee-Jay 585
9/19/64	5	11	2. **Let It Be Me**	Vee-Jay 613
			BETTY EVERETT & JERRY BUTLER	
2/15/69	26	6	3. There'll Come A Time	Uni 55100
			THE EVERLY BROTHERS	
			Donald (real name: Isaac Donald) was born on 2/1/37 in Brownie, Kentucky; Philip on 1/19/39 in Chicago. Vocal duo/guitarists/songwriters. Parents were folk and country singers. Don (beginning at age 8) and Phil (age 6) sang with parents through high school. Invited to Nashville by Chet Atkins and first recorded there for Columbia in 1955. Signed to Archie Bleyer's Cadence Records in 1957. Phil married for a time to the daughter of Archie and Janet (Chordettes) Bleyer. Duo split up in July of 1973, and reunited in September, 1983. Inducted into the Rock And Roll Hall Of Fame in 1986. The #1 duo of the rock era.	
5/27/57	2(4)	22	1. **Bye Bye Love** Best Seller #2 / Top 100 #2 / Jockey #2 / Juke Box #9 end	Cadence 1315
9/30/57	1(4)	20	2. **Wake Up Little Susie** Jockey #1(4) / Top 100 #1(2) / Best Seller #1(1)	Cadence 1337
2/17/58	26	3	3. This Little Girl Of Mine Best Seller #26 / Top 100 #28 written & popularized on R&B charts by Ray Charles in 1955 (POS 9)	Cadence 1342
4/28/58	1(5)	16	4. **All I Have To Do Is Dream/** Jockey #1(5) / Best Seller #1(4) / Top 100 #1(3)	
5/12/58	30	2	5. Claudette written by Roy Orbison	Cadence 1348
8/11/58	1(1)	15	6. **Bird Dog/** Best Seller #1 / Hot 100 #2	
8/18/58	10	11	7. Devoted To You	Cadence 1350
11/24/58	2(1)	11	8. **Problems/**	
12/15/58	40	1	9. Love Of My Life	Cadence 1355
4/20/59	16	8	10. Take A Message To Mary/	
4/20/59	22	6	11. Poor Jenny	Cadence 1364
8/24/59	4	13	12. **('Til) I Kissed You**	Cadence 1369
1/25/60	7	11	13. **Let It Be Me**	Cadence 1376
5/02/60	1(5)	13	14. **Cathy's Clown**	Warner 5151

DATE	POS	WKS	ARTIST—RECORD TITLE	LABEL & NO.
6/27/60	**8**	9	15. **When Will I Be Loved**	Cadence 1380
9/12/60	**7**	10	16. **So Sad (To Watch Good Love Go Bad)/**	
9/12/60	**21**	7	17. Lucille	Warner 5163
11/28/60	**22**	4	18. Like Strangers	Cadence 1388
2/13/61	**7**	10	19. **Walk Right Back/**	
2/13/61	**8**	9	20. Ebony Eyes	Warner 5199
6/12/61	**27**	3	21. Temptation #3 hit for Bing Crosby in 1934	Warner 5220
10/09/61	**20**	6	22. Don't Blame Me #6 hit for Ethel Waters in 1933; released as 7" E.P. with "Muskrat," "Walk Right Back" & "Lucille"	Warner 5501
2/03/62	**6**	9	23. **Crying In The Rain**	Warner 5250
6/02/62	**9**	7	24. **That's Old Fashioned (That's The Way Love Should Be)**	Warner 5273
12/05/64	**31**	2	25. Gone, Gone, Gone	Warner 5478
7/08/67	**40**	2	26. Bowling Green	Warner 7020
			EVERY MOTHERS' SON	
			Quintet formed in Greenwich Village, led by brothers Dennis and Lary Larden.	
5/27/67	**6**	12	1. **Come On Down To My Boat**	MGM 13733
			THE EXCITERS	
			R&B vocal quartet from Jamaica, New York: Herb Rooney, wife Brenda Reid, Carol Johnson and Lillian Walker.	
12/15/62†	**4**	10	1. **Tell Him**	United Art. 544
			EXILE	
			Band formed in Lexington, Kentucky in 1963 as The Exiles; J.P. Pennington, lead singer. Changed name to Exile in 1973. Currently a hot country act.	
8/05/78	**1**(4)	17	● 1. **Kiss You All Over**	Warner 8589
2/03/79	**40**	1	2. You Thrill Me	Warner 8711
			EXPOSÉ	
			Miami-based dance/disco trio: Ann Curless, Jeanette Jurado and Gioia Carmen.	
2/14/87	**5**	12	1. **Come Go With Me**	Arista 9555
5/30/87	**5**	11	2. **Point Of No Return** [R] new version of their 1985 dance/disco hit on Arista 9326	Arista 9579
9/05/87	**7**	13	3. **Let Me Be The One**	Arista 9617
12/05/87†	**1**(1)	16	4. **Seasons Change**	Arista 9640
			EYE TO EYE	
			Pop duo: vocalist Deborah Berg from Seattle and pianist Julian Marshall (of Marshall Hain) from England.	
7/17/82	**37**	3	1. Nice Girls	Warner 50050

DATE	POS	WKS	ARTIST—RECORD TITLE	LABEL & NO.
			F	
			SHELLEY FABARES	
			Born Michele Fabares on 1/19/44 in Santa Monica, California. Niece of actress Nanette Fabray. Starred with Elvis in 3 of his movies. Best known as Mary Stone on "The Donna Reed Show." Married record producer Lou Adler in 1964.	
3/17/62	**1**(2)	13	1. **Johnny Angel**	Colpix 621
6/30/62	**21**	6	2. Johnny Loves Me	Colpix 636
			FABIAN	
			Born Fabian Forte on 2/6/43 in Philadelphia. Discovered at age 14 (because of his good looks and intriguing name) by a chance meeting with Bob Marcucci, owner of Chancellor Records. Began acting career in 1959 with "Hound Dog Man."	
2/02/59	**31**	3	1. I'm A Man	Chancellor 1029
4/06/59	**9**	11	2. **Turn Me Loose**	Chancellor 1033
6/22/59	**3**	10	3. **Tiger**	Chancellor 1037
9/28/59	**29**	3	4. Come On And Get Me	Chancellor 1041
11/30/59	**9**	11	5. **Hound Dog Man/**	
12/07/59	**12**	9	6. This Friendly World above 2: from the film "Hound Dog Man" (starring Fabian)	Chancellor 1044
3/14/60	**31**	3	7. About This Thing Called Love/ all of above: produced by Peter de Angelis	
3/14/60	**39**	2	8. String Along	Chancellor 1047
			BENT FABRIC & His Piano	
			Born Bent Fabricius-Bjerre on 12/7/42 in Copenhagen. Head of Metronome Records in Denmark. Composer/pianist/TV personality/A&R man.	
8/25/62	**7**	12	1. **Alley Cat** [I]	Atco 6226
			THE FABULOUS THUNDERBIRDS	
			Austin, Texas rock and roll group: Kim Wilson (lead singer), Jimmie Vaughan (guitar; brother of Stevie Ray Vaughan), Preston Hubbard (bass) and Fran Christina (drums).	
5/24/86	**10**	10	1. **Tuff Enuff**	CBS Assoc. 05838
			FACE TO FACE	
			Boston rock quintet. Lead singer Laurie Sargent was featured in the film "Streets Of Fire."	
7/21/84	**38**	3	1. 10-9-8	Epic 04430
			TOMMY FACENDA	
			Born on 11/10/39 in Norfolk, Virginia. Back-up vocals with Gene Vincent from 1957-58. Nicknamed "Bubba." First recorded for Nasco in 1958. Later became a firefighter in Virginia.	
11/09/59	**28**	3	1. High School U.S.A. [N] Atlantic released 28 different versions of this record, each mentioning the names of high schools in various cities	Atlantic 51 to 78

DATE	POS	WKS	ARTIST—RECORD TITLE	LABEL & NO.
			FACES	
			Rod Stewart (joined by Ron Wood of the Jeff Beck Group) replaced Steve Marriott as leader of the revamped British group Small Faces in 1969. Wood joined The Rolling Stones in 1975.	
11/27/71	**24**	6	1. (I Know) I'm Losing You **ROD STEWART with FACES**	Mercury 73244
1/15/72	**17**	8	2. Stay With Me	Warner 7545
			FACTS OF LIFE	
			Soul trio formed by Millie Jackson, originally known as The Gospel Truth: Jean Davis (younger sister of Tyrone Davis), Keith Williams (formerly with the Imperials and Flamingos) and Chuck Carter.	
4/09/77	**31**	4	1. Sometimes produced by Millie Jackson	Kayvette 5128
			DONALD FAGEN	
			Born on 1/10/48 in Passaic, New Jersey. Worked as back-up with Jay & The Americans. Fagen and Walter Becker founded Steely Dan.	
10/30/82	**26**	7	1. I.G.Y. (What A Beautiful World) I.G.Y.: International Geophysical Year (Jul '57-Dec '58)	Warner 29900
			BARBARA FAIRCHILD	
			Born on 11/12/50 in Knobel, Arkansas. Country singer/songwriter.	
5/12/73	**32**	5	1. Teddy Bear Song	Columbia 45743
			ADAM FAITH	
			Born Terry Nelhams on 6/23/40 in London. Actor in films and television.	
2/20/65	**31**	2	1. It's Alright with backing band The Roulettes	Amy 913
			PERCY FAITH	
			Born on 4/7/08 in Toronto, Canada. Moved to the United States in 1940. Joined Columbia Records in 1950 as conductor-arranger for their leading singers (Tony Bennett, Doris Day, Rosemary Clooney, Johnny Mathis and others). Died on 2/9/76 (67).	
1/25/60	**1**(9)	17	● 1. **The Theme From "A Summer Place"** **[I]** from the film "A Summer Place"	Columbia 41490
6/27/60	**35**	1	2. Theme For Young Lovers [I]	Columbia 41655
			MARIANNE FAITHFULL	
			English songstress. Discovered by Rolling Stones' manager, Andrew Loog Oldham. Involved in a long, tumultuous relationship with Mick Jagger. Acted in several stage and screen productions.	
12/19/64†	**22**	6	1. As Tears Go By	London 9697
3/27/65	**26**	5	2. Come And Stay With Me	London 9731
6/26/65	**32**	5	3. This Little Bird	London 9759
9/04/65	**24**	5	4. Summer Nights	London 9780
			FALCO	
			Falco (Johann Holzel) was born on 2/19/57 in Vienna, Austria.	
2/22/86	**1**(3)	13	1. **Rock Me Amadeus**	A&M 2821
5/17/86	**18**	8	2. Vienna Calling	A&M 2832

DATE	POS	WKS	ARTIST—RECORD TITLE	LABEL & NO.
			THE FALCONS	
			Detroit R&B group: Eddie Floyd (replaced in 1961 by Wilson Pickett), Bonny Rice, Joe Stubbs (brother of the Four Tops' Levi Stubbs), Willie Schofield and Lance Finnie.	
6/08/59	**17**	10	1. You're So Fine Joe Stubbs, lead singer	Unart 2013
			HAROLD FALTERMEYER	
			West German keyboardist/songwriter/arranger/producer. Arranged and played keyboards on the film scores of "Midnight Express" and "American Gigolo."	
4/13/85	**3**	12	1. **Axel F** **[I]** from the film "Beverly Hills Cop"; Eddie Murphy played Axel Foley	MCA 52536
			AGNETHA FALTSKOG	
			Pronounced: Ag-nyet-ta Felts-kogue. Born on 4/5/50 in Sweden. Member of Abba.	
10/08/83	**29**	5	1. Can't Shake Loose	Polydor 815230
			GEORGIE FAME	
			Born Clive Powell on 6/26/43 in Lancashire, England. Began as a pianist with Billy Fury's back-up group, The Blue Flames.	
2/27/65	**21**	6	1. Yeh, Yeh with The Blue Flames	Imperial 66086
3/02/68	**7**	12	2. **The Ballad Of Bonnie And Clyde**	Epic 10283
			FANCY	
			English rock quartet; Helen Court, lead singer.	
8/03/74	**14**	8	1. Wild Thing	Big Tree 15004
11/16/74	**19**	4	2. Touch Me	Big Tree 16026
			FANNY	
			Female rock quartet from California: sisters June and Jean Millington, Alice DeBuhr, and Nickey Barclay.	
11/06/71	**40**	1	1. Charity Ball	Reprise 1033
3/15/75	**29**	4	2. Butter Boy	Casablanca 814
			THE FANTASTIC JOHNNY C	
			Born Johnny Corley on 4/28/43 in Greenwood, South Carolina. Produced and managed by Jesse James.	
11/04/67	**7**	12	1. **Boogaloo Down Broadway**	Phil-L.A. 305
8/10/68	**34**	2	2. Hitch It To The Horse	Phil-L.A. 315
			DON FARDON	
			Born Don Maughn in Coventry, England. Lead singer of English group The Sorrows.	
9/21/68	**20**	6	1. (The Lament Of The Cherokee) Indian Reservation	GNP Crescendo 405
			DONNA FARGO	
			Born Yvonne Vaughan on 11/10/49 in Mt. Airy, North Carolina. Recorded for Ramco in 1969. Donna was stricken with multiple sclerosis in 1979. Has own music publishing company.	
7/08/72	**11**	10	● 1. The Happiest Girl In The Whole U.S.A.	Dot 17409
11/11/72†	**5**	14	● 2. **Funny Face**	Dot 17429

DATE	POS	WKS	ARTIST—RECORD TITLE	LABEL & NO.
			FAT BOYS	
			Brooklyn-born rap trio: Darren "The Human Beat Box" Robinson, Mark "Prince Markie Dee" Morales and Damon "Kool Rock-ski" Wimbley. Combined weight of over 750 pounds. Appeared in the 1987 film "Disorderlies."	
8/08/87	**12**	11	1. Wipeout backing vocals: The Beach Boys	Tin Pan 885960
7/09/88	**16**	8	2. The Twist **THE FAT BOYS with CHUBBY CHECKER** #1 hit for Chubby in both 1960 and 1962	Tin Pan 887571
			JOSE FELICIANO	
			Born on 9/8/45 in Puerto Rico; raised in New York City. Blind since birth. Virtuoso acoustic guitarist. Has acted in several TV shows. Won the 1968 Best New Artist Grammy Award.	
8/03/68	**3**	11	1. **Light My Fire**	RCA 9550
10/26/68	**25**	7	2. Hi-Heel Sneakers	RCA 9641
			FREDDY FENDER	
			Born Baldemar Huerta on 6/4/37 in San Benito, Texas. Mexican-American singer/ guitarist. First recorded in Spanish under his real name for Falcon in 1956.	
3/08/75	**1**(1)	15	● 1. **Before The Next Teardrop Falls**	ABC/Dot 17540
7/19/75	**8**	14	● 2. **Wasted Days And Wasted Nights** originally recorded by Fender on the Duncan label in 1959	ABC/Dot 17558
11/08/75	**20**	6	3. Secret Love #1 hit for Doris Day in 1954	ABC/Dot 17585
3/20/76	**32**	4	4. You'll Lose A Good Thing	ABC/Dot 17607
			THE FENDERMEN	
			Duo of Phil Humphrey (from Stoughton, WI) and Jim Sundquist (from Niagara, WI); both were born on 11/26/37. Formed at the University of Wisconsin.	
6/13/60	**5**	13	1. **Mule Skinner Blues** written in 1931 by country great Jimmie Rodgers	Soma 1137
			JAY FERGUSON	
			Born on 5/10/43 in San Fernando Valley, California. Before going solo, Jay formed and led the groups Spirit and Jo Jo Gunne.	
1/28/78	**9**	12	1. **Thunder Island**	Asylum 45444
6/09/79	**31**	4	2. Shakedown Cruise	Asylum 46041
			JOHNNY FERGUSON	
			Born on 3/22/37 in Nashville. Worked as a disc jockey in the late 50s.	
4/18/60	**27**	3	1. Angela Jones	MGM 12855
			MAYNARD FERGUSON	
			Jazz trumpeter, born on 5/4/28 in Verdun, Quebec, Canada. Moved to the United States in 1949. Played for Charlie Barnet and then Stan Kenton's Band (1950-56).	
5/28/77	**28**	6	1. Gonna Fly Now (Theme From "Rocky") [I] from the film "Rocky"	Columbia 10468

DATE	POS	WKS	ARTIST—RECORD TITLE		LABEL & NO.
			FERKO STRING BAND		
			Philadelphia string band directed by William Connors. String bands parade annually in Philadelphia's famed New Year's Day Mummers Parade. Also see Nu Tornados.		
6/18/55	**14**	6	1. Alabama Jubilee Juke Box #14 / Best Seller #18 #2 hit for Arthur Collins & Byron Harlan in 1915	[I]	Media 1010
			FERRANTE & TEICHER		
			Piano duo: Arthur Ferrante (b: 9/7/21, New York City) and Louis Teicher (b: 8/24/24, Wilkes-Barre, PA). Met as children while attending the Juilliard School.		
8/08/60	**10**	15	1. **Theme From The Apartment** from the Billy Wilder film "The Apartment"; tune originally entitled "Jealous Lover"	**[I]**	United Art. 231
11/28/60†	**2**(1)	18	2. **Exodus** theme from the Otto Preminger film of the same title	**[I]**	United Art. 274
4/17/61	**37**	1	3. Love Theme From One Eyed Jacks from the Marlon Brando film "One Eyed Jacks"	[I]	United Art. 300
11/13/61	**8**	8	4. **Tonight** from the film "West Side Story"	**[I]**	United Art. 373
11/29/69†	**10**	11	5. **Midnight Cowboy** from the Jon Voight/Dustin Hoffman film of the same title; featuring the "water sound" guitar of Vincent Bell	**[I]**	United Art. 50554
			BRYAN FERRY		
			Born on 9/26/45 in County Durham, England. Lead singer of Roxy Music.		
4/16/88	**31**	3	1. Kiss And Tell from the film "Bright Lights, Big City"		Reprise 28117
			ERNIE FIELDS		
			Born on 8/26/05 in Nacogdoches, Texas. Trombonist/pianist/bandleader/arranger.		
10/12/59	**4**	14	1. **In The Mood** #1 hit for Glenn Miller in 1940	**[I]**	Rendezvous 110
			THE FIESTAS		
			R&B vocal group from Newark: Tommy Bullock (lead), Eddie Morris (tenor), Sam Ingalls (baritone) and Preston Lane (bass).		
4/27/59	**11**	11	1. So Fine		Old Town 1062
			THE 5TH DIMENSION		
			Los Angeles-based group formed in 1966. Consisted of Marilyn McCoo, Florence LaRue, Billy Davis, Jr., Lamont McLemore and Ron Townson. McLemore and McCoo had been in the Hi-Fi's; Townson and Davis had been with groups in St. Louis. First called the Versatiles. Davis and McCoo were married, 1969, and recorded as a duo from 1976.		
2/04/67	**16**	7	1. Go Where You Wanna Go		Soul City 753
6/17/67	**7**	10	2. **Up-Up And Away** above 2: produced by Johnny Rivers (Soul City is his own label)		Soul City 756
12/09/67	**34**	1	3. Paper Cup		Soul City 760
2/24/68	**29**	5	4. Carpet Man		Soul City 762
6/22/68	**3**	12	● 5. **Stoned Soul Picnic**		Soul City 766
10/26/68	**13**	6	6. Sweet Blindness		Soul City 768
1/11/69	**25**	6	7. California Soul		Soul City 770

DATE	POS	WKS	ARTIST—RECORD TITLE	LABEL & NO.
3/15/69	**1**(6)	16	● 8. **Aquarius/Let The Sunshine In** from the Broadway rock musical "Hair"	Soul City 772
8/09/69	**20**	7	9. Workin' On A Groovy Thing	Soul City 776
10/04/69	**1**(3)	14	● 10. **Wedding Bell Blues**	Soul City 779
1/24/70	**21**	6	11. Blowing Away	Soul City 780
5/02/70	**24**	5	12. Puppet Man	Bell 880
6/27/70	**27**	5	13. Save The Country	Bell 895
11/21/70	**2**(2)	15	● 14. **One Less Bell To Answer**	Bell 940
3/13/71	**19**	8	15. Love's Lines, Angles And Rhymes	Bell 965
10/02/71	**12**	9	16. Never My Love	Bell 45134
1/29/72	**37**	3	17. Together Let's Find Love	Bell 45170
4/22/72	**8**	13	● 18. **(Last Night) I Didn't Get To Sleep At All**	Bell 45195
9/30/72	**10**	12	19. **If I Could Reach You**	Bell 45261
2/10/73	**32**	4	20. Living Together, Growing Together from the film "Lost Horizon"; produced by Bones Howe	Bell 45310
			THE FIFTH ESTATE	
			Studio group assembled by producers Steve and Bill Jerome.	
6/10/67	**11**	6	1. Ding Dong! The Witch Is Dead song originally appeared in the 1939 film "The Wizard Of Oz"	Jubilee 5573
			LARRY FINNEGAN	
			Born John Lawrence Finneran in New York City. Moved to Sweden in 1966.	
3/31/62	**11**	8	1. Dear One	Old Town 1113
			THE FIREBALLS	
			Rock and roll band formed while high schoolers in Raton, New Mexico: George Tomsco (b: 4/24/40, lead guitar), Dan Trammell (b: 7/14/40, rhythm guitar), Eric Budd (b: 10/23/38, drums), Stan Lark (b: 7/27/40, bass) and Chuck Tharp (b: 2/3/41, vocalist). First recorded for Kapp in 1958. Trammell left group in 1959. Doug Roberts (d: 11/18/81) replaced Budd in 1962. Tharp quit group in 1960 and was replaced by Jimmy Gilmer (lead vocals, piano). Gilmer was introduced to The Fireballs by their record producer Norman Petty at his famed Clovis, New Mexico studio.	
10/26/59	**39**	2	1. Torquay [I]	Top Rank 2008
2/01/60	**24**	6	2. Bulldog [I]	Top Rank 2026
8/07/61	**27**	3	3. Quite A Party [I]	Warwick 644
			JIMMY GILMER & THE FIREBALLS:	
9/28/63	**1**(5)	13	● 4. **Sugar Shack**	Dot 16487
1/04/64	**15**	8	5. Daisy Petal Pickin'	Dot 16539
			THE FIREBALLS:	
1/27/68	**9**	10	6. **Bottle Of Wine**	Atco 6491
			FIREFALL	
			Mellow rock group formed in Boulder, Colorado by lead singer Rick Roberts.	
9/25/76	**9**	15	1. **You Are The Woman**	Atlantic 3335
4/30/77	**34**	3	2. Cinderella	Atlantic 3392
9/17/77	**11**	12	3. Just Remember I Love You	Atlantic 3420
10/28/78	**11**	10	4. Strange Way	Atlantic 3518
5/10/80	**35**	3	5. Headed For A Fall	Atlantic 3657

DATE	POS	WKS	ARTIST—RECORD TITLE	LABEL & NO.
2/28/81	**37**	3	6. Staying With It lead vocals: Lisa Nemzo and Rick Roberts	Atlantic 3791
			FIREFLIES	
			White doo-wop quartet; Ritchie Adams, lead singer (wrote "Tossin' And Turnin'").	
9/28/59	**21**	10	1. You Were Mine	Ribbon 6901
			THE FIRM	
			British supergroup: Jimmy Page (Led Zeppelin; guitar), Paul Rodgers (Bad Company; vocals), Chris Slade (Manfred Mann; drums) and Tony Franklin (keyboards).	
3/16/85	**28**	6	1. Radioactive	Atlantic 89586
			FIRST CHOICE	
			Female soul trio from Philadelphia, formed as the Debronettes. Consisted of Rochelle Fleming, Annette Guest and Joyce Jones.	
4/28/73	**28**	5	1. Armed And Extremely Dangerous	Philly Groove 175
			FIRST CLASS	
			An assemblage of some of England's leading studio musicians and vocalists.	
8/17/74	**4**	11	1. **Beach Baby**	UK 49022
			THE FIRST EDITION - see KENNY ROGERS	
			EDDIE FISHER	
			Born Edwin Jack Fisher on 8/10/28 in Philadelphia. Radio work while still in high school; at Copacabana night club, New York, at age 17. With Buddy Morrow and Charlie Ventura in 1946. On Eddie Cantor radio show in 1949. Armed Forces Special Services, 1952-53. Married Debbie Reynolds in 1955. Other marriages to Elizabeth Taylor and Connie Stevens. Own "Coke Time" 15-minute TV series, 1953-57. In films "All About Eve" (1950), "Bundle Of Joy" (1956) and "Butterfield 8" (1960). Eddie was the #1 idol of bobbysoxers during the early 1950's.	
3/05/55	**16**	2	1. A Man Chases A Girl (Until She Catches Him)/ Jockey #16 / Juke Box #20 / Best Seller #27 from the film "There's No Business Like Show Business"	
4/02/55	**20**	1	2. (I'm Always Hearing) Wedding Bells Juke Box #20	RCA 6015
5/14/55	**6**	13	3. **Heart** Jockey #6 / Juke Box #13 / Best Seller #15 from the Broadway musical "Damn Yankees"	RCA 6097
8/27/55	**11**	8	4. Song Of The Dreamer Juke Box #11 / Best Seller #16 / Jockey #16 / Top 100 #43 pre	RCA 6196
12/24/55†	**7**	16	5. **Dungaree Doll/** Top 100 #7 / Juke Box #7 / Best Seller #8 / Jockey #9	
12/31/55	**20**	1	6. Everybody's Got A Home But Me Jockey #20 / Top 100 #41 from the Broadway musical "Pipe Dream"	RCA 6337
6/30/56	**18**	7	7. On The Street Where You Live Juke Box #18 / Top 100 #28 from the Broadway musical "My Fair Lady"	RCA 6529
10/20/56	**10**	17	8. **Cindy, Oh Cindy** Best Seller #10 / Top 100 #10 / Jockey #10 / Juke Box #10	RCA 6677
			MISS TONI FISHER	
			Born in Los Angeles in 1931.	
11/23/59	**3**	14	1. **The Big Hurt**	Signet 275

DATE	POS	WKS	ARTIST—RECORD TITLE	LABEL & NO.
7/14/62	**37**	1	2. West Of The Wall shown only as: **TONI FISHER**	Big Top 3097
			ELLA FITZGERALD	
			The most honored jazz singer of all time. Ella Fitzgerald was born on 4/25/18 in Newport News, Virginia. Discovered after winning the Harlem Amateur Hour in 1934, she was hired by Chick Webb and in 1938 created a popular sensation with "A-Tisket, A-Tasket." Following Chick's death in 1939 Ella took over the band for 3 years. Winner of the Down Beat poll as top female vocalist more than 20 times, she remains among the undisputed royalty of 20th century popular music.	
5/30/60	**27**	7	1. Mack The Knife live recording with the Paul Smith Quartet	Verve 10209
			THE FIVE AMERICANS	
			Dallas quintet; Michael Rabon, lead singer.	
2/12/66	**26**	5	1. I See The Light	HBR 454
3/18/67	**5**	9	2. **Western Union**	Abnak 118
6/17/67	**36**	2	3. Sound Of Love	Abnak 120
9/16/67	**36**	1	4. Zip Code	Abnak 123
			THE FIVE BLOBS	
			Studio production; vocals by Bernie Nee.	
11/03/58	**33**	3	1. The Blob from the film of the same title (written by Burt Bacharach)	Columbia 41250
			FIVE FLIGHTS UP	
10/03/70	**37**	5	1. Do What You Wanna Do	T-A 202
			THE FIVE KEYS	
			R&B quintet originally formed as the Sentimental Four in Newport News, Virginia, late 1940s. Consisted of two sets of brothers: Rudy & Bernie West and Ripley & Raphael Ingram. In 1949, added Maryland Pierce and changed group name to The Five Keys. Dickie Smith replaced Raphael Ingram. Smith replaced by Ramon Loper in 1953. Rudy West sings lead on the ballads, Maryland Pierce lead on the rhythm tunes.	
12/25/54†	**28**	2	1. Ling, Ting, Tong Best Seller #28	Capitol 2945
10/06/56	**23**	6	2. Out Of Sight, Out Of Mind Best Seller #23 / Top 100 #27	Capitol 3502
1/12/57	**35**	2	3. Wisdom Of A Fool	Capitol 3597
			FIVE MAN ELECTRICAL BAND	
			Canadian rock group; Les Emmerson, lead singer.	
7/10/71	**3**	12	● 1. **Signs**	Lionel 3213
10/30/71	**26**	6	2. Absolutely Right	Lionel 3220
			THE FIVE SATINS	
			R&B group from New Haven, Connecticut. Consisted of Fred Parris (lead), Al Denby, Jim Freeman, Eddie Martin and Jessie Murphy (piano). Parris was stationed in the Army in Japan when "Still Of The Nite" charted, and the group reformed with Bill Baker as lead singer. Parris returned in January of 1958, replacing Baker.	
9/29/56	**24**	6	1. In The Still Of The Nite Best Seller #24 / Top 100 #29 written by Fred Parris and recorded in a New Haven church basement; originally released on the Standard label, record reportedly had sold multi-millions	Ember 1005

DATE	POS	WKS	ARTIST—RECORD TITLE	LABEL & NO.
8/12/57	**25**	8	2. To The Aisle Best Seller #25 / Top 100 #25	Ember 1019
			THE FIVE STAIRSTEPS	
			Soul group from Chicago, consisting of family members Clarence Jr., James, Alohe, Kenneth and Dennis Burke. Later joined by 5-year old Cubie. Managed by their father and produced by Curtis Mayfield; later became The Invisible Man's Band.	
6/20/70	**8**	11	• 1. **O-o-h Child**	Buddah 165
			5000 VOLTS	
11/15/75	**26**	5	1. I'm On Fire	Philips 40801
			THE FIXX	
			London-based techno-pop group: Cy Curnin (lead singer, piano), Jamie West-Oram (guitars), Rupert Greenall (keyboards), Adam Woods (drums) and Dan K. Brown (bass).	
7/09/83	**20**	8	1. Saved By Zero	MCA 52213
9/10/83	**4**	13	2. **One Thing Leads To Another**	MCA 52264
12/17/83†	**32**	7	3. The Sign Of Fire	MCA 52316
9/08/84	**15**	8	4. Are We Ourselves?	MCA 52444
6/28/86	**19**	6	5. Secret Separation	MCA 52832
			ROBERTA FLACK	
			Born on 2/10/39 in Asheville, North Carolina; raised in Arlington, Virginia. Played piano from an early age. Music scholarship to Howard University at age 15; classmate of Donny Hathaway (soul singer born on 10/1/45 in Chicago). Discovered by Les McCann. Signed to Atlantic in 1969.	
7/03/71	**29**	9	1. You've Got A Friend **ROBERTA FLACK & DONNY HATHAWAY**	Atlantic 2808
3/25/72	**1**(6)	15	• 2. **The First Time Ever I Saw Your Face** popularized because of inclusion in the film "Play Misty For Me"	Atlantic 2864
6/24/72	**5**	11	• 3. **Where Is The Love** **ROBERTA FLACK & DONNY HATHAWAY**	Atlantic 2879
2/03/73	**1**(5)	13	• 4. **Killing Me Softly With His Song**	Atlantic 2940
10/13/73	**30**	5	5. Jesse	Atlantic 2982
7/06/74	**1**(1)	13	• 6. **Feel Like Makin' Love**	Atlantic 3025
3/18/78	**2**(2)	14	• 7. **The Closer I Get To You** **ROBERTA FLACK with DONNY HATHAWAY**	Atlantic 3463
6/24/78	**24**	5	8. If Ever I See You Again	Atlantic 3483
4/17/82	**13**	11	9. Making Love from the film of the same title	Atlantic 4005
9/03/83	**16**	15	10. Tonight, I Celebrate My Love **PEABO BRYSON/ROBERTA FLACK**	Capitol 5242
			THE FLAMING EMBER	
			White soul-rock group from Detroit. Formed as the Flaming Embers: Joe Sladich (guitar), Bill Ellis (piano), Jim Bugnel (bass) and Jerry Plunk (drums).	
11/15/69	**26**	6	1. Mind, Body And Soul	Hot Wax 6902
6/20/70	**24**	10	2. Westbound # 9	Hot Wax 7003
11/28/70	**34**	6	3. I'm Not My Brothers Keeper	Hot Wax 7006

The Critters' biggest hit was the morbidly titled "Mr. Dieingly Sad," which in fact was one of the gentlest songs ever to make the top 20 in the late 60s. Keyboardist Don Ciccone turned up in the 70s lineup of the Four Seasons.

Crowded House evolved from the Australian group Split Enz. The group's critically-acclaimed debut album produced two top-10 singles: "Don't Dream It's Over" and "Something So Strong."

Culture Club's 1983 hit "Time" got to No. 2 and helped them win the Best New Artist Grammy, but time was not so kind to the group. After four more top-10 singles, Culture Club faded from popularity and broke up by 1987.

Vic Dana's best color was red. His biggest hit was "Red Roses For A Blue Lady" (No. 10, 1965), and his last chart entry was a cover of Neil Diamond's "Red Red Wine."

Charlie Daniels' first hit, "Uneasy Rider" (No. 9, 1973), poked fun at redneck conservatives. Ironically, in 1980, his band's "In America" (No. 11) was adopted as an unofficial theme of Ronald Reagan's presidential campaign.

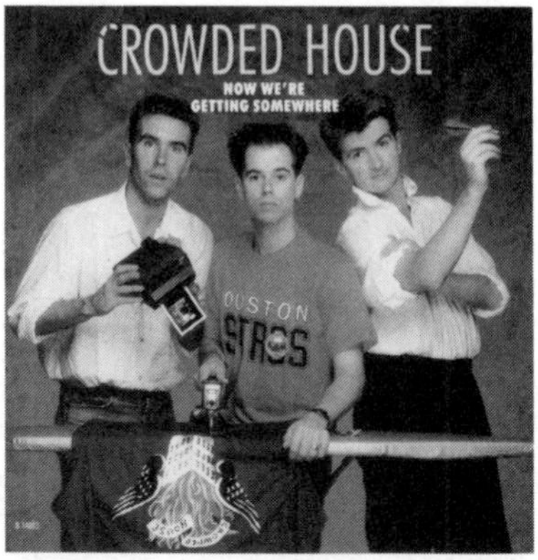

Terence Trent D'Arby lived up to the hype that preceded the release of his album *The Hardline According To . . .* After the first single, "If You Let Me Stay," failed to crack the Top 40, the second, "Wishing Well," went all the way to No. 1.

Bobby Darin's biggest hits were pop show-stoppers like "Mack The Knife," but he never strayed far from his rock roots. His last top-10 hit, "If I Were A Carpenter," was closer to Dylan than Sinatra.

Sammy Davis, Jr. found that two's a crowd on his duets with Frank Sinatra and Dean Martin, both of which failed to crack the top 60. All three men, however, went on to have solo No. 1 hits.

The Spencer Davis Group had something in common with Harold Melvin and the Blues Notes, Paul Revere and the Raiders, and Bo Donaldson and the Heywoods—the group was not named after its lead singer. The Spencer Davis Group's lead singer was the precocious, pre-Michelob Stevie Winwood.

Morris Day's former group the Time broke up during the chart run of its biggest hit, "Jungle Love," in 1984. On his own, he returned to the Top 40 with "The Oak Tree" and "Fishnet."

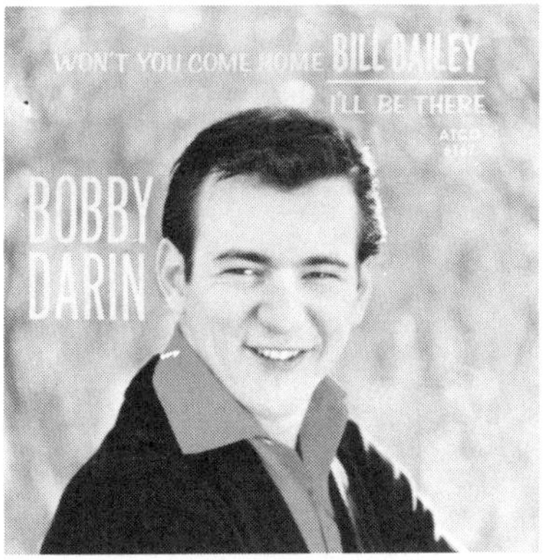

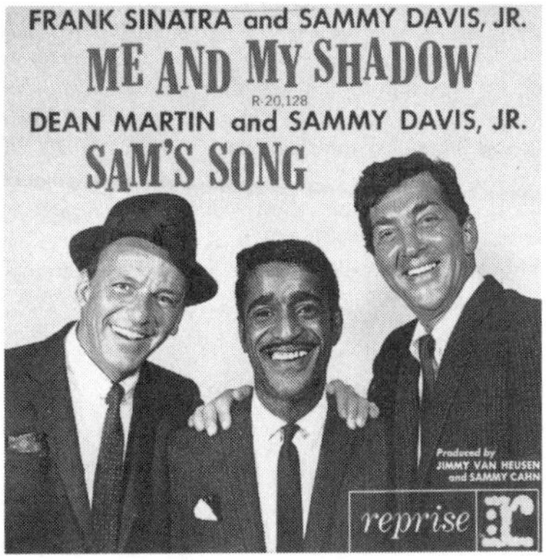

DATE	POS	WKS	ARTIST—RECORD TITLE	LABEL & NO.
			THE FLAMINGOS	
			R&B group formed in Chicago in 1952. Consisted of cousins Zeke & Jake Carey and cousins Paul Wilson & Johnny Carter, with lead singer Sollie McElroy. First recorded for Chance Records in 1953. In 1954, Sollie departed and was replaced by Nate Nelson. Tommy Hunt and Terry Johnson joined in July of 1956, replacing Army-bound Zeke Carey and Johnny Carter. Carey returned in 1958 and group signed with End Records. Nelson joined The Platters in 1966; died of a heart attack on 6/1/84 (52).	
6/08/59	**11**	11	1. I Only Have Eyes For You #2 hit for Ben Selvin in 1934	End 1046
5/23/60	**30**	3	2. Nobody Loves Me Like You written by Sam Cooke	End 1068
			THE FLARES	
			Los Angeles-based R&B quintet, featuring lead singer Aaron Collins of The Cadets/ The Jacks.	
10/09/61	**25**	9	1. Foot Stomping - Part 1	Felsted 8624
			FLASH	
			English rock quartet led by Peter Banks (guitar) and Colin Carter (vocals).	
7/29/72	**29**	6	1. Small Beginnings	Capitol 3345
			FLASH CADILLAC & THE CONTINENTAL KIDS	
			Fifties-styled act formed by 6 students at the University of Colorado.	
10/02/76	**29**	6	1. Did You Boogie (With Your Baby) with spoken interludes by Wolfman Jack	Private S. 45079
			FLEETWOOD MAC	
			Formed as a British blues band in 1967 by ex-John Mayall's Bluesbreakers Peter Green (guitar), Mick Fleetwood (drums) and John McVie (bass), along with guitarist Jeremy Spencer. Many lineup changes followed as group headed toward rock super- stardom. Green and Spencer left in 1970. Christine McVie (keyboards) joined in August, 1970. Bob Welch (guitar) joined in April, 1971, stayed thru 1974. Group relocated to California in 1974, whereupon Lindsey Buckingham (guitar) and Stevie Nicks (vocals) joined in January, 1975. Buckingham left in summer of 1987. Guitarists/vocalists Billy Burnette (son of Dorsey Burnette) and Rick Vito joined in July of 1987.	
12/13/75†	**20**	7	1. Over My Head	Reprise 1339
4/10/76	**11**	11	2. Rhiannon (Will You Ever Win)	Reprise 1345
7/31/76	**11**	13	3. Say You Love Me	Reprise 1356
1/22/77	**10**	11	4. **Go Your Own Way**	Warner 8304
4/30/77	**1**(1)	13	● 5. **Dreams**	Warner 8371
7/23/77	**3**	14	6. **Don't Stop**	Warner 8413
10/29/77	**9**	10	7. **You Make Loving Fun**	Warner 8483
10/13/79	**8**	10	8. **Tusk** with U.S.C. Trojan Marching Band, recorded live at Dodger Stadium	Warner 49077
12/22/79†	**7**	11	9. **Sara**	Warner 49150
3/29/80	**20**	7	10. Think About Me	Warner 49196
6/19/82	**4**	15	11. **Hold Me**	Warner 29966
9/25/82	**12**	8	12. Gypsy	Warner 29918
12/11/82†	**22**	8	13. Love In Store	Warner 29848
4/11/87	**5**	11	14. **Big Love**	Warner 28398

DATE	POS	WKS	ARTIST—RECORD TITLE	LABEL & NO.
7/04/87	**19**	8	15. Seven Wonders	Warner 28317
9/12/87	**4**	13	16. **Little Lies**	Warner 28291
12/26/87†	**14**	10	17. Everywhere	Warner 28143
			THE FLEETWOODS	
			Trio formed while in high school in Olympia, Washington, in 1958: Gary Troxel (b: 11/28/39), Gretchen Christopher (b: 2/29/40) and Barbara Ellis (b: 2/20/40).	
3/16/59	**1**(4)	12	1. **Come Softly To Me**	Dolphin 1
6/22/59	**39**	1	2. Graduation's Here	Dolton 3
9/14/59	**1**(1)	17	3. **Mr. Blue**	Dolton 5
2/29/60	**28**	3	4. Outside My Window	Dolton 15
6/27/60	**23**	4	5. Runaround	Dolton 22
5/08/61	**10**	8	6. **Tragedy**	Dolton 40
10/02/61	**30**	4	7. (He's) The Great Impostor	Dolton 45
11/24/62	**36**	2	8. Lovers By Night, Strangers By Day	Dolton 62
7/13/63	**32**	4	9. Goodnight My Love	Dolton 75
			SHELBY FLINT	
			Singer/songwriter from North Hollywood, California.	
2/06/61	**22**	5	1. Angel On My Shoulder	Valiant 6001
			THE FLIRTATIONS	
			Group consisted of Shirley and Earnestine Pearce from South Carolina, and Viola Billups from Alabama. The Pearce sisters had been in the Gypsies from 1962-65.	
5/24/69	**34**	2	1. Nothing But A Heartache	Deram 85038
			THE FLOATERS	
			Detroit soul group: Charles Clarke (lead), Larry Cunningham, Paul & Ralph Mitchell and Jonathan "Mighty Midget" Murray (joined in 1978).	
7/30/77	**2**(2)	11	• 1. **Float On**	ABC 12284
			A FLOCK OF SEAGULLS	
			British techno-rock group led by vocalist Mike Score. Quartet until 1988 when 3 Philadelphia natives joined the group.	
9/04/82	**9**	10	1. **I Ran (So Far Away)**	Jive 102
1/08/83	**30**	7	2. Space Age Love Song	Jive 2003
6/11/83	**26**	7	3. Wishing (If I Had A Photograph Of You)	Jive 2006
			DICK FLOOD	
			Born on 11/13/32 in Philadelphia. Singer/songwriter.	
9/14/59	**23**	4	1. The Three Bells (The Jimmy Brown Story)	Monument 408
			EDDIE FLOYD	
			Born on 6/25/35 in Montgomery, Alabama; raised in Detroit. Original member of The Falcons, 1955-63. Eddie's uncle, Robert West, founded the Lu Pine record label.	
11/19/66	**28**	6	1. Knock On Wood	Stax 194
9/07/68	**40**	2	2. I've Never Found A Girl (To Love Me Like You Do)	Stax 0002
11/16/68	**17**	9	3. Bring It On Home To Me	Stax 0012

DATE	POS	WKS	ARTIST—RECORD TITLE	LABEL & NO.
			KING FLOYD	
			New Orleans soul-funk singer/songwriter. First recorded for Original Sound in 1965.	
12/12/70†	**6**	13	● 1. **Groove Me**	Chimneyville 435
4/03/71	**29**	7	2. Baby Let Me Kiss You	Chimneyville 437
			THE FLYING MACHINE	
			English pop quintet; Tony Newman, lead singer.	
10/18/69	**5**	12	● 1. **Smile A Little Smile For Me**	Congress 6000
			FOCUS	
			Dutch progressive rock quartet led by guitar virtuoso Jon Akkerman and flutist Thijs Van Leer.	
4/21/73	**9**	11	1. **Hocus Pocus** **[I]**	Sire 704
			DAN FOGELBERG	
			Born on 8/13/51 in Peoria, Illinois. Vocalist/composer. Worked as a folk singer in Los Angeles. With Van Morrison in the early 70s. Session work in Nashville.	
3/01/75	**31**	3	1. Part Of The Plan	Epic 50055
11/04/78	**24**	7	2. The Power Of Gold	Full Moon 50606
			DAN FOGELBERG/TIM WEISBERG	
1/19/80	**2**(2)	13	3. **Longer**	Full Moon 50824
4/19/80	**21**	6	4. Heart Hotels	Full Moon 50862
12/27/80†	**9**	13	5. **Same Old Lang Syne**	Full Moon 50961
9/19/81	**7**	10	6. **Hard To Say**	Full Moon 02488
12/19/81†	**9**	16	7. **Leader Of The Band**	Full Moon 02647
4/24/82	**18**	8	8. Run For The Roses	Full Moon 02821
11/13/82	**23**	9	9. Missing You	Full Moon 03289
3/05/83	**29**	6	10. Make Love Stay	Full Moon 03525
2/11/84	**13**	10	11. The Language Of Love	Full Moon 04314
			JOHN FOGERTY	
			Born on 5/28/45 in Berkeley, California; multi-instrumentalist. With his brother Tom in the Blue Velvets in 1959. Group became the Golliwogs and recorded for Fantasy in 1964. Re-named Creedence Clearwater Revival in 1967. Wrote "Proud Mary," "Have You Ever Seen The Rain," "Bad Moon Risin'," "Lookin' Out My Back Door," and many others. Went solo in 1972 and recorded as "The Blue Ridge Rangers" in 1973.	
			THE BLUE RIDGE RANGERS:	
1/06/73	**16**	10	1. Jambalaya (On The Bayou)	Fantasy 689
5/19/73	**37**	2	2. Hearts Of Stone	Fantasy 700
			JOHN FOGERTY:	
10/04/75	**27**	6	3. Rockin' All Over The World	Asylum 45274
1/19/85	**10**	9	4. **The Old Man Down The Road**	Warner 29100
4/06/85	**20**	6	5. Rock And Roll Girls	Warner 29053
			FOGHAT	
			British rock quartet led by Lonesome Dave Peverett (formerly with Savoy Brown). Settled in New York City in 1975.	
1/10/76	**20**	12	1. Slow Ride	Bearsville 0306
12/25/76†	**34**	4	2. Drivin' Wheel	Bearsville 0313
10/15/77	**33**	3	3. I Just Want To Make Love To You [R] live version of their 1972 hit (POS 83)	Bearsville 0319

DATE	POS	WKS	ARTIST—RECORD TITLE	LABEL & NO.
6/24/78	**36**	2	4. Stone Blue	Bearsville 0325
12/08/79†	**23**	10	5. Third Time Lucky (First Time I Was A Fool)	Bearsville 49125
			WAYNE FONTANA - see THE MINDBENDERS	
			THE FONTANE SISTERS	
			Trio from New Milford, New Jersey: sisters Marge, Bea and Geri, whose family name is Rosse. With Perry Como on radio, TV and recordings from 1945-54.	
12/11/54†	**1**(3)	20	1. **Hearts Of Stone** Juke Box #1(3) / Best Seller #1(1) / Jockey #2	Dot 15265
2/26/55	**13**	8	2. Rock Love Juke Box #13 / Best Seller #19	Dot 15333
6/04/55	**13**	6	3. Rollin' Stone Juke Box #13	Dot 15370
8/20/55	**3**	15	4. **Seventeen** Juke Box #3 / Best Seller #6 / Jockey #7 / Top 100 #15 pre	Dot 15386
11/26/55	**11**	11	5. Daddy-O Top 100 #11 / Juke Box #11 / Best Seller #13 / Jockey #18	Dot 15428
12/31/55	**36**	1	6. Nuttin' For Christmas [N]	Dot 15434
3/17/56	**11**	11	7. Eddie My Love Juke Box #11 / Top 100 #12 / Jockey #13 / Best Seller #15	Dot 15450
7/14/56	**38**	1	8. I'm In Love Again	Dot 15462
1/12/57	**13**	10	9. The Banana Boat Song Jockey #13 / Juke Box #14 / Top 100 #22	Dot 15527
4/28/58	**12**	9	10. Chanson d'Amour (Song Of Love) Jockey #12 / Top 100 #68	Dot 15736
			STEVE FORBERT	
			Born in 1955 in Meridian, Mississippi. Moved to New York City in 1976.	
1/05/80	**11**	12	1. Romeo's Tune	Nemperor 7525
			FORCE M.D.'S	
			Staten Island-based soul/rap quintet. Originally called Dr. Rock & The M.C.'s.	
3/01/86	**10**	11	1. **Tender Love** from the film "Krush Groove"	Warner 28818
			FRANKIE FORD	
			Born Frank Guzzo on 8/4/39 in Gretna, Louisiana. Vocal training since age 6; appeared with Sophie Tucker, Ted Lewis, and Carmen Miranda at local shows at an early age. Appeared in the film "American Hot Wax."	
3/09/59	**14**	12	1. Sea Cruise with Huey "Piano" Smith & The Clowns	Ace 554
			LITA FORD	
			Born in London. Lead guitarist of Los Angeles-based group the Runaways, at age 15, in 1975.	
5/14/88	**12**	10	1. Kiss Me Deadly	RCA 6866

DATE	POS	WKS	ARTIST—RECORD TITLE	LABEL & NO.
			TENNESSEE ERNIE FORD	
			Born Ernest Jennings Ford on 2/13/19 in Bristol, Tennessee. Began career as a disc jockey. Host of musical variety TV shows, 1955-65. America's favorite hymn singer.	
3/19/55	**5**	17	1. **Ballad Of Davy Crockett** Juke Box #5 / Best Seller #6 / Jockey #7 from the Walt Disney film "Davy Crockett"	Capitol 3058
11/12/55	**1**(8)	19	2. **Sixteen Tons** Juke Box #1(8) / Best Seller #1(7) / Top 100 #1(6) / Jockey #1(6)	Capitol 3262
3/10/56	**17**	1	3. That's All Jockey #17 / Top 100 #44	Capitol 3343
9/23/57	**23**	1	4. In The Middle Of An Island Jockey #23 / Top 100 #56	Capitol 3762
			FOREIGNER	
			British/American rock group formed in New York City, 1976. Consisted of Mick Jones (guitar), Lou Gramm (vocals), Ian McDonald (guitar, keyboards), Ed Gagliardi (bass), Al Greenwood (keyboards) and Dennis Elliott (drums). Most of material written by Jones (formerly with Spooky Tooth) and Gramm. Re-formed in 1980 with Jones, Gramm, Elliott and Rick Wills (bass). Gramm, Gagliardi and Greenwood are from New York.	
4/23/77	**4**	13	1. **Feels Like The First Time**	Atlantic 3394
8/13/77	**6**	15	2. **Cold As Ice**	Atlantic 3410
1/14/78	**20**	8	3. Long, Long Way From Home	Atlantic 3439
7/08/78	**3**	14	● 4. **Hot Blooded**	Atlantic 3488
9/30/78	**2**(2)	12	● 5. **Double Vision**	Atlantic 3514
1/20/79	**15**	8	6. Blue Morning, Blue Day	Atlantic 3543
9/22/79	**12**	9	7. Dirty White Boy	Atlantic 3618
11/24/79	**14**	9	8. Head Games	Atlantic 3633
7/11/81	**4**	17	9. **Urgent** sax solo: Jr. Walker	Atlantic 3831
10/17/81	**2**(10)	19	● 10. **Waiting For A Girl Like You**	Atlantic 3868
3/06/82	**26**	6	11. Juke Box Hero	Atlantic 4017
6/05/82	**26**	6	12. Break It Up	Atlantic 4044
12/15/84†	**1**(2)	16	● 13. **I Want To Know What Love Is** vocal backing: New Jersey Mass Choir and Jennifer Holliday	Atlantic 89596
3/23/85	**12**	10	14. That Was Yesterday	Atlantic 89571
12/26/87†	**6**	12	15. **Say You Will**	Atlantic 89169
4/09/88	**5**	11	16. **I Don't Want To Live Without You**	Atlantic 89101
			THE FORTUNES	
			English pop quintet led by Glen Dale and Barry Pritchard.	
9/11/65	**7**	8	1. **You've Got Your Troubles**	Press 9773
11/27/65	**27**	4	2. Here It Comes Again	Press 9798
6/19/71	**15**	9	3. Here Comes That Rainy Day Feeling Again	Capitol 3086
			DAVID FOSTER	
			Canadian keyboardist/composer/arranger. Member of the groups Skylark and Attitudes.	
10/05/85	**15**	10	1. Love Theme From St. Elmo's Fire [I] from the film "St. Elmo's Fire"	Atlantic 89528

DATE	POS	WKS	ARTIST—RECORD TITLE	LABEL & NO.
			THE FOUNDATIONS	
			British integrated R&B-rock group. Lead singer Clem Curtis (from Trinidad) replaced by Colin Young (West Indies) in 1968. Disbanded in 1970.	
1/13/68	**11**	10	1. Baby, Now That I've Found You	Uni 55038
1/18/69	**3**	13	● 2. **Build Me Up Buttercup**	Uni 55101
			FOUR ACES	
			Vocal group from Chester, Pennsylvania: Al Alberts (lead singer), Dave Mahoney (tenor), Sod Vaccaro (baritone) and Lou Silvestri (bass). Worked Ye Olde Mill near Philadelphia, late 1940s. First recorded for Victoria in 1951.	
1/15/55	**3**	21	1. **Melody Of Love** Juke Box #3 / Jockey #9 / Best Seller #11	Decca 29395
5/28/55	**13**	6	2. Heart Jockey #13 / Juke Box #20 / Best Seller #23 from the Broadway musical "Damn Yankees"	Decca 29476
8/27/55	**1**(6)	21	3. **Love Is A Many-Splendored Thing** Jockey #1(6) / Top 100 #1(3) / Juke Box #1(3) / Best Seller #1(2) from the William Holden/Jennifer Jones film of the same title	Decca 29625
12/03/55	**14**	12	4. A Woman In Love Jockey #14 / Top 100 #19 / Best Seller #20 from the film "Guys And Dolls"	Decca 29725
8/04/56	**22**	5	5. I Only Know I Love You Jockey #22 / Top 100 #35	Decca 29989
10/20/56	**20**	2	6. You Can't Run Away From It Jockey #20 / Top 100 #70 from the film of the same title	Decca 30041
			THE FOUR COINS	
			Vocal group of Greek descent from Canonsburg, Pennsylvania: George Mantalis, George Gregorakis, and brothers Michael & George Mahramas. In film "Disc Jockey Jamboree."	
1/15/55	**28**	1	1. I Love You Madly Best Seller #28	Epic 9082
12/10/55	**22**	8	2. Memories Of You Best Seller #22 / Top 10 #28 from the film "The Benny Goodman Story"	Epic 9129
6/17/57	**11**	14	3. Shangri-La Jockey #11 / Best Seller #22 / Top 100 #23	Epic 9213
10/14/57	**28**	4	4. My One Sin Best Seller #28 / Top 100 #29	Epic 9229
11/17/58	**21**	8	5. The World Outside introduced in 1942 film "Suicide Squadron" as "Warsaw Concerto"	Epic 9295
			THE FOUR ESQUIRES	
			Formed group at Boston University: Bill Courtney, Frank Mahoney, Bob Golden and Wally Gold.	
12/16/57	**25**	1	1. Love Me Forever Jockey #25 / Best Seller #44 / Top 100 #51	Paris 509
11/03/58	**21**	6	2. Hideaway	Paris 520

DATE	POS	WKS	ARTIST—RECORD TITLE	LABEL & NO.
			THE FOUR FRESHMEN	
			Jazz-styled vocal and instrumental group formed in 1948 while at Arthur Jordan Conservatory of Music in Indianapolis. Consisted of brothers Ross & Don Barbour, their cousin Bob Flanigan and Ken Errair.	
6/09/56	**17**	7	1. Graduation Day Jockey #17 / Best Seller #25 / Top 100 #27	Capitol 3410
			FOUR JACKS & A JILL	
			South African quintet; Jill is Glenys Lynne (lead singer).	
5/18/68	**18**	7	1. Master Jack	RCA 9473
			THE FOUR KNIGHTS - see NAT KING COLE	
			THE FOUR LADS	
			Vocal group from Toronto, Canada: Bernie Toorish (lead tenor), Jimmie Arnold (second tenor), Frankie Busseri (baritone) and Connie Codarini (bass). Sang in choir at St. Michael's Cathedral in Toronto. Worked local hotels and clubs. Worked Le Ruban Bleu in New York City. Signed as back-up singers by Columbia in 1950. Backed Johnnie Ray on his #1 hit "Cry."	
9/03/55	**2**(6)	25	1. **Moments To Remember** Jockey #2 / Best Seller #3 / Top 100 #3 / Juke Box #4	Columbia 40539
1/28/56	**2**(4)	19	2. **No, Not Much!** Jockey #2 / Top 100 #3 / Best Seller #4 / Juke Box #4	Columbia 40629
4/28/56	**3**	18	3. **Standing On The Corner/** Best Seller #3 / Top 100 #3 / Jockey #3 / Juke Box #3 from the Broadway musical "The Most Happy Fella"	
4/28/56	**22**	12	4. My Little Angel Best Seller #22 / Jockey #24 / Top 100 #30	Columbia 40674
9/15/56	**16**	6	5. A House With Love In It/ Best Seller #16 / Jockey #20 / Top 100 #23	
9/15/56	**17**	6	6. The Bus Stop Song (A Paper Of Pins) Jockey #17 / Best Seller #22 / Top 100 #23 from the Marilyn Monroe film "Bus Stop"	Columbia 40736
2/02/57	**9**	15	7. **Who Needs You** Jockey #9 / Best Seller #13 / Top 100 #14 / Juke Box #17	Columbia 40811
5/20/57	**17**	4	8. I Just Don't Know Jockey #17 / Top 100 #22	Columbia 40914
12/09/57†	**8**	9	9. **Put A Light In The Window** Jockey #8 / Top 100 #35 / Best Seller #39	Columbia 41058
4/07/58	**10**	7	10. **There's Only One Of You** Jockey #10 / Top 100 #41 / Best Seller #43	Columbia 41136
7/14/58	**12**	6	11. Enchanted Island Jockey #12 / Hot 100 #29 / Best Seller #32 from the Jane Powell film of the same title	Columbia 41194
11/24/58	**32**	3	12. The Mocking Bird [R] new version of their 1952 (POS 23) and 1956 (POS 67) hits	Columbia 41266
			THE FOUR PREPS	
			Vocal group formed while at Hollywood High School: Bruce Belland, Glen Larson, Ed Cobb and Marvin Ingraham. Belland was later in duo with Dave Somerville of the Diamonds.	
1/20/58	**2**(3)	14	1. **26 Miles (Santa Catalina)** Jockey #2 / Top 100 #4 / Best Seller #5	Capitol 3845
5/05/58	**3**	14	2. **Big Man** Jockey #3 / Top 100 #5 / Best Seller #6	Capitol 3960

DATE	POS	WKS	ARTIST—RECORD TITLE	LABEL & NO.
9/01/58	**21**	6	3. Lazy Summer Night Hot 100 #21 / Best Seller #34 from the film "Andy Hardy Comes Home"	Capitol 4023
1/11/60	**13**	11	4. Down By The Station	Capitol 4312
5/16/60	**24**	3	5. Got A Girl [N]	Capitol 4362
9/11/61	**17**	4	6. More Money For You And Me [N] Mr. Blue/Alley Oop/Smoke Gets In Your Eyes/In This Whole Wide World/A Worried Man/Tom Dooley/A Teenager In Love	Capitol 4599
			THE 4 SEASONS	
			Vocal group formed in Newark, New Jersey. In 1955, lead singer Frankie Valli (Francis Castelluccio) formed the Variatones with brothers Nick and Tommy DeVito, and Hank Majewski. Changed name to The Four Lovers in 1956. Bob Gaudio (of The Royal Teens) joined as keyboardist and songwriter in 1959, replacing Nick DeVito. Nick Massi replaced Majewski, and their 1961 lineup was set: Valli, Gaudio, Massi and Tommy DeVito. Group had been doing session work for their producer Bob Crewe and took their new name from a New Jersey bowling alley, The Four Seasons. In 1965, Nick Massi was replaced by the group's arranger Charlie Callelo and then by Joe Long. In 1971, Tommy DeVito retired, and Gaudio left (as a performer) the following year. Numerous personnel changes from then on. Also recorded as The Wonder Who?	
9/01/62	**1**(5)	12	1. **Sherry**	Vee-Jay 456
10/27/62	**1**(5)	14	2. **Big Girls Don't Cry**	Vee-Jay 465
12/22/62	**23**	2	3. Santa Claus Is Coming To Town [X] #12 hit for George Hall in 1934	Vee-Jay 478
1/26/63	**1**(3)	12	4. **Walk Like A Man**	Vee-Jay 485
5/04/63	**22**	6	5. Ain't That A Shame!	Vee-Jay 512
7/20/63	**3**	10	6. **Candy Girl/**	
8/10/63	**36**	3	7. Marlena	Vee-Jay 539
11/02/63	**36**	2	8. New Mexican Rose	Vee-Jay 562
2/08/64	**3**	11	9. **Dawn (Go Away)**	Philips 40166
3/07/64	**16**	8	10. Stay	Vee-Jay 582
4/18/64	**6**	8	11. **Ronnie**	Philips 40185
6/27/64	**1**(2)	11	● 12. **Rag Doll**	Philips 40211
6/27/64	**28**	5	13. Alone	Vee-Jay 597
9/05/64	**10**	6	14. **Save It For Me**	Philips 40225
11/21/64	**20**	5	15. Big Man In Town	Philips 40238
1/30/65	**12**	6	16. Bye, Bye, Baby (Baby Goodbye)	Philips 40260
7/10/65	**30**	3	17. Girl Come Running	Philips 40305
10/30/65	**3**	12	18. **Let's Hang On!**	Philips 40317
11/27/65	**12**	8	19. Don't Think Twice **THE WONDER WHO?**	Philips 40324
2/12/66	**9**	6	20. **Working My Way Back To You**	Philips 40350
5/28/66	**13**	7	21. Opus 17 (Don't You Worry 'Bout Me)	Philips 40370
9/17/66	**9**	8	22. **I've Got You Under My Skin** there were 2 top 10 versions of this Cole Porter classic in 1936	Philips 40393
12/24/66†	**10**	8	23. **Tell It To The Rain**	Philips 40412
3/18/67	**16**	7	24. Beggin'	Philips 40433
6/17/67	**9**	8	25. **C'mon Marianne**	Philips 40460
11/18/67	**30**	4	26. Watch The Flowers Grow	Philips 40490
3/09/68	**24**	5	27. Will You Love Me Tomorrow	Philips 40523

DATE	POS	WKS	ARTIST—RECORD TITLE	LABEL & NO.
9/20/75	3	12	28. **Who Loves You**	Warner 8122
1/31/76	1(3)	15	● 29. **December, 1963 (Oh, What a Night)**	Warner 8168
7/04/76	38	2	30. Silver Star above 2: lead vocals by Gerri Polci	Warner 8203
			FOUR TOPS	
			Native Detroit group formed in 1954 as the Four Aims. Consisted of Levi Stubbs (lead singer), Renaldo "Obie" Benson, Lawrence Payton and Abdul "Duke" Fakir. First recorded for Chess in 1956, then Red Top and Columbia, before signing with Motown in 1963. Group has had no personnel changes since its formation. Stubbs is the voice of Audrey II (the voracious vegetation) in the 1986 film "Little Shop of Horrors."	
8/29/64	11	10	1. Baby I Need Your Loving	Motown 1062
2/20/65	24	6	2. Ask The Lonely	Motown 1073
5/22/65	1(2)	13	3. **I Can't Help Myself**	Motown 1076
8/07/65	5	8	4. **It's The Same Old Song**	Motown 1081
11/20/65	19	6	5. Something About You	Motown 1084
3/12/66	18	6	6. Shake Me, Wake Me (When It's Over)	Motown 1090
9/17/66	1(2)	12	7. **Reach Out I'll Be There**	Motown 1098
12/24/66†	6	9	8. **Standing In The Shadows Of Love**	Motown 1102
3/18/67	4	8	9. **Bernadette**	Motown 1104
6/03/67	14	6	10. 7 Rooms Of Gloom	Motown 1110
9/30/67	19	5	11. You Keep Running Away	Motown 1113
2/17/68	14	6	12. Walk Away Renee	Motown 1119
5/11/68	20	6	13. If I Were A Carpenter	Motown 1124
5/30/70	24	8	14. It's All In The Game	Motown 1164
9/26/70	11	10	15. Still Water (Love)	Motown 1170
12/12/70†	14	8	16. River Deep - Mountain High **THE SUPREMES & FOUR TOPS**	Motown 1173
2/27/71	40	2	17. Just Seven Numbers (Can Straighten Out My Life)	Motown 1175
10/02/71	38	3	18. MacArthur Park (Part II)	Motown 1189
12/02/72†	10	9	19. **Keeper Of The Castle**	Dunhill 4330
2/24/73	4	12	● 20. **Ain't No Woman (Like The One I've Got)**	Dunhill 4339
7/28/73	15	8	21. Are You Man Enough from the film "Shaft In Africa"	Dunhill 4354
11/17/73	33	3	22. Sweet Understanding Love	Dunhill 4366
9/19/81	11	11	23. When She Was My Girl	Casablanca 2338
10/01/88	35	2	24. Indestructible tune used by NBC-TV for the 1988 Summer Olympics	Arista 9706
			THE FOUR VOICES	
3/17/56	20	4	1. Lovely One Best Seller #20 / Top 100 #30	Columbia 40643
			SAMANTHA FOX	
			British; born in 1966. Rose to stardom as a topless model for the U.K. "Daily Sun" newspaper.	
12/20/86†	4	13	1. **Touch Me (I Want Your Body)**	Jive 1006
4/02/88	3	14	2. **Naughty Girls (Need Love Too)**	Jive 1089
12/17/88†	8	12	● 3. **I Wanna Have Some Fun** above 2: written, arranged and produced by Full Force	Jive 1154

DATE	POS	WKS	ARTIST—RECORD TITLE	LABEL & NO.
			INEZ FOXX	
			Born on 9/9/42 in Greensboro, North Carolina. Sang with the Gospel Tide Chorus. Accompanied vocally by her brother Charlie Fox (b: 10/23/39).	
8/03/63	**7**	10	1. **Mockingbird**	Symbol 919
			FOXY	
			Miami-based Latino dance band. 4 of 5 members came to Florida with the Cuban emigrees of 1959.	
8/26/78	**9**	13	1. **Get Off**	Dash 5046
4/28/79	**21**	9	2. Hot Number	Dash 5050
			PETER FRAMPTON	
			Born on 4/22/50 in Beckenham, England. Vocalist/guitarist/composer. Joined British band The Herd at age 16, before forming Humble Pie in 1969, which he left in 1971 to form Frampton's Camel.	
3/13/76	**6**	14	1. **Show Me The Way**	A&M 1795
7/17/76	**12**	11	2. Baby, I Love Your Way	A&M 1832
10/09/76	**10**	10	3. **Do You Feel Like We Do** above 3: recorded live at San Francisco's Winterland	A&M 1867
6/11/77	**2**(3)	13	4. **I'm In You**	A&M 1941
9/10/77	**18**	10	5. Signed, Sealed, Delivered (I'm Yours)	A&M 1972
6/09/79	**14**	9	6. I Can't Stand It No More	A&M 2148
			CONNIE FRANCIS	
			Born Concetta Rosa Maria Franconero on 12/12/38 in Newark, New Jersey. First recorded for MGM in 1955. Films: "Where The Boys Are," "Follow The Boys," "Looking For Love" and "When The Boys Meet The Girls," 1961-65. Connie stopped performing after she was raped on 11/8/74, for which she was awarded $3,000,000 in damages. Began comeback with a performance on "Dick Clark's Live Wednesday" TV show in 1978.	
3/03/58	**4**	15	1. **Who's Sorry Now** Top 100 #4 / Best Seller #5 / Jockey #6 there were 5 top 20 versions of this tune in 1923	MGM 12588
6/09/58	**36**	2	2. I'm Sorry I Made You Cry Top 100 #36 / Best Seller #39 #1 hit for Henry Burr in 1918	MGM 12647
8/04/58	**14**	11	3. Stupid Cupid Best Seller #14 / Hot 100 #17	MGM 12683
11/17/58	**30**	1	4. Fallin'	MGM 12713
12/15/58†	**2**(2)	14	5. **My Happiness** there were 5 top 30 versions of this tune in 1948	MGM 12738
3/30/59	**22**	4	6. If I Didn't Care #2 hit for the Ink Spots in 1939	MGM 12769
6/01/59	**5**	12	7. **Lipstick On Your Collar/**	
6/01/59	**9**	11	8. Frankie	MGM 12793
9/21/59	**34**	4	9. You're Gonna Miss Me	MGM 12824
12/07/59	**7**	11	10. **Among My Souvenirs/** there were 4 top 20 versions of this song in 1928	
12/21/59	**36**	2	11. God Bless America the Irving Berlin classic, popularized by Kate Smith in 1939	MGM 12841
3/14/60	**8**	9	12. **Mama/**	
3/28/60	**17**	6	13. Teddy	MGM 12878
5/16/60	**1**(2)	16	14. **Everybody's Somebody's Fool/**	
6/06/60	**19**	8	15. Jealous Of You [F]	MGM 12899

DATE	POS	WKS	ARTIST—RECORD TITLE	LABEL & NO.
8/22/60	**1**(2)	14	16. **My Heart Has A Mind Of Its Own**	MGM 12923
11/21/60	**7**	10	17. **Many Tears Ago**	MGM 12964
1/30/61	**4**	12	18. **Where The Boys Are/** from the film of the same title	
2/20/61	**34**	2	19. No One	MGM 12971
4/24/61	**7**	9	20. **Breakin' In A Brand New Broken Heart**	MGM 12995
7/03/61	**6**	9	21. **Together** #1 hit for Paul Whiteman in 1928	MGM 13019
10/09/61	**14**	7	22. (He's My) Dreamboat	MGM 13039
12/04/61†	**10**	9	23. **When The Boy In Your Arms (Is The Boy In Your Heart)/**	
1/06/62†	**26**	1	24. Baby's First Christmas [X]	MGM 13051
2/24/62	**1**(1)	10	25. **Don't Break The Heart That Loves You**	MGM 13059
5/19/62	**7**	7	26. **Second Hand Love**	MGM 13074
8/11/62	**9**	6	27. **Vacation**	MGM 13087
11/03/62	**24**	4	28. I Was Such A Fool (To Fall In Love With You)	MGM 13096
1/05/63	**18**	6	29. I'm Gonna' Be Warm This Winter	MGM 13116
3/16/63	**17**	7	30. Follow The Boys from the film of the same title	MGM 13127
6/08/63	**23**	5	31. If My Pillow Could Talk	MGM 13143
8/31/63	**36**	3	32. Drownin' My Sorrows	MGM 13160
11/09/63	**28**	4	33. Your Other Love	MGM 13176
3/07/64	**24**	6	34. Blue Winter	MGM 13214
5/30/64	**25**	5	35. Be Anything (But Be Mine)	MGM 13237
			FRANKE & THE KNOCKOUTS	
			Soft-rock quintet led by Franke Previte of New Brunswick, New Jersey.	
3/28/81	**10**	14	1. **Sweetheart**	Millennium 11801
8/01/81	**27**	5	2. You're My Girl	Millennium 11808
5/08/82	**24**	7	3. Without You (Not Another Lonely Night)	Millennium 13105
			FRANKIE GOES TO HOLLYWOOD	
			Rock quintet from Liverpool, England of gay persona; vocals by Holly Johnson and Paul Rutherford.	
2/02/85	**10**	10	1. **Relax** **[R]** originally charted in 1984 (POS 67)	Island 99805
			ARETHA FRANKLIN	
			Born on 3/25/42 in Memphis; raised in Buffalo and Detroit. Daughter of Rev. Cecil L. Franklin, pastor of New Bethel Church in Detroit. First recorded for JVB/Battle in 1956. Signed to Columbia Records in 1960 by John Hammond, then dramatic turn in style and success after signing with Atlantic and working with producer Jerry Wexler. Appeared in the 1980 film "The Blues Brothers." Inducted into the Rock And Roll Hall Of Fame in 1987. The all-time Queen of Soul Music.	
11/20/61	**37**	2	1. Rock-A-Bye Your Baby With A Dixie Melody #1 hit for Al Jolson in 1918	Columbia 42157
3/18/67	**9**	9	• 2. **I Never Loved A Man (The Way I Love You)**	Atlantic 2386
5/06/67	**1**(2)	11	• 3. **Respect**	Atlantic 2403
8/05/67	**4**	8	• 4. **Baby I Love You**	Atlantic 2427
10/07/67	**8**	8	5. **A Natural Woman (You Make Me Feel Like)**	Atlantic 2441
12/16/67†	**2**(2)	11	• 6. **Chain Of Fools**	Atlantic 2464

DATE	POS	WKS	ARTIST—RECORD TITLE	LABEL & NO.
3/02/68	**5**	12	● 7. **(Sweet Sweet Baby) Since You've Been Gone/**	
4/13/68	**16**	7	8. Ain't No Way	Atlantic 2486
			written by Aretha's sister, Carolyn Franklin (d: 4/25/88 [43])	
5/25/68	**7**	9	● 9. **Think**	Atlantic 2518
8/24/68	**6**	8	10. **The House That Jack Built/**	
8/24/68	**10**	10	● 11. I Say A Little Prayer	Atlantic 2546
11/23/68	**14**	8	● 12. See Saw/	
12/28/68†	**31**	2	13. My Song	Atlantic 2574
3/01/69	**19**	6	14. The Weight	Atlantic 2603
4/26/69	**28**	6	15. I Can't See Myself Leaving You	Atlantic 2619
8/09/69	**13**	9	16. Share Your Love With Me	Atlantic 2650
11/15/69	**17**	7	17. Eleanor Rigby	Atlantic 2683
2/28/70	**13**	9	18. Call Me	Atlantic 2706
6/13/70	**23**	5	19. Spirit In The Dark	Atlantic 2731
8/22/70	**11**	8	● 20. Don't Play That Song	Atlantic 2751
			19 & 20: with The Dixie Flyers	
12/19/70	**37**	2	21. Border Song (Holy Moses)	Atlantic 2772
3/06/71	**19**	7	22. You're All I Need To Get By	Atlantic 2787
4/24/71	**6**	11	● 23. **Bridge Over Troubled Water**	Atlantic 2796
8/07/71	**2**(2)	11	● 24. **Spanish Harlem**	Atlantic 2817
11/06/71	**9**	8	● 25. **Rock Steady**	Atlantic 2838
3/25/72	**5**	11	● 26. **Day Dreaming**	Atlantic 2866
6/17/72	**26**	6	27. All The King's Horses	Atlantic 2883
3/10/73	**33**	5	28. Master Of Eyes (The Deepness Of Your Eyes)	Atlantic 2941
7/21/73	**20**	10	29. Angel	Atlantic 2969
12/15/73†	**3**	17	● 30. **Until You Come Back To Me (That's What I'm Gonna Do)**	Atlantic 2995
5/04/74	**19**	8	31. I'm In Love	Atlantic 2999
7/10/76	**28**	6	32. Something He Can Feel	Atlantic 3326
9/11/82	**24**	6	33. Jump To It	Arista 0699
7/06/85	**3**	13	34. **Freeway Of Love**	Arista 9354
10/12/85	**7**	13	35. **Who's Zoomin' Who**	Arista 9410
11/02/85	**18**	8	36. Sisters Are Doin' It For Themselves	RCA 14214
			EURYTHMICS & ARETHA FRANKLIN	
2/15/86	**22**	7	37. Another Night	Arista 9453
10/11/86	**21**	6	38. Jumpin' Jack Flash	Arista 9528
			new version of Rolling Stones' 1968 hit (POS #3); produced by Keith Richards; from the film "Jumpin' Jack Flash"	
1/24/87	**28**	4	39. Jimmy Lee	Arista 9546
3/07/87	**1**(2)	12	40. **I Knew You Were Waiting (For Me)**	Arista 9559
			ARETHA FRANKLIN & GEORGE MICHAEL	

DATE	POS	WKS	ARTIST—RECORD TITLE	LABEL & NO.
			WENDY FRASER - see PATRICK SWAYZE	
			STAN FREBERG	
			Born on 8/7/26 in Los Angeles. Began career doing impersonations on Cliffie Stone's radio show in 1943. Did cartoon voices for the major film studios. His first in a long string of brilliant satirical recordings was "John And Marsha" in 1951. Launched highly successful advertising career, early 60s; winner of 21 Clio awards.	
10/22/55	**16**	2	1. The Yellow Rose Of Texas [C] Jockey #16 / Top 100 #47 pre backing by Jud Conlon's Rhythmaires and Billy May's orchestra; Alvin Stoller, drummer	Capitol 3249
4/27/57	**25**	1	2. Banana Boat (Day-O) [C] Best Seller #25 / Top 100 #43 interruptions by Peter Leeds	Capitol 3687
11/18/57	**32**	3	3. Wun'erful, Wun'erful! (Sides uh-one & uh-two) [C] Best Seller #32 / Top 100 #36 Bubbles In The Wine/Thank You/Louise/Please/Moonlight & Shadows	Capitol 3815
			JOHN FRED & His Playboy Band	
			John Fred Gourrier was born on 5/8/41 in Baton Rouge, Louisiana. Formed The Playboys in 1956 as a white band playing R&B music. John played basketball at LSU, and his father, Fred Gourrier, played baseball with the Detroit Tigers.	
12/16/67†	**1**(2)	13	● 1. **Judy In Disguise (With Glasses)** a parody of The Beatles' "Lucy In The Sky With Diamonds"	Paula 282
			FREDDIE & THE DREAMERS	
			Freddie Garrity was born on 11/14/40 in Manchester, England. Formed The Dreamers in 1961, consisting of Garrity (lead singer), Derek Quinn (lead guitar), Roy Crewsdon (guitar), Peter Birrell (bass) and Bernie Dwyer (drums).	
3/27/65	**1**(2)	8	1. **I'm Telling You Now**	Tower 125
4/24/65	**36**	2	2. I Understand (Just How You Feel)	Mercury 72377
5/15/65	**18**	5	3. Do The Freddie	Mercury 72428
5/15/65	**21**	5	4. You Were Made For Me	Tower 127
			FREE	
			British band formed in 1968: Paul Rodgers (vocals), Paul Kossoff (guitar), Simon Kirke (drums) and Andy Fraser (bass). Kossoff left to form Back Street Crawler, but died of drug-induced heart failure in 1976. Rodgers and Kirke formed Bad Company in 1974.	
9/05/70	**4**	13	1. **All Right Now**	A&M 1206
			THE FREE MOVEMENT	
			Los Angeles-based vocal sextet. Several members formerly with gospel groups.	
9/18/71	**5**	11	1. **I've Found Someone Of My Own**	Decca 32818
			BOBBY FREEMAN	
			Born on 6/13/40 in San Francisco. R&B singer; formed vocal group the Romancers at age 14, and later formed R&B group the Vocaleers.	
5/26/58	**5**	12	1. **Do You Want To Dance** Top 100 #5 / Best Seller #6 / Jockey #11	Josie 835
8/18/58	**37**	1	2. Betty Lou Got A New Pair Of Shoes Hot 100 #37 / Best Seller #40	Josie 841
9/26/60	**37**	3	3. (I Do The) Shimmy Shimmy	King 5373
7/25/64	**5**	10	4. **C'mon And Swim**	Autumn 2

DATE	POS	WKS	ARTIST—RECORD TITLE	LABEL & NO.
			ERNIE FREEMAN	
			Born on 8/16/22 in Cleveland. Died on 5/16/81 in North Hollywood of a heart attack. Pianist/composer/conductor for many top artists, including Frank Sinatra, Dean Martin, Sammy Davis, Jr. and Connie Francis. Also see B. Bumble.	
11/18/57	**4**	12	1. **Raunchy** **[I]** Jockey #4 / Best Seller #11 / Top 100 #12	Imperial 5474
			ACE FREHLEY	
			Born on 4/27/51 in the Bronx. Kiss' lead guitarist until 1983.	
12/02/78†	**13**	12	1. New York Groove	Casablanca 941
			GLENN FREY	
			Born on 11/6/48 in Detroit. Singer/songwriter/guitarist. Founding member of the Eagles. Appeared in episodes of TV's "Miami Vice."	
7/17/82	**31**	5	1. I Found Somebody	Asylum 47466
9/11/82	**15**	11	2. The One You Love	Asylum 69974
7/14/84	**20**	9	3. Sexy Girl	MCA 52413
1/19/85	2(1)	13	4. **The Heat Is On** from the film "Beverly Hills Cop"	MCA 52512
5/04/85	**12**	11	5. Smuggler's Blues	MCA 52546
9/28/85	2(2)	13	6. **You Belong To The City** above 2: from TV's "Miami Vice" soundtrack	MCA 52651
9/10/88	**13**	9	7. True Love	MCA 53363
			FRIDA	
			Born Annifrid Lyngstad on 11/15/45 in Norway. Member of Abba.	
2/12/83	**13**	12	1. I Know There's Something Going On produced by Phil Collins	Atlantic 89984
			DEAN FRIEDMAN	
			Singer/songwriter from New Jersey.	
5/21/77	**26**	10	1. Ariel	Lifesong 45022
			FRIEND AND LOVER	
			Husband and wife duo: James and Cathy Post.	
6/01/68	**10**	11	1. **Reach Out Of The Darkness**	Verve Fore. 5069
			THE FRIENDS OF DISTINCTION	
			Los Angeles-based soul-MOR group. Original lineup: Floyd Butler (b: 6/5/41, San Diego), Harry Elston (b: 11/4/38, Dallas), Jessica Cleaves (b: 12/10/48, Los Angeles) and Barbara Jean Love (b: 7/24/41, Los Angeles). Butler and Elston were in the Hi Fi's with LaMonte McLemore and Marilyn McCoo (later with The Fifth Dimension).	
4/26/69	**3**	13	● 1. **Grazing In The Grass**	RCA 0107
10/11/69	**15**	12	● 2. Going In Circles	RCA 0204
3/21/70	**6**	11	3. **Love Or Let Me Be Lonely**	RCA 0319
			FRIJID PINK	
			Rock group formed in Detroit; Kelly Green, lead singer.	
2/21/70	**7**	11	● 1. **House Of The Rising Sun**	Parrot 341
			MAX FROST & THE TROOPERS	
			Max Frost is actually movie and TV star Christopher Jones.	
9/28/68	**22**	9	1. Shape Of Things To Come from the film "Wild In The Streets" (starring Chris Jones)	Tower 419

DATE	POS	WKS	ARTIST—RECORD TITLE	LABEL & NO.
			BOBBY FULLER FOUR	
			Bobby was born on 10/22/43 in Baytown, Texas and died mysteriously of asphyxiation in Los Angeles on 7/18/66. Band formed in El Paso and featured Bobby (lead vocals, guitar) and his brother Randy (bass).	
2/12/66	**9**	8	1. **I Fought The Law**	Mustang 3014
5/07/66	**26**	3	2. Love's Made A Fool Of You written by Buddy Holly	Mustang 3016
			FUNKADELIC	
			Funk aggregation formed in 1968, consisting of The Parliaments plus a backing band. While recording for Westbound, group also recorded for Invictus as Parliament in 1971. Formed corporation "A Parliafunkadelicament Thang" through which they recorded under both names. By 1974, leader/producer George Clinton reorganized the Parliament/Funkadelic corporation to include varying membership. Also see Parliament and The Parliaments.	
11/04/78	**28**	5	● 1. One Nation Under A Groove (Part 1)	Warner 8618
			RICHIE FURAY	
			Born on 5/9/44 in Yello Springs, Ohio. Member of Buffalo Springfield, Poco, and The Souther, Hillman, Furay Band.	
12/15/79	**39**	3	1. I Still Have Dreams	Asylum 46534
			THE FUZZ	
			Black female trio from Washington, DC: Sheila Young, Barbara Gilliam and Val Williams. Originally called the Passionettes.	
4/17/71	**21**	8	1. I Love You For All Seasons	Calla 174
			G	
			PETER GABRIEL	
			Born on 5/13/50 in London. Lead singer of Genesis from 1966-75.	
12/04/82†	**29**	10	1. Shock The Monkey	Geffen 29883
5/31/86	**1**(1)	14	2. **Sledgehammer**	Geffen 28718
9/27/86	**26**	7	3. In Your Eyes	Geffen 28622
1/24/87	**8**	11	4. **Big Time**	Geffen 28503
			THE GADABOUTS	
8/04/56	**39**	1	1. Stranded In The Jungle [N]	Mercury 70898
			SUNNY GALE	
			Singer from Clayton, New Jersey. Began career with Hal McIntyre's band.	
1/08/55	**17**	1	1. Let Me Go, Lover! Jockey #17	RCA 5952
			GALLERY	
			Pop sextet from Detroit led by Jim Gold (lead singer, guitar).	
4/29/72	**4**	13	● 1. **Nice To Be With You**	Sussex 232
10/07/72	**22**	8	2. I Believe In Music	Sussex 239
2/10/73	**23**	8	3. Big City Miss Ruth Ann	Sussex 248

DATE	POS	WKS	ARTIST—RECORD TITLE	LABEL & NO.
			FRANK GALLOP	
			Best known as the announcer on Perry Como's TV shows during the 50s.	
5/07/66	**34**	5	1. The Ballad Of Irving [C]	Kapp 745
			THE GAP BAND	
			Soul trio from Tulsa, Oklahoma consisting of brothers Charles, Ronnie and Robert Wilson. Named for three streets in Tulsa: Greenwood, Archer and Pine.	
7/03/82	**24**	6	1. Early In The Morning	Total Exp. 8201
9/11/82	**31**	7	2. You Dropped A Bomb On Me	Total Exp. 8203
			DAVE GARDNER	
			Born on 6/11/26 in Jackson, Tennessee. "Brother Dave" had 6 comedy albums chart in the early 60s.	
7/22/57	**22**	4	1. White Silver Sands Best Seller #22 / Top 100 #28	OJ 1002
			DON GARDNER & DEE DEE FORD	
			Black vocal duo from Philadelphia. Gardner formed his own group, the Sonotones, in 1952 and recorded for Gotham and Bruce. Ford also plays organ and piano.	
7/07/62	**20**	7	1. I Need Your Loving	Fire 508
			ART GARFUNKEL	
			Born on 10/13/42 in Queens, New York. Appeared in films "Catch 22," "Carnal Knowledge" and "Bad Timing." Has Masters degree in Math from Columbia University. Also see Simon & Garfunkel.	
10/06/73	**9**	10	1. **All I Know**	Columbia 45926
2/09/74	**38**	1	2. I Shall Sing	Columbia 45983
10/19/74	**34**	3	3. Second Avenue	Columbia 10020
			above 3 shown only as: **GARFUNKEL**	
9/27/75	**18**	12	4. I Only Have Eyes For You	Columbia 10190
1/31/76	**39**	2	5. Break Away	Columbia 10273
2/11/78	**17**	7	6. (What A) Wonderful World **ART GARFUNKEL with JAMES TAYLOR & PAUL SIMON**	Columbia 10676
			FRANK GARI	
			Born on 4/1/42 in New York City. Appeared in several films in the late 50s.	
2/13/61	**27**	5	1. Utopia	Crusade 1020
5/15/61	**23**	6	2. Lullaby Of Love	Crusade 1021
8/14/61	**30**	3	3. Princess	Crusade 1022
			GALE GARNETT	
			Born on 7/17/42 in Auckland, New Zealand. Came to the United States in 1951. Worked as an actress from age 15. Appeared on many TV shows.	
9/05/64	**4**	13	1. **We'll Sing In The Sunshine**	RCA 8388
			LEIF GARRETT	
			Born on 11/8/61 in Hollywood, California. Began film career in 1969; appeared in all 3 "Walking Tall" films.	
9/17/77	**20**	8	1. Surfin' USA	Atlantic 3423
12/03/77†	**13**	9	2. Runaround Sue	Atlantic 3440
12/09/78†	**10**	15	3. **I Was Made For Dancin'**	Scotti Br. 403

DATE	POS	WKS	ARTIST—RECORD TITLE	LABEL & NO.
			DAVID GATES	
			Born on 12/11/40 in Tulsa, Oklahoma. Began career as a session musician, then did songwriting and record producing before becoming the lead singer of Bread. Wrote The Murmaids' hit "Popsicles & Icicles."	
2/15/75	**29**	5	1. Never Let Her Go	Elektra 45223
2/18/78	**15**	12	2. Goodbye Girl title song from the Neil Simon film	Elektra 45450
10/07/78	**30**	5	3. Took The Last Train	Elektra 45500
			MARVIN GAYE	
			Born Marvin Pentz Gay, Jr. on 4/2/39 in Washington, DC. Sang in his father's Apostolic church. In vocal groups the Rainbows and Marquees. Joined Harvey Fuqua in the reformed Moonglows. To Detroit in 1960. Session work as drummer at Motown; married to Berry Gordy's sister Anna, 1961-75. First recorded under own name for Tamla in 1961. In seclusion for several months following the death of Tammi Terrell, 1970. Problems with drugs and the IRS led to his moving to Europe for 3 years. Fatally shot by his father after a quarrel on 4/1/84 in Los Angeles. Inducted into the Rock And Roll Hall Of Fame in 1987. Sang numerous duets with soul singer Tammi Terrell (b: 1946, Philadelphia; d: 3/16/70).	
3/02/63	**30**	3	1. Hitch Hike	Tamla 54075
6/15/63	**10**	10	2. **Pride And Joy**	Tamla 54079
11/23/63	**22**	10	3. Can I Get A Witness	Tamla 54087
3/28/64	**15**	7	4. You're A Wonderful One	Tamla 54093
6/27/64	**15**	8	5. Try It Baby	Tamla 54095
10/10/64	**27**	6	6. Baby Don't You Do It	Tamla 54101
12/12/64†	**6**	11	7. **How Sweet It Is To Be Loved By You**	Tamla 54107
4/10/65	**8**	8	8. **I'll Be Doggone**	Tamla 54112
7/24/65	**25**	5	9. Pretty Little Baby	Tamla 54117
10/23/65	**8**	9	10. **Ain't That Peculiar**	Tamla 54122
3/12/66	**29**	4	11. One More Heartache	Tamla 54129
7/22/67	**33**	3	12. Your Unchanging Love	Tamla 54153
2/03/68	**34**	3	13. You	Tamla 54160
10/19/68	**32**	4	14. Chained	Tamla 54170
11/23/68	**1**(7)	15	15. **I Heard It Through The Grapevine**	Tamla 54176
5/10/69	**4**	13	16. **Too Busy Thinking About My Baby**	Tamla 54181
9/13/69	**7**	9	17. **That's The Way Love Is**	Tamla 54185
7/11/70	**40**	2	18. The End Of Our Road	Tamla 54195
3/06/71	**2**(3)	13	19. **What's Going On**	Tamla 54201
7/17/71	**4**	10	20. **Mercy Mercy Me (The Ecology)**	Tamla 54207
10/16/71	**9**	8	21. **Inner City Blues (Make Me Wanna Holler)**	Tamla 54209
12/30/72†	**7**	9	22. **Trouble Man** from the film of the same title	Tamla 54228
7/28/73	**1**(2)	17	23. **Let's Get It On**	Tamla 54234
11/17/73	**21**	8	24. Come Get To This	Tamla 54241
10/26/74	**28**	3	25. Distant Lover	Tamla 54253
5/08/76	**15**	9	26. I Want You	Tamla 54264
4/23/77	**1**(1)	15	27. **Got To Give It Up (Pt. I)**	Tamla 54280
			DIANA ROSS & MARVIN GAYE:	
10/13/73	**12**	10	28. You're A Special Part Of Me	Motown 1280
3/30/74	**19**	10	29. My Mistake (Was To Love You)	Motown 1269

DATE	POS	WKS	ARTIST—RECORD TITLE	LABEL & NO.
			MARVIN GAYE & TAMMI TERRELL:	
6/03/67	**19**	9	30. Ain't No Mountain High Enough	Tamla 54149
9/30/67	**5**	10	31. **Your Precious Love**	Tamla 54156
12/16/67†	**10**	9	32. **If I Could Build My Whole World Around You**	Tamla 54161
4/27/68	**8**	11	33. **Ain't Nothing Like The Real Thing**	Tamla 54163
8/10/68	**7**	10	34. **You're All I Need To Get By**	Tamla 54169
10/19/68	**24**	6	35. Keep On Lovin' Me Honey	Tamla 54173
2/15/69	**30**	4	36. Good Lovin' Ain't Easy To Come By	Tamla 54179
			MARVIN GAYE & MARY WELLS:	
5/23/64	**19**	6	37. Once Upon A Time/	
6/13/64	**17**	6	38. What's The Matter With You Baby	Motown 1057
11/20/82†	**3**	15	● 39. **Sexual Healing**	Columbia 03302
			MARVIN GAYE & KIM WESTON:	
2/04/67	**14**	7	40. It Takes Two	Tamla 54141
			CRYSTAL GAYLE	
			Born Brenda Gail Webb on 1/9/51 in Paintsville, Kentucky; raised in Wabash, Indiana. Youngest sister of Loretta Lynn. First country artist to tour China (1979).	
9/24/77	**2**(3)	18	● 1. **Don't It Make My Brown Eyes Blue**	United Art. 1016
9/02/78	**18**	11	2. Talking In Your Sleep	United Art. 1214
11/03/79	**15**	10	3. Half The Way	Columbia 11087
11/13/82†	**7**	21	4. **You And I**	Elektra 69936
			EDDIE RABBITT with CRYSTAL GAYLE	
			GLORIA GAYNOR	
			Born on 9/7/49 in Newark, New Jersey. With the Soul Satisfiers group in 1971.	
12/07/74†	**9**	10	1. **Never Can Say Goodbye**	MGM 14748
1/20/79	**1**(3)	17	▲ 2. **I Will Survive**	Polydor 14508
			THE G-CLEFS	
			Group from Roxbury, Massachusetts, consisting of brothers Teddy, Chris, Timmy and Arnold Scott, with Ray Gibson.	
9/15/56	**24**	1	1. Ka-Ding Dong Best Seller #24 / Top 100 #53	Pilgrim 715
10/16/61	**9**	11	2. **I Understand (Just How You Feel)** an adaptation of the "Auld Lang Syne" melody	Terrace 7500
			DAVID GEDDES	
			Formed the group Rock Garden as a teenager, who recorded for Capitol.	
8/23/75	**4**	9	1. **Run Joey Run**	Big Tree 16044
11/22/75	**18**	6	2. The Last Game Of The Season (A Blind Man In The Bleachers)	Big Tree 16052
			THE J. GEILS BAND	
			Rock group formed in Boston, 1967. Consisted of Jerome Geils (guitar), Peter "Wolf" Blankfield (vocals), "Magic Dick" Salwitz (harmonica), Seth Justman (keyboards), Danny Klein (bass) and Stephen Jo Bladd (drums). First recorded for Atlantic in 1969. Wolf left for a solo career in the fall of 1983.	
1/15/72	**39**	2	1. Looking For A Love	Atlantic 2844
5/26/73	**30**	6	2. Give It To Me	Atlantic 2953
11/23/74†	**12**	7	3. Must Of Got Lost	Atlantic 3214

DATE	POS	WKS	ARTIST—RECORD TITLE	LABEL & NO.
1/20/79	**35**	3	4. One Last Kiss	EMI America 8007
3/08/80	**32**	5	5. Come Back	EMI America 8032
5/24/80	**38**	3	6. Love Stinks	EMI America 8039
11/28/81†	**1**(6)	20	● 7. **Centerfold**	EMI America 8102
3/06/82	**4**	12	● 8. **Freeze-Frame**	EMI America 8108
7/03/82	**40**	2	9. Angel In Blue	EMI America 8100
12/11/82†	**24**	7	10. I Do	EMI America 8148
			GENE & DEBBE	
			Gene Thomas (b: 12/4/38, Palestine, TX) and Debbe Nevills.	
3/09/68	**17**	12	1. Playboy	TRX 5006
			GENERAL PUBLIC	
			Fronted by former English Beat vocalists Dave Wakeling and Ranking Roger (Roger Charley). Disbanded in March of 1987. Roger recorded solo in 1988.	
1/26/85	**27**	5	1. Tenderness	I.R.S. 9934
			GENESIS	
			Rock group formed in England in 1967. Consisted of Peter Gabriel (lead vocals), Anthony Phillips (guitar), Tony Banks (keyboards), Michael Rutherford (guitar, bass) and John Mayhew (drums). Phillips and Mayhew left after second album, replaced by Steve Hackett (guitar) and Phil Collins (drums). Gabriel left in June, 1975, with Collins replacing him as new lead singer. Hackett left in 1977, leaving group as a trio: Collins, Rutherford and Banks. Rutherford also in own group, Mike + The Mechanics, formed in 1985.	
6/03/78	**23**	5	1. Follow You Follow Me	Atlantic 3474
6/21/80	**14**	11	2. Misunderstanding	Atlantic 3662
11/07/81	**29**	6	3. No Reply At All	Atlantic 3858
1/23/82	**26**	6	4. Abacab	Atlantic 3891
5/08/82	**40**	2	5. Man On The Corner	Atlantic 4025
7/24/82	**32**	5	6. Paperlate	Atlantic 4053
12/10/83†	**6**	14	7. **That's All!**	Atlantic 89724
6/07/86	**1**(1)	12	8. **Invisible Touch**	Atlantic 89407
8/23/86	**4**	12	9. **Throwing It All Away**	Atlantic 89372
11/15/86†	**4**	15	10. **Land Of Confusion**	Atlantic 89336
2/21/87	**3**	10	11. **Tonight, Tonight, Tonight**	Atlantic 89290
5/02/87	**3**	12	12. **In Too Deep**	Atlantic 89316
			BOBBIE GENTRY	
			Born Roberta Streeter on 7/27/44 in Chickasaw County, Mississippi; raised in Greenwood, Mississippi. Singer/songwriter. Won the 1967 Best New Artist Grammy Award. Married singer Jim Stafford in 1978.	
8/12/67	**1**(4)	12	● 1. **Ode To Billie Joe**	Capitol 5950
			re-charted in 1976 (#54); a new version also charted in 1976 (#65)	
3/08/69	**36**	1	2. Let It Be Me	Capitol 2387
			GLEN CAMPBELL & BOBBIE GENTRY	
1/31/70	**31**	4	3. Fancy	Capitol 2675
3/14/70	**27**	6	4. All I Have To Do Is Dream	Capitol 2745
			BOBBIE GENTRY & GLEN CAMPBELL	

DATE	POS	WKS	ARTIST—RECORD TITLE	LABEL & NO.
			THE GENTRYS	
			Memphis-based rock band formed in 1963. Group featured Larry Raspberry as lead singer.	
9/25/65	**4**	11	1. **Keep On Dancing**	MGM 13379
			BARBARA GEORGE	
			Born on 8/16/42 in New Orleans. R&B singer/songwriter.	
12/18/61†	**3**	11	1. **I Know (You Don't Love Me No More)** cornet solo: Melvin Lastie	A.F.O. 302
			GEORGIA SATELLITES	
			Rock quartet formed in Atlanta in 1980. Led by Dan Baird (lead vocals), Rick Richards (lead guitar, vocals), Rick Price (bass) and Mauro Magellan (drums).	
12/20/86†	**2**(1)	14	1. **Keep Your Hands To Yourself**	Elektra 69502
			GERRY & THE PACEMAKERS	
			Pop-rock group formed in Liverpool, England, 1959: Gerry Marsden (b: 9/24/42; vocals, guitar), Leslie Maguire (piano), Les Chadwick (bass) and Freddie Marsden (drums). The Marsden brothers had been in skiffle bands; Gerry had own rock band, Mars-Bars, in 1958. Signed in 1962 by The Beatles' manager, Brian Epstein.	
6/06/64	**4**	9	1. **Don't Let The Sun Catch You Crying**	Laurie 3251
8/08/64	**9**	7	2. **How Do You Do It?**	Laurie 3261
10/17/64	**17**	6	3. I Like It	Laurie 3271
1/09/65	**14**	5	4. I'll Be There	Laurie 3279
2/13/65	**6**	9	5. **Ferry Across The Mersey**	Laurie 3284
4/24/65	**23**	5	6. It's Gonna Be Alright above 2: from the film "Ferry Cross The Mersey" (starring Gerry & The Pacemakers)	Laurie 3293
10/08/66	**28**	4	7. Girl On A Swing	Laurie 3354
			GET WET	
			Pop band featuring Sherri Beachfront as lead singer.	
5/23/81	**39**	2	1. Just So Lonely	Boardwalk 02018
			STAN GETZ	
			Born on 2/2/27 in Philadelphia. 17-time winner of Down Beat polls as top tenor saxophonist; played with Stan Kenton (1944-45), Jimmy Dorsey (1945-46), Benny Goodman (1946), and most importantly Woody Herman (1947-49).	
10/27/62	**15**	10	1. Desafinado [I] **STAN GETZ/CHARLIE BYRD** (jazz guitarist)	Verve 10260
6/20/64	**5**	10	2. **The Girl From Ipanema** **STAN GETZ/ASTRUD GILBERTO** (Brazilian vocalist) above 2: written by Brazilian composer Antonio Carlos Jobim	Verve 10323
			GIANT STEPS	
			English duo: vocalist Campsie and multi-instrumentalist George McFarlane. Both initially worked together as members of the British band Grand Hotel, then as Quick.	
10/01/88	**13**	10	1. Another Lover	A&M 1226

Taylor Dayne's "Don't Rush Me" was one of four top-10 singles from her self-titled debut LP, the only album to have four top-10 singles without reaching the top 10 itself. It peaked at No. 21.

DeBarge was the last Motown group to reach the top 10 (with "Who's Holding Donna Now") while the company was owned by its legendary founder, Berry Gordy.

Rick Dees was a disc jockey when his "Disco Duck" quacked its way to No. 1 at the height of the disco era in 1976. The follow-ups, "Dis-Gorilla" and "Get Nekkid," fared less well, and Rick went back to his day job.

Neil Diamond's first success was as a songwriter—he wrote Jay and the Americans' No. 18 "Sunday And Me" in 1965. Of Diamond's 33 top-30 hits, only one was written by someone other than himself—the remake of the Hollies' "He Ain't Heavy, He's My Brother."

The Diamonds' "Little Darlin'" stayed at No. 2 for eight weeks, and even that's not a "No. 1" achievement—Foreigner's "Waiting For A Girl Like You" stayed at No. 2 for ten weeks without ever getting to No. 1, which puts the Diamonds in second place, again.

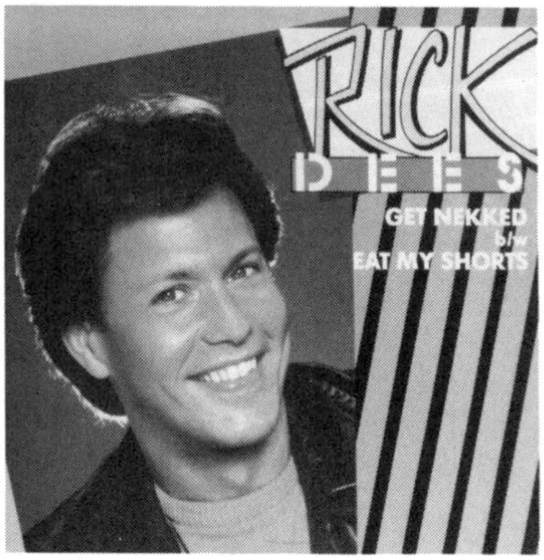

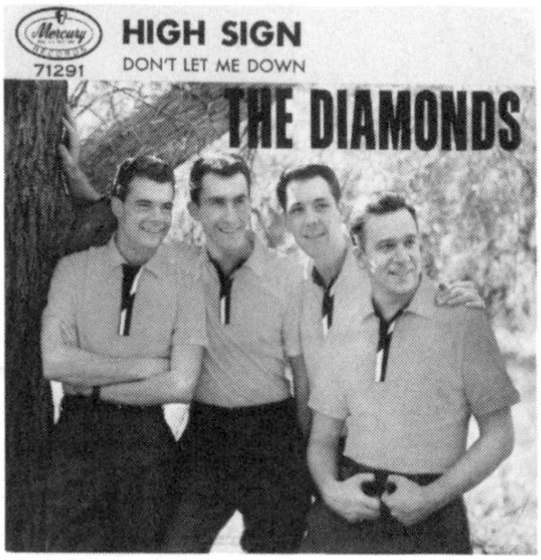

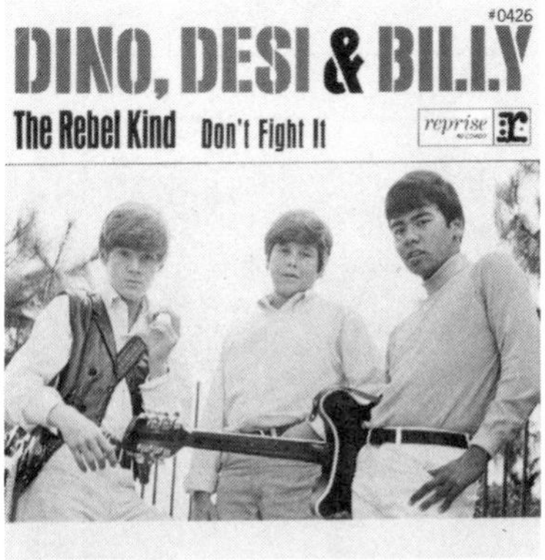

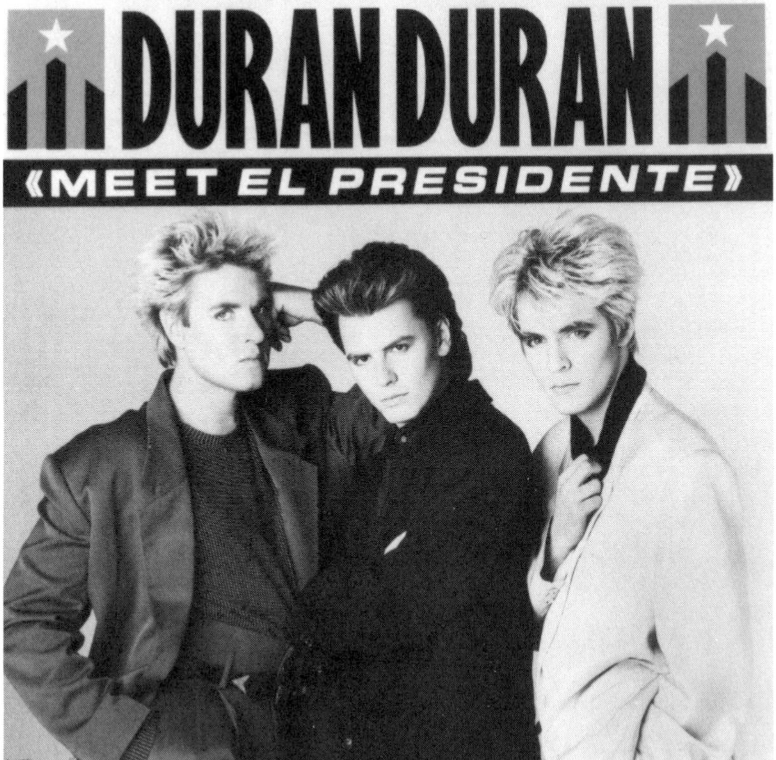

Dino, Desi, & Billy's average age at the time of their first hit was 12 2/3 ("I'm A Fool," 1965). They retired three years later.

Dion blazed a path later followed by Diana Ross and all four Beatles. He hit the top 10 as the lead singer of a group—the Belmonts—and then left and had a No. 1 single on his own—"Runaround Sue," in 1961.

D. J. Jazzy Jeff and the Fresh Prince became the first rap act to win a Grammy (in 1989). That's the kind of success even parents can understand.

Fats Domino never had a No. 1 pop single, much like James Brown, but also like Brown, he is one of rock's most enduring personalities. His biggest hit was "Blueberry Hill" (No. 2, 1956); his last chart single was a remake of the Beatles' "Lady Madonna."

The Dovells' "Bristol Twistin' Annie," in the great tradition of "Old Smokey Locomotion" and "That's What The Nitty Gritty Is," proved that you can't force a sequel—it got to No. 27, while its progenitor, "The Bristol Stomp," got to No. 2.

Duran Duran lasted longer than any of the new British groups of the MTV age. Its first top-10 hit, "Hungry Like The Wolf," came in 1983, and they were still reaching the top 10 in 1988, with "I Don't Want Your Love."

DATE	POS	WKS	ARTIST—RECORD TITLE	LABEL & NO.
			ANDY GIBB	
			Born Andrew Roy Gibb on 3/5/58 in Manchester, England. Moved to Australia when 6 months old, then back to England at age 9. Youngest brother of Barry, Robin and Maurice Gibb - The Bee Gees. Hosted TV's "Solid Gold" from 1981-82. Died on 3/10/88 (30) of an inflammatory heart virus in Oxford, England.	
5/28/77	**1**(4)	23	● 1. **I Just Want To Be Your Everything**	RSO 872
12/10/77†	**1**(2)	22	● 2. **(Love Is) Thicker Than Water**	RSO 883
4/22/78	**1**(7)	19	▲ 3. **Shadow Dancing**	RSO 893
7/22/78	**5**	13	● 4. **An Everlasting Love**	RSO 904
11/04/78	**9**	13	● 5. **(Our Love) Don't Throw It All Away**	RSO 911
2/02/80	**4**	12	6. **Desire**	RSO 1019
4/19/80	**12**	8	7. I Can't Help It **ANDY GIBB & OLIVIA NEWTON-JOHN**	RSO 1026
12/06/80†	**15**	11	8. Time Is Time	RSO 1059
4/11/81	**40**	1	9. Me (Without You)	RSO 1056
			BARRY GIBB	
			Born on 9/1/46 in Manchester, England. Eldest brother of The Bee Gees. Also see Samantha Sang.	
11/15/80†	**3**	15	● 1. **Guilty** **BARBRA STREISAND & BARRY GIBB**	Columbia 11390
2/14/81	**10**	10	2. **What Kind Of Fool** **BARBRA STREISAND & BARRY GIBB**	Columbia 11430
9/29/84	**37**	3	3. Shine Shine	MCA 52443
			ROBIN GIBB	
			Born on 12/22/49 in Manchester, England. Twin brother of The Bee Gees' Maurice Gibb.	
8/19/78	**15**	9	1. Oh! Darling from the film "Sgt. Pepper's Lonely Hearts Club Band"	RSO 907
7/07/84	**37**	4	2. Boys Do Fall In Love	Mirage 99743
			GEORGIA GIBBS	
			Born Fredda Gibbons on 8/17/20 in Worcester, Massachusetts. Sang on Lucky Strike radio show from 1937-38. With Hudson-DeLange band, then with Frankie Trumbauer (1940) and Artie Shaw (1942). On Garry Moore-Jimmy Durante radio show in the late 40s, where Moore dubbed her "Her Nibs, Miss Gibbs."	
1/29/55	**2**(1)	19	1. **Tweedle Dee** Jockey #2 / Best Seller #3 / Juke Box #3	Mercury 70517
3/26/55	**1**(3)	20	2. **Dance With Me Henry (Wallflower)** Juke Box #1 / Best Seller #2 / Jockey #3 revised version of Hank Ballard & The Midnighters' #1 1954 R&B hit "Work With Me Annie," and Etta James' "The Wallflower"	Mercury 70572
7/09/55	**12**	4	3. Sweet And Gentle Jockey #12	Mercury 70647
9/17/55	**14**	4	4. I Want You To Be My Baby Jockey #14 / Best Seller #22 / Top 100 #48 pre	Mercury 70685
4/14/56	**36**	1	5. Rock Right	Mercury 70811
5/26/56	**30**	4	6. Kiss Me Another	Mercury 70850
8/25/56	**20**	8	7. Happiness Street Jockey #20 / Top 100 #25	Mercury 70920

DATE	POS	WKS	ARTIST—RECORD TITLE	LABEL & NO.
12/22/56	**24**	1	8. Tra La La Jockey #24 / Top 100 #39	Mercury 70998
10/20/58	**32**	1	9. The Hula Hoop Song Hot 100 #32 / Best Seller #42 end	Roulette 4106
			TERRI GIBBS	
			Born on 6/15/54 in Augusta, Georgia. Country singer/pianist; blind since birth.	
2/28/81	**13**	12	1. Somebody's Knockin'	MCA 41309
			DEBBIE GIBSON	
			Singer/songwriter/pianist from Long Island. Signed with Atlantic at age 16 in 1987.	
6/27/87	**4**	16	● 1. **Only In My Dreams**	Atlantic 89322
10/24/87	**4**	15	2. **Shake Your Love**	Atlantic 89187
2/06/88	**3**	13	3. **Out Of The Blue**	Atlantic 89129
5/07/88	**1**(1)	14	4. **Foolish Beat**	Atlantic 89109
9/03/88	**22**	6	5. Staying Together	Atlantic 89034
			DON GIBSON	
			Born on 4/3/28 in Shelby, North Carolina. Country singer/songwriter/guitarist.	
3/31/58	**7**	17	1. **Oh Lonesome Me** Best Seller #7 / Top 100 #8 / Jockey #10	RCA 7133
7/14/58	**20**	8	2. Blue Blue Day Jockey #20 / Best Seller #32 / Top 100 #32	RCA 7010
3/28/60	**29**	6	3. Just One Time	RCA 7690
7/10/61	**21**	8	4. Sea Of Heartbreak	RCA 7890
			ASTRUD GILBERTO - see STAN GETZ	
			NICK GILDER	
			Born on 11/7/51 in London, England. Moved to Vancouver, Canada at age 10. Founding member of the rock band Sweeney Todd.	
8/05/78	**1**(1)	18	▲ 1. **Hot Child In The City**	Chrysalis 2226
			TERRY GILKYSON & THE EASY RIDERS	
			Folk trio: Terry Gilkyson, Rick Dehr and Frank Miller. Terry performed with the legendary Weavers folk group in the early 50s. Terry's son, Tony, is the bass guitarist of the group X.	
2/09/57	**4**	14	1. **Marianne** Juke Box #4 / Top 100 #5 / Jockey #5 / Best Seller #6	Columbia 40817
			MICKEY GILLEY	
			Born on 3/9/36 in Ferriday, Louisiana. Country singer/pianist. First cousin to both Jerry Lee Lewis and preacher Jimmy Swaggart. Owner of Gilley's nightclub in Pasadena, Texas. Gilley and the club were featured in the film "Urban Cowboy."	
6/28/80	**22**	9	1. Stand By Me featured in the movie "Urban Cowboy"	Full Moon 46640
			JIMMY GILMER - see THE FIREBALLS	
			JAMES GILREATH	
4/27/63	**21**	6	1. Little Band Of Gold	Joy 274

DATE	POS	WKS	ARTIST—RECORD TITLE	LABEL & NO.
			GINO & GINA	
6/09/58	**20**	1	1. (It's Been A Long Time) Pretty Baby Jockey #20 / Top 100 #34 / Best Seller #39	Mercury 71283
			GIUFFRIA	
			California-based rock quintet led by Gregg Giuffria (keyboardist with Angel) and David Glen Eisley (vocals).	
1/05/85	**15**	7	1. Call To The Heart	MCA 52497
			WILL GLAHE	
			European accordion player/bandleader.	
11/25/57	**16**	15	1. Liechtensteiner Polka [F] Best Seller #16 / Jockey #18 / Top 100 #19	London 1755
			THE GLASS BOTTLE	
			Pop group featuring lead singer Gary Criss.	
9/18/71	**36**	3	1. I Ain't Got Time Anymore	Avco Embassy 4575
			GLASS TIGER	
			Canadian rock quintet: Alan Frew, Sam Reid, Al Connelly, Wayne Parker and Michael Hanson.	
8/09/86	**2**(1)	14	1. **Don't Forget Me (When I'm Gone)**	Manhattan 50037
11/29/86†	**7**	13	2. **Someday**	Manhattan 50048
3/21/87	**34**	5	3. I Will Be There	Manhattan 50066
5/07/88	**31**	5	4. I'm Still Searching	EMI-Man. 50116
			TOM GLAZER & THE DO-RE-MI CHILDREN'S CHORUS	
			Tom is a novelty folk singer from Philadelphia.	
6/15/63	**14**	7	1. On Top Of Spaghetti [N] parody of the tune "On Top Of Old Smokey"	Kapp 526
			THE GLENCOVES	
7/27/63	**38**	2	1. Hootenanny	Select 724
			GARY GLITTER	
			Born Paul Gadd on 5/8/44 in Banbury, England. First recorded as Paul Raven in the early 60s, then as Paul Monday; changed name to Gary Glitter in 1971.	
8/05/72	**7**	9	1. **Rock And Roll Part 2** **[I]**	Bell 45237
12/02/72	**35**	3	2. I Didn't Know I Loved You (Till I Saw You Rock And Roll)	Bell 45276
			GO-GO'S	
			Female rock group formed in 1978 in Los Angeles, consisting of Belinda Carlisle, Jane Wiedlin, Charlotte Caffey, Kathy Valentine and Gina Schock. Disbanded in 1984.	
10/24/81	**20**	13	1. Our Lips Are Sealed	I.R.S. 9901
2/13/82	**2**(3)	15	● 2. **We Got The Beat**	I.R.S. 9903
7/17/82	**8**	9	3. **Vacation**	I.R.S. 9907
3/31/84	**11**	10	4. Head Over Heels	I.R.S. 9926
7/14/84	**32**	5	5. Turn To You	I.R.S. 9928

DATE	POS	WKS	ARTIST—RECORD TITLE	LABEL & NO.
			GO WEST	
			British duo of Peter Cox and Richard Drummie.	
9/26/87	**39**	2	1. Don't Look Down - The Sequel	Chrysalis 43141
			GODLEY & CREME	
			Kevin Godley and Lol Creme formed duo after leaving British group 10cc.	
8/17/85	**16**	10	1. Cry	Polydor 881786
			GODSPELL	
			The original cast as featured in the Broadway rock musical "Godspell" (based upon the gospel according to St. Matthew).	
6/24/72	**13**	9	1. Day By Day lead vocal by original cast member Robin Lamont	Bell 45210
			ANDREW GOLD	
			Born on 8/2/51 in Burbank, California. Son of soundtrack composer Ernest Gold ("Exodus") and singer Marni Nixon. Co-founder of the group Bryndle. Session and arranging work for Linda Ronstadt since early 70s. Member of pop duo Wax, mid-80s.	
4/16/77	**7**	13	1. **Lonely Boy**	Asylum 45384
3/04/78	**25**	9	2. Thank You For Being A Friend	Asylum 45456
			GOLDEN EARRING	
			Rock band from The Netherlands: Barry Hay (vocals), George Kooymans (guitars, vocals), Cesar Zuiderwijk (drums) and Rinus Gerritsen (bass, keyboards).	
6/22/74	**13**	10	1. Radar Love	Track 40202
1/22/83	**10**	15	2. **Twilight Zone**	21 Records 103
			BOBBY GOLDSBORO	
			Born on 1/18/41 in Marianna, Florida. Singer/songwriter/guitarist. To Dothan, Alabama in 1956. Toured with Roy Orbison, 1962-64.	
2/15/64	**9**	8	1. **See The Funny Little Clown**	United Art. 672
5/23/64	**39**	2	2. Whenever He Holds You	United Art. 710
2/20/65	**13**	8	3. Little Things	United Art. 810
6/05/65	**27**	6	4. Voodoo Woman	United Art. 862
3/12/66	**23**	5	5. It's Too Late	United Art. 980
1/14/67	**35**	3	6. Blue Autumn	United Art. 50087
3/30/68	**1**(5)	13	● 7. **Honey**	United Art. 50283
7/13/68	**19**	7	8. Autumn Of My Life	United Art. 50318
11/30/68	**36**	2	9. The Straight Life	United Art. 50461
1/09/71	**11**	11	10. Watching Scotty Grow	United Art. 50727
10/06/73	**21**	8	11. Summer (The First Time)	United Art. 251
			IAN GOMM	
			Born on 3/17/47 in Ealing, England. Member of London band Brinsley Schwarz, 1972-78.	
10/06/79	**18**	5	1. Hold On	Stiff/Epic 50747
			GONE ALL STARS	
			Session band arranged by record company mogul George Goldner.	
3/03/58	**30**	4	1. "7-11" [I] Best Seller #30 / Top 100 #31 version of the tune "Mambo No. 5," written by Perez Prado	Gone 5016

DATE	POS	WKS	ARTIST—RECORD TITLE	LABEL & NO.
			GONZALEZ	
			British soul/disco band.	
2/10/79	**26**	5	1. Haven't Stopped Dancing Yet	Capitol 4674
			BENNY GOODMAN - see ROSEMARY CLOONEY	
			DICKIE GOODMAN	
			Born on 4/19/34 in Hewlett, New York. Dickie and partner Bill Buchanan originated the novelty "break-in" recordings featuring bits of the original versions of Top 40 hits interwoven throughout the recording. Also see Buchanan & Goodman.	
2/23/74	**33**	4	1. Energy Crisis '74 [N]	Rainy Wed. 206
9/13/75	**4**	7	● 2. **Mr. Jaws** **[N]**	Cash 451
			BARRY GORDON	
			Barry was 7 years old at the time of his 1955 hit.	
12/17/55	**6**	4	1. **Nuttin' For Christmas** **[X-N]** Best Seller #6 / Top 100 #7 / Juke Box #9 / Jockey #10 backing by Art Mooney & His Orchestra	MGM 12092
			LESLEY GORE	
			Born on 5/2/46 in New York City; raised in Tenafly, New Jersey. Discovered by Quincy Jones while singing at a hotel in Manhattan. In films "Girls On The Beach," "Ski Party" and "The T.A.M.I. Show."	
5/18/63	**1**(2)	11	1. **It's My Party**	Mercury 72119
7/20/63	**5**	9	2. **Judy's Turn To Cry**	Mercury 72143
10/19/63	**5**	11	3. **She's A Fool**	Mercury 72180
1/11/64	**2**(3)	10	4. **You Don't Own Me**	Mercury 72206
4/04/64	**12**	7	5. That's The Way Boys Are	Mercury 72259
6/20/64	**37**	1	6. I Don't Wanna Be A Loser	Mercury 72270
8/15/64	**14**	6	7. Maybe I Know	Mercury 72309
1/23/65	**27**	5	8. Look Of Love	Mercury 72372
7/17/65	**13**	7	9. Sunshine, Lollipops And Rainbows from the film "Ski Party"	Mercury 72433
10/09/65	**32**	3	10. My Town, My Guy And Me all of above: produced by Quincy Jones	Mercury 72475
3/04/67	**16**	9	11. California Nights	Mercury 72649
			EYDIE GORME	
			Born on 8/16/31 in New York City. Vocalist with big bands of Tommy Tucker and Tex Beneke in the late 40s. Featured on Steve Allen's Tonight Show from 1953. Married Steve Lawrence in December, 1957.	
6/16/56	**39**	1	1. Too Close For Comfort from the Broadway musical "Mr. Wonderful"	ABC-Para. 9684
9/01/56	**34**	3	2. Mama, Teach Me To Dance	ABC-Para. 9722
12/30/57	**24**	1	3. Love Me Forever Jockey #24 / Top 100 #86	ABC-Para. 9863
5/26/58	**11**	9	4. You Need Hands Jockey #11 / Best Seller #32 / Top 100 #32	ABC-Para. 9925
2/09/63	**7**	11	5. **Blame It On The Bossa Nova**	Columbia 42661
8/24/63	**28**	5	6. I Want To Stay Here **STEVE & EYDIE**	Columbia 42815

DATE	POS	WKS	ARTIST—RECORD TITLE	LABEL & NO.
1/25/64	**35**	3	7. I Can't Stop Talking About You **STEVE & EYDIE**	Columbia 42932
			ROBERT GOULET	
			Born on 11/26/33 in Lawrence, Massachusetts. Began concert career in Edmonton, Canada. Launched career as Sir Lancelot in the hit Broadway musical "Camelot." Won the 1962 Best New Artist Grammy Award.	
11/28/64†	**16**	9	1. My Love, Forgive Me (Amore, Scusami)	Columbia 43131
			GQ	
			Bronx, New York soul group: Emmanuel Rahiem LeBlanc (lead singer), Keith Crier, Herb Lane and Paul Service. Group became a trio with the departure of Service, 1980.	
4/14/79	**12**	11	● 1. Disco Nights (Rock-Freak)	Arista 0388
8/11/79	**20**	8	2. I Do Love You	Arista 0426
			CHARLIE GRACIE	
			Born Charles Graci on 5/14/36 in Philadelphia. Vocalist/guitarist. First recorded for Cadillac in 1951. Regular on "Bandstand" (later: American Bandstand), 1952-58.	
2/23/57	**1**(2)	14	1. **Butterfly** Juke Box #1 / Best Seller #3 / Top 100 #7 / Jockey #13	Cameo 105
5/20/57	**16**	6	2. Fabulous Best Seller #16 / Top 100 #26	Cameo 107
			GRAHAM CENTRAL STATION	
			Soul/dance group from Oakland, formed in 1973 by Larry Graham. Originally known as Hot Chocolate. Graham went solo in 1980.	
9/13/75	**38**	2	1. Your Love	Warner 8105
			LARRY GRAHAM	
			Born on 8/14/46 in Beaumont, Texas. To Oakland at the age of 2. Bass player with Sly & The Family Stone from 1966-72. Formed Graham Central Station in 1973.	
8/09/80	**9**	9	● 1. **One In A Million You**	Warner 49221
			LOU GRAMM	
			Born on 5/2/50 in Rochester, New York. Lead singer of Foreigner.	
2/28/87	**5**	11	1. **Midnight Blue**	Atlantic 89304
			BILLY GRAMMER	
			Born on 8/28/25 in Benton, Illinois. Country singer/guitarist. Performed regularly on "The Jimmy Dean Show," CBS-TV, 1957-58. Prominent session musician in Nashville.	
12/08/58†	**4**	15	1. **Gotta Travel On** based on 19th-century tune that originated in the British Isles	Monument 400
			GERRY GRANAHAN	
			Singer/songwriter from New York City. Also see Dicky Doo & The Don'ts.	
6/16/58	**23**	8	1. No Chemise, Please Top 100 #23 / Best Seller #25	Sunbeam 102
			ROCCO GRANATA	
			Born in Italy in 1938; moved to Belgium at age 10. Singer/songwriter/accordionist.	
11/23/59	**31**	7	1. Marina [F]	Laurie 3041

DATE	POS	WKS	ARTIST—RECORD TITLE	LABEL & NO.
			GRAND FUNK RAILROAD	
			Heavy-metal rock group formed in Flint, Michigan in 1968. Consisted of Mark Farner (guitar), Mel Schacher (bass) and Don Brewer (drums). Brewer and Farner had been in Terry Knight & The Pack; Schacher was former bassist with ? & The Mysterians. Knight became producer and manager for Grand Funk, until he was fired in March, 1972. Craig Frost (keyboards) added in 1973. Disbanded in 1976. Re-formed in 1981, with Farner, Brewer and Dennis Bellinger (bass). Disbanded again shortly thereafter.	
9/05/70	**22**	8	1. Closer To Home	Capitol 2877
2/05/72	**29**	5	2. Footstompin' Music	Capitol 3255
11/04/72	**29**	6	3. Rock 'N Roll Soul	Capitol 3363
			GRAND FUNK:	
8/18/73	**1**(1)	13	• 4. **We're An American Band**	Capitol 3660
12/29/73†	**19**	6	5. Walk Like A Man	Capitol 3760
3/30/74	**1**(2)	14	• 6. **The Loco-Motion**	Capitol 3840
7/20/74	**11**	8	7. Shinin' On above 4: produced by Todd Rundgren	Capitol 3917
12/21/74†	**3**	12	8. **Some Kind Of Wonderful**	Capitol 4002
4/19/75	**4**	12	9. **Bad Time**	Capitol 4046
			AMY GRANT	
			Born on 11/25/60 in Augusta, Georgia. The first lady of contemporary Christian music. Married to singer/songwriter Gary Chapman.	
7/06/85	**29**	6	1. Find A Way	A&M 2734
10/11/86	**1**(1)	15	2. **The Next Time I Fall** **PETER CETERA with AMY GRANT**	Full Moon 28597
			EARL GRANT	
			Organist/pianist/vocalist born in Oklahoma City in 1931. First recorded for Decca in 1957. In the films "Tender Is The Night," "Imitation Of Life" and "Tokyo Night." Died in an automobile accident on 6/10/70 (39).	
9/29/58	**7**	13	1. **The End**	Decca 30719
			EDDY GRANT	
			Born Edmond Montague Grant on 3/5/48 in Plaisance, Guyana. Moved to London in 1960. Formed group the Equals in London, 1967. Moved to Barbados in 1982.	
5/21/83	**2**(5)	15	• 1. **Electric Avenue**	Portrait 03793
6/30/84	**26**	6	2. Romancing The Stone written for, but not included in, the film of the same title	Portrait 04433
			GOGI GRANT	
			Born Audrey Brown on 9/20/24 in Philadelphia. Moved to Los Angeles at age 12. Performed vocals for the film "The Helen Morgan Story."	
10/01/55	**9**	10	1. **Suddenly There's A Valley** Jockey #9 / Best Seller #14 / Top 100 #14 / Juke Box #19	Era 1003
5/05/56	**1**(8)	22	2. **The Wayward Wind** Jockey #1(8) / Top 100 #1(7) / Best Seller #1(6) / Juke Box #1(4)	Era 1013
			JANIE GRANT	
			Singer/songwriter born in New York City in 1945. Discovered by recording artist Gerry Granahan.	
5/15/61	**29**	5	1. Triangle	Caprice 104

DATE	POS	WKS	ARTIST—RECORD TITLE	LABEL & NO.
			THE GRASS ROOTS	
			Rock group formed in San Francisco in 1964 by drummer Joel Larson and lead singer Bill Fulton. Originally called The Bedouins. New group recruited in 1966 by pop producer Lou Adler and songwriters Steve Barri and P.F. Sloan (known as the Fantastic Baggies). Consisted of Rob Grill (lead singer, bass), Warren Entner & Creed Bratton (guitars), and Rick Coonce (drums). New lineup in 1971 included Entner, Grill, Reed Kailing, Joel Larson and Virgil Webber.	
7/16/66	**28**	4	1. Where Were You When I Needed You	Dunhill 4029
6/03/67	**8**	9	2. **Let's Live For Today**	Dunhill 4084
9/02/67	**23**	4	3. Things I Should Have Said	Dunhill 4094
9/21/68	**5**	12	• 4. **Midnight Confessions**	Dunhill 4144
1/11/69	**28**	2	5. Bella Linda	Dunhill 4162
5/17/69	**31**	5	6. The River Is Wide	Dunhill 4187
8/09/69	**15**	10	7. I'd Wait A Million Years	Dunhill 4198
11/22/69	**24**	7	8. Heaven Knows	Dunhill 4217
6/13/70	**35**	3	9. Baby Hold On	Dunhill 4237
2/13/71	**15**	11	10. Temptation Eyes	Dunhill 4263
6/19/71	**9**	9	11. **Sooner Or Later**	Dunhill 4279
10/30/71	**16**	8	12. Two Divided By Love	Dunhill 4289
3/18/72	**34**	3	13. Glory Bound	Dunhill 4302
7/22/72	**39**	2	14. The Runway	Dunhill 4316
			GRATEFUL DEAD	
			Psychedelic rock band formed in San Francisco in 1966. Consisted of Jerry Garcia, lead guitar; Bob Weir, rhythm guitar; Ron "Pigpen" McKernan, organ, harmonica; Phil Lesh, bass; and Bill Kreutzmann, drums. Mickey Hart (2nd drummer) and Tom Constanten (keyboards) added in 1968. Constanten left in 1970, Hart in 1971. Keith Godchaux (piano) and his wife Donna (vocals) joined in 1972. Pigpen died of a liver ailment on 3/8/73. Hart returned in 1975. Brent Mydland (keyboards) added in 1979, replacing Keith & Donna Godchaux. Band name derived from the title of an ancient Egyptian prayer.	
8/15/87	**9**	9	1. **Touch Of Grey**	Arista 9606
			DOBIE GRAY	
			Born Leonard Victor Ainsworth on 7/26/42 in Brookshire, Texas. Soul vocalist/ composer/actor. To Los Angeles in 1960. Worked as an actor on Broadway, and in the L.A. production of "Hair." Lead singer of Pollution in 1971.	
1/23/65	**13**	7	1. The "In" Crowd	Charger 105
3/31/73	**5**	15	• 2. **Drift Away**	Decca 33057
2/10/79	**37**	2	3. You Can Do It	Infinity 50003
			THE CHARLES RANDOLPH GREAN SOUNDE	
			Charles is a former artist & repertoire director at RCA and Dot Records. Married to singer Betty Johnson.	
7/05/69	**13**	8	1. Quentin's Theme [I] from the TV series "Dark Shadows"	Ranwood 840
			R.B. GREAVES	
			Born Ronald Bertram Aloysius Greaves on 11/28/44 at the USAF Base in Georgetown, British Guyana. Half American Indian, raised on a Seminole reservation in California. Nephew of Sam Cooke. To England in 1963, as Sonny Childe & The TNT's.	
10/25/69	**2**(1)	13	• 1. **Take A Letter Maria**	Atco 6714

DATE	POS	WKS	ARTIST—RECORD TITLE	LABEL & NO.
2/14/70	**27**	5	2. Always Something There To Remind Me	Atco 6726
			CYNDI GRECCO	
6/12/76	**25**	5	1. Making Our Dreams Come True theme from the TV series "LaVerne & Shirley"	Private S. 45086
			AL GREEN	
			Born on 4/13/46 in Forest City, Arkansas. Singer/songwriter. With gospel group the Greene Brothers. To Grand Rapids, Michigan in 1959. First recorded for Fargo in 1960. In group the Creations from 1964-67. Sang with his brother Robert and Lee Virgins in the group Soul Mates from 1967-68. Went solo in 1969. Wrote most of his songs. Returned to gospel music in 1980.	
8/21/71	**11**	15	• 1. Tired Of Being Alone	Hi 2194
12/11/71†	**1**(1)	15	• 2. **Let's Stay Together**	Hi 2202
4/08/72	**4**	11	• 3. **Look What You Done For Me**	Hi 2211
7/15/72	**3**	11	• 4. **I'm Still In Love With You**	Hi 2216
11/04/72	**3**	12	• 5. **You Ought To Be With Me**	Hi 2227
3/03/73	**10**	9	• 6. **Call Me (Come Back Home)**	Hi 2235
7/21/73	**10**	12	• 7. **Here I Am (Come And Take Me)**	Hi 2247
12/22/73†	**19**	8	8. Livin' For You	Hi 2257
5/11/74	**32**	3	9. Let's Get Married	Hi 2262
11/02/74	**7**	11	• 10. **Sha-La-La (Make Me Happy)**	Hi 2274
3/22/75	**13**	8	11. L-O-V-E (Love)	Hi 2282
11/29/75	**28**	6	12. Full Of Fire	Hi 2300
12/18/76†	**37**	4	13. Keep Me Cryin' all of above: produced by Willie Mitchell	Hi 2319
12/03/88†	**9**	10	14. **Put A Little Love In Your Heart** **ANNIE LENNOX & AL GREEN** from the film "Scrooged"	A&M 1255
			GARLAND GREEN	
			Born on 6/24/42 in Leland, Mississippi. Soul singer/pianist. To Chicago in 1958. Attended Chicago Conservatory of Music. First recorded for Gamma in 1967.	
10/18/69	**20**	4	1. Jealous Kind Of Fella	Uni 55143
			NORMAN GREENBAUM	
			Born on 11/20/42 in Malden, Massachusetts. Moved to the West Coast in 1965 and formed the psychedelic jug band Dr. West's Medicine Show & Junk Band.	
3/07/70	**3**	14	• 1. **Spirit In The Sky**	Reprise 0885
			LORNE GREENE	
			Born on 2/12/15 in Ottawa, Canada; died on 9/11/87 of cardiac arrest. Chief newscaster for CBC radio, 1940-43. Studied acting, appeared in films "The Silver Challice" and "Tight Spot"; starred in TV series "Bonanza" & "Battlestar Galactica."	
11/07/64	**1**(1)	10	1. **Ringo** [S]	RCA 8444
			BOBBY GREGG & His Friends	
			Bobby's real name is Robert Grego; jazz drummer from Philadelphia. Performed with Steve Gibson & The Red Caps from 1955-60.	
4/14/62	**29**	5	1. The Jam - Part 1 [I] featuring Roy Buchanan, guitar	Cotton 1003

DATE	POS	WKS	ARTIST—RECORD TITLE	LABEL & NO.
			ANDY GRIFFITH	
			Born on 6/1/26 in Mount Airy, North Carolina. Screen debut in 1957, "A Face In The Crowd." Best known as sheriff Andy Taylor on the TV series "The Andy Griffith Show"; currently starring in TV's "Matlock."	
4/02/55	**26**	1	1. Make Yourself Comfortable [C] Best Seller #26 vocal: Jean Wilson	Capitol 3057
			LARRY GROCE	
			Born on 4/22/48 in Dallas. Pop-folk singer/songwriter. Wrote children's songs for Walt Disney Records.	
2/07/76	**9**	9	1. **Junk Food Junkie** **[N]** recorded live at McCabe's in Santa Monica	Warner 8165
			HENRY GROSS	
			Rock singer from Brooklyn. Original lead guitarist of Sha-Na-Na.	
4/03/76	**6**	13	● 1. **Shannon**	Lifesong 45002
8/21/76	**37**	2	2. Springtime Mama	Lifesong 45008
			GTR	
			British hard-rock quintet featuring superstar guitarists Steve Hackett (Genesis) and Steve Howe (Yes & Asia), and Max Bacon (vocals).	
5/31/86	**14**	10	1. When The Heart Rules The Mind	Arista 9470
			VINCE GUARALDI TRIO	
			Vince was born on 7/17/32 in San Francisco; died of a heart attack on 2/6/76. Jazz pianist formerly with Woody Herman and Cal Tjader. Wrote the music for the "Charlie Brown" TV specials.	
2/09/63	**22**	6	1. Cast Your Fate To The Wind [I]	Fantasy 563
			THE GUESS WHO	
			Rock group formed in Winnipeg, Canada, 1963. Consisted of Allan "Chad Allan" Kobel (guitar, vocals), Randy Bachman (lead guitar), Garry Peterson (drums), Bob Ashley (piano) and Jim Kale (bass). Recorded as The Reflections, and Chad Allan & The Expressions. Ashley replaced by new lead singer Burton Cummings in 1966. Allan left shortly thereafter. Bachman left in July, 1970, to form Bachman-Turner Overdrive. Replaced by Kurt Winter and Greg Leskiw. Leskiw and Kale left in 1972, replaced by Don McDougall and Bill Wallace. Domenic Troiano replaced both Winter and McDougall in 1974. Group disbanded in 1975; several reformations since then.	
6/05/65	**22**	7	1. Shakin' All Over group is actually Chad Allan & The Expressions	Scepter 1295
4/26/69	**6**	11	● 2. **These Eyes**	RCA 0102
7/26/69	**10**	9	● 3. **Laughing/**	
11/08/69	**22**	6	4. Undun	RCA 0195
1/17/70	**5**	10	5. **No Time**	RCA 0300
3/28/70	**1**(3)	14	● 6. **American Woman/**	
		14	7. No Sugar Tonight	RCA 0325
8/08/70	**17**	8	8. Hand Me Down World	RCA 0367
11/07/70	**10**	8	9. **Share The Land**	RCA 0388
6/12/71	**29**	4	10. Albert Flasher	RCA 0458
9/04/71	**19**	8	11. Rain Dance	RCA 0522
4/20/74	**39**	1	12. Star Baby	RCA 0217
8/10/74	**6**	11	13. **Clap For The Wolfman** featuring bits of dialogue by Wolfman Jack	RCA 0324

DATE	POS	WKS	ARTIST—RECORD TITLE	LABEL & NO.
12/14/74†	**28**	4	14. Dancin' Fool all of above (except #1): produced by Jack Richardson	RCA 10075
			GREG GUIDRY	
			Singer/songwriter/pianist from St. Louis.	
3/20/82	**17**	10	1. Goin' Down	Columbia 02691
			BONNIE GUITAR	
			Born Bonnie Buckingham on 3/25/24 in Seattle. Own group in the early 50s. Worked as session guitarist in Los Angeles in the mid-50s. Owner of Dolphin/Dolton Records in Seattle in 1958. Played on several early Fleetwoods recordings.	
4/27/57	**6**	10	1. **Dark Moon** Jockey #6 / Top 100 #8 / Best Seller #10 / Juke Box #11	Dot 15550
			GUNHILL ROAD	
			Rock trio: Glen Leopolo, Gil Roman and Steve Goldrich.	
6/02/73	**40**	1	1. Back When My Hair Was Short	Kama Sutra 569
			GUNS N' ROSES	
			Los Angeles-based hard-rock quintet: lead singer W. Axl Rose (Bill Bailey) with bassist Duff "Rose" McKagan, guitarists Izzy Stradlin and Slash, and drummer Steven Adler.	
7/23/88	**1**(2)	14	1. **Sweet Child O' Mine** written by Rose for his girlfriend Erin Everly, daughter of Don Everly of The Everly Brothers	Geffen 27963
11/05/88	**7**	12	2. **Welcome To The Jungle**	Geffen 27759
			ARLO GUTHRIE	
			Born on 7/10/47 in Coney Island, New York. Son of legendary folk singer Woody Guthrie.	
9/09/72	**18**	9	1. The City Of New Orleans	Reprise 1103
			H	
			SAMMY HAGAR	
			Born on 10/13/47 in Monterey, California. Rock singer/songwriter/guitarist. Lead singer of Montrose (1973-75). Replaced David Lee Roth as lead singer of Van Halen in 1985.	
12/25/82†	**13**	13	1. Your Love Is Driving Me Crazy	Geffen 29816
8/18/84	**38**	3	2. Two Sides Of Love	Geffen 29246
10/27/84	**26**	6	3. I Can't Drive 55	Geffen 29173
8/01/87	**23**	7	4. Give To Live	Geffen 28314
			MERLE HAGGARD	
			Born on 4/6/37 in Bakersfield, California. Country singer/songwriter/guitarist. Merle's had 38 #1 hits on the country charts.	
1/05/74	**28**	3	1. If We Make It Through December	Capitol 3746
			HAIRCUT ONE HUNDRED	
			British pop-rock sextet founded by vocalist Nick Heyward. Disbanded in 1983.	
7/17/82	**37**	4	1. Love Plus One	Arista 0672

DATE	POS	WKS	ARTIST—RECORD TITLE	LABEL & NO.
			BILL HALEY & His Comets	
			Born William John Clifton Haley Jr. on 7/6/25 in Highland Park, Michigan. Began career as a singer with a New England country band, the Down Homers. Formed the Four Aces of Western Swing in 1948. In 1949, formed the Saddlemen, who recorded on various labels before signing with the Essex label (as Bill Haley & The Comets) in 1952; signed with Decca in 1954. The original Comets band who backed Haley on "Rock Around The Clock" were: Danny Cedrone (lead guitar), Joey D'Ambrose (sax), Billy Williamson (steel guitar), Johnny Grande (piano), Marshall Lytle (bass) and Dick Richards (drums). Comets lineup on subsequent recordings included Williamson, Grande, Rudy Pompilli (sax), Al Rex (bass), Ralph Jones (drums) and Frannie Beecher (lead guitar). Bill died of a heart attack in Harlingen, Texas on 2/9/81. Inducted into the Rock And Roll Hall Of Fame in 1987. Also see The Kingsmen.	
11/20/54†	**11**	15	1. Dim, Dim The Lights (I Want Some Atmosphere) Best Seller #11 / Jockey #16 / Juke Box #16	Decca 29317
3/05/55	**18**	8	2. Mambo Rock/ Best Seller #18	
3/19/55	**17**	2	3. Birth Of The Boogie Juke Box #17 / Best Seller #26	Decca 29418
5/14/55	**1**(8)	24	4. **Rock Around The Clock** Best Seller #1(8) / Juke Box #1(7) / Jockey #1(6) recorded on 4/12/54; featured in the film "Blackboard Jungle"	Decca 29124
7/23/55	**15**	4	5. Razzle-Dazzle Best Seller #15	Decca 29552
11/19/55	**9**	13	6. **Burn That Candle/** Juke Box #9 / Best Seller #16 / Top 100 #20	
11/19/55	**23**	7	7. Rock-A-Beatin' Boogie Best Seller #23 / Top 100 #41	Decca 29713
1/14/56	**6**	15	8. **See You Later, Alligator** Best Seller #6 / Top 100 #6 / Jockey #6 / Juke Box #6	Decca 29791
4/07/56	**16**	5	9. R-O-C-K/ Juke Box #16 / Best Seller #20 / Top 100 #29 featured in the film "Rock Around The Clock"	
4/07/56	**18**	5	10. The Saints Rock 'N Roll Best Seller #18 / Top 100 #42 rock version of the spiritual "When The Saints Go Marching In"	Decca 29870
9/01/56	**25**	4	11. Rip It Up Best Seller #25 / Top 100 #30	Decca 30028
11/24/56	**34**	3	12. Rudy's Rock [I] sax solo by Rudy Pompilli (died on 2/5/76 [47])	Decca 30085
4/21/58	**22**	6	13. Skinny Minnie Top 100 #22 / Best Seller #24	Decca 30592
5/25/74	**39**	1	14. Rock Around The Clock [R] Best Seller #1(8) / Juke Box #1(7) / Jockey #1(6)	MCA 60025
			DARYL HALL	
			Born Daryl Franklin Hohl on 10/11/48 in Philadelphia. Half of Hall & Oates duo.	
8/16/86	**5**	11	1. **Dreamtime**	RCA 14387
11/15/86	**33**	5	2. Foolish Pride	RCA 5038

DATE	POS	WKS	ARTIST—RECORD TITLE	LABEL & NO.
			DARYL HALL & JOHN OATES	
			Daryl Hall (see above) & John Oates (b: 4/7/49 in New York City) met while students at Temple University in 1967. Hall sang back-up for many top soul groups, before teaming up with Oates in 1972. Duo's sophisticated "blue-eyed soul" style has earned them the #2 ranking (behind the Everly Brothers) as the all-time top duo of the rock era.	
4/03/76	**4**	17	• 1. **Sara Smile**	RCA 10530
8/14/76	**7**	16	2. **She's Gone** [R] originally charted in 1974 (POS 60)	Atlantic 3332
12/25/76	**39**	3	3. Do What You Want, Be What You Are	RCA 10808
2/05/77	**1**(2)	14	• 4. **Rich Girl**	RCA 10860
5/28/77	**28**	4	5. Back Together Again	RCA 10970
9/30/78	**20**	7	6. It's A Laugh	RCA 11371
12/01/79†	**18**	10	7. Wait For Me	RCA 11747
8/30/80	**30**	4	8. How Does It Feel To Be Back	RCA 12048
10/11/80	**12**	14	9. You've Lost That Lovin' Feeling	RCA 12103
2/14/81	**1**(3)	17	• 10. **Kiss On My List**	RCA 12142
5/16/81	**5**	14	11. **You Make My Dreams**	RCA 12217
9/12/81	**1**(2)	17	• 12. **Private Eyes**	RCA 12296
11/21/81†	**1**(1)	17	• 13. **I Can't Go For That (No Can Do)**	RCA 12357
4/03/82	**9**	11	14. **Did It In A Minute**	RCA 13065
7/24/82	**33**	5	15. Your Imagination	RCA 13252
11/06/82	**1**(4)	17	• 16. **Maneater**	RCA 13354
2/05/83	**7**	15	17. **One On One**	RCA 13421
5/07/83	**6**	12	18. **Family Man**	RCA 13507
10/29/83	**2**(4)	15	19. **Say It Isn't So**	RCA 13654
2/25/84	**8**	11	20. **Adult Education**	RCA 13714
10/06/84	**1**(2)	16	21. **Out Of Touch**	RCA 13916
1/05/85	**5**	11	22. **Method Of Modern Love**	RCA 13970
3/30/85	**18**	8	23. Some Things Are Better Left Unsaid	RCA 14035
6/15/85	**30**	6	24. Possession Obsession	RCA 14098
9/15/85	**20**	7	25. A Nite At The Apollo Live! The Way You Do The Things You Do/My Girl **DARYL HALL JOHN OATES with DAVID RUFFIN & EDDIE KENDRICK** recorded at the reopening of New York's Apollo Theatre; revival of 2 early Temptations hits	RCA 14178
4/23/88	**3**	11	26. **Everything Your Heart Desires**	Arista 9684
8/06/88	**29**	5	27. Missed Opportunity	Arista 9727
10/29/88	**31**	3	28. Downtown Life	Arista 9753
			JIMMY HALL	
			Mobile, Alabama native. Leader of the Southern rock band Wet Willie.	
11/01/80	**27**	4	1. I'm Happy That Love Has Found You	Epic 50931
			LARRY HALL	
			Born on 6/30/41 in Cincinnati.	
12/07/59†	**15**	11	1. Sandy	Strand 25007

DATE	POS	WKS	ARTIST—RECORD TITLE	LABEL & NO.
			TOM T. HALL	
			Born on 5/25/36 in Olive Hill, Kentucky. Country music storyteller. Wrote "Harper Valley P.T.A." hit for Jeannie C. Riley. Host of "Pop Goes The Country" TV series.	
1/19/74	**12**	9	1. I Love	Mercury 73436
			THE HALOS	
			New York City R&B group. Backing group on Curtis Lee's "Pretty Little Angel Eyes."	
8/28/61	**25**	4	1. "Nag"	7 Arts 709
			HAMILTON, JOE FRANK & REYNOLDS	
			Dan Hamilton, Joe Frank Carollo and Tommy Reynolds. Trio were members of the T-Bones. Reynolds left group in 1972 and was replaced by Alan Dennison. Although Reynolds had left, group still recorded as Hamilton, Joe Frank & Reynolds until July of 1976.	
6/12/71	**4**	11	● 1. **Don't Pull Your Love**	Dunhill 4276
7/19/75	**1**(1)	12	● 2. **Fallin' In Love**	Playboy 6024
12/13/75†	**21**	8	3. Winners And Losers	Playboy 6054
			BOBBY HAMILTON	
8/04/58	**40**	1	1. Crazy Eyes For You	Apt 25002
			GEORGE HAMILTON IV	
			Born on 7/19/37 in Winston-Salem, North Carolina. Country-folk-pop singer/ songwriter/guitarist. Toured with Buddy Holly, Gene Vincent and The Everly Brothers. Moved to Nashville in 1959 and joined the Grand Ole Opry. Own TV series on ABC in 1959, and in Canada in the late 70s.	
11/17/56	**6**	14	1. **A Rose And A Baby Ruth** Top 100 #6 / Best Seller #7 / Jockey #7 / Juke Box #8	ABC-Para. 9765
3/09/57	**33**	4	2. Only One Love	ABC-Para. 9782
12/09/57†	**10**	12	3. **Why Don't They Understand** Jockey #10 / Top 100 #17 / Best Seller #19	ABC-Para. 9862
4/07/58	**25**	1	4. Now And For Always Jockey #25 / Best Seller #37 / Top 100 #37	ABC-Para. 9898
12/15/58†	**29**	5	5. The Teen Commandments [S] **PAUL ANKA-GEORGE HAMILTON IV-JOHNNY NASH** inspirational talk from above 3 ABC-Paramount artists	ABC-Para. 9974
7/20/63	**15**	7	6. Abilene	RCA 8181
			ROY HAMILTON	
			Born on 4/16/29 in Leesburg, Georgia; died of a stroke on 7/20/69. R&B ballad singer. Moved to Jersey City at age 14; sang with the Searchlight Gospel Singers in 1948.	
4/23/55	**6**	16	1. **Unchained Melody** Jockey #6 / Juke Box #6 / Best Seller #9 from the film "Unchained"	Epic 9102
1/27/58	**13**	11	2. Don't Let Go Top 100 #13 / Best Seller #14 / Jockey #16	Epic 9257
2/13/61	**12**	7	3. You Can Have Her	Epic 9434
			RUSS HAMILTON	
			Singer/songwriter, born Ronald Hulme in Liverpool, England.	
8/05/57	**4**	17	1. **Rainbow** Jockey #4 / Best Seller #7 / Top 100 #7	Kapp 184

DATE	POS	WKS	ARTIST—RECORD TITLE	LABEL & NO.
			MARVIN HAMLISCH	
			Born on 6/2/44 in New York City. Pianist/composer/conductor for numerous soundtracks. Won an Oscar and Grammy in the best song category in 1973 for "The Way We Were." Won the 1974 Best New Artist Grammy Award.	
4/20/74	**3**	12	● 1. **The Entertainer** **[I]** written in 1902 by Scott Joplin; featured in the film "The Sting"	MCA 40174
			JAN HAMMER	
			Czechoslovakian-born, jazz-rock keyboard virtuoso. Toured with Sarah Vaughn as conductor/keyboardist. Member of Mahavishnu Orchestra until 1973.	
9/21/85	**1**(1)	13	1. **Miami Vice Theme** **[I]** from TV's "Miami Vice" soundtrack	MCA 52666
			ALBERT HAMMOND	
			Born on 5/18/42 in London; raised in Gibraltar, Spain. Member of the British group Magic Lanterns in 1971.	
11/04/72	**5**	13	● 1. **It Never Rains In Southern California**	Mums 6011
4/13/74	**31**	4	2. I'm A Train	Mums 6026
			THE HAPPENINGS	
			Vocal group from Paterson, New Jersey: Bob Miranda (lead), Tom Giuliano (tenor), Ralph DiVito (baritone) and Dave Libert (bass). Bernie LaPorta replaced DiVito in 1968. Originally the Four Graduates, recorded for Rust in 1963.	
7/30/66	**3**	11	1. **See You In September**	B.T. Puppy 520
10/22/66	**12**	5	2. Go Away Little Girl	B.T. Puppy 522
4/29/67	**3**	9	3. **I Got Rhythm** written in 1930 by George & Ira Gershwin for musical "Girl Crazy"	B.T. Puppy 527
7/22/67	**13**	6	4. My Mammy Al Jolson's theme song; written in 1920	B.T. Puppy 530
			PAUL HARDCASTLE	
			Born in London on 12/10/57. Keyboardist/producer.	
6/22/85	**15**	8	1. 19 title refers to the average age of U.S. soldiers in Vietnam	Chrysalis 42860
			JOE HARNELL	
			Born on 8/2/24 in the Bronx. Conductor/arranger for Frank Sinatra, Peggy Lee and others. Musical director for many TV shows, including the Mike Douglas Show.	
1/26/63	**14**	8	1. Fly Me To The Moon-Bossa Nova [I]	Kapp 497
			HARPERS BIZARRE	
			Santa Cruz, California quintet led by Ted Templeman, who later produced many albums for The Doobie Brothers and Van Halen.	
3/18/67	**13**	7	1. The 59th Street Bridge Song (Feelin' Groovy) written by Paul Simon; arranged by Leon Russell	Warner 5890
6/17/67	**37**	3	2. Come To The Sunshine	Warner 7028
			SLIM HARPO	
			Born James Moore on 1/11/24 in Lobdell, Louisiana (aka: Harmonica Slim). Died of a heart attack on 1/31/70. Blues singer/harmonica player.	
7/10/61	**34**	2	1. Rainin' In My Heart featuring blues guitarist Lightnin' Slim (Otis Hicks)	Excello 2194
3/05/66	**16**	8	2. Baby Scratch My Back [I]	Excello 2273

DATE	POS	WKS	ARTIST—RECORD TITLE	LABEL & NO.
			BETTY HARRIS	
			Born in 1943 in Orlando, Florida. Worked as maid to Big Maybelle, later brought on stage for duets with Maybelle. Worked as road manager for James Carr.	
10/26/63	**23**	6	1. Cry To Me	Jubilee 5456
			EDDIE HARRIS	
			Born in 1936 in Chicago. Jazz tenor saxophonist.	
5/29/61	**36**	3	1. Exodus [I] jazz version of the main theme from the film of the same title	Vee-Jay 378
			EMMYLOU HARRIS	
			Born on 4/2/47 in Birmingham, Alabama. Contemporary country vocalist. Sang back-up with Gram Parsons until his death in 1973. Own band from 1975.	
4/11/81	**37**	3	1. Mister Sandman	Warner 49684
			MAJOR HARRIS	
			Born on 2/9/47 in Richmond, Virginia. Soul singer; sang with The Jarmels, Teenagers, and Impacts in the early 60s. With The Delfonics from 1971-74.	
4/19/75	**5**	14	● 1. **Love Won't Let Me Wait**	Atlantic 3248
			RICHARD HARRIS	
			Born on 10/1/30 in Limerick, Ireland. Began prolific acting career in 1958. Portrayed King Arthur in the film version of "Camelot."	
5/25/68	**2**(1)	10	1. **MacArthur Park**	Dunhill 4134
			ROLF HARRIS	
			Born in Perth, Australia on 3/30/30. Played piano from age 9. Moved to England in the mid-50s. Developed his unique "wobble board sound" out of a sheet of masonite. Had own BBC-TV series from 1970.	
6/22/63	**3**	9	1. **Tie Me Kangaroo Down, Sport** [N]	Epic 9596
			SAM HARRIS	
			Winner of TV's "Star Search" male vocalist category in 1984.	
11/03/84	**36**	3	1. Sugar Don't Bite	Motown 1743
			THURSTON HARRIS	
			Born on 7/11/31 in Indianapolis. First recorded with the Lamplighters in 1953.	
10/28/57	**6**	13	1. **Little Bitty Pretty One** Best Seller #6 / Top 100 #6 / Jockey #12 vocal backing: The Sharps	Aladdin 3398
			GEORGE HARRISON	
			Born on 2/25/43 in Liverpool, England. Formed his first group, the Rebels at age 13. Joined John Lennon and Paul McCartney in The Quarrymen in 1958; group later evolved into The Beatles, with Harrison as lead guitarist. Organized the Bangladesh benefit concerts at Madison Square Garden in 1971. Member of the 1988 supergroup Traveling Wilburys.	
12/05/70	**1**(4)	13	● 1. **My Sweet Lord/**	
		13	2. Isn't It A Pity	Apple 2995
3/06/71	**10**	8	3. **What Is Life**	Apple 1828
8/28/71	**23**	5	4. Bangla-Desh	Apple 1836
5/26/73	**1**(1)	11	5. **Give Me Love (Give Me Peace On Earth)**	Apple 1862
12/14/74†	**15**	6	6. Dark Horse	Apple 1877
2/01/75	**36**	2	7. Ding Dong; Ding Dong	Apple 1879
10/11/75	**20**	6	8. You	Apple 1884

DATE	POS	WKS	ARTIST—RECORD TITLE	LABEL & NO.
12/11/76†	**25**	7	9. This Song	Dark Horse 8294
2/12/77	**19**	7	10. Crackerbox Palace	Dark Horse 8313
3/31/79	**16**	8	11. Blow Away	Dark Horse 8763
5/23/81	**2**(3)	11	12. **All Those Years Ago**	Dark Horse 49725
11/14/87†	**1**(1)	15	13. **Got My Mind Set On You** originally recorded by James Ray in 1962 (Dynamic Sound 503)	Dark Horse 28178
2/27/88	**23**	6	14. When We Was Fab	Dark Horse 28131
			WILBERT HARRISON	
			Born on 1/5/29 in Charlotte, North Carolina. R&B singer; plays several instruments as a one-man band. Joined W.C. Baker band. First recorded for Glades in 1952.	
4/27/59	**1**(2)	12	1. **Kansas City**	Fury 1023
1/24/70	**32**	4	2. Let's Work Together (Part 1)	Sue 11
			COREY HART	
			Born in Montreal, Canada; raised in Spain and Mexico. Singer/songwriter/keyboardist.	
6/23/84	**7**	15	1. **Sunglasses At Night**	EMI America 8203
10/20/84	**17**	9	2. It Ain't Enough	EMI America 8236
6/22/85	**3**	14	3. **Never Surrender**	EMI America 8268
10/05/85	**26**	6	4. Boy In The Box	EMI America 8287
12/28/85†	**30**	7	5. Everything In My Heart	EMI America 8300
10/11/86	**18**	7	6. I Am By Your Side	EMI America 8348
1/31/87	**24**	5	7. Can't Help Falling In Love	EMI America 8368
7/23/88	**38**	2	8. In Your Soul	EMI-Man. 50134
			FREDDIE HART	
			Born on 12/21/26 in Lochapoka, Alabama. Country singer/songwriter/guitarist.	
9/25/71	**17**	12	● 1. Easy Loving	Capitol 3115
			DAN HARTMAN	
			Multi-instrumentalist/songwriter/producer from Harrisburg, Pennsylvania. Member of the Edgar Winter Group from 1972-76. Own studio called the Schoolhouse in Westport, Connecticut.	
12/02/78†	**29**	7	● 1. Instant Replay	Blue Sky 2772
6/02/84	**6**	16	2. **I Can Dream About You** from the film "Streets Of Fire"	MCA 52378
11/03/84	**25**	9	3. We Are The Young	MCA 52471
3/23/85	**39**	2	4. Second Nature	MCA 52519
			HARVEY & THE MOONGLOWS - see THE MOONGLOWS	
			DONNY HATHAWAY - see ROBERTA FLACK	
			RICHIE HAVENS	
			Born on 1/21/41 in Brooklyn. Black folksinger/guitarist.	
4/24/71	**16**	9	1. Here Comes The Sun written by George Harrison (on Beatles' "Abbey Road" album)	Stormy F. 656

DATE	POS	WKS	ARTIST—RECORD TITLE	LABEL & NO.
			DALE HAWKINS	
			Born Delmar Allen Hawkins on 8/22/38 in Goldmine, Louisiana. Rockabilly singer/ guitarist. Toured with R&B package shows. Record production work since 1965.	
7/01/57	**27**	5	1. Susie-Q Best Seller #27 / Top 100 #29	Checker 863
10/13/58	**32**	3	2. La-Do-Dada Hot 100 #32 / Best Seller #44 end	Checker 900
			THE EDWIN HAWKINS' SINGERS	
			Formed by Edwin Hawkins and Betty Watson in Oakland in 1967 as the Northern California State Youth Choir. Member Dorothy Morrison went on to a solo career.	
5/03/69	**4**	9	• 1. **Oh Happy Day** featuring vocalist Dorothy Combs Morrison	Pavilion 20001
5/16/70	**6**	14	2. **Lay Down (Candles In The Rain)** **MELANIE with THE EDWIN HAWKINS' SINGERS**	Buddah 167
			RONNIE HAWKINS	
			Born on 1/10/35 in Huntsville, Arkansas. Formed The Hawks in 1952. To Canada in 1958; assembled group later known as The Band.	
9/21/59	**26**	7	1. Mary Lou	Roulette 4177
			DEANE HAWLEY	
7/04/60	**29**	5	1. Look For A Star from the film "Circus Of Horrors"	Dore 554
			BILL HAYES	
			Born on 6/5/26 in Harvey, Illinois. Bill was a regular on Sid Caesar's TV series "Your Show of Shows." Played Doug Williams on the TV soap opera "Days Of Our Lives."	
2/26/55	**1**(5)	20	1. **The Ballad Of Davy Crockett** Best Seller #1(5) / Jockey #1(3) / Juke Box #1(3)	Cadence 1256
2/16/57	**33**	3	2. Wringle, Wrangle from the movie "Westward Ho, The Wagons"	ABC-Para. 9785
			ISAAC HAYES	
			Born on 8/20/42 in Covington, Tennessee. Soul singer/songwriter/keyboardist/ producer. Session musician for Otis Redding and other artists on the Stax label. Teamed with songwriter David Porter to compose "Soul Man," "Hold On! I'm A Comin'" and many others. Composed film score for "Shaft," "Tough Guys" and "Truck Turner."	
9/27/69	**37**	4	1. By The Time I Get To Phoenix/	
10/18/69	**30**	5	2. Walk On By	Enterprise 9003
6/12/71	**22**	5	3. Never Can Say Goodbye	Enterprise 9031
10/23/71	**1**(2)	12	4. **Theme From Shaft** from the Richard Roundtree film "Shaft"	Enterprise 9038
3/25/72	**30**	5	5. Do Your Thing	Enterprise 9042
12/02/72	**38**	2	6. Theme From The Men [I] from the ABC-TV series "The Men"	Enterprise 9058
1/12/74	**30**	5	7. Joy - Pt. I	Enterprise 9085
12/08/79†	**18**	12	8. Don't Let Go	Polydor 2011

DATE	POS	WKS	ARTIST—RECORD TITLE	LABEL & NO.
			RICHARD HAYMAN & JAN AUGUST	
			Hayman: born on 3/27/20 in Cambridge, Massachusetts. Conductor/arranger/harmonica soloist. August: pianist; died on 1/17/76.	
2/11/56	**11**	11	1. A Theme from "The Three Penny Opera" (Moritat) [I] Jockey #11 / Top 100 #12 / Best Seller #13 / Juke Box #13	Mercury 70781
			LEON HAYWOOD	
			Born on 2/11/42 in Houston. Soul singer/keyboardist. With Big Jay McNeely, and Sam Cooke, early 1960s.	
11/01/75	**15**	8	1. I Want'a Do Something Freaky To You	20th Century 2228
			LEE HAZLEWOOD - see NANCY SINATRA	
			MURRAY HEAD	
			British singer/actor. Played juvenile lead in 1971 film "Sunday, Bloody Sunday."	
5/08/71	**14**	8	1. Superstar [R] with the Trinidad Singers; from "Jesus Christ Superstar - A Rock Opera"; originally charted in 1970 (POS 74)	Decca 32603
3/23/85	**3**	13	2. **One Night In Bangkok** from the Tim Rice, Benny Andersson and Bjorn Ulvaeus musical project "Chess"	RCA 13988
			ROY HEAD	
			Born on 1/9/43 in Three Rivers, Texas. Rock-country singer/guitarist.	
9/18/65	**2**(2)	9	1. **Treat Her Right** **ROY HEAD & THE TRAITS**	Back Beat 546
12/04/65	**39**	1	2. Just A Little Bit	Scepter 12116
12/18/65	**32**	2	3. Apple Of My Eye **ROY HEAD & THE TRAITS**	Back Beat 555
			HEART	
			Rock band formed in Seattle in 1973. Originally known as The Army, then White Heart, shortened to Heart in 1974. Group features Ann Wilson (lead singer) and her sister Nancy (guitar, keyboards). Band moved to Vancouver, Canada in 1975 when their manager Mike Fisher was drafted, and signed with new Mushroom label. When amnesty was declared, group returned to Seattle and signed with the CBS Portrait label in 1976. In addition to the Wilson sisters, the lineup since 1982 includes guitarist Howard Leese, bassist Mark Andes and drummer Denny Carmassi.	
5/29/76	**35**	2	1. Crazy On You re-charted in 1978 (POS 62)	Mushroom 7021
9/04/76	**9**	14	2. **Magic Man**	Mushroom 7011
7/02/77	**11**	12	3. Barracuda	Portrait 70004
5/13/78	**24**	7	4. Heartless	Mushroom 7031
10/28/78	**15**	10	5. Straight On	Portrait 70020
3/17/79	**34**	3	6. Dog & Butterfly	Portrait 70025
3/15/80	**33**	4	7. Even It Up	Epic 50847
11/29/80†	**8**	11	8. **Tell It Like It Is**	Epic 50950
6/19/82	**33**	4	9. This Man Is Mine	Epic 02925
6/29/85	**10**	12	10. **What About Love?**	Capitol 5481
10/05/85	**4**	14	11. **Never**	Capitol 5512
2/01/86	**1**(1)	13	12. **These Dreams**	Capitol 5541
5/03/86	**10**	10	13. **Nothin' At All**	Capitol 5572

DATE	POS	WKS	ARTIST—RECORD TITLE	LABEL & NO.
5/23/87	**1**(3)	15	14. **Alone**	Capitol 44002
8/29/87	**7**	11	15. **Who Will You Run To**	Capitol 44040
11/28/87†	**12**	11	16. There's The Girl	Capitol 44089
			JOEY HEATHERTON	
			Born on 9/14/44 in Rockville Centre, New York. Movie/TV actress. Began career as a child stage performer.	
7/15/72	**24**	7	1. Gone	MGM 14387
			HEATWAVE	
			Multinational, interracial group formed in Germany by Johnnie & Keith Wilder of Dayton, Ohio. Johnnie injured in auto accident in 1979, paralyzed from neck down.	
8/27/77	**2**(2)	17	▲ 1. **Boogie Nights**	Epic 50370
2/04/78	**18**	11	● 2. Always And Forever	Epic 50490
6/03/78	**7**	11	● 3. **The Groove Line**	Epic 50524
			BOBBY HEBB	
			Born on 7/26/41 in Nashville. Singer/songwriter/multi-instrumentalist. Featured on the Grand Ole Opry at age 12. His brother Hal was a member of the Marigolds.	
7/23/66	**2**(2)	11	● 1. **Sunny**	Philips 40365
11/05/66	**39**	1	2. A Satisfied Mind	Philips 40400
			NEAL HEFTI	
			Born on 10/29/22 in Hastings, Nebraska. Trumpeter; most famous as arranger for Woody Herman (1944-46), Harry James and Count Basie, then as composer of TV themes.	
3/05/66	**35**	4	1. Batman Theme [I]	RCA 8755
			BOBBY HELMS	
			Born on 8/15/33 in Bloomington, Indiana. Country singer/guitarist. Appeared on father's local TV show for 6 years.	
10/14/57	**7**	15	1. **My Special Angel** Best Seller #7 / Top 100 #7 / Jockey #8	Decca 30423
10/14/57	**36**	2	2. Fraulein Top 100 #36 / Best Seller #46	Decca 30194
12/23/57	**6**	4	3. **Jingle Bell Rock** **[X]** Top 100 #6 / Best Seller #7 / Jockey #11	Decca 30513
12/28/58	**35**	1	4. Jingle Bell Rock [X-R]	Decca 30513
12/26/60	**36**	1	5. Jingle Bell Rock [X-R]	Decca 30513
			JOE HENDERSON	
			R&B singer, born in 1938 in Como, Mississippi; raised in Gary, Indiana. Moved to Nashville in 1958. With the Fairfield Four gospel group. Died in 1966.	
6/02/62	**8**	10	1. **Snap Your Fingers**	Todd 1072

Bob Dylan is one of the most important American musicians of his generation. Though his chart success has been sporadic (he didn't even have a No. 1 album until 1974's *Planet Waves*), he practically invented folk-rock, protest-rock, soft-rock, country-rock, and singer-songwriter rock. He had one of his biggest hits as a member of the Traveling Wilburys, with their No. 3 LP in 1988.

Earth, Wind & Fire was the leading black/pop act of the late 70s, with two No. 1 albums and nine top-20 singles. The group's much-vaunted 1987 reunion produced a gold album, *Touch the World*, but met with resistance at pop radio, which apparently has a short memory.

Sheena Easton is the queen of reverse crossover. Her first hit, "Morning Train," hit No. 1 on the pop chart in 1981. She later had a No. 1 country single ("We've Got Tonight," with Kenny Rogers), and a top-three Black and Dance hit ("Sugar Walls").

Duane Eddy is rock's leading instrumentalist, with 28 chart singles. He teamed with the Art of Noise in 1986 for a remake of his theme from "Peter Gunn."

Dave Edmunds formed, with Nick Lowe, the seminal rock band Rockpile, and has been a key figure in uncovering important new talent—Elvis Costello and Graham Parker got their first exposure as songwriters on Edmunds' albums.

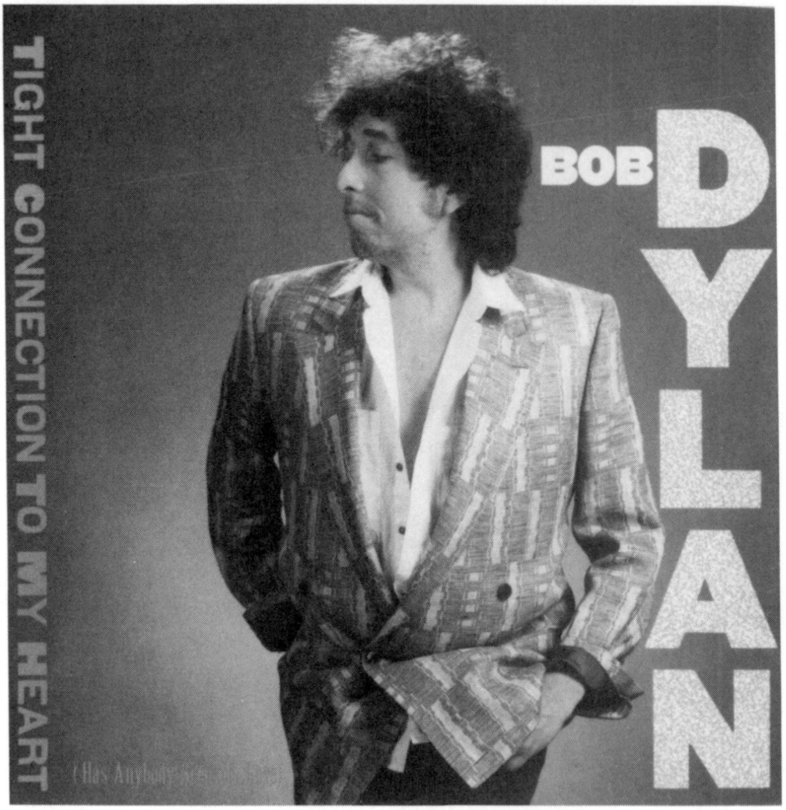

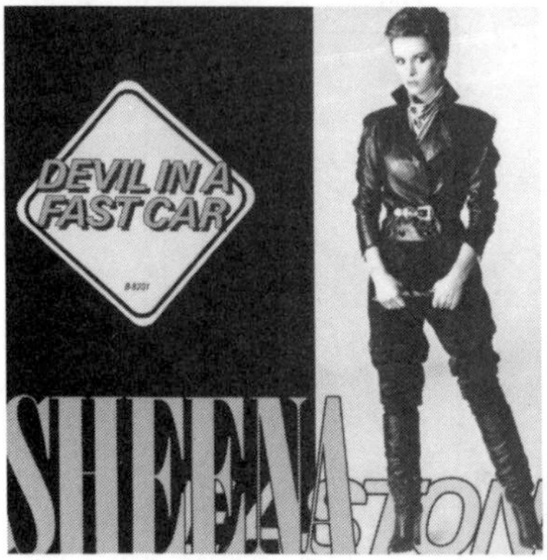

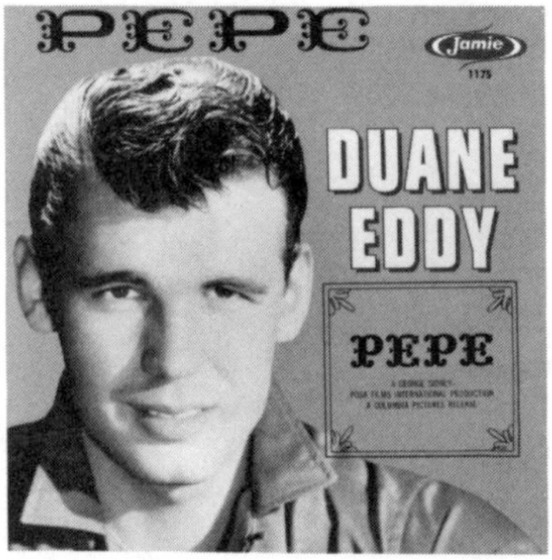

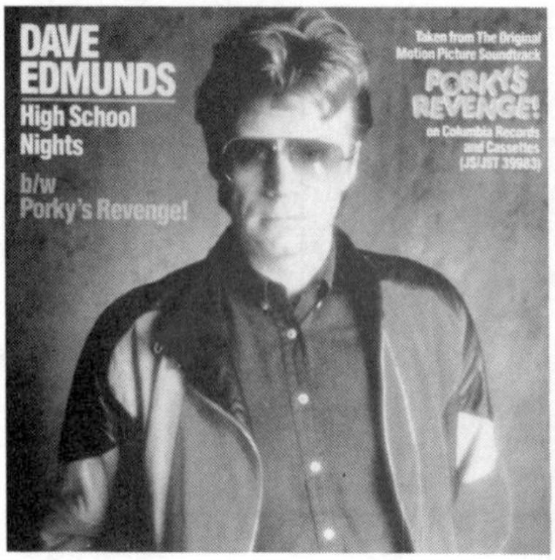

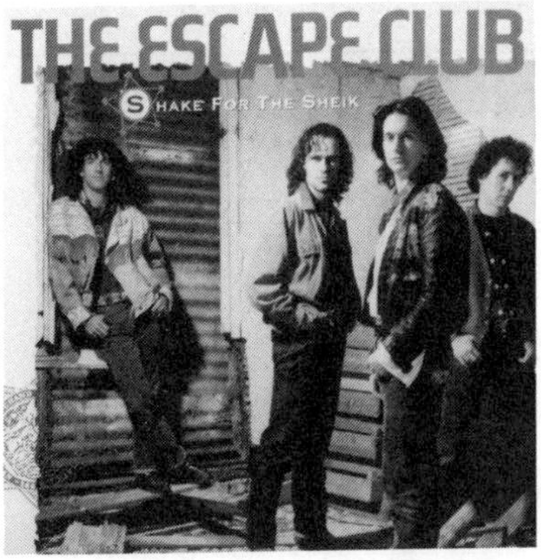

Emerson, Lake & Powell never quite caught on the way Emerson, Lake & Palmer did. Their lone album peaked at No. 23 in 1986, and was forgotten soon after. Apparently they didn't learn anything from Hamilton, Joe Frank & Reynolds.

The Escape Club's "Wild Wild West" hit No. 1, but the follow-up, "Shake for the Sheik," peaked at No. 28, which indicates that they should stay on this side of this hemisphere when looking for subject matter for their songs.

Europe got to No. 8 with the LP *The Final Countdown*, but three "continent" groups did even better. America, Asia, and USA for Africa all had No. 1 albums.

The Eurythmics have been among the most adventurous pop groups of the 80s, from the eerie technopop of "Sweet Dreams (Are Made Of This)" (No. 1, 1983) to the light calypso of "Right By Your Side" (No. 29, 1984) to the hard soul of "Sisters Are Doin' It For Themselves" (No. 16, 1985).

The Everly Brothers had more hits than any other duo of the rock era, including four No. 1s—"Wake Up Little Susie," "Bird Dog," "All I Have To Do Is Dream," and "Cathy's Clown" (the first No. 1 for the Warner Bros. label). The Beatles imitated their harmonies, and Paul McCartney repaid the debt by writing the Everlys' return to the charts, "On The Wings Of A Nightingale," in 1984.

Exposé had four top-10 hits in one year—more than such classic girl groups as the Marvelettes, Crystals, Chiffons, and Shangri-Las had in their entire careers.

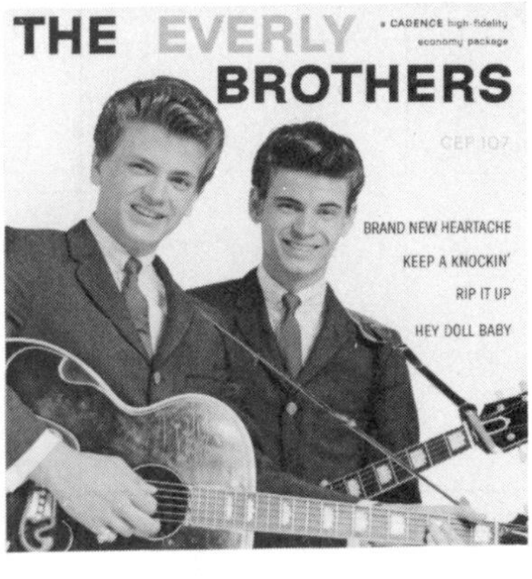

DATE	POS	WKS	ARTIST—RECORD TITLE	LABEL & NO.
			MICHAEL HENDERSON - see NORMAN CONNORS	
			BOBBY HENDRICKS	
			Born on 2/22/38 in Columbus, Ohio. R&B vocalist. With the Swallows in 1956. First recorded with the Flyers for Atco in 1957. With The Drifters, 1958, then went solo.	
9/01/58	**25**	4	1. Itchy Twitchy Feeling Hot 100 #25 / Best Seller #35 backing vocals: The Coasters	Sue 706
			THE JIMI HENDRIX EXPERIENCE	
			Born on 11/27/42 in Seattle. Died of a drug overdose in London on 9/18/70 (27). Legendary psychedelic-blues guitarist. Began career as a studio guitarist. In 1965, formed own band, Jimmy James & The Blue Flames. Created The Jimi Hendrix Experience in 1966, with Noel Redding on bass and Mitch Mitchell on drums. Formed new group in 1969, Band of Gypsys, with Buddy Miles on drums and Billy Cox on bass.	
9/28/68	**20**	8	1. All Along The Watchtower	Reprise 0767
			HENHOUSE FIVE PLUS TOO - see RAY STEVENS	
			DON HENLEY	
			Born on 7/22/47 in Gilmer, Texas. Singer/songwriter/drummer. Own band, Shiloh, in the early 70s. Worked with Glenn Frey in Linda Ronstadt's back-up band, then the two formed the Eagles with Randy Meisner and Bernie Leadon. Went solo in 1982.	
11/07/81†	**6**	15	1. **Leather And Lace** **STEVIE NICKS with DON HENLEY**	Modern 7341
11/13/82†	**3**	14	● 2. **Dirty Laundry**	Asylum 69894
12/08/84†	**5**	14	3. **The Boys Of Summer**	Geffen 29141
3/16/85	**9**	11	4. **All She Wants To Do Is Dance**	Geffen 29065
7/06/85	**34**	5	5. Not Enough Love In The World	Geffen 29012
9/21/85	**22**	8	6. Sunset Grill	Geffen 28906
			CLARENCE "Frogman" HENRY	
			Born on 3/19/37 in Algiers, Louisiana. R&B vocalist/pianist/trombonist. With Bobby Mitchell's R&B band from 1953-55. Nicknamed "Frogman" from hit "Ain't Got No Home."	
1/12/57	**20**	3	1. Ain't Got No Home [N] Best Seller #20 / Top 100 #30	Argo 5259
3/20/61	**4**	11	2. **But I Do** also titled "I Don't Know Why"	Argo 5378
5/29/61	**12**	7	3. You Always Hurt The One You Love #1 hit in 1944 for The Mills Brothers	Argo 5388
			JIM HENSON	
			Creator of The Muppets, that famous crew of puppets starring in TV's "Sesame Street" and "The Muppet Show," also in the films "The Muppet Movie" and "The Great Muppet Caper." Jim is the voice for both Ernie and Kermit.	
8/29/70	**16**	7	1. Rubber Duckie [N] **ERNIE**	Columbia 45207
10/20/79	**25**	7	2. Rainbow Connection **KERMIT** from the original soundtrack of "The Muppet Movie"	Atlantic 3610

DATE	POS	WKS	ARTIST—RECORD TITLE	LABEL & NO.
			HERMAN'S HERMITS	
			Formed in Manchester, England in 1964. Named after a cartoon character in TV's "The Bullwinkle Show." Consisted of Peter "Herman" Noone (b: 11/5/47; vocals), Derek Leckenby and Keith Hopwood (guitars), Karl Green (bass) and Barry Whithman (drums). First called The Heartbeats. Noone left in 1972 for a solo career.	
11/14/64	**13**	9	1. I'm Into Something Good	MGM 13280
2/20/65	**2**(2)	11	2. **Can't You Hear My Heartbeat**	MGM 13310
4/17/65	**1**(3)	11	● 3. **Mrs. Brown You've Got A Lovely Daughter**	MGM 13341
4/17/65	**5**	10	4. **Silhouettes**	MGM 13332
6/05/65	**4**	8	5. **Wonderful World**	MGM 13354
7/10/65	**1**(1)	8	● 6. **I'm Henry VIII, I Am** written in 1911; popularized in England by Harry Champion	MGM 13367
9/25/65	**7**	8	7. **Just A Little Bit Better**	MGM 13398
1/01/66	**8**	8	8. **A Must To Avoid**	MGM 13437
2/26/66	**3**	7	9. **Listen People** from the film "When The Boys Meet The Girls"	MGM 13462
4/16/66	**9**	7	10. **Leaning On The Lamp Post** 8 & 10: from the film "Hold On!"	MGM 13500
7/23/66	**12**	5	11. This Door Swings Both Ways	MGM 13548
10/15/66	**5**	8	12. **Dandy**	MGM 13603
12/24/66	**27**	5	13. East West	MGM 13639
3/04/67	**4**	9	● 14. **There's A Kind Of Hush/**	
3/18/67	**35**	4	15. No Milk Today	MGM 13681
7/08/67	**18**	4	16. Don't Go Out Into The Rain (You're Going To Melt)	MGM 13761
9/16/67	**39**	2	17. Museum	MGM 13787
2/03/68	**22**	6	18. I Can Take Or Leave Your Loving all of above: produced by Mickie Most	MGM 13885
			PATRICK HERNANDEZ	
			Born in 1949 in Paris, France of a Spanish father and Austrian/Italian mother. Rock-disco artist.	
8/04/79	**16**	11	● 1. Born To Be Alive	Columbia 10986
			THE HESITATIONS	
			Soul group from Cleveland. Lead singer George "King" Scott was accidentally killed by a bullet from a gun owned by tenor Fred Deal in February, 1968.	
2/17/68	**38**	2	1. Born Free from the film of the same title	Kapp 878
			EDDIE HEYWOOD	
			Born on 12/4/15 in Atlanta. Black jazz pianist/composer/arranger. Played profes- sionally by age 14. Own band in New York City in 1941. Worked with Billie Holiday. Recorded duet with conductor Hugo Winterhalter (b: 8/15/09; d: 9/17/73 of cancer).	
7/21/56	**11**	18	1. Soft Summer Breeze [I] Best Seller #11 / Top 100 #12 / Juke Box #13 / Jockey #14	Mercury 70863
7/28/56	**2**(2)	23	2. **Canadian Sunset** **[I]** **HUGO WINTERHALTER with EDDIE HEYWOOD** above 2: written by Heywood	RCA 6537

DATE	POS	WKS	ARTIST—RECORD TITLE	LABEL & NO.
			AL HIBBLER	
			Born on 8/16/15 in Little Rock, Arkansas. Blind since birth, studied voice at Little Rock's Conservatory for the Blind. First recorded with Jay McShann for Decca in 1942. With Duke Ellington, 1943-51. Also recorded with Harry Carney, Tab Smith, Mercer Ellington and Billy Strayhorn.	
4/09/55	**3**	19	1. **Unchained Melody** Jockey #3 / Juke Box #3 / Best Seller #5 from the film "Unchained"	Decca 29441
10/15/55	**4**	22	2. **He** Best Seller #4 / Top 100 #7 / Jockey #7 / Juke Box #8	Decca 29660
2/25/56	**21**	5	3. 11th Hour Melody	Decca 29789
7/14/56	**22**	2	4. Never Turn Back Jockey #22 / Top 100 #48	Decca 29950
8/25/56	**10**	12	5. **After The Lights Go Down Low** Jockey #10 / Juke Box #14 / Top 100 #15 / Best Seller #20	Decca 29982
			BERTIE HIGGINS	
			Singer/songwriter, born in 1946 in Tarpon Springs, Florida. First recorded for ABC in 1964. Worked as a drummer with the Roemans from 1964-66.	
1/16/82	**8**	17	1. **Key Largo** inspired by Humphrey Bogart/Lauren Bacall film of the same title	Kat Family 02524
			HIGH INERGY	
			Female soul group from Pasadena, California: Barbara Mitchell, Linda Howard, Michelle Rumph and Vernessa Mitchell (left in 1978; group continued as a trio).	
11/19/77	**12**	11	1. You Can't Turn Me Off (In The Middle Of Turning Me On)	Gordy 7155
			THE HIGHLIGHTS	
			Frank Pizani, lead singer.	
11/10/56	**19**	5	1. City Of Angels Best Seller #19 / Top 100 #30	Bally 1016
			THE HIGHWAYMEN	
			Folk quintet formed at Wesleyan University in Middletown, Connecticut: Dave Fisher, Bob Burnett, Steve Trott, Steve Butts and Chan Daniels (died on 8/2/75).	
7/31/61	**1**(2)	11	1. **Michael** traditional folk song ("Michael Row The Boat Ashore") from the 19th century	United Art. 258
12/25/61†	**13**	13	2. Cotton Fields traditional American ballad, copyrighted in 1850	United Art. 370
			BUNKER HILL	
			Born David Walker on 5/5/41 in Washington, DC. Professional boxer. Ex-lead singer of the gospel group Mighty Clouds Of Joy.	
10/13/62	**33**	3	1. Hide & Go Seek, Part I	Mala 451
			DAN HILL	
			Born on 6/3/54 in Toronto, Canada. Author/singer/songwriter.	
12/24/77†	**3**	15	• 1. **Sometimes When We Touch**	20th Century 2355
7/25/87	**6**	13	2. **Can't We Try** **DAN HILL with VONDA SHEPPARD**	Columbia 07050

DATE	POS	WKS	ARTIST—RECORD TITLE	LABEL & NO.
			JESSIE HILL	
			Born on 12/9/32 in New Orleans. R&B singer/drummer/pianist. With Huey Smith to 1958.	
5/09/60	**28**	4	1. Ooh Poo Pah Doo - Part II [I]	Minit 607
			THE HILLSIDE SINGERS	
			9-member vocal group assembled by producer/arranger Al Ham.	
12/11/71†	**13**	10	1. I'd Like To Teach The World To Sing (In Perfect Harmony)	Metromedia 231
			adapted from a Coca-Cola jingle	
			THE HILLTOPPERS	
			Quartet formed at Western Kentucky College in Bowling Green, Kentucky in 1952. Group named after the school's nickname. Consisted of: Jimmy Sacca (lead singer), Don McGuire, Seymour Spiegelman and Billy Vaughn. Vaughn left in 1955 to become Dot's musical director with a recording career of his own.	
7/30/55	**20**	4	1. The Kentuckian Song	Dot 15375
			Best Seller #20	
			from the Burt Lancaster film "The Kentuckian"	
11/12/55	**8**	13	2. **Only You (And You Alone)**	Dot 15423
			Jockey #8 / Top 100 #9 / Juke Box #10 / Best Seller #16	
1/21/56	**31**	1	3. My Treasure	Dot 15437
10/06/56	**38**	2	4. Ka-Ding-Dong	Dot 15489
2/09/57	**3**	13	5. **Marianne**	Dot 15537
			Juke Box #3 / Jockey #6 / Top 100 #8 / Best Seller #12	
11/25/57	**22**	4	6. The Joker (That's What They Call Me)	Dot 15662
			Jockey #22 / Best Seller #34 / Top 100 #37	
			JOE HINTON	
			Soul singer, born in 1929; died on 8/13/68 in Boston. With Chosen Gospel Singers; lead singer of the Spirits Of Memphis gospel group.	
9/05/64	**13**	9	1. Funny	Back Beat 541
			HIPSWAY	
			Scottish quartet; Grahame Skinner, lead singer.	
3/14/87	**19**	6	1. The Honeythief	Columbia 06579
			AL HIRT	
			Born Alois Maxwell Hirt on 11/7/22 in New Orleans. Trumpet virtuoso. Toured with Jimmy & Tommy Dorsey, Ray McKinley and Horace Heidt. Formed own dixieland combo (with clarinetist Pete Fountain) in the late 50s.	
1/25/64	**4**	13	1. **Java** **[I]**	RCA 8280
5/02/64	**15**	8	2. Cotton Candy [I]	RCA 8346
8/01/64	**30**	4	3. Sugar Lips [I]	RCA 8391
			EDDIE HODGES	
			Born on 3/5/47 in Hattiesburg, Mississippi. Played Frank Sinatra's son in the film "A Hole In The Head."	
7/24/61	**12**	8	1. I'm Gonna Knock On Your Door	Cadence 1397
7/07/62	**14**	8	2. (Girls, Girls, Girls) Made To Love	Cadence 1421
			written by Phil Everly (of The Everly Brothers)	

DATE	POS	WKS	ARTIST—RECORD TITLE	LABEL & NO.
			RON HOLDEN	
			Born on 8/7/39 in Seattle. R&B vocalist. In group The Playboys in 1957. Worked as emcee at Art Laboe's "Oldies But Goodies" club from 1972-77.	
4/25/60	**7**	13	1. **Love You So**	Donna 1315
			instrumental backing by The Thunderbirds	
			AMY HOLLAND	
			Daughter of country singer Esmereldy and opera singer Harry Boersma. Married to singer/keyboardist Michael McDonald.	
9/13/80	**22**	6	1. How Do I Survive	Capitol 4884
			produced by Michael McDonald (of The Doobie Brothers)	
			EDDIE HOLLAND	
			Born on 10/30/39 in Detroit. Singer/songwriter/producer. Member of Motown's hit-production trio with brother Brian Holland and Lamont Dozier; wrote many of Motown's all-time greatest hits. Co-founder of the Invictus/Hot Wax label.	
3/10/62	**30**	4	1. Jamie	Motown 1021
			JENNIFER HOLLIDAY	
			Born on 10/19/60 in Houston. 1982 Tony award winner for Best Actress in Broadway's "Dreamgirls." Also in Broadway's "Your Arm's Too Short To Box With God" (1978) and "Sing, Mahalia Sing" (1985).	
7/31/82	**22**	7	1. And I Am Telling You I'm Not Going	Geffen 29983
			from the original Broadway cast "Dreamgirls"	
			THE HOLLIES	
			Formed in Manchester, England in 1962. Consisted of Allan Clarke (lead vocals), Graham Nash and Tony Hicks (guitars), Eric Haydock (bass) and Don Rathbone (drums). Clarke and Nash had worked as duo, the Guytones, added other members, became the Fourtones, Deltas, then The Hollies. First recorded for Parlophone in 1963. Rathbone left in 1963, replaced by Bobby Elliott. Haydock left in 1966, replaced by Bernie Calvert (first heard on "Bus Stop"). Nash left in December, 1968, replaced by Terry Sylvester, formerly in the Swinging Blue Jeans. Regrouped in 1983 with Clarke, Nash, Hicks and Elliott.	
1/08/66	**32**	4	1. Look Through Any Window	Imperial 66134
8/20/66	**5**	9	2. **Bus Stop**	Imperial 66186
11/12/66	**7**	7	3. **Stop Stop Stop**	Imperial 66214
4/15/67	**11**	9	4. On A Carousel	Imperial 66231
6/24/67	**28**	3	5. Pay You Back With Interest	Imperial 66240
7/08/67	**9**	10	6. **Carrie-Anne**	Epic 10180
5/18/68	**40**	1	7. Jennifer Eccles	Epic 10298
2/07/70	**7**	11	8. **He Ain't Heavy, He's My Brother**	Epic 10532
7/08/72	**2**(2)	13	• 9. **Long Cool Woman (In A Black Dress)**	Epic 10871
12/02/72	**26**	5	10. Long Dark Road	Epic 10920
6/08/74	**6**	11	• 11. **The Air That I Breathe**	Epic 11100
			all of above: produced by Ron Richards	
7/02/83	**29**	6	12. Stop In The Name Of Love	Atlantic 89819
			BRENDA HOLLOWAY	
			Born on 6/21/46 in Atascadero, California. Soul singer/songwriter. Later a back-up singer for Joe Cocker.	
5/23/64	**13**	6	1. Every Little Bit Hurts	Tamla 54094
3/27/65	**25**	5	2. When I'm Gone	Tamla 54111
11/04/67	**39**	1	3. You've Made Me So Very Happy	Tamla 54155

DATE	POS	WKS	ARTIST—RECORD TITLE	LABEL & NO.
			BUDDY HOLLY	
			Born Charles Hardin Holley on 9/7/36 in Lubbock, Texas. Began recording (western & bop) demos with Bob Montgomery in 1954. Signed to Decca label in January, 1956, and recorded in Nashville as Buddy Holly & The Three Tunes (Sonny Curtis, lead guitar; Don Guess, bass; and Jerry Allison, drums). In February of 1957, Buddy assembled his backing group, The Crickets (Allison; Niki Sullivan, rhythm guitar; and Joel B. Mauldin, bass) for recordings at Norman Petty's studio in Clovis, New Mexico. Signed to Brunswick and Coral labels (subsidiaries of Decca Records). Because of contract arrangements, all Brunswick records released as The Crickets, and all Coral records were released as Buddy Holly. Holly split from The Crickets in autumn, 1958. Buddy, Ritchie Valens and the Big Bopper were killed in a plane crash near Mason City, Iowa on 2/3/59 (22). Holly was inducted into the Rock And Roll Hall Of Fame in 1986.	
8/19/57	**1**(1)	16	• 1. **That'll Be The Day** Best Seller #1 / Top 100 #3 / Jockey #3	Brunswick 55009
11/11/57	**3**	16	2. **Peggy Sue** Best Seller #3 / Top 100 #3 / Jockey #3 first known as "Cindy Lou"; renamed after Allison's girlfriend	Coral 61885
12/02/57†	**10**	13	3. **Oh, Boy!** Top 100 #10 / Best Seller #11 / Jockey #20	Brunswick 55035
3/10/58	**17**	8	4. Maybe Baby Jockey #17 / Best Seller #18 / Top 100 #18	Brunswick 55053
6/09/58	**37**	2	5. Rave On Top 100 #37 / Best Seller #41	Coral 61985
8/04/58	**27**	4	6. Think It Over Hot 100 #27 / Best Seller #38 all of above Brunswick records shown only as: **THE CRICKETS**	Brunswick 55072
8/11/58	**32**	4	7. Early In The Morning Hot 100 #32 / Best Seller #45	Coral 62006
3/09/59	**13**	9	8. It Doesn't Matter Anymore written by Paul Anka	Coral 62074
			HOLLYWOOD ARGYLES	
			Gary Paxton recorded "Alley-Oop" as a solo artist; since he was still under contract to Brent Records, where he recorded as Flip of "Skip & Flip," he made up the name of the Hollywood Argyles. After the song was a hit, Gary assembled a Hollywood Argyles group. Gary is now a gospel artist.	
6/13/60	**1**(1)	11	1. **Alley-Oop** **[N]** written by Dallas Frazier	Lute 5905
			HOLLYWOOD FLAMES	
			Los Angeles-based R&B group formed in 1950 by Bobby Day. Known also as The Flames, Four Flames, Hollywood Four Flames, and The Satellites. Many personnel changes.	
12/02/57†	**11**	12	1. Buzz-Buzz-Buzz Top 100 #11 / Best Seller #12 lead vocal: Earl Nelson (of Bob & Earl)	Ebb 119
			EDDIE HOLMAN	
			Born on 6/3/46 in Norfolk, Virginia. Soul singer/songwriter. First recorded for Leopard in the early 60s.	
1/10/70	**2**(1)	12	• 1. **Hey There Lonely Girl** recorded in 1963 by Ruby & The Romantics as "Hey There Lonely Boy"	ABC 11240

DATE	POS	WKS	ARTIST—RECORD TITLE	LABEL & NO.
			CLINT HOLMES	
			Born on 5/9/46 in Bournemouth, England; moved to Buffalo, New York as a child.	
5/05/73	**2**(2)	15	• 1. **Playground In My Mind** child's vocal is by producer Paul Vance's son, Philip	Epic 10891
			RUPERT HOLMES	
			Born on 2/24/47 in Cheshire, England. Moved to New York at age 6. Wrote and arranged for The Drifters, Platters, and Gene Pitney. Arranged/produced for Barbra Streisand.	
11/10/79	**1**(3)	16	• 1. **Escape (The Pina Colada Song)**	Infinity 50035
2/09/80	**6**	12	2. **Him**	MCA 41173
6/14/80	**32**	3	3. Answering Machine	MCA 41235
			THE HOMBRES	
			Memphis, Tennessee foursome.	
10/07/67	**12**	10	1. Let It Out (Let It All Hang Out)	Verve Fore. 5058
			HOMER & JETHRO	
			Henry "Homer" Haynes (b: 7/29/17, Knoxville, TN; d: 8/7/71; guitar) and Kenneth "Jethro" Burns (b: 3/10/23, Knoxville, TN; mandolin). Country music's foremost comedy duo from the 1940s until Homer's death. Jethro went on to work with popular folksinger Steve Goodman.	
9/14/59	**14**	7	1. The Battle Of Kookamonga [C] a parody of "The Battle Of New Orleans"; produced by Chet Atkins	RCA 7585
			THE HONDELLS	
			Southern California-based quartet led by Ritchie Burns.	
10/03/64	**9**	9	1. **Little Honda** written by Brian Wilson of The Beach Boys	Mercury 72324
			THE HONEYCOMBS	
			English rock quintet featuring Dennis D'ell (lead singer) and Ann "Honey" Lantree (drums).	
10/10/64	**5**	9	1. **Have I The Right?**	Interphon 7707
			THE HONEY CONE	
			Female soul trio formed in Los Angeles in 1969. Consisted of prominent back-up singers: Carolyn Willis (member of The Girlfriends and Bob B. Soxx & The Blue Jeans), Edna Wright (sister of Darlene Love; member of The Blossoms and Bob B. Soxx & The Blue Jeans) and Shellie Clark (former Ikette and regular on the TV series "The Jim Nabors Hour" from 1969-70).	
5/01/71	**1**(1)	13	• 1. **Want Ads**	Hot Wax 7011
8/21/71	**11**	10	• 2. Stick-Up	Hot Wax 7106
12/11/71†	**15**	8	3. One Monkey Don't Stop No Show (Part I)	Hot Wax 7110
3/25/72	**23**	6	4. The Day I Found Myself	Hot Wax 7113
			THE HONEYDRIPPERS	
			A rock superstar gathering: Robert Plant, Jimmy Page, Jeff Beck and Nile Rodgers.	
10/27/84†	**3**	14	1. **Sea Of Love**	Es Paranza 99701
1/26/85	**25**	6	2. Rockin' At Midnight recorded by Elvis Presley in 1954 as "Good Rockin' Tonight"	Es Paranza 99686

DATE	POS	WKS	ARTIST—RECORD TITLE	LABEL & NO.
			HONEYMOON SUITE	
			Rock quintet from Toronto, Canada: Johnnie Dee (vocals), Derry Grehan, Rob Preuss, Gary Lalonde and Dave Betts.	
4/26/86	**34**	3	1. Feel It Again	Warner 28779
			HOOTERS	
			Philadelphia rock quintet led by Rob Hyman and Eric Bazilian (arrangers/musicians/ backing vocalists on Cyndi Lauper's platinum album "She's So Unusual"). Hooter: nickname of their keyboard-harmonica.	
9/28/85	**21**	8	1. And We Danced	Columbia 05568
2/01/86	**18**	7	2. Day By Day	Columbia 05730
5/24/86	**38**	1	3. Where Do The Children Go	Columbia 05854
			MARY HOPKIN	
			Born on 5/3/50 in Pontardame, Wales. Discovered by the model Twiggy.	
10/12/68	**2**(3)	12	● 1. **Those Were The Days** melody based on a traditional Russian folk song	Apple 1801
5/03/69	**13**	7	2. Goodbye above 2: produced by Paul McCartney	Apple 1806
3/28/70	**39**	2	3. Temma Harbour	Apple 1816
			JIMMY "BO" HORNE	
			Soul singer/dancer from Miami.	
6/24/78	**38**	1	1. Dance Across The Floor written and produced by Harry "KC" Casey	Sunshine S. 1003
			LENA HORNE	
			Born on 6/30/17 in Brooklyn. Broadway and movie musical star, long married to bandleader Lennie Hayton. Her career reached a new peak in the 1980s with her one-woman Broadway show.	
7/09/55	**19**	1	1. Love Me Or Leave Me Jockey #19 #2 hit for Ruth Etting in 1929	RCA 6073
			BRUCE HORNSBY & THE RANGE	
			Piano-based, jazz-influenced pop quintet led by singer/songwriter/pianist Hornsby, who was raised in Williamsburg, Virginia and moved to Los Angeles in 1980. Formerly the pianist of Sheena Easton's band. Won the 1986 Best New Artist Grammy Award.	
10/18/86	**1**(1)	15	1. **The Way It Is**	RCA 5023
1/31/87	**4**	12	2. **Mandolin Rain**	RCA 5087
5/30/87	**14**	9	3. Every Little Kiss [R]	RCA 5165
5/14/88	**5**	11	4. **The Valley Road**	RCA 7645
8/27/88	**35**	2	5. Look Out Any Window	RCA 8678
			JOHNNY HORTON	
			Country singer, born on 4/3/29 in Tyler, Texas. Married to Billie Jean Jones, widow of country music superstar Hank Williams. Killed in an auto accident on 11/5/60.	
5/04/59	**1**(6)	18	● 1. **The Battle Of New Orleans** original melody written in celebration of the final battle of the War of 1812	Columbia 41339
3/14/60	**3**	13	2. **Sink The Bismarck** inspired by the film of the same title	Columbia 41568
10/17/60	**4**	18	3. **North To Alaska** from the John Wayne film of the same title	Columbia 41782

DATE	POS	WKS	ARTIST—RECORD TITLE	LABEL & NO.
			HOT	
			Integrated female trio consisting of Gwen Owens, Cathy Carson and Juanita Curiel. First known as Sugar & Spice.	
4/02/77	**6**	19	● 1. **Angel In Your Arms**	Big Tree 16085
			HOT BUTTER	
			Stan Free plays the Moog synthesizer.	
8/19/72	**9**	12	1. **Popcorn** [I]	Musicor 1458
			HOT CHOCOLATE	
			Interracial rock-soul group formed in England by lead singer Errol Brown in 1970.	
3/08/75	**8**	9	1. **Emma**	Big Tree 16031
7/05/75	**28**	4	2. Disco Queen	Big Tree 16038
12/06/75†	**3**	15	● 3. **You Sexy Thing**	Big Tree 16047
8/13/77	**31**	5	4. So You Win Again	Big Tree 16096
12/02/78†	**6**	13	● 5. **Every 1's A Winner**	Infinity 50002
			HOTLEGS	
			British trio: Eric Stewart (formerly of The Mindbenders), Kevin Godley and Lol Creme. Graham Gouldman joined the group later on tour. Quartet evolved into 10cc.	
9/05/70	**22**	6	1. Neanderthal Man	Capitol 2886
			DAVID HOUSTON	
			Born on 12/9/38 in Shreveport, Louisiana. Country singer/songwriter/guitarist.	
8/27/66	**24**	8	1. Almost Persuaded	Epic 10025
			THELMA HOUSTON	
			Soul singer/actress from Leland, Mississippi. In films "Norman..Is That You?," "Death Scream" and "The Seventh Dwarf."	
1/29/77	**1**(1)	17	1. **Don't Leave Me This Way**	Tamla 54278
5/19/79	**34**	3	2. Saturday Night, Sunday Morning	Tamla 54297
			WHITNEY HOUSTON	
			Born in 1963 in New Jersey. Billboard's "Artist of the Year" for 1986. Daughter of Cissy Houston and cousin of Dionne Warwick. Began career as a fashion model, then worked as a backing vocalist.	
6/01/85	**3**	13	1. **You Give Good Love**	Arista 9274
8/24/85	**1**(1)	15	2. **Saving All My Love For You**	Arista 9381
12/28/85†	**1**(2)	16	3. **How Will I Know**	Arista 9434
4/05/86	**1**(3)	14	4. **Greatest Love Of All** originally released as the flip side of "You Give Good Love"	Arista 9466
5/16/87	**1**(2)	14	▲ 5. **I Wanna Dance With Somebody (Who Loves Me)**	Arista 9598
8/08/87	**1**(2)	13	6. **Didn't We Almost Have It All**	Arista 9616
11/07/87†	**1**(1)	14	7. **So Emotional**	Arista 9642
3/05/88	**1**(2)	13	8. **Where Do Broken Hearts Go**	Arista 9674
7/09/88	**9**	11	9. **Love Will Save The Day**	Arista 9720
9/24/88	**5**	11	10. **One Moment In Time** tune used by NBC-TV for the 1988 Summer Olympics	Arista 9743

DATE	POS	WKS	ARTIST—RECORD TITLE	LABEL & NO.
			HUDSON BROTHERS	
			Bill, Brett and Mark Hudson from Portland. Own humorous TV variety show, summer of 1974; also hosts of kiddie TV show "The Hudson Brothers Razzle Dazzle Comedy Show." Bill was married to actress Goldie Hawn.	
10/26/74	**21**	5	1. So You Are A Star	Casablanca 0108
8/02/75	**26**	4	2. Rendezvous	Rocket 40417
			THE HUES CORPORATION	
			Black vocal trio formed in Los Angeles in 1969: St. Clair Lee, Fleming Williams and H. Ann Kelley. Williams replaced by Tommy Brown after "Rock The Boat."	
6/15/74	**1**(1)	10	● 1. **Rock The Boat**	RCA 0232
10/26/74	**18**	5	2. Rockin' Soul	RCA 10066
			FRED HUGHES	
			Soul singer from Arkansas. To Los Angeles, formed own band, the Creators.	
6/19/65	**23**	6	1. Oo Wee Baby, I Love You	Vee-Jay 684
			JIMMY HUGHES	
			Soul singer from Florence, Alabama. With Singing Clouds gospel group to 1962. Cousin of Percy Sledge.	
7/11/64	**17**	9	1. Steal Away	Fame 6401
			HUGO & LUIGI	
			Producers, songwriters and label executives Hugo Peretti and Luigi Creator. Hugo died on 5/1/86 (68).	
1/04/60	**35**	3	1. Just Come Home	RCA 7639
			THE HUMAN BEINZ	
			Cleveland bar band.	
1/06/68	**8**	11	1. **Nobody But Me** originally recorded (and written) by The Isley Brothers in 1962	Capitol 5990
			THE HUMAN LEAGUE	
			Electro-pop band from Sheffield, England, featuring lead singer/synthesizer player Philip Oakey, with vocalists Joanne Catherall and Susanne Sulley.	
4/10/82	**1**(3)	21	● 1. **Don't You Want Me**	A&M 2397
7/02/83	**8**	13	2. **(Keep Feeling) Fascination**	A&M 2547
10/29/83	**30**	5	3. Mirror Man	A&M 2587
9/27/86	**1**(1)	15	4. **Human**	A&M 2861
			ENGELBERT HUMPERDINCK	
			Born Arnold George Dorsey on 5/2/36 in Madras, India. To Leicester, England in 1947. First recorded for Decca in 1958. Met Tom Jones' manager, Gordon Mills, in 1965, who suggested his name change to Engelbert Humperdinck (a famous German opera composer). Starred in his own musical variety TV series in 1970.	
4/29/67	**4**	10	1. **Release Me (And Let Me Love Again)**	Parrot 40011
7/15/67	**20**	4	2. There Goes My Everything	Parrot 40015
10/14/67	**25**	5	3. The Last Waltz	Parrot 40019
1/06/68	**18**	7	4. Am I That Easy To Forget	Parrot 40023
6/01/68	**19**	5	5. A Man Without Love	Parrot 40027
11/23/68	**31**	3	6. Les Bicyclettes De Belsize	Parrot 40032
9/27/69	**38**	1	7. I'm A Better Man	Parrot 40040

DATE	POS	WKS	ARTIST—RECORD TITLE	LABEL & NO.
1/03/70	**16**	8	8. Winter World Of Love	Parrot 40044
11/20/76†	**8**	14	● 9. **After The Lovin'**	Epic 50270
			PAUL HUMPHREY & HIS COOL AID CHEMISTS	
			Paul was born on 10/12/35 in Detroit. Black session drummer.	
5/15/71	**29**	7	1. Cool Aid [I]	Lizard 21006
			IVORY JOE HUNTER	
			Born on 10/10/14 in Kirbyville, Texas; died of lung cancer on 11/8/74. R&B singer/ songwriter/pianist. First recorded in 1933 (a cylinder record for the Library Of Congress). Own radio shows, KFDM-Beaumont, Texas, early 40s. Own record companies, Ivory and Pacific in 1944. Signed by King Records in 1947, MGM in 1950.	
12/01/56	**12**	15	1. Since I Met You Baby Best Seller #12 / Top 100 #12 / Jockey #14 / Juke Box #14	Atlantic 1111
			JOHN HUNTER	
			Rock singer/keyboardist from Chicago.	
2/16/85	**39**	2	1. Tragedy	Private I 04643
			TAB HUNTER	
			Born Arthur Andrew Kelm on 7/11/31 in New York City. Sportsman turned actor in 1952. Very popular on film and TV.	
1/19/57	**1**(6)	17	1. **Young Love** Top 100 #1(6) / Jockey #1(6) / Juke Box #1(5) / Best Seller #1(4)	Dot 15533
3/30/57	**11**	8	2. Ninety-Nine Ways Top 100 #11 / Jockey #11 / Best Seller #12 / Juke Box #17	Dot 15548
2/23/59	**31**	4	3. (I'll Be With You In) Apple Blossom Time #2 hit for Charles Harrison in 1920	Warner 5032
			FERLIN HUSKY	
			Born on 12/3/27 in Flat River, Missouri. Country singer/songwriter/ guitarist. Recorded as Terry Preston in the early 50s; also did humorous recordings as Simon Crum.	
3/09/57	**4**	19	1. **Gone** Top 100 #4 / Jockey #4 / Juke Box #4 / Best Seller #5 originally recorded by Husky in 1952 as by Terry Preston	Capitol 3628
12/26/60†	**12**	13	2. Wings Of A Dove	Capitol 4406
			BRIAN HYLAND	
			Born on 11/12/43 in Queens, New York. Own group, the Delphis, at age 12. In production company with Del Shannon in 1970.	
7/11/60	**1**(1)	13	1. **Itsy Bitsy Teenie Weenie Yellow Polkadot Bikini** [N] Brian was a high-school sophomore at the time of this recording	Leader 805
9/04/61	**20**	5	2. Let Me Belong To You	ABC-Para. 10236
4/07/62	**21**	6	3. Ginny Come Lately	ABC-Para. 10294
6/30/62	**3**	11	4. **Sealed With A Kiss**	ABC-Para. 10336
10/13/62	**25**	4	5. Warmed Over Kisses (Left Over Love)	ABC-Para. 10359
8/06/66	**20**	8	6. The Joker Went Wild	Philips 40377
11/26/66	**25**	3	7. Run, Run, Look And See	Philips 40405
10/24/70	**3**	13	● 8. **Gypsy Woman**	Uni 55240

DATE	POS	WKS	ARTIST—RECORD TITLE	LABEL & NO.
			DICK HYMAN	
			Born on 3/8/27 in New York City. Piano playing composer/conductor/arranger who toured Europe with Benny Goodman in 1950. Staff pianist at WMCA and WNBC-New York from 1951-57. Musical director of the Arthur Godfrey Show from 1958-62.	
1/28/56	**8**	15	1. **Moritat (A Theme from "The Three Penny Opera")** **[I]**	MGM 12149
			DICK HYMAN TRIO	
			Jockey #8 / Top 100 #9 / Best Seller #10 / Juke Box #14	
7/05/69	**38**	2	2. The Minotaur [I]	Command 4126
			DICK HYMAN & HIS ELECTRIC ECLECTICS	
			I	
			JANIS IAN	
			Born Janis Eddy Fink on 4/7/51, New York City. Singer/songwriter/pianist/guitarist.	
6/17/67	**14**	8	1. Society's Child (Baby I've Been Thinking)	Verve 5027
7/12/75	**3**	14	2. **At Seventeen**	Columbia 10154
			ICEHOUSE	
			Australian rock quartet led by singer/guitarist Iva Davies. First known as Flowers. "Icehouse" is Australian slang for an insane asylum.	
12/05/87†	**14**	11	1. Crazy	Chrysalis 43156
3/19/88	**7**	13	2. **Electric Blue**	Chrysalis 43201
			co-written by John Oates (of Hall & Oates)	
			ICICLE WORKS	
			Liverpool rock trio: Ian McNabb, Chris Layhe and Chris Sharrock.	
5/26/84	**37**	4	1. Whisper To A Scream (Birds Fly)	Arista 9155
			THE IDES OF MARCH	
			Rock group formed while classmates at a Chicago high school. Named after a line in Shakespeare's "Julius Caesar." Lead singer, Jim Peterik, currently leads Survivor.	
4/11/70	**2**(1)	10	1. **Vehicle**	Warner 7378
			BILLY IDOL	
			Born William Broad on 11/30/55 in London. Leader of the London punk band Generation X from 1977-81.	
8/07/82	**23**	9	1. Hot In The City	Chrysalis 2605
6/25/83	**36**	3	2. White Wedding	Chrysalis 42697
			originally "Bubbled Under" on 11/27/82 (POS 108)	
5/19/84	**4**	14	3. **Eyes Without A Face**	Chrysalis 42786
9/15/84	**29**	6	4. Flesh For Fantasy	Chrysalis 42809
10/25/86	**6**	13	5. **To Be A Lover**	Chrysalis 43024
2/28/87	**37**	2	6. Don't Need A Gun	Chrysalis 43087
5/30/87	**20**	7	7. Sweet Sixteen	Chrysalis 43114
9/26/87	**1**(1)	12	8. **Mony Mony "Live"**	Chrysalis 43161
			studio version hit Bubbling Under chart on 9/26/81 (POS 107)	

DATE	POS	WKS	ARTIST—RECORD TITLE	LABEL & NO.
			FRANK IFIELD	
			Born on 11/30/37 in Coventry, England. Began career as a teenager in Australia with his own radio and TV shows. Signed to Columbia Records in England in 1959.	
9/22/62	**5**	8	1. **I Remember You** #9 hit for Jimmy Dorsey in 1942 (from the film "The Fleet's In")	Vee-Jay 457
			JULIO IGLESIAS	
			Born on 9/23/43 in Madrid, Spain. Immensely popular Spanish singer, worldwide. Soccer goalie for the pro Real Madrid team until temporary paralysis from car crash.	
3/31/84	**5**	12	• 1. **To All The Girls I've Loved Before** **JULIO IGLESIAS & WILLIE NELSON**	Columbia 04217
8/04/84	**19**	8	2. All Of You **JULIO IGLESIAS & DIANA ROSS**	Columbia 04507
			THE IKETTES	
			Female R&B trio formed for the Ike & Tina Turner Revue. Atco group consisted of lead Delores Johnson, Eloise Hester and Joshie Jo Armstead. Modern group consisted of Vanetta Fields, Robbie Montgomery and Jessie Smith; later known as The Mirettes.	
2/03/62	**19**	8	1. I'm Blue (The Gong-Gong Song)	Atco 6212
4/10/65	**36**	4	2. Peaches "N" Cream	Modern 1005
			THE ILLUSION	
			Rock quintet led by John Vinci.	
8/23/69	**32**	6	1. Did You See Her Eyes	Steed 718
			THE IMPALAS	
			Pop vocal quartet from Brooklyn: Joe "Speedo" Frazier, Richard Wagner, Lenny Renda and Tony Carlucci. All members, except black lead singer Frazier, are white.	
4/13/59	2(2)	11	1. **Sorry (I Ran All The Way Home)**	Cub 9022
			THE IMPRESSIONS	
			Soul group formed in Chicago in 1957, originally known as The Roosters. Consisted of Jerry Butler, Curtis Mayfield, Sam Gooden and brothers Arthur and Richard Brooks. Butler left for a solo career in 1958, replaced by Fred Cash. The Brooks brothers left in 1962, leaving Mayfield as the trio's leader. Mayfield left in 1970 for a solo career, replaced by Leroy Hutson. In 1973, Hutson was replaced by Reggie Torian and Ralph Johnson. Johnson joined Mystique in 1976. Did film soundtrack for "Three The Hard Way," 1974. Butler, Mayfield, Gooden and Cash reunited for a tour in 1983.	
6/16/58	**11**	9	1. For Your Precious Love **JERRY BUTLER & THE IMPRESSIONS** Best Seller #11 / Top 100 #11 / Jockey #25	Abner/Falcon 1013
11/20/61	**20**	8	2. Gypsy Woman	ABC-Para. 10241
10/12/63	**4**	11	3. **It's All Right**	ABC-Para. 10487
1/25/64	**12**	7	4. Talking About My Baby	ABC-Para. 10511
4/18/64	**14**	9	5. I'm So Proud	ABC-Para. 10544
6/27/64	**10**	10	6. **Keep On Pushing**	ABC-Para. 10554
9/19/64	**15**	8	7. You Must Believe Me	ABC-Para. 10581
12/12/64†	**7**	7	8. **Amen** song featured in the film "Lilies Of The Field"	ABC-Para. 10602
3/06/65	**14**	5	9. People Get Ready	ABC-Para. 10622
4/24/65	**29**	4	10. Woman's Got Soul	ABC-Para. 10647

DATE	POS	WKS	ARTIST—RECORD TITLE	LABEL & NO.
1/01/66	**33**	2	11. You've Been Cheatin'	ABC-Para. 10750
2/03/68	**14**	8	12. We're A Winner	ABC 11022
10/05/68	**22**	7	13. Fool For You	Curtom 1932
12/28/68†	**25**	6	14. This Is My Country	Curtom 1934
7/12/69	**21**	9	15. Choice Of Colors	Curtom 1943
6/13/70	**28**	8	16. Check Out Your Mind all of above (except #1 & 8): written by Curtis Mayfield	Curtom 1951
6/29/74	**17**	6	17. Finally Got Myself Together (I'm A Changed Man)	Curtom 1997
			THE INDEPENDENTS	
			Soul group consisting of Chuck Jackson, Maurice Jackson, Helen Curry and Eric Thomas. Jackson (no relation to solo singer Chuck Jackson) and Marvin Yancey, Jr. were producers/writers for the group; later teamed in production work, especially for Natalie Cole.	
4/28/73	**21**	9	• 1. Leaving Me	Wand 11252
			INFORMATION SOCIETY	
			Pop/funk/dance outfit formed in Minneapolis in 1985: songwriter Paul Robb, vocalist Kurt Valaquen, keyboardist Amanda Kramer and bassist James Cassidy.	
8/27/88	**3**	14	• 1. **What's On Your Mind (Pure Energy)**	Tommy B. 27826
			JORGEN INGMANN & HIS GUITAR	
			Born Jorgen Ingmann-Pedersen on 4/26/25 in Copenhagen, Denmark.	
2/20/61	**2**(2)	13	1. **Apache** [I]	Atco 6184
			JAMES INGRAM	
			R&B vocalist/multi-instrumentalist/composer from Akron, Ohio. To Los Angeles in the late 70s, with the band Revelation Funk.	
9/19/81	**17**	10	1. Just Once **QUINCY JONES featuring JAMES INGRAM**	A&M 2357
2/13/82	**14**	11	2. One Hundred Ways **QUINCY JONES featuring JAMES INGRAM**	A&M 2387
12/04/82†	**1**(2)	18	• 3. **Baby, Come To Me** **PATTI AUSTIN with JAMES INGRAM** originally charted for 4 weeks (POS 73), then re-entered, 10/16/82	Qwest 50036
1/14/84	**19**	9	4. Yah Mo B There **JAMES INGRAM with MICHAEL McDONALD**	Qwest 29394
10/13/84	**15**	9	5. What About Me? **KENNY ROGERS with KIM CARNES & JAMES INGRAM**	RCA 13899
1/24/87	**2**(1)	12	6. **Somewhere Out There** **LINDA RONSTADT & JAMES INGRAM** from the animated film "An American Tail"	MCA 52973
			LUTHER INGRAM	
			Born on 11/30/44 in Jackson, Tennessee. Soul singer/songwriter. Sang in gospel group with his brothers. First recorded for Smash in 1965. In the film "Wattstax."	
6/24/72	**3**	13	1. **(If Loving You Is Wrong) I Don't Want To Be Right**	KoKo 2111
1/20/73	**40**	2	2. I'll Be Your Shelter (In Time Of Storm)	KoKo 2113

DATE	POS	WKS	ARTIST—RECORD TITLE	LABEL & NO.
			THE INNOCENCE	
			Group is actually the singing, songwriting and record producing duo of Pete Anders and Vinnie Poncia - also recorded as The Trade Winds.	
1/07/67	**34**	3	1. There's Got To Be A Word!	Kama Sutra 214
			THE INNOCENTS	
			Pop trio from Sun Valley, California: James West (lead singer), Al Candelaria (bass) and Darron Stankey (guitar, tenor). First recorded as The Echoes for Andex in 1959. Back-up vocal group for Kathy Young. Group named after their car club.	
9/19/60	**28**	3	1. Honest I Do	Indigo 105
1/09/61	**28**	3	2. Gee Whiz	Indigo 111
			INSTANT FUNK	
			9-man funk ensemble led by James Carmichael. Former back-up band for Bunny Sigler.	
3/31/79	**20**	8	● 1. I Got My Mind Made Up (You Can Get It Girl)	Salsoul 2078
			THE INTRIGUES	
			Soul trio from Philadelphia.	
10/04/69	**31**	4	1. In A Moment	Yew 1001
			THE INTRUDERS	
			Soul group formed in Philadelphia in 1960. Consisted of Sam "Little Sonny" Brown, Eugene "Bird" Daughtry, Phil Terry and Robert "Big Sonny" Edwards. First recorded for Gowen in 1961. Not to be confused with the white rock trio of the same name.	
4/06/68	**6**	11	● 1. **Cowboys To Girls**	Gamble 214
8/10/68	**26**	4	2. (Love Is Like A) Baseball Game	Gamble 217
6/30/73	**36**	6	3. I'll Always Love My Mama (Part 1)	Gamble 2506
			INXS	
			Rock sextet formed in Sydney, Australia: Michael Hutchence (lead singer), Kirk Pengilly, Garry Beers, and brothers Tim, Andy and Jon Farriss. Hutchence starred in the 1987 film "Dogs In Space."	
5/14/83	**30**	5	1. The One Thing	Atco 99905
2/15/86	**5**	14	2. **What You Need**	Atlantic 89460
11/21/87†	**1**(1)	17	3. **Need You Tonight**	Atlantic 89188
2/27/88	**2**(2)	12	4. **Devil Inside**	Atlantic 89144
5/28/88	**3**	12	5. **New Sensation**	Atlantic 89080
9/17/88	**7**	11	6. **Never Tear Us Apart**	Atlantic 89038
			DONNIE IRIS	
			Real name: Dominic Ierace. Native of Beaver Falls, Pennsylvania. Singer/songwriter/ guitarist. Leader of the Pittsburgh rock group The Jaggerz. Toured briefly with the funk group Wild Cherry.	
2/07/81	**29**	6	1. Ah! Leah!	MCA 51025
2/13/82	**37**	2	2. Love Is Like A Rock	MCA 51223
5/01/82	**25**	6	3. My Girl	MCA 52031
			THE IRISH ROVERS	
			Irish-born folk quintet. Group formed in Alberta, Canada in 1964.	
4/06/68	**7**	9	1. **The Unicorn**	Decca 32254
4/18/81	**37**	4	2. Wasn't That A Party **THE ROVERS**	Epic 51007

DATE	POS	WKS	ARTIST—RECORD TITLE	LABEL & NO.
			IRON BUTTERFLY	
			San Diego heavy-metal rock band. Consisted of Doug Ingle (lead vocals, keyboards), Erik Braunn (lead guitar), Lee Dorman (bass) and Ron Bushy (drums). Braunn left in late 1969, replaced by Mike Pinera and Larry Reinhardt.	
9/28/68	30	7	1. In-A-Gadda-Da-Vida 7" version edited down from original 17-minute album cut	Atco 6606
			IRONHORSE	
			Rock band formed by Bachman-Turner Overdrive founder Randy Bachman.	
4/21/79	36	3	1. Sweet Lui-Louise	Scotti Br. 406
			BIG DEE IRWIN	
			Real name: Defosca Ervin. R&B vocalist; former lead singer of The Pastels.	
7/13/63	38	2	1. Swinging On A Star vocal duet with Little Eva; #1 hit for Bing Crosby in 1944 (from the film "Going My Way")	Dimension 1010
			THE ISLANDERS	
			Instrumental duo: Randy Starr (New York City) & Frank Metis (Nuremberg, W. Germany).	
10/19/59	15	8	1. The Enchanted Sea [I]	Mayflower 16
			THE ISLEY BROTHERS	
			R&B trio of brothers from Cincinnati. Formed in early 50s as a gospel group. Consisted of O'Kelly, Ronald and Rudolph Isley. Moved to New York in 1957 and first recorded for Teenage Records. Trio added their younger brothers Ernie (guitar, drums) and Marvin Isley (bass, percussion) and cousin Chris Jasper (keyboards), from 1973-84. Formed own label T-Neck in 1969. Ernie, Marvin and Chris began recording as the trio Isley, Jasper, Isley in 1984. O'Kelly died of a heart attack on 3/31/86 at age 48.	
6/30/62	17	11	1. Twist And Shout	Wand 124
3/19/66	12	8	2. This Old Heart Of Mine (Is Weak For You)	Tamla 54128
3/29/69	2(1)	12	● 3. **It's Your Thing**	T-Neck 901
6/21/69	23	7	4. I Turned You On	T-Neck 902
7/03/71	18	9	5. Love The One You're With	T-Neck 930
8/19/72	24	7	6. Pop That Thang	T-Neck 935
8/18/73	6	15	● 7. **That Lady (Part 1)**	T-Neck 2251
7/12/75	4	13	● 8. **Fight The Power (Part 1)**	T-Neck 2256
11/22/75	22	9	9. For The Love Of You (Part 1 & 2)	T-Neck 2259
8/06/77	40	1	10. Livin' In The Life	T-Neck 2264
5/24/80	39	2	11. Don't Say Goodnight (It's Time For Love) (Parts 1 & 2)	T-Neck 2290
			BURL IVES	
			Born on 6/14/09 in Hunt Township, Illinois. Actor/author/singer. Played semi-pro football. Began Broadway career in the late 30s. Worked in "This Is The Army" service show during World War II. Own CBS network radio show "The Wayfaring Stranger" in 1944. Appeared in many films, including "Our Man In Havana," "East Of Eden," "Smokey," "Cat On A Hot Tin Roof" and "The Big Country." Worked on TV series "The Bold Ones" in the early 70s.	
1/06/62	9	11	1. **A Little Bitty Tear**	Decca 31330
4/21/62	10	8	2. **Funny Way Of Laughin'**	Decca 31371
8/11/62	19	4	3. Call Me Mr. In-Between	Decca 31405
12/08/62	39	1	4. Mary Ann Regrets	Decca 31433

DATE	POS	WKS	ARTIST—RECORD TITLE	LABEL & NO.
			THE IVY THREE	
			Formed in 1959 at Adelphi College in New York. Consisted of Charles Koppelman (lead), Art Berkowitz and Don Rubin.	
8/29/60	**8**	7	1. **Yogi** **[N]**	Shell 720
			based on a character from TV's "Huckleberry Hound" show	
			J	
			TERRY JACKS	
			Native of Winnipeg, Canada. Recorded with wife Susan as The Poppy Family.	
2/09/74	**1**(3)	15	● 1. **Seasons In The Sun**	Bell 45432
			originally recorded by The Kingston Trio in 1964	
			CHUCK JACKSON	
			Born on 7/22/37 in Latta, South Carolina. R&B singer; cousin of singer Ann Sexton. Moved to Pittsburgh as a child. Left college in 1957 to work with the Raspberry Singers gospel group. With The Dell-Vikings from 1957-59. First recorded as a solo for Beltone in 1960.	
3/13/61	**36**	2	1. I Don't Want To Cry	Wand 106
6/02/62	**23**	6	2. Any Day Now (My Wild Beautiful Bird)	Wand 122
			DEON JACKSON	
			Born on 1/26/46 in Ann Arbor, Michigan. Soul singer/clarinetist/drummer. Discovered by producer Ollie McLaughlin.	
2/19/66	**11**	9	1. Love Makes The World Go Round	Carla 2526
			FREDDIE JACKSON	
			Soul singer/songwriter; raised in Harlem. Back-up singer for Melba Moore, Evelyn King and others. Member of Mystic Merlin.	
7/13/85	**18**	8	1. Rock Me Tonight (For Old Times Sake)	Capitol 5459
10/05/85	**12**	11	2. You Are My Lady	Capitol 5495
1/25/86	**25**	6	3. He'll Never Love You (Like I Do)	Capitol 5535
8/15/87	**32**	3	4. Jam Tonight	Capitol 44037
			JANET JACKSON	
			Born on 5/16/66 in Gary, Indiana. Sister of The Jacksons (youngest of 9 children). Debuted at age 7 at the MGM Grand in Las Vegas with her brothers. At age 10, she played Penny Gordon in the TV series "Good Times" (1977-79); in the cast of "Diff'rent Strokes" (1981-82).	
3/22/86	**4**	13	1. **What Have You Done For Me Lately**	A&M 2812
6/07/86	**3**	11	2. **Nasty**	A&M 2830
8/23/86	**1**(2)	13	3. **When I Think Of You**	A&M 2855
11/22/86†	**5**	13	4. **Control**	A&M 2877
2/07/87	**2**(1)	11	5. **Let's Wait Awhile**	A&M 2906
6/20/87	**14**	10	6. The Pleasure Principle	A&M 2927
			JERMAINE JACKSON	
			Born on 12/11/54 in Gary, Indiana. Fourth oldest of the Jackson family. Vocalist/ bassist of The Jackson 5 until group left Motown in 1976. Married Hazel Joy Gordy, daughter of Berry Gordy Jr., on 12/15/73.	
1/13/73	**9**	13	1. **Daddy's Home**	Motown 1216
5/03/80	**9**	14	2. **Let's Get Serious**	Motown 1469

DATE	POS	WKS	ARTIST—RECORD TITLE	LABEL & NO.
8/30/80	**34**	4	3. You're Supposed To Keep Your Love For Me above 2: written, produced and arranged by Stevie Wonder	Motown 1490
8/21/82	**18**	7	4. Let Me Tickle Your Fancy backing vocals: Devo	Motown 1628
8/04/84	**15**	10	5. Dynamite	Arista 9190
11/17/84†	**13**	12	6. Do What You Do	Arista 9279
3/15/86	**16**	9	7. I Think It's Love	Arista 9444
			J.J. JACKSON	
			Born Jerome Louis Jackson on 4/8/41 in Brooklyn. Soul singer/songwriter. Became permanent resident of England in 1969. Not the same person as the MTV VJ.	
11/05/66	**22**	7	1. But It's Alright	Calla 119
			JOE JACKSON	
			Born on 8/11/55 in Burton-on-Trent, England. Singer/songwriter/pianist, featuring an ever changing music style. Moved to New York City in 1982.	
7/07/79	**21**	8	1. Is She Really Going Out With Him?	A&M 2132
10/16/82	**6**	15	2. **Steppin' Out**	A&M 2428
2/05/83	**18**	10	3. Breaking Us In Two	A&M 2510
5/05/84	**15**	9	4. You Can't Get What You Want (Till You Know What You Want)	A&M 2628
			MICHAEL JACKSON	
			Born on 8/29/58 in Gary, Indiana; 7th of 9 children. Became lead singer of his brothers' group, The Jackson 5 (later known as The Jacksons), at age 5. His 1982 "Thriller" album, with sales of 40 million+ copies, is the best-selling album in history. Internationally recognized as the most popular artist since 1983.	
11/06/71	**4**	13	1. **Got To Be There**	Motown 1191
3/18/72	**2**(2)	11	2. **Rockin' Robin**	Motown 1197
6/10/72	**16**	9	3. I Wanna Be Where You Are	Motown 1202
9/09/72	**1**(1)	11	4. **Ben** title song from the film about a trained rat	Motown 1207
7/12/75	**23**	6	5. Just A Little Bit Of You	Motown 1349
9/01/79	**1**(1)	12	▲ 6. **Don't Stop 'Til You Get Enough**	Epic 50742
11/24/79†	**1**(4)	19	▲ 7. **Rock With You**	Epic 50797
2/23/80	**10**	11	• 8. **Off The Wall**	Epic 50838
5/10/80	**10**	11	• 9. **She's Out Of My Life**	Epic 50871
11/13/82†	**2**(3)	14	• 10. **The Girl Is Mine** **MICHAEL JACKSON/PAUL McCARTNEY**	Epic 03288
1/29/83	**1**(7)	17	▲ 11. **Billie Jean**	Epic 03509
3/19/83	**1**(3)	18	▲ 12. **Beat It** featuring lead guitar work by Eddie Van Halen	Epic 03759
6/04/83	**5**	11	13. **Wanna Be Startin' Somethin'**	Epic 03914
7/30/83	**7**	11	14. **Human Nature**	Epic 04026
10/15/83	**1**(6)	18	• 15. **Say Say Say** **PAUL McCARTNEY & MICHAEL JACKSON**	Columbia 04168
10/22/83	**10**	9	16. **P.Y.T. (Pretty Young Thing)**	Epic 04165
2/11/84	**4**	9	17. **Thriller**	Epic 04364
6/23/84	**38**	3	18. Farewell My Summer Love re-mix of a recording from 8/31/73	Motown 1739

DATE	POS	WKS	ARTIST—RECORD TITLE	LABEL & NO.
8/08/87	**1**(1)	11	• 19. **I Just Can't Stop Loving You** backing vocal: Siedah Garrett	Epic 07253
9/19/87	**1**(2)	11	20. **Bad** organ solo: Jimmy Smith	Epic 07418
11/28/87†	**1**(1)	13	21. **The Way You Make Me Feel**	Epic 07645
2/13/88	**1**(2)	13	22. **Man In The Mirror** background vocals: Siedah Garrett, The Winans and The Andrae Crouch Choir	Epic 07668
5/14/88	**1**(1)	11	23. **Dirty Diana** featuring Steve Stevens (Billy Idol's guitarist)	Epic 07739
8/06/88	**11**	8	24. Another Part Of Me	Epic 07962
11/26/88†	**7**	11	25. **Smooth Criminal**	Epic 08044
			MILLIE JACKSON	
			Born on 7/15/44 in Thompson, Georgia. Soul singer/songwriter. To Newark, New Jersey in 1958. Worked as a model in New York City. Professional singing debut at Club Zanzibar in Hoboken, New Jersey, in 1964. First recorded for MGM in 1970.	
5/13/72	**27**	6	1. Ask Me What You Want	Spring 123
9/29/73	**24**	8	2. Hurts So Good from the film "Cleopatra Jones"	Spring 139
			REBBIE JACKSON	
			Born Maureen Jackson on 5/29/50 in Gary, Indiana. Eldest of the 9-sibling Jackson family.	
11/17/84	**24**	8	1. Centipede written and produced by Michael Jackson	Columbia 04547
			STONEWALL JACKSON	
			His real name. Born on 11/6/32 in Tabor City, North Carolina. Country singer/ guitarist/pianist. Descended from General Thomas Jonathan "Stonewall" Jackson.	
6/08/59	**4**	12	1. **Waterloo**	Columbia 41393
			WANDA JACKSON	
			Born on 10/20/37 in Maud, Oklahoma. Country-rockabilly singer/songwriter/guitarist. First recorded for Decca in 1954. Toured with Elvis Presley from 1955-56.	
10/10/60	**37**	1	1. Let's Have A Party	Capitol 4397
8/14/61	**29**	3	2. Right Or Wrong	Capitol 4553
11/27/61	**27**	3	3. In The Middle Of A Heartache	Capitol 4635
			THE JACKSONS	
			Quintet of brothers formed and managed by their father beginning in 1966 in Gary, Indiana. Consisted of Sigmund "Jackie" (b: 5/4/51), Toriano "Tito" (b: 10/15/53), Jermaine (b: 12/11/54), Marlon (b: 3/12/57) and lead singer Michael (b: 8/29/58). First recorded for Steeltown in 1968. Known as The Jackson 5 from 1968-75. Jermaine replaced by Randy (b: 10/29/61) in 1976. Jermaine rejoined the group for 1984's highly publicized "Victory" album and tour. Michael has also recorded solo since 1971. Marlon left for a solo career in 1987. Their sisters Rebbie, La Toya and Janet backed the group; each had a string of solo hits.	
			THE JACKSON 5:	
12/06/69†	**1**(1)	16	1. **I Want You Back**	Motown 1157
3/21/70	**1**(2)	12	2. **ABC**	Motown 1163
6/06/70	**1**(2)	12	3. **The Love You Save**	Motown 1166
9/19/70	**1**(5)	16	4. **I'll Be There**	Motown 1171

DATE	POS	WKS	ARTIST—RECORD TITLE	LABEL & NO.
2/06/71	**2**(2)	9	5. **Mama's Pearl**	Motown 1177
4/10/71	**2**(3)	11	6. **Never Can Say Goodbye**	Motown 1179
7/31/71	**20**	6	7. Maybe Tomorrow	Motown 1186
12/25/71†	**10**	8	8. **Sugar Daddy**	Motown 1194
4/29/72	**13**	8	9. Little Bitty Pretty One	Motown 1199
7/29/72	**16**	8	10. Lookin' Through The Windows	Motown 1205
11/18/72	**18**	8	11. Corner Of The Sky from the Broadway musical "Pippin"	Motown 1214
4/14/73	**28**	4	12. Hallelujah Day	Motown 1224
9/22/73	**28**	7	13. Get It Together	Motown 1277
3/30/74	**2**(2)	16	14. **Dancing Machine**	Motown 1286
11/30/74	**38**	2	15. Whatever You Got, I Want	Motown 1308
2/22/75	**15**	7	16. I Am Love (Parts I & II)	Motown 1310
			THE JACKSONS:	
12/11/76†	**6**	15	▲ 17. **Enjoy Yourself**	Epic 50289
5/07/77	**28**	3	18. Show You The Way To Go	Epic 50350
3/31/79	**7**	14	▲ 19. **Shake Your Body (Down To The Ground)**	Epic 50656
10/11/80	**12**	9	20. Lovely One	Epic 50938
1/10/81	**22**	8	21. Heartbreak Hotel	Epic 50959
6/30/84	**3**	11	● 22. **State Of Shock** lead vocals: Michael Jackson & Mick Jagger	Epic 04503
8/25/84	**17**	8	23. Torture lead vocals: Jermaine & Michael Jackson	Epic 04575
			DICK JACOBS	
			Born on 3/29/18 in New York City. Music director of TV's "Your Hit Parade," 1957-58. A&R director for Coral and Brunswick Records.	
4/07/56	**22**	7	1. "Main Title" And "Molly-O" Jockey #22 / Top 100 #26 from the Otto Preminger film "The Man With The Golden Arm"	Coral 61606
11/03/56	**16**	9	2. Petticoats Of Portugal Jockey #16 / Top 100 #20 / Juke Box #20 / Best Seller #23	Coral 61724
9/16/57	**17**	4	3. Fascination Jockey #17 / Top 100 #52 from the film "Love In The Afternoon"	Coral 61864
			MICK JAGGER	
			Born Michael Phillip Jagger on 7/26/43 in Dartford, England. Lead singer of The Rolling Stones. Also see The Jacksons' "State Of Shock".	
2/16/85	**12**	10	1. Just Another Night	Columbia 04743
5/25/85	**38**	3	2. Lucky In Love	Columbia 04893
9/07/85	**7**	9	3. **Dancing In The Street** **MICK JAGGER/DAVID BOWIE** from the Live-Aid concert	EMI America 8288
10/24/87	**39**	1	4. Let's Work	Columbia 07306
			THE JAGGERZ	
			Rock group formed in Pittsburgh in 1965, featuring lead singer Donnie Iris.	
2/14/70	**2**(1)	11	● 1. **The Rapper**	Kama Sutra 502

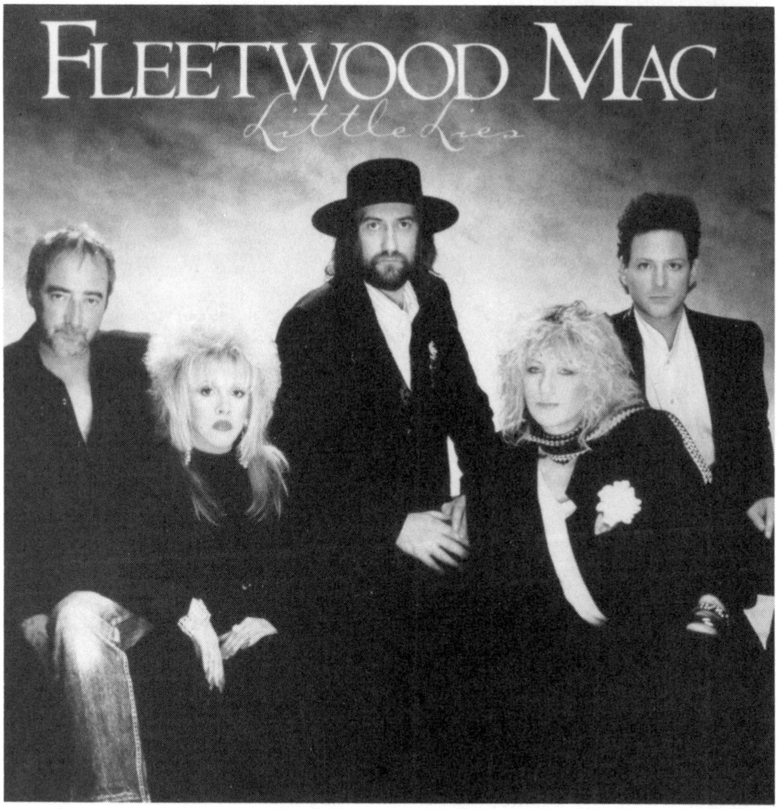

Fabian first hit the Hot 100 prior to his bigger hits of "Turn Me Loose" and "Tiger" with his "I'm A Man" single, which peaked at No. 31. Unlike the later hits sharing the same name by the Yardbirds (1965) and the Spencer Davis Group (1967), the teen idol's 1959 version was penned by Doc Pomus and Mort Schuman.

The Fat Boys-Beach Boys' "Wipeout" in 1987 was a timely enough taste of nostalgia—albeit an admittedly odd taste—to score on the Hot 100 and bring the Beach Boys their first brush with chart action in years.

The Firm, formed by guitarist Jimmy Page after the break-up of Led Zeppelin, never duplicated that group's remarkable success, and quietly disbanded after releasing only two albums. In 1988, Page returned with *Outrider*, the first solo album the legendary guitarist had ever recorded.

Fleetwood Mac continued their pattern of abruptly changing personnel in 1988 when the long-lived band announced the departure of guitarist Lindsey Buckingham. Replacing Buckingham, who apparently preferred the studio to the road, were guitarists Billy Burnette and Rick Vito.

The Fleetwoods continue to inspire covers of their 1959 debut hit, "Come Softly To Me," most recently by pop songster Nick Kamen and by the Roches, whose version appeared in the soundtrack to *Crossing Delancey*.

Force M.D.s first charted in 1986 with "Tender Love" from the *Krush Groove* soundtrack—an album which also featured Chaka Khan, L.L. Cool J, and the Beastie Boys, among other well-known artists.

Lita Ford's successful mid-80s solo career came a decade after she'd already charted with L.A.'s all-girl hard-rockers, the Runaways. In 1989, she dueted with yet another 70s star—former Black Sabbath vocalist Ozzy Osbourne—on her Mike Chapman-penned hit, "Close My Eyes Forever."

David Foster and Olivia Newton-John's duet on "The Best Of Me" was just one of many dual-vocal hits for Newton-John. Count among her other collaborative partners John Travolta, Andy Gibb, Cliff Richard, and the Electric Light Orchestra.

The Four Seasons are receiving significant attention at the close of the 80s now that Rhino Records has reissued a large amount of their 60s back-catalog—including both the group's Christmas album and cult favorite *The Genuine Imitation Life Gazette*.

The Four Tops came on strong in 1988 with the title track to their Arista debut album, *Indestructible*. The fact that the group—featuring Levi Stubbs, Renaldo "Obie" Benson, Lawrence Payton, and Abdul "Duke" Fakir—has had no personnel changes since their 1954 formation gave the song's title added significance.

Samantha Fox made headlines as a model in the U.K. tabloid press prior to launching a career as a singer. Following in the footsteps of U.K. acts the Bay City Rollers and the Tourists, Fox released her own version of Dusty Springfield's 1964 classic, "I Only Want To Be With You," in 1989.

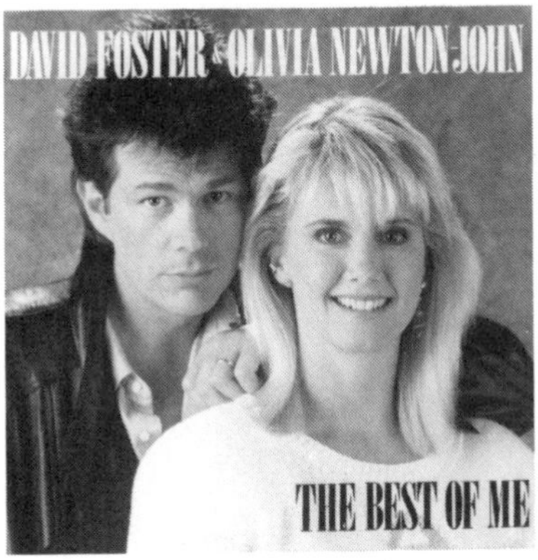

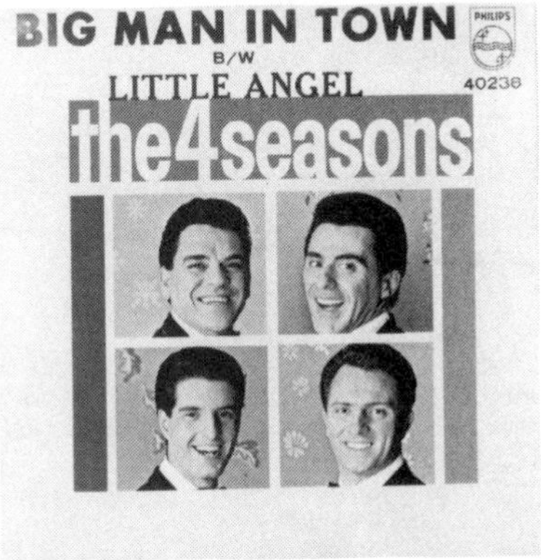

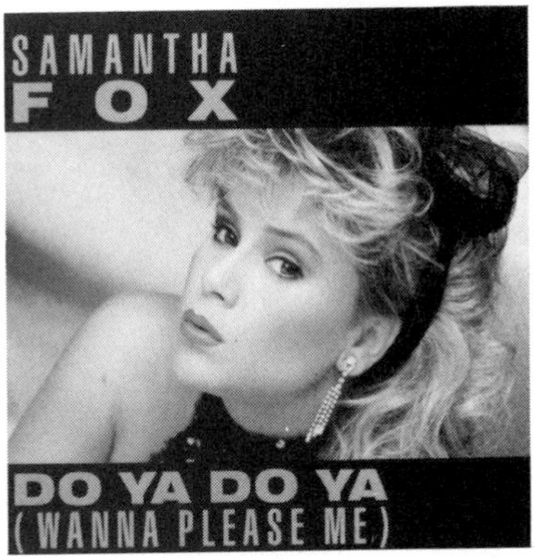

DATE	POS	WKS	ARTIST—RECORD TITLE	LABEL & NO.
			ETTA JAMES	
			Born Jamesetta Hawkins on 1/25/38 in Los Angeles. Nicknamed Miss Peaches. First recorded for Modern in 1954. Frequent bouts with heroin addiction; finally cured in the late 70s. Still active into the 80s, makes many anti-drug abuse appearances.	
6/06/60	**33**	4	1. All I Could Do Was Cry	Argo 5359
11/21/60	**34**	2	2. My Dearest Darling	Argo 5368
4/03/61	**30**	4	3. Trust In Me #5 hit for both Wayne King and Mildred Bailey in 1937	Argo 5385
9/04/61	**39**	2	4. Don't Cry, Baby	Argo 5393
3/31/62	**37**	4	5. Something's Got A Hold On Me	Argo 5409
9/08/62	**34**	2	6. Stop The Wedding	Argo 5418
5/11/63	**25**	6	7. Pushover	Argo 5437
12/30/67†	**23**	7	8. Tell Mama	Cadet 5578
4/06/68	**35**	4	9. Security	Cadet 5594
			JONI JAMES	
			Born Joan Carmello Babbo on 9/22/30 in Chicago. Worked as a dancer from age 12, model during high school. Toured Canada as a dancer, late 1940s. First recorded for Sharp, 1952. Married her orchestral arranger/ conductor Tony Aquaviva (d: 9/27/86).	
2/19/55	**2**(1)	16	1. **How Important Can It Be?** Jockey #2 / Juke Box #6 / Best Seller #8	MGM 11919
10/22/55	**6**	10	2. **You Are My Love** Jockey #6 / Top 100 #15 / Best Seller #18	MGM 12066
8/11/56	**30**	2	3. Give Us This Day	MGM 12288
10/20/58	**19**	8	4. There Goes My Heart #13 hit for Enric Madriguera in 1934	MGM 12706
2/16/59	**33**	4	5. There Must Be A Way #9 hit for both Johnnie Johnston and Charlie Spivak in 1945	MGM 12746
1/25/60	**35**	3	6. Little Things Mean A Lot #1 hit for Kitty Kallen in 1954	MGM 12849
1/23/61	**38**	1	7. My Last Date (With You)	MGM 12933
			RICK JAMES	
			Born James Johnson on 2/1/52 in Buffalo. "Punk funk" singer/songwriter/ guitarist. In Mynah Birds band with Neil Young in the late 60s. To London; formed the band Main Line. Returned to the US and formed Stone City Band; produced Teena Marie, Mary Jane Girls, Eddie Murphy and others.	
8/05/78	**13**	10	1. You And I	Gordy 7156
7/18/81	**40**	2	2. Give It To Me Baby	Gordy 7197
9/05/81	**16**	10	3. Super Freak (Part 1)	Gordy 7205
9/24/83	**40**	1	4. Cold Blooded	Gordy 1687
8/18/84	**36**	3	5. 17	Gordy 1730
			SONNY JAMES	
			Born James Loden on 5/1/29 in Hackleburg, Alabama. Country singer/songwriter/ guitarist. Nicknamed "The Southern Gentleman." Brought to Capitol Records in Nashville by Chet Atkins.	
1/05/57	**1**(1)	17	1. **Young Love** Jockey #1 / Best Seller #2 / Top 100 #2 / Juke Box #4	Capitol 3602
4/20/57	**25**	1	2. First Date, First Kiss, First Love Jockey #25 / Top 100 #39	Capitol 3674

DATE	POS	WKS	ARTIST—RECORD TITLE	LABEL & NO.
			TOMMY JAMES	
			Born Thomas Jackson on 4/29/47 in Dayton, Ohio. To Niles, Michigan at age 11. Formed pop group, The Shondells, at age 12. Recorded "Hanky Panky" on the Snap label in 1963. Tommy re-located to Pittsburgh in 1965 after a disc jockey there popularized "Hanky Panky." Original master was sold to Roulette, whereupon Tommy recruited Pittsburgh group The Raconteurs to become the official Shondells. Consisted of Mike Vale (bass), Pete Lucia (drums), Eddie Gray (guitar) and Ronnie Rosman (organ).	
			TOMMY JAMES & THE SHONDELLS:	
6/18/66	**1**(2)	10	1. **Hanky Panky**	Roulette 4686
8/20/66	**21**	5	2. Say I Am (What I Am)	Roulette 4695
12/10/66	**31**	4	3. It's Only Love	Roulette 4710
3/11/67	**4**	12	4. **I Think We're Alone Now**	Roulette 4720
5/06/67	**10**	8	5. **Mirage**	Roulette 4736
7/15/67	**25**	5	6. I Like The Way	Roulette 4756
9/02/67	**18**	6	7. Gettin' Together	Roulette 4762
5/04/68	**3**	13	8. **Mony Mony**	Roulette 7008
11/23/68	**38**	2	9. Do Something To Me	Roulette 7024
12/21/68†	**1**(2)	15	10. **Crimson And Clover**	Roulette 7028
4/05/69	**7**	8	11. **Sweet Cherry Wine**	Roulette 7039
6/28/69	**2**(3)	12	12. **Crystal Blue Persuasion**	Roulette 7050
10/25/69	**19**	5	13. Ball Of Fire	Roulette 7060
12/20/69†	**23**	7	14. She	Roulette 7066
			TOMMY JAMES:	
6/26/71	**4**	11	15. **Draggin' The Line**	Roulette 7103
10/23/71	**40**	1	16. I'm Comin' Home	Roulette 7110
2/23/80	**19**	9	17. Three Times In Love	Millennium 11785
			THE JAMIES	
			Pop vocal quartet from Dorchester, Massachusetts, led by Tom Jamison and his sister Serena.	
9/15/58	**26**	4	1. Summertime, Summertime Hot 100 #26 / Best Seller #28	Epic 9281
8/04/62	**38**	1	2. Summertime, Summertime [R]	Epic 9281
			JAN & DEAN	
			Jan Berry (b: 4/3/41) and Dean Torrence (b: 3/10/40) formed group called the Barons while attending high school in Los Angeles. Jan & Dean and Barons member Arnie Ginsburg recorded "Jennie Lee" in Jan's garage. Dean left for a 6-month Army Reserve stint, whereupon Jan signed with Doris Day's label, Arwin, and the record was released as by Jan & Arnie. Upon Dean's return from the service, Arnie joined the Navy, and Jan & Dean signed with Herb Alpert's Dore label. Jan was critically injured in an auto accident on 4/19/66. Duo made a comeback in 1978, after their biographical film "Dead Man's Curve" aired on TV.	
5/26/58	**8**	11	1. **Jennie Lee** **JAN & ARNIE** Best Seller #8 / Top 100 #8 / Jockey #17	Arwin 108
8/10/59	**10**	9	2. **Baby Talk**	Dore 522
7/10/61	**25**	4	3. Heart And Soul Larry Clinton hit #1 in 1938 with this Hoagy Carmichael tune	Challenge 9111
4/20/63	**28**	5	4. Linda	Liberty 55531

DATE	POS	WKS	ARTIST—RECORD TITLE	LABEL & NO.
6/22/63	**1**(2)	11	5. **Surf City** Brian Wilson (Beach Boys) helped on words & vocals for this tune	Liberty 55580
9/21/63	**11**	8	6. Honolulu Lulu	Liberty 55613
12/21/63†	**10**	9	7. **Drag City**	Liberty 55641
3/28/64	**8**	11	8. **Dead Man's Curve/**	
4/04/64	**37**	4	9. The New Girl In School	Liberty 55672
7/04/64	**3**	10	10. **The Little Old Lady (From Pasadena)**	Liberty 55704
10/10/64	**16**	5	11. Ride The Wild Surf from the film of the same title	Liberty 55724
11/21/64	**25**	5	12. Sidewalk Surfin'	Liberty 55727
6/26/65	**27**	4	13. You Really Know How To Hurt A Guy	Liberty 55792
11/13/65	**30**	2	14. I Found A Girl	Liberty 55833
6/18/66	**21**	6	15. Popsicle	Liberty 55886
			HORST JANKOWSKI Born on 1/30/36 in Berlin, Germany. Jazz pianist.	
6/05/65	**12**	9	1. A Walk In The Black Forest [I]	Mercury 72425
			THE JARMELS R&B group from Richmond, Virginia: Nathaniel Ruff, Ray Smith, Paul Burnett, Earl Christian and Tom Eldridge.	
8/28/61	**12**	6	1. A Little Bit Of Soap	Laurie 3098
			AL JARREAU Born on 3/12/40 in Milwaukee. Soul-jazz vocalist. Has won 4 Grammys. Has masters degree in psychology from the University of Iowa. Worked clubs in San Francisco with George Duke.	
9/12/81	**15**	11	1. We're In This Love Together	Warner 49746
4/23/83	**21**	6	2. Mornin'	Warner 29720
			shown only as: **JARREAU**	
7/04/87	**23**	5	3. Moonlighting theme from the TV series of the same title	MCA 53124
			JAY & THE AMERICANS Group formed in late 1959 by New York University students as the Harbor-Lites: John "Jay" Traynor (formerly with the Mystics), Sandy Yaguda, Kenny Vance (later a Hollywood musical director) and Howie Kane. Guitarist Marty Sanders joined during production of their first album in 1961. Traynor left after their first hit and was replaced by lead singer Jay Black (real name: David Blatt) in 1962.	
4/07/62	**5**	11	1. **She Cried**	United Art. 415
9/21/63	**25**	4	2. Only In America	United Art. 626
10/03/64	**3**	11	3. **Come A Little Bit Closer**	United Art. 759
1/16/65	**11**	7	4. Let's Lock The Door (And Throw Away The Key)	United Art. 805
6/19/65	**4**	11	5. **Cara, Mia** #10 hit for David Whitfield (with Mantovani's orch.) in 1954	United Art. 881
9/25/65	**13**	6	6. Some Enchanted Evening there were 6 top 10 versions of this "South Pacific" song in 1949	United Art. 919
12/04/65	**18**	6	7. Sunday And Me Neil Diamond's first major hit as a songwriter	United Art. 948
6/11/66	**25**	4	8. Crying	United Art. 50016
1/25/69	**6**	10	● 9. **This Magic Moment**	United Art. 50475

DATE	POS	WKS	ARTIST—RECORD TITLE	LABEL & NO.
1/17/70	**19**	7	10. Walkin' In The Rain	United Art. 50605
			JAY & THE TECHNIQUES	
			Integrated R&B/rock group from Allentown, Pennsylvania: Jay Proctor (lead singer), Karl Landis, Ronnie Goosly, John Walsh, George Lloyd, Chuck Crowl and Dante Dancho.	
8/19/67	**6**	11	1. **Apples, Peaches, Pumpkin Pie**	Smash 2086
11/11/67	**14**	9	2. Keep The Ball Rollin'	Smash 2124
2/10/68	**39**	2	3. Strawberry Shortcake	Smash 2142
			JERRY JAYE	
			Born Jerald Jaye Hatley on 10/19/37 in Manila, Arkansas.	
5/06/67	**29**	6	1. My Girl Josephine	Hi 2120
			THE JAYHAWKS	
			Los Angeles R&B group formed in 1955: James Johnson, Carlton Fisher, Dave Govan and Carver Bunkum. Changed name to The Vibrations in 1960.	
7/28/56	**18**	2	1. Stranded In The Jungle [N] Best Seller #18 / Top 100 #29	Flash 109
			THE JAYNETTS	
			R&B female group from the Bronx, formed by producer/composer Zelma "Zell" Sanders.	
9/07/63	2(2)	9	1. **Sally, Go 'Round The Roses**	Tuff 369
			THE J.B.'s	
			James Brown's super-funk back-up band led by Fred Wesley.	
6/23/73	**22**	6	• 1. Doing It To Death shown as: **FRED WESLEY & THE J.B.'s**	People 621
			JEFFERSON	
			English vocalist.	
1/24/70	**23**	6	1. Baby Take Me In Your Arms	Janus 106
			JEFFERSON STARSHIP	
			Formed as Jefferson Airplane in San Francisco, 1965. Consisted of Marty Balin and Grace Slick (vocals), Paul Kantner (vocals, guitar), Jorma Kaukonen (guitar), Jack Casady (bass) and Spencer Dryden (drums). Slick and Dryden joined in 1966, replacing Signe Anderson and Skip Spence. Slick had been in the Great Society. Spence then formed Moby Grape. Dryden replaced by Joey Covington in 1970. Casady and Kaukonen left by 1974 to go full time with Hot Tuna. Balin left in 1971, rejoined in 1975, by which time group was renamed Jefferson Starship and consisted of Slick, Kantner, Papa John Creach (violin), David Freiberg (bass), Craig Chaquico (guitar), Pete Sears (bass) and John Barbata (drums). Slick left group from June, 1978 to January, 1981 due to personal problems. In 1979, singer Mickey Thomas joined (replaced Balin), along with Aynsley Dunbar who replaced Barbata. Don Baldwin replaced Dunbar in 1982. Kantner left in 1984, and, due to legal difficulties, band's name was shortened to Starship, whose lineup included Slick, Thomas, Sears, Chaquico and Baldwin. Slick left in early 1988.	
			JEFFERSON AIRPLANE:	
5/06/67	**5**	9	1. **Somebody To Love**	RCA 9140
7/01/67	**8**	9	2. **White Rabbit**	RCA 9248
			JEFFERSON STARSHIP:	
9/13/75	**3**	13	3. **Miracles**	Grunt 10367
8/14/76	**12**	11	4. With Your Love	Grunt 10746
3/25/78	**8**	11	5. **Count On Me**	Grunt 11196

DATE	POS	WKS	ARTIST—RECORD TITLE	LABEL & NO.
6/24/78	**12**	8	6. Runaway	Grunt 11274
11/24/79†	**14**	10	7. Jane	Grunt 11750
5/02/81	**29**	6	8. Find Your Way Back	Grunt 12211
11/13/82	**28**	6	9. Be My Lady	Grunt 13350
3/19/83	**38**	2	10. Winds Of Change	Grunt 13439
6/09/84	**23**	8	11. No Way Out	Grunt 13811
			STARSHIP:	
9/28/85	**1**(2)	15	● 12. **We Built This City**	Grunt 14170
1/18/86	**1**(1)	13	13. **Sara**	Grunt 14253
4/26/86	**26**	6	14. Tomorrow Doesn't Matter Tonight	Grunt 14332
2/14/87	**1**(2)	15	● 15. **Nothing's Gonna Stop Us Now** from the film "Mannequin"	Grunt 5109
7/18/87	**9**	10	16. **It's Not Over ('Til It's Over)**	RCA/Grunt 5225
			THE JOE JEFFREY GROUP	
			Joe is an R&B singer/guitarist.	
7/05/69	**14**	8	1. My Pledge Of Love	Wand 11200
			JELLYBEAN	
			John "Jellybean" Benitez is a renowned Manhattan club DJ/remixer/producer.	
12/21/84†	**18**	9	1. Sidewalk Talk written by Madonna	EMI America 8297
8/15/87	**16**	8	2. Who Found Who vocal: Elisa Fiorillo	Chrysalis 43120
			THE JELLY BEANS	
			Black quintet from Jersey City: sisters Elyse & Maxine Herbert, Alma Brewer, Diane Taylor and Charles Thomas.	
7/18/64	**9**	7	1. **I Wanna Love Him So Bad**	Red Bird 10003
			WAYLON JENNINGS	
			Born on 6/15/37 in Littlefield, Texas. While working as a DJ in Lubbock, Texas, Waylon befriended Buddy Holly. Holly produced Waylon's first record "Jole Blon" in 1958. Waylon then joined with Buddy's backing band as bass guitarist on the fateful "Winter Dance Party" tour in 1959. Established himself in the mid-70s as a leader of the "outlaw" movement in country music. Married to Jessi Colter since 1969. In the films "Nashville Rebel," "MacKintosh And T.J." and "Urban Cowboy."	
3/06/76	**25**	5	1. Good Hearted Woman	RCA 10529
			WAYLON & WILLIE (Nelson)	
6/11/77	**25**	7	2. Luckenbach, Texas (Back to the Basics of Love) ending vocal: Willie Nelson	RCA 10924
11/01/80	**21**	10	● 3. Theme From The Dukes Of Hazzard (Good Ol' Boys) shown only as: **WAYLON** from "The Dukes Of Hazzard" TV series	RCA 12067
			KRIS JENSEN	
			Born on 4/4/42 in New Haven, Connecticut. Pop-country singer/guitarist.	
10/06/62	**20**	6	1. Torture	Hickory 1173

DATE	POS	WKS	ARTIST—RECORD TITLE	LABEL & NO.
			JETHRO TULL	
			Progressive rock group formed in 1968 in Blackpool, England. Consisted of Ian Anderson (lead singer, flutist), Mick Abrahams (guitar), Glenn Cornick (bass) and Clive Bunker (drums). Named band after 18th century agriculturist Jethro Tull. Abrahams replaced by Martin Barre in 1968. Added keyboardist John Evans in 1970. Cornick replaced by Jeffrey Hammond-Hammond in 1971. Bunker left in late 1971 and was replaced by Barriemore Barlow, who in turn was replaced by John Glascock (died in 1979). Ian has revamped his lineup several times since then.	
11/25/72†	**11**	10	1. Living In The Past	Chrysalis 2006
11/30/74†	**12**	10	2. Bungle In The Jungle	Chrysalis 2101
			THE JETS	
			Minneapolis-based family band consisting of 8 brothers and sisters: Leroy, Eddie, Eugene, Haini, Rudy, Kathi, Elizabeth and Moana Wolfgramm. Their parents are from the South Pacific country of Tonga. All members play at least two instruments. Eugene left group and formed duo, Boys Club, in 1988.	
5/03/86	**3**	13	1. **Crush On You**	MCA 52774
1/17/87	**3**	12	2. **You Got It All**	MCA 52968
6/27/87	**7**	11	3. **Cross My Broken Heart** from the film "Beverly Hills Cop II"	MCA 53123
11/14/87	**20**	6	4. I Do You	MCA 53193
2/13/88	**6**	13	5. **Rocket 2 U**	MCA 53254
5/07/88	**4**	13	6. **Make It Real**	MCA 53311
			JOAN JETT & THE BLACKHEARTS	
			Joan was born on 9/22/60 in Philadelphia. Played guitar with the Los Angeles female rock band The Runaways, 1975-78. Formed her backing band, The Blackhearts, in 1980. Starred in the 1987 film "Light Of Day" as the leader of a rock band called The Barbusters.	
2/13/82	**1**(7)	16	▲ 1. **I Love Rock 'N Roll**	Boardwalk 135
5/15/82	**7**	10	2. **Crimson And Clover**	Boardwalk 144
8/28/82	**20**	7	3. Do You Wanna Touch Me (Oh Yeah)	Boardwalk 150
7/30/83	**35**	4	4. Fake Friends	Blackheart 52240
10/15/83	**37**	2	5. Everyday People	Blackheart 52272
3/21/87	**33**	5	6. Light Of Day **THE BARBUSTERS** (name of band in film "Light Of Day"; actors Michael J. Fox and Michael McKean are not on the recording); written by Bruce Springsteen	Blackheart 06692
8/13/88	**8**	12	7. **I Hate Myself For Loving You**	Blackheart 07919
12/10/88†	**19**	10	8. Little Liar	Blackheart 08095
			JIGSAW	
			Pop-rock quartet from England: Des Deyer, Clive Scott, Tony Campbell and Barrie Bernard.	
10/11/75	**3**	14	1. **Sky High** from the movie "The Dragon Flies"	Chelsea 3022
3/13/76	**30**	5	2. Love Fire	Chelsea 3037

DATE	POS	WKS	ARTIST—RECORD TITLE	LABEL & NO.
			JOSE JIMENEZ	
			Real name: Bill Dana. Born on 10/5/24 in Quincy, Massachusetts. Head writer for TV's "Steve Allen Show." Star of own TV series from 1963-65. Created the Latin American comic character Jose Jimenez for Steve Allen's TV series.	
9/18/61	**19**	4	1. The Astronaut (Parts 1 & 2) [C] interviewed by Don Hinckley	Kapp 409
			THE JIVE BOMBERS	
			New Jersey-based R&B quartet: Clarence Palmer, Earl Johnson, Al Tinney and William "Pee Wee" Tinney.	
3/16/57	**36**	1	1. Bad Boy	Savoy 1508
			THE JIVE FIVE	
			R&B group formed in Brooklyn in 1959: Eugene Pitt (b: 11/6/37; lead singer; formerly with the Genies), Jerome Hanna and Billy Prophet (tenors), Richard Harris (baritone) and Norman Johnson (bass).	
8/14/61	**3**	12	1. **My True Story**	Beltone 1006
9/11/65	**36**	3	2. I'm A Happy Man	United Art. 853
			J.J. FAD	
			Los Angeles female rap trio: M.C.J.B. (Juana Burns), Baby-D (Dania Birks) and Sassy C (Michelle Franklin).	
6/11/88	**30**	4	● 1. Supersonic	Ruthless 99328
			JO JO GUNNE	
			Los Angeles-based rock quartet formed by Jay Ferguson and Mark Andes (former members of Spirit). Named group after the Chuck Berry hit.	
4/15/72	**27**	6	1. Run Run Run	Asylum 11003
			DAMITA JO	
			Born Damita Jo DuBlanc in Austin, Texas. Featured singer with Steve Gibson & The Red Caps (married to Gibson), 1951-53 and 1959-60. Regular on the Red Foxx TV variety series in 1977.	
11/07/60	**22**	8	1. I'll Save The Last Dance For You answer song to The Drifters' "Save The Last Dance For Me"	Mercury 71690
7/17/61	**12**	7	2. I'll Be There answer song to Ben E. King's "Stand By Me"	Mercury 71840
			SAMI JO	
			Alabama-bred country-pop songstress.	
3/23/74	**21**	7	1. Tell Me A Lie	MGM South 7029
			JoBOXERS	
			Pop-rock quintet from England, led by Dig Wayne.	
11/05/83	**36**	4	1. Just Got Lucky	RCA 13601
			BILLY JOEL	
			Born William Martin Joel on 5/9/49 in Long Island, New York. Formed his first band, the Echoes, in 1964, which later became the Lost Souls. Member of Long Island group The Hassles in the late 60s, then formed a rock duo with The Hassles' drummer Jon Small, called Attila. Signed to Columbia Records in 1973. Involved in a serious motorcycle accident on Long Island in 1982. Married model Christie Brinkley in 1985. Toured and recorded in Russia in 1987.	
4/06/74	**25**	4	1. Piano Man	Columbia 45963
12/28/74†	**34**	5	2. The Entertainer	Columbia 10064
12/10/77†	**3**	18	● 3. **Just The Way You Are**	Columbia 10646

DATE	POS	WKS	ARTIST—RECORD TITLE	LABEL & NO.
4/15/78	**17**	8	4. Movin' Out (Anthony's Song)	Columbia 10708
6/17/78	**24**	5	5. Only The Good Die Young	Columbia 10750
9/09/78	**17**	9	6. She's Always A Woman	Columbia 10788
11/11/78†	**3**	16	● 7. **My Life**	Columbia 10853
3/03/79	**14**	6	8. Big Shot	Columbia 10913
5/12/79	**24**	4	9. Honesty	Columbia 10959
3/22/80	**7**	11	10. **You May Be Right**	Columbia 11231
5/24/80	**1**(2)	19	● 11. **It's Still Rock And Roll To Me**	Columbia 11276
8/16/80	**19**	9	12. Don't Ask Me Why	Columbia 11331
11/01/80	**36**	3	13. Sometimes A Fantasy	Columbia 11379
9/26/81	**17**	8	14. Say Goodbye To Hollywood	Columbia 02518
12/12/81†	**23**	9	15. She's Got A Way	Columbia 02628
10/16/82	**20**	8	16. Pressure	Columbia 03244
12/18/82†	**17**	16	17. Allentown	Columbia 03413
7/30/83	**1**(1)	15	18. **Tell Her About It**	Columbia 04012
10/08/83	**3**	16	● 19. **Uptown Girl**	Columbia 04149
1/07/84	**10**	11	20. **An Innocent Man**	Columbia 04259
4/07/84	**14**	11	21. The Longest Time	Columbia 04400
8/04/84	**27**	7	22. Leave A Tender Moment Alone	Columbia 04514
2/09/85	**18**	10	23. Keeping The Faith	Columbia 04681
7/20/85	**9**	11	24. **You're Only Human (Second Wind)**	Columbia 05417
10/26/85	**34**	3	25. The Night Is Still Young	Columbia 05657
6/21/86	**10**	9	26. **Modern Woman** from the film "Ruthless People"	Epic 06118
9/06/86	**10**	10	27. **A Matter Of Trust**	Columbia 06108
12/20/86†	**18**	9	28. This Is The Time 3-28: produced by Phil Ramone; Billy Joel composed all of his hits	Columbia 06526
			JOHN & ERNEST Duo of John Free and Ernest Smith.	
5/12/73	**31**	4	1. Super Fly Meets Shaft [N] break-in song written and produced by Dickie Goodman	Rainy Wed. 201
			ELTON JOHN Born Reginald Kenneth Dwight on 3/25/47 in Pinner, Middlesex, England. Formed his first group, Bluesology, in 1966. Group backed visiting U.S. soul artists and later became Long John Baldry's backing band. Took the name of Elton John from the first names of Bluesology members Elton Dean and John Baldry. Teamed up with lyricist Bernie Taupin beginning in 1969. Formed own record label, Rocket Records, in 1973. Played the Pinball Wizard in the film version of "Tommy." Recorded duet with New York singer Jennifer Rush. Also see Dionne Warwick.	
12/19/70†	**8**	11	1. **Your Song**	Uni 55265
4/10/71	**34**	4	2. Friends from the British film of the same title	Uni 55277
1/01/72	**24**	7	3. Levon	Uni 55314
5/27/72	**6**	12	4. **Rocket Man**	Uni 55328
8/26/72	**8**	7	5. **Honky Cat**	Uni 55343
12/23/72†	**1**(3)	14	● 6. **Crocodile Rock**	MCA 40000
4/21/73	**2**(1)	12	7. **Daniel**	MCA 40046

DATE	POS	WKS	ARTIST—RECORD TITLE	LABEL & NO.
8/11/73	**12**	9	8. Saturday Night's Alright For Fighting	MCA 40105
11/03/73	**2**(3)	14	• 9. **Goodbye Yellow Brick Road**	MCA 40148
3/02/74	**1**(1)	16	• 10. **Bennie And The Jets**	MCA 40198
7/06/74	**2**(2)	9	• 11. **Don't Let The Sun Go Down On Me**	MCA 40259
9/21/74	**4**	9	12. **The Bitch Is Back**	MCA 40297
12/07/74†	**1**(2)	10	• 13. **Lucy In The Sky With Diamonds** with the reggae guitars of Dr. Winston O'Boogie (John Lennon)	MCA 40344
3/15/75	**1**(2)	17	• 14. **Philadelphia Freedom**	MCA 40364
			ELTON JOHN BAND	
7/12/75	**4**	10	• 15. **Someone Saved My Life Tonight**	MCA 40421
10/18/75	**1**(3)	12	• 16. **Island Girl**	MCA 40461
1/31/76	**14**	5	17. Grow Some Funk Of Your Own/	
		5	18. I Feel Like A Bullet (In The Gun Of Robert Ford)	MCA 40505
7/17/76	**1**(4)	15	• 19. **Don't Go Breaking My Heart**	Rocket 40585
			ELTON JOHN & KIKI DEE	
11/20/76	**6**	11	• 20. **Sorry Seems To Be The Hardest Word**	MCA/Rocket 40645
2/26/77	**28**	3	21. Bite Your Lip (Get up and dance!) all of above: produced by Gus Dudgeon (also #38-39 & 41 below)	MCA/Rocket 40677
4/29/78	**34**	4	22. Ego	MCA 40892
11/18/78	**22**	7	23. Part-Time Love	MCA 40973
6/23/79	**9**	14	• 24. **Mama Can't Buy You Love**	MCA 41042
10/27/79	**31**	4	25. Victim Of Love	MCA 41126
5/10/80	**3**	17	• 26. **Little Jeannie**	MCA 41236
9/20/80	**39**	2	27. (Sartorial Eloquence) Don't Ya Wanna Play This Game No More?	MCA 41293
5/30/81	**21**	6	28. Nobody Wins	Geffen 49722
9/05/81	**34**	3	29. Chloe	Geffen 49788
4/17/82	**13**	10	30. Empty Garden (Hey Hey Johnny)	Geffen 50049
8/14/82	**12**	10	31. Blue Eyes	Geffen 29954
5/14/83	**12**	12	32. I'm Still Standing	Geffen 29639
8/20/83	**25**	8	33. Kiss The Bride	Geffen 29568
11/19/83†	**4**	15	34. **I Guess That's Why They Call It The Blues**	Geffen 29460
6/16/84	**5**	13	35. **Sad Songs (Say So Much)**	Geffen 29292
9/15/84	**16**	10	36. Who Wears These Shoes?	Geffen 29189
1/12/85	**38**	3	37. In Neon	Geffen 29111
11/02/85	**20**	10	38. Wrap Her Up	Geffen 28873
2/08/86	**7**	11	39. **Nikita**	Geffen 28800
7/04/87	**36**	3	40. Flames Of Paradise	Epic 07119
			JENNIFER RUSH with ELTON JOHN	
11/28/87†	**6**	12	41. **Candle In The Wind** with The Melbourne Symphony Orchestra; tribute to Marilyn Monroe; tune first recorded for his "Goodbye Yellow Brick Road" LP in 1973	MCA 53196
7/02/88	**2**(1)	13	42. **I Don't Wanna Go On With You Like That**	MCA 53345

DATE	POS	WKS	ARTIST—RECORD TITLE	LABEL & NO.
10/15/88	**19**	6	43. A Word In Spanish 1-12, 14-22, 30, 32-39, 41-43: written by Elton John and Bernie Taupin	MCA 53408
			LITTLE WILLIE JOHN	
			Born William Edgar John on 11/15/37 in Cullendale, Arkansas; raised in Detroit. R&B singer; brother of Mabel John (of the Raeletts). Convicted of manslaughter in 1966; died of a heart attack in Washington State Prison on 5/26/68.	
7/14/56	**24**	9	1. Fever Best Seller #24 / Top 100 #27	King 4935
4/21/58	**20**	7	2. Talk To Me, Talk To Me Top 100 #20 / Best Seller #22	King 5108
7/25/60	**38**	1	3. Heartbreak (It's Hurtin' Me)	King 5356
10/10/60	**13**	10	4. Sleep #1 hit for Fred Waring's Pennsylvanians in 1924	King 5394
			ROBERT JOHN	
			Born Robert John Pedrick, Jr. in Brooklyn in 1946. First recorded at age 12 for Big Top Records. In 1963, recorded as lead singer with Bobby & The Consoles.	
1/29/72	**3**	13	● 1. **The Lion Sleeps Tonight** adaptation of a South African song (adapted in 1952 as "Wimoweh")	Atlantic 2846
6/30/79	**1**(1)	19	● 2. **Sad Eyes**	EMI America 8015
8/23/80	**31**	4	3. Hey There Lonely Girl	EMI America 8049
			JOHNNIE & JOE	
			R&B duo from the Bronx: Johnnielouise Richardson (d: 10/25/88) and Joe Rivers. Johnnie is the daughter of the late J&S Records owner Zell Sanders.	
5/27/57	**8**	15	1. **Over The Mountain; Across The Sea** Top 100 #8 / Best Seller #9 / Juke Box #17 end	Chess 1654
			JOHNNY & THE HURRICANES	
			Rock and roll instrumental band formed as the Orbits in Toledo, Ohio in 1958. Consisted of leader John Pocisk "Paris" (saxophone), Paul Tesluk (organ), Dave Yorko (guitar), Lionel "Butch" Mattice (bass) and Tony Kaye (drums; replaced in late 1959 by Bo Savich). First recorded for Twirl in 1959. Paris had own label, Attila, from 1965-70.	
6/01/59	**23**	6	1. Crossfire [I]	Warwick 502
8/17/59	**5**	13	2. **Red River Rock** **[I]** rock version of "Red River Valley"	Warwick 509
11/16/59	**25**	6	3. Reveille Rock [I] rock version of the Army bugle call "Reveille"	Warwick 513
2/22/60	**15**	10	4. Beatnik Fly [I] rock version of "Blue Tail Fly"	Warwick 520
			JOHNNY HATES JAZZ	
			U.K.-based trio: Clark Datchler (vocals) and Calvin Hayes (both from England), with American Mike Nocito. Hayes is the son of pop producer Mickie Most. Datchler left group in late 1988.	
4/02/88	**2**(3)	13	1. **Shattered Dreams**	Virgin 99383
8/13/88	**31**	5	2. I Don't Want To Be A Hero	Virgin 99304
			SAMMY JOHNS	
			Born on 2/7/46 in Charlotte, North Carolina. Played guitar from age 10. Own band, the Devilles, from 1963-73.	
3/01/75	**5**	12	● 1. **Chevy Van**	GRC 2046

DATE	POS	WKS	ARTIST—RECORD TITLE	LABEL & NO.
			BETTY JOHNSON	
			Born on 3/16/32 in Charlotte, North Carolina. Married to musical conductor Charles Randolph Grean. Regular on NBC-TV's "Tonight Show" starring Jack Parr.	
12/15/56†	**9**	18	1. **I Dreamed** Jockey #9 / Top 100 #12 / Juke Box #15 / Best Seller #22 featured on an episode of NBC-TV's "Modern Romances"	Bally 1020
6/24/57	**25**	1	2. Little White Lies Jockey #25 / Top 100 #40 #1 hit for Fred Waring's Pennsylvanians in 1930	Bally 1033
2/24/58	**17**	11	3. The Little Blue Man [N] Jockey #17 / Top 100 #19 / Best Seller #20 voice of the Little Blue Man: Hugh Downs (host of TV's "20/20")	Atlantic 1169
6/30/58	**19**	1	4. Dream Jockey #19 / Top 100 #58 #1 hit for the Pied Pipers in 1945	Atlantic 1186
			DON JOHNSON	
			Born on 12/15/49 in Flatt Creek, Missouri. Plays Sonny Crockett on TV's "Miami Vice."	
9/06/86	**5**	10	1. **Heartbeat**	Epic 06285
11/12/88	**25**	5	2. Till I Loved You **BARBRA STREISAND & DON JOHNSON** love theme from "Goya"	Columbia 08062
			MARV JOHNSON	
			Born on 10/15/38 in Detroit. R&B singer/songwriter/pianist. With the Serenaders vocal group, mid-50s. First recorded for Kudo in 1958. Worked in sales and promotion for Motown in the early 70s.	
4/20/59	**30**	6	1. Come To Me released regionally on Tamla 101; Berry Gordy's first release	United Art. 160
11/16/59†	**10**	16	2. **You Got What It Takes**	United Art. 185
3/21/60	**9**	10	3. **I Love The Way You Love**	United Art. 208
10/10/60	**20**	4	4. (You've Got To) Move Two Mountains all of above: female backing by The Rayber Voices	United Art. 241
			MICHAEL JOHNSON	
			Born in 1945 in Alamosa, Colorado; raised in Denver. Studied classical guitar in 1966 in Spain. In the Chad Mitchell Trio with John Denver in 1968.	
5/27/78	**12**	10	1. Bluer Than Blue	EMI America 8001
9/23/78	**32**	5	2. Almost Like Being In Love	EMI America 8004
9/29/79	**19**	9	3. This Night Won't Last Forever	EMI America 8019
			TOM JOHNSTON	
			Lead singer and guitarist of The Doobie Brothers from 1971-78.	
1/12/80	**34**	2	1. Savannah Nights	Warner 49096
			FRANCE JOLI	
			French-Canadian singer from Montreal. Age 16 in 1979.	
9/29/79	**15**	8	1. Come To Me	Prelude 8001
			JON & ROBIN & THE IN CROWD	
			Jon and Robin Abnor.	
5/27/67	**18**	6	1. Do It Again A Little Bit Slower	Abnak 119

DATE	POS	WKS	ARTIST—RECORD TITLE	LABEL & NO.
			THE JONES GIRLS	
			Detroit soul sister trio: Shirley, Brenda and Valorie Jones. Back-up singers for Lou Rawls, Teddy Pendergrass and Aretha Franklin. With Diana Ross from 1975-78. Sang with Le Pamplemousse.	
8/18/79	**38**	1	• 1. You Gonna Make Me Love Somebody Else	Phil. Int. 3680
			ETTA JONES	
			Born on 11/25/28 in Aiken, South Carolina. Jazz singer with Earl Hines' orchestra.	
12/12/60	**36**	1	1. Don't Go To Strangers	Prestige 180
			HOWARD JONES	
			Born on 2/23/55 in Southampton, England. Pop singer/songwriter/synth wizard.	
2/25/84	**27**	6	1. New Song	Elektra 69766
6/02/84	**33**	4	2. What Is Love?	Elektra 69737
4/20/85	**5**	14	3. **Things Can Only Get Better**	Elektra 69651
8/03/85	**19**	8	4. Life In One Day	Elektra 69631
5/03/86	**4**	14	5. **No One Is To Blame**	Elektra 69549
11/08/86	**17**	10	6. You Know I Love You...Don't You?	Elektra 69512
			JACK JONES	
			Born on 1/14/38 in Los Angeles. Son of actor/singer Allan Jones, who had the #8 pop hit "The Donkey Serenade" the year Jack was born.	
11/30/63†	**14**	10	1. Wives And Lovers inspired by the film of the same title	Kapp 551
12/26/64†	**30**	5	2. Dear Heart from the film of the same title	Kapp 635
3/20/65	**15**	7	3. The Race Is On	Kapp 651
7/16/66	**35**	4	4. The Impossible Dream from the musical "Man Of La Mancha"	Kapp 755
3/25/67	**39**	2	5. Lady	Kapp 800
			JIMMY JONES	
			Born on 6/2/37 in Birmingham, Alabama. Joined the R&B group Sparks Of Rhythm in New York, in 1955. Formed own group, the Savoys (later: Pretenders), in 1956.	
1/18/60	**2**(1)	14	1. **Handy Man**	Cub 9049
5/09/60	**3**	10	2. **Good Timin'**	Cub 9067
			JOE JONES	
			Born on 8/12/26 in New Orleans. Pianist/valet for B.B. King in the early 50s. First recorded for Capitol in 1954. Produced The Dixie Cups and Alvin Robinson.	
10/10/60	**3**	9	1. **You Talk Too Much**	Roulette 4304
			LINDA JONES	
			Born on 1/14/44 in Newark, New Jersey; died of diabetes on 3/14/72. R&B singer. First recorded for MGM/Cub as "Linda Lane" in 1963.	
7/22/67	**21**	7	1. Hypnotized	Loma 2070
			ORAN "JUICE" JONES	
			Born in Houston; raised in Harlem. Soul balladeer singer.	
10/11/86	**9**	9	1. **The Rain**	Def Jam 06209

DATE	POS	WKS	ARTIST—RECORD TITLE	LABEL & NO.
			QUINCY JONES	
			Born Quincy Delight Jones, Jr. on 3/14/33 in Chicago. Composer/ conductor/arranger/ producer. Began as a jazz trumpeter, with Lionel Hampton, 1950-53. Music Director for Mercury Records in 1961, then Vice President in 1964. Wrote scores for many films, 1965-73. Scored TV series "Roots" in 1977. Produced Michael Jackson's mega- albums "Thriller" and "Bad." Arranger and producer for hundreds of successful singers and orchestras. Winner of 19 Grammy Awards. Won prestigious NARAS Trustees Award in 1989.	
7/22/78	**21**	7	1. Stuff Like That vocals: Ashford & Simpson and Chaka Khan	A&M 2043
5/09/81	**28**	5	2. Ai No Corrida featuring the vocals of Dune	A&M 2309
9/19/81	**17**	10	3. Just Once **QUINCY JONES featuring JAMES INGRAM**	A&M 2357
2/13/82	**14**	11	4. One Hundred Ways **QUINCY JONES featuring JAMES INGRAM**	A&M 2387
			RICKIE LEE JONES	
			Born on 11/8/54 in Chicago. Pop/jazz-styled singer/songwriter. Moved to Los Angeles in 1977. Won the 1979 Best New Artist Grammy Award.	
5/12/79	**4**	12	1. **Chuck E.'s In Love**	Warner 8825
9/01/79	**40**	1	2. Young Blood	Warner 49018
			TOM JONES	
			Born Thomas Jones Woodward on 6/7/40 in Pontypridd, Wales. Worked local clubs as Tommy Scott; formed own trio, The Senators, in 1963. Began solo career in London in 1964. Won the 1965 Best New Artist Grammy Award. Host of own TV musical variety series from 1969-71.	
5/01/65	**10**	9	1. **It's Not Unusual**	Parrot 9737
7/03/65	**3**	10	2. **What's New Pussycat?** from the film of the same title	Parrot 9765
9/18/65	**27**	5	3. With These Hands #7 hit for Eddie Fisher in 1953	Parrot 9787
1/01/66	**25**	6	4. Thunderball from the James Bond film "Thunderball"	Parrot 9801
1/21/67	**11**	7	5. Green, Green Grass Of Home	Parrot 40009
4/01/67	**27**	4	6. Detroit City	Parrot 40012
4/13/68	**15**	11	7. Delilah	Parrot 40025
10/05/68	**35**	2	8. Help Yourself	Parrot 40029
6/07/69	**13**	9	9. Love Me Tonight	Parrot 40038
8/09/69	**6**	14	● 10. **I'll Never Fall In Love Again** [R] originally charted in 1967 (POS 49)	Parrot 40018
1/03/70	**5**	10	● 11. **Without Love (There Is Nothing)**	Parrot 40045
5/09/70	**13**	7	12. Daughter Of Darkness	Parrot 40048
8/29/70	**14**	7	13. I (Who Have Nothing)	Parrot 40051
11/28/70	**25**	7	14. Can't Stop Loving You	Parrot 40056
2/20/71	**2**(1)	12	● 15. **She's A Lady** written by Paul Anka	Parrot 40058
6/12/71	**26**	6	16. Puppet Man/ written by Neil Sedaka	
7/03/71	**38**	3	17. Resurrection Shuffle	Parrot 40064
2/12/77	**15**	10	18. Say You'll Stay Until Tomorrow	Epic 50308

DATE	POS	WKS	ARTIST—RECORD TITLE	LABEL & NO.
12/24/88†	**31**	6	19. Kiss **THE ART OF NOISE featuring TOM JONES**	China 871038
			JANIS JOPLIN	
			Born on 1/19/43 in Port Arthur, Texas. White blues-rock singer. Nicknamed Pearl. To San Francisco in 1966, joined Big Brother & The Holding Company. Left band to go solo in 1968. Died of a heroin overdose in Hollywood on 10/4/70. The Bette Midler film "The Rose" was inspired by Joplin's life.	
2/20/71	**1**(2)	12	1. **Me And Bobby McGee**	Columbia 45314
			JOURNEY	
			Rock group formed in San Francisco in 1973. Consisted of Neal Schon, George Tickner (guitars), Gregg Rolie (keyboards, vocals), Ross Valory (bass) and Aynsley Dunbar (drums). Schon and Rolie had been in Santana. Tickner left in 1975. Steve Perry (lead vocals) added in 1978. Dunbar was replaced by Steve Smith in 1979. Jonathan Cain (keyboards) added in 1981, replacing Rolie. In 1986 group pared down to a 3-man core: Perry, Schon and Cain.	
8/25/79	**16**	12	1. Lovin', Touchin', Squeezin'	Columbia 11036
3/29/80	**23**	6	2. Any Way You Want It	Columbia 11213
7/05/80	**32**	4	3. Walks Like A Lady	Columbia 11275
4/04/81	**34**	4	4. The Party's Over (Hopelessly In Love)	Columbia 60505
8/01/81	**4**	14	5. **Who's Crying Now**	Columbia 02241
11/07/81	**9**	13	6. **Don't Stop Believin'**	Columbia 02567
1/23/82	**2**(6)	14	7. **Open Arms**	Columbia 02687
6/12/82	**19**	9	8. Still They Ride	Columbia 02883
2/05/83	**8**	16	9. **Separate Ways (Worlds Apart)**	Columbia 03513
4/30/83	**12**	11	10. Faithfully	Columbia 03840
7/23/83	**23**	8	11. After The Fall	Columbia 04004
10/22/83	**23**	7	12. Send Her My Love	Columbia 04151
2/02/85	**9**	11	13. **Only The Young** from the film "Vision Quest"	Geffen 29090
4/19/86	**9**	10	14. **Be Good To Yourself**	Columbia 05869
7/12/86	**17**	7	15. Suzanne	Columbia 06134
9/20/86	**17**	8	16. Girl Can't Help It	Columbia 06302
1/24/87	**14**	9	17. I'll Be Alright Without You	Columbia 06301
			JUMP 'N THE SADDLE	
			Chicago-based band; Peter Quinn, lead singer.	
12/24/83†	**15**	7	1. The Curly Shuffle [N] a Three Stooges parody	Atlantic 89718
			JUNIOR	
			Full name: Junior Giscombe. R&B-funk singer/songwriter from England.	
4/10/82	**30**	3	1. Mama Used To Say	Mercury 76132
			JUST US	
			Consists of New York City record producers Chip Taylor and Al Gorgoni.	
5/07/66	**34**	2	1. I Can't Grow Peaches On A Cherry Tree	Colpix 803

DATE	POS	WKS	ARTIST—RECORD TITLE	LABEL & NO.
			BILL JUSTIS	
			Born on 10/14/26 in Birmingham, Alabama. Died on 7/15/82 in Nashville. Session saxophonist/arranger/producer. Led house band for Sun Records.	
11/18/57	**2**(1)	14	1. **Raunchy** **[I]** Best Seller #2 / Top 100 #3 / Jockey #5 sax: Bill Justis; guitar: Sid Manker	Phillips 3519
			K	
			BERT KAEMPFERT	
			Born on 10/16/23 in Hamburg, Germany. Multi-instrumentalist/bandleader/producer/ composer/arranger for Polydor Records in Germany. Produced the first Beatles recording session. Died on 6/21/80 in Zug, Switzerland.	
11/21/60†	**1**(3)	15	1. **Wonderland By Night** **[I]** trumpet solo: Charly Tabor	Decca 31141
4/10/61	**31**	4	2. Tenderly [I] Rosemary Clooney's theme song (POS 17-1952)	Decca 31236
2/13/65	**11**	10	3. Red Roses For A Blue Lady [I] #3 hit for Vaughn Monroe in 1949	Decca 31722
5/29/65	**33**	3	4. Three O'Clock In The Morning [I] there were 6 top 10 versions of this tune from 1921-30	Decca 31778
			KAJAGOOGOO	
			English pop-synth quintet led by Limahl (Chris Hamill).	
5/21/83	**5**	12	1. **Too Shy**	EMI America 8161
			KALIN TWINS	
			Herbert and Harold Kalin, born on 2/16/39 in Port Jervis, New York.	
6/30/58	**5**	13	1. **When** Hot 100 #5 / Best Seller #7 / Jockey #8	Decca 30642
10/20/58	**12**	9	2. Forget Me Not	Decca 30745
			KITTY KALLEN	
			Born on 5/25/22 in Philadelphia. Big band singer with Jack Teagarden, Jimmy Dorsey and Harry James.	
2/11/56	**39**	1	1. Go On With The Wedding **KITTY KALLEN & GEORGIE SHAW**	Decca 29776
11/09/59	**34**	3	2. If I Give My Heart To You there were 5 top 30 versions of this tune in 1954	Columbia 41473
1/12/63	**18**	6	3. My Coloring Book	RCA 8124
			THE KANE GANG	
			English soul-styled pop trio: Martin Brammer, Paul Woods and David Brewis. Band's name derived from the film "Citizen Kane."	
12/19/87	**36**	3	1. Motortown	Capitol 44062

DATE	POS	WKS	ARTIST—RECORD TITLE	LABEL & NO.
			KANSAS	
			Progressive rock group formed in Topeka in 1970. Consisted of Steve Walsh (lead vocals, keyboards), Kerry Livgren (guitar & keyboards), Phil Ehart (drums), Robby Steinhardt (violin), Rich Williams (guitar) and Dave Hope (bass). Walsh left in 1981 and was replaced by John Elefante. Re-formed lineup in 1986: Walsh, Ehart, Williams, Steve Morse (guitarist from Dixie Dregs) and Billy Greer (bass).	
2/05/77	**11**	13	1. Carry On Wayward Son	Kirshner 4267
12/17/77†	**28**	6	2. Point Of Know Return	Kirshner 4273
2/18/78	**6**	15	• 3. **Dust In The Wind**	Kirshner 4274
6/23/79	**23**	8	4. People Of The South Wind	Kirshner 4284
11/08/80	**40**	1	5. Hold On	Kirshner 4291
5/29/82	**17**	9	6. Play The Game Tonight	Kirshner 02903
11/29/86†	**19**	10	7. All I Wanted	MCA 52958
			KASENETZ-KATZ SINGING ORCHESTRAL CIRCUS	
			Bubblegum rock group assembled by producers Jerry Kasenetz and Jeff Katz. Features members from The 1910 Fruitgum Co./The Ohio Express/The Music Explosion.	
11/09/68	**25**	6	1. Quick Joey Small (Run Joey Run) Joey Levine, lead singer	Buddah 64
			KATRINA & THE WAVES	
			British-based pop/rock quartet fronted by Kansas-born Katrina Leskanich.	
4/20/85	**9**	13	1. **Walking On Sunshine**	Capitol 5466
9/07/85	**37**	2	2. Do You Want Crying	Capitol 5450
			SAMMY KAYE	
			Born on 3/13/10 in Rocky River, Ohio; died on 6/2/87 (cancer). Durable leader of popular "sweet" dance band with the slogan "Swing and Sway with Sammy Kaye." Also played clarinet and alto sax.	
5/02/64	**36**	2	1. Charade [I] from the film of the same title	Decca 31589
			KC	
			Born Harry Wayne Casey on 1/31/51 in Hialeah, Florida. Leader of KC & The Sunshine Band. Seriously injured in an auto accident on 1/15/82. Own label, Meca, in 1983.	
12/22/79†	**2**(2)	16	• 1. **Yes, I'm Ready** **TERI DeSARIO with K.C.**	Casablanca 2227
2/04/84	**18**	10	2. Give It Up	Meca 1001
			KC & THE SUNSHINE BAND	
			Disco/R&B band formed in Florida in 1973 by lead singer/keyboardist Harry "KC" Casey and bassist Richard Finch. Integrated band contained from 7 to 11 members. Casey and Finch wrote, arranged and produced all of their hits.	
8/02/75	**1**(1)	9	1. **Get Down Tonight**	T.K. 1009
11/01/75	**1**(2)	13	2. **That's The Way (I Like It)**	T.K. 1015
7/31/76	**1**(1)	16	3. **(Shake, Shake, Shake) Shake Your Booty**	T.K. 1019
1/29/77	**37**	2	4. I Like To Do It	T.K. 1020
4/02/77	**1**(1)	16	5. **I'm Your Boogie Man**	T.K. 1022
8/13/77	**2**(3)	14	6. **Keep It Comin' Love**	T.K. 1023
3/25/78	**35**	3	7. Boogie Shoes originally released as the B-side of "Shake Your Booty"	T.K. 1025

DATE	POS	WKS	ARTIST—RECORD TITLE	LABEL & NO.
6/24/78	**35**	2	8. It's The Same Old Song	T.K. 1028
9/29/79†	**1**(1)	18	9. **Please Don't Go**	T.K. 1035
			ERNIE K-DOE	
			Born Ernest Kador, Jr. on 2/22/36 in New Orleans. R&B singer/songwriter. Recorded with the Blue Diamonds on Savoy in 1954. First solo recording for Specialty in 1955.	
4/03/61	**1**(1)	12	1. **Mother-In-Law** bass vocal: Benny Spellman	Minit 623
			KEITH	
			Born James Barry Keefer on 5/7/49 in Philadelphia. First recorded as "Keith & The Admirations" on Columbia in 1965.	
11/12/66	**39**	1	1. Ain't Gonna Lie	Mercury 72596
1/07/67	**7**	9	2. **98.6** above 2: featuring backing vocals by The Tokens	Mercury 72639
4/08/67	**37**	2	3. Tell Me To My Face	Mercury 72652
			JERRY KELLER	
			Born on 6/20/37 in Fort Smith, Arkansas. To Tulsa, Oklahoma at age 7.	
7/20/59	**14**	8	1. Here Comes Summer	Kapp 277
			GRACE KELLY - see BING CROSBY	
			MONTY KELLY	
			Arranger/conductor from Oakland. Trumpeter with Paul Whiteman in the early 40s.	
4/04/60	**30**	3	1. Summer Set [I]	Carlton 527
			JOHNNY KEMP	
			Singer/dancer/actor/songwriter, began performing in nightclubs in his native Nassau, Bahamas, at the age of 13. Moved to Harlem in 1979.	
6/25/88	**10**	11	1. **Just Got Paid**	Columbia 07744
			EDDIE KENDRICKS	
			Born on 12/17/39 in Union Springs, Alabama; raised in Birmingham. Joined R&B group the Primes in Detroit in the late 50s. Group later evolved into The Temptations; Eddie sang lead from 1960-71. Eddie later dropped letter "s" from his last name.	
9/15/73	**1**(2)	16	1. **Keep On Truckin' (Part 1)**	Tamla 54238
1/26/74	**2**(2)	13	2. **Boogie Down**	Tamla 54243
6/01/74	**28**	4	3. Son Of Sagittarius	Tamla 54247
4/05/75	**18**	10	4. Shoeshine Boy	Tamla 54257
3/20/76	**36**	3	5. He's A Friend	Tamla 54266
9/14/85	**20**	7	6. A Nite At The Apollo Live! The Way You Do The Things You Do/My Girl **DARYL HALL JOHN OATES with DAVID RUFFIN & EDDIE KENDRICK** recorded at the reopening of New York's Apollo Theatre; revival of 2 early Temptations hits	RCA 14178
			JOYCE KENNEDY - see JEFFREY OSBORNE	
			CHRIS KENNER	
			Born on 12/25/29 in Kenner, Louisiana. Died of a heart attack on 1/25/77. R&B singer/songwriter. First recorded for Baton in 1956.	
7/03/61	**2**(3)	10	1. **I Like It Like That, Part 1**	Instant 3229

DATE	POS	WKS	ARTIST—RECORD TITLE	LABEL & NO.
			KENNY G	
			Kenny Gorelick; fusion saxophonist from Seattle. With Barry White's Love Unlimited Orchestra at age 17. Worked with Jeff Lorber.	
5/16/87	**4**	12	1. **Songbird** **[I]**	Arista 9588
9/26/87	**15**	9	2. Don't Make Me Wait For Love vocal: Lenny Williams (original lead singer for Tower of Power); originally hit Black chart on 12/13/86 (POS 77) on Arista 9544	Arista 9625
11/19/88†	**13**	10	3. Silhouette [I]	Arista 9751
			STAN KENTON	
			Born on 2/19/12 in Wichita, Kansas. Died in Los Angeles on 8/25/79. Organized his first jazz band in 1941. Third person named to the Jazz Hall of Fame.	
11/17/62	**32**	4	1. Mama Sang A Song [S]	Capitol 4847
			KERMIT - see JIM HENSON	
			CHAKA KHAN	
			Born Yvette Marie Stevens on 3/23/53 in Great Lakes, Illinois. Became lead singer of Rufus in 1972. Recorded solo and with Rufus since 1978. Sister of vocalists Taka Boom and Mark Stevens (Jamaica Boys).	
11/18/78	**21**	8	1. I'm Every Woman	Warner 8683
9/29/84	**3**	17	● 2. **I Feel For You** with Grandmaster Melle Mel (rap) and Stevie Wonder (harmonica)	Warner 29195
			GREG KIHN BAND	
			Greg is a rock singer/songwriter/guitarist from Baltimore. Formed band in Berkeley, California, in 1975.	
7/11/81	**15**	13	1. The Breakup Song (They Don't Write 'Em)	Beserkley 47149
3/05/83	**2**(1)	14	2. **Jeopardy**	Beserkley 69847
			GREG KIHN:	
3/23/85	**30**	4	3. Lucky	EMI America 8255
			THEOLA KILGORE	
			Gospel-blues singer from Shreveport, Louisiana; raised in Oakland.	
5/11/63	**21**	8	1. The Love Of My Man	Serock 2004
			ANDY KIM	
			Born Andrew Joachim on 12/5/46 in Montreal, Canada. His parents were from Lebanon. Pop singer/songwriter. Teamed with Jeff Barry to write "Sugar, Sugar."	
6/01/68	**21**	8	1. How'd We Ever Get This Way	Steed 707
10/19/68	**31**	3	2. Shoot'em Up, Baby	Steed 710
6/21/69	**9**	12	● 3. **Baby, I Love You**	Steed 716
11/08/69	**36**	1	4. So Good Together	Steed 720
11/28/70	**17**	8	5. Be My Baby	Steed 729
7/20/74	**1**(1)	13	● 6. **Rock Me Gently**	Capitol 3895
11/23/74	**28**	4	7. Fire, Baby I'm On Fire	Capitol 3962
			ADRIAN KIMBERLY	
7/10/61	**34**	1	1. The Graduation Song... Pomp And Circumstance [I] written in 1901 for the coronation of King Edward VII	Calliope 6501

DATE	POS	WKS	ARTIST—RECORD TITLE	LABEL & NO.
			KING CURTIS	
			Born Curtis Ousley on 2/7/34 in Fort Worth, Texas. Stabbed to death on 8/13/71 in New York City. R&B saxophonist. With Lionel Hampton in 1950. Moved to New York City, did session work. First own recording on Gem in 1953. Played on sessions for Bobby Darin, Aretha Franklin, Brook Benton, Nat King Cole and hundreds of others.	
4/07/62	**17**	8	1. Soul Twist [I]	Enjoy 1000
			KING CURTIS & THE NOBLE KNIGHTS	
9/23/67	**33**	4	2. Memphis Soul Stew [I]	Atco 6511
10/07/67	**28**	4	3. Ode To Billie Joe [I]	Atco 6516
			shown as: **THE KINGPINS**	
			KING HARVEST	
			6-man rock group.	
1/06/73	**13**	11	1. Dancing In The Moonlight	Perception 515
			B.B. KING	
			Born Riley B. King on 9/16/25 in Itta Bena, Mississippi. Moved to Memphis in 1946. Own radio show from 1949-50, where he was dubbed "The Beale Street Blues Boy," later shortened to "Blues Boy," then simply "B.B." First recorded for Bullet in 1949. Inducted into the Rock And Roll Hall Of Fame in 1987. Appeared in the 1987 film "Amazon Women On The Moon." The most famous blues singer/guitarist in the world today.	
6/13/64	**34**	3	1. Rock Me Baby	Kent 393
5/25/68	**39**	1	2. Paying The Cost To Be The Boss	BluesWay 61015
1/31/70	**15**	8	3. The Thrill Is Gone	BluesWay 61032
4/03/71	**40**	1	4. Ask Me No Questions	ABC 11290
9/22/73	**38**	2	5. To Know You Is To Love You	ABC 11373
2/09/74	**28**	6	6. I Like To Live The Love	ABC 11406
			BEN E. KING	
			Born Benjamin Earl Nelson on 9/23/38 in Henderson, North Carolina. To New York in 1947. Worked with The Moonglows for 6 months while still in high school. Joined the Five Crowns in 1957, who became the new Drifters in 1959. Wrote lyrics to "There Goes My Baby," his first lead performance with The Drifters. Went solo in May of 1960.	
1/30/61	**10**	10	1. **Spanish Harlem**	Atco 6185
5/22/61	**4**	11	2. **Stand By Me**	Atco 6194
8/21/61	**18**	5	3. Amor there were 3 top 10 versions in 1944	Atco 6203
5/19/62	**11**	7	4. Don't Play That Song (You Lied)	Atco 6222
8/03/63	**29**	6	5. I (Who Have Nothing)	Atco 6267
3/08/75	**5**	9	6. **Supernatural Thing - Part I**	Atlantic 3241
11/01/86	**9**	13	7. **Stand By Me** **[R]** featured song in the film of the same title	Atlantic 89361
			CAROLE KING	
			Born Carole Klein on 2/9/42 in Brooklyn. Singer/songwriter/pianist. Married lyricist Gerry Goffin in 1958, team wrote 4 #1 hits: "Will You Love Me Tomorrow," "Go Away Little Girl," "Take Good Care Of My Baby" and "The Loco-Motion." Divorced Goffin in 1968, first solo album in 1970. The most successful female songwriter of the rock era.	
9/22/62	**22**	4	1. It Might As Well Rain Until September	Dimension 2000
5/22/71	**1**(5)	15	● 2. **It's Too Late/**	
		15	3. I Feel The Earth Move	Ode 66015
9/04/71	**14**	9	4. So Far Away	Ode 66019

DATE	POS	WKS	ARTIST—RECORD TITLE	LABEL & NO.
2/05/72	**9**	8	5. **Sweet Seasons**	Ode 66022
12/09/72†	**24**	7	6. Been To Canaan	Ode 66031
8/11/73	**28**	5	7. Believe In Humanity	Ode 66035
12/08/73	**37**	2	8. Corazon [I]	Ode 66039
9/14/74	**2**(1)	12	9. **Jazzman**	Ode 66101
1/18/75	**9**	8	10. **Nightingale**	Ode 66106
3/06/76	**28**	6	11. Only Love Is Real 2-11: produced by Lou Adler	Ode 66119
8/20/77	**30**	5	12. Hard Rock Cafe	Capitol 4455
6/14/80	**12**	10	13. One Fine Day	Capitol 4864
			CLAUDE KING	
			Born on 2/5/33 in Shreveport, Louisiana. Country singer/songwriter/guitarist. Acted in the TV mini-series "The Blue And The Gray" in 1982.	
6/16/62	**6**	11	1. **Wolverton Mountain** title is an actual place in Arkansas where Clifton Clowers lives	Columbia 42352
			EVELYN "CHAMPAGNE" KING	
			Born on 6/29/60 in the Bronx. To Philadelphia in 1970. Employed as cleaning woman at Sigma Studios when discovered.	
7/22/78	**9**	10	● 1. **Shame**	RCA 11122
3/03/79	**23**	8	● 2. I Don't Know If It's Right	RCA 11386
9/12/81	**40**	2	3. I'm In Love	RCA 12243
10/02/82	**17**	8	4. Love Come Down above 2 shown as: **EVELYN KING**	RCA 13273
			FREDDY KING	
			Born Freddie Christian on 9/30/34 in Gilmer, Texas. Died on 12/28/76 of a heart attack, hepatitis. Blues vocalist/guitarist.	
4/03/61	**29**	4	1. Hide Away [I] titled after Mel's Hide Away Lounge in Chicago	Federal 12401
			JONATHAN KING	
			Born Kenneth King on 12/6/44 in London. Successful singer/songwriter/producer. Formed U.K. Records in 1972. Produced Hedgehoppers Anonymous.	
10/23/65	**17**	7	1. Everyone's Gone To The Moon	Parrot 9774
			PEGGY KING	
2/05/55	**30**	1	1. Make Yourself Comfortable Best Seller #30	Columbia 40363
			TEDDI KING	
			Born on 9/18/29 in Boston; died on 11/18/77. Jazz-styled vocalist.	
3/03/56	**18**	2	1. Mr. Wonderful Jockey #18 / Top 100 #32 from the Broadway musical of the same title	RCA 6392
			THE KINGSMEN	
			Group is Bill Haley's band, The Comets (minus Haley).	
9/22/58	**35**	2	1. Week End [I] Best Seller #35 / Hot 100 #84	East West 115

Connie Francis, whose career included a role in the classic 60s youth film *Where The Boys Are*—and a 1961 hit of the same name—spent early 1989 in the same Ft. Lauderdale/Miami environs as that film, attempting to resuscitate her career after several well-documented personal tragedies.

Aretha Franklin's strategy for the 80s included several collaborations befitting a true Queen Of Soul. Among her famous partners have been George Michael, George Benson, and the Eurythmics; the producer of her version of the Rolling Stones' "Jumpin' Jack Flash" was no less than that band's guitarist, Keith Richards.

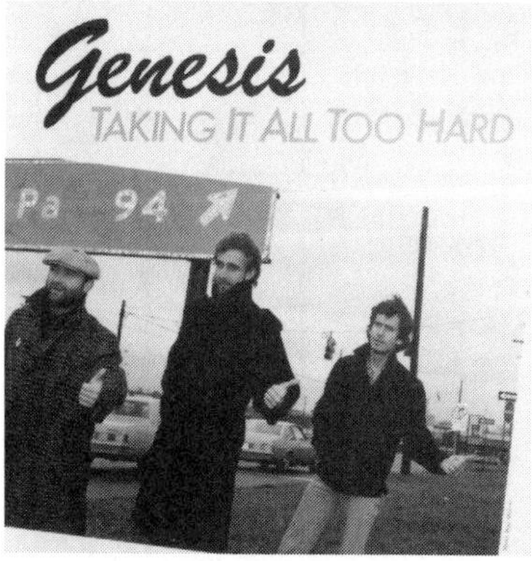

Free's sole appearances in the Hot 100—for "All Right Now" and "Stealer," both in 1971—belie their broad influence in the world of hard rock. Later offshoots from the band included Bad Company, The Firm, Sharks, and Back Street Crawler.

Genesis has spawned a record number of solo artists since the group's 1967 formation in England, including singers Peter Gabriel and Phil Collins, guitarists Steve Hackett, Anthony Phillips, and Mike Rutherford (of Mike + The Mechanics fame), and keyboardist Tony Banks.

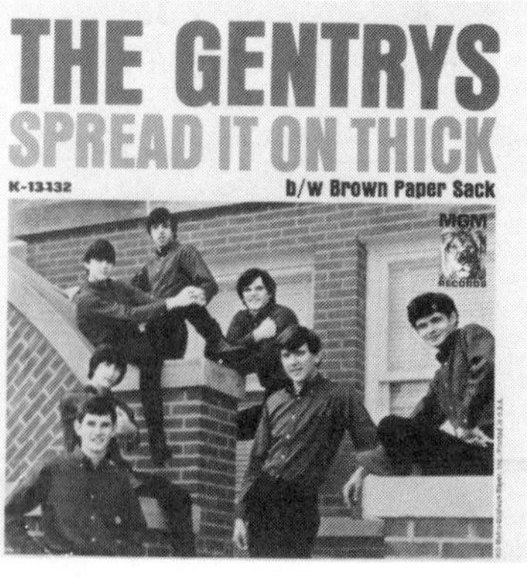

The Gentrys sprang out of Memphis in 1965 with their hit "Keep On Dancing"; by the late 60s, lead singer Larry Raspberry had left the band. He eventually released his own albums with the group Alamo and his own band, the High-Steppers.

Andy Gibb and Victoria Principal were together not only in romance but in song: their duet version of the Everly Brothers hit "All I Have To Do Is Dream" peaked at No. 51 in 1981. It was the last appearance in the Hot 100 for Gibb, who died in 1988.

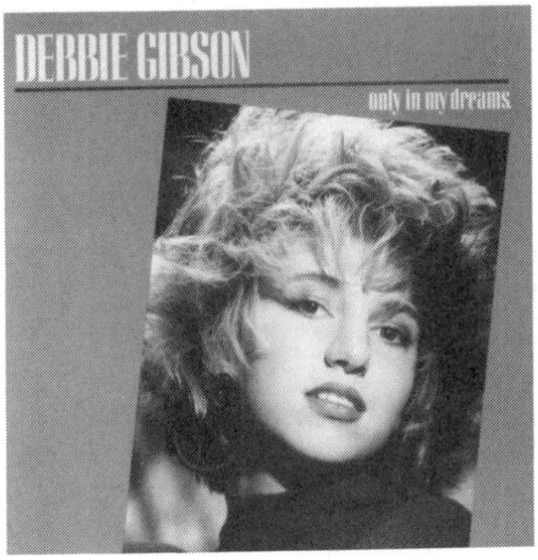

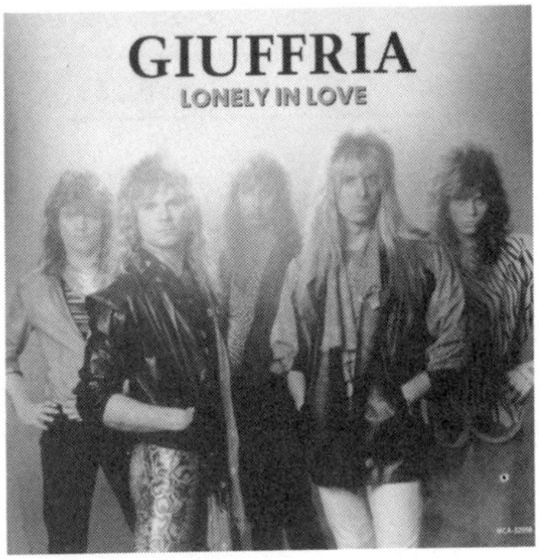

Debbie Gibson became the first teen star to have both the No. 1 album and single simultaneously since Stevie Wonder in the 60s. Her *Electric Youth* album and "Lost In Your Eyes" hit their respective top slots in March, 1989.

Giuffria's namesake, keyboardist Greg Giuffria, has proven to be a persistent figure in the heavy-rock scene: he first hit the charts with Angel in 1975, reappeared with his eponymous band in 1984, and in 1989 returned as a central figure in Simmons Records' debut act House Of Lords.

Robert Goulet's background in theatre brought him his first charting record in 1962—"What Kind Of Fool Am I?" from the musical *Stop The World–I Want To Get Off*—and an eventual acting role in the short-lived network TV series "Blue Light."

The Grass Roots were one of the first 60s bands to demonstrate the power of the compact disk: when MCA saw the group's greatest-hits album enjoying brisk sales in 1988, they quickly rushed to release even more CD titles by the long-defunct band.

The Grateful Dead surprised many with the strong sales success of their *In The Dark* album in 1987; soon after, the group renegotiated its contract with Arista, appeared on a live album with Bob Dylan, and broke several significant attendance records at various US concert venues.

DATE	POS	WKS	ARTIST—RECORD TITLE	LABEL & NO.
			THE KINGSMEN	
			Rock band formed in Portland in 1957. Consisted of Jack Ely (lead singer, guitar), Lynn Easton (drums), Mike Mitchell (guitar), Bob Nordby (bass) and Don Gallucci (keyboards). After release of "Louie Louie" (featuring lead vocal by Ely), Easton took over leadership of band and replaced Ely as lead singer. America's premier Sixties garage band.	
11/30/63	**2**(6)	13	1. **Louie Louie** originally released on the Jerden label	Wand 143
4/04/64	**16**	8	2. Money	Wand 150
1/30/65	**4**	9	3. **The Jolly Green Giant** same tune (different lyrics) as The Olympics' "Big Boy Pete"	Wand 172
			THE KINGSTON TRIO	
			Folk trio formed in San Francisco in 1957. Consisted of Dave Guard (banjo), Bob Shane and Nick Reynolds (guitars). Big break came at San Francisco's Purple Onion, where they stayed for 8 months. Guard left in 1961 to form the Whiskeyhill Singers. John Stewart replaced him. Disbanded in 1968, Shane formed New Kingston Trio. The originators of the folk music craze of the 60s.	
10/06/58	**1**(1)	18	• 1. **Tom Dooley** traditional American folk song written in 1866 as "Tom Dula"	Capitol 4049
3/30/59	**12**	9	2. The Tijuana Jail	Capitol 4167
6/29/59	**15**	6	3. M.T.A. M.T.A.: Metropolitan Transit Authority of Boston	Capitol 4221
9/21/59	**20**	8	4. A Worried Man	Capitol 4271
3/14/60	**32**	5	5. El Matador	Capitol 4338
8/08/60	**37**	2	6. Bad Man Blunder [N]	Capitol 4379
3/03/62	**21**	7	7. Where Have All The Flowers Gone	Capitol 4671
2/23/63	**21**	5	8. Greenback Dollar	Capitol 4898
4/20/63	**8**	8	9. **Reverend Mr. Black**	Capitol 4951
8/31/63	**33**	4	10. Desert Pete	Capitol 5005
			THE KINKS	
			Rock group formed in London in 1963 by Ray Davies (lead singer, guitar) and his brother Dave Davies (lead guitar, vocals). Original lineup also included Peter Quaife (bass) and Mike Avory (drums). Numerous personnel changes during the 70s. Lineup in 1987 consisted of Ray & Dave Davies, Ian Gibbons (keyboards), Bob Henrit (drums) and Jim Rodford (bass).	
10/24/64	**7**	10	1. **You Really Got Me**	Reprise 0306
1/16/65	**7**	9	2. **All Day And All Of The Night**	Reprise 0334
3/27/65	**6**	8	3. **Tired Of Waiting For You**	Reprise 0347
7/10/65	**23**	4	4. Set Me Free	Reprise 0379
9/04/65	**34**	3	5. Who'll Be The Next In Line	Reprise 0366
1/08/66	**13**	9	6. A Well Respected Man	Reprise 0420
6/18/66	**36**	1	7. Dedicated Follower Of Fashion	Reprise 0471
8/27/66	**14**	7	8. Sunny Afternoon	Reprise 0497
9/12/70	**9**	12	9. **Lola** live version charted in 1980 (POS 81)	Reprise 0930
8/19/78	**30**	5	10. A Rock 'N' Roll Fantasy	Arista 0342
5/28/83	**6**	12	11. **Come Dancing**	Arista 1054
9/17/83	**29**	4	12. Don't Forget To Dance	Arista 9075

DATE	POS	WKS	ARTIST—RECORD TITLE	LABEL & NO.
			KISS	
			Hard-rock band formed in New York City in 1973. Consisted of Gene Simmons (bass), Paul Stanley (guitar), Ace Frehley (lead guitar) and Peter Criss (drums). Noted for elaborate makeup and highly theatrical stage shows. Criss replaced by Eric Carr in 1981. Frehley replaced by Vinnie Vincent in 1982. Group appeared without makeup for the first time in 1983 on album cover "Lick It Up." Mark St. John replaced Vincent in 1984. Bruce Kulick replaced St. John in 1985.	
11/29/75†	**12**	10	1. Rock And Roll All Nite [R] live version; original version hit on 5/17/75 (POS 68)	Casablanca 850
4/17/76	**31**	4	2. Shout It Out Loud	Casablanca 854
9/25/76	**7**	13	• 3. **Beth**	Casablanca 863
1/15/77	**15**	8	4. Hard Luck Woman	Casablanca 873
4/09/77	**16**	8	5. Calling Dr. Love	Casablanca 880
7/30/77	**25**	7	6. Christine Sixteen	Casablanca 889
4/15/78	**39**	2	7. Rocket Ride	Casablanca 915
6/16/79	**11**	11	• 8. I Was Made For Lovin' You	Casablanca 983
			MAC & KATIE KISSOON	
			Brother and sister from Trinidad. Moved to England in the late 50s.	
9/04/71	**20**	9	1. Chirpy Chirpy Cheep Cheep	ABC 11306
			KLYMAXX	
			Black female sextet formed in Los Angeles in 1979. Lead vocals and rap by Bernadette Cooper, Joyce "Fenderella" Irby and Lorena Shelby.	
10/26/85	**5**	17	1. **I Miss You**	Constell. 52606
8/02/86	**15**	8	2. Man Size Love from the film "Running Scared"	MCA 52841
6/20/87	**18**	9	3. I'd Still Say Yes	Constell. 53028
			THE KNACK	
			Rock group formed in Los Angeles in 1978. Consisted of Doug Fieger (lead singer, guitar), Berton Averre (guitar), Bruce Gary (drums) and Prescott Niles (bass). Disbanded in 1982.	
7/21/79	**1**(6)	16	• 1. **My Sharona**	Capitol 4731
9/22/79	**11**	11	2. Good Girls Don't	Capitol 4771
3/08/80	**38**	2	3. Baby Talks Dirty	Capitol 4822
			THE KNICKERBOCKERS	
			Rock band formed in Bergenfield, New Jersey in 1964 as the Castle Kings. Lead singer, Buddy Randell, was a member of the Royal Teens. Member Jimmy Walker replaced Bill Medley, for a time, in the Righteous Brothers.	
1/01/66	**20**	9	1. Lies	Challenge 59321
			FREDERICK KNIGHT	
			Born on 8/15/44 in Alabama. Soul singer, record producer.	
5/27/72	**27**	9	1. I've Been Lonely For So Long	Stax 0117

DATE	POS	WKS	ARTIST—RECORD TITLE	LABEL & NO.
			GLADYS KNIGHT & THE PIPS	
			R&B family group from Atlanta. Formed in 1952 when Gladys was 8 years old. Consisted of Gladys (b: 5/28/44 in Atlanta), her brother Merald "Bubba" Knight and sister Brenda, and cousins William & Eleanor Guest. Named "Pips" for their manager, cousin James "Pip" Woods. First recorded for Brunswick in 1958. Brenda and Elenor replaced by cousins Edward Patten and Langston George in 1959. Langston left group in 1962 and group has remained a quartet with the same members ever since. Due to legal problems, Gladys could not record with the Pips from 1977-80. Gladys was a cast member of the 1985 TV series "Charlie & Co." Also see Dionne Warwick.	
6/05/61	**6**	10	1. **Every Beat Of My Heart** shown only as: **PIPS**	Vee-Jay 386
1/20/62	**19**	6	2. Letter Full Of Tears	Fury 1054
7/04/64	**38**	1	3. Giving Up	Maxx 326
8/19/67	**39**	2	4. Everybody Needs Love	Soul 35034
11/04/67	**2**(3)	14	5. **I Heard It Through The Grapevine**	Soul 35039
2/17/68	**15**	8	6. The End Of Our Road	Soul 35042
7/06/68	**40**	1	7. It Should Have Been Me	Soul 35045
8/09/69	**19**	8	8. The Nitty Gritty	Soul 35063
11/15/69	**17**	10	9. Friendship Train	Soul 35068
4/04/70	**25**	5	10. You Need Love Like I Do (Don't You)	Soul 35071
12/19/70†	**9**	12	11. **If I Were Your Woman**	Soul 35078
6/19/71	**17**	9	12. I Don't Want To Do Wrong	Soul 35083
1/08/72	**27**	5	13. Make Me The Woman That You Go Home To	Soul 35091
4/08/72	**33**	6	14. Help Me Make It Through The Night	Soul 35094
2/17/73	**2**(2)	12	15. **Neither One Of Us (Wants To Be The First To Say Goodbye)**	Soul 35098
6/02/73	**19**	8	16. Daddy Could Swear, I Declare	Soul 35105
7/07/73	**28**	7	17. Where Peaceful Waters Flow	Buddah 363
9/15/73	**1**(2)	16	● 18. **Midnight Train To Georgia**	Buddah 383
12/08/73†	**4**	13	● 19. **I've Got To Use My Imagination**	Buddah 393
3/09/74	**3**	13	● 20. **Best Thing That Ever Happened To Me**	Buddah 403
6/01/74	**5**	11	● 21. **On And On** from the film "Claudine"	Buddah 423
11/16/74	**21**	9	22. I Feel A Song (In My Heart)	Buddah 433
5/24/75	**11**	12	23. The Way We Were/Try To Remember	Buddah 463
11/29/75	**22**	7	24. Part Time Love	Buddah 513
1/30/88	**13**	9	25. Love Overboard	MCA 53210
			JEAN KNIGHT	
			Born on 6/26/43 in New Orleans. Soul songstress.	
6/19/71	**2**(2)	13	1. **Mr. Big Stuff**	Stax 0088
			ROBERT KNIGHT	
			Born on 4/21/45 in Franklin, Tennessee. Soul singer. Recorded for Dot in 1960.	
10/28/67	**13**	8	1. Everlasting Love	Rising Sons 705

DATE	POS	WKS	ARTIST—RECORD TITLE	LABEL & NO.
			SONNY KNIGHT	
			Born Joseph C. Smith in 1934 in Maywood, Illinois. R&B singer/songwriter/pianist. Wrote book "The Day The Music Died" in the late 70s under real name.	
11/24/56	**17**	9	1. Confidential	Dot 15507
			Juke Box #17 / Best Seller #19 / Top 100 #20	
			FRED KNOBLOCK	
			Born in Jackson, Mississippi. Performed with the rock band Let's Eat in the late 70s. Member of the country singing songwriter trio of Schuyler, Knobloch & Overstreet (SKO) and Schuyler, Knobloch & Bickhardt (SKB).	
7/26/80	**18**	7	1. Why Not Me	Scotti Br. 518
12/27/80†	**28**	9	2. Killin' Time	Scotti Br. 609
			FRED KNOBLOCK & SUSAN ANTON (TV/film actress)	
			BUDDY KNOX	
			Born Buddy Wayne Knox on 7/20/33 in Happy, Texas. Formed The Rhythm Orchids at West Texas State University: Knox (guitar), Jimmy Bowen (bass), Don Lanier (guitar) and Dave "Dicky Doo" Alldred (drums). Formed own record label, Triple-D, named after KDDD radio in Dumas, Texas. Buddy currently lives near Winnipeg, Canada.	
			BUDDY KNOX with THE RHYTHM ORCHIDS:	
3/02/57	**1**(1)	15	1. **Party Doll**	Roulette 4002
			Best Seller #1 / Top 100 #2 / Juke Box #2 / Jockey #5 originally on Triple-D label (flip side by Jimmy Bowen)	
6/03/57	**17**	7	2. Rock Your Little Baby To Sleep	Roulette 4009
			Jockey #17 / Best Seller #23 / Top 100 #23	
9/09/57	**9**	15	3. **Hula Love**	Roulette 4018
			Jockey #9 / Top 100 #12 / Best Seller #13	
8/04/58	**22**	11	4. Somebody Touched Me	Roulette 4082
			Hot 100 #22 / Best Seller #32	
			BUDDY KNOX:	
1/09/61	**25**	4	5. Lovey Dovey	Liberty 55290
			MOE KOFFMAN QUARTETTE	
			Moe was born on 1/28/28 in Toronto, Canada. Saxophonist with several US big bands from 1950-55.	
2/10/58	**23**	5	1. The Swingin' Shepherd Blues [I]	Jubilee 5311
			Jockey #23 / Best Seller #36 / Top 100 #36	
			KOKOMO	
			Pianist Jimmy Wisner.	
3/06/61	**8**	11	1. **Asia Minor** **[I]**	Felsted 8612
			adapted from the Greig Piano Concerto	
			KOOL & THE GANG	
			R&B group formed in Jersey City, New Jersey in 1964 by bass player Robert "Kool" Bell as the Jazziacs. Session work in New York City, 1964-68. First recorded for De-Lite in 1969. Added lead singer James "J.T." Taylor in 1979. Current lineup consists of brothers Robert and Ronald Bell (sax, keyboards), George Brown (drums), Curtis "Fitz" Williams (keyboards) and Charles Smith (guitar). Taylor left in 1988; replaced by lead singers Gary Brown, Odeen Mays and former Dazz Band lead vocalist Skip Martin.	
10/06/73	**29**	6	1. Funky Stuff	De-Lite 557
1/05/74	**4**	16	● 2. **Jungle Boogie**	De-Lite 559
5/18/74	**6**	11	● 3. **Hollywood Swinging**	De-Lite 561

DATE	POS	WKS	ARTIST—RECORD TITLE	LABEL & NO.
10/12/74	**37**	2	4. Higher Plane	De-Lite 1562
6/28/75	**35**	3	5. Spirit Of The Boogie	De-Lite 1567
11/10/79†	**8**	14	● 6. **Ladies Night**	De-Lite 801
2/09/80	**5**	13	7. **Too Hot**	De-Lite 802
11/22/80†	**1**(2)	21	▲ 8. **Celebration**	De-Lite 807
6/27/81	**39**	2	9. Jones Vs. Jones	De-Lite 813
11/07/81	**17**	12	10. Take My Heart (You Can Have It If You Want It)	De-Lite 815
4/03/82	**10**	9	11. **Get Down On It**	De-Lite 818
9/11/82	**21**	7	12. Big Fun	De-Lite 822
12/04/82†	**30**	7	13. Let's Go Dancin' (Ooh La, La, La) 7-14: produced by Eumir Deodato	De-Lite 824
12/03/83†	**2**(1)	16	14. **Joanna**	De-Lite 829
3/17/84	**13**	10	15. Tonight	De-Lite 830
1/05/85	**10**	13	16. **Misled**	De-Lite 880431
4/20/85	**9**	11	17. **Fresh**	De-Lite 880623
7/27/85	**2**(3)	15	18. **Cherish**	De-Lite 880869
11/23/85	**18**	8	19. Emergency	De-Lite 884199
11/22/86†	**10**	12	20. **Victory**	Mercury 888074
3/14/87	**10**	10	21. **Stone Love**	Mercury 888292
			THE KORGIS	
			British pop duo: James Warren and Andy Davis (both formerly with Stackridge).	
11/08/80	**18**	11	1. Everybody's Got To Learn Sometime	Asylum 47055
			KRAFTWERK	
			German all-electronic duo: Ralf Hutter and Florian Schneider.	
4/12/75	**25**	5	1. Autobahn [I]	Vertigo 203
			BILLY J. KRAMER with The Dakotas	
			Billy was born William Ashton on 8/19/43 near Liverpool, England. Discovered by The Beatles' manager, Brian Epstein, who teamed him with the group The Dakotas.	
5/02/64	**7**	12	1. **Little Children/**	
6/13/64	**9**	8	2. Bad To Me	Imperial 66027
8/15/64	**30**	3	3. I'll Keep You Satisfied	Imperial 66048
9/19/64	**23**	5	4. From A Window above 3: written by John Lennon & Paul McCartney	Imperial 66051
			KRIS KRISTOFFERSON	
			Born on 6/22/36 in Brownsville, Texas. Singer/songwriter/actor. Married to Rita Coolidge from 1973-80. Wrote "Me And Bobby McGee," "For The Good Times" and "Help Me Make It Through The Night." Has starred in many films since 1972.	
10/02/71	**26**	6	1. Loving Her Was Easier (Than Anything I'll Ever Do Again)	Monument 8525
7/07/73	**16**	19	● 2. Why Me	Monument 8571
			BOB KUBAN & THE IN-MEN	
			8-man St. Louis pop-rock band featuring lead singer Walter Scott (real name: Walter Notheis, Jr.), who mysteriously disappeared on 12/27/83, and whose body was found 3 years later with a gunshot wound in the back.	
2/19/66	**12**	7	1. The Cheater	Musicland 20001

DATE	POS	WKS	ARTIST—RECORD TITLE	LABEL & NO.
			L	
			PATTI LaBELLE	
			Patti, born Patricia Holt on 5/24/44 in Philadelphia, began singing career as leader of The Blue Belles. The quartet, formed in Philadelphia in 1962, included Nona Hendryx, Sarah Dash and Cindy Birdsong. Cindy left in 1967 to join The Supremes. Group continued as a trio. In 1971, they shortened their name to LaBelle. In 1977, group disbanded and Patti recorded solo.	
			THE BLUE-BELLES:	
5/12/62	**15**	7	1. I Sold My Heart To The Junkman label incorrectly listed artist as The Blue-Belles; The Starlets are the real vocalists on this song	Newtown 5000
			PATTI LaBELLE & THE BLUE BELLES:	
11/02/63	**37**	3	2. Down The Aisle (Wedding Song)	Newtown 5777
2/08/64	**34**	1	3. You'll Never Walk Alone from the musical "Carousel"	Parkway 896
			LaBELLE:	
2/01/75	**1**(1)	13	4. **Lady Marmalade**	Epic 50048
			PATTI LaBELLE:	
4/06/85	**17**	9	5. New Attitude from the film "Beverly Hills Cop"	MCA 52517
4/19/86	**1**(3)	15	• 6. **On My Own** **PATTI LaBELLE & MICHAEL McDONALD**	MCA 52770
8/23/86	**29**	3	7. Oh, People	MCA 52877
			CHERYL LADD	
			Born Cheryl Stoppelmoor on 7/2/51 in Huron, South Dakota. Played Kris Monroe on the TV series "Charlie's Angels." Married to David Ladd (son of actor Alan Ladd) from 1973-79. Married producer/songwriter Brian Russell (Brian & Brenda) in 1981.	
8/26/78	**34**	3	1. Think It Over	Capitol 4599
			LADY FLASH	
			Barry Manilow's back-up singers: Lorraine "Reparata" Mazzola, Monica Burruss and Debra Byrd. Mazzola was in Reparata & The Delrons.	
8/14/76	**27**	6	1. Street Singin' written, produced and arranged by Barry Manilow	RSO 852
			FRANCIS LAI	
			French composer/conductor.	
2/27/71	**31**	4	1. Theme From Love Story [I] from the film "Love Story"; piano solo: Georges Pludermacher	Paramount 0064
			LAID BACK	
			Danish synth-pop duo: Tim Stahl (keyboards) and John Guldberg (guitar). Highly successful in Europe for 3 years before their US debut.	
4/28/84	**26**	4	1. White Horse	Sire 29346

DATE	POS	WKS	ARTIST—RECORD TITLE	LABEL & NO.
			FRANKIE LAINE	
			Born Frank Paul LoVecchio on 3/30/13 in Chicago. To Los Angeles in the early 40s. First recorded for Exclusive in 1945. With Johnny Moore's Three Blazers. Signed to Mercury label in 1947. Dynamic style found favor with black and white audiences.	
9/03/55	**17**	3	1. Humming Bird Juke Box #17	Columbia 40526
12/17/55	**19**	10	2. A Woman In Love Best Seller #19 / Top 100 #24 from the film "Guys And Dolls"	Columbia 40583
12/08/56†	**3**	18	3. **Moonlight Gambler** Top 100 #3 / Juke Box #3 / Jockey #4 / Best Seller #5	Columbia 40780
4/20/57	**10**	8	4. **Love Is A Golden Ring** Jockey #10 / Best Seller #22 / Top 100 #23 backing vocals and instrumentation: The Easy Riders	Columbia 40856
3/04/67	**39**	2	5. I'll Take Care Of Your Cares	ABC 10891
5/06/67	**35**	3	6. Making Memories	ABC 10924
3/01/69	**24**	7	7. You Gave Me A Mountain written by Marty Robbins; produced by Jimmy Bowen	ABC 11174
			MAJOR LANCE	
			Born on 4/4/42 in Chicago. Soul singer. First recorded for Mercury in 1959. Lived in Britain, 1972-74. Had own label, Osiris, with Al Jackson of the MG's in 1975. In prison for selling cocaine, 1978-81.	
8/10/63	**8**	10	1. **The Monkey Time**	Okeh 7175
11/02/63	**13**	8	2. Hey Little Girl	Okeh 7181
1/11/64	**5**	10	3. **Um, Um, Um, Um, Um, Um**	Okeh 7187
4/11/64	**20**	6	4. The Matador	Okeh 7191
9/19/64	**24**	5	5. Rhythm	Okeh 7203
4/03/65	**40**	1	6. Come See	Okeh 7216
			MICKEY LEE LANE	
11/28/64	**38**	1	1. Shaggy Dog	Swan 4183
			SNOOKY LANSON	
			Born Roy Lanson in Memphis. Star of TV's "Your Hit Parade," 1950-57.	
12/03/55	**20**	6	1. It's Almost Tomorrow Top 100 #20 / Jockey #20 / Juke Box #20	Dot 15424
			THE LARKS	
			Los Angeles R&B group originally named Don Julian & The Meadowlarks: Don Julian (lead singer), Ted Walters and Charles Morrison.	
11/28/64†	**7**	11	1. **The Jerk**	Money 106
			JULIUS LaROSA	
			Born on 1/2/30 in Brooklyn. Regular singer on Arthur Godfrey's TV show until he was fired on-the-air on 10/19/53.	
7/23/55	**13**	7	1. Domani (Tomorrow) Best Seller #13 / Juke Box #13 / Jockey #15	Cadence 1265
10/08/55	**20**	5	2. Suddenly There's A Valley Jockey #20 / Best Seller #22 / Top 100 #29	Cadence 1270
2/18/56	**15**	7	3. Lipstick And Candy And Rubbersole Shoes Jockey #15 / Top 100 #21	RCA 6416
6/16/58	**21**	1	4. Torero Jockey #21	RCA 7227

DATE	POS	WKS	ARTIST—RECORD TITLE	LABEL & NO.
			LARSEN-FEITEN BAND	
			Neil Larsen (keyboards) and Buzz Feiten (guitar). Both are top session musicians. Feiten, a former member of the Paul Butterfield Blues Band and Stevie Wonder's band, joined Mr. Mister in 1989.	
9/13/80	**29**	6	1. Who'll Be The Fool Tonight	Warner 49282
			NICOLETTE LARSON	
			Born on 7/17/52 in Helena, Montana; raised in Kansas City. To San Francisco, 1974. Session vocalist with Neil Young, Linda Ronstadt, Van Halen and many others.	
12/23/78†	**8**	14	1. **Lotta Love** written by Neil Young	Warner 8664
2/16/80	**35**	3	2. Let Me Go, Love duet with Michael McDonald	Warner 49130
			DENISE LaSALLE	
			Born Denise Craig on 7/16/39 in LeFlore County, Mississippi. Soul singer.	
9/25/71	**13**	9	● 1. Trapped By A Thing Called Love	Westbound 182
			DAVID LASLEY	
			Born on 8/20/47 in Sault St. Marie, Michigan. Back-up singer for James Taylor and others. Member of the studio group Roundtree.	
4/24/82	**36**	3	1. If I Had My Wish Tonight	EMI America 8111
			JAMES LAST	
			German producer/arranger/conductor.	
4/26/80	**28**	6	1. The Seduction (Love Theme) [I] from the film "American Gigolo"	Polydor 2071
			LATIMORE	
			Born Benjamin Latimore on 9/7/39 in Charleston, Tennessee. Soul singer/songwriter. With Steve Alaimo in the 60s.	
11/23/74	**31**	3	1. Let's Straighten It Out	Glades 1722
3/26/77	**37**	2	2. Somethin' 'Bout 'Cha	Glades 1739
			STACY LATTISAW	
			Born on 11/25/66 in Washington, DC. Soul singer. Recorded her first album at age 12.	
10/04/80	**21**	10	1. Let Me Be Your Angel	Cotillion 46001
8/01/81	**26**	7	2. Love On A Two Way Street	Cotillion 46015
10/22/83	**40**	1	3. Miracles	Cotillion 99855
			CYNDI LAUPER	
			Born on 6/20/53 in Queens, New York. Recorded an album for Polydor Records in 1980 with the group Blue Angel. Won the 1984 Best New Artist Grammy Award. In the 1988 film "Vibes."	
1/28/84	**2(2)**	14	● 1. **Girls Just Want To Have Fun**	Portrait 04120
4/21/84	**1(2)**	14	2. **Time After Time**	Portrait 04432
7/28/84	**3**	14	3. **She Bop**	Portrait 04516
10/13/84	**5**	14	4. **All Through The Night**	Portrait 04639
1/12/85	**27**	6	5. Money Changes Everything	Portrait 04737
6/01/85	**10**	9	6. **The Goonies 'R' Good Enough** from the film "The Goonies"	Portrait 04918
9/13/86	**1(2)**	12	7. **True Colors**	Portrait 06247
12/13/86†	**3**	13	8. **Change Of Heart**	Portrait 06431
3/21/87	**12**	10	9. What's Going On	Portrait 06970

DATE	POS	WKS	ARTIST—RECORD TITLE	LABEL & NO.
			ROD LAUREN	
			Born on 3/26/40. Rod was groomed by RCA in 1960 to be a hot new teen idol.	
1/11/60	**31**	5	1. If I Had A Girl	RCA 7645
			THE LAURIE SISTERS	
4/16/55	**30**	1	1. Dixie Danny Best Seller #30	Mercury 70548
			EDDIE LAWRENCE	
			Born on 3/2/19 in New York City. Comedian/actor/author/playwright.	
9/01/56	**34**	1	1. The Old Philosopher [C]	Coral 61671
			STEVE LAWRENCE	
			Born Sam Leibowitz on 7/8/35 in Brooklyn. Regular performer on the Steve Allen "Tonight Show" for 5 years. First recorded for King in 1953. Married to singer Eydie Gorme since 12/29/57.	
1/19/57	**18**	8	1. The Banana Boat Song Jockey #18 / Top 100 #30	Coral 61761
3/09/57	**5**	12	2. **Party Doll** Jockey #5 / Top 100 #10 / Juke Box #11 / Best Seller #12	Coral 61792
12/14/59†	**9**	13	3. **Pretty Blue Eyes**	ABC-Para. 10058
3/28/60	**7**	9	4. **Footsteps**	ABC-Para. 10085
4/03/61	**9**	10	5. **Portrait Of My Love**	United Art. 291
12/08/62†	**1**(2)	12	6. **Go Away Little Girl**	Columbia 42601
3/30/63	**26**	6	7. Don't Be Afraid, Little Darlin'	Columbia 42699
6/15/63	**27**	3	8. Poor Little Rich Girl	Columbia 42795
8/24/63	**28**	5	9. I Want To Stay Here **STEVE & EYDIE**	Columbia 42815
11/09/63	**26**	4	10. Walking Proud	Columbia 42865
1/25/64	**35**	3	11. I Can't Stop Talking About You **STEVE & EYDIE**	Columbia 42932
			VICKI LAWRENCE	
			Born on 3/26/49 in Inglewood, California. Regular on Carol Burnett's CBS-TV series from 1967-78. Also starred in TV's "Mama's Family," 1982-83.	
3/17/73	**1**(2)	14	• 1. **The Night The Lights Went Out In Georgia**	Bell 45303
			JOY LAYNE	
2/16/57	**20**	5	1. Your Wild Heart Juke Box #20 / Top 100 #30	Mercury 71038
			LE ROUX	
			6-man Louisiana rock band; Jeff Pollard, lead singer.	
3/20/82	**18**	6	1. Nobody Said It Was Easy (Lookin' For The Lights)	RCA 13059
			LEAPY LEE	
			Born Lee Graham on 7/2/42 in Eastbourne, England. Acted on stage and TV in England. Nicknamed "Leapy" in school because "I was always a leaper!"	
11/09/68	**16**	8	1. Little Arrows	Decca 32380

DATE	POS	WKS	ARTIST—RECORD TITLE	LABEL & NO.
			THE LEAVES	
			Los Angeles garage-rock quintet: John Beck (lead singer), Robert Lee Reiner, Jim Pons, Tom "Ambrose" Ray and Bobby Arlin.	
6/18/66	**31**	4	1. Hey Joe	Mira 222
			LeBLANC & CARR	
			Lenny LeBlanc & Pete Carr (b: 4/22/50, Daytona Beach). Lenny (bass) and Pete (lead guitar) were both session musicians at Muscle Shoals, Alabama.	
2/04/78	**13**	10	1. Falling	Big Tree 16100
			LED ZEPPELIN	
			British heavy-metal rock supergroup formed in October, 1968. Consisted of Robert Plant (lead singer), Jimmy Page (lead guitar), John Paul Jones (bass, keyboards) and John Bonham (drums). First known as the New Yardbirds. Page had been in the Yardbirds, 1966-68. USA tour in 1973 broke many box-office records. Formed own label, Swan Song, in 1974. Plant seriously injured in an auto accident in Greece on 8/4/75. In concert film "The Song Remains The Same" in 1976. Bonham died on 9/25/80 at the age of 33 of asphyxiation. Group disbanded in December, 1980. Their most famous recording, "Stairway To Heaven" (on album "Led Zeppelin IV") was never released as a single.	
12/06/69†	**4**	13	● 1. **Whole Lotta Love**	Atlantic 2690
12/12/70†	**16**	10	2. Immigrant Song	Atlantic 2777
1/15/72	**15**	8	3. Black Dog	Atlantic 2849
11/24/73	**20**	8	4. D'yer Mak'er	Atlantic 2986
5/17/75	**38**	2	5. Trampled Under Foot	Swan Song 70102
1/12/80	**21**	8	6. Fool In The Rain	Swan Song 71003
			BRENDA LEE	
			Born Brenda Mae Tarpley on 12/11/44 in Lithonia, Georgia. Professional singer since age 6. Signed to Decca Records in 1956. Became known as "Little Miss Dynamite." Successful country singer since 1971.	
2/15/60	**4**	15	1. **Sweet Nothin's**	Decca 30967
6/06/60	**1**(3)	18	2. **I'm Sorry/**	
6/20/60	**6**	9	3. That's All You Gotta Do	Decca 31093
9/19/60	**1**(1)	13	4. **I Want To Be Wanted/**	
10/31/60	**40**	1	5. Just A Little	Decca 31149
12/19/60	**14**	3	6. Rockin' Around The Christmas Tree [X] recorded in 1958	Decca 30776
1/16/61	**7**	9	7. **Emotions/**	
2/06/61	**33**	2	8. I'm Learning About Love	Decca 31195
4/03/61	**6**	10	9. **You Can Depend On Me**	Decca 31231
6/26/61	**4**	10	10. **Dum Dum**	Decca 31272
10/09/61	**3**	12	11. **Fool #1/**	
10/16/61	**31**	3	12. Anybody But Me	Decca 31309
1/20/62	**4**	11	13. **Break It To Me Gently**	Decca 31348
4/28/62	**6**	8	14. **Everybody Loves Me But You**	Decca 31379
7/21/62	**15**	7	15. Heart In Hand/	
7/21/62	**29**	4	16. It Started All Over Again	Decca 31407
10/06/62	**3**	12	17. **All Alone Am I**	Decca 31424
2/16/63	**32**	3	18. Your Used To Be	Decca 31454
4/20/63	**6**	10	19. **Losing You**	Decca 31478

DATE	POS	WKS	ARTIST—RECORD TITLE	LABEL & NO.
7/27/63	**24**	6	20. My Whole World Is Falling Down/	
7/27/63	**25**	5	21. I Wonder	Decca 31510
10/12/63	**17**	5	22. The Grass Is Greener	Decca 31539
12/28/63†	**12**	8	23. As Usual	Decca 31570
3/28/64	**25**	5	24. Think	Decca 31599
10/31/64	**17**	7	25. Is It True	Decca 31690
6/26/65	**13**	8	26. Too Many Rivers	Decca 31792
11/13/65	**33**	3	27. Rusty Bells	Decca 31849
10/29/66	**11**	8	28. Coming On Strong	Decca 32018
2/11/67	**37**	2	29. Ride, Ride, Ride	Decca 32079
			CURTIS LEE	
			Born on 10/28/41 in Yuma, Arizona. Pop singer/songwriter.	
7/17/61	**7**	8	1. **Pretty Little Angel Eyes** backing vocals by the Halos	Dunes 2007
			DICKEY LEE	
			Born Dickey Lipscomb on 9/21/41 in Memphis. Pop-country singer/songwriter. First recorded for Sun Records in 1957.	
9/08/62	**6**	11	1. **Patches**	Smash 1758
12/29/62†	**14**	8	2. I Saw Linda Yesterday	Smash 1791
6/19/65	**14**	7	3. Laurie (Strange Things Happen)	TCF Hall 102
			JACKIE LEE	
			Real name: Earl Nelson (of Bob & Earl). Took name from his wife's middle name, Jackie, and his middle name, Lee. Sang lead on Hollywood Flames' "Buzz-Buzz-Buzz."	
12/18/65†	**14**	9	1. The Duck	Mirwood 5502
			JOHNNY LEE	
			Born John Lee Ham on 7/3/46 in Texas City; raised in Alta Loma, Texas. Country singer/songwriter. Married to actress Charlene Tilton from 1982-84.	
8/02/80	**5**	13	● 1. **Lookin' For Love** from the movie "Urban Cowboy"	Full Moon 47004
			LAURA LEE	
			Born Laura Lee Rundless in 1945 in Chicago. Soul singer.	
10/16/71	**36**	4	1. Women's Love Rights	Hot Wax 7105
			PEGGY LEE	
			Born Norma Jean Egstrom on 5/26/20 in Jamestown, North Dakota. Jazz singer with Jack Wardlow band (1936-40), Will Osborne (1940-41) and Benny Goodman (1941-43). Went solo in March of 1943. In films "Mister Music" (1950), "The Jazz Singer" (1953) and "Pete Kelly's Blues" (1955). Co-wrote many songs with husband Dave Barbour.	
3/24/56	**14**	10	1. Mr. Wonderful Jockey #14 / Top 100 #23 / Best Seller #25 from the Broadway musical of the same title	Decca 29834
7/21/58	**8**	13	2. **Fever** Hot 100 #8 / Best Seller #9 / Jockey #10 end	Capitol 3998
10/11/69	**11**	8	3. Is That All There Is	Capitol 2602
			RAYMOND LEFEVRE	
			Conductor/pianist/flutist from Paris, France.	
11/03/58	**30**	5	1. The Day The Rains Came [I]	Kapp 231

DATE	POS	WKS	ARTIST—RECORD TITLE	LABEL & NO.
4/06/68	**37**	5	2. Ame Caline (Soul Coaxing) [I]	Four Corners 147
			THE LEFT BANKE	
			Classical-styled New York rock quintet led by Steve Martin (lead singer) and Mike Brown (keyboards).	
9/24/66	**5**	10	1. **Walk Away Renee**	Smash 2041
2/04/67	**15**	6	2. Pretty Ballerina	Smash 2074
			THE LEMON PIPERS	
			Psychedelic/bubblegum rock quintet from Oxford, Ohio; Ivan Browne, lead singer. Member Bill Bartlett was leader of Ram Jam.	
12/23/67†	**1**(1)	12	● 1. **Green Tambourine**	Buddah 23
			THE LENNON SISTERS	
			Four sisters from Venice, California: Dianne, Peggy, Kathy and Janet Lennon. TV debut on Lawrence Welk's Christmas Eve show in 1955. Left Welk in 1967.	
9/29/56	**15**	10	1. Tonight You Belong To Me Top 100 #15 / Best Seller #16 / Jockey #16 / Juke Box #17 label lists artist as Lawrence Welk; vocals by The Lennon Sisters	Coral 61701
			JOHN LENNON	
			Born on 10/9/40 in Liverpool, England. Founding member of The Beatles. Married Cynthia Powell on 8/23/62, had son Julian. Divorced Cynthia on 11/8/68. Met Yoko Ono (b: 2/18/34 in Japan) in 1966 and married her on 3/20/69. Formed Plastic Ono Band in 1969. To New York City in 1971. Fought deportation from USA, 1972-76, until he was granted a permanent visa. John was shot to death on 12/8/80 in New York City.	
8/09/69	**14**	6	1. Give Peace A Chance **PLASTIC ONO BAND** recorded in a hotel suite in Montreal, Canada	Apple 1809
12/13/69†	**30**	7	2. Cold Turkey **PLASTIC ONO BAND**	Apple 1813
3/07/70	**3**	12	● 3. **Instant Karma (We All Shine On)** **JOHN ONO LENNON**	Apple 1818
4/10/71	**11**	8	4. Power To The People **JOHN LENNON/PLASTIC ONO BAND; YOKO ONO/PLASTIC ONO BAND**	Apple 1830
10/23/71	**3**	9	5. **Imagine** **JOHN LENNON/PLASTIC ONO BAND**	Apple 1840
12/01/73	**18**	8	6. Mind Games **JOHN LENNON**	Apple 1868
10/05/74	**1**(1)	11	7. **Whatever Gets You Thru The Night** **JOHN LENNON with THE PLASTIC ONO NUCLEAR BAND** backing vocal: Elton John	Apple 1874
			JOHN LENNON:	
1/11/75	**9**	8	8. **#9 Dream**	Apple 1878
4/05/75	**20**	5	9. Stand By Me	Apple 1881
11/01/80	**1**(5)	19	● 10. **(Just Like) Starting Over**	Geffen 49604
1/17/81	**2**(3)	17	● 11. **Woman**	Geffen 49644
4/11/81	**10**	10	12. **Watching The Wheels**	Geffen 49695

DATE	POS	WKS	ARTIST—RECORD TITLE	LABEL & NO.
1/21/84	**5**	11	13. **Nobody Told Me** above 4: recorded in 1980	Polydor 817254
			JULIAN LENNON	
			Born John Charles Julian Lennon on 4/8/63. First child to be born to any of The Beatles.	
11/10/84†	**9**	12	1. **Valotte**	Atlantic 89609
2/02/85	**5**	12	2. **Too Late For Goodbyes**	Atlantic 89589
4/27/85	**21**	8	3. Say You're Wrong	Atlantic 89567
4/26/86	**32**	4	4. Stick Around	Atlantic 89437
			ANNIE LENNOX & AL GREEN	
			Annie is the lead singer of the Eurythmics.	
12/03/88†	**9**	10	1. **Put A Little Love In Your Heart** from the film "Scrooged"	A&M 1255
			TOMMY LEONETTI	
			Born on 9/10/29 in Bergen, New Jersey; died on 9/15/79. Vocalist with Charlie Spivak and other bands. Featured singer on TV's "Your Hit Parade."	
7/07/56	**23**	2	1. Free Jockey #23 / Top 100 #40	Capitol 3442
			KETTY LESTER	
			Born Revoyda Frierson on 8/16/34 in Hope, Arkansas. To Los Angeles in 1955. Acted in several TV shows.	
3/10/62	**5**	11	1. **Love Letters** #11 hit for Dick Haymes in 1945	Era 3068
			THE LETTERMEN	
			Harmonic vocal group formed in Los Angeles in 1960. Consisted of Tony Butala (b: 11/20/40), Jim Pike (b: 11/6/38) and Bob Engemann (b: 2/19/36). First recorded for Warner Brothers. Engemann replaced by Gary Pike (Jim's brother), 1968.	
9/25/61	**13**	9	1. The Way You Look Tonight #1 hit for Fred Astaire in 1936	Capitol 4586
12/04/61†	**7**	11	2. **When I Fall In Love** #20 hit for Doris Day in 1952	Capitol 4658
3/10/62	**17**	7	3. Come Back Silly Girl	Capitol 4699
7/17/65	**16**	5	4. Theme From "A Summer Place" from the Sandra Dee/Troy Donahue film	Capitol 5437
1/06/68	**7**	11	5. **Goin' Out Of My Head/Can't Take My Eyes Off You**	Capitol 2054
8/16/69	**12**	10	6. Hurt So Bad	Capitol 2482
			LEVEL 42	
			Pop-soul-jazz foursome from Manchester, England: Mark King (lead vocals), Mike Lindup, and brothers Phil & Boon Gould. The brothers left the band in October, 1987; replaced by Alan Murphy (guitar) and Gary Husband (drums).	
4/05/86	**7**	14	1. **Something About You**	Polydor 883362
5/16/87	**12**	10	2. Lessons In Love	Polydor 883956
			LEVERT	
			Soul trio from Ohio: Gerald & Sean Levert (sons of the O'Jays' Eddie Levert), and Marc Gordon.	
9/05/87	**5**	12	1. **Casanova**	Atlantic 89217

DATE	POS	WKS	ARTIST—RECORD TITLE	LABEL & NO.
			BARBARA LEWIS	
			Born on 2/9/43 in South Lyon, Michigan. R&B singer/multi-instrumentalist/songwriter (since age 9). First recorded in Chicago in 1961. Inactive since the early 70s.	
5/25/63	**3**	10	1. **Hello Stranger** backing vocals: The Dells	Atlantic 2184
3/14/64	**38**	1	2. Puppy Love	Atlantic 2214
7/17/65	**11**	9	3. Baby, I'm Yours	Atlantic 2283
10/09/65	**11**	8	4. Make Me Your Baby	Atlantic 2300
8/13/66	**28**	4	5. Make Me Belong To You	Atlantic 2346
			BOBBY LEWIS	
			Born on 2/17/33 in Indianapolis. R&B singer. Grew up in an orphanage, adopted by a Detroit family at age 12. First recorded for the Parrot label in 1952.	
5/29/61	**1**(7)	17	1. **Tossin' And Turnin'**	Beltone 1002
9/11/61	**9**	7	2. **One Track Mind**	Beltone 1012
			GARY LEWIS & THE PLAYBOYS	
			Pop-rock group formed in Los Angeles in 1964. Consisted of Gary Lewis (vocals, drums), Al Ramsey, John West (guitars), David Walker (keyboards) and David Costell (bass). Lewis (b: 7/31/46) is the son of comedian Jerry Lewis. Group worked regularly at Disneyland in 1964. Lewis inducted into the Army on New Year's Day in 1967, resumed career after discharge in 1968.	
1/23/65	**1**(2)	11	● 1. **This Diamond Ring**	Liberty 55756
4/17/65	**2**(2)	9	2. **Count Me In**	Liberty 55778
7/17/65	**2**(1)	9	3. **Save Your Heart For Me**	Liberty 55809
10/09/65	**4**	8	4. **Everybody Loves A Clown**	Liberty 55818
12/18/65†	**3**	11	5. **She's Just My Style**	Liberty 55846
3/19/66	**9**	7	6. **Sure Gonna Miss Her**	Liberty 55865
5/21/66	**8**	7	7. **Green Grass**	Liberty 55880
8/13/66	**13**	5	8. My Heart's Symphony	Liberty 55898
10/22/66	**15**	6	9. (You Don't Have To) Paint Me A Picture	Liberty 55914
1/07/67	**21**	6	10. Where Will The Words Come From	Liberty 55933
6/10/67	**39**	2	11. Girls In Love	Liberty 55971
7/27/68	**19**	9	12. Sealed With A Kiss	Liberty 56037
			HUEY LEWIS & THE NEWS	
			San Francisco 6-man rock band. Huey was born Hugh Cregg III on 7/5/50 in New York City. Joined the country-rock band Clover in the late 70s. Formed The News in 1980, consisting of Huey (lead singer), Chris Hayes (lead guitar), Mario Cipollina (bass), Bill Gibson (drums), Sean Hopper (keyboards) and Johnny Colla (sax, guitar).	
2/20/82	**7**	13	1. **Do You Believe In Love**	Chrysalis 2589
6/12/82	**36**	4	2. Hope You Love Me Like You Say You Do	Chrysalis 2604
10/08/83	**8**	13	3. **Heart And Soul**	Chrysalis 42726
1/28/84	**6**	13	● 4. **I Want A New Drug**	Chrysalis 42766
4/28/84	**6**	14	5. **The Heart Of Rock & Roll**	Chrysalis 42782
7/28/84	**6**	13	6. **If This Is It**	Chrysalis 42803
10/27/84	**18**	10	7. Walking On A Thin Line	Chrysalis 42825
7/06/85	**1**(2)	15	● 8. **The Power Of Love** from the film "Back To The Future"	Chrysalis 42876

DATE	POS	WKS	ARTIST—RECORD TITLE	LABEL & NO.
8/09/86	**1**(3)	13	9. **Stuck With You**	Chrysalis 43019
10/25/86	**3**	12	10. **Hip To Be Square**	Chrysalis 43065
1/17/87	**1**(1)	12	11. **Jacob's Ladder** written by Bruce Hornsby	Chrysalis 43097
4/11/87	**9**	10	12. **I Know What I Like**	Chrysalis 43108
8/01/87	**6**	11	13. **Doing It All For My Baby**	Chrysalis 43143
7/23/88	**3**	12	14. **Perfect World**	Chrysalis 43265
10/29/88	**25**	6	15. Small World	Chrysalis 43306
			JERRY LEWIS	
			Born Joseph Levitch on 3/16/25 in Newark, New Jersey. Formed comedy team with Dean Martin in 1946 at Atlantic City. Film debut in 1949 in "My Friend Irma." National chairman in campaign against muscular dystrophy.	
11/24/56	**10**	15	1. **Rock-A-Bye Your Baby With A Dixie Melody** Best Seller #10 / Top 100 #12 / Juke Box #13 / Jockey #17 #1 hit for Al Jolson in 1918	Decca 30124
			JERRY LEE LEWIS	
			Born on 9/29/35 in Ferriday, Louisiana. Played piano since age 9, professionally since age 15. First recorded for Sun in 1956. Appeared in the film "Disc Jockey Jamboree" in 1957. Career waned in 1958 after marriage to 13-year-old cousin, Myra Gale Brown, daughter of his bass player. Made comeback in country music beginning in 1968. "The Killer," surrounded by personal tragedies in the past 2 decades, survived several serious illnesses in the past 6 years. Cousin to country singer Mickey Gilley and TV evangelist Jimmy Swaggart.	
7/15/57	**3**	20	1. **Whole Lot Of Shakin' Going On** Best Seller #3 / Top 100 #3 / Jockey #9	Sun 267
12/02/57†	**2**(4)	13	2. **Great Balls Of Fire** Best Seller #2 / Top 100 #2 / Jockey #9	Sun 281
3/10/58	**7**	9	3. **Breathless** Top 100 #7 / Best Seller #9 / Jockey #23	Sun 288
6/02/58	**21**	8	4. High School Confidential Top 100 #21 / Best Seller #22	Sun 296
4/24/61	**30**	4	5. What'd I Say	Sun 356
1/15/72	**40**	1	6. Me And Bobby McGee	Mercury 73248
			RAMSEY LEWIS	
			Ramsey formed the Gentlemen Of Swing, a jazz-oriented trio, in 1956 in Chicago. Consisted of Ramsey (b: 5/27/35, Chicago; piano), Eldee Young (bass) and Isaac "Red" Holt (drums). All had been in The Clefs in the early 50s. First recorded for Chess/Argo in 1956. Disbanded in 1965; Young and Holt then formed the Young-Holt Trio. Lewis re-formed his trio with Cleveland Eaton (bass) and Maurice White (later with Earth, Wind & Fire; drums). Reunited with Young and Holt in 1983.	
			THE RAMSEY LEWIS TRIO:	
8/21/65	**5**	12	1. **The "In" Crowd** **[I]**	Argo 5506
11/27/65	**11**	6	2. Hang On Sloopy [I]	Cadet 5522
2/05/66	**29**	4	3. A Hard Day's Night [I]	Cadet 5525
			RAMSEY LEWIS:	
8/20/66	**19**	6	4. Wade In The Water [I]	Cadet 5541

DATE	POS	WKS	ARTIST—RECORD TITLE	LABEL & NO.
			GORDON LIGHTFOOT	
			Born on 11/17/38 in Orillia, Ontario, Canada. Folk-pop-country singer/songwriter/ guitarist. Worked on "Country Hoedown," CBC-TV series. Teamed with Jim Whalen as the Two Tones in the mid-60s. Wrote hit "Early Mornin' Rain" for Peter, Paul & Mary.	
1/23/71	**5**	11	1. **If You Could Read My Mind**	Reprise 0974
5/11/74	1(1)	11	● 2. **Sundown**	Reprise 1194
10/05/74	**10**	7	3. **Carefree Highway**	Reprise 1309
5/03/75	**26**	4	4. Rainy Day People	Reprise 1328
9/25/76	**2**(2)	13	5. **The Wreck Of The Edmund Fitzgerald** true story of an ore vessel that sunk in Lake Superior on 11/10/75	Reprise 1369
3/25/78	**33**	3	6. The Circle Is Small (I Can See It In Your Eyes)	Warner 8518
			LIGHTHOUSE	
			Rock band from Toronto, Canada; Bob McBride, lead singer.	
10/09/71	**24**	8	1. One Fine Morning	Evolution 1048
11/25/72	**34**	5	2. Sunny Days	Evolution 1069
			LIMAHL	
			Real name: Chris Hamill (Limahl is an anagram of his last name). Ex-leader of Kajagoogoo.	
5/04/85	**17**	9	1. Never Ending Story from the film "The Never Ending Story"	EMI America 8230
			BOB LIND	
			Born on 11/25/44 in Baltimore. Folk-rock singer/songwriter.	
2/12/66	**5**	9	1. **Elusive Butterfly**	World Pac. 77808
			KATHY LINDEN	
			Songstress from Moorestown, New Jersey.	
3/31/58	**7**	11	1. **Billy** Jockey #7 / Top 100 #12 / Best Seller #14 #10 hit for Wee Bonnie Baker (of Orrin Tucker's band) in 1939	Felsted 8510
4/27/59	**11**	10	2. Goodbye Jimmy, Goodbye	Felsted 8571
			LINDISFARNE	
			Folk-rock quintet from England; Alan Hull, lead singer.	
11/25/78	**33**	4	1. Run For Home	Atco 7093
			MARK LINDSAY	
			Born on 3/9/44 in Eugene, Oregon. Lead singer of Paul Revere & The Raiders.	
1/10/70	**10**	11	● 1. **Arizona**	Columbia 45037
7/11/70	**25**	5	2. Silver Bird	Columbia 45180
			LIPPS, INC.	
			Funk project from Minneapolis formed by producer/songwriter/ multi-instrumentalist Steven Greenberg. Vocals by Miss Black Minnesota U.S.A. of 1976, Cynthia Johnson.	
4/19/80	**1**(4)	15	▲ 1. **Funkytown**	Casablanca 2233
			LISA LISA & CULT JAM with FULL FORCE	
			Harlem R&B/rap trio: Lisa Velez, Mike Hughes and Alex "Spanador" Moseley. All of their hits were produced by Full Force.	
8/03/85	**34**	6	1. I Wonder If I Take You Home	Columbia 04886

DATE	POS	WKS	ARTIST—RECORD TITLE	LABEL & NO.
8/30/86	**8**	13	2. **All Cried Out**	Columbia 05844
			featuring Paul Anthony & Bow Legged Lou	
5/02/87	**1**(1)	14	3. **Head To Toe**	Columbia 07008
8/22/87	**1**(1)	13	4. **Lost In Emotion**	Columbia 07267
			above 2 shown only as: **LISA LISA & CULT JAM**	
			LITTLE ANTHONY & THE IMPERIALS	
			R&B group formed in 1957 in Brooklyn. Consisted of Anthony Gourdine (b: 1/8/40), Ernest Wright, Jr., Tracy Lord, Glouster Rogers and Clarence Collins. Anthony first recorded on Winley in 1955 with The DuPonts. Formed The Chesters in 1957, then changed name to The Imperials in 1958. Sammy Strain, who joined group in 1964, left in 1975 to join The O'Jays.	
8/18/58	**4**	14	1. **Tears On My Pillow**	End 1027
			Hot 100 #4 / Best Seller #5 end	
1/18/60	**24**	7	2. Shimmy, Shimmy, Ko-Ko-Bop	End 1060
9/05/64	**15**	8	3. I'm On The Outside (Looking In)	DCP 1104
11/21/64	**6**	12	4. **Goin' Out Of My Head**	DCP 1119
2/13/65	**10**	8	5. **Hurt So Bad**	DCP 1128
7/17/65	**16**	7	6. Take Me Back	DCP 1136
11/06/65	**34**	1	7. I Miss You So	DCP 1149
			LITTLE CAESAR & THE ROMANS	
			Los Angeles R&B quintet led by David "Little Caesar" Johnson (b: 6/16/34, Chicago).	
5/29/61	**9**	9	1. **Those Oldies But Goodies (Remind Me Of You)**	Del-Fi 4158
			THE LITTLE DIPPERS	
			Pop quartet organized by producer Buddy Killen: Delores Dinning, Emily Gilmore, Darrell McCall and Hurshel Wigintin.	
2/08/60	**9**	10	1. **Forever**	University 210
			LITTLE EVA	
			Born Eva Narcissus Boyd on 6/29/45 in Bellhaven, North Carolina. Discovered by songwriters Carole King and Gerry Goffin. Also see Big Dee Irwin.	
7/21/62	**1**(1)	12	1. **The Loco-Motion**	Dimension 1000
11/24/62	**12**	8	2. Keep Your Hands Off My Baby	Dimension 1003
2/23/63	**20**	6	3. Let's Turkey Trot	Dimension 1006
			LITTLE JOE & THE THRILLERS	
			R&B group formed in New York City in 1956. Joe Cook (lead), Farris Hill and Richard Frazier (tenors), Donald Burnett (baritone) and Harry Pascle (bass).	
10/07/57	**22**	9	1. Peanuts	Okeh 7088
			Best Seller #22 / Top 100 #23	
			LITTLE JOEY & THE FLIPS	
			R&B quintet from Philadelphia; Joey Hall, lead singer.	
7/14/62	**33**	3	1. Bongo Stomp	Joy 262
			LITTLE MILTON	
			Born Milton Campbell, Jr. on 9/7/34 in Inverness, Mississippi. Blues singer/ guitarist. Recorded with Ike Turner at Sun Records, 1953-54. In concert film "Wattstax," 1972.	
4/24/65	**25**	7	1. We're Gonna Make It	Checker 1105

DATE	POS	WKS	ARTIST—RECORD TITLE	LABEL & NO.
			LITTLE RICHARD	
			Born Richard Wayne Penniman on 12/5/32 in Macon, Georgia. R&B/rock and roll singer/pianist. Talent contest win led to first recordings for RCA-Victor in 1951. Worked with the Tempo Toppers, 1953-55. Earned degree in Theology in 1961 and was ordained a minister. Left R&B for gospel music, 1959-62 and again in mid-70s. The key figure in the transition from R&B to rock 'n' roll. Appeared in 3 early rock & roll films: "Don't Knock The Rock," "The Girl Can't Help It" and "Mister Rock 'n' Roll"; and the comedy film "Down & Out In Beverly Hills" in 1986. Inducted into the Rock And Roll Hall Of Fame in 1986.	
1/28/56	**17**	5	1. Tutti-Frutti Juke Box #17 / Best Seller #18 / Top 100 #21	Specialty 561
4/07/56	**6**	12	2. **Long Tall Sally/** Best Seller #6 / Top 100 #13 / Juke Box #14 / Jockey #16	
6/30/56	**33**	1	3. Slippin' And Slidin' (Peepin' And Hidin')	Specialty 572
7/14/56	**17**	7	4. Rip It Up Best Seller #17 / Top 100 #27	Specialty 579
4/06/57	**21**	7	5. Lucille Best Seller #21 / Top 100 #27	Specialty 598
6/24/57	**10**	13	6. **Jenny, Jenny** Best Seller #10 / Top 100 #14	Specialty 606
10/07/57	**8**	12	7. **Keep A Knockin'** Top 100 #8 / Best Seller #9 / Jockey #24 from the film "Mister Rock 'n' Roll"	Specialty 611
2/24/58	**10**	10	8. **Good Golly, Miss Molly** Top 100 #10 / Best Seller #13	Specialty 624
6/23/58	**31**	3	9. Ooh! My Soul Best Seller #31 / Top 100 #35	Specialty 633
			LITTLE RIVER BAND	
			Pop-rock group formed in Australia in 1975. Consisted of Glenn Shorrock (lead singer), Rick Formosa, Beeb Birtles and Graham Goble (guitars), Roger McLachlan (bass) and Derek Pellicci (drums). Formosa, McLachlan, replaced by David Briggs (guitar) and George McArdle (bass) after first album. Shorrock replaced by John Farnham in 1983. Numerous personnel changes since 1985. Shorrock replaced Farnham in 1987. 1988 lineup includes: Shorrock, Goble, and Pellicci. Band name after a resort town 30 miles outside Melbourne.	
11/06/76	**28**	6	1. It's A Long Way There	Harvest 4318
9/24/77	**14**	11	2. Help Is On Its Way	Harvest 4428
1/21/78	**16**	9	3. Happy Anniversary	Harvest 4524
8/12/78	**3**	14	4. **Reminiscing**	Harvest 4605
1/27/79	**10**	14	5. **Lady**	Harvest 4667
8/04/79	**6**	14	6. **Lonesome Loser**	Capitol 4748
11/10/79†	**10**	13	7. **Cool Change**	Capitol 4789
9/05/81	**6**	14	8. **The Night Owls**	Capitol 5033
12/26/81†	**10**	15	9. **Take It Easy On Me**	Capitol 5057
5/01/82	**14**	8	10. Man On Your Mind	Capitol 5061
12/04/82†	**11**	13	11. The Other Guy	Capitol 5185
5/28/83	**22**	6	12. We Two	Capitol 5231
8/27/83	**35**	3	13. You're Driving Me Out Of My Mind	Capitol 5256
			LITTLE SISTER	
			Female soul trio organized by Sly Stone for his own record label. Consisted of his sister Vanetta Stewart, Mary Rand and Elva Melton.	
3/28/70	**22**	6	1. You're The One - Part I	Stone Flower 9000

DATE	POS	WKS	ARTIST—RECORD TITLE	LABEL & NO.
1/30/71	**32**	3	2. Somebody's Watching You	Stone Flower 9001
			LIVING IN A BOX	
			Soul-styled pop trio from England: Richard Darbyshire (vocals), Marcus Vere (keyboards) and Anthony "Tich" Critchlow (drums).	
7/25/87	**17**	7	1. Living In A Box	Chrysalis 43104
			L.L. COOL J	
			Real name: James Todd Smith. Rap artist from Queens, New York.	
8/15/87	**14**	8	1. I Need Love	Def Jam 07350
3/26/88	**31**	5	2. Going Back To Cali from the film "Less Than Zero"	Def Jam 07679
			LOBO	
			Born Kent Lavoie on 7/31/43 in Tallahassee, Florida. Pop singer/songwriter/ guitarist. Played with the Legends in Tampa in 1961. This group included Jim Stafford, Gerald Chambers, Gram Parsons and Jon Corneal. Own publishing company, Boo Publishing, in 1974.	
4/24/71	**5**	10	1. **Me And You And A Dog Named Boo**	Big Tree 112
10/14/72	2(2)	10	• 2. **I'd Love You To Want Me**	Big Tree 147
1/13/73	**8**	10	3. **Don't Expect Me To Be Your Friend**	Big Tree 158
5/05/73	**27**	5	4. It Sure Took A Long, Long Time	Big Tree 16001
7/21/73	**22**	8	5. How Can I Tell Her	Big Tree 16004
5/11/74	**37**	2	6. Standing At The End Of The Line	Big Tree 15001
4/26/75	**27**	4	7. Don't Tell Me Goodnight	Big Tree 16033
9/08/79	**23**	8	8. Where Were You When I Was Falling In Love	MCA 41065
			HANK LOCKLIN	
			Born Lawrence Hankins Locklin on 2/15/18 in McLellan, Florida. Country singer/ songwriter/guitarist. Own TV series in Houston and Dallas in the 70s.	
6/13/60	**8**	15	1. **Please Help Me, I'm Falling**	RCA 7692
			LOGGINS & MESSINA	
			Duo of Kenneth Clarke Loggins (b: 1/7/47, Everett, WA) and James Messina (b: 12/5/47, Maywood, CA). Loggins was raised in Alhambra, California and played guitar from age 13. Worked with Second Helping and Gator Creek, and recorded in the late 60s. Wrote "House On Pooh Corner" hit for the Dirt Band. Messina was raised in Harlingen, Texas and played in bands from age 13. Worked as a recording engineer and producer from 1965. Worked with Buffalo Springfield and Poco. Duo formed, 1970.	
12/02/72†	**4**	13	• 1. **Your Mama Don't Dance**	Columbia 45719
4/28/73	**18**	8	2. Thinking Of You	Columbia 45815
11/24/73	**16**	8	3. My Music	Columbia 45952
			DAVE LOGGINS	
			Born on 11/10/47 in Mountain City, Tennessee. Pop/country-styled singer/songwriter. Cousin of Kenny Loggins.	
7/13/74	**5**	10	1. **Please Come To Boston**	Epic 11115
			KENNY LOGGINS	
			Born on 1/7/47 in Everett, Washington. Pop-rock singer/songwriter/ guitarist. Signed as a solo artist with Columbia in 1971 where he met and recorded with Jim Messina from 1972-76.	
8/19/78	**5**	15	1. **Whenever I Call You "Friend"** harmony vocal: Stevie Nicks	Columbia 10794

DATE	POS	WKS	ARTIST—RECORD TITLE	LABEL & NO.
11/24/79†	**11**	16	2. This Is It	Columbia 11109
4/05/80	**36**	2	3. Keep The Fire	Columbia 11215
8/23/80	**7**	12	4. **I'm Alright** theme from the film "Caddyshack"	Columbia 11317
9/25/82	**17**	6	5. Don't Fight It **KENNY LOGGINS with STEVE PERRY**	Columbia 03192
12/11/82†	**15**	13	6. Heart To Heart	Columbia 03377
4/02/83	**24**	7	7. Welcome To Heartlight inspired by the writings of children from Heartlight School	Columbia 03555
2/11/84	**1**(3)	16	● 8. **Footloose**	Columbia 04310
6/23/84	**22**	8	9. I'm Free (Heaven Helps The Man) above 2: from the film "Footloose"	Columbia 04452
4/13/85	**29**	4	10. Vox Humana	Columbia 04849
7/20/85	**40**	1	11. Forever	Columbia 04931
6/07/86	**2**(1)	13	12. **Danger Zone** from the film "Top Gun"	Columbia 05893
4/25/87	**11**	12	13. Meet Me Half Way from the Sylvester Stallone film "Over The Top"	Columbia 06690
7/30/88	**8**	11	14. **Nobody's Fool** theme from the film "Caddyshack II"	Columbia 07971
			LOLITA Lolita Ditta from Vienna, Austria.	
11/14/60	**5**	14	1. **Sailor (Your Home Is The Sea)** [F]	Kapp 349
			LONDON SYMPHONY ORCHESTRA - see JOHN WILLIAMS	
			JULIE LONDON Born on 9/26/26 in Santa Rosa, California. Singer/actress. Played Dixie McCall on the TV series "Emergency."	
12/03/55	**9**	13	1. **Cry Me A River** Jockey #9 / Top 100 #13 / Juke Box #14 / Best Seller #23	Liberty 55006
			LAURIE LONDON Male vocalist, born on 1/19/44 in London. Recorded only hit record at age 13.	
3/24/58	**1**(4)	14	● 1. **He's Got The Whole World (In His Hands)** Jockey #1 / Best Seller #2 / Top 100 #2 traditional black American gospel song	Capitol 3891
			SHORTY LONG Born Frederick Earl Long on 5/20/40 in Birmingham, Alabama. Soul singer/songwriter. Moved to Detroit in 1959. First recorded for Tri-Phi in 1962. Drowned on 6/29/69.	
6/15/68	**8**	8	1. **Here Comes The Judge** [N]	Soul 35044
			LOOKING GLASS Rock quartet formed by Elliot Lurie while at Rutgers University in New Jersey.	
7/01/72	**1**(1)	14	● 1. **Brandy (You're A Fine Girl)**	Epic 10874
9/29/73	**33**	3	2. Jimmy Loves Mary-Anne	Epic 11001

Guns N' Roses are clearly one of the major success stories of the late 80s. *Appetite For Destruction*, the group's Geffen debut album, has been certified platinum seven times over—a success that many say is even more remarkable due to the comparatively small amount of radio airplay the group receives.

Sammy Hagar's work between his stints with Montrose and Van Halen included cover versions of two well-known 60s hits. In 1979, his "(Sittin' On) The Dock Of The Bay" reached No. 65 on the Hot 100; five years later—as part of Hagar, Schon, Aaronson, Shrieve—he sang "Whiter Shade Of Pale" and peaked at No. 94.

Hall & Oates' shift to Arista Records after a lengthy, hit-filled stay at RCA had little effect on the duo's status: *Ooh Yeh!*, their Arista debut, hit the platinum standard set by such previous works as *Voices, Private Eyes, H20, Rock 'N Soul Part 1*, and more.

Roy Hamilton's last appearance in the Top 100 was 1961's "You're Gonna Need Magic"—an unfortunately all-too-accurate title, at least regarding his chances for future hits. The former gospel singer died in 1969.

The Happenings were originally dubbed the Four Graduates—but, wisely, changed their name before scoring with their 1966 hit, "See You In September."

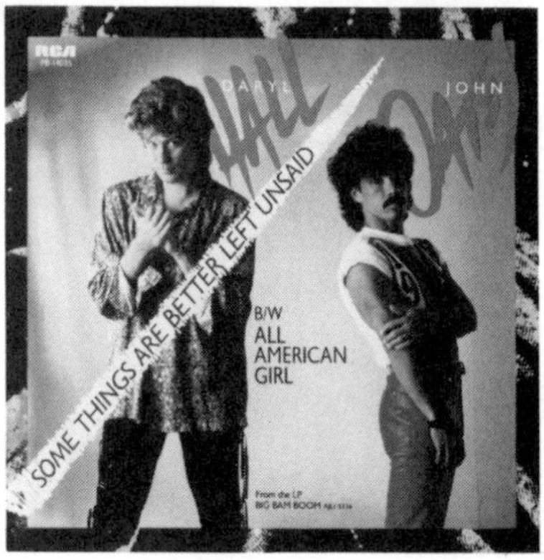

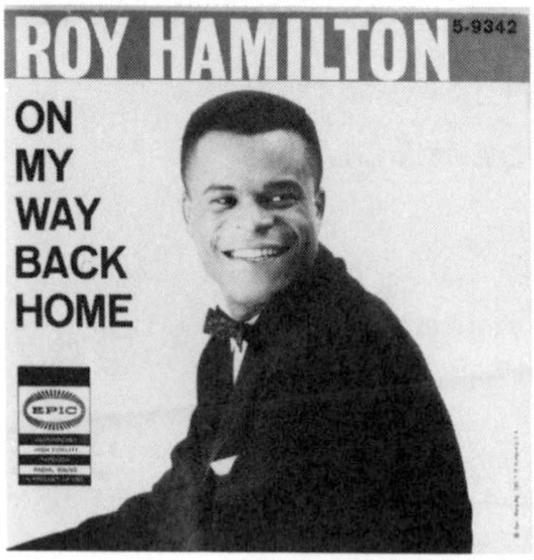

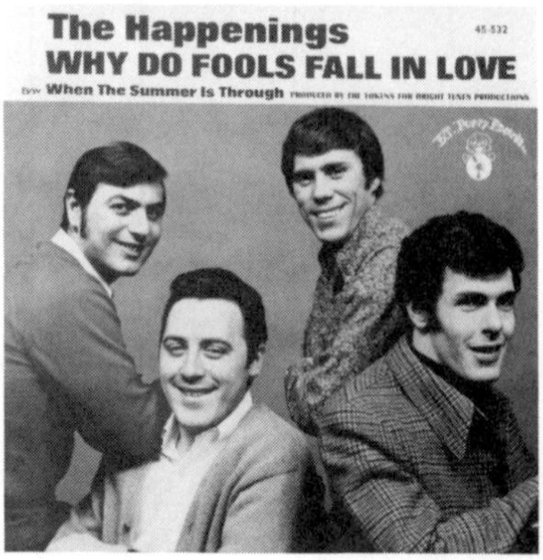

George Harrison's relative semi-retirement came to an abrupt halt in 1988 when the former Beatles guitarist went platinum with *Cloud Nine*—his first solo album in six years—and with his "new" band, the Traveling Wilburys.

Corey Hart made his Canadian homeland proud with dual top-10 hits "Sunglasses At Night" in 1984 and "Never Surrender" in 1985. The first track's title made the selection of an appropriate promotional item especially easy for EMI America.

Heart asked the question "What About Love?" in 1985 and were rewarded with their first top-10 hit since 1980's "Tell It Like It Is." Since the success of *Heart*, the album from which it was drawn, the group—led by the colorful Wilson sisters—has enjoyed a remarkably revitalized career.

Buddy Holly's portrayal in the 1978 film *The Buddy Holly Story* predated a rash of late-80s rock bio-pics, most notably *La Bamba*, the Columbia Pictures film based on 50s rocker Ritchie Valens. In that film, Holly himself was portrayed by singer/songwriter Marshall Crenshaw.

The Honeycombs' "I Can't Stop" followed their top-five hit "Have I The Right?" in 1964—but unlike its predecessor, it peaked at No. 48 and represented the last chart showing the U.K. group would ever make. To this day, the group is noted for its inclusion of a female drummer, Ann "Honey" Lantree, during those relatively unliberated times.

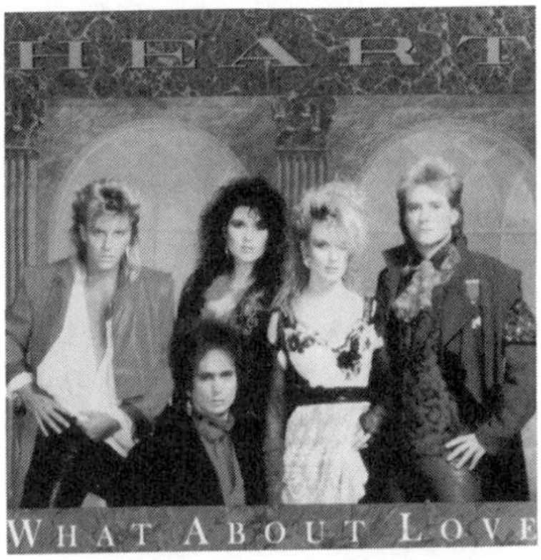

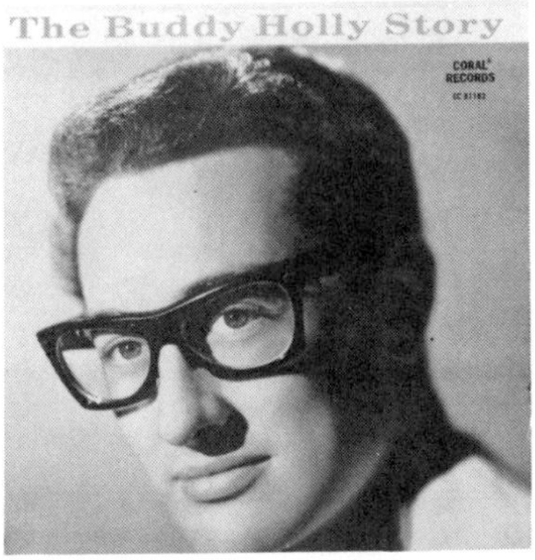

DATE	POS	WKS	ARTIST—RECORD TITLE	LABEL & NO.
			DENISE LOPEZ	
			Dance singer born in Queens, New York. Recorded under the name "Nancy Dee" in 1984.	
8/06/88	**31**	5	1. Sayin' Sorry (Don't Make It Right)	Vendetta 7200
			TRINI LOPEZ	
			Born on 5/15/37 in Dallas. Pop-folk singer/guitarist. Discovered by Don Costa while performing at PJs nightclub in Los Angeles.	
8/10/63	**3**	11	1. **If I Had A Hammer**	Reprise 20198
12/14/63†	**23**	6	2. Kansas City	Reprise 20236
2/06/65	**20**	5	3. Lemon Tree	Reprise 0336
5/07/66	**39**	3	4. I'm Comin' Home, Cindy	Reprise 0455
			JEFF LORBER featuring KARYN WHITE	
			Lorber: jazz fusion keyboardist; White: prominent session singer from Los Angeles.	
2/07/87	**27**	5	1. Facts Of Love	Warner 28588
			GLORIA LORING & CARL ANDERSON	
			Gloria played Liz Curtis on the daytime TV series "Days Of Our Lives."	
8/02/86	**2**(2)	14	1. **Friends And Lovers**	USA Carrere 06122
			LOS BRAVOS	
			Rock quintet consisting of 4 members from Spain and 1 from Germany; Mike Kogel (Kennedy), lead singer.	
9/10/66	**4**	8	1. **Black Is Black**	Press 60002
			LOS INDIOS TABAJARAS	
			Brazilian Indian brothers: Natalicio and Antenor Lima.	
10/12/63	**6**	10	1. **Maria Elena** **[I]** #1 hit for Jimmy Dorsey & His Orchestra in 1941	RCA 8216
			LOS LOBOS	
			Hispanic-American rock quintet based in Los Angeles. Includes: David Hidalgo (lead vocals), Cesar Rosas, Conrad Lozano, Louie Perez and Steve Berlin.	
7/18/87	**1**(3)	14	1. **La Bamba** **[F]**	Slash 28336
10/17/87	**21**	7	2. Come On, Let's Go above 2 from the film "La Bamba"	Slash 28186
			THE LOST GENERATION	
			Chicago soul quartet: Lowrell Simon (lead), his brother Fred Simon, Larry Brownlee (of The C.O.D.'s; d: 1978) and Jesse Dean. Disbanded in 1974. Lowrell began recording solo (as Lowrell) in 1978.	
8/01/70	**30**	5	1. The Sly, Slick, And The Wicked	Brunswick 55436
			BONNIE LOU - see BONNIE	
			JOHN D. LOUDERMILK	
			Born on 3/31/34 in Durham, North Carolina. Pop-country singer/songwriter/multi- instrumentalist. Wrote "Waterloo," "Tobacco Road," "Indian Reservation" and many others. Recorded as "Johnny Dee" and Ebe Sneezer" in 1956.	
4/06/57	**38**	1	1. Sittin' In The Balcony shown as: **JOHNNY DEE**	Colonial 430
12/04/61	**32**	3	2. Language Of Love	RCA 7938

DATE	POS	WKS	ARTIST—RECORD TITLE	LABEL & NO.
			LOVE	
			Los Angeles rock group led by singer/guitarist Arthur Lee.	
9/10/66	**33**	3	1. 7 And 7 Is	Elektra 45605
			LOVE & KISSES	
			Studio group assembled by European disco producer Alec Costandinos.	
6/24/78	**22**	6	1. Thank God It's Friday from the film of the same title	Casablanca 925
			LOVE UNLIMITED	
			Female soul trio from San Pedro, California: sisters Glodean & Linda James, and Diane Taylor. Barry White, who later married Glodean, was their manager and producer.	
5/06/72	**14**	9	• 1. Walkin' In The Rain With The One I Love featuring Barry White's voice on the telephone	Uni 55319
1/04/75	**27**	7	2. I Belong To You	20th Century 2141
			LOVE UNLIMITED ORCHESTRA	
			Studio orchestra conducted and arranged by Barry White.	
12/22/73†	**1**(1)	16	• 1. **Love's Theme** **[I]**	20th Century 2069
3/15/75	**22**	5	2. Satin Soul [I]	20th Century 2162
			DARLENE LOVE	
			Lead singer of backing group The Blossoms. Sang lead on 2 songs by The Crystals and with Bob B. Soxx & The Blue Jeans. Starred in the Off-Broadway show "Leader of The Pack." Appeared in the 1987 film "Lethal Weapon."	
5/11/63	**39**	1	1. (Today I Met) The Boy I'm Gonna Marry	Philles 111
8/24/63	**26**	4	2. Wait Til' My Bobby Gets Home	Philles 114
			LOVERBOY	
			Rock quintet formed in Vancouver, Canada in 1978: Mike Reno (lead singer), Paul Dean (lead guitar), Scott Smith (bass), Matt Frenette (drums) and Doug Johnson (keyboards).	
3/21/81	**35**	6	1. Turn Me Loose	Columbia 11421
1/09/82	**29**	8	2. Working For The Weekend	Columbia 02589
5/15/82	**26**	6	3. When It's Over backing vocal: Nancy Nash	Columbia 02814
7/02/83	**11**	11	4. Hot Girls In Love	Columbia 03941
10/29/83	**34**	3	5. Queen Of The Broken Hearts	Columbia 04096
9/14/85	**9**	11	6. **Lovin' Every Minute Of It**	Columbia 05569
2/15/86	**10**	10	7. **This Could Be The Night**	Columbia 05765
8/23/86	**12**	11	8. Heaven In Your Eyes from the film "Top Gun"	Columbia 06178
10/10/87	**38**	3	9. Notorious	Columbia 07324
			THE LOVIN' SPOONFUL	
			Jug-band rock group formed in New York City in 1965. Consisted of John Sebastian (lead vocals, songwriter, guitarist, harmonica), Zal Yanovsky (lead guitar), Steve Boone (bass) and Joe Butler (drums). Sebastian had been with the Even Dozen Jug Band; did session work at Elektra. Yanovsky and Sebastian were members of the Mugwumps with Cass Elliott and Denny Doherty (later with The Mamas & The Papas). Yanovsky replaced by Jerry Yester (keyboards) in 1967. Disbanded in 1968.	
9/18/65	**9**	8	1. **Do You Believe In Magic**	Kama Sutra 201
12/11/65†	**10**	9	2. **You Didn't Have To Be So Nice**	Kama Sutra 205

DATE	POS	WKS	ARTIST—RECORD TITLE	LABEL & NO.
3/12/66	2(2)	10	3. **Daydream**	Kama Sutra 208
5/14/66	2(2)	9	4. **Did You Ever Have To Make Up Your Mind?**	Kama Sutra 209
7/23/66	1(3)	10	● 5. **Summer In The City**	Kama Sutra 211
10/22/66	**10**	8	6. **Rain On The Roof**	Kama Sutra 216
12/31/66†	**8**	8	7. **Nashville Cats**	Kama Sutra 219
2/25/67	**15**	5	8. Darling Be Home Soon from the Francis Ford Coppola film "You're A Big Boy Now"	Kama Sutra 220
5/20/67	**18**	5	9. Six O'Clock all of above: produced by Erik Jacobsen	Kama Sutra 225
11/11/67	**27**	3	10. She Is Still A Mystery	Kama Sutra 239
			JIM LOWE	
			Born on 5/7/27 in Springfield, Missouri. Vocalist/pianist/composer. Disc jockey in New York City when he recorded "Green Door."	
9/29/56	1(3)	22	1. **The Green Door** Top 100 #1(3) / Juke Box #1(3) / Best Seller #2 / Jockey #2 piano player: Bob Davie	Dot 15486
5/13/57	**15**	6	2. Four Walls/ Juke Box #15 / Jockey #16 / Best Seller #19 / Top 100 #20	
5/13/57	**15**	5	3. Talkin' To The Blues Juke Box #15 / Jockey #20 / Top 100 #21 from the TV production "Modern Romances"	Dot 15569
			NICK LOWE	
			Born on 3/25/49 in England. With Brinsley Schwarz (1970-75) and Rockpile. Married to Carlene Carter. Produced albums for Elvis Costello and Graham Parker & The Rumour.	
8/18/79	**12**	10	1. Cruel To Be Kind	Columbia 11018
			L.T.D.	
			10-man R&B-funk band from Greensboro, North Carolina; Jeffrey Osborne, lead singer. Osborne left in 1980, replaced by Leslie Wilson and Andre Ray. L.T.D. means Love, Togetherness and Devotion.	
11/06/76	**20**	9	1. Love Ballad	A&M 1847
11/12/77	**4**	12	● 2. **(Every Time I Turn Around) Back In Love Again**	A&M 1974
1/31/81	**40**	1	3. Shine On	A&M 2283
			ROBIN LUKE	
			Born on 3/19/42 in Los Angeles. Recorded "Susie Darlin'" in Hawaii, inspired by his younger sister, Susie.	
8/18/58	**5**	15	1. **Susie Darlin'** Hot 100 #5 / Best Seller #6 end	Dot 15781
			LULU	
			Born Marie Lawrie on 11/3/48 near Glasgow, Scotland. Married to Maurice Gibb (Bee Gees) from 1969-73.	
9/23/67	1(5)	15	● 1. **To Sir With Love** from the film of the same title (starring Lulu)	Epic 10187
1/06/68	**32**	3	2. Best Of Both Worlds	Epic 10260
2/07/70	**22**	8	3. Oh Me Oh My (I'm A Fool For You Baby)	Atco 6722
8/22/81	**18**	10	4. I Could Never Miss You (More Than I Do)	Alfa 7006
			BOB LUMAN GROUP	
			Born on 4/15/37 in Nacogdoches, Texas. Died on 12/27/78 in Nashville. Country-rockabilly singer/songwriter/guitarist.	
9/26/60	**7**	9	1. **Let's Think About Living** [N]	Warner 5172

DATE	POS	WKS	ARTIST—RECORD TITLE	LABEL & NO.
			VICTOR LUNDBERG	
			Ex-disc jockey and newsman from Grand Rapids, Michigan.	
11/25/67	**10**	4	1. **An Open Letter To My Teenage Son** [S]	Liberty 55996
			ARTHUR LYMAN	
			Lyman was born on the island of Kauai, Hawaii in 1934. Plays vibraphone, guitar, piano and drums. Formerly with the Martin Denny Trio.	
6/12/61	**4**	10	1. **Yellow Bird** [I]	Hi Fi 5024
			FRANKIE LYMON & THE TEENAGERS	
			R&B group formed as The Premiers in the Bronx, in 1955. Lead singer Lymon was born on 9/30/42 in New York City; died of a drug overdose on 2/28/68 at the age of 25. Other members included Herman Santiago & Jimmy Merchant (tenors), Joe Negroni (baritone; d: 9/5/78) and Sherman Garnes (bass; d: 2/26/77). Group appeared in the films "Rock, Rock, Rock" and "Mister Rock 'n' Roll."	
2/18/56	**6**	16	1. **Why Do Fools Fall In Love**	Gee 1002
			THE TEENAGERS featuring FRANKIE LYMON	
			Best Seller #6 / Top 100 #7 / Juke Box #8 / Jockey #9	
5/12/56	**13**	11	2. I Want You To Be My Girl	Gee 1012
			Best Seller #13 / Top 100 #17 / Juke Box #20 / Jockey #25	
8/26/57	**20**	7	3. Goody Goody	Gee 1039
			Best Seller #20 / Jockey #21 / Top 100 #22	
			BARBARA LYNN	
			Born Barbara Lynn Ozen on 1/16/42 in Beaumont, Texas. R&B singer/songwriter/guitar.	
7/14/62	**8**	8	1. **You'll Lose A Good Thing**	Jamie 1220
			CHERYL LYNN	
			Born on 3/11/57 in Los Angeles. Soul singer. Discovered on TV's "Gong Show."	
1/06/79	**12**	12	● 1. Got To Be Real	Columbia 10808
			GLORIA LYNNE	
			Born on 11/23/31 in New York City. Jazz-styled vocalist.	
2/29/64	**28**	4	1. I Wish You Love	Everest 2036
			LYNYRD SKYNYRD	
			Southern-rock band formed while in high school in Jacksonville, Florida in 1965. Named after their gym teacher Leonard Skinner. Nucleus of band consisted of Ronnie Van Zant (lead singer), Gary Rossington (guitar) and Allen Collins (guitar). Plane crash on 10/20/77 in Gillsburg, Mississippi killed Van Zant and members Steve and Cassie Gaines. Gary and Allen formed the Rossington Collins Band in 1980.	
8/24/74	**8**	11	1. **Sweet Home Alabama**	MCA 40258
1/04/75	**19**	5	2. Free Bird	MCA 40328
7/19/75	**27**	3	3. Saturday Night Special	MCA 40416
1/08/77	**38**	2	4. Free Bird [R]	MCA 40665
			live version of #2 above	
1/07/78	**13**	11	5. What's Your Name	MCA 40819

DATE	POS	WKS	ARTIST—RECORD TITLE	LABEL & NO.
			M	
			M	
			M is British pop musician Robin Scott.	
8/25/79	1(1)	20	● 1. **Pop Muzik**	Sire 49033
			MOMS MABLEY	
			Born Loretta Mary Aiken on 3/19/1894 in Brevard, North Carolina. Died on 5/23/75. Comedienne/actress. Charted 13 comedy albums on Billboard's pop albums charts.	
7/19/69	**35**	2	1. Abraham, Martin And John	Mercury 72935
			BYRON MacGREGOR	
			Canadian narrator of "Americans," Byron was 25 years old and the news director at CKLW-Detroit. The narration was originally written and delivered as an editorial by Gordon Sinclair for CFRB-Toronto on 6/5/73.	
1/12/74	**4**	9	● 1. **Americans** **[S]**	Westbound 222
			backed by instrumental version of "America The Beautiful"	
			MARY MacGREGOR	
			Singer born on 5/6/48 in St. Paul, Minnesota.	
12/25/76†	1(2)	16	● 1. **Torn Between Two Lovers**	Ariola Am. 7638
10/06/79	**39**	2	2. Good Friend	RSO 938
			from the movie "Meatballs"	
			LONNIE MACK	
			Born Lonnie McIntosh on 7/18/41 in Aurora, Indiana. Singer/guitarist (since age 5). Own country band in 1954. With Troy Seals in the early 60s. Re-discovered in 1968. Retired from music, 1971-85.	
6/22/63	**5**	10	1. **Memphis** **[I]**	Fraternity 906
9/21/63	**24**	4	2. Wham! [I]	Fraternity 912
			GISELE MacKENZIE	
			Born Gisele Lefleche on 1/10/27 in Winnipeg, Canada. Popular singing star of TV's "Your Hit Parade" (1953-57).	
6/04/55	**4**	19	1. **Hard To Get**	X 0137
			Jockey #4 / Best Seller #5 / Juke Box #5 with Richard Maltby & his Orchestra; featured on the NBC-TV show "Justice"	
			GORDON MacRAE	
			Born on 3/12/21 in East Orange, New Jersey; died of cancer on 1/24/86. Starred in the film musicals "Oklahoma" and "Carousel."	
10/06/58	**18**	6	1. The Secret	Capitol 4033
			JOHNNY MADDOX & The Rhythm Masters	
			Born in 1929 in Gallatin, Tennessee. Honky-tonk pianist/bandleader.	
2/05/55	2(7)	20	1. **The Crazy Otto** **[I]**	Dot 15325
			cover of original version by honky-tonk piano player Crazy Otto Best Seller #2 / Juke Box #2 / Jockey #7	

DATE	POS	WKS	ARTIST—RECORD TITLE	LABEL & NO.
			BETTY MADIGAN	
			Singer from Washington, DC.	
9/08/58	**31**	3	1. Dance Everyone Dance Best Seller #31 / Hot 100 #34 based on the Israeli harvest song "Hava Nagila"	Coral 62007
			MADNESS	
			Septet from North London, England; led by Graham "Suggs" McPherson, formed as a ska-pop band in 1978. Split up in 1986.	
5/28/83	**7**	13	1. **Our House**	Geffen 29668
9/17/83	**33**	5	2. It Must Be Love	Geffen 29562
			MADONNA	
			Born Madonna Louise Ciccone on 8/16/58 in Bay City, Michigan. To New York in the late 70s; performed with the Pearl Lange and Alvin Ailey dance troupes. Starred in the films "Desperately Seeking Susan," "Shanghai Surprise" and "Who's That Girl?" Appeared in Broadway's "Speed The Plow." Married actor Sean Penn in 1985, divorced in 1989. The top female pop artist of the 80s.	
12/10/83†	**16**	11	1. Holiday	Sire 29478
4/14/84	**10**	15	2. **Borderline**	Sire 29354
9/01/84	**4**	12	3. **Lucky Star**	Sire 29177
11/24/84	**1**(6)	14	● 4. **Like A Virgin**	Sire 29210
2/16/85	**2**(2)	12	5. **Material Girl**	Sire 29083
3/16/85	**1**(1)	14	● 6. **Crazy For You** from the film "Vision Quest"	Geffen 29051
5/11/85	**5**	12	● 7. **Angel**	Sire 29008
8/17/85	**5**	11	8. **Dress You Up**	Sire 28919
4/19/86	**1**(1)	13	9. **Live To Tell** from the film "At Close Range"	Sire 28717
7/05/86	**1**(2)	13	10. **Papa Don't Preach**	Sire 28660
10/04/86	**3**	12	11. **True Blue**	Sire 28591
12/13/86†	**1**(1)	14	12. **Open Your Heart**	Sire 28508
3/28/87	**4**	12	13. **La Isla Bonita**	Sire 28425
7/18/87	**1**(1)	11	14. **Who's That Girl**	Sire 28341
9/19/87	**2**(3)	11	15. **Causing A Commotion** above 2: from the film "Who's That Girl"	Sire 28224
			JOHNNY MAESTRO	
			Born Johnny Mastrangelo on 5/7/39 in New York City. Lead singer of The Crests and Brooklyn Bridge.	
3/20/61	**20**	5	1. Model Girl	Coed 545
5/22/61	**33**	4	2. What A Surprise	Coed 549
			CLEDUS MAGGARD & The Citizen's Band	
			Cledus' real name: Jay Huguely; born in Quick Sand, Kentucky.	
1/24/76	**19**	9	1. The White Knight [N]	Mercury 73751
			MAGIC LANTERNS	
			Rock quintet from Lancashire, England. Albert Hammond was a member in 1971.	
11/30/68	**29**	5	1. Shame, Shame	Atlantic 2560

DATE	POS	WKS	ARTIST—RECORD TITLE	LABEL & NO.
			GEORGE MAHARIS	
			Born on 9/1/33 in New York City. Played Buz Murdock on TV's "Route 66."	
5/26/62	**25**	5	1. Teach Me Tonight there were 5 top 30 versions of this song in 1954	Epic 9504
			THE MAIN INGREDIENT	
			New York soul trio, formed as the Poets in 1964. Consisted of Donald McPherson (d: 7/4/71), Luther Simmons, Jr. and Tony Sylvester. First recorded as the Poets for Red Bird in 1965. McPherson replaced by Cuba Gooding in 1971.	
9/02/72	**3**	10	● 1. **Everybody Plays The Fool**	RCA 0731
3/16/74	**10**	14	● 2. **Just Don't Want To Be Lonely**	RCA 0205
8/10/74	**35**	2	3. Happiness Is Just Around The Bend	RCA 0305
			THE MAJORS	
			Philadelphia R&B group: Ricky Cordo (lead), Eugene Glass, Frank Troutt, Ronald Gathers and Idella Morris. Produced by Jerry Ragavoy.	
9/08/62	**22**	5	1. A Wonderful Dream	Imperial 5855
			MIRIAM MAKEBA	
			Born Zensi Miriam Makeba on 3/4/32 in Johannesburg, South Africa. Married to Hugh Masekela from 1964-66.	
10/28/67	**12**	8	1. Pata Pata [F]	Reprise 0606
			MALO	
			Latin-rock band formed by Jorge Santana (brother of Carlos).	
4/01/72	**18**	8	1. Suavecito	Warner 7559
			RICHARD MALTBY	
			Trumpeter/composer/bandleader born on 6/26/14 in Chicago.	
3/31/56	**14**	8	1. Themes From "The Man With The Golden Arm" [I] Top 100 #14 / Best Seller #15 / Juke Box #19 / Jockey #20 from the film "The Man With The Golden Arm"	Vik 0196
			MAMA CASS	
			Born Ellen Naomi Cohen on 9/19/41 in Baltimore. Died of a heart attack on 7/29/74 in London. Cass Elliot of The Mamas & The Papas.	
7/27/68	**12**	8	1. Dream A Little Dream Of Me with The Mamas & The Papas	Dunhill 4145
8/02/69	**30**	7	2. It's Getting Better	Dunhill 4195
11/15/69	**36**	3	3. Make Your Own Kind Of Music	Dunhill 4214
			MAMA CASS ELLIOT	
			THE MAMAS & THE PAPAS	
			Quartet formed in New York City in 1963. Consisted of John Phillips (b: 8/30/35, Paris Island, SC); Holly Michelle Gilliam Phillips (b: 6/4/45, Long Beach, CA); Dennis Doherty (b: 11/29/41, Halifax, Nova Scotia) and Cass Elliot. Phillips had been in the Journeymen, married Michelle Gilliam in 1962. Elliot had been in the Mugwumps with Doherty and future Lovin' Spoonful member Zal Yanovsky. Group moved to Los Angeles in 1964. Disbanded in 1968, reunited briefly in 1971. Michelle Phillips in films "Dillinger" and "Valentino." Formed new group in 1982: John and daughter, actress MacKenzie Phillips, Dennis Doherty and Spanky McFarlane of Spanky & Our Gang.	
2/05/66	**4**	13	● 1. **California Dreamin'**	Dunhill 4020
4/16/66	**1**(3)	10	● 2. **Monday, Monday**	Dunhill 4026
7/09/66	**5**	8	3. **I Saw Her Again**	Dunhill 4031
11/05/66	**24**	4	4. Look Through My Window	Dunhill 4050

DATE	POS	WKS	ARTIST—RECORD TITLE	LABEL & NO.
12/17/66†	**5**	9	5. **Words Of Love**	Dunhill 4057
3/04/67	**2**(3)	9	6. **Dedicated To The One I Love**	Dunhill 4077
5/13/67	**5**	7	7. **Creeque Alley**	Dunhill 4083
9/02/67	**20**	5	8. Twelve Thirty (Young Girls Are Coming To The Canyon)	Dunhill 4099
11/04/67	**26**	5	9. Glad To Be Unhappy all of above: produced by Lou Adler	Dunhill 4107
			MELISSA MANCHESTER	
			Born on 2/15/51 in the Bronx. Vocalist/pianist/composer. Studied with Paul Simon at University School of the Arts in the early 70s. Former back-up singer for Bette Midler.	
6/14/75	**6**	11	1. **Midnight Blue**	Arista 0116
10/18/75	**30**	5	2. Just Too Many People	Arista 0146
2/28/76	**27**	4	3. Just You And I	Arista 0168
1/06/79	**10**	14	4. **Don't Cry Out Loud**	Arista 0373
11/24/79	**39**	2	5. Pretty Girls	Arista 0456
4/05/80	**32**	5	6. Fire In The Morning	Arista 0485
7/10/82	**5**	15	7. **You Should Hear How She Talks About You**	Arista 0676
			HENRY MANCINI	
			Born on 4/16/24 in Cleveland. Leading film-TV composer/arranger/conductor. Staff composer for Universal Pictures, 1952-58. Won more Oscars (4) and Grammys (20) than any other pop artist.	
4/18/60	**21**	8	1. Mr. Lucky [I]	RCA 7705
11/13/61	**11**	16	2. Moon River from the film "Breakfast At Tiffany's"	RCA 7916
3/02/63	**33**	10	3. Days Of Wine And Roses	RCA 8120
1/25/64	**36**	4	4. Charade	RCA 8256
5/09/64	**31**	2	5. The Pink Panther Theme [I]	RCA 8286
5/24/69	**1**(2)	12	● 6. **Love Theme From Romeo & Juliet** **[I]**	RCA 0131
2/06/71	**13**	8	7. Theme From Love Story [I] above 5: from films and TV shows of the same title	RCA 9927
			STEVE MANDELL - see ERIC WEISSBERG	
			BARBARA MANDRELL	
			Born on 12/25/48 in Houston. Country singer. Host of own TV variety series, "Barbara Mandrell & The Mandrell Sisters," 1980-82.	
5/12/79	**31**	5	1. (If Loving You Is Wrong) I Don't Want To Be Right	ABC 12451
			MANFRED MANN	
			Rock group formed in England in 1964: Manfred Mann (real name: Michael Lubowitz; keyboards), Paul Jones (vocals), Mike Hugg (drums), Michael Vickers (guitar) and Tom McGuiness (bass). Manfred Mann formed his new Earth Band in 1971, featuring Mick Rogers (vocals), Colin Pattenden (bass) and Chris Slade (drums). Mick replaced by Chris Thompson (vocals, guitar) in 1976. Thompson also recorded with own group, Night, in 1979.	
9/12/64	**1**(2)	12	1. **Do Wah Diddy Diddy**	Ascot 2157
11/28/64†	**12**	9	2. Sha La La	Ascot 2165
7/23/66	**29**	5	3. Pretty Flamingo	United Art. 50040
3/09/68	**10**	10	4. **Mighty Quinn (Quinn The Eskimo)**	Mercury 72770

DATE	POS	WKS	ARTIST—RECORD TITLE	LABEL & NO.
			MANFRED MANN'S EARTH BAND:	
12/18/76†	**1(1)**	15	● 5. **Blinded By The Light**	Warner 8252
			written by Bruce Springsteen	
6/04/77	**40**	1	6. Spirit In The Night [R]	Warner 8355
			re-mixed version of their 1976 hit (POS 97)	
2/18/84	**22**	8	7. Runner	Arista 9143
			CHUCK MANGIONE	
			Born on 11/29/40 in Rochester, New York. Flugelhorn/bandleader/composer. Recorded with older brother Gaspare ("Gap") as the Jazz Brothers for Riverside in 1960. To New York City in 1965, with Maynard Ferguson, Kai Winding, and Art Blakey's Jazz Messengers.	
3/18/78	**4**	16	1. **Feels So Good** [I]	A&M 2001
2/16/80	**18**	9	2. Give It All You Got [I]	A&M 2211
			featured song by ABC Sports for the 1980 Winter Olympics	
			THE MANHATTAN TRANSFER	
			Versatile vocal harmony quartet formed in New York City in 1972: Tim Hauser, Alan Paul, Janis Siegel and Cheryl Bentyne (replaced Laurel Masse in 1979).	
11/01/75	**22**	5	1. Operator	Atlantic 3292
5/31/80	**30**	4	2. Twilight Zone/Twilight Tone	Atlantic 3649
6/13/81	**7**	13	3. **Boy From New York City**	Atlantic 3816
11/05/83	**40**	2	4. Spice Of Life	Atlantic 89786
			THE MANHATTANS	
			Soul group from Jersey City, New Jersey. Consisted of George "Smitty" Smith (d: 1970, spinal meningitis; lead), Winfred "Blue" Lovett (bass), Edward "Sonny" Bivins and Kenneth "Wally" Kelly (tenors) and Richard Taylor (baritone). Smith replaced by Gerald Alston in 1971. First recorded for Piney in 1962. Taylor (aka Abdul Rashid Talhah) left in 1976; died 12/7/87 (47) following a lengthy illness. Alston began solo career in 1988.	
2/15/75	**37**	2	1. Don't Take Your Love	Columbia 10045
5/29/76	**1(2)**	17	▲ 2. **Kiss And Say Goodbye**	Columbia 10310
5/31/80	**5**	14	● 3. **Shining Star**	Columbia 11222
			BARRY MANILOW	
			Born Barry Alan Pincus on 6/17/49 in Brooklyn. Vocalist/pianist/composer. Studied at Juilliard, New York College of Music. Wrote jingles. On the WCBS-TV series "Callback." Worked at Continental Baths, New York; in 1972, met Bette Midler, and became her director/arranger/accompanist. Produced her first two albums. Sang jingles for Dr. Pepper, Pepsi and McDonalds ("You Deserve A Break Today").	
12/07/74†	**1(1)**	12	● 1. **Mandy**	Bell 45613
			formerly charted by Scott English as "Brandy"	
3/29/75	**12**	8	2. It's A Miracle	Arista 0108
7/26/75	**6**	13	3. **Could It Be Magic**	Arista 0126
			inspired by Chopin's prelude in C minor	
11/22/75†	**1(1)**	16	● 4. **I Write The Songs**	Arista 0157
4/10/76	**10**	10	5. **Tryin' To Get The Feeling Again**	Arista 0172
10/09/76	**29**	5	6. This One's For You	Arista 0206
12/25/76†	**10**	13	7. **Weekend In New England**	Arista 0212
5/28/77	**1(1)**	13	● 8. **Looks Like We Made It**	Arista 0244
10/22/77	**23**	5	9. Daybreak	Arista 0273
2/18/78	**3**	16	● 10. **Can't Smile Without You**	Arista 0305

DATE	POS	WKS	ARTIST—RECORD TITLE	LABEL & NO.
6/10/78	**19**	4	11. Even Now	Arista 0330
7/08/78	**8**	9	• 12. **Copacabana (At The Copa)**	Arista 0339
10/07/78	**11**	10	13. Ready To Take A Chance Again above 2: from the movie "Foul Play"	Arista 0357
1/06/79	**9**	10	14. **Somewhere In The Night**	Arista 0382
10/20/79	**9**	11	15. **Ships**	Arista 0464
2/02/80	**20**	7	16. When I Wanted You	Arista 0481
5/17/80	**36**	4	17. I Don't Want To Walk Without You	Arista 0501
12/06/80†	**10**	11	18. **I Made It Through The Rain** all of above: produced by Manilow and Ron Dante	Arista 0566
10/17/81	**15**	10	19. The Old Songs	Arista 0633
1/23/82	**21**	7	20. Somewhere Down The Road	Arista 0658
4/24/82	**32**	3	21. Let's Hang On	Arista 0675
9/18/82	**38**	2	22. Oh Julie	Arista 0698
1/15/83	**39**	2	23. Memory theme from the musical "Cats"	Arista 1025
4/09/83	**26**	7	24. Some Kind Of Friend	Arista 1046
11/26/83†	**18**	10	25. Read 'Em And Weep	Arista 9101
			BARRY MANN	
			Born Barry Iberman on 2/9/39 in Brooklyn. One of pop music's most prolific songwriters. Wrote with wife, Cynthia Weil, "You've Lost That Lovin' Feelin'," "(You're My) Soul & Inspiration," "Kicks," "Hungry," "We Gotta Get Out Of This Place," and many others.	
8/21/61	**7**	9	1. **Who Put The Bomp (In The Bomp, Bomp, Bomp)** **[N]**	ABC-Para. 10237
			CARL MANN	
			Born on 8/24/42 in Huntingdon, Tennessee. Rockabilly singer/pianist. Toured with Carl Perkins from 1962-64. Left music from 1967-74.	
7/27/59	**25**	6	1. Mona Lisa	Phillips 3539
			GLORIA MANN	
			Her son, Bob Rosenberg, is the leader of Will To Power.	
2/12/55	**18**	2	1. Earth Angel (Will You Be Mine) Juke Box #18 / Best Seller #24	Sound 109
12/24/55†	**19**	8	2. Teen Age Prayer Best Seller #19 / Top 100 #21	Sound 126
			HERBIE MANN	
			Born Herbert Jay Solomon on 4/16/30 in Brooklyn. Saxophonist/flutist/reeds. First recorded with Mat Mathews Quintet for Brunswick in 1953. First recorded as a solo for Bethlehem in 1954.	
4/26/75	**14**	6	1. Hijack	Atlantic 3246
3/17/79	**26**	6	2. Superman	Atlantic 3547
			MANTOVANI	
			Born Annunzio Paolo Mantovani on 11/15/05 in Venice, Italy. Died on 3/29/80. Played classical violin in England before forming his own orchestra in the early 30s. Achieved international fame 20 years later with his 40-piece orchestra and distinctive "cascading strings" sound.	
7/22/57	**12**	14	1. Around The World [I] Jockey #12 / Best Seller #23 / Top 100 #25 from the film "Around The World In 80 Days"	London 1746

DATE	POS	WKS	ARTIST—RECORD TITLE	LABEL & NO.
1/23/61	**31**	2	2. Main Theme from Exodus (Ari's Theme) [I] from the film "Exodus"	London 1953
			THE MARATHONS - see THE VIBRATIONS	
			THE MARCELS R&B group from Pittsburgh. Consisted of Cornelius "Nini" Harp (lead singer), Ronald "Bingo" Mundy and Gene Bricker (tenors), Richard Knauss (baritone) and Fred Johnson (bass). Knauss replaced by Allen Johnson, and Bricker replaced by Walt Maddox, mid-1961. Mundy left in late 1961.	
3/20/61	**1**(3)	11	1. **Blue Moon** there were 3 Top 10 versions of this classic tune in 1935	Colpix 186
10/30/61	**7**	8	2. **Heartaches** #12 hit for Guy Lombardo in 1931; #1 hit for Ted Weems in 1947	Colpix 612
			LITTLE PEGGY MARCH Born Margaret Battavio on 3/7/48 in Lansdale, Pennsylvania. Lived in Germany from 1969-81. Youngest female singer to have a #1 single on the pop charts.	
4/06/63	**1**(3)	11	1. **I Will Follow Him**	RCA 8139
6/29/63	**32**	3	2. I Wish I Were A Princess	RCA 8189
9/28/63	**26**	4	3. Hello Heartache, Goodbye Love	RCA 8221
			BOBBY MARCHAN Born on 4/30/30 in Youngstown, Ohio. Vocalist with Huey "Piano" Smith & The Clowns.	
7/11/60	**31**	4	1. There's Something On Your Mind, Part 2 [N]	Fire 1022
			BENNY MARDONES Savage, Maryland native.	
7/12/80	**11**	12	1. Into The Night	Polydor 2091
			ERNIE MARESCA Born on 4/21/39 in the Bronx. Songwriter/vocalist. Wrote "Runaround Sue" and "The Wanderer."	
4/21/62	**6**	9	1. **Shout! Shout! (Knock Yourself Out)**	Seville 117
			TEENA MARIE White funk singer/composer/keyboardist/guitarist/producer/actress, born Mary Christine Brockert in Santa Monica in 1957; raised in Venice, California.	
1/17/81	**37**	3	1. I Need Your Lovin'	Gordy 7189
2/02/85	**4**	13	2. **Lovergirl**	Epic 04619
			THE MARK IV Chicago-based pop/rock quartet.	
2/09/59	**24**	7	1. I Got A Wife [N]	Mercury 71403
			THE MARKETTS Hollywood, California instrumental surf quintet.	
2/17/62	**31**	3	1. Surfer's Stomp [I]	Liberty 55401
12/28/63†	**3**	11	2. **Out Of Limits** **[I]** surf-ized version of the "Outer Limits" TV series theme	Warner 5391
2/26/66	**17**	5	3. Batman Theme [I] from the hit TV series	Warner 5696

DATE	POS	WKS	ARTIST—RECORD TITLE	LABEL & NO.
			MAR-KEYS	
			Instrumental group formed in Memphis in 1958. Consisted of Charles Axton (tenor sax), Wayne Jackson (trumpet), Don Nix (baritone sax), Jerry Lee "Smoochie" Smith (keyboards), Steve Cropper (guitar), Donald "Duck" Dunn (bass) and Terry Johnson (drums). Staff musicians at Stax/Volt. Cropper and Dunn later joined Booker T. & The MG's. Also known as the Memphis Horns.	
7/17/61	**3**	12	1. **Last Night** **[I]**	Satellite 107
			PIGMEAT MARKHAM	
			Born Dewey Markham in Durham, North Carolina, in 1906. Died on 12/13/81 in the Bronx. Stage and TV comedian.	
7/06/68	**19**	4	1. Here Comes The Judge [N]	Chess 2049
			ZIGGY MARLEY & THE MELODY MAKERS	
			Kingston, Jamaica reggae group consisting of the late reggae master Bob Marley's children: David (Ziggy), Stephen, Cedella and Sharon.	
7/09/88	**39**	1	1. Tomorrow People	Virgin 99347
			MARION MARLOWE	
7/16/55	**14**	2	1. The Man In The Raincoat Jockey #14 / Juke Box #18	Cadence 1266
			THE MARMALADE	
			Scottish pop quintet led by vocalist Dean Ford (real name: Thomas McAleese).	
4/04/70	**10**	11	1. **Reflections Of My Life**	London 20058
			M/A/R/R/S	
			U.K.-based electro-funk group featuring 2 pairs of brothers: Martyn & Steve Young, with Alex & Rudi Kane. Includes mixers: Chris "CJ" Mackintosh and DJ Dave Dorrell.	
1/16/88	**13**	11	● 1. Pump Up The Volume	4th & B'way 7452
			THE MARSHALL TUCKER BAND	
			Southern rock band formed in South Carolina in 1971: Doug Gray (lead singer), Toy Caldwell (lead guitarist), George McCorkle (rhythm guitar), Paul Riddle (drums), Jerry Eubanks (sax) and Tommy Caldwell (bass; d: 4/28/80). Franklin Wilkie replaced Caldwell.	
12/20/75	**38**	2	1. Fire On The Mountain	Capricorn 0244
4/16/77	**14**	13	2. Heard It In A Love Song	Capricorn 0270
			RALPH MARTERIE	
			Born on 12/24/14 in Naples, Italy (grew up in Chicago). Died on 10/8/78. Very popular early 50s bandleader, played trumpet in the 40s for Enric Madriguera, and other bands.	
3/30/57	**25**	3	1. Tricky [I] Jockey #25 / Top 100 #37	Mercury 71050
5/13/57	**10**	6	2. **Shish-Kebab** **[I]** Jockey #10 / Top 100 #29 same tune as Armenian Jazz Sextet's "Harem Dance"	Mercury 71092

DATE	POS	WKS	ARTIST—RECORD TITLE	LABEL & NO.
			MARTHA & THE VANDELLAS	
			Soul group from Detroit, organized by Martha Reeves (b: 7/18/41) in 1962 with Annette Beard and Rosalind Ashford. Reeves had been in the Del-Phis, recorded for Checkmate. Worked at Motown as A&R secretary, sang back-up. Vandellas did back-up on Marvin Gaye's "Stubborn Kind Of Fellow." Beard left group in 1964, replaced by Betty Kelly. Group disbanded from 1969-71, re-formed with Martha and sister Lois Reeves, and Sandra Tilley in 1971. Martha Reeves went solo in late 1972.	
5/18/63	**29**	8	1. Come And Get These Memories	Gordy 7014
8/17/63	**4**	11	2. **Heat Wave**	Gordy 7022
12/07/63†	**8**	9	3. **Quicksand**	Gordy 7025
9/05/64	**2**(2)	11	4. **Dancing In The Street**	Gordy 7033
12/26/64†	**34**	4	5. Wild One	Gordy 7036
3/13/65	**8**	8	6. **Nowhere To Run**	Gordy 7039
9/11/65	**36**	2	7. You've Been In Love Too Long	Gordy 7045
2/19/66	**22**	7	8. My Baby Loves Me	Gordy 7048
11/12/66	**9**	7	9. **I'm Ready For Love**	Gordy 7056
3/18/67	**10**	10	10. **Jimmy Mack** 1-3, 6, 9-10: written by Holland, Dozier, Holland	Gordy 7058
9/09/67	**25**	6	11. Love Bug Leave My Heart Alone	Gordy 7062
12/02/67	**11**	9	12. Honey Chile	Gordy 7067
			MARTHA REEVES & THE VANDELLAS	
			BOBBI MARTIN	
			Born Barbara Anne Martin on 11/29/43 in Brooklyn; raised in Baltimore. Toured the Far East with Bob Hope's Christmas Shows.	
1/02/65	**19**	7	1. Don't Forget I Still Love You	Coral 62426
4/11/70	**13**	10	2. For The Love Of Him	United Art. 50602
			DEAN MARTIN	
			Born Dino Crocetti on 6/7/17 in Steubenville, Ohio. Vocalist/actor. To California in 1937, worked local clubs. Teamed with comedian Jerry Lewis in Atlantic City in 1946. First film, "My Friend Irma" in 1949. Team broke up after 16th film "Hollywood Or Bust" in 1956. Appeared in many films since then; own TV series from 1965-74.	
12/03/55†	**1**(6)	19	1. **Memories Are Made Of This** Jockey #1(6) / Best Seller #1(5) / Top 100 #1(5) / Juke Box #1(4) backed by The Easy Riders	Capitol 3295
4/07/56	**27**	4	2. Innamorata from the film "Artists & Models"	Capitol 3352
5/26/56	**22**	6	3. Standing On The Corner Jockey #22 / Top 100 #29 from the musical "The Most Happy Fella"	Capitol 3414
4/07/58	**4**	18	4. **Return To Me** Best Seller #4 / Top 100 #4 / Jockey #4	Capitol 3894
8/04/58	**30**	3	5. Angel Baby Hot 100 #30 / Best Seller #43	Capitol 3988
8/11/58	**12**	10	6. Volare (Nel Blu Dipinto Di Blu) Best Seller #12 / Hot 100 #15	Capitol 4028
7/11/64	**1**(1)	13	● 7. **Everybody Loves Somebody**	Reprise 0281
10/17/64	**6**	8	8. **The Door Is Still Open To My Heart**	Reprise 0307
1/09/65	**25**	5	9. You're Nobody Till Somebody Loves You	Reprise 0333
3/13/65	**22**	5	10. Send Me The Pillow You Dream On	Reprise 0344

DATE	POS	WKS	ARTIST—RECORD TITLE	LABEL & NO.
6/12/65	**32**	3	11. (Remember Me) I'm The One Who Loves You	Reprise 0369
8/21/65	**21**	7	12. Houston	Reprise 0393
11/13/65	**10**	8	13. **I Will**	Reprise 0415
3/05/66	**32**	4	14. Somewhere There's A Someone	Reprise 0443
6/11/66	**35**	1	15. Come Running Back	Reprise 0466
7/22/67	**25**	4	16. In The Chapel In The Moonlight	Reprise 0601
9/09/67	**38**	2	17. Little Ole Wine Drinker, Me 7-17: produced by Jimmy Bowen	Reprise 0608
			MARILYN MARTIN	
			Raised in Louisville. Background vocalist for Stevie Nicks, Tom Petty, Kenny Loggins and Joe Walsh.	
10/12/85	**1(1)**	16	1. **Separate Lives** **PHIL COLLINS & MARILYN MARTIN** love theme from the film "White Nights"	Atlantic 89498
2/22/86	**28**	6	2. Night Moves	Atlantic 89465
			MOON MARTIN	
			Real name: John Martin. Singer/songwriter/guitarist from Oklahoma. Wrote Robert Palmer's hit "Bad Case Of Loving You."	
9/22/79	**30**	4	1. Rolene	Capitol 4765
			STEVE MARTIN	
			Born in Waco, Texas in 1945. Raised in California. Popular television and film comedian. Comedy writer for the "Smothers Brothers Comedy Hour" TV show and others.	
7/08/78	**17**	7	● 1. King Tut [N] with The Toot Uncommons	Warner 8577
			TONY MARTIN	
			Born Alvin Morris, Jr. on 12/25/12 in Oakland. Vocalist/actor. In many films from 1936-57, including "Casbah" in 1948. Married to actress Cyd Charisse.	
5/26/56	**10**	11	1. **Walk Hand In Hand** Top 100 #10 / Jockey #13 / Juke Box #16 / Best Seller #21	RCA 6493
			TRADE MARTIN	
			Born on 11/19/43 in Union City, New Jersey.	
11/17/62	**28**	4	1. That Stranger Used To Be My Girl	Coed 570
			VINCE MARTIN with THE TARRIERS	
			Also see The Tarriers.	
10/13/56	**9**	15	1. **Cindy, Oh Cindy** Juke Box #9 / Best Seller #12 / Top 100 #12 / Jockey #12	Glory 247
			WINK MARTINDALE	
			Born Winston Martindale in Jackson, Tennessee in 1933. TV game-show host.	
9/28/59	**7**	12	1. **Deck Of Cards** **[S]**	Dot 15968
			NANCY MARTINEZ	
			Dance singer/actress born in Quebec, Canada.	
12/06/86	**32**	8	1. For Tonight	Atlantic 89371

DATE	POS	WKS	ARTIST—RECORD TITLE	LABEL & NO.
			AL MARTINO	
			Born Alfred Cini on 10/7/27 in Philadelphia. Encouraged by success of boyhood friend, Mario Lanza. Winner on Arthur Godfrey's "Talent Scouts" in 1952. Portrayed singer Johnny Fontane in the 1972 film "The Godfather."	
5/04/63	**3**	11	1. **I Love You Because**	Capitol 4930
8/17/63	**15**	8	2. Painted, Tainted Rose	Capitol 5000
11/16/63	**22**	6	3. Living A Lie	Capitol 5060
2/15/64	**9**	8	4. **I Love You More And More Every Day**	Capitol 5108
5/30/64	**20**	6	5. Tears And Roses	Capitol 5183
9/12/64	**33**	4	6. Always Together	Capitol 5239
12/18/65†	**15**	9	7. Spanish Eyes	Capitol 5542
4/02/66	**30**	4	8. Think I'll Go Somewhere And Cry Myself To Sleep	Capitol 5598
6/17/67	**27**	5	9. Mary In The Morning	Capitol 5904
2/08/75	**17**	8	10. To The Door Of The Sun (Alle Porte Del Sole) 2-4, 6, 8-10: conducted by Peter DeAngelis	Capitol 3987
12/06/75	**33**	4	11. Volare	Capitol 4134
			THE MARVELETTES	
			R&B group from Inkster High School, Inkster, Michigan. Formed in 1960 by Gladys Horton, with Georgeanna Marie Tillman Gordon (d: 1/6/80 of lupus), Wanda Young, Katherine Anderson and Juanita Cowart. Young and Horton both sang lead. Cowart and Gordon left in 1965, Horton left in 1967, replaced by Anne Bogan. Disbanded, 1969.	
10/16/61	**1**(1)	15	1. **Please Mr. Postman**	Tamla 54046
3/03/62	**34**	1	2. Twistin' Postman	Tamla 54054
5/26/62	**7**	11	3. **Playboy**	Tamla 54060
9/01/62	**17**	7	4. Beechwood 4-5789	Tamla 54065
12/05/64†	**25**	8	5. Too Many Fish In The Sea	Tamla 54105
7/03/65	**34**	1	6. I'll Keep Holding On	Tamla 54116
1/29/66	**7**	8	7. **Don't Mess With Bill**	Tamla 54126
2/18/67	**13**	7	8. The Hunter Gets Captured By The Game	Tamla 54143
5/20/67	**23**	5	9. When You're Young And In Love	Tamla 54150
1/06/68	**17**	8	10. My Baby Must Be A Magician	Tamla 54158
			THE MARVELOWS	
			R&B group from Chicago Heights, Illinois. First known as the Mystics. Included Melvin Mason (lead), Willie "Sonny" Stevenson, Frank Paden and Johnny Paden. Added Jesse Smith in 1964.	
7/03/65	**37**	1	1. I Do	ABC-Para. 10629
			RICHARD MARX	
			Chicago-bred, pop-rock singer/songwriter. Professional jingle singer since age 5. Backing singer for Lionel Richie. Co-wrote Kenny Rogers' hit "What About Me." On 1/8/89, married Cynthia Rhodes, lead singer of Animotion.	
7/11/87	**3**	12	1. **Don't Mean Nothing**	Manhattan 50079
10/17/87	**3**	13	2. **Should've Known Better** backing vocals: Fee Waybill (Tubes) & Timothy B. Schmit	Manhattan 50083
1/30/88	**2**(2)	15	3. **Endless Summer Nights**	EMI-Man. 50113
6/11/88	**1**(1)	14	4. **Hold On To The Nights**	EMI-Man. 50106

DATE	POS	WKS	ARTIST—RECORD TITLE	LABEL & NO.
			MARY JANE GIRLS	
			Female "funk & roll" quartet: Joanne McDuffie, Candice Ghant, Kim Wuletick and Yvette Marine. Formed and produced by Rick James.	
4/27/85	**7**	12	1. **In My House**	Gordy 1741
			HUGH MASEKELA	
			Born Hugh Ramapolo Masekela on 4/4/39 in Wilbank, South Africa. Trumpeter/ bandleader/arranger. Played trumpet since age 14. To England in 1959; New York City in 1960. Married to Miriam Makeba from 1964-66. Formed own band in 1964.	
6/22/68	**1**(2)	10	● 1. **Grazing In The Grass** **[I]**	Uni 55066
			MASHMAKHAN	
			Montreal rock quartet led by Pierre Senecal.	
11/07/70	**31**	4	1. As The Years Go By	Epic 10634
			BARBARA MASON	
			Born on 8/9/47 in Philadelphia. First recorded for Crusader in 1964. Wrote all of her Arctic hits.	
6/12/65	**5**	10	1. **Yes, I'm Ready**	Arctic 105
9/04/65	**27**	5	2. Sad, Sad Girl	Arctic 108
2/24/73	**31**	5	3. Give Me Your Love	Buddah 331
12/28/74†	**28**	4	4. From His Woman To You	Buddah 441
			DAVE MASON	
			Born on 5/10/46 in Worchester, England. Vocalist/composer/guitarist. Original member of Traffic.	
10/08/77	**12**	10	1. We Just Disagree	Columbia 10575
7/08/78	**39**	2	2. Will You Still Love Me Tomorrow	Columbia 10749
			TOBIN MATHEWS & Co.	
			Guitarist from Calumet City, Illinois.	
11/14/60	**30**	4	1. Ruby Duby Du [I] from the movie "Key Witness"	Chief 7022
			JOHNNY MATHIS	
			Born on 9/30/35 in San Francisco. Studied opera from age 13. Track scholarship at the San Francisco State College. Invited to Olympic try-outs, chose singing career instead. To New York City in 1956. Ranks behind only Elvis Presley and Frank Sinatra as the top album artist of the rock era.	
5/06/57	**14**	20	1. Wonderful! Wonderful! Jockey #14 / Top 100 #17 / Best Seller #18	Columbia 40784
5/20/57	**5**	23	2. **It's Not For Me To Say** Top 100 #5 / Jockey #5 / Best Seller #6 from the movie "Lizzie"	Columbia 40851
9/16/57	**1**(1)	22	3. **Chances Are/** Jockey #1 / Best Seller #4 / Top 100 #5	
10/14/57	**9**	14	4. The Twelfth Of Never Jockey #9 / Top 100 #51	Columbia 40993
12/16/57	**22**	7	5. Wild Is The Wind/ Jockey #22 / Best Seller #30 / Top 100 #37 from the film of the same title	
1/06/58	**21**	1	6. No Love (But Your Love) Jockey #21 / Best Seller #37 / Top 100 #48	Columbia 41060
2/10/58	**22**	1	7. Come To Me Jockey #22 / Best Seller #40 / Top 100 #43 from the TV production of the same title	Columbia 41082

DATE	POS	WKS	ARTIST—RECORD TITLE	LABEL & NO.
5/05/58	**21**	7	8. All The Time/ Jockey #21 / Best Seller #30 / Top 100 #42 from the Broadway musical "Oh Captain!"	
5/19/58	**21**	2	9. Teacher, Teacher Jockey #21 / Best Seller #30 / Top 100 #43	Columbia 41152
7/14/58	**14**	11	10. A Certain Smile Jockey #14 / Top 100 #19 / Best Seller #21 from the film of the same title	Columbia 41193
10/20/58	**21**	8	11. Call Me	Columbia 41253
5/04/59	**35**	3	12. Someone	Columbia 41355
7/20/59	**20**	8	13. Small World from the Broadway musical "Gypsy"	Columbia 41410
10/19/59	**12**	12	14. Misty the Erroll Garner classic charted at POS 30 in 1954	Columbia 41483
3/28/60	**25**	5	15. Starbright	Columbia 41583
10/13/62	**6**	9	16. **Gina**	Columbia 42582
2/09/63	**9**	10	17. **What Will Mary Say**	Columbia 42666
6/08/63	**30**	4	18. Every Step Of The Way	Columbia 42799
4/22/78	**1**(1)	11	• 19. **Too Much, Too Little, Too Late** **JOHNNY MATHIS/DENIECE WILLIAMS**	Columbia 10693
5/29/82	**38**	3	20. Friends In Love **DIONNE WARWICK & JOHNNY MATHIS**	Arista 0673
			MATTHEWS' SOUTHERN COMFORT English rock sextet; Ian Matthews, lead singer.	
4/24/71	**23**	9	1. Woodstock	Decca 32774
			IAN MATTHEWS Born Ian Matthew MacDonald in Lincolnshire, England in 1946. Founder of Fairport Convention and Matthews' Southern Comfort. From 1984-87 in A&R for Island and Windham Hill record labels.	
12/16/78†	**13**	12	1. Shake It	Mushroom 7039
			PAUL MAURIAT French conductor/arranger; born in 1925.	
1/27/68	**1**(5)	15	• 1. **Love Is Blue** **[I]**	Philips 40495
			ROBERT MAXWELL Born on 4/19/21 in New York City. Jazz harpist/composer. With NBC Symphony under Toscanini at age 17. Also see Mickey Mozart.	
4/18/64	**15**	7	1. Shangri-La [I]	Decca 25622
			NATHANIEL MAYER & The Fabulous Twilights Detroit R&B vocalist.	
5/26/62	**22**	6	1. Village Of Love	Fortune 449
			CURTIS MAYFIELD Born on 6/3/42 in Chicago. Soul singer/songwriter/producer. With Jerry Butler in the gospel group Northern Jubilee Singers. Joined The Impressions in 1957. Wrote most of the hits for The Impressions, Jerry Butler, and himself. Own labels: Windy C, Mayfield, and Curtom. Went solo in 1970. Scored "Superfly," "Claudine," "A Piece Of The Action," "Short Eyes" film soundtracks. Appeared in "Short Eyes."	
1/02/71	**29**	4	1. (Don't Worry) If There's A Hell Below We're All Going To Go	Curtom 1955

DATE	POS	WKS	ARTIST—RECORD TITLE	LABEL & NO.
9/23/72	**4**	11	● 2. **Freddie's Dead**	Curtom 1975
11/25/72†	**8**	13	● 3. **Superfly**	Curtom 1978
			above 2: from the film "Superfly"	
8/25/73	**39**	2	4. Future Shock	Curtom 1987
8/03/74	**40**	1	5. Kung Fu	Curtom 1999
			MAC McANALLY	
			Born Lyman McAnally, Jr. in 1957 in Red Bay, Alabama. Session singer/guitarist.	
8/13/77	**37**	2	1. It's A Crazy World	Ariola Am. 7665
			C.W. McCALL	
			Born William Fries on 11/15/28 in Audubon, Iowa. The character "C.W. McCall" was created for the Metz Bread Company. Fries was their advertising man. Elected mayor of Ouray, Colorado in the early 80s.	
3/22/75	**40**	1	1. Wolf Creek Pass [N]	MGM 14764
12/13/75†	**1**(1)	11	● 2. **Convoy** **[N]**	MGM 14839
			PETER McCANN	
			Connecticut native; staffwriter with ABC Music.	
5/21/77	**5**	16	● 1. **Do You Wanna Make Love**	20th Century 2335
			PAUL McCARTNEY	
			Born James Paul McCartney on 6/18/42 in Liverpool, England. Writer of over 50 top 10 singles. Founding member/bass guitarist of The Beatles. Married Linda Eastman on 3/12/69. First solo album in 1970. Formed group Wings in 1971 with wife Linda (keyboards, backing vocals), Denny Laine (ex-Moody Blues; guitar) and Denny Seiwell (drums). Henry McCullough (guitar) joined in 1972. Seiwell and McCullough left in 1973. In 1975, Joe English (drums) and ex-Thunderclap Newman guitarist James McCulloch (d: 9/27/79 [26] of heart failure) joined; both left in 1977. Wings officially disbanded in April of 1981.	
3/13/71	**5**	11	1. **Another Day**	Apple 1829
8/21/71	**1**(1)	12	● 2. **Uncle Albert/Admiral Halsey**	Apple 1837
			PAUL & LINDA McCARTNEY	
			WINGS:	
3/25/72	**21**	6	3. Give Ireland Back To The Irish	Apple 1847
7/08/72	**28**	3	4. Mary Had A Little Lamb	Apple 1851
12/30/72†	**10**	9	5. **Hi, Hi, Hi**	Apple 1857
4/28/73	**1**(4)	15	● 6. **My Love**	Apple 1861
7/21/73	**2**(3)	12	● 7. **Live And Let Die**	Apple 1863
			from the James Bond film of the same title	
12/08/73†	**10**	10	8. **Helen Wheels**	Apple 1869
2/23/74	**7**	10	9. **Jet**	Apple 1871
5/04/74	**1**(1)	13	● 10. **Band On The Run**	Apple 1873
11/23/74†	**3**	10	11. **Junior's Farm/**	
12/14/74†	**17**	8	12. Sally G	Apple 1875
6/07/75	**1**(1)	11	● 13. **Listen To What The Man Said**	Capitol 4091
10/25/75	**39**	2	14. Letting Go	Capitol 4145
11/15/75	**12**	6	15. Venus And Mars Rock Show	Capitol 4175
4/17/76	**1**(5)	15	● 16. **Silly Love Songs**	Capitol 4256
7/17/76	**3**	11	● 17. **Let 'Em In**	Capitol 4293

DATE	POS	WKS	ARTIST—RECORD TITLE	LABEL & NO.
2/19/77	**10**	11	18. **Maybe I'm Amazed** live version of song from McCartney's first solo album	Capitol 4385
12/24/77†	**33**	4	19. Girls' School flip side "Mull of Kintyre" is one of England's all-time biggest selling singles	Capitol 4504
4/08/78	**1**(2)	12	20. **With A Little Luck**	Capitol 4559
7/15/78	**25**	5	21. I've Had Enough	Capitol 4594
10/14/78	**39**	2	22. London Town	Capitol 4625
3/31/79	**5**	13	• 23. **Goodnight Tonight**	Columbia 10939
6/30/79	**20**	6	24. Getting Closer	Columbia 11020
9/22/79	**29**	4	25. Arrow Through Me	Columbia 11070
5/10/80	**1**(3)	16	• 26. **Coming Up (Live at Glasgow)** 6, 8-12 & 26: **PAUL McCARTNEY & WINGS**	Columbia 11263
4/10/82	**1**(7)	15	• 27. **Ebony And Ivory** **PAUL McCARTNEY with STEVIE WONDER** **PAUL McCARTNEY:**	Columbia 02860
7/17/82	**10**	11	28. **Take It Away**	Columbia 03018
11/13/82†	**2**(3)	14	• 29. **The Girl Is Mine** **MICHAEL JACKSON/PAUL McCARTNEY**	Epic 03288
10/15/83	**1**(6)	18	• 30. **Say Say Say** **PAUL McCARTNEY & MICHAEL JACKSON**	Columbia 04168
1/07/84	**23**	8	31. So Bad	Columbia 04296
10/20/84	**6**	14	32. **No More Lonely Nights** from the film "Give My Regards To Broad Street"; 26-32 (except #29): produced by George Martin	Columbia 04581
12/14/85†	**7**	11	33. **Spies Like Us** from the film of the same title	Capitol 5537
8/23/86	**21**	6	34. Press all of above (except #29): written by McCartney; 1-6, 8-26, 33-34: produced by McCartney	Capitol 5597
			ALTON McCLAIN & DESTINY Black female trio. Destiny: D'Marie Warren & Robyrda Stiger.	
5/19/79	**32**	4	1. It Must Be Love	Polydor 14532
			DELBERT McCLINTON Born on 11/4/40 in Lubbock, Texas. Played harmonica on Bruce Channel's hit "Hey Baby." Leader of the Ron-Dels.	
12/20/80†	**8**	14	1. **Giving It Up For Your Love**	Capitol 4948
			MARILYN McCOO & BILLY DAVIS, JR. Marilyn (b: 9/30/43) and husband Billy (b: 6/26/39) were members of The Fifth Dimension. Marilyn co-hosted TV's "Solid Gold" from 1981-84.	
10/23/76†	**1**(1)	18	• 1. **You Don't Have To Be A Star (To Be In My Show)**	ABC 12208
4/02/77	**15**	8	2. Your Love	ABC 12262

DATE	POS	WKS	ARTIST—RECORD TITLE	LABEL & NO.
			VAN McCOY	
			Pianist/producer/songwriter/singer born on 1/6/44 in Washington, DC; died on 7/6/79 of a heart attack. Formed own Rock'N label in 1960. Produced The Shirelles, Gladys Knight, The Stylistics and Brenda & The Tabulations. Own MAXX label, mid-60s.	
5/31/75	1(1)	12	● 1. **The Hustle** [I] with The Soul City Symphony	Avco 4653
			THE McCOYS	
			Rock band formed in Indiana. Rick Derringer (real name: Zehringer; vocals, guitar), brother Randy Zehringer (drums), Randy Hobbs (bass) and Ronnie Brandon (keyboards).	
9/04/65	1(1)	11	1. **Hang On Sloopy**	Bang 506
11/27/65	7	8	2. **Fever**	Bang 511
5/14/66	22	6	3. Come On Let's Go	Bang 522
			JIMMY McCRACKLIN	
			Born on 8/13/21 in St. Louis. Singer/harmonica player. Settled in Los Angeles. Professional boxer in the mid-40s.	
3/03/58	7	10	1. **The Walk** Top 100 #7 / Best Seller #11 / Jockey #23	Checker 885
			GEORGE McCRAE	
			Born on 10/19/44 in West Palm Beach, Florida. Duets with wife Gwen McCrae, became her manager. Also see Gwen McCrae.	
6/15/74	1(2)	10	1. **Rock Your Baby**	T.K. 1004
3/01/75	37	2	2. I Get Lifted	T.K. 1007
			GWEN McCRAE	
			Born on 12/21/43 in Pensacola, Florida. Married George McCrae, who later became her manager. First recorded with George for Alston in 1969.	
6/21/75	9	8	1. **Rockin' Chair** backing vocal: George McCrae	Cat 1996
			GENE McDANIELS	
			Born Eugene B. McDaniels on 2/12/35 in Kansas City. To Omaha, early 1940s, sang in choirs, attended Omaha Conservatory of Music. Own band, early 50s. Appeared in the film "It's Trad, Dad" in 1962.	
4/03/61	3	12	1. **A Hundred Pounds Of Clay**	Liberty 55308
8/07/61	31	2	2. A Tear	Liberty 55344
10/16/61	5	10	3. **Tower Of Strength**	Liberty 55371
2/10/62	10	7	4. **Chip Chip**	Liberty 55405
9/01/62	21	5	5. Point Of No Return	Liberty 55480
12/15/62	31	2	6. Spanish Lace above 5: with The Johnny Mann Singers	Liberty 55510
			CHAS. McDEVITT Skiffle Group	
			British vocal/instrumental group.	
6/10/57	40	1	1. Freight Train vocal: Nancy Wiskey	Chic 1008
			MICHAEL McDONALD	
			Keyboardist from St. Louis, Missouri. Formerly with Steely Dan and The Doobie Brothers. Married to singer Amy Holland. Also see Nicolette Larson.	
8/28/82	4	13	1. **I Keep Forgettin' (Every Time You're Near)**	Warner 29933

Bruce Hornsby & the Range became a household name with 1986's "The Way It Is," the group's second single for RCA. After that hit, the label remixed the group's initial single, "Every Little Kiss," and watched it garner a second burst of airplay.

Whitney Houston's hit-laden career included a show-stopping performance of "One Moment In Time" on 1989's televised Grammy Awards show.

Engelbert Humperdinck—who changed his name from Arnold Dorsey to that of the well-known German composer on the advice of his manager—must have watched with interest as former crooning rival Tom Jones enhanced his visibility via a 1988 collaboration with U.K. band the Art Of Noise.

Brian Hyland's successful career was topped by three brushes with the top 10: 1960's No. 1 "Itsy Bitsy Teenie Weenie Yellow Polkadot Bikini," 1962's "Sealed With A Kiss," and 1970's "Gypsy Woman."

Billy Idol, former leader of British punk band Generation X, enhanced his career in 1988 via a cameo appearance in comedian Sam Kinison's controversial video, "Wild Thing." Appearing with Idol—and a diverse crew of L.A.-based hard-rockers—was the equally controversial Jessica Hahn.

Julio Iglesias' international superstardom has not diminished his desire to similarly succeed in the US. To that end, duets with established American superstars such as Willie Nelson and Diana Ross have helped him reach the charts' upper tiers.

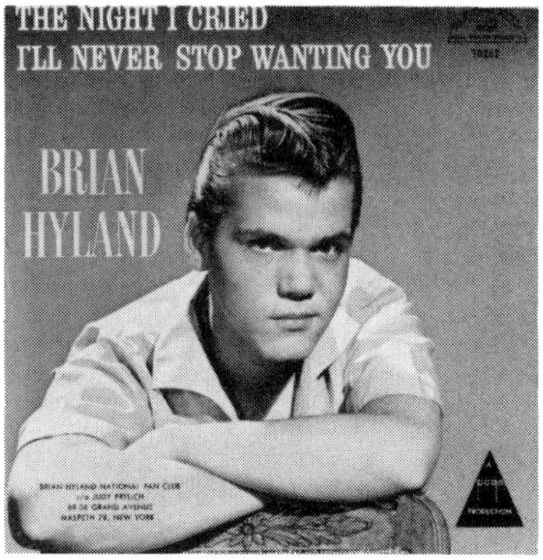

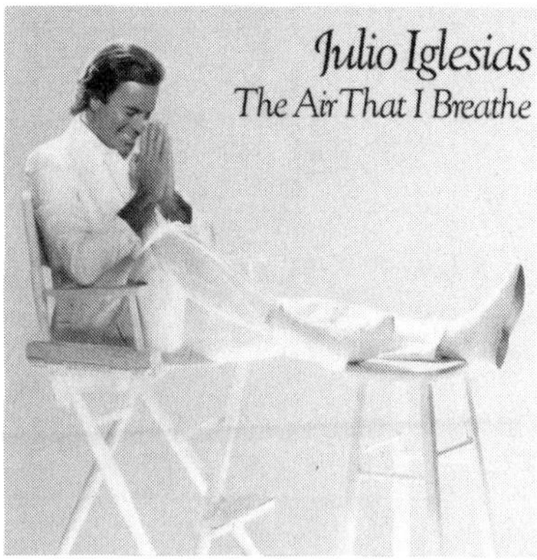

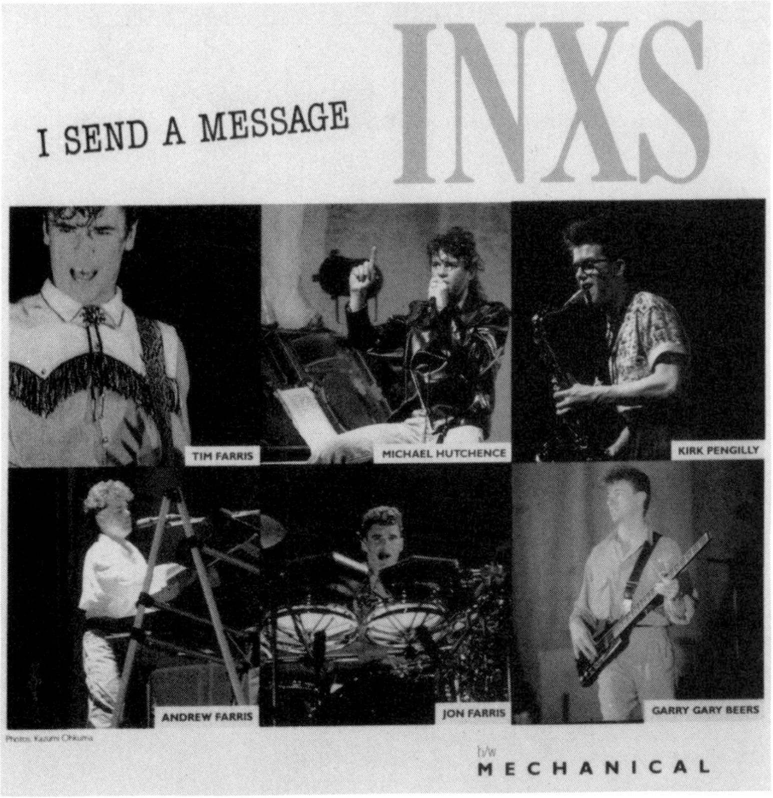

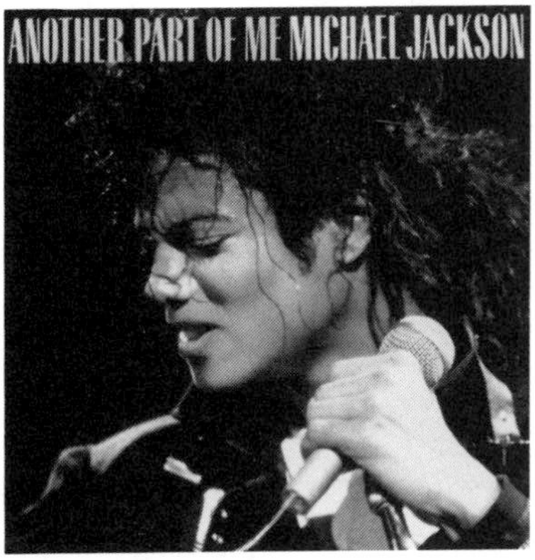

INXS' long career paid off royally in 1988 with the multi-platinum *Kick*. Atlantic Records showed their faith in the Australian group early on by issuing the group's first two albums—*INXS* and *Underneath The Colors*—in the US well after their "official" American debut, third album *Shabooh Shoobah*.

The Isley Brothers are one of very few groups to have appeared in the Hot 100 in a span encompassing *four* decades, beginning with 1959's "Shout–Part 1" and continuing through 1981's "Hurry Up And Wait." In the middle came such hits as "It's Your Thing," "That Lady (Part 1)," and more.

Freddie Jackson has shown that in the age of rap, soul singing still has the power. The former back-up singer for Melba Moore, among others, first hit the top 20 in 1985 with "Rock Me Tonight (For Old Times Sake)."

Janet Jackson's "Come Give Your Love To Me" seemed an impressive hit in 1983 when it reached No. 58—yet that achievement was greatly overshadowed three years later when the singer enjoyed a remarkable streak of *four* consecutive top-10 hits.

Michael Jackson's status as the world's best-known entertainer did not go unchanged in 1989 when his *Moonwalker* video hit the No. 1 spot on *Billboard*'s Top Music Videocassettes chart. Meanwhile, his multi-platinum *Bad* stayed the course—and more—on the Top Pop Albums chart.

DATE	POS	WKS	ARTIST—RECORD TITLE	LABEL & NO.
1/14/84	**19**	9	2. Yah Mo B There	Qwest 29394
			JAMES INGRAM with MICHAEL McDONALD	
8/31/85	**34**	4	3. No Lookin' Back	Warner 28960
4/19/86	**1**(3)	15	● 4. **On My Own**	MCA 52770
			PATTI LaBELLE & MICHAEL McDONALD	
7/12/86	**7**	13	5. **Sweet Freedom** theme from the film "Running Scared"	MCA 52857
			RONNIE McDOWELL	
			Country singer/songwriter from Portland, Tennessee. Sang on the soundtrack for the film "Elvis" in 1979.	
9/17/77	**13**	9	● 1. The King Is Gone a tribute to Elvis Presley	Scorpion 135
			McFADDEN & WHITEHEAD	
			R&B duo of Gene McFadden and John Whitehead from Philadelphia. Wrote songs for many Philadelphia soul acts; defined "The Sound Of Philadelphia."	
6/02/79	**13**	11	▲ 1. Ain't No Stoppin' Us Now	Phil. Int. 3681
			BOB McFADDEN & Dor	
			Bob is from East Liverpool, Ohio. Began career in 1950 as a singing emcee for a special Navy show called "The Bob McFadden Show."	
9/14/59	**39**	1	1. The Mummy [N] "beatnik" comments by Rod McKuen	Brunswick 55140
			BOBBY McFERRIN	
			Unaccompanied, jazz-styled improvisation vocalist born in New York City. Winner of 5 "Best Male Jazz Vocalist" Grammy Awards. Sang 1987 "Cosby Show" theme and Levi's 501 Blues jingle. Father was a baritone with the New York Metropolitan Opera.	
8/13/88	**1**(2)	13	● 1. **Don't Worry Be Happy** from the film "Cocktail"	EMI-Man. 50146
			MAUREEN McGOVERN	
			Born on 7/27/49 in Youngstown, Ohio. Pop singer.	
7/14/73	**1**(2)	11	● 1. **The Morning After** love theme from the film "The Poseidon Adventure"	20th Century 2010
8/11/79	**18**	9	2. Different Worlds theme from the TV series "Angie"	Warner 8835
			JIMMY McGRIFF	
			Born on 4/3/36 in Philadelphia. Jazz-R&B organist/multi-instrumentalist. Toured with Don Gardner and Arthur Prysock.	
10/27/62	**20**	7	1. I've Got A Woman, Part I [I]	Sue 770
			McGUINN, CLARK & HILLMAN	
			Roger McGuinn (b: 7/13/42; vocals, guitar), Gene Clark (b: 11/17/44; guitar) and Chris Hillman (b: 6/4/42; bass). All are former members of The Byrds.	
4/28/79	**33**	4	1. Don't You Write Her Off	Capitol 4693
			THE McGUIRE SISTERS	
			Sisters Christine (b: 7/30/29), Dorothy (b: 2/13/30) and Phyllis (b: 2/14/31) from Middletown, Ohio. Replaced the Chordettes on the Arthur Godfrey Show in 1953. Phyllis went solo in 1964. Reunited in 1986.	
1/08/55	**1**(10)	21	1. **Sincerely/** Jockey #1(10) / Juke Box #1(7) / Best Seller #1(6)	

DATE	POS	WKS	ARTIST—RECORD TITLE	LABEL & NO.
1/29/55	**17**	6	2. No More Jockey #17 / Juke Box #17 / Best Seller #23	Coral 61323
3/26/55	**11**	7	3. It May Sound Silly Jockey #11 / Juke Box #14 / Best Seller #23	Coral 61369
6/04/55	**5**	14	4. **Something's Gotta Give** Jockey #5 / Best Seller #6 / Juke Box #6 from the film "Daddy Long Legs"	Coral 61423
10/29/55	**10**	13	5. **He** Juke Box #10 / Best Seller #12 / Top 100 #12 / Jockey #16	Coral 61501
5/19/56	**13**	12	6. Picnic/ Top 100 #13 / Jockey #14 / Best Seller #15 / Juke Box #18 from the film of the same title	
6/02/56	**37**	1	7. Delilah Jones from the film "The Man With The Golden Arm"	Coral 61627
8/11/56	**32**	3	8. Weary Blues **THE McGUIRE SISTERS & LAWRENCE WELK**	Coral 61670
10/27/56	**37**	3	9. Ev'ry Day Of My Life	Coral 61703
12/22/56†	**32**	3	10. Goodnight My Love, Pleasant Dreams	Coral 61748
1/06/58	**1**(4)	19	11. **Sugartime** Jockey #1 / Top 100 #5 / Best Seller #7	Coral 61924
6/09/58	**25**	1	12. Ding Dong Jockey #25 / Top 100 #43 / Best Seller #44	Coral 61991
1/19/59	**11**	12	13. May You Always	Coral 62059
4/17/61	**20**	7	14. Just For Old Time's Sake 1-7, 9-10, 13-14: orchestra directed by Dick Jacobs	Coral 62249
			BARRY McGUIRE	
			Born on 10/15/37 in Oklahoma City. Member of the New Christy Minstrels.	
8/28/65	**1**(1)	10	1. **Eve Of Destruction**	Dunhill 4009
			BOB & DOUG McKENZIE	
			Canadian comedians Rick Moranis and Dave Thomas of "SCTV."	
2/20/82	**16**	9	1. Take Off [N] with vocals by Geddy Lee of Rush	Mercury 76134
			SCOTT McKENZIE	
			Born in Virginia on 10/1/44. Sang with John Phillips (Mamas & Papas) in The Journeymen.	
6/10/67	**4**	10	1. **San Francisco (Be Sure To Wear Flowers In Your Hair)**	Ode 103
11/11/67	**24**	3	2. Like An Old Time Movie above 2: written and produced by John Phillips	Ode 105
			TOMMY McLAIN	
7/23/66	**15**	7	1. Sweet Dreams	MSL 197
			DON McLEAN	
			Born on 10/02/45 in New Rochelle, New York. Singer/songwriter/poet. The hit "Killing Me Softly With His Song" was written about Don.	
12/04/71†	**1**(4)	17	● 1. **American Pie - Parts I & II** inspired by the death of Buddy Holly	United Art. 50856
4/01/72	**12**	10	2. Vincent/ a tribute to artist Vincent Van Gogh	
		10	3. Castles In The Air	United Art. 50887
1/20/73	**21**	8	4. Dreidel	United Art. 51100

DATE	POS	WKS	ARTIST—RECORD TITLE	LABEL & NO.
1/24/81	**5**	15	5. **Crying**	Millennium 11799
5/02/81	**23**	6	6. Since I Don't Have You	Millennium 11804
12/12/81	**36**	5	7. Castles In The Air [R] new version of Don's 1972 hit	Millennium 11819
			PHIL McLEAN	
			Veteran disc jockey; born in Detroit.	
12/18/61†	**21**	6	1. Small Sad Sam [S-N] a parody of "Big Bad John"	Versatile 107
			ROBIN McNAMARA	
			One of the original cast members of "Hair."	
7/18/70	**11**	8	1. Lay A Little Lovin' On Me	Steed 724
			CLYDE McPHATTER	
			Born Clyde Lensley McPhatter on 11/15/32 in Durham, North Carolina. Died on 6/13/72 in New York City (heart attack). Signed by Billy Ward for the Dominoes in 1950. Left the Dominoes in June, 1953 to form own group, The Drifters. Drafted in 1954, returned to sing solo. One of the most influential and distinctive male voices of the R&B era. Inducted into the Rock And Roll Hall Of Fame in 1987.	
6/09/56	**16**	12	1. Treasure Of Love Best Seller #16 / Juke Box #18 / Top 100 #22	Atlantic 1092
2/23/57	**19**	2	2. Without Love (There Is Nothing) Jockey #19 / Top 100 #38	Atlantic 1117
7/08/57	**26**	3	3. Just To Hold My Hand Best Seller #26 / Top 100 #30	Atlantic 1133
10/20/58†	**6**	20	4. **A Lover's Question**	Atlantic 1199
8/03/59	**38**	2	5. Since You've Been Gone	Atlantic 2028
8/22/60	**23**	5	6. Ta Ta	Mercury 71660
3/24/62	**7**	10	7. **Lover Please**	Mercury 71941
6/30/62	**25**	5	8. Little Bitty Pretty One	Mercury 71987
			CHRISTINE McVIE	
			Born Christine Perfect on 7/12/43 in Birmingham, England. Vocalist with Fleetwood Mac since 1970. Married to Fleetwood Mac bassist John McVie until 1976.	
2/04/84	**10**	11	1. **Got A Hold On Me**	Warner 29372
5/12/84	**30**	6	2. Love Will Show Us How	Warner 29313
			SISTER JANET MEAD	
			Australian nun; born in 1938. Gained prominence through her weekly cathedral rock masses and weekly radio programs.	
3/09/74	**4**	11	● 1. **The Lord's Prayer**	A&M 1491
			MEAT LOAF	
			Born Marvin Lee Aday on 9/27/47 in Dallas. Sang lead vocals on Ted Nugent's 1976 "Free-For-All" LP. Played Eddie in the film "The Rocky Horror Picture Show." Appeared in the films "Americathon" (1979), "Roadie" (1980) & "The Squeeze" (1987).	
4/29/78	**11**	13	● 1. Two Out Of Three Ain't Bad	Epic 50513
9/16/78	**39**	2	2. Paradise By The Dashboard Light [N] female vocal: Ellen Foley; baseball announcer: Phil Rizzuto	Epic 50588
1/20/79	**39**	1	3. You Took The Words Right Out Of My Mouth	Epic 50634

DATE	POS	WKS	ARTIST—RECORD TITLE	LABEL & NO.
			MECO	
			Discofied instrumentals by producer Meco Monardo; born on 11/29/39 in Johnsonburg, Pennsylvania.	
8/27/77	1(2)	13	▲ 1. **Star Wars Theme/Cantina Band** **[I]**	Millennium 604
1/21/78	**25**	6	2. Theme From Close Encounters [I]	Millennium 608
10/21/78	**35**	3	3. Themes From The Wizard Of Oz [N]	Millennium 620
7/05/80	**18**	8	4. Empire Strikes Back [I] Darth Vader/Yoda's Theme; all of above: inspired by films of the same titles	RSO 1038
4/03/82	**35**	3	5. Pop Goes The Movies, Part I [I] 20th Century Fox Trademark/Tara's Theme/The Magnificent Seven/The James Bond Theme/Goldfinger/The Good, The Bad And The Ugly/Theme From The Apartment/Theme From The High & The Mighty	Arista 0660
			GLENN MEDEIROS	
			Born on 6/24/70 and raised in Hawaii.	
4/04/87	**12**	13	1. Nothing's Gonna Change My Love For You	Amherst 311
			BILL MEDLEY - see JENNIFER WARNES	
			RANDY MEISNER	
			Born on 3/8/46 in Scottsbluff, Nebraska. Bassist/vocalist of Poco (1968), Rick Nelson's Stone Canyon Band (1969-71) and the Eagles (1972-76).	
11/08/80	**22**	7	1. Deep Inside My Heart backing vocal: Kim Carnes	Epic 50939
2/07/81	**19**	9	2. Hearts On Fire	Epic 50964
8/28/82	**28**	6	3. Never Been In Love	Epic 03032
			MEL & TIM	
			Cousins Mel Hardin and Tim McPherson, from Holly Springs, Mississippi.	
11/08/69	**10**	11	● 1. **Backfield In Motion**	Bamboo 107
9/16/72	**19**	9	2. Starting All Over Again	Stax 0127
			MELANIE	
			Born Melanie Safka on 2/3/47 in Queens, New York. Neighborhood Records formed by Melanie and her husband/producer Peter Schekeryk.	
5/16/70	**6**	14	1. **Lay Down (Candles In The Rain)** **MELANIE with THE EDWIN HAWKINS' SINGERS**	Buddah 167
9/05/70	**32**	4	2. Peace Will Come (According To Plan)	Buddah 186
11/27/71	1(3)	14	● 3. **Brand New Key**	Neighborhood 4201
2/19/72	**31**	5	4. Ring The Living Bell	Neighborhood 4202
2/26/72	**35**	3	5. The Nickel Song	Buddah 268
4/07/73	**36**	2	6. Bitter Bad	Neighborhood 4210
			JOHN COUGAR MELLENCAMP	
			Born on 10/7/51 in Seymour, Indiana. Rock singer/songwriter/producer. Worked outside of music until 1975. First recorded for MCA in 1976.	
			JOHN COUGAR:	
11/10/79	**28**	8	1. I Need A Lover	Riva 202
11/08/80	**27**	7	2. This Time	Riva 205
3/14/81	**17**	12	3. Ain't Even Done With The Night	Riva 207
5/22/82	2(4)	22	● 4. **Hurts So Good**	Riva 209

DATE	POS	WKS	ARTIST—RECORD TITLE	LABEL & NO.
8/07/82	1(4)	17	● 5. **Jack & Diane**	Riva 210
11/27/82†	**19**	11	6. Hand To Hold On To	Riva 211
			JOHN COUGAR MELLENCAMP:	
10/22/83	**9**	11	7. **Crumblin' Down**	Riva 214
12/17/83†	**8**	11	8. **Pink Houses**	Riva 215
3/31/84	**15**	9	9. Authority Song	Riva 216
8/24/85	**6**	13	10. **Lonely Ol' Night**	Riva 880984
11/16/85	**6**	13	11. **Small Town**	Riva 884202
2/15/86	2(1)	11	12. **R.O.C.K. In The U.S.A.** a salute to 60's rock	Riva 884455
5/17/86	**21**	6	13. Rain On The Scarecrow	Riva 884635
8/02/86	**28**	4	14. Rumbleseat	Riva 884856
8/29/87	**9**	10	15. **Paper In Fire**	Mercury 888763
11/14/87†	**8**	12	16. **Cherry Bomb**	Mercury 888934
2/27/88	**14**	9	17. Check It Out	Mercury 870126
			THE MELLO-TONES	
5/13/57	**24**	1	1. Rosie Lee Best Seller #24 / Top 100 #60	Gee 1037
			HAROLD MELVIN & THE BLUE NOTES	
			Philadelphia soul group formed in 1954: Harold Melvin, Bernard Williams, Jesse Gillis, Jr., Franklin Peaker and Roosevelt Brodie. First recorded for Josie in 1956. Numerous personnel changes until 1970, when Teddy Pendergrass joined as drummer and lead singer. Pendergrass went solo in 1975, relaced by David Ebo.	
10/28/72	**3**	11	● 1. **If You Don't Know Me By Now**	Phil. Int. 3520
10/20/73	**7**	12	● 2. **The Love I Lost (Part 1)**	Phil. Int. 3533
5/03/75	**15**	10	3. Bad Luck (Part 1)	Phil. Int. 3562
12/20/75†	**12**	12	4. Wake Up Everybody (Part 1) all of above: produced by Kenny Gamble & Leon Huff	Phil. Int. 3579
			MEN AT WORK	
			Melbourne, Australia rock quintet formed in 1979. Colin Hay (lead singer, guitar), Ron Strykert (lead guitar), Greg Ham (sax, keyboards), Jerry Speiser (drums) and John Rees (bass). Won the 1982 Best New Artist Grammy Award. Speiser and Rees left in 1984.	
8/07/82	1(1)	17	1. **Who Can It Be Now?**	Columbia 02888
11/27/82†	1(4)	19	● 2. **Down Under**	Columbia 03303
4/09/83	**3**	13	3. **Overkill**	Columbia 03795
7/09/83	**6**	12	4. **It's A Mistake**	Columbia 03959
10/08/83	**28**	5	5. Dr. Heckyll & Mr. Jive	Columbia 04111
			MEN WITHOUT HATS	
			Nucleus of techno-rock band from Montreal, Canada consists of Ivan Doroschuk (singer/songwriter) with his brother Stefan (guitar). Fluctuating personnel included their brother Colin (1983-84).	
7/30/83	**3**	16	1. **The Safety Dance**	Backstreet 52232
12/19/87†	**20**	10	2. Pop Goes The World	Mercury 888859

DATE	POS	WKS	ARTIST—RECORD TITLE	LABEL & NO.
			SERGIO MENDES	
			Born on 2/11/41 in Niteroi, Brazil. Pianist/bandleader. Resident in US since the mid-60s. Originator of the bossa nova style.	
5/14/83	**4**	16	1. **Never Gonna Let You Go** vocals: Joe Pizzulo & Leza Miller	A&M 2540
7/07/84	**29**	7	2. Alibis vocal: Joe Pizzulo	A&M 2639
			SERGIO MENDES & BRASIL '66	
			Latin stylists originating from Brazil and led by pianist Mendes.	
6/01/68	**4**	11	1. **The Look Of Love** from the film "Casino Royale"	A&M 924
8/24/68	**6**	10	2. **The Fool On The Hill** written by John Lennon & Paul McCartney	A&M 961
12/07/68	**16**	6	3. Scarborough Fair written by Paul Simon & Art Garfunkel	A&M 986
			MERCY	
			Florida group led by Jack Sigler, Jr.	
5/03/69	**2**(2)	10	● 1. **Love (Can Make You Happy)**	Sundi 6811
			JIM MESSINA - see LOGGINS & MESSINA	
			THE METERS	
			R&B instrumental group formed in New Orleans in 1966 featuring keyboardist Arthur Neville (brother of Aaron Neville). Group disbanded in 1977, when Art, Aaron, and brothers Charles and Cyril formed The Neville Brothers.	
3/22/69	**34**	1	1. Sophisticated Cissy [I]	Josie 1001
5/24/69	**23**	3	2. Cissy Strut [I]	Josie 1005
			PAT METHENY GROUP - see DAVID BOWIE	
			MFSB featuring THE THREE DEGREES	
			Large racially-mixed studio band formed by producers Kenny Gamble and Leon Huff. Also recorded as The James Boys, and Family. Name means "Mothers, Fathers, Sisters, Brothers."	
3/16/74	**1**(2)	14	● 1. **TSOP (The Sound Of Philadelphia)** **[I]** theme from the TV show "Soul Train"	Phil. Int. 3540
			MIAMI SOUND MACHINE	
			Miami band of Latin American heritage led by singer Gloria Estefan with percussionist husband Emilio Estefan, Jr.	
11/23/85†	**10**	16	1. **Conga**	Epic 05457
3/29/86	**8**	12	2. **Bad Boy**	Epic 05805
7/26/86	**5**	13	3. **Words Get In The Way**	Epic 06120
12/13/86†	**25**	8	4. Falling In Love (Uh-Oh)	Epic 06352
			GLORIA ESTEFAN & MIAMI SOUND MACHINE:	
6/13/87	**5**	12	5. **Rhythm Is Gonna Get You**	Epic 07059
10/24/87	**36**	2	6. Betcha Say That	Epic 07371
1/16/88	**6**	11	7. **Can't Stay Away From You**	Epic 07641
3/26/88	**1**(2)	14	8. **Anything For You**	Epic 07759
6/25/88	**3**	13	9. **1-2-3**	Epic 07921

DATE	POS	WKS	ARTIST—RECORD TITLE	LABEL & NO.
			GEORGE MICHAEL	
			Born Georgios Kyriacos Panayiotou on 6/26/63 in Bushey, England. Former lead singer of Wham!.	
5/10/86	**7**	10	1. **A Different Corner**	Columbia 05888
3/07/87	**1**(2)	12	2. **I Knew You Were Waiting (For Me)**	Arista 9559
			ARETHA FRANKLIN & GEORGE MICHAEL	
6/20/87	**2**(1)	14	3. **I Want Your Sex**	Columbia 07164
			from the film "Beverly Hills Cop II"	
10/31/87	**1**(4)	15	4. **Faith**	Columbia 07623
1/23/88	**1**(2)	13	5. **Father Figure**	Columbia 07682
4/16/88	**1**(3)	14	6. **One More Try**	Columbia 07773
7/16/88	**1**(2)	12	7. **Monkey**	Columbia 07941
10/15/88	**5**	10	8. **Kissing A Fool**	Columbia 08050
			LEE MICHAELS	
			Born on 11/24/45 in Los Angeles. Rock organist/vocalist.	
9/04/71	**6**	12	1. **Do You Know What I Mean**	A&M 1262
12/25/71	**39**	1	2. Can I Get A Witness	A&M 1303
			MICKEY & SYLVIA	
			McHouston "Mickey" Baker and Sylvia Vanderpool. Mickey (b: 10/15/25, Louisville) was a prolific session guitarist. Sylvia began solo career in 1973, recorded as Sylvia.	
1/12/57	**11**	14	1. Love Is Strange	Groove 0175
			Best Seller #11 / Jockey #11 / Top 100 #13 / Juke Box #17	
			BETTE MIDLER	
			Born on 12/1/45 in Paterson, New Jersey. Vocalist/actress. Raised in Hawaii. In the Broadway show "Fiddler On The Roof" for 3 years. Won the 1973 Best New Artist Grammy Award. Nominated for an Oscar in "The Rose" (1979).	
1/20/73	**17**	11	1. Do You Want To Dance?	Atlantic 2928
6/09/73	**8**	11	2. **Boogie Woogie Bugle Boy**	Atlantic 2964
			#6 hit for The Andrews Sisters in 1941	
11/10/73	**40**	1	3. Friends	Atlantic 2980
7/07/79	**40**	2	4. Married Men	Atlantic 3582
3/01/80	**35**	3	5. When A Man Loves A Woman	Atlantic 3643
4/26/80	**3**	16	• 6. **The Rose**	Atlantic 3656
			above 2: from the film "The Rose"	
1/17/81	**39**	2	7. My Mother's Eyes	Atlantic 3771
			from the film "Divine Madness"	
			MIDNIGHT OIL	
			Australian quintet: Peter Garrett (lead vocals), Rob Hirst, Peter Gifford, Martin Rotsey & James Moginie. Garrett was a candidate in the 1984 Australian Senate race.	
5/21/88	**17**	9	1. Beds Are Burning	Columbia 07433
			MIDNIGHT STAR	
			R&B-funk group formed in 1976 at Kentucky State University. Lead vocals by Belinda Lipscomb. Until 1988, band led by brothers Reginald (trumpet) & Vincent (trombone) Calloway.	
1/12/85	**18**	8	1. Operator	Solar 69684

DATE	POS	WKS	ARTIST—RECORD TITLE	LABEL & NO.
			MIKE + THE MECHANICS	
			Rock quintet consisting of Mike Rutherford (Genesis), Paul Carrack (Ace, Squeeze), Paul Young (Sad Cafe), Peter Van Hooke (drummer for Van Morrison) and Adrian Lee.	
1/18/86	**6**	11	1. **Silent Running (On Dangerous Ground)** title track from the movie "On Dangerous Ground"	Atlantic 89488
4/12/86	**5**	12	2. **All I Need Is A Miracle**	Atlantic 89450
8/02/86	**32**	5	3. Taken In	Atlantic 89404
			GARRY MILES	
			Real name: James (Buzz) Cason; lead singer of The Statues. Also see Garry Mills, who is a different artist with another version of the same song.	
7/18/60	**16**	9	1. Look For A Star from the film "Circus Of Horrors"	Liberty 55261
			JOHN MILES	
			Born on 4/23/49 in Jarrow, England. Rock vocalist/guitarist/keyboardist.	
5/14/77	**34**	5	1. Slowdown	London 20092
			CHUCK MILLER	
6/18/55	**9**	14	1. **The House Of Blue Lights** Best Seller #9 / Jockey #18 / Juke Box #19	Mercury 70627
			JODY MILLER	
			Pop/country singer; born in Phoenix on 11/29/41.	
5/15/65	**12**	5	1. Queen Of The House answer song to Roger Miller's "King Of The Road"	Capitol 5402
9/25/65	**25**	5	2. Home Of The Brave	Capitol 5483
			MITCH MILLER	
			Born on 7/4/11 in Rochester, New York. Producer/conductor/arranger. Oboe soloist with the CBS Symphony from 1936-47. A&R executive for both Columbia and Mercury Records. Best known for his sing-along albums and TV show.	
8/06/55	**1**(6)	19	1. **The Yellow Rose Of Texas** Best Seller #1(6) / Jockey #1(6) / Juke Box #1(6) adaptation of a Civil War campfire song	Columbia 40540
2/18/56	**19**	3	2. Lisbon Antigua [I] Jockey #19 / Top 100 #30	Columbia 40635
8/11/56	**8**	12	3. **Theme Song from "Song For A Summer Night"** **[I]** Jockey #8 / Best Seller #9 / Top 100 #10 / Juke Box #10 theme from the Westinghouse TV production of the same title	Columbia 40730
1/27/58	**20**	11	4. March From The River Kwai and Colonel Bogey [I] Jockey #20 / Best Seller #21 / Top 100 #21 from the film "The Bridge On The River Kwai"	Columbia 41066
1/26/59	**16**	10	5. The Children's Marching Song [N] from the film "The Inn of The Sixth Happiness"	Columbia 41317
			NED MILLER	
			Born on 4/12/25 in Rains, Utah. Country singer/songwriter.	
1/26/63	**6**	8	1. **From A Jack To A King**	Fabor 114

DATE	POS	WKS	ARTIST—RECORD TITLE	LABEL & NO.
			ROGER MILLER	
			Country vocalist/humorist/guitarist/composer. Born on 1/2/36 in Fort Worth, Texas; raised in Erick, Oklahoma. To Nashville in the mid-50s, began songwriting career. With Faron Young as writer/drummer in 1962. Won 6 Grammies in 1965. Own TV show in 1966. Songwriter of 1985's Tony Award-winning Broadway musical "Big River."	
7/04/64	**7**	8	1. **Dang Me** **[N]**	Smash 1881
10/03/64	**9**	8	2. **Chug-A-Lug** **[N]**	Smash 1926
1/02/65	**31**	3	3. Do-Wacka-Do [N]	Smash 1947
2/06/65	**4**	12	• 4. **King Of The Road**	Smash 1965
5/22/65	**7**	7	5. **Engine Engine #9**	Smash 1983
8/07/65	**34**	2	6. One Dyin' And A Buryin'	Smash 1994
10/02/65	**31**	3	7. Kansas City Star [N]	Smash 1998
11/27/65	**8**	8	8. **England Swings**	Smash 2010
3/05/66	**26**	5	9. Husbands And Wives	Smash 2024
7/23/66	**40**	1	10. You Can't Roller Skate In A Buffalo Herd [N]	Smash 2043
5/06/67	**37**	1	11. Walkin' In The Sunshine all of above: written by Miller	Smash 2081
3/16/68	**39**	6	12. Little Green Apples	Smash 2148
			STEVE MILLER BAND	
			Steve was born on 10/5/43 in Milwaukee; raised in Dallas. Blues-rock singer/ songwriter/guitarist. While at the University of Wisconsin-Madison, Steve led the blues-rock band the Ardells, later known as the Fabulous Night Trains, featuring Boz Scaggs. To San Francisco in 1966; formed Steve Miller Band, which featured fluctuating lineup.	
11/17/73†	**1**(1)	16	• 1. **The Joker**	Capitol 3732
6/05/76	**11**	9	2. Take The Money And Run	Capitol 4260
9/04/76	**1**(1)	14	3. **Rock'n Me**	Capitol 4323
1/08/77	**2**(2)	15	• 4. **Fly Like An Eagle** above 3: **STEVE MILLER**	Capitol 4372
5/14/77	**8**	13	5. **Jet Airliner**	Capitol 4424
9/03/77	**23**	7	6. Jungle Love	Capitol 4466
11/12/77	**17**	9	7. Swingtown	Capitol 4496
11/14/81	**24**	9	8. Heart Like A Wheel	Capitol 5068
6/19/82	**1**(2)	19	• 9. **Abracadabra**	Capitol 5126
			THE MILLS BROTHERS	
			Smooth vocal group from Piqua, Ohio. Consisted of John Jr. (b: 1911; d: 1936), Herbert (b: 1912; d: 4/12/89 [77]), Harry (b: 1913; d: 6/28/82 [68]) and Donald (b: 1915). Achieved national fame via radio broadcasts and appearances in films. Father, John Sr., joined group in 1936, replacing John Jr.; remained in group until 1956 (d: 12/8/67). Donald and his son, John II, continued as a duo.	
6/17/57	**39**	1	1. Queen Of The Senior Prom	Decca 30299
3/03/58	**21**	2	2. Get A Job Jockey #21	Dot 15695
3/02/68	**23**	10	3. Cab Driver	Dot 17041
			FRANK MILLS	
			Pianist/composer/producer/arranger.	
3/03/79	**3**	12	• 1. **Music Box Dancer** **[I]**	Polydor 14517

DATE	POS	WKS	ARTIST—RECORD TITLE	LABEL & NO.
			GARRY MILLS	
			Also see Garry Miles.	
7/04/60	**26**	6	1. Look For A Star - Part I from the film "Circus Of Horrors"	Imperial 5674
			HAYLEY MILLS	
			Born on 4/18/46 in London. Daughter of English actor John Mills. Disney teen film star.	
9/18/61	**8**	11	1. **Let's Get Together** from the film "The Parent Trap"	Vista 385
4/14/62	**21**	6	2. Johnny Jingo	Vista 395
			STEPHANIE MILLS	
			Born in 1957 in Brooklyn. In 1967, appeared for 4 weeks at the Apollo Theater with The Isley Brothers. At age 15, won starring role of Dorothy in the hit Broadway musical "The Wiz." Briefly married to Jeffrey Daniels of Shalamar in 1980.	
9/01/79	**22**	6	1. What Cha Gonna Do With My Lovin'	20th Century 2403
8/30/80	**6**	16	• 2. **Never Knew Love Like This Before**	20th Century 2460
7/04/81	**40**	2	3. Two Hearts **STEPHANIE MILLS featuring TEDDY PENDERGRASS**	20th Century 2492
			RONNIE MILSAP	
			Born on 1/16/46 in Robbinsville, North Carolina. Country singer/pianist/guitarist. Blind since birth; multi-instrumentalist by age 12. With J.J. Cale band, own band from 1965.	
8/27/77	**16**	10	1. It Was Almost Like A Song	RCA 10976
1/24/81	**24**	9	2. Smoky Mountain Rain	RCA 12084
7/11/81	**5**	15	3. **(There's) No Gettin' Over Me**	RCA 12264
11/28/81†	**20**	11	4. I Wouldn't Have Missed It For The World	RCA 12342
5/29/82	**14**	9	5. Any Day Now	RCA 13216
4/23/83	**23**	8	6. Stranger In My House	RCA 13470
			GARNET MIMMS & THE ENCHANTERS	
			Born Garrett Mimms on 11/16/33 in Ashland, West Virginia. Sang in gospel groups the Evening Stars, Norfolk Four, Harmonizing Four. Formed group the Gainors in 1958. The Enchanters (Zola Pearnell, Sam Bell and Charles Boyer) were formed in 1961.	
9/07/63	**4**	11	1. **Cry Baby**	United Art. 629
12/07/63†	**26**	5	2. For Your Precious Love/	
12/07/63	**30**	4	3. Baby Don't You Weep	United Art. 658
5/07/66	**30**	3	4. I'll Take Good Care Of You **GARNET MIMMS**	United Art. 995
			THE MINDBENDERS	
			Rock group from Manchester, England: Wayne Fontana (born Glyn Geoffrey Ellis on 10/28/45; lead singer), Eric Stewart (lead guitar, vocals), Bob Lang (bass) and Ric Rothwell (drums). Fontana left in October of 1965. Graham Gouldman joined in 1968. Also see Hotlegs and 10cc.	
3/27/65	**1**(1)	10	1. **Game Of Love** **WAYNE FONTANA & THE MINDBENDERS**	Fontana 1509
4/30/66	**2**(2)	10	2. **A Groovy Kind Of Love**	Fontana 1541

DATE	POS	WKS	ARTIST—RECORD TITLE	LABEL & NO.
			SAL MINEO	
			Broadway/Hollywood actor. Born on 1/10/39; stabbed to death on 2/12/76.	
5/20/57	**9**	13	1. **Start Movin' (In My Direction)** Best Seller #9 / Top 100 #10 / Jockey #16 / Juke Box #18 end	Epic 9216
9/23/57	**27**	3	2. Lasting Love Best Seller #27 / Top 100 #35	Epic 9227
			KYLIE MINOGUE	
			Singer/actress from Melbourne, Australia. Began TV acting career at age 11. Cast member of the popular Australian soap "Neighbours."	
7/02/88	**28**	4	1. I Should Be So Lucky	Geffen 27922
9/17/88	**3**	13	2. **The Loco-Motion**	Geffen 27752
			THE MIRACLES	
			R&B group formed at Northern High School in Detroit in 1955. Consisted of William "Smokey" Robinson (lead), Emerson and Bobby Rogers (tenors), Ronnie White (baritone) and Warren "Pete" Moore (bass). Emerson Rogers left in 1956 for US Army, replaced by Claudette Rogers Robinson, Smokey's wife. First recorded for End in 1958. Claudette retired in 1964. Smokey wrote many hit songs for his group and other Motown artists. Smokey went solo in 1972, replaced by William Griffin.	
12/31/60†	**2**(1)	13	1. **Shop Around**	Tamla 54034
2/17/62	**35**	2	2. What's So Good About Good-By	Tamla 54053
6/30/62	**39**	1	3. I'll Try Something New	Tamla 54059
1/12/63	**8**	10	4. **You've Really Got A Hold On Me**	Tamla 54073
5/04/63	**31**	3	5. A Love She Can Count On	Tamla 54078
8/31/63	**8**	9	6. **Mickey's Monkey**	Tamla 54083
1/04/64	**35**	3	7. I Gotta Dance To Keep From Crying	Tamla 54089
7/25/64	**27**	4	8. I Like It Like That	Tamla 54098
10/10/64	**35**	1	9. That's What Love Is Made Of	Tamla 54102
4/17/65	**16**	7	10. Ooo Baby Baby	Tamla 54113
8/07/65	**16**	8	11. The Tracks Of My Tears	Tamla 54118
11/06/65	**14**	6	12. My Girl Has Gone	Tamla 54123
1/22/66	**11**	7	13. Going To A Go-Go	Tamla 54127
11/26/66	**17**	6	14. (Come 'Round Here) I'm The One You Need	Tamla 54140
			SMOKEY ROBINSON & THE MIRACLES:	
3/11/67	**20**	7	15. The Love I Saw In You Was Just A Mirage	Tamla 54145
7/08/67	**23**	8	16. More Love	Tamla 54152
11/25/67	**4**	12	17. **I Second That Emotion**	Tamla 54159
3/09/68	**11**	10	18. If You Can Want	Tamla 54162
6/29/68	**31**	3	19. Yester Love	Tamla 54167
8/31/68	**26**	6	20. Special Occasion	Tamla 54172
1/25/69	**8**	11	21. **Baby, Baby Don't Cry**	Tamla 54178
7/19/69	**33**	2	22. Abraham, Martin And John	Tamla 54184
7/26/69	**32**	4	23. Doggone Right/	
10/04/69	**37**	3	24. Here I Go Again	Tamla 54183
12/27/69†	**37**	4	25. Point It Out	Tamla 54189
10/31/70	**1**(2)	14	26. **The Tears Of A Clown**	Tamla 54199
4/17/71	**18**	8	27. I Don't Blame You At All	Tamla 54205

DATE	POS	WKS	ARTIST—RECORD TITLE	LABEL & NO.
			THE MIRACLES:	
9/14/74	**13**	9	28. Do It Baby	Tamla 54248
12/13/75†	**1**(1)	19	29. **Love Machine (Part 1)**	Tamla 54262
			MR. MISTER	
			Los Angeles-based pop-rock quartet: Richard Page (vocals), Steve George, Pat Mastelotto and Steve Farris (left in 1989; replaced by Buzz Feiten, ex-guitarist of Paul Butterfield Blues Band, Stevie Wonder's band, and the Larsen-Feiten Band).	
10/19/85	**1**(2)	15	1. **Broken Wings**	RCA 14136
1/11/86	**1**(2)	13	2. **Kyrie**	RCA 14258
4/12/86	**8**	11	3. **Is It Love**	RCA 14313
9/19/87	**29**	5	4. Something Real (Inside Me/Inside You)	RCA 5273
			GUY MITCHELL	
			Born Al Cernik on 2/27/27 in Detroit. Sang briefly with Carmen Cavallaro's orchestra in the late 40s. Appearances in several films and TV series.	
2/25/56	**23**	4	1. Ninety Nine Years (Dead Or Alive)	Columbia 40631
11/03/56	**1**(10)	22	2. **Singing The Blues** Juke Box #1(10) / Best Seller #1(9) / Top 100 #1(9) / Jockey #1(9)	Columbia 40769
2/02/57	**16**	8	3. Knee Deep In The Blues Top 100 #16 / Juke Box #16 / Jockey #17 / Best Seller #21	Columbia 40820
4/13/57	**10**	12	4. **Rock-A-Billy** Best Seller #10 / Top 100 #13 / Juke Box #14 / Jockey #15	Columbia 40877
10/19/59	**1**(2)	16	5. **Heartaches By The Number**	Columbia 41476
			JONI MITCHELL	
			Born Roberta Joan Anderson on 11/7/43 in Alberta, Canada. Wrote the hits "Both Sides Now" and "Woodstock." Also see James Taylor.	
12/30/72†	**25**	8	1. You Turn Me On, I'm A Radio	Asylum 11010
4/20/74	**7**	11	2. **Help Me**	Asylum 11034
8/24/74	**22**	7	3. Free Man In Paris	Asylum 11041
1/25/75	**24**	4	4. Big Yellow Taxi [R] live version of Joni's 1970 studio hit	Asylum 45221
			WILLIE MITCHELL	
			Born in Ashland, Mississippi in 1928. Trumpeter/keyboardist/composer/arranger/ producer. To Memphis at an early age. With Tuff Green and Al Jackson in the early 50s. Formed own band in 1954, became house band at Home Of The Blues and Hi Records. Eventually became president of Hi Records.	
10/03/64	**31**	5	1. 20-75 [I] title refers to the record's label number	Hi 2075
4/13/68	**23**	10	2. Soul Serenade [I]	Hi 2140
			MOCEDADES	
			Sextet from Bilbao, Spain, featuring the Amezaga sisters.	
2/16/74	**9**	11	1. **Eres Tu (Touch The Wind)** **[F]** flip side is sung in English	Tara 100
			MODELS	
			Pop-rock quintet from Melbourne, Australia. Led by vocalists/guitarists James Freud and Sean Kelly.	
6/07/86	**37**	4	1. Out Of Mind Out Of Sight	Geffen 28762

DATE	POS	WKS	ARTIST—RECORD TITLE	LABEL & NO.
			DOMENICO MODUGNO	
			Born on 1/9/28 in Polignano a Mare, Italy. Singer/actor.	
8/04/58	**1**(5)	13	1. **Nel Blu Dipinto Di Blu (Volare)** **[F]**	Decca 30677
			Hot 100 #1(5) / Best Seller #1(5)	
			THE MOJO MEN	
			San Francisco-based rock quartet: Jimmy Alaimo, Paul Curcio, Don Metchick and Dennis DeCarr. Originally known as Sly and the Mojo Men, led by Sylvester "Sly Stone" Stewart. Sly did not appear on any of their recordings.	
3/18/67	**36**	3	1. Sit Down, I Think I Love You	Reprise 0539
			THE MOMENTS	
			Soul trio from Hackensack, New Jersey featuring Mark Greene (falsetto lead). Greene left after first record, replaced by William Brown (lead) and Al Goodman. Harry Ray joined after "Love On A Two-Way Street" in 1970. Became Ray, Goodman & Brown in 1978.	
4/18/70	**3**	14	● 1. **Love On A Two-Way Street**	Stang 5012
2/02/74	**17**	9	2. Sexy Mama	Stang 5052
8/02/75	**39**	3	3. Look At Me (I'm In Love)	Stang 5060
			EDDIE MONEY	
			Born Edward Mahoney on 3/2/49 in New York City. Rock singer discovered and subsequently managed by West Coast promoter Bill Graham. Formerly an officer with the New York Police Department.	
4/08/78	**11**	11	1. Baby Hold On	Columbia 10663
7/29/78	**22**	8	2. Two Tickets To Paradise	Columbia 10765
2/24/79	**22**	8	3. Maybe I'm A Fool	Columbia 10900
7/24/82	**16**	12	4. Think I'm In Love	Columbia 02964
9/27/86	**4**	12	5. **Take Me Home Tonight**	Columbia 06231
			Ronnie Spector sings the lead line from "Be My Baby"	
1/24/87	**14**	10	6. I Wanna Go Back	Columbia 06569
5/30/87	**21**	7	7. Endless Nights	Columbia 07035
10/22/88	**9**	13	8. **Walk On Water**	Columbia 08060
			THE MONKEES	
			Formed in Los Angeles in 1965. Chosen from over 400 applicants for new Columbia TV series. Consisted of Davy Jones (b: 12/30/45, Manchester, England; vocals), Michael Nesmith (b: 12/30/42, Houston; guitar, vocals), Peter Tork (b: 2/13/44, Washington, DC; bass, vocals) and Micky Dolenz (b: 3/8/45, Tarzana, CA; drums, vocals). Dolenz had appeared in TV series "Circus Boy," using the name Mickey Braddock in 1956. Jones had been a race-horse jockey, and appeared in London musicals "Oliver" and "Pickwick." Tork had been in the Phoenix Singers; Nesmith had done session work for Stax/Volt. TV show dropped after 58 episodes, 1966-68. Tork left in 1968. Group disbanded in 1969; re-formed (less Nesmith) in 1986.	
9/24/66	**1**(1)	12	● 1. **Last Train To Clarksville**	Colgems 1001
12/17/66	**1**(7)	13	● 2. **I'm A Believer/**	
12/31/66†	**20**	6	3. (I'm Not Your) Steppin' Stone	Colgems 1002
3/25/67	**2**(1)	10	● 4. **A Little Bit Me, A Little Bit You/**	
4/15/67	**39**	1	5. The Girl I Knew Somewhere	Colgems 1004
7/29/67	**3**	9	● 6. **Pleasant Valley Sunday/**	
8/05/67	**11**	7	7. Words	Colgems 1007
11/18/67	**1**(4)	12	● 8. **Daydream Believer**	Colgems 1012

DATE	POS	WKS	ARTIST—RECORD TITLE	LABEL & NO.
3/09/68	**3**	7	● 9. **Valleri/**	
3/30/68	**34**	1	10. Tapioca Tundra	Colgems 1019
6/22/68	**19**	6	11. D. W. Washburn	Colgems 1023
8/02/86	**20**	7	12. That Was Then, This Is Now	Arista 9505
			THE MONOTONES	
			Doo-wop group from Newark, New Jersey. Charles Patrick, lead singer.	
4/07/58	**5**	12	1. **Book Of Love**	Argo 5290
			Top 100 #5 / Best Seller #6 / Jockey #9	
			MATT MONRO	
			British singer; died of liver cancer on 2/7/85 (54).	
6/26/61	**18**	9	1. My Kind Of Girl	Warwick 636
12/26/64†	**23**	5	2. Walk Away	Liberty 55745
			VAUGHN MONROE	
			Born on 10/7/11 in Akron, Ohio; died on 5/21/73. Big-voiced baritone/trumpeter/ bandleader. Very popular on radio, and featured in several movies.	
11/12/55	**38**	1	1. Black Denim Trousers And Motorcycle Boots	RCA 6260
2/18/56	**38**	1	2. Don't Go To Strangers	RCA 6358
9/08/56	**11**	8	3. In The Middle Of The House [N]	RCA 6619
			Jockey #11 / Top 100 #21	
			LOU MONTE	
			Born on 4/2/17 in Lyndhurst, New Jersey. Vocalist/guitarist.	
3/17/58	**12**	11	1. Lazy Mary [F]	RCA 7160
			Best Seller #12 / Top 100 #12 / Jockey #22	
12/15/62†	**5**	9	2. **Pepino The Italian Mouse** **[N]**	Reprise 20106
			HUGO MONTENEGRO	
			Born in 1925; raised in New York City; died on 2/6/81. Conductor/composer.	
4/06/68	**2**(1)	14	1. **The Good, The Bad And The Ugly** **[I]**	RCA 9423
			CHRIS MONTEZ	
			Born Christopher Montanez on 1/17/43 in Los Angeles. Protege of Ritchie Valens.	
9/08/62	**4**	9	1. **Let's Dance**	Monogram 505
2/12/66	**22**	5	2. Call Me	A&M 780
5/28/66	**16**	7	3. The More I See You	A&M 796
9/10/66	**33**	2	4. There Will Never Be Another You	A&M 810
12/03/66	**36**	2	5. Time After Time	A&M 822
			MELBA MONTGOMERY	
			Born on 10/14/38 in Iron City, Tennessee. Country singer.	
6/08/74	**39**	1	1. No Charge [N]	Elektra 45883

DATE	POS	WKS	ARTIST—RECORD TITLE	LABEL & NO.
			THE MOODY BLUES	
			Formed in Birmingham, England in 1964. Consisted of Denny Laine (guitar, vocals), Ray Thomas (flute, vocals), Mike Pinder (keyboards, vocals), Clint Warwick (bass) and Graeme Edge (drums). Laine and Warwick left in the summer of 1966, replaced by Justin Hayward (lead vocals, lead guitar) and John Lodge (vocals, bass). Laine joined Wings in 1971. Patrick Moraz (former Yes keyboardist) replaced Pinder, 1978.	
3/27/65	**10**	8	1. **Go Now!** Denny Laine (Wings), lead singer	London 9726
8/24/68	**24**	6	2. Tuesday Afternoon (Forever Afternoon)	Deram 85028
5/30/70	**21**	8	3. Question	Threshold 67004
9/04/71	**23**	7	4. The Story In Your Eyes	Threshold 67006
5/13/72	**29**	7	5. Isn't Life Strange	Threshold 67009
9/02/72	**2**(2)	14	● 6. **Nights In White Satin** released from their 1968 album "Days of Future Passed"	Deram 85023
2/17/73	**12**	8	7. I'm Just A Singer (In A Rock And Roll Band)	Threshold 67012
9/02/78	**39**	2	8. Steppin' In A Slide Zone	London 270
6/13/81	**12**	9	9. Gemini Dream	Threshold 601
8/15/81	**15**	11	10. The Voice	Threshold 602
9/17/83	**27**	6	11. Sitting At The Wheel	Threshold 604
5/24/86	**9**	12	12. **Your Wildest Dreams**	Polydor 883906
7/23/88	**30**	4	13. I Know You're Out There Somewhere	Polydor 887600
			ART MOONEY	
			Born in Lowell, Massachusetts. Leader of a Detroit-based dance band from the mid-30s to 40s. To New York following WWII service. Biggest hit: "I'm Looking Over A Four- Leaf Clover" in 1948. Also see Barry Gordon.	
4/23/55	**6**	17	1. **Honey-Babe** Best Seller #6 / Juke Box #6 / Jockey #10 from the film "Battle Cry"	MGM 11900
			THE MOONGLOWS	
			R&B group from Louisville. Consisted of lead singers Bobby Lester (d: 10/15/80 [50]) and Harvey Fuqua, with Alexander "Pete" Graves, Prentiss Barnes and Billy Johnson.	
3/26/55	**20**	1	1. Sincerely Juke Box #20	Chess 1581
10/13/56	**25**	1	2. See Saw Best Seller #25 / Top 100 #28	Chess 1629
10/20/58	**22**	4	3. Ten Commandments Of Love **HARVEY & THE MOONGLOWS**	Chess 1705
			BOB MOORE	
			Born on 11/30/32 in Nashville. Top session bass player. Led the band on Roy Orbison's sessions for Monument Records. Also worked as sideman for Elvis Presley, Brenda Lee, Pat Boone and others.	
9/11/61	**7**	10	1. **Mexico** **[I]**	Monument 446
			BOBBY MOORE & THE RHYTHM ACES	
			Formed in Montgomery, Alabama in 1961, featuring leader Bobby Moore (tenor sax) and Chico Jenkins (lead vocals).	
7/30/66	**27**	4	1. Searching For My Love	Checker 1129
			DOROTHY MOORE	
			Born in Jackson, Mississippi in 1946. Lead singer of The Poppies.	
4/10/76	**3**	16	1. **Misty Blue**	Malaco 1029

DATE	POS	WKS	ARTIST—RECORD TITLE	LABEL & NO.
9/10/77	**27**	7	2. I Believe You	Malaco 1042
			JACKIE MOORE	
			R&B singer from Jacksonville, Florida.	
1/23/71	**30**	7	● 1. Precious, Precious	Atlantic 2681
			JANE MORGAN	
			Born Jane Currier in Boston; raised in Florida. Popular singer in France before achieving US fame via TV and nightclub entertaining.	
9/09/57	**7**	21	1. **Fascination** Jockey #7 / Top 100 #11 / Best Seller #12 instrumental intro by The Troubadors; from the film "Love In The Afternoon"	Kapp 191
10/13/58	**21**	10	2. The Day The Rains Came	Kapp 235
8/31/59	**39**	1	3. With Open Arms	Kapp 284
			JAYE P. MORGAN	
			Born Mary Margaret Morgan in Mancos, Colorado. Sang with Frank DeVol's band for 3 years. Featured on many TV variety and game shows from the 1950s-70s.	
11/27/54†	**3**	21	1. **That's All I Want From You** Jockey #3 / Best Seller #5 / Juke Box #5	RCA 5896
3/12/55	**12**	8	2. Danger! Heartbreak Ahead Jockey #12 / Juke Box #13 / Best Seller #18	RCA 6016
6/11/55	**12**	5	3. Chee Chee-OO-Chee (Sang The Little Bird)/ **PERRY COMO & JAYE P. MORGAN** Jockey #12 / Juke Box #14 / Best Seller #24	
6/25/55	**18**	1	4. Two Lost Souls **PERRY COMO & JAYE P. MORGAN** Jockey #18 from the Broadway musical "Damn Yankees"	RCA 6137
8/20/55	**6**	14	5. **The Longest Walk** Jockey #6 / Juke Box #7 / Best Seller #13 / Top 100 #19 pre	RCA 6182
11/12/55	**14**	8	6. Pepper-Hot Baby/ Juke Box #14 / Top 100 #21	
12/03/55	**12**	3	7. If You Don't Want My Love Juke Box #12 / Top 100 #40 all of above: backed by Hugo Winterhalter's Orchestra	RCA 6282
			RUSS MORGAN	
			Born on 4/29/04 in Scranton, Pennsylvania; died on 8/8/69. Trombonist/pianist/ popular sweet-band leader. Biggest hit: "Cruising Down The River" in 1949.	
11/12/55	**30**	4	1. Dogface Soldier from the movie "To Hell And Back"	Decca 29703
3/17/56	**19**	3	2. The Poor People Of Paris [I] Juke Box #19 / Jockey #23 / Top 100 #26	Decca 29835
			THE MORMON TABERNACLE CHOIR	
			375-voice choir directed by Richard P. Condie (died on 12/22/85).	
9/21/59	**13**	11	1. Battle Hymn Of The Republic with the Philadelphia Orchestra, Eugene Ormandy, conductor; written in 1862; a #1 hit for The Columbia Stellar Quartet in 1918	Columbia 41459

DATE	POS	WKS	ARTIST—RECORD TITLE	LABEL & NO.
			GIORGIO MORODER	
			Italian-born electronic composer/conductor/producer for numerous soundtracks. Produced 7 of Donna Summer's albums.	
3/10/79	**33**	4	1. Chase [I] from the film "Midnight Express"	Casablanca 956
			VAN MORRISON	
			Born on 8/31/45 in Belfast, Ireland. Blue-eyed soul singer/songwriter. Leader of Them. Wrote the classic hit "Gloria."	
8/19/67	**10**	10	1. **Brown Eyed Girl**	Bang 545
4/25/70	**39**	2	2. Come Running	Warner 7383
12/05/70†	**9**	9	3. **Domino**	Warner 7434
3/06/71	**23**	8	4. Blue Money	Warner 7462
11/20/71	**28**	4	5. Wild Night	Warner 7518
			THE MOTELS	
			Los Angeles-based quintet led by vocalist Martha Davis. Formed in Berkeley. To Los Angeles in the early 70s. Re-formed in 1978, signed to Capitol in 1979. Disbanded in 1987.	
5/29/82	**9**	15	1. **Only The Lonely**	Capitol 5114
9/17/83	**9**	13	2. **Suddenly Last Summer**	Capitol 5271
1/14/84	**36**	3	3. Remember The Nights	Capitol 5246
8/10/85	**21**	7	4. Shame	Capitol 5497
			MOTHERLODE	
			Canadian pop quartet led by keyboardist William "Smitty" Smith.	
9/13/69	**18**	7	1. When I Die	Buddah 131
			MOTLEY CRUE	
			Los Angeles-based heavy-metal band: "Vince Neil" Wharton (lead vocals), Mick Mars (guitar), Nikki Sixx (bass) and Tommy Lee (drums).	
8/03/85	**16**	9	1. Smokin' In The Boys Room	Elektra 69625
6/13/87	**12**	9	2. Girls, Girls, Girls	Elektra 69465
			MOTT THE HOOPLE	
			British glitter-rock group led by vocalist Ian Hunter; included Bad Company's guitarist Mick Ralphs (left in 1973).	
11/04/72	**37**	3	1. All The Young Dudes produced by David Bowie	Columbia 45673
			MOUNTAIN	
			New York power-rock group led by Leslie West and Felix Pappalardi (fatally shot on 4/17/83 at the age of 44 in New York City).	
6/13/70	**21**	9	1. Mississippi Queen	Windfall 532
			MOUTH & MacNEAL	
			Dutch duo: Willem Duyn and Maggie MacNeal (Sjoukje Van't Spijker).	
6/17/72	**8**	12	● 1. **How Do You Do?**	Philips 40715
			MOVING PICTURES	
			Alex Smith, lead singer of Australian 6-man pop group.	
11/27/82†	**29**	13	1. What About Me	Network 69952

DATE	POS	WKS	ARTIST—RECORD TITLE	LABEL & NO.
			ALISON MOYET	
			Born Genevieve Alison-Jane Moyet in Basildon, Essex, England. Female vocalist of Yaz.	
5/04/85	**31**	6	1. Invisible	Columbia 04781
			THE MICKEY MOZART QUINTET	
			Mickey Mozart is a pseudonym for jazz harpist/composer Robert Maxwell.	
6/08/59	**30**	6	1. Little Dipper [I]	Roulette 4148
			MARIA MULDAUR	
			Maria (b: 9/12/43, New York City) and former husband Geoff Muldaur (divorced, 1972) were members of Jim Kweskin's Jug Band.	
4/13/74	**6**	14	1. **Midnight At The Oasis**	Reprise 1183
1/25/75	**12**	8	2. I'm A Woman	Reprise 1319
			MUNGO JERRY	
			British skiffle quartet: Ray Dorset (lead vocals), Colin Earl, Paul King and Mike Cole.	
7/25/70	**3**	11	● 1. **In The Summertime**	Janus 125
			SHIRLEY MURDOCK	
			Former gospel singer from Toledo. Discovered by Roger Troutman (aka Roger) who hired her as back-up singer for his family funk group, Zapp.	
2/28/87	**23**	7	1. As We Lay	Elektra 69518
			THE MURMAIDS	
			Los Angeles teenage trio: sisters Carol and Terry Fischer, with Sally Gordon.	
12/07/63†	**3**	11	1. **Popsicles And Icicles**	Chattahoochee 628
			MICHAEL MARTIN MURPHEY	
			Progressive country singer/songwriter from Austin, Texas. Half of the duo The Lewis & Clarke Expedition. Appeared in the film "Take This Job And Shove It."	
10/07/72	**37**	2	1. Geronimo's Cadillac	A&M 1368
5/03/75	**3**	13	● 2. **Wildfire**	Epic 50084
9/13/75	**21**	7	3. Carolina In The Pines	Epic 50131
2/21/76	**39**	2	4. Renegade	Epic 50184
8/28/82	**19**	11	5. What's Forever For	Liberty 1466
			EDDIE MURPHY	
			Born on 4/3/61 in Hempstead, New York. Comedian/actor. Former cast member of TV's "Saturday Night Live." Starred in the films "Beverly Hills Cop (I & II)," "Trading Places," "48 Hours," "The Golden Child" and "Coming To America."	
11/09/85	**2**(3)	14	● 1. **Party All The Time** written, produced and arranged by Rick James	Columbia 05609
			WALTER MURPHY	
			Born in 1952 in New York City. Studied classical and jazz piano at Manhattan School of Music. Former arranger for Doc Severinsen and "The Tonight Show" orchestra.	
7/04/76	**1**(1)	22	● 1. **A Fifth Of Beethoven** **[I]** based on Beethoven's Fifth Symphony	Private S. 45073

DATE	POS	WKS	ARTIST—RECORD TITLE	LABEL & NO.
			ANNE MURRAY	
			Born on 6/20/47 in Springhill, Nova Scotia. With CBC-TV show "Sing Along Jubilee." First recorded for Arc in 1969. Regular on Glen Campbell's "Goodtime Hour" TV series. Currently resides in Toronto.	
8/22/70	**8**	11	● 1. **Snowbird**	Capitol 2738
2/10/73	**7**	13	2. **Danny's Song** written by Kenny Loggins for his nephew	Capitol 3481
1/19/74	**12**	10	3. Love Song	Capitol 3776
5/25/74	**8**	10	4. **You Won't See Me** written by John Lennon & Paul McCartney	Capitol 3867
8/19/78	**1**(1)	17	● 5. **You Needed Me**	Capitol 4574
2/10/79	**12**	12	6. I Just Fall In Love Again	Capitol 4675
6/23/79	**25**	7	7. Shadows In The Moonlight	Capitol 4716
10/20/79	**12**	11	8. Broken Hearted Me	Capitol 4773
1/19/80	**12**	11	9. Daydream Believer	Capitol 4813
10/18/80	**33**	4	10. Could I Have This Dance from the film "Urban Cowboy"	Capitol 4920
5/02/81	**34**	4	11. Blessed Are The Believers	Capitol 4987
			THE MUSIC EXPLOSION	
			Jamie Lyons, lead singer of pop-rock quintet from Mansfield, Ohio. Produced by Jerry Kasenetz and Jeff Katz.	
5/27/67	**2**(2)	13	● 1. **Little Bit O' Soul**	Laurie 3380
			THE MUSIC MACHINE	
			Los Angeles rock quintet; Sean Bonniwell, lead singer/songwriter.	
12/10/66†	**15**	8	1. Talk Talk	Original Sound 61
			MUSICAL YOUTH	
			5 schoolboys (ages 11 to 16) from Birmingham, England: Dennis Seaton (lead), with brothers Kelvin (guitar) & Michael Grant (keyboards), and Patrick (bass) & Junior Waite (drums).	
1/15/83	**10**	10	1. **Pass The Dutchie** Dutchie: a Jamaican cooking pot	MCA 52149
			BILLY MYLES	
			New York singer/songwriter. Wrote the Mello-Kings' pop hit "Tonite, Tonite."	
11/25/57	**25**	6	1. The Joker (That's What They Call Me) Best Seller #25 / Top 100 #30	Ember 1026
			THE MYSTICS	
			Quintet from Brooklyn: Phil Cracolici (lead), Bob Ferrante & George Galfo (tenors), Albee Cracolici (baritone) and Allie Contrera (bass).	
6/15/59	**20**	9	1. Hushabye	Laurie 3028
			N	
			NAKED EYES	
			English duo: Pete Byrne (vocals) and Rob Fisher (keyboards, synthesizer). Split in 1984. Fisher later in duo, Climie Fisher.	
4/23/83	**8**	13	1. **Always Something There To Remind Me**	EMI America 8155

DATE	POS	WKS	ARTIST—RECORD TITLE	LABEL & NO.
8/13/83	**11**	12	2. Promises, Promises	EMI America 8170
12/17/83	**37**	3	3. When The Lights Go Out	EMI America 8183
9/29/84	**39**	2	4. (What) In The Name Of Love	EMI America 8219
			NAPOLEON XIV	
			Napoleon is Jerry Samuels, a recording engineer/composer from New York.	
7/30/66	**3**	5	1. **They're Coming To Take Me Away, Ha-Haaa! [N]**	Warner 5831
			GRAHAM NASH	
			Born on 2/2/42 in Blackpool, England. Co-founding member of The Hollies. Formed Crosby, Stills & Nash in 1970.	
7/10/71	**35**	4	1. Chicago	Atlantic 2804
6/10/72	**36**	4	2. Immigration Man	Atlantic 2873
			GRAHAM NASH & DAVID CROSBY	
			JOHNNY NASH	
			Born on 8/19/40 in Houston. Vocalist/guitarist/actor. Appeared on local TV from age 13. With Arthur Godfrey's TV/radio show from 1956-63. In the film "Take A Giant Step" in 1959. Own label, JoDa, in 1965. Began recording in Jamaica, late 60s.	
2/03/58	**23**	1	1. A Very Special Love Jockey #23 / Best Seller #45 / Top 100 #46	ABC-Para. 9874
12/15/58†	**29**	5	2. The Teen Commandments [S] **PAUL ANKA-GEORGE HAMILTON IV-JOHNNY NASH** inspirational talk from above 3 ABC-Paramount artists	ABC-Para. 9974
10/05/68	**5**	12	3. **Hold Me Tight**	JAD 207
1/24/70	**39**	1	4. Cupid	JAD 220
10/07/72	**1**(4)	14	● 5. **I Can See Clearly Now**	Epic 10902
3/03/73	**12**	10	6. Stir It Up	Epic 10949
			THE NASHVILLE TEENS	
			British rock sextet; Arthur Sharp, lead singer.	
10/10/64	**14**	6	1. Tobacco Road	London 9689
			NATURAL FOUR	
			Soul group led by Chris James, formed in 1967 in San Francisco.	
2/09/74	**31**	4	1. Can This Be Real	Curtom 1990
			DAVID NAUGHTON	
			Singer/dancer/actor. Starred in the 1981 film "An American Werewolf In London" and TV show "Makin' It." Cast member of TV's "My Sister Sam."	
5/12/79	**5**	16	● 1. **Makin' It** vocals: Michael Henderson and Jean Cain; from the film "Meatballs"	RSO 916
			NAZARETH	
			Hard-rock group formed in Scotland in 1969. Dan McCafferty, lead singer.	
1/03/76	**8**	14	● 1. **Love Hurts**	A&M 1671
			SAM NEELY	
			Born on 8/22/48 in Cuero, Texas. Pop singer/songwriter.	
10/07/72	**29**	6	1. Loving You Just Crossed My Mind	Capitol 3381
11/09/74	**34**	2	2. You Can Have Her	A&M 1612

Millie Jackson's colorful career includes 1973's "Hurts So Good" single, taken from the soundtrack to *Cleopatra Jones*.

The Jacksons' last single from *Victory*, "Body," was penned by Jackson brother Marlon. Its two predecessors were "State Of Shock" and "Torture"—authored by brother Michael and lyricist Randy Hansen, and brother Jackie and lyricist Kathy Wakefield, respectively.

Rick James' move from Motown to Reprise in 1988 resulted in his hit with "Loosey's Rap," a critical rebirth for the artist. In its 12-inch version, the song also featured rappers Roxanne Shante and Big Daddy Kane.

Jan & Dean's many hits of the 60s tell the story of that decade, by title alone, better than most sociology books—from their initial "Baby Talk" in 1959, through 1963's "Surf City" and "Drag City," 1964's "Sidewalk Surfin'," and 1966's "Batman."

Al Jarreau's "Moonlighting (Theme)" led off an unusual television soundtrack album that also featured Chubby Checker, the Isley Brothers, Linda Ronstadt, Percy Sledge, and Billie Holiday—as well as "Moonlighting" stars Cybill Shepherd and Bruce Willis. The latter two are no strangers themselves to the art of record-making.

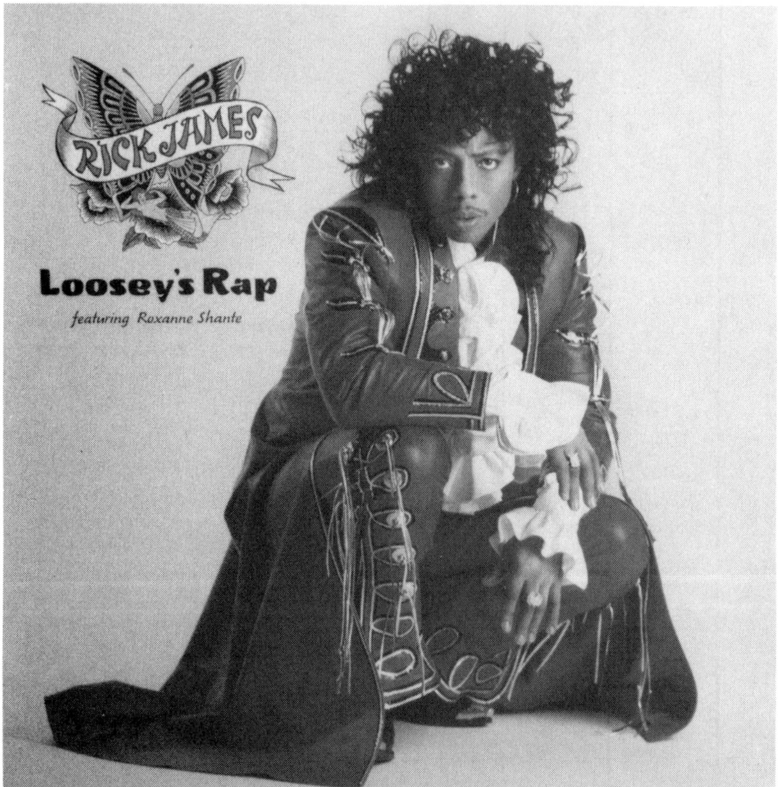

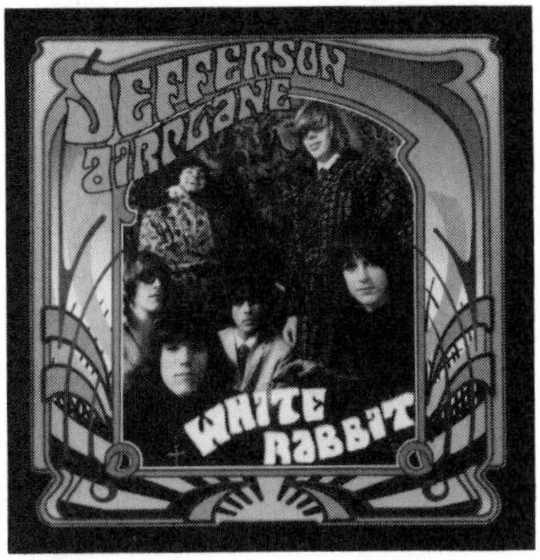

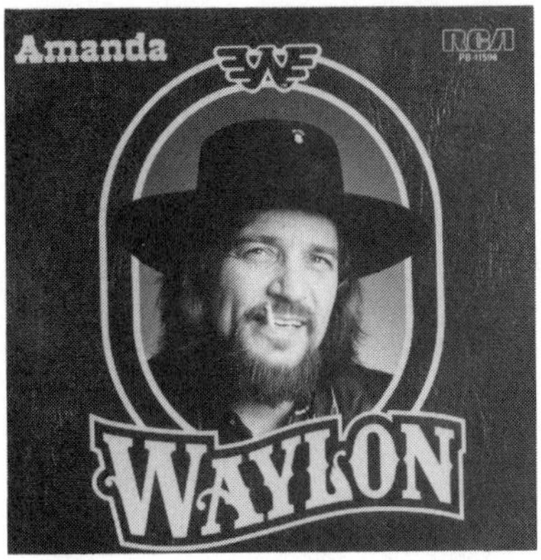

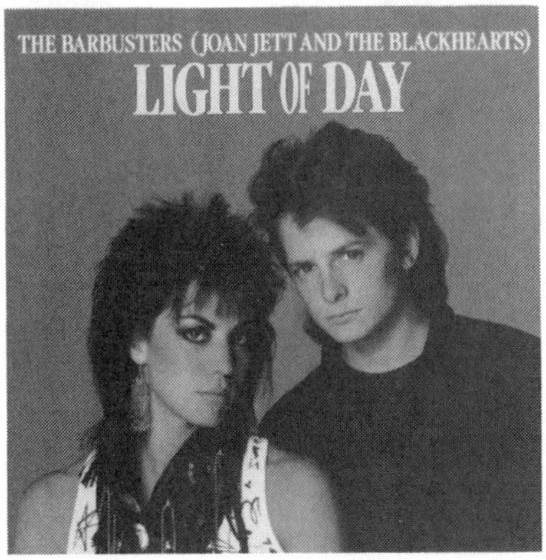

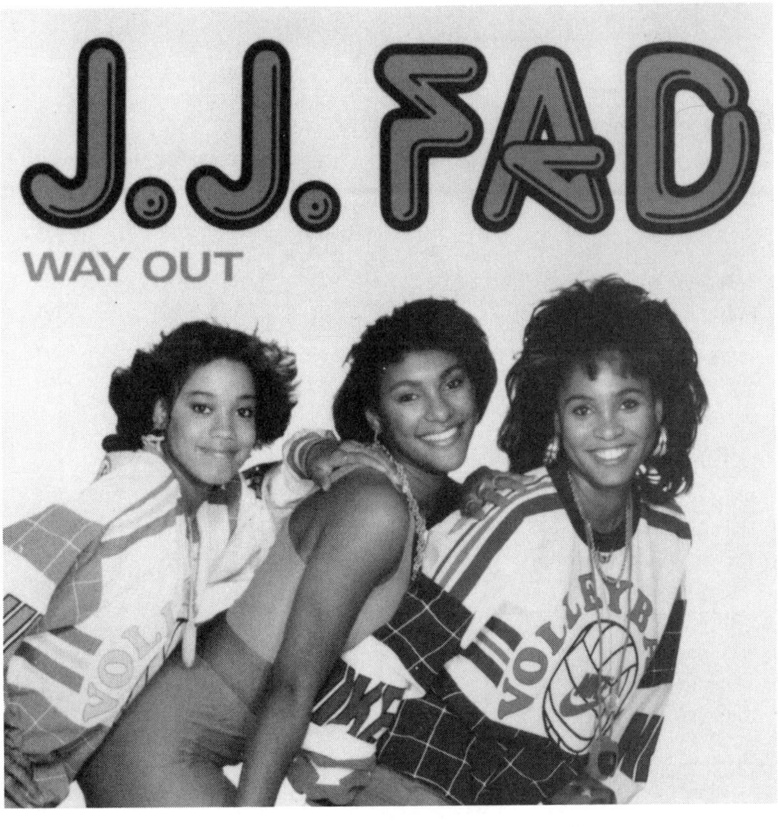

The Jefferson Airplane made headlines in 1989 with word of a planned reunion that would feature past members Grace Slick, Paul Kantner, Jorma Kaukonen, and Jack Casady, among others. At the same time, singer Micky Thomas continues to lead Starship—a group once named Jefferson Starship and, before that, the Jefferson Airplane.

Waylon Jennings' collaboration with his wife Jesse Colter, Willie Nelson, and Tompall Glaser on a 1976 RCA album called *Wanted: The Outlaws* resulted in the first country album ever to be awarded platinum status.

The Jets and MCA Records entered into an unusual marketing agreement with Frito-Lay in 1988: packages of Doritos corn chips bore discount coupons for the group's album, *Magic*.

Joan Jett & the Blackhearts excited many Bruce Springsteen fans when the group, under the name of the Barbusters, issued the first official recording of Springsteen's "Light Of Day," taken from the Paul Schrader-directed film of the same name.

J. J. Fad's "Supersonic" did well enough as an independent single for Atco Records to sign the group and re-release the single nationally. The result? A hit that reached the No. 30 slot on the Hot 100, and a burgeoning career for the young female rap trio.

DATE	POS	WKS	ARTIST—RECORD TITLE	LABEL & NO.
			THE NEIGHBORHOOD	
8/08/70	**29**	4	1. Big Yellow Taxi	Big Tree 102
			RICKY NELSON	
			Born Eric Hilliard Nelson on 5/8/40 in Teaneck, New Jersey. Died on 12/31/85 in a plane crash in DeKalb, Texas. Son of bandleader Ozzie Nelson and vocalist Harriet Hilliard. Rick and brother David appeared on Nelson's radio show from March, 1949, later on TV, 1952 to 1966. Formed own Stone Canyon Band in 1969. Films "Rio Bravo," "Wackiest Ship In The Army," and "Love And Kisses." One of the first teen idols of the rock era. Inducted into the Rock And Roll Hall Of Fame in 1987.	
5/06/57	**4**	15	1. **I'm Walking/** Best Seller #4 / Juke Box #16 / Top 100 #17	
5/13/57	**2**(1)	15	2. A Teenager's Romance Best Seller #2 / Top 100 #8 / Jockey #8 / Juke Box #12	Verve 10047
9/16/57	**14**	7	3. You're My One And Only Love Best Seller #14 / Top 100 #16 above 3: orchestra directed by Barney Kessel	Verve 10070
10/07/57	**3**	18	4. **Be-Bop Baby/** Best Seller #3 / Top 100 #5 / Jockey #10	
10/28/57	**29**	3	5. Have I Told You Lately That I Love You? Bing Crosby & The Andrews Sisters' version hit #24 in 1950	Imperial 5463
12/30/57†	**2**(3)	14	6. **Stood Up/** Best Seller #2 / Top 100 #5 / Jockey #5	
12/30/57†	**18**	9	7. Waitin' In School Top 100 #18 / Jockey #24	Imperial 5483
4/07/58	**4**	10	8. **Believe What You Say/** Best Seller #4 / Top 100 #8 / Jockey #20	
4/07/58	**12**	10	9. My Bucket's Got A Hole In It Best Seller #12 / Top 100 #18 / Jockey #25	Imperial 5503
7/07/58	**1**(2)	15	10. **Poor Little Fool** Hot 100 #1(2) / Best Seller #1(2) / Jockey #2 end	Imperial 5528
10/20/58	**7**	16	11. **Lonesome Town/**	
10/20/58	**10**	13	12. I Got A Feeling	Imperial 5545
3/09/59	**6**	12	13. **Never Be Anyone Else But You/**	
3/16/59	**9**	10	14. It's Late	Imperial 5565
7/13/59	**9**	9	15. **Just A Little Too Much/**	
7/13/59	**9**	8	16. Sweeter Than You	Imperial 5595
12/07/59	**20**	8	17. I Wanna Be Loved/	
12/21/59	**38**	1	18. Mighty Good	Imperial 5614
5/09/60	**12**	9	19. Young Emotions	Imperial 5663
9/19/60	**27**	4	20. I'm Not Afraid/	
9/26/60	**34**	2	21. Yes Sir, That's My Baby #1 hit for Gene Austin in 1925	Imperial 5685
1/09/61	**25**	4	22. You Are The Only One	Imperial 5707
5/01/61	**1**(2)	15	● 23. **Travelin' Man/**	
5/08/61	**9**	13	24. Hello Mary Lou written by Gene Pitney	Imperial 5741
			RICK NELSON:	
10/09/61	**11**	9	25. A Wonder Like You/	
10/09/61	**16**	8	26. Everlovin'	Imperial 5770
3/17/62	**5**	10	27. **Young World**	Imperial 5805

DATE	POS	WKS	ARTIST—RECORD TITLE	LABEL & NO.
8/25/62	**5**	9	28. **Teen Age Idol**	Imperial 5864
12/29/62†	**6**	9	29. **It's Up To You**	Imperial 5901
6/15/63	**25**	5	30. String Along	Decca 31495
10/05/63	**12**	9	31. Fools Rush In #1 hit for Glenn Miller in 1940	Decca 31533
1/11/64	**6**	9	32. **For You** #9 hit for John Boles in 1930	Decca 31574
5/09/64	**26**	5	33. The Very Thought Of You #1 hit for Ray Noble in 1934	Decca 31612
			RICK NELSON & THE STONE CANYON BAND:	
1/03/70	**33**	6	34. She Belongs To Me written by Bob Dylan	Decca 32550
9/16/72	**6**	12	● 35. **Garden Party**	Decca 32980
			SANDY NELSON	
			Born Sander Nelson on 12/1/38 in Santa Monica, California. Rock 'n' roll drummer. Became prominent studio musician. Heard on "Alley Oop," "To Know Him Is To Love Him," "A Thousand Stars," and many others. Lost portion of right leg in a motorcycle accident in 1963. Returned to performing in 1964.	
9/14/59	**4**	12	1. **Teen Beat** **[I]**	Original Sound 5
11/20/61	**7**	12	2. **Let There Be Drums** **[I]**	Imperial 5775
3/03/62	**29**	4	3. Drums Are My Beat [I]	Imperial 5809
			WILLIE NELSON	
			Born on 4/30/33 in Abbott, Texas. Prolific country singer/songwriter. Pioneered "outlaw" country movement. Appeared in several films including "The Electric Horseman" (1979) and "Honeysuckle Rose" (1980).	
10/11/75	**21**	9	1. Blue Eyes Crying In The Rain	Columbia 10176
3/06/76	**25**	5	2. Good Hearted Woman **WAYLON & WILLIE**	RCA 10529
9/27/80	**20**	10	3. On The Road Again from the film "Honeysuckle Rose"	Columbia 11351
4/10/82	**5**	15	4. **Always On My Mind**	Columbia 02741
9/18/82	**40**	3	5. Let It Be Me	Columbia 03073
3/31/84	**5**	12	● 6. **To All The Girls I've Loved Before** **JULIO IGLESIAS & WILLIE NELSON**	Columbia 04217
			NENA	
			Gabriele "Nena" Kerner with 4-member back-up group from West Germany.	
1/21/84	2(1)	13	● 1. **99 Luftballons** **[F]** nuclear protest song	Epic 04108
			THE NEON PHILHARMONIC	
			Chamber-sized orchestra of Nashville Symphony Orchestra musicians. Project headed by Tupper Saussy (composer) and Don Gant (vocals). Gant died on 3/6/87 (44).	
5/10/69	**17**	7	1. Morning Girl	Warner 7261
			PETER NERO	
			Born on 5/22/34 in Brooklyn. Pop-jazz-classical pianist. Won the 1961 Best New Artist Grammy Award.	
11/20/71	**21**	8	1. Theme From "Summer Of '42" [I] from the film of the same title	Columbia 45399

DATE	POS	WKS	ARTIST—RECORD TITLE	LABEL & NO.
			NERVOUS NORVUS	
			Real name: Jimmy Drake.	
6/09/56	**8**	9	1. **Transfusion** **[N]** Best Seller #8 / Top 100 #13 / Jockey #14 / Juke Box #18	Dot 15470
8/11/56	**24**	4	2. Ape Call [N] Best Seller #24 / Top 100 #28 ape calls by Red Blanchard	Dot 15485
			MICHAEL NESMITH & THE FIRST NATIONAL BAND	
			Born on 12/30/43 in Houston. Michael was a professional musician before joining The Monkees. Wrote Linda Ronstadt's hit "Different Drum."	
9/05/70	**21**	7	1. Joanne	RCA 0368
			ROBBIE NEVIL	
			Pop singer/songwriter/guitarist from Los Angeles.	
11/15/86†	**2**(2)	16	1. **C'est La Vie**	Manhattan 50047
3/14/87	**14**	9	2. Dominoes	Manhattan 50053
6/27/87	**10**	9	3. **Wot's It To Ya**	Manhattan 50075
			AARON NEVILLE	
			Born in New Orleans in 1941. Member of the New Orleans R&B family group The Neville Brothers. Brother Art was keyboardist of The Meters. His son Ivan began recording career in 1988.	
12/17/66†	**2**(1)	11	1. **Tell It Like It Is**	Par-Lo 101
			IVAN NEVILLE	
			New Orleans bassist, son of singer Aaron Neville (member of The Neville Brothers). Formerly with Bonnie Raitt's band. Played on The Rolling Stones' "Dirty Work" album.	
11/12/88	**26**	6	1. Not Just Another Girl	Polydor 887814
			THE NEWBEATS	
			Pop trio: Larry Henley (b: 6/30/41, Arp, TX; lead singer) with brothers Dean and Marc Mathis (b: Hahira, GA on 3/17/39 and 2/9/42, respectively).	
8/22/64	**2**(2)	11	1. **Bread And Butter**	Hickory 1269
11/07/64	**16**	7	2. Everything's Alright	Hickory 1282
2/20/65	**40**	1	3. Break Away (From That Boy)	Hickory 1290
10/30/65	**12**	9	4. Run, Baby Run (Back Into My Arms)	Hickory 1332
			THE NEW BIRTH	
			consisted of vocalists Londee Loren, Bobby Downs, Melvin Wilson, Leslie Wilson, Ann Bogan and soloist Alan Frye, with instrumental backing by The Nite-Liters. Melvin, Leslie and Ann recorded as Love, Peace & Happiness in 1972.	
5/05/73	**35**	4	1. I Can Understand It	RCA 0912
8/23/75	**36**	2	2. Dream Merchant	Buddah 470
			THE NEW CHRISTY MINSTRELS	
			Folk/balladeer troupe named after the Christy Minstrels (formed in 1842 by Edwin "Pop" Christy). Group founded and led by Randy Sparks; Barry McGuire, member.	
7/27/63	**14**	7	1. Green, Green	Columbia 42805
11/16/63	**29**	3	2. Saturday Night	Columbia 42887
5/16/64	**17**	9	3. Today from the film "Advance To The Rear"	Columbia 43000

DATE	POS	WKS	ARTIST—RECORD TITLE	LABEL & NO.
			THE NEW COLONY SIX	
			Soft-rock group from Chicago: Patrick McBride, Ronnie Rice, Gerry Van Kollenburg, Les Kummel, Chuck Jobes and William Herman. Ray Graffia joined in 1969.	
5/11/68	**22**	6	1. I Will Always Think About You	Mercury 72775
2/15/69	**16**	9	2. Things I'd Like To Say	Mercury 72858
			NEW EDITION	
			R&B group formed in Boston, consisting of 5 boys (ages 13 to 15 in 1983): Ralph Tresvant, Ronald DeVoe, Michael Bivins, Ricky Bell and Bobby Brown. Brown left for solo career in 1986; replaced by Johnny Gill in 1988.	
10/27/84†	**4**	14	● 1. **Cool It Now**	MCA 52455
1/26/85	**12**	8	2. Mr. Telephone Man	MCA 52484
4/27/85	**35**	4	3. Lost In Love	MCA 52553
4/12/86	**38**	2	4. A Little Bit Of Love (Is All It Takes)	MCA 52768
9/20/86	**21**	6	5. Earth Angel featured in the film "The Karate Kid Part II"	MCA 52905
7/30/88	**7**	13	6. **If It Isn't Love**	MCA 53264
			NEW ENGLAND	
			East Coast melodic rock quartet.	
6/16/79	**40**	1	1. Don't Ever Wanna Lose Ya	Infinity 50013
			NEW KIDS ON THE BLOCK	
			Boston teen quintet formed in the summer of 1984: Joe McIntyre (13-year-old lead singer), Donny Wahlberg, Danny Wood, and brothers Jordan and Jon Knight.	
8/13/88	**10**	12	1. **Please Don't Go Girl**	Columbia 07700
			NEW ORDER	
			Electro-pop group from Manchester, England, formerly known as Joy Division. Lineup since 1986: Bernard Sumner, Stephen Morris, Peter Hook & Gillian Gilbert.	
12/05/87	**32**	8	1. True Faith	Qwest 28271
			THE NEW SEEKERS	
			British-Australian group formed by former Seeker Keith Potger after disbandment of The Seekers in 1969. Consisted of Eve Graham, Lyn Paul, Peter Doyle, Marty Kristian and Paul Layton.	
9/19/70	**14**	9	1. Look What They've Done To My Song Ma	Elektra 45699
12/18/71†	**7**	9	● 2. **I'd Like To Teach The World To Sing (In Perfect Harmony)**	Elektra 45762
4/14/73	**29**	4	3. Pinball Wizard/See Me, Feel Me from the rock opera "Tommy"	Verve 10709
			THE NEW VAUDEVILLE BAND	
			Creation of British composer/record producer Geoff Stephens.	
11/05/66	**1**(3)	13	● 1. **Winchester Cathedral**	Fontana 1562
			NEW YORK CITY	
			New York City R&B quartet: Tim McQueen, John Brown, Ed Shell and Claude Johnston. First recorded for Buddah as Triboro Exchange. Name changed in 1972.	
4/28/73	**17**	12	1. I'm Doin' Fine Now	Chelsea 0113

DATE	POS	WKS	ARTIST—RECORD TITLE	LABEL & NO.
			MICKEY NEWBURY	
			Born Milton Newbury, Jr. on 5/19/40 in Houston. Elected to the Writer's Hall of Fame in Nashville.	
12/04/71†	**26**	7	1. An American Trilogy Dixie/Battle Hymn Of The Republic/All My Trials	Elektra 45750
			JIMMY NEWMAN	
			Born on 8/27/27 in Big Mamou, Louisiana. Cajun-country singer/guitarist.	
7/22/57	**23**	1	1. A Fallen Star Jockey #23 / Top 100 #42	Dot 15574
			RANDY NEWMAN	
			Born on 11/28/43 in New Orleans. Singer/composer/pianist. Nephew of composers Alfred, Emil and Lionel Newman. Scored the films "Ragtime" and "The Natural."	
12/10/77†	**2**(3)	13	● 1. **Short People** **[N]**	Warner 8492
			JUICE NEWTON	
			Born Judy Kay Newton on 2/18/52 in Virginia Beach, Virginia. Pop-country singer.	
3/07/81	**4**	16	● 1. **Angel Of The Morning**	Capitol 4976
6/20/81	**2**(2)	19	● 2. **Queen Of Hearts**	Capitol 4997
11/07/81†	**7**	18	3. **The Sweetest Thing (I've Ever Known)**	Capitol 5046
5/22/82	**7**	13	4. **Love's Been A Little Bit Hard On Me**	Capitol 5120
9/11/82	**11**	10	5. Break It To Me Gently	Capitol 5148
12/18/82†	**25**	10	6. Heart Of The Night	Capitol 5192
9/03/83	**27**	5	7. Tell Her No	Capitol 5265
			WAYNE NEWTON	
			Born on 4/3/42 in Roanoke, Virginia. Singer/multi-instrumentalist. Top Las Vegas entertainer. First big break came in 1962 on TV's "The Jackie Gleason Show." Bobby Darin saw Wayne, signed him up and produced his first charted single.	
8/03/63	**13**	8	1. Danke Schoen with The Newton Brothers (Wayne and his brother Jerry)	Capitol 4989
3/27/65	**23**	5	2. Red Roses For A Blue Lady	Capitol 5366
6/10/72	**4**	13	● 3. **Daddy Don't You Walk So Fast**	Chelsea 0100
3/22/80	**35**	3	4. Years	Aries II 108
			OLIVIA NEWTON-JOHN	
			Born on 9/26/48 in Cambridge, England. To Australia in 1953. At age 16, won talent contest trip to England, sang with Pat Carroll as Pat & Olivia. With the group Toomorrow, in a British film of the same name. Consistent award winner in both pop and country. Granddaughter of Nobel Prize-winning German physicist Max Born. In films "Grease" (1978), "Xanadu" (1980) and "Two Of A Kind" (1983). Married actor Matt Lattanzi in 1985. Also see John Denver.	
7/17/71	**25**	10	1. If Not For You written by Bob Dylan	Uni 55281
12/15/73†	**6**	14	● 2. **Let Me Be There**	MCA 40101
5/11/74	**5**	12	● 3. **If You Love Me (Let Me Know)**	MCA 40209
8/24/74	**1**(2)	10	● 4. **I Honestly Love You**	MCA 40280
2/08/75	**1**(1)	11	● 5. **Have You Never Been Mellow**	MCA 40349
6/21/75	**3**	12	● 6. **Please Mr. Please**	MCA 40418
10/11/75	**13**	7	7. Something Better To Do	MCA 40459

DATE	POS	WKS	ARTIST—RECORD TITLE	LABEL & NO.
1/03/76	**30**	4	8. Let It Shine	MCA 40495
4/17/76	**23**	6	9. Come On Over	MCA 40525
9/04/76	**33**	4	10. Don't Stop Believin'	MCA 40600
2/19/77	**20**	9	11. Sam	MCA 40670
4/08/78	**1**(1)	16	▲ 12. **You're The One That I Want**	RSO 891
			JOHN TRAVOLTA & OLIVIA NEWTON-JOHN	
7/22/78	**3**	15	● 13. **Hopelessly Devoted To You**	RSO 903
8/19/78	**5**	12	● 14. **Summer Nights**	RSO 906
			JOHN TRAVOLTA & OLIVIA NEWTON-JOHN & CAST	
			above 3: from the film "Grease"	
12/09/78†	**3**	17	● 15. **A Little More Love**	MCA 40975
5/05/79	**11**	8	16. Deeper Than The Night	MCA 41009
4/19/80	**12**	8	17. I Can't Help It	RSO 1026
			ANDY GIBB & OLIVIA NEWTON-JOHN	
6/14/80	**1**(4)	16	● 18. **Magic**	MCA 41247
8/30/80	**8**	10	19. **Xanadu**	MCA 41285
			OLIVIA NEWTON-JOHN/ELECTRIC LIGHT ORCHESTRA	
11/22/80†	**20**	11	20. Suddenly	MCA 51007
			OLIVIA NEWTON-JOHN & CLIFF RICHARD	
			above 3: from the film "Xanadu"	
10/17/81	**1**(10)	21	▲ 21. **Physical**	MCA 51182
2/27/82	**5**	10	● 22. **Make A Move On Me**	MCA 52000
9/25/82	**3**	13	23. **Heart Attack**	MCA 52100
2/19/83	**38**	3	24. Tied Up	MCA 52155
			1, 5, 7, 10, 12-13, 15, 18, 20, 22 & 24: written by John Farrar	
11/12/83†	**5**	14	25. **Twist Of Fate**	MCA 52284
2/25/84	**31**	5	26. Livin' In Desperate Times	MCA 52341
			above 2: from the film "Two Of A Kind"	
10/26/85	**20**	7	27. Soul Kiss	MCA 52686
			all of above (except #14, 17, 19, 25-26): produced by John Farrar	
			PAUL NICHOLAS	
			British theater/film actor. Played Billy Shears' brother in film "Sgt. Pepper's Lonely Hearts Club Band."	
9/17/77	**6**	16	● 1. **Heaven On The 7th Floor**	RSO 878
			STEVIE NICKS	
			Born Stephanie Nicks on 5/26/48 in Phoenix; raised in California. Became vocalist of Bay-area group Fritz and subsequently met guitarist Lindsey Buckingham. Teamed up and recorded album "Buckingham-Nicks" in 1973. Vocalist with Fleetwood Mac since January of 1975.	
8/01/81	**3**	15	1. **Stop Draggin' My Heart Around**	Modern 7336
			STEVIE NICKS with TOM PETTY & THE HEARTBREAKERS	
11/07/81†	**6**	15	2. **Leather And Lace**	Modern 7341
			STEVIE NICKS with DON HENLEY	
3/06/82	**11**	11	3. Edge Of Seventeen (Just Like The White Winged Dove)	Modern 7401

DATE	POS	WKS	ARTIST—RECORD TITLE	LABEL & NO.
6/12/82	**32**	4	4. After The Glitter Fades	Modern 7405
6/18/83	**5**	14	5. **Stand Back**	Modern 99863
9/24/83	**14**	9	6. If Anyone Falls	Modern 99832
1/21/84	**33**	4	7. Nightbird	Modern 99799
			with Sandy Stewart (co-writer on above 2)	
11/30/85†	**4**	13	8. **Talk To Me**	Modern 99582
3/01/86	**37**	2	9. Needles And Pins	MCA 52772
			TOM PETTY & THE HEARTBREAKERS with STEVIE NICKS	
3/08/86	**16**	8	10. I Can't Wait	Modern 99565
			all of above: written by Stevie & produced by Jimmy Iovine	
			NIELSEN/PEARSON	
			Sacramento pop duo: Reid Nielsen and Mark Pearson.	
11/15/80	**38**	2	1. If You Should Sail	Capitol 4910
			NIGHT	
			Sextet led by female vocalist Stevie Lange and Chris Thompson, lead singer/ guitarist of Manfred Mann's Earth Band.	
8/04/79	**18**	8	1. Hot Summer Nights	Planet 45903
10/20/79	**17**	8	2. If You Remember Me	Planet 45909
			CHRIS THOMPSON & NIGHT	
			NIGHT RANGER	
			Rock group from California: lead singers Kelly Keagy (drums) and Jack Blades (bass), with guitarists Jeff Watson and Brad Gillis, and keyboardist Alan "Fitz" Gerald. Blades and Gillis were members of Rubicon. Gerald left in 1988; band split up in early 1989.	
2/26/83	**40**	3	1. Don't Tell Me You Love Me	Boardwalk 171
4/21/84	**5**	12	2. **Sister Christian**	MCA/Camel 52350
8/04/84	**14**	11	3. When You Close Your Eyes	MCA/Camel 52420
6/08/85	**8**	11	4. **Sentimental Street**	MCA/Camel 52591
9/21/85	**19**	6	5. Four In The Morning (I Can't Take Any More)	MCA/Camel 52661
12/07/85†	**17**	10	6. Goodbye	MCA/Camel 52729
			all of above (except #2): written by Jack Blades	
			MAXINE NIGHTINGALE	
			Born on 11/2/52 in Wembly, England. First recorded in 1968. In productions of "Hair," "Jesus Christ Superstar," "Godspell" and "Savages," in the early 70s.	
3/13/76	**2**(2)	15	● 1. **Right Back Where We Started From**	United Art. 752
7/07/79	**5**	14	● 2. **Lead Me On**	Windsong 11530
			NILSSON	
			Born Harry Edward Nelson III on 6/15/41 in Brooklyn. Wrote Three Dog Night's hit "One"; scored the film "Skidoo" and TV's "The Courtship Of Eddie's Father." Close friend of John Lennon and Ringo Starr.	
9/06/69	**6**	9	1. **Everybody's Talkin'**	RCA 0161
			theme song from the film "Midnight Cowboy"	
11/29/69	**34**	2	2. I Guess The Lord Must Be In New York City	RCA 0261
5/08/71	**34**	4	3. Me And My Arrow	RCA 0443
1/15/72	**1**(4)	14	● 4. **Without You**	RCA 0604
			written by Badfinger's Pete Ham & Tom Evans	
4/08/72	**27**	6	5. Jump Into The Fire	RCA 0673

DATE	POS	WKS	ARTIST—RECORD TITLE	LABEL & NO.
7/08/72	**8**	10	6. **Coconut**	RCA 0718
10/14/72	**23**	6	7. Spaceman	RCA 0788
5/25/74	**39**	2	8. Daybreak from the film "Son Of Dracula"	RCA 0246
			1910 FRUITGUM CO.	
			New Jersey bubblegum quintet: Mark Gutkowski, Floyd Marcus, Pat Karwan, Steve Mortkowitz and Frank Jeckell. Produced by The Music Explosion and Ohio Express producers Jerry Kasenetz and Jeff Katz.	
2/10/68	**4**	11	● 1. **Simon Says**	Buddah 24
8/10/68	**5**	11	● 2. **1, 2, 3, Red Light**	Buddah 54
12/07/68	**37**	3	3. Goody Goody Gumdrops	Buddah 71
2/08/69	**5**	11	● 4. **Indian Giver**	Buddah 91
6/14/69	**38**	2	5. Special Delivery	Buddah 114
			THE NITE-LITERS	
			R&B band formed in Louisville in 1963 by Harvey Fuqua and Tony Churchill. Expanded to 17 members with 2 vocal groups and band. Renamed New Birth, Inc., with The Nite-Liters making up the instrumental section. Also see The New Birth.	
9/11/71	**39**	1	1. K-Jee [I]	RCA 0461
			NITEFLYTE	
			Disco group led by Howard Johnson and Sandy Torano.	
11/24/79	**37**	2	1. If You Want It	Ariola 7747
			NITTY GRITTY DIRT BAND	
			Country-rock-folk group from Long Beach, California. Led by Jeff Hanna (vocals, guitar) and John McEuen (banjo, mandolin). Changed name to Dirt Band in 1976 when Hanna left the group. Resumed using Nitty Gritty Dirt Band name in 1982. Ex-Eagle member Bernie Leadon replaced McEuen in 1987.	
1/02/71	**9**	13	1. **Mr. Bojangles** prologue: Uncle Charlie and His Dog Teddy	Liberty 56197
			DIRT BAND:	
1/12/80	**13**	11	2. An American Dream harmony vocal: Linda Ronstadt	United Art. 1330
7/12/80	**25**	9	3. Make A Little Magic	United Art. 1356
			JACK NITZSCHE	
			Born Bernard Nitzsche on 4/22/37 in Chicago. Arranger/producer/composer/keyboardist. Arranger for many of Phil Spector's productions. Wrote "Needles And Pins" and scored the film "One Flew Over The Cuckoo's Nest."	
9/07/63	**39**	2	1. The Lonely Surfer [I]	Reprise 20202
			NICK NOBLE	
			Born Nicholas Valkan on 6/21/36 in Chicago.	
8/20/55	**22**	3	1. The Bible Tells Me So Best Seller #22 / Top 100 #61 pre	Wing 90003
3/24/56	**27**	6	2. To You, My Love	Mercury 70821
7/15/57	**20**	1	3. A Fallen Star Jockey #20	Mercury 71124
9/30/57	**37**	1	4. Moonlight Swim	Mercury 71169

DATE	POS	WKS	ARTIST—RECORD TITLE	LABEL & NO.
			CLIFF NOBLES & CO.	
			Cliff was born in Mobile, Alabama in 1944. Soul bandleader/singer.	
6/08/68	**2**(3)	12	● 1. **The Horse** **[I]**	Phil-L.A. 313
			JACKY NOGUEZ	
			Popular European society bandleader from Paris.	
7/27/59	**24**	5	1. Ciao, Ciao Bambina [I]	Jamie 1127
			KENNY NOLAN	
			Los Angeles-based singer/songwriter. Wrote "My Eyes Adored You," "Lady Marmalade" and "Get Dancin'."	
12/11/76†	**3**	20	● 1. **I Like Dreamin'**	20th Century 2287
5/07/77	**20**	11	2. Love's Grown Deep	20th Century 2331
			CHRIS NORMAN - see SUZI QUATRO	
			FREDDIE NORTH	
			Black vocalist from Nashville. Worked in sales and promotion for Nashboro Records. Disc jockey on "Night Train," WLAC-Nashville.	
11/27/71	**39**	1	1. She's All I Got	Mankind 12004
			ALDO NOVA	
			Born Aldo Scarporuscio in Montreal. Rock singer/songwriter/guitarist/keyboardist.	
5/01/82	**23**	7	1. Fantasy	Portrait 02799
			NU SHOOZ	
			Portland, Oregon group centered around husband-and-wife team of guitarist/ songwriter John Smith and lead singer Valerie Day.	
4/05/86	**3**	15	1. **I Can't Wait**	Atlantic 89446
9/06/86	**28**	8	2. Point Of No Return	Atlantic 89392
			THE NU TORNADOS	
			Philadelphia string band; Eddie Dono, leader. Also see Ferko String Band.	
12/15/58	**26**	6	1. Philadelphia U.S.A.	Carlton 492
			TED NUGENT	
			Born on 12/13/48 in Detroit. Heavy-metal rock guitarist; leader of The Amboy Dukes.	
9/10/77	**30**	6	1. Cat Scratch Fever	Epic 50425
			GARY NUMAN	
			Born Gary Webb on 3/8/58 in Hammersmith, England. Synthesized techno-rock artist.	
3/29/80	**9**	17	1. **Cars**	Atco 7211
			THE NUTTY SQUIRRELS	
			Creators and voices: Don Elliot (from Sommerville, NJ) and Sascha Burland (from New York City).	
11/30/59	**14**	7	1. Uh! Oh! Part 2 [N]	Hanover 4540
			THE NYLONS	
			Canadian a cappella quartet formed in 1979: Marc Connors, Paul Cooper, Claude Morrison and Arnold Robinson.	
6/13/87	**12**	10	1. Kiss Him Goodbye	Open Air 0022

DATE	POS	WKS	ARTIST—RECORD TITLE	LABEL & NO.
			# O	
			OAK - see RICK PINETTE	
			THE OAK RIDGE BOYS	
			Country-pop vocal group formed as a gospel quartet in 1940 in Oak Ridge, Tennessee. Disbanded after World War II; reformed in 1957. Many personnel changes. Lineup since early 1970s: Duane Allen (lead), Joe Bonsall (tenor), Richard Sterban (bass) and Bill Golden (baritone; left for a solo career in 1987, replaced by the group's guitarist, Steve Sanders).	
6/06/81	**5**	14	▲ 1. **Elvira**	MCA 51084
2/13/82	**12**	9	2. Bobbie Sue	MCA 51231
			JOHN O'BANION	
			Pop singer from Kokomo, Indiana.	
4/18/81	**24**	7	1. Love You Like I Never Loved Before	Elektra 47125
			RIC OCASEK	
			Born Richard Otcasek in Baltimore. Lead singer/guitarist of The Cars. Appeared in the 1987 film "Made In Heaven."	
10/11/86	**15**	8	1. Emotion In Motion	Geffen 28617
			OCEAN	
			Canadian pop quintet; Janice Morgan, lead singer.	
3/27/71	**2**(1)	12	● 1. **Put Your Hand In The Hand**	Kama Sutra 519
			BILLY OCEAN	
			Born Leslie Sebastian Charles on 1/21/50 in Trinidad. Raised in England.	
5/01/76	**22**	6	1. Love Really Hurts Without You	Ariola 7621
9/08/84	**1**(2)	15	● 2. **Caribbean Queen (No More Love On The Run)**	Jive 9199
12/08/84†	**2**(1)	15	3. **Loverboy**	Jive 9284
4/13/85	**4**	13	4. **Suddenly**	Jive 9323
7/27/85	**24**	8	5. Mystery Lady	Jive 9374
12/21/85†	**2**(1)	14	6. **When The Going Gets Tough, The Tough Get Going** from the film "The Jewel of the Nile"	Jive 9432
5/03/86	**1**(1)	14	7. **There'll Be Sad Songs (To Make You Cry)** above 6: written by Ocean	Jive 9465
8/09/86	**10**	11	8. **Love Zone**	Jive 9510
11/15/86	**16**	11	9. Love Is Forever	Jive 9540
2/20/88	**1**(2)	14	10. **Get Outta My Dreams, Get Into My Car**	Jive 9678
6/25/88	**17**	8	11. The Colour Of Love	Jive 9707
			ALAN O'DAY	
			Born on 10/3/40 in Hollywood. Singer/songwriter/pianist. Wrote Helen Reddy's #1 hit "Angie Baby" and the Righteous Brothers' "Rock And Roll Heaven."	
5/07/77	**1**(1)	17	● 1. **Undercover Angel**	Pacific 001

DATE	POS	WKS	ARTIST—RECORD TITLE	LABEL & NO.
			KENNY O'DELL	
			Born Kenneth Gist, Jr. in Oklahoma (early 1940s). Singer/songwriter/guitarist. Moved to Nashville in 1969. Wrote Charlie Rich's "Behind Closed Doors."	
12/16/67	**38**	2	1. Beautiful People	Vegas 718
			ODYSSEY	
			New York soul/disco trio: Manila-born Tony Reynolds, and sisters Lillian and Louise Lopez, originally from the Virgin Islands.	
12/17/77†	**21**	12	1. Native New Yorker	RCA 11129
			OHIO EXPRESS	
			Bubblegum group from Mansfield, Ohio. Produced by Jerry Kasenetz and Jeff Katz (worked with The Music Explosion and 1910 Fruitgum Co.). Joey Levine (later a member Reunion) was lead singer on most of the hits.	
11/18/67	**29**	5	1. Beg, Borrow And Steal	Cameo 483
5/18/68	**4**	11	● 2. **Yummy Yummy Yummy**	Buddah 38
8/31/68	**33**	5	3. Down At Lulu's	Buddah 56
11/02/68	**15**	10	● 4. Chewy Chewy	Buddah 70
4/26/69	**30**	4	5. Mercy above 4: sung and written by Joey Levine	Buddah 102
			OHIO PLAYERS	
			Originally an R&B instrumental group called the Ohio Untouchables, formed in Dayton in 1959. Back-up on The Falcons' records. First recorded for Lupine in 1962. Members during prime (1974-79): Marshall Jones, Clarence "Satch" Satchell, Jimmy "Diamond" Williams, Marvin "Merv" Pierce, Billy Beck, Ralph "Pee Wee" Middlebrook and Leroy "Sugarfoot" Bonner.	
4/14/73	**15**	9	● 1. Funky Worm [N]	Westbound 214
9/22/73	**31**	6	2. Ecstasy	Westbound 216
9/14/74	**13**	7	● 3. Skin Tight	Mercury 73609
12/28/74†	**1(1)**	12	● 4. **Fire**	Mercury 73643
10/11/75	**33**	3	5. Sweet Sticky Thing	Mercury 73713
11/22/75†	**1(1)**	14	● 6. **Love Rollercoaster**	Mercury 73734
3/27/76	**30**	5	7. Fopp	Mercury 73775
7/31/76	**18**	10	8. Who'd She Coo?	Mercury 73814
			THE O'JAYS	
			R&B group from Canton, Ohio formed in 1958 as the Triumphs. Consisted of Eddie Levert, Walter Williams, William Powell, Bobby Massey and Bill Isles. Recorded as the Mascots for King in 1961. Re-named by Cleveland DJ, Eddie O'Jay. Isles left in 1965. Massey left to become a record producer in 1971, Levert, Williams and Powell continued as a trio. Powell retired from touring due to illness in late 1975 (d: 5/26/77); replaced by Sammy Strain, formerly with Little Anthony & The Imperials.	
8/12/72	**3**	12	● 1. **Back Stabbers**	Phil. Int. 3517
1/27/73	**1(1)**	13	● 2. **Love Train**	Phil. Int. 3524
6/30/73	**33**	2	3. Time To Get Down	Phil. Int. 3531
1/12/74	**10**	11	4. **Put Your Hands Together**	Phil. Int. 3535
5/04/74	**9**	10	● 5. **For The Love Of Money**	Phil. Int. 3544
11/15/75†	**5**	14	● 6. **I Love Music (Part 1)**	Phil. Int. 3577
3/27/76	**20**	6	7. Livin' For The Weekend	Phil. Int. 3587
6/03/78	**4**	11	● 8. **Use Ta Be My Girl**	Phil. Int. 3642

DATE	POS	WKS	ARTIST—RECORD TITLE	LABEL & NO.
1/05/80	**28**	5	9. Forever Mine all of above: written & produced by Kenneth Gamble & Leon Huff	Phil. Int. 3727
			THE O'KAYSIONS	
			R&B sextet from Wilson, North Carolina: Donny Weaver (lead singer), Ron Turner, Jim Spidel, Wayne Pittman, Jimmy Hennant and Bruce Joyner. Originally called The Kays.	
9/07/68	**5**	11	● 1. **Girl Watcher**	ABC 11094
			DANNY O'KEEFE	
			Singer/songwriter born in Spokane, Washington.	
9/23/72	**9**	10	1. **Good Time Charlie's Got The Blues**	Signpost 70006
			MIKE OLDFIELD	
			Born on 5/15/53 in Reading, England. Classical rock multi-instrumentalist/composer.	
3/30/74	**7**	10	1. **Tubular Bells** [I] theme from the film "The Exorcist"	Virgin 55100
			OLIVER	
			Born William Oliver Swofford on 2/22/45 in North Wilkesboro, North Carolina.	
6/07/69	**3**	11	1. **Good Morning Starshine** from the Broadway musical "Hair"	Jubilee 5659
8/30/69	**2**(2)	12	● 2. **Jean** from the film "The Prime Of Miss Jean Brodie"	Crewe 334
12/20/69	**35**	2	3. Sunday Mornin'	Crewe 337
			OLLIE & JERRY	
			Duo of Ollie Brown and Jerry Knight (former member of Raydio).	
6/16/84	**9**	11	1. **Breakin'...There's No Stopping Us** from the film "Breakin'"	Polydor 821708
			NIGEL OLSSON	
			Drummer for Elton John's band from 1971-76.	
1/27/79	**18**	9	1. Dancin' Shoes	Bang 740
5/19/79	**34**	4	2. Little Bit Of Soap	Bang 4800
			THE OLYMPICS	
			R&B group formed at Centennial High School in Compton, California in 1954 as the Challengers. Consisted of Walter Ward (lead), Eddie Lewis (tenor), Charles Fizer (baritone) and Walter Hammond (baritone). Melvin King replaced Fizer in 1958, remained in group as replacement for Hammond when Fizer returned in 1959. Fizer was was killed in Watts rioting.	
8/04/58	**8**	11	1. **Western Movies** [N] Hot 100 #8 / Best Seller #11	Demon 1508
6/08/63	**40**	2	2. The Bounce	Tri Disc 106
			ALEXANDER O'NEAL	
			Minneapolis-based black vocalist, born on 1/23/55 in Mississippi. Co-producer of Janet Jackson's hit "Control." Recorded duets with Cherrelle (born Cheryl Norton in Los Angeles).	
3/29/86	**26**	6	1. Saturday Love	Tabu 05767
			CHERRELLE with ALEXANDER O'NEAL	
9/05/87	**25**	6	2. Fake	Tabu 07100

DATE	POS	WKS	ARTIST—RECORD TITLE	LABEL & NO.
3/05/88	**28**	6	3. Never Knew Love Like This **ALEXANDER O'NEAL featuring CHERRELLE**	Tabu 07646
			100 PROOF Aged In Soul	
			Soul group from Detroit: Clyde Wilson ("Steve Mancha"; lead), Joe Stubbs and Eddie Anderson ("Eddie Holiday"). Stubbs, brother of Levi Stubbs of the Four Tops, had been in the Contours and The Falcons.	
10/03/70	**8**	10	• 1. **Somebody's Been Sleeping**	Hot Wax 7004
			OPUS	
			Australian pop-rock quintet; Herwig Rudisser, lead singer.	
3/15/86	**32**	5	1. Live Is Life	Polydor 883730
			ROY ORBISON	
			Born on 4/23/36 in Vernon, Texas. Had own band, the Wink Westerners in 1952. Attended North Texas University with Pat Boone. First recorded for Je-Wel in early 1956. Toured with Sun Records shows to 1958. Toured with The Beatles in 1963. Wife Claudette killed in a motorcycle accident on 6/7/66; two sons died in a fire in 1986. Resurgence in career beginning in 1985. Inducted into the Rock And Roll Hall Of Fame in 1987. Member of the 1988 supergroup Traveling Wilburys. Died of a heart attack on 12/6/88 (52).	
6/20/60	**2**(1)	15	1. **Only The Lonely (Know How I Feel)**	Monument 421
10/17/60	**9**	8	2. **Blue Angel**	Monument 425
12/31/60†	**27**	3	3. I'm Hurtin'	Monument 433
4/24/61	**1**(1)	15	4. **Running Scared**	Monument 438
8/28/61	**2**(1)	14	5. **Crying/**	
10/09/61	**25**	5	6. Candy Man	Monument 447
3/03/62	**4**	9	7. **Dream Baby (How Long Must I Dream)**	Monument 456
6/23/62	**26**	6	8. The Crowd	Monument 461
10/27/62	**25**	5	9. Leah/	
10/27/62	**33**	4	10. Workin' For The Man all of above: with Bob Moore's Orchestra & Chorus	Monument 467
2/23/63	**7**	10	11. **In Dreams** new version featured in the 1986 film "Blue Velvet"	Monument 806
6/22/63	**22**	5	12. Falling above 4: written by Roy Orbison	Monument 815
9/28/63	**5**	10	13. **Mean Woman Blues/**	
10/12/63	**29**	5	14. Blue Bayou 1-4, 6, 8 & 14: written by Orbison & Joe Melson	Monument 824
12/21/63†	**15**	5	15. Pretty Paper [X]	Monument 830
4/25/64	**9**	9	16. **It's Over**	Monument 837
9/05/64	**1**(3)	14	• 17. **Oh, Pretty Woman** **ROY ORBISON & THE CANDY MEN**	Monument 851
2/20/65	**21**	6	18. Goodnight	Monument 873
8/07/65	**39**	2	19. (Say) You're My Girl	Monument 891
9/18/65	**25**	5	20. Ride Away	MGM 13386
2/12/66	**31**	4	21. Breakin' Up Is Breakin' My Heart	MGM 13446
5/21/66	**39**	2	22. Twinkle Toes above 7: written by Orbison & Bill Dees	MGM 13498

DATE	POS	WKS	ARTIST—RECORD TITLE	LABEL & NO.
			ORCHESTRAL MANOEUVRES IN THE DARK	
			English electro-pop quartet: keyboardists/vocalists Paul Humphreys and Andrew McCluskey with drummer Malcolm Holmes and multi-instrumentalist Martin Cooper.	
10/12/85	**26**	7	1. So In Love	A&M 2746
4/05/86	**4**	13	2. **If You Leave**	A&M 2811
			from the film "Pretty In Pink"	
11/01/86	**19**	7	3. (Forever) Live And Die	A&M 2872
4/16/88	**16**	9	4. Dreaming	A&M 3002
			THE ORIGINAL CASTE	
			Canadian quintet; Dixie Lee Innes, lead singer.	
2/07/70	**34**	2	1. One Tin Soldier	T-A 186
			from the film "Billy Jack"	
			THE ORIGINALS	
			Soul group formed in Detroit in 1966. Consisted of Freddie Gorman (bass), Crathman Spencer & Henry Dixon (tenors) and Walter Gaines (baritone).	
10/18/69	**14**	13	1. Baby, I'm For Real	Soul 35066
3/07/70	**12**	9	2. The Bells	Soul 35069
			above 2: written & produced by Marvin Gaye	
			TONY ORLANDO	
			Born Michael Anthony Orlando Cassavitis on 4/3/44 in New York City. Discovered by producer Don Kirshner. Lead singer of Dawn, 1970-77. Hosted weekly TV variety show "Tony Orlando & Dawn," 1974-76. Also see Wind.	
5/29/61	**39**	2	1. Halfway To Paradise	Epic 9441
9/04/61	**15**	7	2. Bless You	Epic 9452
			ORLEANS	
			Rock group founded in New York City by John Hall with brothers Lawrence and Lance Hoppen, Wells Kelly and Jerry Marotta. Hall and Marotta left in 1977, replaced by Bob Leinbach and R.A. Martin.	
8/30/75	**6**	11	1. **Dance With Me**	Asylum 45261
8/14/76	**5**	12	2. **Still The One**	Asylum 45336
4/07/79	**11**	9	3. Love Takes Time	Infinity 50006
			THE ORLONS	
			R&B group from Philadelphia. Consisted of lead Rosetta Hightower (b: 6/23/44), Marlena Davis (b: 10/4/44), Steve Caldwell (b: 11/22/42) and Shirley Brickley (b: 12/9/44; d: 10/13/77 [gunshot]). Davis and Caldwell left in 1964 and were replaced by Audrey Brickley. Disbanded in 1968, when Hightower moved to England.	
6/23/62	**2**(2)	11	1. **The Wah Watusi**	Cameo 218
11/03/62	**4**	11	2. **Don't Hang Up**	Cameo 231
3/02/63	**3**	10	3. **South Street**	Cameo 243
7/06/63	**12**	7	4. Not Me	Cameo 257
10/19/63	**19**	5	5. Cross Fire!	Cameo 273
			BENJAMIN ORR	
			Bassist/vocalist of The Cars.	
1/17/87	**24**	6	1. Stay The Night	Elektra 69506

DATE	POS	WKS	ARTIST—RECORD TITLE	LABEL & NO.
			ROBERT ELLIS ORRALL with CARLENE CARTER	
			Robert is a Boston-born singer/songwriter/pianist. Carlene, the daughter of June Carter Cash, is married to Nick Lowe.	
5/07/83	**32**	3	1. I Couldn't Say No	RCA 13431
			JEFFREY OSBORNE	
			Born on 3/9/48 in Providence, Rhode Island. Soul singer/songwriter/drummer. Lead singer of L.T.D. until 1980.	
8/14/82	**39**	2	1. I Really Don't Need No Light	A&M 2410
11/20/82	**29**	7	2. On The Wings Of Love	A&M 2434
8/20/83	**25**	6	3. Don't You Get So Mad	A&M 2561
12/17/83†	**30**	8	4. Stay With Me Tonight	A&M 2591
10/06/84	**40**	2	5. The Last Time I Made Love	A&M 2656
			JOYCE KENNEDY & JEFFREY OSBORNE	
3/02/85	**38**	2	6. The Borderlines	A&M 2695
			all of above (except #5): produced by George Duke	
6/28/86	**13**	11	7. You Should Be Mine (The Woo Woo Song)	A&M 2814
7/25/87	**12**	9	8. Love Power	Arista 9567
			DIONNE WARWICK & JEFFREY OSBORNE	
			DONNY OSMOND	
			Born on 12/9/57 in Ogden, Utah. 7th son of George and Olive Osmond, Donny became a member of The Osmonds in 1963. Owner of production company, Night Star. Burst back on to the pop charts in March of 1989.	
5/01/71	**7**	11	● 1. **Sweet And Innocent**	MGM 14227
			recorded in 1958 by Roy Orbison on RCA 7381	
8/21/71	**1**(3)	13	● 2. **Go Away Little Girl**	MGM 14285
12/04/71†	**9**	9	● 3. **Hey Girl**	MGM 14322
3/04/72	**3**	10	● 4. **Puppy Love**	MGM 14367
6/17/72	**13**	8	5. Too Young	MGM 14407
9/16/72	**13**	9	6. Why/	
		9	7. Lonely Boy	MGM 14424
3/24/73	**8**	9	● 8. **The Twelfth Of Never**	MGM 14503
8/04/73	**23**	7	9. A Million To One/	
8/04/73	**25**	7	10. Young Love	MGM 14583
12/15/73†	**14**	8	11. Are You Lonesome Tonight	MGM 14677
			above 8: produced by Mike Curb & Don Costa	
7/24/76	**38**	3	12. C'mon Marianne	Polydor 14320
			DONNY & MARIE OSMOND	
			Co-hosts of own musical/variety TV series from 1976-78.	
7/27/74	**4**	10	● 1. **I'm Leaving It (All) Up To You**	MGM 14735
12/14/74†	**8**	10	2. **Morning Side Of The Mountain**	MGM 14765
1/24/76	**14**	13	3. Deep Purple	MGM 14840
12/25/76†	**21**	8	4. Ain't Nothing Like The Real Thing	Polydor 14363
1/07/78	**38**	3	5. (You're My) Soul And Inspiration	Polydor 14439
11/18/78	**38**	2	6. On The Shelf	Polydor 14510

DATE	POS	WKS	ARTIST—RECORD TITLE	LABEL & NO.
			LITTLE JIMMY OSMOND	
			Born on 4/16/63 in Canoga Park, California. Youngest member of the Osmond family.	
6/03/72	**38**	3	1. Long Haired Lover From Liverpool with the Mike Curb Congregation	MGM 14376
			MARIE OSMOND	
			Born on 10/13/59 in Ogden, Utah. Began performing in concert with her brothers at age 14. Co-hosted the TV series "Ripley's Believe It Or Not" from 1985-86. Emerged as a hit country artist in the 80s.	
10/06/73	**5**	12	● 1. **Paper Roses**	MGM 14609
4/05/75	**40**	2	2. Who's Sorry Now above 2: produced by Sonny James	MGM 14786
6/04/77	**39**	1	3. This Is The Way That I Feel	Polydor 14385
			THE OSMONDS	
			Family group from Ogden, Utah. Alan (b: 6/22/49), Wayne (b: 8/28/51), Merrill (b: 4/30/53), Jay (b: 3/2/55) and Donny (b: 12/9/57). Began as a quartet in 1959, singing religious and barbershop-quartet songs. Regulars on Andy Williams' TV show from 1962-67. Alan, Wayne, Merrill and Jay are currently a hot country act.	
1/23/71	**1**(5)	12	● 1. **One Bad Apple**	MGM 14193
5/29/71	**14**	7	2. Double Lovin'	MGM 14259
9/18/71	**3**	12	● 3. **Yo-Yo**	MGM 14295
1/29/72	**4**	12	● 4. **Down By The Lazy River** written by Alan & Merrill	MGM 14324
7/08/72	**14**	6	5. Hold Her Tight	MGM 14405
11/11/72	**14**	8	6. Crazy Horses	MGM 14450
7/07/73	**36**	2	7. Goin' Home	MGM 14562
10/06/73	**36**	3	8. Let Me In above 4: written by Alan, Merrill & Wayne; above 5: produced by Alan	MGM 14617
9/21/74	**10**	7	9. **Love Me For A Reason**	MGM 14746
8/23/75	**22**	6	10. The Proud One	MGM 14791
			GILBERT O'SULLIVAN	
			Born Raymond O'Sullivan on 12/1/46 in Waterford, Ireland.	
7/01/72	**1**(6)	15	● 1. **Alone Again (Naturally)**	MAM 3619
11/11/72	**2**(2)	14	● 2. **Clair**	MAM 3626
4/07/73	**17**	8	3. Out Of The Question	MAM 3628
7/14/73	**7**	11	● 4. **Get Down**	MAM 3629
11/10/73	**25**	4	5. Ooh Baby	MAM 3633
			THE OTHER ONES	
			Half-Australian (2 brothers and a sister), half-German rock group.	
10/10/87	**29**	4	1. Holiday	Virgin 99428

DATE	POS	WKS	ARTIST—RECORD TITLE	LABEL & NO.
			OTIS & CARLA - see OTIS REDDING and/or CARLA THOMAS	
			THE JOHNNY OTIS SHOW	
			Born John Veliotes (of Greek parents) on 12/8/21 in Vallejo, California. R&B bandleader/composer. Johnny's R&B Caravan featured the top R&B artists of the 50s.	
6/30/58	**9**	15	1. **Willie And The Hand Jive** Hot 100 #9 / Best Seller #14 / Jockey #17	Capitol 3966
			THE OUTFIELD	
			British pop-rock trio: Tony Lewis (lead singer), John Spinks (guitar) and Alan Jackman (drums).	
3/22/86	**6**	12	1. **Your Love**	Columbia 05796
7/12/86	**19**	7	2. All The Love In The World	Columbia 05894
7/25/87	**31**	5	3. Since You've Been Gone	Columbia 07170
			OUTLAWS	
			Southern rock band formed in Tampa in 1974. Consisted of guitarists Hughie Thomasson, Billy Jones & Henry Paul with drummer Monte Yoho and bassist Frank O'Keefe; replaced by Harvey Arnold in 1977. Paul, Yoho and Arnold left by 1980.	
10/11/75	**34**	3	1. There Goes Another Love Song	Arista 0150
2/14/81	**31**	4	2. (Ghost) Riders In The Sky #1 hit for 12 weeks by Vaughn Monroe in 1949	Arista 0582
			THE OUTSIDERS	
			Cleveland rock quintet: Sonny Geraci (lead singer), Tom King (guitar), Bill Bruno (lead guitar), Mert Madsen (bass) and Rick Baker (drums). Geraci later led band Climax.	
3/26/66	**5**	10	1. **Time Won't Let Me**	Capitol 5573
6/04/66	**21**	5	2. Girl In Love	Capitol 5646
8/20/66	**15**	6	3. Respectable	Capitol 5701
12/10/66	**37**	2	4. Help Me Girl	Capitol 5759
			REG OWEN	
			British bandleader born in February of 1928.	
12/22/58†	**10**	13	1. **Manhattan Spiritual** **[I]**	Palette 5005
			BUCK OWENS	
			Born Alvis Edgar Owens on 8/12/29 in Sherman, Texas. Country singer/guitarist/ songwriter. Backing group: The Buckaroos. Co-host of TV's "Hee-Haw," 1969-86.	
2/13/65	**25**	5	1. I've Got A Tiger By The Tail	Capitol 5336
			DONNIE OWENS	
			Pop-country singer born on 10/30/38.	
11/03/58	**25**	8	1. Need You backing vocals: The Ben Denton Singers	Guyden 2001
			OXO	
			West Coast pop-rock quartet led by former Foxy member Ish "Angel" Ledesma.	
4/02/83	**28**	6	1. Whirly Girl	Geffen 29765

DATE	POS	WKS	ARTIST—RECORD TITLE	LABEL & NO.
			THE OZARK MOUNTAIN DAREDEVILS	
			Country-rock group from Springfield, Missouri. Nucleus of band: Larry Lee (keyboards, guitar), Steve Cash (harp), John Dillon (guitar) and Michael Granda (bass).	
6/08/74	**25**	5	1. If You Wanna Get To Heaven	A&M 1515
3/22/75	**3**	12	2. **Jackie Blue**	A&M 1654
			P	
			PABLO CRUISE	
			San Francisco pop-rock quartet formed in 1973. Consisted of Dave Jenkins (vocals, guitar), Bud Cockrell (member of It's A Beautiful Day; vocals, bass), Cory Lerios (keyboards) and Stephen Price (drums). Cockrell replaced by Bruce Day in 1977. John Pierce replaced Day, and guitarist Angelo Rossi joined group in 1980.	
6/11/77	**6**	14	1. **Whatcha Gonna Do?**	A&M 1920
7/01/78	**6**	12	2. **Love Will Find A Way**	A&M 2048
10/21/78	**21**	8	3. Don't Want To Live Without It	A&M 2076
11/10/79	**19**	10	4. I Want You Tonight	A&M 2195
7/25/81	**13**	11	5. Cool Love	A&M 2349
			PACIFIC GAS & ELECTRIC	
			West Coast blues-rock quintet; Charles Allen, lead singer.	
6/20/70	**14**	9	1. Are You Ready? backing vocals: The Blackberries	Columbia 45158
			PATTI PAGE	
			Born Clara Ann Fowler on 11/8/27 in Muskogee, Oklahoma. One of 11 children. Raised in Tulsa. On radio KTUL with Al Klauser & His Oklahomans, as "Ann Fowler," late 40s. Another singer was billed as "Patti Page" for the Page Milk Company show on KTUL. When she left, Fowler took her place and name. With the Jimmy Joy band in 1947. On "Breakfast Club," Chicago radio, 1947; signed by Mercury Records. Used multi-voice effect on records from 1947. Had 42 chart hits from 1948-54. Own TV series "The Patti Page Show," 1955-58 and "The Big Record," 1957-58. In the 1960 film "Elmer Gantry."	
12/18/54†	**8**	7	1. **Let Me Go, Lover!** Jockey #8 / Juke Box #12 / Best Seller #24	Mercury 70511
11/12/55	**16**	8	2. Croce Di Oro (Cross Of Gold) Top 100 #16 / Juke Box #16 / Jockey #17 / Best Seller #20	Mercury 70713
1/14/56	**11**	8	3. Go On With The Wedding Top 100 #11 / Juke Box #12 / Jockey #16 / Best Seller #17 all of above: with Jack Rael & His Orchestra	Mercury 70766
6/16/56	**2**(2)	22	4. **Allegheny Moon** Top 100 #2 / Jockey #2 / Juke Box #2 / Best Seller #5	Mercury 70878
11/03/56	**11**	12	5. Mama From The Train Top 100 #11 / Jockey #12 / Juke Box #12 / Best Seller #17	Mercury 70971
3/23/57	**14**	6	6. A Poor Man's Roses (Or A Rich Man's Gold) Jockey #14 / Top 100 #27	Mercury 71059
6/03/57	**3**	17	7. **Old Cape Cod/** Jockey #3 / Top 100 #7 / Best Seller #8	
6/03/57	**12**	5	8. Wondering Jockey #12 / Top 100 #35	Mercury 71101

DATE	POS	WKS	ARTIST—RECORD TITLE	LABEL & NO.
11/11/57	**23**	3	9. I'll Remember Today Jockey #23 / Best Seller #31 / Top 100 #32	Mercury 71189
2/10/58	**13**	8	10. Belonging To Someone Jockey #13 / Best Seller #32 / Top 100 #34	Mercury 71247
5/05/58	**20**	1	11. Another Time, Another Place Jockey #20 / Top 100 #81 from the film of the same title	Mercury 71294
6/30/58	**9**	10	12. **Left Right Out Of Your Heart** Jockey #9 / Hot 100 #13 / Best Seller #14	Mercury 71331
10/20/58	**39**	1	13. Fibbin' 3-13: orchestra conducted by Vic Schoen	Mercury 71355
7/04/60	**31**	5	14. One Of Us (Will Weep Tonight)	Mercury 71639
5/12/62	**27**	4	15. Most People Get Married	Mercury 71950
5/22/65	**8**	9	16. **Hush, Hush, Sweet Charlotte** from the film of the same title	Columbia 43251
			ROBERT PALMER	
			Born on 1/19/49 in Batley, England; raised on the island of Malta. Lead singer of supergroup The Power Station.	
5/06/78	**16**	9	1. Every Kinda People	Island 100
8/11/79	**14**	10	2. Bad Case Of Loving You (Doctor, Doctor)	Island 49016
3/08/86	**1**(1)	14	● 3. **Addicted To Love**	Island 99570
6/28/86	**33**	5	4. Hyperactive	Island 99545
9/13/86	**2**(1)	13	5. **I Didn't Mean To Turn You On**	Island 99537
7/16/88	**2**(2)	14	6. **Simply Irresistible**	EMI-Man. 50133
11/12/88	**19**	9	7. Early In The Morning	EMI-Man. 50157
			PAPER LACE	
			English quintet formed in 1969; Phil Wright (b: 4/9/48), lead singer.	
7/13/74	**1**(1)	11	● 1. **The Night Chicago Died**	Mercury 73492
			THE PARADE	
			Los Angeles pop-rock group; Jerry Riopelle, leader.	
5/06/67	**20**	5	1. Sunshine Girl	A&M 841
			THE PARADONS	
			R&B vocal group from Bakersfield, California: West Tyler (lead), Chuck Weldon, Billy Myers and William Powers.	
9/26/60	**18**	7	1. Diamonds And Pearls	Milestone 2003
			THE PARIS SISTERS	
			Albeth, Priscilla and Sherrell Paris from San Francisco.	
10/02/61	**5**	11	1. **I Love How You Love Me**	Gregmark 6
3/03/62	**34**	3	2. He Knows I Love Him Too Much	Gregmark 10
			FESS PARKER	
			Born on 8/16/27 in Fort Worth. Starred in the movie "Davy Crockett" and TV's "Daniel Boone" (1964-70).	
3/12/55	**5**	17	1. **Ballad Of Davy Crockett** Best Seller #5 / Jockey #10 from the Disneyland TV production of the same title	Columbia 40449
2/09/57	**12**	6	2. Wringle Wrangle Best Seller #12 / Top 100 #21 from the film "Westward Ho, The Wagons"	Disneyland 43

DATE	POS	WKS	ARTIST—RECORD TITLE	LABEL & NO.
			GRAHAM PARKER & THE SHOT	
			Pub-rock vocalist/guitarist/songwriter, born in London in 1950.	
6/15/85	**39**	3	1. Wake Up (Next To You)	Elektra 69654
			RAY PARKER JR.	
			Born on 5/1/54 in Detroit. Prominent session guitarist in California; worked with Stevie Wonder, Barry White and others. Formed band Raydio in 1977 with Arnell Carmichael, Jerry Knight, Larry Tolbert, Darren Carmichael and Charles Fearing. Parker went solo in 1982. In 1984, Knight recorded in the duo Ollie & Jerry.	
			RAYDIO:	
2/11/78	**8**	16	● 1. **Jack And Jill**	Arista 0283
6/09/79	**9**	14	2. **You Can't Change That**	Arista 0399
			RAY PARKER JR. & RAYDIO:	
6/07/80	**30**	5	3. Two Places At The Same Time	Arista 0494
4/25/81	**4**	15	4. **A Woman Needs Love (Just Like You Do)**	Arista 0592
8/08/81	**21**	6	5. That Old Song	Arista 0616
			RAY PARKER JR.:	
4/10/82	**4**	14	6. **The Other Woman**	Arista 0669
8/21/82	**38**	3	7. Let Me Go	Arista 0695
1/15/83	**35**	4	8. Bad Boy	Arista 1030
12/10/83†	**12**	11	9. I Still Can't Get Over Loving You	Arista 9116
6/30/84	**1**(3)	14	● 10. **Ghostbusters**	Arista 9212
			from 1984's #1 box-office film of the same title	
12/01/84†	**14**	11	11. Jamie	Arista 9293
10/26/85	**34**	4	12. Girls Are More Fun	Arista 9352
			all of above: written and produced by Parker	
			ROBERT PARKER	
			Born on 10/14/30 in New Orleans. Saxophonist/vocalist/bandleader. In Professor Longhair's (Roy Byrd) band from 1949. Led house band at Club Tijuana, New Orleans. Prolific session work.	
5/21/66	**7**	9	1. **Barefootin'**	Nola 721
			MICHAEL PARKS	
			Film and TV actor/singer. In films "The Man Who Came To Dinner," "Night Must Fall," "Wild Seed" and "Back In Town." Starred in the 1963 TV series "Channing"; portrayed Jim Bronson in the 1969 TV series "Then Came Bronson."	
3/28/70	**20**	8	1. Long Lonesome Highway	MGM 14104
			from the TV series "Then Came Bronson"	
			PARLIAMENT	
			Funk aggregation which evolved from The Parliaments. Spearheaded by George Clinton, part of "A Parliafunkadelicament Thang" corporation. The group's nearly 40 members also recorded under the names Funkadelic, P. Funk All Stars and Parlet among others.	
6/12/76	**15**	10	● 1. Tear The Roof Off The Sucker (Give Up The Funk)	Casablanca 856
2/25/78	**16**	12	● 2. Flash Light	Casablanca 909
			THE PARLIAMENTS	
			Soul group consisting of George Clinton (lead), Raymond Davis, Calvin Simon, Clarence "Fuzzy" Haskins and Grady Thomas. Later evolved into Parliament/ Funkadelic.	
8/05/67	**20**	7	1. (I Wanna) Testify	Revilot 207

Billy Joel's lengthy career, decade for decade, has taken him through the Hassles in the 60s, the group Attila in the early 70s, and—as documented on a 1987 live album—the Soviet Union in the 80s.

Elton John and Kiki Dee's "Don't Go Breaking My Heart" held the No. 1 spot for four weeks in 1976. It remains the last hit ever enjoyed by Dee, born Pauline Matthews in England.

Johnny & the Hurricanes claimed their first top-five hit with "Red River Rock" in 1959; a later generation of rock fans heard the group mentioned in a lyric snippet in "One Of The Survivors" by the Kinks, and may well have scratched their heads.

Johnny Hates Jazz were one of the first successes enjoyed by Virgin Records when the label opened its American offices in the late 80s. Members of the group include Clark Datchler, Mike Nocito, Calvin Hayes, and absolutely no one named Johnny.

Jimmy Jones' biggest hit was 1959's "Handy Man," later successfully covered by both Del Shannon and James Taylor; "Good Timin'," the soon-issued follow-up, peaked at No. 3, one chart point short of "Handy Man."

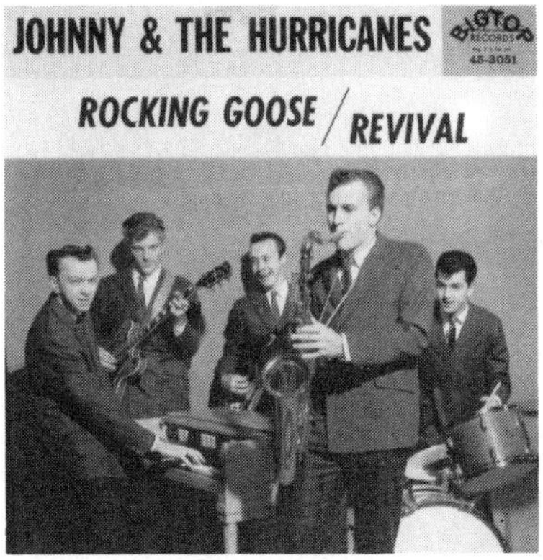

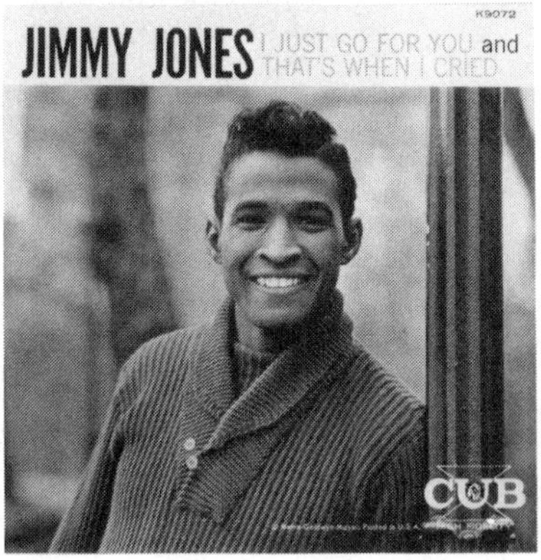

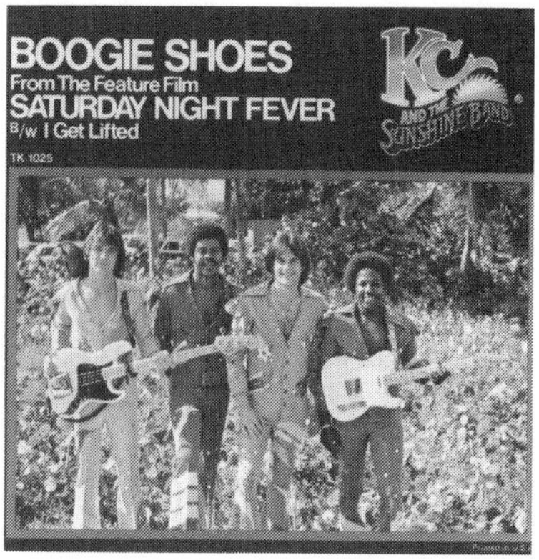

KC & the Sunshine Band were, for many, the pre-eminent disco band of the early 70s. Based around keyboardist Harry "KC" Casey, the group enjoyed five No. 1 hits, including "Get Down Tonight," "That's The Way (I Like It)," "(Shake, Shake, Shake) Your Booty," "I'm Your Boogie Man," and "Please Don't Go." Years after the disco backlash, groups such as Dead Or Alive enjoyed success covering those same songs.

Greg Kihn first came to public attention via Matthew King Kaufman's Beserkley label, for which he recorded "Jeopardy," which peaked at No. 2 in 1983. His first album featured backing by the San Francisco band Earth Quake.

Ben E. King's "Stand By Me" made even more headlines after its mid-80s popularization in the film of the same name. In late 1988, the track was the most requested song in initial test results of the Personics Corporation's in-store custom-taping system.

Kiss celebrated its 15th year in the music business with the release of *Smashes, Thrashes & Hits*—a collection which featured old hits and such new songs as "Let's Put The X In Sex."

Gladys Knight & the Pips' "I Heard It Through The Grapevine" smash stayed in the No. 2 position for three weeks in 1967; within a year, Marvin Gaye's version of the same song claimed the No. 1 spot for a record-setting *seven* weeks. Could they ever have dreamed their hit would later be appropriated by a group of raisins from the West Coast?

DATE	POS	WKS	ARTIST—RECORD TITLE	LABEL & NO.
			JOHN PARR	
			Singer/songwriter, born in Nottingham, England.	
2/02/85	**23**	8	1. Naughty Naughty	Atlantic 89612
7/20/85	**1**(2)	14	2. **St. Elmo's Fire (Man In Motion)** from the film of the same title	Atlantic 89541
			THE ALAN PARSONS PROJECT	
			Duo formed in London in 1975. Consisted of producer Alan Parsons (guitar, keyboards) and lyricist Eric Woolfson (vocals, keyboards). Both had worked at the Abbey Road Studios; Parsons was an engineer, Woolfson a songwriter. Parsons engineered Pink Floyd's "Dark Side Of The Moon" and The Beatles "Abbey Road" albums. Project features varying musicians and vocalists.	
9/11/76	**37**	2	1. (The System Of) Doctor Tarr And Professor Fether	20th Century 2297
9/24/77	**36**	3	2. I Wouldn't Want To Be Like You	Arista 0260
11/17/79	**27**	8	3. Damned If I Do	Arista 0454
1/24/81	**16**	10	4. Games People Play above 3: vocal by Lenny Zakatek	Arista 0573
6/06/81	**15**	12	5. Time	Arista 0598
7/31/82	**3**	17	6. **Eye In The Sky**	Arista 0696
3/24/84	**15**	8	7. Don't Answer Me	Arista 9160
6/23/84	**34**	3	8. Prime Time above 4: vocal by Eric Woolfson; all of above: written by Parsons and Woolfson	Arista 9208
			BILL PARSONS - see BOBBY BARE	
			PARTLAND BROTHERS	
			Canadian duo: Chris (vocals, guitars) and G.P. (vocals, percussion) Partland.	
6/06/87	**27**	5	1. Soul City	Manhattan 50065
			DOLLY PARTON	
			Born on 1/19/46 in Sevier County, Tennessee. Worked on Knoxville radio show at age 11. First recorded for Gold Band in 1957. To Nashville in 1964. Replaced Norma Jean on the Porter Wagoner TV show, 1967-73. Went solo in 1974. Starred in films "Nine To Five," "The Best Little Whorehouse In Texas" and "Rhinestone." Hosted own TV variety show in 1987.	
11/12/77†	**3**	13	● 1. **Here You Come Again**	RCA 11123
4/08/78	**19**	8	2. Two Doors Down	RCA 11240
9/23/78	**37**	4	3. Heartbreaker	RCA 11296
1/13/79	**25**	7	4. Baby I'm Burnin'	RCA 11420
5/03/80	**36**	3	5. Starting Over Again	RCA 11926
12/20/80†	**1**(2)	18	● 6. **9 To 5** from the film of the same title	RCA 12133
9/10/83	**1**(2)	18	▲ 7. **Islands In The Stream** **KENNY ROGERS & DOLLY PARTON** written by The Bee Gees	RCA 13615

DATE	POS	WKS	ARTIST—RECORD TITLE	LABEL & NO.
			THE PARTRIDGE FAMILY	
			Popularized through "The Partridge Family" TV series, with recordings by series stars David Cassidy (lead singer) and real-life stepmother Shirley Jones (backing vocals). David, son of actor Jack Cassidy, was born on 4/12/50 in New York City; raised in California. Shirley was born on 3/31/34 in Smithton, Pennsylvania. Starred in the film musicals "Oklahoma" and "The Music Man." Married David's father in 1956.	
10/31/70	**1**(3)	16	● 1. **I Think I Love You**	Bell 910
2/20/71	**6**	11	● 2. **Doesn't Somebody Want To Be Wanted**	Bell 963
5/15/71	**9**	8	3. **I'll Meet You Halfway**	Bell 996
8/21/71	**13**	10	4. I Woke Up In Love This Morning	Bell 45130
1/01/72	**20**	6	5. It's One Of Those Nights (Yes Love)	Bell 45160
7/29/72	**28**	4	6. Breaking Up Is Hard To Do	Bell 45235
1/27/73	**39**	2	7. Looking Through The Eyes Of Love	Bell 45301
			THE PASTEL SIX	
			California pop septet (ages 18-21 in 1962); headlined at the Cinnamon Cinder club in North Hollywood.	
1/19/63	**25**	5	1. The Cinnamon Cinder (It's A Very Nice Dance)	Zen 102
			THE PASTELS	
			R&B vocal quartet: lead singer "Big Dee Irwin" (DiFosco Ervin), Richard Travis, Tony Thomas and Jimmy Willingham. Formed at Air Force base in Narsarssuak, Greenland in 1954.	
3/03/58	**24**	3	1. Been So Long Top 100 #24 / Best Seller #25	Argo 5287
			PATIENCE & PRUDENCE	
			Los Angeles sister duo: Patience & Prudence McIntyre (ages 11 & 14 in 1956). Hits were backed by their father Mark McIntyre's orchestra.	
8/25/56	**4**	17	1. **Tonight You Belong To Me** Best Seller #4 / Juke Box #4 / Jockey #5 / Top 100 #6	Liberty 55022
12/01/56	**11**	12	2. Gonna Get Along Without Ya Now Jockey #11 / Best Seller #12 / Top 100 #12 / Juke Box #16	Liberty 55040
			ROBBIE PATTON	
			English singer/songwriter. Toured with Fleetwood Mac as a guest in 1979.	
8/01/81	**26**	6	1. Don't Give It Up	Liberty 1420
			PATTY & THE EMBLEMS	
			Soul group from Camden, New Jersey; Pat Russell, lead singer.	
8/15/64	**37**	3	1. Mixed-Up, Shook-Up, Girl	Herald 590
			PAUL & PAULA	
			Real names: Ray Hildebrand (b: 12/21/40, Joshua, TX) and Jill Jackson (b: 5/20/42, McCaney, TX). Formed duo at Howard Payne College, Brownwood, Texas.	
1/12/63	**1**(3)	12	● 1. **Hey Paula** written by Hildebrand, first released on LeCam by "Jill & Ray"	Philips 40084
3/23/63	**6**	8	2. **Young Lovers**	Philips 40096
6/22/63	**27**	4	3. First Quarrel	Philips 40114
			BILLY PAUL	
			Born Paul Williams on 12/1/34 in Philadelphia. Sang on Philadelphia radio broadcasts at age 11. First recorded for Jubilee in 1952.	
11/18/72	**1**(3)	14	● 1. **Me And Mrs. Jones**	Phil. Int. 3521

DATE	POS	WKS	ARTIST—RECORD TITLE	LABEL & NO.
4/20/74	**37**	3	2. Thanks For Saving My Life	Phil. Int. 3538
			LES PAUL & MARY FORD	
			Les was born Lester Polfus on 6/9/16 in Waukesha, Wisconsin. Mary was born Colleen Summer on 7/7/28 in Pasadena; died on 9/30/77. Paul is a self-taught guitarist. Worked local radio stations, then to Chicago, 1932-37. Own trio in 1936. With Fred Waring from 1938-41. Innovator in electric guitar and multi-track recordings. Married vocalist Mary Ford on 12/29/49; divorced in 1963. Les was inducted into the Rock And Roll Hall Of Fame in 1988.	
7/09/55	**7**	13	1. **Hummingbird** Juke Box #7 / Best Seller #8 / Jockey #8	Capitol 3165
11/12/55	**38**	2	2. Amukiriki (The Lord Willing) Top 100 #38	Capitol 3248
2/23/57	**35**	2	3. Cinco Robles	Capitol 3612
9/08/58	**32**	4	4. Put A Ring On My Finger Hot 100 #32 / Best Seller #44	Columbia 41222
7/03/61	**37**	1	5. Jura (I Swear I Love You)	Columbia 41994
			RITA PAVONE	
			Pop singer born in Torino, Italy.	
7/04/64	**26**	4	1. Remember Me	RCA 8365
			FREDA PAYNE	
			Born on 9/19/45 in Detroit. Sister of The Supremes' Scherrie Payne. To New York in 1963. Performed with Pearl Bailey, Duke Ellington and Quincy Jones. First recorded for Impulse in 1965. Hosted the syndicated TV talk show "For You, Black Woman" in the early 80s.	
5/30/70	**3**	15	● 1. **Band Of Gold**	Invictus 9075
10/10/70	**24**	8	2. Deeper & Deeper	Invictus 9080
6/26/71	**12**	10	● 3. Bring The Boys Home	Invictus 9092
			PEACHES & HERB	
			Soul duo from Washington, DC: Herb Fame (born Herbert Feemster, 1942) and Francine Barker (born Francine Hurd, 1947). Fame had been recording solo, Francine sang in vocal group Sweet Things. Marlene Mack filled in for Francine from 1968-69. Re-formed with Fame and Linda Green in 1977.	
2/25/67	**21**	6	1. Let's Fall In Love	Date 1523
4/15/67	**8**	9	2. **Close Your Eyes**	Date 1549
7/08/67	**20**	5	3. For Your Love	Date 1563
10/14/67	**13**	7	4. Love Is Strange	Date 1574
1/13/68	**31**	3	5. Two Little Kids	Date 1586
1/27/79	**5**	13	● 6. **Shake Your Groove Thing**	Polydor 14514
3/31/79	1(4)	15	▲ 7. **Reunited**	Polydor 14547
3/15/80	**19**	8	8. I Pledge My Love	Polydor 2053
			LESLIE PEARL	
			Pop singer/songwriter/producer from Pennsylvania. Wrote jingles for Pepsi, Ford, Gillette and others.	
7/10/82	**28**	7	1. If The Love Fits Wear It	RCA 13235
			PEBBLES	
			Her real name is Perri McKissack. Native of Oakland. Worked with Con Funk Shun in the early 80s while still a teenager. Her cousin is vocalist Cherrelle.	
2/27/88	**5**	12	1. **Girlfriend**	MCA 53185

DATE	POS	WKS	ARTIST—RECORD TITLE	LABEL & NO.
5/28/88	2(2)	11	2. **Mercedes Boy**	MCA 53279
			ANN PEEBLES	
			Born on 4/27/47 in East St. Louis. Sang in family gospel group, the Peebles Choir, from age 8.	
12/22/73	**38**	1	1. I Can't Stand The Rain	Hi 2248
			NIA PEEPLES	
			Singer/actress. Played Nicole Chapman for 3 seasons on the TV series "Fame." Hosted "Top Of The Pops" TV show.	
7/02/88	**35**	3	1. Trouble	Mercury 870154
			TEDDY PENDERGRASS	
			Born on 3/26/50 in Philadelphia. Worked local clubs, became drummer for Harold Melvin's Blue Notes in 1969; vocalist with same group in 1970. Went solo in 1976. Auto accident on 3/18/82 left him partially paralyzed.	
8/12/78	**25**	6	● 1. Close The Door	Phil. Int. 3648
7/04/81	**40**	2	2. Two Hearts **STEPHANIE MILLS featuring TEDDY PENDERGRASS**	20th Century 2492
			THE PENGUINS	
			R&B vocal group formed in Los Angeles in 1954: Cleveland Duncan (lead), Dexter Tisby (tenor), Bruce Tate (baritone) and Curtis Williams (bass). Group named for trademark on Kool cigarettes.	
12/25/54†	**8**	15	1. **Earth Angel (Will You Be Mine)** Best Seller #8 / Juke Box #10 / Jockey #13 considered to be the top R&B record of all time in terms of continuous popularity	DooTone 348
			PEOPLE	
			San Jose, California pop-rock sextet founded by lead guitarist Jeff Levin.	
5/25/68	**14**	10	1. I Love You	Capitol 2078
			PEOPLE'S CHOICE	
			Philadelphia soul group formed in 1971: Frankie Brunson (vocals), Stanley Burton, Roger Andrews, Dave Thompson and Leon Lee.	
9/04/71	**38**	2	1. I Likes To Do It [I]	Phil-L.A. 349
9/13/75	**11**	11	● 2. Do It Any Way You Wanna [I]	TSOP 4769
			THE PEPPERMINT RAINBOW	
4/12/69	**32**	5	1. Will You Be Staying After Sunday	Decca 32410
			EMILIO PERICOLI	
			Singer/actor, born in 1928 in Cesenatico, Italy.	
6/09/62	**6**	10	1. **Al Di La'** **[F]** from the film "Rome Adventure"	Warner 5259
			CARL PERKINS	
			Born on 4/9/32 in Tiptonville, Tennessee. Rockabilly singer/guitarist/songwriter. First recorded for Flip/Sun in 1954. Member of Johnny Cash's touring troupe from 1965-75. The Beatles recorded his songs "Matchbox," "Honey Don't" and "Everybody's Trying To Be My Baby."	
3/10/56	2(4)	17	1. **Blue Suede Shoes** Juke Box #2 / Best Seller #3 / Top 100 #4 / Jockey #5	Sun 234

DATE	POS	WKS	ARTIST—RECORD TITLE	LABEL & NO.
			TONY PERKINS	
			Born on 4/14/32 in New York City. Movie actor. Best Supporting Oscar nominee for "Friendly Persuasion" in 1956.	
10/07/57	**24**	1	1. Moon-Light Swim Jockey #24 / Top 100 #43	RCA 7020
			STEVE PERRY	
			Born on 1/22/49 in Hanford, California. Lead singer of Journey since 1978.	
9/25/82	**17**	6	1. Don't Fight It **KENNY LOGGINS with STEVE PERRY**	Columbia 03192
4/14/84	**3**	13	2. **Oh Sherrie**	Columbia 04391
7/07/84	**21**	8	3. She's Mine	Columbia 04496
10/27/84	**40**	1	4. Strung Out	Columbia 04598
12/22/84†	**18**	11	5. Foolish Heart	Columbia 04693
			THE PERSUADERS	
			Soul group formed in New York City in 1969. Consisted of lead Douglas "Smokey" Scott, Willie Holland, James "B.J." Barnes and Charles Stodghill.	
9/18/71	**15**	9	● 1. Thin Line Between Love & Hate	Atco 6822
12/08/73	**39**	3	2. Some Guys Have All The Luck	Atco 6943
			PET SHOP BOYS	
			British duo: Neil Tennant (vocals) and Chris Lowe (keyboards). Tennant was a writer for the British fan magazine "Smash Hits."	
3/15/86	**1**(1)	14	1. **West End Girls**	EMI America 8307
6/21/86	**10**	9	2. **Opportunities (Let's Make Lots Of Money)**	EMI America 8330
9/26/87	**9**	10	3. **It's A Sin**	EMI America 43027
12/26/87†	**2**(2)	13	4. **What Have I Done To Deserve This?** **PET SHOP BOYS with DUSTY SPRINGFIELD**	EMI-Man. 50107
4/09/88	**4**	10	5. **Always On My Mind** version by Elvis released in 1972 on the flip side of his hit "Separate Ways"; Willie Nelson's version hit #5 in 1982	EMI-Man. 50123
11/05/88	**18**	6	6. Domino Dancing backing vocals: The Voice In Fashion	EMI-Man. 50161
			PETER & GORDON	
			Pop duo formed in London in 1963. Consisted of Peter Asher (b: 6/22/44) and Gordon Waller (b: 6/4/45). Toured USA in 1964, appeared on "Shindig," "Hullabaloo," Ed Sullivan TV shows. Disbanded in 1967. Asher went into production and management, including work with Linda Ronstadt and James Taylor.	
5/16/64	**1**(1)	11	1. **A World Without Love**	Capitol 5175
7/11/64	**12**	6	2. Nobody I Know	Capitol 5211
10/24/64	**16**	6	3. I Don't Want To See You Again above 3: written by John Lennon & Paul McCartney	Capitol 5272
1/23/65	**9**	9	4. **I Go To Pieces**	Capitol 5335
5/08/65	**14**	8	5. True Love Ways	Capitol 5406
7/24/65	**24**	5	6. To Know You Is To Love You	Capitol 5461
3/12/66	**14**	8	7. Woman written by Paul McCartney	Capitol 5579
11/05/66	**6**	10	8. **Lady Godiva**	Capitol 5740
1/14/67	**15**	5	9. Knight In Rusty Armour	Capitol 5808
4/15/67	**31**	3	10. Sunday For Tea	Capitol 5864

DATE	POS	WKS	ARTIST—RECORD TITLE	LABEL & NO.
			PETER, PAUL & MARY	
			Folk group formed in New York City in 1961. Consisted of Mary Travers (b: 11/7/37, Louisville); Peter Yarrow (b: 5/31/38, New York City); & Paul Stookey (b: 11/30/37, Baltimore). Yarrow had worked the Newport Folk Festival in 1960. Stookey had done TV work, and Travers had been in the Broadway musical "The Next President." Disbanded in 1971, reunited in 1978.	
6/09/62	**35**	2	1. Lemon Tree	Warner 5274
9/08/62	**10**	8	2. **If I Had A Hammer**	Warner 5296
3/30/63	**2**(1)	11	3. **Puff The Magic Dragon**	Warner 5348
7/13/63	**2**(1)	12	4. **Blowin' In The Wind**	Warner 5368
9/28/63	**9**	8	5. **Don't Think Twice, It's All Right**	Warner 5385
12/28/63	**35**	2	6. Stewball	Warner 5399
4/04/64	**33**	3	7. Tell It On The Mountain	Warner 5418
2/13/65	**30**	4	8. For Lovin' Me	Warner 5496
9/02/67	**9**	8	9. **I Dig Rock And Roll Music**	Warner 7067
12/23/67	**35**	2	10. Too Much Of Nothing 4-5 & 10: written by Bob Dylan	Warner 7092
5/17/69	**21**	7	11. Day Is Done	Warner 7279
11/08/69	**1**(1)	15	● 12. **Leaving On A Jet Plane** written by John Denver	Warner 7340
			BERNADETTE PETERS	
			Born Bernadette Lazzara on 2/28/48 in Queens, New York. Broadway/TV/film star. Appeared in the films "The Jerk" and "Annie."	
5/10/80	**31**	5	1. Gee Whiz	MCA 41210
			PAUL PETERSEN	
			Born on 9/23/45 in Glendale, California. Member of Disney's "Mouseketeers" and played Jeff Stone on TV's "Donna Reed Show."	
3/31/62	**19**	7	1. She Can't Find Her Keys	Colpix 620
12/15/62†	**6**	10	2. **My Dad**	Colpix 663
			RAY PETERSON	
			Born on 4/23/39 in Denton, Texas. Started singing in his early teens, while being treated for polio at a Texas hospital.	
6/15/59	**25**	7	1. The Wonder Of You	RCA 7513
6/27/60	**7**	11	2. **Tell Laura I Love Her**	RCA 7745
12/19/60†	**9**	9	3. **Corinna, Corinna**	Dunes 2002
9/25/61	**29**	3	4. Missing You	Dunes 2006
			THE PETS	
			Member Richard Polodor became a top producer; worked with Three Dog Night and Steppenwolf, among others.	
6/09/58	**34**	1	1. Cha-Hua-Hua [I] Top 100 #34 / Best Seller #38	Arwin 109
			TOM PETTY & THE HEARTBREAKERS	
			Rock group formed in Los Angeles in 1975. Consisted of Tom Petty (b: 10/20/53, Gainesville, FL; guitar, vocals), Mike Campbell (guitar), Benmont Tench (keyboards), Ron Blair (bass) and Stan Lynch (drums). Petty, Campbell and Tench had been in Florida group Mudcrutch, early 70s. Backed Stevie Nicks on solo LP "Bella Donna." Blair left in 1982, replaced by Howard Epstein. Petty appeared in the 1987 film "Made In Heaven." Member of the 1988 supergroup Traveling Wilburys.	
2/18/78	**40**	1	1. Breakdown	Shelter 62008

DATE	POS	WKS	ARTIST—RECORD TITLE	LABEL & NO.
12/08/79†	**10**	13	2. **Don't Do Me Like That**	Backstreet 41138
2/09/80	**15**	10	3. Refugee	Backstreet 41169
5/16/81	**19**	7	4. The Waiting	Backstreet 51100
8/01/81	**3**	15	5. **Stop Draggin' My Heart Around**	Modern 7336
			STEVIE NICKS with TOM PETTY & THE HEARTBREAKERS	
12/04/82†	**20**	11	6. You Got Lucky	Backstreet 52144
3/12/83	**21**	7	7. Change Of Heart	Backstreet 52181
4/06/85	**13**	9	8. Don't Come Around Here No More	MCA 52496
3/01/86	**37**	2	9. Needles And Pins	MCA 52772
			TOM PETTY & THE HEARTBREAKERS with STEVIE NICKS	
5/23/87	**18**	6	10. Jammin' Me	MCA 53065
			ESTHER PHILLIPS	
			Born Esther Mae Jones on 12/23/35 in Galveston, Texas. One of the first female superstars of R&B. Recorded and toured with The Johnny Otis Orchestra as "Little Esther," 1948-54; scored 7 top 10 hits on the R&B charts in 1950. Bouts with drug addiction interrupted her career and led to her death on 8/7/84.	
11/17/62	**8**	10	1. **Release Me**	Lenox 5555
			re-charted in 1967 at POS 93	
9/20/75	**20**	9	2. What A Diff'rence A Day Makes	Kudu 925
			JOHN PHILLIPS	
			Born on 8/30/35 in Paris Island, South Carolina. Co-founder of The Mamas & The Papas. Father of actress MacKenzie Phillips.	
6/20/70	**32**	7	1. Mississippi	Dunhill 4236
			PHIL PHILLIPS with The Twilights	
			Born John Phillip Baptiste on 3/14/31. Black vocalist from Lake Charles, Louisiana.	
7/20/59	**2**(2)	14	1. **Sea Of Love**	Mercury 71465
			JIM PHOTOGLO	
			Pop vocalist from the South Bay area of Los Angeles.	
5/31/80	**31**	4	1. We Were Meant To Be Lovers	20th Century 2446
			shown only as: **PHOTOGLO**	
5/30/81	**25**	7	2. Fool In Love With You	20th Century 2487
			BOBBY "BORIS" PICKETT & The Crypt-Kickers	
			Born on 2/11/40 in Somerville, Massachusetts. Began recording career in Hollywood while aspiring to be an actor.	
9/15/62	**1**(2)	12	● 1. **Monster Mash** **[N]**	Garpax 44167
12/22/62	**30**	4	2. Monsters' Holiday [X-N]	Garpax 44171
6/30/73	**10**	12	3. **Monster Mash** **[N-R]**	Parrot 348
			WILSON PICKETT	
			Born on 3/18/41 in Prattville, Alabama. Soul singer/songwriter. Sang in local gospel groups. To Detroit in 1955. With The Falcons, 1961-63. Career took off after recording in Memphis with guitarist/producer Steve Cropper.	
8/14/65	**21**	6	1. In The Midnight Hour	Atlantic 2289
3/05/66	**13**	8	2. 634-5789 (Soulsville, U.S.A.)	Atlantic 2320
8/13/66	**6**	8	3. **Land Of 1000 Dances**	Atlantic 2348

DATE	POS	WKS	ARTIST—RECORD TITLE	LABEL & NO.
12/10/66	**23**	6	4. Mustang Sally	Atlantic 2365
2/25/67	**29**	3	5. Everybody Needs Somebody To Love	Atlantic 2381
4/22/67	**32**	2	6. I Found A Love - Part 1	Atlantic 2394
8/26/67	**8**	9	7. **Funky Broadway**	Atlantic 2430
11/11/67	**22**	5	8. Stag-O-Lee	Atlantic 2448
5/11/68	**15**	6	9. She's Lookin' Good	Atlantic 2504
7/06/68	**24**	4	10. I'm A Midnight Mover	Atlantic 2528
1/04/69	**23**	6	11. Hey Jude	Atlantic 2591
5/23/70	**25**	9	12. Sugar Sugar	Atlantic 2722
10/24/70	**14**	9	13. Engine Number 9	Atlantic 2765
2/06/71	**17**	8	● 14. Don't Let The Green Grass Fool You	Atlantic 2781
5/15/71	**13**	9	● 15. Don't Knock My Love - Pt. 1	Atlantic 2797
1/15/72	**24**	8	16. Fire And Water	Atlantic 2852
			WEBB PIERCE	
			Born on 8/8/26 in West Monroe, Louisiana. Top country singer. From 1952-58, had 42 consecutive top 10 hits on Billboard's country charts.	
8/31/59	**24**	7	1. I Ain't Never	Decca 30923
			PILOT	
			Scottish trio: David Paton (lead singer, guitar), Bill Lyall (keyboards) and Stuart Tosh (drums).	
5/10/75	**5**	12	● 1. **Magic**	EMI 3992
			RICK PINETTE & OAK	
			Northeastern pop group led by vocalist Pinette.	
7/12/80	**36**	3	1. King Of The Hill	Mercury 76049
			PINK FLOYD	
			English progressive rock band formed in 1965: David Gilmour (guitar; replaced Syd Barrett in 1968), Roger Waters (bass), Nick Mason (drums) and Rick Wright (keyboards). Waters went solo in 1984. Band inactive, 1984-86. Gilmour, Mason and Wright re-grouped in 1987.	
6/23/73	**13**	9	1. Money	Harvest 3609
2/09/80	**1(4)**	19	● 2. **Another Brick In The Wall (Part II)**	Columbia 11187
			PINK LADY	
			Mei and Kei - Japan's hottest disco duo of the 1970s. Hosted own summer TV variety show in the U.S. in 1979.	
7/21/79	**37**	3	1. Kiss In The Dark	Elektra 46040
			THE PIPKINS	
			British studio group; Tony Burrows, lead singer.	
6/06/70	**9**	10	1. **Gimme Dat Ding** [N] background tune used on TV's "Benny Hill Show"	Capitol 2819
			PIPS - see GLADYS KNIGHT	
			GENE PITNEY	
			Born on 2/17/41 in Rockville, Connecticut. Own band at Rockville High School. Recorded for Decca in 1959, with Ginny Arnell as Jamie & Jane. Recorded for Blaze in 1960 as Billy Bryan. First recorded under own name for Festival in 1960. Wrote "Hello Mary Lou," "He's A Rebel" and "Rubber Ball."	
2/27/61	**39**	1	1. (I Wanna) Love My Life Away	Musicor 1002

DATE	POS	WKS	ARTIST—RECORD TITLE	LABEL & NO.
12/18/61†	**13**	10	2. Town Without Pity from the film of the same title	Musicor 1009
5/19/62	**4**	8	3. **(The Man Who Shot) Liberty Valance** inspired by the film of the same title	Musicor 1020
9/29/62	**2**(1)	11	4. **Only Love Can Break A Heart**	Musicor 1022
1/05/63	**12**	8	5. Half Heaven - Half Heartache	Musicor 1026
4/13/63	**12**	7	6. Mecca	Musicor 1028
8/03/63	**21**	6	7. True Love Never Runs Smooth	Musicor 1032
11/16/63	**17**	6	8. Twenty Four Hours From Tulsa	Musicor 1034
8/29/64	**7**	10	9. **It Hurts To Be In Love**	Musicor 1040
11/07/64	**9**	9	10. **I'm Gonna Be Strong**	Musicor 1045
3/20/65	**31**	4	11. I Must Be Seeing Things	Musicor 1070
5/22/65	**13**	7	12. Last Chance To Turn Around	Musicor 1093
8/21/65	**28**	4	13. Looking Through The Eyes Of Love	Musicor 1103
12/18/65	**37**	2	14. Princess In Rags	Musicor 1130
5/14/66	**25**	5	15. Backstage	Musicor 1171
6/15/68	**16**	8	16. She's A Heartbreaker	Musicor 1306
			THE PIXIES THREE	
			White teenage female trio from Hanover, Pennsylvania.	
10/05/63	**40**	1	1. Birthday Party	Mercury 72130
			ROBERT PLANT	
			Born on 8/20/48 in Bromwich, England. Lead singer of Led Zeppelin and The Honeydrippers.	
9/03/83	**20**	9	1. Big Log	Atlantic 99844
12/24/83†	**39**	5	2. In The Mood	Es Paranza 99820
6/15/85	**36**	4	3. Little By Little	Es Paranza 99644
6/04/88	**25**	7	4. Tall Cool One guitar solo: Jimmy Page	Es Paranza 99348
			PLASTIC ONO BAND - see JOHN LENNON	
			EDDIE PLATT	
			Saxophonist/bandleader from Cleveland.	
3/10/58	**20**	4	1. Tequila [I] Jockey #20 / Best Seller #35 / Top 100 #35	ABC-Para. 9899
			THE PLATTERS	
			R&B group formed in Los Angeles in 1953. Consisted of Tony Williams (lead), David Lynch (tenor), Paul Robi (baritone), Herb Reed (bass) and Zola Taylor. Group first recorded for Federal in 1954, with Alex Hodge instead of Robi, and without Zola Taylor. Hit "Only You" was written by manager Buck Ram and first recorded for Federal, who did not want to use it. To Mercury in 1955, re-recorded "Only You." Williams left to go solo, replaced by Sonny Turner in 1961. Taylor replaced by Sandra Dawn; Robi replaced by Nate Nelson (formerly in The Flamingos) in 1966. Lynch died of cancer on 1/2/81 (61). Robi died of cancer on 2/1/89. Several unrelated groups use The Platters' famous name today.	
10/01/55	**5**	20	1. **Only You (And You Alone)** Best Seller #5 / Top 100 #5 / Jockey #5 / Juke Box #5	Mercury 70633
12/24/55†	**1**(2)	19	2. **The Great Pretender** Top 100 #1(2) / Jockey #1(2) / Juke Box #1(1) / Best Seller #2	Mercury 70753

DATE	POS	WKS	ARTIST—RECORD TITLE	LABEL & NO.
3/31/56	**4**	16	3. **(You've Got) The Magic Touch** Top 100 #4 / Juke Box #4 / Best Seller #5 / Jockey #5	Mercury 70819
7/07/56	**1(5)**	20	4. **My Prayer/** Top 100 #1(5) / Jockey #1(3) / Best Seller #1(2) / Juke Box #1(1) #2 hit for Glenn Miller in 1939	
8/11/56	**39**	1	5. Heaven On Earth	Mercury 70893
10/06/56	**11**	12	6. You'll Never Never Know/ Juke Box #11 / Top 100 #14 / Best Seller #15 / Jockey #18	
10/06/56	**13**	9	7. It Isn't Right Best Seller #13 / Juke Box #13 / Top 100 #23	Mercury 70948
1/12/57	**20**	6	8. On My Word Of Honor/ Juke Box #20 / Best Seller #23 / Top 100 #27	
1/26/57	**20**	2	9. One In A Million Best Seller #20 / Top 100 #31	Mercury 71011
3/23/57	**11**	11	10. I'm Sorry/ Juke Box #11 / Best Seller #14 / Top 100 #19	
4/13/57	**16**	9	11. He's Mine Best Seller #16 / Juke Box #18 / Top 100 #23 / Jockey #24	Mercury 71032
6/10/57	**24**	7	12. My Dream Best Seller #24 / Top 100 #26	Mercury 71093
4/07/58	**1(1)**	14	13. **Twilight Time** Best Seller #1(1) / Top 100 #1(1) / Jockey #1(1) #14 hit for the Three Suns in 1944	Mercury 71289
12/01/58†	**1(3)**	16	14. **Smoke Gets In Your Eyes** #1 hit for Paul Whiteman in 1934	Mercury 71383
4/06/59	**12**	11	15. Enchanted 1-3, 5, 10, 12 & 15: written by Buck Ram	Mercury 71427
2/15/60	**8**	11	16. **Harbor Lights** there were 5 top 10 versions of this tune in 1950	Mercury 71563
8/22/60	**36**	1	17. Red Sails In The Sunset **THE PLATTERS featuring TONY WILLIAMS** Bing Crosby and Guy Lombardo both had #1 versions in 1935	Mercury 71656
10/24/60	**21**	8	18. To Each His Own there were three #1 versions of this tune in 1946	Mercury 71697
1/30/61	**30**	2	19. If I Didn't Care #2 hit for the Ink Spots in 1939	Mercury 71749
8/21/61	**25**	4	20. I'll Never Smile Again #1 hit for Tommy Dorsey in 1940	Mercury 71847
6/04/66	**31**	5	21. I Love You 1000 Times	Musicor 1166
3/25/67	**14**	7	22. With This Ring	Musicor 1229

PLAYER

Pop-rock group formed in Los Angeles: Peter Beckett (vocals, guitar), John Crowley (vocals, guitar), Ronn Moss (bass), John Friesen (drums) and Wayne Cooke (keyboards). Moss joined cast of TV soap "The Bold & The Beautiful." Crowley began solo country career in 1988.

DATE	POS	WKS	ARTIST—RECORD TITLE	LABEL & NO.
11/19/77†	**1(3)**	16	● 1. **Baby Come Back**	RSO 879
4/01/78	**10**	12	2. **This Time I'm In It For Love**	RSO 890
10/21/78	**27**	3	3. Prisoner Of Your Love	RSO 908

DATE	POS	WKS	ARTIST—RECORD TITLE	LABEL & NO.
			THE PLAYMATES	
			Donny Conn (b: 3/29/30), Morey Carr (b: 7/31/32) and Chic Hetti (b: 2/26/30) from Waterbury, Connecticut. Molded nucleus of act at the University of Connecticut, with more emphasis on comedy than singing.	
1/27/58	**19**	7	1. Jo-Ann Best Seller #19 / Top 100 #20	Roulette 4037
6/09/58	**22**	2	2. Don't Go Home Jockey #22 / Top 100 #36 / Best Seller #38	Roulette 4072
11/10/58	**4**	12	3. **Beep Beep** [N]	Roulette 4115
7/27/59	**15**	9	4. What Is Love?	Roulette 4160
11/21/60	**37**	2	5. Wait For Me	Roulette 4276
			POCO	
			Los Angeles country-rock band formed by Rusty Young and Buffalo Springfield members Richie Furay and Jim Messina. Changing personnel included future Eagles members Randy Meisner and Timothy B. Schmit. 1979 lineup: Paul Cotton, Charlie Harrison, Kim Bullard and Steve Chapman.	
2/10/79	**17**	9	1. Crazy Love	ABC 12439
6/16/79	**20**	7	2. Heart Of The Night	MCA 41023
			POINT BLANK	
			6-man rock band from Texas.	
8/29/81	**39**	2	1. Nicole	MCA 51132
			POINTER SISTERS	
			Soul group formed in Oakland in 1971, consisting of sisters Ruth, Anita, Bonnie and June Pointer. Parents were ministers. Group was originally a trio, joined by youngest sister June, in the early 70s. First recorded for Atlantic in 1971. Back-up work for Cold Blood, Elvin Bishop, Boz Scaggs, Grace Slick and many others. Sang in nostalgic 1940s style, 1973-77. In the film "Car Wash," 1976. Bonnie went solo in 1978, group continued as trio in new musical style.	
9/08/73	**11**	12	1. Yes We Can Can	Blue Thumb 229
11/09/74	**13**	8	2. Fairytale	Blue Thumb 254
8/23/75	**20**	8	3. How Long (Betcha' Got A Chick On The Side)	Blue Thumb 265
12/16/78†	2(2)	16	● 4. **Fire** written by Bruce Springsteen	Planet 45901
4/14/79	**30**	4	5. Happiness	Planet 45902
8/30/80	**3**	17	● 6. **He's So Shy**	Planet 47916
6/27/81	2(3)	16	● 7. **Slow Hand**	Planet 47929
2/13/82	**13**	10	8. Should I Do It	Planet 47960
7/24/82	**16**	8	9. American Music	Planet 13254
10/30/82	**30**	6	10. I'm So Excited	Planet 13327
2/11/84	**5**	14	11. **Automatic**	Planet 13730
5/12/84	**3**	15	12. **Jump (For My Love)**	Planet 13780
9/08/84	**9**	12	13. **I'm So Excited** [R] slightly different mix than #10 above	Planet 13857
12/22/84†	**6**	14	14. **Neutron Dance** from the film "Beverly Hills Cop"	Planet 13951
7/27/85	**11**	13	15. Dare Me	RCA 14126
12/06/86	**33**	3	16. Goldmine 4-16: produced by Richard Perry	RCA 5062

DATE	POS	WKS	ARTIST—RECORD TITLE	LABEL & NO.
			BONNIE POINTER	
			Born on 7/11/51 in East Oakland, California. One of the Pointer Sisters.	
7/28/79	**11**	15	1. Heaven Must Have Sent You	Motown 1459
2/16/80	**40**	2	2. I Can't Help Myself (Sugar Pie, Honey Bunch)	Motown 1478
			POISON	
			Hard-rock quartet formed in Harrisburg, Pennsylvania: Bret Michaels (vocals), Bobby Dall, Rikki Rockett and CC Deville.	
4/11/87	**9**	9	1. **Talk Dirty To Me**	Capitol 5686
10/17/87	**13**	9	2. I Won't Forget You	Enigma 44038
5/21/88	**6**	11	3. **Nothin' But A Good Time**	Capitol 44145
8/27/88	**12**	9	4. Fallen Angel	Enigma 44191
11/12/88	**1**(3)	14	● 5. **Every Rose Has Its Thorn**	Enigma 44203
			POLICE	
			Rock trio formed in England in 1977: Gordon "Sting" Sumner (b: 10/2/51; vocals, bass), Andy Summers (b: 12/31/42; guitar) and Stewart Copeland (b: 7/16/52; drums). First guitarist was Henri Padovani, replaced by Summers in 1977. Copeland had been with Curved Air. Inactive as a group since appearance at "Amnesty '86." Sting began recording solo in 1985.	
4/07/79	**32**	5	1. Roxanne	A&M 2096
11/22/80†	**10**	13	2. **De Do Do Do, De Da Da Da**	A&M 2275
2/21/81	**10**	13	3. **Don't Stand So Close To Me**	A&M 2301
10/10/81	**3**	15	4. **Every Little Thing She Does Is Magic**	A&M 2371
1/30/82	**11**	10	5. Spirits In The Material World	A&M 2390
6/04/83	**1**(8)	20	● 6. **Every Breath You Take**	A&M 2542
8/27/83	**3**	13	7. **King Of Pain**	A&M 2569
11/19/83	**16**	9	8. Synchronicity II	A&M 2571
1/21/84	**8**	10	9. **Wrapped Around Your Finger** all of above: written by Sting	A&M 2614
			PONI-TAILS	
			Pop female trio from Brush High School in Lyndhurst, Ohio. Consisted of Toni Cistone (lead), LaVerne Novak (high harmony) and Patti McCabe. First recorded for Point in 1957.	
7/28/58	**7**	12	1. **Born Too Late** Hot 100 #7 / Best Seller #11	ABC-Para. 9934
			THE POPPY FAMILY	
			Canadian pop quartet: Susan (vocals) and husband Terry Jacks (guitar, composer); Craig MacCaw (guitar) and Satwan Singh (percussion). Group and marriage broke up in 1973; Susan and Terry began solo careers.	
4/25/70	**2**(2)	13	● 1. **Which Way You Goin' Billy?**	London 129
9/19/70	**29**	6	2. That's Where I Went Wrong	London 139
			SANDY POSEY	
			Born on 6/18/47 in Jasper, Alabama; raised in West Memphis, Arkansas. Worked as a session singer in Nashville and Memphis in the early 60s. Left music from 1968-70. Back-up singer on the Nashville Network.	
8/06/66	**12**	12	1. Born A Woman	MGM 13501
12/10/66	**12**	8	2. Single Girl	MGM 13612
4/08/67	**31**	2	3. What A Woman In Love Won't Do	MGM 13702
7/01/67	**12**	8	4. I Take It Back	MGM 13744

DATE	POS	WKS	ARTIST—RECORD TITLE		LABEL & NO.
			MIKE POST		
			Record producer/composer of numerous television and film scores.		
6/21/75	**10**	10	1. **The Rockford Files**	**[I]**	MGM 14772
10/03/81	**10**	10	2. **The Theme From Hill Street Blues**	**[I]**	Elektra 47186
			featuring Larry Carlton, guitar		
4/03/82	**25**	7	3. Theme From Magnum P.I.	[I]	Elektra 47400
			all of above: from TV series of the same titles		
			FRANCK POURCEL'S FRENCH FIDDLES		
			Frank was born on 1/1/15 in Marseilles, France. String orchestra leader/composer/ arranger/violinist.		
4/27/59	**9**	11	1. **Only You**	**[I]**	Capitol 4165
			JANE POWELL		
			Born Suzanne Burce on 4/1/29 in Portland. Star of many movie musicals, mid-40s through 50s.		
10/06/56	**15**	9	1. True Love		Verve 2018
			Best Seller #15 / Top 100 #24		
			THE POWER STATION		
			Superstar quartet: Robert Palmer (lead singer), Chic's Tony Thompson (drums), and Duran Duran's John Taylor (bass) and Andy Taylor (guitar).		
3/30/85	**6**	12	1. **Some Like It Hot**		Capitol 5444
6/22/85	**9**	10	2. **Get It On**		Capitol 5479
			revival of 1972's "Bang A Gong" by T. Rex (Marc Bolan)		
10/05/85	**34**	3	3. Communication		Capitol 5511
			above 3: produced by Chic's Bernard Edwards		
			JOEY POWERS		
			Born in Canonsburg, Pennsylvania. Produced "The John Hills Exercise Show" for NBC-TV. Wrestling instructor at Ohio State University.		
12/07/63†	**10**	9	1. **Midnight Mary**		Amy 892
			POZO-SECO SINGERS		
			Native Texan trio: Susan Taylor, Lofton Kline and country star Don Williams (lead singer).		
10/08/66	**32**	6	1. I Can Make It With You		Columbia 43784
1/14/67	**32**	4	2. Look What You've Done		Columbia 43927
			PEREZ PRADO		
			Domase Perez Pradio, born on 11/13/18 in Mantanzas, Cuba. Moved to Mexico City in 1948 and formed a big band. Toured and worked in the USA beginning in 1954. In the film "Underwater!" "The King Of Mambo" died on 12/4/83 (65).		
3/05/55	**1**(10)	26	1. **Cherry Pink And Apple Blossom White**	**[I]**	RCA 5965
			Best Seller #1(10) / Juke Box #1(8) / Jockey #1(6) trumpet solo: Billy Regis; from the film "Underwater!"		
6/23/58	**1**(1)	17	● 2. **Patricia**	**[I]**	RCA 7245
			Top 100 #1(1) / Jockey #1(1) / Best Seller #2		
			PRATT & McCLAIN		
			Truett Pratt and Jerry McClain, with backing group Brother Love.		
4/24/76	**5**	10	1. **Happy Days**		Reprise 1351
			from the TV series of the same title		

DATE	POS	WKS	ARTIST—RECORD TITLE	LABEL & NO.
			PRELUDE	
			English folk-based trio: Ian Vardy with Brian and Irene Hume (husband & wife).	
11/02/74	**22**	5	1. After The Goldrush	Island 002
			THE PREMIERS	
			Latin-rock band from San Gabriel, California.	
7/04/64	**19**	6	1. Farmer John	Warner 5443
			THE PRESIDENTS	
			Soul group consisting of Archie Powell, Bill Shorter and Tony Boyd.	
11/14/70	**11**	9	1. 5-10-15-20 (25-30 Years Of Love)	Sussex 207
			ELVIS PRESLEY	
			"The King of Rock & Roll." Born on 1/8/35 in Tupelo, Mississippi. Died on 8/16/77 in Memphis at the age of 42 due to heart failure caused by drug abuse. Won talent contest at age 8, singing "Old Shep." First played guitar at age 11. Moved to Memphis in 1948. Sang in high school shows. Worked as an usher and truck driver after graduation. First recorded for Sun in 1954. Signed to RCA Records on 11/22/55. First film, "Love Me Tender" in 1956. In US Army from 3/24/58 to 3/5/60. In many films thereafter. NBC-TV special in 1968. Married Priscilla Beaulieu on 5/1/67; divorced on 10/11/73. Only child Lisa Marie, born on 2/1/68. Elvis' last live performance was in Indianapolis on 6/26/77. Inducted into the Rock And Roll Hall Of Fame in 1986.	
3/10/56	**1**(8)	22	1. **Heartbreak Hotel/** Best Seller #1(8) / Juke Box #1(8) / Top 100 #1(7) / Jockey #1(3)	
3/17/56	**19**	10	2. I Was The One Jockey #19 / Top 100 #23	RCA 47-6420
4/28/56	**20**	5	3. Blue Suede Shoes Best Seller #20 / Top 100 #24 / Jockey #24 from the E.P. "Elvis Presley"	RCA EPA-747
6/02/56	**1**(1)	19	4. **I Want You, I Need You, I Love You/** Best Seller #1 / Top 100 #3 / Juke Box #3 / Jockey #6	
6/09/56	**31**	3	5. My Baby Left Me written and recorded on RCA by Arthur "Big Boy" Crudup in 1950	RCA 47-6540
8/04/56	**1**(11)	24	6. **Don't Be Cruel/** Best Seller #1(11)/Juke Box #1(11)/Jockey #1(8)/Top 100 #1(7)	
		24	7. Hound Dog Juke Box #1(11)/Best Seller #1(11)/Top 100 #2/Jockey #4 most popular 2-sided hit single in history; because of the enormous strength of each side, and with Billboard alternating the sides shown first, its 11 weeks at #1 are a combined total of the 2 sides as they flip-flopped at #1 on both the Best Seller and Juke Box charts	RCA 47-6604
10/20/56	**1**(5)	19	8. **Love Me Tender/** Best Seller #1(5) / Jockey #1(5) / Top 100 #1(4) / Juke Box #1(1) from Elvis' first movie; tune adapted from "Aura Lee" of 1861	
11/10/56	**20**	4	9. Anyway You Want Me (That's How I Will Be) Jockey #20 / Top 100 #27	RCA 47-6643
11/24/56†	**2**(2)	14	10. **Love Me/** Jockey #2 / Top 100 #6 / Best Seller #7 / Juke Box #8	
12/29/56	**19**	4	11. When My Blue Moon Turns To Gold Again Jockey #19 / Top 100 #27 above 2: from the E.P. "Elvis"	RCA EPA-992

DATE	POS	WKS	ARTIST—RECORD TITLE	LABEL & NO.
1/05/57	**24**	3	12. Poor Boy Jockey #24 / Top 100 #35 from the film and the E.P. "Love Me Tender"	RCA EPA-4006
1/26/57	**1**(3)	14	13. **Too Much/** Best Seller #1(3) / Juke Box #1(1) / Top 100 #2 / Jockey #2	
2/09/57	**21**	4	14. Playing For Keeps Jockey #21 / Top 100 #34	RCA 47-6800
4/06/57	**1**(9)	22	15. **All Shook Up** Juke Box #1(9) end/Best Seller #1(8)/Top 100 #1(8)/Jockey #1(7)	RCA 47-6870
4/29/57	**25**	1	16. (There'll Be) Peace In The Valley (For Me) Best Seller #25 / Top 100 #39 from the E.P. "Peace In The Valley"; #7 Country hit for Red Foley in 1951	RCA EPA-4054
6/24/57	**1**(7)	18	17. **(Let Me Be Your) Teddy Bear/** Best Seller #1(7) / Top 100 #1(7) / Jockey #1(3)	
7/08/57	**20**	13	18. Loving You Jockey #20 / Top 100 #28 above 2: from the film "Loving You"	RCA 47-7000
10/14/57	**1**(7)	19	19. **Jailhouse Rock/** Best Seller #1(7) / Top 100 #1(6) / Jockey #1(2)	
10/21/57	**18**	6	20. Treat Me Nice Jockey #18 / Top 100 #27 above 2: from the film "Jailhouse Rock"	RCA 47-7035
1/27/58	**1**(5)	16	• 21. **Don't/** Best Seller #1(5) / Top 100 #1(1) / Jockey #1(1)	
2/03/58	**8**	7	22. I Beg Of You Top 100 #8 / Jockey #11	RCA 47-7150
4/21/58	**2**(1)	13	• 23. **Wear My Ring Around Your Neck/** Best Seller #2 / Top 100 #3 / Jockey #3	
5/05/58	**15**	2	24. Doncha' Think It's Time Jockey #15 / Top 100 #21	RCA 47-7240
6/30/58	**1**(2)	14	• 25. **Hard Headed Woman/** Best Seller #1(2) / Jockey #1(1) / Top 100 #2	
7/14/58	**25**	4	26. Don't Ask Me Why Jockey #25 / Top 100 #28 above 2: from the film "King Creole"	RCA 47-7280
11/10/58	**4**	14	27. **One Night/** #11 hit on the R&B charts for Smiley Lewis in 1956	
11/10/58	**8**	12	• 28. I Got Stung	RCA 47-7410
3/30/59	**2**(1)	11	• 29. **(Now And Then There's) A Fool Such As I/** #4 hit on the Country charts for Hank Snow in 1953	
3/30/59	**4**	10	30. I Need Your Love Tonight	RCA 47-7506
7/13/59	**1**(2)	10	31. **A Big Hunk O' Love/** above 4: Elvis' only recordings during his Army hitch	
7/13/59	**12**	10	32. My Wish Came True	RCA 47-7600
4/11/60	**1**(4)	13	33. **Stuck On You/**	
4/25/60	**17**	7	34. Fame And Fortune above 2: recorded 15 days after his Army discharge	RCA 47-7740
7/25/60	**1**(5)	16	• 35. **It's Now Or Never/** adapted from the Italian song "O Sole Mio" of 1899	
8/01/60	**32**	2	36. A Mess Of Blues	RCA 47-7777

DATE	POS	WKS	ARTIST—RECORD TITLE	LABEL & NO.
11/14/60	**1**(6)	14	● 37. **Are You Lonesome To-night?/** #4 hit for Vaughn Deleath in 1927	
11/28/60	**20**	8	38. I Gotta Know	RCA 47-7810
2/20/61	**1**(2)	11	39. **Surrender/** adapted from the Italian song "Come Back To Sorrento"	
3/13/61	**32**	2	40. Lonely Man from the film "Wild In The Country"	RCA 47-7850
4/24/61	**14**	5	41. Flaming Star from the film of the same title and the E.P. "Elvis By Request"	RCA LPC-128
5/22/61	**5**	7	42. **I Feel So Bad/** #8 hit on the R&B charts for Chuck Willis in 1954	
6/19/61	**26**	2	43. Wild In The Country from the film of the same title	RCA 47-7880
8/28/61	**5**	10	44. **Little Sister/**	
9/04/61	**4**	7	45. (Marie's the Name) His Latest Flame	RCA 47-7908
12/18/61†	**2**(1)	12	● 46. **Can't Help Falling In Love/**	
12/18/61†	**23**	5	47. Rock-A-Hula Baby above 2: from the film "Blue Hawaii"	RCA 47-7968
3/24/62	**1**(2)	11	48. **Good Luck Charm/**	
4/07/62	**31**	5	49. Anything That's Part Of You	RCA 47-7992
5/19/62	**15**	7	50. Follow That Dream from the film and the E.P. of the same title	RCA EPA-4368
8/11/62	**5**	9	51. **She's Not You**	RCA 47-8041
10/06/62	**30**	4	52. King Of The Whole Wide World from the film and the E.P. "Kid Galahad"	RCA EPA-4371
10/27/62	**2**(5)	14	● 53. **Return To Sender** from the film "Girls! Girls! Girls!"	RCA 47-8100
2/23/63	**11**	7	54. One Broken Heart For Sale from the film "It Happened At The World's Fair"	RCA 47-8134
7/13/63	**3**	8	55. **(You're the) Devil In Disguise**	RCA 47-8188
11/02/63	**8**	7	56. **Bossa Nova Baby/** from the film "Fun In Acapulco"	
11/09/63	**32**	3	57. Witchcraft #5 hit on the R&B charts for The Spiders in 1956	RCA 47-8243
3/07/64	**12**	7	58. Kissin' Cousins/ from the film of the same title	
3/14/64	**29**	4	59. It Hurts Me	RCA 47-8307
5/23/64	**34**	2	60. Kiss Me Quick recorded on June 25, 1961 (on the "Pot Luck" LP)	RCA 447-0639
5/30/64	**21**	5	61. What'd I Say/ written and recorded by Ray Charles (POS 6) ... 1959;	
5/30/64	**29**	4	62. Viva Las Vegas above 2: from the film "Viva Las Vegas"	RCA 47-8360
8/08/64	**16**	6	63. Such A Night recorded on April 4, 1960 (on the "Elvis Is Back!" LP); #2 hit on the R&B charts for The Drifters in 1954	RCA 47-8400
10/24/64	**12**	8	64. Ask Me/	
10/24/64	**16**	8	65. Ain't That Loving You Baby recorded June 10, 1958	RCA 47-8440
3/13/65	**21**	6	66. Do The Clam from the film "Girl Happy"	RCA 47-8500

DATE	POS	WKS	ARTIST—RECORD TITLE	LABEL & NO.
5/08/65	**3**	11	67. **Crying In The Chapel** recorded on 10/31/60; there were 5 top 20 versions in 1953	RCA 447-0643
7/03/65	**11**	6	68. (Such An) Easy Question recorded on March 18, 1962 (on the "Pot Luck" LP); from the film "Tickle Me"	RCA 47-8585
9/18/65	**11**	7	69. I'm Yours recorded on June 26, 1961 (on the "Pot Luck" LP)	RCA 47-8657
12/04/65	**14**	6	70. Puppet On A String from the film "Girl Happy"	RCA 447-0650
1/22/66	**33**	3	71. Tell Me Why recorded on January 12, 1957; The Crew Cuts and Gale Storm both had hit versions in 1956	RCA 47-8740
4/09/66	**25**	5	72. Frankie And Johnny version of classic song written around 1850; from the film of the same title	RCA 47-8780
7/09/66	**19**	5	73. Love Letters #11 hit for Dick Haymes in 1945	RCA 47-8870
11/05/66	**40**	2	74. Spinout from the film of the same title	RCA 47-8941
2/18/67	**33**	4	75. Indescribably Blue	RCA 47-9056
11/04/67	**38**	2	76. Big Boss Man #78 hit for Jimmy Reed in 1961	RCA 47-9341
4/20/68	**28**	4	77. U.S. Male written and originally recorded by Jerry Reed	RCA 47-9465
12/14/68†	**12**	11	78. If I Can Dream	RCA 47-9670
4/12/69	**35**	2	79. Memories from the NBC-TV special "Elvis"	RCA 47-9731
5/17/69	**3**	11	● 80. **In The Ghetto**	RCA 47-9741
8/02/69	**35**	4	81. Clean Up Your Own Back Yard from the film "The Trouble With Girls (and how to get into it)"	RCA 47-9747
9/20/69	**1**(1)	13	● 82. **Suspicious Minds**	RCA 47-9764
12/13/69†	**6**	11	● 83. **Don't Cry Daddy**	RCA 47-9768
2/21/70	**16**	8	84. Kentucky Rain	RCA 47-9791
5/23/70	**9**	11	● 85. **The Wonder Of You** recorded live at Las Vegas; #25 hit for Ray Peterson in 1959	RCA 47-9835
8/22/70	**32**	3	86. I've Lost You/	
		3	87. The Next Step Is Love	RCA 47-9873
11/07/70	**11**	8	88. You Don't Have To Say You Love Me #4 hit for Dusty Springfield in 1966	RCA 47-9916
1/02/71	**21**	8	89. I Really Don't Want To Know/ #11 hit for Les Paul & Mary Ford in 1954	
		8	90. There Goes My Everything #20 hit for Engelbert Humperdinck in 1967	RCA 47-9960
3/27/71	**33**	4	91. Where Did They Go, Lord/	
		4	92. Rags To Riches #1 hit (8 weeks) for Tony Bennett in 1953	RCA 47-9980
8/14/71	**36**	2	93. I'm Leavin'	RCA 47-9998
3/11/72	**40**	1	94. Until It's Time For You To Go #53 hit for Neil Diamond in 1970	RCA 74-0619
9/09/72	**2**(1)	12	● 95. **Burning Love**	RCA 74-0769
12/23/72†	**20**	8	96. Separate Ways featured in the film "Elvis On Tour"	RCA 74-0815

DATE	POS	WKS	ARTIST—RECORD TITLE	LABEL & NO.
5/05/73	**17**	7	97. Steamroller Blues recorded live in Hawaii (written by James Taylor in 1970)	RCA 74-0910
3/23/74	**39**	2	98. I've Got A Thing About You Baby #93 hit for Billy Lee Riley in 1972	RCA APBO-0196
6/29/74	**17**	7	99. If You Talk In Your Sleep	RCA APBO-0280
11/09/74	**14**	9	100. Promised Land #41 hit for Chuck Berry in 1965	RCA PB-10074
2/15/75	**20**	6	101. My Boy #41 hit for Richard Harris in 1972	RCA PB-10191
6/07/75	**35**	3	102. T-R-O-U-B-L-E	RCA PB-10278
5/01/76	**28**	5	103. Hurt #4 hit for Timi Yuro in 1961	RCA PB-10601
2/05/77	**31**	5	104. Moody Blue	RCA PB-10857
7/16/77	**18**	12	● 105. Way Down	RCA PB-10998
12/03/77	**22**	7	● 106. My Way recorded live from Elvis' tour; written by Paul Anka in 1969	RCA PB-11165
2/28/81	**28**	5	107. Guitar Man [R] re-mix by Felton Jarvis (d: 1/3/81) of Elvis' 1968 hit (POS 43)	RCA PB-12158
			BILLY PRESTON	
			Born on 9/9/46 in Houston. R&B vocalist/keyboardist. To Los Angeles at an early age. With Mahalia Jackson in 1956. Played piano in film "St. Louis Blues," 1958. Regular on "Shindig" TV show. Recorded with The Beatles on "Get Back" and "Let It Be"; worked Concert For Bangladesh in 1969. Prominent session man, played on Sly & The Family Stone hits. With The Rolling Stones USA tour in 1975.	
5/13/72	**2**(1)	14	● 1. **Outa-Space** **[I]**	A&M 1320
5/19/73	**1**(2)	14	● 2. **Will It Go Round In Circles**	A&M 1411
10/13/73	**4**	13	● 3. **Space Race** **[I]**	A&M 1463
8/03/74	**1**(1)	14	● 4. **Nothing From Nothing**	A&M 1544
1/04/75	**22**	6	5. Struttin' [I] all of above: written by Preston	A&M 1644
3/01/80	**4**	15	6. **With You I'm Born Again** **BILLY PRESTON & SYREETA** Syreeta (Wright) was married to Stevie Wonder	Motown 1477
			JOHNNY PRESTON	
			Born John Preston Courville on 8/18/39 in Port Arthur, Texas. Discovered by J.P. "Big Bopper" Richardson in Beaumont, Texas.	
12/21/59†	**1**(3)	14	1. **Running Bear** Indian sounds by the Big Bopper & George Jones; written by the Big Bopper (J.P. Richardson)	Mercury 71474
4/04/60	**7**	12	2. **Cradle Of Love**	Mercury 71598
7/25/60	**14**	7	3. Feel So Fine Shirley & Lee's version "Feel So Good" hit POS 2-R&B in 1955	Mercury 71651
			THE PRETENDERS	
			Rock quartet featuring lead singer/songwriter/guitarist Chrissie Hynde (b: 9/7/51, Akron, OH). Formed in 1978, early British lineup included guitarist James Honeyman- Scott (d: 6/16/82; replaced by Robbie MacIntosh), bassist Pete Farndon (d: 4/14/83; replaced in 1982 by Malcolm Foster) and drummer Martin Chambers. Hynde married Jim Kerr of Simple Minds in 1984. With the exception of Hynde, numerous personnel changes since 1985. Also see UB40.	
4/12/80	**14**	12	1. Brass In Pocket (I'm Special)	Sire 49181

DATE	POS	WKS	ARTIST—RECORD TITLE	LABEL & NO.
1/29/83	**5**	14	2. **Back On The Chain Gang** from the film "The King Of Comedy"	Sire 29840
1/07/84	**19**	9	3. Middle Of The Road	Sire 29444
4/07/84	**28**	6	4. Show Me	Sire 29317
11/01/86	**10**	13	5. **Don't Get Me Wrong** all of above: written by Hynde	Sire 28630
			PRETTY POISON	
			Five-piece Philadelphia dance band founded by Camden, New Jersey natives: Jade Starling (vocals) and Whey Cooler.	
10/31/87	**8**	14	1. **Catch Me (I'm Falling)** from the film "Hiding Out"	Virgin 99416
5/07/88	**36**	4	2. Nightime remake of Svengali 8403 (hit Black charts on 10/27/84 [POS 82])	Virgin 99350
			LLOYD PRICE	
			Born on 3/9/33 in Kenner, Louisiana. R&B vocalist/pianist/composer. First recording was the #1 R&B hit "Lawdy Miss Clawdy" on Specialty in 1952. In US Army, 1953-56. Formed own record company, KRC, in 1957; leased "Just Because" to ABC Records. Signed to ABC in 1958. Formed Double-L label in 1963. In later years has continued in music, production, and booking agency work.	
4/06/57	**29**	6	1. Just Because	ABC-Para. 9792
1/05/59	**1**(4)	15	2. **Stagger Lee**	ABC-Para. 9972
3/30/59	**23**	4	3. Where Were You (On Our Wedding Day)?	ABC-Para. 9997
5/11/59	**2**(3)	14	4. **Personality**	ABC-Para. 10018
8/17/59	**3**	12	5. **I'm Gonna Get Married**	ABC-Para. 10032
11/23/59	**20**	9	6. Come Into My Heart	ABC-Para. 10062
2/15/60	**14**	9	7. Lady Luck	ABC-Para. 10075
5/30/60	**40**	1	8. No If's - No And's	ABC-Para. 10102
7/18/60	**19**	7	9. Question all of above: written by Price	ABC-Para. 10123
10/26/63	**21**	6	10. Misty	Double-L 722
			RAY PRICE	
			Country singer, born on 1/12/26 in Perryville, Texas. Ray charted over 80 top 40 hits on Billboard's country charts.	
11/07/70†	**11**	14	1. For The Good Times written by Kris Kristofferson	Columbia 45178
			CHARLEY PRIDE	
			Born on 3/18/38 in Sledge, Mississippi. First black country superstar. Had 29 #1 hits on the country charts.	
12/18/71†	**21**	11	● 1. Kiss An Angel Good Mornin'	RCA 0550
			MAXI PRIEST	
			25-year old reggae singer, born and raised in England.	
12/10/88†	**25**	7	1. Wild World	Virgin 99269
			LOUIS PRIMA & KEELY SMITH	
			Jazz trumpeter/singer/composer/bandleader. Louis Prima (b: 12/7/11, New Orleans; d: 8/24/78) married jazz-styled vocalist Dorothy Keely Smith (b: 3/9/32, Norfolk, VA) in 1952; divorced in 1961. Duo backed by Sam Butera & The Witnesses.	
11/24/58	**18**	7	1. That Old Black Magic from the film "Senior Prom"	Capitol 4063

DATE	POS	WKS	ARTIST—RECORD TITLE	LABEL & NO.
12/12/60†	**15**	8	2. Wonderland By Night [I]	Dot 16151
			LOUIS PRIMA	
			PRINCE	
			Born Prince Roger Nelson on 6/7/58 in Minneapolis. R&B vocalist/multi-instrumentalist/composer/producer/actor. Named for the Prince Roger Trio, led by his father. Starred in the films "Purple Rain" (1984), "Under The Cherry Moon" (1986) and "Sign 'O' The Times" (1987). Founded own label, Paisley Park. Prince's backing band, The Revolution, featured Lisa Coleman (keyboards), Wendy Melvoin (guitar), Bobby "Z" Rivkin (percussion), Matt "Dr." Fink (keyboards), Eric Leeds (saxophone) and Andre Cymone (bass; replaced by Brownmark in 1981). Disbanded in late 1986 and formed new backing band of which Sheila E. was a member.	
12/08/79†	**11**	12	● 1. I Wanna Be Your Lover	Warner 49050
3/19/83	**6**	15	2. **Little Red Corvette**	Warner 29746
6/18/83	**12**	10	3. 1999 originally charted for 12 weeks (POS 44), then re-entered, 6/4/83	Warner 29896
9/17/83	**8**	11	4. **Delirious**	Warner 29503
6/09/84	**1(5)**	16	▲ 5. **When Doves Cry**	Warner 29286
			PRINCE & THE REVOLUTION:	
8/11/84	**1(2)**	14	● 6. **Let's Go Crazy**	Warner 29216
10/06/84	**2(2)**	11	● 7. **Purple Rain**	Warner 29174
12/22/84†	**8**	10	8. **I Would Die 4 U**	Warner 29121
3/02/85	**25**	6	9. Take Me With U female vocals: Apollonia; above 5: from the film "Purple Rain"	Warner 29079
5/18/85	**2(1)**	14	10. **Raspberry Beret**	Paisley P. 28972
8/03/85	**7**	10	11. **Pop Life**	Paisley P. 28998
3/08/86	**1(2)**	13	● 12. **Kiss**	Paisley P. 28751
6/14/86	**23**	6	13. Mountains above 2: from the film "Under The Cherry Moon"	Paisley P. 28711
3/14/87	**3**	11	14. **Sign 'O' The Times**	Paisley P. 28399
8/29/87	**2(1)**	13	15. **U Got The Look** backing vocal: Sheena Easton	Paisley P. 28289
12/05/87†	**10**	12	16. **I Could Never Take The Place Of Your Man**	Paisley P. 28288
5/14/88	**8**	9	17. **Alphabet St.** all of above: written and produced by Prince	Paisley P. 27900
			PRISM	
			Canadian rock group; Ron Tabak, lead singer (replaced by Henry Small in 1981).	
3/13/82	**39**	2	1. Don't Let Him Know	Capitol 5082
			P.J. PROBY	
			Born James Marcus Smith on 11/6/38 in Houston.	
2/25/67	**23**	5	1. Niki Hoeky	Liberty 55936
			PROCOL HARUM	
			British rock group led by Gary Brooker (vocals/piano) and Robin Trower (guitar). Translation of Latin group name: "beyond these things."	
7/01/67	**5**	10	1. **A Whiter Shade Of Pale**	Deram 7507
11/11/67	**34**	2	2. Homburg	A&M 885
6/24/72	**16**	8	3. Conquistador	A&M 1347

Kool & the Gang's "Celebration," a No. 1 hit for two weeks in 1980, was an exercise-class favorite of many; ironically, after 20 full years on the charts, the group has yet to have a bigger hit.

Frankie Laine's last charting record was the unusually-titled "Dammit Isn't God's Last Name," issued by ABC Records in 1969. Peak position? An ungodly 86.

Stacy Lattisaw beat the Tiffanies and Debbie Gibsons of the world back in 1980 when she released her first album, *Young And In Love*, at the ripe old age of 12.

Cyndi Lauper drew significant critical praise as lead singer of Polydor's Blue Angel in the early 80s. Following the success of her multi-platinum Portrait solo debut *She's No Angel*, Polydor quickly reissued the Blue Angel album.

John Lennon & the Plastic Ono Band's "Power To The People" peaked at No. 11 in 1971, while the ex-Beatle's next single, "Imagine," peaked at No. 3 a few months later. As a solo artist, Lennon's only No. 1 hits were 1974's "Whatever Gets You Thru The Night" and 1980's "(Just Like) Starting Over."

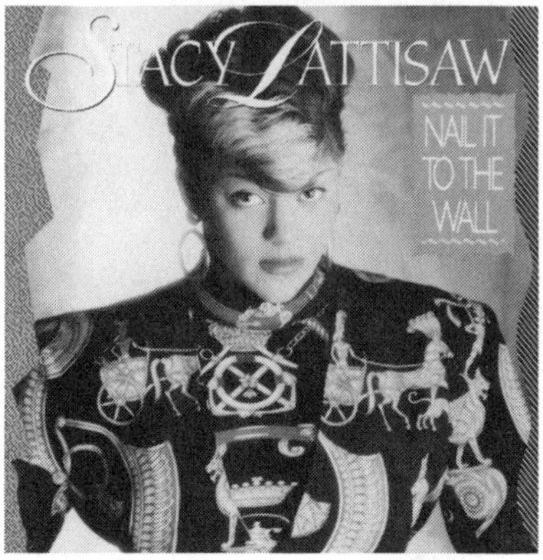

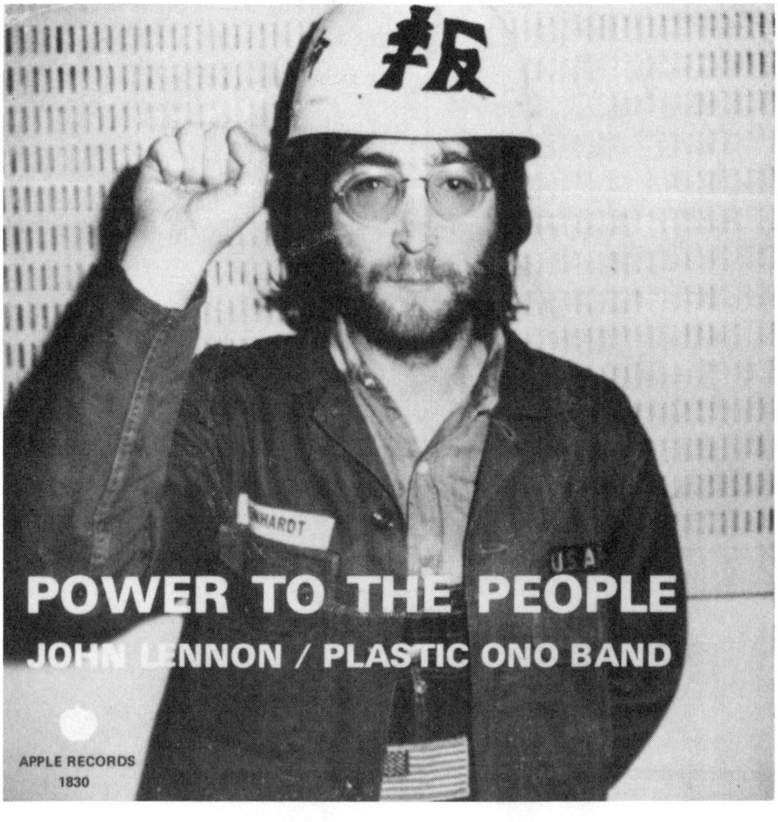

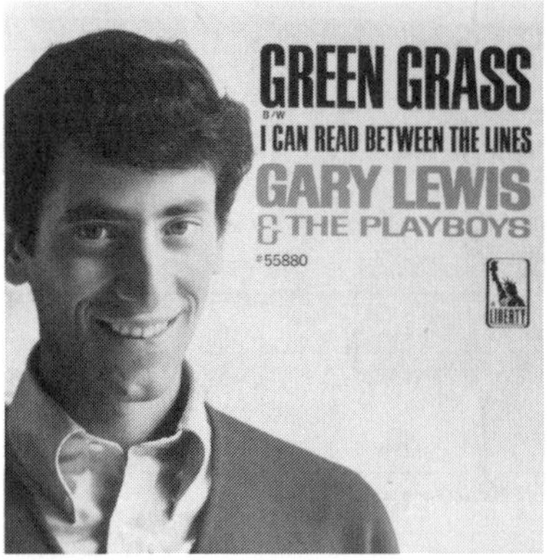

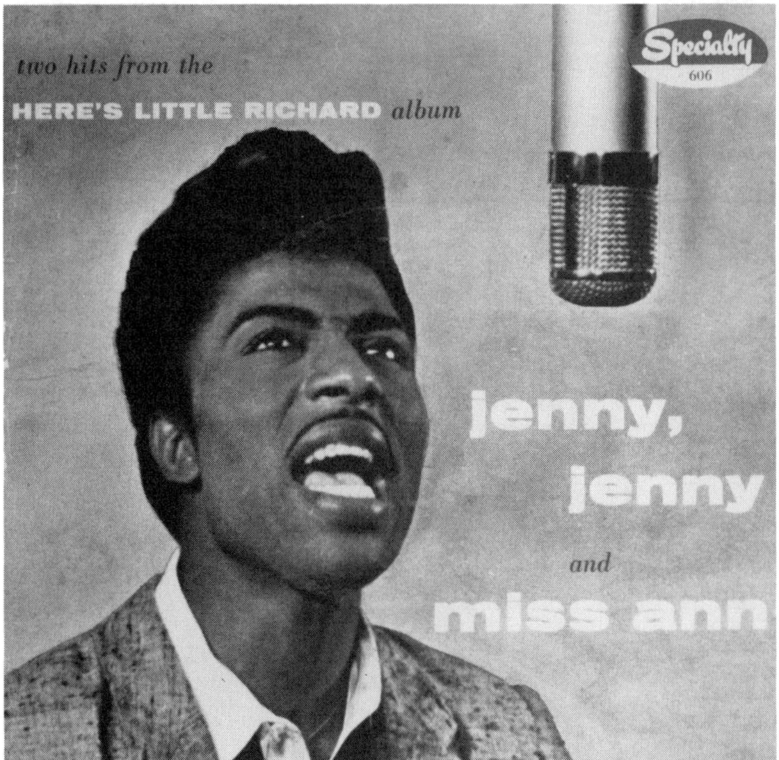

LeVert, a trio consisting of Marc Gordon and brothers Gerald and Sean LeVert—sons of the O'Jays' Eddie LeVert—enjoyed two No. 1 hits on *Billboard*'s Black Singles chart, with "Casanova" crossing over to No. 5 on the Hot 100.

Gary Lewis & the Playboys' first charting single, "This Diamond Ring," stayed in the No. 1 slot for two weeks in 1965. Lewis—a singing drummer and son of comedian Jerry Lewis—interrupted his rock career for a stint in the Army that effectively ended his hit-making career.

Huey Lewis & the News are local boys who made good, according to many San Franciscans. Singer Lewis emerged in the 70s with the already-established rock group Clover; bassist Mario Cippollina was brother of John, the near-legendary guitarist from Quicksilver Messenger Service. Lewis and the News quickly made headlines.

Lisa Lisa & Cult Jam's first top-10 single made for an interesting artist billing: "All Cried Out," which peaked at No. 8 in 1986, was officially credited to Lisa Lisa & Cult Jam featuring Paul Anthony & Bow Legged Lou.

Little Richard's colorful career has shown no sign of letting up in the 80s. Increased activity in the film world saw him sing on two hit film soundtracks, including "Great Gosh A'Mighty! It's A Matter of Time" in 1986's *Down And Out In Beverly Hills*, and, with singer Philip Bailey, the title track from 1988's *Twins*.

DATE	POS	WKS	ARTIST—RECORD TITLE	LABEL & NO.
			JEANNE PRUETT	
			Country singer/songwriter, born Norma Jean Bowman on 1/30/37 in Pell City, Alabama. Songwriter for Marty Robbins since 1963.	
6/23/73	**28**	5	1. Satin Sheets	MCA 40015
			PSEUDO ECHO	
			Techno-rock quartet from Melbourne, Australia; Brian Canham, lead singer.	
6/06/87	**6**	10	1. **Funky Town**	RCA 5217
			PSYCHEDELIC FURS	
			British techno-rock group. Nucleus consists of brothers Richard (vocals) and Tim Butler (bass) with John Ashton (guitar).	
5/02/87	**26**	5	1. Heartbreak Beat	Columbia 06420
			GARY PUCKETT & THE UNION GAP	
			Singer/guitarist Puckett (b: 10/17/42, Hibbing, MN) formed group in San Diego in 1967; named after the town of Union Gap, Washington. Included Kerry Chater (bass), Paul Whitebread (drums), Dwight Bement (sax) & Gary Withem (keyboards).	
12/02/67†	**4**	15	● 1. **Woman, Woman**	Columbia 44297
3/16/68	**2**(3)	13	● 2. **Young Girl**	Columbia 44450
6/22/68	**2**(2)	11	● 3. **Lady Willpower**	Columbia 44547
9/28/68	**7**	10	● 4. **Over You**	Columbia 44644
3/22/69	**15**	8	5. Don't Give In To Him all of above: produced by Jerry Fuller	Columbia 44788
9/06/69	**9**	9	6. **This Girl Is A Woman Now**	Columbia 44967
			PURE PRAIRIE LEAGUE	
			Country-rock group formed in Cincinnati in 1971. Numerous personnel changes.	
4/12/75	**27**	3	1. Amie	RCA 10184
5/24/80	**10**	11	2. **Let Me Love You Tonight**	Casablanca 2266
10/04/80	**34**	4	3. I'm Almost Ready	Casablanca 2294
5/23/81	**28**	6	4. Still Right Here In My Heart	Casablanca 2332
			JAMES & BOBBY PURIFY	
			R&B duo: cousins James Purify (b: 5/12/44, Pensacola, FL) and Robert Lee Dickey (b: 9/2/39, Tallahassee, FL). Dickey left in the late 60s. Purify worked solo until 1974, when Ben Moore became "Bobby Purify."	
10/22/66	**6**	10	1. **I'm Your Puppet**	Bell 648
2/25/67	**38**	1	2. Wish You Didn't Have To Go	Bell 660
5/13/67	**25**	5	3. Shake A Tail Feather	Bell 669
10/07/67	**23**	5	4. Let Love Come Between Us	Bell 685
			BILL PURSELL	
			Pianist from Tulare, California. Appeared with the Nashville Symphony Orchestra. Taught musical composition at Vanderbilt University.	
2/16/63	**9**	10	1. **Our Winter Love** **[I]**	Columbia 42619
			THE PYRAMIDS	
			Surf band from Long Beach, California.	
2/22/64	**18**	6	1. Penetration [I]	Best 13002

DATE	POS	WKS	ARTIST—RECORD TITLE	LABEL & NO.
			Q	
			Q	
4/09/77	**23**	7	1. Dancin' Man	Epic 50335
			QUAKER CITY BOYS	
			Philadelphia string band; Tommy Reilly, leader.	
1/26/59	**39**	1	1. Teasin'	Swan 4023
			QUARTERFLASH	
			Rock group from Portland, led by the husband-and-wife team of Marv (guitar) and and Rindy (vocals, saxophone) Ross. Originally known as Seafood Mama.	
11/07/81†	**3**	19	1. **Harden My Heart**	Geffen 49824
3/13/82	**16**	7	2. Find Another Fool	Geffen 50006
7/02/83	**14**	11	3. Take Me To Heart	Geffen 29603
			SUZI QUATRO & CHRIS NORMAN	
			Rock singer Suzi was born on 6/3/50 in Detroit. Portrayed Leather Tuscadero on TV's "Happy Days" in 1977. Chris Norman is lead singer of Smokie.	
2/24/79	**4**	15	● 1. **Stumblin' In**	RSO 917
			QUEEN	
			Rock group formed in England in 1972. Consisted of Freddie Mercury (vocals), Brian May (guitar), John Deacon (bass) and Roger Taylor (drums). May and Taylor had been in the group Smile. Mercury had recorded as Larry Lurex. Wrote soundtrack for the film "Flash Gordon" in 1980.	
3/29/75	**12**	11	1. Killer Queen	Elektra 45226
2/07/76	**9**	17	● 2. **Bohemian Rhapsody**	Elektra 45297
6/12/76	**16**	11	3. You're My Best Friend	Elektra 45318
12/04/76†	**13**	12	4. Somebody To Love	Elektra 45362
11/26/77†	**4**	17	▲ 5. **We Are The Champions/**	
		17	6. We Will Rock You	Elektra 45441
12/09/78†	**24**	6	7. Bicycle Race/	
		6	8. Fat Bottomed Girls	Elektra 45541
1/12/80	**1**(4)	17	● 9. **Crazy Little Thing Called Love**	Elektra 46579
8/30/80	**1**(3)	21	▲ 10. **Another One Bites The Dust**	Elektra 47031
12/05/81†	**29**	8	11. Under Pressure	Elektra 47235
			QUEEN & DAVID BOWIE	
5/15/82	**11**	8	12. Body Language	Elektra 47452
3/03/84	**16**	8	13. Radio Ga-Ga	Capitol 5317
			? (QUESTION MARK) & THE MYSTERIANS	
			Early punk-rock quintet. Lead singer Rudy Martinez ("?") was born in Mexico and raised in Saginaw, Michigan.	
9/17/66	**1**(1)	12	● 1. **96 Tears**	Cameo 428
12/10/66	**22**	6	2. I Need Somebody	Cameo 441

DATE	POS	WKS	ARTIST—RECORD TITLE	LABEL & NO.
			QUIET RIOT	
			Heavy-metal rock quartet from Los Angeles: Kevin DuBrow (lead singer), Carlos Cavazo (guitar), Frankie Banali (drums) and Rudy Sarzo (bass; replaced by Chuck Wright in 1985). Dubrow and Wright left group in 1987; replaced by Paul Shortino (vocals) and Sean McNabb (bass).	
10/15/83	**5**	14	● 1. **Cum On Feel The Noize**	Pasha 04005
1/28/84	**31**	4	2. Bang Your Head (Metal Health)	Pasha 04267
			THE QUIN-TONES	
			York, Pennsylvania group consisting of Roberta Haymon (lead singer), Ronnie Scott, Phyllis Carr, Caroline Holmes, Kenneth Sexton and Eunice Cristi.	
9/08/58	**18**	6	1. Down The Aisle Of Love Best Seller #18 / Hot 100 #20	Hunt 321
			R	
			EDDIE RABBITT	
			Born Edward Thomas on 11/27/44 in Brooklyn; raised in East Orange, New Jersey. Country singer/songwriter/guitarist. First recorded for 20th Century in 1964. Moved to Nashville in 1968. Became established after Elvis Presley recorded his song "Kentucky Rain."	
3/03/79	**30**	4	1. Every Which Way But Loose from the film of the same title	Elektra 45554
7/14/79	**13**	10	2. Suspicions	Elektra 46053
7/26/80	**5**	15	● 3. **Drivin' My Life Away** from the film "Roadie"	Elektra 46656
12/06/80†	**1**(2)	18	● 4. **I Love A Rainy Night**	Elektra 47066
8/08/81	**5**	15	5. **Step By Step**	Elektra 47174
12/05/81†	**15**	10	6. Someone Could Lose A Heart Tonight	Elektra 47239
5/22/82	**35**	4	7. I Don't Know Where To Start	Elektra 47435
11/13/82†	**7**	21	8. **You And I** **EDDIE RABBITT with CRYSTAL GAYLE**	Elektra 69936
			GERRY RAFFERTY	
			Born on 4/16/47 in Paisley, Scotland. Singer/songwriter/guitarist. Co-leader of Stealers Wheel.	
5/13/78	**2**(6)	15	● 1. **Baker Street** sax solo: Raphael Ravenscroft	United Art. 1192
8/26/78	**12**	10	2. Right Down The Line	United Art. 1233
1/06/79	**28**	6	3. Home And Dry	United Art. 1266
6/16/79	**17**	7	4. Days Gone Down (Still Got The Light In Your Eyes)	United Art. 1298
9/08/79	**21**	8	5. Get It Right Next Time	United Art. 1316

DATE	POS	WKS	ARTIST—RECORD TITLE	LABEL & NO.
			RAIDERS - see PAUL REVERE & THE RAIDERS	
			RAINBOW	
			Hard-rock band led by British guitarist Ritchie Blackmore and bassist Roger Glover, both members of Deep Purple. Group disbanded upon re-formation of Deep Purple, 1984.	
6/19/82	**40**	1	1. Stone Cold	Mercury 76146
			THE RAINDROPS	
			Songwriting team of Ellie Greenwich (b: 10/23/40) and husband Jeff Barry (b: 4/3/38). Barry wrote "Tell Laura I Love Her"; team wrote "Be My Baby," "Da Doo Ron Ron," "Chapel Of Love," "River Deep-Mountain High," "Hanky Panky," "Leader of The Pack" and many others.	
8/31/63	**17**	7	1. The Kind Of Boy You Can't Forget	Jubilee 5455
			MARVIN RAINWATER	
			Born Marvin Karlton Percy on 7/2/25 in Wichita, Kansas. Rockabilly singer of Cherokee Indian heritage.	
6/10/57	**18**	12	1. Gonna Find Me A Bluebird Juke Box #18 end / Best Seller #19 / Top 100 #22	MGM 12412
			RAM JAM	
			East Coast rock quartet led by Bill Bartlett (lead guitarist of The Lemon Pipers). Member Howie Blauvelt played bass in Billy Joel's group The Hassles.	
7/23/77	**18**	8	1. Black Betty	Epic 50357
			EDDIE RAMBEAU	
			Born Edward Flurie on 6/30/43 in Hazleton, Pennsylvania. Pop singer/songwriter.	
6/05/65	**35**	2	1. Concrete And Clay	DynoVoice 204
			RAMRODS	
			Instrumental rock quartet from Connecticut; Vincent Bell, lead guitar.	
2/20/61	**30**	1	1. (Ghost) Riders In The Sky [I]	Amy 813
			THE RAN-DELLS	
			Cousins Steve Rappaport and John Spirt from Villas, New Jersey.	
8/31/63	**16**	8	1. Martian Hop [N]	Chairman 4403
			BOOTS RANDOLPH	
			Born Homer Louis Randolph III in Paducah, Kentucky. Premier Nashville session saxophonist.	
3/30/63	**35**	3	1. Yakety Sax [I]	Monument 804
			RANDY & THE RAINBOWS	
			Pop group from Queens, New York; Dominick "Randy" Safuto, lead singer.	
7/27/63	**10**	10	1. **Denise**	Rust 5059
			RARE EARTH	
			Nucleus of Detroit rock group: Gil Bridges (saxophone, flute), John Persh (trombone, bass) and Pete Rivera (drums). Worked as the Sunliners in the 60s. In 1970, added Ed Guzman (percussion) and Ray Monette (replaced guitarist Rob Richards). Mark Olson replaced Kenneth James (keyboards) in 1971. Many changes thereafter.	
4/04/70	**4**	17	1. **Get Ready**	Rare Earth 5012
8/22/70	**7**	11	2. **(I Know) I'm Losing You**	Rare Earth 5017

DATE	POS	WKS	ARTIST—RECORD TITLE	LABEL & NO.
1/02/71	**17**	8	3. Born To Wander	Rare Earth 5021
8/07/71	**7**	10	4. **I Just Want To Celebrate**	Rare Earth 5031
12/18/71†	**19**	7	5. Hey Big Brother	Rare Earth 5038
6/17/78	**39**	2	6. Warm Ride written by The Bee Gees	Prodigal 0640
			THE RASCALS	
			Blue-eyed soul/pop quartet formed in New York City in 1964. Consisted of Felix Cavaliere, Dino Danelli, Eddie Brigati and Gene Cornish. All except Danelli had been in Joey Dee's Starliters. Brigati and Cornish left in 1971, replaced by Robert Popwell, Buzzy Feiten and Ann Sutton. Group disbanded in 1972. Cavaliere, Cornish and Danelli reunited in June of 1988.	
			THE YOUNG RASCALS:	
3/26/66	**1**(1)	12	1. **Good Lovin'**	Atlantic 2321
7/09/66	**20**	4	2. You Better Run	Atlantic 2338
2/25/67	**16**	9	3. I've Been Lonely Too Long	Atlantic 2377
5/06/67	**1**(4)	11	● 4. **Groovin'**	Atlantic 2401
7/22/67	**10**	8	5. **A Girl Like You**	Atlantic 2424
9/23/67	**4**	9	6. **How Can I Be Sure**	Atlantic 2438
12/23/67†	**20**	5	7. It's Wonderful	Atlantic 2463
			THE RASCALS:	
4/20/68	**3**	11	● 8. **A Beautiful Morning**	Atlantic 2493
7/27/68	**1**(5)	13	● 9. **People Got To Be Free**	Atlantic 2537
12/14/68†	**24**	6	10. A Ray Of Hope above 9: written by Cavaliere & Brigati	Atlantic 2584
3/01/69	**39**	2	11. Heaven	Atlantic 2599
6/07/69	**27**	5	12. See	Atlantic 2634
9/20/69	**26**	6	13. Carry Me Back	Atlantic 2664
			RASPBERRIES	
			Cleveland pop-rock quartet: Eric Carmen (lead singer, guitar), Wally Bryson (lead guitar), David Smalley (bass) and Jim Bonfanti (drums). Smalley and Bonfanti replaced by Scott McCarl and Michael McBride in 1974. Carmen went solo in 1975.	
8/19/72	**5**	11	● 1. **Go All The Way**	Capitol 3348
12/09/72†	**16**	9	2. I Wanna Be With You	Capitol 3473
5/12/73	**35**	7	3. Let's Pretend	Capitol 3546
10/12/74	**18**	6	4. Overnight Sensation (Hit Record)	Capitol 3946
			RATT	
			Hard-rock quintet from Los Angeles; Stephen Pearcy, lead singer.	
7/14/84	**12**	10	1. Round And Round	Atlantic 89693
8/17/85	**40**	1	2. Lay It Down	Atlantic 89546
			LOU RAWLS	
			Born on 12/1/35 in Chicago. With the Pilgrim Travelers gospel group, 1957-59. Summer replacement TV show "Lou Rawls & The Golddiggers" in 1969. In films "Angel Angel, Down We Go" and "Believe In Me." Voice of many Budweiser beer ads. Also see Sam Cooke.	
10/15/66	**13**	8	1. Love Is A Hurtin' Thing	Capitol 5709
5/06/67	**29**	4	2. Dead End Street	Capitol 5869
8/30/69	**18**	8	3. Your Good Thing (Is About To End)	Capitol 2550

DATE	POS	WKS	ARTIST—RECORD TITLE	LABEL & NO.
10/16/71	**17**	11	4. A Natural Man	MGM 14262
7/10/76	**2**(2)	13	● 5. **You'll Never Find Another Love Like Mine**	Phil. Int. 3592
2/25/78	**24**	8	6. Lady Love	Phil. Int. 3634
			RAY, GOODMAN & BROWN	
			Soul group consisting of Harry Ray (tenor), Al Goodman (bass) and Billy Brown (falsetto). Formerly known as The Moments.	
2/16/80	**5**	14	● 1. **Special Lady**	Polydor 2033
			DIANE RAY	
			Born on 9/1/42 in Gastonia, North Carolina.	
9/07/63	**31**	3	1. Please Don't Talk To The Lifeguard	Mercury 72117
			JAMES RAY	
			R&B singer, born in 1941 in Washington, DC.	
12/25/61†	**22**	7	1. If You Gotta Make A Fool Of Somebody with the Hutch Davie Orchestra	Caprice 110
			JOHNNIE RAY	
			Born on 1/10/27 in Dallas, Oregon. Has worn hearing aid since age 14. First recorded for Okeh in 1951. Famous for emotion-packed delivery, with R&B influences. Appeared in three films. Active into the 80s. Now lives in Hollywood.	
9/08/56	**2**(1)	23	1. **Just Walking In The Rain** Top 100 #2 / Juke Box #2 / Best Seller #3 / Jockey #3	Columbia 40729
1/19/57	**10**	10	2. **You Don't Owe Me A Thing/** Best Seller #10 / Top 100 #10 / Jockey #10 / Juke Box #12	
2/02/57	**36**	2	3. Look Homeward, Angel	Columbia 40803
5/06/57	**12**	5	4. Yes Tonight, Josephine Jockey #12 / Top 100 #18 all of above: backed by Ray Conniff & His Orchestra	Columbia 40893
			MARGIE RAYBURN	
			Born in Madera, California. Member of The Sunnysiders, also sang with Ray Anthony's Orchestra.	
11/11/57	**9**	13	1. **I'm Available** Jockey #9 / Best Seller #15 / Top 100 #16	Liberty 55102
			RAYDIO - see RAY PARKER JR.	
			THE RAYS	
			R&B group formed in New York City in 1955: Harold Miller (lead), Walter Ford and David Jones (tenors) and Harry James (baritone). First recorded for Chess in 1955.	
10/21/57	**3**	17	1. **Silhouettes** Top 100 #3 / Best Seller #4 / Jockey #5	Cameo 117
			CHRIS REA	
			Born in Middlesbrough, England in 1951. Pop singer/songwriter.	
7/29/78	**12**	10	1. Fool (If You Think It's Over)	United Art. 1198
			READY FOR THE WORLD	
			Black sextet from Flint, Michigan, formed in 1982: Melvin Riley, Jr. (lead singer), Gordon Strozier, Gregory Potts, Willie Triplett, John Eaton and Gerald Valentine.	
8/24/85	**1**(1)	13	1. **Oh Sheila**	MCA 52636
1/25/86	**21**	6	2. Digital Display	MCA 52734
12/27/86†	**9**	12	3. **Love You Down**	MCA 52947

DATE	POS	WKS	ARTIST—RECORD TITLE	LABEL & NO.
			REAL LIFE	
			Australian quartet; David Sterry, lead singer.	
1/14/84	**29**	6	1. Send Me An Angel	Curb 52287
5/05/84	**40**	1	2. Catch Me I'm Falling	Curb 52362
			THE REBELS	
			Buffalo disc jockey Tom Shannon and producer Phil Todaro (Shan-Todd label) recruited the Buffalo group, The Rebels (aka: The Rockin' Rebels) to record Shannon's theme song "Wild Weekend." Consisted of twins Mickey & Jim Kipler, Paul Balon and Tom Gorman. Later Swan recordings, which were billed as The Rockin' Rebels, were by a different group that recorded in 1959 as the Hot-Toddys.	
1/26/63	**8**	12	1. **Wild Weekend** [I]	Swan 4125
			REDBONE	
			American Indian "swamp rock" group formed in Los Angeles in 1968. Consisted of brothers Lolly (lead vocals, guitar) and Pat Vegas (bass), Anthony Bellamy (guitar) and Peter De Poe (drums). The Vegas brothers had been session musicians and worked the "Shindig" TV show. Wrote P.J. Proby's hit "Niki Hoeky."	
1/08/72	**21**	7	1. The Witch Queen Of New Orleans	Epic 10749
2/09/74	**5**	18	● 2. **Come And Get Your Love**	Epic 11035
			GENE REDDING	
			Born in Anderson, Indiana in 1945. Discovered by Etta James at a USO Club in Anchorage, Alaska.	
7/06/74	**24**	5	1. This Heart	Haven 7000
			OTIS REDDING	
			Born on 9/9/41 in Dawson, Georgia. Killed in a plane crash in Lake Monona in Madison, Wisconsin on 12/10/67. Soul singer/songwriter/producer/pianist. First recorded with Johnny Jenkins & The Pinetoppers on Confederate in 1960. Own label, Jotis. Plane crash also killed 4 members of the Bar-Kays. Otis was inducted into the Rock And Roll Hall Of Fame in 1989.	
6/19/65	**21**	6	1. I've Been Loving You Too Long (To Stop Now)	Volt 126
10/23/65	**35**	3	2. Respect	Volt 128
4/02/66	**31**	3	3. Satisfaction	Volt 132
10/29/66	**29**	4	4. Fa-Fa-Fa-Fa-Fa (Sad Song)	Volt 138
12/31/66†	**25**	6	5. Try A Little Tenderness	Volt 141
6/03/67	**26**	4	6. Tramp	Stax 216
			OTIS & CARLA (Thomas)	
9/23/67	**30**	2	7. Knock On Wood	Stax 228
			OTIS & CARLA (Thomas)	
2/10/68	1(4)	14	● 8. **(Sittin' On) The Dock Of The Bay**	Volt 157
			recorded 3 days before his death	
5/11/68	**25**	5	9. The Happy Song (Dum-Dum)	Volt 163
7/27/68	**36**	1	10. Amen	Atco 6592
12/14/68†	**21**	5	11. Papa's Got A Brand New Bag	Atco 6636

DATE	POS	WKS	ARTIST—RECORD TITLE	LABEL & NO.
			HELEN REDDY	
			Born on 10/25/42 in Melbourne, Australia. Family was in show business, Helen made stage debut at age 4. Own TV series in the early 60s. Migrated to New York in 1966. To Los Angeles in 1968. Acted in the films "Airport 1975" (1974), "Pete's Dragon" (1977) and "Sgt. Pepper's Lonely Hearts Club Band" (1978).	
5/08/71	**13**	9	1. I Don't Know How To Love Him from the rock opera "Jesus Christ Superstar"	Capitol 3027
10/14/72	1(1)	14	● 2. **I Am Woman** originally charted for 3 weeks (POS 97), then re-entered, 9/16/72; from the film "Stand Up And Be Counted"	Capitol 3350
3/10/73	**12**	10	3. Peaceful	Capitol 3527
7/28/73	1(1)	14	● 4. **Delta Dawn**	Capitol 3645
11/17/73	**3**	13	● 5. **Leave Me Alone (Ruby Red Dress)**	Capitol 3768
3/30/74	**15**	9	6. Keep On Singing	Capitol 3845
7/20/74	**9**	12	7. **You And Me Against The World**	Capitol 3897
11/02/74	1(1)	13	● 8. **Angie Baby**	Capitol 3972
3/01/75	**22**	5	9. Emotion	Capitol 4021
7/26/75	**35**	2	10. Bluebird	Capitol 4108
8/30/75	**8**	9	11. **Ain't No Way To Treat A Lady**	Capitol 4128
12/27/75†	**19**	9	12. Somewhere In The Night	Capitol 4192
8/21/76	**29**	5	13. I Can't Hear You No More	Capitol 4312
6/11/77	**18**	12	14. You're My World	Capitol 4418
			REDEYE	
			Rock quartet led by Dave Hodgkins and Douglas "Red" Mark.	
12/26/70†	**27**	7	1. Games	Pentagram 204
			DAN REED NETWORK	
			Portland-based, funk-rock quintet led by singer/composer Dan Reed.	
4/30/88	**38**	2	1. Ritual	Mercury 870183
			JERRY REED	
			Born Jerry Reed Hubbard on 3/20/37 in Atlanta. Country singer/guitarist/songwriter/ actor. Among his many films, co-starred in "Gator" and "Smokey & The Bandit." Elvis Presley recorded 2 of Reed's songs: "U.S. Male" and "Guitar Man."	
1/09/71	**8**	14	● 1. **Amos Moses** [N]	RCA 9904
5/29/71	**9**	9	2. **When You're Hot, You're Hot** [N]	RCA 9976
			JIMMY REED	
			Born Mathis James Reed on 9/6/25 in Dunleith, Mississippi; died from an epileptic seizure on 8/29/76. R&B vocalist/guitarist/harmonica player/songwriter. Taught guitar by Eddie Taylor at age 7. First recorded for Chance in 1953. Afflicted with epilepsy since 1957. Distinctive and influential blues singer, active until death.	
11/04/57	**32**	3	1. Honest I Do Top 100 #32 / Best Seller #36	Vee-Jay 253
2/29/60	**37**	2	2. Baby What You Want Me To Do	Vee-Jay 333
			LOU REED	
			Born Louis Firbank on 3/2/44 in the New York City area. Lead singer/songwriter of the New York seminal rock band the Velvet Underground.	
3/31/73	**16**	8	1. Walk On The Wild Side produced by David Bowie & Mick Ronson	RCA 0887

DATE	POS	WKS	ARTIST—RECORD TITLE	LABEL & NO.
			DELLA REESE	
			Born Delloreese Patricia Early on 7/6/31 in Detroit. With Mahalia Jackson troupe from 1945-49, and Erskine Hawkins in the early 50s. Solo since 1957. Actress/singer on many TV shows. Own series "Della" in 1970. Played "Della Rogers" on the TV series "Chico & The Man" from 1976-78. Appeared in the 1958 film "Let's Rock."	
9/09/57	**12**	13	1. And That Reminds Me Jockey #12 / Best Seller #23 / Top 100 #29	Jubilee 5292
10/05/59	**2**(1)	15	2. **Don't You Know**	RCA 7591
12/28/59†	**16**	8	3. Not One Minute More	RCA 7644
			JIM REEVES	
			Born on 8/20/24 in Panola County, Texas. Killed in a plane crash on 7/31/64 in Nashville. Aspirations of a professional baseball career cut short by an ankle injury. DJ at KWKH-Shreveport, Louisiana, home of the "Louisiana Hayride," early 50s. First recorded for Macy's in 1950. Joined "Hayride" cast following first country hit "Mexican Joe" in 1953. Joined the Grand Ole Opry in 1955. Own ABC-TV series in 1957. In the 1963 film "Kimberley Jim." Posthumously, he continued to have many top 10 country hits into the 80s.	
5/06/57	**11**	14	1. Four Walls Jockey #11 / Top 100 #12 / Juke Box #13 / Best Seller #14	RCA 6874
1/11/60	**2**(3)	20	2. **He'll Have To Go**	RCA 7643
7/11/60	**37**	1	3. I'm Gettin' Better	RCA 7756
11/28/60	**31**	4	4. Am I Losing You	RCA 7800
			MARTHA REEVES - see MARTHA & THE VANDELLAS	
			THE REFLECTIONS	
			Detroit rock quartet: Tony Micale (lead vocals), Dan Bennie, Phil Castrodale and John Dean.	
5/02/64	**6**	9	1. **(Just Like) Romeo & Juliet**	Golden World 9
			RE-FLEX	
			British techno-rock quartet founded by computer keyboardist Paul Fishman.	
2/18/84	**24**	5	1. The Politics Of Dancing	Capitol 5301
			THE REGENTS	
			Bronx vocal group formed as the Desires in 1958. Consisted of Guy Villari (lead), Sal Cuomo, Charles Fassert, Don Jacobucci and Tony "Hot Rod" Gravagna. "Barbara- Ann," written for Fassert's sister, was first recorded as a demo in 1958. Group had disbanded by the time "Barbara-Ann" was released.	
5/22/61	**13**	7	1. Barbara-Ann	Gee 1065
7/31/61	**28**	4	2. Runaround	Gee 1071
			REGINA	
			New York native, Regina Richards.	
7/19/86	**10**	12	1. **Baby Love**	Atlantic 89417
			CLARENCE REID	
			Born on 2/14/45 in Cochran, Georgia. Soul singer/composer/arranger/producer. With the Miami vocal group, the Delmiros, in the early 60s. Also recorded as "Blowfly."	
9/13/69	**40**	2	1. Nobody But You Babe	Alston 4574

DATE	POS	WKS	ARTIST—RECORD TITLE	LABEL & NO.
			R.E.M.	
			Athens, Georgia rock quartet formed in 1980: Michael Stipe (vocals), Peter Buck, Mike Mills and Bill Berry.	
10/17/87	**9**	10	1. **The One I Love**	I.R.S. 53171
			DIANE RENAY	
			Philadelphian Renee Diane Kushner.	
2/15/64	**6**	8	1. **Navy Blue**	20th Century 456
4/25/64	**29**	4	2. Kiss Me Sailor	20th Century 477
			RENE & RENE	
			Mexican-American duo from Laredo, Texas: Rene Ornelas and Rene Herrera.	
12/14/68†	**14**	9	1. Lo Mucho Que Te Quiero (The More I Love You)	White Whale 287
			MIKE RENO & ANN WILSON	
			Lead singers of Loverboy and Heart, respectively.	
5/19/84	**7**	13	1. **Almost Paradise...Love Theme From Footloose** from the film "Footloose"	Columbia 04418
			REO SPEEDWAGON	
			Rock quintet from Champaign, Illinois: Kevin Cronin (lead vocals, rhythm guitar), Gary Richrath (lead guitar), Neal Doughty (keyboards), Bruce Hall (bass) and Alan Gratzer (drums). Gratzer left in 1988, replaced by former Santana drummer Graham Lear. Group named after a 1911 fire truck.	
12/27/80†	**1**(1)	20	● 1. **Keep On Loving You**	Epic 50953
3/28/81	**5**	15	2. **Take It On The Run**	Epic 01054
7/04/81	**24**	6	3. Don't Let Him Go	Epic 02127
8/29/81	**20**	7	4. In Your Letter	Epic 02457
6/19/82	**7**	13	5. **Keep The Fire Burnin'**	Epic 02967
10/02/82	**26**	6	6. Sweet Time	Epic 03175
11/17/84	**29**	5	7. I Do'wanna Know	Epic 04659
1/26/85	**1**(3)	14	8. **Can't Fight This Feeling**	Epic 04713
4/20/85	**19**	9	9. One Lonely Night	Epic 04848
8/17/85	**34**	3	10. Live Every Moment	Epic 05412
2/28/87	**16**	7	11. That Ain't Love	Epic 06656
9/19/87	**19**	8	12. In My Dreams	Epic 07255
7/30/88	**20**	9	13. Here With Me	Epic 07901
			RESTLESS HEART	
			Nashville country-rock quintet led by vocalist Larry Stewart.	
5/30/87	**33**	5	1. I'll Still Be Loving You	RCA 5065
			REUNION	
			RCA studio group; Joey Levine (Ohio Express), lead singer.	
9/28/74	**8**	10	1. **Life Is A Rock (But The Radio Rolled Me)** [N]	RCA 10056
			THE REVELS	
			Philadelphia group formed in high school, led by John Kelly.	
11/23/59	**35**	2	1. Midnight Stroll	Norgolde 103

DATE	POS	WKS	ARTIST—RECORD TITLE	LABEL & NO.
			PAUL REVERE & THE RAIDERS	
			Pop-rock group formed in Portland in 1960. Band formed around Paul Revere (keyboards) and Mark Lindsay (lead singer). To Los Angeles in 1965. On daily ABC-TV show "Where The Action Is" in 1965. Group had many personnel changes throughout their career.	
4/17/61	**38**	1	1. Like, Long Hair [I]	Gardena 116
12/25/65†	**11**	11	2. Just Like Me	Columbia 43461
3/26/66	**4**	12	3. **Kicks**	Columbia 43556
7/09/66	**6**	7	4. **Hungry**	Columbia 43678
10/15/66	**20**	5	5. The Great Airplane Strike	Columbia 43810
12/17/66†	**4**	10	6. **Good Thing**	Columbia 43907
3/04/67	**22**	6	7. Ups And Downs	Columbia 44018
5/06/67	**5**	8	8. **Him Or Me - What's It Gonna Be?**	Columbia 44094
9/02/67	**17**	5	9. I Had A Dream	Columbia 44227
2/24/68	**19**	6	10. Too Much Talk	Columbia 44444
7/13/68	**27**	6	11. Don't Take It So Hard	Columbia 44553
3/08/69	**18**	9	12. Mr. Sun, Mr. Moon	Columbia 44744
6/14/69	**20**	8	13. Let Me	Columbia 44854
			RAIDERS:	
5/29/71	**1**(1)	15	• 14. **Indian Reservation (The Lament Of The Cherokee Reservation Indian)**	Columbia 45332
10/02/71	**23**	6	15. Birds Of A Feather	Columbia 45453
			DEBBIE REYNOLDS	
			Born Mary Reynolds on 4/1/32 in El Paso, Texas. Leading lady of 50s musicals and later in comedies. Married Eddie Fisher on 9/26/55; divorced by 1959. Mother of actress Carrie Fisher.	
7/22/57	**1**(5)	23	1. **Tammy** Top 100 #1(5) / Jockey #1(5) / Best Seller #1(3) from the film "Tammy & The Bachelor"	Coral 61851
1/20/58	**20**	1	2. A Very Special Love Jockey #20 / Top 100 #83	Coral 61897
2/22/60	**25**	8	3. Am I That Easy To Forget	Dot 15985
			JODY REYNOLDS	
			Rockabilly singer/guitarist from Yuma, Arizona.	
5/26/58	**5**	14	1. **Endless Sleep** Best Seller #5 / Top 100 #5 / Jockey #7	Demon 1507
			LAWRENCE REYNOLDS	
10/11/69	**28**	6	1. Jesus Is A Soul Man	Warner 7322
			RHYTHM HERITAGE	
			Los Angeles studio group assembled by producers Steve Barri and Michael Omartian (keyboards). Vocals by Oren and Luther Waters.	
1/10/76	**1**(1)	12	• 1. **Theme From S.W.A.T.** [I] from the ABC-TV series "S.W.A.T."	ABC 12135
5/08/76	**20**	8	2. Barretta's Theme ("Keep Your Eye On The Sparrow") from the Robert Blake TV series "Baretta"	ABC 12177

DATE	POS	WKS	ARTIST—RECORD TITLE	LABEL & NO.
			CHARLIE RICH	
			Born on 12/14/32 in Colt, Arkansas. Rockabilly-country singer/pianist/songwriter. First played jazz and blues. Own jazz group, the Velvetones, mid-1950s, while in the US Air Force. Session work with Sun Records in 1958. Known as the "Silver Fox."	
5/02/60	**22**	9	1. Lonely Weekends	Phillips 3552
9/25/65	**21**	7	2. Mohair Sam	Smash 1993
6/09/73	**15**	12	● 3. Behind Closed Doors	Epic 10950
10/27/73	**1**(2)	17	● 4. **The Most Beautiful Girl**	Epic 11040
2/23/74	**18**	8	5. There Won't Be Anymore	RCA 0195
3/09/74	**11**	9	6. A Very Special Love Song	Epic 11091
8/24/74	**24**	7	7. I Love My Friend	Epic 20006
6/28/75	**19**	6	8. Every Time You Touch Me (I Get High)	Epic 50103
			CLIFF RICHARD	
			Born Harry Rodger Webb on 10/14/40 in Lucknow, India, of British parentage. Vocalist/actor/guitarist. To England in 1948. Worked in skiffle groups, mid-1950s. Backing band: The Drifters (later: The Shadows). The Shadows disbanded in 1969. Superstar in England, with over 80 charted hits, including ten #1 singles. British films "Expresso Bongo," "The Young Ones," "Summer Holiday" and "Wonderful Life."	
11/02/59	**30**	4	1. Living Doll **CLIFF RICHARD & The Drifters** from the film "Serious Charge"	ABC-Para. 10042
1/18/64	**25**	7	2. It's All In The Game	Epic 9633
8/14/76	**6**	12	● 3. **Devil Woman**	Rocket 40574
11/17/79†	**7**	14	4. **We Don't Talk Anymore**	EMI America 8025
4/05/80	**34**	3	5. Carrie	EMI America 8035
9/27/80	**10**	13	6. **Dreaming**	EMI America 8057
11/22/80†	**20**	11	7. Suddenly **OLIVIA NEWTON-JOHN & CLIFF RICHARD**	MCA 51007
1/24/81	**17**	11	8. A Little In Love	EMI America 8068
2/06/82	**23**	8	9. Daddy's Home	EMI America 8103
			LIONEL RICHIE	
			Born on 6/20/49 in Tuskegee, Alabama. Grew up on the campus of Tuskegee Institute where his grandfather worked. Former lead singer of the Commodores. Appeared in the film "Thank God It's Friday" (1978).	
7/18/81	**1**(9)	19	▲ 1. **Endless Love** **DIANA ROSS & LIONEL RICHIE** from the film of the same title; written by Richie	Motown 1519
10/23/82	**1**(2)	13	● 2. **Truly**	Motown 1644
1/22/83	**4**	16	3. **You Are**	Motown 1657
4/16/83	**5**	12	4. **My Love**	Motown 1677
10/01/83	**1**(4)	17	● 5. **All Night Long (All Night)**	Motown 1698
12/03/83†	**7**	14	6. **Running With The Night**	Motown 1710
3/10/84	**1**(2)	17	● 7. **Hello**	Motown 1722
7/07/84	**3**	14	8. **Stuck On You**	Motown 1746
10/13/84	**8**	13	9. **Penny Lover**	Motown 1762
11/09/85	**1**(4)	16	● 10. **Say You, Say Me** featured in the film (not album) "White Nights"	Motown 1819
7/19/86	**2**(2)	14	11. **Dancing On The Ceiling**	Motown 1843

DATE	POS	WKS	ARTIST—RECORD TITLE	LABEL & NO.
10/18/86	**9**	10	12. **Love Will Conquer All**	Motown 1866
1/10/87	**7**	10	13. **Ballerina Girl**	Motown 1873
4/18/87	**20**	7	14. Se La	Motown 1883
			NELSON RIDDLE	
			Born on 6/1/21 in Oradell, New Jersey; died on 10/6/85. Trombonist/arranger with Charlie Spivak and Tommy Dorsey in the 40s. One of the most in-demand of all arranger-conductors for many top artists, including Frank Sinatra (several classic 50s albums), Nat King Cole, Ella Mae Morse, and, more recently, Linda Ronstadt; also arranger/musical director for many films.	
12/31/55†	**1**(4)	24	1. **Lisbon Antigua** **[I]** Best Seller #1(4) / Jockey #1(2) / Top 100 #2 / Juke Box #2	Capitol 3287
3/31/56	**20**	4	2. Port Au Prince [I] Jockey #20 / Top 100 #32	Capitol 3374
8/04/56	**39**	2	3. Theme From "The Proud Ones" [I] from the film of the same title	Capitol 3472
8/04/62	**30**	3	4. Route 66 Theme [I] from the hit TV series	Capitol 4741
			THE RIGHTEOUS BROTHERS	
			Blue-eyed soul duo: Bill Medley (b: 9/19/40, Santa Ana, CA; baritone) and Bobby Hatfield (b: 8/10/40, Beaver Dam, WI; tenor). Formed duo in 1962. First recorded as the Paramours for Smash in 1962. On "Hullabaloo" and "Shindig" TV shows. Split up from 1968-74. Medley went solo, replaced by Billy Walker; rejoined Hatfield in 1974. Also see Bill Medley.	
12/26/64†	**1**(2)	13	1. **You've Lost That Lovin' Feelin'**	Philles 124
4/17/65	**9**	10	2. **Just Once In My Life**	Philles 127
7/31/65	**4**	11	3. **Unchained Melody**	Philles 129
12/11/65†	**5**	8	4. **Ebb Tide** all of above: produced by Phil Spector	Philles 130
3/19/66	**1**(3)	11	● 5. **(You're My) Soul And Inspiration**	Verve 10383
6/18/66	**18**	5	6. He	Verve 10406
8/27/66	**30**	3	7. Go Ahead And Cry	Verve 10430
6/15/74	**3**	10	8. **Rock And Roll Heaven**	Haven 7002
10/05/74	**20**	4	9. Give It To The People	Haven 7004
12/07/74	**32**	3	10. Dream On	Haven 7006
			CHERYL PEPSII RILEY	
			Black singer, native of Brooklyn. Discovered by the group Full Force. Worked as a nurse and backing singer.	
12/10/88	**32**	5	1. Thanks For My Child written, produced and arranged by Full Force	Columbia 07996
			JEANNIE C. RILEY	
			Born Jeannie Carolyn Stephenson on 10/19/45 in Anson, Texas. Country singer.	
8/31/68	**1**(1)	12	● 1. **Harper Valley P.T.A.** written by Tom T. Hall	Plantation 3

DATE	POS	WKS	ARTIST—RECORD TITLE	LABEL & NO.
			THE RINKY-DINKS - see BOBBY DARIN	
			MIGUEL RIOS	
			Born in Granada, Spain in 1944.	
6/20/70	**14**	8	1. A Song Of Joy based on the last movement of Beethoven's 9th Symphony; Waldo de los Rios, conductor	A&M 1193
			THE RIP CHORDS	
			California group featuring the duo of Terry Melcher (Doris Day's son; produced The Byrds, Paul Revere & The Raiders) and Bruce Johnston (Beach Boys). Touring group featured a different foursome.	
1/04/64	**4**	11	1. **Hey Little Cobra**	Columbia 42921
5/23/64	**28**	5	2. Three Window Coupe	Columbia 43035
			MINNIE RIPERTON	
			Born on 11/8/47 in Chicago; died of cancer on 7/12/79 in Los Angeles. Recorded as "Andrea Davis" on Chess in 1966. Lead singer of the rock-R&B sextet, Rotary Connection, from 1967-70. In Stevie Wonder's back-up group, Wonderlove, in 1973.	
2/15/75	**1**(1)	13	● 1. **Lovin' You**	Epic 50057
			THE RITCHIE FAMILY	
			Philadelphia disco group named for arranger/producer Ritchie Rome. Group featured various session singers and musicians.	
9/06/75	**11**	12	1. Brazil [I]	20th Century 2218
10/02/76	**17**	11	2. The Best Disco In Town	Marlin 3306
			LEE RITENOUR	
			Born on 1/11/52 in Los Angeles. Guitarist/composer/arranger. Top session guitarist, has appeared on more than 200 albums. Nicknamed "Captain Fingers."	
5/23/81	**15**	9	1. Is It You vocal: Eric Tagg	Elektra 47124
			TEX RITTER	
			Born Woodward Ritter on 1/12/05 in Murvaul, Texas; died of a heart attack on 1/3/74. Country singer/actor. Starred in over 80 Hollywood westerns from 1935-45. Father of actor John Ritter.	
7/07/56	**28**	6	1. The Wayward Wind	Capitol 3430
8/14/61	**20**	4	2. I Dreamed Of A Hill-Billy Heaven [S]	Capitol 4567
			JOHNNY RIVERS	
			Born John Ramistella on 11/7/42 in New York City; raised in Baton Rouge. Rock and roll singer/guitarist/songwriter/producer. Recorded with the Spades for Suede in 1956. Named Johnny Rivers by DJ Alan Freed in 1958. To Los Angeles in 1961. Own Soul City label, 1966.	
6/13/64	**2**(2)	10	1. **Memphis**	Imperial 66032
8/22/64	**12**	7	2. Maybelline	Imperial 66056
11/14/64	**9**	9	3. **Mountain Of Love**	Imperial 66075
2/27/65	**20**	4	4. Midnight Special	Imperial 66087
6/19/65	**7**	8	5. **Seventh Son**	Imperial 66112
10/30/65	**26**	4	6. Where Have All The Flowers Gone	Imperial 66133
1/15/66	**35**	3	7. Under Your Spell Again	Imperial 66144
3/26/66	**3**	10	8. **Secret Agent Man** from the TV series of the same title	Imperial 66159
6/25/66	**19**	6	9. (I Washed My Hands In) Muddy Water	Imperial 66175

DATE	POS	WKS	ARTIST—RECORD TITLE	LABEL & NO.
10/08/66	**1**(1)	12	10. **Poor Side Of Town**	Imperial 66205
2/18/67	**3**	8	11. **Baby I Need Your Lovin'**	Imperial 66227
6/17/67	**10**	6	12. **The Tracks Of My Tears**	Imperial 66244
12/02/67†	**14**	8	13. Summer Rain	Imperial 66267
11/11/72†	**6**	14	● 14. **Rockin' Pneumonia - Boogie Woogie Flu**	United Art. 50960
5/05/73	**38**	2	15. Blue Suede Shoes	United Art. 198
8/09/75	**22**	5	16. Help Me Rhonda	Epic 50121
7/30/77	**10**	15	● 17. **Swayin' To The Music (Slow Dancin')**	Big Tree 16094
			THE RIVIERAS	
			Rock and roll sextet from Indiana; Bill Dobslaw, lead singer.	
2/01/64	**5**	9	1. **California Sun**	Riviera 1401
			THE ROAD APPLES	
12/27/75†	**35**	4	1. Let's Live Together	Polydor 14285
			ROB BASE & D.J. E-Z ROCK	
			Harlem rap duo: Robert Ginyard with deejay Rodney "Skip" Bryce.	
10/15/88	**36**	3	● 1. It Takes Two	Profile 5186
			MARTY ROBBINS	
			Born Martin Robinson on 9/26/25 in Glendale, Arizona; died of a heart attack on 12/8/82. Country singer/guitarist/songwriter. Own radio show with K-Bar Cowboys, late 1940s. Own TV show, "Western Caravan," KPHO-Phoenix, 1951. First recorded for Columbia in 1952. Regular on the Grand Ole Opry since 1953. Own label, Robbins, in 1958. Stock car racer. Films "Road To Nashville" and "Guns Of A Stranger."	
11/24/56	**17**	7	1. Singing The Blues Juke Box #17 / Top 100 #26	Columbia 21545
4/27/57	**2**(1)	21	2. **A White Sport Coat (And A Pink Carnation)** Best Seller #2 / Top 100 #3 / Jockey #4 / Juke Box #4 end	Columbia 40864
12/09/57†	**15**	9	3. The Story Of My Life Jockey #15 / Top 100 #30 / Best Seller #31	Columbia 41013
5/05/58	**26**	5	4. Just Married Best Seller #26 / Top 100 #35	Columbia 41143
8/25/58	**27**	5	5. She Was Only Seventeen (He Was One Year More)	Columbia 41208
3/16/59	**38**	3	6. The Hanging Tree from the film of the same title; 2-6: with Ray Conniff & His Orchestra	Columbia 41325
11/30/59†	**1**(2)	16	7. **El Paso**	Columbia 41511
4/11/60	**26**	4	8. Big Iron	Columbia 41589
8/01/60	**31**	3	9. Is There Any Chance	Columbia 41686
12/05/60	**34**	5	10. Ballad Of The Alamo from the film "The Alamo"	Columbia 41809
2/13/61	**3**	12	11. **Don't Worry**	Columbia 41922
8/18/62	**16**	7	12. Devil Woman	Columbia 42486
12/08/62	**18**	5	13. Ruby Ann	Columbia 42614
			ROBERT & JOHNNY	
			Bronx R&B duo: Robert Carr and Johnny Mitchell.	
3/03/58	**32**	6	1. We Belong Together Best Seller #32 / Top 100 #33	Old Town 1047

DATE	POS	WKS	ARTIST—RECORD TITLE	LABEL & NO.
			AUSTIN ROBERTS	
			Born on 9/19/45 in Newport News, Virginia. Collaborator on cartoon series "Scooby Doo" and "Josie & The Pussycats."	
11/11/72	**12**	10	1. Something's Wrong With Me	Chelsea 0101
8/30/75	**9**	9	2. **Rocky**	Private S. 45020
			DON ROBERTSON	
			Born on 12/5/22 in Peking, China; moved to Chicago at age 4. Pianist/composer. Created the Nashville piano style. Wrote several of Elvis Presley's hits.	
5/05/56	**6**	14	1. **The Happy Whistler** [I] Jockey #6 / Best Seller #9 / Top 100 #9 / Juke Box #12	Capitol 3391
			IVO ROBIC	
			Born near Zagreb, Yugoslavia in 1927. Name pronounced Eevo Robish.	
8/31/59	**13**	11	1. Morgen [F]	Laurie 3033
			FLOYD ROBINSON	
			Born in 1937 in Nashville. Singer/guitarist/composer. Worked on local radio with his high school band the Eagle Rangers, at age 12. Own programs on WLAC and WSM- Nashville.	
8/03/59	**20**	12	1. Makin' Love	RCA 7529
			SMOKEY ROBINSON	
			Born William Robinson on 2/19/40 in Detroit. Formed The Miracles (then called the Matadors) at Northern High School in 1955. First recorded for End in 1958. Married Miracles' member Claudette Rogers in 1963. Left The Miracles on 1/29/72. Wrote dozens of hit songs for Motown artists. Vice President of Motown Records until 1988. Inducted into the Rock And Roll Hall Of Fame in 1987.	
1/19/74	**27**	6	1. Baby Come Close	Tamla 54239
5/31/75	**26**	6	2. Baby That's Backatcha	Tamla 54258
10/18/75	**36**	3	3. The Agony And The Ecstasy	Tamla 54261
11/17/79†	**4**	17	4. **Cruisin'**	Tamla 54306
5/03/80	**31**	4	5. Let Me Be The Clock	Tamla 54311
3/21/81	**2**(3)	16	● 6. **Being With You**	Tamla 54321
2/27/82	**33**	5	7. Tell Me Tomorrow - Part I	Tamla 1601
5/09/87	**8**	12	8. **Just To See Her**	Motown 1877
8/15/87	**10**	11	9. **One Heartbeat**	Motown 1897
			VICKI SUE ROBINSON	
			Born in Philadelphia in 1955. Disco vocalist. Appeared in the original Broadway productions of "Hair" and "Jesus Christ Superstar."	
6/19/76	**10**	13	1. **Turn The Beat Around**	RCA 10562
			ROCHELL & THE CANDLES	
			Los Angeles R&B group consisting of lead Johnny Wyatt, Rochell Henderson, Melvin Sasso and T.C. Henderson.	
3/27/61	**26**	4	1. Once Upon A Time	Swingin' 623
			ROCK-A-TEENS	
			Rock and roll sextet from New York City.	
10/12/59	**16**	9	1. Woo-Hoo [I]	Roulette 4192

DATE	POS	WKS	ARTIST—RECORD TITLE	LABEL & NO.
			ROCKETS	
			Detroit rock band led by David Gilbert (vocals), Jim McCarty (guitar) and John Badanjek (drums).	
8/11/79	**30**	6	1. Oh Well	RSO 935
			ROCKWELL	
			Born Kennedy Gordy on 3/15/64 in Detroit. Son of Motown chairman, Berry Gordy, Jr.	
2/11/84	2(3)	14	● 1. **Somebody's Watching Me** backing vocal: Michael Jackson	Motown 1702
6/23/84	**35**	2	2. Obscene Phone Caller	Motown 1731
			THE ROCKY FELLERS	
			Consists of a father and his four sons from Manila, The Philippines.	
4/27/63	**16**	8	1. Killer Joe	Scepter 1246
			EILEEN RODGERS	
			Born in Pittsburgh in 1933. Featured vocalist in Charlie Spivak's band, 1954-56.	
9/08/56	**18**	10	1. Miracle Of Love Jockey #18 / Top 100 #19 / Best Seller #23	Columbia 40708
9/29/58	**26**	4	2. Treasure Of Your Love	Columbia 41214
			JIMMIE RODGERS	
			Born on 9/18/33 in Camas, Washington. Vocalist/guitarist/pianist. Formed first group while in the Air Force. Own NBC-TV variety series in 1959. Career hampered following mysterious assault in Los Angeles on 12/1/67, which left him with a fractured skull. Returned to performing on 1/28/69.	
8/19/57	1(4)	23	1. **Honeycomb** Jockey #1(4) / Best Seller #1(2) / Top 100 #1(2)	Roulette 4015
11/18/57	**3**	14	2. **Kisses Sweeter Than Wine** Jockey #3 / Top 100 #7 / Best Seller #8	Roulette 4031
2/24/58	**7**	9	3. **Oh-Oh, I'm Falling In Love Again** Jockey #7 / Top 100 #22 / Best Seller #23	Roulette 4045
5/19/58	**3**	15	4. **Secretly/** Best Seller #3 / Jockey #3 / Top 100 #4	
5/26/58	**16**	1	5. Make Me A Miracle Jockey #16 / Top 100 #54	Roulette 4070
8/11/58	**10**	10	6. **Are You Really Mine** Hot 100 #10 / Best Seller #10	Roulette 4090
12/01/58	**11**	10	7. Bimbombey	Roulette 4116
3/30/59	**36**	3	8. I'm Never Gonna Tell	Roulette 4129
6/15/59	**32**	4	9. Ring-A-Ling-A-Lario/	
7/06/59	**40**	1	10. Wonderful You	Roulette 4158
10/12/59	**32**	3	11. Tucumcari	Roulette 4191
2/01/60	**24**	5	12. T.L.C. Tender Love And Care above 4: with Joe Reisman's Orchestra	Roulette 4218
6/18/66	**37**	2	13. It's Over	Dot 16861
10/14/67	**31**	4	14. Child Of Clay	A&M 871

DATE	POS	WKS	ARTIST—RECORD TITLE	LABEL & NO.
			TOMMY ROE	
			Born on 5/9/42 in Atlanta. Pop-rock singer/guitarist/composer. Formed band, The Satins, at Brown High School, worked local dances in the late 50s. Group recorded for Judd in 1960. Moved to Britain in the mid-60s, returned in 1969.	
8/11/62	**1**(2)	11	● 1. **Sheila**	ABC-Para. 10329
11/03/62	**35**	2	2. Susie Darlin'	ABC-Para. 10362
10/26/63	**3**	11	3. **Everybody**	ABC-Para. 10478
2/08/64	**36**	4	4. Come On	ABC-Para. 10515
7/02/66	**8**	10	● 5. **Sweet Pea**	ABC-Para. 10762
10/01/66	**6**	11	6. **Hooray For Hazel**	ABC 10852
1/28/67	**23**	5	7. It's Now Winters Day	ABC 10888
2/15/69	**1**(4)	13	● 8. **Dizzy**	ABC 11164
5/17/69	**29**	3	9. Heather Honey	ABC 11211
12/06/69†	**8**	11	● 10. **Jam Up Jelly Tight**	ABC 11247
9/25/71	**25**	7	11. Stagger Lee	ABC 11307
			ROGER	
			Roger Troutman from Hamilton, Ohio. Leader of the family group Zapp. Worked with Sly Stone and George Clinton.	
12/12/87†	**3**	13	1. **I Want To Be Your Man**	Reprise 28229
			JULIE ROGERS	
			Born Julie Rolls on 4/6/43 in London.	
12/05/64†	**10**	9	1. **The Wedding**	Mercury 72332
			KENNY ROGERS	
			Born on 8/21/38 in Houston. With high school band the Scholars in 1958. Bass player of jazz group, the Bobby Doyle Trio, recorded for Columbia. In Kirby Stone Four and The New Christy Minstrels, mid-1960s. Formed and fronted The First Edition in 1967. Original lineup included Thelma Camacho, Mike Settle, Terry Williams and Mickey Jones. All but Jones were members of The New Christy Minstrels. Group hosted own syndicated TV variety show, "Rollin'," in 1972. Rogers split from group in 1973. Starred in films "The Gambler," "Coward Of The County" and "Six Pack." Also see Dottie West.	
			THE FIRST EDITION:	
2/24/68	**5**	8	1. **Just Dropped In (To See What Condition My Condition Was In)**	Reprise 0655
2/08/69	**19**	8	2. But You Know I Love You	Reprise 0799
			KENNY ROGERS & THE FIRST EDITION:	
7/05/69	**6**	9	3. **Ruby, Don't Take Your Love To Town**	Reprise 0829
10/25/69	**26**	6	4. Ruben James	Reprise 0854
3/14/70	**11**	12	5. Something's Burning	Reprise 0888
7/25/70	**17**	8	6. Tell It All Brother	Reprise 0923
11/14/70	**33**	5	7. Heed The Call	Reprise 0953
			KENNY ROGERS:	
4/23/77	**5**	13	● 8. **Lucille**	United Art. 929
9/10/77	**28**	4	9. Daytime Friends	United Art. 1027
7/15/78	**32**	3	10. Love Or Something Like It	United Art. 1210
12/23/78†	**16**	13	11. The Gambler	United Art. 1250
5/12/79	**5**	13	● 12. **She Believes In Me**	United Art. 1273

DATE	POS	WKS	ARTIST—RECORD TITLE	LABEL & NO.
9/22/79	7	12	13. **You Decorated My Life**	United Art. 1315
12/01/79†	3	15	● 14. **Coward Of The County**	United Art. 1327
4/12/80	4	14	15. **Don't Fall In Love With A Dreamer**	United Art. 1345
			KENNY ROGERS with KIM CARNES	
6/28/80	14	8	16. Love The World Away from the film "Urban Cowboy"; above 9: produced by Larry Butler	United Art. 1359
10/04/80	1(6)	19	● 17. **Lady** written by Lionel Richie	Liberty 1380
6/13/81	3	14	18. **I Don't Need You**	Liberty 1415
9/12/81	14	10	19. Share Your Love With Me	Liberty 1430
1/16/82	13	11	20. Through The Years above 4: produced by Lionel Richie	Liberty 1444
7/24/82	13	10	21. Love Will Turn You Around from the film "Six Pack"	Liberty 1471
1/29/83	6	15	22. **We've Got Tonight**	Liberty 1492
			KENNY ROGERS & SHEENA EASTON	
5/28/83	37	3	23. All My Life	Liberty 1495
9/10/83	1(2)	18	▲ 24. **Islands In The Stream**	RCA 13615
			KENNY ROGERS & DOLLY PARTON written by The Bee Gees	
2/04/84	23	6	25. This Woman	RCA 13710
10/13/84	15	9	26. What About Me?	RCA 13899
			KENNY ROGERS with KIM CARNES & JAMES INGRAM	
			TIMMIE "Oh Yeah" ROGERS	
			Born on 7/4/15 in Detroit. Black vaudeville and nightclub comedian.	
11/04/57	36	4	1. Back To School Again Top 100 #36 / Best Seller #37	Cameo 116
			THE ROLLING STONES	
			British R&B-influenced rock group formed in London in January, 1963. Consisted of Mick Jagger (b: 7/26/43; vocals), Keith Richards (b: 12/18/43; lead guitar), Brian Jones (b: 2/28/42; guitar), Bill Wyman (b: 10/24/36; bass) and Charlie Watts (b: 6/2/41; drums). Jagger was the lead singer of Blues, Inc. Took name from a Muddy Waters song. Promoted as the "bad boys" in contrast to The Beatles. First UK tour, with Ronettes in 1964. Jones left group shortly before drowning on 7/3/69. Replaced by Mick Taylor (b: 1/17/48). In 1975, Ron Wood (ex-Jeff Beck Group, ex-Faces) replaced Taylor. Film "Gimme Shelter" is a documentary of their controversial Altamont concert on 12/6/69. Considered by many as the world's greatest rock band of all-time. Inducted into the Rock And Roll Hall Of Fame in 1989.	
8/01/64	24	5	1. Tell Me (You're Coming Back)	London 9682
8/22/64	26	6	2. It's All Over Now	London 9687
11/07/64	6	9	3. **Time Is On My Side**	London 9708
1/30/65	19	5	4. Heart Of Stone	London 9725
4/10/65	9	8	5. **The Last Time**	London 9741
6/19/65	1(4)	12	● 6. **(I Can't Get No) Satisfaction**	London 9766
10/16/65	1(2)	11	7. **Get Off Of My Cloud**	London 9792
1/08/66	6	6	8. **As Tears Go By**	London 9808
3/05/66	2(3)	9	9. **19th Nervous Breakdown**	London 9823

DATE	POS	WKS	ARTIST—RECORD TITLE	LABEL & NO.
5/21/66	**1**(2)	10	10. **Paint It, Black**	London 901
7/16/66	**8**	8	11. **Mothers Little Helper/**	
8/06/66	**24**	4	12. Lady Jane	London 902
10/08/66	**9**	6	13. **Have You Seen Your Mother, Baby, Standing In The Shadow?**	London 903
2/04/67	**1**(1)	9	● 14. **Ruby Tuesday**	London 904
9/23/67	**14**	6	15. Dandelion all of above: produced by Andrew Loog Oldham	London 905
1/13/68	**25**	4	16. She's A Rainbow	London 906
6/15/68	**3**	11	17. **Jumpin' Jack Flash**	London 908
7/26/69	**1**(4)	14	● 18. **Honky Tonk Women**	London 910
5/01/71	**1**(2)	12	19. **Brown Sugar**	Rolling S. 19100
7/03/71	**28**	5	20. Wild Horses	Rolling S. 19101
5/06/72	**7**	9	21. **Tumbling Dice**	Rolling S. 19103
7/29/72	**22**	4	22. Happy	Rolling S. 19104
9/22/73	**1**(1)	13	● 23. **Angie**	Rolling S. 19105
2/02/74	**15**	6	24. Doo Doo Doo Doo Doo (Heartbreaker)	Rolling S. 19109
8/17/74	**16**	7	25. It's Only Rock 'N Roll (But I Like It)	Rolling S. 19301
11/16/74	**17**	7	26. Ain't Too Proud To Beg	Rolling S. 19302
5/08/76	**10**	7	27. **Fool To Cry**	Rolling S. 19304
6/10/78	**1**(1)	16	● 28. **Miss You**	Rolling S. 19307
9/23/78	**8**	9	29. **Beast Of Burden**	Rolling S. 19309
1/13/79	**31**	4	30. Shattered	Rolling S. 19310
7/05/80	**3**	14	31. **Emotional Rescue**	Rolling S. 20001
10/18/80	**26**	5	32. She's So Cold	Rolling S. 21001
8/29/81	**2**(3)	19	33. **Start Me Up**	Rolling S. 21003
12/12/81†	**13**	12	34. Waiting On A Friend	Rolling S. 21004
4/10/82	**20**	6	35. Hang Fire	Rolling S. 21300
7/03/82	**25**	5	36. Going To A Go-Go	Rolling S. 21301
11/19/83	**9**	10	37. **Undercover Of The Night**	Rolling S. 99813
3/22/86	**5**	10	38. **Harlem Shuffle**	Rolling S. 05802
6/14/86	**28**	4	39. One Hit (To The Body) 1, 4-25, 27-35, 37 & 39: written by Jagger & Richards; above 15: produced by The Glimmer Twins (Jagger & Richards)	Rolling S. 05906
			THE ROMANTICS	
			Rock quartet from Detroit; Wally Palmar, lead singer.	
12/03/83†	**3**	15	1. **Talking In Your Sleep**	Nemperor 04135
3/31/84	**37**	3	2. One In A Million	Nemperor 04373
			ROMEO VOID	
			San Francisco new-wave quintet; Debora Iyall, lead singer.	
10/20/84	**35**	2	1. A Girl In Trouble (Is A Temporary Thing)	Columbia 04534
			RONALD & RUBY	
3/24/58	**20**	3	1. Lollipop Jockey #20 / Top 100 #39 / Best Seller #40	RCA 7174

L. L. Cool J's multi-platinum *Bigger And Deffer* was one of 1987's most surprising hits; the young rapper's crossover base was further solidified when his "Going Back To Cali," from the film *Less Than Zero*, reached No. 31 on the Hot 100.

Kenny Loggins has informally been dubbed the "soundtrack king" due to his presence on many such hit albums of the 80s. Among his best known are "I'm Alright" from *Caddyshack*, "Footloose" and "I'm Free (Heaven Help The Man)" from *Footloose*, and "Danger Zone" and "Playing With the Boys" from *Top Gun*.

Trini Lopez was one of many artists who covered Ritchie Valens' "La Bamba." Unfortunately, his 1966 version, titled "La Bamba–Part One," peaked at No. 86.

Madonna's staggering success was clearly indicated by the debut of her 1989 single "Like A Prayer." The first single from the album of the same name, it was her 14th consecutive single to top all new entries on its initial week of charting.

George Maharis was one of several 60s artists who managed to maintain a dual singing and acting career. "Baby Has Gone Bye Bye" was his third single to hit the Top 100; appropriately, it peaked at No. 62 *in* '62.

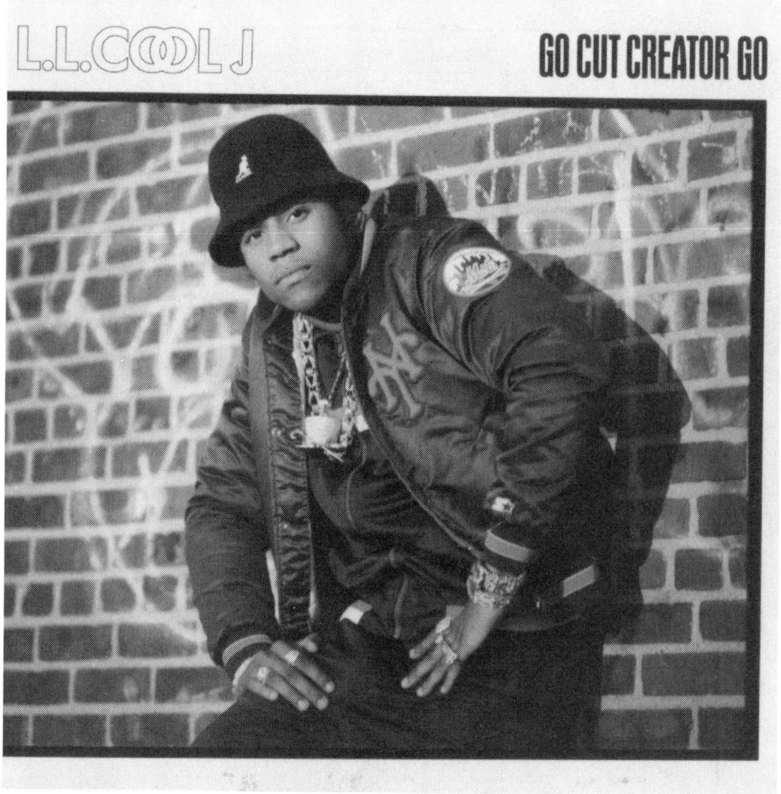

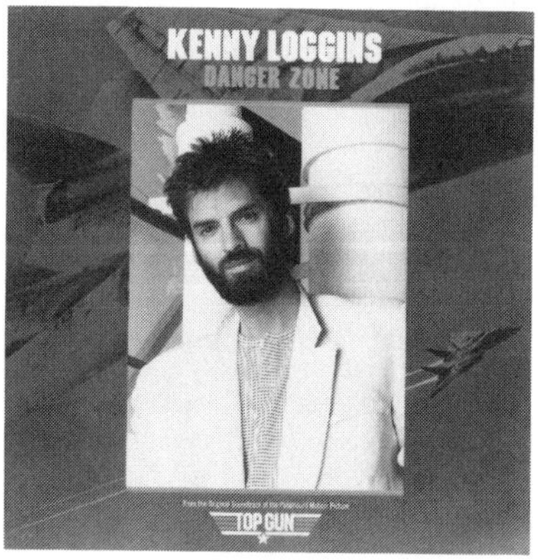

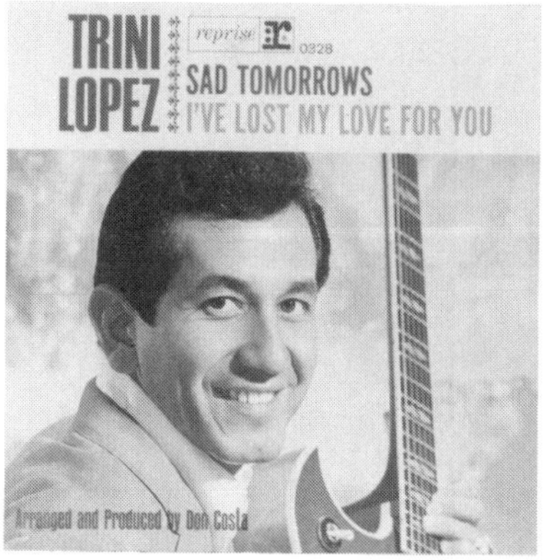

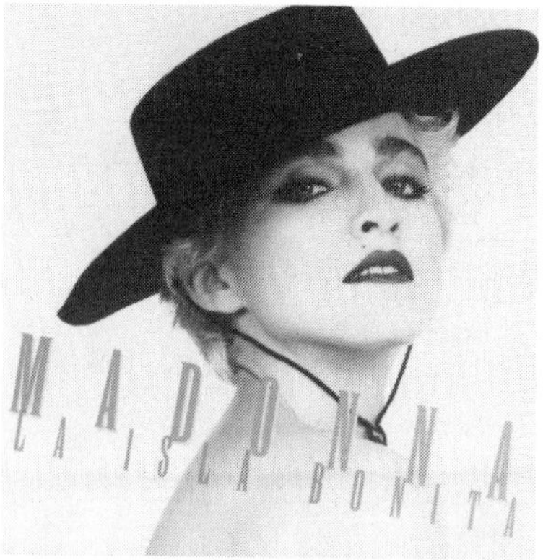

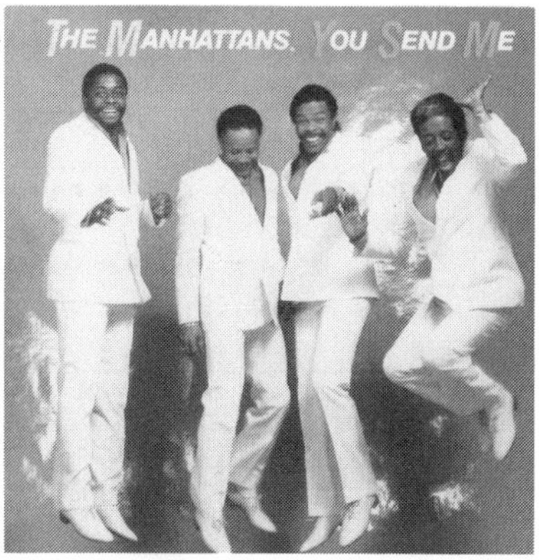

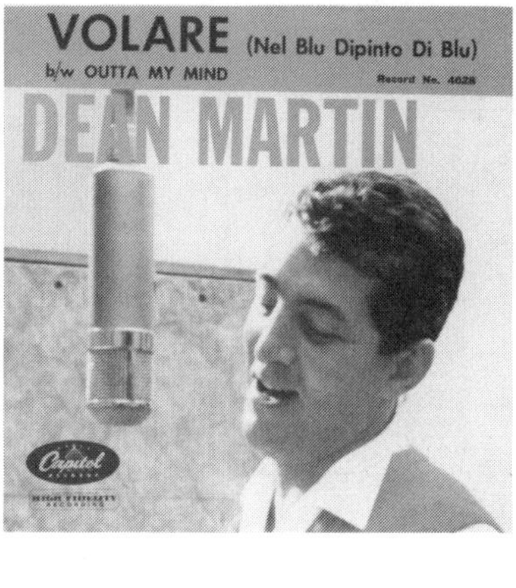

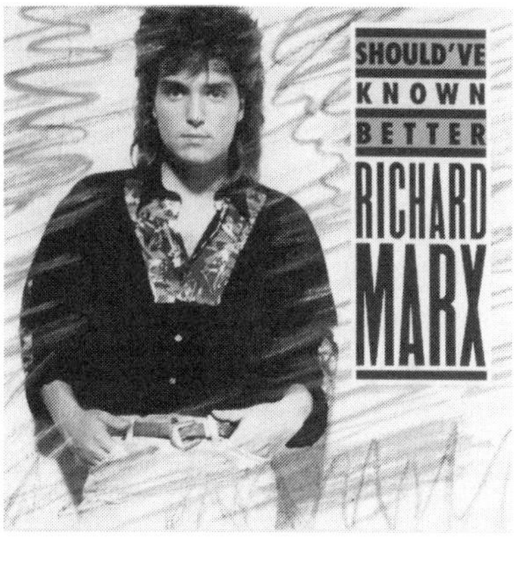

Barbara Mandrell and Lee Greenwood's respective debuts on the Hot 100 were five years apart: Mandrell's "Woman To Woman" on Dot Records reached No. 92 in 1978; Greenwood's MCA single "I.O.U." hit No. 53 in 1983.

The Manhattans' "Kiss And Say Goodbye" was the Jersey City, N. J.-based vocal group's biggest seller ever; entering the Hot 100 in April 1976, it held the No. 1 spot for two weeks and was later certified platinum.

Barry Manilow's 1979 single "Ships" threw some hardcore rock 'n' roll fans for a loop: the track, which peaked at No. 9, was penned and sung earlier by none other than Ian Hunter, leader of rock group Mott The Hoople.

Dean Martin's first gold single was officially 1964's No. 1 "Everybody Loves Somebody"; his last appearance on the Hot 100 came five years later with "I Take A Lot Of Pride In What I Am."

Richard Marx set more than a few records with his 1987 Manhattan Records debut—like being the first new act ever played on 117 radio stations nationwide during his initial week on the charts.

DATE	POS	WKS	ARTIST—RECORD TITLE	LABEL & NO.
			DON RONDO	
			Baritone singer from New York City. Sang on TV/radio commercials.	
11/03/56	**11**	12	1. Two Different Worlds Jockey #11 / Top 100 #19 / Best Seller #23	Jubilee 5256
7/29/57	**7**	15	2. **White Silver Sands** Jockey #7 / Best Seller #9 / Top 100 #10	Jubilee 5288
			THE RONETTES	
			Formed in New York City as the Darling Sisters in 1958. Consisted of Veronica "Ronnie" Bennett Spector (b: 8/10/45), sister Estelle Bennett Vann (b: 7/22/44) and cousin Nedra Talley Ross (b: 1/27/46). Sang professionally since junior high school. Back-up work for Phil Spector in 1962. Group disbanded in 1966. Veronica married to Phil Spector, 1968-74.	
9/14/63	**2**(3)	10	1. **Be My Baby**	Philles 116
1/11/64	**24**	6	2. Baby, I Love You	Philles 118
5/16/64	**39**	1	3. (The Best Part Of) Breakin' Up	Philles 120
7/18/64	**34**	4	4. Do I Love You?	Philles 121
11/21/64	**23**	7	5. Walking In The Rain all of above: produced by Phil Spector	Philles 123
			RONNIE & THE HI-LITES	
			R&B vocal quintet from Jersey City. Lead singer Ronnie Goodson, born in 1947, died of a brain tumor on 11/4/80.	
4/21/62	**16**	8	1. I Wish That We Were Married	Joy 260
			RONNY & THE DAYTONAS	
			Nashville quartet specializing in hot-rod music. Ronny is Bucky Wilkin.	
8/22/64	**4**	10	1. **G.T.O.**	Mala 481
1/08/66	**27**	5	2. Sandy	Mala 513
			LINDA RONSTADT	
			Born on 7/15/46 in Tucson, Arizona. While in high school formed folk trio, The Three Ronstadts (with sister and brother). To Los Angeles in 1964. Formed the Stone Poneys with Bobby Kimmel (guitar) and Ken Edwards (keyboards); recorded for Sidewalk in 1965. Went solo in 1968. In 1971 formed backing band with Glenn Frey, Don Henley, Randy Meisner and Bernie Leadon (later became the Eagles). In "Pirates Of Penzance" operetta in New York City, in 1980, also in film of same name in 1983. Also see The Nitty Gritty Dirt Band.	
12/09/67†	**13**	13	1. Different Drum **STONE PONEYS featuring LINDA RONSTADT**	Capitol 2004
9/12/70	**25**	7	2. Long Long Time	Capitol 2846
1/04/75	**1**(1)	10	3. **You're No Good**	Capitol 3990
4/26/75	**2**(2)	13	4. **When Will I Be Loved**	Capitol 4050
10/04/75	**5**	10	5. **Heat Wave**	Asylum 45282
1/24/76	**25**	6	6. Tracks Of My Tears	Asylum 45295
9/04/76	**11**	11	7. That'll Be The Day	Asylum 45340
10/08/77	**3**	16	● 8. **Blue Bayou**	Asylum 45431
10/29/77	**5**	12	9. **It's So Easy**	Asylum 45438
2/25/78	**31**	3	10. Poor Poor Pitiful Me	Asylum 45462
5/20/78	**32**	3	11. Tumbling Dice	Asylum 45479
9/09/78	**16**	8	12. Back In The U.S.A.	Asylum 45519
11/18/78†	**7**	13	13. **Ooh Baby Baby**	Asylum 45546
2/09/80	**10**	12	14. **How Do I Make You**	Asylum 46602

DATE	POS	WKS	ARTIST—RECORD TITLE	LABEL & NO.
4/19/80	**8**	11	15. **Hurt So Bad**	Asylum 46624
7/19/80	**31**	4	16. I Can't Let Go	Asylum 46654
10/23/82	**29**	5	17. Get Closer	Asylum 69948
1/29/83	**37**	3	18. I Knew You When	Asylum 69853
1/24/87	**2**(1)	12	19. **Somewhere Out There**	MCA 52973
			LINDA RONSTADT & JAMES INGRAM	
			from the animated film "An American Tail"; 3-19: produced by Peter Asher (Peter & Gordon)	
			THE ROOFTOP SINGERS	
			Folk trio from New York City: Erik Darling, Willard Svanoe and Lynne Taylor (d: 1982). Disbanded in 1967. Darling was a member of The Tarriers in 1956, and The Weavers, 1958-62. Taylor was a vocalist with Benny Goodman and Buddy Rich.	
1/12/63	**1**(2)	11	1. **Walk Right In**	Vanguard 35017
4/20/63	**20**	5	2. Tom Cat	Vanguard 35019
			THE ROSE GARDEN	
			West Virginia quintet; Diana Di Rose, lead singer.	
12/09/67	**17**	7	1. Next Plane To London	Atco 6510
			ROSE ROYCE	
			Eight-member backing band formed in Los Angeles, early 70s. Backed Edwin Starr as Total Concept Unlimited in 1973. Backed The Temptations, became regular band for Undisputed Truth. Lead vocalist Gwen Dickey added, name changed to Rose Royce in 1976. Did soundtrack for the film "Car Wash."	
12/11/76†	**1**(1)	14	▲ 1. **Car Wash**	MCA 40615
3/19/77	**10**	10	2. **I Wanna Get Next To You**	MCA 40662
			above 2: from the film "Car Wash"	
10/22/77	**39**	2	3. Do Your Dance - Part 1	Whitfield 8440
1/13/79	**32**	4	4. Love Don't Live Here Anymore	Whitfield 8712
			DAVID ROSE	
			Born on 6/15/10 in London; moved to Chicago at an early age. Conductor/composer/ arranger for numerous films. Scored many TV series, such as "The Red Skelton Show," "Bonanza" and "Little House On The Prairie" TV series. Married briefly to Martha Raye and Judy Garland.	
6/02/62	**1**(1)	13	1. **The Stripper** **[I]**	MGM 13064
			ROSIE & THE ORIGINALS	
			San Diego group; Rosalie Hamlin, lead singer.	
12/12/60†	**5**	12	1. **Angel Baby**	Highland 1011
			DIANA ROSS	
			Born Diane Earle on 3/26/44 in Detroit. In vocal group, the Primettes, first recorded for LuPine in 1960. Lead singer of The Supremes from 1961-69. Went solo in late 1969. Oscar nominee for the 1972 film "Lady Sings The Blues." Appeared in the films "Mahogany" and "The Wiz." Also see The Supremes.	
5/02/70	**20**	8	1. Reach Out And Touch (Somebody's Hand)	Motown 1165
8/15/70	**1**(3)	13	2. **Ain't No Mountain High Enough**	Motown 1169
1/09/71	**16**	8	3. Remember Me	Motown 1176
5/15/71	**29**	5	4. Reach Out I'll Be There	Motown 1184
9/11/71	**38**	3	5. Surrender	Motown 1188
3/03/73	**34**	4	6. Good Morning Heartache	Motown 1211
			from the film "Lady Sings The Blues"	

DATE	POS	WKS	ARTIST—RECORD TITLE	LABEL & NO.
7/07/73	**1**(1)	16	7. **Touch Me In The Morning**	Motown 1239
10/13/73	**12**	10	8. You're A Special Part Of Me	Motown 1280
			DIANA ROSS & MARVIN GAYE	
1/26/74	**14**	8	9. Last Time I Saw Him	Motown 1278
3/30/74	**19**	10	10. My Mistake (Was To Love You)	Motown 1269
			DIANA ROSS & MARVIN GAYE	
11/22/75†	**1**(1)	13	11. **Theme From Mahogany (Do You Know Where You're Going To)**	Motown 1377
4/24/76	**1**(2)	13	12. **Love Hangover**	Motown 1392
8/21/76	**25**	8	13. One Love In My Lifetime	Motown 1398
12/03/77†	**27**	7	14. Gettin' Ready For Love	Motown 1427
8/18/79	**19**	9	15. The Boss	Motown 1462
8/09/80	**1**(4)	17	● 16. **Upside Down**	Motown 1494
10/04/80	**5**	14	17. **I'm Coming Out**	Motown 1491
11/15/80†	**9**	15	18. **It's My Turn** from the film of the same title	Motown 1496
7/18/81	**1**(9)	19	▲ 19. **Endless Love**	Motown 1519
			DIANA ROSS & LIONEL RICHIE from the film of the same title; written by Richie	
10/24/81	**7**	14	20. **Why Do Fools Fall In Love**	RCA 12349
1/30/82	**8**	10	21. **Mirror, Mirror**	RCA 13021
10/16/82	**10**	10	22. **Muscles** written by Michael Jackson	RCA 13348
3/19/83	**40**	2	23. So Close	RCA 13424
7/23/83	**31**	3	24. Pieces Of Ice	RCA 13549
8/04/84	**19**	8	25. All Of You	Columbia 04507
			JULIO IGLESIAS & DIANA ROSS	
9/22/84	**19**	8	26. Swept Away written & produced by Daryl Hall	RCA 13864
3/09/85	**10**	9	27. **Missing You** dedicated to Marvin Gaye; produced & written by Lionel Richie	RCA 13966
			JACK ROSS	
			West Coast nightclub entertainer/trumpet player. Died on 12/16/82 (66).	
4/07/62	**16**	6	1. Cinderella [C]	Dot 16333
			JACKIE ROSS	
			Born on 1/30/46 in St. Louis. Sang gospel on parent's radio show at age 3. Moved to Chicago in 1954. First recorded for Sar in 1962.	
8/15/64	**11**	8	1. Selfish One	Chess 1903
			SPENCER ROSS	
1/18/60	**13**	10	1. Tracy's Theme [I] from the TV production "Philadelphia Story"; saxophone: Jimmy Abato	Columbia 41532
			DAVID LEE ROTH	
			Born on 10/10/55 in Bloomington, Indiana. Former lead singer of Van Halen.	
1/26/85	**3**	11	1. **California Girls**	Warner 29102

DATE	POS	WKS	ARTIST—RECORD TITLE	LABEL & NO.
4/20/85	**12**	10	2. Just A Gigolo/I Ain't Got Nobody "Just A Gigolo": #1 hit for Ted Lewis in 1931; "I Ain't Got Nobody": #3 hit for Marion Harris in 1921	Warner 29040
7/26/86	**16**	8	3. Yankee Rose	Warner 28656
1/30/88	**6**	11	4. **Just Like Paradise**	Warner 28119
			THE ROUTERS	
			Rock and roll instrumental quintet led by Mike Gordon.	
11/24/62	**19**	7	1. Let's Go [I]	Warner 5283
			THE ROVER BOYS	
			Canadian group featuring Billy Albert, lead singer.	
5/19/56	**16**	7	1. Graduation Day Jockey #16 / Best Seller #19 / Top 100 #20	ABC-Para. 9700
			ROVERS - see IRISH ROVERS	
			ROXY MUSIC	
			English art-rock band. Nucleus consisted of Bryan Ferry (vocals, keyboards), Phil Manzanera (guitar) and Andy Mackay (horns).	
2/21/76	**30**	5	1. Love Is The Drug	Atco 7042
			THE ROYAL GUARDSMEN	
			Novelty-pop sextet from Ocala, Florida. Consisted of Barry Winslow (vocals, guitar), Chris Nunley (vocals), Tom Richards (lead guitar), Bill Balough (bass) and Billy Taylor (organ).	
12/17/66	**2**(4)	11	● 1. **Snoopy Vs. The Red Baron** **[N]**	Laurie 3366
3/11/67	**15**	5	2. The Return Of The Red Baron [N]	Laurie 3379
1/04/69	**35**	5	3. Baby Let's Wait	Laurie 3461
			THE ROYAL PHILHARMONIC ORCHESTRA	
			British; Louis Clark, conductor (born in Birmingham, England; arranger for ELO).	
11/28/81†	**10**	12	1. **Hooked On Classics** **[I]** Tchaikovsky Piano Concerto No. 1/Flight of the Bumble Bee/Mozart Symphony No. 40 in G Minor/Rhapsody In Blue/Karelia Suite/The Marriage of Figaro/Romeo & Juliet/Trumpet Voluntary/Hallelujah Chorus/Grieg Piano Concerto in A Minor/March of the Toreadors	RCA 12304
			THE ROYAL SCOTS DRAGOON GUARDS	
			The Pipes and Drums and The Military Band of Scotland's armored regiment.	
5/27/72	**11**	8	1. Amazing Grace [I] bagpipes solo: Pipe Major Tony Crease	RCA 0709
			ROYAL TEENS	
			Quartet from Fort Lee, New Jersey. Consisted of Bob Gaudio, Bill Crandall, Billy Dalton and Tom Austin. Crandall was replaced by Larry Qualiano, and Joseph "Joe Villa" Francavilla joined as vocalist in late 1958. In 1960, Gaudio joined The 4 Seasons. Al Kooper joined the group for a short time in 1959.	
2/03/58	**3**	12	1. **Short Shorts** Top 100 #3 / Best Seller #4 / Jockey #6	ABC-Para. 9882
11/16/59	**26**	6	2. Believe Me	Capitol 4261

DATE	POS	WKS	ARTIST—RECORD TITLE	LABEL & NO.
			THE ROYALTONES	
			Rock and roll instrumental group from Dearborn, Michigan. Formed in 1957 as the Paragons. Featuring tenor saxophonist George Katsakis.	
11/10/58	**17**	10	1. Poor Boy [I]	Jubilee 5338
			BILLY JOE ROYAL	
			Born on 4/3/42 in Valdosta, Georgia; raised in Marietta, Georgia. Began performing on radio at age 11. His close friend Joe South wrote many of his hits.	
7/31/65	**9**	8	1. **Down In The Boondocks**	Columbia 43305
10/09/65	**14**	8	2. I Knew You When	Columbia 43390
1/15/66	**38**	1	3. I've Got To Be Somebody	Columbia 43465
11/01/69	**15**	10	4. Cherry Hill Park	Columbia 44902
			THE RUBETTES	
			British quintet featuring Paul DaVinci, lead singer.	
8/31/74	**37**	2	1. Sugar Baby Love	Polydor 15089
			RUBICON	
			Bay area septet led by horn player Jerry Martini (member of Sly & The Family Stone 1966-76). Group included Jack Blades and Brad Gillis of Night Ranger.	
4/08/78	**28**	3	1. I'm Gonna Take Care Of Everything	20th Century 2362
			RUBY & THE ROMANTICS	
			Akron, Ohio R&B quintet: Ruby Nash Curtis (b: 11/12/39, New York City; lead), Ed Roberts & George Lee (tenors), Ronald Mosley (baritone) and Leroy Fann (bass; d: 1973).	
2/23/63	**1**(1)	10	1. **Our Day Will Come**	Kapp 501
6/15/63	**16**	6	2. My Summer Love	Kapp 525
8/31/63	**27**	5	3. Hey There Lonely Boy	Kapp 544
			DAVID RUFFIN	
			Born on 1/18/41 in Meridian, Mississippi. Brother of Jimmy Ruffin. With the Dixie Nightingales gospel group. Recorded for Anna in 1960. Co-lead singer of The Temptations from 1963-68.	
2/22/69	**9**	9	1. **My Whole World Ended (The Moment You Left Me)**	Motown 1140
11/29/75†	**9**	11	2. **Walk Away From Love**	Motown 1376
9/14/85	**20**	7	3. A Nite At The Apollo Live! The Way You Do The Things You Do/My Girl **DARYL HALL JOHN OATES with DAVID RUFFIN & EDDIE KENDRICK** recorded at the reopening of New York's Apollo Theatre; revival of 2 early Temptations hits	RCA 14178
			JIMMY RUFFIN	
			Born on 5/7/39 in Collinsville, Mississippi. Brother of David Ruffin. Back-up work at Motown in the early 60s. First recorded for Miracle in 1961.	
9/10/66	**7**	14	1. **What Becomes Of The Brokenhearted**	Soul 35022
12/24/66†	**17**	8	2. I've Passed This Way Before	Soul 35027
4/08/67	**29**	3	3. Gonna Give Her All The Love I've Got	Soul 35032
3/22/80	**10**	9	4. **Hold On To My Love** written and produced by Robin Gibb	RSO 1021

DATE	POS	WKS	ARTIST—RECORD TITLE	LABEL & NO.
			RUFUS Featuring CHAKA KHAN	
			Soul group from Chicago. Band was first known as Smoke, then Ask Rufus. Varying membership. Included Tony Maiden (guitar), Nate Morgan, Kevin Murphy (keyboards), Bobby Watson (bass), Andre Fischer (drums) and Chaka Khan (lead singer). After Khan went solo in 1978, vocals were by Maiden and David Wolinski.	
7/13/74	**3**	12	● 1. **Tell Me Something Good**	ABC 11427
			RUFUS	
			written by Stevie Wonder	
11/02/74	**11**	11	2. You Got The Love	ABC 12032
3/08/75	**10**	7	3. **Once You Get Started**	ABC 12066
2/14/76	**5**	12	● 4. **Sweet Thing**	ABC 12149
6/12/76	**39**	1	5. Dance Wit Me	ABC 12179
3/12/77	**30**	6	6. At Midnight (My Love Will Lift You Up)	ABC 12239
6/04/77	**32**	3	7. Hollywood	ABC 12269
			RUFUS & CHAKA KHAN:	
5/27/78	**38**	3	8. Stay	ABC 12349
1/19/80	**30**	4	9. Do You Love What You Feel	MCA 41131
11/12/83	**22**	8	10. Ain't Nobody	Warner 29555
			THE RUGBYS	
			Glenn Howerton, Mike Morner, Steve McNichol and Ed Vernon.	
9/20/69	**24**	7	1. You, I	Amazon 1
			RUN-D.M.C.	
			Rap trio from Queens, New York: Rappers Joseph Simmons (Run), Darryl McDaniels (DMC) with DJ Jason Mizell (Jam Master Jay).	
8/16/86	**4**	10	1. **Walk This Way**	Profile 5112
			with Aerosmith's Steve Tyler (vocals) and Joe Perry (guitar)	
11/29/86	**29**	7	2. You Be Illin'	Profile 5119
			TODD RUNDGREN	
			Born on 6/22/48 in Upper Darby, Pennsylvania. Virtuoso musician/ songwriter/producer/ engineer. Leader of groups Nazz and Utopia. Produced Meat Loaf's "Bat Out Of Hell" album and produced albums for Badfinger, Grand Funk Railroad, The Tubes, Patti Smith and many others.	
12/26/70†	**20**	9	1. We Gotta Get You A Woman	Ampex 31001
			RUNT	
5/06/72	**16**	9	2. I Saw The Light	Bearsville 0003
11/10/73	**5**	12	3. **Hello It's Me**	Bearsville 0009
			original version by Nazz charted in 1969	
6/26/76	**34**	3	4. Good Vibrations	Bearsville 0309
7/08/78	**29**	5	5. Can We Still Be Friends	Bearsville 0324
			RUSH	
			Canadian power-rock trio: Geddy Lee (vocals, bass), Alex Lifeson (guitar) and Neil Peart (drums). Also see Bob & Doug McKenzie.	
10/09/82	**21**	6	1. New World Man	Mercury 76179

DATE	POS	WKS	ARTIST—RECORD TITLE	LABEL & NO.
			JENNIFER RUSH - see ELTON JOHN	
			MERRILEE RUSH & THE TURNABOUTS	
			From Seattle, Washington. Discovered by another Northwest band, Paul Revere & The Raiders.	
6/01/68	**7**	12	1. **Angel Of The Morning**	Bell 705
			PATRICE RUSHEN	
			Born on 9/30/54 in Los Angeles. Jazz-soul vocalist/pianist/songwriter. Much session work with Jean Luc-Ponty, Lee Ritenour and Stanley Turrentine.	
6/05/82	**23**	7	1. Forget Me Nots	Elektra 47427
			BOBBY RUSSELL	
			Born on 4/19/41 in Nashville. Wrote "Honey," "Little Green Apples" and "The Night The Lights Went Out In Georgia."	
11/23/68	**36**	2	1. 1432 Franklin Pike Circle Hero	Elf 90020
8/28/71	**28**	7	2. Saturday Morning Confusion [N]	United Art. 50788
			BRENDA RUSSELL	
			Soul singer/keyboardist/composer, born Brenda Gordon in Brooklyn. To Toronto at age 12. Recorded as duo, Brian & Brenda, with former husband Brian Russell in 1978; co-hosted the Canadian TV series "Music Machine." Session work for Barbra Streisand, Elton John, Bette Midler and many others.	
10/13/79	**30**	6	1. So Good, So Right	Horizon 123
4/02/88	**6**	13	2. **Piano In The Dark**	A&M 3003
			featuring male vocalist Joe Esposito (Brooklyn Dreams)	
			LEON RUSSELL	
			Born on 4/2/41 in Lawton, Oklahoma. Vocalist/songwriter/top multi-instrumentalist sessionman. Formed Shelter Records with British producer Denny Cordell in 1970. Recorded as Hank Wilson in 1973. Married Mary McCreary (vocalist with Little Sister, part of Sly Stone's "family") in 1976. Own label, Paradise, 1976. Wrote "Superstar" and "This Masquerade." Also see Joe Cocker.	
9/23/72	**11**	7	1. Tight Rope	Shelter 7325
9/13/75	**14**	10	2. Lady Blue	Shelter 40378
			CHARLIE RYAN & The Timberline Riders	
			Born in Graceville, Minnesota; raised in Montana. Country singer.	
8/08/60	**33**	4	1. Hot Rod Lincoln [S-N]	4 Star 7047
			BOBBY RYDELL	
			Born Robert Ridarelli on 4/26/42 in Philadelphia. Regular on Paul Whiteman's amateur TV show, 1951-54. Drummer with Rocco & The Saints, which included Frankie Avalon on trumpet in 1956. First recorded for Veko in 1957. Films "Bye Bye Birdie" and "That Lady From Peking."	
8/10/59	**11**	9	1. Kissin' Time	Cameo 167
10/26/59	**6**	14	2. **We Got Love**	Cameo 169
2/08/60	**2**(1)	13	3. **Wild One/**	
2/22/60	**19**	10	4. Little Bitty Girl	Cameo 171
5/16/60	**5**	8	5. **Swingin' School/**	
			from the film "Because They're Young"	
5/16/60	**18**	8	6. Ding-A-Ling	Cameo 175
8/01/60	**4**	11	7. **Volare**	Cameo 179
11/14/60	**14**	10	8. Sway	Cameo 182
2/06/61	**11**	8	9. Good Time Baby	Cameo 186

DATE	POS	WKS	ARTIST—RECORD TITLE	LABEL & NO.
5/08/61	**21**	5	10. That Old Black Magic #1 hit for Glenn Miller in 1943	Cameo 190
7/10/61	**25**	5	11. The Fish	Cameo 192
11/06/61	**21**	6	12. I Wanna Thank You	Cameo 201
12/25/61	**21**	3	13. Jingle Bell Rock [X] **BOBBY RYDELL/CHUBBY CHECKER**	Cameo 205
3/10/62	**18**	7	14. I've Got Bonnie	Cameo 209
6/23/62	**14**	7	15. I'll Never Dance Again	Cameo 217
10/27/62	**10**	8	16. **The Cha-Cha-Cha**	Cameo 228
2/23/63	**23**	6	17. Butterfly Baby	Cameo 242
6/01/63	**17**	5	18. Wildwood Days	Cameo 252
12/07/63†	**4**	12	19. **Forget Him**	Cameo 280
			MITCH RYDER & THE DETROIT WHEELS	
			White soul-rock group. Leader Ryder was born William Levise, Jr. on 2/26/45 in Detroit. Group was originally known as Billy Lee & The Rivieras. Renamed by their producer Bob Crewe. Ryder went solo in 1967. Formed new rock group, Detroit, in 1971.	
1/08/66	**10**	8	1. **Jenny Take A Ride!**	New Voice 806
3/26/66	**17**	6	2. Little Latin Lupe Lu	New Voice 808
10/22/66	**4**	14	3. **Devil With A Blue Dress On & Good Golly Miss Molly**	New Voice 817
2/18/67	**6**	9	4. **Sock It To Me-Baby!**	New Voice 820
5/13/67	**24**	4	5. Too Many Fish In The Sea & Three Little Fishes	New Voice 822
9/30/67	**30**	4	6. What Now My Love **MITCH RYDER**	DynoVoice 901

DATE	POS	WKS	ARTIST—RECORD TITLE	LABEL & NO.
			S	
			SADE	
			Born Helen Folasade Adu on 1/16/59 in Nigeria; moved to London at age 4. Appeared in the 1986 film "Absolute Beginners." A former designer of menswear. Won the 1985 Best New Artist Grammy Award.	
3/30/85	**5**	13	1. **Smooth Operator**	Portrait 04807
12/28/85†	**5**	13	2. **The Sweetest Taboo**	Portrait 05713
4/19/86	**20**	7	3. Never As Good As The First Time	Portrait 05846
6/11/88	**16**	8	4. Paradise	Epic 07904
			SSGT BARRY SADLER	
			Born in New Mexico in 1941. Staff Sergeant of the US Army Special Forces (aka Green Berets). Served in Vietnam until injuring leg in booby trap. Shot in the head during a 1988 robbery attempt at his Guatemala home; suffered brain damage.	
2/19/66	**1**(5)	11	● 1. **The Ballad Of The Green Berets**	RCA 8739
5/14/66	**28**	4	2. The "A" Team	RCA 8804
			SAFARIS	
			Los Angeles-born pop quartet formed in 1959. Jim Stephens (lead singer), Richard Clasky, Marvin Rosenberg and Shelly Briar.	
7/11/60	**6**	11	1. **Image Of A Girl**	Eldo 101
			SAGA	
			Canadian rock quintet: Michael Sadler (lead singer), brothers Jim & Ian Crichton, Jim Gilmour and Steve Negus.	
1/29/83	**26**	8	1. On The Loose	Portrait 03359
			CAROLE BAYER SAGER	
			Born on 3/8/47 in New York City. Prolific pop lyricist. Married Burt Bacharach in 1982. Collaborated in writing "A Groovy Kind Of Love," "Midnight Blue," "Nobody Does It Better," "When I Need You" and many others. Wrote lyrics for many film scores.	
6/13/81	**30**	7	1. Stronger Than Before	Boardwalk 02054
			SAILCAT	
			Country-rock duo: Court Pickett and John Wyker.	
7/15/72	**12**	10	1. Motorcycle Mama	Elektra 45782
			BUFFY SAINTE-MARIE	
			Born on 2/20/41 of Cree Indian parents on Piapot Reserve, Saskatchewan, Canada. Folksinger/songwriter. Co-writer of "Up Where We Belong."	
4/29/72	**38**	2	1. Mister Can't You See	Vanguard 35151
			CRISPIAN ST. PETERS	
			Born Peter Smith on 4/5/44 in Swanley, Kent, England. Pop singer/guitarist.	
7/09/66	**4**	8	1. **The Pied Piper**	Jamie 1320
7/22/67	**36**	2	2. You Were On My Mind	Jamie 1310

DATE	POS	WKS	ARTIST—RECORD TITLE	LABEL & NO.
			KYU SAKAMOTO	
			Native of Kawasaki, Japan. One of 520 people killed in the crash of the Japan Airlines 747 near Tokyo on 8/12/85 (43).	
5/25/63	**1**(3)	12	1. **Sukiyaki** **[F]**	Capitol 4945
			released in Japan as "Ue O Muite Aruko" (I Look Up When I Walk)	
			SALSOUL ORCHESTRA	
			Disco orchestra conducted by Philadelphia producer/arranger Vincent Montana, Jr. Vocalists included Phyllis Rhodes, Ronni Tyson, Carl Helm and Philip Hurt.	
2/14/76	**18**	9	1. Tangerine [I]	Salsoul 2004
			#1 hit for Jimmy Dorsey in 1942	
10/30/76	**30**	5	2. Nice 'N' Naasty	Salsoul 2011
			SALT-N-PEPA	
			Queens-based female rap trio: Cheryl "Salt" James and Sandy "Pepa" Denton (from Kingston, Jamaica) with DJ Spinderella (LaToya).	
12/26/87†	**19**	13	● 1. Push It	Next Plateau 315
			SAMMY SALVO	
			Pop vocalist from Birmingham, Alabama.	
3/03/58	**23**	1	1. Oh Julie	RCA 7097
			Jockey #23 / Top 100 #78	
			SAM & DAVE	
			Samuel Moore (b: 10/12/35, Miami) and David Prater (b: 5/9/37, Ocilla, GA). Sam had been with the Melionaires gospel group, and Dave was a solo artist prior to their meeting in Miami in 1961. First recorded for Alston in 1962. Duo produced by Isaac Hayes and David Porter. Dave was killed in a car crash on 4/9/88.	
6/04/66	**21**	7	1. Hold On! I'm A Comin'	Stax 189
9/30/67	**2**(3)	11	● 2. **Soul Man**	Stax 231
2/17/68	**9**	9	3. **I Thank You**	Stax 242
			SAM THE SHAM & THE PHAROAHS	
			Dallas rock & roll group formed in the early 60s featuring lead singer Domingo "Sam" Samudio (b: 1940, Dallas). First recorded for Dingo in 1965. Samudio went solo in 1970. Formed new band in 1974. On the 1982 film soundtrack "The Border." Sam is currently a street preacher in Memphis.	
5/01/65	**2**(2)	14	● 1. **Wooly Bully**	MGM 13322
8/21/65	**26**	4	2. Ju Ju Hand	MGM 13364
11/13/65	**33**	3	3. Ring Dang Doo	MGM 13397
7/02/66	**2**(2)	11	● 4. **Lil' Red Riding Hood**	MGM 13506
10/15/66	**22**	5	5. The Hair On My Chinny Chin Chin	MGM 13581
1/21/67	**27**	4	6. How Do You Catch A Girl	MGM 13649
			SAN REMO GOLDEN STRINGS	
			Group of master violinists.	
10/09/65	**27**	5	1. Hungry For Love [I]	Ric-Tic 104

DATE	POS	WKS	ARTIST—RECORD TITLE	LABEL & NO.
			FELICIA SANDERS	
			Born in New York City; raised in California. Died on 2/7/75. Vocalist on Percy Faith's 1953 #1 hit "Song From Moulin Rouge."	
5/28/55	**29**	3	1. Blue Star Best Seller #29 theme from the mid-50s "Medic" TV series	Columbia 40508
			THE SANDPEBBLES	
			Consisted of Calvin White, Andrea Bolden and Lonzine Wright. White had been lead singer of the Gospel Wonders. Group name changed to C & The Shells in 1968.	
1/06/68	**22**	6	1. Love Power	Calla 141
			THE SANDPIPERS	
			Los Angeles-based trio: Jim Brady (b: 8/24/44), Michael Piano (b: 10/26/44) and Richard Shoff (b: 4/30/44); met while in the Mitchell Boys Choir.	
8/13/66	**9**	9	1. **Guantanamera** **[F]**	A&M 806
11/12/66	**30**	4	2. Louie, Louie [F]	A&M 819
5/02/70	**17**	8	3. Come Saturday Morning from the film "The Sterile Cuckoo"	A&M 1134
			JODIE SANDS	
			Philadelphia pop songstress.	
6/10/57	**15**	9	1. With All My Heart Jockey #15 / Top 100 #20 / Best Seller #21	Chancellor 1003
			TOMMY SANDS	
			Born on 8/27/37 in Chicago. Pop singer/actor. Mother was a vocalist with Art Kassel's band. Married Nancy Sinatra in 1960; divorced in 1965. In the films "Sing Boy Sing," "Mardi Gras," "Babes In Toyland" and "The Longest Day."	
2/23/57	**2**(2)	12	1. **Teen-Age Crush** Best Seller #2 / Top 100 #3 / Jockey #4 / Juke Box #7 from the 1957 TV play "The Singing Idol" (starring Sands)	Capitol 3639
5/27/57	**16**	8	2. Goin' Steady Jockey #16 / Best Seller #18 / Top 100 #19	Capitol 3723
2/24/58	**24**	2	3. Sing Boy Sing Jockey #24 / Best Seller #46 / Top 100 #46 from the film of the same title	Capitol 3867
			THE SANFORD/TOWNSEND BAND	
			Los Angeles-based rock band led by Ed Sanford and John Townsend.	
7/16/77	**9**	12	1. **Smoke From A Distant Fire**	Warner 8370
			SAMANTHA SANG	
			Born Cheryl Gray on 8/5/53 in Melbourne, Australia. Began career on Melbourne radio at age 8.	
1/07/78	**3**	17	▲ 1. **Emotion** backing vocal: Barry Gibb; written by Barry & Robin Gibb	Private S. 45178
			SANTA ESMERALDA	
			Spanish-flavored disco studio project produced by Nicolas Skorsky and Jean-Manuel De Scarano.	
12/10/77†	**15**	12	1. Don't Let Me Be Misunderstood vocal: Leroy Gomez	Casablanca 902

DATE	POS	WKS	ARTIST—RECORD TITLE	LABEL & NO.
			MONGO SANTAMARIA	
			Cuban-born bandleader/conga, bongo and percussion player. Member of bands led by Perez Prado, Tito Puente and Cal Tjader.	
4/13/63	**10**	6	1. **Watermelon Man** **[I]**	Battle 45909
3/08/69	**32**	2	2. Cloud Nine [I]	Columbia 44740
			SANTANA	
			Latin-rock group formed in San Francisco in 1966. Consisted of Carlos Santana (b: 7/20/47, Autlan de Navarro, Mexico; vocals, guitar), Gregg Rolie (keyboards) and David Brown (bass). Added percussionists Michael Carabello, Jose Chepitos Areas and Michael Shrieve in 1969. Worked Fillmore West and Woodstock in 1969. Neal Schon (guitar) added in 1971. Santana began solo work in 1972. Schon and Rolie formed Journey.	
2/07/70	**9**	11	1. **Evil Ways**	Columbia 45069
11/21/70†	**4**	12	2. **Black Magic Woman**	Columbia 45270
3/06/71	**13**	8	3. Oye Como Va [F]	Columbia 45330
10/30/71	**12**	8	4. Everybody's Everything	Columbia 45472
3/11/72	**36**	4	5. No One To Depend On	Columbia 45552
11/19/77	**27**	5	6. She's Not There	Columbia 10616
2/17/79	**32**	3	7. Stormy	Columbia 10873
1/19/80	**35**	3	8. You Know That I Love You	Columbia 11144
5/16/81	**17**	11	9. Winning	Columbia 01050
8/28/82	**15**	10	10. Hold On	Columbia 03160
			SANTO & JOHNNY	
			Brooklyn-born guitar duo: Santo Farina (b: 10/24/37; steel guitar) and his brother Johnny (b: 4/30/41; rhythm guitar).	
8/17/59	**1**(2)	13	1. **Sleep Walk** **[I]**	Canadian A. 103
12/14/59	**23**	7	2. Tear Drop [I]	Canadian A. 107
			LARRY SANTOS	
			Born on 6/2/41 in Oneonto, New York.	
4/03/76	**36**	2	1. We Can't Hide It Anymore	Casablanca 844
			THE SAPPHIRES	
			Philadelphia R&B trio: Carol Jackson (lead singer), George Gainer & Joe Livingston.	
2/22/64	**25**	5	1. Who Do You Love	Swan 4162
			LEO SAYER	
			Born Gerard Sayer on 5/21/48 in Shoreham, England. With Patches in the early 70s. Songwriting team with David Courtney, 1972-75. Own TV show in England, early 80s.	
3/22/75	**9**	9	1. **Long Tall Glasses (I Can Dance)**	Warner 8043
11/06/76†	**1**(1)	17	● 2. **You Make Me Feel Like Dancing**	Warner 8283
3/26/77	**1**(1)	14	● 3. **When I Need You**	Warner 8332
7/23/77	**17**	10	4. How Much Love	Warner 8319
11/05/77	**38**	2	5. Thunder In My Heart	Warner 8465
1/28/78	**36**	2	6. Easy To Love	Warner 8502
10/18/80	**2**(5)	15	● 7. **More Than I Can Say**	Warner 49565
2/14/81	**23**	6	8. Living In A Fantasy	Warner 49657

DATE	POS	WKS	ARTIST—RECORD TITLE	LABEL & NO.
			BOZ SCAGGS	
			Born William Royce Scaggs on 6/8/44 in Ohio; raised in Texas. Joined Steve Miller's band, The Marksmen, in 1959. Joined R&B band, The Wigs, in 1963. To Europe in 1964, toured as a folksinger. Rejoined Miller in 1967, solo since 1969.	
5/22/76	**38**	3	1. It's Over	Columbia 10319
8/07/76	**3**	15	● 2. **Lowdown**	Columbia 10367
3/19/77	**11**	12	3. Lido Shuffle	Columbia 10491
4/19/80	**15**	9	4. Breakdown Dead Ahead	Columbia 11241
7/12/80	**17**	9	5. JoJo	Columbia 11281
9/06/80	**14**	10	6. Look What You've Done To Me	Columbia 11349
12/27/80†	**14**	9	7. Miss Sun backing vocal: Lisa Dal Bello	Columbia 11406
6/11/88	**35**	4	8. Heart Of Mine	Columbia 07780
			SCANDAL	
			New York-based rock band led by Patty Smyth and Zack Smith.	
7/21/84	**7**	15	1. **The Warrior**	Columbia 04424
			JOEY SCARBURY	
			Born on 6/7/55 in Ontario, California. Session singer for producer Mike Post and others.	
6/13/81	**2**(2)	18	● 1. **Theme From "Greatest American Hero" (Believe It or Not)** from the TV series of the same title	Elektra 47147
			SCARLETT & BLACK	
			Keyboardist/singer/songwriter Robin Wild and songwriter Sue West (former backing vocalist for Doctor & The Medics).	
3/12/88	**20**	8	1. You Don't Know	Virgin 99405
			PETER SCHILLING	
			Born on 1/28/56 in Stuttgart, Germany. Pop singer/songwriter.	
11/12/83	**14**	10	1. Major Tom (Coming Home)	Elektra 69811
			TIMOTHY B. SCHMIT	
			Born on 10/30/47 in Sacramento. Member of Poco, 1970-77, and the Eagles, 1977-82.	
10/24/87	**25**	5	1. Boys Night Out	MCA 53137
			JOHN SCHNEIDER	
			Born on 4/8/54 in Mount Kisco, New York. Country singer/actor. Played "Bo Duke" on TV's "The Dukes Of Hazzard." Appeared in many TV films.	
6/27/81	**14**	11	1. It's Now Or Never	Scotti Br. 02105
			THE VOICES OF WALTER SCHUMANN	
			A choral group led by Schumann.	
4/09/55	**14**	6	1. The Ballad Of Davy Crockett Jockey #14 / Best Seller #29 from the Disney TV series of the same title	RCA 6041
			EDDIE SCHWARTZ	
			Canadian singer/songwriter. Wrote Pat Benatar's "Hit Me With Your Best Shot."	
1/16/82	**28**	7	1. All Our Tomorrows	Atco 7342

DATE	POS	WKS	ARTIST—RECORD TITLE	LABEL & NO.
			SCORPIONS	
			German heavy-metal rock quintet: Rudolf Schenker (lead guitar), Klaus Meine (lead singer), Matthias Jabs (guitar), Francis Buchholz (bass) and Herman Rarebell (drums).	
4/28/84	**25**	7	1. Rock You Like A Hurricane	Mercury 818440
			BOBBY SCOTT	
			Born on 1/29/37 in the Bronx. Vocalist/jazz pianist/composer/arranger. Wrote Herb Alpert's hit "Taste Of Honey."	
1/21/56	**13**	10	1. Chain Gang Jockey #13 / Juke Box #13 / Top 100 #15 / Best Seller #17	ABC-Para. 9658
			FREDDIE SCOTT	
			Born on 4/24/33 in Providence, Rhode Island. Recorded first hit while working as a songwriter for Columbia Music.	
8/10/63	**10**	9	1. **Hey, Girl**	Colpix 692
2/18/67	**39**	2	2. Are You Lonely For Me	Shout 207
			JACK SCOTT	
			Born Jack Scafone, Jr. on 1/24/36 in Windsor, Canada. Rock and roll-ballad singer/ songwriter/guitarist. Moved to Hazel Park, Michigan in 1946. First recorded for ABC-Paramount in 1957. Still active into the 80s in Detroit area.	
6/16/58	**11**	18	1. Leroy/ Best Seller #11 / Top 100 #25	
7/07/58	**3**	16	2. My True Love Hot 100 #3 / Best Seller #7 / Jockey #13 end	Carlton 462
10/20/58	**28**	4	3. With Your Love	Carlton 483
12/28/58†	**8**	13	4. **Goodbye Baby**	Carlton 493
8/03/59	**35**	4	5. The Way I Walk	Carlton 514
1/18/60	**5**	13	6. **What In The World's Come Over You**	Top Rank 2028
5/09/60	**3**	12	7. **Burning Bridges/**	
5/30/60	**34**	2	8. Oh, Little One	Top Rank 2041
9/05/60	**38**	2	9. It Only Happened Yesterday	Top Rank 2055
			LINDA SCOTT	
			Born Linda Joy Sampson on 6/1/45 in Queens, New York. Moved to Teaneck, New Jersey at age 11.	
4/03/61	**3**	10	1. **I've Told Every Little Star** from the 1932 stage production "Music In The Air"	Canadian A. 123
7/24/61	**9**	10	2. **Don't Bet Money Honey**	Canadian A. 127
11/27/61	**12**	8	3. I Don't Know Why #2 hit for Wayne King in 1931	Canadian A. 129
			PEGGY SCOTT & JO JO BENSON	
			Soul duo; Jo Jo formerly sang with Chuck Willis and The Blue Notes.	
7/06/68	**31**	7	1. Lover's Holiday	SSS Int'l. 736
11/30/68	**27**	4	2. Pickin' Wild Mountain Berries	SSS Int'l. 748
2/15/69	**37**	3	3. Soul Shake	SSS Int'l. 761
			SCRITTI POLITTI	
			British trio: Green Gartside (vocals), Fred Maher (drums) and David Gamson (keyboards). Italian name means "political writing."	
10/26/85	**11**	13	1. Perfect Way	Warner 28949

DATE	POS	WKS	ARTIST—RECORD TITLE	LABEL & NO.
			JOHNNY SEA	
			Born on 7/15/40 in Atlanta. Singer/guitarist, joined the Louisiana Hayride while still in high school.	
6/25/66	**35**	2	1. Day For Decision [S] patriotic answer to "Eve Of Destruction"	Warner 5820
			SEALS & CROFTS	
			Pop duo: Jim Seals (b: 10/17/41, Sidney, TX; guitar, fiddle, saxophone) and Dash Crofts (b: 8/14/40, Cisco, TX; drums, mandolin, keyboards, guitar). With Dean Beard, recorded for Edmoral and Atlantic in 1957. To Los Angeles in 1958. With the Champs from 1958-65. Own group, the Dawnbreakers, late 60s; entire band converted to Baha'i faith in 1969.	
10/21/72	**6**	11	1. **Summer Breeze**	Warner 7606
2/17/73	**20**	9	2. Hummingbird	Warner 7671
6/16/73	**6**	12	3. **Diamond Girl**	Warner 7708
10/13/73	**21**	8	4. We May Never Pass This Way (Again)	Warner 7740
5/17/75	**18**	8	5. I'll Play For You	Warner 8075
6/05/76	**6**	15	6. **Get Closer** featuring Carolyn Willis (Honey Cone/Bob B. Soxx & The Blue Jeans)	Warner 8190
10/22/77	**28**	5	7. My Fair Share love theme from the film "One On One"	Warner 8405
5/27/78	**18**	7	8. You're The Love	Warner 8551
			THE SEARCHERS	
			Liverpool, England rock quartet formed in 1960: Mike Pender and John McNally (vocals, guitars), Tony Jackson (vocals, bass) and Chris Curtis (drums). Worked as back-up band for Johnny Sandon; toured England and worked Star Club in Hamburg, Germany. Left Sandon in 1962. Jackson replaced by Frank Allen in 1965. Curtis replaced by Billy Adamson in 1969. Active into the 80s.	
3/21/64	**13**	8	1. Needles And Pins	Kapp 577
6/20/64	**16**	8	2. Don't Throw Your Love Away	Kapp 593
9/12/64	**34**	3	3. Some Day We're Gonna Love Again	Kapp 609
11/14/64	**35**	2	4. When You Walk In The Room	Kapp 618
12/19/64†	**3**	11	5. **Love Potion Number Nine**	Kapp 27
2/20/65	**29**	3	6. What Have They Done To The Rain	Kapp 644
4/10/65	**21**	4	7. Bumble Bee	Kapp 49
			JOHN SEBASTIAN	
			Born on 3/17/44 in New York City. Played with the Even Dozen Jug Band as "John Benson" in 1964. Did session work for Elektra Records and toured with Mississippi John Hurt. Formed Lovin' Spoonful in 1965. Went solo in 1968.	
4/10/76	**1**(1)	11	● 1. **Welcome Back** from the ABC-TV series "Welcome Back Kotter"	Reprise 1349
			THE SECRETS	
			Cleveland female quartet: Kragen Gray, Josie Allen, Carole Raymont and Pat Miller.	
12/07/63	**18**	6	1. The Boy Next Door	Philips 40146

DATE	POS	WKS	ARTIST—RECORD TITLE	LABEL & NO.
			NEIL SEDAKA	
			Born on 3/13/39 in Brooklyn. Pop singer/songwriter/pianist. Studied piano since elementary school. Formed songwriting team with lyricist Howard Greenfield while attending Lincoln High School (partnership lasted over 20 years). Recorded with The Tokens on Melba in 1956. Attended Juilliard School for classical piano. Prolific hit songwriter. Career revived in 1974 after singing with Elton John's new Rocket label.	
12/28/58†	**14**	9	1. The Diary	RCA 7408
10/26/59	**9**	13	2. **Oh! Carol** written for singer/songwriter Carole King	RCA 7595
4/18/60	**9**	9	3. **Stairway To Heaven**	RCA 7709
8/29/60	**17**	9	4. You Mean Everything To Me/	
10/03/60	**28**	3	5. Run Samson Run	RCA 7781
12/31/60†	**4**	12	6. **Calendar Girl**	RCA 7829
5/08/61	**11**	7	7. Little Devil	RCA 7874
11/27/61†	**6**	11	8. **Happy Birthday, Sweet Sixteen**	RCA 7957
7/07/62	**1**(2)	12	9. **Breaking Up Is Hard To Do**	RCA 8046
10/20/62	**5**	9	10. **Next Door To An Angel**	RCA 8086
2/16/63	**17**	7	11. Alice In Wonderland	RCA 8137
5/18/63	**26**	5	12. Let's Go Steady Again	RCA 8169
12/07/63	**33**	4	13. Bad Girl all of above: produced by Al Nevins & Don Kirshner; all of above & 18: written by Sedaka & Greenfield	RCA 8254
11/16/74†	**1**(1)	15	14. **Laughter In The Rain**	Rocket 40313
4/26/75	**22**	5	15. The Immigrant	Rocket 40370
8/02/75	**27**	4	16. That's When The Music Takes Me	Rocket 40426
9/20/75	**1**(3)	12	● 17. **Bad Blood** backing vocal: Elton John	Rocket 40460
12/27/75†	**8**	11	18. **Breaking Up Is Hard To Do** **[R]** slow version of Neil's 1962 hit	Rocket 40500
5/01/76	**16**	7	19. Love In The Shadows	Rocket 40543
7/24/76	**36**	2	20. Steppin' Out	Rocket 40582
5/10/80	**19**	10	21. Should've Never Let You Go **NEIL SEDAKA & DARA SEDAKA** (Neil's daughter) 14-15, 17, 19-20: written by Sedaka & Phil Cody	Elektra 46615
			THE SEEDS	
			Los Angeles garage-rock quartet: Sky Saxon (b: Richard Marsh; lead singer, bass), Jan Savage (guitar), Rick Aldridge (drums) and Daryl Hooper (keyboards).	
2/11/67	**36**	3	1. Pushin' Too Hard	GNP Crescendo 372
			THE SEEKERS	
			Pop-folk Australian-born quartet: Judith Durham (b: 7/3/43; lead singer), Keith Potger (guitar), Bruce Woodley (Spanish guitar) and Athol Guy (standup bass). Potger formed the New Seekers in 1970.	
4/10/65	**4**	10	1. **I'll Never Find Another You**	Capitol 5383
6/26/65	**19**	7	2. A World Of Our Own	Capitol 5430
12/31/66†	**2**(2)	12	● 3. **Georgy Girl** from the film of the same title	Capitol 5756

DATE	POS	WKS	ARTIST—RECORD TITLE	LABEL & NO.
			BOB SEGER	
			Born on 5/6/45 in Ann Arbor, Michigan; raised in Detroit. Rock singer/songwriter/ guitarist. First recorded in 1966, formed the System in 1968. Left music to attend college in 1969, returned in 1971. Formed own backing group, The Silver Bullet Band in 1976: Alto Reed (horns), Robyn Robbins (keyboards), Drew Abbott (guitar), Chris Campbell (bass) and Charlie Allen Martin (drums). Various personnel changes since then; Campbell is the only remaining original member.	
1/25/69	**17**	9	1. Ramblin' Gamblin' Man	Capitol 2297
			shown as: **BOB SEGER SYSTEM**	
1/15/77	**4**	13	2. **Night Moves**	Capitol 4369
5/14/77	**24**	4	3. Mainstreet	Capitol 4422
			BOB SEGER & The Silver Bullet Band:	
6/03/78	**4**	11	4. **Still The Same**	Capitol 4581
8/19/78	**12**	10	5. Hollywood Nights	Capitol 4618
11/25/78†	**13**	11	6. We've Got Tonite	Capitol 4653
5/05/79	**28**	5	7. Old Time Rock & Roll	Capitol 4702
			BOB SEGER:	
3/01/80	**6**	12	8. **Fire Lake**	Capitol 4836
5/10/80	**5**	11	9. **Against The Wind**	Capitol 4863
8/16/80	**14**	9	10. You'll Accomp'ny Me	Capitol 4904
9/26/81	**5**	12	11. **Tryin' To Live My Life Without You**	Capitol 5042
			BOB SEGER & The Silver Bullet Band:	
12/18/82†	**2**(4)	19	12. **Shame On The Moon**	Capitol 5187
3/26/83	**12**	9	13. Even Now	Capitol 5213
6/11/83	**27**	6	14. Roll Me Away	Capitol 5235
12/01/84†	**17**	8	15. Understanding from the film "Teachers"	Capitol 5413
3/29/86	**13**	9	16. American Storm	Capitol 5532
5/31/86	**12**	9	17. Like A Rock	Capitol 5592
5/30/87	**1**(1)	14	18. **Shakedown** **BOB SEGER** from the film "Beverly Hills Cop II"	MCA 53094
			MARILYN SELLARS	
			Country singer from Northfield, Minnesota. Worked as an airline stewardess.	
9/28/74	**37**	2	1. One Day At A Time	Mega 1205
			MICHAEL SEMBELLO	
			Born on 4/17/54 in Philadelphia. Session guitarist/producer/composer/ arranger/ vocalist. Guitarist on Stevie Wonder's albums from 1974-79.	
7/02/83	**1**(2)	16	1. **Maniac** from the film "Flashdance"	Casablanca 812516
10/29/83	**34**	2	2. Automatic Man	Warner 29485
			SENATOR BOBBY	
			Senator Bobby is Bill Minkin of a comedy troupe called The Hardly-Worthit Players. Another of the members is talk-show host Dennis Wholey.	
1/21/67	**20**	4	1. Wild Thing [C]	Parkway 127

DATE	POS	WKS	ARTIST—RECORD TITLE	LABEL & NO.
			THE SENSATIONS	
			Philadelphia R&B vocal quartet: Yvonne Mills Baker (lead), Sam Armstrong (baritone), Richard Curtain (tenor) and Alphonso Howell (bass).	
2/10/62	**4**	12	1. **Let Me In**	Argo 5405
			THE SERENDIPITY SINGERS	
			Pop-folk group organized at the University of Colorado.	
3/21/64	**6**	11	1. **Don't Let The Rain Come Down (Crooked Little Man)**	Philips 40175
6/13/64	**30**	5	2. Beans In My Ears [N]	Philips 40198
			DAVID SEVILLE	
			Born Ross Bagdasarian on 1/27/19 in Fresno, California; died on 1/16/72. To Los Angeles in 1950. Appeared in the films "Viva Zapata," "Stalag 17" and "Rear Window." Wrote "Come On-a My House." Creator of The Chipmunks.	
4/14/58	**1**(3)	18	1. **Witch Doctor** **[N]** Top 100 #1(3) / Best Seller #1(2) / Jockey #2	Liberty 55132
7/14/58	**34**	2	2. The Bird On My Head [N] Best Seller #34 / Top 100 #36	Liberty 55140
			CHARLIE SEXTON	
			Austin, Texas rock singer/guitarist. Lead guitarist for Joe Ely's band at age 13 in 1982.	
2/08/86	**17**	10	1. Beat's So Lonely	MCA 52715
			PHIL SEYMOUR	
			Vocalist/drummer formerly with the Dwight Twilley Band. Originally from Tulsa, Oklahoma.	
2/21/81	**22**	7	1. Precious To Me	Boardwalk 5703
			SHADES OF BLUE	
			White coed quartet, discovered by Edwin Starr.	
5/28/66	**12**	8	1. Oh How Happy	Impact 1007
			THE SHADOWS OF KNIGHT	
			Chicago-area "garage band": Jim Sohns (lead singer), Joe Kelley (lead guitarist), Warren Rogers (bass), Jerry McGeorge (rhythm guitar) and Tom Schiffour (drums).	
4/16/66	**10**	8	1. **Gloria** written by Van Morrison	Dunwich 116
7/02/66	**39**	1	2. Oh Yeah	Dunwich 122
			SHALAMAR	
			Black vocal trio formed in 1977 by Don Cornelius, the producer/host of TV's "Soul Train." Consisted of vocalists/dancers Jody Watley and Jeffrey Daniels with Gerald Brown. Howard Hewett replaced Brown in early 1978. Watley and Daniels (former husband of Stephanie Mills) pursued solo careers in 1984; replaced by Delisa Davis and Micki Free. Hewett left in 1985, replaced by Sidney Justin.	
4/16/77	**25**	8	1. Uptown Festival Going To A Go-Go/I Can't Help Myself/Uptight (Everything's Alright)/Stop! In The Name Of Love/It's The Same Old Song	Soul Train 10885
2/02/80	**8**	13	● 2. **The Second Time Around**	Solar 11709
8/06/83	**22**	10	3. Dead Giveaway	Solar 69819
4/14/84	**17**	10	4. Dancing In The Sheets from the film "Footloose"	Columbia 04372

DATE	POS	WKS	ARTIST—RECORD TITLE	LABEL & NO.
			THE SHANGRI-LAS	
			"Girl group" formed at Andrew Jackson High School in Queens, New York. Consisted of two sets of sisters: Mary (lead singer) & Betty Weiss and twins Mary Ann & Marge Ganser. Mary Ann died of encephalitis in 1971 and Marge died of a drug overdose.	
9/05/64	**5**	9	1. **Remember (Walkin' In The Sand)**	Red Bird 008
10/24/64	**1**(1)	10	2. **Leader Of The Pack**	Red Bird 014
1/16/65	**18**	5	3. Give Him A Great Big Kiss	Red Bird 018
6/19/65	**29**	4	4. Give Us Your Blessings	Red Bird 030
11/20/65	**6**	8	5. **I Can Never Go Home Anymore**	Red Bird 043
2/26/66	**33**	2	6. Long Live Our Love	Red Bird 048
			SHANNON	
			Brenda Shannon Greene from Washington, DC. Began singing career at York University.	
1/07/84	**8**	12	● 1. **Let The Music Play**	Mirage 99810
			DEL SHANNON	
			Born Charles Westover on 12/30/39 in Coopersville, Michigan. With US Army "Get Up And Go" radio show in Germany. Discovered by Ann Arbor DJ/producer Ollie McLaughlin. Formed own label, Berlee, in 1963. Wrote "I Go To Pieces" for Peter & Gordon. To Los Angeles in 1966, production work.	
3/27/61	**1**(4)	12	1. **Runaway** electric organ (musitron) solo by co-writer Max Crook	Big Top 3067
6/19/61	**5**	11	2. **Hats Off To Larry**	Big Top 3075
10/09/61	**28**	5	3. So Long Baby	Big Top 3083
1/06/62	**38**	2	4. Hey! Little Girl	Big Top 3091
1/26/63	**12**	7	5. Little Town Flirt	Big Top 3131
7/25/64	**22**	7	6. Handy Man	Amy 905
12/19/64†	**9**	10	7. **Keep Searchin' (We'll Follow The Sun)**	Amy 915
3/13/65	**30**	4	8. Stranger In Town	Amy 919
1/23/82	**33**	4	9. Sea Of Love produced by Tom Petty	Network 47951
			DEE DEE SHARP	
			Born Dione LaRue on 9/9/45 in Philadelphia. Backing vocalist at Cameo Records in 1961. Married record producer Kenny Gamble in 1967, recorded as Dee Dee Sharp Gamble. Also see Chubby Checker.	
3/17/62	**2**(2)	15	1. **Mashed Potato Time**	Cameo 212
6/23/62	**9**	9	2. **Gravy (For My Mashed Potatoes)**	Cameo 219
11/10/62	**5**	9	3. **Ride!**	Cameo 230
3/09/63	**10**	9	4. **Do The Bird**	Cameo 244
11/02/63	**33**	5	5. Wild!	Cameo 274
			GEORGIE SHAW	
			Pop singer styled after Eddie Fisher.	
11/12/55	**23**	6	1. No Arms Can Ever Hold You (Like These Arms Of Mine) Top 100 #23 / Best Seller #25	Decca 29679
2/11/56	**39**	1	2. Go On With The Wedding **KITTY KALLEN & GEORGIE SHAW**	Decca 29776

DATE	POS	WKS	ARTIST—RECORD TITLE	LABEL & NO.
			TOMMY SHAW	
			Born in Montgomery, Alabama. Lead guitarist of Styx since joining in 1976.	
11/03/84	**33**	3	1. Girls With Guns	A&M 2676
			SHEILA E.	
			Born Sheila Escovedo on 12/12/59 in San Francisco. Singer/percussionist. With father Pete Escovedo in the band, Azteca, in the mid-70s. Toured with Lionel Richie, recorded with Prince. Brother Peto was in Con Funk Shun.	
7/21/84	**7**	16	1. **The Glamorous Life**	Warner 29285
12/08/84	**34**	5	2. The Belle Of St. Mark	Warner 29180
12/28/85†	**11**	12	3. A Love Bizarre from the film "Krush Groove"; backing vocals: Prince	Paisley P. 28890
			THE SHELLS	
			Brooklyn R&B vocal quintet: Nathaniel "Little Nate" Bouknight (lead), Gus Geter (baritone), Bobby Nurse and Randy Alston (tenors) and Danny Small (bass).	
12/31/60†	**21**	5	1. Baby Oh Baby	Johnson 104
			SHEP & THE LIMELITES	
			R&B vocal trio from New York City: James "Shep" Sheppard, lead (formerly with the Heartbeats) and tenors Clarence Bassett and Charles Baskerville (formerly in the Videos).	
4/10/61	**2**(1)	11	1. **Daddy's Home** answer to the Heartbeats' "A Thousand Miles Away"	Hull 740
			SHEPHERD SISTERS	
			New York-based family trio.	
11/04/57	**18**	7	1. Alone (Why Must I Be Alone) Best Seller #18 / Top 100 #20 / Jockey #22	Lance 125
			T.G. SHEPPARD	
			Born William Browder on 7/20/44 in Humbolt, Tennessee. Country singer.	
5/16/81	**37**	2	1. I Loved 'Em Every One	Warner 49690
			VONDA SHEPPARD - see DAN HILL	
			SHERIFF	
			Canadian rock quintet; Freddy Curci, lead singer. Disbanded in 1983. Members Wolf Hassell and Arnold Lanni are now the duo Frozen Ghost.	
12/17/88†	**1**(1)	13	1. **When I'm With You** **[R]**	Capitol 44302
			ALLAN SHERMAN	
			Born on 11/30/24 in Chicago; died on 11/21/73. Began as a professional comedy writer for Jackie Gleason, Joe E. Lewis and others. Creator/producer of TV's "I've Got A Secret."	
8/10/63	**2**(3)	8	1. **Hello Mudduh, Hello Fadduh! (A Letter From Camp)** **[C]** adaptation of Ponchielli's "Dance Of The Hours"	Warner 5378
5/08/65	**40**	1	2. Crazy Downtown [C] parody of Petula Clark's "Downtown"	Warner 5614
			BOBBY SHERMAN	
			Born on 7/22/44 in Santa Monica, California. Regular on TV's "Shindig"; played Jeremy Bolt on TV's "Here Come The Brides." Currently involved in TV production.	
9/06/69	**3**	11	● 1. **Little Woman**	Metromedia 121
12/06/69†	**9**	9	● 2. **La La La (If I Had You)**	Metromedia 150

Michael McDonald's "Sweet Freedom," from the soundtrack to the film *Running Scared*, held the Hot 100's No. 7 spot in 1986. The former Doobie Brother had already scored heavily with separate duets with James Ingram ("Yah Mo B There") and Patti LaBelle ("On My Own").

The McGuire Sisters' "Sincerely" held the No. 1 slots on *Billboard's* Jockey, Juke Box, and Best Seller charts in 1955 prior to the establishment of the Hot 100. Their final appearance on the latter chart came six years later with "Just Because"—which reached the minimal ranking of No. 99.

Clyde McPhatter left the Dominoes in 1953 to form his own group, known the world over as the hit-making Drifters. His historic work with that group was ably documented in 1988 by Atlantic Records, who issued two double-album sets of classic Drifters material that included McPhatter's contributions.

Meat Loaf and John Parr's team-up on "Rock 'N' Roll Mercenaries" was not the former's first charting duet; in 1971, Motown subsidiary Rare Earth Records issued "What You See Is What You Get" by label act Stoney & Meatloaf, who also recorded an album for the label.

Harold Melvin & the Blue Notes' "Yesterday I Had the Blues" came directly between two gold singles for the Philly soul group: 1972's "If You Don't Know Me By Now," which reached No. 3 on the Hot 100, and the next year's "The Love I Lost (Part 1)," which hit No. 7.

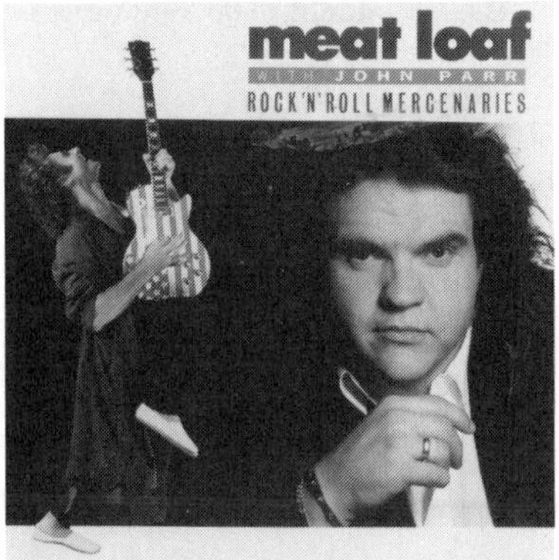

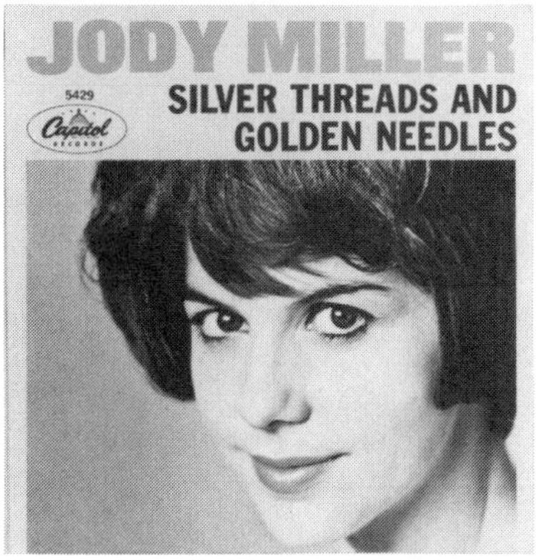

Sergio Mendes & Brasil '66 knew a good song when they heard it; their cover of Otis Redding's "(Sittin' On) The Dock Of The Bay" reached No. 66 in 1969. Later cover versions would follow by Sammy Hagar and Michael Bolton, among others.

The Miami Sound Machine's "Falling In Love (Uh-Oh)" broke a winning top-10 streak for the band when it peaked at No. 25. Its predecessors included 1985's "Conga" (which held the No. 10 slot), "Bad Boy" (No. 8), and "Words Get In The Way" (No. 5).

George Michael's year was clearly 1988: the British artist held the year-end No. 1 slots for single and album of the year with *Faith* and its title track, among many other top rankings.

Jody Miller's "Silver Threads And Golden Needles" peaked at No. 54 in 1965—a comparative disappointment for the artist, whose previous single, "Queen Of The House," reached No. 12 months earlier.

Mitch Miller's "Tunes Of Glory" was apparently the producer/conductor's last noteworthy tune of glory; the track was his last to appear on the Hot 100, peaking at the No. 88 position in 1961.

DATE	POS	WKS	ARTIST—RECORD TITLE	LABEL & NO.
2/28/70	**9**	11	● 3. **Easy Come, Easy Go**	Metromedia 177
6/06/70	**24**	5	4. Hey, Mister Sun	Metromedia 188
8/15/70	**5**	13	● 5. **Julie, Do Ya Love Me**	Metromedia 194
2/27/71	**16**	7	6. Cried Like A Baby	Metromedia 206
5/15/71	**29**	5	7. The Drum	Metromedia 217
			THE SHERRYS	
			Female R&B group from Philadelphia. Formed by Joe Cook, included his daughters Dinell and Delphine. Cook had own hit in 1957, "Peanuts," as "Little Joe."	
11/10/62	**35**	2	1. Pop Pop Pop-Pie	Guyden 2068
			THE SHIELDS	
			R&B group formed by Jesse Belvin solely to record "You Cheated." Frankie Ervin (lead), Jesse Belvin (falsetto), Johnny Watson, Mel Williams & Charles Wright.	
9/15/58	**12**	9	1. You Cheated Best Seller #12 end / Hot 100 #15	Dot 15805
			THE SHIRELLES	
			R&B "girl group" from Passaic, New Jersey. Consisted of Shirley Owens Alston (b: 6/10/41), Beverly Lee (b: 8/3/41), Doris Kenner (b: 8/2/41) and Addie "Micki" Harris (b: 1/22/40; d: 6/10/82). Formed in junior high school as the Poquellos. First recorded for Tiara in 1958. Kenner left group in 1968; returned in 1975. Alston left for solo career in 1975, recorded as "Lady Rose."	
10/17/60	**39**	3	1. Tonights The Night	Scepter 1208
12/12/60†	**1**(2)	15	2. **Will You Love Me Tomorrow** first #1 song for writers Carole King & Gerry Goffin	Scepter 1211
2/06/61	**3**	14	3. **Dedicated To The One I Love** **[R]** originally charted in 1959 (POS 83)	Scepter 1203
5/01/61	**4**	8	4. **Mama Said**	Scepter 1217
10/23/61	**21**	5	5. Big John	Scepter 1223
1/06/62	**8**	11	6. **Baby It's You**	Scepter 1227
3/31/62	**1**(3)	13	7. **Soldier Boy**	Scepter 1228
7/07/62	**22**	6	8. Welcome Home Baby	Scepter 1234
10/06/62	**36**	3	9. Stop The Music	Scepter 1237
12/15/62†	**19**	9	10. Everybody Loves A Lover	Scepter 1243
4/20/63	**4**	9	11. **Foolish Little Girl**	Scepter 1248
7/13/63	**26**	4	12. Don't Say Goodnight And Mean Goodbye	Scepter 1255
			SHIRLEY & COMPANY	
			Shirley Goodman (formerly of Shirley & Lee), and a group of studio musicians. Included Kenny Jeremiah of the Soul Survivors.	
2/22/75	**12**	8	1. Shame, Shame, Shame male vocal: Jesus Alvarez	Vibration 532
			SHIRLEY & LEE	
			New Orleans R&B duo formed in the early 50s. Shirley Goodman (b: 6/19/36) and Leonard Lee (b: 6/29/36; d: 10/23/76). First recorded for Aladdin in 1952. Billed as "The Sweethearts Of The Blues," recorded together until 1963.	
9/08/56	**20**	9	1. Let The Good Times Roll Best Seller #20 / Top 100 #27	Aladdin 3325
1/05/57	**38**	1	2. I Feel Good	Aladdin 3338

DATE	POS	WKS	ARTIST—RECORD TITLE	LABEL & NO.
			DON SHIRLEY TRIO	
			Pianist, organist. Born in Kingston, Jamaica on 1/27/27.	
10/09/61	**40**	1	1. Water Boy [I]	Cadence 1392
			THE SHOCKING BLUE	
			Dutch rock quartet: Mariska Veres (lead singer), Robbie van Leeuwen (guitar), Cor van Beek (drums) and Klaasje van der Wal (bass). Disbanded in 1974.	
12/20/69†	**1**(1)	13	● 1. **Venus**	Colossus 108
			TROY SHONDELL	
			Born on 5/14/44 in Fort Wayne, Indiana. Pop-country singer/songwriter.	
9/25/61	**6**	12	1. **This Time**	Liberty 55353
			DINAH SHORE	
			Born Frances Shore on 3/1/17 in Winchester, Tennessee. One of the most popular female vocalists of the 1940 to mid-50s era. Own TV variety show, 1951-62; own morning talk show "Dinah's Place," 1970-74. Married to actor George Montgomery from 1943-62.	
5/21/55	**12**	2	1. Whatever Lola Wants (Lola Gets) Jockey #12 / Best Seller #28 from the Broadway musical "Damn Yankees"	RCA 6077
12/10/55	**20**	1	2. Love And Marriage Jockey #20 / Top 100 #42	RCA 6266
2/23/57	**19**	10	3. Chantez-Chantez Jockey #19 / Top 100 #27	RCA 6792
9/09/57	**15**	7	4. Fascination Jockey #15 / Top 100 #98 from the film "Love In The Afternoon"	RCA 6980
12/02/57	**24**	1	5. I'll Never Say "Never Again" Again Jockey #24 #4 hit for Ozzie Nelson & His Orchestra in 1935	RCA 7056
			BUNNY SIGLER	
			Born Walter Sigler on 3/27/41 in Philadelphia. R&B vocalist/multi-instrumentalist/composer/producer. First recorded for V-Tone in 1959.	
7/22/67	**22**	7	1. Let The Good Times Roll & Feel So Good	Parkway 153
			THE SILHOUETTES	
			Philadelphia R&B doo-wop group formed as the Tornadoes by William Horton (lead), Richard Lewis (tenor), Earl Beal (baritone) and Raymond Edwards (bass).	
1/20/58	**1**(2)	13	1. **Get A Job** Top 100 #1 / Best Seller #2 / Jockey #3 first released on the Junior label (#391) in 1957	Ember 1029
			THE SILKIE	
			Folk quartet formed in 1963 at Hull University in Hull, England; Silvia Tatler, lead singer.	
11/06/65	**10**	7	1. **You've Got To Hide Your Love Away** Beatles contributed musical accompaniment & production assistance	Fontana 1525
			SILVER	
			Country-rock quintet led by John Batdorf of Batdorf & Rodney.	
8/07/76	**16**	12	1. Wham Bam (Shang-A-Lang)	Arista 0189

DATE	POS	WKS	ARTIST—RECORD TITLE	LABEL & NO.
			SILVER CONDOR	
			Rock quintet led by Joe Cerisano and Earl Slick (Phantom, Rocker & Slick).	
8/29/81	**32**	4	1. You Could Take My Heart Away	Columbia 02268
			SILVER CONVENTION	
			German studio disco act assembled by producer Michael Kunze and writer/arranger Silvester Levay. Female vocal trio formed in 1976 consisting of Penny McLean, Ramona Wolf and Linda Thompson.	
10/25/75	**1**(3)	13	● 1. **Fly, Robin, Fly**	Midland I. 10339
4/17/76	**2**(3)	15	● 2. **Get Up And Boogie (That's Right)**	Midland I. 10571
			SILVETTI	
			Argentinian Bebu Silvetti.	
3/19/77	**39**	3	1. Spring Rain [I]	Salsoul 2014
			THE HARRY SIMEONE CHORALE	
			Harry was born on 5/9/11 in Newark, New Jersey. Began career in 1939 as an arranger for Fred Waring. Arranger/conductor for film and TV shows.	
12/28/58	**13**	6	1. The Little Drummer Boy [X]	20th Fox 121
12/28/59	**15**	3	2. The Little Drummer Boy [X-R]	20th Fox 121
12/19/60	**24**	3	3. The Little Drummer Boy [X-R]	20th Fox 121
12/25/61	**22**	2	4. The Little Drummer Boy [X-R]	20th Fox 121
12/15/62	**28**	3	5. The Little Drummer Boy [X-R]	20th Fox 121
			GENE SIMMONS	
			Born in Tupelo, Mississippi in 1933. Nicknamed "Jumpin' Gene."	
8/29/64	**11**	8	1. Haunted House	Hi 2076
			PATRICK SIMMONS	
			Born on 1/23/50 in Aberdeen, Washington; raised in San Jose, California. Vocalist/ guitarist. Original member of The Doobie Brothers; wrote their hit "Black Water."	
4/16/83	**30**	5	1. So Wrong	Elektra 69839
			SIMON & GARFUNKEL	
			Folk-rock duo from New York City: Paul Simon and Art Garfunkel. Recorded as Tom & Jerry in 1957. Duo split in 1964; Simon was working solo in England, Garfunkel was in graduate school. They re-formed in 1965 and stayed together until 1971. Reunited in 1981 for national tour.	
12/04/65†	**1**(2)	12	● 1. **The Sounds Of Silence**	Columbia 43396
2/26/66	**5**	10	2. **Homeward Bound**	Columbia 43511
5/14/66	**3**	10	3. **I Am A Rock**	Columbia 43617
8/27/66	**25**	4	4. The Dangling Conversation	Columbia 43728
11/19/66	**13**	6	5. A Hazy Shade Of Winter	Columbia 43873
4/01/67	**16**	7	6. At The Zoo	Columbia 44046
8/12/67	**23**	5	7. Fakin' It	Columbia 44232
3/16/68	**11**	9	8. Scarborough Fair/Canticle song also known as "Parsley, Sage, Rosemary And Thyme"	Columbia 44465
5/04/68	**1**(3)	12	● 9. **Mrs. Robinson** above 2: from the film "The Graduate"	Columbia 44511
4/19/69	**7**	9	10. **The Boxer**	Columbia 44785
2/14/70	**1**(6)	13	● 11. **Bridge Over Troubled Water**	Columbia 45079
4/18/70	**4**	12	● 12. **Cecilia**	Columbia 45133

DATE	POS	WKS	ARTIST—RECORD TITLE	LABEL & NO.
9/26/70	**18**	8	13. El Condor Pasa	Columbia 45237
11/01/75	**9**	9	14. **My Little Town** all of above: written by Paul Simon	Columbia 10230
5/01/82	**27**	6	15. Wake Up Little Susie recorded live in New York's Central Park on 9/19/81	Warner 50053
			CARLY SIMON	
			Born on 6/25/45 in New York City. Pop vocalist/songwriter. Father is co-founder of Simon & Schuster publishing. Won the 1971 Best New Artist Grammy Award. Married James Taylor on 11/3/72; filed for divorce in 1982.	
6/05/71	**10**	10	1. **That's The Way I've Always Heard It Should Be**	Elektra 45724
1/01/72	**13**	10	2. Anticipation	Elektra 45759
12/16/72†	**1**(3)	14	● 3. **You're So Vain** backing vocal: Mick Jagger	Elektra 45824
4/21/73	**17**	9	4. The Right Thing To Do	Elektra 45843
2/16/74	**5**	13	● 5. **Mockingbird** **CARLY SIMON & JAMES TAYLOR**	Elektra 45880
6/01/74	**14**	6	6. Haven't Got Time For The Pain	Elektra 45887
5/24/75	**21**	5	7. Attitude Dancing	Elektra 45246
8/27/77	**2**(3)	15	● 8. **Nobody Does It Better** from the film "The Spy Who Loved Me"	Elektra 45413
5/06/78	**6**	11	9. **You Belong To Me**	Elektra 45477
9/23/78	**36**	3	10. Devoted To You **CARLY SIMON & JAMES TAYLOR**	Elektra 45506
8/23/80	**11**	13	● 11. Jesse	Warner 49518
12/06/86†	**18**	9	12. Coming Around Again from the film "Heartburn"	Arista 9525
			JOE SIMON	
			Born on 9/2/43 in Simmesport, Louisiana. Moved to Oakland in 1959. First recorded with vocal group, the Golden Tones, for Hush in 1960.	
6/08/68	**25**	7	1. (You Keep Me) Hangin' On	Sound Stage 2608
3/29/69	**13**	11	● 2. The Chokin' Kind	Sound Stage 2628
2/06/71	**40**	3	3. Your Time To Cry	Spring 108
12/11/71†	**11**	11	● 4. Drowning In The Sea Of Love	Spring 120
8/19/72	**11**	8	● 5. Power Of Love	Spring 128
4/14/73	**37**	2	6. Step By Step	Spring 133
8/25/73	**18**	8	7. Theme From Cleopatra Jones featuring The Mainstreeters; from the film of the same title	Spring 138
5/10/75	**8**	11	8. **Get Down, Get Down (Get On The Floor)**	Spring 156
			PAUL SIMON	
			Born on 11/5/41 in Newark, New Jersey; raised in Queens, New York. Vocalist/ composer/guitarist. Met Art Garfunkel in high school, recorded together as Tom & Jerry in 1957. Worked as Jerry Landis, Paul Kane, Harrison Gregory and True Taylor in the early 60s. To England from 1963-64. Returned to USA and recorded first album with Garfunkel in 1965. Went solo in 1971. Married to actress Carrie Fisher from 1983-85. In the films "Annie Hall" and "One-Trick Pony."	
2/19/72	**4**	11	1. **Mother And Child Reunion**	Columbia 45547
4/22/72	**22**	8	2. Me And Julio Down By The Schoolyard	Columbia 45585
6/02/73	**2**(2)	11	3. **Kodachrome**	Columbia 45859

DATE	POS	WKS	ARTIST—RECORD TITLE	LABEL & NO.
8/18/73	**2**(1)	14	● 4. **Loves Me Like A Rock** vocal backing: The Dixie Hummingbirds	Columbia 45907
1/05/74	**35**	3	5. American Tune	Columbia 45900
9/06/75	**23**	6	6. Gone At Last **PAUL SIMON/PHOEBE SNOW** vocal backing: The Jessy Dixon Singers	Columbia 10197
1/03/76	**1**(3)	13	● 7. **50 Ways To Leave Your Lover**	Columbia 10270
5/29/76	**40**	2	8. Still Crazy After All These Years	Columbia 10332
11/05/77†	**5**	14	9. **Slip Slidin' Away**	Columbia 10630
2/11/78	**17**	7	10. (What A) Wonderful World **ART GARFUNKEL with JAMES TAYLOR & PAUL SIMON**	Columbia 10676
8/16/80	**6**	12	11. **Late In The Evening**	Warner 49511
11/22/80	**40**	2	12. One-Trick Pony from the film of the same title	Warner 49601
4/25/87	**23**	7	13. You Can Call Me Al initially charted for 14 wks. (POS 44), then re-entered on 3/28/87	Warner 28667
			NINA SIMONE	
			Born Eunice Waymon on 2/21/33 in Tryon, South Carolina. Jazz-influenced vocalist/ pianist/composer. Attended Juilliard School of Music in New York City. Devoted more time to political activism in the 70s, infrequent recording.	
8/24/59	**18**	11	1. I Loves You, Porgy from the film "Porgy And Bess"	Bethlehem 11021
			SIMPLE MINDS	
			Scottish rock group; nucleus of group: Jim Kerr (lead singer; married to Chrissie Hynde of the Pretenders), Michael MacNeil (keyboards), Charles Burchill (guitar), Mel Gaynor (drums) and John Giblin (bass).	
3/23/85	**1**(1)	14	1. **Don't You (Forget About Me)** from the film "The Breakfast Club"	A&M 2703
10/26/85	**3**	16	2. **Alive & Kicking**	A&M 2783
2/08/86	**14**	9	3. Sanctify Yourself	A&M 2810
5/03/86	**28**	6	4. All The Things She Said	A&M 2828
			SIMPLY RED	
			British pop sextet led by vocalist Mick "Red" Hucknall. Includes Tony Bowers, Chris Joyce, Fritz McIntyre, Sylvan Richardson and Tim Kellett.	
5/10/86	**1**(1)	14	1. **Holding Back The Years**	Elektra 69564
8/30/86	**28**	6	2. Money$ Too Tight (To Mention) originally released in August of 1985	Elektra 69528
4/18/87	**27**	6	3. The Right Thing	Elektra 69487

DATE	POS	WKS	ARTIST—RECORD TITLE	LABEL & NO.
			FRANK SINATRA	
			Born Francis Albert Sinatra on 12/12/15 in Hoboken, New Jersey. With Harry James from 1939-40, first recorded for Brunswick in 1939; with Tommy Dorsey, 1940-42. Went solo in late 1942 and charted 40 top 10 hits through 1954. Appeared in many films from 1941 on. Won an Oscar for the film "From Here To Eternity" in 1953. Own TV show in 1957. Own record company, Reprise, 1961, sold to Warner Bros. in 1963. Announced his retirement in 1970, but made comeback in 1973. Regarded by many as the greatest popular singer of the 20th century.	
1/22/55	**19**	4	1. Melody Of Love **FRANK SINATRA & RAY ANTHONY** Jockey #19	Capitol 3018
5/07/55	**1**(2)	21	2. **Learnin' The Blues** Jockey #1 / Best Seller #2 / Juke Box #2	Capitol 3102
9/24/55	**13**	5	3. Same Old Saturday Night Jockey #13 / Top 100 #65 pre	Capitol 3218
11/05/55	**5**	15	4. **Love And Marriage** Top 100 #5 / Jockey #5 / Best Seller #6 / Juke Box #7 from the TV production "Our Town"	Capitol 3260
12/17/55†	**7**	9	5. **(Love Is) The Tender Trap** Jockey #7 / Top 100 #23 / Best Seller #24 from the film "The Tender Trap"	Capitol 3290
3/24/56	**21**	3	6. Flowers Mean Forgiveness Jockey #21 / Top 100 #35	Capitol 3350
6/02/56	**13**	6	7. (How Little It Matters) How Little We Know Jockey #13 / Top 100 #30	Capitol 3423
11/03/56†	**3**	17	8. **Hey! Jealous Lover** Jockey #3 / Top 100 #6 / Juke Box #7 / Best Seller #8	Capitol 3552
2/09/57	**15**	6	9. Can I Steal A Little Love Jockey #15 / Top 100 #20 from the film "Rock Pretty Baby"	Capitol 3608
7/22/57	**25**	1	10. You're Cheatin' Yourself (If You're Cheatin' On Me) Jockey #25	Capitol 3744
10/28/57†	**2**(1)	17	11. **All The Way** from the film "The Joker Is Wild" Jockey #2 / Best Seller #15 / Top 100 #15	Capitol 3793
1/20/58	**6**	14	12. **Witchcraft** Jockey #6 / Best Seller #20 / Top 100 #20	Capitol 3859
5/12/58	**22**	1	13. How Are Ya' Fixed For Love? **FRANK SINATRA & KEELY SMITH** Jockey #22 / Top 100 #97	Capitol 3952
9/07/59	**30**	1	14. High Hopes from the film "A Hole In The Head"	Capitol 4214
11/16/59	**38**	3	15. Talk To Me	Capitol 4284
11/28/60	**25**	2	16. Ol' MacDonald all of above (except #1 & 13): with Nelson Riddle & His Orchestra	Capitol 4466
1/20/62	**34**	3	17. Pocketful Of Miracles from the film of the same title	Reprise 20040
10/10/64	**27**	6	18. Softly, As I Leave You	Reprise 0301
1/30/65	**32**	3	19. Somewhere In Your Heart	Reprise 0332
1/15/66	**28**	4	20. It Was A Very Good Year	Reprise 0429
5/28/66	**1**(1)	11	21. **Strangers In The Night** from the film "A Man Could Get Killed"	Reprise 0470

DATE	POS	WKS	ARTIST—RECORD TITLE	LABEL & NO.
9/17/66	**25**	5	22. Summer Wind	Reprise 0509
12/03/66	**4**	9	23. **That's Life**	Reprise 0531
3/25/67	**1**(4)	11	• 24. **Somethin' Stupid**	Reprise 0561
			NANCY SINATRA & FRANK SINATRA	
8/26/67	**30**	4	25. The World We Knew (Over And Over)	Reprise 0610
11/16/68	**23**	5	26. Cycles	Reprise 0764
4/12/69	**27**	6	27. My Way	Reprise 0817
5/31/80	**32**	6	28. Theme From New York, New York from the film "New York, New York"	Reprise 49233
			NANCY SINATRA	
			Born on 6/8/40 in Jersey City, New Jersey. First child of Frank and Nancy Sinatra. Moved to Los Angeles while a child. Made national TV debut with father and Elvis Presley in 1959. Married to Tommy Sands, 1960-65. Appeared on "Hullabaloo," "American Bandstand," and own specials, mid-60s. In films "For Those Who Think Young," "Get Yourself A College Girl," "The Oscar" and "Speedway."	
2/05/66	**1**(1)	12	• 1. **These Boots Are Made For Walkin'**	Reprise 0432
4/30/66	**7**	7	2. **How Does That Grab You, Darlin'?**	Reprise 0461
7/30/66	**36**	2	3. Friday's Child	Reprise 0491
12/10/66	**5**	9	• 4. **Sugar Town**	Reprise 0527
3/25/67	**1**(4)	11	• 5. **Somethin' Stupid**	Reprise 0561
			NANCY SINATRA & FRANK SINATRA	
4/08/67	**15**	5	6. Love Eyes	Reprise 0559
7/08/67	**14**	7	7. Jackson	Reprise 0595
			NANCY SINATRA & LEE HAZLEWOOD	
10/07/67	**24**	4	8. Lightning's Girl	Reprise 0620
11/04/67	**20**	4	9. Lady Bird	Reprise 0629
			NANCY SINATRA & LEE HAZLEWOOD	
1/27/68	**26**	5	10. Some Velvet Morning	Reprise 0651
			NANCY SINATRA & LEE HAZLEWOOD	
			GORDON SINCLAIR	
			Born on 6/3/1900 in Toronto; died on 5/17/84. Canadian broadcaster/author.	
1/26/74	**24**	4	1. The Americans (A Canadian's Opinion) [S] originally broadcast as an editorial on 6/5/73 on CFRB-Toronto	Avco 4628
			THE SINGING DOGS	
			An actual recording of dogs barking, produced by Don Charles in Copenhagen.	
12/17/55	**22**	2	1. Oh! Susanna [N] Best Seller #22 / Top 100 #37 written in 1848 by Stephen Foster; DJ copies labeled as "Dolly's Oh! Susanna"	RCA 6344
			THE SINGING NUN	
			Sister Luc-Gabrielle (real name: Jeanine Deckers) from the Fichermont, Belgium nuns convent. Recorded under the name Soeur Sourire ("Sister Smile"). Committed suicide on 3/31/85 (52).	
11/16/63	**1**(4)	12	1. **Dominique** **[F]**	Philips 40152

DATE	POS	WKS	ARTIST—RECORD TITLE	LABEL & NO.
			SIR DOUGLAS QUINTET	
			"Tex-Mex" rock band led by Doug Sahm (b: 11/6/41) from San Antonio. Co-founded by country singer Augie Meyers.	
4/17/65	13	9	1. She's About A Mover	Tribe 8308
3/05/66	31	5	2. The Rains Came	Tribe 8314
3/15/69	27	6	3. Mendocino	Smash 2191
			SISTER SLEDGE	
			Sisters Debra, Joan, Kim and Kathie Sledge from North Philadelphia. First recorded as Sisters Sledge for Money Back label in 1971. Worked as back-up vocalists.	
3/10/79	9	13	1. **He's The Greatest Dancer**	Cotillion 44245
5/12/79	2(2)	11	● 2. **We Are Family**	Cotillion 44251
3/06/82	23	6	3. My Guy	Cotillion 47000
			THE SIX TEENS	
			Los Angeles R&B sextet: Trudy Williams and Ed Wells (leads), Richard Owens, Darryl Lewis, Beverly Pecot and Louise Williams. In 1956, members ranged in age from 14 to 19.	
9/01/56	25	1	1. A Casual Look Best Seller #25 / Top 100 #48	Flip 315
			SKIP & FLIP	
			Gary "Flip" Paxton and Clyde "Skip" Battin. Met at the University of Arizona, and appeared on "Arizona Jubilee" in 1958 as the Rockabillies. Paxton formed The Hollywood Argyles, and later started own Garpax record label.	
7/27/59	11	9	1. It Was I	Brent 7002
4/25/60	11	10	2. Cherry Pie	Brent 7010
			SKYLARK	
			Group from Vancouver: lead singers Donny Gerrard & B.J. (Bonnie Jean) Cook, with David Foster, Duris Maxwell, Norman McPherson, Steven Pugsley and Carl Graves. Keyboardist Foster later joined Attitudes; recorded solo in the mid-80s.	
3/31/73	9	14	1. **Wildflower**	Capitol 3511
			THE SKYLINERS	
			Pittsburgh vocal quintet: Jimmy Beaumont (b: 10/21/40; lead), Janet Vogel (d: 2/21/80, suicide) & Wally Lester (tenors), Joe VerScharen (baritone) and Jackie Taylor (bass voice/guitarist).	
3/23/59	12	10	1. Since I Don't Have You	Calico 103
6/15/59	26	7	2. This I Swear	Calico 106
6/20/60	24	6	3. Pennies From Heaven #1 hit for Bing Crosby in 1936	Calico 117
			SKYY	
			Brooklyn R&B-pop-funk octet. Vocals by sisters Denise, Delores and Bonnie Dunning. Organized by Randy Muller, former leader of Brass Construction.	
2/20/82	26	4	1. Call Me	Salsoul 2152
			SLADE	
			English hard-rock quartet: Noddy Holder (b: 6/15/50; lead singer), David Hill (guitar), Jim Lea (bass, keyboards) and Don Powell (drums).	
5/05/84	20	8	1. Run Runaway	CBS Assoc. 04398
8/11/84	37	3	2. My Oh My	CBS Assoc. 04528

DATE	POS	WKS	ARTIST—RECORD TITLE	LABEL & NO.
			SLAVE	
			Funk band from Dayton, Ohio formed by Steve Washington (trumpet) in 1975. Studio vocalist Steve Arrington was a member from 1978-82. Numerous personnel changes.	
7/23/77	**32**	6	1. Slide [I]	Cotillion 44218
			PERCY SLEDGE	
			Born in 1941 in Leighton, Alabama. Worked local clubs with Esquires Combo until going solo.	
4/30/66	**1**(2)	10	● 1. **When A Man Loves A Woman**	Atlantic 2326
8/06/66	**17**	6	2. Warm And Tender Love	Atlantic 2342
11/19/66	**20**	7	3. It Tears Me Up	Atlantic 2358
7/22/67	**40**	1	4. Love Me Tender	Atlantic 2414
4/06/68	**11**	11	5. Take Time To Know Her	Atlantic 2490
			SLY & THE FAMILY STONE	
			San Francisco interracial "psychedelic soul" group formed by Sylvester "Sly Stone" Stewart (b: 3/15/44, Dallas; lead singer, keyboards), Sly's brother Freddie Stone (guitar), Cynthia Robinson (trumpet), Jerry Martini (saxophone), Sly's sister Rosie Stone (piano, vocals), Larry Graham (bass) and Gregg Errico (drums). Sly recorded gospel at age 4. With vocal group the Viscanes while in high school. Producer and writer for Bobby Freeman, the Mojo Men, the Beau Brummels. Formed own groups, The Stoners in 1966 and the Family Stone in 1967. Worked Woodstock Festival in 1969. Career waned in the mid-70s. Worked with George Clinton (Parliament/Funkadelic) in 1982.	
3/02/68	**8**	12	1. **Dance To The Music**	Epic 10256
1/04/69	**1**(4)	14	● 2. **Everyday People**	Epic 10407
4/26/69	**22**	6	3. Stand!	Epic 10450
8/30/69	**2**(2)	13	4. **Hot Fun In The Summertime**	Epic 10497
1/10/70	**1**(2)	12	● 5. **Thank You (Falettinme Be Mice Elf Agin)/**	
		12	6. Everybody Is A Star	Epic 10555
6/20/70	**38**	3	7. I Want To Take You Higher [R] originally charted in 1969 (POS 60)	Epic 10450
11/13/71	**1**(3)	13	● 8. **Family Affair**	Epic 10805
2/26/72	**23**	6	9. Runnin' Away	Epic 10829
7/14/73	**12**	13	● 10. If You Want Me To Stay	Epic 11017
8/17/74	**32**	3	11. Time For Livin'	Epic 11140
			SLY FOX	
			Black-and-white duo: Gary "Mudbone" Cooper (P-Funk) and Michael Camacho.	
2/15/86	**7**	14	1. **Let's Go All The Way** based on the same groove as the Boogie Boys' "Fly Girl"	Capitol 5552
			SMALL FACES	
			British rock quartet: Steve Marriott (guitar), Ronnie Lane (bass), Ian McLagan (organ) and Kenny Jones (drums). In 1968, Marriott formed Humble Pie. Remaining members evolved into Faces in 1969; disbanded in 1975. Jones joined The Who in 1979.	
1/13/68	**16**	8	1. Itchycoo Park	Immediate 501
			MILLIE SMALL	
			Born Millicent Smith on 10/6/46 in Jamaica. Nicknamed "The Blue Beat Girl."	
6/06/64	**2**(1)	9	1. **My Boy Lollipop**	Smash 1893

DATE	POS	WKS	ARTIST—RECORD TITLE	LABEL & NO.
9/05/64	**40**	2	2. Sweet William	Smash 1920
			SMITH	
			Los Angeles-based rock quintet fronted by St. Louis blues rocker Gayle McCormick.	
10/04/69	**5**	11	1. **Baby It's You**	Dunhill 4206
			FRANKIE SMITH	
			Philadelphia native. Wrote and produced for Philadelphia International in the late 70s, and later for WMOT.	
7/11/81	**30**	7	● 1. Double Dutch Bus	WMOT 5356
			based on the double-dutch jump rope game; certified gold for both 7" and 12" singles	
			HUEY "PIANO" SMITH & THE CLOWNS	
			Huey was born on 1/26/34 in New Orleans. With Earl King in the early 50s. Recorded with Eddie "Guitar Slim" Jones' band from 1951-54. Much session work in New Orleans. Own band, The Clowns, in 1957, with Bobby Marchan (vocals). Marchan left in 1960, replaced by Curly Smith. Also see Frankie Ford.	
3/31/58	**9**	9	1. **Don't You Just Know It**	Ace 545
			Top 100 #9 / Best Seller #13	
			HURRICANE SMITH	
			Born Norman Smith in northern England, 1923. Vocalist/producer/engineer/session musician. Produced early Pink Floyd albums and did some engineering for The Beatles.	
12/23/72†	**3**	12	1. **Oh, Babe, What Would You Say?**	Capitol 3383
			JIMMY SMITH	
			Born on 12/8/25 in Norristown, Pennsylvania. Pioneer jazz organist. Won Major Bowes Amateur Show in 1934. With father (James, Sr.) in song-and-dance team, 1942. With Don Gardner & The Sonotones, recorded for Bruce in 1953. Smith first recorded with own trio for Blue Note in 1956. Began doing vocals in 1966.	
6/09/62	**21**	7	1. Walk On The Wild Side - Part 1 [I]	Verve 10255
			from the film of the same title	
			KEELY SMITH - see LOUIS PRIMA and FRANK SINATRA	
			O.C. SMITH	
			Born Ocie Lee Smith on 6/21/36 in Mansfield, Louisiana; raised in Los Angeles. Sang while in US Air Force from 1953-57. First recorded for Cadence in 1956. With Count Basie from 1961-63.	
4/20/68	**40**	2	1. The Son Of Hickory Holler's Tramp	Columbia 44425
9/21/68	**2**(1)	12	● 2. **Little Green Apples**	Columbia 44616
9/20/69	**34**	2	3. Daddy's Little Man	Columbia 44948
			PATTI SMITH GROUP	
			Born on 12/31/46 in Chicago; raised in New Jersey. Poet-turned-punk-rocker.	
5/13/78	**13**	9	1. Because The Night	Arista 0318
			written by Smith and Bruce Springsteen	
			RAY SMITH	
			Born on 10/31/34 in Melber, Kentucky; committed suicide on 11/29/79.	
2/01/60	**22**	8	1. Rockin' Little Angel	Judd 1016

DATE	POS	WKS	ARTIST—RECORD TITLE	LABEL & NO.
			REX SMITH	
			Born in Jacksonville, Florida. Vocalist/actor. Starred in several Broadway musicals and in TV film "Sooner Or Later." Appeared in the films "Pirates Of Penzance" and and "Streethawk." Recorded duet with rock singer Rachel Sweet (b: 1963, Akron, OH).	
5/12/79	**10**	10	● 1. **You Take My Breath Away** from the TV film "Sooner Or Later"	Columbia 10908
8/08/81	**32**	4	2. Everlasting Love **REX SMITH/RACHEL SWEET**	Columbia 02169
			SAMMI SMITH	
			Born on 8/5/43 in Orange, California; raised in Oklahoma. Country singer.	
2/20/71	**8**	11	● 1. **Help Me Make It Through The Night**	Mega 0015
			SOMETHIN' SMITH & THE REDHEADS	
			Trio from UCLA: Smith (vocals, guitar), Saul Striks (piano), Major Short (violin).	
4/02/55	**7**	23	1. **It's A Sin To Tell A Lie** Best Seller #7 / Juke Box #8 / Jockey #9 #1 hit for Fats Waller in 1936	Epic 9093
7/14/56	**27**	3	2. In A Shanty In Old Shanty Town #1 hit for Ted Lewis in 1932	Epic 9168
			VERDELLE SMITH	
			Black songstress from St. Petersburg, Florida.	
8/13/66	**38**	2	1. Tar And Cement	Capitol 5632
			WHISTLING JACK SMITH	
			Born Billy Moeller on 2/2/46 in Liverpool, England.	
5/13/67	**20**	5	1. I Was Kaiser Bill's Batman [I]	Deram 85005
			SMOKIE	
			British pop-rock quartet featuring lead singer Chris Norman. Also see Suzi Quatro.	
1/22/77	**25**	8	1. Living Next Door To Alice	RSO 860
			SNEAKER	
			Los Angeles-based pop-rock sextet.	
12/19/81†	**34**	6	1. More Than Just The Two Of Us	Handshake 02557
			SNIFF 'n' the TEARS	
			British rock group led by Paul Roberts (vocals) and Loz Netto (guitar).	
8/18/79	**15**	9	1. Driver's Seat	Atlantic 3604
			PHOEBE SNOW	
			Born Phoebe Laub on 7/17/52 in New York City; raised in New Jersey. Vocalist/ guitarist/songwriter. Began performing in Greenwich Village in the early 70s.	
2/08/75	**5**	11	1. **Poetry Man**	Shelter 40353
9/06/75	**23**	6	2. Gone At Last **PAUL SIMON/PHOEBE SNOW** vocal backing: The Jessy Dixon Singers	Columbia 10197

DATE	POS	WKS	ARTIST—RECORD TITLE	LABEL & NO.
			SOFT CELL	
			British electro-rock duo: Marc Almond (vocals) & David Ball (synthesizer). Almond began solo career in late 1988.	
5/22/82	**8**	15	1. **Tainted Love**	Sire 49855
			JOANIE SOMMERS	
			Born on 2/24/41 in Buffalo, moved to California in 1954. Vocalist for Pepsi-Cola jingles in early and mid-60s.	
6/16/62	**7**	11	1. **Johnny Get Angry**	Warner 5275
			SONNY	
			Born Salvatore Bono on 2/16/35 in Detroit. Sonny Bono of Sonny & Cher. With Specialty Records as A&R man and writer from 1957-59. Co-wrote The Searchers' hit "Needles And Pins." Elected mayor of Palm Springs, California on 4/12/88. Appeared in the 1988 film "Hairspray."	
9/04/65	**10**	8	1. **Laugh At Me**	Atco 6369
			SONNY & CHER	
			Husband and wife duo: Sonny and Cher Bono. Session singers for Phil Spector. First recorded as Caesar & Cleo for Vault in 1963. Married in 1963; divorced in 1974. In the films "Good Times" (1966) and "Chastity" (1968). Own CBS-TV variety series from 1971-74. Brief TV reunion in 1975. Each recorded solo.	
7/31/65	**1**(3)	10	● 1. **I Got You Babe**	Atco 6359
9/11/65	**8**	9	2. **Baby Don't Go**	Reprise 0309
9/25/65	**20**	4	3. Just You	Atco 6345
10/23/65	**15**	6	4. But You're Mine	Atco 6381
2/12/66	**14**	6	5. What Now My Love	Atco 6395
10/15/66	**21**	4	6. Little Man	Atco 6440
1/28/67	**6**	8	7. **The Beat Goes On**	Atco 6461
11/13/71	**7**	11	8. **All I Ever Need Is You**	Kapp 2151
3/11/72	**8**	11	9. **A Cowboys Work Is Never Done**	Kapp 2163
8/05/72	**32**	5	10. When You Say Love adapted from the "Budweiser" jingle; all of above: written (except #5, 8 & 10) and produced (except #8 & 10) by Sonny	Kapp 2176
			THE SOPWITH "CAMEL"	
			San Francisco quintet; Peter Kraemer, lead singer.	
1/28/67	**26**	4	1. Hello Hello	Kama Sutra 217
			THE S.O.S. BAND	
			Atlanta funk-R&B band formed by Mary Davis (vocals, keyboards). Name means "Sounds Of Success."	
6/28/80	**3**	14	▲ 1. **Take Your Time (Do It Right) Part 1**	Tabu 5522
			THE SOUL CHILDREN	
			Group formed by songwriters Isaac Hayes and David Porter. Consisted of Anita Louis, Shelbra Bennett, John Colbert and Norman West. Colbert later recorded as J. Blackfoot.	
3/23/74	**36**	2	1. I'll Be The Other Woman	Stax 0182
			SOUL SURVIVORS	
			White-soul band from New York City and Philadelphia. Formed by the Ingui brothers, Charles & Richard, and Kenny Jeremiah. Re-formed by the Inguis in 1972. Jeremiah was later with Shirley Goodman in Shirley & Company.	
9/23/67	**4**	12	1. **Expressway To Your Heart**	Crimson 1010

DATE	POS	WKS	ARTIST—RECORD TITLE	LABEL & NO.
1/20/68	**33**	3	2. Explosion In Your Soul	Crimson 1012
			DAVID SOUL	
			Born David Solberg on 8/28/43 in Chicago. Ken Hutchinson of TV's "Starsky & Hutch." Began career as a folksinger and appeared several times on "The Merv Griffin Show" as "The Covered Man" (wore a ski mask).	
2/19/77	**1**(1)	13	● 1. **Don't Give Up On Us**	Private S. 45129
			JIMMY SOUL	
			Born James McCleese in New York City in 1942; raised in North Carolina and Portsmouth, Virginia. Worked with gospel groups, including the Nightingales, billed as "The Wonder Boy."	
5/05/62	**22**	8	1. Twistin' Matilda	S.P.Q.R. 3300
4/20/63	**1**(2)	11	2. **If You Wanna Be Happy**	S.P.Q.R. 3305
			SOUNDS OF SUNSHINE	
7/24/71	**39**	2	1. Love Means (You Never Have To Say You're Sorry)	Ranwood 896
			SOUNDS ORCHESTRAL	
			English; Johnny Pearson, piano.	
4/10/65	**10**	11	1. **Cast Your Fate To The Wind** [I]	Parkway 942
			JOE SOUTH	
			Born on 2/28/40 in Atlanta. Successful Nashville session guitarist/songwriter in the mid-60s. Wrote "Down In The Boondocks," "Hush" and "Rose Garden." Producer for Billy Joe Royal.	
2/01/69	**12**	9	1. Games People Play	Capitol 2248
1/17/70	**12**	9	2. Walk A Mile In My Shoes	Capitol 2704
			JOE SOUTH & THE BELIEVERS	
			THE SOUTHER, HILLMAN, FURAY BAND	
			Country-rock sextet formed as a supergroup featuring veterans J.D. Souther, Chris Hillman and Richie Furay.	
9/21/74	**27**	4	1. Fallin' In Love	Asylum 45201
			J.D. SOUTHER	
			Born John David Souther in Detroit; raised in Amarillo, Texas.	
10/20/79	**7**	13	1. **You're Only Lonely**	Columbia 11079
3/14/81	**11**	10	2. Her Town Too	Columbia 60514
			JAMES TAYLOR & J.D. SOUTHER	
			RED SOVINE	
			Born Woodrow Wilson Sovine on 7/17/18 in Charleston, West Virginia; died on 4/14/80. Country singer/songwriter/guitarist.	
8/28/76	**40**	1	● 1. Teddy Bear [S]	Starday 142
			SPANDAU BALLET	
			English quintet: Tony Hadley (lead singer), Gary Kemp (guitar), Steve Norman (sax), Martin Kemp (bass) and John Keeble (drums).	
8/27/83	**4**	13	1. **True**	Chrysalis 42720
12/17/83†	**29**	6	2. Gold	Chrysalis 42743
9/01/84	**34**	4	3. Only When You Leave	Chrysalis 42792

DATE	POS	WKS	ARTIST—RECORD TITLE	LABEL & NO.
			SPANKY & OUR GANG	
			Folk-pop group formed in Chicago in 1966 featuring lead singer Elaine "Spanky" McFarlane (b: 6/19/42, Peoria, IL). Spanky became lead singer of the new Mamas & The Papas, early 80s.	
6/03/67	**9**	5	1. **Sunday Will Never Be The Same**	Mercury 72679
9/16/67	**31**	2	2. Making Every Minute Count	Mercury 72714
10/28/67	**14**	9	3. Lazy Day	Mercury 72732
2/03/68	**30**	4	4. Sunday Mornin'	Mercury 72765
5/18/68	**17**	7	5. Like To Get To Know You	Mercury 72795
			JUDSON SPENCE	
			Singer/songwriter/multi-instrumentalist born in Pascagoula, Mississippi.	
11/26/88	**32**	4	1. Yeah, Yeah, Yeah	Atlantic 88999
			TRACIE SPENCER	
			Native of Waterloo, Iowa. 12 years old at time of first hit in 1988.	
11/19/88	**38**	3	1. Symptoms Of True Love	Capitol 44140
			SPIDER	
			New York-based rock quintet. South African native Amanda Blue, lead singer.	
6/07/80	**39**	2	1. New Romance (It's A Mystery)	Dreamland 100
			SPINNERS	
			R&B vocal group from Ferndale High School near Detroit, originally known as the Domingoes. Discovered by producer/lead singer of The Moonglows, Harvey Fuqua, and became the Spinners in 1961. First recorded on Fuqua's Tri-Phi label. Many personnel changes. G.C. Cameron was lead singer from 1968-72. 1972 hit lineup included Phillippe Wynne (tenor; d: 7/14/84), Bobby Smith (tenor), Billy Henderson (tenor), Henry Fambrough (baritone) and Pervis Jackson (bass). Wynne left group in 1977 and toured with Parliament/Funkadelic; replaced by John Edwards.	
7/17/61	**27**	5	1. That's What Girls Are Made For lead vocal: Harvey Fuqua (of The Moonglows)	Tri-Phi 1001
8/14/65	**35**	2	2. I'll Always Love You	Motown 1078
8/22/70	**14**	10	3. It's A Shame	V.I.P. 25057
10/07/72	**3**	11	• 4. **I'll Be Around**	Atlantic 2904
1/20/73	**4**	12	• 5. **Could It Be I'm Falling In Love**	Atlantic 2927
5/19/73	**11**	11	• 6. One Of A Kind (Love Affair)	Atlantic 2962
9/08/73	**29**	3	7. Ghetto Child	Atlantic 2973
2/23/74	**20**	8	8. Mighty Love - Pt. 1	Atlantic 3006
6/08/74	**18**	6	9. I'm Coming Home	Atlantic 3027
8/03/74	**1**(1)	15	• 10. **Then Came You** **DIONNE WARWICKE & SPINNERS**	Atlantic 3202
10/26/74	**15**	5	11. Love Don't Love Nobody - Pt. I	Atlantic 3206
4/05/75	**37**	2	12. Living A Little, Laughing A Little	Atlantic 3252
8/30/75	**5**	13	• 13. **They Just Can't Stop It the (Games People Play)**	Atlantic 3284
1/24/76	**36**	3	14. Love Or Leave	Atlantic 3309
10/02/76	**2**(3)	17	• 15. **The Rubberband Man** above 12: produced & arranged by Thom Bell	Atlantic 3355
1/26/80	**2**(2)	16	• 16. **Working My Way Back To You/Forgive Me, Girl**	Atlantic 3637
5/24/80	**4**	14	17. **Cupid/I've Loved You For A Long Time**	Atlantic 3664

DATE	POS	WKS	ARTIST—RECORD TITLE	LABEL & NO.
			SPIRAL STARECASE	
			Sacramento pop-rock quintet featuring lead singer Pat Upton.	
5/03/69	**12**	11	1. More Today Than Yesterday	Columbia 44741
			SPIRIT	
			Los Angeles eclectic rock group: Jay Ferguson (lead singer), Mark Andes (bass), Ed Cassidy (drums), Randy California (guitar) and John Locke (keyboards). Ferguson and Andes left to form Jo Jo Gunne, mid-1971. Andes became an original member of Firefall in 1975; joined Heart in 1983.	
3/08/69	**25**	5	1. I Got A Line On You	Ode 115
			THE SPOKESMEN	
			Johnny Madara, Dave White and Roy Gilmore. White was with Danny & The Juniors.	
10/09/65	**36**	3	1. The Dawn Of Correction answer to "Eve Of Destruction"	Decca 31844
			DUSTY SPRINGFIELD	
			Born Mary O'Brien on 4/16/39 in London. Vocalist/guitarist. In The Lana Sisters vocal group. With brother Tom Springfield and Tim Feild in folk trio, The Springfields, 1960-63. Didn't record from 1973-78 except for back-up work for Anne Murray in 1975. Began recording again in 1978.	
2/15/64	**12**	7	1. I Only Want To Be With You	Philips 40162
5/02/64	**38**	2	2. Stay Awhile	Philips 40180
7/11/64	**6**	10	3. **Wishin' And Hopin'**	Philips 40207
6/04/66	**4**	10	4. **You Don't Have To Say You Love Me**	Philips 40371
10/01/66	**20**	5	5. All I See Is You	Philips 40396
4/22/67	**40**	2	6. I'll Try Anything	Philips 40439
10/14/67	**22**	5	7. The Look Of Love from the film "Casino Royale"	Philips 40465
12/14/68†	**10**	10	8. **Son-Of-A Preacher Man**	Atlantic 2580
5/24/69	**31**	4	9. The Windmills Of Your Mind	Atlantic 2623
11/29/69	**24**	9	10. A Brand New Me	Atlantic 2685
12/26/87†	**2**(2)	13	11. **What Have I Done To Deserve This?** **PET SHOP BOYS with DUSTY SPRINGFIELD**	EMI America 50107
			RICK SPRINGFIELD	
			Born on 8/23/49 in Sydney, Australia. Singer/actor/songwriter. With top Australian teen-idol band Zoot before going solo in 1972. Turned to acting in the late 70s, played Noah Drake on the TV soap opera "General Hospital" in the early 80s. Starred in the film "Hard To Hold" in 1984.	
9/02/72	**14**	9	1. Speak To The Sky	Capitol 3340
5/09/81	**1**(2)	22	● 2. **Jessie's Girl**	RCA 12201
9/12/81	**8**	12	3. **I've Done Everything For You** written by Sammy Hagar	RCA 12166
12/26/81†	**20**	10	4. Love Is Alright Tonite	RCA 13008
3/13/82	**2**(4)	16	5. **Don't Talk To Strangers**	RCA 13070
6/19/82	**21**	9	6. What Kind Of Fool Am I	RCA 13245
10/09/82	**32**	5	7. I Get Excited	RCA 13303
4/23/83	**9**	13	8. **Affair Of The Heart**	RCA 13497
7/23/83	**18**	11	9. Human Touch	RCA 13576
11/12/83	**23**	6	10. Souls	RCA 13650
3/17/84	**5**	12	11. **Love Somebody**	RCA 13738

DATE	POS	WKS	ARTIST—RECORD TITLE	LABEL & NO.
6/09/84	**26**	6	12. Don't Walk Away	RCA 13813
9/08/84	**20**	9	13. Bop 'Til You Drop above 3: from the film "Hard To Hold"	RCA 13861
12/15/84†	**27**	6	14. Bruce [N] recorded in 1978; an autobiographical song about Springfield being mistaken for Bruce Springsteen	Mercury 880405
4/20/85	**26**	6	15. Celebrate Youth	RCA 14047
7/13/85	**22**	8	16. State Of The Heart	RCA 14120
3/05/88	**22**	6	17. Rock Of Life all of above (except #3): written by Springfield	RCA 6853
			THE SPRINGFIELDS	
			English folk trio: Dusty and brother Tom Springfield and Tim Feild.	
9/01/62	**20**	6	1. Silver Threads And Golden Needles	Philips 40038
			BRUCE SPRINGSTEEN	
			Born on 9/23/49 in Freehold, New Jersey. Rock singer/songwriter/guitarist. Worked local clubs in New Jersey and Greenwich Village, mid-60s. Own E-Street Band in 1973, consisted of Clarence Clemons (saxophone), David Sancious and Danny Federici (keyboards), Gary Tallent (bass) and Vini Lopez (drums). Sancious and Lopez replaced by Roy Bittan and Max Weinberg. Miami Steve Van Zandt (guitar) joined group in 1975. Wrote Earth Band's "Blinded By The Light" and the Pointer Sisters' "Fire." After "Born To Run," a court injunction prevented the release of any new albums until 1978. Married to model/actress Julianne Phillips from 1985-89. Appeared in the 1987 film "Hail! Hail! Rock 'N' Roll." "The Boss" is America's #1 rock star of the past decade.	
10/11/75	**23**	5	1. Born To Run	Columbia 10209
7/15/78	**33**	2	2. Prove It All Night	Columbia 10763
11/08/80	**5**	14	3. **Hungry Heart**	Columbia 11391
2/21/81	**20**	6	4. Fade Away	Columbia 11431
5/26/84	**2**(4)	15	5. **Dancing In The Dark**	Columbia 04463
8/18/84	**7**	13	6. **Cover Me**	Columbia 04561
11/24/84†	**9**	11	7. **Born In The U.S.A.**	Columbia 04680
3/02/85	**6**	12	8. **I'm On Fire**	Columbia 04772
6/08/85	**5**	13	9. **Glory Days**	Columbia 04924
9/14/85	**9**	9	10. **I'm Goin' Down**	Columbia 05603
12/21/85†	**6**	9	11. **My Hometown**	Columbia 05728
			BRUCE SPRINGSTEEN & THE E STREET BAND:	
11/29/86	**8**	9	12. **War**	Columbia 06432
10/03/87	**5**	11	13. **Brilliant Disguise**	Columbia 07595
12/19/87†	**9**	11	14. **Tunnel Of Love**	Columbia 07663
3/19/88	**13**	8	15. One Step Up all of above (except #12): written by Springsteen	Columbia 07726
			SPYRO GYRA	
			Jazz-pop band formed in 1975 in Buffalo, New York. Led by saxophonist Jay Beckenstein (b: 5/14/51).	
7/28/79	**24**	8	1. Morning Dance [I]	Infinity 50011

DATE	POS	WKS	ARTIST—RECORD TITLE	LABEL & NO.
			SQUEEZE	
			English pop-rock quintet led by Chris Difford & Glenn Tilbrook. Originally known as UK Squeeze due to confusion with American band, Tight Squeeze. Paul Carrack (Ace, Mike + The Mechanics) was lead singer of fluctuating lineup in 1981.	
10/17/87	**15**	10	1. Hourglass	A&M 2967
1/23/88	**32**	5	2. 853-5937	A&M 2994
			BILLY SQUIER	
			Born on 5/12/50 in Wellesley, Massachusetts. Hard-rock singer/songwriter/guitarist.	
6/20/81	**17**	11	1. The Stroke	Capitol 5005
10/17/81	**35**	3	2. In The Dark	Capitol 5040
11/27/82	**32**	6	3. Everybody Wants You	Capitol 5163
7/14/84	**15**	12	4. Rock Me Tonite	Capitol 5370
			STACEY Q	
			Dance/disco singer from Los Angeles. Real name: Stacey Swain.	
8/16/86	**3**	13	1. **Two Of Hearts**	Atlantic 89381
2/21/87	**35**	4	2. We Connect	Atlantic 89331
			JIM STAFFORD	
			Born on 1/15/44 in Eloise, Florida. Singer/songwriter/guitarist. Own summer variety TV show in 1975, and co-host of "Those Amazing Animals" from 1980-81.	
7/14/73	**39**	1	1. Swamp Witch	MGM 14496
12/29/73†	**3**	15	● 2. **Spiders & Snakes**	MGM 14648
5/04/74	**12**	9	3. My Girl Bill [N]	MGM 14718
7/20/74	**7**	11	4. **Wildwood Weed** **[N]**	MGM 14737
1/18/75	**24**	5	5. Your Bulldog Drinks Champagne [N]	MGM 14775
9/27/75	**37**	2	6. I Got Stoned And I Missed It [N] all of above: produced by Lobo and Phil Gernhard	MGM 14819
			JO STAFFORD	
			Born on 11/12/20 in Coalinga, California. Member of Tommy Dorsey's vocal group, the Pied Pipers, 1940-42. Married to orchestra leader Paul Weston.	
10/15/55	**13**	7	1. Suddenly There's A Valley Jockey #13 / Top 100 #16 / Juke Box #18 / Best Seller #21	Columbia 40559
12/03/55†	**14**	14	2. It's Almost Tomorrow Juke Box #14 / Top 100 #19 / Jockey #20 / Best Seller #25	Columbia 40595
12/22/56	**38**	1	3. On London Bridge all of above: with Paul Weston & His Orchestra	Columbia 40782
			TERRY STAFFORD	
			Born in Hollis, Oklahoma and raised in Amarillo, Texas. Elvis Presley sound-alike.	
3/21/64	**3**	10	1. **Suspicion**	Crusader 101
6/06/64	**25**	6	2. I'll Touch A Star	Crusader 105
			STALLION	
			Denver-based quintet; Buddy Stephens, lead singer.	
4/23/77	**37**	2	1. Old Fashioned Boy (You're The One)	Casablanca 877

DATE	POS	WKS	ARTIST—RECORD TITLE	LABEL & NO.
			FRANK STALLONE	
			Philadelphia singer; brother of actor Sylvester Stallone.	
8/20/83	**10**	10	1. **Far From Over**	RSO 815023
			from the film "Staying Alive"	
			STAMPEDERS	
			Pop-rock trio from Calgary, Canada: Rick Dodson, Ronnie King and Kim Berly.	
9/11/71	**8**	10	1. **Sweet City Woman**	Bell 45120
4/03/76	**40**	2	2. Hit The Road Jack	Quality 501
			featuring a telephone conversation with Wolfman Jack	
			JOE STAMPLEY	
			Born on 6/6/43 in Springhill, Louisiana. Country singer. Leader of The Uniques.	
3/03/73	**37**	3	1. Soul Song	Dot 17442
			THE STANDELLS	
			Los Angeles-area punk-rock quartet: Dick Dodd (lead singer, drums), Larry Tamblyn and Tony Valentino (guitars) and Gary Lane (bass). Dodd was an original Mouseketeer.	
6/11/66	**11**	9	1. Dirty Water	Tower 185
			MICHAEL STANLEY BAND	
			Cleveland rock group: Michael Stanley (vocals, guitar), Kevin Raleigh (vocals, keyboards), Bob Pelander (keyboards), Tommy Dobeck (drums), Michael Gismondi (bass), Rick Bell (sax) and Gary Markashy (lead guitar; replaced by Danny Powers in 1983).	
1/10/81	**33**	5	1. He Can't Love You	EMI America 8063
11/12/83	**39**	1	2. My Town	EMI America 8178
			THE STAPLE SINGERS	
			Family soul group consisting of Roebuck "Pop" Staples (b: 12/28/15, Winoma, MS), with his son Pervis (who left in 1971) and daughters Cleotha, Yvonne, and lead singer Mavis Staples. Roebuck was a blues guitarist in his teens, later with the Golden Trumpets gospel group. Moved to Chicago in 1935. Formed own gospel group in the early 50s. First recorded for United in 1953. Mavis recorded solo, early 70s.	
3/20/71	**27**	5	1. Heavy Makes You Happy (Sha-Na-Boom Boom)	Stax 0083
11/13/71	**12**	10	2. Respect Yourself	Stax 0104
4/15/72	**1**(1)	14	3. **I'll Take You There**	Stax 0125
8/26/72	**38**	3	4. This World	Stax 0137
4/14/73	**33**	3	5. Oh La De Da	Stax 0156
11/10/73	**9**	11	• 6. **If You're Ready (Come Go With Me)**	Stax 0179
3/23/74	**23**	7	7. Touch A Hand, Make A Friend	Stax 0196
11/01/75	**1**(1)	12	• 8. **Let's Do It Again**	Curtom 0109
			from the film of the same title	
			CYRIL STAPLETON	
			Born on 12/31/14 in Nottingham, England; died on 2/25/74. British bandleader. BBC showband maestro, 1952-57.	
9/29/56	**25**	2	1. The Italian Theme [I]	London 1672
1/19/59	**13**	10	2. The Children's Marching Song [N]	London 1851
			with the children from the film "The Inn Of The Sixth Happiness"	

DATE	POS	WKS	ARTIST—RECORD TITLE	LABEL & NO.
			STARBUCK	
			Atlanta pop-rock septet; Bruce Blackman, lead singer.	
5/29/76	**3**	14	1. **Moonlight Feels Right**	Private S. 45039
5/21/77	**38**	2	2. Everybody Be Dancin'	Private S. 45144
			BUDDY STARCHER	
			Born on 3/16/10 in Ripley, West Virginia. Worked on WFBR-Baltimore in 1928. Worked as a DJ on WCAU, WIBG-Philadelphia. Own band from 1937. Manager of WNBM-Miami.	
5/14/66	**39**	1	1. History Repeats Itself [S]	Boone 1038
			STARGARD	
			Disco trio: Rochelle Runnells, Debra Anderson and Janice Williams. Appeared as "The Diamonds" in film "Sgt. Pepper's Lonely Hearts Club Band."	
3/04/78	**21**	7	1. Theme Song From "Which Way Is Up" from the film of the same title	MCA 40825
			STARLAND VOCAL BAND	
			Pop quartet: Bill and wife Taffy Danoff, John Carroll and Margot Chapman. Bill and Taffy had fronted Fat City folk quintet. Bill co-wrote "Take Me Home, Country Roads" with friend, John Denver. Denver owned Windsong record label. Won the 1976 Best New Artist Grammy Award.	
6/05/76	**1**(2)	14	• 1. **Afternoon Delight**	Windsong 10588
			THE STARLETS	
			Female R&B group from Chicago. Dynetta Boone ("Liz Walker"), lead singer. Although record label listed The Blue-Belles, The Starlets actually recorded "I Sold My Heart To The Junkman." Also see Patti LaBelle & The Blue Belles.	
6/12/61	**38**	2	1. Better Tell Him No	Pam 1003
			STARPOINT	
			Black sextet from Maryland: brothers Ernest, George, Orlando and Gregory Phillips, with Renee Diggs and Kayode Adeyemo. Formed as Lycindiana, did session work for Motown and All-Platinum Records.	
11/16/85	**25**	9	1. Object Of My Desire	Elektra 69621
			BRENDA K. STARR	
			Real name: Brenda Kaplan. Singer/film actress from New York City of Puerto Rican heritage. Daughter of Harvey Kaplan (member of Spiral Staircase).	
5/07/88	**13**	12	1. I Still Believe	MCA 53288
9/03/88	**24**	7	2. What You See Is What You Get	MCA 53367
			EDWIN STARR	
			Born Charles Hatcher on 1/21/42 in Nashville; raised in Cleveland. Brother of singers Roger and Willie Hatcher. In vocal group, the Futuretones; recorded for Tress in 1957. With Bill Doggett Combo from 1963-65.	
9/04/65	**21**	6	1. Agent Double-O-Soul	Ric-Tic 103
3/22/69	**6**	9	2. **Twenty-Five Miles**	Gordy 7083
7/25/70	**1**(3)	13	3. **War**	Gordy 7101
1/02/71	**26**	4	4. Stop The War Now	Gordy 7104

DATE	POS	WKS	ARTIST—RECORD TITLE	LABEL & NO.
			KAY STARR	
			Born Katherine Starks on 7/21/22 in Dougherty, Oklahoma. With Joe Venuti's orchestra at age 15, and sang briefly with Glenn Miller, Charlie Barnet and Bob Crosby before launching solo career.	
8/06/55	**17**	1	1. Good And Lonesome Juke Box #17	RCA 6146
1/07/56	**1**(6)	20	2. **Rock And Roll Waltz** Juke Box #1(6) / Top 100 #1(4) / Best Seller #1(1) / Jockey #1(1)	RCA 6359
6/30/56	**40**	1	3. Second Fiddle	RCA 6541
9/16/57	**9**	10	4. **My Heart Reminds Me** Jockey #9 / Top 100 #53	RCA 6981
			RANDY STARR	
			Born Warren Nadel on 7/2/30 in New York City. Pop singer/songwriter/guitarist. Member of instrumental duo The Islanders.	
5/06/57	**32**	2	1. After School	Dale 100
			RINGO STARR	
			Born Richard Starkey on 7/7/40 in Liverpool, England. Ringo joined The Beatles following ousting of drummer Pete Best in 1962. First solo album in 1970. Films "Candy" (made in 1967, released in 1969), "The Magic Christian," "200 Motels," "Born To Boogie," "Blindman," "That'll Be The Day" and "Cave Man." Married actress Barbara Bach in 1982.	
5/08/71	**4**	11	● 1. **It Don't Come Easy**	Apple 1831
4/15/72	**9**	7	2. **Back Off Boogaloo** above 2: written by Ringo; produced by George Harrison	Apple 1849
10/20/73	**1**(1)	12	● 3. **Photograph** written by Ringo & George Harrison	Apple 1865
12/29/73†	**1**(1)	12	● 4. **You're Sixteen**	Apple 1870
3/23/74	**5**	11	5. **Oh My My**	Apple 1872
11/30/74†	**6**	10	6. **Only You**	Apple 1876
2/22/75	**3**	10	7. **No No Song**	Apple 1880
7/05/75	**31**	3	8. It's All Down To Goodnight Vienna written by John Lennon	Apple 1882
10/16/76	**26**	6	9. A Dose Of Rock 'N' Roll	Atlantic 3361
12/05/81	**38**	2	10. Wrack My Brain written and produced by George Harrison	Boardwalk 130
			STARS on 45	
			Dutch session vocalists and musicians assembled by producer Jaap Eggermont.	
5/02/81	**1**(1)	14	● 1. **Stars on 45** Venus/Sugar Sugar/No Reply/I'll Be Back/Drive My Car/Do You Want To Know A Secret/We Can Work It Out/I Should Have Known Better/Nowhere Man/You're Going To Lose That Girl	Radio 3810
4/17/82	**28**	5	2. Stars on 45 III Uptight Everything's All Right/My Cherie Amour/Yester Me, Yester You/Master Blaster/You Are The Sunshine Of My Life/Isn't She Lovely/Sir Duke/I Wish/I Was Made To Love Her/Superstition/Fingertips	Radio 4019

Hayley Mills' "Ching Ching And A Ding Ding Ding" never managed an appearance in the Hot 100 despite its memorable name. However, the Disney star's "Let's Get Together" from the film *The Parent Trap* hit the top 10 in 1961, and her "Johnny Jingo" reached No. 21 the following year.

Stephanie Mills' initial claim to fame came via her role as Dorothy in Broadway's *The Wiz*, a part she played for five years.

Ronnie Milsap's 1984 single "She Loves My Car" struck some fans as unusual if only for its title; this country artist has been blind since birth.

Sal Mineo's "Start Movin' (In My Direction)" was the biggest single in the well-known actor's career. Between 1957 and 1958, Mineo also charted with "Love Affair," "Lasting Love," "You Shouldn't Do That," "Party Time," and "Little Pigeon."

Kylie Minogue, originally the petite star of the Australian soap opera "Neighbours," sailed to No. 3 in 1988 with a remake of "The Loco-Motion," a 1962 No. 1 record by an equally diminutive pop vocalist—Little Eva.

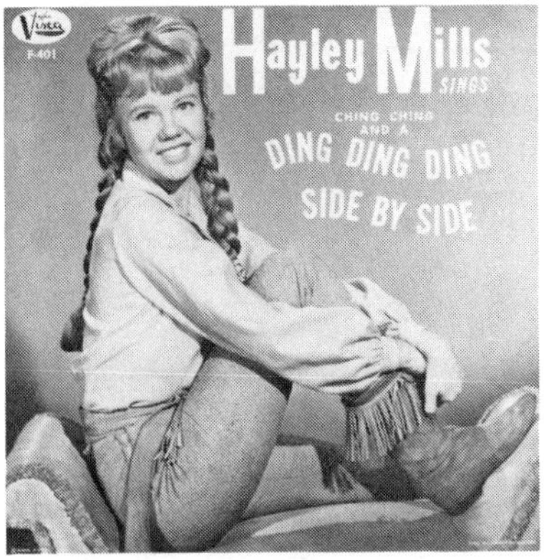

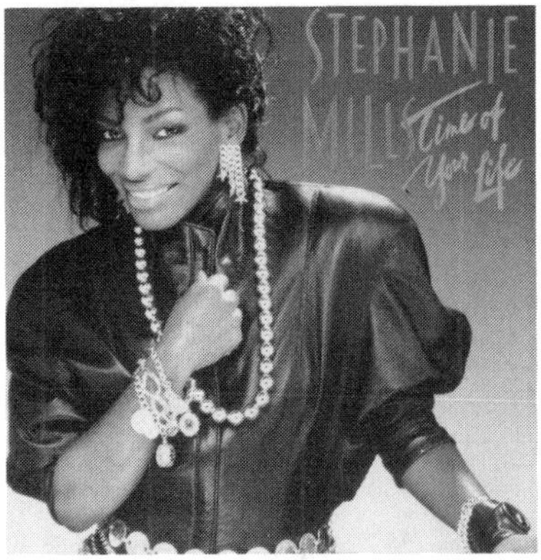

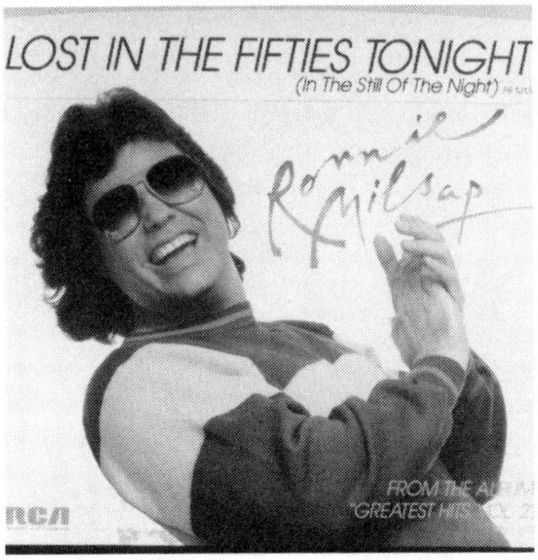

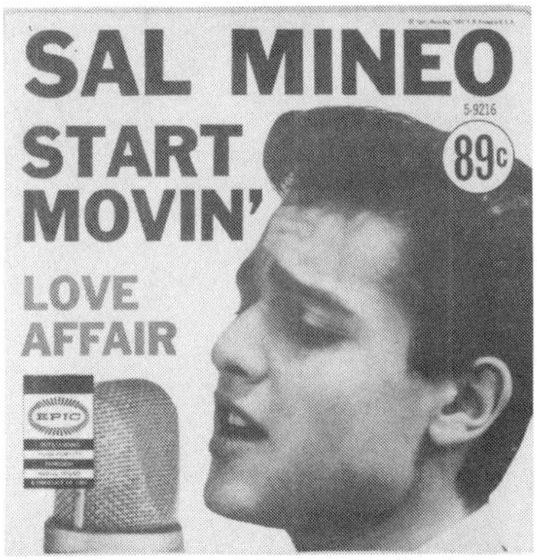

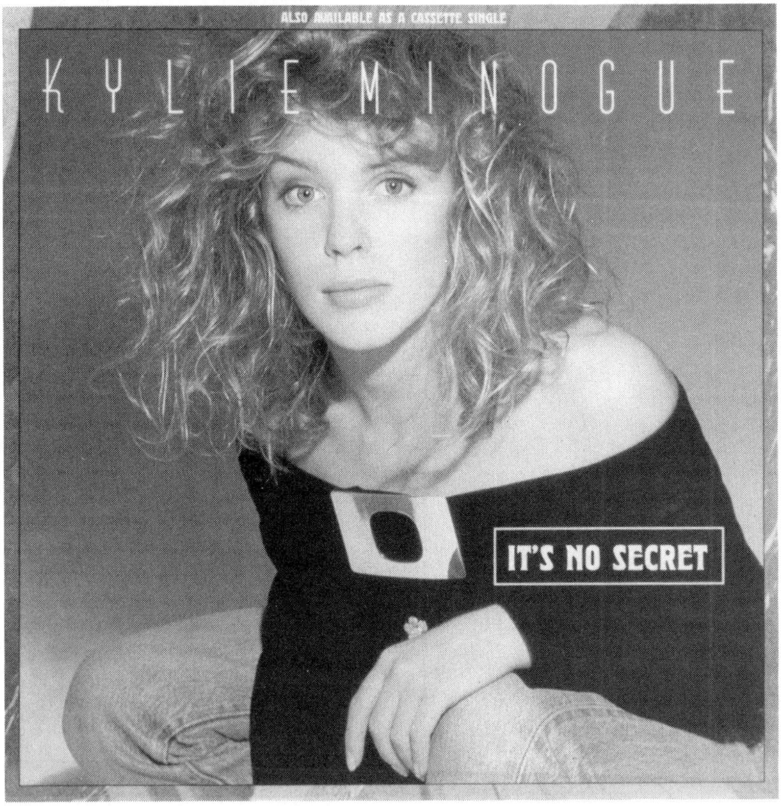

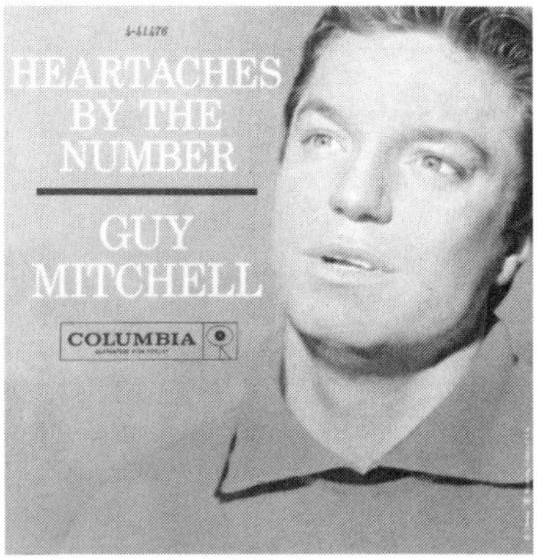

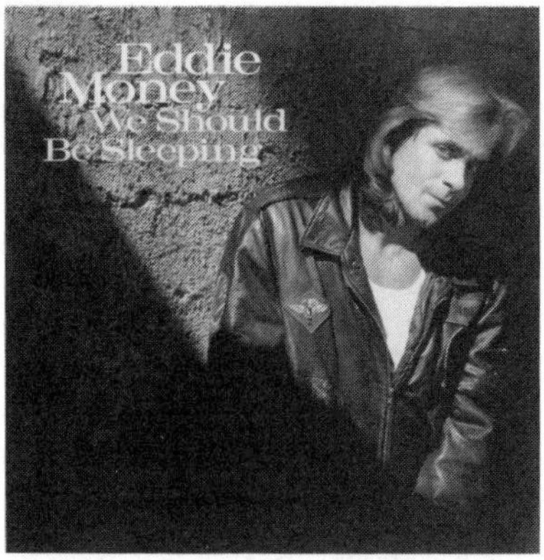

Guy Mitchell may not be remembered as the star of the short-lived TV detective series "Whispering Smith." Yet Mitchell recorded the fourth biggest song of the years 1955–88, a 1956 remake of Marty Robbins' "Singing The Blues" that stayed at No. 1 for 10 weeks.

Eddie Money was on his way to becoming a policeman like his father, but he dropped out of the academy, changed his name, and made rock 'n' roll his new beat. In his career, Money has copped five Top-40 singles. "Take Me Home Tonight," which hit No. 4, featured vocals by Ronnie Spector.

The Moody Blues charted highest with a song from their *Days Of Future Passed* album: "Nights in White Satin," which spent seven weeks in the top 10, peaking at No. 2. It was also a Hit Of Albums Passed, since *Days Of Future Passed* had been released fully five years earlier.

Motley Crue brought some of the glitter back to rock 'n' roll, emulating their mascara-ed idols from the early 70s. At a time when Kiss decided to take off their makeup, Motley Crue was just starting to smear it on.

Michael Martin Murphey's 1972 Top-40 hit "Geronimo's Cadillac" was covered by two double-threat recording-and-movie stars, Hoyt Axton and Cher. In 1981, Murphey appeared on the silver screen himself, in the film based on the Johnny Paycheck song "Take This Job And Shove It."

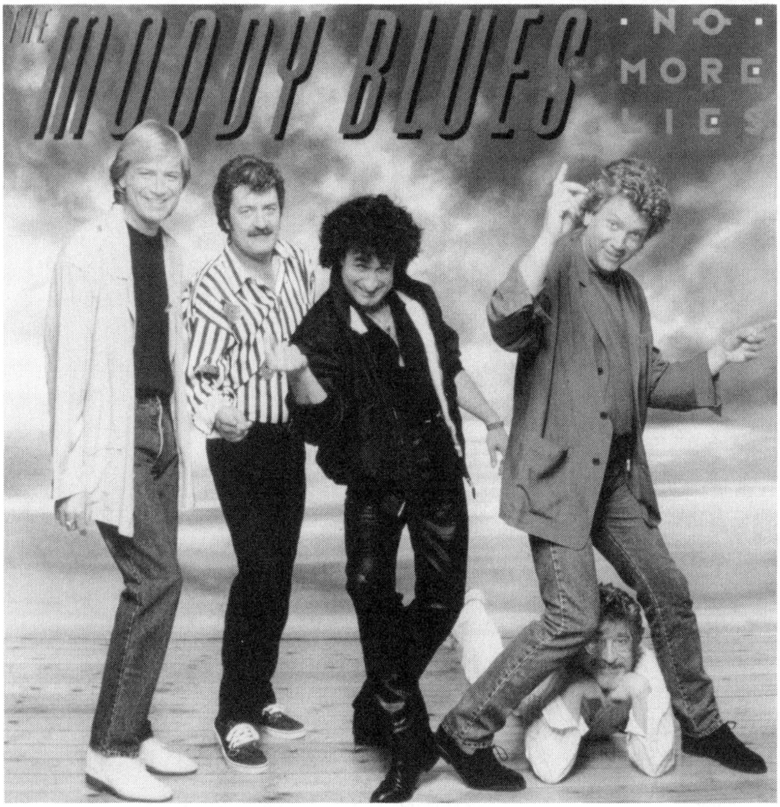

DATE	POS	WKS	ARTIST—RECORD TITLE	LABEL & NO.
			STARSHIP - see JEFFERSON STARSHIP	
			STARZ	
			New York-based rock quintet: Michael Lee Smith (lead singer), Peter Sweval (bassist), Richie Ranno (guitar), Brenden Harkin (guitar) and Joe X. Dube (drums).	
4/30/77	**33**	2	1. Cherry Baby	Capitol 4399
			THE STATLER BROTHERS	
			Country vocal quartet from Staunton, Virginia. Consisted of brothers Harold & Don Reid, Phil Balsley and Lew DeWitt (replaced by Jimmy Fortune in 1983).	
12/11/65†	**4**	9	1. **Flowers On The Wall**	Columbia 43315
			CANDI STATON	
			Born in Hanceville, Alabama. Sang with the Jewel Gospel Trio from age 10. Went solo in 1968. Married for a time to Clarence Carter.	
10/03/70	**24**	9	1. Stand By Your Man	Fame 1472
6/26/76	**20**	11	2. Young Hearts Run Free	Warner 8181
			THE STATUS QUO	
			English rock quintet: Francis Rossi, Rick Parfitt, Roy Lynes, John Coghlan and Alan Lancaster.	
6/29/68	**12**	11	1. Pictures Of Matchstick Men	Cadet Con. 7001
			STEALERS WHEEL	
			English group led by Gerry Rafferty (vocals, guitar) & Joe Egan (vocals, keyboards).	
3/31/73	**6**	13	1. **Stuck In The Middle With You**	A&M 1416
3/09/74	**29**	3	2. Star	A&M 1483
			STEAM	
			New York City studio group assembled by producer Paul Leka.	
11/08/69	**1**(2)	13	● 1. **Na Na Hey Hey Kiss Him Goodbye**	Fontana 1667
			STEEL BREEZE	
			Ric Jacobs, lead singer of 6-man pop band from California.	
9/18/82	**16**	11	1. You Don't Want Me Anymore	RCA 13283
2/19/83	**30**	6	2. Dreamin' Is Easy	RCA 13427
			STEELY DAN	
			Los Angeles-based pop/jazz-styled group formed by Donald Fagen (keyboards, vocals) and Walter Becker (bass, vocals). Group, primarily known as a studio unit, featured Fagen and Becker with various studio musicians. Duo went their separate ways, 1981.	
12/30/72†	**6**	11	1. **Do It Again**	ABC 11338
4/07/73	**11**	11	2. Reeling In The Years	ABC 11352
6/08/74	**4**	11	3. **Rikki Don't Lose That Number**	ABC 11439
6/21/75	**37**	2	4. Black Friday	ABC 12101
1/07/78	**11**	11	5. Peg	ABC 12320
5/06/78	**19**	8	6. Deacon Blues	ABC 12355
7/01/78	**22**	5	7. FM (No Static At All) from the film "FM"	MCA 40894
9/23/78	**26**	5	8. Josie	ABC 12404
12/13/80†	**10**	13	9. **Hey Nineteen**	MCA 51036

DATE	POS	WKS	ARTIST—RECORD TITLE	LABEL & NO.
3/28/81	**22**	7	10. Time Out Of Mind all of above: written by Fagen & Becker and produced by Gary Katz	MCA 51082
			LOU STEIN	
			Born on 4/22/22 in Philadelphia. Pianist with Ray McKinley, 1941-42 & 1946-47. Studio and free-lance musician into the 70s.	
3/30/57	**31**	3	1. Almost Paradise [I] with Bill Fontaine's orchestra	RKO Unique 385
			JIM STEINMAN	
			Born in New York City. Wrote, arranged all cuts on Meat Loaf's "Bat Out Of Hell" LP.	
7/18/81	**32**	6	1. Rock And Roll Dreams Come Through featured vocal: Rory Dodd	Epic 02111
			VAN STEPHENSON	
			Pop singer/songwriter from Nashville.	
5/12/84	**22**	10	1. Modern Day Delilah	MCA 52376
			STEPPENWOLF	
			Hard-rock quintet formed in Los Angeles in 1967. Original lineup: John Kay (born Joachim Krauledat on 4/12/44 in Tilsit, East Germany), vocals, guitar; Michael Monarch, guitar; Goldy McJohn, keyboards; Nick St. Nicholas, bass; Mars Bonfire (Dennis Edmonton), guitar, and brother Jerry Edmonton, drums. All but Monarch were members of the Canadian group Sparrow. Many personnel changes except for Kay.	
7/20/68	**2**(3)	12	● 1. **Born To Be Wild**	Dunhill 4138
10/26/68	**3**	13	● 2. **Magic Carpet Ride**	Dunhill 4161
3/15/69	**10**	8	3. **Rock Me**	Dunhill 4182
9/06/69	**31**	5	4. Move Over	Dunhill 4205
2/07/70	**39**	1	5. Monster	Dunhill 4221
5/09/70	**35**	3	6. Hey Lawdy Mama all of above: produced by Gabriel Mekler	Dunhill 4234
10/05/74	**29**	3	7. Straight Shootin' Woman	Mums 6031
			THE STEREOS	
			R&B quintet from Steubenville, Ohio. Originally called the Buckeyes. Consisted of Bruce Robinson (lead), Nathaniel Hicks, Sam Profit, George Otis and Ronnie Collins.	
10/16/61	**29**	3	1. I Really Love You	Cub 9095
			STEVE & EYDIE - see STEVE LAWRENCE and/or EYDIE GORME	
			APRIL STEVENS - see NINO TEMPO	
			CAT STEVENS	
			Born Steven Georgiou on 7/21/47 in London. Began career playing folk music at Hammersmith College in 1966. Contracted tuberculosis in 1968, and spent over a year recuperating. Adopted new style when he re-emerged. Lived in Brazil in the mid-70s. Converted to Muslim religion in late 1979, took name "Yusef Islam."	
3/06/71	**11**	10	1. Wild World	A&M 1231
7/10/71	**30**	7	2. Moon Shadow	A&M 1265
10/09/71	**7**	10	3. **Peace Train**	A&M 1291
4/22/72	**6**	11	4. **Morning Has Broken**	A&M 1335
12/02/72†	**16**	9	5. Sitting	A&M 1396

DATE	POS	WKS	ARTIST—RECORD TITLE	LABEL & NO.
8/04/73	**31**	5	6. The Hurt	A&M 1418
4/20/74	**10**	11	7. **Oh Very Young**	A&M 1503
8/24/74	**6**	9	8. **Another Saturday Night**	A&M 1602
1/11/75	**26**	4	9. Ready	A&M 1645
8/16/75	**33**	4	10. Two Fine People	A&M 1700
7/23/77	**33**	3	11. (Remember The Days Of The) Old Schoolyard	A&M 1948
			CONNIE STEVENS	
			Born Concetta Ingolia on 4/8/38 in Brooklyn. Played Cricket Blake on TV's "Hawaiian Eye" from 1959-63. Appeared in the films "Eighteen And Anxious," "Rockabye Baby," "Parrish," "Never Too Late" and others.	
4/27/59	**4**	11	1. **Kookie, Kookie (Lend Me Your Comb)** **[N]** **EDWARD BYRNES & CONNIE STEVENS**	Warner 5047
3/14/60	**3**	17	2. **Sixteen Reasons**	Warner 5137
			DODIE STEVENS	
			Born Geraldine Pasquale on 2/17/46 in Chicago; raised in California.	
3/09/59	**3**	14	1. **Pink Shoe Laces**	Crystalette 724
			RAY STEVENS	
			Born Ray Ragsdale on 1/24/41 in Clarkdale, Georgia. Attended Georgia State University, studied music theory and composition. Production work, mid-60s. Numerous appearances on Andy Williams TV show, late 60s. Own TV show in summer of 1970. Featured on "Music Country" TV show, 1973-74. The #1 novelty recording artist of the rock era.	
9/18/61	**35**	1	1. Jeremiah Peabody's Poly Unsaturated Quick Dissolving Fast Acting Pleasant Tasting Green And Purple Pills [N]	Mercury 71843
7/14/62	**5**	9	2. **Ahab, The Arab** **[N]**	Mercury 71966
6/29/63	**17**	6	3. Harry The Hairy Ape [N]	Mercury 72125
8/31/68	**28**	3	4. Mr. Businessman	Monument 1083
4/26/69	**8**	10	● 5. **Gitarzan** **[N]**	Monument 1131
7/26/69	**27**	4	6. Along Came Jones [N]	Monument 1150
4/18/70	**1**(2)	13	● 7. **Everything Is Beautiful**	Barnaby 2011
4/27/74	**1**(3)	12	● 8. **The Streak** **[N]**	Barnaby 600
5/24/75	**14**	10	9. Misty	Barnaby 614
2/05/77	**40**	1	10. In The Mood [N] **HENHOUSE FIVE PLUS TOO**	Warner 8301
			B.W. STEVENSON	
			Born Louis Stevenson on 10/5/49 in Dallas; died on 4/28/88, after heart surgery.	
8/25/73	**9**	12	1. **My Maria**	RCA 0030
			AL STEWART	
			Born on 9/5/45 in Glasgow, Scotland. Pop-rock singer/composer/guitarist.	
1/22/77	**8**	10	1. **Year Of The Cat** written about British comedian Tony Hancock	Janus 266
10/21/78	**7**	13	2. **Time Passages**	Arista 0362
2/17/79	**29**	4	3. Song On The Radio above 3: produced by Alan Parsons	Arista 0389
9/27/80	**24**	6	4. Midnight Rocks	Arista 0552

DATE	POS	WKS	ARTIST—RECORD TITLE	LABEL & NO.
			AMII STEWART	
			Born in Washington, DC in 1956. Disco singer/dancer/actress. In the Broadway musical "Bubbling Brown Sugar."	
2/24/79	**1**(1)	14	▲ 1. **Knock On Wood**	Ariola 7736
			BILLY STEWART	
			Born on 3/24/37 in Washington, DC; died in an auto accident on 1/17/70. R&B vocalist/composer/keyboardist. Discovered by Bo Diddley in 1956. First recorded for Chess/Argo in 1956. Nicknamed "Fat Boy."	
5/01/65	**26**	4	1. I Do Love You	Chess 1922
7/10/65	**24**	5	2. Sitting In The Park	Chess 1932
8/06/66	**10**	7	3. **Summertime** from the musical "Porgy & Bess"	Chess 1966
11/05/66	**29**	5	4. Secret Love revival of Doris Day's 1954 hit (POS 1)	Chess 1978
			JERMAINE STEWART	
			Chicago-bred singer. Former dancer on TV's "Soul Train." Worked as back-up vocalist for Shalamar and Boy George.	
6/28/86	**5**	13	1. **We Don't Have To Take Our Clothes Off**	Arista 9424
4/16/88	**27**	5	2. Say It Again	Arista 9636
			JOHN STEWART	
			Born on 9/5/39 in San Diego. Member of the Kingston Trio from 1961-67. Wrote "Daydream Believer."	
6/02/79	**5**	13	1. **Gold**	RSO 931
9/29/79	**28**	5	2. Midnight Wind above 2: backing vocals by Stevie Nicks & Lindsey Buckingham	RSO 1000
1/26/80	**34**	4	3. Lost Her In The Sun	RSO 1016
			ROD STEWART	
			Born on 1/10/45 in London. Worked as a folksinger in Europe, early 60s. Recorded for English Decca in 1964. With the Hoochie Coochie Men, Steampacket and Shotgun Express. Joined Jeff Beck Group, 1967-69. With Faces from 1969-75, also recorded solo during this time. Left Faces in December, 1975.	
8/28/71	**1**(5)	15	● 1. **Maggie May**	Mercury 73224
11/27/71	**24**	6	2. (I Know) I'm Losing You	Mercury 73244
			ROD STEWART with FACES	
9/16/72	**13**	7	3. You Wear It Well	Mercury 73330
12/16/72	**40**	1	4. Angel	Mercury 73344
10/23/76	**1**(8)	17	● 5. **Tonight's The Night (Gonna Be Alright)**	Warner 8262
2/26/77	**21**	9	6. The First Cut Is The Deepest written by Cat Stevens	Warner 8321
7/02/77	**30**	4	7. The Killing Of Georgie (Part I & II)	Warner 8396
11/26/77†	**4**	15	● 8. **You're In My Heart (The Final Acclaim)**	Warner 8475
3/11/78	**28**	4	9. Hot Legs	Warner 8535
5/27/78	**22**	6	10. I Was Only Joking	Warner 8568
12/23/78†	**1**(4)	18	▲ 11. **Da Ya Think I'm Sexy?**	Warner 8724
5/12/79	**22**	6	12. Ain't Love A Bitch	Warner 8810
11/29/80†	**5**	17	13. **Passion**	Warner 49617
10/31/81	**5**	15	14. **Young Turks**	Warner 49843
2/13/82	**20**	8	15. Tonight I'm Yours (Don't Hurt Me)	Warner 49886

DATE	POS	WKS	ARTIST—RECORD TITLE	LABEL & NO.
6/11/83	**14**	9	16. Baby Jane	Warner 29608
10/01/83	**35**	3	17. What Am I Gonna Do (I'm So In Love With You)	Warner 29564
6/02/84	**6**	13	18. **Infatuation**	Warner 29256
9/15/84	**10**	10	19. **Some Guys Have All The Luck**	Warner 29215
6/14/86	**6**	12	20. **Love Touch** theme from the film "Legal Eagles"	Warner 28668
6/04/88	**12**	9	21. Lost In You	Warner 27927
9/10/88	**12**	10	22. Forever Young	Warner 27796
			SANDY STEWART	
			Born Sandra Galitz on 7/10/37 in Philadelphia. Regular on the Eddie Fisher and Perry Como TV shows.	
1/12/63	**20**	5	1. My Coloring Book	Colpix 669
			STEPHEN STILLS	
			Born on 1/3/45 in Dallas. Member of Buffalo Springfield and Crosby, Stills & Nash.	
12/19/70†	**14**	10	1. Love The One You're With	Atlantic 2778
3/27/71	**37**	2	2. Sit Yourself Down	Atlantic 2790
			STING	
			Born Gordon Sumner on 10/2/51 in Wallsend, England. Lead singer/bass guitarist of the Police. In the films "Quadrophenia," "Dune," "The Bride," "Plenty" and others. Nicknamed Sting because of a yellow and black jersey he liked to wear.	
6/15/85	**3**	14	1. **If You Love Somebody Set Them Free**	A&M 2738
9/07/85	**8**	11	2. **Fortress Around Your Heart**	A&M 2767
11/23/85	**17**	9	3. Love Is The Seventh Wave	A&M 2787
2/01/86	**16**	8	4. Russians	A&M 2799
10/24/87	**7**	12	5. **We'll Be Together**	A&M 2983
2/06/88	**15**	8	6. Be Still My Beating Heart	A&M 2992
			GARY STITES	
			Born on 7/23/40 in Denver. Pop singer/songwriter/guitarist.	
5/18/59	**24**	5	1. Lonely For You	Carlton 508
			MORRIS STOLOFF	
			Born on 8/1/98 in Philadelphia; died on 4/16/80. Composer/conductor/violinist. Became musical director for Columbia Pictures in 1936. Winner of 3 Academy Awards.	
4/21/56	**1**(3)	22	1. **Moonglow and Theme From "Picnic"** **[I]** Jockey #1 / Best Seller #2 / Top 100 #2 / Juke Box #4 with the Columbia Pictures Orchestra; from the film "Picnic"; 4 top 10 versions of "Moonglow" charted in 1934	Decca 29888
			STONE PONEYS - see LINDA RONSTADT	
			CLIFFIE STONE	
			Born Clifford Snyder on 3/1/17 in Burbank, California. Bass player/orchestra and square dance band leader. Worked with the Anson Weeks and Freddie Slack bands in the late 30s. Became a country DJ in the mid-40s. Songwriter of many country songs.	
8/13/55	**14**	4	1. The Popcorn Song [N] Juke Box #14 / Best Seller #25 vocal: Bob Roubian	Capitol 3131

DATE	POS	WKS	ARTIST—RECORD TITLE	LABEL & NO.
			THE KIRBY STONE FOUR	
			Kirby Stone (b: 4/27/18 in New York City), Eddie Hall, Larry Foster and Mike Gardner. Kirby was musical director for various TV shows.	
7/28/58	**25**	1	1. Baubles, Bangles And Beads Jockey #25 end / Hot 100 #50 with Jimmy Carroll's orchestra; from Broadway's "Kismet"	Columbia 41183
			STONEBOLT	
			Pacific Northwest pop-rock quintet; David Wills, lead singer.	
9/30/78	**29**	5	1. I Will Still Love You	Parachute 512
			PAUL STOOKEY	
			Born on 11/30/37 in Baltimore. Paul of Peter, Paul & Mary.	
9/04/71	**24**	9	1. Wedding Song (There Is Love)	Warner 7511
			STORIES	
			New York rock quartet: Ian Lloyd (lead singer, bass), Michael Brown (founding member of Left Banke; keyboards), Steve Love (guitar) and Bryan Madey (drums). Brown left group in 1973, replaced by Ken Aaronson (bass) and Ken Bichel (keyboards).	
7/14/73	**1**(2)	15	● 1. **Brother Louie**	Kama Sutra 577
			BILLY STORM	
			Born on 6/29/38 in Dayton, Ohio. Lead singer of The Valiants.	
5/18/59	**28**	6	1. I've Come Of Age	Columbia 41356
			GALE STORM	
			Born Josephine Cottle on 4/5/22 in Bloomington, Texas. Moved to Hollywood in 1939, leading lady in films during the 40s and early 50s. Own TV series "My Little Margie" from 1952-55, also "The Gale Storm Show," 1956-62.	
10/22/55	**2**(3)	17	1. **I Hear You Knocking** Top 100 #2 / Juke Box #2 / Best Seller #3 / Jockey #4	Dot 15412
12/24/55†	**6**	12	2. **Teen Age Prayer/** Jockey #6 / Juke Box #6 / Top 100 #9 / Best Seller #13	
12/31/55†	**5**	9	3. Memories Are Made Of This Jockey #5 / Top 100 #16	Dot 15436
3/03/56	**9**	14	4. **Why Do Fools Fall In Love** Jockey #9 / Juke Box #14 / Best Seller #15 / Top 100 #15	Dot 15448
5/05/56	**6**	14	5. **Ivory Tower** Jockey #6 / Juke Box #6 / Top 100 #10 / Best Seller #15	Dot 15458
4/29/57	**4**	18	6. **Dark Moon** Juke Box #4 end / Top 100 #5 / Best Seller #6 / Jockey #6	Dot 15558
			THE STRANGELOVES	
			Writers/producers Bob Feldman, Jerry Goldstein and Richard Gottehrer. Team wrote and produced the Angels' "My Boyfriends Back," also produced McCoys' "Hang On Sloopy." Gottehrer became a partner in Sire Records, and produced the Go-Go's' first 2 albums and Blondie's debut album.	
7/10/65	**11**	8	1. I Want Candy	Bang 501
10/23/65	**39**	1	2. Cara-Lin	Bang 508
2/05/66	**30**	4	3. Night Time	Bang 514

DATE	POS	WKS	ARTIST—RECORD TITLE	LABEL & NO.
			STRAWBERRY ALARM CLOCK	
			West Coast psychedelic rock sextet: Ed King (lead guitar), Mark Weitz (keyboards), Lee Freeman (guitar), Gary Lovetro (bass), George Bunnel (bass) and Randy Seol (drums). King joined Lynyrd Skynyrd, 1973-75. Originally known as the Sixpence.	
10/14/67	**1**(1)	14	• 1. **Incense And Peppermints**	Uni 55018
			lead vocal: Greg Munford (16-year-old leader of L.A. band the Shapes)	
1/27/68	**23**	6	2. Tomorrow	Uni 55046
			STRAY CATS	
			Long Island, New York rockabilly trio: Brian Setzer (b: 4/10/60; lead singer, guitar), Lee Rocker (born Leon Drucher; string bass) and Slim Jim Phantom (born Jim McDonell; drums). Group disbanded in 1985; reunited in 1988. Setzer portrayed Eddie Cochran in the film "La Bamba."	
10/23/82	**9**	13	1. **Rock This Town**	EMI America 8132
1/08/83	**3**	14	2. **Stray Cat Strut**	EMI America 8122
			originally "Bubbled Under" for 6 weeks beginning 7/17/82	
8/20/83	**5**	12	3. **(She's) Sexy + 17**	EMI America 8168
12/03/83	**35**	3	4. I Won't Stand In Your Way	EMI America 8185
			STREET PEOPLE	
			Studio group; Rupert Holmes, member.	
2/21/70	**36**	5	1. Jennifer Tomkins	Musicor 1365
			BARBRA STREISAND	
			Born Barbara Joan Streisand on 4/24/42 in Brooklyn. Made Broadway debut in "I Can Get It For You Wholesale," 1962. Lead role in Broadway's "Funny Girl," 1964. Film debut in "Funny Girl," 1968 (tied with Katharine Hepburn for Best Actress Oscar), also starred in "A Star Is Born," "Hello Dolly," "Funny Lady," "The Way We Were" and many others. Produced, directed, starred and co-wrote the 1983 film "Yentl."	
5/23/64	**5**	12	1. **People**	Columbia 42965
			from Broadway's "Funny Girl"	
1/22/66	**32**	3	2. Second Hand Rose	Columbia 43469
12/12/70†	**6**	12	3. **Stoney End**	Columbia 45236
8/28/71	**40**	1	4. Where You Lead	Columbia 45414
8/12/72	**37**	4	5. Sweet Inspiration/Where You Lead	Columbia 45626
12/22/73†	**1**(3)	17	• 6. **The Way We Were**	Columbia 45944
			from the film of the same title	
1/08/77	**1**(3)	18	• 7. **Evergreen**	Columbia 10450
			love theme from the film "A Star Is Born"	
5/28/77	**4**	14	8. **My Heart Belongs To Me**	Columbia 10555
7/01/78	**25**	5	9. Songbird	Columbia 10756
8/26/78	**21**	6	10. Love Theme From "Eyes Of Laura Mars" (Prisoner)	Columbia 10777
			from the film "Eyes Of Laura Mars"	
11/04/78	**1**(2)	15	• 11. **You Don't Bring Me Flowers**	Columbia 10840
			BARBRA STREISAND & NEIL DIAMOND	
7/07/79	**3**	13	• 12. **The Main Event/Fight**	Columbia 11008
			from the film "The Main Event"	
10/27/79	**1**(2)	13	• 13. **No More Tears (Enough Is Enough)**	Columbia 11125
			BARBRA STREISAND/DONNA SUMMER	
2/23/80	**37**	3	14. Kiss Me In The Rain	Columbia 11179

DATE	POS	WKS	ARTIST—RECORD TITLE	LABEL & NO.
9/13/80	**1**(3)	19	● 15. **Woman In Love**	Columbia 11364
11/15/80†	**3**	15	● 16. **Guilty**	Columbia 11390
			BARBRA STREISAND & BARRY GIBB	
2/14/81	**10**	10	17. **What Kind Of Fool**	Columbia 11430
			BARBRA STREISAND & BARRY GIBB	
11/28/81†	**11**	11	18. Comin' In And Out Of Your Life	Columbia 02621
12/10/83	**40**	2	19. The Way He Makes Me Feel	Columbia 04177
			from the film "Yentl"	
11/12/88	**25**	5	20. Till I Loved You	Columbia 08062
			BARBRA STREISAND & DON JOHNSON	
			love theme from "Goya"	
			THE STRING-A-LONGS	
			Instrumental quintet: Keith McCormack, Aubrey Lee de Cordova, Richard Stephens & Jimmy Torres (guitars), and Don Allen (drums).	
1/23/61	**3**	13	1. **Wheels** **[I]**	Warwick 603
4/17/61	**35**	2	2. Brass Buttons [I]	Warwick 625
			BARRETT STRONG	
			Born on 2/5/41 in Mississippi. R&B singer/songwriter. Wrote many of The Temptations' hits with Norman Whitfield, including "Just My Imagination," "Papa Was A Rollin' Stone," "Ball Of Confusion" and "Cloud Nine."	
3/21/60	**23**	8	1. Money (That's What I Want)	Anna 1111
			JUD STRUNK	
			Born Justin Strunk, Jr. on 6/11/36 in Jamestown, New York. Regular on TV's "Laugh In." Killed in a plane crash on 10/15/81.	
3/24/73	**14**	10	1. Daisy A Day	MGM 14463
			STRYPER	
			Christian heavy-metal band from Orange County, California: Michael Sweet (vocals), Robert Sweet, Oz Fox and Tim Gaines.	
12/26/87†	**23**	8	1. Honestly	Enigma 75009
			THE STYLE COUNCIL	
			English duo: Paul Weller (ex-vocalist of The Jam) and Mick Talbot (keyboards). Expanded to a trio in 1988 with the addition of female vocalist Dee C. Lee.	
5/12/84	**29**	6	1. My Ever Changing Moods	Geffen 29359
			THE STYLISTICS	
			Soul group from Philadelphia, formed in 1968. Consisted of Russell Thompkins, Jr. (b: 3/21/51; lead), Airron Love, James Smith, James Dunn and Herbie Murrell. Thompkins, Love and Smith sang with the Percussions; Murrell and Dunn with the Monarchs from 1965-68. First recorded for Sebring in 1969.	
7/17/71	**39**	1	1. Stop, Look, Listen (To Your Heart)	Avco Embassy 4572
11/27/71†	**9**	13	● 2. **You Are Everything**	Avco 4581
3/11/72	**3**	14	● 3. **Betcha By Golly, Wow**	Avco 4591
7/01/72	**25**	6	4. People Make The World Go Round	Avco 4595
11/11/72	**10**	8	● 5. **I'm Stone In Love With You**	Avco 4603
3/03/73	**5**	9	● 6. **Break Up To Make Up**	Avco 4611
6/09/73	**23**	5	7. You'll Never Get To Heaven (If You Break My Heart)	Avco 4618
11/17/73	**14**	11	8. Rockin' Roll Baby	Avco 4625

DATE	POS	WKS	ARTIST—RECORD TITLE	LABEL & NO.
4/13/74	**2**(2)	14	● 9. **You Make Me Feel Brand New** all of above: produced by Thom Bell	Avco 4634
8/17/74	**18**	7	10. Let's Put It All Together	Avco 4640
			STYX	
			Chicago-based rock quintet: Dennis DeYoung (vocals, keyboards), Tommy Shaw (lead guitar), James Young (guitar), and twin brothers John (drums) and Chuck Panozzo (bass). Shaw replaced John Curulewski in 1976. Most songs written by Dennis DeYoung and/or Tommy Shaw.	
1/18/75	**6**	11	1. **Lady**	Wooden N. 10102
3/27/76	**27**	5	2. Lorelei	A&M 1786
12/18/76	**36**	3	3. Mademoiselle	A&M 1877
10/29/77†	**8**	15	4. **Come Sail Away**	A&M 1977
4/01/78	**29**	4	5. Fooling Yourself (The Angry Young Man)	A&M 2007
10/21/78	**21**	7	6. Blue Collar Man (Long Nights)	A&M 2087
4/07/79	**16**	13	7. Renegade	A&M 2110
10/20/79	**1**(2)	14	● 8. **Babe**	A&M 2188
1/19/80	**26**	5	9. Why Me	A&M 2206
1/24/81	**3**	15	10. **The Best Of Times**	A&M 2300
3/28/81	**9**	13	11. **Too Much Time On My Hands**	A&M 2323
2/12/83	**3**	16	● 12. **Mr. Roboto**	A&M 2525
4/30/83	**6**	13	13. **Don't Let It End**	A&M 2543
6/02/84	**40**	2	14. Music Time	A&M 2625
			SUAVÉ	
			Los Angeles native, born on 2/22/66. Son of Waymond Anderson, Sr. (member of GQ)	
4/23/88	**20**	7	1. My Girl	Capitol 44124
			SUGARHILL GANG	
			New York rap trio formed in Harlem. Consisted of Michael "Wonder Mike" Wright, Guy "Master Gee" O'Brien and Henry "Big Bank Hank" Jackson. One of the first commercially-successful rap acts.	
1/05/80	**36**	2	1. Rapper's Delight issued commercially only as a 12" single	Sugar Hill 542
			SUGARLOAF	
			Denver rock quartet: Jerry Corbetta (lead singer, keyboards), Bob Webber (guitar), Bob Raymond (bass) and Bob MacVittie (drums). Robert Yeazel (guitar, vocals) joined in 1971. By 1974, Myron Pollock replaced MacVittie, and Yeazel had left.	
9/19/70	**3**	12	1. **Green-Eyed Lady**	Liberty 56183
2/01/75	**9**	11	2. **Don't Call Us, We'll Call You** **SUGARLOAF/JERRY CORBETTA**	Claridge 402
			DONNA SUMMER	
			Born Adrian Donna Gaines on 12/31/48 in Boston. With group Crow, played local clubs. In German production of "Hair," European productions of "Godspell," "The Me Nobody Knows" and "Porgy And Bess." Settled in Germany, where she recorded "Love To Love You Baby." In the film "Thank God It's Friday" in 1979. Married Bruce Sudano of Brooklyn Dreams in 1980. Dubbed "The Queen of Disco."	
12/20/75†	**2**(2)	14	● 1. **Love To Love You Baby**	Oasis 401
9/03/77	**6**	14	● 2. **I Feel Love**	Casablanca 884
1/28/78	**37**	3	3. I Love You	Casablanca 907

DATE	POS	WKS	ARTIST—RECORD TITLE	LABEL & NO.
6/03/78	**3**	14	● 4. **Last Dance** from the film "Thank God It's Friday"	Casablanca 926
9/30/78	**1**(3)	15	● 5. **MacArthur Park**	Casablanca 939
1/20/79	**4**	14	● 6. **Heaven Knows** **DONNA SUMMER with BROOKLYN DREAMS**	Casablanca 959
4/28/79	**1**(3)	17	▲ 7. **Hot Stuff**	Casablanca 978
6/09/79	**1**(5)	15	▲ 8. **Bad Girls**	Casablanca 988
9/15/79	**2**(2)	14	● 9. **Dim All The Lights**	Casablanca 2201
10/27/79	**1**(2)	13	● 10. **No More Tears (Enough Is Enough)** **BARBRA STREISAND/DONNA SUMMER**	Columbia 11125
1/26/80	**5**	12	● 11. **On The Radio**	Casablanca 2236
9/27/80	**3**	13	● 12. **The Wanderer**	Geffen 49563
10/11/80	**36**	3	13. Walk Away	Casablanca 2300
1/10/81	**33**	3	14. Cold Love	Geffen 49634
3/28/81	**40**	2	15. Who Do You Think You're Foolin'	Geffen 49664
7/17/82	**10**	11	16. **Love Is In Control (Finger On The Trigger)**	Geffen 29982
2/05/83	**33**	6	17. The Woman In Me	Geffen 29805
6/18/83	**3**	17	18. **She Works Hard For The Money**	Mercury 812370
9/01/84	**21**	8	19. There Goes My Baby	Geffen 29291
			HENRY LEE SUMMER Rock singer from Brazil, Indiana.	
4/02/88	**20**	7	1. I Wish I Had A Girl	CBS Assoc. 07720
			SUNNY & THE SUNGLOWS San Antonio band formed in 1959: led by Sunny Ozuna.	
9/28/63	**11**	9	1. Talk To Me	Tear Drop 3014
			THE SUNNYSIDERS Group included vocalist Margie Rayburn.	
5/21/55	**12**	10	1. Hey, Mr. Banjo Juke Box #12 / Jockey #19 / Best Seller #20	Kapp 113
			THE SUNSHINE COMPANY Southern California pop quintet featuring lead singer Mary Nance.	
11/18/67	**36**	3	1. Back On The Street Again	Imperial 66260
			SUPERTRAMP British rock quintet: Roger Hodgson (vocals, guitar), Rick Davies (vocals, keyboards), John Helliwell (sax), Dougie Thomson (bass) and Bob Siebenberg (drums). Hodgson went solo in 1983.	
5/17/75	**35**	2	1. Bloody Well Right	A&M 1660
7/02/77	**15**	11	2. Give A Little Bit	A&M 1938
4/28/79	**6**	13	3. **The Logical Song**	A&M 2128
8/04/79	**15**	8	4. Goodbye Stranger	A&M 2162
11/03/79	**10**	11	5. **Take The Long Way Home**	A&M 2193
10/04/80	**15**	8	6. Dreamer from their 1974 album "Crime Of The Century"	A&M 2269
10/30/82	**11**	11	7. It's Raining Again	A&M 2502
2/26/83	**31**	5	8. My Kind Of Lady all of above: written by Davies and Hodgson	A&M 2517

DATE	POS	WKS	ARTIST—RECORD TITLE	LABEL & NO.
6/08/85	**28**	7	9. Cannonball	A&M 2731
			THE SUPREMES	
			R&B vocal group from Detroit, formed as the Primettes in 1959. Consisted of lead singer Diana Ross (b: 3/26/44), Mary Wilson (b: 3/6/44) and Florence Ballard (b: 6/30/43; d: 2/22/76 of cardiac arrest). Recorded for LuPine in 1960. Signed to Motown's Tamla label in 1960. Changed name to The Supremes in 1961. Ballard discharged from group in 1967, replaced by Cindy Birdsong, formerly with Patti LaBelle's Blue Belles. Ross left in 1969 for solo career, replaced by Jean Terrell. Birdsong left in 1972, replaced by Lynda Lawrence. Terrell and Lawrence left in 1973. Mary Wilson re-formed group with Scherrie Payne (sister of Freda Payne) and Cindy Birdsong. Birdsong left again in 1976, replaced by Susaye Greene. In 1978, Wilson toured England with Karen Ragland and Karen Jackson, but lost rights to the name "Supremes" thereafter. Inducted into the Rock And Roll Hall Of Fame in 1988.	
12/28/63†	**23**	7	1. When The Lovelight Starts Shining Through His Eyes	Motown 1051
7/18/64	1(2)	13	2. **Where Did Our Love Go**	Motown 1060
10/10/64	1(4)	12	3. **Baby Love**	Motown 1066
11/21/64	1(2)	13	4. **Come See About Me**	Motown 1068
3/06/65	1(2)	10	5. **Stop! In The Name Of Love**	Motown 1074
5/08/65	1(1)	10	6. **Back In My Arms Again**	Motown 1075
8/14/65	**11**	7	7. Nothing But Heartaches	Motown 1080
10/30/65	1(2)	10	8. **I Hear A Symphony**	Motown 1083
1/29/66	**5**	8	9. **My World Is Empty Without You**	Motown 1089
5/07/66	**9**	7	10. **Love Is Like An Itching In My Heart**	Motown 1094
8/20/66	1(2)	11	11. **You Can't Hurry Love**	Motown 1097
11/05/66	1(2)	10	12. **You Keep Me Hangin' On**	Motown 1101
2/04/67	1(1)	10	13. **Love Is Here And Now You're Gone**	Motown 1103
4/15/67	1(1)	10	14. **The Happening** from the film of the same title	Motown 1107
			DIANA ROSS & THE SUPREMES:	
8/19/67	2(2)	10	15. **Reflections**	Motown 1111
11/25/67	**9**	6	16. **In And Out Of Love**	Motown 1116
4/06/68	**28**	5	17. Forever Came Today all of above: written by Eddie Holland, Lamont Dozier and Brian Holland	Motown 1122
7/06/68	**30**	3	18. Some Things You Never Get Used To	Motown 1126
10/26/68	1(2)	15	19. **Love Child**	Motown 1135
12/14/68†	2(2)	12	20. **I'm Gonna Make You Love Me** **DIANA ROSS & THE SUPREMES & THE TEMPTATIONS**	Motown 1137
2/01/69	**10**	7	21. **I'm Livin' In Shame**	Motown 1139
3/22/69	**25**	6	22. I'll Try Something New **DIANA ROSS & THE SUPREMES & THE TEMPTATIONS**	Motown 1142
4/26/69	**27**	5	23. The Composer	Motown 1146
6/14/69	**31**	4	24. No Matter What Sign You Are	Motown 1148
11/15/69	1(1)	15	25. **Someday We'll Be Together**	Motown 1156
			THE SUPREMES:	
3/14/70	**10**	10	26. **Up The Ladder To The Roof**	Motown 1162
8/01/70	**21**	8	27. Everybody's Got The Right To Love	Motown 1167

DATE	POS	WKS	ARTIST—RECORD TITLE	LABEL & NO.
11/21/70	**7**	12	28. **Stoned Love**	Motown 1172
12/12/70†	**14**	8	29. River Deep - Mountain High	Motown 1173
			THE SUPREMES & FOUR TOPS	
5/22/71	**16**	8	30. Nathan Jones	Motown 1182
1/29/72	**16**	9	31. Floy Joy	Motown 1195
6/03/72	**37**	3	32. Automatically Sunshine	Motown 1200
8/07/76	**40**	1	33. I'm Gonna Let My Heart Do The Walking	Motown 1391
			SURFACE	
			Soul trio from New Jersey: Bernard Jackson (lead singer), David Townsend (son of producer/songwriter Ed Townsend) and Dave Conley.	
6/20/87	**20**	8	1. Happy	Columbia 06611
			THE SURFARIS	
			Teenage surf band from Glendora, California. Consisted of Ron Wilson (drummer), Jim Fuller (lead guitar), Bob Berryhill (rhythm guitar), Pat Connolly (bass) and Jim Pash (sax, clarinet).	
7/06/63	**2**(1)	10	1. **Wipe Out** **[I]**	Dot 16479
8/27/66	**16**	10	2. Wipe Out [I-R]	Dot 144
			SURVIVOR	
			Midwest rock group: Dave Bickler (lead singer), Jim Peterik (keyboards; former lead singer of Ides Of March), Frankie Sullivan (guitar), Gary Smith (drums) and Dennis Johnson (bass). Smith and Johnson replaced by Marc Doubray and Stephan Ellis in 1981. Bickler replaced by Jimi Jamison in 1984. Droubay and Ellis left in 1988.	
11/21/81	**33**	4	1. Poor Man's Son	Scotti Br. 02560
6/26/82	**1**(6)	18	▲ 2. **Eye Of The Tiger** from the film "Rocky III"	Scotti Br. 02912
10/16/82	**17**	7	3. American Heartbeat	Scotti Br. 03213
10/20/84	**13**	13	4. I Can't Hold Back	Scotti Br. 04603
2/09/85	**8**	11	5. **High On You**	Scotti Br. 04685
5/11/85	**4**	14	6. **The Search Is Over**	Scotti Br. 04871
11/23/85†	**2**(2)	16	7. **Burning Heart** from the film "Rocky IV"	Scotti Br. 05663
11/15/86†	**9**	13	8. **Is This Love**	Scotti Br. 06381
			BILLY SWAN	
			Born on 5/12/42 in Cape Girardeau, Missouri. Singer/songwriter/ keyboardist/ guitarist. Produced Tony Joe White's first 3 albums.	
10/26/74	**1**(2)	12	● 1. **I Can Help**	Monument 8621
			BETTYE SWANN	
			Born Betty Jean Champion on 10/24/44 in Shreveport, Louisiana. Moved to Los Angeles in the late 50s. In vocal group the Fawns, recorded for Money in 1964.	
7/01/67	**21**	7	1. Make Me Yours	Money 126
4/19/69	**38**	2	2. Don't Touch Me	Capitol 2382
			PATRICK SWAYZE featuring WENDY FRASER	
			Film actor Swayze was born on 8/18/52 in Houston, Texas. Starred in "The Outsiders," "Uncommon Valor," "Red Dawn," "Dirty Dancing" and others.	
1/16/88	**3**	13	1. **She's Like The Wind** from the film "Dirty Dancing"	RCA 5363

DATE	POS	WKS	ARTIST—RECORD TITLE	LABEL & NO.
			KEITH SWEAT	
			Singer/songwriter born and raised in Harlem.	
2/06/88	**5**	13	1. **I Want Her**	Vintertn. 69431
			SWEATHOG	
12/11/71	**33**	4	1. Hallelujah	Columbia 45492
			SWEET	
			English rock band: Brian Connolly (lead singer), Steve Priest (bass, vocals), Andy Scott (guitar, keyboards) and Mick Tucker (drums).	
3/17/73	**3**	15	● 1. **Little Willy**	Bell 45251
8/02/75	**5**	14	2. **Ballroom Blitz**	Capitol 4055
11/22/75†	**5**	11	● 3. **Fox On The Run**	Capitol 4157
3/06/76	**20**	7	4. Action	Capitol 4220
4/15/78	**8**	14	5. **Love Is Like Oxygen**	Capitol 4549
			THE SWEET INSPIRATIONS	
			R&B vocal quartet: Cissy Houston, Estelle Brown, Sylvia Shemwell and Myrna Smith. Spent nearly 6 years as studio group, primarily for Atlantic. Work included backing Aretha Franklin and Elvis Presley. Cissy, mother of Whitney Houston, recorded solo in 1970.	
3/30/68	**18**	10	1. Sweet Inspiration	Atlantic 2476
			SWEET SENSATION	
			8-member soul group from Manchester, England led by Marcel King (vocals), with additional vocals by St. Clair Palmer, Vincent James and Junior Daye.	
2/15/75	**14**	8	1. Sad Sweet Dreamer	Pye 71002
			RACHEL SWEET - see REX SMITH	
			SWING OUT SISTER	
			British jazz-pop trio: Corinne Drewery (vocals), Andy Connell and Martin Jackson. Drewery was a fashion designer.	
9/26/87	**6**	11	1. **Breakout**	Mercury 888016
2/20/88	**31**	3	2. Twilight World	Mercury 888484
			THE SWINGING BLUE JEANS	
			Liverpool, England rock quartet: Ray Ennis and Ralph Ellis (guitars), Norman Kuhlke (drums) and Les Braid (bass).	
3/28/64	**24**	5	1. Hippy Hippy Shake	Imperial 66021
			SWINGIN' MEDALLIONS	
			8-man rock and roll band from Greenwood, South Carolina led by John McElrath.	
6/04/66	**17**	6	1. Double Shot (Of My Baby's Love)	Smash 2033
			SWITCH	
			Soul-funk sextet from Mansfield, Ohio. Discovered by Jermaine Jackson. Consisted of Bobby DeBarge, Phillip Ingram (lead vocals), Greg Williams, Tommy DeBarge, Eddie Fluellen and Jody Sims. Williams, Sims and Bobby DeBarge were in White Heat. Brothers Bobby and Tommy DeBarge were later in family group DeBarge.	
12/02/78	**36**	3	1. There'll Never Be	Gordy 7159

DATE	POS	WKS	ARTIST—RECORD TITLE	LABEL & NO.
			THE SYLVERS	
			Memphis family of 10 brothers and sisters: Olympia-Ann, Leon, Charmaine, James, Edmund, Ricky, Angelia, Pat, Foster and Jonathon Sylvers.	
3/13/76	**1**(1)	15	● 1. **Boogie Fever**	Capitol 4179
11/13/76†	**5**	17	● 2. **Hot Line**	Capitol 4336
5/21/77	**17**	10	3. High School Dance	Capitol 4405
			FOSTER SYLVERS	
			Born on 2/25/62 in Memphis. Youngest member of The Sylvers family group.	
6/30/73	**22**	8	1. Misdemeanor	MGM 14580
			SYLVESTER	
			Born Sylvester James in Los Angeles. Moved to San Francisco in 1967. With vocal group, the Cockettes. In film "The Rose." Backing vocals by Martha Wash, Izora Rhodes (later known as Two Tons O' Fun and The Weather Girls), and Jeanie Tracy. Died on 12/16/88 (40) of AIDS-related complications.	
9/30/78	**19**	10	1. Dance (Disco Heat)	Fantasy 827
2/17/79	**36**	3	2. You Make Me Feel (Mighty Real)	Fantasy 846
5/05/79	**40**	2	3. I (Who Have Nothing)	Fantasy 855
			SYLVIA	
			Country singer Sylvia Kirby Allen born in 1957 in Kokomo, Indiana. Moved to Nashville in 1975.	
10/09/82	**15**	9	● 1. Nobody	RCA 13223
			SYLVIA	
			Born Sylvia Vanderpool on 5/6/36 in New York City. Singer/songwriter/producer. First recorded with Hot Lips Page for Columbia in 1950, as Little Sylvia. Half of Mickey & Sylvia duo. Married Joe Robinson, owner of All-Platinum/Vibration Records (later known as Sugar Hill). Their son Joe was leader of West Street Mob.	
4/21/73	**3**	13	● 1. **Pillow Talk**	Vibration 521
			SYLVIA SYMS	
			Nightclub singer from the Bronx.	
6/16/56	**20**	2	1. I Could Have Danced All Night Jockey #20 / Top 100 #35 from the musical "My Fair Lady"	Decca 29903
9/01/56	**21**	3	2. English Muffins And Irish Stew Jockey #21 / Top 100 #51	Decca 29969
			SYNDICATE OF SOUND	
			San Jose garage-rock quintet: Don Baskin (lead singer), Jim Sawyers (guitar), Bob Gonzalez (bass), John Sharkey (rhythm guitar) and John Duckworth (drums).	
6/25/66	**8**	6	1. **Little Girl**	Bell 640
			SYREETA - see BILLY PRESTON	
			THE SYSTEM	
			New York City-based, techno-funk duo: Mic Murphy (b: Raleigh, NC; vocals, guitar) and David Frank (b: Dayton, OH; synthesizer).	
5/16/87	**4**	13	1. **Don't Disturb This Groove**	Atlantic 89320

DATE	POS	WKS	ARTIST—RECORD TITLE	LABEL & NO.
			T	
			TACO	
			Born Taco Ockerse in 1955 to Dutch parents in Jaharta, Indonesia. German-based singer.	
7/23/83	**4**	14	● 1. **Puttin' On The Ritz**	RCA 13574
			written in 1929 by Irving Berlin; #1 hit for Harry Richman in 1930	
			TALK TALK	
			British rock band; Mark Hollis, lead singer.	
4/21/84	**31**	6	1. It's My Life	EMI America 8195
			TALKING HEADS	
			New York City-based new-wave quartet: David Byrne (lead singer, guitar), Jerry Harrison (keyboards, guitar), Tina Weymouth (bass) and husband Chris Frantz (drums). Formed as a trio of Byrne, Weymouth & Frantz at the Rhode Island School of Design. Harrison was member of The Modern Lovers. Also see Tom Tom Club.	
12/23/78†	**26**	9	1. Take Me To The River	Sire 1032
9/03/83	**9**	11	2. **Burning Down The House**	Sire 29565
11/08/86	**25**	7	3. Wild Wild Life	Sire 28629
			TA MARA & THE SEEN	
			Minneapolis quintet led by Margaret Cox, a veteran Minneapolis night club singer. Group includes guitarist Oliver Leiber, son of songwriter Jerry Leiber.	
11/30/85†	**24**	10	1. Everybody Dance	A&M 2768
			THE TAMS	
			Atlanta R&B quintet: brothers Charles and Joseph (lead singer) Pope, with Robert Smith, Floyd Ashton and Horace Key.	
1/18/64	**9**	9	1. **What Kind Of Fool (Do You Think I Am)**	ABC-Para. 10502
			NORMA TANEGA	
			Born on 1/30/39 in Vallejo, California. Singer/songwriter/pianist/guitarist.	
3/19/66	**22**	6	1. Walkin' My Cat Named Dog	New Voice 807
			THE TARRIERS	
			Folk trio: Erik Darling (tenor, banjo), Bob Carey (bass, guitar) and movie actor Alan Arkin (baritone, guitar). Darling became a member of The Rooftop Singers.	
10/13/56	**9**	15	1. **Cindy, Oh Cindy**	Glory 247
			VINCE MARTIN with THE TARRIERS	
			Juke Box #9 / Best Seller #12 / Top 100 #12 / Jockey #12	
12/22/56†	**4**	16	2. **The Banana Boat Song**	Glory 249
			Juke Box #4 / Best Seller #5 / Top 100 #6 / Jockey #6	
			A TASTE OF HONEY	
			Soul/disco quartet, formed in Los Angeles in 1972. Consisted of Janice Marie Johnson (vocals, guitar), Hazel Payne (vocals, bass), Perry Kimble (keyboards) and Donald Johnson (drums). Re-formed in 1980 with Janice Johnson and Hazel Payne. Won the 1978 Best New Artist Grammy Award.	
7/22/78	**1**(3)	17	▲ 1. **Boogie Oogie Oogie**	Capitol 4565
4/11/81	**3**	16	● 2. **Sukiyaki**	Capitol 4953

DATE	POS	WKS	ARTIST—RECORD TITLE	LABEL & NO.
			TAVARES	
			Family R&B group from New Bedford, Massachusetts. Consisted of brothers Ralph, Antone "Chubby," Feliciano "Butch," Arthur "Pooch" and Perry Lee "Tiny" Tavares. Worked as Chubby & The Turnpikes from 1964-69.	
11/03/73	**35**	3	1. Check It Out	Capitol 3674
5/17/75	**25**	5	2. Remember What I Told You To Forget	Capitol 4010
8/23/75	**10**	13	3. **It Only Takes A Minute**	Capitol 4111
7/10/76	**15**	12	● 4. Heaven Must Be Missing An Angel (Part 1)	Capitol 4270
12/11/76	**34**	2	5. Don't Take Away The Music	Capitol 4348
4/23/77	**22**	7	6. Whodunit	Capitol 4398
4/15/78	**32**	4	7. More Than A Woman from the film "Saturday Night Fever"	Capitol 4500
11/20/82	**33**	9	8. A Penny For Your Thoughts	RCA 13292
			ANDY TAYLOR	
			Born on 2/16/61 in Dolver-Hampton, England. Lead guitarist of Duran Duran and The Power Station.	
7/05/86	**24**	7	1. Take It Easy from the film "American Anthem"	Atlantic 89414
			BOBBY TAYLOR & THE VANCOUVERS	
			Interracial sextet based in Vancouver, Canada. Included guitarist Tommy Chong, of Cheech & Chong fame, Wes Henderson, Robbie King, Ted Lewis and Eddie Patterson. Bobby Taylor discovered The Jackson 5.	
5/18/68	**29**	5	1. Does Your Mama Know About Me	Gordy 7069
			JAMES TAYLOR	
			Born on 3/12/48 in Boston. Singer/songwriter/guitarist. With older brother Alex in the Fabulous Corsairs in 1964. In New York group, The Flying Machine, in 1967, with friend Danny Kortchmar. Moved to England in 1968, recorded for Peter Asher. Married Carly Simon on 11/3/72; filed for divorce in 1982. In film "Two Lane Blacktop" with Dennis Wilson in 1973. Sister Kate and brothers Alex and Livingston also recorded.	
9/26/70	**3**	14	1. **Fire And Rain**	Warner 7423
3/20/71	**37**	1	2. Country Road	Warner 7460
6/19/71	**1**(1)	12	● 3. **You've Got A Friend**	Warner 7498
10/16/71	**31**	5	4. Long Ago And Far Away above 2: backing vocals by Joni Mitchell	Warner 7521
12/16/72†	**14**	9	5. Don't Let Me Be Lonely Tonight	Warner 7655
2/16/74	**5**	13	● 6. **Mockingbird** **CARLY SIMON & JAMES TAYLOR**	Elektra 45880
7/19/75	**5**	10	7. **How Sweet It Is (To Be Loved By You)**	Warner 8109
8/07/76	**22**	8	8. Shower The People	Warner 8222
7/09/77	**4**	13	9. **Handy Man**	Columbia 10557
11/05/77	**20**	9	10. Your Smiling Face	Columbia 10602
2/11/78	**17**	7	11. (What A) Wonderful World **ART GARFUNKEL with JAMES TAYLOR & PAUL SIMON**	Columbia 10676
9/23/78	**36**	3	12. Devoted To You **CARLY SIMON & JAMES TAYLOR**	Elektra 45506
6/30/79	**28**	5	13. Up On The Roof	Columbia 11005

DATE	POS	WKS	ARTIST—RECORD TITLE	LABEL & NO.
3/14/81	**11**	10	14. Her Town Too **JAMES TAYLOR & J.D. SOUTHER**	Columbia 60514
			JOHN TAYLOR	
			Born on 6/20/60 in Birmingham, England. Bass guitarist of Duran Duran and The Power Station.	
4/05/86	**23**	6	1. I Do What I Do... theme from the film "9 1/2 Weeks"	Capitol 5551
			JOHNNIE TAYLOR	
			Born on 5/5/38 in Crawfordsville, Arkansas. With gospel group the Highway QC's in Chicago, early 50s. In vocal group the Five Echoes, recorded for Sabre in 1954. In The Soul Stirrers gospel group before going solo. First solo recording for Sar in 1961.	
11/02/68	**5**	13	● 1. **Who's Making Love**	Stax 0009
1/25/69	**20**	8	2. Take Care Of Your Homework	Stax 0023
5/31/69	**36**	5	3. Testify (I Wonna)	Stax 0033
7/18/70	**37**	2	4. Steal Away	Stax 0068
11/14/70	**39**	2	5. I Am Somebody, Part II	Stax 0078
2/13/71	**28**	5	6. Jody's Got Your Girl And Gone	Stax 0085
7/14/73	**11**	12	● 7. I Believe In You (You Believe In Me)	Stax 0161
10/27/73	**15**	8	8. Cheaper To Keep Her	Stax 0176
3/16/74	**34**	2	9. We're Getting Careless With Our Love	Stax 0193
3/06/76	**1**(4)	13	▲ 10. **Disco Lady** first single certified platinum by R.I.A.A.	Columbia 10281
6/26/76	**33**	3	11. Somebody's Gettin' It	Columbia 10334
			LITTLE JOHNNY TAYLOR	
			Born Johnny Young on 2/11/43 in Memphis. Blues singer/harmonica player. Moved to Los Angeles in 1950. With Mighty Clouds Of Joy and Stars Of Bethel gospel groups. Duets with Ted Taylor (no relation) in the 70s.	
9/14/63	**19**	8	1. Part Time Love	Galaxy 722
			LIVINGSTON TAYLOR	
			Born on 11/21/50 in Boston. James Taylor's younger brother.	
12/16/78†	**30**	5	1. I Will Be In Love With You	Epic 50604
9/13/80	**38**	2	2. First Time Love	Epic 50894
			R. DEAN TAYLOR	
			Born in Toronto, Canada, in 1939. First recorded for Barry in 1960. Own label, Jane. Co-wrote hit "Love Child" for The Supremes.	
9/19/70	**5**	13	1. **Indiana Wants Me**	Rare Earth 5013
			THE T-BONES	
			A Joe Saraceno studio production. Also see Hamilton, Joe Frank & Reynolds.	
12/25/65†	**3**	11	1. **No Matter What Shape (Your Stomach's In)** [I] tune is from an "Alka Seltzer" jingle	Liberty 55836
			BRAM TCHAIKOVSKY	
			Bram (real name: Peter Bramall) formed rock group in Lincolnshire, England.	
8/18/79	**37**	3	1. Girl Of My Dreams	Polydor 14575

DATE	POS	WKS	ARTIST—RECORD TITLE	LABEL & NO.
			TEARS FOR FEARS	
			British duo: Roland Orzabal (vocals, guitar, keyboards) and Curt Smith (vocals, bass). Adopted name from Arthur Janev's book "Prisoners Of Pain." Assisted by Manny Elias (drums) and Ian Stanley (keyboards).	
4/13/85	**1**(2)	14	1. **Everybody Wants To Rule The World**	Mercury 880659
6/29/85	**1**(3)	13	2. **Shout**	Mercury 880294
9/21/85	**3**	12	3. **Head Over Heels**	Mercury 880899
5/03/86	**27**	6	4. Mothers Talk all of above: produced by Chris Hughes	Mercury 884638
			TECHNIQUES	
11/25/57	**29**	2	1. Hey! Little Girl Best Seller #29 / Top 100 #33	Roulette 4030
			THE TEDDY BEARS	
			Los Angeles trio: Phil Spector (b: 12/26/40 in the Bronx), Carol Connors (lead singer; real name: Annette Kleinbard) and Marshall Leib. Spector became a well- known writer and producer; owner of Philles Records.	
10/13/58	**1**(3)	18	1. **To Know Him, Is To Love Him**	Dore 503
			THE TEE SET	
			Dutch quintet led by vocalist Peter Tetteroo.	
2/07/70	**5**	10	1. **Ma Belle Amie**	Colossus 107
			TEEGARDEN & VAN WINKLE	
			David Teegarden (drums) and Skip Knape (keyboards). Teegarden later joined Bob Seger's band, 1978-81.	
10/17/70	**22**	5	1. God, Love And Rock & Roll	Westbound 170
			THE TEENAGERS - see FRANKIE LYMON	
			THE TEEN QUEENS	
			R&B duo formed in Los Angeles in 1955 by Betty and Rosie Collins, sisters of Aaron Collins of the Cadets/Jacks.	
3/10/56	**14**	8	1. Eddie My Love Best Seller #14 / Juke Box #16 / Top 100 #22	RPM 453
			NINO TEMPO & APRIL STEVENS	
			Nino (b: 1/6/35) and sister April (b: 4/29/36) from Niagara Falls, New York. Prior to teaming up, Nino was a session saxophonist and April had recorded solo.	
10/05/63	**1**(1)	12	1. **Deep Purple** #1 hit for Larry Clinton & His Orchestra in 1939	Atco 6273
12/28/63†	**11**	7	2. Whispering #1 hit for Paul Whiteman & His Orchestra in 1920	Atco 6281
3/14/64	**32**	3	3. Stardust #1 hit for Isham Jones & His Orchestra in 1931	Atco 6286
10/01/66	**26**	5	4. All Strung Out	White Whale 236
			THE TEMPOS	
			Pittsburgh vocal quartet: Mike Lazo, Gene Schachter, Jim Drake and Tom Minoto.	
8/10/59	**23**	6	1. See You In September	Climax 102
			THE TEMPTATIONS	
			White quartet from Flushing, New York. Consisted of Neil Stevens, Larry Curtis, Artie Sands and Artie Marin.	
5/09/60	**29**	3	1. Barbara	Goldisc 3001

DATE	POS	WKS	ARTIST—RECORD TITLE	LABEL & NO.
			THE TEMPTATIONS	
			Soul group formed in Detroit in 1960. Consisted of Eddie Kendricks, Paul Williams (d: 8/17/73), Melvin Franklin, Otis Williams and Elbridge Bryant, who was replaced by David Ruffin in 1964. Originally called the Primes and Elgins, first recorded for Miracle in 1961. Ruffin (cousin of Billy Stewart) replaced by Dennis Edwards (ex-Contours) in 1968. Kendricks and Paul Williams left in 1971, replaced by Ricky Owens (ex-Vibrations) and Richard Street. Owens was replaced by Damon Harris. Harris left in 1975, replaced by Glenn Leonard. Edwards left group, 1977-79, replaced by Louis Price. Ali Ollie Woodson replaced Edwards from 1984-87. 1988 lineup: Williams, Franklin, Street, Edwards and Ron Tyson. Recognized as America's all-time favorite soul group. Inducted into the Rock And Roll Hall Of Fame in 1989.	
3/21/64	**11**	8	1. The Way You Do The Things You Do	Gordy 7028
7/04/64	**33**	4	2. I'll Be In Trouble	Gordy 7032
9/26/64	**26**	6	3. Girl (Why You Wanna Make Me Blue)	Gordy 7035
1/30/65	**1**(1)	11	4. **My Girl**	Gordy 7038
4/17/65	**18**	7	5. It's Growing	Gordy 7040
8/07/65	**17**	7	6. Since I Lost My Baby	Gordy 7043
11/06/65	**13**	6	7. My Baby	Gordy 7047
3/26/66	**29**	3	8. Get Ready all of above (except #3): produced by Smokey Robinson	Gordy 7049
6/11/66	**13**	10	9. Ain't Too Proud To Beg	Gordy 7054
9/03/66	**3**	9	10. **Beauty Is Only Skin Deep**	Gordy 7055
12/03/66	**8**	8	11. **(I Know) I'm Losing You**	Gordy 7057
5/13/67	**8**	8	12. **All I Need**	Gordy 7061
8/12/67	**6**	9	13. **You're My Everything**	Gordy 7063
10/21/67	**14**	8	14. (Loneliness Made Me Realize) It's You That I Need	Gordy 7065
1/27/68	**4**	11	15. **I Wish It Would Rain**	Gordy 7068
5/18/68	**13**	8	16. I Could Never Love Another (After Loving You)	Gordy 7072
8/17/68	**26**	5	17. Please Return Your Love To Me	Gordy 7074
11/23/68†	**6**	11	18. **Cloud Nine**	Gordy 7081
12/14/68†	**2**(2)	12	19. **I'm Gonna Make You Love Me** **DIANA ROSS & THE SUPREMES & THE TEMPTATIONS**	Motown 1137
2/22/69	**6**	11	20. **Run Away Child, Running Wild**	Gordy 7084
3/22/69	**25**	6	21. I'll Try Something New **DIANA ROSS & THE SUPREMES & THE TEMPTATIONS**	Motown 1142
5/31/69	**20**	6	22. Don't Let The Joneses Get You Down	Gordy 7086
8/30/69	**1**(2)	15	23. **I Can't Get Next To You**	Gordy 7093
1/24/70	**7**	10	24. **Psychedelic Shack**	Gordy 7096
6/06/70	**3**	13	25. **Ball Of Confusion (That's What The World Is Today)**	Gordy 7099
10/17/70	**33**	4	26. Ungena Za Ulimwengu (Unite The World)	Gordy 7102
2/20/71	**1**(2)	13	27. **Just My Imagination (Running Away With Me)**	Gordy 7105
11/20/71	**18**	8	28. Superstar (Remember How You Got Where You Are)	Gordy 7111
3/18/72	**30**	4	29. Take A Look Around 15-18, 20, 22-29: written by Norman Whitfield & Barrett Strong	Gordy 7115
10/28/72	**1**(1)	12	30. **Papa Was A Rollin' Stone**	Gordy 7121

DATE	POS	WKS	ARTIST—RECORD TITLE	LABEL & NO.
3/10/73	**7**	11	31. **Masterpiece**	Gordy 7126
7/07/73	**40**	2	32. The Plastic Man	Gordy 7129
9/08/73	**35**	4	33. Hey Girl (I Like Your Style)	Gordy 7131
1/12/74	**27**	4	34. Let Your Hair Down 9-11, 13-18, 20, 22-34: produced by Norman Whitfield	Gordy 7133
2/01/75	**40**	1	35. Happy People	Gordy 7138
4/19/75	**26**	9	36. Shakey Ground	Gordy 7142
8/23/75	**37**	2	37. Glasshouse	Gordy 7144
			10cc	
			English art-rock group which evolved from Hotlegs. Consisted of Eric Stewart (guitar), Graham Gouldman (bass), Lol Creme (guitar, keyboards) and Kevin Godley (drums). Stewart and Gouldman were members of The Mindbenders. Godley and Creme left in 1976, replaced by drummer Paul Burgess. Added members Rick Fenn, Stuart Tosh and Duncan MacKay in 1978. Gouldman later in duo, Wax. Also see Godley & Creme.	
6/14/75	**2**(3)	11	1. **I'm Not In Love**	Mercury 73678
1/29/77	**5**	14	● 2. **The Things We Do For Love**	Mercury 73875
6/25/77	**40**	1	3. People In Love	Mercury 73917
			TEN YEARS AFTER	
			British blues-rock quartet: Alvin Lee (vocals, guitar), Leo Lyons (bass) Chick Churchill (keyboards) and Ric Lee (drums).	
11/20/71	**40**	2	1. I'd Love To Change The World	Columbia 45457
			ROBERT TEPPER	
			Native of Baylor, New Jersey.	
3/01/86	**22**	7	1. No Easy Way Out from the film "Rocky IV"	Scotti Br. 05750
			TAMMI TERRELL - see MARVIN GAYE	
			JOE TEX	
			Born Joseph Arrington, Jr. on 8/8/33 in Rogers, Texas; died of a heart attack on 8/13/82. Sang with local gospel groups. Won recording contract at Apollo Theater talent contest in 1954. First recorded for King in 1955. Became a convert to Muslim faith, changed name to "Joseph Hazziez" in July, 1972.	
1/02/65	**5**	8	1. **Hold What You've Got**	Dial 4001
10/16/65	**23**	5	2. I Want To (Do Everything For You)	Dial 4016
1/01/66	**29**	4	3. A Sweet Woman Like You	Dial 4022
6/18/66	**39**	1	4. S.Y.S.L.J.F.M. (The Letter Song)	Dial 4028
4/08/67	**35**	3	5. Show Me	Dial 4055
11/25/67	**10**	10	● 6. **Skinny Legs And All**	Dial 4063
3/02/68	**33**	3	7. Men Are Gettin' Scarce	Dial 4069
2/26/72	**2**(2)	16	● 8. **I Gotcha**	Dial 1010
4/23/77	**12**	10	● 9. Ain't Gonna Bump No More (With No Big Fat Woman) all of above: produced by Buddy Killen	Epic 50313
			THEM	
			Belfast, Northern Ireland rock quintet: Van Morrison (lead singer), Billy Harrison, Alan Henderson, John McAuley and Peter Bardens. Disbanded in late 1966. Morrison went on to solo career. Bardens formed Camel in 1972; recorded solo in 1987.	
6/26/65	**24**	6	1. Here Comes The Night	Parrot 9749

Eddie Murphy's Rick James-produced pop album *How Could It Be* reached No. 26 on the chart, while his previous album, *Eddie Murphy: Comedian*, only hit No. 35. He's the only comedian ever to chart higher as a singer.

Johnny Nash's 1972 No. 1, "I Can See Clearly Now," was the first reggae-influenced song to hit the top of the American pop charts. The owner of a recording studio in Jamaica who often employed the young Bob Marley as a songwriter, Nash was actually born in Texas.

Ricky Nelson, despite the lack of respect shown him as a teen-heartthrob TV star, earned 35 Top-40 hits in the 50s, 60s, and 70s, nearly half of which went top 10. He also had the fastest moving record of the 50s: "Lonesome Town" jumped from No. 86 to No. 18 in one week.

New Colony Six came out of Chicago to record a total of ten charting songs by 1972, including Top 40s "I Will Always Think About You" and "Things I'd Like To Say." Was it self-centered for them to include the pronoun "I" in the titles of half of their hits?

New Edition were considered Jackson 5 clones with their debut, the No. 1 R & B hit "Candy Girl." The resemblance faded, yet like the Jacksons, this Boston-based vocal quintet appeals to white and black audiences alike, as proven by the No. 1 crossover hit of 1988, "If It Isn't Love."

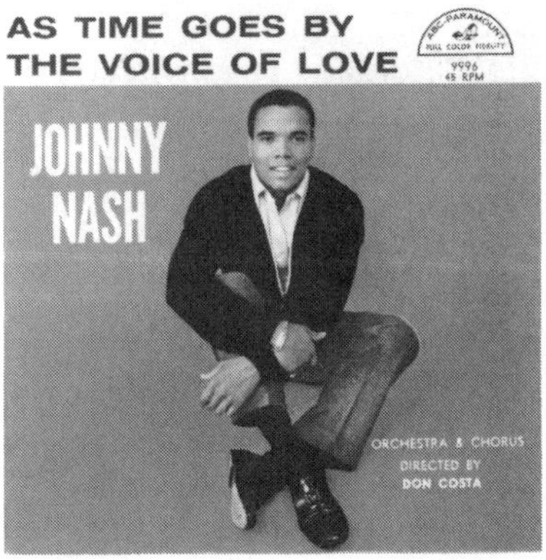

NEVER BE ANYONE ELSE BUT YOU
IT'S LATE
RICKY
NELSON

Stevie Nicks is the only female artist in the 80s to have No. 1 albums as both a solo act and as a part of a group: Nicks' *Bella Donna* album and Fleetwood Mac's *Mirage*. The only male to perform the feat is former Wham! vocalist George Michael.

Nu Shooz are Portland, Oregon's husband-and-wife team of John Smith and Valerie Day, whose 1986 smash "I Can't Wait" spent five weeks in the top 10, peaking at No. 3. That kind of success could even pay for some Nu Cloz, too.

The Oak Ridge Boys enjoyed their first No. 1 country single in 1978 with "I'll Be True To You," taken from their *Room Service* LP. The album, which went to No. 3 on the Country chart, also yielded subsequent hits "Cryin' Again" and "Come On In," falling into line at No. 3 each.

Billy Ocean had No. 1 hits with "Caribbean Queen (No More Love On The Run)" and "There'll Be Sad Songs (To Make You Cry)." His 1988 No. 1, "Get Outta My Dreams, Get Into My Car," had no parentheses in the title, but it was his fastest No. 1 ever, hitting the pop summit in just nine weeks.

Alexander O'Neal and Cherelle's 1988 single "Never Knew Love Like This" was their second to reach No. 2 on the R & B charts, following their "Saturday Love" duet of two years before. For Cherelle, they were her biggest R & B hits—but O'Neal topped them both with his own No. 1, "Fake."

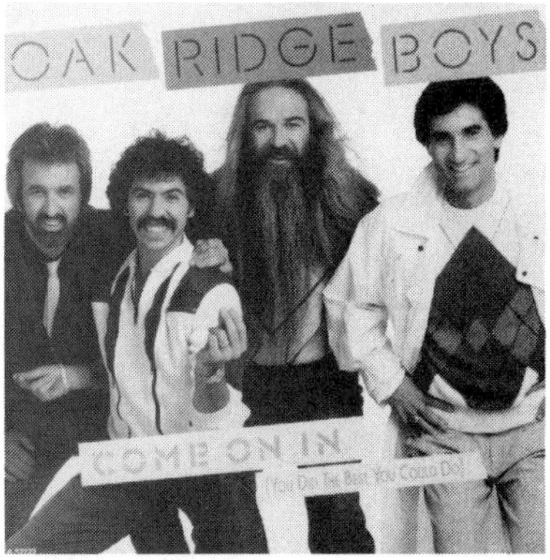

DATE	POS	WKS	ARTIST—RECORD TITLE	LABEL & NO.
12/04/65	**33**	2	2. Mystic Eyes [I]	Parrot 9796
			THIN LIZZY	
			Dublin, Ireland rock quartet led by Phil Lynott (d: 1/4/86 [35]).	
6/05/76	**12**	9	1. The Boys Are Back In Town	Mercury 73786
			THINK	
			Studio group assembled by producers Lou Stallman and Bobby Susser.	
1/01/72	**23**	5	1. Once You Understand featuring dialogue between a teenager and his parents	Laurie 3583
			38 SPECIAL	
			Florida Southern-rock sextet: Donnie Van Zant (younger brother of Lynyrd Skynyrd's Ronnie Van Zant; lead singer), Don Barnes, Jeff Carlisi, Steve Brookins, Jack Grondin and Larry Jungstrom (replaced Ken Lyons in 1979). By 1988, Barnes and Brookins replaced by Danny Chauncey and Max Carl.	
4/18/81	**27**	6	1. Hold On Loosely	A&M 2316
5/22/82	**10**	12	2. **Caught Up In You**	A&M 2412
10/02/82	**38**	2	3. You Keep Runnin' Away	A&M 2431
12/03/83†	**19**	9	4. If I'd Been The One	A&M 2594
2/18/84	**20**	8	5. Back Where You Belong	A&M 2615
10/27/84	**25**	5	6. Teacher Teacher from the film "Teachers"; all of above: produced by Rodney Mills	Capitol 5405
5/24/86	**14**	9	7. Like No Other Night	A&M 2831
			B.J. THOMAS	
			Born Billy Joe Thomas on 8/7/42 in Hugo, Oklahoma; raised in Roseburg, Texas (near Houston). With the Triumphs, worked local clubs; recorded for Hickory in 1964. Went solo in 1966. Became a born-again Christian in 1976 and began a successful gospel recording career.	
3/12/66	**8**	10	1. **I'm So Lonesome I Could Cry** **B.J. THOMAS & THE TRIUMPHS**	Scepter 12129
6/04/66	**22**	5	2. Mama	Scepter 12139
7/23/66	**34**	4	3. Billy And Sue **B.J. THOMAS & THE TRIUMPHS**	Hickory 1395
8/03/68	**28**	7	4. The Eyes Of A New York Woman	Scepter 12219
12/14/68†	**5**	12	● 5. **Hooked On A Feeling**	Scepter 12230
11/22/69†	**1**(4)	19	● 6. **Raindrops Keep Fallin' On My Head** from the film "Butch Cassidy & The Sundance Kid"	Scepter 12265
4/11/70	**26**	6	7. Everybody's Out Of Town	Scepter 12277
7/11/70	**9**	10	8. **I Just Can't Help Believing**	Scepter 12283
1/09/71	**38**	3	9. Most Of All	Scepter 12299
3/13/71	**16**	9	10. No Love At All	Scepter 12307
8/14/71	**34**	3	11. Mighty Clouds Of Joy	Scepter 12320
2/26/72	**15**	9	12. Rock And Roll Lullaby featuring Duane Eddy, guitar	Scepter 12344
3/01/75	**1**(1)	14	● 13. **(Hey Won't You Play) Another Somebody Done Somebody Wrong Song**	ABC 12054
8/06/77	**17**	10	14. Don't Worry Baby	MCA 40735

DATE	POS	WKS	ARTIST—RECORD TITLE	LABEL & NO.
			CARLA THOMAS	
			Born on 12/21/42 in Memphis. Daughter of Rufus Thomas. First recorded with Rufus for Satellite in 1960.	
2/20/61	**10**	10	1. **Gee Whiz (Look At His Eyes)**	Atlantic 2086
9/24/66	**14**	10	2. B-A-B-Y	Stax 195
6/03/67	**26**	4	3. Tramp	Stax 216
			OTIS (Redding) **& CARLA**	
9/23/67	**30**	2	4. Knock On Wood	Stax 228
			OTIS & CARLA	
			IAN THOMAS	
			Canadian singer/songwriter.	
12/29/73†	**34**	3	1. Painted Ladies	Janus 224
			IRMA THOMAS	
			Born Irma Lee on 2/18/41 in Ponchatoula, Louisiana. The Soul Queen of New Orleans. Discovered by New Orleans bandleader Tommy Ridgley.	
4/25/64	**17**	7	1. Wish Someone Would Care	Imperial 66013
			RUFUS THOMAS	
			Born on 3/26/17 in Cayce, Mississippi. R&B singer/songwriter/choreographer. Father of singers Carla and Vaneese Thomas. First recorded for Talent in 1950. Disc jockey at WDIA-Memphis from 1953-74.	
11/02/63	**10**	9	1. **Walking The Dog**	Stax 140
2/28/70	**28**	8	2. Do The Funky Chicken	Stax 0059
1/23/71	**25**	8	3. (Do The) Push And Pull, Part I	Stax 0079
9/18/71	**31**	4	4. The Breakdown (Part I)	Stax 0098
			TIMMY THOMAS	
			Born on 11/13/44 in Evansville, Indiana. Soul singer/songwriter/keyboardist. Studio musician at Gold Wax Records in Memphis. Session work for Betty Wright and KC & The Sunshine Band.	
12/23/72†	**3**	11	1. **Why Can't We Live Together**	Glades 1703
			THOMPSON TWINS	
			British trio: Tom Bailey (b: 1/18/56, England; lead singer, synthesizer), Alannah Currie (b: 9/28/57, New Zealand; xylophone, percussion) and Joe Leeway (b: England; conga, synthesizer). Leeway left in 1986.	
3/12/83	**30**	5	1. Lies	Arista 1024
2/25/84	**3**	15	2. **Hold Me Now**	Arista 9164
6/09/84	**11**	9	3. Doctor! Doctor!	Arista 9209
10/05/85	**6**	14	4. **Lay Your Hands On Me**	Arista 9396
1/25/86	**8**	11	5. **King For A Day**	Arista 9450
4/25/87	**31**	5	6. Get That Love	Arista 9577
			CHRIS THOMPSON - see NIGHT	
			KAY THOMPSON	
			Born on 11/9/13 in St. Louis. Wrote "Eloise" series of children's books. In the film musical "Funny Face," 1956.	
3/17/56	**39**	2	1. Eloise [N]	Cadence 3

DATE	POS	WKS	ARTIST—RECORD TITLE	LABEL & NO.
			SUE THOMPSON	
			Born Eva Sue McKee on 7/19/26 in Nevada, Missouri; raised in San Jose, California.	
9/25/61	**5**	11	1. **Sad Movies (Make Me Cry)**	Hickory 1153
1/13/62	**3**	11	2. **Norman**	Hickory 1159
7/21/62	**31**	5	3. Have A Good Time	Hickory 1174
10/20/62	**17**	6	4. James (Hold The Ladder Steady)	Hickory 1183
2/06/65	**23**	4	5. Paper Tiger all of above (except #3): written by John D. Loudermilk	Hickory 1284
			ALI THOMSON	
			Scottish singer/songwriter. Younger brother of Supertramp's Dougie Thomson.	
7/12/80	**15**	9	1. Take A Little Rhythm	A&M 2243
			THE THREE DEGREES	
			Philadelphia R&B trio discovered by Richard Barrett. Originally consisted of Fayette Pinkney, Linda Turner and Shirley Porter. Turner and Porter replaced by Sheila Ferguson and Valerie Holiday in 1966.	
7/25/70	**29**	4	1. Maybe	Roulette 7079
3/16/74	**1**(2)	14	● 2. **TSOP (The Sound Of Philadelphia)** [I] theme from the TV show "Soul Train"	Phil. Int. 3540
10/19/74	**2**(1)	13	● 3. **When Will I See You Again**	Phil. Int. 3550
			THREE DOG NIGHT	
			Los Angeles pop-rock group formed in 1968 featuring lead singers Danny Hutton (b: 9/10/42), Cory Wells (b: 2/5/42) and Chuck Negron (b: 6/8/42). Disbanded in the mid-70s. Re-formed in the mid-80s to tour.	
3/29/69	**29**	4	1. Try A Little Tenderness	Dunhill 4177
5/31/69	**5**	12	● 2. **One** written by Nilsson	Dunhill 4191
8/16/69	**4**	12	3. **Easy To Be Hard**	Dunhill 4203
11/08/69	**10**	12	4. **Eli's Coming** written by Laura Nyro	Dunhill 4215
3/07/70	**15**	8	5. Celebrate	Dunhill 4229
6/06/70	**1**(2)	13	● 6. **Mama Told Me (Not To Come)** written by Randy Newman	Dunhill 4239
9/12/70	**15**	8	7. Out In The Country	Dunhill 4250
12/05/70†	**19**	9	8. One Man Band	Dunhill 4262
3/27/71	**1**(6)	15	● 9. **Joy To The World**	Dunhill 4272
7/17/71	**7**	11	10. **Liar** written by Russ Ballard	Dunhill 4282
11/20/71	**4**	10	● 11. **An Old Fashioned Love Song** written by Paul Williams	Dunhill 4294
1/08/72	**5**	10	12. **Never Been To Spain** 9 & 12: written by Hoyt Axton	Dunhill 4299
4/01/72	**12**	8	13. The Family Of Man	Dunhill 4306
8/26/72	**1**(1)	9	● 14. **Black & White**	Dunhill 4317
12/09/72†	**19**	9	15. Pieces Of April	Dunhill 4331
6/02/73	**3**	10	● 16. **Shambala**	Dunhill 4352
11/17/73	**17**	6	17. Let Me Serenade You	Dunhill 4370
4/13/74	**4**	12	● 18. **The Show Must Go On**	Dunhill 4382

DATE	POS	WKS	ARTIST—RECORD TITLE	LABEL & NO.
7/13/74	**16**	8	19. Sure As I'm Sittin' Here	Dunhill 15001
11/02/74	**33**	3	20. Play Something Sweet (Brickyard Blues)	Dunhill 15013
8/09/75	**32**	3	21. Til The World Ends 15 & 21: written by Dave Loggins	ABC 12114
			JOHNNY THUNDER	
			R&B singer from Leesburg, Florida. Discovered by Teddy Vann.	
1/05/63	**4**	9	1. **Loop De Loop**	Diamond 129
			THUNDERCLAP NEWMAN	
			British trio: Andy Newman, Speedy Keen (lead singer) and Jimmy McCulloch (member of Wings, 1975-77; died on 9/27/79 [26]). Group put together by Pete Townshend.	
10/25/69	**37**	2	1. Something In The Air from the film "The Magic Christian"	Track 2656
			TIERRA	
			East Los Angeles group led by brothers Steve (trombone, timbales) and Rudy (guitar) Salas. Both formerly with El Chicano.	
12/13/80†	**18**	15	1. Together	Boardwalk 5702
			TIFFANY	
			Tiffany Darwisch, born on 10/2/71. California pop singer, originally from Oklahoma.	
9/26/87	**1**(2)	13	1. **I Think We're Alone Now**	MCA 53167
12/12/87†	**1**(2)	14	2. **Could've Been**	MCA 53231
3/12/88	**7**	9	3. **I Saw Him Standing There**	MCA 53285
12/03/88†	**6**	14	4. **All This Time**	MCA 53371
			TIJUANA BRASS - see HERB ALPERT	
			'TIL TUESDAY	
			Boston pop quartet: Aimee Mann (lead singer, bass), Michael Hausmann (drums), Robert Holmes (guitar) and Joey Pesce (keyboards - replaced by Michael Montes in 1988).	
5/18/85	**8**	13	1. **Voices Carry**	Epic 04795
11/01/86	**26**	5	2. What About Love	Epic 06289
			JOHNNY TILLOTSON	
			Born on 4/20/39 in Jacksonville, Florida; raised in Palatka, Florida. On local radio "Young Folks Revue" from age 9. Worked as a disc jockey on WWPF. Appeared on the "Toby Dowdy" TV show in Jacksonville, then own show. Signed by Cadence Records in 1958. In the film "Just For Fun."	
10/24/60	**2**(1)	12	1. **Poetry In Motion**	Cadence 1384
2/06/61	**25**	5	2. Jimmy's Girl	Cadence 1391
8/28/61	**7**	8	3. **Without You**	Cadence 1404
1/20/62	**35**	1	4. Dreamy Eyes [R] originally charted in 1958 (POS 63)	Cadence 1409
5/19/62	**3**	12	5. **It Keeps Right On A-Hurtin'**	Cadence 1418
8/25/62	**17**	6	6. Send Me The Pillow You Dream On	Cadence 1424
11/17/62	**24**	5	7. I Can't Help It (If I'm Still In Love With You) classic country hit by Hank Williams	Cadence 1432
3/23/63	**24**	6	8. Out Of My Mind	Cadence 1434
8/24/63	**18**	7	9. You Can Never Stop Me Loving You	Cadence 1437
11/30/63†	**7**	10	10. **Talk Back Trembling Lips**	MGM 13181
3/14/64	**37**	2	11. Worried Guy	MGM 13193

DATE	POS	WKS	ARTIST—RECORD TITLE	LABEL & NO.
6/06/64	**36**	2	12. I Rise, I Fall	MGM 13232
11/28/64	**31**	6	13. She Understands Me	MGM 13284
10/02/65	**35**	2	14. Heartaches By The Number	MGM 13376
			TIMBUK 3	
			Austin-based husband-and-wife duo: Pat and Barbara Kooyman MacDonald. Met while Barbara was attending the University of Wisconsin in 1978.	
11/22/86	**19**	9	1. The Future's So Bright, I Gotta Wear Shades	I.R.S. 52940
			THE TIME	
			Funk group formed in Minneapolis by Prince in 1981. Original lineup: Morris Day (lead singer), Terry Lewis, Jimmy "Jam" Harris, Monte Moir, Jesse Johnson and Jellybean Johnson. Disbanded in 1984. Day and Jesse Johnson went solo; Lewis and Harris became a highly successful songwriting/producing team.	
1/05/85	**20**	10	1. Jungle Love	Warner 29181
4/13/85	**36**	2	2. The Bird	Warner 29094
			above 2: from the film "Purple Rain"	
			TIMES TWO	
			Male duo of vocalists/keyboardists from Pt. Reyes, California: Shanti Jones and Johnny Dollar.	
4/23/88	**21**	8	1. Strange But True	Reprise 27998
			TIMEX SOCIAL CLUB	
			Berkeley, California rap group led by vocalist Michael Marshall; produced by Jay King, who later formed and fronted Club Nouveau.	
7/12/86	**8**	12	1. **Rumors**	Jay 7001
			TIN TIN	
			Australian duo: Steve Kipner (keyboards) and Steve Groves (guitar).	
5/08/71	**20**	6	1. Toast And Marmalade For Tea	Atco 6794
			TINY TIM	
			Born Herbert Khaury on 4/12/30 in New York City. Novelty singer/ukulele player. National phenomenon when he married "Miss Vicki" on "The Tonight Show" on 12/18/69.	
6/08/68	**17**	6	1. Tip-Toe Thru' The Tulips With Me [N]	Reprise 0679
			#1 hit (10 weeks) for Nick Lucas in 1929	
			TOBY BEAU	
			Texas pop quintet: Danny McKenna, Rob Young, Balde Silva, Steve Zipper and Ron Rose.	
7/01/78	**13**	12	1. My Angel Baby	RCA 11250
			ART & DOTTY TODD	
			Pop duo consisting of Arthur W. Todd (b: 3/11/20) and Dotty Todd (b: 6/22/23), both from Elizabeth, New Jersey. Married in 1941.	
4/21/58	**6**	11	1. **Chanson d'Amour (Song Of Love)**	Era 1064
			Jockey #6 / Best Seller #13 / Top 100 #13	
			NICK TODD	
			Pat Boone's younger brother.	
2/10/58	**21**	2	1. At The Hop	Dot 15675
			Jockey #21 / Top 100 #70	

DATE	POS	WKS	ARTIST—RECORD TITLE	LABEL & NO.
			THE TOKENS	
			Vocal group originally formed as the Linc-Tones at Lincoln High School in Brooklyn in 1955. Consisted of Hank Medress, Neil Sedaka, Eddie Rabkin and Cynthia Zolitin. First recorded for Melba in 1956. Rabkin replaced by Jay Siegel in 1956. Zolitin and Sedaka left in 1958. Medress then formed Darrell & The Oxfords, 1958-59, then re-formed The Tokens with brothers Phil and Mitch Margo and recorded for Warwick in 1960. Formed own label B.T. Puppy in 1964. Medress produced Tony Orlando & Dawn in 1970, and then left The Tokens, who continued as a trio and recorded as Cross Country in 1973.	
4/24/61	**15**	6	1. Tonight I Fell In Love	Warwick 615
11/27/61	**1**(3)	13	● 2. **The Lion Sleeps Tonight**	RCA 7954
			also known as "Wimoweh"; a South African Zulu song	
4/09/66	**30**	5	3. I Hear Trumpets Blow	B.T. Puppy 518
5/20/67	**36**	2	4. Portrait Of My Love	Warner 5900
			TOM TOM CLUB	
			Studio project headed by Chris Frantz and wife Tina Weymouth of Talking Heads.	
4/10/82	**31**	4	1. Genius Of Love	Sire 49882
			TOMMY TUTONE	
			San Francisco rock band led by Tommy Heath (lead singer) & Jim Keller (lead guitar).	
6/21/80	**38**	2	1. Angel Say No	Columbia 11278
3/13/82	**4**	16	2. **867-5309/Jenny**	Columbia 02646
			TONE LOC	
			L.A.-based rapper, born Anthony Smith.	
12/24/88†	**2**(1)	14	▲ 1. **Wild Thing**	Delicious 102
			OSCAR TONEY, JR.	
			Born on 5/26/39 in Selma, Alabama; raised in Columbus, Georgia. Own gospel group, Sensational Melodies Of Joy, while in high school. Own group, the Searchers, first recorded for Max in 1957. Recorded solo for King in 1958. Oscar's 3 sisters sang as the Tonettes.	
6/17/67	**23**	5	1. For Your Precious Love	Bell 672
			TONY & JOE	
			Tony Savonne & Joe Saraceno.	
8/04/58	**33**	1	1. The Freeze	Era 1075
			Hot 100 #33 / Best Seller #39	
			MEL TORME	
			Born Melvin Howard on 9/13/25 in Chicago. Jazz singer/songwriter/ pianist/drummer/ actor. Wrote Nat King Cole's "The Christmas Song."	
12/15/62	**36**	3	1. Comin' Home Baby	Atlantic 2165
			THE TORNADOES	
			English surf-rock instrumental quintet organized by producer Joe Meek in 1962. Original lineup: Alan Caddy (lead guitar), George Bellamy, Roger LaVerne Jackson, Heinz Burt and Clem Cattini. Meek committed suicide on 2/3/67.	
11/17/62	**1**(3)	13	1. **Telstar** **[I]**	London 9561

DATE	POS	WKS	ARTIST—RECORD TITLE	LABEL & NO.
			MITCHELL TOROK	
			Born on 10/28/29 in Houston. Singer/songwriter/guitarist.	
4/29/57	**25**	3	1. Pledge Of Love Best Seller #25 / Top 100 #26	Decca 30230
8/31/59	**27**	6	2. Caribbean [R] same version charted in 1953 (POS 26) on Abbott 140	Guyden 2018
			TOTO	
			Pop-rock group formed in Los Angeles in 1978. Consisted of Bobby Kimball (vocals), Steve Lukather (guitar), David Paich and Steve Porcaro (keyboards), David Hungate (bass) and Jeff Porcaro (drums). Prominent session musicians, most notably behind Boz Scaggs in the late 70s. Hungate was replaced by Mike Porcaro in 1983. Kimball replaced by Fergie Frederiksen in 1984; Frederiksen replaced by Joseph Williams (conductor John's son) in 1986. Steve Porcaro left in 1988. Paich and his father Marty won an Emmy for writing the theme to the TV series "Ironside."	
11/11/78†	**5**	14	● 1. **Hold The Line**	Columbia 10830
2/09/80	**26**	8	2. 99	Columbia 11173
5/08/82	**2**(5)	18	3. **Rosanna**	Columbia 02811
9/11/82	**30**	5	4. Make Believe	Columbia 03143
11/20/82†	**1**(1)	16	5. **Africa**	Columbia 03335
3/26/83	**10**	12	6. **I Won't Hold You Back**	Columbia 03597
11/24/84	**30**	6	7. Stranger In Town	Columbia 04672
9/27/86	**11**	12	8. I'll Be Over You	Columbia 06280
2/07/87	**38**	2	9. Without Your Love	Columbia 06570
3/26/88	**22**	8	10. Pamela	Columbia 07715
			TOWER OF POWER	
			Integrated Oakland-based R&B-funk band formed by sax player Emilio "Mimi" Castillo in the late 60s. Lenny Williams sang lead from 1972-75. Originally known as the Motowns.	
8/26/72	**29**	5	1. You're Still A Young Man	Warner 7612
6/16/73	**17**	11	2. So Very Hard To Go	Warner 7687
8/24/74	**26**	4	3. Don't Change Horses (In The Middle Of A Stream)	Warner 7828
			ED TOWNSEND	
			Born on 4/16/29 in Fayetteville, Tennessee. R&B singer/songwriter.	
4/28/58	**13**	13	1. For Your Love Jockey #13 / Best Seller #15 / Top 100 #15	Capitol 3926
			PETE TOWNSHEND	
			Born on 5/19/45 in London. Lead guitarist/songwriter of The Who.	
7/05/80	**9**	12	1. **Let My Love Open The Door**	Atco 7217
12/21/85†	**26**	7	2. Face The Face	Atco 99590
			THE TOYS	
			Trio from Woodrow Wilson High School, Jamaica, New York: Barbara Harris, June Montiero and Barbara Parritt. Appearances on "Shindig" TV show in 1965. In film "The Girl In Daddy's Bikini."	
10/02/65	**2**(3)	11	● 1. **A Lover's Concerto** adapted from Bach: Minuet In G	DynoVoice 209
1/01/66	**18**	6	2. Attack	DynoVoice 214

DATE	POS	WKS	ARTIST—RECORD TITLE	LABEL & NO.
			T'PAU	
			Group from Shrewsbury, England; Carol Decker, lead singer. Band named after a Vulcan Princess in an episode of the TV series "Star Trek."	
6/06/87	**4**	16	1. **Heart And Soul**	Virgin 99466
			THE TRADE WINDS	
			New York City pop singing/songwriting/production duo: Pete Anders (Andreoli) and Vini Poncia. First recorded with the group, The Videls. Recorded in 1966-67 as The Trade Winds, The Innocence and The Videls. Poncia produced several albums for Ringo Starr and Melissa Manchester.	
2/27/65	**32**	4	1. New York's A Lonely Town	Red Bird 020
			THE TRAMMPS	
			Philadelphia disco group. Key members: Jimmy Ellis (lead tenor), Earl Young (lead bass), Harold and Stanley Wade (tenors) and Robert Upchurch (baritone). Had own label, Golden Fleece, in 1973.	
2/21/76	**35**	4	1. Hold Back The Night	Buddah 507
6/05/76	**27**	5	2. That's Where The Happy People Go	Atlantic 3306
3/25/78	**11**	13	3. Disco Inferno in the film "Saturday Night Fever"	Atlantic 3389
			THE TRASHMEN	
			Minneapolis/St. Paul surf-rock quartet: Tony Andreason, Dal Winslow, Bob Reed and Steve Wahrer. Both hits taken from tunes by The Rivingtons: "Papa-Oom-Mow-Mow" and "The Bird's The Word." Wahrer died of throat cancer on 1/21/89 (47).	
12/28/63†	**4**	10	1. **Surfin' Bird**	Garrett 4002
2/29/64	**30**	4	2. Bird Dance Beat	Garrett 4003
			TRAVIS & BOB	
			Travis Pritchett and Bob Weaver from Jackson, Alabama.	
4/06/59	**8**	9	1. **Tell Him No**	Sandy 1017
			JOHN TRAVOLTA	
			Born on 2/18/54 in Englewood, New Jersey. Vinnie Barbarino on the TV series "Welcome Back Kotter." Starred in the films "Saturday Night Fever," "Grease," "Urban Cowboy," "Blow Out" and others.	
6/12/76	**10**	10	1. **Let Her In**	Midland I. 10623
11/27/76	**38**	2	2. Whenever I'm Away From You	Midland I. 10780
3/19/77	**34**	3	3. All Strung Out On You	Midland I. 10907
4/08/78	**1**(1)	16	▲ 4. **You're The One That I Want** **JOHN TRAVOLTA & OLIVIA NEWTON-JOHN**	RSO 891
8/19/78	**5**	12	• 5. **Summer Nights** **JOHN TRAVOLTA & OLIVIA NEWTON-JOHN & CAST** above 2: from the film "Grease"	RSO 906
			THE TREMELOES	
			British pop-rock quartet: Alan Blakely, Dave Munden, Ricky West and Len Hawkes. Group originally formed by Brian Poole (went solo in 1966).	
5/06/67	**13**	8	1. Here Comes My Baby	Epic 10139
7/15/67	**11**	10	2. Silence Is Golden	Epic 10184
10/21/67	**36**	4	3. Even The Bad Times Are Good	Epic 10233

DATE	POS	WKS	ARTIST—RECORD TITLE	LABEL & NO.
			T. REX	
			British rock group led by Marc Bolan (born Marc Feld on 9/30/48 in London; killed in an auto accident on 9/16/77).	
1/29/72	**10**	11	1. **Bang A Gong (Get It On)**	Reprise 1032
			TRIUMPH	
			Canadian hard-rock trio formed in Toronto in 1975. Consisted of Gil Moore (drums, vocals), Rik Emmett (guitar, vocals) and Mike Levine (keyboards, bass).	
8/25/79	**38**	3	1. Hold On	RCA 11569
10/18/86	**27**	5	2. Somebody's Out There	MCA 52898
			THE TRIUMPHS - see B.J. THOMAS	
			THE TROGGS	
			British rock quartet from Andover, England. Consisted of Reg Presley (lead singer), Chris Britton (guitar), Pete Staples (bass) and Ronnie Bond (drums).	
7/09/66	**1**(2)	9	1. **Wild Thing**	Fontana 1548
9/03/66	**29**	2	2. With A Girl Like You	Fontana 1552
			above 2: also released on Atco 6415	
3/23/68	**7**	12	3. **Love Is All Around**	Fontana 1607
			DORIS TROY	
			Born Doris Payne on 1/6/37 in New York City. R&B vocalist/songwriter. Backing vocalist on Pink Floyd's album "Dark Side Of The Moon."	
7/06/63	**10**	8	1. **Just One Look**	Atlantic 2188
			ANDREA TRUE CONNECTION	
			Disco act led by white Nashville-born vocalist Andrea True. Andrea moved to New York in 1968 and wrote commercials for radio and TV. Her break came while singing at the Riverboat in the Empire State Building, 1974.	
4/24/76	**4**	16	● 1. **More, More, More (Pt. 1)**	Buddah 515
3/26/77	**27**	5	2. N.Y., You Got Me Dancing	Buddah 564
			THE TUBES	
			San Francisco theatre rock troupe led by Fee Waybill.	
8/01/81	**35**	3	1. Don't Want To Wait Anymore	Capitol 5007
5/07/83	**10**	12	2. **She's A Beauty**	Capitol 5217
			TANYA TUCKER	
			Born on 10/10/58 in Seminole, Texas. Bit part in the film "Jeremiah Johnson" in 1972. Prominent country singer.	
6/07/75	**37**	2	1. Lizzie And The Rainman	MCA 40402
			TOMMY TUCKER	
			Born Robert Higginbotham on 3/5/39 in Springfield, Ohio. Vocalist/pianist. First recorded for Hi in 1959. Died of poisoning on 1/22/82.	
2/29/64	**11**	8	1. Hi-Heel Sneakers	Checker 1067
			THE TUNE WEAVERS	
			Boston R&B quintet consisting of Margo Sylvia (lead), husband John Sylvia (bass), Gilbert Lopez (Margo's brother; tenor) and Charlotte Davis (Margo's cousin).	
9/23/57	**5**	14	1. **Happy, Happy Birthday Baby**	Checker 872
			Top 100 #5 / Best Seller #8 / Jockey #12	

DATE	POS	WKS	ARTIST—RECORD TITLE	LABEL & NO.
			THE TURBANS	
			Philadelphia R&B quartet: Al Banks (lead), Matthew Platt (tenor), Charles Williams (baritone) and Andrew "Chet" Jones (bass). Jones wrote hit "When You Dance." Disbanded in 1961.	
1/14/56	**33**	1	1. When You Dance	Herald 458
			IKE & TINA TURNER	
			Husband-and-wife duo: guitarist Ike Turner (b: 11/5/31 in Clarksdale, MS) and vocalist Tina (born Anna Mae Bullock on 11/26/38 in Brownsville, TN). Married from 1958-76. At age 11, Ike was backing pianist for bluesmen Sonny Boy Williamson (Aleck Ford) and Robert Nighthawk (of the Nighthawks). Formed own band, the Kings of Rhythm, while in high school; backed Jackie Brenston's hit "Rocket '88'." Prolific session, production and guitar work during the 1950s. In 1960, developed a dynamic stage show around Tina; "The Ike & Tina Turner Revue" featured her backing vocalists, The Ikettes, and Ike's Kings Of Rhythm. Disbanded in 1974. In the mid-80s, Tina emerged as a successful solo artist.	
10/03/60	**27**	6	1. A Fool In Love	Sue 730
9/04/61	**14**	5	2. It's Gonna Work Out Fine	Sue 749
1/13/62	**38**	2	3. Poor Fool	Sue 753
8/08/70	**34**	6	4. I Want To Take You Higher	Liberty 56177
			IKE & TINA TURNER & THE IKETTES	
2/13/71	**4**	11	• 5. **Proud Mary**	Liberty 56216
10/27/73	**22**	7	6. Nutbush City Limits	United Art. 298
			JESSE LEE TURNER	
			Rockabilly singer from Bowling, Texas.	
1/26/59	**20**	6	1. The Little Space Girl [N]	Carlton 496
			SAMMY TURNER	
			Born Samuel Black on 6/2/32 in Paterson, New Jersey. Tommy Edwards-styled vocalist.	
7/06/59	**3**	14	1. **Lavender-Blue** old traditional folk song from England, 1750	Big Top 3016
11/16/59	**19**	7	2. Always 4 versions hit the top 10 in 1926	Big Top 3029
			SPYDER TURNER	
			Born Dwight D. Turner in 1947 in Beckley, West Virginia. Soul vocalist.	
1/14/67	**12**	8	1. Stand By Me [N] vocal impressions of Jackie Wilson, David Ruffin, Billy Stewart, Smokey Robinson and Chuck Jackson	MGM 13617
			TINA TURNER	
			Born Anna Mae Bullock on 11/26/38 in Brownsville, Tennessee. R&B-rock vocalist/ actress. Half of Ike & Tina Turner duo. In films "Tommy" and "Mad Max Beyond Thunderdome."	
2/18/84	**26**	7	1. Let's Stay Together	Capitol 5322
6/23/84	**1**(3)	18	• 2. **What's Love Got To Do With It** Grammy winner: Record of The Year & Song of The Year	Capitol 5354
10/06/84	**5**	13	3. **Better Be Good To Me**	Capitol 5387
1/26/85	**7**	12	4. **Private Dancer**	Capitol 5433
5/18/85	**37**	3	5. Show Some Respect	Capitol 5461
7/20/85	**2**(1)	12	6. **We Don't Need Another Hero (Thunderdome)**	Capitol 5491
10/12/85	**15**	10	7. One Of The Living above 2: from the film "Mad Max Beyond Thunderdome"	Capitol 5518

DATE	POS	WKS	ARTIST—RECORD TITLE	LABEL & NO.
12/07/85†	**15**	9	8. It's Only Love **BRYAN ADAMS/TINA TURNER**	A&M 2791
9/06/86	**2**(3)	12	9. **Typical Male**	Capitol 5615
12/20/86†	**30**	6	10. Two People	Capitol 5644
3/07/87	**13**	7	11. What You Get Is What You See	Capitol 5668
			THE TURTLES	
			Pop-folk-rock group formed at Westchester High School in Los Angeles in 1961. Led by Mark Volman (b: 4/19/47, Los Angeles) and Howard Kaylan (b: Howard Kaplan on 6/22/47, New York City). First called the Nightriders; then the Crossfires. Recorded for Capco in 1963. Name changed to The Turtles in 1965. Many personnel changes except for Volman and Kaylan. Group disbanded in 1970. Volman and Kaylan joined the Mothers Of Invention. Went out as a duo in 1972 and recorded as Phlorescent Leech & Eddie and later as Flo & Eddie. Did soundtrack for the film "Strawberry Shortcake." Toured again as The Turtles in 1985.	
8/21/65	**8**	8	1. **It Ain't Me Babe** written by Bob Dylan	White Whale 222
11/20/65	**29**	4	2. Let Me Be	White Whale 224
2/19/66	**20**	9	3. You Baby	White Whale 227
3/04/67	**1**(3)	12	● 4. **Happy Together**	White Whale 244
5/27/67	**3**	8	5. **She'd Rather Be With Me**	White Whale 249
8/26/67	**12**	7	6. You Know What I Mean	White Whale 254
12/02/67	**14**	7	7. She's My Girl	White Whale 260
10/12/68	**6**	9	8. **Elenore**	White Whale 276
1/25/69	**6**	9	9. **You Showed Me**	White Whale 292
			TUXEDO JUNCTION	
			Female disco studio group assembled by producers W. Michael Lewis & Lauren Rinder.	
7/01/78	**32**	2	1. Chattanooga Choo Choo revival of Glenn Miller's 1941 hit (POS 1)	Butterfly 1205
			DWIGHT TWILLEY	
			Born on 6/6/51 in Tulsa, Oklahoma. Rock singer/songwriter/pianist. Formed the Dwight Twilley Band with Phil Seymour (bass, drums) in 1974.	
6/21/75	**16**	8	1. I'm On Fire **DWIGHT TWILLEY BAND**	Shelter 40380
3/03/84	**16**	10	2. Girls	EMI America 8196
			TWISTED SISTER	
			Long Island, New York heavy-metal quintet led by Dee Snider. Disbanded in late 1987.	
8/18/84	**21**	7	1. We're Not Gonna Take It	Atlantic 89641
			CONWAY TWITTY	
			Born Harold Jenkins on 9/1/33 in Friars Point, Mississippi. Superstar country singer. Conway's charted over 30 #1 solo country hits. Raised in Helena, Arkansas. Formed own group, the Phillips County Ramblers, at age 10. Offered a professional career with the Philadelphia Phillies when drafted. With service band, Cimmarons, in Japan, early 50s. Changed his name in 1957 and first recorded for Mercury. In the films "Sexpot Goes To College" and "College Confidential." Switched from pop to country music in 1965. Moved to Nashville in 1968. Owns tourist complex, Twitty City, in Hendersonville, Tennessee.	
9/29/58	**1**(2)	17	1. **It's Only Make Believe**	MGM 12677
2/16/59	**28**	7	2. The Story Of My Love	MGM 12748

DATE	POS	WKS	ARTIST—RECORD TITLE	LABEL & NO.
8/24/59	**29**	3	3. Mona Lisa #1 hit for Nat King Cole in 1950	MGM 12804
10/12/59	**10**	13	4. **Danny Boy** based on traditional Irish song "Londonderry Air" of 1855	MGM 12826
1/18/60	**6**	10	5. **Lonely Blue Boy** originally recorded (unreleased) by Elvis Presley as "Danny"; from the film "King Creole"	MGM 12857
4/25/60	**26**	5	6. What Am I Living For	MGM 12886
7/11/60	**35**	5	7. Is A Blue Bird Blue	MGM 12911
1/16/61	**22**	5	8. C'est Si Bon (It's So Good) #21 hit for Danny Kaye in 1950	MGM 12969
9/15/73	**22**	7	9. You've Never Been This Far Before	MCA 40094
			TYCOON	
			New York-based pop-rock sextet; Norman Mershon, lead singer.	
4/28/79	**26**	5	1. Such A Woman	Arista 0398
			BONNIE TYLER	
			Born Gaynor Hopkins on 6/8/53 in Swansea, Wales. Distinctive raspy vocals caused by operation to remove throat nodules in 1976.	
4/22/78	**3**	15	● 1. **It's A Heartache**	RCA 11249
8/13/83	**1**(4)	18	● 2. **Total Eclipse Of The Heart**	Columbia 03906
4/07/84	**34**	4	3. Holding Out For A Hero from the film "Footloose"	Columbia 04370
			THE TYMES	
			Soul group formed in Philadelphia in 1956. Consisted of George Williams (lead), George Hilliard, Donald Banks, Albert Berry and Norman Burnett. First called the Latineers. Berry and Hilliard were replaced by female singers Terri Gonzalez and Melanie Moore in the early 70s.	
6/22/63	**1**(1)	12	1. **So Much In Love**	Parkway 871
8/31/63	**7**	8	2. **Wonderful! Wonderful!**	Parkway 884
1/04/64	**19**	6	3. Somewhere	Parkway 891
12/28/68	**39**	1	4. People from the film "Funny Girl"	Columbia 44630
9/07/74	**12**	8	5. You Little Trustmaker	RCA 10022
			U	
			UB40	
			British integrated reggae octet; Ali Campbell, lead singer. Took name from a British unemployment benefit form.	
3/17/84	**34**	4	● 1. Red Red Wine	A&M 2600
9/07/85	**28**	4	2. I Got You Babe **UB40 with CHRISSIE HYNDE** (lead singer of the Pretenders)	A&M 2758
9/03/88	**1**(1)	12	3. **Red Red Wine** **[R]**	A&M 1244

DATE	POS	WKS	ARTIST—RECORD TITLE	LABEL & NO.
			TRACEY ULLMAN	
			Born on 12/30/59 in England. Actress/singer/comedienne. Own variety-style TV show on new Fox Broadcasting Co. network in 1987.	
3/17/84	**8**	11	1. **They Don't Know**	MCA 52347
			UNDERGROUND SUNSHINE	
			Rock quartet: Chris Connors and Jane Little (both from Wisconsin), with Frank and Betty Kohl (from Germany).	
8/23/69	**26**	5	1. Birthday written by John Lennon & Paul McCartney	Intrepid 75002
			THE UNDISPUTED TRUTH	
			Soul group consisting of Joe Harris, Billie Calvin and Brenda Evans. Many personnel changes thereafter.	
7/31/71	**3**	13	1. **Smiling Faces Sometimes**	Gordy 7108
			THE UNIFICS	
			Soul vocal group formed at Howard University in Washington, DC; Al Johnson, lead singer.	
10/19/68	**25**	5	1. Court Of Love	Kapp 935
1/18/69	**36**	4	2. The Beginning Of My End	Kapp 957
			UNION GAP - see GARY PUCKETT	
			UNIT FOUR plus TWO	
			English pop-rock sextet; Tommy Moeller, lead singer.	
5/29/65	**28**	4	1. Concrete And Clay	London 9751
			PHILIP UPCHURCH COMBO	
			Philip was born on 7/19/41 in Chicago. R&B guitarist. Session player for George Benson, Quincy Jones, The Jacksons and many others.	
6/26/61	**29**	3	1. You Can't Sit Down, Part 2 [I]	Boyd 3398
			URIAH HEEP	
			British hard-rock band. Key members: David Byron (lead singer), Mick Box (lead guitar) and Ken Hensley (keyboards).	
9/16/72	**39**	3	1. Easy Livin	Mercury 73307
			USA for AFRICA	
			USA: United Support of Artists - a collection of 46 major artists formed to help the suffering people of Africa and the USA	
3/23/85	**1**(4)	12	▲ 1. **We Are The World** soloists (in order): Lionel Richie, Stevie Wonder, Paul Simon, Kenny Rogers, James Ingram, Tina Turner, Billy Joel, Michael Jackson, Diana Ross, Dionne Warwick, Willie Nelson, Al Jarreau, Bruce Springsteen, Kenny Loggins, Steve Perry, Daryl Hall, Huey Lewis, Cyndi Lauper, Kim Carnes, Bob Dylan, and Ray Charles; written by Michael Jackson & Lionel Richie	Columbia 04839
			UTOPIA	
			Veteran pop-rock group with own recording studio near Woodstock, New York. Consists of Todd Rundgren (guitar), Kasim Sulton (bass), Roger Powell (keyboards) and Willie Wilcox (drums).	
3/29/80	**27**	5	1. Set Me Free	Bearsville 49180

DATE	POS	WKS	ARTIST—RECORD TITLE	LABEL & NO.
			U2	
			Rock band formed in Dublin, Ireland in 1976. Consists of Paul "Bono" Hewson (vocals), Dave "The Edge" Evans (guitar), Adam Clayton (bass) and Larry Mullen Jr. (drums). Emerged as 1987's leading rock act. 1988 film "Rattle And Hum" based on band.	
12/01/84	**33**	5	1. Pride (In The Name Of Love)	Island 99704
4/04/87	**1**(3)	13	2. **With Or Without You**	Island 99469
6/20/87	**1**(2)	13	3. **I Still Haven't Found What I'm Looking For**	Island 99430
10/03/87	**13**	9	4. Where The Streets Have No Name	Island 99408
10/08/88	**3**	13	● 5. **Desire**	Island 99250
			V	
			JERRY VALE	
			Born Genero Vitaliano on 7/8/32 in the Bronx. Pop ballad singer.	
3/24/56	**30**	5	1. Innamorata (Sweetheart) from the film "Artists & Models"	Columbia 40634
7/28/56	**14**	17	2. You Don't Know Me Best Seller #14 / Top 100 #14 / Juke Box #14 / Jockey #15	Columbia 40710
1/23/65	**24**	4	3. Have You Looked Into Your Heart	Columbia 43181
			RITCHIE VALENS	
			Born Richard Valenzuela on 5/13/41 in Pacoima, California. Latin rock and roll singer/songwriter/guitarist. Killed in the plane crash that also took the lives of Buddy Holly and the Big Bopper on 2/3/59. In the film "Go Johnny Go." The 1987 film "La Bamba" was based on his life.	
12/15/58†	**2**(2)	18	1. **Donna/**	
1/19/59	**22**	8	2. La Bamba [F]	Del-Fi 4110
			CATERINA VALENTE	
			Born in Paris of Italian parentage. Popular European singer/dancer.	
4/09/55	**8**	14	1. **The Breeze And I** Jockey #8 / Best Seller #13 #1 hit for Jimmy Dorsey in 1940	Decca 29467
			JOHN VALENTI	
			Blue-eyed soul singer from Chicago.	
10/30/76	**37**	2	1. Anything You Want	Ariola Am. 7625
			MARK VALENTINO	
			Born Anthony Busillo on 3/12/42 in Philadelphia.	
12/08/62	**27**	3	1. The Push And Kick	Swan 4121
			JOE VALINO	
10/27/56	**12**	14	1. Garden Of Eden Top 100 #12 / Jockey #12 / Best Seller #13 / Juke Box #13	Vik 0226
			VALJEAN	
			Born Valjean Johns on 11/19/34 in Shattuck, Oklahoma. Pianist.	
6/16/62	**28**	4	1. Theme From Ben Casey [I] from the TV series of the same title	Carlton 573

DATE	POS	WKS	ARTIST—RECORD TITLE	LABEL & NO.
			FRANKIE VALLI	
			Born Francis Castellucio on 5/3/37 in Newark, New Jersey. Recorded his first solo single in 1953 as Frank Valley on the Corona label. Formed own group the Variatones in 1955, and changed their name to the Four Lovers in 1956, which evolved into The 4 Seasons by 1961. Began solo work in 1965.	
2/12/66	**39**	1	1. (You're Gonna) Hurt Yourself	Smash 2015
6/03/67	**2**(1)	14	● 2. **Can't Take My Eyes Off You**	Philips 40446
9/16/67	**18**	5	3. I Make A Fool Of Myself	Philips 40484
1/20/68	**29**	4	4. To Give (The Reason I Live)	Philips 40510
1/18/75	**1**(1)	14	● 5. **My Eyes Adored You**	Private S. 45003
6/14/75	**6**	9	6. **Swearin' To God**	Private S. 45021
11/08/75	**11**	8	7. Our Day Will Come	Private S. 45043
5/08/76	**36**	2	8. Fallen Angel	Private S. 45074
6/17/78	**1**(2)	15	▲ 9. **Grease** from the film of the same title	RSO 897
			JUNE VALLI	
			Born on 6/30/30 in the Bronx. Married to Chicago disc jockey Howard Miller.	
5/14/55	**29**	1	1. Unchained Melody Best Seller #29 from the film "Unchained"	RCA 6078
4/18/60	**29**	4	2. Apple Green	Mercury 71588
			LEROY VAN DYKE	
			Born on 10/4/29 in Spring Fork, Missouri. Former livestock auctioneer.	
12/08/56†	**19**	7	1. Auctioneer [N] Juke Box #19 / Best Seller #21 / Top 100 #29	Dot 15503
11/20/61	**5**	12	2. **Walk On By**	Mercury 71834
3/31/62	**35**	2	3. If A Woman Answers (Hang Up The Phone)	Mercury 71926
			VAN HALEN	
			Hard-rock band formed in Pasadena, California in 1974. Consisted of David Lee Roth (b: 10/10/55; vocals), Eddie Van Halen (b: 1/26/57; guitar), Michael Anthony (b: 6/20/55; bass) and Alex Van Halen (b: 5/8/55; drums). The Van Halen brothers were born in Nijmegen, The Netherlands, and moved to Pasadena in 1968. Sammy Hagar replaced Roth as lead singer in 1985.	
3/11/78	**36**	3	1. You Really Got Me	Warner 8515
5/26/79	**15**	9	2. Dance The Night Away	Warner 8823
3/13/82	**12**	10	3. (Oh) Pretty Woman	Warner 50003
6/26/82	**38**	3	4. Dancing In The Street	Warner 29986
1/21/84	**1**(5)	15	● 5. **Jump**	Warner 29384
4/21/84	**13**	10	6. I'll Wait	Warner 29307
6/30/84	**13**	10	7. Panama	Warner 29250
3/29/86	**3**	11	8. **Why Can't This Be Love**	Warner 28740
6/14/86	**22**	7	9. Dreams	Warner 28702
8/30/86	**22**	9	10. Love Walks In	Warner 28626
6/18/88	**34**	2	11. Black And Blue	Warner 27891
7/23/88	**5**	12	12. **When It's Love**	Warner 27827
11/05/88	**13**	10	13. Finish What Ya Started	Warner 27746

DATE	POS	WKS	ARTIST—RECORD TITLE	LABEL & NO.
			VANDENBERG	
			Dutch hard-rock quartet: led by Adrian Vandenberg (guitar, keyboards), Bert Heerink (lead singer), Dick Kemper (bass) and Jos Zoomer (drums).	
3/12/83	**39**	2	1. Burning Heart	Atco 99947
			LUTHER VANDROSS	
			Born on 4/20/51 in New York City. Soul singer/producer/songwriter. Commercial jingle singer, then a top session vocalist/arranger.	
11/14/81	**33**	4	1. Never Too Much	Epic 02409
10/29/83	**27**	5	2. How Many Times Can We Say Goodbye	Arista 9073
			DIONNE WARWICK & LUTHER VANDROSS	
4/27/85	**29**	6	3. 'Til My Baby Comes Home	Epic 04760
12/27/86†	**15**	11	4. Stop To Love	Epic 06523
			VANGELIS	
			Born Evangelos Papathanassiou in Greece. Keyboardist/composer. Moved to Paris during the late 60s, then to London in the mid-70s. Formed rock band, Aphrodite's Child, in France with Demis Roussos, 1968-early 70s.	
2/20/82	**1**(1)	15	1. **Chariots Of Fire - Titles** **[I]** from the Academy Award-winning film of the same title	Polydor 2189
			VANILLA FUDGE	
			Psychedelic rock quartet formed in New York in 1966. Consisted of Mark Stein (lead singer, keyboards), Vinnie Martell (guitar), Tim Bogert (bass) and Carmine Appice (drums).	
8/03/68	**6**	9	1. **You Keep Me Hangin' On** **[R]** originally charted in 1967 (POS 67)	Atco 6590
10/26/68	**38**	4	2. Take Me For A Little While	Atco 6616
			VANITY FARE	
			British pop quintet featuring lead singer Trevor Brice.	
12/20/69†	**12**	9	1. Early In The Morning	Page One 21027
5/16/70	**5**	14	● 2. **Hitchin' A Ride**	Page One 21029
			GINO VANNELLI	
			Born on 6/16/52 in Montreal, Canada. Pop/soul-styled singer/songwriter.	
10/26/74	**22**	5	1. People Gotta Move	A&M 1614
10/14/78	**4**	13	2. **I Just Wanna Stop**	A&M 2072
4/04/81	**6**	14	3. **Living Inside Myself**	Arista 0588
			RANDY VANWARMER	
			Born Randall Van Wormer on 3/30/55 in Denver. Pop singer/songwriter/guitarist.	
4/21/79	**4**	14	● 1. **Just When I Needed You Most**	Bearsville 0334
			THE VAPORS	
			British pub-rock quartet; David Fenton, lead singer.	
11/15/80	**36**	3	1. Turning Japanese	Liberty 1364
			FRANKIE VAUGHAN	
			English pop singer/actor. In film "Let's Make Love" (1960).	
7/28/58	**22**	1	1. Judy Jockey #22 / Top 100 #100	Epic 9273

DATE	POS	WKS	ARTIST—RECORD TITLE	LABEL & NO.
			SARAH VAUGHAN	
			Born on 3/27/24 in Newark, New Jersey. Jazz singer. Studied piano from 1931-39. Won amateur contest at the Apollo Theater in 1942, which led to her joining Earl Hines' band as vocalist and second pianist. First recorded solo for Continental in 1944. With Billy Eckstine from 1944-45. Married manager/trumpet player George Treadwell in 1947. Dubbed "The Divine One." Still active in the 80s.	
11/27/54†	**6**	15	1. **Make Yourself Comfortable** Jockey #6 / Best Seller #8 / Juke Box #8	Mercury 70469
2/26/55	**12**	9	2. How Important Can It Be? Jockey #12 / Best Seller #18 / Juke Box #20	Mercury 70534
4/23/55	**6**	11	3. **Whatever Lola Wants** Jockey #6 / Juke Box #9 / Best Seller #12 from the Broadway musical "Damn Yankees"	Mercury 70595
7/16/55	**14**	1	4. Experience Unnecessary Jockey #14	Mercury 70646
12/03/55	**11**	7	5. C'est La Vie Jockey #11 / Top 100 #22	Mercury 70727
3/03/56	**13**	7	6. Mr. Wonderful Jockey #13 / Top 100 #38	Mercury 70777
7/21/56	**19**	6	7. Fabulous Character Jockey #19 / Top 100 #27 all of above: with Hugo Peretti & His Orchestra	Mercury 70885
1/12/57	**19**	5	8. The Banana Boat Song Jockey #19 / Top 100 #31	Mercury 71020
8/17/59	**7**	11	9. **Broken-Hearted Melody**	Mercury 71477
			BILLY VAUGHN	
			Born Richard Vaughn on 4/12/19 in Glasgow, Kentucky. Organized the Hilltoppers vocal group in 1952. Music director for Dot Records. Arranger/conductor for Pat Boone, Gale Storm, The Fontane Sisters and many other Dot artists. Billy had more pop hits than any other orchestra leader during the rock era.	
12/11/54†	**2**(1)	27	1. **Melody Of Love** **[I]** Best Seller #2 / Jockey #2 / Juke Box #3 tune written in 1903	Dot 15247
9/24/55	**5**	15	2. **The Shifting Whispering Sands (Parts 1 & 2)** **[S]** Best Seller #5 / Top 100 #5 pre / Jockey #5 / Juke Box #10 narration by Ken Nordine	Dot 15409
2/25/56	**37**	2	3. A Theme From The Three Penny Opera "Moritat" [I] written in 1928; later known as "Mack The Knife"	Dot 15444
9/08/56	**18**	6	4. When The White Lilacs Bloom Again [I] Juke Box #18 / Jockey #21 / Top 100 #22	Dot 15491
12/16/57	**10**	7	5. **Raunchy/** **[I]** Jockey #10 / Best Seller #25 / Top 100 #33	
1/13/58	**5**	18	6. Sail Along Silvery Moon [I] Best Seller #5 / Top 100 #5 / Jockey #6 #4 hit for Bing Crosby in 1937	Dot 15661
4/14/58	**30**	4	7. Tumbling Tumbleweeds [I] Best Seller #30 / Top 100 #35 #13 hit for the Sons of The Pioneers in 1934	Dot 15710
8/25/58	**20**	8	8. La Paloma [I] Best Seller #20 / Hot 100 #26 Spanish tango written in 1864	Dot 15795
2/02/59	**37**	1	9. Blue Hawaii [I] #5 hit for Bing Crosby in 1937	Dot 15879

DATE	POS	WKS	ARTIST—RECORD TITLE	LABEL & NO.
7/18/60	**19**	7	10. Look For A Star [I] from the film "Circus Of Horrors"	Dot 16106
3/06/61	**28**	3	11. Wheels [I]	Dot 16174
8/11/62	**13**	8	12. A Swingin' Safari [I]	Dot 16374
			BOBBY VEE	
			Born Robert Velline on 4/30/43 in Fargo, North Dakota. Formed band, The Shadows, with his brother and a friend in 1959. After Buddy Holly's death in a plane crash, The Shadows filled in on Buddy's next scheduled show in Fargo. First recorded for Soma in 1959. In the films "Swingin' Along," "It's Trad, Dad," "Play It Cool," "C'mon Let's Live A Little" and "Just For Fun."	
9/05/60	**6**	13	1. **Devil Or Angel**	Liberty 55270
12/12/60†	**6**	11	2. **Rubber Ball** co-written by Gene Pitney	Liberty 55287
2/27/61	**33**	3	3. Stayin' In	Liberty 55296
8/21/61	**1**(3)	11	4. **Take Good Care Of My Baby**	Liberty 55354
11/20/61	**2**(1)	13	5. **Run To Him**	Liberty 55388
3/17/62	**15**	6	6. Please Don't Ask About Barbara	Liberty 55419
6/09/62	**15**	6	7. Sharing You	Liberty 55451
9/15/62	**20**	6	8. Punish Her	Liberty 55479
12/22/62†	**3**	11	9. **The Night Has A Thousand Eyes**	Liberty 55521
4/13/63	**13**	7	10. Charms	Liberty 55530
7/20/63	**34**	2	11. Be True To Yourself with The Johnny Mann Singers	Liberty 55581
8/12/67	**3**	13	● 12. **Come Back When You Grow Up** **BOBBY VEE & THE STRANGERS**	Liberty 55964
12/16/67	**37**	2	13. Beautiful People **BOBBY VEE & THE STRANGERS**	Liberty 56009
5/18/68	**35**	4	14. My Girl/Hey Girl	Liberty 56033
			SUZANNE VEGA	
			New York vocalist/acoustic guitarist/songwriter.	
7/04/87	**3**	12	1. **Luka**	A&M 2937
			THE VELVETS	
			R&B doo-wop quintet from Odessa, Texas; Virgil Johnson, lead singer.	
6/26/61	**26**	4	1. Tonight (Could Be The Night)	Monument 441
			THE VENTURES	
			Guitar-based instrumental rock and roll band formed in the Seattle/Tacoma, Washington area. Consisted of lead guitarist Nokie Edwards (b: 5/9/39; bass) and lead guitarist Bob Bogle (b: 1/16/37), rhythm guitarist Don Wilson (b: 2/10/37), and drummer Howie Johnson. First recorded for own label, Blue Horizon, in 1959. Johnson was injured in an auto accident, and was replaced by Mel Taylor in 1963. Taylor went solo in 1967, returned in 1978. Edwards left in 1968, replaced by Gerry McGee, returned in 1972. Added keyboardist John Durrill in 1969. Latest recordings featured Edwards, Bogle, Wilson and Taylor. McGee again replaced Edwards.	
7/25/60	**2**(1)	14	1. **Walk—Don't Run** **[I]**	Dolton 25
11/14/60	**15**	10	2. Perfidia [I] 5 versions hit the top 15 in 1941	Dolton 28
2/13/61	**29**	5	3. Ram-Bunk-Shush [I]	Dolton 32
8/01/64	**8**	7	4. **Walk-Don't Run '64** **[I-R]** new version of their 1960 hit	Dolton 96

DATE	POS	WKS	ARTIST—RECORD TITLE	LABEL & NO.
11/21/64	**35**	3	5. Slaughter On Tenth Avenue [I] written by Richard Rodgers in 1936	Dolton 300
4/12/69	**4**	9	6. **Hawaii Five-O** **[I]** from the TV series of the same title	Liberty 56068
			VIK VENUS	
7/26/69	**38**	3	1. Moonflight [N] a Dickie Goodman type recording	Buddah 118
			BILLY VERA	
			Born William McCord, Jr. on 5/28/44 in Riverside, California. Raised in Westchester County, New York. Wrote hit songs for many pop, R&B and country artists. Formed The Beaters in Los Angeles in 1979, an R&B-based, 10-piece band.	
3/23/68	**36**	1	1. Country Girl - City Man **BILLY VERA & JUDY CLAY**	Atlantic 2480
6/06/81	**39**	2	2. I Can Take Care Of Myself	Alfa 7002
12/06/86†	**1**(2)	15	● 3. **At This Moment** **[R]** **BILLY VERA & THE BEATERS** recorded at the Roxy in January of 1981; originally charted in 1981 on Alfa 7005 (POS 79); newly popularized through play on TV's "Family Ties"	Rhino 74403
			LARRY VERNE	
			Born on 2/8/36 in Minneapolis.	
9/05/60	**1**(1)	10	1. **Mr. Custer** **[N]**	Era 3024
			THE VIBRATIONS	
			Los Angeles R&B vocal group. Originally recorded as The Jayhawks. Consisted of James Johnson, Carl Fisher, Richard Owens, Dave Govan and Don Bradley. Also recorded as The Marathons. Owens joined The Temptations for a short time in 1971.	
3/13/61	**25**	4	1. The Watusi	Checker 969
5/22/61	**20**	7	2. Peanut Butter **THE MARATHONS**	Arvee 5027
4/25/64	**26**	5	3. My Girl Sloopy	Atlantic 2221
			VILLAGE PEOPLE	
			New York campy disco group: Victor Willis, Randy Jones, David Hodo, Felipe Rose, Glenn Hughes and Alexander Briley. In the film "Can't Stop The Music" (1980).	
7/29/78	**25**	6	● 1. Macho Man	Casablanca 922
11/11/78†	**2**(3)	20	▲ 2. **Y.M.C.A.**	Casablanca 945
3/31/79	**3**	13	● 3. **In The Navy**	Casablanca 973
			THE VILLAGE STOMPERS	
			Greenwich Village, New York dixieland-styled band.	
10/05/63	**2**(1)	12	1. **Washington Square** **[I]**	Epic 9617

DATE	POS	WKS	ARTIST—RECORD TITLE	LABEL & NO.
			GENE VINCENT & His Blue Caps	
			Born Vincent Eugene Craddock on 2/11/35 in Norfolk, Virginia; died from an ulcer hemorrhage on 10/12/71. Innovative rock and roll singer/songwriter/guitarist. Injured left leg in motorcycle accident in 1953, had to wear steel brace thereafter. Formed own band, The Bluecaps, in Norfolk in 1956. Appeared in films "The Girl Can't Help It" and "Hot Rod Gang." To England from 1960-67. Injured in car crash that killed Eddie Cochran in England in 1960.	
6/23/56	**7**	15	1. **Be-Bop-A-Lula** Best Seller #7 / Top 100 #9 / Juke Box #10 / Jockey #11	Capitol 3450
9/16/57	**13**	12	2. Lotta Lovin' Best Seller #13 / Top 100 #14 / Jockey #18	Capitol 3763
1/13/58	**23**	1	3. Dance To The Bop Jockey #23 / Top 100 #43 / Best Seller #44	Capitol 3839
			BOBBY VINTON	
			Born Stanley Robert Vinton on 4/16/35 in Canonsburg, Pennsylvania. Father was a bandleader. Formed own band while in high school; toured as backing band for Dick Clark's "Caravan of Stars" in 1960. Left band for a singing career in 1962. Own TV series from 1975-78.	
6/16/62	**1**(4)	13	● 1. **Roses Are Red (My Love)**	Epic 9509
9/15/62	**12**	7	2. Rain Rain Go Away	Epic 9532
9/22/62	**38**	2	3. I Love You The Way You Are	Diamond 121
1/05/63	**33**	3	4. Trouble Is My Middle Name/	
1/12/63	**38**	2	5. Let's Kiss And Make Up	Epic 9561
3/30/63	**21**	6	6. Over The Mountain (Across The Sea)	Epic 9577
6/01/63	**3**	10	7. **Blue On Blue**	Epic 9593
8/24/63	**1**(3)	12	8. **Blue Velvet** #16 hit for Tony Bennett in 1951	Epic 9614
12/07/63†	**1**(4)	12	9. **There! I've Said It Again** #1 hit for Vaughn Monroe in 1945	Epic 9638
3/07/64	**9**	8	10. **My Heart Belongs To Only You**	Epic 9662
5/30/64	**13**	6	11. Tell Me Why 2 versions hit the top 10 in 1952	Epic 9687
8/22/64	**17**	6	12. Clinging Vine	Epic 9705
11/07/64	**1**(1)	14	13. **Mr. Lonely**	Epic 9730
3/20/65	**17**	5	14. Long Lonely Nights	Epic 9768
5/22/65	**22**	6	15. L-O-N-E-L-Y	Epic 9791
10/16/65	**38**	1	16. What Color (Is A Man)	Epic 9846
12/25/65†	**23**	6	17. Satin Pillows	Epic 9869
5/28/66	**40**	1	18. Dum-De-Da aka "She Understands Me"	Epic 10014
12/17/66†	**11**	8	19. Coming Home Soldier	Epic 10090
10/14/67	**6**	11	20. **Please Love Me Forever**	Epic 10228
1/27/68	**24**	4	21. Just As Much As Ever	Epic 10266
4/13/68	**33**	6	22. Take Good Care Of My Baby	Epic 10305
8/03/68	**23**	5	23. Halfway To Paradise	Epic 10350
11/16/68	**9**	12	● 24. **I Love How You Love Me**	Epic 10397
5/03/69	**34**	2	25. To Know You Is To Love You	Epic 10461
7/12/69	**34**	2	26. The Days Of Sand And Shovels	Epic 10485
3/18/72	**24**	8	27. Every Day Of My Life	Epic 10822
7/08/72	**19**	10	28. Sealed With A Kiss	Epic 10861

Roy Orbison ended 1965 with the No. 25 song "Ride Away," and would only break the Top 40 two more times before his 1967–80 retirement. His subsequent solo work, as well as that with super-group Traveling Wilburys, continued to top the charts even after his death in 1988.

Robert Palmer has scaled the pop charts with three top R & B hits of the 80s: the System's "You Are In My System" at No. 78, the Gap Band's "Early In The Morning" at No. 19, and Cherelle's "I Didn't Mean To Turn You On" at No. 2. Palmer did better when he left himself un-covered, as proven by his original No. 1 hit "Simply Irresistible."

The Paris Sisters, Albeth, Priscilla and Sherrell, had their fifth and final chart single with "Dream Lover" in 1964. They suffered from the loss of the producer responsible for their previous hits, including the No. 5 "I Love How You Love Me"—girl-group hitmaker Phil Spector.

Ray Parker, Jr. was a Motown session man when he was 16 and played on the Honey Cone's No. 1 hit "Want Ads" at 17, but he was 30 when "Ghostbusters" floated up to No. 1 in 1984—with a little help from the No. 1 box-office hit of the year.

Dolly Parton and Kenny Rogers made a duet of "Real Love," as they had with their 1983 No. 1 "Islands In The Stream." Rogers had never gone that far with a female partner before—he only got to No. 4 with Kim Carnes on "Don't Fall In Love With A Dreamer" and to No. 6 with Sheena Easton on "We've Got Tonight."

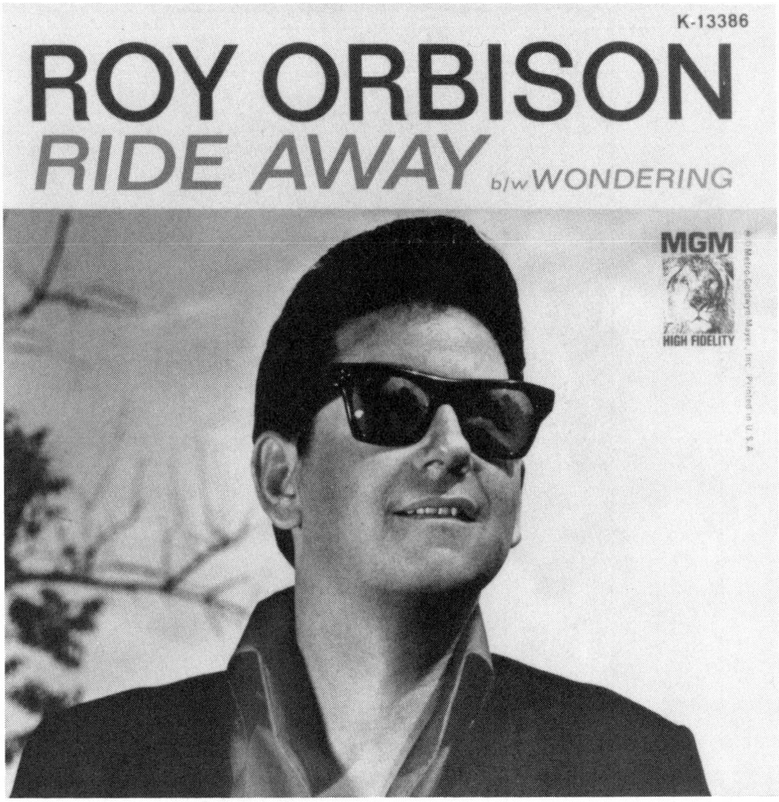

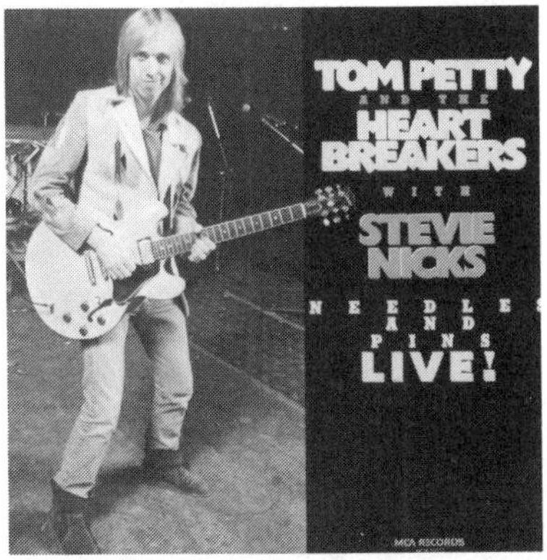

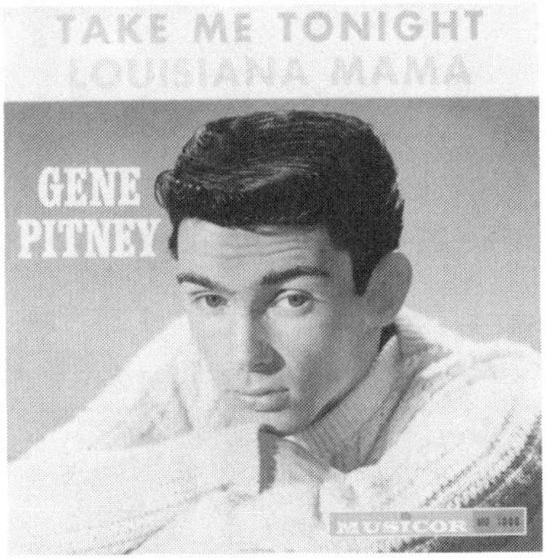

Les Paul and Mary Ford were No. 1 artists in the early 50s with "How High The Moon" and "Vaya Con Dios," and Paul became part of music's vocabulary with his self-named hollow-body electric guitar. He was also known as Hot Rod Red and Rhubarb Red, but his real name was Lester Polfus.

Pebbles, who like her cousin Cherelle has no last name, topped the R & B charts in 1988 with "Girlfriend," also a No. 5 pop hit that year. But for Pebbles, "Mercedes Boy" would be a better vehicle: her second R & B No. 1 was a No. 2 pop hit as well.

Tom Petty and the Heartbreakers and Stevie Nicks went to No. 37 in 1986 with "Needles And Pins," another collaboration after their No. 3 smash "Stop Draggin' My Heart Around." Apart, neither could top that chart peak, although Nicks came closest with the No. 6 "Leather And Lace," the No. 5 "Stand Back," and the No. 4 "Talk To Me."

Gene Pitney's 24 chart hits included material from no less diverse a group of songwriting teams as Bacharach-David, Goffin-King, and Jagger-Richards. Of course, Pitney could return the favor, penning Ricky Nelson's "Hello Mary Lou" and the Crystals' "He's A Rebel."

Robert Plant's first Top-40 hit was in 1969 with Led Zeppelin's "Whole Lotta Love," but nearly 20 years later, in 1988, he scored two hit singles—"Tall Cool One" and "Ship Of Fools"—making him the No. 9 pop album artist of that year.

DATE	POS	WKS	ARTIST—RECORD TITLE	LABEL & NO.
10/12/74	**3**	11	● 29. **My Melody Of Love**	ABC 12022
4/19/75	**33**	2	30. Beer Barrel Polka #1 hit for Will Glahe in 1939	ABC 12056
			THE VIRTUES	
			Philadelphia rock and roll instrumental trio led by Frank ("Virtue") Virtuoso.	
3/23/59	**5**	12	1. **Guitar Boogie Shuffle** [I]	Hunt 324
			THE VISCOUNTS	
			New Jersey instrumental quintet: Harry Haller (tenor saxophone), Bobby Spievak (guitar), Larry Vecchio (organ), Joe Spievak (bass) and Clark Smith (drums).	
1/01/66	**39**	1	1. Harlem Nocturne [I-R] originally charted in 1959 (POS 52)	Amy 940
			VIXEN	
			L.A.-based, female heavy-metal quartet: Janet Kuehnemund, Janet Gardner (vocals), Roxy Petrucci and Share Pedersen.	
10/29/88	**26**	5	1. Edge Of A Broken Heart written, produced and arranged by Richard Marx	EMI-Man. 50141
			THE VOGUES	
			Vocal group formed in Turtle Creek, Pennsylvania in 1960. Consisted of Bill Burkette (lead), Hugh Geyer & Chuck Blasko (tenors) and Don Miller (baritone). Met in high school.	
10/09/65	**4**	9	1. **You're The One**	Co & Ce 229
12/11/65†	**4**	12	2. **Five O'Clock World**	Co & Ce 232
3/19/66	**21**	6	3. Magic Town	Co & Ce 234
6/25/66	**29**	4	4. The Land Of Milk And Honey	Co & Ce 238
7/13/68	**7**	11	● 5. **Turn Around, Look At Me**	Reprise 0686
9/21/68	**7**	8	6. **My Special Angel**	Reprise 0766
12/07/68	**27**	4	7. Till	Reprise 0788
3/29/69	**34**	2	8. No, Not Much	Reprise 0803
			THE VOLUME'S	
			Detroit R&B quintet featuring lead singer Ed Union.	
6/02/62	**22**	6	1. I Love You	Chex 1002
			ROGER VOUDOURIS	
			Born on 12/29/54 in Sacramento, California. Pop singer/songwriter/guitarist.	
4/28/79	**21**	10	1. Get Used To It	Warner 8762
			THE VOXPOPPERS	
5/05/58	**18**	1	1. Wishing For Your Love Jockey #18 / Best Seller #41 / Top 100 #44	Mercury 71282

DATE	POS	WKS	ARTIST—RECORD TITLE	LABEL & NO.
			W	
			WA WA NEE	
			Australian-based dance band. Includes: Steve Williams, brothers Mark and Paul Gray, (from Australia), Chris Sweeney (from the US), & Phil Witchett (from New Zealand).	
10/31/87	**35**	3	1. Sugar Free	Epic 07283
			ADAM WADE	
			Born on 3/17/37 in Pittsburgh. Attended Virginia State College and worked as lab assistant with Dr. Jonas Salk team. TV actor/host of the 1976 game show "Musical Chairs." Worked in "Guys & Dolls" musical in Las Vegas, in 1978. TV talk-show host in Los Angeles, in the 80s.	
3/27/61	**7**	10	1. **Take Good Care Of Her**	Coed 546
5/29/61	**5**	9	2. **The Writing On The Wall**	Coed 550
8/07/61	**10**	7	3. **As If I Didn't Know**	Coed 553
			all of above: with George Paxton & His Orchestra	
			WADSWORTH MANSION	
			Quartet: Steve Jablecki (lead vocals), Wayne Gagnon, John Poole and Mike Jablecki.	
2/13/71	**7**	7	1. **Sweet Mary**	Sussex 209
			JACK WAGNER	
			Born and raised in Washington, Missouri. Played Frisco Jones on the TV soap opera "General Hospital."	
11/24/84†	**2**(2)	12	1. **All I Need**	Qwest 29238
			THE WAIKIKIS	
			Belgian instrumental group.	
1/09/65	**33**	3	1. Hawaii Tattoo [I]	Kapp 30
			THE WAILERS	
			Teenage rock and roll instrumental quintet from Tacoma, Washington; formed in 1958. Consisted of John Greek, Rick Dangel, Mark Marush, Kent Morrill (lead vocals) and Mike Burk.	
6/01/59	**36**	2	1. Tall Cool One [I]	Golden Crest 518
5/30/64	**38**	1	2. Tall Cool One [I-R]	Golden Crest 518
			LOUDON WAINWRIGHT III	
			Born on 9/5/46 in Durham, North Carolina. Satirical folksinger/songwriter.	
2/24/73	**16**	9	1. Dead Skunk [N]	Columbia 45726
			JOHN WAITE	
			Born on 7/4/55 in England. Lead singer of The Babys.	
7/21/84	**1**(1)	16	1. **Missing You**	EMI America 8212
11/10/84	**37**	4	2. Tears	EMI America 8238
8/31/85	**25**	6	3. Every Step Of The Way	EMI America 8282
			JOHNNY WAKELIN & THE KINSHASA BAND	
			British group led by singer/songwriter Wakelin.	
8/16/75	**21**	6	1. Black Superman - "Muhammad Ali" [N]	Pye 71012

DATE	POS	WKS	ARTIST—RECORD TITLE	LABEL & NO.
			THE WALKER BROS.	
			Los Angeles pop trio: Scott Engel, Gary Leeds and John Maus. More popular in England than U.S. (charted 10 hits in U.K.).	
11/13/65	**16**	6	1. Make It Easy On Yourself	Smash 2009
4/30/66	**13**	7	2. The Sun Ain't Gonna Shine (Anymore)	Smash 2032
			JR. WALKER & THE ALL STARS	
			R&B group formed in South Bend, Indiana by Walker (born Autry DeWalt II in Blythesville, Arkansas, 1942). Included Walker (sax, vocals), Willie Woods (guitar), Vic Thomas (organ) and James Graves (drums). First recorded for Harvey in 1962. Most recent group included son Autry DeWalt, Jr. on drums.	
3/06/65	**4**	10	1. **Shotgun**	Soul 35008
7/03/65	**36**	2	2. Do The Boomerang	Soul 35012
8/21/65	**29**	5	3. Shake And Fingerpop	Soul 35013
5/21/66	**20**	6	4. (I'm A) Road Runner	Soul 35015
9/03/66	**18**	5	5. How Sweet It Is (To Be Loved By You)	Soul 35024
3/11/67	**31**	4	6. Pucker Up Buttercup	Soul 35030
12/23/67†	**24**	6	7. Come See About Me	Soul 35041
9/14/68	**31**	6	8. Hip City - Pt. 2	Soul 35048
6/21/69	**4**	11	9. **What Does It Take (To Win Your Love)**	Soul 35062
11/22/69	**16**	9	10. These Eyes	Soul 35067
2/28/70	**21**	9	11. Gotta Hold On To This Feeling	Soul 35070
8/01/70	**32**	4	12. Do You See My Love (For You Growing)	Soul 35073
			JERRY WALLACE	
			Born on 12/15/28 in Kansas City, Missouri; raised in Glendale, Arizona. Pop-country singer/guitarist. First recorded for Allied in 1951. Appeared on the TV shows "Night Gallery" and "Hec Ramsey."	
9/15/58	**11**	9	1. How The Time Flies Hot 100 #11 / Best Seller #33 end	Challenge 59013
9/07/59	**8**	15	2. **Primrose Lane** **JERRY WALLACE with The Jewels**	Challenge 59047
2/01/60	**36**	2	3. Little Coco Palm	Challenge 59060
1/09/61	**26**	4	4. There She Goes	Challenge 59098
12/22/62†	**24**	7	5. Shutters And Boards	Challenge 9171
8/22/64	**19**	7	6. In The Misty Moonlight	Challenge 59246
9/30/72	**38**	2	7. If You Leave Me Tonight I'll Cry from TV's Night Gallery: "The Tune In Dan's Cafe"	Decca 32989
			JOE WALSH	
			Born on 11/20/47 in Wichita, Kansas. Rock singer/songwriter/guitarist. Member of The James Gang (1969-71) and the Eagles (1975-82).	
9/22/73	**23**	7	1. Rocky Mountain Way	Dunhill 4361
7/01/78	**12**	9	2. Life's Been Good	Asylum 45493
6/14/80	**19**	8	3. All Night Long from the film "Urban Cowboy"	Full Moon 46639
6/27/81	**34**	4	4. A Life Of Illusion	Asylum 47144
			TRAVIS WAMMACK	
			Muscle Shoals' session guitarist.	
8/09/75	**38**	2	1. (Shu-Doo-Pa-Poo-Poop) Love Being Your Fool	Capricorn 0239

DATE	POS	WKS	ARTIST—RECORD TITLE	LABEL & NO.
			WALTER WANDERLEY	
			Brazilian organist/pianist/composer. Died of cancer on 9/4/86 (55).	
10/01/66	**26**	4	1. Summer Samba (So Nice) [I]	Verve 10421
			WANG CHUNG	
			British pop/rock group: Jack Hues (lead singer, guitar, keyboards), Nick Feldman (bass, keyboards) and Darren Costin (drums). Costin left in 1985.	
3/10/84	**38**	3	1. Don't Let Go	Geffen 29377
5/26/84	**16**	10	2. Dance Hall Days	Geffen 29310
10/25/86	**2**(2)	15	3. **Everybody Have Fun Tonight**	Geffen 28562
2/14/87	**9**	11	4. **Let's Go!**	Geffen 28531
7/25/87	**36**	2	5. Hypnotize Me from the film "Innerspace"	Geffen 28359
			WAR	
			Band formed in Long Beach, California in 1969. Consisted of Leroy "Lonnie" Jordan (keyboards), Howard Scott (guitar), Charles Miller (saxophone; murdered in 1980), Morris "B.B." Dickerson (bass), Harold Brown & Thomas "Papa Dee" Allen (percussion) and Lee Oskar (harmonica). Eric Burdon's back-up band until 1971. Dickerson was replaced by Luther Rabb. Lee Oskar recorded solo, beginning in 1976. Alice Tweed Smyth (vocals) added in 1978. Pat Rizzo (horns) and Ron Hammond (former member of Aalon; percussion) added in 1979. Smyth left group in 1982.	
7/11/70	**3**	13	● 1. **Spill The Wine** **ERIC BURDON & WAR**	MGM 14118
9/25/71	**35**	2	2. All Day Music	United Art. 50815
4/01/72	**16**	10	● 3. Slippin' Into Darkness	United Art. 50867
12/30/72†	**7**	9	● 4. **The World Is A Ghetto**	United Art. 50975
3/24/73	**2**(2)	12	● 5. **The Cisco Kid**	United Art. 163
8/04/73	**8**	10	6. **Gypsy Man**	United Art. 281
12/08/73†	**15**	10	7. Me And Baby Brother	United Art. 350
7/13/74	**33**	2	8. Ballero [I]	United Art. 432
6/14/75	**6**	13	● 9. **Why Can't We Be Friends?**	United Art. 629
10/11/75	**7**	11	10. **Low Rider**	United Art. 706
7/31/76	**7**	12	● 11. **Summer**	United Art. 834
2/11/78	**39**	2	12. Galaxy	MCA 40820
			ANITA WARD	
			Born on 12/20/57 in Memphis. R&B/disco vocalist.	
5/26/79	**1**(2)	15	1. **Ring My Bell**	Juana 3422
			BILLY WARD & HIS DOMINOES	
			R&B group formed as The Dominoes in New York in 1950 by Ward (b: Los Angeles) and talent agent Rose Marks. Consisted of Ward (piano), Clyde McPhatter (lead), Charlie White (tenor), Joe Lamont (baritone) and Bill Brown (bass). Signed by King/Federal in 1950. Lead singers, at various times: Clyde McPhatter (1950-53), Jackie Wilson (1953-57) and Eugene Mumford.	
9/15/56	**13**	6	1. St. Therese Of The Roses Jockey #13 / Best Seller #20 / Top 100 #27 Jackie Wilson, lead singer	Decca 29933

DATE	POS	WKS	ARTIST—RECORD TITLE	LABEL & NO.
7/15/57	**12**	17	2. Star Dust Jockey #12 / Top 100 #13 / Best Seller #14 there have been 19 charted versions of this Hoagy Carmichael tune	Liberty 55071
10/07/57	**20**	8	3. Deep Purple Best Seller #20 / Top 100 #22 3 versions of this tune hit the top 10 in 1939	Liberty 55099
			DALE WARD	
			Lead singer of The Crescendos. Pop-country vocalist.	
2/01/64	**25**	5	1. Letter From Sherry Dale's version of "Oh Julie" is on the flip side	Dot 16520
			JOE WARD	
12/24/55	**20**	3	1. Nuttin For Xmas [N-X] Juke Box #20 / Best Seller #22 / Top 100 #22	King 4854
			ROBIN WARD	
			Real name: Jackie Ward. Pop female singer originally from Nebraska.	
11/16/63	**14**	7	1. Wonderful Summer	Dot 16530
			JENNIFER WARNES	
			Born in Seattle; raised in Orange County, California. Pop/MOR-styled vocalist. Lead actress in the Los Angeles production of "Hair." Recorded duet with Bill Medley (baritone of The Righteous Brothers).	
2/26/77	**6**	14	1. **Right Time Of The Night**	Arista 0223
9/22/79	**19**	8	2. I Know A Heartache When I See One	Arista 0430
10/02/82	**1**(3)	15	▲ 3. **Up Where We Belong** **JOE COCKER & JENNIFER WARNES** love theme from the film "An Officer & A Gentleman"	Island 99996
10/10/87	**1**(1)	15	● 4. **(I've Had) The Time Of My Life** **BILL MEDLEY & JENNIFER WARNES** love theme from the film "Dirty Dancing"	RCA 5224
			DIONNE WARWICK	
			Born Marie Dionne Warwick on 12/12/40 in East Orange, New Jersey. In church choir from age 6. With the Drinkard Singers gospel group. Formed trio, the Gospelaires, with sister Dee Dee and their aunt Cissy Houston. Attended Hartt College Of Music, Hartford, Connecticut. Much backup studio work in New York during the late 50s. Added an "e" to her last name for a time in the early 70s. She was Burt Bacharach and Hal David's main "voice" for the songs they composed. Co-hosted TV's "Solid Gold" from 1980-81.	
1/05/63	**21**	7	1. Don't Make Me Over	Scepter 1239
1/04/64	**8**	9	2. **Anyone Who Had A Heart**	Scepter 1262
5/09/64	**6**	11	3. **Walk On By**	Scepter 1274
9/19/64	**34**	3	4. You'll Never Get To Heaven (If You Break My Heart)	Scepter 1282
11/07/64	**20**	6	5. Reach Out For Me	Scepter 1285
1/22/66	**39**	1	6. Are You There (With Another Girl)	Scepter 12122
4/23/66	**8**	8	7. **Message To Michael**	Scepter 12133
7/16/66	**22**	5	8. Trains And Boats And Planes	Scepter 12153
10/22/66	**26**	5	9. I Just Don't Know What To Do With Myself	Scepter 12167
5/27/67	**15**	9	10. Alfie written for, but not included in, the film of the same title	Scepter 12187
8/26/67	**32**	3	11. The Windows Of The World	Scepter 12196

DATE	POS	WKS	ARTIST—RECORD TITLE	LABEL & NO.
11/04/67	**4**	10	● 12. **I Say A Little Prayer/**	
2/03/68	**2**(4)	11	13. (Theme From) Valley Of The Dolls from the film of the same title	Scepter 12203
4/27/68	**10**	9	14. **Do You Know The Way To San Jose**	Scepter 12216
9/21/68	**33**	4	15. Who Is Gonna Love Me?	Scepter 12226
11/23/68	**19**	6	16. Promises, Promises from the Broadway musical of the same title	Scepter 12231
2/08/69	**7**	11	17. **This Girl's In Love With You**	Scepter 12241
6/07/69	**37**	3	18. The April Fools	Scepter 12249
10/11/69	**16**	7	19. You've Lost That Lovin' Feeling	Scepter 12262
1/03/70	**6**	10	20. **I'll Never Fall In Love Again** from the Broadway musical "Promises, Promises"	Scepter 12273
5/09/70	**32**	3	21. Let Me Go To Him 1-6, 8-21: produced by Burt Bacharach & Hal David	Scepter 12276
10/31/70	**37**	2	22. Make It Easy On Yourself 1-12, 14-18, 20-22: written by Burt Bacharach & Hal David	Scepter 12294
8/03/74	**1**(1)	15	● 23. **Then Came You** **DIONNE WARWICKE & SPINNERS**	Atlantic 3202
7/28/79	**5**	17	● 24. **I'll Never Love This Way Again**	Arista 0419
12/15/79†	**15**	11	25. Deja Vu produced by Barry Manilow	Arista 0459
9/06/80	**23**	6	26. No Night So Long	Arista 0527
5/29/82	**38**	3	27. Friends In Love **DIONNE WARWICK & JOHNNY MATHIS**	Arista 0673
11/06/82†	**10**	13	28. **Heartbreaker** backing vocal: Barry Gibb	Arista 1015
10/29/83	**27**	5	29. How Many Times Can We Say Goodbye **DIONNE WARWICK & LUTHER VANDROSS**	Arista 9073
11/23/85†	**1**(4)	17	● 30. **That's What Friends Are For** **DIONNE & FRIENDS** with Friends: Elton John, Gladys Knight and Stevie Wonder; Dionne sings lead for over one minute, with each "friend" contributing about 30-40 seconds of solo vocals	Arista 9422
7/25/87	**12**	9	31. Love Power **DIONNE WARWICK & JEFFREY OSBORNE**	Arista 9567
			WAS (NOT WAS) Detroit rock-funk ensemble fronted by composer/bassist Don Fagenson and lyricist/ flutist David Weiss. Includes vocalists Sweet Pea Atkinson and Sir Harry Bowens.	
11/05/88	**16**	10	1. Spy In The House Of Love	Chrysalis 43266
			BABY WASHINGTON Born Justine Washington (aka: Jeanette Washington) on 11/13/40 in Bamberg, South Carolina; raised in Harlem. R&B vocalist/pianist. Sang in 50s vocal group, The Hearts. First recorded solo for J&S in 1957.	
6/01/63	**40**	1	1. That's How Heartaches Are Made	Sue 783

DATE	POS	WKS	ARTIST—RECORD TITLE	LABEL & NO.
			DINAH WASHINGTON	
			Born Ruth Lee Jones on 8/29/24 in Tuscaloosa, Alabama; died on 12/14/63 (overdose of alcohol and pills). Jazz-blues vocalist/pianist. Moved to Chicago in 1927. With Sallie Martin Gospel Singers, 1940-41; local club work in Chicago, 1941-43. With Lionel Hampton, 1943-46. First recorded for Keynote in 1943. Solo touring from 1946. Married 7 times, once to singer Eddie Chamblee.	
6/22/59	**8**	14	1. **What A Diff'rence A Day Makes** #5 hit for the Dorsey Brothers in 1934	Mercury 71435
10/26/59	**17**	8	2. Unforgettable #12 hit for Nat King Cole in 1952	Mercury 71508
2/08/60	**5**	12	3. **Baby (You've Got What It Takes)** **DINAH WASHINGTON & BROOK BENTON**	Mercury 71565
6/06/60	**7**	10	4. **A Rockin' Good Way (To Mess Around And Fall In Love)** **DINAH WASHINGTON & BROOK BENTON**	Mercury 71629
7/18/60	**24**	6	5. This Bitter Earth	Mercury 71635
11/07/60	**30**	2	6. Love Walked In 3 versions hit the top 10 in 1938	Mercury 71696
11/06/61	**23**	6	7. September In The Rain #1 hit for Guy Lombardo in 1937	Mercury 71876
6/23/62	**36**	3	8. Where Are You #5 hit for Mildred Bailey in 1937	Roulette 4424
			GROVER WASHINGTON, JR. - see BILL WITHERS	
			JODY WATLEY	
			Born on 1/30/59 in Chicago. Female vocalist of Shalamar (1977-84) and former dancer on TV's "Soul Train." Her godfather was Jackie Wilson. Won the 1987 Best New Artist Grammy Award.	
3/21/87	**2**(4)	14	1. **Looking For A New Love**	MCA 52956
10/24/87	**6**	14	2. **Don't You Want Me**	MCA 53162
2/27/88	**10**	10	3. **Some Kind Of Lover** production and instruments by Andre Cymone	MCA 53235
			WATTS 103rd STREET RHYTHM BAND - see CHARLES WRIGHT	
			THOMAS WAYNE	
			Born Thomas Wayne Perkins on 7/22/40 in Battsville, Mississippi. Killed in an auto accident on 8/15/71. Brother of guitarist Luther Perkins of Johnny Cash's band.	
2/16/59	**5**	13	1. **Tragedy** backing band: The DeLons	Fernwood 109
			WE FIVE	
			California pop quintet: Beverly Bivens (lead singer), Mike Stewart (brother of John Stewart), Pete Fullerton, Bob Jones and Jerry Burgan.	
8/07/65	**3**	13	1. **You Were On My Mind**	A&M 770
12/25/65	**31**	2	2. Let's Get Together	A&M 784
			JIM WEATHERLY	
			Pop-country songwriter/singer born on 3/17/43 in Pontotoc, Mississippi. Wrote Gladys Knight's hits "Neither One Of Us," "Midnight Train To Georgia" and "Best Thing That Ever Happened To Me."	
10/12/74	**11**	8	1. The Need To Be	Buddah 420

DATE	POS	WKS	ARTIST—RECORD TITLE	LABEL & NO.
			JOAN WEBER	
			New Jersey songstress, born in 1936; died on 5/13/81 (45).	
12/04/54†	**1**(4)	16	1. **Let Me Go Lover** Jockey #1(4) / Juke Box #1(4) / Best Seller #1(2) from a "Studio One" CBS-TV production	Columbia 40366
			WEDNESDAY	
			Pop quartet; Mike O'Neil, lead singer.	
2/16/74	**34**	4	1. Last Kiss	Sussex 507
			TIM WEISBERG - see DAN FOGELBERG	
			ERIC WEISSBERG & STEVE MANDELL	
			Prominent session musicians. Both had worked with Judy Collins and John Denver.	
2/03/73	**2**(4)	11	● 1. **Dueling Banjos** **[I]** tune written in 1955; featured in the film "Deliverance"	Warner 7659
			BOB WELCH	
			Born on 7/31/46 in Los Angeles. Guitarist/vocalist with Fleetwood Mac (1971-74). Formed the British rock group Paris in 1976.	
11/19/77†	**8**	11	1. **Sentimental Lady** backing vocals: Christine McVie & Lindsey Buckingham	Capitol 4479
2/25/78	**14**	10	2. Ebony Eyes	Capitol 4543
7/01/78	**31**	3	3. Hot Love, Cold World	Capitol 4588
3/17/79	**19**	8	4. Precious Love	Capitol 4685
			LENNY WELCH	
			Born on 5/15/38 in Asbury Park, New Jersey. Black MOR vocalist.	
11/23/63	**4**	12	1. **Since I Fell For You** #20 hit for Paul Gayten in 1947	Cadence 1439
4/11/64	**25**	5	2. Ebb Tide featured in the film "Sweet Bird Of Youth"; both Frank Chacksfield & Vic Damone had top 10 versions in 1953; above 2: conducted by Archie Bleyer	Cadence 1422
2/14/70	**34**	4	3. Breaking Up Is Hard To Do	Common. U. 3004
			LAWRENCE WELK	
			Born on 3/11/03 in Strasburg, North Dakota. Accordionist and polka/sweet bandleader since the mid-20s. Band's style labeled "champagne music." Own national TV musical variety show began on 7/2/55 and ran into the 70s.	
3/03/56	**17**	2	1. Moritat (A Theme From "The Threepenny Opera") [I] Juke Box #17 / Top 100 #31	Coral 61574
4/07/56	**17**	2	2. The Poor People Of Paris [I] Juke Box #17 / Top 100 #45	Coral 61592
8/11/56	**32**	3	3. Weary Blues **THE McGUIRE SISTERS & LAWRENCE WELK**	Coral 61670
9/29/56	**15**	10	4. Tonight You Belong To Me vocals: The Lennon Sisters and The Sparklers	Coral 61701
12/05/60	**21**	3	5. Last Date [I]	Dot 16145
12/31/60†	**1**(2)	13	● 6. **Calcutta** **[I]** featuring Frank Scott, harpsichord	Dot 16161

DATE	POS	WKS	ARTIST—RECORD TITLE	LABEL & NO.
			MARY WELLS	
			R&B vocalist born on 5/13/43 in Detroit. At age 17, presented "Bye Bye Love," a tune she had written for Jackie Wilson, to Wilson's songwriter, Berry Gordy, Jr. Gordy signed her to his new label and she became the first artist to record for Motown. Also was the first to have a top 10 and #1 single for that label. Married for a time to Cecil Womack (brother of Bobby Womack).	
8/21/61	**33**	3	1. I Don't Want To Take A Chance	Motown 1011
5/05/62	**8**	10	2. **The One Who Really Loves You**	Motown 1024
8/25/62	**9**	9	3. **You Beat Me To The Punch**	Motown 1032
12/15/62†	**7**	10	4. **Two Lovers**	Motown 1035
3/09/63	**15**	6	5. Laughing Boy	Motown 1039
7/06/63	**40**	1	6. Your Old Stand By	Motown 1042
10/12/63	**22**	7	7. You Lost The Sweetest Boy/	
1/25/64	**29**	6	8. What's Easy For Two Is So Hard For One	Motown 1048
4/11/64	**1**(2)	13	9. **My Guy**	Motown 1056
			2-6, 8-9: written and produced by Smokey Robinson	
5/23/64	**19**	6	10. Once Upon A Time/	
6/13/64	**17**	6	11. What's The Matter With You Baby	Motown 1057
			above 2: **MARVIN GAYE & MARY WELLS**	
1/30/65	**34**	2	12. Use Your Head	20th Century 555
			FRED WESLEY - see THE JB's	
			DOTTIE WEST	
			Born Dorothy Marsh on 10/11/32 in McMinnville, Tennessee. Country singer.	
4/25/81	**14**	12	1. What Are We Doin' In Love	Liberty 1404
			backing vocal: Kenny Rogers	
			KIM WESTON - see MARVIN GAYE	
			WET WILLIE	
			Mobile, Alabama rock band led by brothers Jimmy and Jack Hall.	
7/06/74	**10**	11	1. **Keep On Smilin'**	Capricorn 0043
1/28/78	**30**	4	2. Street Corner Serenade	Epic 50478
6/30/79	**29**	5	3. Weekend	Epic 50714
			WHAM!	
			Pop duo from Bushey, England: George Michael (b: Georgios Kyriacos Panayiotou on 6/26/63; lead singer) and Andrew Ridgely (b: 1/26/63; guitarist). Disbanded in 1986. Michael recorded solo. Ridgely pursued race car driving.	
10/06/84	**1**(3)	14	● 1. **Wake Me Up Before You Go-Go**	Columbia 04552
12/22/84†	**1**(3)	17	● 2. **Careless Whisper**	Columbia 04691
			released in England as a solo single by George Michael	
4/06/85	**1**(2)	14	3. **Everything She Wants**	Columbia 04840
8/03/85	**3**	12	4. **Freedom**	Columbia 05409
12/14/85†	**3**	12	5. **I'm Your Man**	Columbia 05721
7/19/86	**10**	8	6. **The Edge Of Heaven**	Columbia 06182
			all of above: written and produced by George Michael	

DATE	POS	WKS	ARTIST—RECORD TITLE	LABEL & NO.
			WHEN IN ROME	
			U.K.-based trio fomed in 1984: Clive Farrington (vocals), Michael Floreale (keyboards) and Andrew Mann (vocals).	
10/22/88	**11**	13	1. The Promise	Virgin 99323
			THE WHISPERS	
			Los Angeles soul group formed in 1964. Consisted of Gordy Harmon, twin brothers Walter and Wallace "Scotty" Scott, Marcus Hutson and Nicholas Caldwell. First recorded for Dore in 1964. Harmon replaced by Leaveil Degree in 1973.	
3/15/80	**19**	8	• 1. And The Beat Goes On	Solar 11894
5/24/80	**28**	4	2. Lady	Solar 11928
3/28/81	**28**	5	3. It's A Love Thing	Solar 12154
7/11/87	**7**	12	4. **Rock Steady**	Solar 70006
			IAN WHITCOMB & BLUESVILLE	
			Born on 7/10/41 in Woking, England. Pop singer/songwriter/author.	
6/19/65	**8**	8	1. **You Turn Me On (Turn On Song)**	Tower 134
			WHITE LION	
			New York-based rock band: Mike Tramp (vocals), James Lomenzo, Vito Bratta and Greg D'Angelo. Tramp is a native of Denmark.	
4/09/88	**8**	11	1. **Wait**	Atlantic 89126
12/17/88†	**3**	12	2. **When The Children Cry**	Atlantic 89015
			WHITE PLAINS	
			English production by Roger Greenaway & Roger Cook. Tony Burrows, lead singer.	
5/23/70	**13**	10	1. My Baby Loves Lovin'	Deram 85058
			WHITESNAKE	
			British heavy-metal band. 1987 lineup: David Coverdale (vocals), John Sykes (guitar), Neil Murray (bass) and Aynsley Dunbar (drums). Coverdale and early Whitesnake members Jon Lord and Ian Paice were members of Deep Purple.	
8/08/87	**1**(1)	14	1. **Here I Go Again**	Geffen 28339
11/07/87	**2**(1)	13	2. **Is This Love**	Geffen 28233
			BARRY WHITE	
			Born on 9/12/44 in Galveston, Texas; raised in Los Angeles. Soul singer/songwriter/ keyboardist/producer/arranger. With Upfronts vocal group, recorded for Lummtone in 1960. A&R man for Mustang/Bronco, 1966-67. Formed Love Unlimited in 1969, which included future wife Glodean James. Leader of 40-piece Love Unlimited Orchestra.	
5/05/73	**3**	12	• 1. **I'm Gonna Love You Just A Little More Baby**	20th Century 2018
9/01/73	**32**	6	2. I've Got So Much To Give	20th Century 2042
11/17/73†	**7**	15	• 3. **Never, Never Gonna Give Ya Up**	20th Century 2058
8/10/74	**1**(1)	9	• 4. **Can't Get Enough Of Your Love, Babe**	20th Century 2120
11/16/74†	**2**(2)	12	• 5. **You're The First, The Last, My Everything**	20th Century 2133
3/22/75	**8**	7	6. **What Am I Gonna Do With You**	20th Century 2177
6/21/75	**40**	2	7. I'll Do For You Anything You Want Me To	20th Century 2208
1/24/76	**32**	4	8. Let The Music Play	20th Century 2265
10/01/77	**4**	12	• 9. **It's Ecstasy When You Lay Down Next To Me**	20th Century 2350
5/27/78	**24**	5	10. Oh What A Night For Dancing	20th Century 2365

DATE	POS	WKS	ARTIST—RECORD TITLE	LABEL & NO.
			KARYN WHITE	
			Prominent session singer from Los Angeles. Touring vocalist with O'Bryan in 1984. Recorded with jazz/fusion keyboardist Jeff Lorber in 1986.	
2/07/87	**27**	5	1. Facts Of Love	Warner 28588
			JEFF LORBER featuring KARYN WHITE	
11/26/88†	**7**	14	2. **The Way You Love Me**	Warner 27773
			TONY JOE WHITE	
			Born on 7/23/43 in Oak Grove, Louisiana. Bayou rock singer/songwriter. Wrote Brook Benton's hit "Rainy Night In Georgia."	
7/26/69	**8**	8	1. **Polk Salad Annie**	Monument 1104
			MARGARET WHITING	
			Born on 7/22/24 in Detroit; raised in Hollywood. Daughter of popular composer Richard Whiting. Very popular from 1946-54, she had over 40 charted hits.	
12/08/56	**20**	5	1. The Money Tree Jockey #20 / Top 100 #49	Capitol 3586
11/19/66	**26**	5	2. The Wheel Of Hurt	London 101
			ROGER WHITTAKER	
			Born on 3/22/36 in Nairobi, Kenya. British MOR singer.	
5/10/75	**19**	9	1. The Last Farewell	RCA 50030
			THE WHO	
			Rock group formed in London in 1964. Consisted of Roger Daltrey (b: 3/1/44, lead singer), Pete Townshend (b: 5/19/45; guitar, vocals), John Entwistle (b: 10/9/44; bass) and Keith Moon (b: 8/23/47; drums). Originally known as the High Numbers in 1964. All but Moon had been in The Detours. Developed stage antics of destroying their instruments. 1969 rock opera album "Tommy" became a film in 1975. Solo work by members began in 1972. Moon died of a drug overdose on 9/7/78, replaced by Kenney Jones. 1973 rock opera album "Quadrophenia" became a film in 1979. The Who's biographical film "The Kids Are Alright" was released in 1979. 11 fans trampled to death at their concert in Cincinnati on 12/3/79. Group's status is currently in limbo. Re-grouped at "Live Aid" in 1986.	
5/20/67	**24**	4	1. Happy Jack	Decca 32114
10/28/67	**9**	9	2. **I Can See For Miles**	Decca 32206
5/04/68	**40**	2	3. Call Me Lightning	Decca 32288
8/31/68	**25**	6	4. Magic Bus	Decca 32362
5/03/69	**19**	5	5. Pinball Wizard	Decca 32465
8/23/69	**37**	2	6. I'm Free	Decca 32519
8/01/70	**27**	6	7. Summertime Blues	Decca 32708
10/17/70	**12**	9	8. See Me, Feel Me	Decca 32729
8/07/71	**15**	10	9. Won't Get Fooled Again from the film "Lifehouse"	Decca 32846
12/04/71	**34**	5	10. Behind Blue Eyes	Decca 32888
8/05/72	**17**	8	11. Join Together	Decca 32983
1/13/73	**39**	2	12. The Relay	Track 33041
1/03/76	**16**	10	13. Squeeze Box	MCA 40475
9/16/78	**14**	9	14. Who Are You	MCA 40948
4/04/81	**18**	10	15. You Better You Bet	Warner 49698
10/09/82	**28**	6	16. Athena all of above (except #7): written by Pete Townshend	Warner 29905

DATE	POS	WKS	ARTIST—RECORD TITLE	LABEL & NO.
			JANE WIEDLIN	
			Born on 5/20/58 in Oconomowoc, Wisconsin; raised in California. Former rhythm guitarist of the Go-Go's.	
6/11/88	**9**	10	1. **Rush Hour**	EMI-Man. 50118
			HARLOW WILCOX & THE OAKIES	
			Harlow is a top session guitarist from Norman, Oklahoma.	
11/22/69	**30**	6	1. Groovy Grubworm [I]	Plantation 28
			WILD CHERRY	
			White funk band formed in Steubenville, Ohio in the early 70s. Consisted of Bob Parissi (lead vocals, guitar), Bryan Bassett (guitar), Mark Avsec (keyboards), Allen Wentz (bass) and Ron Beitle (drums).	
7/31/76	**1(3)**	18	▲ 1. **Play That Funky Music**	Epic 50225
			KIM WILDE	
			Born Kim Smith on 11/18/60 in Chiswick, England. Pop-rock singer. Daughter of singer Marty Wilde.	
7/17/82	**25**	8	1. Kids In America	EMI America 8110
4/18/87	**1(1)**	13	2. **You Keep Me Hangin' On**	MCA 53024
			MATTHEW WILDER	
			Born and raised in Manhattan; moved to Los Angeles in the late 70s. Singer/ songwriter/keyboardist. Session singer for Rickie Lee Jones and Bette Midler.	
11/26/83†	**5**	14	1. **Break My Stride**	Private I 04113
3/24/84	**33**	4	2. The Kid's American	Private I 04363
			WILL TO POWER	
			Florida-based trio formed and fronted by producer Bob Rosenberg with Dr. J. and Maria Mendez. Rosenberg is the son of singer Gloria Mann.	
10/15/88	**1(1)**	15	● 1. **Baby, I Love Your Way/Freebird Medley (Free Baby)**	Epic 08034
			ANDY WILLIAMS	
			Born Howard Andrew Williams on 12/3/28 in Wall Lake, Iowa. Formed quartet with his brothers and eventually moved to Los Angeles. With Bing Crosby on hit "Swingin' On A Star," 1944. With comedienne Kay Thompson in the mid-40s. Went solo in 1952. On Steve Allen's "Tonight Show" from 1952-55. Own NBC-TV variety series from 1962-67; 1969-71. Appeared in the film "I'd Rather Be Rich" in 1964. One of America's greatest pop-MOR singers. Formerly married to singer/actress Claudine Longet.	
8/18/56	**7**	17	1. **Canadian Sunset** Jockey #7 / Top 100 #8 / Juke Box #9 / Best Seller #10	Cadence 1297
12/22/56	**33**	3	2. Baby Doll from the film of the same title	Cadence 1303
3/02/57	**1(3)**	14	3. **Butterfly** Top 100 #1(3) / Jockey #1(2) / Juke Box #2 / Best Seller #4	Cadence 1308
6/03/57	**8**	14	4. **I Like Your Kind Of Love** Jockey #8 / Top 100 #9 / Best Seller #10 / Juke Box #19 end female vocal: Peggy Powers	Cadence 1323
10/14/57	**17**	3	5. Lips Of Wine Jockey #17 / Top 100 #39	Cadence 1336
2/24/58	**3**	14	6. **Are You Sincere** Jockey #3 / Top 100 #10 / Best Seller #11	Cadence 1340
9/22/58	**17**	6	7. Promise Me, Love	Cadence 1351

DATE	POS	WKS	ARTIST—RECORD TITLE	LABEL & NO.
1/12/59	**11**	15	8. The Hawaiian Wedding Song song written in 1926, with new lyrics added	Cadence 1358
9/28/59	**5**	11	9. **Lonely Street**	Cadence 1370
12/28/59†	**7**	9	10. **The Village Of St. Bernadette**	Cadence 1374
6/05/61	**37**	2	11. The Bilbao Song	Cadence 1398
7/14/62	**38**	1	12. Stranger On The Shore	Columbia 42451
11/03/62	**39**	1	13. Don't You Believe It	Columbia 42523
3/23/63	**2**(4)	12	14. **Can't Get Used To Losing You/**	
4/13/63	**26**	7	15. Days Of Wine And Roses from the film of the same title	Columbia 42674
7/06/63	**13**	8	16. Hopeless	Columbia 42784
1/25/64	**13**	8	17. A Fool Never Learns	Columbia 42950
5/16/64	**34**	4	18. Wrong For Each Other	Columbia 43015
10/03/64	**28**	5	19. On The Street Where You Live from the Broadway musical "My Fair Lady"	Columbia 43128
12/19/64†	**24**	7	20. Dear Heart from the film of the same title	Columbia 43180
4/24/65	**36**	3	21. And Roses And Roses	Columbia 43257
10/16/65	**40**	1	22. Ain't It True	Columbia 43358
4/22/67	**34**	3	23. Music To Watch Girls By	Columbia 44065
11/30/68	**33**	4	24. Battle Hymn Of The Republic backed by St. Charles Borromeo Choir; recorded at St. Patrick's Cathedral on 6/8/68 as a eulogy to Senator Robert F. Kennedy	Columbia 44650
5/03/69	**22**	7	25. Happy Heart	Columbia 44818
2/27/71	**9**	10	26. **(Where Do I Begin) Love Story** from the film "Love Story"	Columbia 45317
5/20/72	**34**	4	27. Love Theme From "The Godfather" (Speak Softly Love) from the film of the same title	Columbia 45579
			BILLY WILLIAMS	
			Born on 12/28/10 in Waco, Texas; died on 10/17/72 in Chicago. Lead singer of The Charioteers from 1930-50. Formed own Billy Williams Quartet with Eugene Dixon, Claude Riddick and John Ball in 1950. Many appearances on TV, especially "Your Show Of Shows" with Sid Caesar. By early 60s, had lost voice due to diabetes. Moved to Chicago and worked as social worker until his death.	
6/17/57	**3**	18	1. **I'm Gonna Sit Right Down And Write Myself A Letter** Jockey #3 / Top 100 #6 / Best Seller #7 #5 hit for Fats Waller in 1935	Coral 61830
2/16/59	**39**	3	2. Nola #3 instrumental hit for bandleader Vincent Lopez in 1922	Coral 62069
			DANNY WILLIAMS	
			Born in Port Elizabeth, South Africa. Moved to England as a youngster.	
4/04/64	**9**	10	1. **White On White**	United Art. 685
			DENIECE WILLIAMS	
			Born Deniece Chandler on 6/3/51 in Gary, Indiana. Soul vocalist/songwriter. Recorded for Toddlin' Town, early 60s. Member of Wonderlove, Stevie Wonder's back-up group, from 1972-75.	
3/05/77	**25**	7	1. Free	Columbia 10429

DATE	POS	WKS	ARTIST—RECORD TITLE	LABEL & NO.
4/22/78	**1**(1)	11	• 2. **Too Much, Too Little, Too Late**	Columbia 10693
			JOHNNY MATHIS/DENIECE WILLIAMS	
5/01/82	**10**	9	3. It's Gonna Take A Miracle	ARC 02812
4/14/84	**1**(2)	14	• 4. **Let's Hear It For The Boy** from the film "Footloose"	Columbia 04417
			DON WILLIAMS	
			Born on 5/27/39 in Floydada, Texas. Country singer/songwriter/guitarist. Charted over 15 #1 country hits. Leader of the Pozo-Seco Singers. In films "W.W. & The Dixie Dancekings" and "Smokey & The Bandit II."	
11/15/80	**24**	9	1. I Believe In You	MCA 41304
			JOHN WILLIAMS	
			Born on 2/8/32 in New York City. Noted composer/conductor of many top box-office film hits. Succeeded Arthur Fiedler as conductor of the Boston Pops in 1980.	
9/13/75	**32**	4	1. Theme From "Jaws" (Main Title) [I]	MCA 40439
8/13/77	**10**	7	2. **Star Wars (Main Title)** [I] performed by The London Symphony Orchestra	20th Century 2345
1/21/78	**13**	8	3. Theme From "Close Encounters Of The Third Kind" [I] all of above: from film soundtracks composed by John Williams	Arista 0300
			LARRY WILLIAMS	
			Born on 5/10/35 in New Orleans; committed suicide on 1/7/80 in Los Angeles. R&B-rock and roll singer/songwriter/pianist. With Lloyd Price in the early 50s. Convicted of narcotics dealing in 1960, jail term interrupted his career.	
7/08/57	**5**	17	1. **Short Fat Fannie** Best Seller #5 / Top 100 #6 / Jockey #15	Specialty 608
11/11/57	**14**	14	2. Bony Moronie Best Seller #14 / Top 100 #18	Specialty 615
			MASON WILLIAMS	
			Born on 8/24/38 in Abilene, Texas. Folk guitarist/songwriter/author/ photographer/ TV comedy writer ("The Smothers Brothers Comedy Hour").	
7/13/68	**2**(2)	11	1. **Classical Gas** **[I]**	Warner 7190
			MAURICE WILLIAMS & THE ZODIACS	
			R&B vocal group from Lancaster, South Carolina, led by pianist/songwriter Maurice Williams. Originally recorded as The Gladiolas, became The Zodiacs in 1959. Williams re-formed group with Wiley Bennett, Henry Gaston, Charles Thomas, Albert Hill and Little Willie Morrow in 1960.	
10/10/60	**1**(1)	14	1. **Stay**	Herald 552
			OTIS WILLIAMS - see CHARMS	
			ROGER WILLIAMS	
			Born Louis Weertz in 1925 in Omaha. Learned to play the piano by age 3. Educated at Drake University, Idaho State University, and Juilliard School of Music. Took lessons from Lenny Tristano and Teddy Wilson. Win on the TV show "Arthur Godfrey's Talent Scouts" led to recording contract.	
8/20/55	**1**(4)	26	1. **Autumn Leaves** **[I]** Best Seller #1 / Top 100 #2 pre / Juke Box #2 / Jockey #3	Kapp 116
1/14/56	**38**	1	2. Wanting You [I] from the 1928 musical "The New Moon"	Kapp 127

DATE	POS	WKS	ARTIST—RECORD TITLE	LABEL & NO.
3/24/56	37	1	3. La Mer (Beyond The Sea) [I] #26 hit for Benny Goodman in 1948	Kapp 138
3/16/57	15	10	4. Almost Paradise [I] Jockey #15 / Best Seller #22 / Top 100 #26	Kapp 175
11/11/57	22	7	5. Till Jockey #22 / Top 100 #27 / Best Seller #28	Kapp 197
9/08/58	**10**	11	6. **Near You** **[I]** Hot 100 #10 / Best Seller #16 end #1 hit (17 weeks) for Francis Craig in 1947	Kapp 233
10/15/66	**7**	14	7. **Born Free** from the film of the same title	Kapp 767
			BRUCE WILLIS	
			Plays David Addison on the TV series "Moonlighting." Married actress Demi Moore on 11/21/87. Appeared in the films "Blind Date" (1987) and "Die Hard" (1988).	
1/31/87	**5**	10	1. **Respect Yourself**	Motown 1876
			CHUCK WILLIS	
			Born on 1/31/28 in Atlanta; died on 4/10/58 (peritonitis). R&B singer/songwriter.	
5/13/57	12	8	1. C. C. Rider Top 100 #12 / Best Seller #13 inspired the "Stroll" dance craze	Atlantic 1130
3/10/58	33	3	2. Betty And Dupree Best Seller #33 / Top 100 #33	Atlantic 1168
5/12/58	**9**	17	3. **What Am I Living For/** Jockey #9 / Best Seller #15 / Top 100 #15	
5/26/58	24	2	4. Hang Up My Rock And Roll Shoes	Atlantic 1179
			AL WILSON	
			Born on 6/19/39 in Meridian, Mississippi. Soul singer/drummer. Moved to San Bernadino, California in the late 50s. Member of The Rollers from 1960-62.	
9/21/68	27	5	1. The Snake	Soul City 767
11/24/73†	**1**(1)	16	● 2. **Show And Tell**	Rocky Road 30073
11/09/74	30	3	3. La La Peace Song	Rocky Road 30200
5/01/76	29	4	4. I've Got A Feeling (We'll Be Seeing Each Other Again)	Playboy 6062
			ANN WILSON - see MIKE RENO	
			BRIAN WILSON	
			Born on 6/20/42 in Hawthorne, California. Leader/bassist/composer/producer of the legendary surf-rock group, The Beach Boys. Due to nervous exhaustion, he quit touring in late 1965, but continued to produce much of the group's material until the early 1970s. In semi-retirement until 1987.	
4/23/66	32	3	1. Caroline, No	Capitol 5610
			DANNY WILSON - see DANNY	
			J. FRANK WILSON & THE CAVALIERS	
			J. Frank was born in 1941 in Lufkin, Texas. Band formed in San Angelo, Texas. The Cavaliers: Phil Trungo, Jerry Graham, Bobby Woods and George Croyle.	
9/26/64	**2**(1)	12	1. **Last Kiss**	Josie 923

DATE	POS	WKS	ARTIST—RECORD TITLE	LABEL & NO.
			JACKIE WILSON	
			Born on 6/9/34 in Detroit; died on 1/21/84. Sang with local gospel groups; became an amateur boxer. Worked as solo singer until 1953, then joined Billy Ward's Dominoes as Clyde McPhatter's replacement. Solo since 1957. His goddaughter is Jody Watley. Jackie collapsed from a stroke, on stage, at the Latin Casino in Camden, New Jersey, on 9/25/75; spent rest of his life in hospitals. Inducted into the Rock And Roll Hall Of Fame in 1987.	
4/21/58	**22**	10	1. To Be Loved Top 100 #22 / Best Seller #23	Brunswick 55052
12/08/58†	**7**	16	2. **Lonely Teardrops**	Brunswick 55105
4/13/59	**13**	9	3. That's Why (I Love You So)	Brunswick 55121
7/06/59	**20**	6	4. I'll Be Satisfied	Brunswick 55136
10/12/59	**37**	1	5. You Better Know It from the film "Go Johnny Go"	Brunswick 55149
1/04/60	**34**	3	6. Talk That Talk	Brunswick 55165
4/11/60	**4**	12	7. **Night/**	
4/25/60	**15**	9	8. Doggin' Around	Brunswick 55166
8/01/60	**12**	9	9. (You Were Made For) All My Love/	
8/01/60	**15**	8	10. A Woman, A Lover, A Friend	Brunswick 55167
10/24/60	**8**	12	11. **Alone At Last/** based on Tchaikovsky's Piano Concerto in B Flat	
11/28/60	**32**	2	12. Am I The Man	Brunswick 55170
1/16/61	**9**	6	13. **My Empty Arms**	Brunswick 55201
3/27/61	**20**	5	14. Please Tell Me Why/	
3/27/61	**40**	1	15. Your One And Only Love	Brunswick 55208
6/26/61	**19**	5	16. I'm Comin' On Back To You	Brunswick 55216
9/11/61	**37**	2	17. Years From Now	Brunswick 55219
2/03/62	**34**	4	18. The Greatest Hurt	Brunswick 55221
3/23/63	**5**	9	19. **Baby Workout** all of above (except #18): orchestra directed by Dick Jacobs	Brunswick 55239
8/10/63	**33**	1	20. Shake! Shake! Shake!	Brunswick 55246
11/19/66	**11**	8	21. Whispers (Gettin' Louder)	Brunswick 55300
9/02/67	**6**	9	22. **(Your Love Keeps Lifting Me) Higher And Higher**	Brunswick 55336
12/16/67	**32**	2	23. Since You Showed Me How To Be Happy	Brunswick 55354
8/31/68	**34**	2	24. I Get The Sweetest Feeling	Brunswick 55381
			MERI WILSON	
			Dallas-based song stylist.	
7/02/77	**18**	10	● 1. Telephone Man [N]	GRT 127
			NANCY WILSON	
			Born on 2/20/37 in Chillicothe, Ohio. Jazz stylist with Rusty Bryant's Carolyn Club Band in Columbus. First recorded for Dot in 1956.	
7/18/64	**11**	7	1. (You Don't Know) How Glad I Am	Capitol 5198
6/15/68	**29**	9	2. Face It Girl, It's Over	Capitol 2136
			WILTON PLACE STREET BAND	
			Los Angeles studio project produced and arranged by Trevor Lawrence (resided on Wilton Place in Los Angeles).	
3/12/77	**24**	7	1. Disco Lucy (I Love Lucy Theme) [I] discofied theme from the TV series "I Love Lucy"	Island 078

DATE	POS	WKS	ARTIST—RECORD TITLE	LABEL & NO.
			JESSE WINCHESTER	
			Born on 5/17/44 in Shreveport, Louisiana. Pop-MOR singer/songwriter/guitarist. Became Canadian in 1973.	
5/30/81	**32**	5	1. Say What	Bearsville 49711
			WIND	
			New York studio group featuring Tony Orlando as lead singer.	
10/04/69	**28**	4	1. Make Believe	Life 200
			KAI WINDING	
			Born on 5/18/22 in Aarhus, Denmark; died on 5/6/83. Jazz trombonist. With Benny Goodman and Stan Kenton in the mid-40s.	
7/27/63	**8**	9	1. **More** [I] theme from the film "Mondo Cane"	Verve 10295
			THE WING & A PRAYER FIFE & DRUM CORPS.	
			Big band from New York City, with vocals by Linda November, Vivian Cherry, Arlene Martell and Helen Miles.	
12/20/75†	**14**	12	1. Baby Face 4 versions hit the top 10 in 1926	Wing & Prayer 103
			PETE WINGFIELD	
			Keyboardist from England. Worked with Freddie King, Jimmy Witherspoon and Van Morrison. In Olympic Runners band.	
10/25/75	**15**	8	1. Eighteen With A Bullet hit #18 with a bullet on the 11/22/75 "Hot 100" chart	Island 026
			WINGS - see PAUL McCARTNEY	
			THE WINSTONS	
			Washington, DC soul septet featuring lead singer Richard Spencer. Toured as back-up band for The Impressions.	
6/14/69	**7**	10	● 1. **Color Him Father**	Metromedia 117
			EDGAR WINTER	
			Born on 12/28/46 in Beaumont, Texas. Rock singer/keyboardist/saxophonist. Younger brother of rock guitarist Johnny Winter. Group included Rick Derringer and Dan Hartman, 1972-75.	
			THE EDGAR WINTER GROUP:	
4/21/73	**1**(1)	14	● 1. **Frankenstein** [I] featuring lead guitar work by Ronnie Montrose	Epic 10967
9/08/73	**14**	9	2. Free Ride	Epic 11024
8/10/74	**33**	2	3. River's Risin'	Epic 11143
			HUGO WINTERHALTER - see EDDIE HEYWOOD	
			STEVE WINWOOD	
			Born on 5/12/48 in Birmingham, England. Rock singer/keyboardist/guitarist. Lead singer of rock bands The Spencer Davis Group, Blind Faith and Traffic.	
2/28/81	**7**	12	1. **While You See A Chance**	Island 49656
7/05/86	**1**(1)	14	2. **Higher Love**	Island 28710
10/25/86	**20**	7	3. Freedom Overspill	Island 28595
3/14/87	**8**	12	4. **The Finer Things**	Island 28498
7/04/87	**13**	10	5. Back In The High Life Again	Island 28472

DATE	POS	WKS	ARTIST—RECORD TITLE	LABEL & NO.
11/07/87	**9**	12	6. **Valerie** **[R]** remix of his 1982 hit (POS 70)	Island 28231
6/18/88	**1**(4)	14	7. **Roll With It**	Virgin 99326
9/10/88	**6**	11	8. **Don't You Know What The Night Can Do?**	Virgin 99290
12/10/88†	**11**	11	9. Holding On	Virgin 99261
			BILL WITHERS	
			Born on 7/4/38 in Slab Fork, West Virginia. Black vocalist/guitarist/composer. Moved to California in 1967 and made demo records of his songs. First recorded for Sussex in 1970, produced by Booker T. Jones. Made professional singing debut in 1971. Married to actress Denise Nicholas. Recorded duet with jazz-R&B saxophonist Grover Washington, Jr. (b: 12/13/43, Buffalo).	
8/14/71	**3**	12	● 1. **Ain't No Sunshine**	Sussex 219
5/27/72	**1**(3)	14	● 2. **Lean On Me**	Sussex 235
9/09/72	**2**(2)	10	● 3. **Use Me**	Sussex 241
3/03/73	**31**	5	4. Kissing My Love	Sussex 250
1/21/78	**30**	4	5. Lovely Day	Columbia 10627
3/07/81	**2**(3)	16	6. **Just The Two Of Us** **GROVER WASHINGTON, JR. with BILL WITHERS**	Elektra 47103
			PETER WOLF	
			Born Peter Blankfield on 3/7/46 in the Bronx. Lead singer of The J. Geils Band until 1983. Married to actress Faye Dunaway from 1975-79.	
7/28/84	**12**	10	1. Lights Out	EMI America 8208
11/17/84	**36**	2	2. I Need You Tonight	EMI America 8241
3/21/87	**15**	9	3. Come As You Are	EMI America 8350
			WOLFMAN JACK - see GUESS WHO and STAMPEDERS	
			BOBBY WOMACK	
			Born on 3/4/44 in Cleveland. Soul vocalist/guitarist/songwriter. Sang in family gospel group, the Womack Brothers. Group recorded for Sar as The Valentinos and The Lovers, 1962-64. Toured as guitarist with Sam Cooke. Solo recording for Him label in 1965. Back-up guitarist on many sessions, including Wilson Pickett, Box Tops, Joe Tex, Aretha Franklin and Janis Joplin. Married for a time to Sam Cooke's widow.	
1/08/72	**27**	7	1. That's The Way I Feel About Cha	United Art. 50847
1/13/73	**31**	6	● 2. Harry Hippie with backing group, Peace	United Art. 50946
8/11/73	**29**	6	3. Nobody Wants You When You're Down And Out	United Art. 255
3/09/74	**10**	11	● 4. **Lookin' For A Love**	United Art. 375

DATE	POS	WKS	ARTIST—RECORD TITLE	LABEL & NO.
			THE WONDER WHO? - see THE 4 SEASONS	
			STEVIE WONDER	
			Born Steveland Morris on 5/13/50 in Saginaw, Michigan. Singer/songwriter/ multi-instrumentalist/producer. Blind since birth. Signed to Motown in 1960, did back-up work. First recorded in 1962, renamed "Little Stevie Wonder" by Berry Gordy, Jr. Married to Syreeta Wright from 1970-72. Near-fatal auto accident on 8/16/73. Winner of 16 Grammy Awards. In the films "Bikini Beach" and "Muscle Beach Party." Inducted into the Rock And Roll Hall Of Fame in 1989. Also see Dionne Warwick.	
			LITTLE STEVIE WONDER:	
7/06/63	**1**(3)	12	1. **Fingertips - Pt 2**	Tamla 54080
10/19/63	**33**	4	2. Workout Stevie, Workout	Tamla 54086
			STEVIE WONDER:	
7/11/64	**29**	4	3. Hey Harmonica Man	Tamla 54096
1/22/66	**3**	9	4. **Uptight (Everything's Alright)**	Tamla 54124
5/07/66	**20**	4	5. Nothing's Too Good For My Baby	Tamla 54130
7/30/66	**9**	8	6. **Blowin In The Wind**	Tamla 54136
11/26/66	**9**	8	7. **A Place In The Sun**	Tamla 54139
4/01/67	**32**	3	8. Travlin' Man	Tamla 54147
6/24/67	**2**(2)	12	9. **I Was Made To Love Her**	Tamla 54151
10/21/67	**12**	5	10. I'm Wondering	Tamla 54157
4/27/68	**9**	9	11. **Shoo-Be-Doo-Be-Doo-Da-Day**	Tamla 54165
8/17/68	**35**	3	12. You Met Your Match	Tamla 54168
11/09/68	**2**(2)	11	13. **For Once In My Life**	Tamla 54174
3/22/69	**39**	1	14. I Don't Know Why/	
6/21/69	**4**	11	15. My Cherie Amour	Tamla 54180
11/01/69	**7**	12	16. **Yester-Me, Yester-You, Yesterday**	Tamla 54188
2/21/70	**26**	5	17. Never Had A Dream Come True	Tamla 54191
7/04/70	**3**	13	18. **Signed, Sealed, Delivered I'm Yours**	Tamla 54196
10/31/70	**9**	8	19. **Heaven Help Us All**	Tamla 54200
3/27/71	**13**	9	20. We Can Work It Out	Tamla 54202
9/04/71	**8**	11	21. **If You Really Love Me** written by Wonder & Syreeta Wright	Tamla 54208
6/24/72	**33**	5	22. Superwoman (Where Were You When I Needed You)	Tamla 54216
12/09/72†	**1**(1)	13	23. **Superstition**	Tamla 54226
3/31/73	**1**(1)	13	24. **You Are The Sunshine Of My Life**	Tamla 54232
9/01/73	**4**	12	25. **Higher Ground**	Tamla 54235
11/24/73†	**8**	14	26. **Living For The City**	Tamla 54242
4/27/74	**16**	9	27. Don't You Worry 'Bout A Thing	Tamla 54245
8/17/74	**1**(1)	14	28. **You Haven't Done Nothin** backing vocals: Jackson 5	Tamla 54252
11/30/74†	**3**	14	29. **Boogie On Reggae Woman**	Tamla 54254
12/04/76†	**1**(1)	15	30. **I Wish**	Tamla 54274
4/16/77	**1**(3)	13	31. **Sir Duke** a tribute to Duke Ellington	Tamla 54281
9/17/77	**32**	4	32. Another Star	Tamla 54286

DATE	POS	WKS	ARTIST—RECORD TITLE	LABEL & NO.
12/03/77†	**36**	5	33. As	Tamla 54291
11/10/79	**4**	14	34. **Send One Your Love**	Tamla 54303
10/04/80	**5**	16	35. **Master Blaster (Jammin')**	Tamla 54317
1/17/81	**11**	11	36. I Ain't Gonna Stand For It	Tamla 54320
1/30/82	**4**	13	37. **That Girl**	Tamla 1602
4/10/82	**1**(7)	15	● 38. **Ebony And Ivory**	Columbia 02860
			PAUL McCARTNEY with STEVIE WONDER	
6/19/82	**13**	9	39. Do I Do	Tamla 1612
9/01/84	**1**(3)	15	● 40. **I Just Called To Say I Love You**	Motown 1745
12/15/84†	**17**	10	41. Love Light In Flight above 2: from the film "The Woman In Red"	Motown 1769
9/14/85	**1**(1)	14	42. **Part-Time Lover**	Tamla 1808
12/14/85†	**10**	11	43. **Go Home**	Tamla 1817
3/22/86	**24**	6	44. Overjoyed	Tamla 1832
11/07/87	**19**	7	45. Skeletons	Motown 1907
			BRENTON WOOD	
			Born Alfred Smith on 7/26/41 in Shreveport. Raised in San Pedro, California. Soul singer/songwriter/pianist. First recorded with Little Freddy & The Rockets in 1958.	
6/24/67	**34**	1	1. The Oogum Boogum Song	Double Shot 111
9/09/67	**9**	10	2. **Gimme Little Sign**	Double Shot 116
12/16/67	**34**	3	3. Baby You Got It	Double Shot 121
			LAUREN WOOD	
			Pop singer/songwriter/keyboardist; originally from Pittsburgh.	
10/27/79	**24**	6	1. Please Don't Leave harmony vocal: Michael McDonald	Warner 49043
			STEVIE WOODS	
			Black vocalist based in Los Angeles. Originally from Columbus, Ohio.	
11/14/81	**25**	10	1. Steal The Night	Cotillion 46016
3/20/82	**38**	3	2. Just Can't Win 'Em All	Cotillion 46030
			SHEB WOOLEY	
			Born on 4/10/21 in Erick, Oklahoma. Singer/songwriter/actor. Played Pete Nolan in the TV series "Rawhide." Also made comical recordings under pseudonym "Ben Colder." Appeared in the films "Rocky Mountain" and "Giant."	
6/02/58	**1**(6)	14	1. **The Purple People Eater** [N] Best Seller #1(6) / Top 100 #1(6) / Jockey #1(4)	MGM 12651
			WORLD PARTY	
			London-based group featuring keyboardist/vocalist/producer/engineer Karl Wallinger from North Wales (formerly of The Waterboys).	
4/04/87	**27**	5	1. Ship Of Fools (Save Me From Tomorrow)	Chrysalis 43052
			LINK WRAY & HIS RAY MEN	
			Link was born on 5/2/35 in Dunn, North Carolina. Rock and roll guitarist. Part American Indian. Joined family band the Palomino Ranch Gang in the early 50s. First recorded as "Lucky" Wray for Starday in 1956. Active into the late 70s. Recorded album with rockabilly singer Robert Gordon in 1977.	
5/12/58	**16**	10	1. Rumble [I] Best Seller #16 / Top 100 #16	Cadence 1347

Poison is anything but on the charts, as evidenced by the heavy-metal quartet's No. 13 single "I Won't Forget You," which was surpassed by other Poisonings: "Fallen Angel" (No. 12), "Nothin' But A Good Time," (No. 6) and "Every Rose Has Its Thorn" (No. 1).

Elvis Presley's "All Shook Up" held the No. 1 spot for nine weeks in 1957, his best assault on the incredible 11-week reign of "Don't Be Cruel." His career would ultimately encompass nine No. 1 albums and 18 No. 1 songs, a singles record surpassed only by the Beatles.

Prince was being typically risque with his enticement to "Let's Pretend We're Married," one of the four charting singles from his album *1999*, which arrived 17 years early in 1982. His biggest album at the time, it was bested by 1984's *Purple Rain*, which spent an incredible 24 weeks at No. 1.

The Rascals began when Felix Cavaliere, Eddie Brigati, and Gene Cornish defected from Joey Dee & the Starlighters in 1965. Their eight-year career spawned 13 Top-40 hits, including No. 1s "Good Lovin'," "Groovin'," and—dropping the "Young" from their name—"People Got To Be Free."

Lou Rawls' roots may go back to the 50s gospel group the Pilgrim Travelers, but the soul veteran's biggest hit didn't come along for decades. In 1976, his Gamble & Huff-produced "You'll Never Find A Love Like Mine" spent 13 weeks in the Top 40, peaking at No. 2 for two weeks.

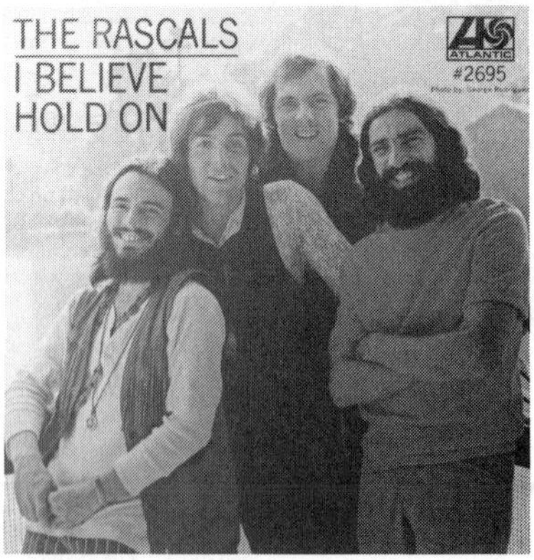

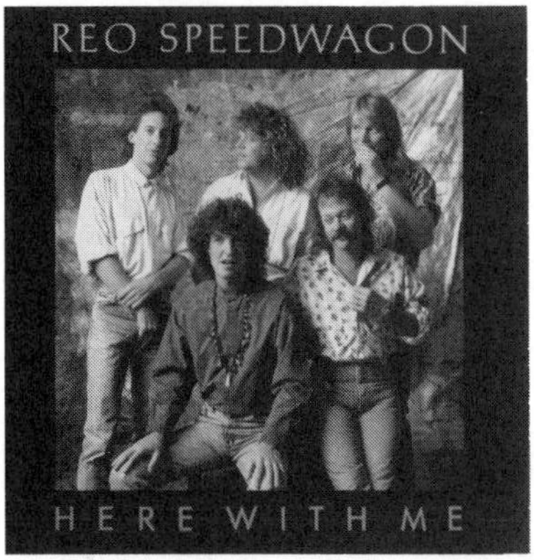

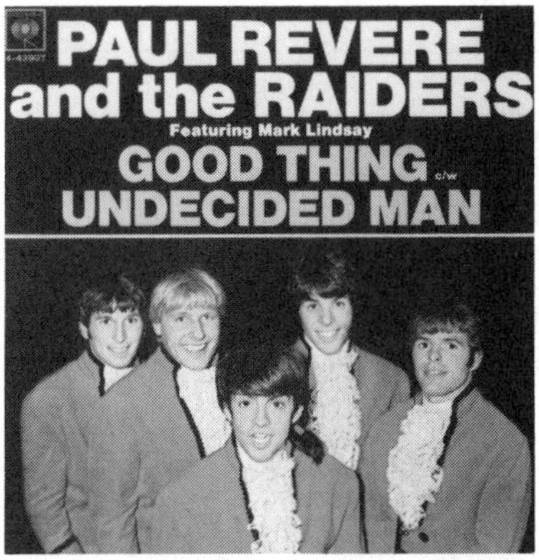

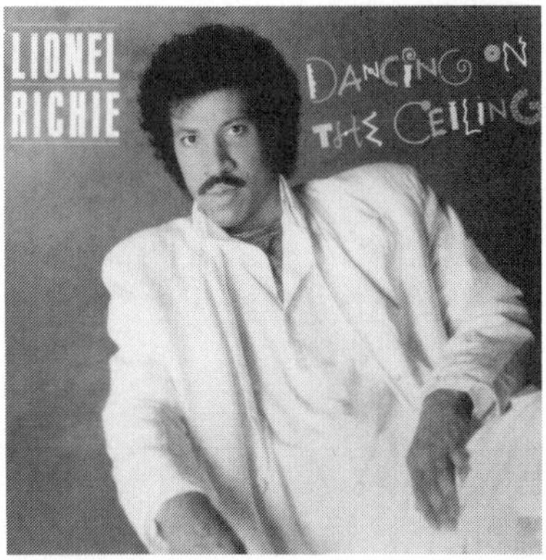

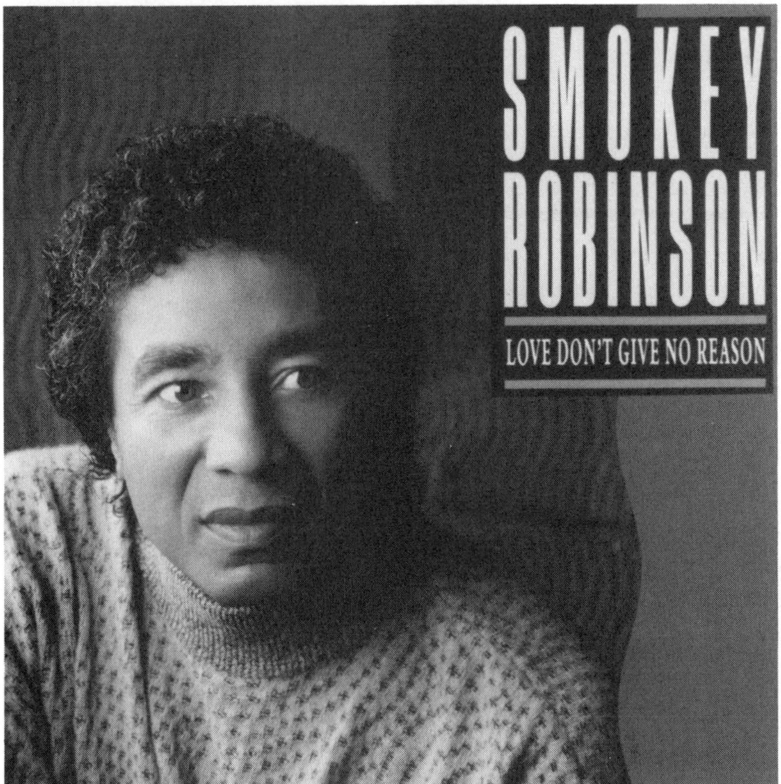

REO Speedwagon's lucky 13th Top-40 hit was the No. 20 "Here With Me." Yet the Illinois quintet's biggest song was 1985's "Can't Fight This Feeling," a title which presumably had nothing to do with the place where REO's Kevin Cronin completed the song: the Hawaiian island of Molokai, a former leper colony.

Paul Revere and the Raiders were well-known to America's living rooms from Dick Clark's "Where The Action Is" when "Good Thing" cracked the top five in 1967. Yet their only No. 1 hit came years after they left the tube: "Indian Reservation," by the subsequently-abbreviated Raiders.

Debbie Reynolds' "Tammy," from her film *Tammy And The Bachelor,* held the No. 1 spot for five weeks in 1957—awarding the unlikely actress-turned-hit-maker with the No. 58 song of the years 1955-88.

Lionel Richie's gravity-defying video further enhanced the success of "Dancing On The Ceiling," which spent eight weeks of 1986 in the top 10, peaking at No. 2. The album of the same name actually went *through* the ceiling, and became his second No. 1 album.

Smokey Robinson's "Love Don't Give No Reason" was one of a series of hits that the Motown standard-bearer recorded with the seemingly incongruous Motown upstart Rick James. Their partnership reached its height with the song "17," which rose to No. 36 on the pop charts.

DATE	POS	WKS	ARTIST—RECORD TITLE	LABEL & NO.
3/16/59	**23**	3	2. Raw-Hide [I]	Epic 9300
			BETTY WRIGHT	
			Born on 12/21/53 in Miami. Soul singer. In family gospel group Echoes Of Joy, from 1956. First recorded for Deep City in 1966. Hostess of TV talk shows in Miami. Also see Peter Brown.	
9/07/68	**33**	2	1. Girls Can't Do What The Guys Do	Alston 4569
12/11/71†	**6**	12	● 2. **Clean Up Woman**	Alston 4601
			CHARLES WRIGHT & THE WATTS 103rd STREET RHYTHM BAND	
			Charles was born in 1942 in Clarksdale, Mississippi. Vocalist/pianist/guitarist/producer/leader of an 8-man, soul-funk band from the Watts section of Los Angeles. Evolved from the Soul Runners. Big break came through assistance by comedian Bill Cosby.	
3/22/69	**11**	10	1. Do Your Thing	Warner 7250
			THE WATTS 103RD STREET RHYTHM BAND:	
5/30/70	**16**	10	2. Love Land	Warner 7365
9/12/70	**12**	10	3. Express Yourself	Warner 7417
			DALE WRIGHT with the Rock-Its	
			Rockabilly singer from Cincinnati.	
2/24/58	**38**	2	1. She's Neat Best Seller #38 / Top 100 #39	Fraternity 792
			GARY WRIGHT	
			Born on 4/26/43 in Creskill, New Jersey. Pop-rock singer/songwriter/keyboardist. Appeared in "Captain Video" TV series at age 7. In the Broadway play "Fanny." Co-leader of the rock group Spooky Tooth.	
1/31/76	**2**(3)	14	● 1. **Dream Weaver**	Warner 8167
5/15/76	**2**(2)	18	2. **Love Is Alive**	Warner 8143
8/01/81	**16**	10	3. Really Wanna Know You	Warner 49769
			PRISCILLA WRIGHT	
6/25/55	**16**	9	1. The Man In The Raincoat Jockey #16 / Best Seller #18 / Juke Box #20 backing vocals: Don Wright & The Septette	Unique 303
			TAMMY WYNETTE	
			Born Virginia Wynette Pugh on 5/5/42 in Tupelo, Mississippi. With over 15 #1 country hits, dubbed "The First Lady Of Country Music." Discovered by producer Billy Sherrill. Married to country star George Jones from 1968-75.	
12/28/68†	**19**	9	1. Stand By Your Man	Epic 10398
			Y	
			"WEIRD AL" YANKOVIC	
			Los Angeles novelty singer/accordionist. Specializes in song parodies.	
3/17/84	**12**	7	1. Eat It [N] parody of Michael Jackson's "Beat It"; guitar: Rick Derringer	Rock 'n' R. 04374

DATE	POS	WKS	ARTIST—RECORD TITLE	LABEL & NO.
			YARBROUGH & PEOPLES	
			Dallas soul duo: Cavin Yarbrough and Alisa Peoples. Discovered by The Gap Band.	
3/14/81	**19**	7	● 1. Don't Stop The Music	Mercury 76085
			GLENN YARBROUGH	
			Born on 1/12/30 in Milwaukee. Lead singer of The Limeliters (1959-63).	
4/17/65	**12**	9	1. Baby The Rain Must Fall from the film of the same title	RCA 8498
			THE YARDBIRDS	
			Legendary rock group formed in Surrey, England in 1963. Consisted of Keith Relf (d: 5/14/76; vocals, harmonica), Anthony "Top" Topham and Chris Dreja (guitars), Paul "Sam" Samwell-Smith (bass, keyboards) and Jim McCarty (drums). Formed as the Metropolitan Blues Quartet at Kingston Art School. Topham replaced by Eric Clapton in 1963. Clapton replaced by Jeff Beck in 1965. Samwell-Smith replaced by Chris Dreja (bass) and Jimmy Page (guitar) added in 1966. Beck left in December of 1966. Group disbanded in July, 1968. Page formed the New Yardbirds in October of 1968, which evolved into Led Zeppelin. Relf and McCarty formed Renaissance in 1969. Keith Relf later in Armageddon, 1975. McCarty later in Illusion, 1977.	
6/05/65	**6**	9	1. **For Your Love**	Epic 9790
8/21/65	**9**	8	2. **Heart Full Of Soul** above 2: written by Graham Gouldman (10cc)	Epic 9823
11/20/65	**17**	7	3. I'm A Man	Epic 9857
4/09/66	**11**	8	4. Shapes Of Things	Epic 10006
7/16/66	**13**	7	5. Over Under Sideways Down	Epic 10035
12/24/66	**30**	4	6. Happenings Ten Years Time Ago	Epic 10094
			THE YELLOW BALLOON	
			Quintet from Oregon and Arizona formed by Don Grady (Robbie Douglas of "My Three Sons"). Alex Valdez, lead singer.	
4/29/67	**25**	5	1. Yellow Balloon	Canterbury 508
			YES	
			Progressive rock group formed in London in 1968. Consisted of Jon Anderson (vocals), Peter Banks (guitar), Tony Kaye (keyboards), Chris Squire (bass) and Bill Bruford (drums). Banks replaced by Steve Howe in 1971. Kaye (joined Badfinger in 1978) replaced by Rick Wakeman in 1971. Bruford left to join King Crimson, replaced by Alan White, late 1972. Wakeman replaced by Patrick Moraz in 1974, rejoined in 1976 when Moraz left. Wakeman and Anderson left in 1980, replaced by The Buggles' Trevor Horne (guitar) and Geoff Downes (keyboards). Group disbanded in 1980. Howe and Downes went with Asia. Re-formed in 1983 with Anderson, Kaye, Squire, White, and South African guitarist Trevor Rabin. Anderson left group in 1988.	
12/04/71	**40**	2	1. Your Move	Atlantic 2819
3/04/72	**13**	10	2. Roundabout	Atlantic 2854
11/19/83†	1(2)	17	3. **Owner Of A Lonely Heart**	Atco 99817
3/24/84	**24**	7	4. Leave It	Atco 99787
10/31/87	**30**	6	5. Love Will Find A Way	Atco 99449
2/06/88	**40**	1	6. Rhythm Of Love	Atco 99419

DATE	POS	WKS	ARTIST—RECORD TITLE	LABEL & NO.
			DENNIS YOST - see CLASSICS IV	
			THE YOUNGBLOODS	
			Folk-rock group led by vocalist Jesse Colin Young (born Perry Miller on 11/11/44). Band formed in Boston, then moved to California in late 1967.	
8/02/69	**5**	12	● 1. **Get Together** **[R]**	RCA 9752
			re-popularized as theme for National Council of Christians & Jews; originally charted in 1967 (POS 62)	
			YOUNG-HOLT UNLIMITED	
			Chicago instrumental soul group: Eldee Young (bass), Isaac "Red" Holt (drums; both of the Ramsey Lewis Trio) and Don Walker (piano). Walker left by 1968.	
1/21/67	**40**	2	1. Wack Wack [I]	Brunswick 55305
			THE YOUNG HOLT TRIO	
12/07/68†	**3**	12	● 2. **Soulful Strut** **[I]**	Brunswick 55391
			exact same recording as Barbara Acklin's "Am I The Same Girl," except vocal part replaced by piano	
			THE YOUNG RASCALS - see THE RASCALS	
			BARRY YOUNG	
12/04/65†	**13**	7	1. One Has My Name (The Other Has My Heart)	Dot 16756
			FARON YOUNG	
			Born on 2/25/32 in Shreveport, Louisiana. Country singer/guitarist. Charted over 30 top 10 country hits. In films "The Young Sheriff," "Daniel Boone" and "Hidden Guns." Publisher of the Music City News magazine in Nashville.	
5/01/61	**12**	11	1. Hello Walls	Capitol 4533
			written by Willie Nelson	
			JOHN PAUL YOUNG	
			Australian pop singer/songwriter/pianist.	
8/05/78	**7**	15	1. **Love Is In The Air**	Scotti Br. 402
			KATHY YOUNG with THE INNOCENTS	
			Born on 10/21/45 in Santa Ana, California. Pop singer. Also see The Innocents.	
10/31/60	**3**	15	1. **A Thousand Stars**	Indigo 108
3/06/61	**30**	6	2. Happy Birthday Blues	Indigo 115
			NEIL YOUNG	
			Born on 11/12/45 in Toronto, Canada. Rock singer/songwriter/guitarist. Formed rock band the Mynah Birds featuring lead singer Rick James, early 60s. Moved to Los Angeles in 1966 and formed Buffalo Springfield. Went solo in 1969 with backing band, Crazy Horse. Joined with Crosby, Stills & Nash in 1970. Appeared in the 1987 film "Made In Heaven."	
12/05/70	**33**	3	1. Only Love Can Break Your Heart	Reprise 0958
2/12/72	**1**(1)	13	● 2. **Heart Of Gold**	Reprise 1065
			backing vocals: Linda Ronstadt and James Taylor	
5/20/72	**31**	4	3. Old Man	Reprise 1084
			PAUL YOUNG	
			Born on 1/17/56 in Bedfordshire, England. Pop-rock vocalist/guitarist.	
3/03/84	**22**	8	1. Come Back And Stay	Columbia 04313
6/01/85	**1**(1)	15	2. **Everytime You Go Away**	Columbia 04867
9/21/85	**13**	9	3. I'm Gonna Tear Your Playhouse Down	Columbia 05577

DATE	POS	WKS	ARTIST—RECORD TITLE	LABEL & NO.
			VICTOR YOUNG	
			Born on 8/8/1900 in Chicago; died on 11/11/56. Conductor/composer/violinist.	
7/08/57	**13**	9	1. Around The World [I]	Decca 30262
			Jockey #13 / Best Seller #20 / Top 100 #26 from the film "Around The World In 80 Days"; flip side is Bing Crosby's vocal version	
			TIMI YURO	
			Born Rosemarie Timothy Aurro Yuro on 8/4/40 in Chicago. Moved to Los Angeles in 1952. First recorded for Liberty in 1959. Lost voice in 1980 and underwent 3 throat operations.	
7/31/61	**4**	10	1. **Hurt**	Liberty 55343
8/11/62	**12**	6	2. What's A Matter Baby (Is It Hurting You)	Liberty 55469
8/10/63	**24**	7	3. Make The World Go Away	Liberty 55587
			Z	
			HELMUT ZACHARIAS	
			German violinist.	
9/08/56	**12**	7	1. When The White Lilacs Bloom Again [I]	Decca 30039
			Jockey #12 / Top 100 #16 / Best Seller #19 / Juke Box #19	
			JOHN ZACHERLE	
			Born on 9/26/18 in Philadelphia. "The Cool Ghoul." During the late 1950s, hosted horror movies on WCAU-TV in Philadelphia.	
3/10/58	**6**	7	1. **Dinner With Drac - Part 1** **[N]**	Cameo 130
			Top 100 #6 / Best Seller #8	
			PIA ZADORA	
			Born Pia Schipani in 1955 in New York City. Actress/singer. In the films "Butterfly," "The Lonely Lady" and "Hairspray."	
2/12/83	**36**	3	1. The Clapping Song	Elektra 69889
			ZAGER & EVANS	
			Lincoln, Nebraska duo: Denny Zager and Rick Evans. Disbanded in 1969.	
6/28/69	**1**(6)	12	● 1. **In The Year 2525 (Exordium & Terminus)**	RCA 0174
			released regionally in 1968 on Truth Records	
			THE MICHAEL ZAGER BAND	
			Disco studio group led by keyboardist/writer/arranger Michael Zager (b: 1943 in Jersey City, NJ). Member of Ten Wheel Drive from 1968-73.	
4/29/78	**36**	4	1. Let's All Chant [I]	Private S. 45184
			RICKY ZAHND & The Blue Jeaners	
12/24/55	**21**	2	1. (I'm Gettin') Nuttin' For Christmas [N-X]	Columbia 40576
			Best Seller #21 / Top 100 #40	
			FRANK ZAPPA	
			Born on 12/21/40 in Baltimore, Maryland. Singer/songwriter/guitarist. Rock music's leading satirist. Formed The Mothers Of Invention in 1965. In the films "2000 Motels" and "Baby Snakes." Father of Dweezil and Moon Unit.	
9/04/82	**32**	3	1. Valley Girl [N]	Barking P. 02972
			featuring Frank's daughter, Moon Unit Zappa	

DATE	POS	WKS	ARTIST—RECORD TITLE	LABEL & NO.
			WARREN ZEVON	
			Born on 1/24/47 in Canada. Parents were Russian immigrants. Singer/songwriter/ pianist. Wrote Linda Ronstadt's "Poor Poor Pitiful Me."	
4/22/78	**21**	6	1. Werewolves Of London	Asylum 45472
			THE ZODIACS - see MAURICE WILLIAMS	
			THE ZOMBIES	
			British rock quintet: Rod Argent (keyboards), Colin Blunstone (vocals), Paul Atkinson (guitar), Chris White (bass) and Hugh Grundy (drums). Group disbanded in late 1967. Rod formed Argent in 1969.	
11/07/64	**2**(1)	12	1. **She's Not There**	Parrot 9695
1/30/65	**6**	8	2. **Tell Her No**	Parrot 9723
2/22/69	**3**	11	● 3. **Time Of The Season** recorded in 1967	Date 1628
			ZZ TOP	
			Boogie-rock trio formed in Houston in 1969. Consisted of Billy Gibbons (vocals, guitar), Dusty Hill (vocals, bass) and Frank Beard (drums). All were born in 1949 in Texas. Gibbons had been lead guitarist in Moving Sidewalks, a Houston psychedelic rock band. Hill and Beard had played in American Blues, based in Dallas. Inactive from 1977-79.	
8/16/75	**20**	4	1. Tush	London 220
3/01/80	**34**	3	2. I Thank You	Warner 49163
5/07/83	**37**	3	3. Gimme All Your Lovin	Warner 29693
6/02/84	**8**	12	4. **Legs**	Warner 29272
10/26/85	**8**	13	5. **Sleeping Bag**	Warner 28884
2/08/86	**21**	7	6. Stages	Warner 28810
4/19/86	**22**	7	7. Rough Boy	Warner 28733
8/30/86	**35**	3	8. Velcro Fly	Warner 28650

THE SONGS

THE SONGS

This section lists, alphabetically, all titles in the artist section. The artist's name is listed next to each title along with the highest position attained and year of peak popularity. Some titles show the letter F as a position, indicating the title was listed as a flip side and did not chart on its own.

A song with more than one charted version is listed once, with the artists' names listed below in chronological order. Many songs that have the same title, but are different tunes, are listed separately, with the most popular title listed first. This will make it easy to determine which songs are the same composition; the amount of charted versions of a particular song; and which versions were the most popular.

Cross references have been used throughout to aid in finding a title. If you have trouble, please keep the following in mind: titles in which an apostrophe is used within a word will come before a title using the complete spelling (Lovin' comes before Loving), etc. Titles beginning with a contraction follow titles that begin with a similar non-contracted word (Can't follows Can). Titles such as I.O.U., D.O.A., and SOS will be found at the beginning of their respective letters; however, titles such as R.O.C.K. and B-A-B-Y, which are spellings of words, are listed with their regular spellings.

POS/YR	RECORD TITLE/ARTIST

A

POS/YR	RECORD TITLE/ARTIST
28/66	**"A" Team** . . . SSgt Barry Sadler
1/70	**ABC** . . . Jackson 5
26/82	**Abacab** . . . Genesis
16/64	**Abigail Beecher** . . . Freddy Cannon
15/63	**Abilene** . . . George Hamilton IV
31/60	**About This Thing Called Love** . . . Fabian
32/74	**Abra-Ca-Dabra** . . . DeFranco Family
1/82	**Abracadabra** . . . Steve Miller Band
	Abraham, Martin And John
4/68	Dion
33/69	Miracles
35/69	Moms Mabley
8/71	Tom Clay (medley)
26/71	**Absolutely Right** . . . Five Man Electrical Band
13/65	**Action** . . . Freddy Cannon
20/76	**Action** . . . Sweet
1/86	**Addicted To Love** . . . Robert Palmer
	Admiral Halsey ..see: Uncle Albert
8/84	**Adult Education** . . . Daryl Hall-John Oates
9/83	**Affair Of The Heart** . . . Rick Springfield
16/57	**Affair To Remember (Our Love Affair)** . . . Vic Damone
1/83	**Africa** . . . Toto
18/70	**After Midnight** . . . Eric Clapton
32/57	**After School** . . . Randy Starr
23/83	**After The Fall** . . . Journey
32/82	**After The Glitter Fades** . . . Stevie Nicks
22/74	**After The Goldrush** . . . Prelude
10/56	**After The Lights Go Down Low** . . . Al Hibbler
2/79	**After The Love Has Gone** . . . Earth, Wind & Fire
8/77	**After The Lovin'** . . . Engelbert Humperdinck
1/76	**Afternoon Delight** . . . Starland Vocal Band
1/84	**Against All Odds (Take A Look At Me Now)** . . . Phil Collins
5/80	**Against The Wind** . . . Bob Seger
21/65	**Agent Double-O-Soul** . . . Edwin Starr

POS/YR	RECORD TITLE/ARTIST
36/75	**Agony And The Ecstasy** . . . Smokey Robinson
29/81	**Ah! Leah!** . . . Donnie Iris
5/62	**Ahab, The Arab** . . . Ray Stevens
28/81	**Ai No Corrida** . . . Quincy Jones
17/81	**Ain't Even Done With The Night** . . . John Cougar
12/77	**Ain't Gonna Bump No More (With No Big Fat Woman)** . . . Joe Tex
39/66	**Ain't Gonna Lie** . . . Keith
20/57	**Ain't Got No Home** . . . Clarence "Frogman" Henry
24/70	**Ain't It Funky Now** . . . James Brown
40/65	**Ain't It True** . . . Andy Williams
22/79	**Ain't Love A Bitch** . . . Rod Stewart
	Ain't No Mountain High Enough
19/67	Marvin Gaye & Tammi Terrell
1/70	Diana Ross
13/79	**Ain't No Stoppin' Us Now** . . . McFadden & Whitehead
3/71	**Ain't No Sunshine** . . . Bill Withers
16/68	**Ain't No Way** . . . Aretha Franklin
8/75	**Ain't No Way To Treat A Lady** . . . Helen Reddy
4/73	**Ain't No Woman (Like The One I've Got)** . . . Four Tops
22/83	**Ain't Nobody** . . . Rufus & Chaka Khan
	Ain't Nothing Like The Real Thing
8/68	Marvin Gaye & Tammi Terrell
21/77	Donny & Marie Osmond
20/64	**Ain't Nothing You Can Do** . . . Bobby Bland
19/64	**Ain't She Sweet** . . . Beatles
	Ain't That A Shame
1/55	Pat Boone
10/55	Fats Domino
22/63	4 Seasons
35/79	Cheap Trick
33/61	**Ain't That Just Like A Woman** . . . Fats Domino
16/64	**Ain't That Loving You Baby** . . . Elvis Presley
8/65	**Ain't That Peculiar** . . . Marvin Gaye
	Ain't Too Proud To Beg
13/66	Temptations
17/74	Rolling Stones
21/72	**Ain't Understanding Mellow** . . . Jerry Butler & Brenda Lee Eager
6/74	**Air That I Breathe** . . . Hollies
31/70	**Airport Love Theme** . . . Vincent Bell

POS/YR	RECORD TITLE/ARTIST
	Al Di La'
6/62	Emilio Pericoli
29/64	Ray Charles Singers
14/55	**Alabama Jubilee** . . . Ferko String Band
	Alamo ..see: Ballad Of The
29/71	**Albert Flasher** . . . Guess Who
	Alfie
32/66	Cher
15/67	Dionne Warwick
29/84	**Alibis** . . . Sergio Mendes
17/63	**Alice In Wonderland** . . . Neil Sedaka
27/68	**Alice Long (You're Still My Favorite Girlfriend)** . . . Tommy Boyce & Bobby Hart
29/81	**Alien** . . . Atlanta Rhythm Section
34/72	**Alive** . . . Bee Gees
3/85	**Alive & Kicking** . . . Simple Minds
14/78	**Alive Again** . . . Chicago
35/67	**All** . . . James Darren
3/62	**All Alone Am I** . . . Brenda Lee
20/68	**All Along The Watchtower** . . . Jimi Hendrix
2/59	**All American Boy** . . . Bill Parsons
11/56	**All At Once You Love Her** . . . Perry Como
2/76	**All By Myself** . . . Eric Carmen
8/86	**All Cried Out** . . . Lisa Lisa & Cult Jam
7/65	**All Day And All Of The Night** . . . Kinks
35/71	**All Day Music** . . . War
19/88	**All Fired Up** . . . Pat Benatar
33/60	**All I Could Do Was Cry** . . . Etta James
7/71	**All I Ever Need Is You** . . . Sonny & Cher
	All I Have To Do Is Dream
1/58	Everly Brothers
14/63	Richard Chamberlain
27/70	Bobbie Gentry & Glen Campbell
9/73	**All I Know** . . . Art Garfunkel
2/85	**All I Need** . . . Jack Wagner
8/67	**All I Need** . . . Temptations
5/86	**All I Need Is A Miracle** . . . Mike + The Mechanics
	All I Really Want To Do
15/65	Cher
40/65	Byrds
20/66	**All I See Is You** . . . Dusty Springfield
19/87	**All I Wanted** . . . Kansas
19/61	**All In My Mind** . . . Maxine Brown
37/83	**All My Life** . . . Kenny Rogers
	All My Love ..see: (You Were Made For)

POS/YR	RECORD TITLE/ARTIST
19/80	**All Night Long** . . . Joe Walsh
1/83	**All Night Long (All Night)** . . . Lionel Richie
	(All Of A Sudden) My Heart Sings
15/59	Paul Anka
38/65	Mel Carter
19/84	**All Of You** . . . Julio Iglesias & Diana Ross
28/82	**All Our Tomorrows** . . . Eddie Schwartz
2/80	**All Out Of Love** . . . Air Supply
38/58	**All Over Again** . . . Johnny Cash
13/80	**All Over The World** . . . Electric Light Orchestra
12/83	**All Right** . . . Christopher Cross
4/70	**All Right Now** . . . Free
22/89	**All She Wants Is** . . . Duranduran
9/85	**All She Wants To Do Is Dance** . . . Don Henley
1/57	**All Shook Up** . . . Elvis Presley
	All Strung Out
26/66	Nino Tempo & April Stevens
34/77	John Travolta
26/72	**All The King's Horses** . . . Aretha Franklin
19/86	**All The Love In The World** . . . Outfield
28/86	**All The Things She Said** . . . Simple Minds
21/58	**All The Time** . . . Johnny Mathis
2/58	**All The Way** . . . Frank Sinatra
37/72	**All The Young Dudes** . . . Mott The Hoople
17/83	**All This Love** . . . DeBarge
6/89	**All This Time** . . . Tiffany
2/81	**All Those Years Ago** . . . George Harrison
5/84	**All Through The Night** . . . Cyndi Lauper
36/83	**All Time High** . . . Rita Coolidge
35/77	**All You Get From Love Is A Love Song** . . . Carpenters
1/67	**All You Need Is Love** . . . Beatles
2/56	**Allegheny Moon** . . . Patti Page
17/83	**Allentown** . . . Billy Joel
7/62	**Alley Cat** . . . Bent Fabric
	Alley-Oop
1/60	Hollywood Argyles
15/60	Dante & The Evergreens
32/59	**Almost Grown** . . . Chuck Berry
32/78	**Almost Like Being In Love** . . . Michael Johnson
25/84	**Almost Over You** . . . Sheena Easton
	Almost Paradise
15/57	Roger Williams

POS/YR	RECORD TITLE/ARTIST
31/57	Lou Stein
7/84	**Almost Paradise...Love Theme From Footloose** . . . Mike Reno & Ann Wilson
24/66	**Almost Persuaded** . . . David Houston
28/78	**Almost Summer** . . . Celebration featuring Mike Love
1/87	**Alone** . . . Heart
1/72	**Alone Again (Naturally)** . . . Gilbert O'Sullivan
8/60	**Alone At Last** . . . Jackie Wilson
	Alone (Why Must I Be Alone)
18/57	Shepherd Sisters
28/64	4 Seasons
	Along Came Jones
9/59	Coasters
27/69	Ray Stevens
14/85	**Along Comes A Woman** . . . Chicago
7/66	**Along Comes Mary** . . . Association
8/88	**Alphabet St.** . . . Prince
32/74	**Already Gone** . . . Eagles
2/73	**Also Sprach Zarathustra (2001)** . . . Deodato
40/62	**Alvin Twist** . . . Chipmunks
3/59	**Alvin's Harmonica** . . . Chipmunks
33/60	**Alvin's Orchestra** . . . Chipmunks
1/87	**Always** . . . Atlantic Starr
19/59	**Always** . . . Sammy Turner
18/78	**Always And Forever** . . . Heatwave
	Always On My Mind
5/82	Willie Nelson
4/88	Pet Shop Boys
	Always Something There To Remind Me ..see: (There's)
18/68	**Always Together** . . . Dells
33/64	**Always Together** . . . Al Martino
31/60	**Am I Losing You** . . . Jim Reeves
	Am I That Easy To Forget
25/60	Debbie Reynolds
18/68	Engelbert Humperdinck
32/60	**Am I The Man** . . . Jackie Wilson
1/86	**Amanda** . . . Boston
	Amazing Grace
15/71	Judy Collins
11/72	Royal Scots Dragoon Guards
37/68	**Ame Caline (Soul Coaxing)** . . . Raymond Lefevre
	Amen
7/65	Impressions
36/68	Otis Redding

POS/YR	RECORD TITLE/ARTIST
8/81	**America** . . . Neil Diamond
27/72	**American City Suite** . . . Cashman & West
13/80	**American Dream** . . . Dirt Band
17/82	**American Heartbeat** . . . Survivor
16/82	**American Music** . . . Pointer Sisters
1/72	**American Pie** . . . Don McLean
13/86	**American Storm** . . . Bob Seger
26/72	**American Trilogy** . . . Mickey Newbury
35/74	**American Tune** . . . Paul Simon
1/70	**American Woman** . . . Guess Who
	Americans
4/74	Byron MacGregor
24/74	Gordon Sinclair
27/75	**Amie** . . . Pure Prairie League
7/59	**Among My Souvenirs** . . . Connie Francis
18/61	**Amor** . . . Ben E. King
	(Amos & Andy Song) ..see: Like A Sunday In Salem
8/71	**Amos Moses** . . . Jerry Reed
38/55	**Amukiriki (The Lord Willing)** . . . Les Paul & Mary Ford
37/57	**Anastasia** . . . Pat Boone
22/67	**And Get Away** . . . Esquires
22/82	**And I Am Telling You I'm Not Going** . . . Jennifer Holliday
12/64	**And I Love Her (Him)** . . . Beatles
29/73	**And I Love You So** . . . Perry Como
36/65	**And Roses And Roses** . . . Andy Williams
	And That Reminds Me
9/57	Kay Starr
12/57	Della Reese
19/80	**And The Beat Goes On** . . . Whispers
21/85	**And We Danced** . . . Hooters
2/69	**And When I Die** . . . Blood, Sweat & Tears
3/88	**Angel** . . . Aerosmith
5/85	**Angel** . . . Madonna
20/73	**Angel** . . . Aretha Franklin
40/72	**Angel** . . . Rod Stewart
5/61	**Angel Baby** . . . Rosie & The Originals
30/58	**Angel Baby** . . . Dean Martin
40/82	**Angel In Blue** . . . J. Geils Band
6/77	**Angel In Your Arms** . . . Hot
14/89	**Angel Of Harlem** . . . U2
	Angel Of The Morning
7/68	Merrilee Rush
4/81	Juice Newton
22/61	**Angel On My Shoulder** . . . Shelby Flint
38/80	**Angel Say No** . . . Tommy Tutone

POS/YR	RECORD TITLE/ARTIST
33/58	**Angel Smile** . . . Nat King Cole
27/60	**Angela Jones** . . . Johnny Ferguson
11/56	**Angels In The Sky** . . . Crew-Cuts
22/59	**Angels Listened In** . . . Crests
1/73	**Angie** . . . Rolling Stones *(also see: Different Worlds)*
1/74	**Angie Baby** . . . Helen Reddy
	(Angry Young Man) ..see: Fooling Yourself
19/87	**Animal** . . . Def Leppard
1/74	**Annie's Song** . . . John Denver
1/80	**Another Brick In The Wall (Part II)** . . . Pink Floyd
5/71	**Another Day** . . . Paul McCartney
13/88	**Another Lover** . . . Giant Steps
22/86	**Another Night** . . . Aretha Franklin
1/80	**Another One Bites The Dust** . . . Queen
32/74	**Another Park, Another Sunday** . . . Doobie Brothers
11/88	**Another Part Of Me** . . . Michael Jackson
32/76	**Another Rainy Day In New York City** . . . Chicago
	Another Saturday Night
10/63	Sam Cooke
6/74	Cat Stevens
22/60	**Another Sleepless Night** . . . Jimmy Clanton
	Another Somebody Done Somebody Wrong Song ..see: (Hey Won't You Play)
32/77	**Another Star** . . . Stevie Wonder
20/58	**Another Time, Another Place** . . . Patti Page
32/80	**Answering Machine** . . . Rupert Holmes
	(Anthony's Song) ..see: Movin' Out
13/72	**Anticipation** . . . Carly Simon
	Any Day Now
23/62	Chuck Jackson
14/82	Ronnie Milsap
14/65	**Any Way You Want It** . . . Dave Clark Five
23/80	**Any Way You Want It** . . . Journey
31/61	**Anybody But Me** . . . Brenda Lee
31/60	**Anymore** . . . Teresa Brewer
8/64	**Anyone Who Had A Heart** . . . Dionne Warwick
1/88	**Anything For You** . . . Gloria Estefan & Miami Sound Machine
31/62	**Anything That's Part Of You** . . . Elvis Presley
37/76	**Anything You Want** . . . John Valenti

POS/YR	RECORD TITLE/ARTIST
33/76	**Anytime (I'll Be There)** . . . Paul Anka
20/56	**Anyway You Want Me (That's How I Will Be)** . . . Elvis Presley
2/61	**Apache** . . . Jorgen Ingmann
	Apartment ..see: Theme From The
24/56	**Ape Call** . . . Nervous Norvus
	Apple Blossom Time ..see: (I'll Be With You In)
29/60	**Apple Green** . . . June Valli
32/65	**Apple Of My Eye** . . . Roy Head
6/67	**Apples, Peaches, Pumpkin Pie** . . . Jay & The Techniques
37/69	**April Fools** . . . Dionne Warwick
28/56	**April In Paris** . . . Count Basie
1/57	**April Love** . . . Pat Boone
1/69	**Aquarius (medley)** . . . 5th Dimension
15/84	**Are We Ourselves?** . . . Fixx
39/69	**Are You Happy** . . . Jerry Butler
39/67	**Are You Lonely For Me** . . . Freddie Scott
	Are You Lonesome To-night?
1/60	Elvis Presley
14/74	Donny Osmond
15/73	**Are You Man Enough** . . . Four Tops
14/70	**Are You Ready?** . . . Pacific Gas & Electric
10/58	**Are You Really Mine** . . . Jimmie Rodgers
11/56	**Are You Satisfied?** . . . Rusty Draper
3/58	**Are You Sincere** . . . Andy Williams
39/66	**Are You There (With Another Girl)** . . . Dionne Warwick
26/77	**Ariel** . . . Dean Friedman
10/70	**Arizona** . . . Mark Lindsay
28/73	**Armed And Extremely Dangerous** . . . First Choice
	Around The World In 80 Days
12/57	Mantovani
13/57	Victor Young
25/57	Bing Crosby
29/79	**Arrow Through Me** . . . Wings
1/81	**Arthur's Theme (Best That You Can Do)** . . . Christopher Cross
20/60	**Artificial Flowers** . . . Bobby Darin
36/78	**As** . . . Stevie Wonder
10/61	**As If I Didn't Know** . . . Adam Wade
	As Tears Go By
22/65	Marianne Faithfull
6/66	Rolling Stones
31/70	**As The Years Go By** . . . Mashmakhan
12/64	**As Usual** . . . Brenda Lee

POS/YR	RECORD TITLE/ARTIST
23/87	**As We Lay** . . . Shirley Murdock
37/80	**Ashes By Now** . . . Rodney Crowell
8/61	**Asia Minor** . . . Kokomo
12/64	**Ask Me** . . . Elvis Presley
18/56	**Ask Me** . . . Nat King Cole
40/71	**Ask Me No Questions** . . . B.B. King
27/72	**Ask Me What You Want** . . . Millie Jackson
24/65	**Ask The Lonely** . . . Four Tops
19/61	**Astronaut** . . . Jose Jimenez
30/77	**At Midnight (My Love Will Lift You Up)** . . . Rufus Featuring Chaka Khan
	At My Front Door
7/55	Pat Boone
17/55	El Dorados
3/75	**At Seventeen** . . . Janis Ian
	(At The Copa) ..see: Copacabana
	At The Hop
1/58	Danny & The Juniors
21/58	Nick Todd
18/66	**At The Scene** . . . Dave Clark Five
16/67	**At The Zoo** . . . Simon & Garfunkel
1/87	**At This Moment** . . . Billy Vera & The Beaters
28/82	**Athena** . . . Who
27/81	**Atlanta Lady (Something About Your Love)** . . . Marty Balin
7/69	**Atlantis** . . . Donovan
39/80	**Atomic** . . . Blondie
18/66	**Attack** . . . Toys
21/75	**Attitude Dancing** . . . Carly Simon
15/73	**Aubrey** . . . Bread
19/57	**Auctioneer** . . . Leroy Van Dyke
15/84	**Authority Song** . . . John Cougar Mellencamp
25/75	**Autobahn** . . . Kraftwerk
5/84	**Automatic** . . . Pointer Sisters
34/83	**Automatic Man** . . . Michael Sembello
37/72	**Automatically Sunshine** . . . Supremes
	Autumn Leaves
1/55	Roger Williams
35/55	Steve Allen
19/68	**Autumn Of My Life** . . . Bobby Goldsboro
18/56	**Autumn Waltz** . . . Tony Bennett
3/85	**Axel F** . . . Harold Faltermeyer

POS/YR	RECORD TITLE/ARTIST
	B
1/79	**Babe** . . . Styx
14/66	**B-A-B-Y** . . . Carla Thomas
8/69	**Baby, Baby Don't Cry** . . . Miracles
12/61	**Baby Blue** . . . Echoes
14/72	**Baby Blue** . . . Badfinger
1/78	**Baby Come Back** . . . Player
32/68	**Baby, Come Back** . . . Equals
27/74	**Baby Come Close** . . . Smokey Robinson
1/83	**Baby, Come To Me** . . . Patti Austin with James Ingram
33/56	**Baby Doll** . . . Andy Williams
1/72	**Baby Don't Get Hooked On Me** . . . Mac Davis
8/65	**Baby Don't Go** . . . Sonny & Cher
39/64	**Baby, Don't You Cry** . . . Ray Charles
27/64	**Baby Don't You Do It** . . . Marvin Gaye
30/63	**Baby Don't You Weep** . . . Garnet Mimms & The Enchanters
14/76	**Baby Face** . . . Wing & A Prayer Fife & Drum Corps.
11/78	**Baby Hold On** . . . Eddie Money
35/70	**Baby Hold On** . . . Grass Roots
26/84	**Baby I Lied** . . . Deborah Allen
4/67	**Baby I Love You** . . . Aretha Franklin
	Baby, I Love You
24/64	Ronettes
9/69	Andy Kim
	Baby, I Love Your Way
12/76	Peter Frampton
1/88	Will To Power (medley)
	Baby I Need Your Loving
11/64	Four Tops
3/67	Johnny Rivers
3/71	**Baby I'm-A Want You** . . . Bread
25/79	**Baby I'm Burnin'** . . . Dolly Parton
14/69	**Baby, I'm For Real** . . . Originals
11/65	**Baby, I'm Yours** . . . Barbara Lewis
	Baby It's You
8/62	Shirelles
5/69	Smith
14/83	**Baby Jane** . . . Rod Stewart
29/71	**Baby Let Me Kiss You** . . . King Floyd

POS/YR	RECORD TITLE/ARTIST
24/72	**Baby Let Me Take You (In My Arms)** . . . Detroit Emeralds
35/69	**Baby Let's Wait** . . . Royal Guardsmen
1/64	**Baby Love** . . . Supremes
10/86	**Baby Love** . . . Regina
25/82	**Baby Makes Her Blue Jeans Talk** . . . Dr. Hook
11/68	**Baby, Now That I've Found You** . . . Foundations
21/61	**Baby Oh Baby** . . . Shells
16/66	**Baby Scratch My Back** . . . Slim Harpo
6/61	**Baby Sittin' Boogie** . . . Buzz Clifford
23/70	**Baby Take Me In Your Arms** . . . Jefferson
10/59	**Baby Talk** . . . Jan & Dean
38/80	**Baby Talks Dirty** . . . Knack
26/75	**Baby That's Backatcha** . . . Smokey Robinson
12/65	**Baby The Rain Must Fall** . . . Glenn Yarbrough
4/77	**Baby, What A Big Surprise** . . . Chicago
37/60	**Baby What You Want Me To Do** . . . Jimmy Reed
5/63	**Baby Workout** . . . Jackie Wilson
34/67	**Baby You Got It** . . . Brenton Wood
34/67	**Baby You're A Rich Man** . . . Beatles
5/60	**Baby (You've Got What It Takes)** . . . Dinah Washington & Brook Benton
26/61	**Baby's First Christmas** . . . Connie Francis
5/74	**Back Home Again** . . . John Denver
37/81	**Back In Black** . . . AC/DC
	Back In Love Again ..see: (Every Time I Turn Around)
1/65	**Back In My Arms Again** . . . Supremes
13/87	**Back In The High Life Again** . . . Steve Winwood
38/77	**Back In The Saddle** . . . Aerosmith
	Back In The U.S.A.
37/59	Chuck Berry
16/78	Linda Ronstadt
9/72	**Back Off Boogaloo** . . . Ringo Starr
34/89	**Back On Holiday** . . . Robbie Nevil
33/80	**Back On My Feet Again** . . . Babys
5/83	**Back On The Chain Gang** . . . Pretenders
36/67	**Back On The Street Again** . . . Sunshine Company
3/72	**Back Stabbers** . . . O'Jays
36/57	**Back To School Again** . . . Timmie "Oh Yeah" Rogers
28/77	**Back Together Again** . . . Daryl Hall & John Oates
40/73	**Back When My Hair Was Short** . . . Gunhill Road
20/84	**Back Where You Belong** . . . 38 Special
10/69	**Backfield In Motion** . . . Mel & Tim
25/66	**Backstage** . . . Gene Pitney
1/87	**Bad** . . . Michael Jackson
1/73	**Bad, Bad Leroy Brown** . . . Jim Croce
1/75	**Bad Blood** . . . Neil Sedaka
8/86	**Bad Boy** . . . Miami Sound Machine
35/83	**Bad Boy** . . . Ray Parker Jr.
36/57	**Bad Boy** . . . Jive Bombers
14/79	**Bad Case Of Loving You (Doctor, Doctor)** . . . Robert Palmer
33/63	**Bad Girl** . . . Neil Sedaka
1/79	**Bad Girls** . . . Donna Summer
15/75	**Bad Luck** . . . Harold Melvin & The Blue Notes
37/60	**Bad Man Blunder** . . . Kingston Trio
1/88	**Bad Medicine** . . . Bon Jovi
2/69	**Bad Moon Rising** . . . Creedence Clearwater Revival
4/75	**Bad Time** . . . Grand Funk Railroad
9/64	**Bad To Me** . . . Billy J. Kramer
2/78	**Baker Street** . . . Gerry Rafferty
3/70	**Ball Of Confusion (That's What The World Is Today)** . . . Temptations
19/69	**Ball Of Fire** . . . Tommy James & The Shondells
14/58	**Ballad Of A Teenage Queen** . . . Johnny Cash
7/68	**Ballad Of Bonnie And Clyde** . . . Georgie Fame
	Ballad Of Davy Crockett
1/55	Bill Hayes
5/55	Tennessee Ernie Ford
5/55	Fess Parker
14/55	Voices Of Walter Schumann
34/66	**Ballad Of Irving** . . . Frank Gallop
8/69	**Ballad Of John And Yoko** . . . Beatles
33/62	**Ballad Of Paladin** . . . Duane Eddy
34/60	**Ballad Of The Alamo** . . . Marty Robbins
1/66	**Ballad Of The Green Berets** . . . SSgt Barry Sadler
18/57	**Ballerina** . . . Nat King Cole
7/87	**Ballerina Girl** . . . Lionel Richie
33/74	**Ballero** . . . War
5/75	**Ballroom Blitz** . . . Sweet

POS/YR	RECORD TITLE/ARTIST
	Banana Boat (Day-O)
5/57	Harry Belafonte
25/57	Stan Freberg
	Banana Boat Song
4/57	Tarriers
13/57	Fontane Sisters
18/57	Steve Lawrence
19/57	Sarah Vaughan
3/70	**Band Of Gold** . . . Freda Payne
	Band Of Gold
4/56	Don Cherry
11/56	Kit Carson
32/66	Mel Carter
1/74	**Band On The Run** . . . Paul McCartney
35/67	**Banda, A** . . . Herb Alpert
18/55	**Bandit (O'Cangaceiro)** . . . Eddie Barclay
	Bang A Gong (Get It On)
10/72	T. Rex
9/85	Power Station
2/66	**Bang Bang (My Baby Shot Me Down)** . . . Cher
22/68	**Bang-Shang-A-Lang** . . . Archies
31/84	**Bang Your Head (Metal Health)** . . . Quiet Riot
23/71	**Bangla-Desh** . . . George Harrison
15/55	**Banjo's Back In Town** . . . Teresa Brewer
29/60	**Barbara** . . . Temptations
	Barbara-Ann
13/61	Regents
2/66	Beach Boys
7/66	**Barefootin'** . . . Robert Parker
20/76	**Baretta's Theme ("Keep Your Eye On The Sparrow")** . . . Rhythm Heritage
11/77	**Barracuda** . . . Heart
	Baseball Game ..see: (Love Is Like A)
15/73	**Basketball Jones Featuring Tyrone Shoelaces** . . . Cheech & Chong *(also see: Love Jones)*
	Batman Theme
17/66	Marketts
35/66	Neal Hefti
37/71	**Battle Hymn Of Lt. Calley** . . . C Company Featuring Terry Nelson
	Battle Hymn Of The Republic
13/59	Mormon Tabernacle Choir
33/68	Andy Williams
14/59	**Battle Of Kookamonga** . . . Homer & Jethro
1/59	**Battle Of New Orleans** . . . Johnny Horton
25/58	**Baubles, Bangles And Beads** . . . Kirby Stone Four
34/73	**Be** . . . Neil Diamond
25/64	**Be Anything (But Be Mine)** . . . Connie Francis
7/56	**Be-Bop-A-Lula** . . . Gene Vincent
3/57	**Be-Bop Baby** . . . Ricky Nelson
31/63	**Be Careful Of Stones That You Throw** . . . Dion
9/86	**Be Good To Yourself** . . . Journey
35/82	**Be Mine Tonight** . . . Neil Diamond
	Be My Baby
2/63	Ronettes
17/70	Andy Kim
8/59	**Be My Guest** . . . Fats Domino
28/82	**Be My Lady** . . . Jefferson Starship
9/85	**Be Near Me** . . . ABC
15/88	**Be Still My Beating Heart** . . . Sting
4/74	**Be Thankful For What You Got** . . . William DeVaughn
6/63	**Be True To Your School** . . . Beach Boys
34/63	**Be True To Yourself** . . . Bobby Vee
4/74	**Beach Baby** . . . First Class
12/81	**Beach Boys Medley** . . . Beach Boys
30/64	**Beans In My Ears** . . . Serendipity Singers
8/78	**Beast Of Burden** . . . Rolling Stones
6/67	**Beat Goes On** . . . Sonny & Cher
1/83	**Beat It** . . . Michael Jackson *(also see: Eat It)*
17/86	**Beat's So Lonely** . . . Charlie Sexton
12/82	**Beatles' Movie Medley** . . . Beatles
15/60	**Beatnik Fly** . . . Johnny & The Hurricanes
3/68	**Beautiful Morning** . . . Rascals
	Beautiful People
37/67	Bobby Vee
38/67	Kenny O'Dell
15/72	**Beautiful Sunday** . . . Daniel Boone
3/66	**Beauty Is Only Skin Deep** . . . Temptations
3/64	**Because** . . . Dave Clark Five
27/88	**Because Of You** . . . Cover Girls
13/78	**Because The Night** . . . Patti Smith Group
4/60	**Because They're Young** . . . Duane Eddy
17/88	**Beds Are Burning** . . . Midnight Oil
17/62	**Beechwood 4-5789** . . . Marvelettes
24/58	**Been So Long** . . . Pastels
24/73	**Been To Canaan** . . . Carole King
4/58	**Beep Beep** . . . Playmates

POS/YR	RECORD TITLE/ARTIST
33/75	**Beer Barrel Polka** . . . Bobby Vinton
17/65	**Before And After** . . . Chad & Jeremy
23/78	**Before My Heart Finds Out** . . . Gene Cotton
1/75	**Before The Next Teardrop Falls** . . . Freddy Fender
29/67	**Beg, Borrow And Steal** . . . Ohio Express
16/67	**Beggin'** . . . 4 Seasons
36/69	**Beginning Of My End** . . . Unifics
7/71	**Beginnings** . . . Chicago
34/71	**Behind Blue Eyes** . . . Who
15/73	**Behind Closed Doors** . . . Charlie Rich
2/81	**Being With You** . . . Smokey Robinson
28/73	**Believe In Humanity** . . . Carole King
26/59	**Believe Me** . . . Royal Teens
4/58	**Believe What You Say** . . . Ricky Nelson
28/69	**Bella Linda** . . . Grass Roots
34/84	**Belle Of St. Mark** . . . Sheila E.
12/70	**Bells, The** . . . Originals
13/58	**Belonging To Someone** . . . Patti Page
1/72	**Ben** . . . Michael Jackson
	Ben Casey ..see: Theme From
5/68	**Bend Me, Shape Me** . . . American Breed
1/74	**Bennie And The Jets** . . . Elton John
4/67	**Bernadette** . . . Four Tops
14/57	**Bernardine** . . . Pat Boone
16/75	**Bertha Butt Boogie** . . . Jimmy Castor Bunch
17/76	**Best Disco In Town** . . . Ritchie Family
32/68	**Best Of Both Worlds** . . . Lulu
1/77	**Best Of My Love** . . . Emotions
1/75	**Best Of My Love** . . . Eagles
3/81	**Best Of Times** . . . Styx
39/64	**(Best Part Of) Breakin' Up** . . . Ronettes
3/74	**Best Thing That Ever Happened To Me** . . . Gladys Knight & The Pips
3/72	**Betcha By Golly, Wow** . . . Stylistics
	(Betcha Got A Chick On The Side) ..see: How Long
36/87	**Betcha Say That** . . . Gloria Estefan & Miami Sound Machine
7/76	**Beth** . . . Kiss
1/81	**Bette Davis Eyes** . . . Kim Carnes
5/84	**Better Be Good To Me** . . . Tina Turner
12/80	**Better Love Next Time** . . . Dr. Hook
38/61	**Better Tell Him No** . . . Starlets
33/58	**Betty And Dupree** . . . Chuck Willis
37/58	**Betty Lou Got A New Pair Of Shoes** . . . Bobby Freeman
40/61	**Bewildered** . . . James Brown
	Beyond The Sea
37/56	Roger Williams
6/60	Bobby Darin
	Bible Tells Me So
7/55	Don Cornell
22/55	Nick Noble
24/79	**Bicycle Race** . . . Queen
1/61	**Big Bad John** . . . Jimmy Dean
26/58	**Big Beat** . . . Fats Domino
38/58	**Big Bopper's Wedding** . . . Big Bopper
38/67	**Big Boss Man** . . . Elvis Presley
23/73	**Big City Miss Ruth Ann** . . . Gallery
19/61	**Big Cold Wind** . . . Pat Boone
21/82	**Big Fun** . . . Kool & The Gang
1/62	**Big Girls Don't Cry** . . . 4 Seasons
1/59	**Big Hunk O' Love** . . . Elvis Presley
3/59	**Big Hurt** . . . Miss Toni Fisher
26/60	**Big Iron** . . . Marty Robbins
21/61	**Big John** . . . Shirelles
20/83	**Big Log** . . . Robert Plant
5/87	**Big Love** . . . Fleetwood Mac
3/58	**Big Man** . . . Four Preps
20/64	**Big Man In Town** . . . 4 Seasons
14/79	**Big Shot** . . . Billy Joel
8/87	**Big Time** . . . Peter Gabriel
	Big Yellow Taxi
29/70	Neighborhood
24/75	Joni Mitchell
3/80	**Biggest Part Of Me** . . . Ambrosia
37/61	**Bilbao Song** . . . Andy Williams
1/83	**Billie Jean** . . . Michael Jackson
7/58	**Billy** . . . Kathy Linden
34/66	**Billy And Sue** . . . B.J. Thomas
1/74	**Billy, Don't Be A Hero** . . . Bo Donaldson & The Heywoods
	Billy Jack ..see: One Tin Soldier
11/58	**Bimbombey** . . . Jimmie Rodgers
36/85	**Bird** . . . Time *(also see: Do The)*
30/64	**Bird Dance Beat** . . . Trashmen
1/58	**Bird Dog** . . . Everly Brothers
34/58	**Bird On My Head** . . . David Seville
12/63	**Birdland** . . . Chubby Checker
3/65	**Birds And The Bees** . . . Jewel Akens
23/71	**Birds Of A Feather** . . . Raiders

POS/YR	RECORD TITLE/ARTIST
17/55	**Birth Of The Boogie** . . . Bill Haley
26/69	**Birthday** . . . Underground Sunshine
40/63	**Birthday Party** . . . Pixies Three
4/74	**Bitch Is Back** . . . Elton John
28/77	**Bite Your Lip (Get up and dance!)** . . . Elton John
4/64	**Bits And Pieces** . . . Dave Clark Five
36/73	**Bitter Bad** . . . Melanie
34/88	**Black And Blue** . . . Van Halen
1/72	**Black & White** . . . Three Dog Night
18/77	**Black Betty** . . . Ram Jam
	Black Denim Trousers
6/55	Cheers
38/55	Vaughn Monroe
15/72	**Black Dog** . . . Led Zeppelin
37/75	**Black Friday** . . . Steely Dan
4/66	**Black Is Black** . . . Los Bravos
4/71	**Black Magic Woman** . . . Santana
13/69	**Black Pearl** . . . Sonny Charles & The Checkmates, Ltd.
17/57	**Black Slacks** . . . Joe Bennett
21/75	**Black Superman - "Muhammad Ali"** . . . Johnny Wakelin
1/75	**Black Water** . . . Doobie Brothers
7/63	**Blame It On The Bossa Nova** . . . Eydie Gorme
39/64	**Bless Our Love** . . . Gene Chandler
15/61	**Bless You** . . . Tony Orlando
34/81	**Blessed Are The Believers** . . . Anne Murray
	Blind Man In The Bleachers ..see: Last Game Of The Season
1/77	**Blinded By The Light** . . . Manfred Mann's Earth Band
33/58	**Blob, The** . . . Five Blobs
35/75	**Bloody Well Right** . . . Supertramp
2/55	**Blossom Fell** . . . Nat King Cole
16/79	**Blow Away** . . . George Harrison
	Blowin' In The Wind
2/63	Peter, Paul & Mary
9/66	Stevie Wonder
21/70	**Blowing Away** . . . 5th Dimension
9/60	**Blue Angel** . . . Roy Orbison
35/67	**Blue Autumn** . . . Bobby Goldsboro
	Blue Bayou
29/63	Roy Orbison
3/77	Linda Ronstadt
20/58	**Blue Blue Day** . . . Don Gibson

POS/YR	RECORD TITLE/ARTIST
21/78	**Blue Collar Man (Long Nights)** . . . Styx
12/82	**Blue Eyes** . . . Elton John
21/75	**Blue Eyes Crying In The Rain** . . . Willie Nelson
37/59	**Blue Hawaii** . . . Billy Vaughn
8/84	**Blue Jean** . . . David Bowie
5/57	**Blue Monday** . . . Fats Domino
23/71	**Blue Money** . . . Van Morrison
1/61	**Blue Moon** . . . Marcels
15/79	**Blue Morning, Blue Day** . . . Foreigner
3/63	**Blue On Blue** . . . Bobby Vinton
29/55	**Blue Star** . . . Felicia Sanders
	Blue Suede Shoes
2/56	Carl Perkins
20/56	Elvis Presley
38/73	Johnny Rivers
16/60	**Blue Tango** . . . Bill Black's Combo
1/63	**Blue Velvet** . . . Bobby Vinton
24/64	**Blue Winter** . . . Connie Francis
	Blueberry Hill
29/56	Louis Armstrong
2/57	Fats Domino
35/75	**Bluebird** . . . Helen Reddy
12/78	**Bluer Than Blue** . . . Michael Johnson
36/62	**Blues (Stay Away From Me)** . . . Ace Cannon
37/67	**Blue's Theme** . . . Davie Allan & The Arrows
	Bo Weevil
17/56	Teresa Brewer
35/56	Fats Domino
	(also see: Boll Weevil)
12/82	**Bobbie Sue** . . . Oak Ridge Boys
8/59	**Bobby Sox To Stockings** . . . Frankie Avalon
3/62	**Bobby's Girl** . . . Marcie Blane
11/82	**Body Language** . . . Queen
9/76	**Bohemian Rhapsody** . . . Queen
2/61	**Boll Weevil Song** . . . Brook Benton
19/61	**Bonanza** . . . Al Caiola
14/59	**Bongo Rock** . . . Preston Epps
33/62	**Bongo Stomp** . . . Little Joey & The Flips
	Bonnie And Clyde ..see: Ballad Of
26/60	**Bonnie Came Back** . . . Duane Eddy
	(also see: My Bonnie)
14/57	**Bony Moronie** . . . Larry Williams
7/67	**Boogaloo Down Broadway** . . . Fantastic Johnny C
12/77	**Boogie Child** . . . Bee Gees

POS/YR	RECORD TITLE/ARTIST
2/74	**Boogie Down** . . . Eddie Kendricks
1/76	**Boogie Fever** . . . Sylvers
2/77	**Boogie Nights** . . . Heatwave
3/75	**Boogie On Reggae Woman** . . . Stevie Wonder
1/78	**Boogie Oogie Oogie** . . . A Taste Of Honey
35/78	**Boogie Shoes** . . . KC & The Sunshine Band
6/79	**Boogie Wonderland** . . . Earth, Wind & Fire with The Emotions
8/73	**Boogie Woogie Bugle Boy** . . . Bette Midler
5/58	**Book Of Love** . . . Monotones
17/55	**Boom Boom Boomerang** . . . DeCastro Sisters
	Boomerang ..see: Do The
36/71	**Booty Butt** . . . Ray Charles Orchestra
20/84	**Bop 'Til You Drop** . . . Rick Springfield
33/83	**Border, The** . . . America
37/70	**Border Song** . . . Aretha Franklin
10/84	**Borderline** . . . Madonna
38/85	**Borderlines** . . . Jeffrey Osborne
12/66	**Born A Woman** . . . Sandy Posey
	Born Free
7/66	Roger Williams
38/68	Hesitations
9/85	**Born In The U.S.A.** . . . Bruce Springsteen
16/79	**Born To Be Alive** . . . Patrick Hernandez
3/89	**Born To Be My Baby** . . . Bon Jovi
2/68	**Born To Be Wild** . . . Steppenwolf
5/56	**Born To Be With You** . . . Chordettes
23/75	**Born To Run** . . . Bruce Springsteen
17/71	**Born To Wander** . . . Rare Earth
7/58	**Born Too Late** . . . Poni-Tails
19/79	**Boss, The** . . . Diana Ross
28/63	**Boss Guitar** . . . Duane Eddy
8/63	**Bossa Nova Baby** . . . Elvis Presley
8/68	**Both Sides Now** . . . Judy Collins
9/68	**Bottle Of Wine** . . . Fireballs
19/80	**Boulevard** . . . Jackson Browne
40/63	**Bounce, The** . . . Olympics
40/67	**Bowling Green** . . . Everly Brothers
7/69	**Boxer, The** . . . Simon & Garfunkel
	Boy From New York City
8/65	Ad Libs
7/81	Manhattan Transfer
	Boy I'm Gonna Marry ..see: (Today I Met)
26/85	**Boy In The Box** . . . Corey Hart

POS/YR	RECORD TITLE/ARTIST
2/69	**Boy Named Sue** . . . Johnny Cash
18/63	**Boy Next Door** . . . Secrets
10/59	**Boy Without A Girl** . . . Frankie Avalon
12/76	**Boys Are Back In Town** . . . Thin Lizzy
37/84	**Boys Do Fall In Love** . . . Robin Gibb
25/87	**Boys Night Out** . . . Timothy B. Schmit
5/85	**Boys Of Summer** . . . Don Henley
1/71	**Brand New Key** . . . Melanie
15/87	**Brand New Lover** . . . Dead Or Alive
24/69	**Brand New Me** . . . Dusty Springfield
1/72	**Brandy (You're A Fine Girl)** . . . Looking Glass
35/61	**Brass Buttons** . . . String-A-Longs
14/80	**Brass In Pocket (I'm Special)** . . . Pretenders
11/75	**Brazil** . . . Ritchie Family
2/64	**Bread And Butter** . . . Newbeats
39/76	**Break Away** . . . Art Garfunkel
40/65	**Break Away (From That Boy)** . . . Newbeats
	Break It To Me Gently
4/62	Brenda Lee
11/82	Juice Newton
26/82	**Break It Up** . . . Foreigner
5/84	**Break My Stride** . . . Matthew Wilder
5/73	**Break Up To Make Up** . . . Stylistics
35/68	**Break Your Promise** . . . Delfonics
8/84	**Breakdance** . . . Irene Cara
31/71	**Breakdown, The** . . . Rufus Thomas
40/78	**Breakdown** . . . Tom Petty
15/80	**Breakdown Dead Ahead** . . . Boz Scaggs
7/61	**Breakin' In A Brand New Broken Heart** . . . Connie Francis
9/84	**Breakin'...There's No Stopping Us** . . . Ollie & Jerry
	Breakin' Up ..also see: (Best Part Of)
31/66	**Breakin' Up Is Breakin' My Heart** . . . Roy Orbison
22/81	**Breaking Away** . . . Balance
	Breaking Up Is Hard To Do
1/62	Neil Sedaka
34/70	Lenny Welch
28/72	Partridge Family
8/76	Neil Sedaka
18/83	**Breaking Us In Two** . . . Joe Jackson
6/87	**Breakout** . . . Swing Out Sister
15/81	**Breakup Song (They Don't Write 'Em)** . . . Greg Kihn Band

POS/YR	RECORD TITLE/ARTIST
7/58	**Breathless** . . . Jerry Lee Lewis
8/55	**Breeze And I** . . . Caterina Valente
5/77	**Brick House** . . . Commodores
	Bridge Over Troubled Water
1/70	Simon & Garfunkel
6/71	Aretha Franklin
5/87	**Brilliant Disguise** . . . Bruce Springsteen
	Bring It On Home To Me
13/62	Sam Cooke
32/65	Animals
17/68	Eddie Floyd
29/67	**Bring It Up** . . . James Brown
12/71	**Bring The Boys Home** . . . Freda Payne
2/61	**Bristol Stomp** . . . Dovells
27/62	**Bristol Twistin' Annie** . . . Dovells
12/79	**Broken Hearted Me** . . . Anne Murray
7/59	**Broken-Hearted Melody** . . . Sarah Vaughan
1/85	**Broken Wings** . . . Mr. Mister
1/73	**Brother Louie** . . . Stories
22/69	**Brother Love's Travelling Salvation Show** . . . Neil Diamond
32/70	**Brother Rapp** . . . James Brown
10/67	**Brown Eyed Girl** . . . Van Morrison
1/71	**Brown Sugar** . . . Rolling Stones
27/85	**Bruce** . . . Rick Springfield
3/69	**Build Me Up Buttercup** . . . Foundations
24/60	**Bulldog** . . . Fireballs
21/65	**Bumble Bee** . . . Searchers
21/61	**Bumble Boogie** . . . B. Bumble & The Stingers
12/75	**Bungle In The Jungle** . . . Jethro Tull
9/55	**Burn That Candle** . . . Bill Haley
40/81	**Burnin' For You** . . . Blue Oyster Cult
3/60	**Burning Bridges** . . . Jack Scott
34/71	**Burning Bridges** . . . Mike Curb Congregation
9/83	**Burning Down The House** . . . Talking Heads
2/86	**Burning Heart** . . . Survivor
39/83	**Burning Heart** . . . Vandenberg
2/72	**Burning Love** . . . Elvis Presley
5/66	**Bus Stop** . . . Hollies
17/56	**Bus Stop Song (A Paper Of Pins)** . . . Four Lads
25/63	**Bust Out** . . . Busters
4/63	**Busted** . . . Ray Charles
34/79	**Bustin' Loose** . . . Chuck Brown
4/61	**But I Do** . . . Clarence "Frogman" Henry
22/66	**But It's Alright** . . . J.J. Jackson
19/69	**But You Know I Love You** . . . First Edition
15/65	**But You're Mine** . . . Sonny & Cher
29/75	**Butter Boy** . . . Fanny
	Butterfly
1/57	Charlie Gracie
1/57	Andy Williams
23/63	**Butterfly Baby** . . . Bobby Rydell
11/58	**Buzz-Buzz-Buzz** . . . Hollywood Flames
	By The Time I Get To Phoenix
26/67	Glen Campbell
37/69	Isaac Hayes
12/65	**Bye, Bye, Baby (Baby Goodbye)** . . . 4 Seasons
2/57	**Bye Bye Love** . . . Everly Brothers

C

POS/YR	RECORD TITLE/ARTIST
	C.C. Rider
12/57	Chuck Willis
34/63	LaVern Baker
10/66	Animals
	(also see: Jenny Take A Ride)
2/87	**C'est La Vie** . . . Robbie Nevil
11/55	**C'est La Vie** . . . Sarah Vaughan
22/61	**C'est Si Bon (It's So Good)** . . . Conway Twitty
22/57	**Ca, C'est L'amour** . . . Tony Bennett
23/68	**Cab Driver** . . . Mills Brothers
22/62	**Cajun Queen** . . . Jimmy Dean
1/61	**Calcutta** . . . Lawrence Welk
4/61	**Calendar Girl** . . . Neil Sedaka
4/66	**California Dreamin'** . . . Mamas & The Papas
	California Girls
3/65	Beach Boys
3/85	David Lee Roth
16/67	**California Nights** . . . Lesley Gore
25/69	**California Soul** . . . 5th Dimension
5/64	**California Sun** . . . Rivieras
1/80	**Call Me** . . . Blondie
13/70	**Call Me** . . . Aretha Franklin
21/58	**Call Me** . . . Johnny Mathis

Jimmie Rodgers was given a guitar while serving in Korea for the Air Force. A lucky transfer to a base in Nashville paved the way for the 14 Top-40 hits he'd enjoy between 1957 and 1967, including his initial No. 1 smash, "Honeycomb."

Tommy Roe's debut single "Sheila" hit No. 3 in England, leading Roe to tour the country, sometimes with the Beatles as an opening act. One of his 11 Top-40 songs, "It's Now Winter's Day," rose to No. 23—quite appropriately—in the winter of 1966–67.

Kenny Rogers, despite his grey beard, leads the pop pack for the greatest number of Top-40 albums in the 80s, with 11. Those comparative youngsters tied for second place include Prince, Elvis Costello, Pat Benatar, and Rush.

The Rolling Stones boast eight No. 1 songs in their generation-spanning career, but "(I Can't Get No) Satisfaction" is tied with "Honky Tonk Women" for the group's all-time chart-topping single. Both held the prime spot for four weeks, which had to have been at least a little satisfying.

Linda Ronstadt's turn at "When You Wish Upon A Star" didn't scorch the charts, but a song from another Walt Disney cartoon, *An American Tail*, was her second biggest hit. "Somewhere Out There," a 1987 duet with James Ingram, rose to No. 2, matching 1975's "When Will I Be Loved."

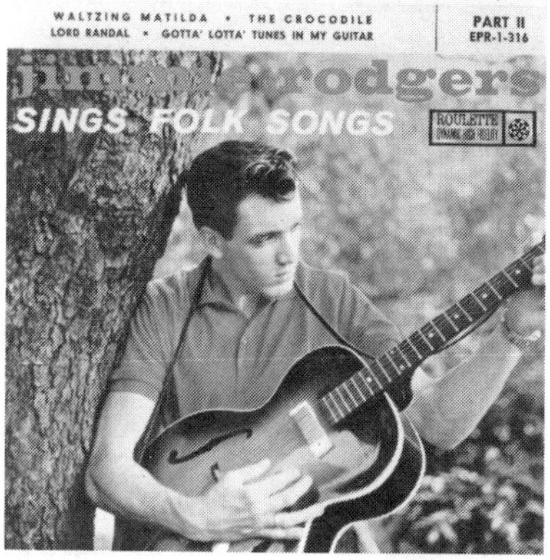

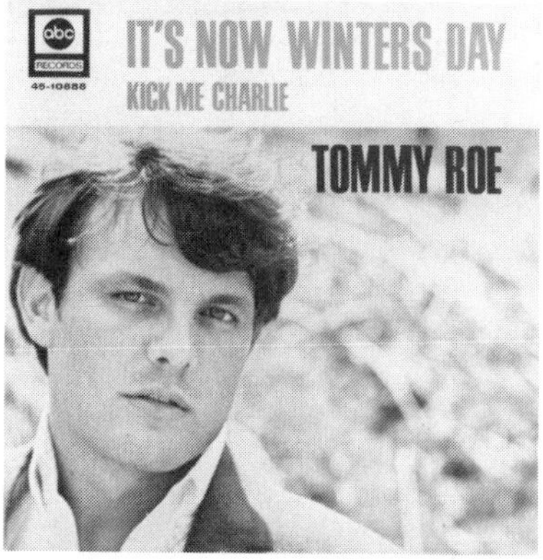

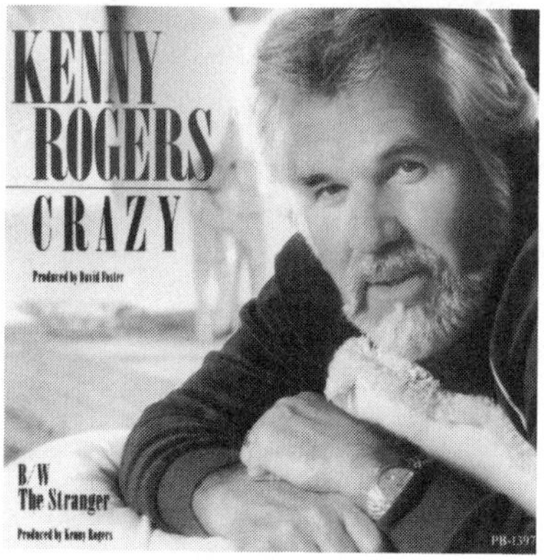

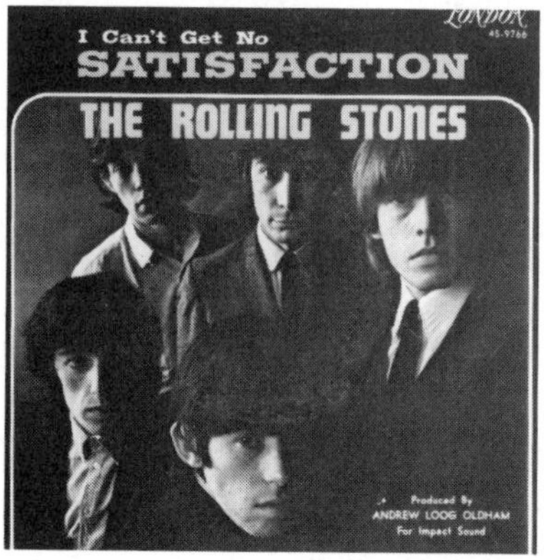

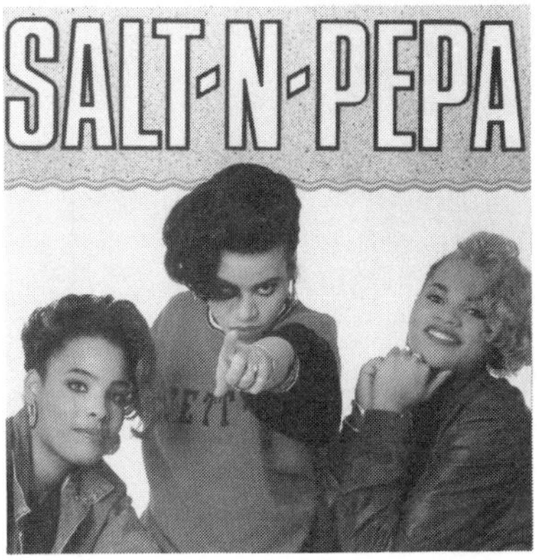

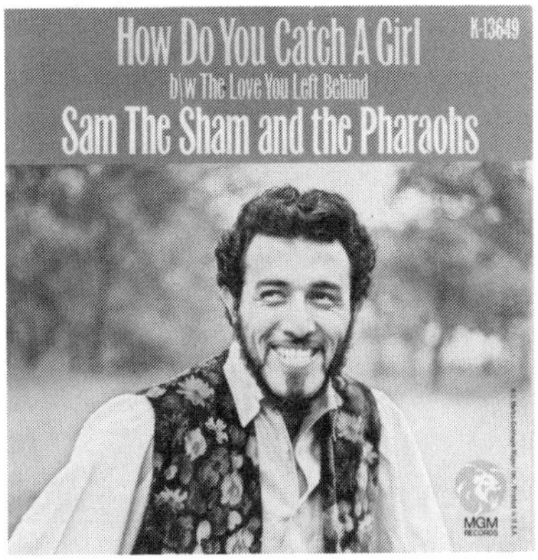

David Lee Roth confounded expectations by recording songs no heavy-metal screamer would dare touch: remakes of Frank Sinatra's "That's Life," the Beach Boys' "California Girls," and Louis Prima's "Just A Gigolo/I Ain't Got Nobody." His seven chart singles include four unlikely cover songs.

Bobby Rydell, one of the best musicians of the clean-cut pre-Beatles era, hit No. 4 with a remake of "Volare," Sicilian crooner Domenico Modugno's No. 1 of two years before. Rydell covered the song with honest Mediterranean flair, as Bobby Rydell was born Robert Ridarelli.

Sade's "Hang On To Your Love" reached No. 14 on the R & B charts. The Nigerian-born British songstress continued her R & B chart ascendancy with the No. 5 "Smooth Operator" and the No. 3 "The Sweetest Taboo." But for Sade, a #1 R & B hit was "Paradise."

Salt-n-Pepa, the New York-based rap trio, ended 1988 with Top-40 pop hit "Push It" and a powerhouse album as well. Their *Hot, Cool & Vicious* album lived up to its name on the year-end album charts, scoring in the Top 40 for 1988, just as it had the year before.

Sam the Sham and the Pharaohs had their final Top-40 hit, "How Do You Catch A Girl," during the winter of 1966–67. Sam ended the Sham in 1967, and later recorded under his real name, Sam Samudio—as he did on the 1981 soundtrack *The Border* with Ry Cooder, John Hiatt, and Freddy Fender.

POS/YR	RECORD TITLE/ARTIST
22/66	**Call Me** . . . Chris Montez
26/82	**Call Me** . . . Skyy
10/73	**Call Me (Come Back Home)** . . . Al Green
40/68	**Call Me Lightning** . . . Who
19/62	**Call Me Mr. In-Between** . . . Burl Ives
6/74	**Call On Me** . . . Chicago
22/63	**Call On Me** . . . Bobby Bland
15/85	**Call To The Heart** . . . Giuffria
18/86	**Calling America** . . . Electric Light Orchestra
16/77	**Calling Dr. Love** . . . Kiss
32/77	**Calling Occupants Of Interplanetary Craft** . . . Carpenters
2/75	**Calypso** . . . John Denver
5/69	**Can I Change My Mind** . . . Tyrone Davis
	Can I Get A Witness
22/63	Marvin Gaye
39/71	Lee Michaels
15/57	**Can I Steal A Little Love** . . . Frank Sinatra
31/74	**Can This Be Real** . . . Natural Four
29/78	**Can We Still Be Friends** . . . Todd Rundgren
16/56	**Can You Find It In Your Heart** . . . Tony Bennett
38/78	**Can You Fool** . . . Glen Campbell
1/64	**Can't Buy Me Love** . . . Beatles
1/85	**Can't Fight This Feeling** . . . REO Speedwagon
5/74	**Can't Get Enough** . . . Bad Company
1/74	**Can't Get Enough Of Your Love, Babe** . . . Barry White
9/75	**Can't Get It Out Of My Head** . . . Electric Light Orchestra
2/63	**Can't Get Used To Losing You** . . . Andy Williams
	Can't Help Falling In Love
2/62	Elvis Presley
24/87	Corey Hart
39/76	**Can't Hide Love** . . . Earth, Wind & Fire
29/83	**Can't Shake Loose** . . . Agnetha Faltskog
3/78	**Can't Smile Without You** . . . Barry Manilow
6/88	**Can't Stay Away From You** . . . Gloria Estefan & Miami Sound Machine
13/77	**Can't Stop Dancin'** . . . Captain & Tennille
25/70	**Can't Stop Loving You** . . . Tom Jones
	Can't Take My Eyes Off You
2/67	Frankie Valli
7/68	Lettermen (medley)

POS/YR	RECORD TITLE/ARTIST
6/87	**Can't We Try** . . . Dan Hill with Vonda Sheppard
	Can't You ..also see: Can'tcha
2/65	**Can't You Hear My Heartbeat** . . . Herman's Hermits
4/64	**Can't You See That She's Mine** . . . Dave Clark Five
20/87	**Can'tcha Say (You Believe In Me) (medley)** . . . Boston
	Canadian Sunset
2/56	Hugo Winterhalter with Eddie Heywood
7/56	Andy Williams
3/70	**Candida** . . . Dawn
6/88	**Candle In The Wind** . . . Elton John
	(Candles In The Rain) ..see: Lay Down
21/87	**Candy** . . . Cameo
3/63	**Candy Girl** . . . 4 Seasons
1/72	**Candy Man** . . . Sammy Davis, Jr.
25/61	**Candy Man** . . . Roy Orbison
15/58	**Cannonball** . . . Duane Eddy
28/85	**Cannonball** . . . Supertramp
16/86	**Captain Of Her Heart** . . . Double
1/77	**Car Wash** . . . Rose Royce
39/65	**Cara-Lin** . . . Strangeloves
4/65	**Cara, Mia** . . . Jay & The Americans
10/74	**Carefree Highway** . . . Gordon Lightfoot
1/85	**Careless Whisper** . . . Wham!
27/59	**Caribbean** . . . Mitchell Torok
1/84	**Caribbean Queen (No More Love On The Run)** . . . Billy Ocean
18/58	**Carol** . . . Chuck Berry
21/75	**Carolina In The Pines** . . . Michael Martin Murphey
32/66	**Caroline, No** . . . Brian Wilson
29/68	**Carpet Man** . . . 5th Dimension
3/87	**Carrie** . . . Europe
34/80	**Carrie** . . . Cliff Richard
9/67	**Carrie-Anne** . . . Hollies
26/69	**Carry Me Back** . . . Rascals
11/77	**Carry On Wayward Son** . . . Kansas
9/80	**Cars** . . . Gary Numan
5/87	**Casanova** . . . Levert
27/67	**Casino Royale** . . . Herb Alpert
	Cast Your Fate To The Wind
22/63	Vince Guaraldi Trio
10/65	Sounds Orchestral
	Castles In The Air
F/72	Don McLean

POS/YR	RECORD TITLE/ARTIST
36/81	Don McLean
25/56	**Casual Look** . . . Six Teens
26/67	**Cat In The Window (The Bird In The Sky)** . . . Petula Clark
30/77	**Cat Scratch Fever** . . . Ted Nugent
1/74	**Cat's In The Cradle** . . . Harry Chapin
1/58	**Catch A Falling Star** . . . Perry Como
8/87	**Catch Me (I'm Falling)** . . . Pretty Poison
40/84	**Catch Me I'm Falling** . . . Real Life
23/65	**Catch The Wind** . . . Donovan
4/65	**Catch Us If You Can** . . . Dave Clark Five
23/62	**Caterina** . . . Perry Como
1/60	**Cathy's Clown** . . . Everly Brothers
37/87	**Caught Up In The Rapture** . . . Anita Baker
10/82	**Caught Up In You** . . . 38 Special
2/87	**Causing A Commotion** . . . Madonna
	(Cave Man) ..see: Troglodyte
4/70	**Cecilia** . . . Simon & Garfunkel
15/70	**Celebrate** . . . Three Dog Night
26/85	**Celebrate Youth** . . . Rick Springfield
1/81	**Celebration** . . . Kool & The Gang
1/82	**Centerfold** . . . J. Geils Band
24/84	**Centipede** . . . Rebbie Jackson
14/58	**Certain Smile** . . . Johnny Mathis
23/58	**Cerveza** . . . Boots Brown
10/62	**Cha-Cha-Cha** . . . Bobby Rydell
34/58	**Cha-Hua-Hua** . . . Pets
2/60	**Chain Gang** . . . Sam Cooke
13/56	**Chain Gang** . . . Bobby Scott
2/68	**Chain Of Fools** . . . Aretha Franklin
32/68	**Chained** . . . Marvin Gaye
17/62	**Chains** . . . Cookies
10/56	**Chains Of Love** . . . Pat Boone
12/88	**Chains Of Love** . . . Erasure
1/57	**Chances Are** . . . Johnny Mathis
31/65	**Change Is Gonna Come** . . . Sam Cooke
3/87	**Change Of Heart** . . . Cyndi Lauper
19/78	**Change Of Heart** . . . Eric Carmen
21/83	**Change Of Heart** . . . Tom Petty
37/77	**Changes In Latitudes, Changes In Attitudes** . . . Jimmy Buffett
	Chanson d'Amour (Song Of Love)
6/58	Art & Dotty Todd
12/58	Fontane Sisters
19/57	**Chantez-Chantez** . . . Dinah Shore
6/58	**Chantilly Lace** . . . Big Bopper

POS/YR	RECORD TITLE/ARTIST
	Chapel In The Moonlight
32/65	Bachelors
25/67	Dean Martin
1/64	**Chapel Of Love** . . . Dixie Cups
	Charade
36/64	Sammy Kaye
36/64	Henry Mancini
1/82	**Chariots Of Fire - Titles** . . . Vangelis
40/71	**Charity Ball** . . . Fanny
2/59	**Charlie Brown** . . . Coasters
13/63	**Charms** . . . Bobby Vee
33/79	**Chase** . . . Giorgio Moroder
	Chattanooga Choo Choo
36/62	Floyd Cramer
32/78	Tuxedo Junction
34/60	**Chattanooga Shoe Shine Boy** . . . Freddy Cannon
15/73	**Cheaper To Keep Her** . . . Johnnie Taylor
12/66	**Cheater, The** . . . Bob Kuban
14/88	**Check It Out** . . . John Cougar Mellencamp
35/73	**Check It Out** . . . Tavares
28/70	**Check Out Your Mind** . . . Impressions
12/55	**Chee Chee-OO-Chee (Sang The Little Bird)** . . . Perry Como & Jaye P. Morgan
32/78	**Cheeseburger In Paradise** . . . Jimmy Buffett
	Cherchez La Femme ..see: Whispering
	Cherish
1/66	Association
9/71	David Cassidy
2/85	**Cherish** . . . Kool & The Gang
33/77	**Cherry Baby** . . . Starz
8/88	**Cherry Bomb** . . . John Cougar Mellencamp
	Cherry, Cherry
6/66	Neil Diamond
31/73	Neil Diamond
15/69	**Cherry Hill Park** . . . Billy Joe Royal
11/60	**Cherry Pie** . . . Skip & Flip
	Cherry Pink And Apple Blossom White
1/55	Perez Prado
14/55	Alan Dale
5/75	**Chevy Van** . . . Sammy Johns
15/68	**Chewy Chewy** . . . Ohio Express
35/71	**Chicago** . . . Graham Nash
9/71	**Chick-A-Boom (Don't Ya Jes' Love It)** . . . Daddy Dewdrop
31/67	**Child Of Clay** . . . Jimmie Rodgers

POS/YR	RECORD TITLE/ARTIST
	Children's Marching Song
13/59	Cyril Stapleton
16/59	Mitch Miller
38/60	**China Doll** . . . Ames Brothers
10/83	**China Girl** . . . David Bowie
15/73	**China Grove** . . . Doobie Brothers
10/62	**Chip Chip** . . . Gene McDaniels
	Chipmunk Song
1/58	Chipmunks
39/61	Chipmunks
40/62	Chipmunks
29/80	**Chiquitita** . . . Abba
20/71	**Chirpy Chirpy Cheep Cheep** . . . Mac & Katie Kissoon
34/81	**Chloe** . . . Elton John
21/69	**Choice Of Colors** . . . Impressions
13/69	**Chokin' Kind** . . . Joe Simon
26/68	**Choo Choo Train** . . . Box Tops
25/77	**Christine Sixteen** . . . Kiss
4/79	**Chuck E.'s In Love** . . . Rickie Lee Jones
9/64	**Chug-A-Lug** . . . Roger Miller
14/56	**Church Bells May Ring** . . . Diamonds
10/83	**Church Of The Poison Mind** . . . Culture Club
24/59	**Ciao, Ciao Bambina** . . . Jacky Noguez
	Cinco Robles (Five Oaks)
22/57	Russell Arms
35/57	Les Paul & Mary Ford
16/62	**Cinderella** . . . Jack Ross
34/77	**Cinderella** . . . Firefall
	Cindy, Oh Cindy
9/56	Vince Martin with The Tarriers
10/56	Eddie Fisher
8/62	**Cindy's Birthday** . . . Johnny Crawford
11/69	**Cinnamon** . . . Derek
25/63	**Cinnamon Cinder (It's A Very Nice Dance)** . . . Pastel Six
7/88	**Circle In The Sand** . . . Belinda Carlisle
33/78	**Circle Is Small (I Can See It In Your Eyes)** . . . Gordon Lightfoot
38/82	**Circles** . . . Atlantic Starr
2/73	**Cisco Kid** . . . War
23/69	**Cissy Strut** . . . Meters
18/85	**C-I-T-Y** . . . John Cafferty/Beaver Brown Band
19/56	**City Of Angels** . . . Highlights
18/72	**City Of New Orleans** . . . Arlo Guthrie
2/72	**Clair** . . . Gilbert O'Sullivan
	Clam ..see: Do The

POS/YR	RECORD TITLE/ARTIST
6/74	**Clap For The Wolfman** . . . Guess Who
36/83	**Clapping Song** . . . Pia Zadora
8/65	**Clapping Song (Clap Pat Clap Slap)** . . . Shirley Ellis
38/59	**Class, The** . . . Chubby Checker
2/68	**Classical Gas** . . . Mason Williams
30/58	**Claudette** . . . Everly Brothers
6/72	**Clean Up Woman** . . . Betty Wright
35/69	**Clean Up Your Own Back Yard** . . . Elvis Presley
21/60	**Clementine** . . . Bobby Darin
	Cleopatra Jones ..see: Theme From
28/58	**Click-Clack** . . . Dicky Doo & The Don'ts
17/64	**Clinging Vine** . . . Bobby Vinton
40/80	**Clones (We're All)** . . . Alice Cooper
	Close Encounters ..see: Theme From
25/78	**Close The Door** . . . Teddy Pendergrass
12/62	**Close To Cathy** . . . Mike Clifford
	Close To You ..see: (They Long To Be)
8/67	**Close Your Eyes** . . . Peaches & Herb
37/73	**Close Your Eyes** . . . Edward Bear
2/78	**Closer I Get To You** . . . Roberta Flack with Donny Hathaway
22/70	**Closer To Home** . . . Grand Funk Railroad
38/83	**Closer You Get** . . . Alabama
	Cloud Nine
6/69	Temptations
32/69	Mongo Santamaria
	C'mon ..see: Come On
F/80	**Cocaine** . . . Eric Clapton
25/57	**Cocoanut Woman** . . . Harry Belafonte
8/72	**Coconut** . . . Nilsson
6/77	**Cold As Ice** . . . Foreigner
40/83	**Cold Blooded** . . . Rick James
33/81	**Cold Love** . . . Donna Summer
7/67	**Cold Sweat** . . . James Brown
30/70	**Cold Turkey** . . . John Lennon/Plastic Ono Band
	Colonel Bogey ..see: March From The River Kwai
7/69	**Color Him Father** . . . Winstons
16/67	**Color My World** . . . Petula Clark
F/71	**Colour My World** . . . Chicago
17/88	**Colour Of Love** . . . Billy Ocean
3/64	**Come A Little Bit Closer** . . . Jay & The Americans
7/70	**Come And Get It** . . . Badfinger

POS/YR	RECORD TITLE/ARTIST
29/63	**Come And Get These Memories** . . . Martha & The Vandellas
5/74	**Come And Get Your Love** . . . Redbone
26/65	**Come And Stay With Me** . . . Marianne Faithfull
15/87	**Come As You Are** . . . Peter Wolf
32/80	**Come Back** . . . J. Geils Band
22/84	**Come Back And Stay** . . . Paul Young
17/62	**Come Back Silly Girl** . . . Lettermen
3/67	**Come Back When You Grow Up** . . . Bobby Vee
38/58	**Come Closer To Me** . . . Nat King Cole
6/83	**Come Dancing** . . . Kinks
21/73	**Come Get To This** . . . Marvin Gaye
	Come Go With Me
4/57	Dell-Vikings
18/82	Beach Boys
5/87	**Come Go With Me** . . . Expose
14/65	**Come Home** . . . Dave Clark Five
20/59	**Come Into My Heart** . . . Lloyd Price
30/74	**Come Monday** . . . Jimmy Buffett
36/64	**Come On** . . . Tommy Roe
29/59	**Come On And Get Me** . . . Fabian
5/64	**C'mon And Swim** . . . Bobby Freeman
6/67	**Come On Down To My Boat** . . . Every Mothers' Son
1/83	**Come On Eileen** . . . Dexys Midnight Runners
35/59	**C'mon Everybody** . . . Eddie Cochran
	Come On Let's Go
22/66	McCoys
21/87	Los Lobos
28/62	**Come On Little Angel** . . . Belmonts
	C'mon Marianne
9/67	4 Seasons
38/76	Donny Osmond
23/76	**Come On Over** . . . Olivia Newton-John
17/66	**(Come 'Round Here) I'm The One You Need** . . . Miracles
39/70	**Come Running** . . . Van Morrison
35/66	**Come Running Back** . . . Dean Martin
8/78	**Come Sail Away** . . . Styx
17/70	**Come Saturday Morning** . . . Sandpipers
40/65	**Come See** . . . Major Lance
	Come See About Me
1/64	Supremes
24/68	Jr. Walker & The All Stars
1/59	**Come Softly To Me** . . . Fleetwoods
15/79	**Come To Me** . . . France Joli

POS/YR	RECORD TITLE/ARTIST
22/58	**Come To Me** . . . Johnny Mathis
30/59	**Come To Me** . . . Marv Johnson
37/67	**Come To The Sunshine** . . . Harpers Bizarre
	Come Together
1/69	Beatles
23/78	Aerosmith
36/62	**Comin' Home Baby** . . . Mel Torme
11/82	**Comin' In And Out Of Your Life** . . . Barbra Streisand
18/87	**Coming Around Again** . . . Carly Simon
11/67	**Coming Home Soldier** . . . Bobby Vinton
11/66	**Coming On Strong** . . . Brenda Lee
1/80	**Coming Up (Live at Glasgow)** . . . Paul McCartney
30/69	**Commotion** . . . Creedence Clearwater Revival
34/85	**Communication** . . . Power Station
27/69	**Composer, The** . . . Supremes
	Concrete And Clay
28/65	Unit Four plus Two
35/65	Eddie Rambeau
17/56	**Confidential** . . . Sonny Knight
37/79	**Confusion** . . . Electric Light Orchestra
10/86	**Conga** . . . Miami Sound Machine
16/72	**Conquistador** . . . Procol Harum
11/62	**Conscience** . . . James Darren
33/61	**Continental Walk** . . . Hank Ballard *(also see: Do The, & Do The New)*
5/87	**Control** . . . Janet Jackson
8/72	**Convention '72** . . . Delegates
1/76	**Convoy** . . . C.W. McCall
32/73	**Cook With Honey** . . . Judy Collins
29/71	**Cool Aid** . . . Paul Humphrey
10/80	**Cool Change** . . . Little River Band
4/85	**Cool It Now** . . . New Edition
7/66	**Cool Jerk** . . . Capitols
13/81	**Cool Love** . . . Pablo Cruise
11/82	**Cool Night** . . . Paul Davis
12/57	**Cool Shake** . . . Dell-Vikings
8/78	**Copacabana (At The Copa)** . . . Barry Manilow
37/73	**Corazon** . . . Carole King
9/61	**Corinna, Corinna** . . . Ray Peterson
18/72	**Corner Of The Sky** . . . Jackson 5
15/64	**Cotton Candy** . . . Al Hirt
13/62	**Cotton Fields** . . . Highwaymen

POS/YR	RECORD TITLE/ARTIST
33/80	**Could I Have This Dance** . . . Anne Murray
37/72	**Could It Be Forever** . . . David Cassidy
4/73	**Could It Be I'm Falling In Love** . . . Spinners
6/75	**Could It Be Magic** . . . Barry Manilow
23/57	**Could This Be Magic** . . . Dubs
1/88	**Could've Been** . . . Tiffany
3/77	**Couldn't Get It Right** . . . Climax Blues Band
35/61	**Count Every Star** . . . Donnie & The Dreamers
2/65	**Count Me In** . . . Gary Lewis & The Playboys
8/78	**Count On Me** . . . Jefferson Starship
25/60	**Country Boy** . . . Fats Domino
11/76	**Country Boy (You Got Your Feet In L.A.)** . . . Glen Campbell
36/68	**Country Girl - City Man** . . . Billy Vera & Judy Clay
37/71	**Country Road** . . . James Taylor
25/68	**Court Of Love** . . . Unifics
31/64	**Cousin Of Mine** . . . Sam Cooke
7/84	**Cover Me** . . . Bruce Springsteen
6/73	**Cover Of "Rolling Stone"** . . . Dr. Hook
3/80	**Coward Of The County** . . . Kenny Rogers
6/68	**Cowboys To Girls** . . . Intruders
8/72	**Cowboys Work Is Never Done** . . . Sonny & Cher
19/77	**Crackerbox Palace** . . . George Harrison
1/70	**Cracklin' Rosie** . . . Neil Diamond
7/60	**Cradle Of Love** . . . Johnny Preston
9/61	**Crazy** . . . Patsy Cline
14/88	**Crazy** . . . Icehouse
36/60	**Crazy Arms** . . . Bob Beckham
	Crazy Downtown ..see: Downtown
40/58	**Crazy Eyes For You** . . . Bobby Hamilton
1/85	**Crazy For You** . . . Madonna
14/72	**Crazy Horses** . . . Osmonds
15/85	**Crazy In The Night (Barking At Airplanes)** . . . Kim Carnes
	Crazy Little Mama ..see: At My Front Door
1/80	**Crazy Little Thing Called Love** . . . Queen
15/58	**Crazy Love** . . . Paul Anka
17/79	**Crazy Love** . . . Poco
29/79	**Crazy Love** . . . Allman Brothers Band
22/72	**Crazy Mama** . . . J.J. Cale

POS/YR	RECORD TITLE/ARTIST
35/76	**Crazy On You** . . . Heart
2/55	**Crazy Otto** . . . Johnny Maddox
5/67	**Creeque Alley** . . . Mamas & The Papas
16/71	**Cried Like A Baby** . . . Bobby Sherman
	Crimson And Clover
1/69	Tommy James & The Shondells
7/82	Joan Jett
16/55	**Croce Di Oro (Cross Of Gold)** . . . Patti Page
1/73	**Crocodile Rock** . . . Elton John
	Crooked Little Man ..see: Don't Let The Rain Come Down
19/63	**Cross Fire!** . . . Orlons
7/87	**Cross My Broken Heart** . . . Jets
	Cross Of Gold ..see: Croce Di Oro
23/59	**Crossfire** . . . Johnny & The Hurricanes
28/69	**Crossroads** . . . Cream
26/62	**Crowd, The** . . . Roy Orbison
9/84	**Cruel Summer** . . . Bananarama
12/79	**Cruel To Be Kind** . . . Nick Lowe
4/80	**Cruisin'** . . . Smokey Robinson
9/83	**Crumblin' Down** . . . John Cougar Mellencamp
3/86	**Crush On You** . . . Jets
16/85	**Cry** . . . Godley & Creme
18/66	**Cry** . . . Ronnie Dove
4/63	**Cry Baby** . . . Garnet Mimms & The Enchanters
18/56	**Cry Baby** . . . Bonnie Sisters
38/62	**Cry Baby Cry** . . . Angels
2/68	**Cry Like A Baby** . . . Box Tops
	Cry Me A River
9/55	Julie London
11/70	Joe Cocker
23/63	**Cry To Me** . . . Betty Harris
	Crying
2/61	Roy Orbison
25/66	Jay & The Americans
5/81	Don McLean
3/65	**Crying In The Chapel** . . . Elvis Presley
6/62	**Crying In The Rain** . . . Everly Brothers
6/66	**Crying Time** . . . Ray Charles
2/69	**Crystal Blue Persuasion** . . . Tommy James & The Shondells
5/83	**Cum On Feel The Noize** . . . Quiet Riot
	Cupid
17/61	Sam Cooke
39/70	Johnny Nash
22/76	Dawn

POS/YR	RECORD TITLE/ARTIST
4/80	Spinners (medley)
	Curious Mind ..see: Um, Um, Um, Um, Um, Um
15/84	**Curly Shuffle** . . . Jump 'N The Saddle
10/75	**Cut The Cake** . . . AWB
15/83	**Cuts Like A Knife** . . . Bryan Adams
23/68	**Cycles** . . . Frank Sinatra

D

POS/YR	RECORD TITLE/ARTIST
36/71	**D.O.A.** . . . Bloodrock
19/68	**D. W. Washburn** . . . Monkees
20/73	**D'yer Mak'er** . . . Led Zeppelin
	Da Doo Ron Ron
3/63	Crystals
1/77	Shaun Cassidy
1/79	**Da Ya Think I'm Sexy?** . . . Rod Stewart
35/88	**Da'Butt** . . . E.U.
19/73	**Daddy Could Swear, I Declare** . . . Gladys Knight & The Pips
4/72	**Daddy Don't You Walk So Fast** . . . Wayne Newton
	Daddy-O
11/55	Fontane Sisters
14/55	Bonnie Lou
	Daddy's Home
2/61	Shep & The Limelites
9/73	Jermaine Jackson
23/82	Cliff Richard
34/69	**Daddy's Little Man** . . . O.C. Smith
14/73	**Daisy A Day** . . . Jud Strunk
20/75	**Daisy Jane** . . . America
15/64	**Daisy Petal Pickin'** . . . Jimmy Gilmer & The Fireballs
27/79	**Damned If I Do** . . . Alan Parsons Project
38/78	**Dance Across The Floor** . . . Jimmy "Bo" Horne
8/64	**Dance, Dance, Dance** . . . Beach Boys
6/78	**Dance, Dance, Dance (Yowsah, Yowsah, Yowsah)** . . . Chic
19/78	**Dance (Disco Heat)** . . . Sylvester
31/58	**Dance Everyone Dance** . . . Betty Madigan
16/84	**Dance Hall Days** . . . Wang Chung

POS/YR	RECORD TITLE/ARTIST
30/88	**Dance Little Sister** . . . Terence Trent D'Arby
10/61	**Dance On Little Girl** . . . Paul Anka
19/58	**Dance Only With Me** . . . Perry Como
24/61	**Dance The Mess Around** . . . Chubby Checker
15/79	**Dance The Night Away** . . . Van Halen
23/58	**Dance To The Bop** . . . Gene Vincent
8/68	**Dance To The Music** . . . Sly & The Family Stone
39/76	**Dance Wit Me** . . . Rufus Featuring Chaka Khan
6/75	**Dance With Me** . . . Orleans
8/78	**Dance With Me** . . . Peter Brown
15/59	**Dance With Me** . . . Drifters
1/55	**Dance With Me Henry (Wallflower)** . . . Georgia Gibbs
12/62	**(Dance With The) Guitar Man** . . . Duane Eddy
28/75	**Dancin' Fool** . . . Guess Who
23/77	**Dancin' Man** . . . Q
12/62	**Dancin' Party** . . . Chubby Checker
18/79	**Dancin' Shoes** . . . Nigel Olsson
2/84	**Dancing In The Dark** . . . Bruce Springsteen
13/73	**Dancing In The Moonlight** . . . King Harvest
17/84	**Dancing In The Sheets** . . . Shalamar
	Dancing In The Street
2/64	Martha & The Vandellas
38/82	Van Halen
7/85	Mick Jagger/David Bowie
2/74	**Dancing Machine** . . . Jackson 5
2/86	**Dancing On The Ceiling** . . . Lionel Richie
1/77	**Dancing Queen** . . . Abba
14/67	**Dandelion** . . . Rolling Stones
5/66	**Dandy** . . . Herman's Hermits
7/64	**Dang Me** . . . Roger Miller
12/55	**Danger! Heartbreak Ahead** . . . Jaye P. Morgan
2/86	**Danger Zone** . . . Kenny Loggins
25/66	**Dangling Conversation** . . . Simon & Garfunkel
	Dangling On A String ..see: (You've Got Me)
2/73	**Daniel** . . . Elton John
13/63	**Danke Schoen** . . . Wayne Newton
10/59	**Danny Boy** . . . Conway Twitty
7/73	**Danny's Song** . . . Anne Murray

POS/YR	RECORD TITLE/ARTIST
11/85	**Dare Me** . . . Pointer Sisters
15/75	**Dark Horse** . . . George Harrison
1/74	**Dark Lady** . . . Cher
	Dark Moon
4/57	Gale Storm
6/57	Bonnie Guitar
19/68	**Darlin'** . . . Beach Boys
15/67	**Darling Be Home Soon** . . . Lovin' Spoonful
7/55	**Darling Je Vous Aime Beaucoup** . . . Nat King Cole
13/70	**Daughter Of Darkness** . . . Tom Jones
	Davy Crockett ..see: Ballad Of
3/64	**Dawn (Go Away)** . . . 4 Seasons
36/65	**Dawn Of Correction** . . . Spokesmen
4/72	**Day After Day** . . . Badfinger
13/72	**Day By Day** . . . Godspell
18/86	**Day By Day** . . . Hooters
5/72	**Day Dreaming** . . . Aretha Franklin
35/66	**Day For Decision** . . . Johnny Sea
23/72	**Day I Found Myself** . . . Honey Cone
21/87	**Day-In Day-Out** . . . David Bowie
21/69	**Day Is Done** . . . Peter, Paul & Mary
	Day-O ..see: Banana Boat
	Day The Rains Came
21/58	Jane Morgan
30/58	Raymond Lefevre
5/66	**Day Tripper** . . . Beatles
23/77	**Daybreak** . . . Barry Manilow
39/74	**Daybreak** . . . Nilsson
2/66	**Daydream** . . . Lovin' Spoonful
	Daydream Believer
1/67	Monkees
12/80	Anne Murray
17/79	**Days Gone Down (Still Got The Light In Your Eyes)** . . . Gerry Rafferty
34/69	**Days Of Sand And Shovels** . . . Bobby Vinton
	Days Of Wine And Roses
26/63	Andy Williams
33/63	Henry Mancini
28/77	**Daytime Friends** . . . Kenny Rogers
3/77	**Dazz** . . . Brick
10/81	**De Do Do Do, De Da Da Da** . . . Police
19/78	**Deacon Blues** . . . Steely Dan
29/67	**Dead End Street** . . . Lou Rawls
22/83	**Dead Giveaway** . . . Shalamar
8/64	**Dead Man's Curve** . . . Jan & Dean

POS/YR	RECORD TITLE/ARTIST
16/73	**Dead Skunk** . . . Loudon Wainwright III
	Dear Heart
24/65	Andy Williams
30/65	Jack Jones
24/62	**Dear Ivan** . . . Jimmy Dean
9/62	**Dear Lady Twist** . . . Gary U.S. Bonds
13/62	**Dear Lonely Hearts** . . . Nat King Cole
11/62	**Dear One** . . . Larry Finnegan
1/76	**December, 1963 (Oh, What a Night)** . . . 4 Seasons
7/59	**Deck Of Cards** . . . Wink Martindale
7/58	**Dede Dinah** . . . Frankie Avalon
36/66	**Dedicated Follower Of Fashion** . . . Kinks
	Dedicated To The One I Love
3/61	Shirelles
2/67	Mamas & The Papas
22/80	**Deep Inside My Heart** . . . Randy Meisner
	Deep Purple
20/57	Billy Ward & His Dominoes
1/63	Nino Tempo & April Stevens
14/76	Donny & Marie Osmond
24/70	**Deeper & Deeper** . . . Freda Payne
11/79	**Deeper Than The Night** . . . Olivia Newton-John
15/80	**Deja Vu** . . . Dionne Warwick
22/60	**Delaware** . . . Perry Como
40/58	**Delicious!** . . . Jim Backus & Friend
15/68	**Delilah** . . . Tom Jones
	Delilah Jones ..see: Man With The Golden Arm
8/83	**Delirious** . . . Prince
1/73	**Delta Dawn** . . . Helen Reddy
10/63	**Denise** . . . Randy & The Rainbows
25/79	**Dependin' On You** . . . Doobie Brothers
5/83	**Der Kommissar** . . . After The Fire
15/62	**Desafinado** . . . Stan Getz/Charlie Byrd
10/84	**Desert Moon** . . . Dennis DeYoung
33/63	**Desert Pete** . . . Kingston Trio
8/71	**Desiderata** . . . Les Crane
3/88	**Desire** . . . U2
4/80	**Desire** . . . Andy Gibb
16/78	**Desiree** . . . Neil Diamond
	Detroit City
16/63	Bobby Bare
27/67	Tom Jones
	Devil In Disguise ..see: (You're the)
2/88	**Devil Inside** . . . INXS
6/60	**Devil Or Angel** . . . Bobby Vee

POS/YR	RECORD TITLE/ARTIST
3/79	**Devil Went Down To Georgia** . . . Charlie Daniels Band
4/66	**Devil With A Blue Dress On (medley)** . . . Mitch Ryder & The Detroit Wheels
6/76	**Devil Woman** . . . Cliff Richard
16/62	**Devil Woman** . . . Marty Robbins
36/77	**Devil's Gun** . . . C.J. & Co.
	Devoted To You
10/58	Everly Brothers
36/78	Carly Simon & James Taylor
33/74	**Devotion** . . . Earth, Wind & Fire
13/89	**Dial My Heart** . . . Boys
24/72	**Dialogue** . . . Chicago
6/73	**Diamond Girl** . . . Seals & Crofts
5/87	**Diamonds** . . . Herb Alpert
18/60	**Diamonds And Pearls** . . . Paradons
35/75	**Diamonds And Rust** . . . Joan Baez
1/57	**Diana** . . . Paul Anka
10/64	**Diane** . . . Bachelors
14/59	**Diary, The** . . . Neil Sedaka
15/72	**Diary** . . . Bread
9/82	**Did It In A Minute** . . . Daryl Hall & John Oates
29/76	**Did You Boogie (With Your Baby)** . . . Flash Cadillac & The Continental Kids
2/66	**Did You Ever Have To Make Up Your Mind?** . . . Lovin' Spoonful
32/69	**Did You See Her Eyes** . . . Illusion
10/70	**Didn't I (Blow Your Mind This Time)** . . . Delfonics
1/87	**Didn't We Almost Have It All** . . . Whitney Houston
	Died In Your Arms ..see: (I Just)
7/86	**Different Corner** . . . George Michael
13/68	**Different Drum** . . . Stone Poneys/Linda Ronstadt
18/79	**Different Worlds** . . . Maureen McGovern
14/86	**Digging Your Scene** . . . Blow Monkeys
21/86	**Digital Display** . . . Ready For The World
2/79	**Dim All The Lights** . . . Donna Summer
11/55	**Dim, Dim The Lights (I Want Some Atmosphere)** . . . Bill Haley
18/60	**Ding-A-Ling** . . . Bobby Rydell
25/58	**Ding Dong** . . . McGuire Sisters
36/75	**Ding Dong; Ding Dong** . . . George Harrison

POS/YR	RECORD TITLE/ARTIST
11/67	**Ding Dong! The Witch Is Dead** . . . Fifth Estate
6/58	**Dinner With Drac** . . . John Zacherle
1/88	**Dirty Diana** . . . Michael Jackson
3/83	**Dirty Laundry** . . . Don Henley
11/66	**Dirty Water** . . . Standells
12/79	**Dirty White Boy** . . . Foreigner
36/67	**Dis-Advantages Of You** . . . Brass Ring
1/76	**Disco Duck** . . . Rick Dees
11/78	**Disco Inferno** . . . Trammps
1/76	**Disco Lady** . . . Johnnie Taylor
24/77	**Disco Lucy (I Love Lucy Theme)** . . . Wilton Place Street Band
12/79	**Disco Nights (Rock-Freak)** . . . GQ
28/75	**Disco Queen** . . . Hot Chocolate
	(Disco Round) ..see: I Love The Nightlife
28/74	**Distant Lover** . . . Marvin Gaye
30/66	**Distant Shores** . . . Chad & Jeremy
	Dixie ..also see: Theme From
30/55	**Dixie Danny** . . . Laurie Sisters
1/69	**Dizzy** . . . Tommy Roe
	Do ..also see: Doo
13/82	**Do I Do** . . . Stevie Wonder
34/64	**Do I Love You?** . . . Ronettes
36/70	**Do It** . . . Neil Diamond
6/73	**Do It Again** . . . Steely Dan
20/68	**Do It Again** . . . Beach Boys
18/67	**Do It Again A Little Bit Slower** . . . Jon & Robin & The In Crowd
11/75	**Do It Any Way You Wanna** . . . People's Choice
13/74	**Do It Baby** . . . Miracles
29/85	**Do It For Love** . . . Sheena Easton
19/79	**Do It Or Die** . . . Atlanta Rhythm Section
2/74	**Do It ('Til You're Satisfied)** . . . B.T. Express
27/62	**Do-Re-Mi** . . . Lee Dorsey
23/80	**Do Right** . . . Paul Davis
38/68	**Do Something To Me** . . . Tommy James & The Shondells
1/80	**Do That To Me One More Time** . . . Captain & Tennille
10/63	**Do The Bird** . . . Dee Dee Sharp
36/65	**Do The Boomerang** . . . Jr. Walker & The All Stars
21/65	**Do The Clam** . . . Elvis Presley
18/65	**Do The Freddie** . . . Freddie & The Dreamers

POS/YR	RECORD TITLE/ARTIST
	(also see: Let's Do The Freddie)
28/70	**Do The Funky Chicken** . . . Rufus Thomas
37/62	**Do The New Continental** . . . Dovells
25/71	**(Do The) Push And Pull** . . . Rufus Thomas
13/85	**Do They Know It's Christmas?** . . . Band Aid
31/65	**Do-Wacka-Do** . . . Roger Miller
1/64	**Do Wah Diddy Diddy** . . . Manfred Mann
13/85	**Do What You Do** . . . Jermaine Jackson
37/70	**Do What You Wanna Do** . . . Five Flights Up
39/76	**Do What You Want, Be What You Are** . . . Daryl Hall & John Oates
24/77	**Do Ya** . . . Electric Light Orchestra
	Do Ya Think I'm Sexy? ..see: Da Ya
18/77	**Do Ya Wanna Get Funky With Me** . . . Peter Brown
7/82	**Do You Believe In Love** . . . Huey Lewis & The News
	Do You Believe In Magic
9/65	Lovin' Spoonful
31/78	Shaun Cassidy
10/76	**Do You Feel Like We Do** . . . Peter Frampton
10/68	**Do You Know The Way To San Jose** . . . Dionne Warwick
6/71	**Do You Know What I Mean** . . . Lee Michaels
	Do You Know Where You're Going To ..see: Theme From Mahogany
	Do You Love Me
3/62	Contours
11/64	Dave Clark Five
11/88	Contours
30/80	**Do You Love What You Feel** . . . Rufus Featuring Chaka Khan
2/83	**Do You Really Want To Hurt Me** . . . Culture Club
32/70	**Do You See My Love (For You Growing)** . . . Jr. Walker & The All Stars
5/77	**Do You Wanna Make Love** . . . Peter McCann
20/82	**Do You Wanna Touch Me (Oh Yeah)** . . . Joan Jett
37/85	**Do You Want Crying** . . . Katrina & The Waves
	Do You Want To Dance
5/58	Bobby Freeman
12/65	Beach Boys

POS/YR	RECORD TITLE/ARTIST
17/73	Bette Midler
2/64	**Do You Want To Know A Secret** . . . Beatles
39/77	**Do Your Dance** . . . Rose Royce
11/69	**Do Your Thing** . . . Watts 103rd St. Band
30/72	**Do Your Thing** . . . Isaac Hayes
	Dock Of The Bay ..see: (Sittin' On)
11/84	**Doctor! Doctor!** . . . Thompson Twins
	(Doctor, Doctor) ..see: Bad Case Of Loving You
28/83	**Dr. Heckyll & Mr. Jive** . . . Men At Work
	Doctor Kildare ..see: Theme From
8/72	**Doctor My Eyes** . . . Jackson Browne
	Doctor Tarr ..see: (System Of)
	Doctor Zhivago ..see: Somewhere My Love
11/75	**Doctor's Orders** . . . Carol Douglas
38/69	**Does Anybody Know I'm Here** . . . Dells
7/71	**Does Anybody Really Know What Time It Is?** . . . Chicago
36/83	**Does It Make You Remember** . . . Kim Carnes
5/61	**Does Your Chewing Gum Lose It's Flavor (On The Bedpost Over Night)** . . . Lonnie Donegan
29/68	**Does Your Mama Know About Me** . . . Bobby Taylor
19/79	**Does Your Mother Know** . . . Abba
6/71	**Doesn't Somebody Want To Be Wanted** . . . Partridge Family
34/79	**Dog & Butterfly** . . . Heart
30/55	**Dogface Soldier** . . . Russ Morgan
15/60	**Doggin' Around** . . . Jackie Wilson
32/69	**Doggone Right** . . . Miracles
6/87	**Doing It All For My Baby** . . . Huey Lewis & The News
22/73	**Doing It To Death** . . . Fred Wesley & The J.B.'s
31/60	**Doll House** . . . Donnie Brooks
13/55	**Domani (Tomorrow)** . . . Julius LaRosa
1/63	**Dominique** . . . Singing Nun
9/71	**Domino** . . . Van Morrison
18/88	**Domino Dancing** . . . Pet Shop Boys
14/87	**Dominoes** . . . Robbie Nevil
1/58	**Don't** . . . Elvis Presley
15/84	**Don't Answer Me** . . . Alan Parsons Project
19/80	**Don't Ask Me Why** . . . Billy Joel

POS/YR	RECORD TITLE/ARTIST
25/58	**Don't Ask Me Why** . . . Elvis Presley
26/63	**Don't Be Afraid, Little Darlin'** . . . Steve Lawrence
	Don't Be Angry
14/55	Crew-Cuts
25/55	Nappy Brown
	Don't Be Cruel
1/56	Elvis Presley
11/60	Bill Black's Combo
4/88	Cheap Trick
8/88	**Don't Be Cruel** . . . Bobby Brown
9/61	**Don't Bet Money Honey** . . . Linda Scott
20/61	**Don't Blame Me** . . . Everly Brothers
37/67	**Don't Blame The Children** . . . Sammy Davis, Jr.
1/62	**Don't Break The Heart That Loves You** . . . Connie Francis
4/79	**Don't Bring Me Down** . . . Electric Light Orchestra
12/66	**Don't Bring Me Down** . . . Animals
9/75	**Don't Call Us, We'll Call You** . . . Sugarloaf
	Don't Cha ..see: Don'tcha
26/74	**Don't Change Horses (In The Middle Of A Stream)** . . . Tower Of Power
36/71	**Don't Change On Me** . . . Ray Charles
13/85	**Don't Come Around Here No More** . . . Tom Petty
21/60	**Don't Come Knockin'** . . . Fats Domino
35/73	**Don't Cross The River** . . . America
10/83	**Don't Cry** . . . Asia
39/61	**Don't Cry, Baby** . . . Etta James
6/70	**Don't Cry Daddy** . . . Elvis Presley
10/79	**Don't Cry Out Loud** . . . Melissa Manchester
4/87	**Don't Disturb This Groove** . . . System
34/72	**Don't Do It** . . . Band
10/80	**Don't Do Me Like That** . . . Tom Petty
2/87	**Don't Dream It's Over** . . . Crowded House
23/72	**Don't Ever Be Lonely (A Poor Little Fool Like Me)** . . . Cornelius Brothers & Sister Rose
40/79	**Don't Ever Wanna Lose Ya** . . . New England
8/73	**Don't Expect Me To Be Your Friend** . . . Lobo
4/80	**Don't Fall In Love With A Dreamer** . . . Kenny Rogers with Kim Carnes
12/76	**(Don't Fear) The Reaper** . . . Blue Oyster Cult
17/82	**Don't Fight It** . . . Kenny Loggins with Steve Perry
1/57	**Don't Forbid Me** . . . Pat Boone
19/65	**Don't Forget I Still Love You** . . . Bobbi Martin
2/86	**Don't Forget Me (When I'm Gone)** . . . Glass Tiger
29/83	**Don't Forget To Dance** . . . Kinks
10/86	**Don't Get Me Wrong** . . . Pretenders
15/69	**Don't Give In To Him** . . . Gary Puckett & The Union Gap
26/81	**Don't Give It Up** . . . Robbie Patton
37/68	**Don't Give Up** . . . Petula Clark
1/77	**Don't Give Up On Us** . . . David Soul
1/76	**Don't Go Breaking My Heart** . . . Elton John & Kiki Dee
22/58	**Don't Go Home** . . . Playmates
17/62	**Don't Go Near The Indians** . . . Rex Allen
18/67	**Don't Go Out Into The Rain (You're Going To Melt)** . . . Herman's Hermits
	Don't Go To Strangers
38/56	Vaughn Monroe
36/60	Etta Jones
4/62	**Don't Hang Up** . . . Orlons
21/79	**Don't Hold Back** . . . Chanson
2/77	**Don't It Make My Brown Eyes Blue** . . . Crystal Gayle
8/65	**Don't Just Stand There** . . . Patty Duke
13/71	**Don't Knock My Love** . . . Wilson Pickett
12/88	**Don't Know What You Got (Till It's Gone)** . . . Cinderella
	Don't Leave Me This Way
1/77	Thelma Houston
40/87	Communards
	Don't Let Go
13/58	Roy Hamilton
18/80	Isaac Hayes
38/84	**Don't Let Go** . . . Wang Chung
24/81	**Don't Let Him Go** . . . REO Speedwagon
39/82	**Don't Let Him Know** . . . Prism
6/83	**Don't Let It End** . . . Styx
14/73	**Don't Let Me Be Lonely Tonight** . . . James Taylor
	Don't Let Me Be Misunderstood
15/65	Animals
15/78	Santa Esmeralda
35/69	**Don't Let Me Down** . . . Beatles

POS/YR	RECORD TITLE/ARTIST
17/71	**Don't Let The Green Grass Fool You** . . . Wilson Pickett
20/69	**Don't Let The Joneses Get You Down** . . . Temptations
6/64	**Don't Let The Rain Come Down (Crooked Little Man)** . . . Serendipity Singers
39/67	**Don't Let The Rain Fall Down On Me** . . . Critters
4/64	**Don't Let The Sun Catch You Crying** . . . Gerry & The Pacemakers
2/74	**Don't Let The Sun Go Down On Me** . . . Elton John
4/78	**Don't Look Back** . . . Boston
39/87	**Don't Look Down - The Sequel** . . . Go West
4/85	**Don't Lose My Number** . . . Phil Collins
21/63	**Don't Make Me Over** . . . Dionne Warwick
15/87	**Don't Make Me Wait For Love** . . . Kenny G/Lenny Williams
3/87	**Don't Mean Nothing** . . . Richard Marx
33/65	**Don't Mess Up A Good Thing** . . . Fontella Bass & Bobby McClure
7/66	**Don't Mess With Bill** . . . Marvelettes
37/87	**Don't Need A Gun** . . . Billy Idol
34/83	**Don't Pay The Ferryman** . . . Chris DeBurgh
40/59	**Don't Pity Me** . . . Dion & The Belmonts
	Don't Play That Song
11/62	Ben E. King
11/70	Aretha Franklin
	Don't Pull Your Love
4/71	Hamilton, Joe Frank & Reynolds
27/76	Glen Campbell (medley)
2/89	**Don't Rush Me** . . . Taylor Dayne
26/63	**Don't Say Goodnight And Mean Goodbye** . . . Shirelles
39/80	**Don't Say Goodnight (It's Time For Love)** . . . Isley Brothers
7/63	**Don't Say Nothin' Bad (About My Baby)** . . . Cookies
15/72	**Don't Say You Don't Remember** . . . Beverly Bremers
20/63	**Don't Set Me Free** . . . Ray Charles
9/88	**Don't Shed A Tear** . . . Paul Carrack
5/67	**Don't Sleep In The Subway** . . . Petula Clark
10/81	**Don't Stand So Close To Me** . . . Police
3/77	**Don't Stop** . . . Fleetwood Mac

POS/YR	RECORD TITLE/ARTIST
9/81	**Don't Stop Believin'** . . . Journey
33/76	**Don't Stop Believin'** . . . Olivia Newton-John
19/81	**Don't Stop The Music** . . . Yarbrough & Peoples
1/79	**Don't Stop 'Til You Get Enough** . . . Michael Jackson
34/76	**Don't Take Away The Music** . . . Tavares
27/68	**Don't Take It So Hard** . . . Paul Revere & The Raiders
32/59	**Don't Take Your Guns To Town** . . . Johnny Cash
37/75	**Don't Take Your Love** . . . Manhattans
2/82	**Don't Talk To Strangers** . . . Rick Springfield
27/75	**Don't Tell Me Goodnight** . . . Lobo
40/83	**Don't Tell Me You Love Me** . . . Night Ranger
	Don't Think Twice, It's All Right
9/63	Peter, Paul & Mary
12/65	Wonder Who?
22/60	**Don't Throw Away All Those Teardrops** . . . Frankie Avalon
	Don't Throw It All Away ..see: (Our Love)
16/64	**Don't Throw Your Love Away** . . . Searchers
38/69	**Don't Touch Me** . . . Bettye Swann
26/84	**Don't Walk Away** . . . Rick Springfield
21/78	**Don't Want To Live Without It** . . . Pablo Cruise
35/81	**Don't Want To Wait Anymore** . . . Tubes
3/61	**Don't Worry** . . . Marty Robbins
	Don't Worry Baby
24/64	Beach Boys
17/77	B.J. Thomas
1/88	**Don't Worry Be Happy** . . . Bobby McFerrin
29/71	**(Don't Worry) If There's A Hell Below We're All Going To Go** . . . Curtis Mayfield
	Don't Ya Wanna Play This Game No More ..see: (Sartorial Eloquence)
	Don't You ..also see: Don'tcha, Doncha'
39/62	**Don't You Believe It** . . . Andy Williams
6/67	**Don't You Care** . . . Buckinghams
1/85	**Don't You (Forget About Me)** . . . Simple Minds
	Don't You Forget It ..see: (I Love You)
25/83	**Don't You Get So Mad** . . . Jeffrey Osborne

POS/YR	RECORD TITLE/ARTIST
9/58	**Don't You Just Know It** . . . Huey "Piano" Smith
2/59	**Don't You Know** . . . Della Reese
6/88	**Don't You Know What The Night Can Do?** . . . Steve Winwood
1/82	**Don't You Want Me** . . . Human League
6/87	**Don't You Want Me** . . . Jody Watley
16/74	**Don't You Worry 'Bout A Thing** . . . Stevie Wonder
	Don't You Worry 'Bout Me ..see: Opus 17
33/79	**Don't You Write Her Off** . . . McGuinn, Clark & Hillman
15/58	**Doncha' Think It's Time** . . . Elvis Presley
2/59	**Donna** . . . Ritchie Valens
6/63	**Donna The Prima Donna** . . . Dion
15/74	**Doo Doo Doo Doo Doo (Heartbreaker)** . . . Rolling Stones
6/64	**Door Is Still Open To My Heart** . . . Dean Martin
35/74	**Doraville** . . . Atlanta Rhythm Section
26/76	**Dose Of Rock 'N' Roll** . . . Ringo Starr
39/58	**Dottie** . . . Danny & The Juniors
22/71	**Double Barrel** . . . Dave & Ansil Collins
30/81	**Double Dutch Bus** . . . Frankie Smith
14/71	**Double Lovin'** . . . Osmonds
17/66	**Double Shot (Of My Baby's Love)** . . . Swingin' Medallions
2/78	**Double Vision** . . . Foreigner
33/68	**Down At Lulu's** . . . Ohio Express
9/63	**(Down At) Papa Joe's** . . . Dixiebelles
4/72	**Down By The Lazy River** . . . Osmonds
13/60	**Down By The Station** . . . Four Preps
9/65	**Down In The Boondocks** . . . Billy Joe Royal
3/69	**Down On The Corner** . . . Creedence Clearwater Revival
18/58	**Down The Aisle Of Love** . . . Quin-Tones
37/63	**Down The Aisle (Wedding Song)** . . . Patti LaBelle
1/83	**Down Under** . . . Men At Work
	Downtown
1/65	Petula Clark
40/65	Allan Sherman (Crazy Downtown)
31/88	**Downtown Life** . . . Daryl Hall John Oates
	Dr. ..see: Doctor
10/64	**Drag City** . . . Jan & Dean
4/71	**Draggin' The Line** . . . Tommy James
28/81	**Draw Of The Cards** . . . Kim Carnes

POS/YR	RECORD TITLE/ARTIST
19/58	**Dream** . . . Betty Johnson
12/68	**Dream A Little Dream Of Me** . . . Mama Cass
	Dream Baby (How Long Must I Dream)
4/62	Roy Orbison
31/71	Glen Campbell
37/84	**Dream (Hold On To Your Dream)** . . . Irene Cara
2/59	**Dream Lover** . . . Bobby Darin
	Dream Merchant
38/67	Jerry Butler
36/75	New Birth
6/76	**Dream On** . . . Aerosmith
32/74	**Dream On** . . . Righteous Brothers
25/65	**Dream On Little Dreamer** . . . Perry Como
26/79	**Dream Police** . . . Cheap Trick
2/76	**Dream Weaver** . . . Gary Wright
	Dreamboat ..see: (He's My)
15/80	**Dreamer** . . . Supertramp
11/60	**Dreamin'** . . . Johnny Burnette
30/83	**Dreamin' Is Easy** . . . Steel Breeze
10/80	**Dreaming** . . . Cliff Richard
16/88	**Dreaming** . . . Orchestral Manoeuvres In The Dark
27/79	**Dreaming** . . . Blondie
1/77	**Dreams** . . . Fleetwood Mac
22/86	**Dreams** . . . Van Halen
32/68	**Dreams Of The Everyday Housewife** . . . Glen Campbell
5/86	**Dreamtime** . . . Daryl Hall
35/62	**Dreamy Eyes** . . . Johnny Tillotson
21/73	**Dreidel** . . . Don McLean
5/85	**Dress You Up** . . . Madonna
5/73	**Drift Away** . . . Dobie Gray
6/63	**Drip Drop** . . . Dion
3/84	**Drive** . . . Cars
15/79	**Driver's Seat** . . . Sniff 'n' the Tears
5/80	**Drivin' My Life Away** . . . Eddie Rabbitt
34/77	**Drivin' Wheel** . . . Foghat
36/63	**Drownin' My Sorrows** . . . Connie Francis
11/72	**Drowning In The Sea Of Love** . . . Joe Simon
29/71	**Drum, The** . . . Bobby Sherman
29/62	**Drums Are My Beat** . . . Sandy Nelson
20/67	**Dry Your Eyes** . . . Brenda & The Tabulations
14/66	**Duck, The** . . . Jackie Lee
14/87	**Dude (Looks Like A Lady)** . . . Aerosmith

POS/YR	RECORD TITLE/ARTIST
2/73	**Dueling Banjos** . . . Eric Weissberg & Steve Mandell
1/62	**Duke Of Earl** . . . Gene Chandler
	Dukes Of Hazzard ..see: Theme From The
	Dum-De-Da ..see: She Understands Me
4/61	**Dum Dum** . . . Brenda Lee *(also see: Happy Song)*
7/56	**Dungaree Doll** . . . Eddie Fisher
18/77	**Dusic** . . . Brick
6/78	**Dust In The Wind** . . . Kansas
30/60	**Dutchman's Gold** . . . Walter Brennan
15/84	**Dynamite** . . . Jermaine Jackson
10/75	**Dynomite** . . . Bazuka

E

POS/YR	RECORD TITLE/ARTIST
9/74	**Earache My Eye Featuring Alice Bowie** . . . Cheech & Chong
12/70	**Early In The Morning** . . . Vanity Fare
	Early In The Morning
24/58	Rinky-Dinks
32/58	Buddy Holly
	Early In The Morning
24/82	Gap Band
19/88	Robert Palmer
	Earth Angel
3/55	Crew-Cuts
8/55	Penguins
18/55	Gloria Mann
21/86	New Edition
1/63	**Easier Said Than Done** . . . Essex
27/66	**East West** . . . Herman's Hermits
4/77	**Easy** . . . Commodores
9/70	**Easy Come, Easy Go** . . . Bobby Sherman
39/72	**Easy Livin** . . . Uriah Heep
2/85	**Easy Lover** . . . Philip Bailey with Phil Collins
17/71	**Easy Loving** . . . Freddie Hart
	Easy Question ..see: (Such An)
4/69	**Easy To Be Hard** . . . Three Dog Night
36/78	**Easy To Love** . . . Leo Sayer
12/84	**Eat It** . . . "Weird Al" Yankovic
	Ebb Tide
25/64	Lenny Welch

POS/YR	RECORD TITLE/ARTIST
5/66	Righteous Brothers
1/82	**Ebony And Ivory** . . . Paul McCartney with Stevie Wonder
8/61	**Ebony Eyes** . . . Everly Brothers
14/78	**Ebony Eyes** . . . Bob Welch
40/69	**Echo Park** . . . Keith Barbour
31/73	**Ecstasy** . . . Ohio Players
	Eddie My Love
11/56	Fontane Sisters
14/56	Chordettes
14/56	Teen Queens
26/88	**Edge Of A Broken Heart** . . . Vixen
10/86	**Edge Of Heaven** . . . Wham!
11/82	**Edge Of Seventeen (Just Like The White Winged Dove)** . . . Stevie Nicks
26/77	**Edge Of The Universe** . . . Bee Gees
34/78	**Ego** . . . Elton John
1/65	**Eight Days A Week** . . . Beatles
32/88	**853-5937** . . . Squeeze
14/66	**Eight Miles High** . . . Byrds
4/82	**867-5309/Jenny** . . . Tommy Tutone
21/71	**Eighteen** . . . Alice Cooper
15/75	**Eighteen With A Bullet** . . . Pete Wingfield
10/63	**18 Yellow Roses** . . . Bobby Darin
	Ein Schiff Wird Kommen ..see: Never On Sunday
18/70	**El Condor Pasa** . . . Simon & Garfunkel
32/60	**El Matador** . . . Kingston Trio
1/60	**El Paso** . . . Marty Robbins
30/58	**El Rancho Rock** . . . Champs
17/63	**El Watusi** . . . Ray Barretto *(also see: Wah Watusi, & Watusi)*
	Eleanor Rigby
11/66	Beatles
35/68	Ray Charles
17/69	Aretha Franklin
26/72	**Elected** . . . Alice Cooper
6/85	**Election Day** . . . Arcadia
2/83	**Electric Avenue** . . . Eddy Grant
7/88	**Electric Blue** . . . Icehouse
6/68	**Elenore** . . . Turtles
	11th Hour Melody
21/56	Al Hibbler
35/56	Lou Busch
10/69	**Eli's Coming** . . . Three Dog Night
39/56	**Eloise** . . . Kay Thompson
5/66	**Elusive Butterfly** . . . Bob Lind
5/81	**Elvira** . . . Oak Ridge Boys

POS/YR	RECORD TITLE/ARTIST
18/85	**Emergency** . . . Kool & The Gang
8/75	**Emma** . . . Hot Chocolate
3/78	**Emotion** . . . Samantha Sang
22/75	**Emotion** . . . Helen Reddy
15/86	**Emotion In Motion** . . . Ric Ocasek
3/80	**Emotional Rescue** . . . Rolling Stones
7/61	**Emotions** . . . Brenda Lee
18/80	**Empire Strikes Back (medley)** . . . Meco
13/57	**Empty Arms** . . . Teresa Brewer
13/82	**Empty Garden (Hey Hey Johnny)** . . . Elton John
12/59	**Enchanted** . . . Platters
12/58	**Enchanted Island** . . . Four Lads
	Enchanted Sea
15/59	Islanders
28/59	Martin Denny
7/58	**End, The** . . . Earl Grant
	End Of Our Road
15/68	Gladys Knight & The Pips
40/70	Marvin Gaye
2/63	**End Of The World** . . . Skeeter Davis
1/81	**Endless Love** . . . Diana Ross & Lionel Richie
21/87	**Endless Nights** . . . Eddie Money
5/58	**Endless Sleep** . . . Jody Reynolds
2/88	**Endless Summer Nights** . . . Richard Marx
12/59	**Endlessly** . . . Brook Benton
33/74	**Energy Crisis '74** . . . Dickie Goodman
7/65	**Engine Engine #9** . . . Roger Miller
14/70	**Engine Number 9** . . . Wilson Pickett
8/65	**England Swings** . . . Roger Miller
21/56	**English Muffins And Irish Stew** . . . Sylvia Syms
6/77	**Enjoy Yourself** . . . Jacksons
	Enough Is Enough ..see: No More Tears
3/74	**Entertainer, The** . . . Marvin Hamlisch
31/65	**Entertainer, The** . . . Tony Clarke
34/75	**Entertainer, The** . . . Billy Joel
19/67	**Epistle To Dippy** . . . Donovan
9/74	**Eres Tu (Touch The Wind)** . . . Mocedades
1/79	**Escape (The Pina Colada Song)** . . . Rupert Holmes
35/71	**Escape-ism** . . . James Brown
19/62	**Eso Beso (That Kiss!)** . . . Paul Anka
1/65	**Eve Of Destruction** . . . Barry McGuire
33/80	**Even It Up** . . . Heart
12/83	**Even Now** . . . Bob Seger
19/78	**Even Now** . . . Barry Manilow

POS/YR	RECORD TITLE/ARTIST
36/67	**Even The Bad Times Are Good** . . . Tremeloes
5/82	**Even The Nights Are Better** . . . Air Supply
1/77	**Evergreen** . . . Barbra Streisand
5/78	**Everlasting Love** . . . Andy Gibb
	Everlasting Love
13/67	Robert Knight
6/74	Carl Carlton
32/81	Rex Smith/Rachel Sweet
16/61	**Everlovin'** . . . Rick Nelson
6/61	**Every Beat Of My Heart** . . . Pips
1/83	**Every Breath You Take** . . . Police
	Every Day ..also see: Everyday
	Every Day Of My Life
37/56	McGuire Sisters
24/72	Bobby Vinton
16/78	**Every Kinda People** . . . Robert Palmer
13/64	**Every Little Bit Hurts** . . . Brenda Holloway
14/87	**Every Little Kiss** . . . Bruce Hornsby & The Range
3/81	**Every Little Thing She Does Is Magic** . . . Police
39/58	**Every Night (I Pray)** . . . Chantels
1/88	**Every Rose Has Its Thorn** . . . Poison
25/85	**Every Step Of The Way** . . . John Waite
30/63	**Every Step Of The Way** . . . Johnny Mathis
13/79	**Every Time I Think Of You** . . . Babys
4/77	**(Every Time I Turn Around) Back In Love Again** . . . L.T.D.
19/75	**Every Time You Touch Me (I Get High)** . . . Charlie Rich
30/79	**Every Which Way But Loose** . . . Eddie Rabbitt
5/81	**Every Woman In The World** . . . Air Supply
3/63	**Everybody** . . . Tommy Roe
38/77	**Everybody Be Dancin'** . . . Starbuck
24/86	**Everybody Dance** . . . Ta Mara & The Seen
38/78	**Everybody Dance** . . . Chic
2/86	**Everybody Have Fun Tonight** . . . Wang Chung
F/70	**Everybody Is A Star** . . . Sly & The Family Stone
15/64	**Everybody Knows (I Still Love You)** . . . Dave Clark Five
31/59	**Everybody Likes To Cha Cha Cha** . . . Sam Cooke

POS/YR	RECORD TITLE/ARTIST
4/65	**Everybody Loves A Clown** . . . Gary Lewis & The Playboys
	Everybody Loves A Lover
6/58	Doris Day
19/63	Shirelles
6/62	**Everybody Loves Me But You** . . . Brenda Lee
1/64	**Everybody Loves Somebody** . . . Dean Martin
32/78	**Everybody Needs Love** . . . Stephen Bishop
39/67	**Everybody Needs Love** . . . Gladys Knight & The Pips
29/67	**Everybody Needs Somebody To Love** . . . Wilson Pickett
3/72	**Everybody Plays The Fool** . . . Main Ingredient
1/85	**Everybody Wants To Rule The World** . . . Tears For Fears
32/82	**Everybody Wants You** . . . Billy Squier
12/71	**Everybody's Everything** . . . Santana
20/55	**Everybody's Got A Home But Me** . . . Eddie Fisher
21/70	**Everybody's Got The Right To Love** . . . Supremes
18/80	**Everybody's Got To Learn Sometime** . . . Korgis
26/70	**Everybody's Out Of Town** . . . B.J. Thomas
1/60	**Everybody's Somebody's Fool** . . . Connie Francis
6/69	**Everybody's Talkin'** . . . Nilsson
36/83	**Everyday I Write The Book** . . . Elvis Costello
	Everyday People
1/69	Sly & The Family Stone
37/83	Joan Jett
19/69	**Everyday With You Girl** . . . Classics IV
6/79	**Every 1's A Winner** . . . Hot Chocolate
17/65	**Everyone's Gone To The Moon** . . . Jonathan King
5/72	**Everything I Own** . . . Bread
30/86	**Everything In My Heart** . . . Corey Hart
1/70	**Everything Is Beautiful** . . . Ray Stevens
1/85	**Everything She Wants** . . . Wham!
10/68	**Everything That Touches You** . . . Association
3/88	**Everything Your Heart Desires** . . . Daryl Hall John Oates
16/64	**Everything's Alright** . . . Newbeats

POS/YR	RECORD TITLE/ARTIST
38/70	**Everything's Tuesday** . . . Chairmen Of The Board
1/85	**Everytime You Go Away** . . . Paul Young
14/88	**Everywhere** . . . Fleetwood Mac
9/70	**Evil Ways** . . . Santana
10/76	**Evil Woman** . . . Electric Light Orchestra
19/70	**Evil Woman Don't Play Your Games With Me** . . . Crow
	Exodus
2/61	Ferrante & Teicher
31/61	Mantovani
36/61	Eddie Harris
	Exorcist, Theme From ..see: Tubular Bells
14/55	**Experience Unnecessary** . . . Sarah Vaughan
33/68	**Explosion In Your Soul** . . . Soul Survivors
4/75	**Express** . . . B.T. Express
12/70	**Express Yourself** . . . Charles Wright
4/67	**Expressway To Your Heart** . . . Soul Survivors
3/82	**Eye In The Sky** . . . Alan Parsons Project
1/82	**Eye Of The Tiger** . . . Survivor
28/68	**Eyes Of A New York Woman** . . . B.J. Thomas
	Eyes Of Laura Mars ..see: Love Theme From
4/84	**Eyes Without A Face** . . . Billy Idol

F

POS/YR	RECORD TITLE/ARTIST
22/78	**FM (No Static At All)** . . . Steely Dan
29/66	**Fa-Fa-Fa-Fa-Fa (Sad Song)** . . . Otis Redding
16/57	**Fabulous** . . . Charlie Gracie
19/56	**Fabulous Character** . . . Sarah Vaughan
29/68	**Face It Girl, It's Over** . . . Nancy Wilson
26/86	**Face The Face** . . . Pete Townshend
27/87	**Facts Of Love** . . . Jeff Lorber/Karyn White
20/81	**Fade Away** . . . Bruce Springsteen
13/74	**Fairytale** . . . Pointer Sisters
1/87	**Faith** . . . George Michael
12/83	**Faithfully** . . . Journey
25/87	**Fake** . . . Alexander O'Neal
35/83	**Fake Friends** . . . Joan Jett

POS/YR	RECORD TITLE/ARTIST
23/67	**Fakin' It** . . . Simon & Garfunkel
17/83	**Fall In Love With Me** . . . Earth, Wind & Fire
12/88	**Fallen Angel** . . . Poison
36/76	**Fallen Angel** . . . Frankie Valli
	Fallen Star
20/57	Nick Noble
23/57	Jimmy Newman
30/58	**Fallin'** . . . Connie Francis
1/75	**Fallin' In Love** . . . Hamilton, Joe Frank & Reynolds
27/74	**Fallin' In Love** . . . Souther, Hillman, Furay Band
13/78	**Falling** . . . LeBlanc & Carr
22/63	**Falling** . . . Roy Orbison
25/87	**Falling In Love (Uh-Oh)** . . . Miami Sound Machine
1/75	**Fame** . . . David Bowie
4/80	**Fame** . . . Irene Cara
17/60	**Fame And Fortune** . . . Elvis Presley
1/71	**Family Affair** . . . Sly & The Family Stone
6/83	**Family Man** . . . Daryl Hall & John Oates
12/72	**Family Of Man** . . . Three Dog Night
31/70	**Fancy** . . . Bobbie Gentry
39/77	**Fancy Dancer** . . . Commodores
38/60	**Fannie Mae** . . . Buster Brown
12/76	**Fanny (Be Tender With My Love)** . . . Bee Gees
23/82	**Fantasy** . . . Aldo Nova
32/78	**Fantasy** . . . Earth, Wind & Fire
10/83	**Far From Over** . . . Frank Stallone
38/84	**Farewell My Summer Love** . . . Michael Jackson
19/64	**Farmer John** . . . Premiers
21/87	**Fascinated** . . . Company B
	Fascination
7/57	Jane Morgan
15/57	Dinah Shore
17/57	Dick Jacobs
	(also see: Keep Feeling)
6/88	**Fast Car** . . . Tracy Chapman
F/79	**Fat Bottomed Girls** . . . Queen
1/88	**Father Figure** . . . George Michael
34/86	**Feel It Again** . . . Honeymoon Suite
1/74	**Feel Like Makin' Love** . . . Roberta Flack
10/75	**Feel Like Makin' Love** . . . Bad Company
	Feel So Fine
14/60	Johnny Preston
22/67	Bunny Sigler (medley)
	Feelin' Groovy ..see: 59th Street Bridge
10/73	**Feelin' Stronger Every Day** . . . Chicago
33/72	**Feeling Alright** . . . Joe Cocker
6/75	**Feelings** . . . Morris Albert
4/77	**Feels Like The First Time** . . . Foreigner
4/78	**Feels So Good** . . . Chuck Mangione
20/81	**Feels So Right** . . . Alabama
32/61	**Fell In Love On Monday** . . . Fats Domino
13/76	**Fernando** . . . Abba
6/65	**Ferry Across The Mersey** . . . Gerry & The Pacemakers
	Fever
24/56	Little Willie John
8/58	Peggy Lee
7/65	McCoys
23/78	**Ffun** . . . Con Funk Shun
39/58	**Fibbin'** . . . Patti Page
1/76	**Fifth Of Beethoven** . . . Walter Murphy
1/76	**50 Ways To Leave Your Lover** . . . Paul Simon
13/67	**59th Street Bridge Song (Feelin' Groovy)** . . . Harpers Bizarre
3/79	**Fight (medley)** . . . Barbra Streisand
	Fight For Your Right ..see: (You Gotta)
4/75	**Fight The Power** . . . Isley Brothers
	(Final Acclaim) ..see: You're In My Heart
8/87	**Final Countdown** . . . Europe
17/74	**Finally Got Myself Together (I'm A Changed Man)** . . . Impressions
29/85	**Find A Way** . . . Amy Grant
16/82	**Find Another Fool** . . . Quarterflash
27/61	**Find Another Girl** . . . Jerry Butler
29/81	**Find Your Way Back** . . . Jefferson Starship
22/84	**Fine Fine Day** . . . Tony Carey
8/87	**Finer Things** . . . Steve Winwood
7/60	**Finger Poppin' Time** . . . Hank Ballard
1/63	**Fingertips** . . . Little Stevie Wonder
13/88	**Finish What Ya Started** . . . Van Halen
35/79	**Fins** . . . Jimmy Buffett
1/75	**Fire** . . . Ohio Players
2/68	**Fire** . . . Crazy World Of Arthur Brown
2/79	**Fire** . . . Pointer Sisters
17/81	**Fire And Ice** . . . Pat Benatar
3/70	**Fire And Rain** . . . James Taylor
24/72	**Fire And Water** . . . Wilson Pickett
28/74	**Fire, Baby I'm On Fire** . . . Andy Kim
32/80	**Fire In The Morning** . . . Melissa Manchester

POS/YR	RECORD TITLE/ARTIST
6/80	**Fire Lake** . . . Bob Seger
38/75	**Fire On The Mountain** . . . Marshall Tucker Band
20/58	**Firefly** . . . Tony Bennett
21/77	**First Cut Is The Deepest** . . . Rod Stewart
25/57	**First Date, First Kiss, First Love** . . . Sonny James
33/84	**First Day Of Summer** . . . Tony Carey
20/60	**First Name Initial** . . . Annette
37/69	**First Of May** . . . Bee Gees
27/63	**First Quarrel** . . . Paul & Paula
1/72	**First Time Ever I Saw Your Face** . . . Roberta Flack
	(First Time I Was A Fool) ..see: Third Time Lucky
38/80	**First Time Love** . . . Livingston Taylor
25/61	**Fish, The** . . . Bobby Rydell
26/74	**Fish Ain't Bitin'** . . . Lamont Dozier
23/88	**Fishnet** . . . Morris Day
10/63	**500 Miles Away From Home** . . . Bobby Bare
4/66	**Five O'Clock World** . . . Vogues
	Five Oaks ..see: Cinco Robles
27/78	**5.7.0.5.** . . . City Boy
11/70	**5-10-15-20 (25-30 Years Of Love)** . . . Presidents
1/88	**Flame, The** . . . Cheap Trick
36/87	**Flames Of Paradise** . . . Jennifer Rush/Elton John
14/61	**Flaming Star** . . . Elvis Presley
28/66	**Flamingo** . . . Herb Alpert
16/78	**Flash Light** . . . Parliament
1/83	**Flashdance...What A Feeling** . . . Irene Cara
29/84	**Flesh For Fantasy** . . . Billy Idol
2/77	**Float On** . . . Floaters
21/56	**Flowers Mean Forgiveness** . . . Frank Sinatra
4/66	**Flowers On The Wall** . . . Statler Brothers
16/72	**Floy Joy** . . . Supremes
7/61	**Fly, The** . . . Chubby Checker
13/76	**Fly Away** . . . John Denver
2/77	**Fly Like An Eagle** . . . Steve Miller
14/63	**Fly Me To The Moon** . . . Joe Harnell
1/75	**Fly, Robin, Fly** . . . Silver Convention
38/78	**Flying High** . . . Commodores
3/56	**Flying Saucer** . . . Buchanan & Goodman

POS/YR	RECORD TITLE/ARTIST
18/57	**Flying Saucer The 2nd** . . . Buchanan & Goodman
	Foggy Mountain Breakdown ..see: Ballad Of Bonnie & Clyde
15/62	**Follow That Dream** . . . Elvis Presley
17/63	**Follow The Boys** . . . Connie Francis
23/78	**Follow You Follow Me** . . . Genesis
32/68	**Folsom Prison Blues** . . . Johnny Cash
7/56	**Fool, The** . . . Sanford Clark
22/68	**Fool For You** . . . Impressions
12/78	**Fool (If You Think It's Over)** . . . Chris Rea
27/60	**Fool In Love** . . . Ike & Tina Turner
25/81	**Fool In Love With You** . . . Jim Photoglo
21/80	**Fool In The Rain** . . . Led Zeppelin
13/64	**Fool Never Learns** . . . Andy Williams
3/61	**Fool #1** . . . Brenda Lee
6/68	**Fool On The Hill** . . . Sergio Mendes & Brasil '66
2/59	**Fool Such As I** . . . Elvis Presley
10/76	**Fool To Cry** . . . Rolling Stones
20/55	**Fooled** . . . Perry Como
3/76	**Fooled Around And Fell In Love** . . . Elvin Bishop
28/83	**Foolin'** . . . Def Leppard
29/78	**Fooling Yourself (The Angry Young Man)** . . . Styx
1/88	**Foolish Beat** . . . Debbie Gibson
18/85	**Foolish Heart** . . . Steve Perry
4/63	**Foolish Little Girl** . . . Shirelles
33/86	**Foolish Pride** . . . Daryl Hall
29/59	**Fools Hall Of Fame** . . . Pat Boone
	Fools Rush In
24/60	Brook Benton
12/63	Rick Nelson
25/61	**Foot Stomping** . . . Flares
1/84	**Footloose** . . . Kenny Loggins
7/60	**Footsteps** . . . Steve Lawrence
29/72	**Footstompin' Music** . . . Grand Funk Railroad
30/76	**Fopp** . . . Ohio Players
23/59	**For A Penny** . . . Pat Boone
3/71	**For All We Know** . . . Carpenters
30/86	**For America** . . . Jackson Browne
26/71	**(For God's Sake) Give More Power To The People** . . . Chi-Lites
30/65	**For Lovin' Me** . . . Peter, Paul & Mary
28/61	**For My Baby** . . . Brook Benton
23/58	**For My Good Fortune** . . . Pat Boone

POS/YR	RECORD TITLE/ARTIST
2/68	**For Once In My Life** . . . Stevie Wonder
	For Sentimental Reasons ..see: (I Love You)
11/71	**For The Good Times** . . . Ray Price
13/70	**For The Love Of Him** . . . Bobbi Martin
9/74	**For The Love Of Money** . . . O'Jays
22/75	**For The Love Of You** . . . Isley Brothers
32/86	**For Tonight** . . . Nancy Martinez
7/67	**For What It's Worth** . . . Buffalo Springfield
6/64	**For You** . . . Rick Nelson
4/81	**For Your Eyes Only** . . . Sheena Easton
6/65	**For Your Love** . . . Yardbirds
	For Your Love
13/58	Ed Townsend
20/67	Peaches & Herb
	For Your Precious Love
11/58	Jerry Butler & The Impressions
26/64	Garnet Mimms & The Enchanters
23/67	Oscar Toney, Jr.
	Forever
9/60	Little Dippers
25/64	Pete Drake
40/85	**Forever** . . . Kenny Loggins
28/68	**Forever Came Today** . . . Supremes
35/56	**Forever Darling** . . . Ames Brothers
20/79	**Forever In Blue Jeans** . . . Neil Diamond
19/86	**(Forever) Live And Die** . . . Orchestral Manoeuvres In The Dark
26/85	**Forever Man** . . . Eric Clapton
28/80	**Forever Mine** . . . O'Jays
12/88	**Forever Young** . . . Rod Stewart
4/64	**Forget Him** . . . Bobby Rydell
12/58	**Forget Me Not** . . . Kalin Twins
23/82	**Forget Me Nots** . . . Patrice Rushen
2/80	**Forgive Me, Girl (medley)** . . . Spinners
13/55	**Forgive My Heart** . . . Nat King Cole
8/85	**Fortress Around Your Heart** . . . Sting
14/69	**Fortunate Son** . . . Creedence Clearwater Revival
9/59	**Forty Miles Of Bad Road** . . . Duane Eddy
36/79	**Found A Cure** . . . Ashford & Simpson
19/85	**Four In The Morning (I Can't Take Any More)** . . . Night Ranger
	Four Walls
11/57	Jim Reeves
15/57	Jim Lowe
36/68	**1432 Franklin Pike Circle Hero** . . . Bobby Russell
5/76	**Fox On The Run** . . . Sweet

POS/YR	RECORD TITLE/ARTIST
1/73	**Frankenstein** . . . Edgar Winter
9/59	**Frankie** . . . Connie Francis
	Frankie And Johnny
20/61	Brook Benton
14/63	Sam Cooke
25/66	Elvis Presley
36/57	**Fraulein** . . . Bobby Helms
4/72	**Freddie's Dead** . . . Curtis Mayfield
20/71	**Free** . . . Chicago
23/56	**Free** . . . Tommy Leonetti
25/77	**Free** . . . Deniece Williams
	Free Bird
19/75	Lynyrd Skynyrd
38/77	Lynyrd Skynyrd (Live)
22/74	**Free Man In Paris** . . . Joni Mitchell
14/73	**Free Ride** . . . Edgar Winter Group
3/85	**Freedom** . . . Wham!
20/86	**Freedom Overspill** . . . Steve Winwood
3/85	**Freeway Of Love** . . . Aretha Franklin
33/58	**Freeze, The** . . . Tony & Joe
4/82	**Freeze-Frame** . . . J. Geils Band
	Freight Train
6/57	Rusty Draper
40/57	Chas. McDevitt Skiffle Group
9/85	**Fresh** . . . Kool & The Gang
	(Friday Night) ..see: Livin' It Up
16/67	**Friday On My Mind** . . . Easybeats
36/66	**Friday's Child** . . . Nancy Sinatra
5/56	**Friendly Persuasion (Thee I Love)** . . . Pat Boone
34/71	**Friends** . . . Elton John
40/73	**Friends** . . . Bette Midler
2/86	**Friends And Lovers** . . . Gloria Loring & Carl Anderson
38/82	**Friends In Love** . . . Dionne Warwick & Johnny Mathis
17/69	**Friendship Train** . . . Gladys Knight & The Pips
32/61	**Frogg** . . . Brothers Four
6/63	**From A Jack To A King** . . . Ned Miller
23/64	**From A Window** . . . Billy J. Kramer
28/75	**From His Woman To You** . . . Barbara Mason
39/72	**From The Beginning** . . . Emerson, Lake & Palmer
11/56	**From The Candy Store On The Corner To The Chapel On The Hill** . . . Tony Bennett
28/75	**Full Of Fire** . . . Al Green

POS/YR	RECORD TITLE/ARTIST
	Fun ..also see: Ffun
5/64	**Fun, Fun, Fun** . . . Beach Boys
8/67	**Funky Broadway** . . . Wilson Pickett
39/68	**Funky Judge** . . . Bull & The Matadors
15/71	**Funky Nassau** . . . Beginning Of The End
14/68	**Funky Street** . . . Arthur Conley
29/73	**Funky Stuff** . . . Kool & The Gang
6/87	**Funky Town** . . . Pseudo Echo
15/73	**Funky Worm** . . . Ohio Players
1/80	**Funkytown** . . . Lipps, Inc.
25/61	**Funny** . . . Maxine Brown
5/73	**Funny Face** . . . Donna Fargo
	Funny How Time Slips Away
22/62	Jimmy Elledge
13/64	Joe Hinton
10/62	**Funny Way Of Laughin'** . . . Burl Ives
39/73	**Future Shock** . . . Curtis Mayfield
19/86	**Future's So Bright, I Gotta Wear Shades** . . . Timbuk 3

G

POS/YR	RECORD TITLE/ARTIST
4/64	**G.T.O.** . . . Ronny & The Daytonas
39/78	**Galaxy** . . . War
29/67	**Gallant Men** . . . Senator Everett McKinley Dirksen
4/69	**Galveston** . . . Glen Campbell
16/79	**Gambler, The** . . . Kenny Rogers
1/65	**Game Of Love** . . . Mindbenders
27/71	**Games** . . . Redeye
12/69	**Games People Play** . . . Joe South
16/81	**Games People Play** . . . Alan Parsons Project *(also see: They Just Can't Stop It)*
12/56	**Garden Of Eden** . . . Joe Valino
6/72	**Garden Party** . . . Ricky Nelson
21/58	**Gee, But It's Lonely** . . . Pat Boone
19/56	**Gee Whittakers!** . . . Pat Boone
28/61	**Gee Whiz** . . . Innocents
	Gee Whiz (Look At His Eyes)
10/61	Carla Thomas
31/80	Bernadette Peters
12/81	**Gemini Dream** . . . Moody Blues
33/81	**General Hospi-Tale** . . . Afternoon Delights
31/82	**Genius Of Love** . . . Tom Tom Club
39/68	**Gentle On My Mind** . . . Glen Campbell
33/72	**George Jackson** . . . Bob Dylan
1/60	**Georgia On My Mind** . . . Ray Charles
2/67	**Georgy Girl** . . . Seekers
37/72	**Geronimo's Cadillac** . . . Michael Martin Murphey
	Get A Job
1/58	Silhouettes
21/58	Mills Brothers
1/69	**Get Back** . . . Beatles
6/76	**Get Closer** . . . Seals & Crofts
29/82	**Get Closer** . . . Linda Ronstadt
10/75	**Get Dancin'** . . . Disco Tex & The Sex-O-Lettes
7/73	**Get Down** . . . Gilbert O'Sullivan
8/75	**Get Down, Get Down (Get On The Floor)** . . . Joe Simon
10/82	**Get Down On It** . . . Kool & The Gang
1/75	**Get Down Tonight** . . . K.C. & The Sunshine Band
24/71	**Get It On** . . . Chase *(also see: Bang A Gong)*
21/79	**Get It Right Next Time** . . . Gerry Rafferty
28/73	**Get It Together** . . . Jackson 5
40/67	**Get It Together** . . . James Brown
27/67	**Get Me To The World On Time** . . . Electric Prunes
9/78	**Get Off** . . . Foxy
1/65	**Get Off Of My Cloud** . . . Rolling Stones
18/72	**Get On The Good Foot** . . . James Brown
11/67	**Get On Up** . . . Esquires
1/88	**Get Outta My Dreams, Get Into My Car** . . . Billy Ocean
	Get Ready
29/66	Temptations
4/70	Rare Earth
31/87	**Get That Love** . . . Thompson Twins
30/76	**Get The Funk Out Ma Face** . . . Brothers Johnson
	Get Together
31/65	We Five
5/69	Youngbloods
2/76	**Get Up And Boogie (That's Right)** . . . Silver Convention
	(Get Up And Dance) ..see: Bite Your Lip

POS/YR	RECORD TITLE/ARTIST
34/71	**Get Up, Get Into It, Get Involved** . . . James Brown
	Get Up (I Feel Like Being A) Sex Machine ..see: Sex Machine
21/79	**Get Used To It** . . . Roger Voudouris
12/76	**Getaway** . . . Earth, Wind & Fire
26/85	**Getcha Back** . . . Beach Boys
27/78	**Gettin' Ready For Love** . . . Diana Ross
18/67	**Gettin' Together** . . . Tommy James & The Shondells
20/79	**Getting Closer** . . . Wings
29/73	**Ghetto Child** . . . Spinners
	(Ghost) Riders In The Sky
30/61	Ramrods
31/81	Outlaws
22/56	**Ghost Town** . . . Don Cherry
33/88	**Ghost Town** . . . Cheap Trick
1/84	**Ghostbusters** . . . Ray Parker Jr.
37/83	**Gimme All Your Lovin** . . . ZZ Top
9/70	**Gimme Dat Ding** . . . Pipkins
12/69	**Gimme Gimme Good Lovin'** . . . Crazy Elephant
9/67	**Gimme Little Sign** . . . Brenton Wood
	Gimme Some Lovin'
7/67	Spencer Davis Group
18/80	Blues Brothers
6/62	**Gina** . . . Johnny Mathis
9/58	**Ginger Bread** . . . Frankie Avalon
38/61	**Ginnie Bell** . . . Paul Dino
21/62	**Ginny Come Lately** . . . Brian Hyland
17/86	**Girl Can't Help It** . . . Journey
30/65	**Girl Come Running** . . . 4 Seasons
5/64	**Girl From Ipanema** . . . Stan Getz/Astrud Gilberto
39/67	**Girl I Knew Somewhere** . . . Monkees
21/66	**Girl In Love** . . . Outsiders
35/84	**Girl In Trouble (Is A Temporary Thing)** . . . Romeo Void
2/83	**Girl Is Mine** . . . Michael Jackson/Paul McCartney
10/67	**Girl Like You** . . . Rascals
19/61	**Girl Of My Best Friend** . . . Ral Donner
37/79	**Girl Of My Dreams** . . . Bram Tchaikovsky
28/66	**Girl On A Swing** . . . Gerry & The Pacemakers
5/68	**Girl Watcher** . . . O'Kaysions
26/64	**Girl (Why You Wanna Make Me Blue)** . . . Temptations

POS/YR	RECORD TITLE/ARTIST
13/57	**Girl With The Golden Braids** . . . Perry Como
10/67	**Girl, You'll Be A Woman Soon** . . . Neil Diamond
5/88	**Girlfriend** . . . Pebbles
16/84	**Girls** . . . Dwight Twilley
34/85	**Girls Are More Fun** . . . Ray Parker Jr.
34/80	**Girls Can Get It** . . . Dr. Hook
33/68	**Girls Can't Do What The Guys Do** . . . Betty Wright
12/87	**Girls, Girls, Girls** . . . Motley Crue
14/62	**(Girls, Girls, Girls) Made To Love** . . . Eddie Hodges
33/64	**Girls Grow Up Faster Than Boys** . . . Cookies
39/67	**Girls In Love** . . . Gary Lewis & The Playboys
2/84	**Girls Just Want To Have Fun** . . . Cyndi Lauper
33/78	**Girls' School** . . . Wings
33/84	**Girls With Guns** . . . Tommy Shaw
8/69	**Gitarzan** . . . Ray Stevens
15/77	**Give A Little Bit** . . . Supertramp
18/65	**Give Him A Great Big Kiss** . . . Shangri-Las
21/72	**Give Ireland Back To The Irish** . . . Wings
18/80	**Give It All You Got** . . . Chuck Mangione
30/73	**Give It To Me** . . . J. Geils Band
40/81	**Give It To Me Baby** . . . Rick James
20/74	**Give It To The People** . . . Righteous Brothers
18/84	**Give It Up** . . . KC
15/69	**Give It Up Or Turnit A Loose** . . . James Brown
38/76	**Give It Up (Turn It Loose)** . . . Tyrone Davis
40/75	**Give It What You Got** . . . B.T. Express
	Give Me ..also see: Gimme
3/70	**Give Me Just A Little More Time** . . . Chairmen Of The Board
1/73	**Give Me Love (Give Me Peace On Earth)** . . . George Harrison
4/80	**Give Me The Night** . . . George Benson
31/73	**Give Me Your Love** . . . Barbara Mason
	Give More Power To The People ..see: (For God's Sake)
14/69	**Give Peace A Chance** . . . John Lennon/Plastic Ono Band
23/87	**Give To Live** . . . Sammy Hagar

Santo & Johnny Farina sailed all the way to No. 1 with the dreamy guitar instrumental "Sleepwalk" in 1959. As a testament to its timelessness, the song was covered in the 80s by latter-day Latino rockers Los Lobos, making it a live-performance encore favorite.

Boz Scaggs, a member of the Steve Miller Band, knew Miller since high school. The two collaborated in the 60s and had their greatest solo hits in the 70s. By the 80s, Miller recorded an album of jazz standards and Scaggs hit the Top 40 on the year-end Adult Contemporary chart with "Heart of Mine."

Neil Sedaka's "Next Door To An Angel" hit No. 5 in 1962, and it would be his last top-10 hit of the 60s. His incredible career rebound of the 70s peaked with "Bad Blood," which seized the No. 1 spot from "Fame" by comparative neophyte David Bowie.

Bob Seger scaled the Top 40 for the 17th time with "Like A Rock." His 1979 Top-40 hit "Old Time Rock 'N' Roll" charted again in 1983, with a little help from Tom Cruise's pantless lip-synching version in the movie *Risky Business*.

Carly Simon's "Why" was one of her few film songs that didn't make the Top 40. Still, she has done boffo box-office with "Nobody Does It Better" from *The Spy Who Loved Me*, "Coming Around Again" from *Heartburn*, and "Let The River Run," the theme from *Working Girl*.

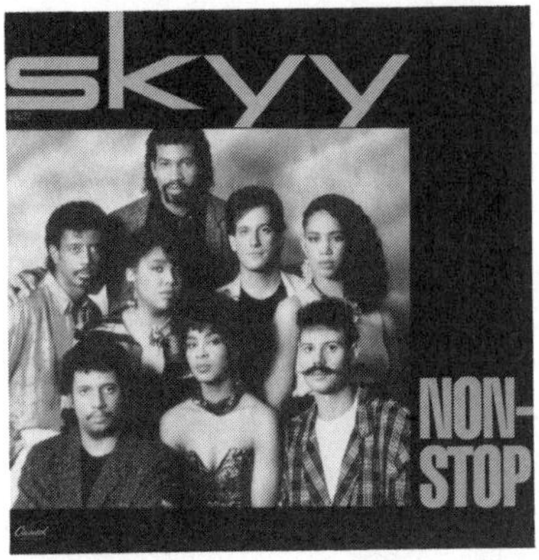

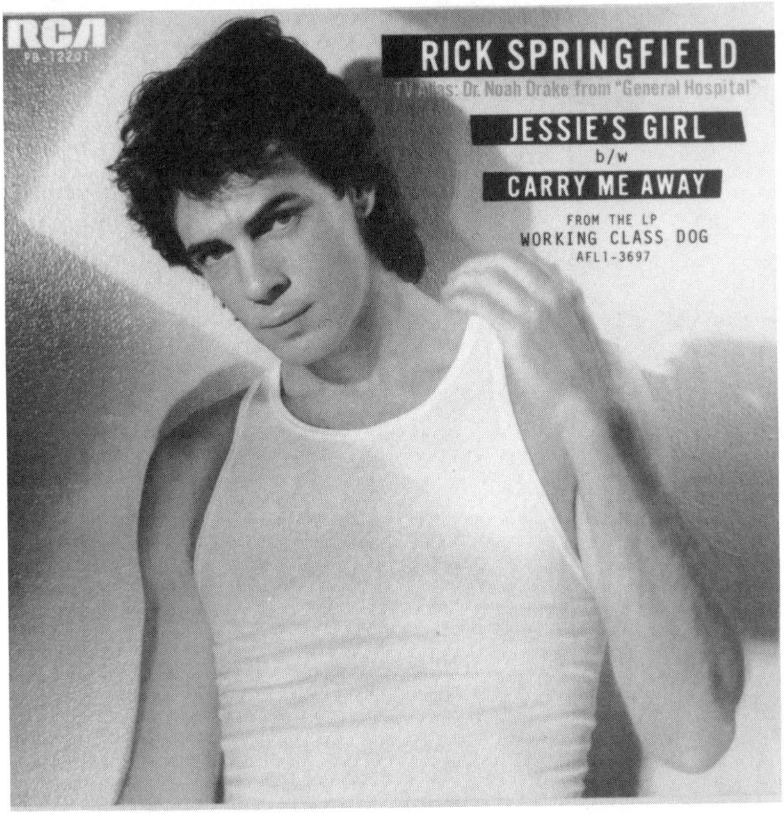

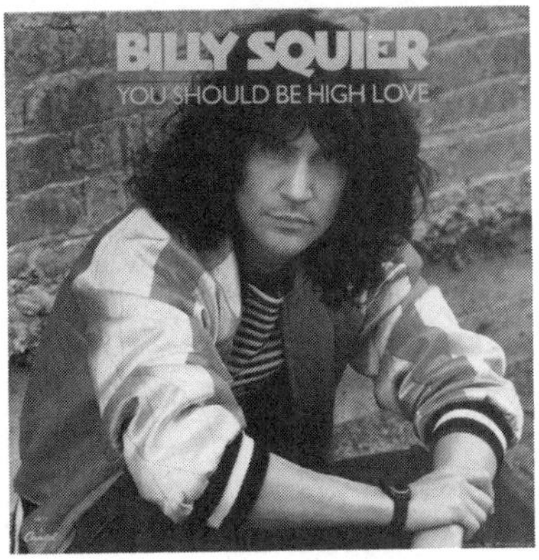

Frank Sinatra released 67 chart songs, 28 Top-40 hits, and three No. 1s from 1955 onward. Yet during the entire decade of the 70s, he never crossed into the Top 40—leaving it in 1969 with "My Way," and re-entering it in 1980 with "Theme From New York, New York."

Skyy, led by the Dunning sisters Denise, Delores, and Bonnie, had a No. 1 R & B hit with "Call Me," which reached No. 26 on the pop charts. Aretha Franklin, Johnny Mathis, and Chris Montez all charted higher with songs by that same name, but Blondie topped them all in 1980 with their No. 1 "Call Me."

Rick Springfield came to America's attention in the late 70s as Noah Drake on the soap opera "General Hospital," but he'd had a Top-40 hit in 1972 and was signed to RCA Records even before he debuted on the show. His return to Top 40 was big, with the 1981 No. 1 "Jessie's Girl."

Bruce Springsteen's "Fire" just missed the Top 40, but the Pointer Sisters' cover version shot to No. 2 in 1979. No Springsteen single has ever risen above No. 2, and he's actually distinguished as having the *most* top-10 records for an artist who's never had a No. 1.

Billy Squier was part of the wave of heavy-metal/pop singers championed by young listeners in the early 80s. But would kids really want to know that when Squier's "The Stroke" entered the Top 40, Squier was already past his 31st birthday?

POS/YR	RECORD TITLE/ARTIST
30/56	**Give Us This Day** . . . Joni James
29/65	**Give Us Your Blessings** . . . Shangri-Las
34/73	**Give Your Baby A Standing Ovation** . . . Dells
8/81	**Giving It Up For Your Love** . . . Delbert McClinton
38/64	**Giving Up** . . . Gladys Knight & The Pips
3/88	**Giving You The Best That I Got** . . . Anita Baker
6/64	**Glad All Over** . . . Dave Clark Five
19/55	**Glad Rag Doll** . . . Crazy Otto
26/67	**Glad To Be Unhappy** . . . Mamas & The Papas
7/84	**Glamorous Life** . . . Sheila E.
37/75	**Glasshouse** . . . Temptations
8/56	**Glendora** . . . Perry Como
2/82	**Gloria** . . . Laura Branigan
10/66	**Gloria** . . . Shadows Of Knight
25/77	**Gloria** . . . Enchantment
34/72	**Glory Bound** . . . Grass Roots
5/85	**Glory Days** . . . Bruce Springsteen
1/86	**Glory Of Love** . . . Peter Cetera
30/66	**Go Ahead And Cry** . . . Righteous Brothers
5/72	**Go All The Way** . . . Raspberries
	Go Away Little Girl
1/63	Steve Lawrence
12/66	Happenings
1/71	Donny Osmond
36/70	**Go Back** . . . Crabby Appleton
32/71	**Go Down Gamblin'** . . . Blood, Sweat & Tears
10/86	**Go Home** . . . Stevie Wonder
23/84	**Go Insane** . . . Lindsey Buckingham
5/60	**Go, Jimmy, Go** . . . Jimmy Clanton
10/65	**Go Now!** . . . Moody Blues
	Go On With The Wedding
11/56	Patti Page
39/56	Kitty Kallen & Georgie Shaw
16/67	**Go Where You Wanna Go** . . . 5th Dimension
10/77	**Go Your Own Way** . . . Fleetwood Mac
36/59	**God Bless America** . . . Connie Francis
18/61	**God, Country And My Baby** . . . Johnny Burnette
22/70	**God, Love And Rock & Roll** . . . Teegarden & Van Winkle
39/66	**God Only Knows** . . . Beach Boys
	Godfather ..see: Love Theme From The

POS/YR	RECORD TITLE/ARTIST
17/82	**Goin' Down** . . . Greg Guidry
36/73	**Goin' Home** . . . Osmonds
	Goin' Out Of My Head
6/64	Little Anthony & The Imperials
7/68	Lettermen (medley)
16/57	**Goin' Steady** . . . Tommy Sands
31/88	**Going Back To Cali** . . . L.L. Cool J
35/64	**Going Going Gone** . . . Brook Benton
15/69	**Going In Circles** . . . Friends Of Distinction
	Going To A Go-Go
11/66	Miracles
25/82	Rolling Stones
11/69	**Going Up The Country** . . . Canned Heat
5/79	**Gold** . . . John Stewart
29/84	**Gold** . . . Spandau Ballet
10/76	**Golden Years** . . . David Bowie
8/65	**Goldfinger** . . . Shirley Bassey
33/86	**Goldmine** . . . Pointer Sisters
	Gone
4/57	Ferlin Husky
24/72	Joey Heatherton
23/75	**Gone At Last** . . . Paul Simon/Phoebe Snow
31/64	**Gone, Gone, Gone** . . . Everly Brothers
23/77	**Gone Too Far** . . . England Dan & John Ford Coley
18/57	**Gonna Find Me A Bluebird** . . . Marvin Rainwater
	Gonna Fly Now (Theme From "Rocky")
1/77	Bill Conti
28/77	Maynard Ferguson
11/56	**Gonna Get Along Without Ya Now** . . . Patience & Prudence
29/67	**Gonna Give Her All The Love I've Got** . . . Jimmy Ruffin
36/69	**Goo Goo Barabajagal (Love Is Hot)** . . . Donovan
17/55	**Good And Lonesome** . . . Kay Starr
	Good Foot ..see: Get On The
39/79	**Good Friend** . . . Mary MacGregor
11/79	**Good Girls Don't** . . . Knack
	Good Golly, Miss Molly
10/58	Little Richard
4/76	Mitch Ryder (medley)
25/76	**Good Hearted Woman** . . . Waylon & Willie
18/63	**Good Life** . . . Tony Bennett
1/66	**Good Lovin'** . . . Rascals

POS/YR	RECORD TITLE/ARTIST
30/69	**Good Lovin' Ain't Easy To Come By** . . . Marvin Gaye & Tammi Terrell
36/75	**Good Lovin' Gone Bad** . . . Bad Company
1/62	**Good Luck Charm** . . . Elvis Presley
34/73	**Good Morning Heartache** . . . Diana Ross
3/69	**Good Morning Starshine** . . . Oliver
11/64	**Good News** . . . Sam Cooke
21/69	**Good Old Rock 'N Roll (medley)** . . . Cat Mother & the All Night News Boys
2/68	**Good, The Bad And The Ugly** . . . Hugo Montenegro
4/67	**Good Thing** . . . Paul Revere & The Raiders
11/61	**Good Time Baby** . . . Bobby Rydell
9/72	**Good Time Charlie's Got The Blues** . . . Danny O'Keefe
1/79	**Good Times** . . . Chic
11/64	**Good Times** . . . Sam Cooke
3/60	**Good Timin'** . . . Jimmy Jones
40/79	**Good Timin'** . . . Beach Boys
	Good Vibrations
1/66	Beach Boys
34/76	Todd Rundgren
13/69	**Goodbye** . . . Mary Hopkin
17/86	**Goodbye** . . . Night Ranger
8/59	**Goodbye Baby** . . . Jack Scott
33/64	**Goodbye Baby (Baby Goodbye)** . . . Solomon Burke
3/61	**Goodbye Cruel World** . . . James Darren
15/78	**Goodbye Girl** . . . David Gates
33/86	**Goodbye Is Forever** . . . Arcadia
11/59	**Goodbye Jimmy, Goodbye** . . . Kathy Linden
31/68	**Goodbye My Love** . . . James Brown
15/79	**Goodbye Stranger** . . . Supertramp
7/72	**Goodbye To Love** . . . Carpenters
2/73	**Goodbye Yellow Brick Road** . . . Elton John
21/65	**Goodnight** . . . Roy Orbison
	Goodnight My Love
32/57	McGuire Sisters
32/63	Fleetwoods
27/69	Paul Anka
5/79	**Goodnight Tonight** . . . Wings
20/57	**Goody Goody** . . . Frankie Lymon & The Teenagers
37/68	**Goody Goody Gumdrops** . . . 1910 Fruitgum Co.
12/83	**Goody Two Shoes** . . . Adam Ant

POS/YR	RECORD TITLE/ARTIST
10/85	**Goonies 'R' Good Enough** . . . Cyndi Lauper
24/60	**Got A Girl** . . . Four Preps
10/84	**Got A Hold On Me** . . . Christine McVie
39/58	**Got A Match?** . . . Daddy-O's
1/88	**Got My Mind Set On You** . . . George Harrison
12/79	**Got To Be Real** . . . Cheryl Lynn
4/71	**Got To Be There** . . . Michael Jackson
	Got To Get You Into My Life
7/76	Beatles
9/78	Earth, Wind & Fire
22/65	**Got To Get You Off My Mind** . . . Solomon Burke
1/77	**Got To Give It Up** . . . Marvin Gaye
21/70	**Gotta Hold On To This Feeling** . . . Jr. Walker & The All Stars
24/79	**Gotta Serve Somebody** . . . Bob Dylan
4/59	**Gotta Travel On** . . . Billy Grammer
	Graduation Day
16/56	Rover Boys
17/56	Four Freshmen
34/61	**Graduation Song...Pomp And Circumstance** . . . Adrian Kimberly
39/59	**Graduation's Here** . . . Fleetwoods
17/63	**Grass Is Greener** . . . Brenda Lee
9/62	**Gravy (For My Mashed Potatoes)** . . . Dee Dee Sharp
	Grazing In The Grass
1/68	Hugh Masekela
3/69	Friends Of Distinction
1/78	**Grease** . . . Frankie Valli
20/66	**Great Airplane Strike** . . . Paul Revere & The Raiders
2/58	**Great Balls Of Fire** . . . Jerry Lee Lewis
	Great Imposter ..see: (He's) The
1/56	**Great Pretender** . . . Platters
	Greatest American Hero ..see: Theme From
34/62	**Greatest Hurt** . . . Jackie Wilson
	Greatest Love Of All
24/77	George Benson
1/86	Whitney Houston
	Green Berets ..see: Ballad Of
1/56	**Green Door** . . . Jim Lowe
3/70	**Green-Eyed Lady** . . . Sugarloaf
8/66	**Green Grass** . . . Gary Lewis & The Playboys
14/63	**Green, Green** . . . New Christy Minstrels

POS/YR	RECORD TITLE/ARTIST
11/67	**Green, Green Grass Of Home** . . . Tom Jones
39/68	**Green Light** . . . American Breed
3/62	**Green Onions** . . . Booker T. & The MG's
2/69	**Green River** . . . Creedence Clearwater Revival
1/68	**Green Tambourine** . . . Lemon Pipers
21/63	**Greenback Dollar** . . . Kingston Trio
2/60	**Greenfields** . . . Brothers Four
7/78	**Groove Line** . . . Heatwave
6/71	**Groove Me** . . . King Floyd
	Groovin'
1/67	Rascals
21/67	Booker T. & The MG's
30/69	**Groovy Grubworm** . . . Harlow Wilcox
	Groovy Kind Of Love
2/66	Mindbenders
1/88	Phil Collins
12/70	**Groovy Situation** . . . Gene Chandler
14/76	**Grow Some Funk Of Your Own** . . . Elton John
9/66	**Guantanamera** . . . Sandpipers
11/58	**Guess Things Happen That Way** . . . Johnny Cash
31/59	**Guess Who** . . . Jesse Belvin
3/81	**Guilty** . . . Barbra Streisand & Barry Gibb
5/59	**Guitar Boogie Shuffle** . . . Virtues
11/72	**Guitar Man** . . . Bread
28/81	**Guitar Man** . . . Elvis Presley
	Guitar Man ..see: (Dance With The)
10/55	**Gum Drop** . . . Crew-Cuts
12/82	**Gypsy** . . . Fleetwood Mac
24/63	**Gypsy Cried** . . . Lou Christie
8/73	**Gypsy Man** . . . War
	Gypsy Woman
20/61	Impressions
3/70	Brian Hyland
1/71	**Gypsys, Tramps & Thieves** . . . Cher

H

POS/YR	RECORD TITLE/ARTIST
2/69	**Hair** . . . Cowsills
22/66	**Hair On My Chinny Chin Chin** . . . Sam The Sham & The Pharoahs
1/73	**Half-Breed** . . . Cher
12/63	**Half Heaven - Half Heartache** . . . Gene Pitney
15/79	**Half The Way** . . . Crystal Gayle
	Halfway To Paradise
39/61	Tony Orlando
23/68	Bobby Vinton
33/71	**Hallelujah** . . . Sweathog
28/73	**Hallelujah Day** . . . Jackson 5
	Hand Jive ..see: Willie And The Hand Jive
17/70	**Hand Me Down World** . . . Guess Who
19/83	**Hand To Hold On To** . . . John Cougar
2/88	**Hands To Heaven** . . . Breathe
	Handy Man
2/60	Jimmy Jones
22/64	Del Shannon
4/77	James Taylor
9/69	**Hang 'Em High** . . . Booker T. & The MG's
20/82	**Hang Fire** . . . Rolling Stones
8/74	**Hang On In There Baby** . . . Johnny Bristol
	Hang On Sloopy
26/64	Vibrations (My Girl)
1/65	McCoys
11/65	Ramsey Lewis Trio
24/58	**Hang Up My Rock And Roll Shoes** . . . Chuck Willis
	Hangin' On ..see: (You Keep Me)
35/86	**Hanging On A Heart Attack** . . . Device
38/59	**Hanging Tree** . . . Marty Robbins
1/66	**Hanky Panky** . . . Tommy James & The Shondells
	Happening
1/67	Supremes
32/67	Herb Alpert
30/66	**Happenings Ten Years Time Ago** . . . Yardbirds
11/72	**Happiest Girl In The Whole U.S.A.** . . . Donna Fargo
30/79	**Happiness** . . . Pointer Sisters
35/74	**Happiness Is Just Around The Bend** . . . Main Ingredient
	Happiness Street
20/56	Georgia Gibbs
38/56	Tony Bennett
20/87	**Happy** . . . Surface
22/72	**Happy** . . . Rolling Stones
16/78	**Happy Anniversary** . . . Little River Band

POS/YR	RECORD TITLE/ARTIST
30/61	**Happy Birthday Blues** . . . Kathy Young with The Innocents
6/62	**Happy Birthday, Sweet Sixteen** . . . Neil Sedaka
5/76	**Happy Days** . . . Pratt & McClain
10/60	**Happy-Go-Lucky-Me** . . . Paul Evans
5/57	**Happy, Happy Birthday Baby** . . . Tune Weavers
22/69	**Happy Heart** . . . Andy Williams
24/67	**Happy Jack** . . . Who
19/76	**Happy Music** . . . Blackbyrds
1/59	**Happy Organ** . . . Dave "Baby" Cortez
40/75	**Happy People** . . . Temptations
34/59	**Happy Reindeer** . . . Dancer, Prancer & Nervous
25/68	**Happy Song (Dum-Dum)** . . . Otis Redding
27/66	**Happy Summer Days** . . . Ronnie Dove
1/67	**Happy Together** . . . Turtles
6/56	**Happy Whistler** . . . Don Robertson
8/60	**Harbor Lights** . . . Platters
	Hard Day's Night
1/64	Beatles
29/66	Ramsey Lewis
3/84	**Hard Habit To Break** . . . Chicago
1/58	**Hard Headed Woman** . . . Elvis Presley
15/77	**Hard Luck Woman** . . . Kiss
30/77	**Hard Rock Cafe** . . . Carole King
4/55	**Hard To Get** . . . Gisele MacKenzie
7/81	**Hard To Say** . . . Dan Fogelberg
1/82	**Hard To Say I'm Sorry** . . . Chicago
3/82	**Harden My Heart** . . . Quarterflash
39/66	**Harlem Nocturne** . . . Viscounts
5/86	**Harlem Shuffle** . . . Rolling Stones
1/68	**Harper Valley P.T.A.** . . . Jeannie C. Riley
31/73	**Harry Hippie** . . . Bobby Womack
17/63	**Harry The Hairy Ape** . . . Ray Stevens
13/75	**Harry Truman** . . . Chicago
5/61	**Hats Off To Larry** . . . Del Shannon
11/64	**Haunted House** . . . Gene Simmons
31/62	**Have A Good Time** . . . Sue Thompson
5/64	**Have I The Right?** . . . Honeycombs
29/57	**Have I Told You Lately That I Love You?** . . . Ricky Nelson
8/71	**Have You Ever Seen The Rain** . . . Creedence Clearwater Revival
18/63	**Have You Heard** . . . Duprees

POS/YR	RECORD TITLE/ARTIST
24/65	**Have You Looked Into Your Heart** . . . Jerry Vale
1/75	**Have You Never Been Mellow** . . . Olivia Newton-John
3/71	**Have You Seen Her** . . . Chi-Lites
9/66	**Have You Seen Your Mother, Baby, Standing In The Shadow?** . . . Rolling Stones
14/74	**Haven't Got Time For The Pain** . . . Carly Simon
26/79	**Haven't Stopped Dancing Yet** . . . Gonzalez
17/62	**Having A Party** . . . Sam Cooke
	Having My Baby ..see: (You're)
4/69	**Hawaii Five-O** . . . Ventures
33/65	**Hawaii Tattoo** . . . Waikikis
11/59	**Hawaiian Wedding Song** . . . Andy Williams
	Hazy Shade Of Winter
13/66	Simon & Garfunkel
2/88	Bangles
	He
4/55	Al Hibbler
10/55	McGuire Sisters
18/66	Righteous Brothers
	He Ain't Heavy, He's My Brother
7/70	Hollies
20/70	Neil Diamond
33/81	**He Can't Love You** . . . Michael Stanley Band
	He Don't Love You (Like I Love You)
7/60	Jerry Butler
1/75	Dawn
34/62	**He Knows I Love Him Too Much** . . . Paris Sisters
	He Will Break Your Heart ..see: He Don't Love You
	He'll Have To Go (Stay)
2/60	Jim Reeves
4/60	Jeanne Black
25/86	**He'll Never Love You (Like I Do)** . . . Freddie Jackson
36/76	**He's A Friend** . . . Eddie Kendricks
30/81	**He's A Liar** . . . Bee Gees
1/62	**He's A Rebel** . . . Crystals
1/58	**He's Got The Whole World (In His Hands)** . . . Laurie London
16/57	**He's Mine** . . . Platters
14/61	**(He's My) Dreamboat** . . . Connie Francis
1/63	**He's So Fine** . . . Chiffons

POS/YR	RECORD TITLE/ARTIST
3/80	**He's So Shy** . . . Pointer Sisters
11/63	**He's Sure The Boy I Love** . . . Crystals
30/61	**(He's) The Great Impostor** . . . Fleetwoods
9/79	**He's The Greatest Dancer** . . . Sister Sledge
14/79	**Head Games** . . . Foreigner
3/85	**Head Over Heels** . . . Tears For Fears
11/84	**Head Over Heels** . . . Go-Go's
1/87	**Head To Toe** . . . Lisa Lisa & Cult Jam
35/80	**Headed For A Fall** . . . Firefall
14/77	**Heard It In A Love Song** . . . Marshall Tucker Band
	Heart
6/55	Eddie Fisher
13/55	Four Aces
4/87	**Heart And Soul** . . . T'Pau
8/83	**Heart And Soul** . . . Huey Lewis & The News
	Heart And Soul
18/61	Cleftones
25/61	Jan & Dean
3/82	**Heart Attack** . . . Olivia Newton-John
9/65	**Heart Full Of Soul** . . . Yardbirds
21/80	**Heart Hotels** . . . Dan Fogelberg
15/62	**Heart In Hand** . . . Brenda Lee
24/81	**Heart Like A Wheel** . . . Steve Miller Band
1/79	**Heart Of Glass** . . . Blondie
1/72	**Heart Of Gold** . . . Neil Young
35/88	**Heart Of Mine** . . . Boz Scaggs
6/84	**Heart Of Rock & Roll** . . . Huey Lewis & The News
19/65	**Heart Of Stone** . . . Rolling Stones
20/79	**Heart Of The Night** . . . Poco
25/83	**Heart Of The Night** . . . Juice Newton
15/83	**Heart To Heart** . . . Kenny Loggins
1/79	**Heartache Tonight** . . . Eagles
7/61	**Heartaches** . . . Marcels
	Heartaches By The Number
1/59	Guy Mitchell
35/65	Johnny Tillotson
5/86	**Heartbeat** . . . Don Johnson
3/73	**Heartbeat - It's A Lovebeat** . . . DeFranco Family
26/87	**Heartbreak Beat** . . . Psychedelic Furs
1/56	**Heartbreak Hotel** . . . Elvis Presley
22/81	**Heartbreak Hotel** . . . Jacksons
38/60	**Heartbreak (It's Hurtin' Me)** . . . Little Willie John

POS/YR	RECORD TITLE/ARTIST
39/74	**Heartbreak Kid** . . . Bo Donaldson & The Heywoods
10/83	**Heartbreaker** . . . Dionne Warwick
23/80	**Heartbreaker** . . . Pat Benatar
37/78	**Heartbreaker** . . . Dolly Parton
	(Heartbreaker) ..see: Doo Doo Doo Doo
24/78	**Heartless** . . . Heart
5/82	**Heartlight** . . . Neil Diamond
8/81	**Hearts** . . . Marty Balin
	Hearts Of Stone
1/55	Fontane Sisters
15/55	Charms
20/61	Bill Black's Combo
37/73	Blue Ridge Rangers
19/81	**Hearts On Fire** . . . Randy Meisner
26/87	**Hearts On Fire** . . . Bryan Adams
2/85	**Heat Is On** . . . Glenn Frey
4/82	**Heat Of The Moment** . . . Asia
6/87	**Heat Of The Night** . . . Bryan Adams
	Heat Wave
4/63	Martha & The Vandellas
5/75	Linda Ronstadt
29/69	**Heather Honey** . . . Tommy Roe
1/85	**Heaven** . . . Bryan Adams
39/69	**Heaven** . . . Rascals
9/70	**Heaven Help Us All** . . . Stevie Wonder
12/86	**Heaven In Your Eyes** . . . Loverboy
1/87	**Heaven Is A Place On Earth** . . . Belinda Carlisle
4/79	**Heaven Knows** . . . Donna Summer
24/69	**Heaven Knows** . . . Grass Roots
15/76	**Heaven Must Be Missing An Angel** . . . Tavares
11/79	**Heaven Must Have Sent You** . . . Bonnie Pointer
39/56	**Heaven On Earth** . . . Platters
6/77	**Heaven On The 7th Floor** . . . Paul Nicholas
40/59	**Heavenly Lover** . . . Teresa Brewer
27/71	**Heavy Makes You Happy (Sha-Na-Boom Boom)** . . . Staple Singers
33/70	**Heed The Call** . . . Kenny Rogers
10/74	**Helen Wheels** . . . Paul McCartney
1/84	**Hello** . . . Lionel Richie
6/81	**Hello Again** . . . Neil Diamond
20/84	**Hello Again** . . . Cars
1/64	**Hello, Dolly!** . . . Louis Armstrong
1/67	**Hello Goodbye** . . . Beatles

POS/YR	RECORD TITLE/ARTIST
26/63	**Hello Heartache, Goodbye Love** . . . Little Peggy March
26/67	**Hello Hello** . . . Sopwith "Camel"
35/73	**Hello Hurray** . . . Alice Cooper
1/68	**Hello, I Love You** . . . Doors
5/73	**Hello It's Me** . . . Todd Rundgren
9/61	**Hello Mary Lou** . . . Ricky Nelson
2/63	**Hello Mudduh, Hello Fadduh! (A Letter From Camp)** . . . Allan Sherman
24/76	**Hello Old Friend** . . . Eric Clapton
	Hello Stranger
3/63	Barbara Lewis
15/77	Yvonne Elliman
12/61	**Hello Walls** . . . Faron Young
23/60	**Hello Young Lovers** . . . Paul Anka
1/65	**Help!** . . . Beatles
14/77	**Help Is On Its Way** . . . Little River Band
7/74	**Help Me** . . . Joni Mitchell
	Help Me Girl
29/66	Animals
37/66	Outsiders
	Help Me Make It Through The Night
8/71	Sammi Smith
33/72	Gladys Knight & The Pips
	Help Me, Rhonda
1/65	Beach Boys
22/75	Johnny Rivers
35/68	**Help Yourself** . . . Tom Jones
6/62	**Her Royal Majesty** . . . James Darren
11/81	**Her Town Too** . . . James Taylor & J.D. Souther
23/77	**Here Come Those Tears Again** . . . Jackson Browne
13/67	**Here Comes My Baby** . . . Tremeloes
14/59	**Here Comes Summer** . . . Jerry Keller
15/71	**Here Comes That Rainy Day Feeling Again** . . . Fortunes
	Here Comes The Judge
8/68	Shorty Long
19/68	Pigmeat Markham
24/65	**Here Comes The Night** . . . Them
4/84	**Here Comes The Rain Again** . . . Eurythmics
16/71	**Here Comes The Sun** . . . Richie Havens
10/73	**Here I Am (Come And Take Me)** . . . Al Green
5/81	**Here I Am (Just When I Thought I Was Over You)** . . . Air Supply
1/87	**Here I Go Again** . . . Whitesnake

POS/YR	RECORD TITLE/ARTIST
37/69	**Here I Go Again** . . . Miracles
27/65	**Here It Comes Again** . . . Fortunes
15/67	**Here We Go Again** . . . Ray Charles
20/88	**Here With Me** . . . REO Speedwagon
3/78	**Here You Come Again** . . . Dolly Parton
12/67	**Heroes And Villains** . . . Beach Boys
1/62	**Hey! Baby** . . . Bruce Channel
12/67	**Hey Baby (They're Playing Our Song)** . . . Buckinghams
19/72	**Hey Big Brother** . . . Rare Earth
23/64	**Hey, Bobba Needle** . . . Chubby Checker
7/78	**Hey Deanie** . . . Shaun Cassidy
	Hey, Girl
10/63	Freddie Scott
35/68	Bobby Vee (medley)
9/72	Donny Osmond
35/73	**Hey Girl (I Like Your Style)** . . . Temptations
29/64	**Hey Harmonica Man** . . . Stevie Wonder
3/57	**Hey! Jealous Lover** . . . Frank Sinatra
32/64	**Hey Jean, Hey Dean** . . . Dean & Jean
31/66	**Hey Joe** . . . Leaves
	Hey Jude
1/68	Beatles
23/69	Wilson Pickett
35/70	**Hey Lawdy Mama** . . . Steppenwolf
31/67	**Hey, Leroy, Your Mama's Callin' You** . . . Jimmy Castor
20/62	**Hey, Let's Twist** . . . Joey Dee
4/64	**Hey Little Cobra** . . . Rip Chords
13/63	**Hey Little Girl** . . . Major Lance
20/59	**Hey Little Girl** . . . Dee Clark
29/57	**Hey! Little Girl** . . . Techniques
38/62	**Hey! Little Girl** . . . Del Shannon
12/55	**Hey, Mr. Banjo** . . . Sunnysiders
24/70	**Hey, Mister Sun** . . . Bobby Sherman
10/81	**Hey Nineteen** . . . Steely Dan
1/63	**Hey Paula** . . . Paul & Paula
	Hey There Lonely Girl (Boy)
27/63	Ruby & The Romantics
2/70	Eddie Holman
31/80	Robert John
16/68	**Hey, Western Union Man** . . . Jerry Butler
1/75	**(Hey Won't You Play) Another Somebody Done Somebody Wrong Song** . . . B.J. Thomas
21/75	**Hey You** . . . Bachman-Turner Overdrive
14/70	**Hi-De-Ho** . . . Blood, Sweat & Tears

POS/YR	RECORD TITLE/ARTIST
	Hi-Heel Sneakers
11/64	Tommy Tucker
25/68	Jose Feliciano
10/73	**Hi, Hi, Hi** . . . Wings
33/62	**Hide & Go Seek** . . . Bunker Hill
29/61	**Hide Away** . . . Freddy King
20/62	**Hide 'Nor Hair** . . . Ray Charles
21/58	**Hideaway** . . . Four Esquires
	High-Heel ..see: Hi-Heel
30/59	**High Hopes** . . . Frank Sinatra
8/85	**High On You** . . . Survivor
21/58	**High School Confidential** . . . Jerry Lee Lewis
17/77	**High School Dance** . . . Sylvers
28/59	**High School U.S.A.** . . . Tommy Facenda
37/58	**High Sign** . . . Diamonds
22/71	**High Time We Went** . . . Joe Cocker
	Higher & Higher ..see: (Your Love Keeps Lifting Me)
4/73	**Higher Ground** . . . Stevie Wonder
1/86	**Higher Love** . . . Steve Winwood
37/74	**Higher Plane** . . . Kool & The Gang
26/79	**Highway Song** . . . Blackfoot
14/75	**Hijack** . . . Herbie Mann
	Hill Street Blues ..see: Theme From
6/80	**Him** . . . Rupert Holmes
5/67	**Him Or Me - What's It Gonna Be?** . . . Paul Revere & The Raiders
31/68	**Hip City** . . . Jr. Walker & The All Stars
37/67	**Hip Hug-Her** . . . Booker T. & The MG's
3/86	**Hip To Be Square** . . . Huey Lewis & The News
24/64	**Hippy Hippy Shake** . . . Swinging Blue Jeans
	His Latest Flame ..see: Marie's The Name
39/66	**History Repeats Itself** . . . Buddy Starcher
9/80	**Hit Me With Your Best Shot** . . . Pat Benatar
	(Hit Record) ..see: Overnight Sensation
	Hit The Road Jack
1/61	Ray Charles
40/76	Stampeders
30/63	**Hitch Hike** . . . Marvin Gaye
34/68	**Hitch It To The Horse** . . . Fantastic Johnny C
5/70	**Hitchin' A Ride** . . . Vanity Fare
9/73	**Hocus Pocus** . . . Focus
35/76	**Hold Back The Night** . . . Trammps

POS/YR	RECORD TITLE/ARTIST
14/72	**Hold Her Tight** . . . Osmonds
4/82	**Hold Me** . . . Fleetwood Mac
3/84	**Hold Me Now** . . . Thompson Twins
8/65	**Hold Me, Thrill Me, Kiss Me** . . . Mel Carter
5/68	**Hold Me Tight** . . . Johnny Nash
40/83	**Hold Me 'Til The Mornin' Comes** . . . Paul Anka
15/82	**Hold On** . . . Santana
18/79	**Hold On** . . . Ian Gomm
38/79	**Hold On** . . . Triumph
40/80	**Hold On** . . . Kansas
21/66	**Hold On! I'm A Comin'** . . . Sam & Dave
27/81	**Hold On Loosely** . . . 38 Special
10/81	**Hold On Tight** . . . ELO
10/80	**Hold On To My Love** . . . Jimmy Ruffin
1/88	**Hold On To The Nights** . . . Richard Marx
5/79	**Hold The Line** . . . Toto
5/65	**Hold What You've Got** . . . Joe Tex
5/72	**Hold Your Head Up** . . . Argent
37/82	**Holdin' On** . . . Tane Cain
17/75	**Holdin' On To Yesterday** . . . Ambrosia
1/86	**Holding Back The Years** . . . Simply Red
11/89	**Holding On** . . . Steve Winwood
34/84	**Holding Out For A Hero** . . . Bonnie Tyler
16/67	**Holiday** . . . Bee Gees
16/84	**Holiday** . . . Madonna
29/87	**Holiday** . . . Other Ones
6/69	**Holly Holy** . . . Neil Diamond
32/77	**Hollywood** . . . Rufus Featuring Chaka Khan
12/78	**Hollywood Nights** . . . Bob Seger
6/74	**Hollywood Swinging** . . . Kool & The Gang
23/66	**Holy Cow** . . . Lee Dorsey
34/67	**Homburg** . . . Procol Harum
28/79	**Home And Dry** . . . Gerry Rafferty
25/65	**Home Of The Brave** . . . Jody Miller
5/66	**Homeward Bound** . . . Simon & Garfunkel
28/60	**Honest I Do** . . . Innocents
32/57	**Honest I Do** . . . Jimmy Reed
23/88	**Honestly** . . . Stryper
24/79	**Honesty** . . . Billy Joel
1/68	**Honey** . . . Bobby Goldsboro
6/55	**Honey-Babe** . . . Art Mooney
11/67	**Honey Chile** . . . Martha & The Vandellas
19/70	**Honey Come Back** . . . Glen Campbell

POS/YR	RECORD TITLE/ARTIST
27/74	**Honey, Honey** . . . Abba
1/57	**Honeycomb** . . . Jimmie Rodgers
19/87	**Honeythief** . . . Hipsway
8/72	**Honky Cat** . . . Elton John
2/56	**Honky Tonk** . . . Bill Doggett
1/69	**Honky Tonk Women** . . . Rolling Stones
11/63	**Honolulu Lulu** . . . Jan & Dean
23/61	**Hoochi Coochi Coo** . . . Hank Ballard
17/64	**Hooka Tooka** . . . Chubby Checker
	Hooked On A Feeling
5/69	B.J. Thomas
1/74	Blue Swede
10/82	**Hooked On Classics** . . . Royal Philharmonic Orchestra
31/82	**Hooked On Swing (medley)** . . . Larry Elgart
6/66	**Hooray For Hazel** . . . Tommy Roe
38/63	**Hootenanny** . . . Glencoves
36/82	**Hope You Love Me Like You Say You Do** . . . Huey Lewis & The News
13/63	**Hopeless** . . . Andy Williams
3/78	**Hopelessly Devoted To You** . . . Olivia Newton-John
2/68	**Horse, The** . . . Cliff Nobles & Co.
1/72	**Horse With No Name** . . . America
3/78	**Hot Blooded** . . . Foreigner
1/78	**Hot Child In The City** . . . Nick Gilder
1/56	**Hot Diggity (Dog Ziggity Boom)** . . . Perry Como
2/69	**Hot Fun In The Summertime** . . . Sly & The Family Stone
11/83	**Hot Girls In Love** . . . Loverboy
23/82	**Hot In The City** . . . Billy Idol
28/78	**Hot Legs** . . . Rod Stewart
5/77	**Hot Line** . . . Sylvers
31/78	**Hot Love, Cold World** . . . Bob Welch
21/79	**Hot Number** . . . Foxy
15/71	**Hot Pants** . . . James Brown
11/63	**Hot Pastrami** . . . Dartells
36/63	**Hot Pastrami With Mashed Potatoes** . . . Joey Dee
15/80	**Hot Rod Hearts** . . . Robbie Dupree
	Hot Rod Lincoln
26/60	Johnny Bond
33/60	Charlie Ryan
9/72	Commander Cody
14/69	**Hot Smoke & Sasafrass** . . . Bubble Puppy
1/79	**Hot Stuff** . . . Donna Summer

POS/YR	RECORD TITLE/ARTIST
18/79	**Hot Summer Nights** . . . Night
1/77	**Hotel California** . . . Eagles
3/63	**Hotel Happiness** . . . Brook Benton
F/56	**Hound Dog** . . . Elvis Presley
9/59	**Hound Dog Man** . . . Fabian
15/87	**Hourglass** . . . Squeeze
9/55	**House Of Blue Lights** . . . Chuck Miller
	House Of The Rising Sun
1/64	Animals
7/70	Frijid Pink
6/68	**House That Jack Built** . . . Aretha Franklin
16/56	**House With Love In It** . . . Four Lads
21/65	**Houston** . . . Dean Martin
33/60	**How About That** . . . Dee Clark
12/83	**How Am I Supposed To Live Without You** . . . Laura Branigan
22/58	**How Are Ya' Fixed For Love?** . . . Frank Sinatra & Keely Smith
12/81	**How 'Bout Us** . . . Champaign
	How Can I Be Sure
4/67	Young Rascals
25/72	David Cassidy
3/88	**How Can I Fall?** . . . Breathe
22/73	**How Can I Tell Her** . . . Lobo
1/71	**How Can You Mend A Broken Heart** . . . Bee Gees
1/77	**How Deep Is Your Love** . . . Bee Gees
10/80	**How Do I Make You** . . . Linda Ronstadt
22/80	**How Do I Survive** . . . Amy Holland
27/67	**How Do You Catch A Girl** . . . Sam The Sham & The Pharoahs
8/72	**How Do You Do?** . . . Mouth & MacNeal
9/64	**How Do You Do It?** . . . Gerry & The Pacemakers
30/80	**How Does It Feel To Be Back** . . . Daryl Hall & John Oates
7/66	**How Does That Grab You, Darlin'?** . . . Nancy Sinatra
	How Glad I Am ..see: (You Don't Know)
	How Important Can It Be?
2/55	Joni James
12/55	Sarah Vaughan
13/56	**(How Little It Matters) How Little We Know** . . . Frank Sinatra
3/75	**How Long** . . . Ace
20/75	**How Long (Betcha' Got A Chick On The Side)** . . . Pointer Sisters

POS/YR	RECORD TITLE/ARTIST
27/83	**How Many Times Can We Say Goodbye** . . . Dionne Warwick & Luther Vandross
3/78	**How Much I Feel** . . . Ambrosia
17/77	**How Much Love** . . . Leo Sayer
	How Sweet It Is (To Be Loved By You)
6/65	Marvin Gaye
18/66	Jr. Walker & The All Stars
5/75	James Taylor
11/58	**How The Time Flies** . . . Jerry Wallace
20/86	**(How To Be A) Millionaire** . . . ABC
1/86	**How Will I Know** . . . Whitney Houston
12/78	**How You Gonna See Me Now** . . . Alice Cooper
21/68	**How'd We Ever Get This Way** . . . Andy Kim
14/60	**Hucklebuck, The** . . . Chubby Checker
	Hula Hoop Song
32/58	Georgia Gibbs
38/58	Teresa Brewer
9/57	**Hula Love** . . . Buddy Knox
25/62	**Hully Gully Baby** . . . Dovells
1/86	**Human** . . . Human League
7/83	**Human Nature** . . . Michael Jackson
18/83	**Human Touch** . . . Rick Springfield
	Hummingbird
7/55	Les Paul & Mary Ford
17/55	Frankie Laine
20/73	**Hummingbird** . . . Seals & Crofts
3/61	**Hundred Pounds Of Clay** . . . Gene McDaniels
6/66	**Hungry** . . . Paul Revere & The Raiders
4/88	**Hungry Eyes** . . . Eric Carmen
27/65	**Hungry For Love** . . . San Remo Golden Strings
5/80	**Hungry Heart** . . . Bruce Springsteen
3/83	**Hungry Like The Wolf** . . . Duran Duran
13/67	**Hunter Gets Captured By The Game** . . . Marvelettes
5/68	**Hurdy Gurdy Man** . . . Donovan
33/76	**Hurricane** . . . Bob Dylan
	Hurt
4/61	Timi Yuro
28/76	Elvis Presley
31/73	**Hurt, The** . . . Cat Stevens
	Hurt So Bad
10/65	Little Anthony & The Imperials
12/69	Lettermen
8/80	Linda Ronstadt

POS/YR	RECORD TITLE/ARTIST
	Hurt Yourself ..see: (You're Gonna)
2/72	**Hurting Each Other** . . . Carpenters
2/82	**Hurts So Good** . . . John Cougar
24/73	**Hurts So Good** . . . Millie Jackson
26/66	**Husbands And Wives** . . . Roger Miller
4/68	**Hush** . . . Deep Purple
8/65	**Hush, Hush, Sweet Charlotte** . . . Patti Page
20/59	**Hushabye** . . . Mystics
1/75	**Hustle, The** . . . Van McCoy
33/86	**Hyperactive** . . . Robert Palmer
36/87	**Hypnotize Me** . . . Wang Chung
21/67	**Hypnotized** . . . Linda Jones
10/88	**Hysteria** . . . Def Leppard
26/82	**I.G.Y. (What A Beautiful World)** . . . Donald Fagen
35/76	**I.O.U.** . . . Jimmy Dean
25/63	**I Adore Him** . . . Angels
11/81	**I Ain't Gonna Stand For It** . . . Stevie Wonder
12/85	**I Ain't Got Nobody (medley)** . . . David Lee Roth
36/71	**I Ain't Got Time Anymore** . . . Glass Bottle
24/59	**I Ain't Never** . . . Webb Pierce
1/56	**I Almost Lost My Mind** . . . Pat Boone
3/66	**I Am A Rock** . . . Simon & Garfunkel
18/86	**I Am By Your Side** . . . Corey Hart
4/71	**I Am...I Said** . . . Neil Diamond
15/75	**I Am Love** . . . Jackson 5
39/70	**I Am Somebody** . . . Johnnie Taylor
1/72	**I Am Woman** . . . Helen Reddy
8/58	**I Beg Of You** . . . Elvis Presley
15/89	**I Beg Your Pardon** . . . Kon Kan
33/64	**I Believe** . . . Bachelors
33/82	**I Believe** . . . Chilliwack
22/72	**I Believe In Music** . . . Gallery
24/80	**I Believe In You** . . . Don Williams
11/73	**I Believe In You (You Believe In Me)** . . . Johnnie Taylor

POS/YR	RECORD TITLE/ARTIST
15/75	**(I Believe) There's Nothing Stronger Than Our Love** . . . Paul Anka
27/77	**I Believe You** . . . Dorothy Moore
27/75	**I Belong To You** . . . Love Unlimited
	I Can Dance ..see: Long Tall Glasses
6/84	**I Can Dream About You** . . . Dan Hartman
24/69	**I Can Hear Music** . . . Beach Boys
1/74	**I Can Help** . . . Billy Swan
32/66	**I Can Make It With You** . . . Pozo-Seco Singers
6/65	**I Can Never Go Home Anymore** . . . Shangri-Las
1/72	**I Can See Clearly Now** . . . Johnny Nash
9/67	**I Can See For Miles** . . . Who
	(I Can See It In Your Eyes) ..see: Circle Is Small
22/69	**I Can Sing A Rainbow (medley)** . . . Dells
39/81	**I Can Take Care Of Myself** . . . Billy & The Beaters
22/68	**I Can Take Or Leave Your Loving** . . . Herman's Hermits
35/73	**I Can Understand It** . . . New Birth
26/84	**I Can't Drive 55** . . . Sammy Hagar
1/69	**I Can't Get Next To You** . . . Temptations
	(I Can't Get No) Satisfaction
1/65	Rolling Stones
31/66	Otis Redding
1/82	**I Can't Go For That (No Can Do)** . . . Daryl Hall & John Oates
34/66	**I Can't Grow Peaches On A Cherry Tree** . . . Just Us
29/76	**I Can't Hear You No More** . . . Helen Reddy
12/80	**I Can't Help It** . . . Andy Gibb & Olivia Newton-John
24/62	**I Can't Help It (If I'm Still In Love With You)** . . . Johnny Tillotson
	I Can't Help Myself
1/65	Four Tops
22/72	Donnie Elbert
40/80	Bonnie Pointer
39/60	**(I Can't Help You) I'm Falling Too** . . . Skeeter Davis *(also see: Please Help Me, I'm Falling)*
13/84	**I Can't Hold Back** . . . Survivor
31/80	**I Can't Let Go** . . . Linda Ronstadt
22/56	**I Can't Love You Enough** . . . LaVern Baker
28/69	**I Can't See Myself Leaving You** . . . Aretha Franklin

POS/YR	RECORD TITLE/ARTIST
10/81	**I Can't Stand It** . . . Eric Clapton
14/79	**I Can't Stand It No More** . . . Peter Frampton
28/68	**I Can't Stand Myself (When You Touch Me)** . . . James Brown
	I Can't Stand The Rain
38/73	Ann Peebles
18/78	Eruption
7/63	**I Can't Stay Mad At You** . . . Skeeter Davis
9/68	**I Can't Stop Dancing** . . . Archie Bell
1/62	**I Can't Stop Loving You** . . . Ray Charles
35/64	**I Can't Stop Talking About You** . . . Steve & Eydie
8/80	**I Can't Tell You Why** . . . Eagles
37/68	**I Can't Turn You Loose** . . . Chambers Brothers
3/86	**I Can't Wait** . . . Nu Shooz
16/86	**I Can't Wait** . . . Stevie Nicks
32/66	**I Chose To Sing The Blues** . . . Ray Charles
20/56	**I Could Have Danced All Night** . . . Sylvia Syms
13/68	**I Could Never Love Another (After Loving You)** . . . Temptations
18/81	**I Could Never Miss You (More Than I Do)** . . . Lulu
10/88	**I Could Never Take The Place Of Your Man** . . . Prince
9/66	**I Couldn't Live Without Your Love** . . . Petula Clark
32/83	**I Couldn't Say No** . . . Robert Ellis Orrall with Carlene Carter
17/61	**I Count The Tears** . . . Drifters
6/59	**I Cried A Tear** . . . LaVern Baker
	I Didn't Get To Sleep At All ..see: (Last Night)
35/72	**I Didn't Know I Loved You (Till I Saw You Rock And Roll)** . . . Gary Glitter
2/86	**I Didn't Mean To Turn You On** . . . Robert Palmer
9/67	**I Dig Rock And Roll Music** . . . Peter, Paul & Mary
	I Do
37/65	Marvelows
24/83	J. Geils Band
15/76	**I Do, I Do, I Do, I Do, I Do** . . . Abba
	I Do Love You
26/65	Billy Stewart
20/79	GQ
	(I Do The) ..see: Shimmy Shimmy

POS/YR	RECORD TITLE/ARTIST
29/84	**I Do'wanna Know** . . . REO Speedwagon
23/86	**I Do What I Do...** . . . John Taylor
20/87	**I Do You** . . . Jets
18/71	**I Don't Blame You At All** . . . Miracles
39/83	**I Don't Care Anymore** . . . Phil Collins
	I Don't Know How To Love Him
13/71	Helen Reddy
28/71	Yvonne Elliman
23/79	**I Don't Know If It's Right** . . . Evelyn "Champagne" King
35/82	**I Don't Know Where To Start** . . . Eddie Rabbitt
12/61	**I Don't Know Why** . . . Linda Scott *(also see: But I Do)*
39/69	**I Don't Know Why** . . . Stevie Wonder
8/75	**I Don't Like To Sleep Alone** . . . Paul Anka
38/87	**I Don't Mind At All** . . . Bourgeois Tagg
3/81	**I Don't Need You** . . . Kenny Rogers
37/64	**I Don't Wanna Be A Loser** . . . Lesley Gore
2/88	**I Don't Wanna Go On With You Like That** . . . Elton John
3/88	**I Don't Wanna Live Without Your Love** . . . Chicago
35/65	**I Don't Wanna Lose You Baby** . . . Chad & Jeremy
20/69	**I Don't Want Nobody To Give Me Nothing** . . . James Brown
31/88	**I Don't Want To Be A Hero** . . . Johnny Hates Jazz
22/64	**I Don't Want To Be Hurt Anymore** . . . Nat King Cole
	I Don't Want To Be Right ..see: (If Loving You Is Wrong)
36/61	**I Don't Want To Cry** . . . Chuck Jackson
17/71	**I Don't Want To Do Wrong** . . . Gladys Knight & The Pips
5/88	**I Don't Want To Live Without You** . . . Foreigner
34/64	**I Don't Want To See Tomorrow** . . . Nat King Cole
16/64	**I Don't Want To See You Again** . . . Peter & Gordon
39/65	**I Don't Want To Spoil The Party** . . . Beatles
33/61	**I Don't Want To Take A Chance** . . . Mary Wells
36/80	**I Don't Want To Walk Without You** . . . Barry Manilow
4/88	**I Don't Want Your Love** . . . Duranduran

POS/YR	RECORD TITLE/ARTIST
9/57	**I Dreamed** . . . Betty Johnson
20/61	**I Dreamed Of A Hill-Billy Heaven** . . . Tex Ritter
12/61	**I Fall To Pieces** . . . Patsy Cline
21/74	**I Feel A Song (In My Heart)** . . . Gladys Knight & The Pips
1/64	**I Feel Fine** . . . Beatles
3/84	**I Feel For You** . . . Chaka Khan
38/57	**I Feel Good** . . . Shirley & Lee
F/76	**I Feel Like A Bullet (In The Gun Of Robert Ford)** . . . Elton John
6/77	**I Feel Love** . . . Donna Summer
5/61	**I Feel So Bad** . . . Elvis Presley
F/71	**I Feel The Earth Move** . . . Carole King
9/66	**I Fought The Law** . . . Bobby Fuller Four
30/65	**I Found A Girl** . . . Jan & Dean
32/67	**I Found A Love** . . . Wilson Pickett
31/82	**I Found Somebody** . . . Glenn Frey
10/88	**I Found Someone** . . . Cher
1/64	**I Get Around** . . . Beach Boys
32/82	**I Get Excited** . . . Rick Springfield
37/75	**I Get Lifted** . . . George McCrae
34/68	**I Get The Sweetest Feeling** . . . Jackie Wilson
2/88	**I Get Weak** . . . Belinda Carlisle
7/78	**I Go Crazy** . . . Paul Davis
9/65	**I Go To Pieces** . . . Peter & Gordon
10/58	**I Got A Feeling** . . . Ricky Nelson
25/69	**I Got A Line On You** . . . Spirit
10/73	**I Got A Name** . . . Jim Croce
24/59	**I Got A Wife** . . . Mark IV
20/62	**I Got A Woman** . . . Jimmy McGriff
27/73	**I Got Ants In My Pants** . . . James Brown
	I Got Life ..see: Ain't Got No
20/79	**I Got My Mind Made Up (You Can Get It Girl)** . . . Instant Funk
3/67	**I Got Rhythm** . . . Happenings
37/75	**I Got Stoned And I Missed It** . . . Jim Stafford
8/58	**I Got Stung** . . . Elvis Presley
6/68	**I Got The Feelin'** . . . James Brown
16/66	**I Got The Feelin' (Oh No No)** . . . Neil Diamond
28/63	**I Got What I Wanted** . . . Brook Benton
	I Got You Babe
1/65	Sonny & Cher
28/85	UB40 with Chrissie Hynde
3/65	**I Got You (I Feel Good)** . . . James Brown

POS/YR	RECORD TITLE/ARTIST
2/72	**I Gotcha** . . . Joe Tex
35/64	**I Gotta Dance To Keep From Crying** . . . Miracles
20/60	**I Gotta Know** . . . Elvis Presley
4/84	**I Guess That's Why They Call It The Blues** . . . Elton John
34/69	**I Guess The Lord Must Be In New York City** . . . Nilsson
17/67	**I Had A Dream** . . . Paul Revere & The Raiders
11/67	**I Had Too Much To Dream (Last Night)** . . . Electric Prunes
8/88	**I Hate Myself For Loving You** . . . Joan Jett
36/64	**I Have A Boyfriend** . . . Chiffons
1/65	**I Hear A Symphony** . . . Supremes
30/66	**I Hear Trumpets Blow** . . . Tokens
	I Hear You Knocking
2/55	Gale Storm
4/71	Dave Edmunds
4/87	**I Heard A Rumour** . . . Bananarama
	I Heard It Through The Grapevine
2/67	Gladys Knight & The Pips
1/68	Marvin Gaye
1/74	**I Honestly Love You** . . . Olivia Newton-John
1/84	**I Just Called To Say I Love You** . . . Stevie Wonder
9/70	**I Just Can't Help Believing** . . . B.J. Thomas
1/87	**I Just Can't Stop Loving You** . . . Michael Jackson with Siedah Garrett
1/87	**(I Just) Died In Your Arms** . . . Cutting Crew
17/57	**I Just Don't Know** . . . Four Lads
26/66	**I Just Don't Know What To Do With Myself** . . . Dionne Warwick
17/61	**I Just Don't Understand** . . . Ann-Margret
12/79	**I Just Fall In Love Again** . . . Anne Murray
4/78	**I Just Wanna Stop** . . . Gino Vannelli
1/77	**I Just Want To Be Your Everything** . . . Andy Gibb
7/71	**I Just Want To Celebrate** . . . Rare Earth
33/77	**I Just Want To Make Love To You** . . . Foghat
4/82	**I Keep Forgettin' (Every Time You're Near)** . . . Michael McDonald
	I Kissed You ..see: ('Til)
1/87	**I Knew You Were Waiting (For Me)** . . . Aretha Franklin & George Michael

POS/YR	RECORD TITLE/ARTIST
	I Knew You When
14/65	Billy Joe Royal
37/83	Linda Ronstadt
19/79	**I Know A Heartache When I See One** . . . Jennifer Warnes
3/65	**I Know A Place** . . . Petula Clark
	(I Know) I'm Losing You
8/66	Temptations
7/70	Rare Earth
24/71	Rod Stewart with Faces
13/83	**I Know There's Something Going On** . . . Frida
9/87	**I Know What I Like** . . . Huey Lewis & The News
3/62	**I Know (You Don't Love Me No More)** . . . Barbara George
30/88	**I Know You're Out There Somewhere** . . . Moody Blues
19/62	**I Left My Heart In San Francisco** . . . Tony Bennett
3/77	**I Like Dreamin'** . . . Kenny Nolan
17/64	**I Like It** . . . Gerry & The Pacemakers
31/83	**I Like It** . . . DeBarge
	I Like It Like That
2/61	Chris Kenner
7/65	Dave Clark Five
27/64	**I Like It Like That** . . . Miracles
25/67	**I Like The Way** . . . Tommy James & The Shondells
37/77	**I Like To Do It** . . . KC & The Sunshine Band
28/74	**I Like To Live The Love** . . . B.B. King
8/57	**I Like Your Kind Of Love** . . . Andy Williams
38/71	**I Likes To Do It** . . . People's Choice
13/88	**I Live For Your Love** . . . Natalie Cole
12/74	**I Love** . . . Tom T. Hall
1/81	**I Love A Rainy Night** . . . Eddie Rabbitt
	I Love How You Love Me
5/61	Paris Sisters
9/68	Bobby Vinton
	I Love Lucy ..see: Disco Lucy
5/76	**I Love Music** . . . O'Jays
21/57	**I Love My Baby (My Baby Loves Me)** . . . Jill Corey
24/74	**I Love My Friend** . . . Charlie Rich
1/82	**I Love Rock 'N Roll** . . . Joan Jett
5/78	**I Love The Nightlife (Disco 'Round)** . . . Alicia Bridges

POS/YR	RECORD TITLE/ARTIST
9/60	**I Love The Way You Love** . . . Marv Johnson
12/81	**I Love You** . . . Climax Blues Band
14/68	**I Love You** . . . People
22/62	**I Love You** . . . Volume's
37/78	**I Love You** . . . Donna Summer
3/63	**I Love You Because** . . . Al Martino
39/63	**(I Love You) Don't You Forget It** . . . Perry Como
30/66	**I Love You Drops** . . . Vic Dana
21/71	**I Love You For All Seasons** . . . Fuzz
17/58	**(I Love You) For Sentimental Reasons** . . . Sam Cooke
40/60	**I Love You In The Same Old Way** . . . Paul Anka
28/55	**I Love You Madly** . . . Four Coins
9/64	**I Love You More And More Every Day** . . . Al Martino
31/66	**I Love You 1000 Times** . . . Platters
38/62	**I Love You The Way You Are** . . . Bobby Vinton
37/81	**I Loved 'Em Every One** . . . T.G. Sheppard
18/59	**I Loves You, Porgy** . . . Nina Simone
10/81	**I Made It Through The Rain** . . . Barry Manilow
18/67	**I Make A Fool Of Myself** . . . Frankie Valli
37/68	**I Met Her In Church** . . . Box Tops
5/85	**I Miss You** . . . Klymaxx
	I Miss You So
34/57	Chris Connor
33/59	Paul Anka
34/65	Little Anthony & The Imperials
19/81	**I Missed Again** . . . Phil Collins
31/65	**I Must Be Seeing Things** . . . Gene Pitney
28/79	**I Need A Lover** . . . John Cougar
14/87	**I Need Love** . . . L.L. Cool J
22/66	**I Need Somebody** . . . ? & The Mysterians
25/76	**I Need To Be In Love** . . . Carpenters
9/72	**I Need You** . . . America
37/82	**I Need You** . . . Paul Carrack
36/84	**I Need You Tonight** . . . Peter Wolf
4/59	**I Need Your Love Tonight** . . . Elvis Presley
20/62	**I Need Your Lovin'** . . . Don Gardner & Dee Dee Ford
37/81	**I Need Your Lovin'** . . . Teena Marie
12/77	**I Never Cry** . . . Alice Cooper

POS/YR	RECORD TITLE/ARTIST
9/67	**I Never Loved A Man (The Way I Love You)** . . . Aretha Franklin
	I Only Have Eyes For You
11/59	Flamingos
18/75	Art Garfunkel
22/56	**I Only Know I Love You** . . . Four Aces
	I Only Want To Be With You
12/64	Dusty Springfield
12/76	Bay City Rollers
25/71	**I Play And Sing** . . . Dawn
19/80	**I Pledge My Love** . . . Peaches & Herb
9/82	**I Ran (So Far Away)** . . . A Flock Of Seagulls
39/82	**I Really Don't Need No Light** . . . Jeffrey Osborne
	I Really Don't Want To Know
18/60	Tommy Edwards
22/66	Ronnie Dove
21/71	Elvis Presley
29/61	**I Really Love You** . . . Stereos
8/89	**I Remember Holding You** . . . Boys Club
5/62	**I Remember You** . . . Frank Ifield
36/64	**I Rise, I Fall** . . . Johnny Tillotson
5/66	**I Saw Her Again** . . . Mamas & The Papas
	I Saw Her (Him) Standing There
14/64	Beatles
7/88	Tiffany
14/63	**I Saw Linda Yesterday** . . . Dickey Lee
16/72	**I Saw The Light** . . . Todd Rundgren
	I Say A Little Prayer
4/67	Dionne Warwick
10/68	Aretha Franklin
4/67	**I Second That Emotion** . . . Miracles
26/66	**I See The Light** . . . Five Americans
38/74	**I Shall Sing** . . . Art Garfunkel
1/74	**I Shot The Sheriff** . . . Eric Clapton
28/88	**I Should Be So Lucky** . . . Kylie Minogue
15/62	**I Sold My Heart To The Junkman** . . . Blue-Belles
6/69	**I Started A Joke** . . . Bee Gees
13/88	**I Still Believe** . . . Brenda K. Starr
12/84	**I Still Can't Get Over Loving You** . . . Ray Parker Jr.
39/79	**I Still Have Dreams** . . . Richie Furay
1/87	**I Still Haven't Found What I'm Looking For** . . . U2
12/67	**I Take It Back** . . . Sandy Posey
13/67	**I Thank The Lord For The Night Time** . . . Neil Diamond

POS/YR	RECORD TITLE/ARTIST
	I Thank You
9/68	Sam & Dave
34/80	ZZ Top
1/70	**I Think I Love You** . . . Partridge Family
16/86	**I Think It's Love** . . . Jermaine Jackson
	I Think We're Alone Now
4/67	Tommy James & The Shondells
1/87	Tiffany
23/69	**I Turned You On** . . . Isley Brothers
	I Understand (Just How You Feel)
9/61	G-Clefs
36/65	Freddie & The Dreamers
33/59	**I Waited Too Long** . . . LaVern Baker
17/56	**I Walk The Line** . . . Johnny Cash
12/86	**I Wanna Be A Cowboy** . . . Boys Don't Cry
14/63	**I Wanna Be Around** . . . Tony Bennett
20/59	**I Wanna Be Loved** . . . Ricky Nelson
16/72	**I Wanna Be Where You Are** . . . Michael Jackson
16/73	**I Wanna Be With You** . . . Raspberries
11/80	**I Wanna Be Your Lover** . . . Prince
23/75	**I Wanna Dance Wit' Choo** . . . Disco Tex & The Sex-O-Lettes
1/87	**I Wanna Dance With Somebody (Who Loves Me)** . . . Whitney Houston
10/77	**I Wanna Get Next To You** . . . Rose Royce
14/87	**I Wanna Go Back** . . . Eddie Money
8/89	**I Wanna Have Some Fun** . . . Samantha Fox
35/85	**I Wanna Hear It From Your Lips** . . . Eric Carmen
36/68	**I Wanna Live** . . . Glen Campbell
9/64	**I Wanna Love Him So Bad** . . . Jelly Beans
39/61	**(I Wanna) Love My Life Away** . . . Gene Pitney
	(I Wanna) Testify
20/67	Parliaments
36/69	Johnnie Taylor
21/61	**I Wanna Thank You** . . . Bobby Rydell
6/84	**I Want A New Drug** . . . Huey Lewis & The News
11/65	**I Want Candy** . . . Strangeloves
5/88	**I Want Her** . . . Keith Sweat
	I Want To ..also see: I Wanna, & I Want'a
1/60	**I Want To Be Wanted** . . . Brenda Lee
3/88	**I Want To Be Your Man** . . . Roger
23/65	**I Want To (Do Everything For You)** . . . Joe Tex
36/66	**I Want To Go With You** . . . Eddy Arnold

POS/YR	RECORD TITLE/ARTIST
1/64	**I Want To Hold Your Hand** . . . Beatles
1/85	**I Want To Know What Love Is** . . . Foreigner
28/63	**I Want To Stay Here** . . . Steve & Eydie
	I Want To Take You Higher
34/70	Ike & Tina Turner
38/70	Sly & The Family Stone
8/59	**I Want To Walk You Home** . . . Fats Domino
15/76	**I Want You** . . . Marvin Gaye
20/66	**I Want You** . . . Bob Dylan
1/70	**I Want You Back** . . . Jackson 5
37/81	**I Want You, I Need You** . . . Chris Christian
1/56	**I Want You, I Need You, I Love You** . . . Elvis Presley
	I Want You To Be My Baby
14/55	Georgia Gibbs
18/55	Lillian Briggs
13/56	**I Want You To Be My Girl** . . . Frankie Lymon & The Teenagers
32/58	**I Want You To Know** . . . Fats Domino
7/79	**I Want You To Want Me** . . . Cheap Trick
19/79	**I Want You Tonight** . . . Pablo Cruise
7/79	**I Want Your Love** . . . Chic
2/87	**I Want Your Sex** . . . George Michael
15/75	**I Want'a Do Something Freaky To You** . . . Leon Haywood
29/73	**I Was Checkin' Out She Was Checkin' In** . . . Don Covay
20/67	**I Was Kaiser Bill's Batman** . . . Whistling Jack Smith
10/79	**I Was Made For Dancin'** . . . Leif Garrett
11/79	**I Was Made For Lovin' You** . . . Kiss
2/67	**I Was Made To Love Her** . . . Stevie Wonder
22/78	**I Was Only Joking** . . . Rod Stewart
24/62	**I Was Such A Fool (To Fall In Love With You)** . . . Connie Francis
19/56	**I Was The One** . . . Elvis Presley
19/66	**(I Washed My Hands In) Muddy Water** . . . Johnny Rivers
	I (Who Have Nothing)
29/63	Ben E. King
14/70	Tom Jones
40/79	Sylvester
10/65	**I Will** . . . Dean Martin
22/68	**I Will Always Think About You** . . . New Colony Six

POS/YR	RECORD TITLE/ARTIST
30/79	**I Will Be In Love With You** . . . Livingston Taylor
34/87	**I Will Be There** . . . Glass Tiger
1/63	**I Will Follow Him** . . . Little Peggy March
29/78	**I Will Still Love You** . . . Stonebolt
1/79	**I Will Survive** . . . Gloria Gaynor
1/77	**I Wish** . . . Stevie Wonder
20/88	**I Wish I Had A Girl** . . . Henry Lee Summer
32/63	**I Wish I Were A Princess** . . . Little Peggy March
4/68	**I Wish It Would Rain** . . . Temptations
16/62	**I Wish That We Were Married** . . . Ronnie & The Hi-Lites
28/64	**I Wish You Love** . . . Gloria Lynne
13/71	**I Woke Up In Love This Morning** . . . Partridge Family
13/87	**I Won't Forget You** . . . Poison
10/83	**I Won't Hold You Back** . . . Toto
11/74	**I Won't Last A Day Without You** . . . Carpenters
35/83	**I Won't Stand In Your Way** . . . Stray Cats
25/63	**I Wonder** . . . Brenda Lee
34/85	**I Wonder If I Take You Home** . . . Lisa Lisa & Cult Jam
8/68	**I Wonder What She's Doing Tonite** . . . Tommy Boyce & Bobby Hart
21/63	**I Wonder What She's Doing Tonight** . . . Barry & The Tamerlanes
22/58	**I Wonder Why** . . . Dion & The Belmonts
8/85	**I Would Die 4 U** . . . Prince
20/82	**I Wouldn't Have Missed It For The World** . . . Ronnie Milsap
22/56	**I Wouldn't Know Where To Begin** . . . Eddy Arnold
36/77	**I Wouldn't Want To Be Like You** . . . Alan Parsons
1/76	**I Write The Songs** . . . Barry Manilow
	I'd Like To Teach The World To Sing (In Perfect Harmony)
7/72	New Seekers
13/72	Hillside Singers
40/71	**I'd Love To Change The World** . . . Ten Years After
2/72	**I'd Love You To Want Me** . . . Lobo
38/80	**I'd Rather Leave While I'm In Love** . . . Rita Coolidge

POS/YR	RECORD TITLE/ARTIST
2/76	**I'd Really Love To See You Tonight** . . . England Dan & John Ford Coley
18/87	**I'd Still Say Yes** . . . Klymaxx
15/69	**I'd Wait A Million Years** . . . Grass Roots
36/73	**I'll Always Love My Mama** . . . Intruders
3/88	**I'll Always Love You** . . . Taylor Dayne
35/65	**I'll Always Love You** . . . Spinners
14/87	**I'll Be Alright Without You** . . . Journey
3/72	**I'll Be Around** . . . Spinners
8/65	**I'll Be Doggone** . . . Marvin Gaye
3/76	**I'll Be Good To You** . . . Brothers Johnson
4/56	**I'll Be Home** . . . Pat Boone
33/64	**I'll Be In Trouble** . . . Temptations
11/86	**I'll Be Over You** . . . Toto
20/59	**I'll Be Satisfied** . . . Jackie Wilson
36/74	**I'll Be The Other Woman** . . . Soul Children
1/70	**I'll Be There** . . . Jackson 5
12/61	**I'll Be There** . . . Damita Jo *(also see: Stand By Me)*
14/65	**I'll Be There** . . . Gerry & The Pacemakers
31/59	**(I'll Be With You In) Apple Blossom Time** . . . Tab Hunter
40/73	**I'll Be Your Shelter (In Time Of Storm)** . . . Luther Ingram
18/58	**I'll Come Running Back To You** . . . Sam Cooke
25/64	**I'll Cry Instead** . . . Beatles
40/75	**I'll Do For You Anything You Want Me To** . . . Barry White
9/74	**I'll Have To Say I Love You In A Song** . . . Jim Croce
34/65	**I'll Keep Holding On** . . . Marvelettes
30/64	**I'll Keep You Satisfied** . . . Billy J. Kramer
21/65	**I'll Make All Your Dreams Come True** . . . Ronnie Dove
9/71	**I'll Meet You Halfway** . . . Partridge Family
14/62	**I'll Never Dance Again** . . . Bobby Rydell
6/69	**I'll Never Fall In Love Again** . . . Tom Jones
6/70	**I'll Never Fall In Love Again** . . . Dionne Warwick
4/65	**I'll Never Find Another You** . . . Seekers
5/79	**I'll Never Love This Way Again** . . . Dionne Warwick
24/57	**I'll Never Say "Never Again" Again** . . . Dinah Shore

POS/YR	RECORD TITLE/ARTIST
25/61	**I'll Never Smile Again** . . . Platters
13/55	**I'll Never Stop Loving You** . . . Doris Day
18/75	**I'll Play For You** . . . Seals & Crofts
	(I'll Remember) ..see: In The Still Of The Nite
23/57	**I'll Remember Today** . . . Patti Page
34/58	**I'll Remember Tonight** . . . Pat Boone
22/60	**I'll Save The Last Dance For You** . . . Damita Jo *(also see: Save The Last Dance For Me)*
32/62	**I'll See You In My Dreams** . . . Pat Boone
33/87	**I'll Still Be Loving You** . . . Restless Heart
39/67	**I'll Take Care Of Your Cares** . . . Frankie Laine
30/66	**I'll Take Good Care Of You** . . . Garnet Mimms
25/63	**I'll Take You Home** . . . Drifters
1/72	**I'll Take You There** . . . Staple Singers
25/64	**I'll Touch A Star** . . . Terry Stafford
40/67	**I'll Try Anything** . . . Dusty Springfield
	I'll Try Something New
39/62	Miracles
25/69	Supremes & Temptations
9/83	**I'll Tumble 4 Ya** . . . Culture Club
13/84	**I'll Wait** . . . Van Halen
15/58	**I'll Wait For You** . . . Frankie Avalon
1/66	**I'm A Believer** . . . Monkees
38/69	**I'm A Better Man** . . . Engelbert Humperdinck
17/65	**I'm A Fool** . . . Dino, Desi & Billy
24/61	**I'm A Fool To Care** . . . Joe Barry
35/71	**I'm A Greedy Man** . . . James Brown
36/65	**I'm A Happy Man** . . . Jive Five
38/59	**I'm A Hog For You** . . . Coasters
10/67	**I'm A Man** . . . Spencer Davis Group
17/65	**I'm A Man** . . . Yardbirds
31/59	**I'm A Man** . . . Fabian
24/68	**I'm A Midnight Mover** . . . Wilson Pickett
20/66	**(I'm A) Road Runner** . . . Jr. Walker & The All Stars
25/61	**I'm A Telling You** . . . Jerry Butler
31/74	**I'm A Train** . . . Albert Hammond
12/75	**I'm A Woman** . . . Maria Muldaur
16/80	**I'm Alive** . . . Electric Light Orchestra
35/83	**I'm Alive** . . . Neil Diamond
34/80	**I'm Almost Ready** . . . Pure Prairie League
7/80	**I'm Alright** . . . Kenny Loggins
20/55	**(I'm Always Hearing) Wedding Bells** . . . Eddie Fisher
9/57	**I'm Available** . . . Margie Rayburn
19/62	**I'm Blue (The Gong-Gong Song)** . . . Ikettes
40/71	**I'm Comin' Home** . . . Tommy James
39/66	**I'm Comin' Home, Cindy** . . . Trini Lopez
19/61	**I'm Comin' On Back To You** . . . Jackie Wilson
18/74	**I'm Coming Home** . . . Spinners
5/80	**I'm Coming Out** . . . Diana Ross
19/64	**I'm Crying** . . . Animals
17/73	**I'm Doin' Fine Now** . . . New York City
17/76	**I'm Easy** . . . Keith Carradine
21/78	**I'm Every Woman** . . . Chaka Khan
	I'm Falling Too ..see: (I Can't Help You)
37/69	**I'm Free** . . . Who
22/84	**I'm Free (Heaven Helps The Man)** . . . Kenny Loggins
	(I'm Gettin') ..also see: Nuttin' For Christmas
37/60	**I'm Gettin' Better** . . . Jim Reeves
9/85	**I'm Goin' Down** . . . Bruce Springsteen
17/59	**I'm Gonna Be A Wheel Some Day** . . . Fats Domino
9/64	**I'm Gonna Be Strong** . . . Gene Pitney
18/63	**I'm Gonna' Be Warm This Winter** . . . Connie Francis
3/59	**I'm Gonna Get Married** . . . Lloyd Price
12/61	**I'm Gonna Knock On Your Door** . . . Eddie Hodges
40/76	**I'm Gonna Let My Heart Do The Walking** . . . Supremes
3/73	**I'm Gonna Love You Just A Little More Baby** . . . Barry White
	I'm Gonna Make You Love Me
26/68	Madeline Bell
2/69	Supremes & Temptations
10/69	**I'm Gonna Make You Mine** . . . Lou Christie
3/57	**I'm Gonna Sit Right Down And Write Myself A Letter** . . . Billy Williams
28/78	**I'm Gonna Take Care Of Everything** . . . Rubicon
13/85	**I'm Gonna Tear Your Playhouse Down** . . . Paul Young
27/80	**I'm Happy That Love Has Found You** . . . Jimmy Hall

POS/YR	RECORD TITLE/ARTIST
1/65	**I'm Henry VIII, I Am** . . . Herman's Hermits
27/61	**I'm Hurtin'** . . . Roy Orbison
19/74	**I'm In Love** . . . Aretha Franklin
40/81	**I'm In Love** . . . Evelyn King
	I'm In Love Again
3/56	Fats Domino
38/56	Fontane Sisters
38/61	**I'm In The Mood For Love** . . . Chimes
2/77	**I'm In You** . . . Peter Frampton
	I'm Into Something Good
13/64	Herman's Hermits
38/64	Earl-Jean
12/73	**I'm Just A Singer (In A Rock And Roll Band)** . . . Moody Blues
33/61	**I'm Learning About Love** . . . Brenda Lee
36/71	**I'm Leavin'** . . . Elvis Presley
	I'm Leaving It Up To You
1/63	Dale & Grace
4/74	Donny & Marie Osmond
10/69	**I'm Livin' In Shame** . . . Supremes
	I'm Losing You ..see: (I Know)
40/59	**I'm Movin' On** . . . Ray Charles
37/73	**I'm Never Gonna Be Alone Anymore** . . . Cornelius Brothers & Sister Rose
36/59	**I'm Never Gonna Tell** . . . Jimmie Rodgers
27/60	**I'm Not Afraid** . . . Ricky Nelson
14/78	**I'm Not Gonna Let It Bother Me Tonight** . . . Atlanta Rhythm Section
2/75	**I'm Not In Love** . . . 10cc
4/75	**I'm Not Lisa** . . . Jessi Colter
34/70	**I'm Not My Brothers Keeper** . . . Flaming Ember
32/86	**I'm Not The One** . . . Cars
20/67	**(I'm Not Your) Steppin' Stone** . . . Monkees
6/85	**I'm On Fire** . . . Bruce Springsteen
16/75	**I'm On Fire** . . . Dwight Twilley
26/75	**I'm On Fire** . . . 5000 Volts
15/64	**I'm On The Outside (Looking In)** . . . Little Anthony & The Imperials
16/59	**I'm Ready** . . . Fats Domino
9/66	**I'm Ready For Love** . . . Martha & The Vandellas
	I'm So Excited
30/82	Pointer Sisters
9/84	Pointer Sisters

POS/YR	RECORD TITLE/ARTIST
8/66	**I'm So Lonesome I Could Cry** . . . B.J. Thomas
14/64	**I'm So Proud** . . . Impressions
1/60	**I'm Sorry** . . . Brenda Lee
1/75	**I'm Sorry** . . . John Denver
11/57	**I'm Sorry** . . . Platters
36/58	**I'm Sorry I Made You Cry** . . . Connie Francis
14/57	**I'm Stickin' With You** . . . Jimmy Bowen with The Rhythm Orchids
3/72	**I'm Still In Love With You** . . . Al Green
31/88	**I'm Still Searching** . . . Glass Tiger
12/83	**I'm Still Standing** . . . Elton John
10/72	**I'm Stone In Love With You** . . . Stylistics
1/65	**I'm Telling You Now** . . . Freddie & The Dreamers
38/62	**(I'm The Girl On) Wolverton Mountain** . . . Jo Ann Campbell
	I'm The One Who Loves You ..see: (Remember Me)
	I'm The One You Need ..see: (Come 'Round Here)
27/57	**I'm Waiting Just For You** . . . Pat Boone
	I'm Walkin'
4/57	Fats Domino
4/57	Ricky Nelson
12/67	**I'm Wondering** . . . Stevie Wonder
1/77	**I'm Your Boogie Man** . . . KC & The Sunshine Band
3/86	**I'm Your Man** . . . Wham!
6/66	**I'm Your Puppet** . . . James & Bobby Purify
11/65	**I'm Yours** . . . Elvis Presley
33/59	**I've Been Around** . . . Fats Domino
35/69	**I've Been Hurt** . . . Bill Deal
9/87	**I've Been In Love Before** . . . Cutting Crew
27/72	**I've Been Lonely For So Long** . . . Frederick Knight
16/67	**I've Been Lonely Too Long** . . . Young Rascals
21/65	**I've Been Loving You Too Long (To Stop Now)** . . . Otis Redding
9/74	**(I've Been) Searchin' So Long** . . . Chicago
34/75	**I've Been This Way Before** . . . Neil Diamond
28/59	**I've Come Of Age** . . . Billy Storm
8/81	**I've Done Everything For You** . . . Rick Springfield
5/71	**I've Found Someone Of My Own** . . . Free Movement

POS/YR	RECORD TITLE/ARTIST
29/76	**I've Got A Feeling (We'll Be Seeing Each Other Again)** . . . Al Wilson
18/83	**I've Got A Rock N' Roll Heart** . . . Eric Clapton
39/74	**I've Got A Thing About You Baby** . . . Elvis Presley
25/65	**I've Got A Tiger By The Tail** . . . Buck Owens
	I've Got A Woman ..see: I Got A Woman
18/62	**I've Got Bonnie** . . . Bobby Rydell
5/77	**I've Got Love On My Mind** . . . Natalie Cole
33/64	**I've Got Sand In My Shoes** . . . Drifters
32/73	**I've Got So Much To Give** . . . Barry White
12/74	**I've Got The Music In Me** . . . Kiki Dee
	I've Got To ..also see: I've Gotta
38/66	**I've Got To Be Somebody** . . . Billy Joe Royal
4/74	**I've Got To Use My Imagination** . . . Gladys Knight & The Pips
9/66	**I've Got You Under My Skin** . . . 4 Seasons
11/69	**I've Gotta Be Me** . . . Sammy Davis, Jr.
8/68	**I've Gotta Get A Message To You** . . . Bee Gees
25/78	**I've Had Enough** . . . Wings
6/59	**I've Had It** . . . Bell Notes
1/87	**(I've Had) The Time Of My Life** . . . Bill Medley & Jennifer Warnes
32/70	**I've Lost You** . . . Elvis Presley
4/80	**I've Loved You For A Long Time (medley)** . . . Spinners
3/82	**I've Never Been To Me** . . . Charlene
40/68	**I've Never Found A Girl (To Love Me Like You Do)** . . . Eddie Floyd
17/67	**I've Passed This Way Before** . . . Jimmy Ruffin
3/61	**I've Told Every Little Star** . . . Linda Scott
4/71	**If** . . . Bread
32/62	**If A Man Answers** . . . Bobby Darin
35/62	**If A Woman Answers (Hang Up The Phone)** . . . Leroy Van Dyke
14/83	**If Anyone Falls** . . . Stevie Nicks
7/58	**If Dreams Came True** . . . Pat Boone
24/78	**If Ever I See You Again** . . . Roberta Flack
10/84	**If Ever You're In My Arms Again** . . . Peabo Bryson
12/69	**If I Can Dream** . . . Elvis Presley

POS/YR	RECORD TITLE/ARTIST
1/78	**If I Can't Have You** . . . Yvonne Elliman
10/68	**If I Could Build My Whole World Around You** . . . Marvin Gaye & Tammi Terrell
10/72	**If I Could Reach You** . . . 5th Dimension
	If I Didn't Care
22/59	Connie Francis
30/61	Platters
39/75	**If I Ever Lose This Heaven** . . . AWB
34/59	**If I Give My Heart To You** . . . Kitty Kallen
31/60	**If I Had A Girl** . . . Rod Lauren
	If I Had A Hammer
10/62	Peter, Paul & Mary
3/63	Trini Lopez
36/82	**If I Had My Wish Tonight** . . . David Lasley
23/65	**If I Loved You** . . . Chad & Jeremy
8/55	**If I May** . . . Nat King Cole
34/65	**If I Ruled The World** . . . Tony Bennett
39/79	**If I Said You Have A Beautiful Body Would You Hold It Against Me** . . . Bellamy Brothers
	If I Were A Carpenter
8/66	Bobby Darin
20/68	Four Tops
36/70	Johnny Cash & June Carter
9/71	**If I Were Your Woman** . . . Gladys Knight & The Pips
19/84	**If I'd Been The One** . . . 38 Special
7/88	**If It Isn't Love** . . . New Edition
	(If Loving You Is Wrong) I Don't Want To Be Right
3/72	Luther Ingram
31/79	Barbara Mandrell
23/63	**If My Pillow Could Talk** . . . Connie Francis
25/71	**If Not For You** . . . Olivia Newton-John
29/86	**If She Knew What She Wants** . . . Bangles
17/87	**If She Would Have Been Faithful...** . . . Chicago
28/82	**If The Love Fits Wear It** . . . Leslie Pearl
	If There's A Hell Below ..see: (Don't Worry)
6/84	**If This Is It** . . . Huey Lewis & The News
28/74	**If We Make It Through December** . . . Merle Haggard
11/68	**If You Can Want** . . . Miracles
5/71	**If You Could Read My Mind** . . . Gordon Lightfoot

POS/YR	RECORD TITLE/ARTIST
33/59	**(If You Cry) True Love, True Love** . . . Drifters
3/72	**If You Don't Know Me By Now** . . . Harold Melvin & The Bluenotes
12/55	**If You Don't Want My Love** . . . Jaye P. Morgan
22/62	**If You Gotta Make A Fool Of Somebody** . . . James Ray
11/76	**If You Know What I Mean** . . . Neil Diamond
4/86	**If You Leave** . . . Orchestral Manoeuvres In The Dark
1/76	**If You Leave Me Now** . . . Chicago
38/72	**If You Leave Me Tonight I'll Cry** . . . Jerry Wallace
8/70	**(If You Let Me Make Love To You Then) Why Can't I Touch You?** . . . Ronnie Dyson
5/74	**If You Love Me (Let Me Know)** . . . Olivia Newton-John
3/85	**If You Love Somebody Set Them Free** . . . Sting
37/63	**If You Need Me** . . . Solomon Burke
8/71	**If You Really Love Me** . . . Stevie Wonder
17/79	**If You Remember Me** . . . Chris Thompson & Night
38/80	**If You Should Sail** . . . Nielsen/Pearson
17/74	**If You Talk In Your Sleep** . . . Elvis Presley
1/63	**If You Wanna Be Happy** . . . Jimmy Soul
25/74	**If You Wanna Get To Heaven** . . . Ozark Mountain Daredevils
37/79	**If You Want It** . . . Niteflyte
12/73	**If You Want Me To Stay** . . . Sly & The Family Stone
9/73	**If You're Ready (Come Go With Me)** . . . Staple Singers
20/65	**Iko Iko** . . . Dixie Cups
6/60	**Image Of A Girl** . . . Safaris
7/78	**Imaginary Lover** . . . Atlanta Rhythm Section
3/71	**Imagine** . . . John Lennon/Plastic Ono Band
22/75	**Immigrant, The** . . . Neil Sedaka
16/71	**Immigrant Song** . . . Led Zeppelin
36/72	**Immigration Man** . . . Graham Nash & David Crosby
35/66	**Impossible Dream** . . . Jack Jones
17/83	**In A Big Country** . . . Big Country

POS/YR	RECORD TITLE/ARTIST
30/68	**In-A-Gadda-Da-Vida** . . . Iron Butterfly
31/69	**In A Moment** . . . Intrigues
27/56	**In A Shanty In Old Shanty Town** . . . Somethin' Smith & The Redheads
11/80	**In America** . . . Charlie Daniels Band
9/67	**In And Out Of Love** . . . Supremes
	"In" Crowd
5/65	Ramsey Lewis Trio
13/65	Dobie Gray
7/63	**In Dreams** . . . Roy Orbison
19/87	**In My Dreams** . . . REO Speedwagon
7/85	**In My House** . . . Mary Jane Girls
10/60	**In My Little Corner Of The World** . . . Anita Bryant
23/63	**In My Room** . . . Beach Boys
38/85	**In Neon** . . . Elton John
19/81	**In The Air Tonight** . . . Phil Collins
	In The Chapel In The Moonlight ..see: Chapel
35/81	**In The Dark** . . . Billy Squier
3/69	**In The Ghetto** . . . Elvis Presley
33/67	**In The Heat Of The Night** . . . Ray Charles
27/61	**In The Middle Of A Heartache** . . . Wanda Jackson
	In The Middle Of An Island
9/57	Tony Bennett
23/57	Tennessee Ernie Ford
	In The Middle Of The House
11/56	Vaughn Monroe
20/56	Rusty Draper
	In The Midnight Hour
21/65	Wilson Pickett
30/73	Cross Country
19/64	**In The Misty Moonlight** . . . Jerry Wallace
	In The Mood
4/59	Ernie Fields
40/77	Henhouse Five Plus Too
39/84	**In The Mood** . . . Robert Plant
	In The Name Of Love ..see: (What)
3/79	**In The Navy** . . . Village People
5/72	**In The Rain** . . . Dramatics
38/60	**In The Still Of The Night** . . . Dion & The Belmonts
24/56	**In The Still Of The Nite** . . . Five Satins
3/70	**In The Summertime** . . . Mungo Jerry
1/69	**In The Year 2525 (Exordium & Terminus)** . . . Zager & Evans
3/87	**In Too Deep** . . . Genesis

POS/YR	RECORD TITLE/ARTIST
26/86	**In Your Eyes** . . . Peter Gabriel
20/81	**In Your Letter** . . . REO Speedwagon
5/89	**In Your Room** . . . Bangles
38/88	**In Your Soul** . . . Corey Hart
1/67	**Incense And Peppermints** . . . Strawberry Alarm Clock
33/67	**Indescribably Blue** . . . Elvis Presley
35/88	**Indestructible** . . . Four Tops
5/69	**Indian Giver** . . . 1910 Fruitgum Co.
10/68	**Indian Lake** . . . Cowsills
	Indian Reservation
20/68	Don Fardon
1/71	Raiders
5/70	**Indiana Wants Me** . . . R. Dean Taylor
6/84	**Infatuation** . . . Rod Stewart
	Innamorata
27/56	Dean Martin
30/56	Jerry Vale
9/71	**Inner City Blues (Make Me Wanna Holler)** . . . Marvin Gaye
10/84	**Innocent Man** . . . Billy Joel
32/76	**Inseparable** . . . Natalie Cole
34/66	**Inside-Looking Out** . . . Animals
3/70	**Instant Karma** . . . John Ono Lennon
29/79	**Instant Replay** . . . Dan Hartman
11/80	**Into The Night** . . . Benny Mardones
10/85	**Invincible** . . . Pat Benatar
31/85	**Invisible** . . . Alison Moyet
40/83	**Invisible Hands** . . . Kim Carnes
1/86	**Invisible Touch** . . . Genesis
15/62	**Irresistible You** . . . Bobby Darin
	Irving ..see: Ballad Of
35/60	**Is A Blue Bird Blue** . . . Conway Twitty
8/86	**Is It Love** . . . Mr. Mister
34/69	**Is It Something You've Got** . . . Tyrone Davis
17/64	**Is It True** . . . Brenda Lee
15/81	**Is It You** . . . Lee Ritenour
21/79	**Is She Really Going Out With Him?** . . . Joe Jackson
11/69	**Is That All There Is** . . . Peggy Lee
31/60	**Is There Any Chance** . . . Marty Robbins
4/83	**Is There Something I Should Know** . . . Duran Duran
2/87	**Is This Love** . . . Whitesnake
9/87	**Is This Love** . . . Survivor
1/75	**Island Girl** . . . Elton John
30/57	**Island In The Sun** . . . Harry Belafonte

POS/YR	RECORD TITLE/ARTIST
37/82	**Island Of Lost Souls** . . . Blondie
1/83	**Islands In The Stream** . . . Kenny Rogers & Dolly Parton
F/70	**Isn't It A Pity** . . . George Harrison
13/77	**Isn't It Time** . . . Babys
29/72	**Isn't Life Strange** . . . Moody Blues
9/69	**Israelites** . . . Desmond Dekker & The Aces
17/84	**It Ain't Enough** . . . Corey Hart
8/65	**It Ain't Me Babe** . . . Turtles
13/59	**It Doesn't Matter Anymore** . . . Buddy Holly
4/71	**It Don't Come Easy** . . . Ringo Starr
10/70	**It Don't Matter To Me** . . . Bread
29/64	**It Hurts Me** . . . Elvis Presley
7/64	**It Hurts To Be In Love** . . . Gene Pitney
13/56	**It Isn't Right** . . . Platters
23/61	**It Keeps Rainin'** . . . Fats Domino
3/62	**It Keeps Right On A-Hurtin'** . . . Johnny Tillotson
37/77	**It Keeps You Runnin'** . . . Doobie Brothers
11/55	**It May Sound Silly** . . . McGuire Sisters
22/62	**It Might As Well Rain Until September** . . . Carole King
25/83	**It Might Be You** . . . Stephen Bishop
3/67	**It Must Be Him** . . . Vikki Carr
32/79	**It Must Be Love** . . . Alton McClain & Destiny
33/83	**It Must Be Love** . . . Madness
5/72	**It Never Rains In Southern California** . . . Albert Hammond
38/60	**It Only Happened Yesterday** . . . Jack Scott
11/56	**It Only Hurts For A Little While** . . . Ames Brothers
10/75	**It Only Takes A Minute** . . . Tavares
40/68	**It Should Have Been Me** . . . Gladys Knight & The Pips
29/62	**It Started All Over Again** . . . Brenda Lee
27/73	**It Sure Took A Long, Long Time** . . . Lobo
14/67	**It Takes Two** . . . Marvin Gaye & Kim Weston
36/88	**It Takes Two** . . . Rob Base & D.J. E-Z Rock
20/66	**It Tears Me Up** . . . Percy Sledge
28/66	**It Was A Very Good Year** . . . Frank Sinatra
16/77	**It Was Almost Like A Song** . . . Ronnie Milsap
11/59	**It Was I** . . . Skip & Flip

Brenda K. Starr made her first foray into chartdom with her 1985 R & B single "Pickin' Up The Pieces." Yet her biggest year was 1988, when she was recognized as the No. 12 female pop singles artist of the year with Top-40 hits "I Still Believe" and "What You See Is What You Get."

Starship's "Beat Patrol" was the eighth charting single since the San Francisco veterans dropped the "Jefferson" from their name. The first two Starship singles went all the way to No. 1: 1985's "We Built This City" and 1986's "Sara."

Rod Stewart has been topping the charts for nearly two decades, with No. 1 hits "Maggie May," "Tonight's The Night (Gonna Be Alright)," and "Do Ya Think I'm Sexy." Yet none of his albums featured any more than two top-20 singles—until 1987's *Out Of Order*.

Sting, a musician with a short name who likes his titles long, hit the Top 40 with 'Love Is The Seventh Wave," "Fortress Around Your Heart," and "If You Love Somebody, Set Them Free." The album they came from? *The Dream Of The Blue Turtles*.

The Stray Cats led the rockabilly revival by scoring top-10 hits "Rock This Town," "Stray Cat Strut," and "(She's) Sexy + 17" before their 1985 break-up. Revivalists that they were, the Stray Cats actually revived *themselves* in 1988 and reformed.

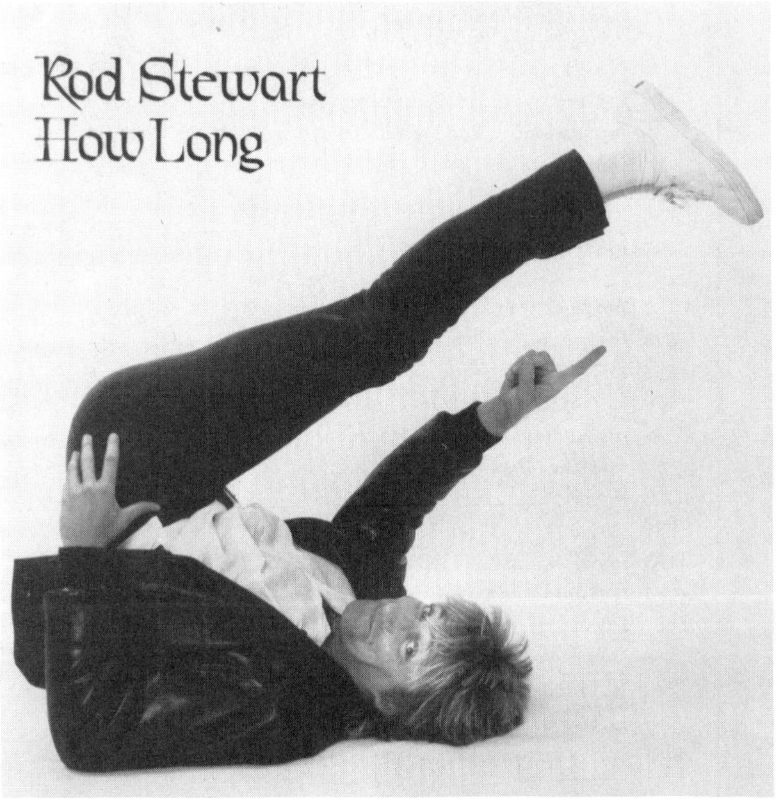

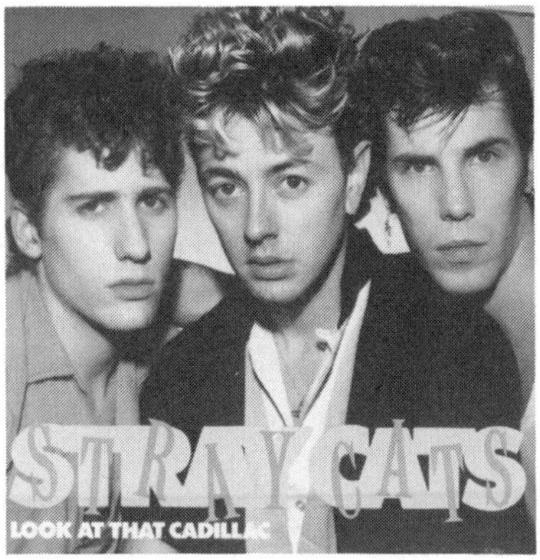

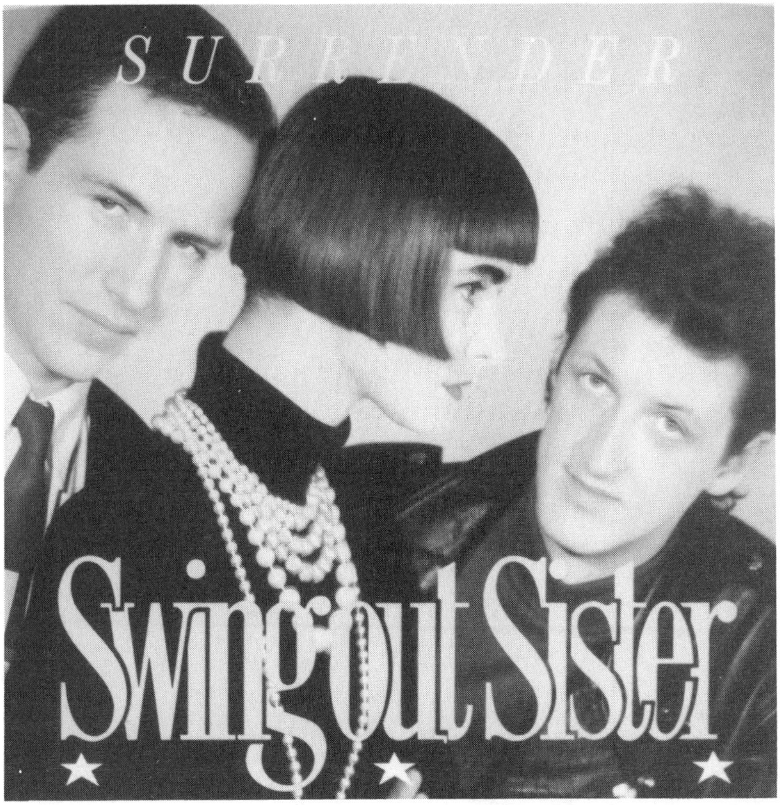

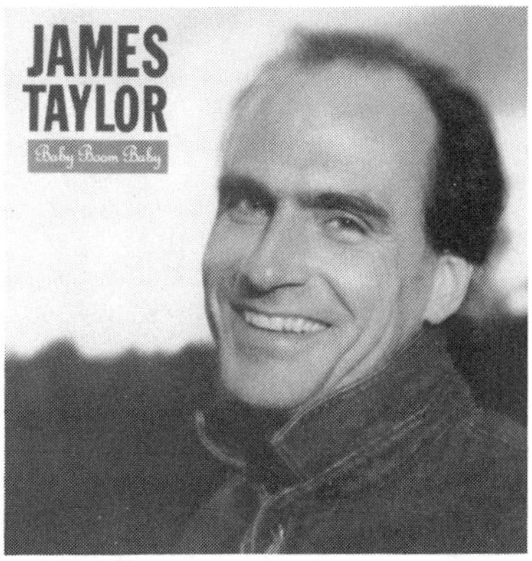

Barbara Streisand and Kim Carnes have both held the No. 1 pop-singles spot for nine weeks—Streisand with three three-week stints for "The Way We Were," "Evergreen," and "Woman In Love," and Carnes with the nine-week reign of smash hit "Bette Davis Eyes."

Donna Summer's "Supernatural Love" was her eighth charting single with the word "love" in the title. Of course, the song that introduced her as the Queen of Disco had the most "love" in it—the 1976 dance-floor blitz "Love To Love You Baby."

Swing Out Sister's "Surrender" couldn't match the No. 6 success of their "Breakout," but it was in interesting company. There are 20 different in-print songs entitled "Surrender," including Cheap Trick's chart hit, Diana Ross' Top-40 single, and Elvis Presley's No. 1.

James Taylor hit it big in 1971 with No. 1 single "You've Got A Friend." In the years to come, he had quite a few friends record with him, including Carly Simon, Joni Mitchell, Simon & Garfunkel, and J. D. Souther. In all, six out of his 14 Top-40 hits featured celebrity appearances.

The Temptations have failed to crack the pop Top 40 since "Glasshouse" in 1975, but their influence continues to be strong on the R & B charts, where they earned Top-40 hits in the late 80s with "To Be Continued," "I Wonder Who She's Seeing Now," and "Look What You Started."

POS/YR	RECORD TITLE/ARTIST
10/88	**It Would Take A Strong Strong Man** . . . Rick Astley
37/77	**It's A Crazy World** . . . Mac McAnally
3/78	**It's A Heartache** . . . Bonnie Tyler
20/78	**It's A Laugh** . . . Daryl Hall & John Oates
28/76	**It's A Long Way There** . . . Little River Band
28/81	**It's A Love Thing** . . . Whispers
8/66	**It's A Man's Man's Man's World** . . . James Brown
12/75	**It's A Miracle** . . . Barry Manilow
13/84	**It's A Miracle** . . . Culture Club
6/83	**It's A Mistake** . . . Men At Work
32/70	**It's A New Day** . . . James Brown
14/70	**It's A Shame** . . . Spinners
9/87	**It's A Sin** . . . Pet Shop Boys
7/55	**It's A Sin To Tell A Lie** . . . Somethin' Smith & The Redheads
31/75	**It's All Down To Goodnight Vienna** . . . Ringo Starr
	It's All In The Game
1/58	Tommy Edwards
25/64	Cliff Richard
24/70	Four Tops
26/64	**It's All Over Now** . . . Rolling Stones
4/63	**It's All Right** . . . Impressions
	It's Almost Tomorrow
20/55	David Carroll
20/55	Snooky Lanson
7/56	Dream Weavers
14/56	Jo Stafford
31/65	**It's Alright** . . . Adam Faith
20/58	**(It's Been A Long Time) Pretty Baby** . . . Gino & Gina
4/77	**It's Ecstasy When You Lay Down Next To Me** . . . Barry White
30/69	**It's Getting Better** . . . Mama Cass
12/72	**It's Going To Take Some Time** . . . Carpenters
23/65	**It's Gonna Be Alright** . . . Gerry & The Pacemakers
10/82	**It's Gonna Take A Miracle** . . . Deniece Williams
14/61	**It's Gonna Work Out Fine** . . . Ike & Tina Turner
18/65	**It's Growing** . . . Temptations
10/71	**It's Impossible** . . . Perry Como
	It's In His Kiss ..see: Shoop Shoop Song
38/83	**It's Inevitable** . . . Charlie

POS/YR	RECORD TITLE/ARTIST
3/59	**It's Just A Matter Of Time** . . . Brook Benton
9/59	**It's Late** . . . Ricky Nelson
23/66	**It's My Life** . . . Animals
31/84	**It's My Life** . . . Talk Talk
1/63	**It's My Party** . . . Lesley Gore
9/81	**It's My Turn** . . . Diana Ross
37/89	**It's No Secret** . . . Kylie Minogue
5/57	**It's Not For Me To Say** . . . Johnny Mathis
9/87	**It's Not Over ('Til It's Over)** . . . Starship
10/65	**It's Not Unusual** . . . Tom Jones
	It's Now Or Never
1/60	Elvis Presley
14/81	John Schneider
23/67	**It's Now Winters Day** . . . Tommy Roe
29/76	**It's O.K.** . . . Beach Boys
20/72	**It's One Of Those Nights (Yes Love)** . . . Partridge Family
15/86	**It's Only Love** . . . Bryan Adams/Tina Turner
31/66	**It's Only Love** . . . Tommy James & The Shondells
	It's Only Make Believe
1/58	Conway Twitty
10/70	Glen Campbell
16/74	**It's Only Rock 'N Roll (But I Like It)** . . . Rolling Stones
9/64	**It's Over** . . . Roy Orbison
37/66	**It's Over** . . . Jimmie Rodgers
38/76	**It's Over** . . . Boz Scaggs
11/82	**It's Raining Again** . . . Supertramp
21/77	**It's Sad To Belong** . . . England Dan & John Ford Coley
5/77	**It's So Easy** . . . Linda Ronstadt
1/80	**It's Still Rock And Roll To Me** . . . Billy Joel
	It's The Same Old Song
5/65	Four Tops
35/78	KC & The Sunshine Band
4/59	**It's Time To Cry** . . . Paul Anka
1/71	**It's Too Late** . . . Carole King
23/66	**It's Too Late** . . . Bobby Goldsboro
4/58	**It's Too Soon To Know** . . . Pat Boone
6/63	**It's Up To You** . . . Rick Nelson
20/68	**It's Wonderful** . . . Rascals
6/57	**It's You I Love** . . . Fats Domino
33/78	**It's You That I Need** . . . Enchantment
	It's You That I Need ..see: (Loneliness Made Me Realize)

POS/YR	RECORD TITLE/ARTIST
2/69	**It's Your Thing** . . . Isley Brothers
25/56	**Italian Theme** . . . Cyril Stapleton
25/58	**Itchy Twitchy Feeling** . . . Bobby Hendricks
16/68	**Itchycoo Park** . . . Small Faces
1/60	**Itsy Bitsy Teenie Weenie Yellow Polkadot Bikini** . . . Brian Hyland
	Ivory Tower
2/56	Cathy Carr
6/56	Gale Storm
11/56	Charms
18/57	**Ivy Rose** . . . Perry Como

J

POS/YR	RECORD TITLE/ARTIST
1/82	**Jack & Diane** . . . John Cougar
8/78	**Jack And Jill** . . . Raydio
3/75	**Jackie Blue** . . . Ozark Mountain Daredevils
14/67	**Jackson** . . . Nancy Sinatra & Lee Hazlewood
1/87	**Jacob's Ladder** . . . Huey Lewis & The News
1/57	**Jailhouse Rock** . . . Elvis Presley
29/62	**Jam, The** . . . Bobby Gregg
32/87	**Jam Tonight** . . . Freddie Jackson
8/70	**Jam Up Jelly Tight** . . . Tommy Roe
14/57	**Jamaica Farewell** . . . Harry Belafonte
	Jambalaya (On The Bayou)
30/62	Fats Domino
16/73	Blue Ridge Rangers
17/62	**James (Hold The Ladder Steady)** . . . Sue Thompson
14/85	**Jamie** . . . Ray Parker Jr.
30/62	**Jamie** . . . Eddie Holland
18/87	**Jammin' Me** . . . Tom Petty
14/80	**Jane** . . . Jefferson Starship
4/64	**Java** . . . Al Hirt
	Jaws ..see: Theme From, & Mr. Jaws
2/74	**Jazzman** . . . Carole King
20/69	**Jealous Kind Of Fella** . . . Garland Green
19/60	**Jealous Of You** . . . Connie Francis
2/69	**Jean** . . . Oliver
17/77	**Jeans On** . . . David Dundas

POS/YR	RECORD TITLE/ARTIST
8/58	**Jennie Lee** . . . Jan & Arnie
40/68	**Jennifer Eccles** . . . Hollies
26/68	**Jennifer Juniper** . . . Donovan
36/70	**Jennifer Tomkins** . . . Street People
	Jenny ..see: 867-5309
10/57	**Jenny, Jenny** . . . Little Richard
10/66	**Jenny Take A Ride!** . . . Mitch Ryder & The Detroit Wheels
2/83	**Jeopardy** . . . Greg Kihn Band
35/61	**Jeremiah Peabody's Poly Unsaturated Pills** . . . Ray Stevens
7/65	**Jerk, The** . . . Larks
11/80	**Jesse** . . . Carly Simon
30/73	**Jesse** . . . Roberta Flack
1/81	**Jessie's Girl** . . . Rick Springfield
	Jesus Christ Superstar ..see: Superstar
28/69	**Jesus Is A Soul Man** . . . Lawrence Reynolds
35/73	**Jesus Is Just Alright** . . . Doobie Brothers
7/74	**Jet** . . . Paul McCartney
8/77	**Jet Airliner** . . . Steve Miller Band
	Jim Dandy
17/57	LaVern Baker
25/74	Black Oak Arkansas
28/87	**Jimmy Lee** . . . Aretha Franklin
33/73	**Jimmy Loves Mary-Anne** . . . Looking Glass
10/67	**Jimmy Mack** . . . Martha & The Vandellas
25/61	**Jimmy's Girl** . . . Johnny Tillotson
	Jingle Bell Rock
6/57	Bobby Helms
35/58	Bobby Helms
36/60	Bobby Helms
21/61	Bobby Rydell/Chubby Checker
10/70	**Jingle Jangle** . . . Archies
1/75	**Jive Talkin'** . . . Bee Gees
19/58	**Jo-Ann** . . . Playmates
17/80	**JoJo** . . . Boz Scaggs
2/84	**Joanna** . . . Kool & The Gang
21/70	**Joanne** . . . Michael Nesmith
28/71	**Jody's Got Your Girl And Gone** . . . Johnnie Taylor
	John And Yoko ..see: Ballad Of
1/62	**Johnny Angel** . . . Shelley Fabares
8/58	**Johnny B. Goode** . . . Chuck Berry
7/62	**Johnny Get Angry** . . . Joanie Sommers
21/62	**Johnny Jingo** . . . Hayley Mills
21/62	**Johnny Loves Me** . . . Shelley Fabares

POS/YR	RECORD TITLE/ARTIST
35/62	**Johnny Will** . . . Pat Boone
17/72	**Join Together** . . . Who
1/74	**Joker, The** . . . Steve Miller Band
	Joker (That's What They Call Me)
22/57	Hilltoppers
25/57	Billy Myles
20/66	**Joker Went Wild** . . . Brian Hyland
4/65	**Jolly Green Giant** . . . Kingsmen
39/81	**Jones Vs. Jones** . . . Kool & The Gang
18/60	**Josephine** . . . Bill Black's Combo
26/78	**Josie** . . . Steely Dan
16/68	**Journey To The Center Of The Mind** . . . Amboy Dukes
6/72	**Joy** . . . Apollo 100
30/74	**Joy** . . . Isaac Hayes
1/71	**Joy To The World** . . . Three Dog Night
26/65	**Ju Ju Hand** . . . Sam The Sham & The Pharoahs
22/58	**Judy** . . . Frankie Vaughan
	Judy Blue Eyes ..see: Suite
1/68	**Judy In Disguise (With Glasses)** . . . John Fred
33/75	**Judy Mae** . . . Boomer Castleman
5/63	**Judy's Turn To Cry** . . . Lesley Gore
10/56	**Juke Box Baby** . . . Perry Como
26/82	**Juke Box Hero** . . . Foreigner
5/70	**Julie, Do Ya Love Me** . . . Bobby Sherman
1/84	**Jump** . . . Van Halen
3/84	**Jump (For My Love)** . . . Pointer Sisters
27/72	**Jump Into The Fire** . . . Nilsson
28/60	**Jump Over** . . . Freddy Cannon
13/87	**Jump Start** . . . Natalie Cole
24/82	**Jump To It** . . . Aretha Franklin
	Jumpin' Jack Flash
3/68	Rolling Stones
21/86	Aretha Franklin
21/57	**June Night** . . . Jimmy Dorsey
4/74	**Jungle Boogie** . . . Kool & The Gang
8/72	**Jungle Fever** . . . Chakachas
20/85	**Jungle Love** . . . Time
23/77	**Jungle Love** . . . Steve Miller Band
3/75	**Junior's Farm** . . . Paul McCartney
9/76	**Junk Food Junkie** . . . Larry Groce
37/61	**Jura (I Swear I Love You)** . . . Les Paul & Mary Ford
4/58	**Just A Dream** . . . Jimmy Clanton
12/85	**Just A Gigolo (medley)** . . . David Lee Roth

POS/YR	RECORD TITLE/ARTIST
8/65	**Just A Little** . . . Beau Brummels
40/60	**Just A Little** . . . Brenda Lee
39/65	**Just A Little Bit** . . . Roy Head
7/65	**Just A Little Bit Better** . . . Herman's Hermits
23/75	**Just A Little Bit Of You** . . . Michael Jackson
9/59	**Just A Little Too Much** . . . Ricky Nelson
7/77	**Just A Song Before I Go** . . . Crosby, Stills & Nash
12/85	**Just Another Night** . . . Mick Jagger
19/85	**Just As I Am** . . . Air Supply
	Just As Much As Ever
32/59	Bob Beckham
24/68	Bobby Vinton
7/59	**Just Ask Your Heart** . . . Frankie Avalon
19/64	**Just Be True** . . . Gene Chandler
29/57	**Just Because** . . . Lloyd Price
8/57	**Just Between You And Me** . . . Chordettes
21/81	**Just Between You And Me** . . . April Wine
12/57	**Just Born (To Be Your Baby)** . . . Perry Como
38/82	**Just Can't Win 'Em All** . . . Stevie Woods
35/60	**Just Come Home** . . . Hugo & Luigi
10/74	**Just Don't Want To Be Lonely** . . . Main Ingredient
5/68	**Just Dropped In (To See What Condition My Condition Was In)** . . . First Edition
20/61	**Just For Old Time's Sake** . . . McGuire Sisters
36/83	**Just Got Lucky** . . . JoBoxers
10/88	**Just Got Paid** . . . Johnny Kemp
18/59	**Just Keep It Up** . . . Dee Clark
33/66	**Just Like A Woman** . . . Bob Dylan
40/88	**Just Like Heaven** . . . Cure
11/66	**Just Like Me** . . . Paul Revere & The Raiders
6/88	**Just Like Paradise** . . . David Lee Roth
6/64	**(Just Like) Romeo & Juliet** . . . Reflections
1/80	**(Just Like) Starting Over** . . . John Lennon
26/58	**Just Married** . . . Marty Robbins
1/71	**Just My Imagination** . . . Temptations
17/81	**Just Once** . . . Quincy Jones/James Ingram
9/65	**Just Once In My Life** . . . Righteous Brothers
10/63	**Just One Look** . . . Doris Troy
29/60	**Just One Time** . . . Don Gibson

POS/YR	RECORD TITLE/ARTIST
24/61	**Just Out Of Reach (Of My Two Open Arms)** . . . Solomon Burke
11/77	**Just Remember I Love You** . . . Firefall
40/71	**Just Seven Numbers (Can Straighten Out My Life)** . . . Four Tops
39/81	**Just So Lonely** . . . Get Wet
2/81	**Just The Two Of Us** . . . Grover Washington, Jr./Bill Withers
3/78	**Just The Way You Are** . . . Billy Joel
7/76	**Just To Be Close To You** . . . Commodores
26/57	**Just To Hold My Hand** . . . Clyde McPhatter
8/87	**Just To See Her** . . . Smokey Robinson
30/75	**Just Too Many People** . . . Melissa Manchester
2/56	**Just Walking In The Rain** . . . Johnnie Ray
27/78	**Just What I Needed** . . . Cars
4/79	**Just When I Needed You Most** . . . Randy Vanwarmer
20/65	**Just You** . . . Sonny & Cher
27/76	**Just You And I** . . . Melissa Manchester
4/73	**Just You 'N' Me** . . . Chicago

K

POS/YR	RECORD TITLE/ARTIST
39/71	**K-Jee** . . . Nite-Liters
	Ka-Ding Dong
24/56	G-Clefs
35/56	Diamonds
38/56	Hilltoppers
	Kansas City
1/59	Wilbert Harrison
23/64	Trini Lopez
31/65	**Kansas City Star** . . . Roger Miller
1/84	**Karma Chameleon** . . . Culture Club
16/58	**Kathy-O** . . . Diamonds
16/69	**Keem-O-Sabe** . . . Electric Indian
8/57	**Keep A Knockin'** . . . Little Richard
8/83	**(Keep Feeling) Fascination** . . . Human League
2/77	**Keep It Comin' Love** . . . KC & The Sunshine Band
37/77	**Keep Me Cryin'** . . . Al Green
4/65	**Keep On Dancing** . . . Gentrys

POS/YR	RECORD TITLE/ARTIST
24/68	**Keep On Lovin' Me Honey** . . . Marvin Gaye & Tammi Terrell
1/81	**Keep On Loving You** . . . REO Speedwagon
10/64	**Keep On Pushing** . . . Impressions
15/74	**Keep On Singing** . . . Helen Reddy
10/74	**Keep On Smilin'** . . . Wet Willie
1/73	**Keep On Truckin'** . . . Eddie Kendricks
9/65	**Keep Searchin'** . . . Del Shannon
14/67	**Keep The Ball Rollin'** . . . Jay & The Techniques
36/80	**Keep The Fire** . . . Kenny Loggins
7/82	**Keep The Fire Burnin'** . . . REO Speedwagon
	Keep Your Eye On The Sparrow ..see: Baretta's Theme
12/62	**Keep Your Hands Off My Baby** . . . Little Eva
2/87	**Keep Your Hands To Yourself** . . . Georgia Satellites
10/73	**Keeper Of The Castle** . . . Four Tops
18/85	**Keeping The Faith** . . . Billy Joel
20/55	**Kentuckian Song** . . . Hilltoppers
16/70	**Kentucky Rain** . . . Elvis Presley
	Kentucky Woman
22/67	Neil Diamond
38/68	Deep Purple
6/58	**Kewpie Doll** . . . Perry Como
8/82	**Key Largo** . . . Bertie Higgins
4/66	**Kicks** . . . Paul Revere & The Raiders
33/84	**Kid's American** . . . Matthew Wilder
7/60	**Kiddio** . . . Brook Benton
25/82	**Kids In America** . . . Kim Wilde
16/63	**Killer Joe** . . . Rocky Fellers
12/75	**Killer Queen** . . . Queen
28/81	**Killin' Time** . . . Fred Knoblock & Susan Anton
1/73	**Killing Me Softly With His Song** . . . Roberta Flack
30/77	**Killing Of Georgie** . . . Rod Stewart
1/67	**Kind Of A Drag** . . . Buckinghams
17/63	**Kind Of Boy You Can't Forget** . . . Raindrops
8/86	**King For A Day** . . . Thompson Twins
40/72	**King Heroin** . . . James Brown
13/77	**King Is Gone** . . . Ronnie McDowell
3/83	**King Of Pain** . . . Police
36/80	**King Of The Hill** . . . Rick Pinette & Oak

POS/YR	RECORD TITLE/ARTIST
4/65	**King Of The Road** . . . Roger Miller *(also see: Queen Of The House)*
30/62	**King Of The Whole Wide World** . . . Elvis Presley
17/78	**King Tut** . . . Steve Martin
31/74	**Kings Of The Party** . . . Brownsville Station
	Kiss
1/86	Prince
31/89	Art Of Noise featuring Tom Jones
21/72	**Kiss An Angel Good Mornin'** . . . Charley Pride
1/76	**Kiss And Say Goodbye** . . . Manhattans
31/88	**Kiss And Tell** . . . Bryan Ferry
25/65	**Kiss Away** . . . Ronnie Dove
12/87	**Kiss Him Goodbye** . . . Nylons
37/79	**Kiss In The Dark** . . . Pink Lady
30/56	**Kiss Me Another** . . . Georgia Gibbs
12/88	**Kiss Me Deadly** . . . Lita Ford
15/68	**Kiss Me Goodbye** . . . Petula Clark
37/80	**Kiss Me In The Rain** . . . Barbra Streisand
34/64	**Kiss Me Quick** . . . Elvis Presley
29/64	**Kiss Me Sailor** . . . Diane Renay
1/81	**Kiss On My List** . . . Daryl Hall & John Oates
25/83	**Kiss The Bride** . . . Elton John
1/78	**Kiss You All Over** . . . Exile
3/57	**Kisses Sweeter Than Wine** . . . Jimmie Rodgers
12/64	**Kissin' Cousins** . . . Elvis Presley
35/61	**Kissin' On The Phone** . . . Paul Anka
11/59	**Kissin' Time** . . . Bobby Rydell
5/88	**Kissing A Fool** . . . George Michael
31/73	**Kissing My Love** . . . Bill Withers
16/57	**Knee Deep In The Blues** . . . Guy Mitchell
15/67	**Knight In Rusty Armour** . . . Peter & Gordon
	Knock On Wood
28/66	Eddie Floyd
30/67	Otis & Carla
1/79	Amii Stewart
1/71	**Knock Three Times** . . . Dawn
12/73	**Knockin' On Heaven's Door** . . . Bob Dylan
14/77	**Knowing Me, Knowing You** . . . Abba
	Ko Ko Mo (I Love You So)
2/55	Perry Como
6/55	Crew-Cuts
2/73	**Kodachrome** . . . Paul Simon

POS/YR	RECORD TITLE/ARTIST
1/88	**Kokomo** . . . Beach Boys
4/59	**Kookie, Kookie (Lend Me Your Comb)** . . . Edward Byrnes & Connie Stevens
40/74	**Kung Fu** . . . Curtis Mayfield
1/74	**Kung Fu Fighting** . . . Carl Douglas
1/86	**Kyrie** . . . Mr. Mister

L

POS/YR	RECORD TITLE/ARTIST
	La Bamba
22/59	Ritchie Valens
1/87	Los Lobos
9/58	**La Dee Dah** . . . Billy & Lillie
32/58	**La-Do-Dada** . . . Dale Hawkins
4/87	**La Isla Bonita** . . . Madonna
9/70	**La La La (If I Had You)** . . . Bobby Sherman
4/68	**La-La Means I Love You** . . . Delfonics
30/74	**La La Peace Song** . . . Al Wilson
	La Mer ..see: Beyond The Sea
20/58	**La Paloma** . . . Billy Vaughn
8/80	**Ladies Night** . . . Kool & The Gang
1/80	**Lady** . . . Kenny Rogers
6/75	**Lady** . . . Styx
10/79	**Lady** . . . Little River Band
28/80	**Lady** . . . Whispers
39/67	**Lady** . . . Jack Jones
20/67	**Lady Bird** . . . Nancy Sinatra & Lee Hazlewood
14/75	**Lady Blue** . . . Leon Russell
6/66	**Lady Godiva** . . . Peter & Gordon
3/87	**Lady In Red** . . . Chris DeBurgh
24/66	**Lady Jane** . . . Rolling Stones
24/78	**Lady Love** . . . Lou Rawls
30/83	**Lady Love Me (One More Time)** . . . George Benson
14/60	**Lady Luck** . . . Lloyd Price
4/68	**Lady Madonna** . . . Beatles
1/75	**Lady Marmalade** . . . LaBelle
2/68	**Lady Willpower** . . . Gary Puckett & The Union Gap
8/81	**Lady (You Bring Me Up)** . . . Commodores

POS/YR	RECORD TITLE/ARTIST
33/68	**Lalena** . . . Donovan
	Lament Of Cherokee ..see: Indian Reservation
4/87	**Land Of Confusion** . . . Genesis
29/66	**Land Of Milk And Honey** . . . Vogues
	Land Of 1000 Dances
30/65	Cannibal & The Headhunters
6/66	Wilson Pickett
13/84	**Language Of Love** . . . Dan Fogelberg
32/61	**Language Of Love** . . . John D. Loudermilk
	Lara's Theme ..see: Somewhere My Love
13/65	**Last Chance To Turn Around** . . . Gene Pitney
21/76	**Last Child** . . . Aerosmith
3/78	**Last Dance** . . . Donna Summer
	Last Date
2/60	Floyd Cramer
21/60	Lawrence Welk
	(also see: My Last Date (With You))
19/75	**Last Farewell** . . . Roger Whittaker
18/75	**Last Game Of The Season (A Blind Man In The Bleachers)** . . . David Geddes
	Last Kiss
2/64	J. Frank Wilson
34/74	Wednesday
3/61	**Last Night** . . . Mar-Keys
8/72	**(Last Night) I Didn't Get To Sleep At All** . . . 5th Dimension
3/73	**Last Song** . . . Edward Bear
9/65	**Last Time** . . . Rolling Stones
40/84	**Last Time I Made Love** . . . Joyce Kennedy & Jeffrey Osborne
14/74	**Last Time I Saw Him** . . . Diana Ross
1/66	**Last Train To Clarksville** . . . Monkees
39/80	**Last Train To London** . . . Electric Light Orchestra
25/67	**Last Waltz** . . . Engelbert Humperdinck
40/66	**Last Word In Lonesome Is Me** . . . Eddy Arnold
27/57	**Lasting Love** . . . Sal Mineo
6/80	**Late In The Evening** . . . Paul Simon
10/65	**Laugh At Me** . . . Sonny
15/65	**Laugh, Laugh** . . . Beau Brummels
10/69	**Laughing** . . . Guess Who
15/63	**Laughing Boy** . . . Mary Wells
1/75	**Laughter In The Rain** . . . Neil Sedaka
14/65	**Laurie (Strange Things Happen)** . . . Dickey Lee

POS/YR	RECORD TITLE/ARTIST
3/59	**Lavender-Blue** . . . Sammy Turner
	LaVerne & Shirley Theme ..see: Making Our Dreams Come True
13/83	**Lawyers In Love** . . . Jackson Browne
11/70	**Lay A Little Lovin' On Me** . . . Robin McNamara
6/70	**Lay Down (Candles In The Rain)** . . . Melanie
3/78	**Lay Down Sally** . . . Eric Clapton
16/56	**Lay Down Your Arms** . . . Chordettes
40/85	**Lay It Down** . . . Ratt
7/69	**Lay Lady Lay** . . . Bob Dylan
6/85	**Lay Your Hands On Me** . . . Thompson Twins
10/72	**Layla** . . . Derek & The Dominos
14/67	**Lazy Day** . . . Spanky & Our Gang
40/64	**Lazy Elsie Molly** . . . Chubby Checker
12/58	**Lazy Mary** . . . Lou Monte
14/61	**Lazy River** . . . Bobby Darin
21/58	**Lazy Summer Night** . . . Four Preps
1/78	**Le Freak** . . . Chic
5/79	**Lead Me On** . . . Maxine Nightingale
9/82	**Leader Of The Band** . . . Dan Fogelberg
19/65	**Leader Of The Laundromat** . . . Detergents
1/64	**Leader Of The Pack** . . . Shangri-Las
25/62	**Leah** . . . Roy Orbison
	Lean On Me
1/72	Bill Withers
1/87	Club Nouveau
9/66	**Leaning On The Lamp Post** . . . Herman's Hermits
1/55	**Learnin' The Blues** . . . Frank Sinatra
6/82	**Leather And Lace** . . . Stevie Nicks with Don Henley
27/84	**Leave A Tender Moment Alone** . . . Billy Joel
24/84	**Leave It** . . . Yes
3/73	**Leave Me Alone (Ruby Red Dress)** . . . Helen Reddy
21/73	**Leaving Me** . . . Independents
1/69	**Leaving On A Jet Plane** . . . Peter, Paul & Mary
9/58	**Left Right Out Of Your Heart** . . . Patti Page
	Legend Of Billy Jack ..see: One Tin Soldier
31/80	**Legend Of Wooley Swamp** . . . Charlie Daniels Band

POS/YR	RECORD TITLE/ARTIST
8/84	**Legs** . . . ZZ Top
	Lemon Tree
35/62	Peter, Paul & Mary
20/65	Trini Lopez
11/58	**Leroy** . . . Jack Scott
31/68	**Les Bicyclettes De Belsize** . . . Engelbert Humperdinck
34/68	**Lesson, The** . . . Vikki Carr
12/87	**Lessons In Love** . . . Level 42
	Let A Man Come In And Do The Popcorn
21/69	James Brown (Part One)
40/70	James Brown (Part Two)
36/69	**Let A Woman Be A Woman - Let A Man Be A Man** . . . Dyke & The Blazers
3/76	**Let 'Em In** . . . Wings
10/76	**Let Her In** . . . John Travolta
39/85	**Let Him Go** . . . Animotion
1/70	**Let It Be** . . . Beatles
	Let It Be Me
7/60	Everly Brothers
5/64	Betty Everett & Jerry Butler
36/69	Glen Campbell & Bobbie Gentry
40/82	Willie Nelson
12/67	**Let It Out (Let It All Hang Out)** . . . Hombres
23/74	**Let It Ride** . . . Bachman-Turner Overdrive
30/76	**Let It Shine** . . . Olivia Newton-John
5/82	**Let It Whip** . . . Dazz Band
23/67	**Let Love Come Between Us** . . . James & Bobby Purify
20/69	**Let Me** . . . Paul Revere & The Raiders
29/65	**Let Me Be** . . . Turtles
31/80	**Let Me Be The Clock** . . . Smokey Robinson
7/87	**Let Me Be The One** . . . Expose
6/74	**Let Me Be There** . . . Olivia Newton-John
21/80	**Let Me Be Your Angel** . . . Stacy Lattisaw
1/57	**(Let Me Be Your) Teddy Bear** . . . Elvis Presley
20/61	**Let Me Belong To You** . . . Brian Hyland
38/82	**Let Me Go** . . . Ray Parker Jr.
35/80	**Let Me Go, Love** . . . Nicolette Larson
	Let Me Go, Lover!
1/55	Joan Weber
6/55	Teresa Brewer
8/55	Patti Page
17/55	Sunny Gale
32/70	**Let Me Go To Him** . . . Dionne Warwick
4/62	**Let Me In** . . . Sensations

POS/YR	RECORD TITLE/ARTIST
36/73	**Let Me In** . . . Osmonds
10/80	**Let Me Love You Tonight** . . . Pure Prairie League
17/73	**Let Me Serenade You** . . . Three Dog Night
18/82	**Let Me Tickle Your Fancy** . . . Jermaine Jackson
9/80	**Let My Love Open The Door** . . . Pete Townshend
16/58	**Let The Bells Keep Ringing** . . . Paul Anka
	Let The Four Winds Blow
29/57	Roy Brown
15/61	Fats Domino
	Let The Good Times Roll
20/56	Shirley & Lee
22/67	Bunny Sigler (medley)
7/60	**Let The Little Girl Dance** . . . Billy Bland
8/84	**Let The Music Play** . . . Shannon
32/76	**Let The Music Play** . . . Barry White
1/69	**Let The Sunshine In (medley)** . . . 5th Dimension
	Let Them ..see: Let 'Em
7/61	**Let There Be Drums** . . . Sandy Nelson
27/74	**Let Your Hair Down** . . . Temptations
1/76	**Let Your Love Flow** . . . Bellamy Brothers
28/71	**Let Your Love Go** . . . Bread
36/78	**Let's All Chant** . . . Michael Zager Band
1/83	**Let's Dance** . . . David Bowie
4/62	**Let's Dance** . . . Chris Montez
1/75	**Let's Do It Again** . . . Staple Singers
40/65	**Let's Do The Freddie** . . . Chubby Checker *(also see: Do The Freddie)*
21/67	**Let's Fall In Love** . . . Peaches & Herb
1/73	**Let's Get It On** . . . Marvin Gaye
32/74	**Let's Get Married** . . . Al Green
9/80	**Let's Get Serious** . . . Jermaine Jackson
8/61	**Let's Get Together** . . . Hayley Mills *(also see: Get Together)*
9/87	**Let's Go!** . . . Wang Chung
14/79	**Let's Go** . . . Cars
19/62	**Let's Go** . . . Routers
39/61	**Let's Go Again** . . . Hank Ballard
7/86	**Let's Go All The Way** . . . Sly Fox
1/84	**Let's Go Crazy** . . . Prince
30/83	**Let's Go Dancin' (Ooh La, La, La)** . . . Kool & The Gang
31/66	**Let's Go Get Stoned** . . . Ray Charles
6/60	**Let's Go, Let's Go, Let's Go** . . . Hank Ballard

POS/YR	RECORD TITLE/ARTIST
26/63	**Let's Go Steady Again** . . . Neil Sedaka
3/81	**Let's Groove** . . . Earth, Wind & Fire
	Let's Hang On!
3/65	4 Seasons
32/82	Barry Manilow
37/60	**Let's Have A Party** . . . Wanda Jackson
1/84	**Let's Hear It For The Boy** . . . Deniece Williams
38/63	**Let's Kiss And Make Up** . . . Bobby Vinton
20/63	**Let's Limbo Some More** . . . Chubby Checker
8/67	**Let's Live For Today** . . . Grass Roots
35/76	**Let's Live Together** . . . Road Apples
11/65	**Let's Lock The Door** . . . Jay & The Americans
35/73	**Let's Pretend** . . . Raspberries
18/74	**Let's Put It All Together** . . . Stylistics
20/66	**Let's Start All Over Again** . . . Ronnie Dove
	Let's Stay Together
1/72	Al Green
26/84	Tina Turner
31/74	**Let's Straighten It Out** . . . Latimore
7/60	**Let's Think About Living** . . . Bob Luman
20/63	**Let's Turkey Trot** . . . Little Eva
8/61	**Let's Twist Again** . . . Chubby Checker
2/87	**Let's Wait Awhile** . . . Janet Jackson
39/87	**Let's Work** . . . Mick Jagger
	Let's Work Together
26/70	Canned Heat
32/70	Wilbert Harrison
	Letter, The
1/67	Box Tops
20/69	Arbors
7/70	Joe Cocker
25/64	**Letter From Sherry** . . . Dale Ward
19/62	**Letter Full Of Tears** . . . Gladys Knight & The Pips
	Letter Song ..see: S.Y.S.L.J.F.M.
25/58	**Letter To An Angel** . . . Jimmy Clanton
33/73	**Letter To Myself** . . . Chi-Lites
39/75	**Letting Go** . . . Wings
24/72	**Levon** . . . Elton John
7/71	**Liar** . . . Three Dog Night
12/65	**Liar, Liar** . . . Castaways
	Liberty Valance ..see: (Man Who Shot)
14/68	**Licking Stick - Licking Stick** . . . James Brown
11/77	**Lido Shuffle** . . . Boz Scaggs

POS/YR	RECORD TITLE/ARTIST
13/62	**Lie To Me** . . . Brook Benton
16/57	**Liechtensteiner Polka** . . . Will Glahe
20/66	**Lies** . . . Knickerbockers
27/87	**Lies** . . . Jonathan Butler
30/83	**Lies** . . . Thompson Twins
7/86	**Life In A Northern Town** . . . Dream Academy
19/85	**Life In One Day** . . . Howard Jones
11/77	**Life In The Fast Lane** . . . Eagles
8/74	**Life Is A Rock (But The Radio Rolled Me)** . . . Reunion
34/81	**Life Of Illusion** . . . Joe Walsh
12/78	**Life's Been Good** . . . Joe Walsh
	Light My Fire
1/67	Doors
3/68	Jose Feliciano
33/87	**Light Of Day** . . . Barbusters (Joan Jett)
1/66	**Lightnin' Strikes** . . . Lou Christie
24/67	**Lightning's Girl** . . . Nancy Sinatra
12/84	**Lights Out** . . . Peter Wolf
11/67	**(Lights Went Out In) Massachusetts** . . . Bee Gees
27/66	**Like A Baby** . . . Len Barry
12/86	**Like A Rock** . . . Bob Seger
2/65	**Like A Rolling Stone** . . . Bob Dylan
36/76	**Like A Sad Song** . . . John Denver
40/78	**Like A Sunday In Salem (The Amos & Andy Song)** . . . Gene Cotton
1/84	**Like A Virgin** . . . Madonna
24/67	**Like An Old Time Movie** . . . Scott McKenzie
38/61	**Like, Long Hair** . . . Paul Revere & The Raiders
14/86	**Like No Other Night** . . . 38 Special
22/60	**Like Strangers** . . . Everly Brothers
17/68	**Like To Get To Know You** . . . Spanky & Our Gang
	Limbo Rock
2/62	Chubby Checker
40/62	Champs
28/63	**Linda** . . . Jan & Dean
	Ling, Ting, Tong
26/55	Charms
28/55	Five Keys
	Lion Sleeps Tonight
1/61	Tokens
3/72	Robert John
17/57	**Lips Of Wine** . . . Andy Williams

POS/YR	RECORD TITLE/ARTIST
15/56	**Lipstick And Candy And Rubbersole Shoes** . . . Julius LaRosa
5/59	**Lipstick On Your Collar** . . . Connie Francis
	Lisbon Antigua
1/56	Nelson Riddle
19/56	Mitch Miller
3/66	**Listen People** . . . Herman's Hermits
11/72	**Listen To The Music** . . . Doobie Brothers
1/75	**Listen To What The Man Said** . . . Wings
	Little ..also see: Lil'
16/68	**Little Arrows** . . . Leapy Lee
21/63	**Little Band Of Gold** . . . James Gilreath
2/67	**Little Bit Me, A Little Bit You** . . . Monkees
11/76	**Little Bit More** . . . Dr. Hook
16/65	**Little Bit Of Heaven** . . . Ronnie Dove
38/86	**Little Bit Of Love (Is All It Takes)** . . . New Edition
	Little Bit Of Soap
12/61	Jarmels
34/79	Nigel Olsson
2/67	**Little Bit O' Soul** . . . Music Explosion
19/60	**Little Bitty Girl** . . . Bobby Rydell
	Little Bitty Pretty One
6/57	Thurston Harris
25/62	Clyde McPhatter
13/72	Jackson 5
9/62	**Little Bitty Tear** . . . Burl Ives
29/62	**Little Black Book** . . . Jimmy Dean
17/58	**Little Blue Man** . . . Betty Johnson
17/61	**Little Boy Sad** . . . Johnny Burnette
36/85	**Little By Little** . . . Robert Plant
7/64	**Little Children** . . . Billy J. Kramer
36/60	**Little Coco Palm** . . . Jerry Wallace
2/57	**Little Darlin'** . . . Diamonds
15/63	**Little Deuce Coupe** . . . Beach Boys
11/61	**Little Devil** . . . Neil Sedaka
8/62	**Little Diane** . . . Dion
30/59	**Little Dipper** . . . Mickey Mozart Quintet
	Little Drummer Boy
13/58	Harry Simeone Chorale
15/59	Harry Simeone Chorale
24/60	Harry Simeone Chorale
22/61	Harry Simeone Chorale
28/62	Harry Simeone Chorale
23/61	**Little Egypt (Ying-Yang)** . . . Coasters
8/66	**Little Girl** . . . Syndicate Of Sound
20/66	**Little Girl I Once Knew** . . . Beach Boys

POS/YR	RECORD TITLE/ARTIST
	Little Green Apples
2/68	O.C. Smith
39/68	Roger Miller
21/70	**Little Green Bag** . . . George Baker Selection
9/64	**Little Honda** . . . Hondells
17/81	**Little In Love** . . . Cliff Richard
3/80	**Little Jeannie** . . . Elton John
17/66	**Little Latin Lupe Lu** . . . Mitch Ryder & The Detroit Wheels
19/89	**Little Liar** . . . Joan Jett
4/87	**Little Lies** . . . Fleetwood Mac
33/56	**Little Love Can Go A Long, Long Way** . . . Dream Weavers
21/66	**Little Man** . . . Sonny & Cher
3/79	**Little More Love** . . . Olivia Newton-John
3/64	**Little Old Lady (From Pasadena)** . . . Jan & Dean
38/67	**Little Old Wine Drinker, Me** . . . Dean Martin
4/67	**Little Ole Man (Uptight-Everything's Alright)** . . . Bill Cosby
6/83	**Little Red Corvette** . . . Prince
23/62	**Little Red Rented Rowboat** . . . Joe Dowell
2/66	**Lil' Red Riding Hood** . . . Sam The Sham & The Pharoahs
11/63	**Little Red Rooster** . . . Sam Cooke
14/89	**Little Respect** . . . Erasure
32/57	**Little Sandy Sleighfoot** . . . Jimmy Dean
5/61	**Little Sister** . . . Elvis Presley
20/59	**Little Space Girl** . . . Jesse Lee Turner
1/58	**Little Star** . . . Elegants
13/65	**Little Things** . . . Bobby Goldsboro
35/60	**Little Things Mean A Lot** . . . Joni James
20/83	**Little Too Late** . . . Pat Benatar
12/63	**Little Town Flirt** . . . Del Shannon
25/57	**Little White Lies** . . . Betty Johnson
3/73	**Little Willy** . . . Sweet
3/69	**Little Woman** . . . Bobby Sherman
	Live And Die ..see: (Forever)
2/73	**Live And Let Die** . . . Wings
34/85	**Live Every Moment** . . . REO Speedwagon
32/86	**Live Is Life** . . . Opus
40/88	**Live My Life** . . . Boy George
1/86	**Live To Tell** . . . Madonna
20/76	**Livin' For The Weekend** . . . O'Jays
19/74	**Livin' For You** . . . Al Green

POS/YR	RECORD TITLE/ARTIST
31/84	**Livin' In Desperate Times** . . . Olivia Newton-John
40/77	**Livin' In The Life** . . . Isley Brothers
15/79	**Livin' It Up (Friday Night)** . . . Bell & James
1/87	**Livin' On A Prayer** . . . Bon Jovi
13/77	**Livin' Thing** . . . Electric Light Orchestra
22/63	**Living A Lie** . . . Al Martino
37/75	**Living A Little, Laughing A Little** . . . Spinners
30/59	**Living Doll** . . . Cliff Richard
8/74	**Living For The City** . . . Stevie Wonder
17/87	**Living In A Box** . . . Living In A Box
23/81	**Living In A Fantasy** . . . Leo Sayer
22/72	**Living In A House Divided** . . . Cher
4/86	**Living In America** . . . James Brown
11/73	**Living In The Past** . . . Jethro Tull
6/81	**Living Inside Myself** . . . Gino Vannelli
25/77	**Living Next Door To Alice** . . . Smokie
32/73	**Living Together, Growing Together** . . . 5th Dimension
37/75	**Lizzie And The Rainman** . . . Tanya Tucker
14/69	**Lo Mucho Que Te Quiero** . . . Rene & Rene
F/78	**Load-Out, The** . . . Jackson Browne
	Loco-Motion
1/62	Little Eva
1/74	Grand Funk
3/88	Kylie Minogue
12/63	**Loddy Lo** . . . Chubby Checker
6/79	**Logical Song** . . . Supertramp
9/70	**Lola** . . . Kinks
	Lollipop
2/58	Chordettes
20/58	Ronald & Ruby
39/78	**London Town** . . . Wings
14/67	**(Loneliness Made Me Realize) It's You That I Need** . . . Temptations
22/65	**L-O-N-E-L-Y** . . . Bobby Vinton
6/60	**Lonely Blue Boy** . . . Conway Twitty
	Lonely Boy
1/59	Paul Anka
F/72	Donny Osmond
7/77	**Lonely Boy** . . . Andrew Gold
6/62	**Lonely Bull** . . . Herb Alpert
3/71	**Lonely Days** . . . Bee Gees
24/59	**Lonely For You** . . . Gary Stites
26/58	**Lonely Island** . . . Sam Cooke

POS/YR	RECORD TITLE/ARTIST
32/61	**Lonely Man** . . . Elvis Presley
3/76	**Lonely Night (Angel Face)** . . . Captain & Tennille
6/85	**Lonely Ol' Night** . . . John Cougar Mellencamp
23/59	**Lonely One** . . . Duane Eddy
5/75	**Lonely People** . . . America
5/59	**Lonely Street** . . . Andy Williams
39/63	**Lonely Surfer** . . . Jack Nitzsche
7/59	**Lonely Teardrops** . . . Jackie Wilson
12/60	**Lonely Teenager** . . . Dion
22/60	**Lonely Weekends** . . . Charlie Rich
6/79	**Lonesome Loser** . . . Little River Band
7/58	**Lonesome Town** . . . Ricky Nelson
31/71	**Long Ago And Far Away** . . . James Taylor
1/70	**Long And Winding Road** . . . Beatles
2/72	**Long Cool Woman (In A Black Dress)** . . . Hollies
26/72	**Long Dark Road** . . . Hollies
38/72	**Long Haired Lover From Liverpool** . . . Little Jimmy Osmond
33/66	**Long Live Our Love** . . . Shangri-Las
17/65	**Long Lonely Nights** . . . Bobby Vinton
20/70	**Long Lonesome Highway** . . . Michael Parks
25/70	**Long Long Time** . . . Linda Ronstadt
20/78	**Long, Long Way From Home** . . . Foreigner
	(Long Nights) ..see: Blue Collar Man
8/80	**Long Run** . . . Eagles
9/75	**Long Tall Glasses (I Can Dance)** . . . Leo Sayer
	Long Tall Sally
6/56	Little Richard
8/56	Pat Boone
22/77	**Long Time** . . . Boston
8/73	**Long Train Runnin'** . . . Doobie Brothers
2/80	**Longer** . . . Dan Fogelberg
14/84	**Longest Time** . . . Billy Joel
6/55	**Longest Walk** . . . Jaye P. Morgan
5/74	**Longfellow Serenade** . . . Neil Diamond
39/75	**Look At Me (I'm In Love)** . . . Moments
1/88	**Look Away** . . . Chicago
	Look For A Star
16/60	Garry Miles
19/60	Billy Vaughn
26/60	Garry Mills
29/60	Deane Hawley

POS/YR	RECORD TITLE/ARTIST
36/57	**Look Homeward, Angel** . . . Johnnie Ray
14/61	**Look In My Eyes** . . . Chantels
11/75	**Look In My Eyes Pretty Woman** . . . Dawn
18/83	**Look Of Love** . . . ABC
	Look Of Love
22/67	Dusty Springfield
4/68	Sergio Mendes & Brasil '66
27/65	**Look Of Love** . . . Lesley Gore
35/88	**Look Out Any Window** . . . Bruce Hornsby & The Range
32/66	**Look Through Any Window** . . . Hollies
24/66	**Look Through My Window** . . . Mamas & The Papas
14/70	**Look What They've Done To My Song Ma** . . . New Seekers
4/72	**Look What You Done For Me** . . . Al Green
32/67	**Look What You've Done** . . . Pozo-Seco Singers
14/80	**Look What You've Done To Me** . . . Boz Scaggs
	Lookin' For A Love
39/72	J. Geils Band
10/74	Bobby Womack
5/80	**Lookin' For Love** . . . Johnny Lee
2/70	**Lookin' Out My Back Door** . . . Creedence Clearwater Revival
16/72	**Lookin' Through The Windows** . . . Jackson 5
5/58	**Looking Back** . . . Nat King Cole
2/87	**Looking For A New Love** . . . Jody Watley
39/83	**Looking For A Stranger** . . . Pat Benatar
29/76	**Looking For Space** . . . John Denver
	Looking Through The Eyes Of Love
28/65	Gene Pitney
39/73	Partridge Family
1/77	**Looks Like We Made It** . . . Barry Manilow
4/63	**Loop De Loop** . . . Johnny Thunder
4/74	**Lord's Prayer** . . . Sister Janet Mead
27/76	**Lorelei** . . . Styx
6/63	**Losing You** . . . Brenda Lee
34/80	**Lost Her In The Sun** . . . John Stewart
1/87	**Lost In Emotion** . . . Lisa Lisa & Cult Jam
3/80	**Lost In Love** . . . Air Supply
35/85	**Lost In Love** . . . New Edition
12/88	**Lost In You** . . . Rod Stewart
35/61	**Lost Love** . . . H.B. Barnum
9/77	**Lost Without Your Love** . . . Bread
8/79	**Lotta Love** . . . Nicolette Larson

POS/YR	RECORD TITLE/ARTIST
13/57	**Lotta Lovin'** . . . Gene Vincent
	Louie Louie
2/63	Kingsmen
30/66	Sandpipers
	Love And Marriage
5/55	Frank Sinatra
20/55	Dinah Shore
	Love Ballad
20/76	L.T.D.
18/79	George Benson
	Love Being Your Fool ..see: (Shu-Doo-Pa-Poo-Poop)
1/88	**Love Bites** . . . Def Leppard
11/86	**Love Bizarre** . . . Sheila E.
25/67	**Love Bug Leave My Heart Alone** . . . Martha & The Vandellas
10/62	**Love Came To Me** . . . Dion
2/69	**Love (Can Make You Happy)** . . . Mercy
23/88	**Love Changes (Everything)** . . . Climie Fisher
1/68	**Love Child** . . . Supremes
17/82	**Love Come Down** . . . Evelyn King
32/79	**Love Don't Live Here Anymore** . . . Rose Royce
15/74	**Love Don't Love Nobody** . . . Spinners
15/67	**Love Eyes** . . . Nancy Sinatra
30/76	**Love Fire** . . . Jigsaw
5/70	**Love Grows (Where My Rosemary Goes)** . . . Edison Lighthouse
1/76	**Love Hangover** . . . Diana Ross
11/71	**Love Her Madly** . . . Doors
8/76	**Love Hurts** . . . Nazareth
7/73	**Love I Lost** . . . Harold Melvin & The Bluenotes
20/67	**Love I Saw In You Was Just A Mirage** . . . Miracles
36/77	**Love In 'C' Minor** . . . Cerrone
22/83	**Love In Store** . . . Fleetwood Mac
15/82	**Love In The First Degree** . . . Alabama
16/76	**Love In The Shadows** . . . Neil Sedaka
5/83	**Love Is A Battlefield** . . . Pat Benatar
10/57	**Love Is A Golden Ring** . . . Frankie Laine
13/66	**Love Is A Hurtin' Thing** . . . Lou Rawls
	Love Is A Many-Splendored Thing
1/55	Four Aces
26/55	Don Cornell
23/83	**Love Is A Stranger** . . . Eurythmics
2/76	**Love Is Alive** . . . Gary Wright
7/68	**Love Is All Around** . . . Troggs

POS/YR	RECORD TITLE/ARTIST
15/58	**Love Is All We Need** . . . Tommy Edwards
20/82	**Love Is Alright Tonite** . . . Rick Springfield
	Love Is Blue
1/68	Paul Mauriat
22/69	Dells (medley)
16/86	**Love Is Forever** . . . Billy Ocean
1/67	**Love Is Here And Now You're Gone** . . . Supremes
10/82	**Love Is In Control (Finger On The Trigger)** . . . Donna Summer
7/78	**Love Is In The Air** . . . John Paul Young
26/68	**(Love Is Like A) Baseball Game** . . . Intruders
37/82	**Love Is Like A Rock** . . . Donnie Iris
9/66	**Love Is Like An Itching In My Heart** . . . Supremes
8/78	**Love Is Like Oxygen** . . . Sweet
	Love Is Strange
11/57	Mickey & Sylvia
13/67	Peaches & Herb
10/79	**Love Is The Answer** . . . England Dan & John Ford Coley
30/76	**Love Is The Drug** . . . Roxy Music
17/85	**Love Is The Seventh Wave** . . . Sting
7/56	**(Love Is) The Tender Trap** . . . Frank Sinatra
1/78	**(Love Is) Thicker Than Water** . . . Andy Gibb
16/73	**Love Jones** . . . Brighter Side Of Darkness *(also see: Basketball Jones)*
16/70	**Love Land** . . . Charles Wright
	Love Letters
5/62	Ketty Lester
19/66	Elvis Presley
1/57	**Love Letters In The Sand** . . . Pat Boone
17/85	**Love Light In Flight** . . . Stevie Wonder
13/75	**L-O-V-E (Love)** . . . Al Green
	Love, Love, Love
30/56	Clovers
30/56	Diamonds
1/76	**Love Machine** . . . Miracles
15/68	**Love Makes A Woman** . . . Barbara Acklin
11/66	**Love Makes The World Go Round** . . . Deon Jackson
26/63	**Love (Makes The World Go 'Round)** . . . Paul Anka
33/58	**Love Makes The World Go 'Round** . . . Perry Como
2/57	**Love Me** . . . Elvis Presley
14/76	**Love Me** . . . Yvonne Elliman
1/64	**Love Me Do** . . . Beatles
10/74	**Love Me For A Reason** . . . Osmonds
	Love Me Forever
24/57	Eydie Gorme
25/57	Four Esquires
	Love Me Or Leave Me
12/55	Sammy Davis, Jr.
19/55	Lena Horne
	Love Me Tender
1/56	Elvis Presley
21/62	Richard Chamberlain
40/67	Percy Sledge
11/57	**Love Me To Pieces** . . . Jill Corey
22/82	**Love Me Tomorrow** . . . Chicago
13/69	**Love Me Tonight** . . . Tom Jones
25/68	**Love Me Two Times** . . . Doors
12/62	**Love Me Warm And Tender** . . . Paul Anka
	Love Me With All Your Heart
3/64	Ray Charles Singers
38/66	Bachelors
39/71	**Love Means (You Never Have To Say You're Sorry)** . . . Sounds Of Sunshine
	Love My Life Away ..see: (I Wanna)
40/58	**Love Of My Life** . . . Everly Brothers
21/63	**Love Of My Man** . . . Theola Kilgore
	Love On A Two-Way Street
3/70	Moments
26/81	Stacy Lattisaw
2/81	**Love On The Rocks** . . . Neil Diamond
36/76	**Love Or Leave** . . . Spinners
	Love Or Let Me Be Lonely
6/70	Friends Of Distinction
40/82	Paul Davis
32/78	**Love Or Something Like It** . . . Kenny Rogers
13/88	**Love Overboard** . . . Gladys Knight & The Pips
34/79	**Love Pains** . . . Yvonne Elliman
36/86	**Love Parade** . . . Dream Academy
37/82	**Love Plus One** . . . Haircut One Hundred
	Love Potion Number Nine
23/59	Clovers
3/65	Searchers
12/87	**Love Power** . . . Dionne Warwick & Jeffrey Osborne
22/68	**Love Power** . . . Sandpebbles
22/76	**Love Really Hurts Without You** . . . Billy Ocean
1/76	**Love Rollercoaster** . . . Ohio Players

POS/YR	RECORD TITLE/ARTIST
31/63	**Love She Can Count On** . . . Miracles
40/63	**Love So Fine** . . . Chiffons
3/76	**Love So Right** . . . Bee Gees
5/84	**Love Somebody** . . . Rick Springfield
12/74	**Love Song** . . . Anne Murray
38/80	**Love Stinks** . . . J. Geils Band
	Love Story ..see: Theme From
11/79	**Love Takes Time** . . . Orleans
	Love The One You're With
14/71	Stephen Stills
18/71	Isley Brothers
14/80	**Love The World Away** . . . Kenny Rogers
21/78	**Love Theme From Eyes Of Laura Mars (Prisoner)** . . . Barbra Streisand
37/61	**Love Theme From One Eyed Jacks** . . . Ferrante & Teicher
	Love Theme From One On One ..see: My Fair Share
1/69	**Love Theme From Romeo & Juliet** . . . Henry Mancini
15/85	**Love Theme From St. Elmo's Fire** . . . David Foster
34/72	**Love Theme From The Godfather** . . . Andy Williams
2/76	**Love To Love You Baby** . . . Donna Summer
6/86	**Love Touch** . . . Rod Stewart
1/73	**Love Train** . . . O'Jays
30/60	**Love Walked In** . . . Dinah Washington
22/86	**Love Walks In** . . . Van Halen
30/71	**Love We Had (Stays On My Mind)** . . . Dells
9/86	**Love Will Conquer All** . . . Lionel Richie
6/78	**Love Will Find A Way** . . . Pablo Cruise
30/87	**Love Will Find A Way** . . . Yes
40/69	**Love Will Find A Way** . . . Jackie DeShannon
1/75	**Love Will Keep Us Together** . . . Captain & Tennille
9/88	**Love Will Save The Day** . . . Whitney Houston
30/84	**Love Will Show Us How** . . . Christine McVie
13/82	**Love Will Turn You Around** . . . Kenny Rogers
5/75	**Love Won't Let Me Wait** . . . Major Harris
9/87	**Love You Down** . . . Ready For The World
1/79	**Love You Inside Out** . . . Bee Gees

POS/YR	RECORD TITLE/ARTIST
24/81	**Love You Like I Never Loved Before** . . . John O'Banion
26/58	**Love You Most Of All** . . . Sam Cooke
1/70	**Love You Save** . . . Jackson 5
7/60	**Love You So** . . . Ron Holden
10/86	**Love Zone** . . . Billy Ocean
7/82	**Love's Been A Little Bit Hard On Me** . . . Juice Newton
20/77	**Love's Grown Deep** . . . Kenny Nolan
19/71	**Love's Lines, Angles And Rhymes** . . . 5th Dimension
26/66	**Love's Made A Fool Of You** . . . Bobby Fuller Four
1/74	**Love's Theme** . . . Love Unlimited Orchestra
30/78	**Lovely Day** . . . Bill Withers
12/80	**Lovely One** . . . Jacksons
20/56	**Lovely One** . . . Four Voices
2/89	**Lover In Me** . . . Sheena Easton
7/62	**Lover Please** . . . Clyde McPhatter
2/65	**Lover's Concerto** . . . Toys
31/68	**Lover's Holiday** . . . Peggy Scott & Jo Jo Benson
40/80	**Lover's Holiday** . . . Change
31/61	**Lover's Island** . . . Blue Jays
6/59	**Lover's Question** . . . Clyde McPhatter
2/85	**Loverboy** . . . Billy Ocean
4/85	**Lovergirl** . . . Teena Marie
36/62	**Lovers By Night, Strangers By Day** . . . Fleetwoods
3/62	**Lovers Who Wander** . . . Dion
2/73	**Loves Me Like A Rock** . . . Paul Simon
25/61	**Lovey Dovey** . . . Buddy Knox
9/85	**Lovin' Every Minute Of It** . . . Loverboy
16/79	**Lovin', Touchin', Squeezin'** . . . Journey
1/75	**Lovin' You** . . . Minnie Riperton
32/67	**Lovin' You** . . . Bobby Darin
26/71	**Loving Her Was Easier (Than Anything I'll Ever Do Again)** . . . Kris Kristofferson
20/57	**Loving You** . . . Elvis Presley
29/72	**Loving You Just Crossed My Mind** . . . Sam Neely
7/75	**Low Rider** . . . War
3/76	**Lowdown** . . . Boz Scaggs
35/71	**Lowdown** . . . Chicago
	Lt. Calley ..see: Battle Hymn Of
5/77	**Lucille** . . . Kenny Rogers

POS/YR	RECORD TITLE/ARTIST
	Lucille
21/57	Little Richard
21/60	Everly Brothers
25/77	**Luckenbach, Texas** . . . Waylon Jennings
30/85	**Lucky** . . . Greg Kihn Band
25/60	**Lucky Devil** . . . Carl Dobkins, Jr.
38/85	**Lucky In Love** . . . Mick Jagger
14/59	**Lucky Ladybug** . . . Billy & Lillie
25/57	**Lucky Lips** . . . Ruth Brown
20/84	**Lucky One** . . . Laura Branigan
4/84	**Lucky Star** . . . Madonna
29/70	**Lucretia Mac Evil** . . . Blood, Sweat & Tears
1/75	**Lucy In The Sky With Diamonds** . . . Elton John
3/87	**Luka** . . . Suzanne Vega
16/56	**Lullaby Of Birdland** . . . Blue Stars
23/61	**Lullaby Of Love** . . . Frank Gari
2/75	**Lyin' Eyes** . . . Eagles

M

POS/YR	RECORD TITLE/ARTIST
15/59	**M.T.A.** . . . Kingston Trio
5/70	**Ma Belle Amie** . . . Tee Set
	MacArthur Park
2/68	Richard Harris
38/71	Four Tops
1/78	Donna Summer
22/74	**Machine Gun** . . . Commodores
25/78	**Macho Man** . . . Village People
	Mack The Knife
8/56	Dick Hyman
11/56	Richard Hayman & Jan August
17/56	Lawrence Welk
20/56	Louis Armstrong
37/56	Billy Vaughn
1/59	Bobby Darin
27/60	Ella Fitzgerald
3/86	**Mad About You** . . . Belinda Carlisle
	Made To Love ..see: (Girls, Girls, Girls)
36/76	**Mademoiselle** . . . Styx
23/60	**Madison, The** . . . Al Brown's Tunetoppers
30/60	**Madison Time** . . . Ray Bryant Combo
1/71	**Maggie May** . . . Rod Stewart

POS/YR	RECORD TITLE/ARTIST
1/80	**Magic** . . . Olivia Newton-John
5/75	**Magic** . . . Pilot
12/84	**Magic** . . . Cars
25/68	**Magic Bus** . . . Who
3/68	**Magic Carpet Ride** . . . Steppenwolf
9/76	**Magic Man** . . . Heart
4/58	**Magic Moments** . . . Perry Como
	Magic Touch ..see: (You've Got)
21/66	**Magic Town** . . . Vogues
39/77	**Magical Mystery Tour** . . . Ambrosia
8/78	**Magnet And Steel** . . . Walter Egan
35/61	**Magnificent Seven** . . . Al Caiola
	Magnum P.I. ..see: Theme From
	Mahogany ..see: Theme From
3/79	**Main Event (medley)** . . . Barbra Streisand
	Main Theme From Exodus ..see: Exodus
	Main Title And Molly-O ..see: Man With The Golden Arm
24/77	**Mainstreet** . . . Bob Seger
36/61	**Majestic, The** . . . Dion
14/83	**Major Tom (Coming Home)** . . . Peter Schilling
25/80	**Make A Little Magic** . . . Dirt Band
5/82	**Make A Move On Me** . . . Olivia Newton-John
28/69	**Make Believe** . . . Wind
30/82	**Make Believe** . . . Toto
	Make It Easy On Yourself
20/62	Jerry Butler
16/65	Walker Bros.
37/70	Dionne Warwick
22/71	**Make It Funky** . . . James Brown
4/88	**Make It Real** . . . Jets
1/70	**Make It With You** . . . Bread
29/83	**Make Love Stay** . . . Dan Fogelberg
16/58	**Make Me A Miracle** . . . Jimmie Rodgers
28/66	**Make Me Belong To You** . . . Barbara Lewis
3/88	**Make Me Lose Control** . . . Eric Carmen
9/70	**Make Me Smile** . . . Chicago
27/72	**Make Me The Woman That You Go Home To** . . . Gladys Knight & The Pips
11/65	**Make Me Your Baby** . . . Barbara Lewis
21/67	**Make Me Yours** . . . Bettye Swann
	Make The World Go Away
24/63	Timi Yuro
6/65	Eddy Arnold

POS/YR	RECORD TITLE/ARTIST
36/69	**Make Your Own Kind Of Music** . . . Mama Cass Elliot
	Make Yourself Comfortable
6/55	Sarah Vaughan
26/55	Andy Griffith
30/55	Peggy King
5/79	**Makin' It** . . . David Naughton
20/59	**Makin' Love** . . . Floyd Robinson
31/67	**Making Every Minute Count** . . . Spanky & Our Gang
13/82	**Making Love** . . . Roberta Flack
35/87	**Making Love In The Rain** . . . Herb Alpert/Lisa Keith
2/83	**Making Love Out Of Nothing At All** . . . Air Supply
35/67	**Making Memories** . . . Frankie Laine
25/76	**Making Our Dreams Come True** . . . Cyndi Grecco
	Mama ..also see: Mamma
8/60	**Mama** . . . Connie Francis
22/66	**Mama** . . . B.J. Thomas
9/79	**Mama Can't Buy You Love** . . . Elton John
14/63	**Mama Didn't Lie** . . . Jan Bradley
11/56	**Mama From The Train** . . . Patti Page
11/57	**Mama Look At Bubu** . . . Harry Belafonte
4/61	**Mama Said** . . . Shirelles
	Mama Sang A Song
32/62	Stan Kenton
38/62	Walter Brennan
34/56	**Mama, Teach Me To Dance** . . . Eydie Gorme
1/70	**Mama Told Me (Not To Come)** . . . Three Dog Night
30/82	**Mama Used To Say** . . . Junior
2/71	**Mama's Pearl** . . . Jackson 5
18/55	**Mambo Rock** . . . Bill Haley
19/66	**Mame** . . . Herb Alpert
32/76	**Mamma Mia** . . . Abba
16/55	**Man Chases A Girl** . . . Eddie Fisher
31/79	**Man I'll Never Be** . . . Boston
1/88	**Man In The Mirror** . . . Michael Jackson
	Man In The Raincoat
14/55	Marion Marlowe
16/55	Priscilla Wright
40/82	**Man On The Corner** . . . Genesis
14/82	**Man On Your Mind** . . . Little River Band
15/86	**Man Size Love** . . . Klymaxx
4/62	**(Man Who Shot) Liberty Valance** . . . Gene Pitney

POS/YR	RECORD TITLE/ARTIST
	Man With The Golden Arm (Main Title/Molly-O/Delilah Jones)
14/56	Richard Maltby
16/56	Elmer Bernstein
22/56	Dick Jacobs
37/56	McGuire Sisters
19/68	**Man Without Love** . . . Engelbert Humperdinck
4/87	**Mandolin Rain** . . . Bruce Hornsby & The Range
1/75	**Mandy** . . . Barry Manilow
1/82	**Maneater** . . . Daryl Hall & John Oates
10/57	**Mangos** . . . Rosemary Clooney
10/59	**Manhattan Spiritual** . . . Reg Owen
1/83	**Maniac** . . . Michael Sembello
2/86	**Manic Monday** . . . Bangles
7/60	**Many Tears Ago** . . . Connie Francis
20/58	**March From The River Kwai and Colonel Bogey** . . . Mitch Miller
8/77	**Margaritaville** . . . Jimmy Buffett
6/63	**Maria Elena** . . . Los Indios Tabajaras
	Marianne
3/57	Hilltoppers
4/57	Terry Gilkyson & The Easy Riders
15/65	**Marie** . . . Bachelors
4/61	**(Marie's the Name) His Latest Flame** . . . Elvis Presley
31/59	**Marina** . . . Rocco Granata
36/63	**Marlena** . . . 4 Seasons
28/69	**Marrakesh Express** . . . Crosby, Stills & Nash
40/79	**Married Men** . . . Bette Midler
16/63	**Martian Hop** . . . Ran-Dells
39/62	**Mary Ann Regrets** . . . Burl Ives
28/72	**Mary Had A Little Lamb** . . . Wings
27/67	**Mary In The Morning** . . . Al Martino
26/59	**Mary Lou** . . . Ronnie Hawkins
12/56	**Mary's Boy Child** . . . Harry Belafonte
39/62	**Mary's Little Lamb** . . . James Darren
23/87	**Mary's Prayer** . . . Danny Wilson
2/62	**Mashed Potato Time** . . . Dee Dee Sharp
	Massachusetts ..see: (Lights Went Out In)
5/80	**Master Blaster (Jammin')** . . . Stevie Wonder
18/68	**Master Jack** . . . Four Jacks & A Jill
33/73	**Master Of Eyes** . . . Aretha Franklin
7/73	**Masterpiece** . . . Temptations
20/64	**Matador, The** . . . Major Lance

POS/YR	RECORD TITLE/ARTIST
17/64	**Matchbox** . . . Beatles
2/85	**Material Girl** . . . Madonna
10/86	**Matter Of Trust** . . . Billy Joel
39/69	**May I** . . . Bill Deal
15/65	**May The Bird Of Paradise Fly Up Your Nose** . . . "Little" Jimmy Dickens
11/59	**May You Always** . . . McGuire Sisters
	Maybe
15/58	Chantels
29/70	Three Degrees
17/58	**Maybe Baby** . . . Crickets
14/64	**Maybe I Know** . . . Lesley Gore
22/79	**Maybe I'm A Fool** . . . Eddie Money
10/77	**Maybe I'm Amazed** . . . Wings
20/71	**Maybe Tomorrow** . . . Jackson 5
	Maybellene
5/55	Chuck Berry
12/64	Johnny Rivers
15/74	**Me And Baby Brother** . . . War
	Me And Bobby McGee
1/71	Janis Joplin
40/72	Jerry Lee Lewis
22/72	**Me And Julio Down By The Schoolyard** . . . Paul Simon
1/72	**Me And Mrs. Jones** . . . Billy Paul
34/71	**Me And My Arrow** . . . Nilsson
5/71	**Me And You And A Dog Named Boo** . . . Lobo
40/81	**Me (Without You)** . . . Andy Gibb
5/63	**Mean Woman Blues** . . . Roy Orbison
12/63	**Mecca** . . . Gene Pitney
	"Medic" Theme ..see: Blue Star
22/69	**Medicine Man** . . . Buchanan Brothers
11/87	**Meet Me Half Way** . . . Kenny Loggins
2/66	**Mellow Yellow** . . . Donovan
5/57	**Melodie D'Amour** . . . Ames Brothers
	Melody Of Love
2/55	Billy Vaughn
3/55	Four Aces
8/55	David Carroll
19/55	Frank Sinatra & Ray Anthony
30/55	Leo Diamond
35/69	**Memories** . . . Elvis Presley
	Memories Are Made Of This
1/56	Dean Martin
5/56	Gale Storm
	Memories Of You
22/55	Four Coins
20/56	Benny Goodman/Rosemary Clooney

POS/YR	RECORD TITLE/ARTIST
39/83	**Memory** . . . Barry Manilow
	Memphis
5/63	Lonnie Mack
2/64	Johnny Rivers
33/67	**Memphis Soul Stew** . . . King Curtis
	Men ..also see: Theme From The
33/68	**Men Are Gettin' Scarce** . . . Joe Tex
6/66	**Men In My Little Girl's Life** . . . Mike Douglas
27/69	**Mendocino** . . . Sir Douglas Quintet
2/88	**Mercedes Boy** . . . Pebbles
30/69	**Mercy** . . . Ohio Express
35/64	**Mercy, Mercy** . . . Don Covay
4/71	**Mercy Mercy Me (The Ecology)** . . . Marvin Gaye
	Mercy, Mercy, Mercy
5/67	Buckinghams
11/67	Cannonball Adderley
32/60	**Mess Of Blues** . . . Elvis Presley
8/66	**Message To Michael** . . . Dionne Warwick
5/85	**Method Of Modern Love** . . . Daryl Hall & John Oates
16/58	**Mexican Hat Rock** . . . Applejacks
7/61	**Mexico** . . . Bob Moore
1/85	**Miami Vice Theme** . . . Jan Hammer
1/61	**Michael** . . . Highwaymen
18/66	**Michelle** . . . David & Jonathan
1/82	**Mickey** . . . Toni Basil
8/63	**Mickey's Monkey** . . . Miracles
19/84	**Middle Of The Road** . . . Pretenders
6/74	**Midnight At The Oasis** . . . Maria Muldaur
5/87	**Midnight Blue** . . . Lou Gramm
6/75	**Midnight Blue** . . . Melissa Manchester
5/68	**Midnight Confessions** . . . Grass Roots
10/70	**Midnight Cowboy** . . . Ferrante & Teicher
	Midnight Hour ..see: In The
2/62	**Midnight In Moscow** . . . Kenny Ball
10/64	**Midnight Mary** . . . Joey Powers
	Midnight Rider
27/72	Joe Cocker
19/74	Gregg Allman
24/80	**Midnight Rocks** . . . Al Stewart
	Midnight Special
16/60	Paul Evans
20/65	Johnny Rivers
35/59	**Midnight Stroll** . . . Revels

POS/YR	RECORD TITLE/ARTIST
1/73	**Midnight Train To Georgia** . . . Gladys Knight & The Pips
28/79	**Midnight Wind** . . . John Stewart
34/71	**Mighty Clouds Of Joy** . . . B.J. Thomas
38/59	**Mighty Good** . . . Ricky Nelson
20/74	**Mighty Love** . . . Spinners
29/74	**Mighty Mighty** . . . Earth, Wind & Fire
10/68	**Mighty Quinn (Quinn The Eskimo)** . . . Manfred Mann
33/64	**Miller's Cave** . . . Bobby Bare
	Million To One
5/60	Jimmy Charles
23/73	Donny Osmond
	Millionaire ..see: (How To Be A)
26/69	**Mind, Body And Soul** . . . Flaming Ember
18/73	**Mind Games** . . . John Lennon
38/69	**Minotaur, The** . . . Dick Hyman
14/79	**Minute By Minute** . . . Doobie Brothers
18/56	**Miracle Of Love** . . . Eileen Rodgers
3/75	**Miracles** . . . Jefferson Starship
40/83	**Miracles** . . . Stacy Lattisaw
10/67	**Mirage** . . . Tommy James & The Shondells
30/83	**Mirror Man** . . . Human League
8/82	**Mirror, Mirror** . . . Diana Ross
22/73	**Misdemeanor** . . . Foster Sylvers
10/85	**Misled** . . . Kool & The Gang
5/84	**Miss Me Blind** . . . Culture Club
14/81	**Miss Sun** . . . Boz Scaggs
1/78	**Miss You** . . . Rolling Stones
29/88	**Missed Opportunity** . . . Daryl Hall John Oates
1/84	**Missing You** . . . John Waite
10/85	**Missing You** . . . Diana Ross
23/82	**Missing You** . . . Dan Fogelberg
29/61	**Missing You** . . . Ray Peterson
7/60	**Mission Bell** . . . Donnie Brooks
14/86	**Missionary Man** . . . Eurythmics
32/70	**Mississippi** . . . John Phillips
21/70	**Mississippi Queen** . . . Mountain
33/85	**Mistake No. 3** . . . Culture Club
	Mister ..see: Mr.
	Misty
12/59	Johnny Mathis
21/63	Lloyd Price
14/75	Ray Stevens
3/76	**Misty Blue** . . . Dorthy Moore
14/80	**Misunderstanding** . . . Genesis

POS/YR	RECORD TITLE/ARTIST
37/64	**Mixed-Up, Shook-Up, Girl** . . . Patty & The Emblems
32/58	**Mocking Bird, The** . . . Four Lads
	Mockingbird
7/63	Inez Foxx
5/74	Carly Simon & James Taylor
20/61	**Model Girl** . . . Johnny Maestro
22/84	**Modern Day Delilah** . . . Van Stephenson
18/81	**Modern Girl** . . . Sheena Easton
14/83	**Modern Love** . . . David Bowie
10/86	**Modern Woman** . . . Billy Joel
21/65	**Mohair Sam** . . . Charlie Rich
	Molly-O ..see: Man With The Golden Arm
2/55	**Moments To Remember** . . . Four Lads
	Mona Lisa
25/59	Carl Mann
29/59	Conway Twitty
1/66	**Monday, Monday** . . . Mamas & The Papas
13/73	**Money** . . . Pink Floyd
27/85	**Money Changes Everything** . . . Cyndi Lauper
1/85	**Money For Nothing** . . . Dire Straits
9/76	**Money Honey** . . . Bay City Rollers
	Money (That's What I Want)
23/60	Barrett Strong
16/64	Kingsmen
20/56	**Money Tree** . . . Margaret Whiting
28/86	**Money$ Too Tight (To Mention)** . . . Simply Red
1/88	**Monkey** . . . George Michael
8/63	**Monkey Time** . . . Major Lance
39/70	**Monster** . . . Steppenwolf
	Monster Mash
1/62	Bobby "Boris" Pickett
10/73	Bobby "Boris" Pickett
30/62	**Monsters' Holiday** . . . Bobby "Boris" Pickett
8/70	**Montego Bay** . . . Bobby Bloom
15/68	**Monterey** . . . Animals
	Mony Mony
3/68	Tommy James & The Shondells
1/87	Billy Idol
31/77	**Moody Blue** . . . Elvis Presley
1/61	**Moody River** . . . Pat Boone
24/69	**Moody Woman** . . . Jerry Butler
	Moon River
11/61	Jerry Butler
11/61	Henry Mancini

POS/YR	RECORD TITLE/ARTIST
30/71	**Moon Shadow** . . . Cat Stevens
28/58	**Moon Talk** . . . Perry Como
38/69	**Moonflight** . . . Vik Venus
	Moonglow and Theme From "Picnic"
1/56	Morris Stoloff
4/56	George Cates
13/56	McGuire Sisters (Picnic)
3/76	**Moonlight Feels Right** . . . Starbuck
3/57	**Moonlight Gambler** . . . Frankie Laine
	Moonlight Swim
24/57	Tony Perkins
37/57	Nick Noble
23/87	**Moonlighting** . . . Al Jarreau
4/56	**More** . . . Perry Como
8/63	**More** . . . Kai Winding
16/66	**More I See You** . . . Chris Montez
	More Love
23/67	Miracles
10/80	Kim Carnes
17/61	**More Money For You And Me** . . . Four Preps
4/76	**More, More, More** . . . Andrea True Connection
5/76	**More Than A Feeling** . . . Boston
32/78	**More Than A Woman** . . . Tavares
2/80	**More Than I Can Say** . . . Leo Sayer
34/82	**More Than Just The Two Of Us** . . . Sneaker
18/89	**More Than You Know** . . . Martika
12/69	**More Today Than Yesterday** . . . Spiral Starecase
13/59	**Morgen** . . . Ivo Robic
	Moritat ..see: Mack The Knife
21/83	**Mornin'** . . . Jarreau
14/75	**Mornin' Beautiful** . . . Dawn
1/73	**Morning After** . . . Maureen McGovern
24/79	**Morning Dance** . . . Spyro Gyra
17/69	**Morning Girl** . . . Neon Philharmonic
6/72	**Morning Has Broken** . . . Cat Stevens
	Morning Side Of The Mountain
27/59	Tommy Edwards
8/75	Donny & Marie Osmond
1/81	**Morning Train (Nine To Five)** . . . Sheena Easton
1/73	**Most Beautiful Girl** . . . Charlie Rich
14/55	**Most Of All** . . . Don Cornell
38/71	**Most Of All** . . . B.J. Thomas
27/62	**Most People Get Married** . . . Patti Page
31/56	**Mostly Martha** . . . Crew-Cuts

POS/YR	RECORD TITLE/ARTIST
4/72	**Mother And Child Reunion** . . . Paul Simon
37/71	**Mother Freedom** . . . Bread
1/61	**Mother-In-Law** . . . Ernie K-Doe
11/69	**Mother Popcorn** . . . James Brown
8/66	**Mothers Little Helper** . . . Rolling Stones
27/86	**Mothers Talk** . . . Tears For Fears
12/72	**Motorcycle Mama** . . . Sailcat
36/87	**Motortown** . . . Kane Gang
	Mountain Of Love
21/60	Harold Dorman
9/64	Johnny Rivers
2/61	**Mountain's High** . . . Dick & DeeDee
23/86	**Mountains** . . . Prince
12/86	**Move Away** . . . Culture Club
31/69	**Move Over** . . . Steppenwolf
	Move Two Mountains ..see: (You've Got To)
14/76	**Movin'** . . . Brass Construction
19/75	**Movin' On** . . . Bad Company
17/78	**Movin' Out (Anthony's Song)** . . . Billy Joel
16/63	**Mr. Bass Man** . . . Johnny Cymbal
2/71	**Mr. Big Stuff** . . . Jean Knight
1/59	**Mr. Blue** . . . Fleetwoods
35/78	**Mr. Blue Sky** . . . Electric Light Orchestra
9/71	**Mr. Bojangles** . . . Nitty Gritty Dirt Band
28/68	**Mr. Businessman** . . . Ray Stevens
38/72	**Mr. Can't You See** . . . Buffy Sainte-Marie
1/60	**Mr. Custer** . . . Larry Verne
17/66	**Mr. Dieingly Sad** . . . Critters
	Mr. Dream Merchant ..see: Dream Merchant
4/75	**Mr. Jaws** . . . Dickie Goodman
6/57	**Mr. Lee** . . . Bobbettes
1/64	**Mr. Lonely** . . . Bobby Vinton
21/60	**Mr. Lucky** . . . Henry Mancini
3/83	**Mr. Roboto** . . . Styx
37/81	**Mr. Sandman** . . . Emmylou Harris
36/66	**Mr. Spaceman** . . . Byrds
18/69	**Mr. Sun, Mr. Moon** . . . Paul Revere & The Raiders
1/65	**Mr. Tambourine Man** . . . Byrds
12/85	**Mr. Telephone Man** . . . New Edition
	Mr. Wonderful
13/56	Sarah Vaughan
14/56	Peggy Lee
18/56	Teddi King

POS/YR	RECORD TITLE/ARTIST
1/65	**Mrs. Brown You've Got A Lovely Daughter** . . . Herman's Hermits
	Mrs. Robinson
1/68	Simon & Garfunkel
37/69	Booker T. & The MG's
	Muddy Water ..see: (I Washed My Hands In)
	Muhammad Ali ..see: Black Superman
5/60	**Mule Skinner Blues** . . . Fendermen
30/62	**Multiplication** . . . Bobby Darin
39/59	**Mummy, The** . . . Bob McFadden & Dor
39/82	**Murphy's Law** . . . Cheri
10/82	**Muscles** . . . Diana Ross
39/67	**Museum** . . . Herman's Hermits
3/79	**Music Box Dancer** . . . Frank Mills
40/84	**Music Time** . . . Styx
	Music To Watch Girls By
15/67	Bob Crewe Generation
34/67	Andy Williams
4/76	**Muskrat Love** . . . Captain & Tennille
12/75	**Must Of Got Lost** . . . J. Geils Band
8/66	**Must To Avoid** . . . Herman's Hermits
23/66	**Mustang Sally** . . . Wilson Pickett
21/56	**Mutual Admiration Society** . . . Teresa Brewer
13/78	**My Angel Baby** . . . Toby Beau
13/65	**My Baby** . . . Temptations
	(My Baby Don't Love Me) ..see: No More
31/56	**My Baby Left Me** . . . Elvis Presley
13/70	**My Baby Loves Lovin'** . . . White Plains
22/66	**My Baby Loves Me** . . . Martha & The Vandellas
17/68	**My Baby Must Be A Magician** . . . Marvelettes
30/67	**My Back Pages** . . . Byrds
35/78	**My Best Friend's Girl** . . . Cars
19/56	**My Blue Heaven** . . . Fats Domino
26/64	**My Bonnie** . . . Beatles with Tony Sheridan *(also see: Bonnie Came Back)*
11/55	**My Bonnie Lassie** . . . Ames Brothers
21/62	**My Boomerang Won't Come Back** . . . Charlie Drake
20/75	**My Boy** . . . Elvis Presley
	My Boy - Flat Top
16/55	Dorothy Collins
39/55	Boyd Bennett
2/64	**My Boy Lollipop** . . . Millie Small
1/63	**My Boyfriend's Back** . . . Angels

POS/YR	RECORD TITLE/ARTIST
12/58	**My Bucket's Got A Hole In It** . . . Ricky Nelson
4/69	**My Cherie Amour** . . . Stevie Wonder
	My Coloring Book
18/63	Kitty Kallen
20/63	Sandy Stewart
8/67	**My Cup Runneth Over** . . . Ed Ames
6/63	**My Dad** . . . Paul Petersen
34/60	**My Dearest Darling** . . . Etta James
1/72	**My Ding-A-Ling** . . . Chuck Berry *(also see: Ding-A-Ling)*
24/57	**My Dream** . . . Platters
9/61	**My Empty Arms** . . . Jackie Wilson
29/84	**My Ever Changing Moods** . . . Style Council
1/75	**My Eyes Adored You** . . . Frankie Valli
28/77	**My Fair Share** . . . Seals & Crofts
	My Girl
1/65	Temptations
35/68	Bobby Vee (medley)
20/85	Hall & Oates/David Ruffin/Eddie Kendrick (medley)
20/88	Suave'
25/82	**My Girl** . . . Donnie Iris
12/74	**My Girl Bill** . . . Jim Stafford
22/81	**My Girl (Gone, Gone, Gone)** . . . Chilliwack
14/65	**My Girl Has Gone** . . . Miracles
	My Girl Josephine
14/60	Fats Domino
29/67	Jerry Jaye
	My Girl Sloopy ..see: Hang On Sloopy
	My Guy
1/64	Mary Wells
23/82	Sister Sledge
2/59	**My Happiness** . . . Connie Francis
4/77	**My Heart Belongs To Me** . . . Barbra Streisand
9/64	**My Heart Belongs To Only You** . . . Bobby Vinton
4/89	**My Heart Can't Tell You No** . . . Rod Stewart
38/64	**My Heart Cries For You** . . . Ray Charles
1/60	**My Heart Has A Mind Of Its Own** . . . Connie Francis
3/59	**My Heart Is An Open Book** . . . Carl Dobkins, Jr.
	My Heart Reminds Me ..see: And That Reminds Me
	My Heart Sings ..see: (All Of A Sudden)

POS/YR	RECORD TITLE/ARTIST
13/66	**My Heart's Symphony** . . . Gary Lewis & The Playboys
8/60	**My Home Town** . . . Paul Anka
6/86	**My Hometown** . . . Bruce Springsteen
18/61	**My Kind Of Girl** . . . Matt Monro
31/83	**My Kind Of Lady** . . . Supertramp
	My Last Date (With You)
26/61	Skeeter Davis
38/61	Joni James
	(also see: Last Date)
3/79	**My Life** . . . Billy Joel
22/56	**My Little Angel** . . . Four Lads
9/75	**My Little Town** . . . Simon & Garfunkel
1/66	**My Love** . . . Petula Clark
1/73	**My Love** . . . Paul McCartney
5/83	**My Love** . . . Lionel Richie
16/65	**My Love, Forgive Me** . . . Robert Goulet
13/67	**My Mammy** . . . Happenings
9/73	**My Maria** . . . B.W. Stevenson
26/59	**My Melancholy Baby** . . . Tommy Edwards
3/74	**My Melody Of Love** . . . Bobby Vinton
19/74	**My Mistake (Was To Love You)** . . . Diana Ross & Marvin Gaye
39/81	**My Mother's Eyes** . . . Bette Midler
16/73	**My Music** . . . Loggins & Messina
37/84	**My Oh My** . . . Slade
	My One Sin
24/55	Nat King Cole
28/57	Four Coins
	My Own True Love
33/59	Jimmy Clanton
13/62	Duprees
21/57	**My Personal Possession** . . . Nat King Cole
14/69	**My Pledge Of Love** . . . Joe Jeffrey Group
1/56	**My Prayer** . . . Platters
1/89	**My Prerogative** . . . Bobby Brown
1/79	**My Sharona** . . . Knack
31/69	**My Song** . . . Aretha Franklin
	My Special Angel
7/57	Bobby Helms
7/68	Vogues
16/63	**My Summer Love** . . . Ruby & The Romantics
	My Sweet Lady
17/74	Cliff DeYoung
32/77	John Denver
1/70	**My Sweet Lord** . . . George Harrison

POS/YR	RECORD TITLE/ARTIST
29/74	**My Thang** . . . James Brown
39/83	**My Town** . . . Michael Stanley Band
32/65	**My Town, My Guy And Me** . . . Lesley Gore
31/56	**My Treasure** . . . Hilltoppers
22/63	**My True Confession** . . . Brook Benton
3/58	**My True Love** . . . Jack Scott
3/61	**My True Story** . . . Jive Five
	My Way
27/69	Frank Sinatra
22/77	Elvis Presley
9/69	**My Whole World Ended (The Moment You Left Me)** . . . David Ruffin
24/63	**My Whole World Is Falling Down** . . . Brenda Lee
12/59	**My Wish Came True** . . . Elvis Presley
16/72	**My World** . . . Bee Gees
5/66	**My World Is Empty Without You** . . . Supremes
24/85	**Mystery Lady** . . . Billy Ocean
33/65	**Mystic Eyes** . . . Them

N

POS/YR	RECORD TITLE/ARTIST
1/69	**Na Na Hey Hey Kiss Him Goodbye** . . . Steam
8/76	**Nadia's Theme (The Young And The Restless)** . . . Barry DeVorzon & Parry Botkin, Jr.
23/64	**Nadine (Is It You?)** . . . Chuck Berry
25/61	**"Nag"** . . . Halos
3/65	**Name Game** . . . Shirley Ellis
12/78	**Name Of The Game** . . . Abba
8/67	**Nashville Cats** . . . Lovin' Spoonful
3/86	**Nasty** . . . Janet Jackson
16/71	**Nathan Jones** . . . Supremes
21/78	**Native New Yorker** . . . Odyssey
38/60	**Natural Born Lover** . . . Fats Domino
10/73	**Natural High** . . . Bloodstone
17/71	**Natural Man** . . . Lou Rawls
8/67	**Natural Woman** . . . Aretha Franklin
40/68	**Naturally Stoned** . . . Avant-Garde
40/61	**Nature Boy** . . . Bobby Darin

Joe Tex had a No. 2 hit with "I Gotcha" in 1972. Among Top-40 artists that took the name of their home states, his hits beat out Tex Ritter's No. 20 "I Dreamed Of A Hill-Billy Heaven," but were edged out by Tennessee Ernie Ford and his No. 1 "Sixteen Tons."

B. J. Thomas went to No. 1 on the pop charts twice, with "Raindrops Keep Fallin' On My Head," and then again with "(Hey Won't You Play) Another Somebody Done Somebody Wrong Song." The latter tune has the longest title of any No. 1 hit, excluding the multiple-song medleys.

Tiffany, at 16, is the third youngest chart-topping artist, after Little Peggy March and Brenda Lee. With Tommy James' nugget "I Think We're Alone Now" and "Could've Been," she became the only female artist of the rock era to have her first two singles hit No. 1.

'Til Tuesday's lead singer, Aimee Mann, either wrote or co-wrote every one of the group's hits, including their 1985 top 10 "Voices Carry." On later recordings, 'Til Tuesday would perform material by Mann and estimable fellow songwriters Elvis Costello, Jules Shear, and Matthew Sweet.

The Tokens used a South African folk song—originally recorded by Miriam Makeba—in their 1961 No. 1 hit "The Lion Sleeps Tonight." They later charted with the folk-based "La Bomba," a cover version of Ritchie Valens' "La Bamba." In 1972, they were covered themselves, with Robert John's No. 3 version of "The Lion Sleeps Tonight."

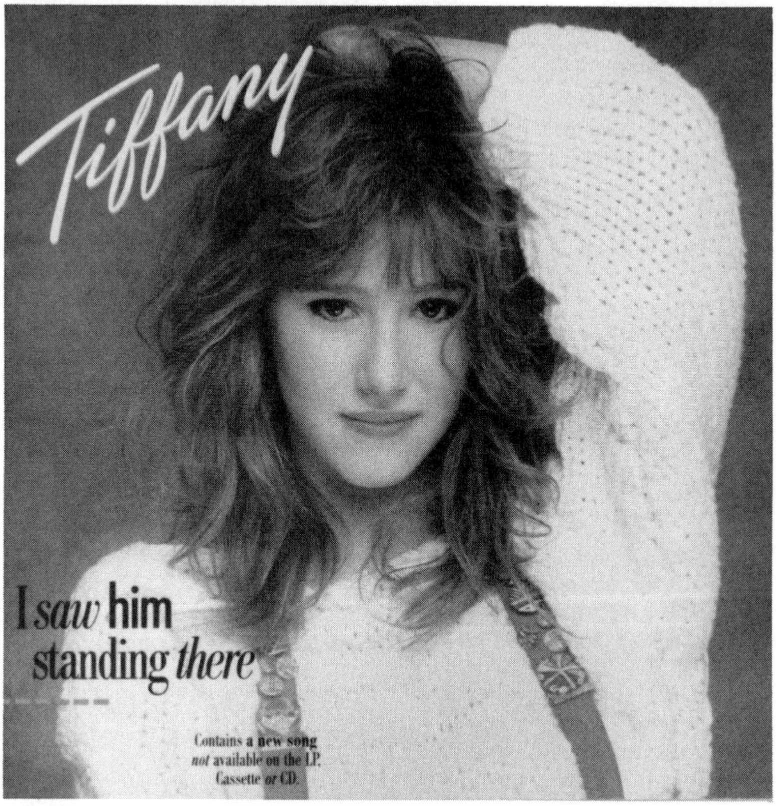

Tina Turner's "Better Be Good To Me" in 1984 was her fourth highest hit (at No. 5) as a solo artist, and one of the five Top-40 hits on the *Private Dancer* album. 11 years earlier to the month, Ike and Tina Turner had their final Top-40 song, 1973's "Nutbush City Limits."

Utopia, Todd Rundgren's virtuoso ensemble, had only one Top-40 song in the 80s, "Set Me Free." Yet in the 70s and 80s alike, he's produced other artists' chart hits, including those by Meat Loaf, Patti Smith, and The Pursuit Of Happiness.

Ritchie Valens and Buddy Holly had more in common than the fatal flight in 1959 and subsequent Hollywood versions of their lives—both had two posthumous chart hits. For Valens, they were "That's My Little Suzie" and "Little Girl."

Van Halen's "Love Walks In" was the third of the six Top-40 singles the group would earn after the departure of David Lee Roth. For Van Halen albums, the numbers were good: Roth's last album with the group was the No. 2 *1984*; their-next, 5150, went to No. 1.

Luther Vandross' "Stop To Love" went to No. 15 on the pop charts, making it his biggest Top-40 pop single ever—it was also his second R & B No. 1, and the top R & B song of 1987.

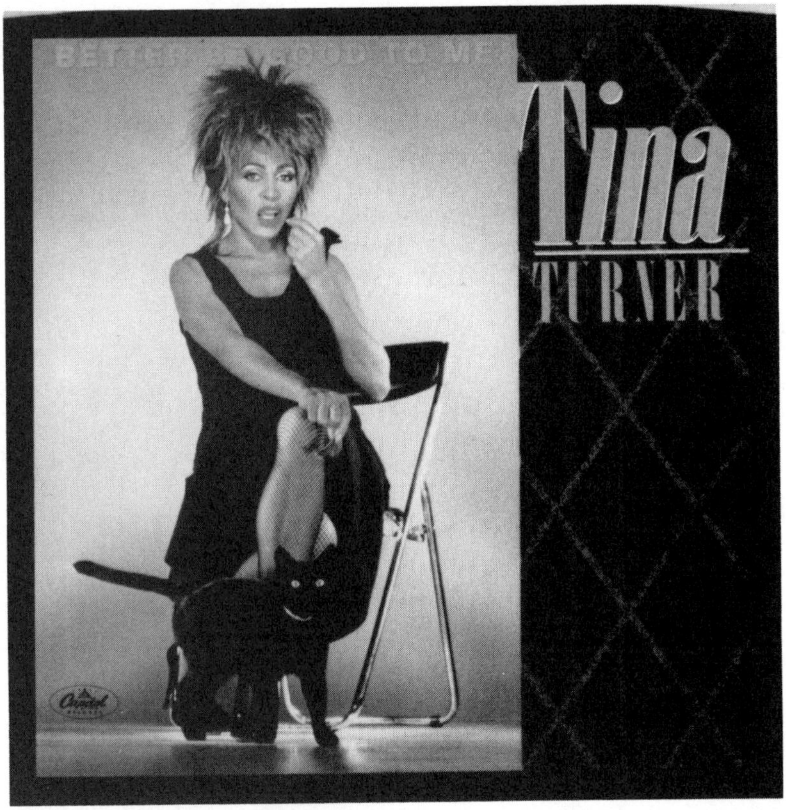

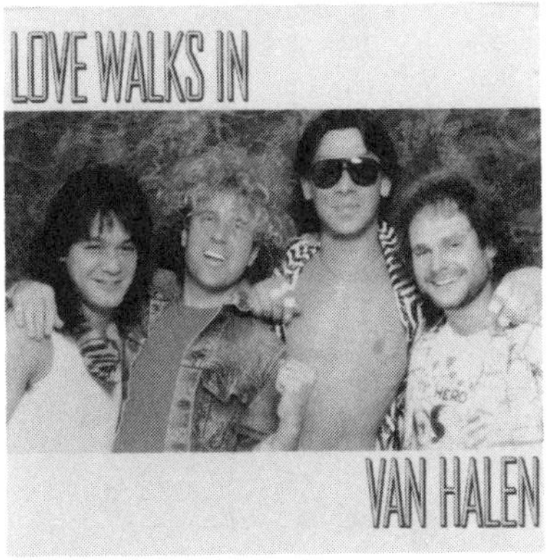

POS/YR	RECORD TITLE/ARTIST
3/88	**Naughty Girls (Need Love Too)** . . . Samantha Fox
	Naughty Lady Of Shady Lane
3/55	Ames Brothers
17/55	Archie Bleyer
23/85	**Naughty Naughty** . . . John Parr
6/64	**Navy Blue** . . . Diane Renay
22/70	**Neanderthal Man** . . . Hotlegs
10/58	**Near You** . . . Roger Williams
40/58	**Nee Nee Na Na Na Na Nu Nu** . . . Dicky Doo & The Don'ts
11/74	**Need To Be** . . . Jim Weatherly
31/64	**Need To Belong** . . . Jerry Butler
25/58	**Need You** . . . Donnie Owens
1/88	**Need You Tonight** . . . INXS
	Needles And Pins
13/64	Searchers
37/86	Tom Petty/Stevie Nicks
2/73	**Neither One Of Us (Wants To Be The First To Say Goodbye)** . . . Gladys Knight & The Pips
	Nel Blu Dipinto Di Blu ..see: Volare
24/67	**Neon Rainbow** . . . Box Tops
6/85	**Neutron Dance** . . . Pointer Sisters
4/85	**Never** . . . Heart
20/86	**Never As Good As The First Time** . . . Sade
6/59	**Never Be Anyone Else But You** . . . Ricky Nelson
15/80	**Never Be The Same** . . . Christopher Cross
28/82	**Never Been In Love** . . . Randy Meisner
5/72	**Never Been To Spain** . . . Three Dog Night
	Never Can Say Goodbye
2/71	Jackson 5
22/71	Isaac Hayes
9/75	Gloria Gaynor
13/71	**Never Ending Song Of Love** . . . Delaney & Bonnie & Friends
17/85	**Never Ending Story** . . . Limahl
20/68	**Never Give You Up** . . . Jerry Butler
11/76	**Never Gonna Fall In Love Again** . . . Eric Carmen
1/88	**Never Gonna Give You Up** . . . Rick Astley
4/83	**Never Gonna Let You Go** . . . Sergio Mendes
26/70	**Never Had A Dream Come True** . . . Stevie Wonder
28/88	**Never Knew Love Like This** . . . Alexander O'Neal/Cherrelle
6/80	**Never Knew Love Like This Before** . . . Stephanie Mills
29/75	**Never Let Her Go** . . . David Gates
27/87	**Never Let Me Down** . . . David Bowie
	Never My Love
2/67	Association
12/71	5th Dimension
7/74	Blue Swede
7/74	**Never, Never Gonna Give Ya Up** . . . Barry White
	Never On Sunday
19/60	Don Costa
13/61	Chordettes
3/85	**Never Surrender** . . . Corey Hart
7/88	**Never Tear Us Apart** . . . INXS
33/81	**Never Too Much** . . . Luther Vandross
22/56	**Never Turn Back** . . . Al Hibbler
17/85	**New Attitude** . . . Patti LaBelle
37/64	**New Girl In School** . . . Jan & Dean
1/77	**New Kid In Town** . . . Eagles
	New Lovers ..see: (Welcome)
36/63	**New Mexican Rose** . . . 4 Seasons
10/84	**New Moon On Monday** . . . Duran Duran
6/60	**New Orleans** . . . Gary U.S. Bonds
39/80	**New Romance (It's A Mystery)** . . . Spider
3/88	**New Sensation** . . . INXS
27/84	**New Song** . . . Howard Jones
21/82	**New World Man** . . . Rush
13/79	**New York Groove** . . . Ace Frehley
14/67	**New York Mining Disaster 1941** . . . Bee Gees
	New York, New York ..see: Theme From
27/77	**New York, You Got Me Dancing** . . . Andrea True Connection
32/65	**New York's A Lonely Town** . . . Trade Winds
5/62	**Next Door To An Angel** . . . Neil Sedaka
17/67	**Next Plane To London** . . . Rose Garden
F/7	**Next Step Is Love** . . . Elvis Presley
1/86	**Next Time I Fall** . . . Peter Cetera with Amy Grant
37/82	**Nice Girls** . . . Eye To Eye
30/76	**Nice 'N' Naasty** . . . Salsoul Orchestra
4/72	**Nice To Be With You** . . . Gallery
35/72	**Nickel Song** . . . Melanie
39/81	**Nicole** . . . Point Blank
4/60	**Night** . . . Jackie Wilson
1/74	**Night Chicago Died** . . . Paper Lace

POS/YR	RECORD TITLE/ARTIST
1/78	**Night Fever** . . . Bee Gees
3/63	**Night Has A Thousand Eyes** . . . Bobby Vee
34/85	**Night Is Still Young** . . . Billy Joel
11/56	**Night Lights** . . . Nat King Cole
4/77	**Night Moves** . . . Bob Seger
28/86	**Night Moves** . . . Marilyn Martin
6/81	**Night Owls** . . . Little River Band
1/73	**Night The Lights Went Out In Georgia** . . . Vicki Lawrence
3/71	**Night They Drove Old Dixie Down** . . . Joan Baez
30/66	**Night Time** . . . Strangeloves
35/62	**Night Train** . . . James Brown
33/84	**Nightbird** . . . Stevie Nicks
36/88	**Nightime** . . . Pretty Poison
9/75	**Nightingale** . . . Carole King
15/88	**Nightmare On My Street** . . . D.J. Jazzy Jeff & The Fresh Prince
10/76	**Nights Are Forever Without You** . . . England Dan & John Ford Coley
2/72	**Nights In White Satin** . . . Moody Blues
7/75	**Nights On Broadway** . . . Bee Gees
3/85	**Nightshift** . . . Commodores
23/67	**Niki Hoeky** . . . P.J. Proby
7/86	**Nikita** . . . Elton John
1/81	**9 To 5** . . . Dolly Parton
15/85	**19** . . . Paul Hardcastle
2/66	**19th Nervous Breakdown** . . . Rolling Stones
1/66	**96 Tears** . . . ? & The Mysterians
7/67	**98.6** . . . Keith
26/80	**99** . . . Toto
2/84	**99 Luftballons** . . . Nena
11/57	**Ninety-Nine Ways** . . . Tab Hunter
23/56	**Ninety Nine Years (Dead Or Alive)** . . . Guy Mitchell
33/71	**1900 Yesterday** . . . Liz Damon's Orient Express
12/83	**1999** . . . Prince
7/88	**Nite And Day** . . . Al B. Sure!
	Nitty Gritty
8/64	Shirley Ellis
19/69	Gladys Knight & The Pips
	No Arms Can Ever Hold You
23/55	Georgie Shaw
26/55	Pat Boone
27/65	Bachelors

POS/YR	RECORD TITLE/ARTIST
39/74	**No Charge** . . . Melba Montgomery
23/58	**No Chemise, Please** . . . Gerry Granahan
22/86	**No Easy Way Out** . . . Robert Tepper
	No Gettin' Over Me ..see: (There's)
40/60	**No If's - No And's** . . . Lloyd Price
34/85	**No Lookin' Back** . . . Michael McDonald
16/71	**No Love At All** . . . B.J. Thomas
21/58	**No Love (But Your Love)** . . . Johnny Mathis
8/70	**No Matter What** . . . Badfinger
3/66	**No Matter What Shape (Your Stomach's In)** . . . T-Bones
31/69	**No Matter What Sign You Are** . . . Supremes
35/67	**No Milk Today** . . . Herman's Hermits
	No More
6/55	DeJohn Sisters
17/55	McGuire Sisters
6/84	**No More Lonely Nights** . . . Paul McCartney
25/73	**No More Mr. Nice Guy** . . . Alice Cooper
1/79	**No More Tears (Enough Is Enough)** . . . Barbra Streisand/Donna Summer
23/84	**No More Words** . . . Berlin
23/80	**No Night So Long** . . . Dionne Warwick
3/75	**No No Song** . . . Ringo Starr
	No, Not Much!
2/56	Four Lads
34/69	Vogues
	No One
34/61	Connie Francis
21/63	Ray Charles
4/86	**No One Is To Blame** . . . Howard Jones
19/58	**No One Knows** . . . Dion & The Belmonts
36/72	**No One To Depend On** . . . Santana
	No Other Arms ..see: No Arms Can Ever Hold You
27/59	**No Other Arms, No Other Lips** . . . Chordettes
10/64	**No Particular Place To Go** . . . Chuck Berry
29/81	**No Reply At All** . . . Genesis
F/70	**No Sugar Tonight** . . . Guess Who
14/79	**No Tell Lover** . . . Chicago
5/70	**No Time** . . . Guess Who
33/83	**No Time For Talk** . . . Christopher Cross
23/84	**No Way Out** . . . Jefferson Starship
15/82	**Nobody** . . . Sylvia

POS/YR	RECORD TITLE/ARTIST
8/68	**Nobody But Me** . . . Human Beinz
21/59	**Nobody But You** . . . Dee Clark
40/69	**Nobody But You Babe** . . . Clarence Reid
2/77	**Nobody Does It Better** . . . Carly Simon
12/64	**Nobody I Know** . . . Peter & Gordon
30/60	**Nobody Loves Me Like You** . . . Flamingos
18/82	**Nobody Said It Was Easy** . . . Le Roux
5/84	**Nobody Told Me** . . . John Lennon
29/73	**Nobody Wants You When You're Down And Out** . . . Bobby Womack
21/81	**Nobody Wins** . . . Elton John
8/88	**Nobody's Fool** . . . Kenny Loggins
13/87	**Nobody's Fool** . . . Cinderella
39/59	**Nola** . . . Billy Williams
3/62	**Norman** . . . Sue Thompson
4/60	**North To Alaska** . . . Johnny Horton
34/85	**Not Enough Love In The World** . . . Don Henley
26/88	**Not Just Another Girl** . . . Ivan Neville
12/63	**Not Me** . . . Orlons
16/60	**Not One Minute More** . . . Della Reese
25/65	**Not The Lovin' Kind** . . . Dino, Desi & Billy
10/86	**Nothin' At All** . . . Heart
6/88	**Nothin' But A Good Time** . . . Poison
	Nothin' Yet ..see: (We Ain't Got)
34/69	**Nothing But A Heartache** . . . Flirtations
11/65	**Nothing But Heartaches** . . . Supremes
12/62	**Nothing Can Change This Love** . . . Sam Cooke
18/65	**Nothing Can Stop Me** . . . Gene Chandler
	Nothing For Xmas ..see: Nuttin'
1/74	**Nothing From Nothing** . . . Billy Preston
12/87	**Nothing's Gonna Change My Love For You** . . . Glenn Medeiros
1/87	**Nothing's Gonna Stop Us Now** . . . Starship
20/66	**Nothing's Too Good For My Baby** . . . Stevie Wonder
2/87	**Notorious** . . . Duran Duran
38/87	**Notorious** . . . Loverboy
25/58	**Now And For Always** . . . George Hamilton IV
	(Now And Then There's) A ..see: Fool Such As I
3/66	**Nowhere Man** . . . Beatles
8/65	**Nowhere To Run** . . . Martha & The Vandellas
9/75	**#9 Dream** . . . John Lennon
22/73	**Nutbush City Limits** . . . Ike & Tina Turner
23/62	**Nutrocker** . . . B. Bumble & The Stingers
	Nuttin' For Christmas
6/55	Barry Gordon
20/55	Joe Ward
21/55	Ricky Zahnd
36/55	Fontane Sisters

O

POS/YR	RECORD TITLE/ARTIST
10/60	**O Dio Mio** . . . Annette
25/85	**Object Of My Desire** . . . Starpoint
35/84	**Obscene Phone Caller** . . . Rockwell
6/85	**Obsession** . . . Animotion
	Ode To Billie Joe
1/67	Bobbie Gentry
28/67	Kingpins
10/80	**Off The Wall** . . . Michael Jackson
	Oh ..also see: O
3/73	**Oh, Babe, What Would You Say?** . . . Hurricane Smith
23/64	**Oh Baby Don't You Weep** . . . James Brown
10/58	**Oh, Boy!** . . . Crickets
9/59	**Oh! Carol** . . . Neil Sedaka
15/78	**Oh! Darling** . . . Robin Gibb
1/72	**Oh Girl** . . . Chi-Lites
39/85	**Oh Girl** . . . Boy Meets Girl
	Oh Happy Day
4/69	Edwin Hawkins' Singers
40/70	Glen Campbell
12/66	**Oh How Happy** . . . Shades Of Blue
	Oh Julie
5/58	Crescendos
23/58	Sammy Salvo
38/82	**Oh Julie** . . . Barry Manilow
33/73	**Oh La De Da** . . . Staple Singers
34/60	**Oh, Little One** . . . Jack Scott
7/58	**Oh Lonesome Me** . . . Don Gibson
22/70	**Oh Me Oh My (I'm A Fool For You Baby)** . . . Lulu

POS/YR	RECORD TITLE/ARTIST
5/74	**Oh My My** . . . Ringo Starr
4/81	**Oh No** . . . Commodores
24/65	**Oh No Not My Baby** . . . Maxine Brown
7/58	**Oh-Oh, I'm Falling In Love Again** . . . Jimmie Rodgers
29/86	**Oh, People** . . . Patti LaBelle
	Oh, Pretty Woman
1/64	Roy Orbison
12/82	Van Halen
1/85	**Oh Sheila** . . . Ready For The World
3/84	**Oh Sherrie** . . . Steve Perry
22/55	**Oh! Susanna** . . . Singing Dogs
10/74	**Oh Very Young** . . . Cat Stevens
30/79	**Oh Well** . . . Rockets
10/69	**Oh, What A Night** . . . Dells *(also see: December, 1963)*
24/78	**Oh What A Night For Dancing** . . . Barry White
39/66	**Oh Yeah** . . . Shadows Of Knight
14/70	**Ohio** . . . Crosby, Stills, Nash & Young
3/57	**Old Cape Cod** . . . Patti Page
5/75	**Old Days** . . . Chicago
20/80	**Old-Fashion Love** . . . Commodores
37/77	**Old Fashioned Boy (You're The One)** . . . Stallion
4/71	**Old Fashioned Love Song** . . . Three Dog Night
5/60	**Old Lamplighter** . . . Browns
25/60	**Ol' MacDonald** . . . Frank Sinatra
31/72	**Old Man** . . . Neil Young
10/85	**Old Man Down The Road** . . . John Fogerty
34/56	**Old Philosopher** . . . Eddie Lawrence
5/62	**Old Rivers** . . . Walter Brennan
	Old Schoolyard ..see: (Remember The Days Of The)
15/81	**Old Songs** . . . Barry Manilow
28/79	**Old Time Rock & Roll** . . . Bob Seger
25/61	**Ole Buttermilk Sky** . . . Bill Black's Combo
11/67	**On A Carousel** . . . Hollies
5/74	**On And On** . . . Gladys Knight & The Pips
11/77	**On And On** . . . Stephen Bishop
	On Broadway
9/63	Drifters
7/78	George Benson
38/56	**On London Bridge** . . . Jo Stafford
1/86	**On My Own** . . . Patti LaBelle & Michael McDonald

POS/YR	RECORD TITLE/ARTIST
20/57	**On My Word Of Honor** . . . Platters
7/84	**On The Dark Side** . . . John Cafferty
26/83	**On The Loose** . . . Saga
5/80	**On The Radio** . . . Donna Summer
4/61	**On The Rebound** . . . Floyd Cramer
16/68	**On The Road Again** . . . Canned Heat
20/80	**On The Road Again** . . . Willie Nelson
38/78	**On The Shelf** . . . Donny & Marie Osmond
	On The Street Where You Live
4/56	Vic Damone
18/56	Eddie Fisher
28/64	Andy Williams
27/82	**On The Way To The Sky** . . . Neil Diamond
29/82	**On The Wings Of Love** . . . Jeffrey Osborne
14/63	**On Top Of Spaghetti** . . . Tom Glazer
11/61	**Once In Awhile** . . . Chimes
19/64	**Once Upon A Time** . . . Marvin Gaye & Mary Wells
26/61	**Once Upon A Time** . . . Rochell & The Candles
10/75	**Once You Get Started** . . . Rufus Featuring Chaka Khan
23/72	**Once You Understand** . . . Think
5/69	**One** . . . Three Dog Night
1/71	**One Bad Apple** . . . Osmonds
11/63	**One Broken Heart For Sale** . . . Elvis Presley
37/74	**One Day At A Time** . . . Marilyn Sellars
34/65	**One Dyin' And A Buryin'** . . . Roger Miller
	One Eyed Jacks ..see: Love Theme From
	One Fine Day
5/63	Chiffons
12/80	Carole King
24/71	**One Fine Morning** . . . Lighthouse
38/87	**One For The Mockingbird** . . . Cutting Crew
28/88	**One Good Reason** . . . Paul Carrack
4/88	**One Good Woman** . . . Peter Cetera
13/66	**One Has My Name (The Other Has My Heart)** . . . Barry Young
10/87	**One Heartbeat** . . . Smokey Robinson
11/74	**One Hell Of A Woman** . . . Mac Davis
28/86	**One Hit (To The Body)** . . . Rolling Stones
14/82	**One Hundred Ways** . . . Quincy Jones/James Ingram
9/87	**One I Love** . . . R.E.M.

POS/YR	RECORD TITLE/ARTIST
20/57	**One In A Million** . . . Platters
37/84	**One In A Million** . . . Romantics
9/80	**One In A Million You** . . . Larry Graham
14/65	**One Kiss For Old Times' Sake** . . . Ronnie Dove
35/79	**One Last Kiss** . . . J. Geils Band
2/70	**One Less Bell To Answer** . . . 5th Dimension
37/73	**One Less Set Of Footsteps** . . . Jim Croce
19/85	**One Lonely Night** . . . REO Speedwagon
25/76	**One Love In My Lifetime** . . . Diana Ross
19/71	**One Man Band** . . . Three Dog Night
28/73	**One Man Band (Plays All Alone)** . . . Ronnie Dyson
7/75	**One Man Woman/One Woman Man** . . . Paul Anka
8/61	**One Mint Julep** . . . Ray Charles
5/88	**One Moment In Time** . . . Whitney Houston
15/72	**One Monkey Don't Stop No Show** . . . Honey Cone
29/66	**One More Heartache** . . . Marvin Gaye
1/85	**One More Night** . . . Phil Collins
	One More Sunrise ..see: Morgen
32/65	**One More Time** . . . Ray Charles Singers
1/88	**One More Try** . . . George Michael
28/78	**One Nation Under A Groove** . . . Funkadelic
4/58	**One Night** . . . Elvis Presley
3/85	**One Night In Bangkok** . . . Murray Head
13/85	**One Night Love Affair** . . . Bryan Adams
11/73	**One Of A Kind (Love Affair)** . . . Spinners
15/85	**One Of The Living** . . . Tina Turner
1/75	**One Of These Nights** . . . Eagles
31/60	**One Of Us (Will Weep Tonight)** . . . Patti Page
7/83	**One On One** . . . Daryl Hall & John Oates
	One On One, Love Theme From ..see: My Fair Share
29/76	**One Piece At A Time** . . . Johnny Cash
24/81	**One Step Closer** . . . Doobie Brothers
22/86	**One Step Closer To You** . . . Gavin Christopher
13/88	**One Step Up** . . . Bruce Springsteen
	One Summer Night
7/58	Danleers
22/61	Diamonds
1/81	**One That You Love** . . . Air Supply

POS/YR	RECORD TITLE/ARTIST
30/83	**One Thing** . . . INXS
4/83	**One Thing Leads To Another** . . . Fixx
	One Tin Soldier (The Legend Of Billy Jack)
34/70	Original Caste
26/71	Coven
10/71	**One Toke Over The Line** . . . Brewer & Shipley
9/61	**One Track Mind** . . . Bobby Lewis
40/80	**One-Trick Pony** . . . Paul Simon
2/65	**1-2-3** . . . Len Barry
3/88	**1-2-3** . . . Gloria Estefan & Miami Sound Machine
5/68	**1, 2, 3, Red Light** . . . 1910 Fruitgum Co.
24/79	**One Way Or Another** . . . Blondie
8/62	**One Who Really Loves You** . . . Mary Wells
15/82	**One You Love** . . . Glenn Frey
36/80	**Only A Lonely Heart Sees** . . . Felix Cavaliere
25/63	**Only In America** . . . Jay & The Americans
4/87	**Only In My Dreams** . . . Debbie Gibson
2/62	**Only Love Can Break A Heart** . . . Gene Pitney
33/70	**Only Love Can Break Your Heart** . . . Neil Young
28/76	**Only Love Is Real** . . . Carole King
33/57	**Only One Love** . . . George Hamilton IV
	Only Sixteen
28/59	Sam Cooke
6/76	Dr. Hook
24/78	**Only The Good Die Young** . . . Billy Joel
2/60	**Only The Lonely** . . . Roy Orbison
9/82	**Only The Lonely** . . . Motels
4/69	**Only The Strong Survive** . . . Jerry Butler
9/85	**Only The Young** . . . Journey
17/82	**Only Time Will Tell** . . . Asia
34/84	**Only When You Leave** . . . Spandau Ballet
12/75	**Only Women** . . . Alice Cooper
4/75	**Only Yesterday** . . . Carpenters
	Only You
5/55	Platters
8/55	Hilltoppers
9/59	Franck Pourcel's French Fiddles
6/75	Ringo Starr
20/71	**Only You Know And I Know** . . . Delaney & Bonnie
23/65	**Oo Wee Baby, I Love You** . . . Fred Hughes
34/67	**Oogum Boogum Song** . . . Brenton Wood
25/73	**Ooh Baby** . . . Gilbert O'Sullivan

POS/YR	RECORD TITLE/ARTIST
	Ooh Baby Baby
16/65	Miracles
7/79	Linda Ronstadt
8/70	**O-o-h Child** . . . Five Stairsteps
31/58	**Ooh! My Soul** . . . Little Richard
36/85	**Ooh Ooh Song** . . . Pat Benatar
28/60	**Ooh Poo Pah Doo** . . . Jessie Hill
2/82	**Open Arms** . . . Journey
10/67	**Open Letter To My Teenage Son** . . . Victor Lundberg
27/66	**Open The Door To Your Heart** . . . Darrell Banks
8/55	**Open Up Your Heart (And Let The Sunshine In)** . . . Cowboy Church Sunday School
1/87	**Open Your Heart** . . . Madonna
18/85	**Operator** . . . Midnight Star
22/75	**Operator** . . . Manhattan Transfer
17/72	**Operator (That's Not The Way It Feels)** . . . Jim Croce
10/86	**Opportunities (Let's Make Lots Of Money)** . . . Pet Shop Boys
13/66	**Opus 17 (Don't You Worry 'Bout Me)** . . . 4 Seasons
11/83	**Other Guy** . . . Little River Band
31/67	**Other Man's Grass Is Always Greener** . . . Petula Clark
4/82	**Other Woman** . . . Ray Parker Jr.
	Our Day Will Come
1/63	Ruby & The Romantics
11/75	Frankie Valli
7/83	**Our House** . . . Madness
30/70	**Our House** . . . Crosby, Stills, Nash & Young
20/81	**Our Lips Are Sealed** . . . Go-Go's
10/78	**Our Love** . . . Natalie Cole
	Our Love Affair ..see: Affair To Remember
9/78	**(Our Love) Don't Throw It All Away** . . . Andy Gibb
9/63	**Our Winter Love** . . . Bill Pursell
39/67	**Out & About** . . . Tommy Boyce & Bobby Hart
19/80	**Out Here On My Own** . . . Irene Cara
15/70	**Out In The Country** . . . Three Dog Night
3/64	**Out Of Limits** . . . Marketts
37/86	**Out Of Mind Out Of Sight** . . . Models
24/63	**Out Of My Mind** . . . Johnny Tillotson
24/64	**Out Of Sight** . . . James Brown

POS/YR	RECORD TITLE/ARTIST
23/56	**Out Of Sight, Out Of Mind** . . . Five Keys
3/88	**Out Of The Blue** . . . Debbie Gibson
17/73	**Out Of The Question** . . . Gilbert O'Sullivan
1/84	**Out Of Touch** . . . Daryl Hall John Oates
21/82	**Out Of Work** . . . Gary U.S. Bonds
2/72	**Outa-Space** . . . Billy Preston
28/60	**Outside My Window** . . . Fleetwoods
34/74	**Outside Woman** . . . Bloodstone
1/65	**Over And Over** . . . Dave Clark Five
20/76	**Over My Head** . . . Fleetwood Mac
	Over The Mountain; Across The Sea
8/57	Johnnie & Joe
21/63	Bobby Vinton
16/60	**Over The Rainbow** . . . Demensions
13/66	**Over Under Sideways Down** . . . Yardbirds
7/68	**Over You** . . . Gary Puckett & The Union Gap
24/86	**Overjoyed** . . . Stevie Wonder
3/83	**Overkill** . . . Men At Work
18/74	**Overnight Sensation (Hit Record)** . . . Raspberries
16/70	**Overture From Tommy (A Rock Opera)** . . . Assembled Multitude
1/84	**Owner Of A Lonely Heart** . . . Yes
13/71	**Oye Como Va** . . . Santana

P

POS/YR	RECORD TITLE/ARTIST
10/64	**P.S. I Love You** . . . Beatles
8/62	**P.T. 109** . . . Jimmy Dean
10/83	**P.Y.T. (Pretty Young Thing)** . . . Michael Jackson
9/82	**Pac-Man Fever** . . . Buckner & Garcia
13/58	**Padre** . . . Toni Arden
1/66	**Paint It, Black** . . . Rolling Stones
	Paint Me A Picture ..see: (You Don't Have To)
34/74	**Painted Ladies** . . . Ian Thomas
15/63	**Painted, Tainted Rose** . . . Al Martino
	Paladin ..see: Ballad Of
3/62	**Palisades Park** . . . Freddy Cannon
26/76	**Paloma Blanca** . . . George Baker Selection

POS/YR	RECORD TITLE/ARTIST
22/88	**Pamela** . . . Toto
13/84	**Panama** . . . Van Halen
35/66	**Pandora's Golden Heebie Jeebies** . . . Association
1/86	**Papa Don't Preach** . . . Madonna
31/74	**Papa Don't Take No Mess** . . . James Brown
	Papa Joe's ..see: (Down At)
1/72	**Papa Was A Rollin' Stone** . . . Temptations
	Papa's Got A Brand New Bag
8/65	James Brown
21/69	Otis Redding
34/67	**Paper Cup** . . . 5th Dimension
9/87	**Paper In Fire** . . . John Cougar Mellencamp
	Paper Roses
5/60	Anita Bryant
5/73	Marie Osmond
23/65	**Paper Tiger** . . . Sue Thompson
1/66	**Paperback Writer** . . . Beatles
32/82	**Paperlate** . . . Genesis
16/88	**Paradise** . . . Sade
39/78	**Paradise By The Dashboard Light** . . . Meat Loaf
34/86	**Paranoimia** . . . Art Of Noise
12/88	**Parents Just Don't Understand** . . . D.J. Jazzy Jeff & The Fresh Prince
38/58	**Part Of Me** . . . Jimmy Clanton
31/75	**Part Of The Plan** . . . Dan Fogelberg
19/63	**Part Time Love** . . . Little Johnny Taylor
22/75	**Part Time Love** . . . Gladys Knight & The Pips
22/78	**Part-Time Love** . . . Elton John
1/85	**Part-Time Lover** . . . Stevie Wonder
2/85	**Party All The Time** . . . Eddie Murphy
	Party Doll
1/57	Buddy Knox
5/57	Steve Lawrence
5/62	**Party Lights** . . . Claudine Clark
34/81	**Party's Over (Hopelessly In Love)** . . . Journey
10/83	**Pass The Dutchie** . . . Musical Youth
5/81	**Passion** . . . Rod Stewart
12/67	**Pata Pata** . . . Miriam Makeba
4/70	**Patches** . . . Clarence Carter
6/62	**Patches** . . . Dickey Lee
1/58	**Patricia** . . . Perez Prado
13/71	**Pay To The Piper** . . . Chairmen Of The Board

POS/YR	RECORD TITLE/ARTIST
28/67	**Pay You Back With Interest** . . . Hollies
26/74	**Payback, The** . . . James Brown
39/68	**Paying The Cost To Be The Boss** . . . B.B. King
	Peace In The Valley ..see: (There'll Be)
38/77	**Peace Of Mind** . . . Boston
31/75	**Peace Pipe** . . . B.T. Express
7/71	**Peace Train** . . . Cat Stevens
32/70	**Peace Will Come (According To Plan)** . . . Melanie
12/73	**Peaceful** . . . Helen Reddy
22/73	**Peaceful Easy Feeling** . . . Eagles
36/65	**Peaches "N" Cream** . . . Ikettes
20/61	**Peanut Butter** . . . Marathons
22/57	**Peanuts** . . . Little Joe & The Thrillers
28/59	**Peek-A-Boo** . . . Cadillacs
11/78	**Peg** . . . Steely Dan
3/57	**Peggy Sue** . . . Buddy Holly
18/64	**Penetration** . . . Pyramids
24/60	**Pennies From Heaven** . . . Skyliners
33/82	**Penny For Your Thoughts** . . . Tavares
1/67	**Penny Lane** . . . Beatles
8/84	**Penny Lover** . . . Lionel Richie
	People
5/64	Barbra Streisand
39/68	Tymes
13/85	**People Are People** . . . Depeche Mode
12/67	**People Are Strange** . . . Doors
14/65	**People Get Ready** . . . Impressions
1/68	**People Got To Be Free** . . . Rascals
22/74	**People Gotta Move** . . . Gino Vannelli
40/77	**People In Love** . . . 10cc
25/72	**People Make The World Go Round** . . . Stylistics
23/79	**People Of The South Wind** . . . Kansas
12/64	**People Say** . . . Dixie Cups
18/61	**"Pepe"** . . . Duane Eddy
5/63	**Pepino The Italian Mouse** . . . Lou Monte
14/56	**Pepper-Hot Baby** . . . Jaye P. Morgan
1/62	**Peppermint Twist** . . . Joey Dee
10/62	**Percolator (Twist)** . . . Billy Joe & The Checkmates
11/85	**Perfect Way** . . . Scritti Politti
3/88	**Perfect World** . . . Huey Lewis & The News
15/60	**Perfidia** . . . Ventures
2/59	**Personality** . . . Lloyd Price

POS/YR	RECORD TITLE/ARTIST
19/82	**Personally** . . . Karla Bonoff
	Peter Gunn
8/59	Ray Anthony
27/60	Duane Eddy
5/59	**Petite Fleur** . . . Chris Barber's Jazz Band
16/56	**Petticoats Of Portugal** . . . Dick Jacobs
1/75	**Philadelphia Freedom** . . . Elton John
26/58	**Philadelphia U.S.A.** . . . Nu Tornados
32/66	**Phoenix Love Theme** . . . Brass Ring
1/73	**Photograph** . . . Ringo Starr
12/83	**Photograph** . . . Def Leppard
1/81	**Physical** . . . Olivia Newton-John
6/88	**Piano In The Dark** . . . Brenda Russell
25/74	**Piano Man** . . . Billy Joel
1/75	**Pick Up The Pieces** . . . AWB
27/68	**Pickin' Wild Mountain Berries** . . . Peggy Scott & Jo Jo Benson
	Picnic ..see: Moonglow
12/68	**Pictures Of Matchstick Men** . . . Status Quo
12/68	**Piece Of My Heart** . . . Big Brother & The Holding Company
19/73	**Pieces Of April** . . . Three Dog Night
31/83	**Pieces Of Ice** . . . Diana Ross
4/66	**Pied Piper** . . . Crispian St. Peters
3/73	**Pillow Talk** . . . Sylvia
13/80	**Pilot Of The Airwaves** . . . Charlie Dore
	(Pina Colada Song) ..see: Escape
	Pinball Wizard
19/69	Who
29/73	New Seekers (medley)
11/60	**Pineapple Princess** . . . Annette
5/88	**Pink Cadillac** . . . Natalie Cole
8/84	**Pink Houses** . . . John Cougar Mellencamp
31/64	**Pink Panther Theme** . . . Henry Mancini
3/59	**Pink Shoe Laces** . . . Dodie Stevens
	Piove ..see: Ciao, Ciao Bambina
4/63	**Pipeline** . . . Chantay's
9/66	**Place In The Sun** . . . Stevie Wonder
38/59	**Plain Jane** . . . Bobby Darin
19/55	**Plantation Boogie** . . . Lenny Dee
40/73	**Plastic Man** . . . Temptations
11/72	**Play Me** . . . Neil Diamond
6/55	**Play Me Hearts And Flowers (I Wanna Cry)** . . . Johnny Desmond
33/74	**Play Something Sweet (Brickyard Blues)** . . . Three Dog Night

POS/YR	RECORD TITLE/ARTIST
1/76	**Play That Funky Music** . . . Wild Cherry
17/82	**Play The Game Tonight** . . . Kansas
7/62	**Playboy** . . . Marvelettes
17/68	**Playboy** . . . Gene & Debbe
2/73	**Playground In My Mind** . . . Clint Holmes
21/57	**Playing For Keeps** . . . Elvis Presley
3/67	**Pleasant Valley Sunday** . . . Monkees
18/78	**Please Come Home For Christmas** . . . Eagles
5/74	**Please Come To Boston** . . . Dave Loggins
15/62	**Please Don't Ask About Barbara** . . . Bobby Vee
1/80	**Please Don't Go** . . . K.C. & The Sunshine Band
39/61	**Please Don't Go** . . . Ral Donner
10/88	**Please Don't Go Girl** . . . New Kids On The Block
24/79	**Please Don't Leave** . . . Lauren Wood
31/63	**Please Don't Talk To The Lifeguard** . . . Diane Ray
8/60	**Please Help Me, I'm Falling** . . . Hank Locklin *(also see: (I Can't Help You))*
	Please Love Me Forever
12/61	Cathy Jean & The Roommates
6/67	Bobby Vinton
3/75	**Please Mr. Please** . . . Olivia Newton-John
	Please Mr. Postman
1/61	Marvelettes
1/75	Carpenters
11/59	**Please Mr. Sun** . . . Tommy Edwards
3/64	**Please Please Me** . . . Beatles
26/68	**Please Return Your Love To Me** . . . Temptations
14/61	**Please Stay** . . . Drifters
20/61	**Please Tell Me Why** . . . Jackie Wilson
28/66	**Please Tell Me Why** . . . Dave Clark Five
14/87	**Pleasure Principle** . . . Janet Jackson
	Pledge Of Love
12/57	Ken Copeland
25/57	Mitchell Torok
	Pledging My Love
17/55	Johnny Ace
17/55	Teresa Brewer
34/62	**Pocketful Of Miracles** . . . Frank Sinatra
2/60	**Poetry In Motion** . . . Johnny Tillotson
5/75	**Poetry Man** . . . Phoebe Snow
37/70	**Point It Out** . . . Miracles
28/78	**Point Of Know Return** . . . Kansas

POS/YR	RECORD TITLE/ARTIST
5/87	**Point Of No Return** . . . Expose
21/62	**Point Of No Return** . . . Gene McDaniels
28/86	**Point Of No Return** . . . Nu Shooz
25/83	**Poison Arrow** . . . ABC
7/59	**Poison Ivy** . . . Coasters
24/84	**Politics Of Dancing** . . . Re-Flex
8/69	**Polk Salad Annie** . . . Tony Joe White
	Pomp & Circumstance ..see: Graduation Song
1/61	**Pony Time** . . . Chubby Checker
17/58	**Poor Boy** . . . Royaltones
24/57	**Poor Boy** . . . Elvis Presley
38/62	**Poor Fool** . . . Ike & Tina Turner
22/59	**Poor Jenny** . . . Everly Brothers
1/58	**Poor Little Fool** . . . Ricky Nelson
27/63	**Poor Little Rich Girl** . . . Steve Lawrence
14/57	**Poor Man's Roses (Or A Rich Man's Gold)** . . . Patti Page
33/81	**Poor Man's Son** . . . Survivor
	Poor People Of Paris
1/56	Les Baxter
17/56	Lawrence Welk
19/56	Russ Morgan
31/78	**Poor Poor Pitiful Me** . . . Linda Ronstadt
1/66	**Poor Side Of Town** . . . Johnny Rivers
35/82	**Pop Goes The Movies** . . . Meco
20/88	**Pop Goes The World** . . . Men Without Hats
7/85	**Pop Life** . . . Prince
1/79	**Pop Muzik** . . . M
35/62	**Pop Pop Pop-Pie** . . . Sherrys
24/72	**Pop That Thang** . . . Isley Brothers
9/72	**Popcorn** . . . Hot Butter
30/69	**Popcorn, The** . . . James Brown
14/55	**Popcorn Song** . . . Cliffie Stone
10/62	**Popeye The Hitchhiker** . . . Chubby Checker
21/66	**Popsicle** . . . Jan & Dean
3/64	**Popsicles And Icicles** . . . Murmaids
20/56	**Port Au Prince** . . . Nelson Riddle
	Portrait Of My Love
9/61	Steve Lawrence
36/67	Tokens
19/56	**Portuguese Washerwomen** . . . Joe "Fingers" Carr
	Poseidon Adventure ..see: Morning After
7/65	**Positively 4th Street** . . . Bob Dylan

POS/YR	RECORD TITLE/ARTIST
30/85	**Possession Obsession** . . . Daryl Hall & John Oates
2/88	**Pour Some Sugar On Me** . . . Def Leppard
24/78	**Power Of Gold** . . . Dan Fogelberg/Tim Weisberg
1/85	**Power Of Love** . . . Huey Lewis & The News
11/72	**Power Of Love** . . . Joe Simon
26/88	**Power Of Love** . . . Laura Branigan
11/71	**Power To The People** . . . John Lennon/Plastic Ono Band
3/72	**Precious And Few** . . . Climax
19/79	**Precious Love** . . . Bob Welch
30/71	**Precious, Precious** . . . Jackie Moore
22/81	**Precious To Me** . . . Phil Seymour
21/86	**Press** . . . Paul McCartney
20/82	**Pressure** . . . Billy Joel
	Pretty Baby ..see: (It's Been A Long Time)
15/67	**Pretty Ballerina** . . . Left Banke
9/60	**Pretty Blue Eyes** . . . Steve Lawrence
29/66	**Pretty Flamingo** . . . Manfred Mann
39/79	**Pretty Girls** . . . Melissa Manchester
36/59	**Pretty Girls Everywhere** . . . Eugene Church
7/61	**Pretty Little Angel Eyes** . . . Curtis Lee
25/65	**Pretty Little Baby** . . . Marvin Gaye
15/64	**Pretty Paper** . . . Roy Orbison
	Pretty Woman ..see: (Oh)
10/63	**Pride And Joy** . . . Marvin Gaye
33/84	**Pride (In The Name Of Love)** . . . U2
34/84	**Prime Time** . . . Alan Parsons Project
8/59	**Primrose Lane** . . . Jerry Wallace
30/61	**Princess** . . . Frank Gari
37/65	**Princess In Rags** . . . Gene Pitney
20/56	**Priscilla** . . . Eddie Cooley
	(Prisoner) ..also see: Love Theme From Eyes Of Laura Mars
18/63	**Prisoner Of Love** . . . James Brown
27/78	**Prisoner Of Your Love** . . . Player
7/85	**Private Dancer** . . . Tina Turner
1/81	**Private Eyes** . . . Daryl Hall & John Oates
2/58	**Problems** . . . Everly Brothers
11/88	**Promise** . . . When In Rome
40/88	**Promise Me** . . . Cover Girls
17/58	**Promise Me, Love** . . . Andy Williams
14/74	**Promised Land** . . . Elvis Presley
9/79	**Promises** . . . Eric Clapton

POS/YR	RECORD TITLE/ARTIST
38/81	**Promises In The Dark** . . . Pat Benatar
11/83	**Promises, Promises** . . . Naked Eyes
19/68	**Promises, Promises** . . . Dionne Warwick
29/63	**Proud** . . . Johnny Crawford
	Proud Mary
2/69	Creedence Clearwater Revival
4/71	Ike & Tina Turner
22/75	**Proud One** . . . Osmonds
	Proud Ones ..see: Theme From
33/78	**Prove It All Night** . . . Bruce Springsteen
7/88	**Prove Your Love** . . . Taylor Dayne
7/70	**Psychedelic Shack** . . . Temptations
5/66	**Psychotic Reaction** . . . Count Five
31/67	**Pucker Up Buttercup** . . . Jr. Walker & The All Stars
2/63	**Puff The Magic Dragon** . . . Peter, Paul & Mary
13/88	**Pump Up The Volume** . . . M/A/R/R/S
20/62	**Punish Her** . . . Bobby Vee
	Puppet Man
24/70	5th Dimension
26/71	Tom Jones
14/65	**Puppet On A String** . . . Elvis Presley
	Puppy Love
2/60	Paul Anka
3/72	Donny Osmond
38/64	**Puppy Love** . . . Barbara Lewis
1/58	**Purple People Eater** . . . Sheb Wooley
2/84	**Purple Rain** . . . Prince
27/62	**Push And Kick** . . . Mark Valentino
	Push And Pull ..see: (Do The)
19/88	**Push It** . . . Salt-N-Pepa
36/67	**Pushin' Too Hard** . . . Seeds
25/63	**Pushover** . . . Etta James
17/58	**Pussy Cat** . . . Ames Brothers
8/58	**Put A Light In The Window** . . . Four Lads
	Put A Little Love In Your Heart
4/69	Jackie DeShannon
9/89	Annie Lennox & Al Green
32/58	**Put A Ring On My Finger** . . . Les Paul & Mary Ford
40/83	**Put It In A Magazine** . . . Sonny Charles
2/71	**Put Your Hand In The Hand** . . . Ocean
10/74	**Put Your Hands Together** . . . O'Jays
2/59	**Put Your Head On My Shoulder** . . . Paul Anka
4/83	**Puttin' On The Ritz** . . . Taco

POS/YR	RECORD TITLE/ARTIST

Q

1/61	**Quarter To Three** . . . Gary U.S. Bonds
2/56	**Que Sera, Sera (Whatever Will Be, Will Be)** . . . Doris Day
2/81	**Queen Of Hearts** . . . Juice Newton
40/76	**Queen Of My Soul** . . . Average White Band
34/83	**Queen Of The Broken Hearts** . . . Loverboy
9/58	**Queen Of The Hop** . . . Bobby Darin
12/65	**Queen Of The House** . . . Jody Miller *(also see: King Of The Road)*
39/57	**Queen Of The Senior Prom** . . . Mills Brothers
13/69	**Quentin's Theme** . . . Charles Randolph Grean Sounde
19/60	**Question** . . . Lloyd Price
21/70	**Question** . . . Moody Blues
37/68	**Question Of Temperature** . . . Balloon Farm
24/71	**Questions 67 And 68** . . . Chicago
25/68	**Quick Joey Small (Run Joey Run)** . . . Kasenetz-Katz Singing Orchestral Circus
8/64	**Quicksand** . . . Martha & The Vandellas
4/59	**Quiet Village** . . . Martin Denny
27/61	**Quite A Party** . . . Fireballs

R

15/65	**Race Is On** . . . Jack Jones
13/74	**Radar Love** . . . Golden Earring
16/84	**Radio Ga-Ga** . . . Queen
28/85	**Radioactive** . . . Firm
1/64	**Rag Doll** . . . 4 Seasons
17/88	**Rag Doll** . . . Aerosmith
F/71	**Rags To Riches** . . . Elvis Presley
16/59	**Ragtime Cowboy Joe** . . . Chipmunks
9/86	**Rain, The** . . . Oran "Juice" Jones

POS/YR	RECORD TITLE/ARTIST
23/66	**Rain** . . . Beatles
19/71	**Rain Dance** . . . Guess Who
10/66	**Rain On The Roof** . . . Lovin' Spoonful
21/86	**Rain On The Scarecrow** . . . John Cougar Mellencamp
12/62	**Rain Rain Go Away** . . . Bobby Vinton
2/67	**Rain, The Park & Other Things** . . . Cowsills
4/57	**Rainbow** . . . Russ Hamilton
25/79	**Rainbow Connection** . . . Kermit
2/61	**Raindrops** . . . Dee Clark *(also see: Cloudy Summer Afternoon)*
1/70	**Raindrops Keep Fallin' On My Head** . . . B.J. Thomas
34/61	**Rainin' In My Heart** . . . Slim Harpo
31/66	**Rains Came** . . . Sir Douglas Quintet
26/75	**Rainy Day People** . . . Gordon Lightfoot
2/66	**Rainy Day Women #12 & 35** . . . Bob Dylan
2/71	**Rainy Days And Mondays** . . . Carpenters
4/70	**Rainy Night In Georgia** . . . Brook Benton
29/61	**Ram-Bunk-Shush** . . . Ventures
21/61	**Rama Lama Ding Dong** . . . Edsels
17/69	**Ramblin' Gamblin' Man** . . . Bob Seger
2/73	**Ramblin Man** . . . Allman Brothers Band
2/62	**Ramblin' Rose** . . . Nat King Cole
27/58	**Ramrod** . . . Duane Eddy
2/70	**Rapper, The** . . . Jaggerz
36/80	**Rapper's Delight** . . . Sugarhill Gang
1/81	**Rapture** . . . Blondie
2/85	**Raspberry Beret** . . . Prince
	Raunchy
2/57	Bill Justis
4/57	Ernie Freeman
10/57	Billy Vaughn
37/58	**Rave On** . . . Buddy Holly
23/59	**Raw-Hide** . . . Link Wray
24/69	**Ray Of Hope** . . . Rascals
15/55	**Razzle-Dazzle** . . . Bill Haley
20/70	**Reach Out And Touch (Somebody's Hand)** . . . Diana Ross
20/64	**Reach Out For Me** . . . Dionne Warwick
	Reach Out I'll Be There
1/66	Four Tops
29/71	Diana Ross
10/68	**Reach Out Of The Darkness** . . . Friend And Lover
18/84	**Read 'Em And Weep** . . . Barry Manilow

POS/YR	RECORD TITLE/ARTIST
26/75	**Ready** . . . Cat Stevens
35/69	**Ready Or Not Here I Come (Can't Hide From Love)** . . . Delfonics
11/78	**Ready To Take A Chance Again** . . . Barry Manilow
5/80	**Real Love** . . . Doobie Brothers
16/81	**Really Wanna Know You** . . . Gary Wright
	Reaper, The ..see: (Don't Fear)
6/58	**Rebel-'Rouser** . . . Duane Eddy
28/69	**Reconsider Me** . . . Johnny Adams
37/66	**Recovery** . . . Fontella Bass
	Red Red Wine
34/84	UB40
1/88	UB40
5/59	**Red River Rock** . . . Johnny & The Hurricanes
37/59	**Red River Rose** . . . Ames Brothers
	Red Roses For A Blue Lady
10/65	Vic Dana
11/65	Bert Kaempfert
23/65	Wayne Newton
2/66	**Red Rubber Ball** . . . Cyrkle
	Red Sails In The Sunset
36/60	Platters
35/63	Fats Domino
	Reelin' And Rockin'
23/65	Dave Clark Five
27/73	Chuck Berry
11/73	**Reeling In The Years** . . . Steely Dan
2/67	**Reflections** . . . Supremes
10/70	**Reflections Of My Life** . . . Marmalade
1/84	**Reflex, The** . . . Duran Duran
15/80	**Refugee** . . . Tom Petty
10/85	**Relax** . . . Frankie Goes To Hollywood
39/73	**Relay, The** . . . Who
	Release Me
8/62	Esther Phillips
4/67	Engelbert Humperdinck
39/63	**Remember Diana** . . . Paul Anka
16/71	**Remember Me** . . . Diana Ross
26/64	**Remember Me** . . . Rita Pavone
32/65	**(Remember Me) I'm The One Who Loves You** . . . Dean Martin
33/77	**(Remember The Days Of The) Old Schoolyard** . . . Cat Stevens
36/84	**Remember The Nights** . . . Motels
24/63	**Remember Then** . . . Earls
5/64	**Remember (Walkin' In The Sand)** . . . Shangri-Las

POS/YR	RECORD TITLE/ARTIST
25/75	**Remember What I Told You To Forget** . . . Tavares
6/57	**Remember You're Mine** . . . Pat Boone
3/78	**Reminiscing** . . . Little River Band
26/75	**Rendezvous** . . . Hudson Brothers
16/79	**Renegade** . . . Styx
39/76	**Renegade** . . . Michael Martin Murphey
4/65	**Rescue Me** . . . Fontella Bass
	Respect
35/65	Otis Redding
1/67	Aretha Franklin
	Respect Yourself
12/71	Staple Singers
5/87	Bruce Willis
15/66	**Respectable** . . . Outsiders
	Resurrection Shuffle
38/71	Tom Jones
40/71	Ashton, Gardner & Dyke
15/67	**Return Of The Red Baron** . . . Royal Guardsmen
4/58	**Return To Me** . . . Dean Martin
2/62	**Return To Sender** . . . Elvis Presley
	Reuben ..see: Ruben
1/79	**Reunited** . . . Peaches & Herb
25/59	**Reveille Rock** . . . Johnny & The Hurricanes
15/62	**Revenge** . . . Brook Benton
8/63	**Reverend Mr. Black** . . . Kingston Trio
12/68	**Revolution** . . . Beatles
16/66	**Rhapsody In The Rain** . . . Lou Christie
11/76	**Rhiannon (Will You Ever Win)** . . . Fleetwood Mac
1/75	**Rhinestone Cowboy** . . . Glen Campbell
24/64	**Rhythm** . . . Major Lance
5/87	**Rhythm Is Gonna Get You** . . . Gloria Estefan & Miami Sound Machine
40/88	**Rhythm Of Love** . . . Yes
3/85	**Rhythm Of The Night** . . . DeBarge
3/63	**Rhythm Of The Rain** . . . Cascades
1/77	**Rich Girl** . . . Daryl Hall & John Oates
5/62	**Ride!** . . . Dee Dee Sharp
25/65	**Ride Away** . . . Roy Orbison
4/70	**Ride Captain Ride** . . . Blues Image
23/75	**Ride 'Em Cowboy** . . . Paul Davis
2/80	**Ride Like The Wind** . . . Christopher Cross
37/67	**Ride, Ride, Ride** . . . Brenda Lee
16/64	**Ride The Wild Surf** . . . Jan & Dean

POS/YR	RECORD TITLE/ARTIST
28/65	**Ride Your Pony** . . . Lee Dorsey
	Riders In The Sky ..see: (Ghost)
14/71	**Riders On The Storm** . . . Doors
2/76	**Right Back Where We Started From** . . . Maxine Nightingale
29/84	**Right By Your Side** . . . Eurythmics
12/78	**Right Down The Line** . . . Gerry Rafferty
23/71	**Right On The Tip Of My Tongue** . . . Brenda & The Tabulations
7/87	**Right On Track** . . . Breakfast Club
	Right Or Wrong
29/61	Wanda Jackson
14/64	Ronnie Dove
9/73	**Right Place Wrong Time** . . . Dr. John
27/87	**Right Thing** . . . Simply Red
17/73	**Right Thing To Do** . . . Carly Simon
6/77	**Right Time Of The Night** . . . Jennifer Warnes
4/74	**Rikki Don't Lose That Number** . . . Steely Dan
32/59	**Ring-A-Ling-A-Lario** . . . Jimmie Rodgers
33/65	**Ring Dang Doo** . . . Sam The Sham & The Pharoahs
1/79	**Ring My Bell** . . . Anita Ward
17/63	**Ring Of Fire** . . . Johnny Cash
31/72	**Ring The Living Bell** . . . Melanie
1/64	**Ringo** . . . Lorne Greene
17/71	**Rings** . . . Cymarron
10/62	**Rinky Dink** . . . Baby Cortez
14/83	**Rio** . . . Duran Duran
	Rip It Up
17/56	Little Richard
25/56	Bill Haley
36/64	**Rip Van Winkle** . . . Devotions
1/79	**Rise** . . . Herb Alpert
38/88	**Ritual** . . . Dan Reed Network
14/71	**River Deep - Mountain High** . . . Supremes & Four Tops
31/69	**River Is Wide** . . . Grass Roots
	River Kwai March ..see: March From
33/74	**River's Risin'** . . . Edgar Winter
30/78	**Rivers Of Babylon** . . . Boney M
	Road Runner ..see: (I'm A)
25/59	**Robbin' The Cradle** . . . Tony Bellus
16/56	**R-O-C-K** . . . Bill Haley
23/55	**Rock-A-Beatin' Boogie** . . . Bill Haley
10/57	**Rock-A-Billy** . . . Guy Mitchell

POS/YR	RECORD TITLE/ARTIST
	Rock-A-Bye Your Baby With A Dixie Melody
10/56	Jerry Lewis
37/61	Aretha Franklin
23/62	**Rock-A-Hula Baby** . . . Elvis Presley
	Rock And Roll ..also see: Rock 'N' Roll, Rockin' Roll
7/72	**Rock And Roll** . . . Gary Glitter
12/76	**Rock And Roll All Nite** . . . Kiss
32/81	**Rock And Roll Dreams Come Through** . . . Jim Steinman
20/85	**Rock And Roll Girls** . . . John Fogerty
3/74	**Rock And Roll Heaven** . . . Righteous Brothers
23/74	**Rock And Roll, Hoochie Koo** . . . Rick Derringer
19/58	**Rock And Roll Is Here To Stay** . . . Danny & The Juniors
28/76	**Rock And Roll Love Letter** . . . Bay City Rollers
15/72	**Rock And Roll Lullaby** . . . B.J. Thomas
	Rock And Roll Music
8/57	Chuck Berry
5/76	Beach Boys
1/56	**Rock And Roll Waltz** . . . Kay Starr
	Rock Around The Clock
1/55	Bill Haley
39/74	Bill Haley
2/86	**R.O.C.K. In The U.S.A.** . . . John Cougar Mellencamp
8/56	**Rock Island Line** . . . Lonnie Donegan
13/55	**Rock Love** . . . Fontane Sisters
10/69	**Rock Me** . . . Steppenwolf
1/86	**Rock Me Amadeus** . . . Falco
34/64	**Rock Me Baby** . . . B.B. King
38/72	**Rock Me Baby** . . . David Cassidy
1/74	**Rock Me Gently** . . . Andy Kim
18/85	**Rock Me Tonight (For Old Times Sake)** . . . Freddie Jackson
15/84	**Rock Me Tonite** . . . Billy Squier
	Rock 'N' Roll ..also see: Rock And Roll, Rockin' Roll
13/79	**Rock 'N' Roll Fantasy** . . . Bad Company
30/78	**Rock 'N' Roll Fantasy** . . . Kinks
15/75	**Rock N' Roll (I Gave You The Best Years Of My Life)** . . . Mac Davis
19/83	**Rock 'N' Roll Is King** . . . ELO
29/72	**Rock 'N Roll Soul** . . . Grand Funk Railroad

POS/YR	RECORD TITLE/ARTIST
16/83	**Rock Of Ages** . . . Def Leppard
22/88	**Rock Of Life** . . . Rick Springfield
5/74	**Rock On** . . . David Essex
36/56	**Rock Right** . . . Georgia Gibbs
7/87	**Rock Steady** . . . Whispers
9/71	**Rock Steady** . . . Aretha Franklin
1/74	**Rock The Boat** . . . Hues Corporation
8/83	**Rock The Casbah** . . . Clash
30/87	**Rock The Night** . . . Europe
9/82	**Rock This Town** . . . Stray Cats
1/80	**Rock With You** . . . Michael Jackson
25/84	**Rock You Like A Hurricane** . . . Scorpions
1/74	**Rock Your Baby** . . . George McCrae
17/57	**Rock Your Little Baby To Sleep** . . . Buddy Knox
38/59	**Rocka-Conga** . . . Applejacks
6/72	**Rocket Man** . . . Elton John
39/78	**Rocket Ride** . . . Kiss
6/88	**Rocket 2 U** . . . Jets
10/75	**Rockford Files** . . . Mike Post
27/75	**Rockin' All Over The World** . . . John Fogerty
14/60	**Rockin' Around The Christmas Tree** . . . Brenda Lee
25/85	**Rockin' At Midnight** . . . Honeydrippers
9/75	**Rockin' Chair** . . . Gwen McCrae
7/60	**Rockin' Good Way (To Mess Around And Fall In Love)** . . . Dinah Washington & Brook Benton
22/60	**Rockin' Little Angel** . . . Ray Smith
1/76	**Rockin' Me** . . . Steve Miller
6/73	**Rockin' Pneumonia And The Boogie Woogie Flu** . . . Johnny Rivers
	Rockin' Robin
2/58	Bobby Day
2/72	Michael Jackson
	Rockin' Roll ..also see: Rock And Roll, Rock 'N' Roll
14/73	**Rockin' Roll Baby** . . . Stylistics
18/74	**Rockin' Soul** . . . Hues Corporation
9/75	**Rocky** . . . Austin Roberts
9/73	**Rocky Mountain High** . . . John Denver
23/73	**Rocky Mountain Way** . . . Joe Walsh
	Rocky, Theme From ..see: Gonna Fly Now
30/79	**Rolene** . . . Moon Martin
27/83	**Roll Me Away** . . . Bob Seger

POS/YR	RECORD TITLE/ARTIST
14/75	**Roll On Down The Highway** . . . Bachman-Turner Overdrive
29/56	**Roll Over Beethoven** . . . Chuck Berry
1/88	**Roll With It** . . . Steve Winwood
34/79	**Roller** . . . April Wine
13/55	**Rollin' Stone** . . . Fontane Sisters
26/84	**Romancing The Stone** . . . Eddy Grant
	Romeo & Juliet ..see: Love Theme, (Just Like)
11/80	**Romeo's Tune** . . . Steve Forbert
6/64	**Ronnie** . . . 4 Seasons
2/82	**Rosanna** . . . Toto
3/80	**Rose, The** . . . Bette Midler
6/56	**Rose And A Baby Ruth** . . . George Hamilton IV
3/71	**Rose Garden** . . . Lynn Anderson
	Roses And Roses ..see: And Roses
1/62	**Roses Are Red (My Love)** . . . Bobby Vinton
24/57	**Rosie Lee** . . . Mello-Tones
30/80	**Rotation** . . . Herb Alpert
22/86	**Rough Boy** . . . ZZ Top
1/57	**Round And Round** . . . Perry Como
12/84	**Round And Round** . . . Ratt
21/65	**Round Every Corner** . . . Petula Clark
13/72	**Roundabout** . . . Yes
30/62	**Route 66 Theme** . . . Nelson Riddle
37/82	**Route 101** . . . Herb Alpert
32/79	**Roxanne** . . . Police
16/74	**Rub It In** . . . Billy "Crash" Craddock
6/61	**Rubber Ball** . . . Bobby Vee
37/79	**Rubber Biscuit** . . . Blues Brothers
16/70	**Rubber Duckie** . . . Ernie
2/76	**Rubberband Man** . . . Spinners
26/69	**Ruben James** . . . Kenny Rogers
28/60	**Ruby** . . . Ray Charles
18/62	**Ruby Ann** . . . Marty Robbins
	Ruby Baby
2/63	Dion
33/75	Billy "Crash" Craddock
6/69	**Ruby, Don't Take Your Love To Town** . . . Kenny Rogers
30/60	**Ruby Duby Du** . . . Tobin Mathews & Co.
	Ruby Red Dress ..see: Leave Me Alone
1/67	**Ruby Tuesday** . . . Rolling Stones
21/60	**Rudolph The Red Nosed Reindeer** . . . Chipmunks

POS/YR	RECORD TITLE/ARTIST
34/56	**Rudy's Rock** . . . Bill Haley
16/58	**Rumble** . . . Link Wray
28/86	**Rumbleseat** . . . John Cougar Mellencamp
8/86	**Rumors** . . . Timex Social Club
12/62	**Rumors** . . . Johnny Crawford
6/69	**Run Away Child, Running Wild** . . . Temptations
12/65	**Run, Baby Run (Back Into My Arms)** . . . Newbeats
33/78	**Run For Home** . . . Lindisfarne
18/82	**Run For The Roses** . . . Dan Fogelberg
4/75	**Run Joey Run** . . . David Geddes
36/60	**Run Red Run** . . . Coasters
25/66	**Run, Run, Look And See** . . . Brian Hyland
27/72	**Run Run Run** . . . Jo Jo Gunne
20/84	**Run Runaway** . . . Slade
28/60	**Run Samson Run** . . . Neil Sedaka
2/61	**Run To Him** . . . Bobby Vee
16/72	**Run To Me** . . . Bee Gees
6/85	**Run To You** . . . Bryan Adams
23/60	**Runaround** . . . Fleetwoods
28/61	**Runaround** . . . Regents
	Runaround Sue
1/61	Dion
13/78	Leif Garrett
1/61	**Runaway** . . . Del Shannon
12/78	**Runaway** . . . Jefferson Starship
39/84	**Runaway** . . . Bon Jovi
22/84	**Runner** . . . Manfred Mann's Earth Band
23/72	**Runnin' Away** . . . Sly & The Family Stone
1/60	**Running Bear** . . . Johnny Preston
11/78	**Running On Empty** . . . Jackson Browne
1/61	**Running Scared** . . . Roy Orbison
30/85	**Running Up That Hill** . . . Kate Bush
7/84	**Running With The Night** . . . Lionel Richie
39/72	**Runway, The** . . . Grass Roots
9/88	**Rush Hour** . . . Jane Wiedlin
16/86	**Russians** . . . Sting
33/65	**Rusty Bells** . . . Brenda Lee

POS/YR	RECORD TITLE/ARTIST

S

POS/YR	RECORD TITLE/ARTIST
15/75	**S.O.S.** . . . Abba
	S.W.A.T. ..see: Theme From
39/66	**S.Y.S.L.J.F.M. (The Letter Song)** . . . Joe Tex
20/61	**Sacred** . . . Castells
1/79	**Sad Eyes** . . . Robert John
29/60	**Sad Mood** . . . Sam Cooke
5/61	**Sad Movies (Make Me Cry)** . . . Sue Thompson
27/65	**Sad, Sad Girl** . . . Barbara Mason
5/84	**Sad Songs (Say So Much)** . . . Elton John
14/75	**Sad Sweet Dreamer** . . . Sweet Sensation
3/83	**Safety Dance** . . . Men Without Hats
5/58	**Sail Along Silvery Moon** . . . Billy Vaughn
4/79	**Sail On** . . . Commodores
1/80	**Sailing** . . . Christopher Cross
5/60	**Sailor (Your Home Is The Sea)** . . . Lolita
	Saint ..see: St.
	Saints Rock 'N Roll ..see: When The Saints Go Marchin' In
17/75	**Sally G** . . . Paul McCartney
2/63	**Sally, Go 'Round The Roses** . . . Jaynetts
36/83	**Salt In My Tears** . . . Martin Briley
20/77	**Sam** . . . Olivia Newton-John
9/81	**Same Old Lang Syne** . . . Dan Fogelberg
13/55	**Same Old Saturday Night** . . . Frank Sinatra
16/60	**Same One** . . . Brook Benton
8/61	**San Antonio Rose** . . . Floyd Cramer
9/67	**San Franciscan Nights** . . . Animals
4/67	**San Francisco (Be Sure To Wear Flowers In Your Hair)** . . . Scott McKenzie
14/86	**Sanctify Yourself** . . . Simple Minds
23/55	**Sand And The Sea** . . . Nat King Cole
15/60	**Sandy** . . . Larry Hall
21/63	**Sandy** . . . Dion
27/66	**Sandy** . . . Ronny & The Daytonas
32/57	**Santa & The Satellite** . . . Buchanan & Goodman
23/62	**Santa Claus Is Coming To Town** . . . 4 Seasons
1/86	**Sara** . . . Starship

POS/YR	RECORD TITLE/ARTIST
7/80	**Sara** . . . Fleetwood Mac
4/76	**Sara Smile** . . . Daryl Hall & John Oates
39/80	**(Sartorial Eloquence) Don't Ya Wanna Play This Game No More?** . . . Elton John
23/66	**Satin Pillows** . . . Bobby Vinton
28/73	**Satin Sheets** . . . Jeanne Pruett
22/75	**Satin Soul** . . . Love Unlimited Orchestra
	Satisfaction ..see: (I Can't Get No)
39/66	**Satisfied Mind** . . . Bobby Hebb
3/72	**Saturday In The Park** . . . Chicago
26/86	**Saturday Love** . . . Cherrelle with Alexander O'Neal
28/71	**Saturday Morning Confusion** . . . Bobby Russell
1/76	**Saturday Night** . . . Bay City Rollers
29/63	**Saturday Night** . . . New Christy Minstrels
18/64	**Saturday Night At The Movies** . . . Drifters
27/75	**Saturday Night Special** . . . Lynyrd Skynyrd
34/79	**Saturday Night, Sunday Morning** . . . Thelma Houston
12/73	**Saturday Night's Alright For Fighting** . . . Elton John
21/77	**Saturday Nite** . . . Earth, Wind & Fire
35/79	**Saturdaynight** . . . Herman Brood
25/81	**Sausalito Summernight** . . . Diesel
34/80	**Savannah Nights** . . . Tom Johnston
16/85	**Save A Prayer** . . . Duran Duran
22/77	**Save It For A Rainy Day** . . . Stephen Bishop
10/64	**Save It For Me** . . . 4 Seasons
27/70	**Save The Country** . . . 5th Dimension
	Save The Last Dance For Me
1/60	Drifters
18/74	DeFranco Family *(also see: I'll Save The Last Dance)*
2/65	**Save Your Heart For Me** . . . Gary Lewis & The Playboys
27/76	**Save Your Kisses For Me** . . . Brotherhood Of Man
37/61	**Saved** . . . LaVern Baker
20/83	**Saved By Zero** . . . Fixx
1/85	**Saving All My Love For You** . . . Whitney Houston
17/81	**Say Goodbye To Hollywood** . . . Billy Joel
3/73	**Say, Has Anybody Seen My Sweet Gypsy Rose** . . . Dawn

POS/YR	RECORD TITLE/ARTIST
21/66	**Say I Am (What I Am)** . . . Tommy James & The Shondells
27/88	**Say It Again** . . . Jermaine Stewart
2/83	**Say It Isn't So** . . . Daryl Hall-John Oates
10/68	**Say It Loud - I'm Black And I'm Proud** . . . James Brown
20/59	**Say Man** . . . Bo Diddley
1/83	**Say Say Say** . . . Paul McCartney & Michael Jackson
22/65	**Say Something Funny** . . . Patty Duke
32/81	**Say What** . . . Jesse Winchester
40/64	**Say You** . . . Ronnie Dove
11/76	**Say You Love Me** . . . Fleetwood Mac
1/85	**Say You, Say Me** . . . Lionel Richie
6/88	**Say You Will** . . . Foreigner
20/81	**Say You'll Be Mine** . . . Christopher Cross
15/77	**Say You'll Stay Until Tomorrow** . . . Tom Jones
39/65	**(Say) You're My Girl** . . . Roy Orbison
21/85	**Say You're Wrong** . . . Julian Lennon
31/88	**Sayin' Sorry (Don't Make It Right)** . . . Denise Lopez
	Scarborough Fair
11/68	Simon & Garfunkel
16/68	Sergio Mendes & Brasil '66
13/59	**Scarlet Ribbons (For Her Hair)** . . . Browns
33/75	**School Boy Crush** . . . Average White Band
3/57	**School Day** . . . Chuck Berry
28/61	**School Is In** . . . Gary U.S. Bonds
5/61	**School Is Out** . . . Gary U.S. Bonds
7/72	**School's Out** . . . Alice Cooper
6/72	**Scorpio** . . . Dennis Coffey
20/87	**Se La** . . . Lionel Richie
	Se Si Bon ..see: Whispering
14/59	**Sea Cruise** . . . Frankie Ford
21/61	**Sea Of Heartbreak** . . . Don Gibson
	Sea Of Love
2/59	Phil Phillips with The Twilights
33/82	Del Shannon
3/85	Honeydrippers
	Sealed With A Kiss
3/62	Brian Hyland
19/68	Gary Lewis & The Playboys
19/72	Bobby Vinton
4/85	**Search Is Over** . . . Survivor
3/57	**Searchin'** . . . Coasters
	Searchin' So Long ..see: (I've Been)

POS/YR	RECORD TITLE/ARTIST
27/66	**Searching For My Love** . . . Bobby Moore
1/88	**Seasons Change** . . . Expose
1/74	**Seasons In The Sun** . . . Terry Jacks
38/69	**Seattle** . . . Perry Como
34/74	**Second Avenue** . . . Garfunkel
40/56	**Second Fiddle** . . . Kay Starr
7/62	**Second Hand Love** . . . Connie Francis
32/66	**Second Hand Rose** . . . Barbra Streisand
39/85	**Second Nature** . . . Dan Hartman
8/80	**Second Time Around** . . . Shalamar
18/58	**Secret, The** . . . Gordon MacRae
3/66	**Secret Agent Man** . . . Johnny Rivers
	Secret Love
29/66	Billy Stewart
20/75	Freddy Fender
3/86	**Secret Lovers** . . . Atlantic Starr
19/86	**Secret Separation** . . . Fixx
3/58	**Secretly** . . . Jimmie Rodgers
35/68	**Security** . . . Etta James
28/80	**Seduction, The** . . . James Last Band
27/69	**See** . . . Rascals
	See Me, Feel Me
12/70	Who
29/73	New Seekers (medley)
25/56	**See Saw** . . . Moonglows
14/68	**See Saw** . . . Aretha Franklin
	See See ..see: C.C.
9/64	**See The Funny Little Clown** . . . Bobby Goldsboro
	See You In September
23/59	Tempos
3/66	Happenings
6/56	**See You Later, Alligator** . . . Bill Haley
4/84	**Self Control** . . . Laura Branigan
11/64	**Selfish One** . . . Jackie Ross
6/57	**Send For Me** . . . Nat King Cole
23/83	**Send Her My Love** . . . Journey
	Send In The Clowns
36/75	Judy Collins
19/77	Judy Collins
29/84	**Send Me An Angel** . . . Real Life
13/63	**Send Me Some Lovin'** . . . Sam Cooke
	Send Me The Pillow You Dream On
17/62	Johnny Tillotson
22/65	Dean Martin
4/79	**Send One Your Love** . . . Stevie Wonder
8/78	**Sentimental Lady** . . . Bob Welch
8/85	**Sentimental Street** . . . Night Ranger

POS/YR	RECORD TITLE/ARTIST
1/85	**Separate Lives** . . . Phil Collins & Marilyn Martin
20/73	**Separate Ways** . . . Elvis Presley
8/83	**Separate Ways (Worlds Apart)** . . . Journey
8/79	**September** . . . Earth, Wind & Fire
23/61	**September In The Rain** . . . Dinah Washington
17/80	**September Morn'** . . . Neil Diamond
23/80	**Sequel** . . . Harry Chapin
21/87	**Serious** . . . Donna Allen
13/78	**Serpentine Fire** . . . Earth, Wind & Fire
23/65	**Set Me Free** . . . Kinks
27/80	**Set Me Free** . . . Utopia
33/66	**7 And 7 Is** . . . Love
21/81	**Seven Bridges Road** . . . Eagles
27/62	**Seven Day Weekend** . . . Gary U.S. Bonds
	Seven Days
17/56	Dorothy Collins
18/56	Crew-Cuts
30/58	**"7-11" (Mambo No. 5)** . . . Gone All Stars
9/59	**Seven Little Girls Sitting In The Back Seat** . . . Paul Evans
14/67	**7 Rooms Of Gloom** . . . Four Tops
19/87	**Seven Wonders** . . . Fleetwood Mac
22/81	**Seven Year Ache** . . . Rosanne Cash
7/65	**Seventh Son** . . . Johnny Rivers
	Seventeen
3/55	Fontane Sisters
5/55	Boyd Bennett
18/55	Rusty Draper
36/84	**17** . . . Rick James
28/86	**Sex As A Weapon** . . . Pat Benatar
15/70	**Sex Machine** . . . James Brown
3/83	**Sexual Healing** . . . Marvin Gaye
	Sexy + 17 ..see: (She's)
5/80	**Sexy Eyes** . . . Dr. Hook
20/84	**Sexy Girl** . . . Glenn Frey
17/74	**Sexy Mama** . . . Moments
12/65	**Sha La La** . . . Manfred Mann
7/74	**Sha-La-La (Make Me Happy)** . . . Al Green
1/78	**Shadow Dancing** . . . Andy Gibb
25/79	**Shadows In The Moonlight** . . . Anne Murray
13/82	**Shadows Of The Night** . . . Pat Benatar
19/62	**Shadrack** . . . Brook Benton
	Shaft ..see: Theme From
38/64	**Shaggy Dog** . . . Mickey Lee Lane

POS/YR	RECORD TITLE/ARTIST
7/65	**Shake** . . . Sam Cooke
25/67	**Shake A Tail Feather** . . . James & Bobby Purify
29/65	**Shake And Fingerpop** . . . Jr. Walker & The All Stars
28/89	**Shake For The Sheik** . . . Escape Club
13/79	**Shake It** . . . Ian Matthews
4/82	**Shake It Up** . . . Cars
18/66	**Shake Me, Wake Me (When It's Over)** . . . Four Tops
31/67	**Shake, Rattle & Roll** . . . Arthur Conley
33/63	**Shake! Shake! Shake!** . . . Jackie Wilson
1/76	**(Shake, Shake, Shake) Shake Your Booty** . . . KC & The Sunshine Band
1/87	**Shake You Down** . . . Gregory Abbott
7/79	**Shake Your Body (Down To The Ground)** . . . Jacksons
5/79	**Shake Your Groove Thing** . . . Peaches & Herb
4/87	**Shake Your Love** . . . Debbie Gibson
23/77	**Shake Your Rump To The Funk** . . . Bar-Kays
1/87	**Shakedown** . . . Bob Seger
31/79	**Shakedown Cruise** . . . Jay Ferguson
26/75	**Shakey Ground** . . . Temptations
22/65	**Shakin' All Over** . . . Guess Who
3/73	**Shambala** . . . Three Dog Night
9/78	**Shame** . . . Evelyn "Champagne" King
21/85	**Shame** . . . Motels
23/62	**Shame On Me** . . . Bobby Bare
2/83	**Shame On The Moon** . . . Bob Seger
29/68	**Shame, Shame** . . . Magic Lanterns
12/75	**Shame, Shame, Shame** . . . Shirley & Company
31/82	**Shanghai Breezes** . . . John Denver
	Shangri-La
11/57	Four Coins
15/64	Robert Maxwell
27/64	Vic Dana
6/76	**Shannon** . . . Henry Gross
22/68	**Shape Of Things To Come** . . . Max Frost
11/66	**Shapes Of Things** . . . Yardbirds
10/70	**Share The Land** . . . Guess Who
	Share Your Love With Me
13/69	Aretha Franklin
14/81	Kenny Rogers
6/79	**Sharing The Night Together** . . . Dr. Hook
15/62	**Sharing You** . . . Bobby Vee

POS/YR	RECORD TITLE/ARTIST
31/79	**Shattered** . . . Rolling Stones
2/88	**Shattered Dreams** . . . Johnny Hates Jazz
30/75	**Shaving Cream** . . . Benny Bell
23/70	**She** . . . Tommy James & The Shondells
5/79	**She Believes In Me** . . . Kenny Rogers
33/70	**She Belongs To Me** . . . Rick Nelson
5/83	**She Blinded Me With Science** . . . Thomas Dolby
3/84	**She Bop** . . . Cyndi Lauper
30/70	**She Came In Through The Bathroom Window** . . . Joe Cocker
19/62	**She Can't Find Her Keys** . . . Paul Petersen
	She Comes To Me ..see: (When She Needs Good Lovin')
5/62	**She Cried** . . . Jay & The Americans
23/77	**She Did It** . . . Eric Carmen
27/67	**She Is Still A Mystery** . . . Lovin' Spoonful
1/64	**She Loves You** . . . Beatles
18/59	**She Say (Oom Dooby Doom)** . . . Diamonds
	She Understands Me
31/64	Johnny Tillotson
40/66	Bobby Vinton (Dum-De-Da)
6/89	**She Wants To Dance With Me** . . . Rick Astley
27/58	**She Was Only Seventeen (He Was One Year More)** . . . Marty Robbins
3/83	**She Works Hard For The Money** . . . Donna Summer
3/67	**She'd Rather Be With Me** . . . Turtles
22/81	**She's A Bad Mama Jama (She's Built, She's Stacked)** . . . Carl Carlton
10/83	**She's A Beauty** . . . Tubes
5/63	**She's A Fool** . . . Lesley Gore
16/68	**She's A Heartbreaker** . . . Gene Pitney
2/71	**She's A Lady** . . . Tom Jones
25/68	**She's A Rainbow** . . . Rolling Stones
4/64	**She's A Woman** . . . Beatles
13/65	**She's About A Mover** . . . Sir Douglas Quintet
39/71	**She's All I Got** . . . Freddie North
17/78	**She's Always A Woman** . . . Billy Joel
18/62	**She's Everything (I Wanted You To Be)** . . . Ral Donner
7/76	**She's Gone** . . . Daryl Hall & John Oates
23/82	**She's Got A Way** . . . Billy Joel
14/62	**She's Got You** . . . Patsy Cline

POS/YR	RECORD TITLE/ARTIST
3/66	**She's Just My Style** . . . Gary Lewis & The Playboys
3/88	**She's Like The Wind** . . . Patrick Swayze/Wendy Fraser
15/68	**She's Lookin' Good** . . . Wilson Pickett
21/84	**She's Mine** . . . Steve Perry
14/67	**She's My Girl** . . . Turtles
38/58	**She's Neat** . . . Dale Wright
11/71	**She's Not Just Another Woman** . . . 8th Day
	She's Not There
2/64	Zombies
27/77	Santana
5/62	**She's Not You** . . . Elvis Presley
10/80	**She's Out Of My Life** . . . Michael Jackson
5/83	**(She's) Sexy + 17** . . . Stray Cats
26/80	**She's So Cold** . . . Rolling Stones
33/64	**She's The One** . . . Chartbusters
1/62	**Sheila** . . . Tommy Roe
17/64	**Shelter Of Your Arms** . . . Sammy Davis, Jr.
1/62	**Sherry** . . . 4 Seasons
	Shifting, Whispering Sands
3/55	Rusty Draper
5/55	Billy Vaughn
24/70	**Shilo** . . . Neil Diamond
37/60	**Shimmy Shimmy** . . . Bobby Freeman
24/60	**Shimmy, Shimmy, Ko-Ko-Bop** . . . Little Anthony & The Imperials
8/79	**Shine A Little Love** . . . Electric Light Orchestra
40/81	**Shine On** . . . L.T.D.
37/84	**Shine Shine** . . . Barry Gibb
11/74	**Shinin' On** . . . Grand Funk
1/75	**Shining Star** . . . Earth, Wind & Fire
5/80	**Shining Star** . . . Manhattans
27/87	**Ship Of Fools (Save Me From Tomorrow)** . . . World Party
9/79	**Ships** . . . Barry Manilow
10/57	**Shish-Kebab** . . . Ralph Marterie
29/83	**Shock The Monkey** . . . Peter Gabriel
18/75	**Shoeshine Boy** . . . Eddie Kendricks
9/68	**Shoo-Be-Doo-Be-Doo-Da-Day** . . . Stevie Wonder *(also see: Shu)*
6/64	**Shoop Shoop Song (It's In His Kiss)** . . . Betty Everett
31/68	**Shoot'em Up, Baby** . . . Andy Kim

POS/YR	RECORD TITLE/ARTIST
	Shop Around
2/61	Miracles
4/76	Captain & Tennille
5/57	**Short Fat Fannie** . . . Larry Williams
2/78	**Short People** . . . Randy Newman
3/58	**Short Shorts** . . . Royal Teens
4/65	**Shotgun** . . . Jr. Walker & The All Stars
13/82	**Should I Do It** . . . Pointer Sisters
3/87	**Should've Known Better** . . . Richard Marx
19/80	**Should've Never Let You Go** . . . Neil Sedaka & Dara Sedaka
1/85	**Shout** . . . Tears For Fears
6/62	**Shout** . . . Joey Dee
31/76	**Shout It Out Loud** . . . Kiss
6/62	**Shout! Shout! (Knock Yourself Out)** . . . Ernie Maresca
1/74	**Show And Tell** . . . Al Wilson
28/84	**Show Me** . . . Pretenders
35/67	**Show Me** . . . Joe Tex
6/76	**Show Me The Way** . . . Peter Frampton
4/74	**Show Must Go On** . . . Three Dog Night
37/85	**Show Some Respect** . . . Tina Turner
28/77	**Show You The Way To Go** . . . Jacksons
22/76	**Shower The People** . . . James Taylor
38/75	**(Shu-Doo-Pa-Poo-Poop) Love Being Your Fool** . . . Travis Wammack
32/61	**Shu Rah** . . . Fats Domino
23/63	**Shut Down** . . . Beach Boys
24/63	**Shutters And Boards** . . . Jerry Wallace
22/58	**Sick And Tired** . . . Fats Domino
8/74	**Sideshow** . . . Blue Magic
25/64	**Sidewalk Surfin'** . . . Jan & Dean
18/86	**Sidewalk Talk** . . . Jellybean
3/87	**Sign 'O' The Times** . . . Prince
32/84	**Sign Of Fire** . . . Fixx
11/66	**Sign Of The Times** . . . Petula Clark
4/88	**Sign Your Name** . . . Terence Trent D'Arby
3/70	**Signed, Sealed, Delivered I'm Yours** . . . Stevie Wonder
18/77	**Signed, Sealed, Delivered (I'm Yours)** . . . Peter Frampton
3/71	**Signs** . . . Five Man Electrical Band
11/67	**Silence Is Golden** . . . Tremeloes
6/86	**Silent Running (On Dangerous Ground)** . . . Mike + The Mechanics
13/89	**Silhouette** . . . Kenny G

POS/YR	RECORD TITLE/ARTIST
	Silhouettes
3/57	Rays
10/57	Diamonds
5/65	Herman's Hermits
1/76	**Silly Love Songs** . . . Wings
25/70	**Silver Bird** . . . Mark Lindsay
20/55	**Silver Dollar** . . . Teresa Brewer
38/76	**Silver Star** . . . 4 Seasons
20/62	**Silver Threads And Golden Needles** . . . Springfields
4/68	**Simon Says** . . . 1910 Fruitgum Co.
2/88	**Simply Irresistible** . . . Robert Palmer
	Since I Don't Have You
12/59	Skyliners
23/81	Don McLean
4/63	**Since I Fell For You** . . . Lenny Welch
17/65	**Since I Lost My Baby** . . . Temptations
	Since I Met You Baby
12/56	Ivory Joe Hunter
34/57	Mindy Carson
32/67	**Since You Showed Me How To Be Happy** . . . Jackie Wilson
31/87	**Since You've Been Gone** . . . Outfield
38/59	**Since You've Been Gone** . . . Clyde McPhatter
	Since You've Been Gone ..see: (Sweet Sweet Baby)
	Sincerely
1/55	McGuire Sisters
20/55	Moonglows
3/73	**Sing** . . . Carpenters
5/76	**Sing A Song** . . . Earth, Wind & Fire
24/58	**Sing Boy Sing** . . . Tommy Sands
	Singing The Blues
1/56	Guy Mitchell
17/56	Marty Robbins
12/66	**Single Girl** . . . Sandy Posey
3/60	**Sink The Bismarck** . . . Johnny Horton
1/77	**Sir Duke** . . . Stevie Wonder
5/84	**Sister Christian** . . . Night Ranger
1/75	**Sister Golden Hair** . . . America
24/74	**Sister Mary Elephant (Shudd-Up!)** . . . Cheech & Chong
18/85	**Sisters Are Doin' It For Themselves** . . . Eurythmics & Aretha Franklin
36/67	**Sit Down, I Think I Love You** . . . Mojo Men
37/71	**Sit Yourself Down** . . . Stephen Stills

POS/YR	RECORD TITLE/ARTIST
	Sittin' In The Balcony
18/57	Eddie Cochran
38/57	Johnny Dee
	(Sittin' On) The Dock Of The Bay
1/68	Otis Redding
11/88	Michael Bolton
16/73	**Sitting** . . . Cat Stevens
27/83	**Sitting At The Wheel** . . . Moody Blues
24/65	**Sitting In The Park** . . . Billy Stewart
32/63	**Six Days On The Road** . . . Dave Dudley
28/59	**Six Nights A Week** . . . Crests
18/67	**Six O'Clock** . . . Lovin' Spoonful
13/66	**634-5789 (Soulsville, U.S.A.)** . . . Wilson Pickett
	(also see: Beechwood 4-5789)
2/59	**16 Candles** . . . Crests
3/60	**Sixteen Reasons** . . . Connie Stevens
	Sixteen Tons
1/55	Tennessee Ernie Ford
17/55	Johnny Desmond
6/82	**'65 Love Affair** . . . Paul Davis
19/87	**Skeletons** . . . Stevie Wonder
13/74	**Skin Tight** . . . Ohio Players
39/87	**Skin Trade** . . . Duran Duran
10/67	**Skinny Legs And All** . . . Joe Tex
22/58	**Skinny Minnie** . . . Bill Haley
25/68	**Skip A Rope** . . . Henson Cargill
3/75	**Sky High** . . . Jigsaw
14/68	**Sky Pilot** . . . Animals
35/64	**Slaughter On Tenth Avenue** . . . Ventures
1/86	**Sledgehammer** . . . Peter Gabriel
13/60	**Sleep** . . . Little Willie John
1/59	**Sleep Walk** . . . Santo & Johnny
8/85	**Sleeping Bag** . . . ZZ Top
	Sleeping Beauty ..see: To A
32/77	**Slide** . . . Slave
6/68	**Slip Away** . . . Clarence Carter
5/78	**Slip Slidin' Away** . . . Paul Simon
33/56	**Slipin' And Slidin'** . . . Little Richard
19/75	**Slippery When Wet** . . . Commodores
16/72	**Slippin' Into Darkness** . . . War
39/83	**Slipping Away** . . . Dave Edmunds
3/66	**Sloop John B** . . . Beach Boys
20/77	**Slow Dancin' Don't Turn Me On** . . . Addrisi Bros.
10/77	**Slow Dancing (Swayin' To The Music)** . . . Johnny Rivers
25/64	**Slow Down** . . . Beatles

POS/YR	RECORD TITLE/ARTIST
2/81	**Slow Hand** . . . Pointer Sisters
20/76	**Slow Ride** . . . Foghat
3/62	**Slow Twistin'** . . . Chubby Checker
	Slow Walk
17/56	Sil Austin
26/57	Bill Doggett
34/77	**Slowdown** . . . John Miles
30/70	**Sly, Slick, And The Wicked** . . . Lost Generation
29/72	**Small Beginnings** . . . Flash
21/62	**Small Sad Sam** . . . Phil McLean
6/85	**Small Town** . . . John Cougar Mellencamp
20/59	**Small World** . . . Johnny Mathis
25/88	**Small World** . . . Huey Lewis & The News
5/69	**Smile A Little Smile For Me** . . . Flying Machine
34/83	**Smile Has Left Your Eyes** . . . Asia
21/55	**Smiles** . . . Crazy Otto
3/71	**Smiling Faces Sometimes** . . . Undisputed Truth
9/77	**Smoke From A Distant Fire** . . . Sanford/Townsend Band
	Smoke Gets In Your Eyes
1/59	Platters
27/73	Blue Haze
4/73	**Smoke On The Water** . . . Deep Purple
17/60	**Smokie** . . . Bill Black's Combo
	Smokin' In The Boy's Room
3/74	Brownsville Station
16/85	Motley Crue
22/87	**Smoking Gun** . . . Robert Cray Band
24/81	**Smoky Mountain Rain** . . . Ronnie Milsap
12/62	**Smoky Places** . . . Corsairs
7/89	**Smooth Criminal** . . . Michael Jackson
5/85	**Smooth Operator** . . . Sade
12/85	**Smuggler's Blues** . . . Glenn Frey
27/68	**Snake, The** . . . Al Wilson
8/62	**Snap Your Fingers** . . . Joe Henderson
31/69	**Snatching It Back** . . . Clarence Carter
2/66	**Snoopy Vs. The Red Baron** . . . Royal Guardsmen
	(also see: Return Of The Red Baron)
8/70	**Snowbird** . . . Anne Murray
23/84	**So Bad** . . . Paul McCartney
38/59	**So Close** . . . Brook Benton
40/83	**So Close** . . . Diana Ross
1/88	**So Emotional** . . . Whitney Houston
14/71	**So Far Away** . . . Carole King

Gino Vannelli had his ninth and final charting single with "Hurts To Be In Love." The 70s were his heyday, peaking with "I Just Wanna Stop" in 1978 (No. 4). Yet even into the late 80s, the Canadian singer-songwriter regularly charted in the middle of the Hot 100.

Bobby Vee, born Robert Thomas Velline, had only a modest chart hit with "How Many Tears." But his next single, "Take Good Care of My Baby," shot all the way to No. 1 for three weeks in 1961, making it the chart pinnacle of his career.

The Ventures' "Green Hornet Theme" came from the crime-stopping radio program, later produced as a TV series after the success of "Batman." Chart-wise, the "Green Hornet Theme" got thwacked by the "Batman Theme," which went to No. 17 for the Marketts and No. 35 for its composer, Neal Hefti.

Bobby Vinton would chart 44 times in his career, and hit No. 1 four times with "Roses Are Red (My Love)," "Blue Velvet," "There! I've Said It Again," and "Mr. Lonely." Oddly, his first and fourth chart-topping singles were recorded at the same session, but charted over two years apart.

Billy Ward and his Dominoes' biggest pop hit ever was the No. 12 "Star Dust," also a No. 5 R & B hit. On the R & B charts, the Dominoes proved their extraordinary staying power with "Sixty-Minute Man," which held its own at No. 1 for an amazing 14 weeks.

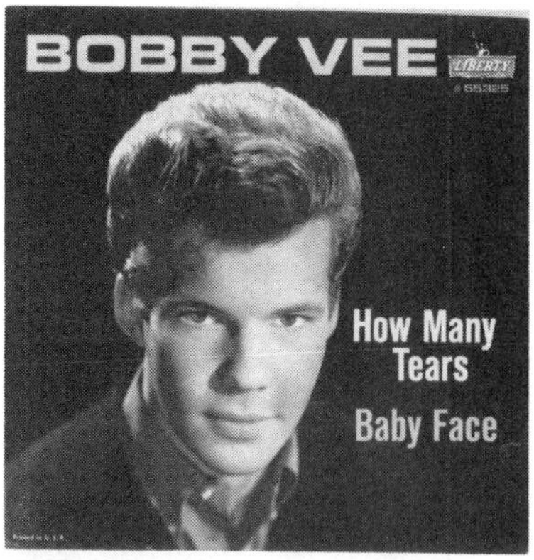

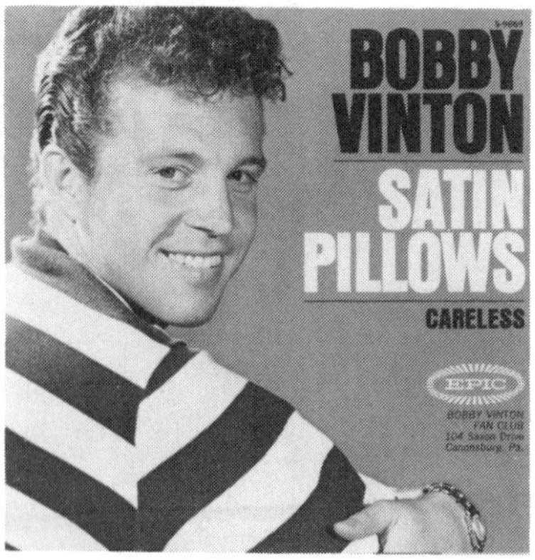

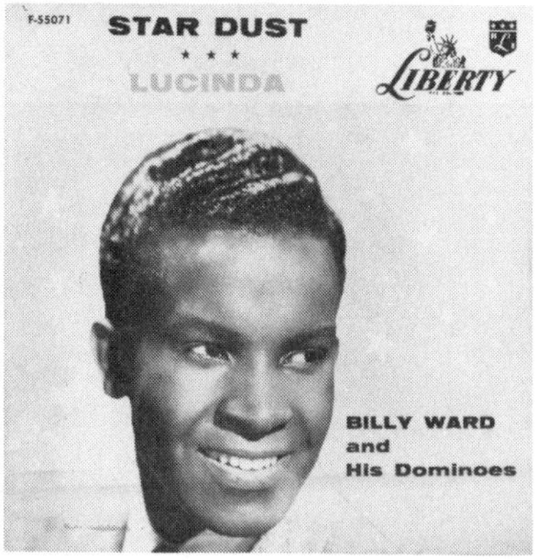

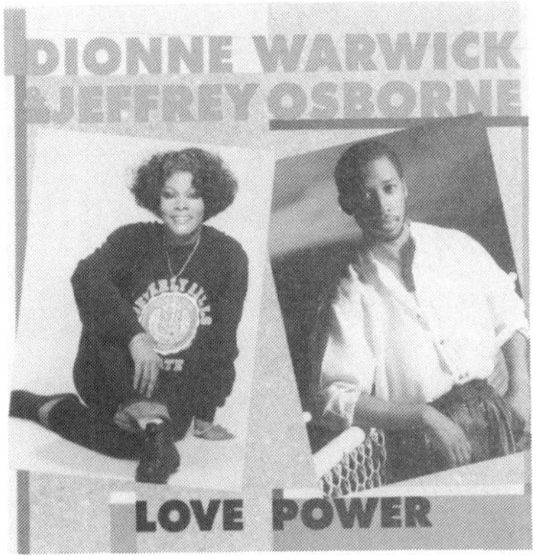

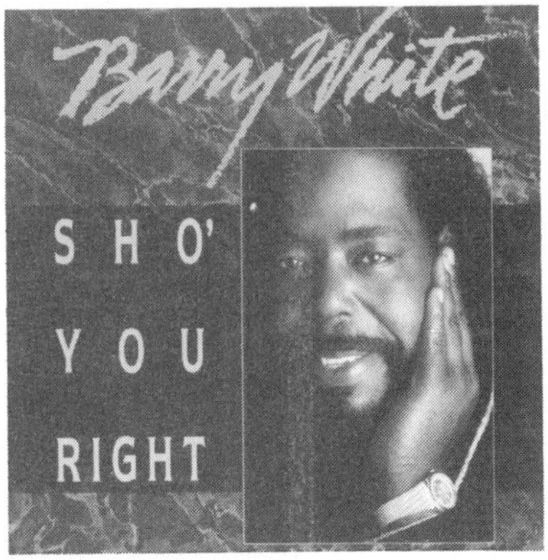

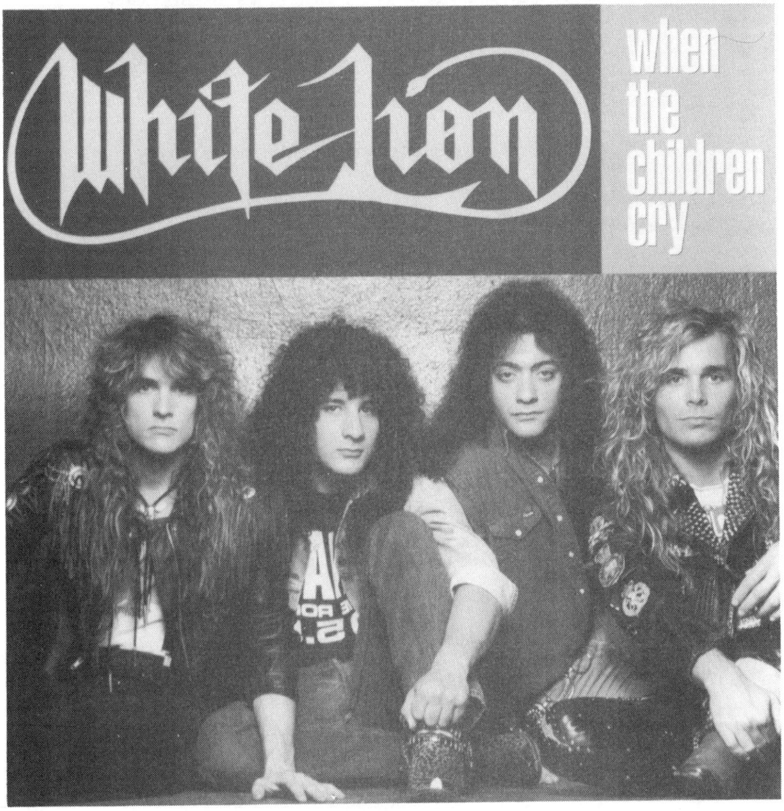

Dionne Warwick and Jeffrey Osborne's "Love Power" was a No. 5 R & B hit, but despite Warwick's many duets, her most successful singles were with larger groups—"Then Came You" with the Spinners, and "That's What Friends Are For" with Elton John, Gladys Knight, and Stevie Wonder. Both were No. 1 hits.

Jody Watley went to No. 6 on the pop charts with "Don't You Want Me." Her successes since leaving Shalamar are estimable—in 1987 and 1988, she scored as many Top-40 singles as her old group had in the entire decade of the 80s.

Wham! is the only 80s group to land three Top-40 hits in the year-end chart: 1985's "Careless Whisper," "Wake Me Up Before You Go-Go," and "Everything She Wants." The only solo artists to do so were Lionel Richie and Cyndi Lauper in 1984, and Wham!'s George Michael in 1988.

Barry White became synonymous with the glittering, sensual sound of 70s disco/soul, and hit the R & B Top 40 20 times until 1982. "Sho' You Right" marked his return to the R & B charts at No. 17—after a nearly five-year absence.

White Lion, like other lions, travels in a pride. In White Lion's case, the *Pride* in question was their Top-40 album that spawned the hits "When The Children Cry" and "Wait."

POS/YR	RECORD TITLE/ARTIST
19/86	**So Far Away** . . . Dire Straits
11/59	**So Fine** . . . Fiestas
30/79	**So Good, So Right** . . . Brenda Russell
36/69	**So Good Together** . . . Andy Kim
39/69	**So I Can Love You** . . . Emotions
26/85	**So In Love** . . . Orchestral Manoeuvres In The Dark
7/77	**So In To You** . . . Atlanta Rhythm Section
28/61	**So Long Baby** . . . Del Shannon
6/59	**So Many Ways** . . . Brook Benton
1/63	**So Much In Love** . . . Tymes
2/57	**So Rare** . . . Jimmy Dorsey
7/60	**So Sad (To Watch Good Love Go Bad)** . . . Everly Brothers
21/62	**So This Is Love** . . . Castells
17/73	**So Very Hard To Go** . . . Tower Of Power
30/83	**So Wrong** . . . Patrick Simmons
21/74	**So You Are A Star** . . . Hudson Brothers
29/67	**So You Want To Be A Rock 'N' Roll Star** . . . Byrds
31/77	**So You Win Again** . . . Hot Chocolate
14/67	**Society's Child (Baby I've Been Thinking)** . . . Janis Ian
6/67	**Sock It To Me-Baby!** . . . Mitch Ryder & The Detroit Wheels
35/57	**Soft** . . . Bill Doggett
	Soft Summer Breeze
11/56	Eddie Heywood
34/56	Diamonds
27/64	**Softly, As I Leave You** . . . Frank Sinatra
29/72	**Softly Whispering I Love You** . . . English Congregation
1/62	**Soldier Boy** . . . Shirelles *(also see: To A)*
12/85	**Solid** . . . Ashford & Simpson
7/83	**Solitaire** . . . Laura Branigan
17/75	**Solitaire** . . . Carpenters
21/70	**Solitary Man** . . . Neil Diamond
34/64	**Some Day We're Gonna Love Again** . . . Searchers
36/81	**Some Days Are Diamonds (Some Days Are Stone)** . . . John Denver
13/65	**Some Enchanted Evening** . . . Jay & The Americans
	Some Guys Have All The Luck
39/73	Persuaders
10/84	Rod Stewart
37/59	**Some Kind-A Earthquake** . . . Duane Eddy

POS/YR	RECORD TITLE/ARTIST
26/83	**Some Kind Of Friend** . . . Barry Manilow
10/88	**Some Kind Of Lover** . . . Jody Watley
3/75	**Some Kind Of Wonderful** . . . Grand Funk
32/61	**Some Kind Of Wonderful** . . . Drifters
6/85	**Some Like It Hot** . . . Power Station
18/85	**Some Things Are Better Left Unsaid** . . . Daryl Hall & John Oates
30/68	**Some Things You Never Get Used To** . . . Supremes
26/68	**Some Velvet Morning** . . . Nancy Sinatra & Lee Hazlewood
11/85	**Somebody** . . . Bryan Adams
5/67	**Somebody To Love** . . . Jefferson Airplane
13/77	**Somebody To Love** . . . Queen
22/58	**Somebody Touched Me** . . . Buddy Knox
18/56	**Somebody Up There Likes Me** . . . Perry Como
7/82	**Somebody's Baby** . . . Jackson Browne
8/70	**Somebody's Been Sleeping** . . . 100 Proof Aged In Soul
33/76	**Somebody's Gettin' It** . . . Johnnie Taylor
13/81	**Somebody's Knockin'** . . . Terri Gibbs
27/86	**Somebody's Out There** . . . Triumph
2/84	**Somebody's Watching Me** . . . Rockwell
32/71	**Somebody's Watching You** . . . Little Sister
7/87	**Someday** . . . Glass Tiger
25/72	**Someday Never Comes** . . . Creedence Clearwater Revival
36/82	**Someday, Someway** . . . Marshall Crenshaw
1/69	**Someday We'll Be Together** . . . Supremes
35/59	**Someone** . . . Johnny Mathis
15/82	**Someone Could Lose A Heart Tonight** . . . Eddie Rabbitt
4/75	**Someone Saved My Life Tonight** . . . Elton John
21/80	**Someone That I Used To Love** . . . Natalie Cole
13/55	**Someone You Love** . . . Nat King Cole
37/77	**Somethin' 'Bout 'Cha** . . . Latimore
1/67	**Somethin' Stupid** . . . Nancy Sinatra
3/69	**Something** . . . Beatles
7/86	**Something About You** . . . Level 42
19/65	**Something About You** . . . Four Tops
13/75	**Something Better To Do** . . . Olivia Newton-John
28/76	**Something He Can Feel** . . . Aretha Franklin

POS/YR	RECORD TITLE/ARTIST
37/69	**Something In The Air** . . . Thunderclap Newman
29/87	**Something Real (Inside Me/Inside You)** . . . Mr. Mister
7/87	**Something So Strong** . . . Crowded House
11/70	**Something's Burning** . . . Kenny Rogers
37/62	**Something's Got A Hold On Me** . . . Etta James
	Something's Gotta Give
5/55	McGuire Sisters
9/55	Sammy Davis, Jr.
12/72	**Something's Wrong With Me** . . . Austin Roberts
31/77	**Sometimes** . . . Facts Of Life
36/80	**Sometimes A Fantasy** . . . Billy Joel
3/78	**Sometimes When We Touch** . . . Dan Hill
19/64	**Somewhere** . . . Tymes
26/66	**Somewhere** . . . Len Barry
21/82	**Somewhere Down The Road** . . . Barry Manilow
	Somewhere In The Night
19/76	Helen Reddy
9/79	Barry Manilow
32/65	**Somewhere In Your Heart** . . . Frank Sinatra
9/66	**Somewhere, My Love** . . . Ray Conniff
2/87	**Somewhere Out There** . . . Linda Ronstadt & James Ingram
32/66	**Somewhere There's A Someone** . . . Dean Martin
10/69	**Son-Of-A Preacher Man** . . . Dusty Springfield
40/68	**Son Of Hickory Holler's Tramp** . . . O.C. Smith
28/74	**Son Of Sagittarius** . . . Eddie Kendricks
8/56	**Song For A Summer Night** . . . Mitch Miller
14/70	**Song Of Joy** . . . Miguel Rios *(also see: Joy)*
11/55	**Song Of The Dreamer** . . . Eddie Fisher
29/79	**Song On The Radio** . . . Al Stewart
1/72	**Song Sung Blue** . . . Neil Diamond
4/87	**Songbird** . . . Kenny G
25/78	**Songbird** . . . Barbra Streisand
30/70	**Soolaimon (African Trilogy II)** . . . Neil Diamond
9/71	**Sooner Or Later** . . . Grass Roots
34/69	**Sophisticated Cissy** . . . Meters

POS/YR	RECORD TITLE/ARTIST
25/76	**Sophisticated Lady (She's A Different Lady)** . . . Natalie Cole
2/59	**Sorry (I Ran All The Way Home)** . . . Impalas
6/76	**Sorry Seems To Be The Hardest Word** . . . Elton John
	Soul And Inspiration ..see: (You're My)
27/87	**Soul City** . . . Partland Brothers
	Soul Coaxing ..see: Ame Caline
18/69	**Soul Deep** . . . Box Tops
17/67	**Soul Finger** . . . Bar-Kays
20/85	**Soul Kiss** . . . Olivia Newton-John
17/68	**Soul-Limbo** . . . Booker T. & The MG's
35/73	**Soul Makossa** . . . Manu Dibango
	Soul Man
2/67	Sam & Dave
14/79	Blues Brothers
29/71	**Soul Power** . . . James Brown
23/68	**Soul Serenade** . . . Willie Mitchell
37/69	**Soul Shake** . . . Peggy Scott & Jo Jo Benson
37/73	**Soul Song** . . . Joe Stampley
17/62	**Soul Twist** . . . King Curtis
3/69	**Soulful Strut** . . . Young-Holt Unlimited
23/83	**Souls** . . . Rick Springfield
36/67	**Sound Of Love** . . . Five Americans
1/66	**Sounds Of Silence** . . . Simon & Garfunkel
3/63	**South Street** . . . Orlons
29/75	**South's Gonna Do It** . . . Charlie Daniels Band
18/82	**Southern Cross** . . . Crosby, Stills & Nash
1/77	**Southern Nights** . . . Glen Campbell
15/64	**Southtown, U.S.A.** . . . Dixiebelles
30/83	**Space Age Love Song** . . . A Flock Of Seagulls
15/73	**Space Oddity** . . . David Bowie
4/73	**Space Race** . . . Billy Preston
23/72	**Spaceman** . . . Nilsson
40/85	**Spanish Eddie** . . . Laura Branigan
15/66	**Spanish Eyes** . . . Al Martino
27/66	**Spanish Flea** . . . Herb Alpert
	Spanish Harlem
10/61	Ben E. King
2/71	Aretha Franklin
31/62	**Spanish Lace** . . . Gene McDaniels
	(Speak Softly Love) ..see: Love Theme From The Godfather
14/72	**Speak To The Sky** . . . Rick Springfield

POS/YR	RECORD TITLE/ARTIST
38/69	**Special Delivery** . . . 1910 Fruitgum Co.
5/80	**Special Lady** . . . Ray, Goodman & Brown
26/68	**Special Occasion** . . . Miracles
17/56	**Speedoo** . . . Cadillacs
6/62	**Speedy Gonzales** . . . Pat Boone
40/83	**Spice Of Life** . . . Manhattan Transfer
3/74	**Spiders & Snakes** . . . Jim Stafford
7/86	**Spies Like Us** . . . Paul McCartney
3/70	**Spill The Wine** . . . Eric Burdon & War
2/69	**Spinning Wheel** . . . Blood, Sweat & Tears
40/66	**Spinout** . . . Elvis Presley
23/70	**Spirit In The Dark** . . . Aretha Franklin
40/77	**Spirit In The Night** . . . Manfred Mann's Earth Band
3/70	**Spirit In The Sky** . . . Norman Greenbaum
35/75	**Spirit Of The Boogie** . . . Kool & The Gang
11/82	**Spirits In The Material World** . . . Police
3/58	**Splish Splash** . . . Bobby Darin
	Spooky
3/68	Classics IV
17/79	Atlanta Rhythm Section
39/77	**Spring Rain** . . . Silvetti
37/76	**Springtime Mama** . . . Henry Gross
16/88	**Spy In The House Of Love** . . . Was (Not Was)
16/76	**Squeeze Box** . . . Who
1/85	**St. Elmo's Fire (Man In Motion)** . . . John Parr *(also see: Love Theme)*
13/56	**St. Therese Of The Roses** . . . Billy Ward & His Dominoes
21/86	**Stages** . . . ZZ Top
	Stagger Lee
1/59	Lloyd Price
22/67	Wilson Pickett
25/71	Tommy Roe
9/60	**Stairway To Heaven** . . . Neil Sedaka
22/69	**Stand!** . . . Sly & The Family Stone
5/83	**Stand Back** . . . Stevie Nicks
	Stand By Me
4/61	Ben E. King
12/67	Spyder Turner
20/75	John Lennon
22/80	Mickey Gilley
9/86	Ben E. King *(also see: I'll Be There)*

POS/YR	RECORD TITLE/ARTIST
	Stand By Your Man
19/69	Tammy Wynette
24/70	Candi Staton
10/77	**Stand Tall** . . . Burton Cummings
37/74	**Standing At The End Of The Line** . . . Lobo
6/67	**Standing In The Shadows Of Love** . . . Four Tops
	Standing On The Corner
3/56	Four Lads
22/56	Dean Martin
29/74	**Star** . . . Stealers Wheel
39/74	**Star Baby** . . . Guess Who
	Star Is Born, Love Theme From A ..see: Evergreen
	Star Wars Theme
1/77	Meco
10/77	John Williams
25/60	**Starbright** . . . Johnny Mathis
	Stardust
12/57	Billy Ward & His Dominoes
32/64	Nino Tempo & April Stevens
1/81	**Stars on 45** . . . Stars on 45
28/82	**Stars on 45 III** . . . Stars on 45
2/81	**Start Me Up** . . . Rolling Stones
9/57	**Start Movin' (In My Direction)** . . . Sal Mineo
19/72	**Starting All Over Again** . . . Mel & Tim
	Starting Over ..see: (Just Like)
36/80	**Starting Over Again** . . . Dolly Parton
3/84	**State Of Shock** . . . Jacksons
22/85	**State Of The Heart** . . . Rick Springfield
	Stay
1/60	Maurice Williams
16/64	4 Seasons
20/78	Jackson Browne
38/78	**Stay** . . . Rufus/Chaka Khan
7/71	**Stay Awhile** . . . Bells
38/64	**Stay Awhile** . . . Dusty Springfield
10/68	**Stay In My Corner** . . . Dells
16/84	**Stay The Night** . . . Chicago
24/87	**Stay The Night** . . . Benjamin Orr
17/72	**Stay With Me** . . . Faces
30/84	**Stay With Me Tonight** . . . Jeffrey Osborne
1/78	**Stayin' Alive** . . . Bee Gees
33/61	**Stayin' In** . . . Bobby Vee
22/88	**Staying Together** . . . Debbie Gibson
37/81	**Staying With It** . . . Firefall

POS/YR	RECORD TITLE/ARTIST
	Steal Away
17/64	Jimmy Hughes
37/70	Johnnie Taylor
6/80	**Steal Away** . . . Robbie Dupree
25/81	**Steal The Night** . . . Stevie Woods
17/73	**Steamroller Blues** . . . Elvis Presley
13/62	**Steel Guitar And A Glass Of Wine** . . . Paul Anka
5/81	**Step By Step** . . . Eddie Rabbitt
14/60	**Step By Step** . . . Crests
37/73	**Step By Step** . . . Joe Simon
24/67	**Step Out Of Your Mind** . . . American Breed
39/78	**Steppin' In A Slide Zone** . . . Moody Blues
6/82	**Steppin' Out** . . . Joe Jackson
36/76	**Steppin' Out** . . . Neil Sedaka
7/74	**Steppin' Out (Gonna Boogie Tonight)** . . . Dawn
	Steppin' Stone ..see: (I'm Not Your)
35/63	**Stewball** . . . Peter, Paul & Mary
32/86	**Stick Around** . . . Julian Lennon
25/61	**Stick Shift** . . . Duals
11/71	**Stick-Up** . . . Honey Cone
40/60	**Sticks And Stones** . . . Ray Charles
1/79	**Still** . . . Commodores
8/63	**Still** . . . Bill Anderson
40/76	**Still Crazy After All These Years** . . . Paul Simon
20/87	**Still In Love (medley)** . . . Boston
22/82	**Still In Saigon** . . . Charlie Daniels Band
28/81	**Still Right Here In My Heart** . . . Pure Prairie League
5/76	**Still The One** . . . Orleans
4/78	**Still The Same** . . . Bob Seger
19/82	**Still They Ride** . . . Journey
11/70	**Still Water (Love)** . . . Four Tops
12/73	**Stir It Up** . . . Johnny Nash
7/80	**Stomp!** . . . Brothers Johnson
36/78	**Stone Blue** . . . Foghat
40/82	**Stone Cold** . . . Rainbow
10/87	**Stone Love** . . . Kool & The Gang
7/70	**Stoned Love** . . . Supremes
30/73	**Stoned Out Of My Mind** . . . Chi-Lites
3/68	**Stoned Soul Picnic** . . . 5th Dimension
14/71	**Stones** . . . Neil Diamond
6/71	**Stoney End** . . . Barbra Streisand
2/58	**Stood Up** . . . Ricky Nelson

POS/YR	RECORD TITLE/ARTIST
9/74	**Stop And Smell The Roses** . . . Mac Davis
8/64	**Stop And Think It Over** . . . Dale & Grace
3/81	**Stop Draggin' My Heart Around** . . . Stevie Nicks with Tom Petty
	Stop! In The Name Of Love
1/65	Supremes
29/83	Hollies
39/71	**Stop, Look, Listen (To Your Heart)** . . . Stylistics
7/66	**Stop Stop Stop** . . . Hollies
36/62	**Stop The Music** . . . Shirelles
26/71	**Stop The War Now** . . . Edwin Starr
34/62	**Stop The Wedding** . . . Etta James
15/87	**Stop To Love** . . . Luther Vandross
	Stormy
5/68	Classics IV
32/79	Santana
23/71	**Story In Your Eyes** . . . Moody Blues
15/58	**Story Of My Life** . . . Marty Robbins
16/61	**Story Of My Love** . . . Paul Anka
28/59	**Story Of My Love** . . . Conway Twitty
16/55	**Story Untold** . . . Crew-Cuts
10/83	**Straight From The Heart** . . . Bryan Adams
39/81	**Straight From The Heart** . . . Allman Brothers Band
36/68	**Straight Life** . . . Bobby Goldsboro
15/78	**Straight On** . . . Heart
29/74	**Straight Shootin' Woman** . . . Steppenwolf
1/89	**Straight Up** . . . Paula Abdul
	Stranded In The Jungle
15/56	Cadets
18/56	Jayhawks
39/56	Gadabouts
21/88	**Strange But True** . . . Times Two
14/76	**Strange Magic** . . . Electric Light Orchestra
11/78	**Strange Way** . . . Firefall
23/83	**Stranger In My House** . . . Ronnie Milsap
30/65	**Stranger In Town** . . . Del Shannon
30/84	**Stranger In Town** . . . Toto
	Stranger On The Shore
1/62	Mr. Acker Bilk
38/62	Andy Williams
1/66	**Strangers In The Night** . . . Frank Sinatra
8/67	**Strawberry Fields Forever** . . . Beatles
5/77	**Strawberry Letter 23** . . . Brothers Johnson
39/68	**Strawberry Shortcake** . . . Jay & The Techniques
3/83	**Stray Cat Strut** . . . Stray Cats

POS/YR	RECORD TITLE/ARTIST
1/74	**Streak, The** . . . Ray Stevens
30/78	**Street Corner Serenade** . . . Wet Willie
36/79	**Street Life** . . . Crusaders/Randy Crawford
27/76	**Street Singin'** . . . Lady Flash
	String Along
39/60	Fabian
25/63	Rick Nelson
1/62	**Stripper, The** . . . David Rose
17/81	**Stroke** . . . Billy Squier
4/58	**Stroll, The** . . . Diamonds
30/81	**Stronger Than Before** . . . Carole Bayer Sager
40/84	**Strung Out** . . . Steve Perry
7/84	**Strut** . . . Sheena Easton
22/75	**Struttin'** . . . Billy Preston
6/73	**Stuck In The Middle With You** . . . Stealers Wheel
1/60	**Stuck On You** . . . Elvis Presley
3/84	**Stuck On You** . . . Lionel Richie
1/86	**Stuck With You** . . . Huey Lewis & The News
21/78	**Stuff Like That** . . . Quincy Jones
4/79	**Stumblin' In** . . . Suzi Quatro & Chris Norman
14/58	**Stupid Cupid** . . . Connie Francis
18/72	**Suavecito** . . . Malo
39/65	**Subterranean Homesick Blues** . . . Bob Dylan
16/64	**Such A Night** . . . Elvis Presley
26/79	**Such A Woman** . . . Tycoon
11/65	**(Such An) Easy Question** . . . Elvis Presley
4/85	**Suddenly** . . . Billy Ocean
20/81	**Suddenly** . . . Olivia Newton-John & Cliff Richard
9/83	**Suddenly Last Summer** . . . Motels
	Suddenly There's A Valley
9/55	Gogi Grant
13/55	Jo Stafford
20/55	Julius LaRosa
37/74	**Sugar Baby Love** . . . Rubettes
10/72	**Sugar Daddy** . . . Jackson 5
36/84	**Sugar Don't Bite** . . . Sam Harris
32/65	**Sugar Dumpling** . . . Sam Cooke
35/87	**Sugar Free** . . . Wa Wa Nee
30/64	**Sugar Lips** . . . Al Hirt
5/58	**Sugar Moon** . . . Pat Boone
22/69	**Sugar On Sunday** . . . Clique

POS/YR	RECORD TITLE/ARTIST
1/63	**Sugar Shack** . . . Jimmy Gilmer & The Fireballs
	Sugar, Sugar
1/69	Archies
25/70	Wilson Pickett
5/66	**Sugar Town** . . . Nancy Sinatra
9/85	**Sugar Walls** . . . Sheena Easton
1/58	**Sugartime** . . . McGuire Sisters
21/69	**Suite: Judy Blue Eyes** . . . Crosby, Stills & Nash
	Sukiyaki
1/63	Kyu Sakamoto
3/81	A Taste Of Honey
4/79	**Sultans Of Swing** . . . Dire Straits
7/76	**Summer** . . . War
6/72	**Summer Breeze** . . . Seals & Crofts
1/66	**Summer In The City** . . . Lovin' Spoonful
	Summer Night ..see: Song For A
5/78	**Summer Nights** . . . John Travolta & Olivia Newton-John
24/65	**Summer Nights** . . . Marianne Faithfull
	Summer Of '42 ..see: Theme From
5/85	**Summer Of '69** . . . Bryan Adams
	Summer Place ..see: Theme From A
14/68	**Summer Rain** . . . Johnny Rivers
26/66	**Summer Samba (So Nice)** . . . Walter Wanderley
33/71	**Summer Sand** . . . Dawn
30/60	**Summer Set** . . . Monty Kelly
7/64	**Summer Song** . . . Chad & Jeremy
21/73	**Summer (The First Time)** . . . Bobby Goldsboro
25/66	**Summer Wind** . . . Frank Sinatra
11/60	**Summer's Gone** . . . Paul Anka
10/66	**Summertime** . . . Billy Stewart
	Summertime Blues
8/58	Eddie Cochran
14/68	Blue Cheer
27/70	Who
	Summertime, Summertime
26/58	Jamies
38/62	Jamies
13/66	**Sun Ain't Gonna Shine (Anymore)** . . . Walker Bros.
20/86	**Sun Always Shines On T.V.** . . . a-ha
38/85	**Sun City** . . . Artists United Against Apartheid
18/65	**Sunday And Me** . . . Jay & The Americans
31/67	**Sunday For Tea** . . . Peter & Gordon

POS/YR	RECORD TITLE/ARTIST
	Sunday Mornin'
30/68	Spanky & Our Gang
35/69	Oliver
9/67	**Sunday Will Never Be The Same** . . . Spanky & Our Gang
1/74	**Sundown** . . . Gordon Lightfoot
39/77	**Sunflower** . . . Glen Campbell
7/84	**Sunglasses At Night** . . . Corey Hart
2/66	**Sunny** . . . Bobby Hebb
14/66	**Sunny Afternoon** . . . Kinks
34/72	**Sunny Days** . . . Lighthouse
34/76	**Sunrise** . . . Eric Carmen
22/85	**Sunset Grill** . . . Don Henley
4/72	**Sunshine** . . . Jonathan Edwards
20/67	**Sunshine Girl** . . . Parade
13/65	**Sunshine, Lollipops And Rainbows** . . . Lesley Gore
5/68	**Sunshine Of Your Love** . . . Cream
1/74	**Sunshine On My Shoulders** . . . John Denver
1/66	**Sunshine Superman** . . . Donovan
13/70	**Super Bad** . . . James Brown
31/73	**Super Fly Meets Shaft** . . . John & Ernest
16/81	**Super Freak** . . . Rick James
8/73	**Superfly** . . . Curtis Mayfield *(also see: Freddie's Dead)*
26/79	**Superman** . . . Herbie Mann
5/75	**Supernatural Thing** . . . Ben E. King
30/88	**Supersonic** . . . J.J. Fad
2/71	**Superstar** . . . Carpenters
35/76	**Superstar** . . . Paul Davis
14/71	**Superstar - Jesus Christ Superstar** . . . Murray Head
18/71	**Superstar (Remember How You Got Where You Are)** . . . Temptations
1/73	**Superstition** . . . Stevie Wonder
31/88	**Superstitious** . . . Europe
33/72	**Superwoman (Where Were You When I Needed You)** . . . Stevie Wonder
16/74	**Sure As I'm Sittin' Here** . . . Three Dog Night
9/66	**Sure Gonna Miss Her** . . . Gary Lewis & The Playboys
1/63	**Surf City** . . . Jan & Dean
7/63	**Surfer Girl** . . . Beach Boys
31/62	**Surfer's Stomp** . . . Mar-Kets
4/64	**Surfin' Bird** . . . Trashmen
14/62	**Surfin' Safari** . . . Beach Boys

POS/YR	RECORD TITLE/ARTIST
	Surfin' U.S.A.
3/63	Beach Boys
36/74	Beach Boys
20/77	Leif Garrett
1/61	**Surrender** . . . Elvis Presley
38/71	**Surrender** . . . Diana Ross
6/89	**Surrender To Me** . . . Ann Wilson & Robin Zander
11/68	**Susan** . . . Buckinghams
	Susie Darlin'
5/58	Robin Luke
35/62	Tommy Roe
3/64	**Suspicion** . . . Terry Stafford
13/79	**Suspicions** . . . Eddie Rabbitt
1/69	**Suspicious Minds** . . . Elvis Presley
1/85	**Sussudio** . . . Phil Collins
17/86	**Suzanne** . . . Journey
	Suzie-Q
27/57	Dale Hawkins
11/68	Creedence Clearwater Revival
39/73	**Swamp Witch** . . . Jim Stafford
34/57	**Swanee River Rock (Talkin' 'Bout That River)** . . . Ray Charles
14/60	**Sway** . . . Bobby Rydell
6/75	**Swearin' To God** . . . Frankie Valli
	Sweet And Gentle
10/55	Alan Dale
12/55	Georgia Gibbs
7/71	**Sweet And Innocent** . . . Donny Osmond
19/81	**Sweet Baby** . . . Stanley Clarke/George Duke
13/68	**Sweet Blindness** . . . 5th Dimension
4/69	**Sweet Caroline (Good Times Never Seemed So Good)** . . . Neil Diamond
7/69	**Sweet Cherry Wine** . . . Tommy James & The Shondells
1/88	**Sweet Child O' Mine** . . . Guns N' Roses
8/71	**Sweet City Woman** . . . Stampeders
28/69	**Sweet Cream Ladies, Forward March** . . . Box Tops
5/82	**Sweet Dreams** . . . Air Supply
15/66	**Sweet Dreams** . . . Tommy McLain
1/83	**Sweet Dreams (Are Made of This)** . . . Eurythmics
36/75	**Sweet Emotion** . . . Aerosmith
7/86	**Sweet Freedom** . . . Michael McDonald
6/71	**Sweet Hitch-Hiker** . . . Creedence Clearwater Revival

POS/YR	RECORD TITLE/ARTIST
8/74	**Sweet Home Alabama** . . . Lynyrd Skynyrd
	Sweet Inspiration
18/68	Sweet Inspirations
37/72	Barbra Streisand (medley)
17/78	**Sweet Life** . . . Paul Davis
2/58	**Sweet Little Sixteen** . . . Chuck Berry
5/76	**Sweet Love** . . . Commodores
8/86	**Sweet Love** . . . Anita Baker
36/79	**Sweet Lui-Louise** . . . Ironhorse
7/71	**Sweet Mary** . . . Wadsworth Mansion
40/75	**Sweet Maxine** . . . Doobie Brothers
4/60	**Sweet Nothin's** . . . Brenda Lee
7/56	**Sweet Old Fashioned Girl** . . . Teresa Brewer
8/66	**Sweet Pea** . . . Tommy Roe
9/72	**Sweet Seasons** . . . Carole King
20/87	**Sweet Sixteen** . . . Billy Idol
2/67	**Sweet Soul Music** . . . Arthur Conley
33/75	**Sweet Sticky Thing** . . . Ohio Players
13/75	**Sweet Surrender** . . . John Denver
15/72	**Sweet Surrender** . . . Bread
5/68	**(Sweet Sweet Baby) Since You've Been Gone** . . . Aretha Franklin
10/66	**Sweet Talkin' Guy** . . . Chiffons
17/78	**Sweet Talkin' Woman** . . . Electric Light Orchestra
5/76	**Sweet Thing** . . . Rufus Featuring Chaka Khan
26/82	**Sweet Time** . . . REO Speedwagon
33/73	**Sweet Understanding Love** . . . Four Tops
40/64	**Sweet William** . . . Millie Small
29/66	**Sweet Woman Like You** . . . Joe Tex
9/59	**Sweeter Than You** . . . Ricky Nelson
5/86	**Sweetest Taboo** . . . Sade
7/82	**Sweetest Thing (I've Ever Known)** . . . Juice Newton
32/67	**Sweetest Thing This Side Of Heaven** . . . Chris Bartley
10/81	**Sweetheart** . . . Franke & The Knockouts
16/61	**Sweets For My Sweet** . . . Drifters
19/84	**Swept Away** . . . Diana Ross
39/60	**Swingin' On A Rainbow** . . . Frankie Avalon
13/62	**Swingin' Safari** . . . Billy Vaughn
5/60	**Swingin' School** . . . Bobby Rydell
23/58	**Swingin' Shepherd Blues** . . . Moe Koffman Quartette

POS/YR	RECORD TITLE/ARTIST
38/63	**Swinging On A Star** . . . Big Dee Irwin/Little Eva
17/77	**Swingtown** . . . Steve Miller Band
26/61	**Switch-A-Roo** . . . Hank Ballard
5/72	**Sylvia's Mother** . . . Dr. Hook
38/88	**Symptoms Of True Love** . . . Tracie Spencer
16/83	**Synchronicity II** . . . Police
37/76	**(System Of) Doctor Tarr And Professor Fether** . . . Alan Parsons Project

T

POS/YR	RECORD TITLE/ARTIST
24/60	**T.L.C. Tender Love And Care** . . . Jimmie Rodgers
1/74	**TSOP (The Sound Of Philadelphia)** . . . MFSB featuring The Three Degrees
23/60	**Ta Ta** . . . Clyde McPhatter
8/82	**Tainted Love** . . . Soft Cell
3/78	**Take A Chance On Me** . . . Abba
2/69	**Take A Letter Maria** . . . R.B. Greaves
15/80	**Take A Little Rhythm** . . . Ali Thomson
30/72	**Take A Look Around** . . . Temptations
16/59	**Take A Message To Mary** . . . Everly Brothers
20/69	**Take Care Of Your Homework** . . . Johnnie Taylor
25/61	**Take Five** . . . Dave Brubeck Quartet
7/61	**Take Good Care Of Her** . . . Adam Wade
	Take Good Care Of My Baby
1/61	Bobby Vee
33/68	Bobby Vinton
10/82	**Take It Away** . . . Paul McCartney
12/72	**Take It Easy** . . . Eagles
24/86	**Take It Easy** . . . Andy Taylor
10/82	**Take It Easy On Me** . . . Little River Band
33/76	**Take It Like A Man** . . . Bachman-Turner Overdrive
5/81	**Take It On The Run** . . . REO Speedwagon
4/76	**Take It To The Limit** . . . Eagles
16/65	**Take Me Back** . . . Little Anthony & The Imperials
18/82	**Take Me Down** . . . Alabama

POS/YR	RECORD TITLE/ARTIST
38/68	**Take Me For A Little While** . . . Vanilla Fudge
7/86	**Take Me Home** . . . Phil Collins
8/79	**Take Me Home** . . . Cher
2/71	**Take Me Home, Country Roads** . . . John Denver
4/86	**Take Me Home Tonight** . . . Eddie Money
11/75	**Take Me In Your Arms (Rock Me)** . . . Doobie Brothers
14/83	**Take Me To Heart** . . . Quarterflash
26/79	**Take Me To The River** . . . Talking Heads
25/85	**Take Me With U** . . . Prince
1/86	**Take My Breath Away** . . . Berlin
17/81	**Take My Heart (You Can Have It If You Want It)** . . . Kool & The Gang
16/82	**Take Off** . . . Bob & Doug McKenzie
1/85	**Take On Me** . . . a-ha
10/79	**Take The Long Way Home** . . . Supertramp
11/76	**Take The Money And Run** . . . Steve Miller
8/63	**Take These Chains From My Heart** . . . Ray Charles
11/68	**Take Time To Know Her** . . . Percy Sledge
3/80	**Take Your Time (Do It Right)** . . . S.O.S. Band
32/86	**Taken In** . . . Mike + The Mechanics
12/74	**Takin' Care Of Business** . . . Bachman-Turner Overdrive
13/76	**Takin' It To The Streets** . . . Doobie Brothers
7/64	**Talk Back Trembling Lips** . . . Johnny Tillotson
9/87	**Talk Dirty To Me** . . . Poison
15/67	**Talk Talk** . . . Music Machine
34/60	**Talk That Talk** . . . Jackie Wilson
4/86	**Talk To Me** . . . Stevie Nicks
21/87	**Talk To Me** . . . Chico DeBarge
38/59	**Talk To Me** . . . Frank Sinatra
	Talk To Me, Talk To Me
20/58	Little Willie John
11/63	Sunny & The Sunglows
15/57	**Talkin' To The Blues** . . . Jim Lowe
12/64	**Talking About My Baby** . . . Impressions
3/84	**Talking In Your Sleep** . . . Romantics
18/78	**Talking In Your Sleep** . . . Crystal Gayle
27/72	**Talking Loud And Saying Nothing** . . . James Brown

POS/YR	RECORD TITLE/ARTIST
25/88	**Tall Cool One** . . . Robert Plant
	Tall Cool One
36/59	Wailers
38/64	Wailers
	Tall Oak Tree ..see: (There Was A)
7/59	**Tall Paul** . . . Annette
6/59	**Tallahassee Lassie** . . . Freddy Cannon
	Tammy
1/57	Debbie Reynolds
5/57	Ames Brothers
18/76	**Tangerine** . . . Salsoul Orchestra
31/75	**Tangled Up In Blue** . . . Bob Dylan
34/68	**Tapioca Tundra** . . . Monkees
38/66	**Tar And Cement** . . . Verdelle Smith
13/86	**Tarzan Boy** . . . Baltimora
7/65	**Taste Of Honey** . . . Herb Alpert
18/72	**Taurus** . . . Dennis Coffey
24/72	**Taxi** . . . Harry Chapin
7/58	**Tea For Two** . . . Tommy Dorsey Orchestra
25/62	**Teach Me Tonight** . . . George Maharis
16/70	**Teach Your Children** . . . Crosby, Stills, Nash & Young
21/58	**Teacher, Teacher** . . . Johnny Mathis
25/84	**Teacher Teacher** . . . 38 Special
31/61	**Tear, A** . . . Gene McDaniels
23/59	**Tear Drop** . . . Santo & Johnny
20/57	**Tear Drops** . . . Lee Andrews & The Hearts
5/56	**Tear Fell** . . . Teresa Brewer
15/76	**Tear The Roof Off The Sucker (Give Up The Funk)** . . . Parliament
37/84	**Tears** . . . John Waite
20/64	**Tears And Roses** . . . Al Martino
1/70	**Tears Of A Clown** . . . Miracles
4/58	**Tears On My Pillow** . . . Little Anthony & The Imperials
39/59	**Teasin'** . . . Quaker City Boys
17/60	**Teddy** . . . Connie Francis
40/76	**Teddy Bear** . . . Red Sovine *(also see: (Let Me Be Your))*
32/73	**Teddy Bear Song** . . . Barbara Fairchild
	Teen Age ..also see: Teenage
2/57	**Teen-Age Crush** . . . Tommy Sands
5/62	**Teen Age Idol** . . . Rick Nelson
	Teen Age Prayer
6/56	Gale Storm
19/56	Gloria Mann
1/60	**Teen Angel** . . . Mark Dinning
4/59	**Teen Beat** . . . Sandy Nelson

POS/YR	RECORD TITLE/ARTIST
29/59	**Teen Commandments** . . . Paul Anka-George Hamilton IV-Johnny Nash
	Teenage Queen ..see: Ballad Of
5/59	**Teenager In Love** . . . Dion & The Belmonts
2/57	**Teenager's Romance** . . . Ricky Nelson
9/83	**Telefone (Long Distance Love Affair)** . . . Sheena Easton
7/77	**Telephone Line** . . . Electric Light Orchestra
18/77	**Telephone Man** . . . Meri Wilson
1/83	**Tell Her About It** . . . Billy Joel
	Tell Her No
6/65	Zombies
27/83	Juice Newton
40/73	**Tell Her She's Lovely** . . . El Chicano
4/63	**Tell Him** . . . Exciters
8/59	**Tell Him No** . . . Travis & Bob
17/70	**Tell It All Brother** . . . Kenny Rogers
	Tell It Like It Is
2/67	Aaron Neville
8/81	Heart
33/64	**Tell It On The Mountain** . . . Peter, Paul & Mary
7/88	**Tell It To My Heart** . . . Taylor Dayne
10/67	**Tell It To The Rain** . . . 4 Seasons
7/60	**Tell Laura I Love Her** . . . Ray Peterson
23/68	**Tell Mama** . . . Etta James
22/62	**Tell Me** . . . Dick & DeeDee
21/74	**Tell Me A Lie** . . . Sami Jo
3/74	**Tell Me Something Good** . . . Rufus Featuring Chaka Khan
37/67	**Tell Me To My Face** . . . Keith
33/82	**Tell Me Tomorrow** . . . Smokey Robinson
13/64	**Tell Me Why** . . . Bobby Vinton
18/61	**Tell Me Why** . . . Belmonts
33/66	**Tell Me Why** . . . Elvis Presley
24/64	**Tell Me (You're Coming Back)** . . . Rolling Stones
1/62	**Telstar** . . . Tornadoes
39/70	**Temma Harbour** . . . Mary Hopkin
27/61	**Temptation** . . . Everly Brothers
15/71	**Temptation Eyes** . . . Grass Roots
22/58	**Ten Commandments Of Love** . . . Harvey & The Moonglows *(also see: Teen Commandments)*
38/84	**10-9-8** . . . Face To Face
25/83	**Tender Is The Night** . . . Jackson Browne

POS/YR	RECORD TITLE/ARTIST
10/86	**Tender Love** . . . Force M.D.'s
	Tender, Love and Care ..see: T.L.C.
	Tender Trap ..see: (Love Is)
31/85	**Tender Years** . . . John Cafferty
31/61	**Tenderly** . . . Bert Kaempfert
27/85	**Tenderness** . . . General Public
23/70	**Tennessee Bird Walk** . . . Jack Blanchard & Misty Morgan
35/64	**Tennessee Waltz** . . . Sam Cooke
	Tequila
1/58	Champs
20/58	Eddie Platt
	Testify ..see: (I Wanna)
1/75	**Thank God I'm A Country Boy** . . . John Denver
22/78	**Thank God It's Friday** . . . Love & Kisses
1/70	**Thank You (Falettinme Be Mice Elf Agin)** . . . Sly & The Family Stone
25/78	**Thank You For Being A Friend** . . . Andrew Gold
35/64	**Thank You Girl** . . . Beatles
16/59	**Thank You Pretty Baby** . . . Brook Benton
32/88	**Thanks For My Child** . . . Cheryl Pepsii Riley
37/74	**Thanks For Saving My Life** . . . Billy Paul
16/87	**That Ain't Love** . . . REO Speedwagon
4/82	**That Girl** . . . Stevie Wonder
22/80	**That Girl Could Sing** . . . Jackson Browne
6/73	**That Lady** . . . Isley Brothers
20/64	**That Lucky Old Sun** . . . Ray Charles
	That Old Black Magic
13/55	Sammy Davis, Jr.
18/58	Louis Prima & Keely Smith
21/61	Bobby Rydell
21/81	**That Old Song** . . . Ray Parker Jr. & Raydio
28/62	**That Stranger Used To Be My Girl** . . . Trade Martin
12/63	**That Sunday, That Summer** . . . Nat King Cole
20/86	**That Was Then, This Is Now** . . . Monkees
12/85	**That Was Yesterday** . . . Foreigner
	That'll Be The Day
1/57	Crickets
11/76	Linda Ronstadt
6/84	**That's All!** . . . Genesis
17/56	**That's All** . . . Tennessee Ernie Ford
3/55	**That's All I Want From You** . . . Jaye P. Morgan

POS/YR	RECORD TITLE/ARTIST
16/56	**That's All There Is To That** . . . Nat King Cole
6/60	**That's All You Gotta Do** . . . Brenda Lee
40/63	**That's How Heartaches Are Made** . . . Baby Washington
39/58	**That's How Much I Love You** . . . Pat Boone
31/61	**That's It-I Quit-I'm Movin' On** . . . Sam Cooke
4/66	**That's Life** . . . Frank Sinatra
28/83	**That's Love** . . . Jim Capaldi
9/62	**That's Old Fashioned (That's The Way Love Should Be)** . . . Everly Brothers
3/77	**That's Rock 'N' Roll** . . . Shaun Cassidy
12/64	**That's The Way Boys Are** . . . Lesley Gore
27/72	**That's The Way I Feel About Cha** . . . Bobby Womack
1/75	**That's The Way (I Like It)** . . . KC & The Sunshine Band
10/71	**That's The Way I've Always Heard It Should Be** . . . Carly Simon
7/69	**That's The Way Love Is** . . . Marvin Gaye
33/63	**That's The Way Love Is** . . . Bobby Bland
12/75	**That's The Way Of The World** . . . Earth, Wind & Fire
1/86	**That's What Friends Are For** . . . Dionne & Friends
27/61	**That's What Girls Are Made For** . . . Spinners
19/87	**That's What Love Is All About** . . . Michael Bolton
35/64	**That's What Love Is Made Of** . . . Miracles
27/75	**That's When The Music Takes Me** . . . Neil Sedaka
29/70	**That's Where I Went Wrong** . . . Poppy Family
27/76	**That's Where The Happy People Go** . . . Trammps
13/59	**That's Why (I Love You So)** . . . Jackie Wilson
35/60	**Theme For Young Lovers** . . . Percy Faith
	Theme From A Summer Place
1/60	Percy Faith
16/65	Lettermen
28/62	**Theme From Ben Casey** . . . Valjean
18/73	**Theme From Cleopatra Jones** . . . Joe Simon
	Theme From Close Encounters
13/78	John Williams
25/78	Meco

POS/YR	RECORD TITLE/ARTIST
39/61	**Theme From Dixie** . . . Duane Eddy
10/62	**Theme From Dr. Kildare (Three Stars Will Shine Tonight)** . . . Richard Chamberlain
	Theme From Exorcist ..see: Tubular Bells
2/81	**Theme From Greatest American Hero (Believe It Or Not)** . . . Joey Scarbury
10/81	**Theme From Hill Street Blues** . . . Mike Post
32/75	**Theme From Jaws (Main Title)** . . . John Williams
	Theme From Love Story
9/71	Andy Williams (Where Do I Begin)
13/71	Henry Mancini
31/71	Francis Lai
25/82	**Theme From Magnum P.I.** . . . Mike Post
1/76	**Theme From Mahogany (Do You Know Where You're Going To)** . . . Diana Ross
32/80	**Theme From New York, New York** . . . Frank Sinatra
	Theme From Picnic ..see: Moonglow
	Theme From Pink Panther ..see: Pink Panther Theme
	Theme From Rocky ..see: Gonna Fly Now
1/71	**Theme From Shaft** . . . Isaac Hayes
21/71	**Theme From Summer Of '42** . . . Peter Nero
	Theme From Superfly ..see: Freddie's Dead
1/76	**Theme From S.W.A.T.** . . . Rhythm Heritage
10/60	**Theme From The Apartment** . . . Ferrante & Teicher
21/80	**Theme From The Dukes Of Hazzard (Good Ol' Boys)** . . . Waylon Jennings
	Theme From The Man With The Golden Arm ..see: Man With The Golden Arm
38/72	**Theme From The Men** . . . Isaac Hayes
39/56	**Theme From The Proud Ones** . . . Nelson Riddle
	Theme From The Three Penny Opera ..see: Mack The Knife
27/60	**Theme From The Unforgiven (The Need For Love)** . . . Don Costa
2/68	**Theme From Valley Of The Dolls** . . . Dionne Warwick
21/78	**Theme From Which Way Is Up** . . . Stargard
35/78	**Themes From The Wizard Of Oz** . . . Meco

POS/YR	RECORD TITLE/ARTIST
1/74	**Then Came You** . . . Dionne Warwicke & Spinners
6/63	**Then He Kissed Me** . . . Crystals
	Then You Can Tell Me Goodbye
6/67	Casinos
27/76	Glen Campbell (medley)
34/75	**There Goes Another Love Song** . . . Outlaws
	There Goes My Baby
2/59	Drifters
21/84	Donna Summer
	There Goes My Everything
20/67	Engelbert Humperdinck
F/71	Elvis Presley
19/58	**There Goes My Heart** . . . Joni James
1/64	**There! I've Said It Again** . . . Bobby Vinton
20/68	**There Is** . . . Dells
11/67	**There Is A Mountain** . . . Donovan
	There Is Love ..see: Wedding Song
32/73	**There It Is** . . . Tyrone Davis
33/59	**There Must Be A Way** . . . Joni James
22/85	**There Must Be An Angel (Playing With My Heart)** . . . Eurythmics
26/61	**There She Goes** . . . Jerry Wallace
23/60	**(There Was A) Tall Oak Tree** . . . Dorsey Burnette
36/68	**There Was A Time** . . . James Brown
33/66	**There Will Never Be Another You** . . . Chris Montez
18/74	**There Won't Be Anymore** . . . Charlie Rich
25/57	**(There'll Be) Peace In The Valley (For Me)** . . . Elvis Presley
1/86	**There'll Be Sad Songs (To Make You Cry)** . . . Billy Ocean
26/69	**There'll Come A Time** . . . Betty Everett
36/78	**There'll Never Be** . . . Switch
14/57	**There's A Gold Mine In The Sky** . . . Pat Boone
	There's A Kind Of Hush (All Over The World)
4/67	Herman's Hermits
12/76	Carpenters
3/61	**There's A Moon Out Tonight** . . . Capris
	(There's) Always Something There To Remind Me
27/70	R.B. Greaves
8/83	Naked Eyes
21/69	**There's Gonna Be A Showdown** . . . Archie Bell

POS/YR	RECORD TITLE/ARTIST
34/67	**There's Got To Be A Word!** . . . Innocence
5/81	**(There's) No Gettin' Over Me** . . . Ronnie Milsap
20/62	**There's No Other (Like My Baby)** . . . Crystals
	There's Nothing Stronger Than Our Love ..see: (I Believe)
10/58	**There's Only One Of You** . . . Four Lads
31/60	**There's Something On Your Mind** . . . Bobby Marchan
12/88	**There's The Girl** . . . Heart
1/66	**These Boots Are Made For Walkin'** . . . Nancy Sinatra
1/86	**These Dreams** . . . Heart
	These Eyes
6/69	Guess Who
16/69	Jr. Walker & The All Stars
8/84	**They Don't Know** . . . Tracey Ullman
5/75	**They Just Can't Stop It the (Games People Play)** . . . Spinners
1/70	**(They Long To Be) Close To You** . . . Carpenters
3/66	**They're Coming To Take Me Away, Ha-Haaa!** . . . Napoleon XIV
	Thicker Than Water ..see: (Love Is)
15/71	**Thin Line Between Love & Hate** . . . Persuaders
3/62	**Things** . . . Bobby Darin
5/85	**Things Can Only Get Better** . . . Howard Jones
23/67	**Things I Should Have Said** . . . Grass Roots
16/69	**Things I'd Like To Say** . . . New Colony Six
5/77	**Things We Do For Love** . . . 10cc
7/68	**Think** . . . Aretha Franklin
25/64	**Think** . . . Brenda Lee
33/60	**Think** . . . James Brown
20/80	**Think About Me** . . . Fleetwood Mac
30/66	**Think I'll Go Somewhere And Cry Myself To Sleep** . . . Al Martino
16/82	**Think I'm In Love** . . . Eddie Money
27/58	**Think It Over** . . . Crickets
34/78	**Think It Over** . . . Cheryl Ladd
9/84	**Think Of Laura** . . . Christopher Cross
11/61	**Think Twice** . . . Brook Benton
18/73	**Thinking Of You** . . . Loggins & Messina
14/75	**Third Rate Romance** . . . Amazing Rhythm Aces

POS/YR	RECORD TITLE/ARTIST
23/80	**Third Time Lucky (First Time I Was A Fool)** . . . Foghat
24/60	**This Bitter Earth** . . . Dinah Washington
10/86	**This Could Be The Night** . . . Loverboy
1/65	**This Diamond Ring** . . . Gary Lewis & The Playboys
12/66	**This Door Swings Both Ways** . . . Herman's Hermits
12/59	**This Friendly World** . . . Fabian
9/69	**This Girl Is A Woman Now** . . . Gary Puckett & The Union Gap
	This Guy's (Girl's) In Love With You
1/68	Herb Alpert
7/69	Dionne Warwick
24/74	**This Heart** . . . Gene Redding
26/59	**This I Swear** . . . Skyliners
11/80	**This Is It** . . . Kenny Loggins
35/78	**This Is Love** . . . Paul Anka
25/69	**This Is My Country** . . . Impressions
3/67	**This Is My Song** . . . Petula Clark
32/85	**This Is Not America** . . . David Bowie/Pat Metheny Group
18/87	**This Is The Time** . . . Billy Joel
39/77	**This Is The Way That I Feel** . . . Marie Osmond
32/65	**This Little Bird** . . . Marianne Faithfull
11/81	**This Little Girl** . . . Gary U.S. Bonds
21/63	**This Little Girl** . . . Dion
26/58	**This Little Girl Of Mine** . . . Everly Brothers
24/58	**This Little Girl's Gone Rockin'** . . . Ruth Brown
	This Magic Moment
16/60	Drifters
6/69	Jay & The Americans
33/82	**This Man Is Mine** . . . Heart
10/76	**This Masquerade** . . . George Benson
19/79	**This Night Won't Last Forever** . . . Michael Johnson
12/66	**This Old Heart Of Mine** . . . Isley Brothers
29/76	**This One's For You** . . . Barry Manilow
20/59	**This Should Go On Forever** . . . Rod Bernard
25/77	**This Song** . . . George Harrison
6/61	**This Time** . . . Troy Shondell
24/83	**This Time** . . . Bryan Adams
27/80	**This Time** . . . John Cougar
10/78	**This Time I'm In It For Love** . . . Player
6/75	**This Will Be** . . . Natalie Cole

POS/YR	RECORD TITLE/ARTIST
23/84	**This Woman** . . . Kenny Rogers
38/72	**This World** . . . Staple Singers
6/63	**Those Lazy-Hazy-Crazy Days Of Summer** . . . Nat King Cole
9/61	**Those Oldies But Goodies (Remind Me Of You)** . . . Little Caesar & The Romans
2/68	**Those Were The Days** . . . Mary Hopkin
13/65	**Thou Shalt Not Steal** . . . Dick & DeeDee
3/60	**Thousand Stars** . . . Kathy Young with The Innocents
	Three Bells
1/59	Browns
23/59	Dick Flood
35/61	**Three Hearts In A Tangle** . . . Roy Drusky
24/67	**Three Little Fishes (medley)** . . . Mitch Ryder & The Detroit Wheels
15/60	**Three Nights A Week** . . . Fats Domino
33/65	**Three O'Clock In The Morning** . . . Bert Kaempfert
	Three Penny Opera ..see: Mack The Knife
36/74	**Three Ring Circus** . . . Blue Magic
11/59	**Three Stars** . . . Tommy Dee
1/78	**Three Times A Lady** . . . Commodores
19/80	**Three Times In Love** . . . Tommy James
28/64	**Three Window Coupe** . . . Rip Chords
15/70	**Thrill Is Gone** . . . B.B. King
4/84	**Thriller** . . . Michael Jackson
13/82	**Through The Years** . . . Kenny Rogers
4/86	**Throwing It All Away** . . . Genesis
17/72	**Thunder And Lightning** . . . Chi Coltrane
38/77	**Thunder In My Heart** . . . Leo Sayer
9/78	**Thunder Island** . . . Jay Ferguson
25/66	**Thunderball** . . . Tom Jones
1/65	**Ticket To Ride** . . . Beatles
1/81	**Tide Is High** . . . Blondie
1/73	**Tie A Yellow Ribbon Round The Ole Oak Tree** . . . Dawn
3/63	**Tie Me Kangaroo Down, Sport** . . . Rolf Harris
38/83	**Tied Up** . . . Olivia Newton-John
37/60	**Ties That Bind** . . . Brook Benton
3/59	**Tiger** . . . Fabian
11/72	**Tight Rope** . . . Leon Russell
1/68	**Tighten Up** . . . Archie Bell
7/70	**Tighter, Tighter** . . . Alive & Kicking
12/59	**Tijuana Jail** . . . Kingston Trio
38/66	**Tijuana Taxi** . . . Herb Alpert
4/59	**('Til) I Kissed You** . . . Everly Brothers

POS/YR	RECORD TITLE/ARTIST
29/85	**'Til My Baby Comes Home** . . . Luther Vandross
32/75	**Til The World Ends** . . . Three Dog Night
	Till
22/57	Roger Williams
14/62	Angels
27/68	Vogues
26/62	**Till Death Do Us Part** . . . Bob Braun
25/88	**Till I Loved You** . . . Barbra Streisand & Don Johnson
20/63	**Till Then** . . . Classics
30/59	**Till There Was You** . . . Anita Bryant
15/81	**Time** . . . Alan Parsons Project
1/84	**Time After Time** . . . Cyndi Lauper
36/66	**Time After Time** . . . Chris Montez
30/60	**Time And The River** . . . Nat King Cole
26/88	**Time And Tide** . . . Basia
2/83	**Time (Clock Of The Heart)** . . . Culture Club
32/74	**Time For Livin'** . . . Sly & The Family Stone
39/68	**Time For Livin'** . . . Association
	Time For Us ..see: Romeo & Juliet
11/68	**Time Has Come Today** . . . Chambers Brothers
1/73	**Time In A Bottle** . . . Jim Croce
6/64	**Time Is On My Side** . . . Rolling Stones
6/69	**Time Is Tight** . . . Booker T. & The MG's
15/81	**Time Is Time** . . . Andy Gibb
	Time Of My Life ..see: (I've Had)
3/69	**Time Of The Season** . . . Zombies
22/81	**Time Out Of Mind** . . . Steely Dan
7/78	**Time Passages** . . . Al Stewart
33/73	**Time To Get Down** . . . O'Jays
	Time To Love-A Time To Cry ..see: Petite Fleur
18/84	**Time Will Reveal** . . . DeBarge
5/66	**Time Won't Let Me** . . . Outsiders
7/76	**Times Of Your Life** . . . Paul Anka
17/71	**Timothy** . . . Buoys
4/74	**Tin Man** . . . America
5/55	**Tina Marie** . . . Perry Como
17/68	**Tip-Toe Thru' The Tulips With Me** . . . Tiny Tim
11/71	**Tired Of Being Alone** . . . Al Green
8/80	**Tired Of Toein' The Line** . . . Rocky Burnette
6/65	**Tired Of Waiting For You** . . . Kinks

POS/YR	RECORD TITLE/ARTIST
	To ..also see: Too
26/62	**To A Sleeping Beauty** . . . Jimmy Dean
5/84	**To All The Girls I've Loved Before** . . . Julio Iglesias & Willie Nelson
6/86	**To Be A Lover** . . . Billy Idol
22/58	**To Be Loved** . . . Jackie Wilson
21/60	**To Each His Own** . . . Platters
29/68	**To Give (The Reason I Live)** . . . Frankie Valli
	To Know Him Is To Love Him
1/58	Teddy Bears
24/65	Peter & Gordon
34/69	Bobby Vinton
38/73	**To Know You Is To Love You** . . . B.B. King
17/67	**To Love Somebody** . . . Bee Gees
1/67	**To Sir With Love** . . . Lulu
35/69	**To Susan On The West Coast Waiting** . . . Donovan
25/57	**To The Aisle** . . . Five Satins
17/75	**To The Door Of The Sun (Alle Porte Del Sole)** . . . Al Martino
25/56	**To The Ends Of The Earth** . . . Nat King Cole
27/56	**To You, My Love** . . . Nick Noble
20/71	**Toast And Marmalade For Tea** . . . Tin Tin
14/64	**Tobacco Road** . . . Nashville Teens
17/64	**Today** . . . New Christy Minstrels
39/63	**(Today I Met) The Boy I'm Gonna Marry** . . . Darlene Love
23/76	**Today's The Day** . . . America
6/61	**Together** . . . Connie Francis
18/81	**Together** . . . Tierra
19/66	**Together Again** . . . Ray Charles
1/88	**Together Forever** . . . Rick Astley
37/72	**Together Let's Find Love** . . . 5th Dimension
26/60	**Togetherness** . . . Frankie Avalon
20/63	**Tom Cat** . . . Rooftop Singers
1/58	**Tom Dooley** . . . Kingston Trio
29/59	**Tomboy** . . . Perry Como
23/68	**Tomorrow** . . . Strawberry Alarm Clock
26/86	**Tomorrow Doesn't Matter Tonight** . . . Starship
39/88	**Tomorrow People** . . . Ziggy Marley & The Melody Makers
8/61	**Tonight** . . . Ferrante & Teicher
13/84	**Tonight** . . . Kool & The Gang
26/61	**Tonight (Could Be The Night)** . . . Velvets

POS/YR	RECORD TITLE/ARTIST
16/83	**Tonight, I Celebrate My Love** . . . Peabo Bryson/Robert Flack
15/61	**Tonight I Fell In Love** . . . Tokens
20/82	**Tonight I'm Yours (Don't Hurt Me)** . . . Rod Stewart
13/61	**Tonight My Love, Tonight** . . . Paul Anka
7/86	**Tonight She Comes** . . . Cars
3/87	**Tonight, Tonight, Tonight** . . . Genesis
	Tonight You Belong To Me
4/56	Patience & Prudence
15/56	Lawrence Welk with The Lennon Sisters
28/65	**Tonight's The Night** . . . Solomon Burke
39/60	**Tonight's The Night** . . . Shirelles
1/76	**Tonight's The Night (Gonna Be Alright)** . . . Rod Stewart
4/69	**Too Busy Thinking About My Baby** . . . Marvin Gaye
39/56	**Too Close For Comfort** . . . Eydie Gorme
5/80	**Too Hot** . . . Kool & The Gang
24/78	**Too Hot Ta Trot** . . . Commodores
5/85	**Too Late For Goodbyes** . . . Julian Lennon
2/72	**Too Late To Turn Back Now** . . . Cornelius Brothers & Sister Rose
	Too Many Fish In The Sea
25/65	Marvelettes
24/67	Mitch Ryder & The Detroit Wheels (medley)
13/65	**Too Many Rivers** . . . Brenda Lee
1/57	**Too Much** . . . Elvis Presley
1/79	**Too Much Heaven** . . . Bee Gees
35/67	**Too Much Of Nothing** . . . Peter, Paul & Mary
19/68	**Too Much Talk** . . . Paul Revere & The Raiders
30/60	**Too Much Tequila** . . . Champs
9/81	**Too Much Time On My Hands** . . . Styx
1/78	**Too Much, Too Little, Too Late** . . . Johnny Mathis/Deniece Williams
5/83	**Too Shy** . . . Kajagoogoo
	Too Soon To Know ..see: It's Too Soon
40/81	**Too Tight** . . . Con Funk Shun
13/69	**Too Weak To Fight** . . . Clarence Carter
13/72	**Too Young** . . . Donny Osmond
21/56	**Too Young To Go Steady** . . . Nat King Cole
30/78	**Took The Last Train** . . . David Gates
1/73	**Top Of The World** . . . Carpenters
27/58	**Topsy I** . . . Cozy Cole

POS/YR	RECORD TITLE/ARTIST
3/58	**Topsy II** . . . Cozy Cole
	Torero
18/58	Renato Carosone
21/58	Julius LaRosa
1/77	**Torn Between Two Lovers** . . . Mary MacGregor
39/59	**Torquay** . . . Fireballs
17/84	**Torture** . . . Jacksons
20/62	**Torture** . . . Kris Jensen
1/61	**Tossin' And Turnin'** . . . Bobby Lewis
1/83	**Total Eclipse Of The Heart** . . . Bonnie Tyler
23/74	**Touch A Hand, Make A Friend** . . . Staple Singers
37/80	**Touch And Go** . . . Cars
3/69	**Touch Me** . . . Doors
19/74	**Touch Me** . . . Fancy
4/87	**Touch Me (I Want Your Body)** . . . Samantha Fox
1/73	**Touch Me In The Morning** . . . Diana Ross
16/81	**Touch Me When We're Dancing** . . . Carpenters
9/87	**Touch Of Grey** . . . Grateful Dead
	Touch The Wind ..see: Eres Tu
	Tough ..also see: Tuff
22/85	**Tough All Over** . . . John Cafferty
5/61	**Tower Of Strength** . . . Gene McDaniels
13/62	**Town Without Pity** . . . Gene Pitney
24/56	**Tra La La** . . . Georgia Gibbs
35/64	**Tra La La La Suzy** . . . Dean & Jean
2/69	**Traces** . . . Classics IV
	Tracks Of My Tears
16/65	Miracles
10/67	Johnny Rivers
25/76	Linda Ronstadt
9/69	**Tracy** . . . Cuff Links
13/60	**Tracy's Theme** . . . Spencer Ross
1/79	**Tragedy** . . . Bee Gees
	Tragedy
5/59	Thomas Wayne
10/61	Fleetwoods
39/85	**Tragedy** . . . John Hunter
23/80	**Train In Vain (Stand By Me)** . . . Clash
36/60	**Train Of Love** . . . Annette
27/74	**Train Of Thought** . . . Cher
38/79	**Train, Train** . . . Blackfoot
22/66	**Trains And Boats And Planes** . . . Dionne Warwick

POS/YR	RECORD TITLE/ARTIST
26/67	**Tramp** . . . Otis & Carla
38/75	**Trampled Under Foot** . . . Led Zeppelin
8/56	**Transfusion** . . . Nervous Norvus
35/61	**Transistor Sister** . . . Freddy Cannon
13/71	**Trapped By A Thing Called Love** . . . Denise LaSalle
2/70	**Travelin' Band** . . . Creedence Clearwater Revival
1/61	**Travelin' Man** . . . Ricky Nelson
32/67	**Travlin' Man** . . . Stevie Wonder
16/56	**Treasure Of Love** . . . Clyde McPhatter
26/58	**Treasure Of Your Love** . . . Eileen Rodgers
3/71	**Treat Her Like A Lady** . . . Cornelius Brothers & Sister Rose
2/65	**Treat Her Right** . . . Roy Head
18/57	**Treat Me Nice** . . . Elvis Presley
18/81	**Treat Me Right** . . . Pat Benatar
29/61	**Triangle** . . . Janie Grant
25/57	**Tricky** . . . Ralph Marterie
6/72	**Troglodyte (Cave Man)** . . . Jimmy Castor Bunch
9/82	**Trouble** . . . Lindsey Buckingham
35/75	**T-R-O-U-B-L-E** . . . Elvis Presley
35/88	**Trouble** . . . Nia Peeples
20/60	**Trouble In Paradise** . . . Crests
33/63	**Trouble Is My Middle Name** . . . Bobby Vinton
7/73	**Trouble Man** . . . Marvin Gaye
4/83	**True** . . . Spandau Ballet
3/86	**True Blue** . . . Madonna
1/86	**True Colors** . . . Cyndi Lauper
32/87	**True Faith** . . . New Order
35/69	**True Grit** . . . Glen Campbell
	True Love
3/56	Bing Crosby & Grace Kelly
15/56	Jane Powell
13/88	**True Love** . . . Glenn Frey
21/63	**True Love Never Runs Smooth** . . . Gene Pitney
	True Love, True Love ..see: (If You Cry)
14/65	**True Love Ways** . . . Peter & Gordon
1/82	**Truly** . . . Lionel Richie
30/61	**Trust In Me** . . . Etta James
23/69	**Try A Little Kindness** . . . Glen Campbell
	Try A Little Tenderness
25/67	Otis Redding
29/69	Three Dog Night
23/83	**Try Again** . . . Champaign
15/64	**Try It Baby** . . . Marvin Gaye
33/58	**Try The Impossible** . . . Lee Andrews & The Hearts
11/75	**Try To Remember (medley)** . . . Gladys Knight & The Pips
12/66	**Try Too Hard** . . . Dave Clark Five
10/76	**Tryin' To Get The Feeling Again** . . . Barry Manilow
5/81	**Tryin' To Live My Life Without You** . . . Bob Seger
10/77	**Tryin' To Love Two** . . . William Bell
15/74	**Trying To Hold On To My Woman** . . . Lamont Dozier
40/70	**Trying To Make A Fool Of Me** . . . Delfonics
7/74	**Tubular Bells** . . . Mike Oldfield
32/59	**Tucumcari** . . . Jimmie Rodgers
24/68	**Tuesday Afternoon (Forever Afternoon)** . . . Moody Blues
17/62	**Tuff** . . . Ace Cannon
10/86	**Tuff Enuff** . . . Fabulous Thunderbirds
30/80	**Tulsa Time** . . . Eric Clapton
	Tumbling Dice
7/72	Rolling Stones
32/78	Linda Ronstadt
30/58	**Tumbling Tumbleweeds** . . . Billy Vaughn
9/88	**Tunnel Of Love** . . . Bruce Springsteen
27/64	**Turn Around** . . . Dick & DeeDee
7/68	**Turn Around, Look At Me** . . . Vogues
3/70	**Turn Back The Hands Of Time** . . . Tyrone Davis
16/66	**Turn-Down Day** . . . Cyrkle
9/59	**Turn Me Loose** . . . Fabian
35/81	**Turn Me Loose** . . . Loverboy
28/62	**Turn On Your Love Light** . . . Bobby Bland
10/76	**Turn The Beat Around** . . . Vicki Sue Robinson
13/78	**Turn To Stone** . . . Electric Light Orchestra
32/84	**Turn To You** . . . Go-Go's
1/65	**Turn! Turn! Turn!** . . . Byrds
29/85	**Turn Up The Radio** . . . Autograph
5/82	**Turn Your Love Around** . . . George Benson
36/80	**Turning Japanese** . . . Vapors
36/58	**Turvy II** . . . Cozy Cole
20/75	**Tush** . . . ZZ Top
8/79	**Tusk** . . . Fleetwood Mac

POS/YR	RECORD TITLE/ARTIST
	Tutti' Frutti
12/56	Pat Boone
17/56	Little Richard
	Tweedlee Dee
2/55	Georgia Gibbs
14/55	LaVern Baker
	Twelfth Of Never
9/57	Johnny Mathis
8/73	Donny Osmond
20/67	**Twelve Thirty (Young Girls Are Coming To The Canyon)** . . . Mamas & The Papas
15/63	**Twenty Miles** . . . Chubby Checker
31/64	**20-75** . . . Willie Mitchell
17/63	**Twenty Four Hours From Tulsa** . . . Gene Pitney
6/69	**Twenty-Five Miles** . . . Edwin Starr
4/70	**25 Or 6 To 4** . . . Chicago
2/58	**26 Miles (Santa Catalina)** . . . Four Preps
38/81	**Twilight** . . . ELO
1/58	**Twilight Time** . . . Platters
31/88	**Twilight World** . . . Swing Out Sister
10/83	**Twilight Zone** . . . Golden Earring
30/80	**Twilight Zone/Twilight Tone** . . . Manhattan Transfer
14/65	**Twine Time** . . . Alvin Cash
39/66	**Twinkle Toes** . . . Roy Orbison
	Twist
1/60	Chubby Checker
28/60	Hank Ballard
1/62	Chubby Checker
16/88	Fat Boys with Chubby Checker
	Twist And Shout
17/62	Isley Brothers
2/64	Beatles
23/86	Beatles
26/62	**Twist-Her** . . . Bill Black's Combo
25/63	**Twist It Up** . . . Chubby Checker
5/84	**Twist Of Fate** . . . Olivia Newton-John
9/62	**Twist, Twist Senora** . . . Gary U.S. Bonds
22/62	**Twistin' Matilda** . . . Jimmy Soul
34/62	**Twistin' Postman** . . . Marvelettes
9/62	**Twistin' The Night Away** . . . Sam Cooke
27/60	**Twistin' U.S.A.** . . . Danny & The Juniors
	Twistin' White Silver Sands ..see: White Silver Sands
17/59	**Twixt Twelve And Twenty** . . . Pat Boone
11/56	**Two Different Worlds** . . . Don Rondo
16/71	**Two Divided By Love** . . . Grass Roots

POS/YR	RECORD TITLE/ARTIST
19/78	**Two Doors Down** . . . Dolly Parton
6/63	**Two Faces Have I** . . . Lou Christie
33/75	**Two Fine People** . . . Cat Stevens
1/89	**Two Hearts** . . . Phil Collins
16/55	**Two Hearts** . . . Pat Boone
40/81	**Two Hearts** . . . Stephanie Mills/Teddy Pendergrass
38/83	**Two Less Lonely People In The World** . . . Air Supply
31/68	**Two Little Kids** . . . Peaches & Herb
18/55	**Two Lost Souls** . . . Perry Como & Jaye P. Morgan
7/63	**Two Lovers** . . . Mary Wells
10/88	**Two Occasions** . . . Deele
3/86	**Two Of Hearts** . . . Stacey Q
11/78	**Two Out Of Three Ain't Bad** . . . Meat Loaf
30/87	**Two People** . . . Tina Turner
30/80	**Two Places At The Same Time** . . . Ray Parker Jr. & Raydio
38/84	**Two Sides Of Love** . . . Sammy Hagar
22/78	**Two Tickets To Paradise** . . . Eddie Money
32/63	**Two Tickets To Paradise** . . . Brook Benton
	2001 Space Odyssey ..see: Also Sprach Zarathustra
2/86	**Typical Male** . . . Tina Turner

U

POS/YR	RECORD TITLE/ARTIST
2/87	**U Got The Look** . . . Prince
28/68	**U.S. Male** . . . Elvis Presley
14/59	**Uh! Oh! (Part 2)** . . . Nutty Squirrels
5/64	**Um, Um, Um, Um, Um, Um** . . . Major Lance
9/62	**Unchain My Heart** . . . Ray Charles
	Unchained Melody
1/55	Les Baxter
3/55	Al Hibbler
6/55	Roy Hamilton
29/55	June Valli
4/65	Righteous Brothers
1/71	**Uncle Albert/Admiral Halsey** . . . Paul & Linda McCartney
29/82	**Under Pressure** . . . Queen & David Bowie

POS/YR	RECORD TITLE/ARTIST
4/64	**Under The Boardwalk** . . . Drifters
24/88	**Under The Milky Way** . . . Church
35/66	**Under Your Spell Again** . . . Johnny Rivers
1/77	**Undercover Angel** . . . Alan O'Day
9/83	**Undercover Of The Night** . . . Rolling Stones
35/64	**Understand Your Man** . . . Johnny Cash
17/85	**Understanding** . . . Bob Seger
22/69	**Undun** . . . Guess Who
9/73	**Uneasy Rider** . . . Charlie Daniels
17/59	**Unforgettable** . . . Dinah Washington
	Unforgiven ..see: Theme From The
33/70	**Ungena Za Ulimwengu (Unite The World)** . . . Temptations
7/68	**Unicorn, The** . . . Irish Rovers
24/76	**Union Man** . . . Cate Bros.
3/83	**Union Of The Snake** . . . Duran Duran
13/70	**United We Stand** . . . Brotherhood Of Man
39/68	**Unknown Soldier** . . . Doors
40/72	**Until It's Time For You To Go** . . . Elvis Presley
3/74	**Until You Come Back To Me (That's What I'm Gonna Do)** . . . Aretha Franklin
	Up A Lazy River ..see: Lazy River
4/70	**Up Around The Bend** . . . Creedence Clearwater Revival
16/75	**Up In A Puff Of Smoke** . . . Polly Brown
25/70	**Up On Cripple Creek** . . . Band
	Up On The Roof
5/63	Drifters
28/79	James Taylor
10/70	**Up The Ladder To The Roof** . . . Supremes
7/67	**Up-Up And Away** . . . 5th Dimension
1/82	**Up Where We Belong** . . . Joe Cocker & Jennifer Warnes
22/67	**Ups And Downs** . . . Paul Revere & The Raiders
1/80	**Upside Down** . . . Diana Ross
3/66	**Uptight (Everything's Alright)** . . . Stevie Wonder *(also see: Little Ole Man)*
13/62	**Uptown** . . . Crystals
25/77	**Uptown Festival (Motown Medley)** . . . Shalamar
3/83	**Uptown Girl** . . . Billy Joel
4/81	**Urgent** . . . Foreigner
2/72	**Use Me** . . . Bill Withers
4/78	**Use Ta Be My Girl** . . . O'Jays
34/65	**Use Your Head** . . . Mary Wells
27/61	**Utopia** . . . Frank Gari

V

POS/YR	RECORD TITLE/ARTIST
8/82	**Vacation** . . . Go-Go's
9/62	**Vacation** . . . Connie Francis
9/87	**Valerie** . . . Steve Winwood
3/68	**Valleri** . . . Monkees
32/82	**Valley Girl** . . . Frank Zappa
8/57	**Valley Of Tears** . . . Fats Domino
	Valley Of The Dolls ..see: Theme From
5/88	**Valley Road** . . . Bruce Hornsby & The Range
9/85	**Valotte** . . . Julian Lennon
2/70	**Vehicle** . . . Ides Of March
35/86	**Velcro Fly** . . . ZZ Top
8/72	**Ventura Highway** . . . America
1/59	**Venus** . . . Frankie Avalon
	Venus
1/70	Shocking Blue
1/86	Bananarama
12/75	**Venus And Mars Rock Show** . . . Wings
7/62	**Venus In Blue Jeans** . . . Jimmy Clanton
23/58	**Very Precious Love** . . . Ames Brothers
	Very Special Love
20/58	Debbie Reynolds
23/58	Johnny Nash
11/74	**Very Special Love Song** . . . Charlie Rich
26/64	**Very Thought Of You** . . . Ricky Nelson
31/79	**Victim Of Love** . . . Elton John
32/87	**Victim Of Love** . . . Bryan Adams
10/87	**Victory** . . . Kool & The Gang
40/79	**Video Killed The Radio Star** . . . Buggles
18/86	**Vienna Calling** . . . Falco
1/85	**View To A Kill** . . . Duran Duran
22/62	**Village Of Love** . . . Nathaniel Mayer
7/60	**Village Of St. Bernadette** . . . Andy Williams
12/72	**Vincent** . . . Don McLean
29/64	**Viva Las Vegas** . . . Elvis Presley
28/70	**Viva Tirado** . . . El Chicano
15/81	**Voice** . . . Moody Blues

POS/YR	RECORD TITLE/ARTIST
32/80	**Voices** . . . Cheap Trick
8/85	**Voices Carry** . . . 'Til Tuesday
	Volare (Nel Blu Dipinto Di Blu)
1/58	Domenico Modugno
12/58	Dean Martin
4/60	Bobby Rydell
33/75	Al Martino
27/65	**Voodoo Woman** . . . Bobby Goldsboro
29/85	**Vox Humana** . . . Kenny Loggins
29/82	**Voyeur** . . . Kim Carnes

W

POS/YR	RECORD TITLE/ARTIST
36/74	**W-O-L-D** . . . Harry Chapin
40/67	**Wack Wack** . . . Young-Holt Unlimited
	Wade In The Water
19/66	Ramsey Lewis
37/67	Herb Alpert
2/62	**Wah Watusi** . . . Orlons *(also see: El Watusi, Watusi)*
8/88	**Wait** . . . White Lion
37/61	**Wait A Minute** . . . Coasters
23/57	**Wait And See** . . . Fats Domino
18/80	**Wait For Me** . . . Daryl Hall & John Oates
37/60	**Wait For Me** . . . Playmates
26/63	**Wait Til' My Bobby Gets Home** . . . Darlene Love
18/58	**Waitin' In School** . . . Ricky Nelson
19/81	**Waiting** . . . Tom Petty
2/81	**Waiting For A Girl Like You** . . . Foreigner
5/88	**Waiting For A Star To Fall** . . . Boy Meets Girl
13/82	**Waiting On A Friend** . . . Rolling Stones
1/84	**Wake Me Up Before You Go-Go** . . . Wham!
	Wake The Town And Tell The People
5/55	Les Baxter
13/55	Mindy Carson
12/76	**Wake Up Everybody** . . . Harold Melvin & The Blue Notes
	Wake Up Little Susie
1/57	Everly Brothers
27/82	Simon & Garfunkel
39/85	**Wake Up (Next To You)** . . . Graham Parker

POS/YR	RECORD TITLE/ARTIST
7/58	**Walk, The** . . . Jimmy McCracklin
12/70	**Walk A Mile In My Shoes** . . . Joe South
23/65	**Walk Away** . . . Matt Monro
36/80	**Walk Away** . . . Donna Summer
9/76	**Walk Away From Love** . . . David Ruffin
	Walk Away Renee
5/66	Left Banke
14/68	Four Tops
	Walk Don't Run
2/60	Ventures
8/64	Ventures ('64)
10/56	**Walk Hand In Hand** . . . Tony Martin
12/65	**Walk In The Black Forest** . . . Horst Jankowski
1/63	**Walk Like A Man** . . . 4 Seasons
19/74	**Walk Like A Man** . . . Grand Funk
1/86	**Walk Like An Egyptian** . . . Bangles
7/86	**Walk Of Life** . . . Dire Straits
5/61	**Walk On By** . . . Leroy Van Dyke
	Walk On By
6/64	Dionne Warwick
30/69	Isaac Hayes
16/73	**Walk On The Wild Side** . . . Lou Reed
21/62	**Walk On The Wild Side** . . . Jimmy Smith
9/88	**Walk On Water** . . . Eddie Money
17/72	**Walk On Water** . . . Neil Diamond
7/61	**Walk Right Back** . . . Everly Brothers
1/63	**Walk Right In** . . . Rooftop Singers
	Walk This Way
10/77	Aerosmith
4/86	Run-D.M.C.
12/57	**Walkin' After Midnight** . . . Patsy Cline
	Walkin' In The Rain
23/64	Ronettes
19/70	Jay & The Americans
14/72	**Walkin' In The Rain With The One I Love** . . . Love Unlimited
	Walkin' In The Sand ..see: Remember
37/67	**Walkin' In The Sunshine** . . . Roger Miller
12/63	**Walkin' Miracle** . . . Essex
22/66	**Walkin' My Cat Named Dog** . . . Norma Tanega
29/58	**Walking Along** . . . Diamonds
9/89	**Walking Away** . . . Information Society
11/87	**Walking Down Your Street** . . . Bangles
6/75	**Walking In Rhythm** . . . Blackbyrds
18/84	**Walking On A Thin Line** . . . Huey Lewis & The News

POS/YR	RECORD TITLE/ARTIST
9/85	**Walking On Sunshine** . . . Katrina & The Waves
26/63	**Walking Proud** . . . Steve Lawrence
10/63	**Walking The Dog** . . . Rufus Thomas
	Walking The Floor ..see: I'm Walking
6/60	**Walking To New Orleans** . . . Fats Domino
32/80	**Walks Like A Lady** . . . Journey
2/62	**Wanderer, The** . . . Dion
3/80	**Wanderer, The** . . . Donna Summer
5/83	**Wanna Be Startin' Somethin'** . . . Michael Jackson
1/71	**Want Ads** . . . Honey Cone
7/87	**Wanted Dead Or Alive** . . . Bon Jovi
38/56	**Wanting You** . . . Roger Williams
	War
1/70	Edwin Starr
8/86	Bruce Springsteen
17/84	**War Song** . . . Culture Club
17/66	**Warm And Tender Love** . . . Percy Sledge
39/78	**Warm Ride** . . . Rare Earth
25/62	**Warmed Over Kisses (Left Over Love)** . . . Brian Hyland
7/84	**Warrior, The** . . . Scandal
2/63	**Washington Square** . . . Village Stompers
37/81	**Wasn't That A Party** . . . Irish Rovers
8/75	**Wasted Days And Wasted Nights** . . . Freddy Fender
9/82	**Wasted On The Way** . . . Crosby, Stills & Nash
40/79	**Watch Out For Lucy** . . . Eric Clapton
30/67	**Watch The Flowers Grow** . . . 4 Seasons
11/71	**Watching Scotty Grow** . . . Bobby Goldsboro
10/81	**Watching The Wheels** . . . John Lennon
40/61	**Water Boy** . . . Don Shirley Trio
4/59	**Waterloo** . . . Stonewall Jackson
6/74	**Waterloo** . . . Abba
10/63	**Watermelon Man** . . . Mongo Santamaria
25/61	**Watusi, The** . . . Vibrations *(also see: El Watusi, Wah Watusi)*
18/77	**Way Down** . . . Elvis Presley
3/60	**Way Down Yonder In New Orleans** . . . Freddie Cannon
40/83	**Way He Makes Me Feel** . . . Barbra Streisand
24/78	**Way I Feel Tonight** . . . Bay City Rollers
35/59	**Way I Walk** . . . Jack Scott

POS/YR	RECORD TITLE/ARTIST
4/75	**Way I Want To Touch You** . . . Captain & Tennille
1/86	**Way It Is** . . . Bruce Hornsby
7/72	**Way Of Love** . . . Cher
	Way We Were
1/74	Barbra Streisand
11/75	Gladys Knight & The Pips (medley)
	Way You Do The Things You Do
11/64	Temptations
20/78	Rita Coolidge
20/85	Hall & Oates/David Ruffin/Eddie Kendrick (medley)
13/61	**Way You Look Tonight** . . . Lettermen
7/89	**Way You Love Me** . . . Karyn White
1/88	**Way You Make Me Feel** . . . Michael Jackson
24/58	**Ways Of A Woman In Love** . . . Johnny Cash
	Wayward Wind
1/56	Gogi Grant
28/56	Tex Ritter
5/67	**(We Ain't Got) Nothin' Yet** . . . Blues Magoos
	We All Shine On ..see: Instant Karma
14/88	**We All Sleep Alone** . . . Cher
2/79	**We Are Family** . . . Sister Sledge
4/78	**We Are The Champions** . . . Queen
1/85	**We Are The World** . . . USA for Africa
25/84	**We Are The Young** . . . Dan Hartman
5/85	**We Belong** . . . Pat Benatar
32/58	**We Belong Together** . . . Robert & Johnny
1/85	**We Built This City** . . . Starship
21/68	**We Can Fly** . . . Cowsills
	We Can Work It Out
1/66	Beatles
13/71	Stevie Wonder
36/76	**We Can't Hide It Anymore** . . . Larry Santos
35/87	**We Connect** . . . Stacey Q
5/86	**We Don't Have To Take Our Clothes Off** . . . Jermaine Stewart
2/85	**We Don't Need Another Hero (Thunderdome)** . . . Tina Turner
7/80	**We Don't Talk Anymore** . . . Cliff Richard
6/59	**We Got Love** . . . Bobby Rydell
35/69	**We Got More Soul** . . . Dyke & The Blazers
2/82	**We Got The Beat** . . . Go-Go's
13/65	**We Gotta Get Out Of This Place** . . . Animals

POS/YR	RECORD TITLE/ARTIST
20/71	**We Gotta Get You A Woman** . . . Todd Rundgren
12/77	**We Just Disagree** . . . Dave Mason
27/80	**We Live For Love** . . . Pat Benatar
39/64	**We Love You Beatles** . . . Carefrees
21/73	**We May Never Pass This Way (Again)** . . . Seals & Crofts
22/83	**We Two** . . . Little River Band
31/80	**We Were Meant To Be Lovers** . . . Jim Photoglo
F/78	**We Will Rock You** . . . Queen
7/87	**We'll Be Together** . . . Sting
9/78	**We'll Never Have To Say Goodbye Again** . . . England Dan & John Ford Coley
4/64	**We'll Sing In The Sunshine** . . . Gale Garnett
14/68	**We're A Winner** . . . Impressions
7/77	**We're All Alone** . . . Rita Coolidge
1/73	**We're An American Band** . . . Grand Funk
40/72	**We're Free** . . . Beverly Bremers
34/74	**We're Getting Careless With Our Love** . . . Johnnie Taylor
	(We're Gonna) ..also see: Rock Around The Clock
25/65	**We're Gonna Make It** . . . Little Milton
15/81	**We're In This Love Together** . . . Al Jarreau
21/84	**We're Not Gonna Take It** . . . Twisted Sister
9/87	**We're Ready** . . . Boston
25/72	**We've Got To Get It On Again** . . . Addrisi Brothers
	We've Got Tonite
13/79	Bob Seger
6/83	Kenny Rogers & Sheena Easton
2/70	**We've Only Just Begun** . . . Carpenters
2/58	**Wear My Ring Around Your Neck** . . . Elvis Presley
23/67	**Wear Your Love Like Heaven** . . . Donovan
32/56	**Weary Blues** . . . McGuire Sisters
10/65	**Wedding, The** . . . Julie Rogers
1/69	**Wedding Bell Blues** . . . 5th Dimension
	Wedding Bells ..see: (I'm Always Hearing)
24/71	**Wedding Song (There Is Love)** . . . Paul Stookey *(also see: Down The Aisle)*
35/58	**Week End** . . . Kingsmen
29/79	**Weekend** . . . Wet Willie
10/77	**Weekend In New England** . . . Barry Manilow
19/69	**Weight, The** . . . Aretha Franklin
1/76	**Welcome Back** . . . John Sebastian
22/62	**Welcome Home Baby** . . . Shirelles
18/60	**(Welcome) New Lovers** . . . Pat Boone
24/83	**Welcome To Heartlight** . . . Kenny Loggins
37/86	**Welcome To The Boomtown** . . . David & David
7/88	**Welcome To The Jungle** . . . Guns N' Roses
29/61	**Well, I Told You** . . . Chantels
13/66	**Well Respected Man** . . . Kinks
21/78	**Werewolves Of London** . . . Warren Zevon
1/86	**West End Girls** . . . Pet Shop Boys
37/62	**West Of The Wall** . . . Toni Fisher
24/70	**Westbound # 9** . . . Flaming Ember
8/58	**Western Movies** . . . Olympics
5/67	**Western Union** . . . Five Americans
24/63	**Wham!** . . . Lonnie Mack
16/76	**Wham Bam (Shang-A-Lang)** . . . Silver
	What A Beautiful World ..see: I.G.Y.
	What A Diff'rence A Day Makes
8/59	Dinah Washington
20/75	Esther Phillips
	What A Feeling ..see: Flashdance
1/79	**What A Fool Believes** . . . Doobie Brothers
22/61	**What A Party** . . . Fats Domino
22/61	**What A Price** . . . Fats Domino
33/61	**What A Surprise** . . . Johnny Maestro
31/67	**What A Woman In Love Won't Do** . . . Sandy Posey
32/88	**What A Wonderful World** . . . Louis Armstrong *(also see: Wonderful World)*
10/85	**What About Love?** . . . Heart
26/86	**What About Love** . . . 'Til Tuesday
15/84	**What About Me?** . . . Kenny Rogers/Kim Carnes/James Ingram
29/83	**What About Me** . . . Moving Pictures
39/72	**What Am I Crying For?** . . . Classics IV
35/83	**What Am I Gonna Do (I'm So In Love With You)** . . . Rod Stewart
8/75	**What Am I Gonna Do With You** . . . Barry White

Whitesnake's "Is This Love" rose to the No. 2 spot at the end of 1987, but it holds another record. Survivor's top-10 success earlier that year with "Is This Love" made them the only two different singles with the same title to hit the top 10 in the same year.

Kim Wilde's cover of the Supremes' "You Keep Me Hangin' On" went to No. 1 in 1987, as it originally had in 1966. There was one other No. 1-charting remake that year of a No. 1 hit: Club Nouveau's "Lean On Me," which initially topped the chart for Bill Withers in 1972.

Deniece Williams had her first No. 1 hit in "Too Much, Too Little, Too Late," the 1978 duet with Johnny Mathis, whose previous chart-topping single was "Chances Are," from over 30 years before. Williams had no such wait for her second No. 1, 1984's "Let's Hear It For The Boy."

Bruce Willis recorded versions of Top-40 hits "Young Blood" by the Coasters and "Under The Boardwalk" by the Drifters, but didn't crack the Top 40 himself until he covered the Staple Singers' "Respect Yourself" in 1987. At No. 5, it was his first cover to top the original version, which peaked at No. 12 in 1971.

Wings' "Mull Of Kintyre" single was a big hit in England, but it never even charted in this country. It was the flip side of 1978's Top-40 hit "Girls School." McCartney came back stronger with his next charting single, "With A Little Luck," a No. 1 smash. Duets included, Macca would ultimately top the chart nine times.

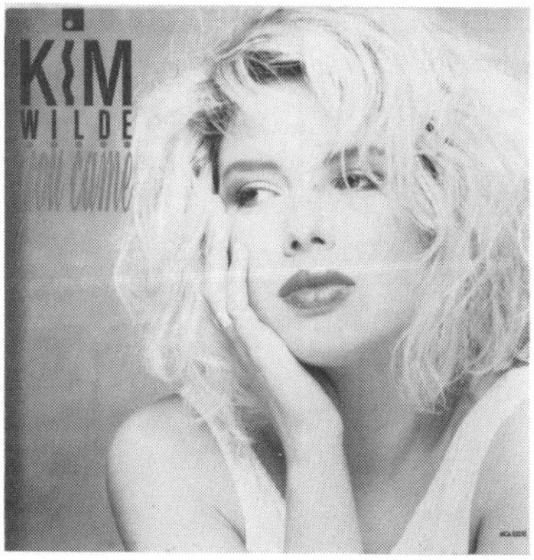

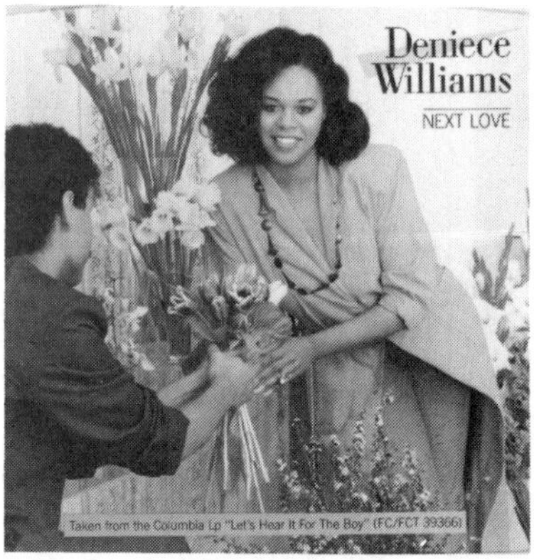

Deniece
Williams
NEXT LOVE
Taken from the Columbia Lp "Let's Hear It For The Boy" (FC/FCT 39366)

Steve Winwood's No. 1 album success *Roll With It* marked an auspicious event in a career that began back in the 60s. As lead vocalist on the No. 1 album *Blind Faith* in 1969, it would take Winwood 19 years to hit No. 1 again.

Bill Withers was in an egocentric groove for his two biggest hits of the 70s, the No. 1 "Lean On Me" and No. 2 "Use Me." For his next biggest hit, he had to expand to "Just The Two Of Us," a 1981 duet with Grover Washington, Jr. that peaked at No. 2.

Stevie Wonder has had 58 chart hits and 44 Top 40s as a solo artist and in collaboration with others. With 26 top-10 songs, he's had the third greatest success, after Elvis Presley and the Beatles (as well as the third most charted records, following the same two).

Paul Young has made big hits out of cover songs, like his No. 1 version of Daryl Hall's "Everytime You Go Away." He also went top 20 with Ann Peebles' "I'm Gonna Tear Your Playhouse Down," a song that has been recorded by Graham Parker and even by Fletcher Henderson, back in the 20s.

POS/YR	RECORD TITLE/ARTIST
	What Am I Living For
9/58	Chuck Willis
26/60	Conway Twitty
14/81	**What Are We Doin' In Love** . . . Dottie West
39/71	**What Are You Doing Sunday** . . . Dawn
7/66	**What Becomes Of The Brokenhearted** . . . Jimmy Ruffin
	What Cha ..see: What You, Whatcha
38/65	**What Color (Is A Man)** . . . Bobby Vinton
4/69	**What Does It Take (To Win Your Love)** . . . Jr. Walker & The All Stars
2/88	**What Have I Done To Deserve This?** . . . Pet Shop Boys & Dusty Springfield
29/65	**What Have They Done To The Rain** . . . Searchers
4/86	**What Have You Done For Me Lately** . . . Janet Jackson
7/89	**What I Am** . . . Edie Brickell & New Bohemians
39/84	**(What) In The Name Of Love** . . . Naked Eyes
5/60	**What In The World's Come Over You** . . . Jack Scott
10/71	**What Is Life** . . . George Harrison
15/59	**What Is Love?** . . . Playmates
33/84	**What Is Love?** . . . Howard Jones
19/70	**What Is Truth** . . . Johnny Cash
10/81	**What Kind Of Fool** . . . Barbra Streisand & Barry Gibb
17/62	**What Kind Of Fool Am I** . . . Sammy Davis, Jr.
21/82	**What Kind Of Fool Am I** . . . Rick Springfield
	What Kind Of Fool Do You Think I Am
9/64	Tams
23/69	Bill Deal
18/62	**What Kind Of Love Is This** . . . Joey Dee
40/65	**What Now** . . . Gene Chandler
	What Now My Love
14/66	Sonny & Cher
24/66	Herb Alpert
30/67	Mitch Ryder
	What The World Needs Now Is Love
7/65	Jackie DeShannon
8/71	Tom Clay (medley)
9/63	**What Will Mary Say** . . . Johnny Mathis
	What You ..also see: Whatcha

POS/YR	RECORD TITLE/ARTIST
13/87	**What You Get Is What You See** . . . Tina Turner
5/86	**What You Need** . . . INXS
24/88	**What You See Is What You Get** . . . Brenda K. Starr
9/79	**What You Won't Do For Love** . . . Bobby Caldwell
	What'd I Say
6/59	Ray Charles
30/61	Jerry Lee Lewis
24/62	Bobby Darin
21/64	Elvis Presley
	What's ..also see: Wot's
12/62	**What's A Matter Baby** . . . Timi Yuro
29/64	**What's Easy For Two Is So Hard For One** . . . Mary Wells
19/82	**What's Forever For** . . . Michael Martin Murphey
	What's Going On
2/71	Marvin Gaye
12/87	Cyndi Lauper
1/84	**What's Love Got To Do With It** . . . Tina Turner
3/65	**What's New Pussycat?** . . . Tom Jones
3/88	**What's On Your Mind (Pure Energy)** . . . Information Society
35/62	**What's So Good About Good-By** . . . Miracles
17/64	**What's The Matter With You Baby** . . . Marvin Gaye & Mary Wells
20/69	**What's The Use Of Breaking Up** . . . Jerry Butler
7/62	**What's Your Name** . . . Don & Juan
13/78	**What's Your Name** . . . Lynyrd Skynyrd
	Whatcha ..also see: What You
6/77	**Whatcha Gonna Do** . . . Pablo Cruise
22/79	**Whatcha Gonna Do With My Lovin'** . . . Stephanie Mills
9/71	**Whatcha See Is Whatcha Get** . . . Dramatics
1/74	**Whatever Gets You Thru The Night** . . . John Lennon/Plastic Ono Band
	Whatever Lola Wants
6/55	Sarah Vaughan
12/55	Dinah Shore
	Whatever Will Be, Will Be ..see: Que Sera, Sera
38/74	**Whatever You Got, I Want** . . . Jackson 5
26/66	**Wheel Of Hurt** . . . Margaret Whiting

POS/YR	RECORD TITLE/ARTIST
	Wheels
3/61	String-A-Longs
28/61	Billy Vaughn
5/58	**When** . . . Kalin Twins
	When A Man (Woman) Loves A Woman (Man)
1/66	Percy Sledge
35/80	Bette Midler
27/82	**When All Is Said And Done** . . . Abba
1/84	**When Doves Cry** . . . Prince
30/82	**When He Shines** . . . Sheena Easton
18/69	**When I Die** . . . Motherlode
7/62	**When I Fall In Love** . . . Lettermen
9/64	**When I Grow Up (To Be A Man)** . . . Beach Boys
1/77	**When I Need You** . . . Leo Sayer
29/57	**When I See You** . . . Fats Domino
1/86	**When I Think Of You** . . . Janet Jackson
20/80	**When I Wanted You** . . . Barry Manilow
15/67	**When I Was Young** . . . Animals
25/65	**When I'm Gone** . . . Brenda Holloway
1/89	**When I'm With You** . . . Sheriff
5/88	**When It's Love** . . . Van Halen
26/82	**When It's Over** . . . Loverboy
18/66	**When Liking Turns To Loving** . . . Ronnie Dove
19/56	**When My Blue Moon Turns To Gold Again** . . . Elvis Presley
14/56	**When My Dreamboat Comes Home** . . . Fats Domino
28/62	**When My Little Girl Is Smiling** . . . Drifters
37/66	**(When She Needs Good Lovin') She Comes To Me** . . . Chicago Loop
11/81	**When She Was My Girl** . . . Four Tops
5/87	**When Smokey Sings** . . . ABC
10/62	**When The Boy In Your Arms (Is The Boy In Your Heart)** . . . Connie Francis
19/58	**When The Boys Talk About The Girls** . . . Valerie Carr
3/89	**When The Children Cry** . . . White Lion
2/86	**When The Going Gets Tough, The Tough Get Going** . . . Billy Ocean
14/86	**When The Heart Rules The Mind** . . . GTR
37/83	**When The Lights Go Out** . . . Naked Eyes
23/64	**When The Lovelight Starts Shining Through His Eyes** . . . Supremes

POS/YR	RECORD TITLE/ARTIST
18/56	**When The Saints Go Marching In** . . . Bill Haley
	When The White Lilacs Bloom Again
12/56	Helmut Zacharias
18/56	Billy Vaughn
10/61	**When We Get Married** . . . Dreamlovers
36/88	**When We Kiss** . . . Bardeux
23/88	**When We Was Fab** . . . George Harrison
	When Will I Be Loved
8/60	Everly Brothers
2/75	Linda Ronstadt
2/74	**When Will I See You Again** . . . Three Degrees
14/84	**When You Close Your Eyes** . . . Night Ranger
33/56	**When You Dance** . . . Turbans
32/72	**When You Say Love** . . . Sonny & Cher
35/64	**When You Walk In The Room** . . . Searchers
30/60	**When You Wish Upon A Star** . . . Dion & The Belmonts
9/71	**When You're Hot, You're Hot** . . . Jerry Reed
6/79	**When You're In Love With A Beautiful Woman** . . . Dr. Hook
23/67	**When You're Young And In Love** . . . Marvelettes
35/85	**When Your Heart Is Weak** . . . Cock Robin
39/64	**Whenever He Holds You** . . . Bobby Goldsboro
5/78	**Whenever I Call You "Friend"** . . . Kenny Loggins
38/76	**Whenever I'm Away From You** . . . John Travolta
32/60	**Where Are You** . . . Frankie Avalon
36/62	**Where Are You** . . . Dinah Washington
	Where Did Our Love Go
1/64	Supremes
15/71	Donnie Elbert
33/71	**Where Did They Go, Lord** . . . Elvis Presley
1/88	**Where Do Broken Hearts Go** . . . Whitney Houston
	(Where Do I Begin) ..see: Theme From Love Story
38/86	**Where Do The Children Go** . . . Hooters
25/65	**Where Do You Go** . . . Cher
	Where Have All The Flowers Gone
21/62	Kingston Trio
26/65	Johnny Rivers

POS/YR	RECORD TITLE/ARTIST
5/72	**Where Is The Love** . . . Roberta Flack & Donny Hathaway
3/60	**Where Or When** . . . Dion & The Belmonts
28/73	**Where Peaceful Waters Flow** . . . Gladys Knight & The Pips
	Where The Action Is ..see: Action
4/61	**Where The Boys Are** . . . Connie Francis
13/87	**Where The Streets Have No Name** . . . U2
23/59	**Where Were You (On Our Wedding Day)?** . . . Lloyd Price
28/66	**Where Were You When I Needed You** . . . Grass Roots
23/79	**Where Were You When I Was Falling In Love** . . . Lobo
21/67	**Where Will The Words Come From** . . . Gary Lewis & The Playboys
	Where You Lead
40/71	Barbra Streisand
37/72	Barbra Streisand (medley)
26/69	**Where's The Playground Susie** . . . Glen Campbell
	Which Way Is Up ..see: Theme From
2/70	**Which Way You Goin' Billy?** . . . Poppy Family
7/81	**While You See A Chance** . . . Steve Winwood
14/80	**Whip It** . . . Devo
28/83	**Whirly Girl** . . . Oxo
37/84	**Whisper To A Scream (Birds Fly)** . . . Icicle Works
	Whispering
11/64	Nino Tempo & April Stevens
27/77	Dr. Buzzard's Original "Savannah" Band
9/57	**Whispering Bells** . . . Dell-Vikings
11/66	**Whispers (Gettin' Louder)** . . . Jackie Wilson
	White Christmas
7/55	Bing Crosby
34/57	Bing Crosby
26/60	Bing Crosby
12/61	Bing Crosby
38/62	Bing Crosby
26/84	**White Horse** . . . Laid Back
19/76	**White Knight** . . . Cledus Maggard
28/72	**White Lies, Blue Eyes** . . . Bullet
9/64	**White On White** . . . Danny Williams
8/67	**White Rabbit** . . . Jefferson Airplane
6/68	**White Room** . . . Cream
	White Silver Sands
7/57	Don Rondo

POS/YR	RECORD TITLE/ARTIST
18/57	Owen Bradley Quintet
22/57	Dave Gardner
9/60	Bill Black's Combo
2/57	**White Sport Coat (And A Pink Carnation)** . . . Marty Robbins
36/83	**White Wedding** . . . Billy Idol
5/67	**Whiter Shade Of Pale** . . . Procol Harum
21/66	**Who Am I** . . . Petula Clark
14/78	**Who Are You** . . . Who
33/64	**Who Can I Turn To** . . . Tony Bennett
1/82	**Who Can It Be Now?** . . . Men At Work
25/64	**Who Do You Love** . . . Sapphires
15/74	**Who Do You Think You Are** . . . Bo Donaldson & The Heywoods
40/81	**Who Do You Think You're Foolin'** . . . Donna Summer
16/87	**Who Found Who** . . . Jellybean/Elisa Fiorillo
33/68	**Who Is Gonna Love Me?** . . . Dionne Warwick
3/75	**Who Loves You** . . . 4 Seasons
9/57	**Who Needs You** . . . Four Lads
7/61	**Who Put The Bomp (In The Bomp, Bomp, Bomp)** . . . Barry Mann
16/84	**Who Wears These Shoes?** . . . Elton John
19/68	**Who Will Answer?** . . . Ed Ames
7/87	**Who Will You Run To** . . . Heart
18/76	**Who'd She Coo?** . . . Ohio Players
29/80	**Who'll Be The Fool Tonight** . . . Larsen-Feiten Band
34/65	**Who'll Be The Next In Line** . . . Kinks
F/70	**Who'll Stop The Rain** . . . Creedence Clearwater Revival
4/81	**Who's Crying Now** . . . Journey
6/85	**Who's Holding Donna Now** . . . DeBarge
27/73	**Who's In The Strawberry Patch With Sally** . . . Dawn
3/86	**Who's Johnny** . . . El DeBarge
	Who's Making Love
5/68	Johnnie Taylor
39/81	Blues Brothers
	Who's Sorry Now
4/58	Connie Francis
40/75	Marie Osmond
1/87	**Who's That Girl** . . . Madonna
21/84	**Who's That Girl?** . . . Eurythmics
40/70	**Who's Your Baby?** . . . Archies
7/85	**Who's Zoomin' Who** . . . Aretha Franklin
22/77	**Whodunit** . . . Tavares

POS/YR	RECORD TITLE/ARTIST
3/57	**Whole Lot Of Shakin' Going On** . . . Jerry Lee Lewis
4/70	**Whole Lotta Love** . . . Led Zeppelin
6/59	**Whole Lotta Loving** . . . Fats Domino
	Why
1/59	Frankie Avalon
13/72	Donny Osmond
5/57	**Why Baby Why** . . . Pat Boone
33/85	**Why Can't I Have You** . . . Cars
	Why Can't I Touch You ..see: (If You Let Me Make Love To You Then)
3/86	**Why Can't This Be Love** . . . Van Halen
6/75	**Why Can't We Be Friends?** . . . War
3/73	**Why Can't We Live Together** . . . Timmy Thomas
	Why Do Fools Fall In Love
6/56	Frankie Lymon & The Teenagers
9/56	Gale Storm
12/56	Diamonds
7/81	Diana Ross
38/63	**Why Do Lovers Break Each Other's Heart?** . . . Bob B. Soxx & The Blue Jeans
10/58	**Why Don't They Understand** . . . George Hamilton IV
37/63	**Why Don't You Believe Me** . . . Duprees
13/83	**Why Me?** . . . Irene Cara
16/73	**Why Me** . . . Kris Kristofferson
26/80	**Why Me** . . . Styx
18/80	**Why Not Me** . . . Fred Knoblock
39/87	**Why You Treat Me So Bad** . . . Club Nouveau
3/69	**Wichita Lineman** . . . Glen Campbell
22/63	**Wiggle Wobble** . . . Les Cooper
33/63	**Wild!** . . . Dee Dee Sharp
2/84	**Wild Boys** . . . Duran Duran
29/56	**Wild Cherry** . . . Don Cherry
31/67	**Wild Honey** . . . Beach Boys
28/71	**Wild Horses** . . . Rolling Stones
26/61	**Wild In The Country** . . . Elvis Presley
22/57	**Wild Is The Wind** . . . Johnny Mathis
28/71	**Wild Night** . . . Van Morrison
2/60	**Wild One** . . . Bobby Rydell
34/65	**Wild One** . . . Martha & The Vandellas
	Wild Thing
1/66	Troggs
20/67	Senator Bobby
14/74	Fancy
2/89	**Wild Thing** . . . Tone Loc
8/63	**Wild Weekend** . . . Rebels

POS/YR	RECORD TITLE/ARTIST
25/86	**Wild Wild Life** . . . Talking Heads
1/88	**Wild, Wild West** . . . Escape Club
	Wild World
11/71	Cat Stevens
25/89	Maxi Priest
3/75	**Wildfire** . . . Michael Murphey
9/73	**Wildflower** . . . Skylark
17/63	**Wildwood Days** . . . Bobby Rydell
7/74	**Wildwood Weed** . . . Jim Stafford
1/73	**Will It Go Round In Circles** . . . Billy Preston
32/69	**Will You Be Staying After Sunday** . . . Peppermint Rainbow
	Will You Love Me Tomorrow
1/61	Shirelles
24/68	4 Seasons
39/78	Dave Mason
3/87	**Will You Still Love Me?** . . . Chicago
	Willie And The Hand Jive
9/58	Johnny Otis Show
26/74	Eric Clapton
15/65	**Willow Weep For Me** . . . Chad & Jeremy
22/58	**Win Your Love For Me** . . . Sam Cooke
1/66	**Winchester Cathedral** . . . New Vaudeville Band
31/69	**Windmills Of Your Mind** . . . Dusty Springfield
32/67	**Windows Of The World** . . . Dionne Warwick
38/83	**Winds Of Change** . . . Jefferson Starship
1/67	**Windy** . . . Association
12/61	**Wings Of A Dove** . . . Ferlin Husky
8/81	**Winner Takes It All** . . . Abba
21/76	**Winners And Losers** . . . Hamilton, Joe Frank & Reynolds
17/81	**Winning** . . . Santana
16/70	**Winter World Of Love** . . . Engelbert Humperdinck
	Wipe Out
2/63	Surfaris
16/66	Surfaris
12/87	Fat Boys/Beach Boys
35/57	**Wisdom Of A Fool** . . . Five Keys
17/64	**Wish Someone Would Care** . . . Irma Thomas
38/67	**Wish You Didn't Have To Go** . . . James & Bobby Purify
6/64	**Wishin' And Hopin'** . . . Dusty Springfield
18/58	**Wishing For Your Love** . . . Voxpoppers

POS/YR	RECORD TITLE/ARTIST
26/83	**Wishing (If I Had A Photograph Of You)** . . . A Flock Of Seagulls
1/88	**Wishing Well** . . . Terence Trent D'Arby
11/74	**Wishing You Were Here** . . . Chicago
1/58	**Witch Doctor** . . . David Seville
21/72	**Witch Queen Of New Orleans** . . . Redbone
6/58	**Witchcraft** . . . Frank Sinatra
32/63	**Witchcraft** . . . Elvis Presley
9/72	**Witchy Woman** . . . Eagles
29/66	**With A Girl Like You** . . . Troggs
1/78	**With A Little Luck** . . . Wings
15/57	**With All My Heart** . . . Jodie Sands
39/59	**With Open Arms** . . . Jane Morgan
1/87	**With Or Without You** . . . U2
35/69	**With Pen In Hand** . . . Vikki Carr
21/59	**With The Wind And The Rain In Your Hair** . . . Pat Boone
27/65	**With These Hands** . . . Tom Jones
14/67	**With This Ring** . . . Platters
4/80	**With You I'm Born Again** . . . Billy Preston & Syreeta
30/57	**With You On My Mind** . . . Nat King Cole
12/76	**With Your Love** . . . Jefferson Starship
28/58	**With Your Love** . . . Jack Scott
	Without Love (There Is Nothing)
19/57	Clyde McPhatter
29/63	Ray Charles
5/70	Tom Jones
1/72	**Without You** . . . Nilsson
7/61	**Without You** . . . Johnny Tillotson
24/82	**Without You (Not Another Lonely Night)** . . . Franke & The Knockouts
20/80	**Without Your Love** . . . Roger Daltrey
38/87	**Without Your Love** . . . Toto
14/64	**Wives And Lovers** . . . Jack Jones
	Wizard Of Oz ..see: Themes From The
40/75	**Wolf Creek Pass** . . . C.W. McCall
6/62	**Wolverton Mountain** . . . Claude King *(also see: (I'm The Girl On))*
2/81	**Woman** . . . John Lennon
14/66	**Woman** . . . Peter & Gordon
15/60	**Woman, A Lover, A Friend** . . . Jackie Wilson
1/80	**Woman In Love** . . . Barbra Streisand
	Woman In Love
14/55	Four Aces
19/55	Frankie Laine
33/83	**Woman In Me** . . . Donna Summer
24/83	**Woman In You** . . . Bee Gees
4/81	**Woman Needs Love (Just Like You Do)** . . . Ray Parker Jr. & Raydio
22/74	**Woman To Woman** . . . Shirley Brown
4/68	**Woman, Woman** . . . Gary Puckett & The Union Gap
29/65	**Woman's Got Soul** . . . Impressions
36/71	**Women's Love Rights** . . . Laura Lee
15/71	**Won't Get Fooled Again** . . . Who
19/60	**Won't You Come Home Bill Bailey** . . . Bobby Darin
11/61	**Wonder Like You** . . . Rick Nelson
	Wonder Of You
25/59	Ray Peterson
9/70	Elvis Presley
22/62	**Wonderful Dream** . . . Majors
14/63	**Wonderful Summer** . . . Robin Ward
4/58	**Wonderful Time Up There** . . . Pat Boone
16/78	**Wonderful Tonight** . . . Eric Clapton
	Wonderful! Wonderful!
14/57	Johnny Mathis
7/63	Tymes *(also see: Wun'erful, Wun'erful!)*
	Wonderful World
12/60	Sam Cooke
4/65	Herman's Hermits
17/78	Art Garfunkel with James Taylor & Paul Simon *(also see: What A)*
25/70	**Wonderful World, Beautiful People** . . . Jimmy Cliff
40/59	**Wonderful You** . . . Jimmie Rodgers
12/57	**Wondering** . . . Patti Page
21/80	**Wondering Where The Lions Are** . . . Bruce Cockburn
25/80	**Wonderland** . . . Commodores
	Wonderland By Night
1/61	Bert Kaempfert
15/61	Louis Prima
18/61	Anita Bryant
16/59	**Woo-Hoo** . . . Rock-A-Teens
	Woo Woo Song ..see: You Should Be Mine
1/61	**Wooden Heart** . . . Joe Dowell
	Woodstock
11/70	Crosby, Stills, Nash & Young
23/71	Matthews' Southern Comfort
2/65	**Wooly Bully** . . . Sam The Sham & The Pharoahs
19/88	**Word In Spanish** . . . Elton John

POS/YR	RECORD TITLE/ARTIST
6/86	**Word Up** . . . Cameo
11/67	**Words** . . . Monkees
15/68	**Words** . . . Bee Gees
5/86	**Words Get In The Way** . . . Miami Sound Machine
5/67	**Words Of Love** . . . Mamas & The Papas
13/57	**Words Of Love** . . . Diamonds
18/66	**Work Song** . . . Herb Alpert
32/74	**Workin' At The Car Wash Blues** . . . Jim Croce
33/62	**Workin' For The Man** . . . Roy Orbison
20/69	**Workin' On A Groovy Thing** . . . 5th Dimension
29/82	**Working For The Weekend** . . . Loverboy
8/66	**Working In The Coal Mine** . . . Lee Dorsey
	Working My Way Back To You
9/66	4 Seasons
2/80	Spinners (medley)
33/63	**Workout Stevie, Workout** . . . Stevie Wonder
37/69	**World** . . . James Brown
7/73	**World Is A Ghetto** . . . War
19/65	**World Of Our Own** . . . Seekers
21/58	**World Outside** . . . Four Coins
30/67	**World We Knew (Over And Over)** . . . Frank Sinatra
1/64	**World Without Love** . . . Peter & Gordon
37/64	**Worried Guy** . . . Johnny Tillotson
20/59	**Worried Man** . . . Kingston Trio
3/69	**Worst That Could Happen** . . . Brooklyn Bridge
10/87	**Wot's It To Ya** . . . Robbie Nevil
5/85	**Would I Lie To You?** . . . Eurythmics
8/66	**Wouldn't It Be Nice** . . . Beach Boys
38/81	**Wrack My Brain** . . . Ringo Starr
20/85	**Wrap Her Up** . . . Elton John
8/84	**Wrapped Around Your Finger** . . . Police
2/76	**Wreck Of The Edmund Fitzgerald** . . . Gordon Lightfoot
	Wringle Wrangle
12/57	Fess Parker
33/57	Bill Hayes
5/61	**Writing On The Wall** . . . Adam Wade
34/64	**Wrong For Each Other** . . . Andy Williams
32/57	**Wun'erful, Wun'erful!** . . . Stan Freberg

X

POS/YR	RECORD TITLE/ARTIST
8/80	**Xanadu** . . . Olivia Newton-John/Electric Light Orchestra

Y

POS/YR	RECORD TITLE/ARTIST
2/79	**Y.M.C.A.** . . . Village People
7/61	**Ya Ya** . . . Lee Dorsey
19/84	**Yah Mo B There** . . . James Ingram with Michael McDonald
35/63	**Yakety Sax** . . . Boots Randolph
1/58	**Yakety Yak** . . . Coasters
16/86	**Yankee Rose** . . . David Lee Roth
32/88	**Yeah, Yeah, Yeah** . . . Judson Spence
8/77	**Year Of The Cat** . . . Al Stewart
35/80	**Years** . . . Wayne Newton
37/61	**Years From Now** . . . Jackie Wilson
21/65	**Yeh, Yeh** . . . Georgie Fame
25/67	**Yellow Balloon** . . . Yellow Balloon
4/61	**Yellow Bird** . . . Arthur Lyman Group
23/70	**Yellow River** . . . Christie
	Yellow Rose Of Texas
1/55	Mitch Miller
3/55	Johnny Desmond
16/55	Stan Freberg
2/66	**Yellow Submarine** . . . Beatles
30/59	**"Yep!"** . . . Duane Eddy
	Yes, I'm Ready
5/65	Barbara Mason
2/80	Teri DeSario with K.C.
34/60	**Yes Sir, That's My Baby** . . . Ricky Nelson
12/57	**Yes Tonight, Josephine** . . . Johnnie Ray
11/73	**Yes We Can Can** . . . Pointer Sisters
31/68	**Yester Love** . . . Miracles
7/69	**Yester-Me, Yester-You, Yesterday** . . . Stevie Wonder
	Yesterday
1/65	Beatles
25/67	Ray Charles

POS/YR	RECORD TITLE/ARTIST
2/73	**Yesterday Once More** . . . Carpenters
19/69	**Yesterday, When I Was Young** . . . Roy Clark
21/64	**Yesterday's Gone** . . . Chad & Jeremy
11/82	**Yesterday's Songs** . . . Neil Diamond
3/71	**Yo-Yo** . . . Osmonds
8/60	**Yogi** . . . Ivy Three
	You ..also see: U
20/75	**You** . . . George Harrison
21/58	**You** . . . Aquatones
25/78	**You** . . . Rita Coolidge
34/68	**You** . . . Marvin Gaye
1/74	**You Ain't Seen Nothing Yet** . . . Bachman-Turner Overdrive
12/61	**You Always Hurt The One You Love** . . . Clarence Henry
7/83	**You And I** . . . Eddie Rabbitt with Crystal Gayle
13/78	**You And I** . . . Rick James
9/77	**You And Me** . . . Alice Cooper
9/74	**You And Me Against The World** . . . Helen Reddy
4/83	**You Are** . . . Lionel Richie
9/72	**You Are Everything** . . . Stylistics
26/62	**You Are Mine** . . . Frankie Avalon
7/58	**You Are My Destiny** . . . Paul Anka
12/85	**You Are My Lady** . . . Freddie Jackson
6/55	**You Are My Love** . . . Joni James
27/76	**You Are My Starship** . . . Norman Connors/Michael Henderson
7/62	**You Are My Sunshine** . . . Ray Charles
5/75	**You Are So Beautiful** . . . Joe Cocker
17/87	**You Are The Girl** . . . Cars
25/61	**You Are The Only One** . . . Ricky Nelson
1/73	**You Are The Sunshine Of My Life** . . . Stevie Wonder
9/76	**You Are The Woman** . . . Firefall
20/66	**You Baby** . . . Turtles
29/86	**You Be Illin'** . . . Run-D.M.C.
9/62	**You Beat Me To The Punch** . . . Mary Wells
6/78	**You Belong To Me** . . . Carly Simon
7/62	**You Belong To Me** . . . Duprees
2/85	**You Belong To The City** . . . Glenn Frey
37/59	**You Better Know It** . . . Jackie Wilson
24/62	**You Better Move On** . . . Arthur Alexander
20/66	**You Better Run** . . . Rascals
9/67	**You Better Sit Down Kids** . . . Cher

POS/YR	RECORD TITLE/ARTIST
18/81	**You Better You Bet** . . . Who
23/87	**You Can Call Me Al** . . . Paul Simon
6/61	**You Can Depend On Me** . . . Brenda Lee
37/79	**You Can Do It** . . . Dobie Gray
8/82	**You Can Do Magic** . . . America
	You Can Have Her
12/61	Roy Hamilton
34/74	Sam Neely
36/58	**You Can Make It If You Try** . . . Gene Allison
18/63	**You Can Never Stop Me Loving You** . . . Johnny Tillotson
9/79	**You Can't Change That** . . . Raydio
15/84	**You Can't Get What You Want (Till You Know What You Want)** . . . Joe Jackson
	You Can't Hurry Love
1/66	Supremes
10/83	Phil Collins
40/66	**You Can't Roller Skate In A Buffalo Herd** . . . Roger Miller
20/56	**You Can't Run Away From It** . . . Four Aces
	You Can't Sit Down
29/61	Philip Upchurch Combo
3/63	Dovells
12/77	**You Can't Turn Me Off (In The Middle Of Turning Me On)** . . . High Inergy
12/58	**You Cheated** . . . Shields
32/72	**You Could Have Been A Lady** . . . April Wine
15/82	**You Could Have Been With Me** . . . Sheena Easton
32/81	**You Could Take My Heart Away** . . . Silver Condor
7/79	**You Decorated My Life** . . . Kenny Rogers
10/66	**You Didn't Have To Be So Nice** . . . Lovin' Spoonful
1/78	**You Don't Bring Me Flowers** . . . Barbra Streisand & Neil Diamond
3/63	**You Don't Have To Be A Baby To Cry** . . . Caravelles
1/77	**You Don't Have To Be A Star (To Be In My Show)** . . . Marilyn McCoo & Billy Davis, Jr.
15/66	**(You Don't Have To) Paint Me A Picture** . . . Gary Lewis & The Playboys
	You Don't Have To Say You Love Me
4/66	Dusty Springfield
11/70	Elvis Presley
20/88	**You Don't Know** . . . Scarlett & Black

POS/YR	RECORD TITLE/ARTIST
11/64	**(You Don't Know) How Glad I Am** . . . Nancy Wilson
	You Don't Know Me
14/56	Jerry Vale
2/62	Ray Charles
4/61	**You Don't Know What You've Got (Until You Lose It)** . . . Ral Donner
8/72	**You Don't Mess Around With Jim** . . . Jim Croce
10/57	**You Don't Owe Me A Thing** . . . Johnnie Ray
2/64	**You Don't Own Me** . . . Lesley Gore
16/82	**You Don't Want Me Anymore** . . . Steel Breeze
31/82	**You Dropped A Bomb On Me** . . . Gap Band
24/69	**You Gave Me A Mountain** . . . Frankie Laine
3/85	**You Give Good Love** . . . Whitney Houston
1/86	**You Give Love A Bad Name** . . . Bon Jovi
38/79	**You Gonna Make Me Love Somebody Else** . . . Jones Girls
3/87	**You Got It All** . . . Jets
3/89	**You Got It (The Right Stuff)** . . . New Kids On The Block
20/83	**You Got Lucky** . . . Tom Petty
11/74	**You Got The Love** . . . Rufus Featuring Chaka Khan
18/67	**You Got To Me** . . . Neil Diamond
	You Got What It Takes
10/60	Marv Johnson
7/67	Dave Clark Five
40/69	**You Got Yours And I'll Get Mine** . . . Delfonics
7/87	**(You Gotta) Fight For Your Right (To Party!)** . . . Beastie Boys
1/74	**You Haven't Done Nothin** . . . Stevie Wonder
24/69	**You, I** . . . Rugbys
	You Keep Me Hangin' On
1/66	Supremes
6/68	Vanilla Fudge
1/87	Kim Wilde
25/68	**(You Keep Me) Hangin' On** . . . Joe Simon
38/82	**You Keep Runnin' Away** . . . 38 Special
19/67	**You Keep Running Away** . . . Four Tops
17/86	**You Know I Love You...Don't You?** . . . Howard Jones
35/80	**You Know That I Love You** . . . Santana

POS/YR	RECORD TITLE/ARTIST
12/67	**You Know What I Mean** . . . Turtles
1/77	**You Light Up My Life** . . . Debby Boone
12/74	**You Little Trustmaker** . . . Tymes
22/63	**You Lost The Sweetest Boy** . . . Mary Wells
10/77	**You Made Me Believe In Magic** . . . Bay City Rollers
9/77	**You Make Loving Fun** . . . Fleetwood Mac
2/74	**You Make Me Feel Brand New** . . . Stylistics
1/77	**You Make Me Feel Like Dancing** . . . Leo Sayer
36/79	**You Make Me Feel (Mighty Real)** . . . Sylvester
5/81	**You Make My Dreams** . . . Daryl Hall & John Oates
7/80	**You May Be Right** . . . Billy Joel
17/60	**You Mean Everything To Me** . . . Neil Sedaka
35/68	**You Met Your Match** . . . Stevie Wonder
7/84	**You Might Think** . . . Cars
15/64	**You Must Believe Me** . . . Impressions
	You Must Have Been A Beautiful Baby
5/61	Bobby Darin
35/67	Dave Clark Five
40/79	**You Need A Woman Tonight** . . . Captain & Tennille
11/58	**You Need Hands** . . . Eydie Gorme
25/70	**You Need Love Like I Do (Don't You)** . . . Gladys Knight & The Pips
1/78	**You Needed Me** . . . Anne Murray
14/64	**You Never Can Tell** . . . Chuck Berry
10/78	**You Never Done It Like That** . . . Captain & Tennille
3/72	**You Ought To Be With Me** . . . Al Green
	You Really Got A Hold On Me ..see: You've Really
	You Really Got Me
7/64	Kinks
36/78	Van Halen
27/65	**You Really Know How To Hurt A Guy** . . . Jan & Dean
37/81	**You Saved My Soul** . . . Burton Cummings
	You Send Me
1/57	Sam Cooke
8/57	Teresa Brewer
3/76	**You Sexy Thing** . . . Hot Chocolate
35/80	**You Shook Me All Night Long** . . . AC/DC
1/76	**You Should Be Dancing** . . . Bee Gees

POS/YR	RECORD TITLE/ARTIST
13/86	**You Should Be Mine (The Woo Woo Song)** . . . Jeffrey Osborne
39/64	**You Should Have Seen The Way He Looked At Me** . . . Dixie Cups
5/82	**You Should Hear How She Talks About You** . . . Melissa Manchester
6/69	**You Showed Me** . . . Turtles
11/85	**You Spin Me Round (Like A Record)** . . . Dead Or Alive
10/79	**You Take My Breath Away** . . . Rex Smith
3/60	**You Talk Too Much** . . . Joe Jones
38/65	**You Tell Me Why** . . . Beau Brummels
40/79	**You Thrill Me** . . . Exile
39/79	**You Took The Words Right Out Of My Mouth** . . . Meat Loaf
8/65	**You Turn Me On** . . . Ian Whitcomb
25/73	**You Turn Me On, I'm A Radio** . . . Joni Mitchell
36/72	**You Want It, You Got It** . . . Detroit Emeralds
13/72	**You Wear It Well** . . . Rod Stewart
12/60	**(You Were Made For) All My Love** . . . Jackie Wilson
21/65	**You Were Made For Me** . . . Freddie & The Dreamers
27/58	**You Were Made For Me** . . . Sam Cooke
21/59	**You Were Mine** . . . Fireflies
	You Were On My Mind
3/65	We Five
36/67	Crispian St. Peters
30/65	**You Were Only Fooling (While I Was Falling In Love)** . . . Vic Damone
22/62	**You Win Again** . . . Fats Domino
8/74	**You Won't See Me** . . . Anne Murray
22/65	**You'd Better Come Home** . . . Petula Clark
14/80	**You'll Accomp'ny Me** . . . Bob Seger
	You'll Lose A Good Thing
8/62	Barbara Lynn
32/76	Freddy Fender
2/76	**You'll Never Find Another Love Like Mine** . . . Lou Rawls
	You'll Never Get To Heaven (If You Break My Heart)
34/64	Dionne Warwick
23/73	Stylistics
11/56	**You'll Never Never Know** . . . Platters
34/64	**You'll Never Walk Alone** . . . Patti LaBelle & Her Blue Belles
	You're ..also see: Your

POS/YR	RECORD TITLE/ARTIST
18/86	**You're A Friend Of Mine** . . . Clarence Clemons & Jackson Browne
36/78	**You're A Part Of Me** . . . Gene Cotton with Kim Carnes
12/73	**You're A Special Part Of Me** . . . Diana Ross & Marvin Gaye
15/64	**You're A Wonderful One** . . . Marvin Gaye
	You're All I Need To Get By
7/68	Marvin Gaye & Tammi Terrell
19/71	Aretha Franklin
34/75	Dawn
25/57	**You're Cheatin' Yourself (If You're Cheatin' On Me)** . . . Frank Sinatra
35/83	**You're Driving Me Out Of My Mind** . . . Little River Band
39/66	**(You're Gonna) Hurt Yourself** . . . Frankie Valli
34/59	**You're Gonna Miss Me** . . . Connie Francis
1/74	**(You're) Having My Baby** . . . Paul Anka
4/78	**You're In My Heart (The Final Acclaim)** . . . Rod Stewart
16/76	**You're My Best Friend** . . . Queen
6/67	**You're My Everything** . . . Temptations
27/81	**You're My Girl** . . . Franke & The Knockouts
	You're My Girl ..see: (Say)
14/57	**You're My One And Only Love** . . . Ricky Nelson
	(You're My) Soul And Inspiration
1/66	Righteous Brothers
38/78	Donny & Marie Osmond
	You're My World
26/64	Cilla Black
18/77	Helen Reddy
1/75	**You're No Good** . . . Linda Ronstadt
25/65	**You're Nobody Till Somebody Loves You** . . . Dean Martin
9/85	**You're Only Human (Second Wind)** . . . Billy Joel
7/79	**You're Only Lonely** . . . J.D. Souther
	You're Sixteen
8/60	Johnny Burnette
1/74	Ringo Starr
17/59	**You're So Fine** . . . Falcons
1/73	**You're So Vain** . . . Carly Simon
29/72	**You're Still A Young Man** . . . Tower Of Power
34/80	**You're Supposed To Keep Your Love For Me** . . . Jermaine Jackson

POS/YR	RECORD TITLE/ARTIST
3/63	**(You're the) Devil In Disguise** . . . Elvis Presley
2/75	**You're The First, The Last, My Everything** . . . Barry White
3/85	**You're The Inspiration** . . . Chicago
18/78	**You're The Love** . . . Seals & Crofts
4/65	**You're The One** . . . Vogues
22/70	**You're The One** . . . Little Sister
1/78	**You're The One That I Want** . . . John Travolta & Olivia Newton-John
13/80	**You're The Only Woman (You & I)** . . . Ambrosia
11/61	**You're The Reason** . . . Bobby Edwards
3/63	**You're The Reason I'm Living** . . . Bobby Darin
33/66	**You've Been Cheatin'** . . . Impressions
36/65	**You've Been In Love Too Long** . . . Martha & The Vandellas
	(You've Got) ..see: Personality
	You've Got A Friend
1/71	James Taylor
29/71	Roberta Flack & Donny Hathaway
38/70	**(You've Got Me) Dangling On A String** . . . Chairmen Of The Board
33/77	**You've Got Me Runnin'** . . . Gene Cotton
4/56	**(You've Got) The Magic Touch** . . . Platters
28/71	**You've Got To Crawl (Before You Walk)** . . . 8th Day
10/65	**You've Got To Hide Your Love Away** . . . Silkie
20/60	**(You've Got To) Move Two Mountains** . . . Marv Johnson
	(You've Got What It Takes) ..see: Baby
7/65	**You've Got Your Troubles** . . . Fortunes
	You've Lost That Lovin' Feelin'
1/65	Righteous Brothers
16/69	Dionne Warwick
12/80	Daryl Hall & John Oates
	You've Made Me So Very Happy
39/67	Brenda Holloway
2/69	Blood, Sweat & Tears
22/73	**You've Never Been This Far Before** . . . Conway Twitty
8/63	**You've Really Got A Hold On Me** . . . Miracles
25/55	**Young Abe Lincoln** . . . Don Cornell
28/75	**Young Americans** . . . David Bowie
17/63	**Young And In Love** . . . Dick & DeeDee
	Young And The Restless ..see: Nadia's Theme
23/58	**Young And Warm And Wonderful** . . . Tony Bennett
	Young Blood
8/57	Coasters
20/76	Bad Company
40/79	**Young Blood** . . . Rickie Lee Jones
12/60	**Young Emotions** . . . Ricky Nelson
2/68	**Young Girl** . . . Gary Puckett & The Union Gap
20/76	**Young Hearts Run Free** . . . Candi Staton
	Young Love
1/57	Tab Hunter
1/57	Sonny James
17/57	Crew-Cuts
25/73	Donny Osmond
38/82	**Young Love** . . . Air Supply
6/63	**Young Lovers** . . . Paul & Paula
	Young Lovers ..see: Theme For
5/81	**Young Turks** . . . Rod Stewart
5/62	**Young World** . . . Rick Nelson
	Your ..also see: You're
24/75	**Your Bulldog Drinks Champagne** . . . Jim Stafford
29/62	**Your Cheating Heart** . . . Ray Charles
34/61	**Your Friends** . . . Dee Clark
18/69	**Your Good Thing (Is About To End)** . . . Lou Rawls
33/82	**Your Imagination** . . . Daryl Hall & John Oates
6/86	**Your Love** . . . Outfield
15/77	**Your Love** . . . Marilyn McCoo & Billy Davis, Jr.
38/75	**Your Love** . . . Graham Central Station
13/83	**Your Love Is Driving Me Crazy** . . . Sammy Hagar
	(Your Love Keeps Lifting Me) Higher And Higher
6/67	Jackie Wilson
2/77	Rita Coolidge
24/61	**Your Ma Said You Cried In Your Sleep Last Night** . . . Kenny Dino
4/73	**Your Mama Don't Dance** . . . Loggins & Messina
40/71	**Your Move** . . . Yes
14/62	**Your Nose Is Gonna Grow** . . . Johnny Crawford
40/63	**Your Old Stand By** . . . Mary Wells
40/61	**Your One And Only Love** . . . Jackie Wilson
28/63	**Your Other Love** . . . Connie Francis

POS/YR	RECORD TITLE/ARTIST
5/67	**Your Precious Love** . . . Marvin Gaye & Tammi Terrell *(also see: For Your Precious Love)*
20/77	**Your Smiling Face** . . . James Taylor
8/71	**Your Song** . . . Elton John
40/71	**Your Time To Cry** . . . Joe Simon
33/67	**Your Unchanging Love** . . . Marvin Gaye
32/63	**Your Used To Be** . . . Brenda Lee
20/57	**Your Wild Heart** . . . Joy Layne
9/86	**Your Wildest Dreams** . . . Moody Blues
	(Yowsah, Yowsah, Yowsah) ..see: Dance, Dance, Dance
4/68	**Yummy Yummy Yummy** . . . Ohio Express

POS/YR	RECORD TITLE/ARTIST

Z

POS/YR	RECORD TITLE/ARTIST
8/63	**Zip-A-Dee Doo-Dah** . . . Bob B. Soxx & The Blue Jeans
36/67	**Zip Code** . . . Five Americans
16/57	**Zip Zip** . . . Diamonds
11/66	**Zorba The Greek** . . . Herb Alpert
	Zorro
17/58	Chordettes

THE RECORD HOLDERS

TOP ARTIST AND RECORD ACHIEVEMENTS

	WEEKS				THE TOP 100 RECORDS 1955-1988
YR	CHR	T40	T10	#1	TITLE/ARTIST
56	28	24	21	11	1. DON'T BE CRUEL/HOUND DOG Elvis Presley
55	26	26	20	10	2. CHERRY PINK AND APPLE BLOSSOM WHITE Perez Prado
55	21	21	18	10	3. SINCERELY The McGuire Sisters
56	26	22	17	10	4. SINGING THE BLUES Guy Mitchell
81	26	21	15	10	5. PHYSICAL Olivia Newton-John
77	25	21	14	10	6. YOU LIGHT UP MY LIFE Debby Boone
59	26	22	16	9	7. MACK THE KNIFE Bobby Darin
57	30	22	15	9	8. ALL SHOOK UP Elvis Presley
81	26	20	14	9	9. BETTE DAVIS EYES Kim Carnes
68	19	19	14	9	10. HEY JUDE The Beatles
81	27	19	13	9	11. ENDLESS LOVE Diana Ross & Lionel Richie
60	21	17	12	9	12. THE THEME FROM "A SUMMER PLACE" Percy Faith
55	38	25	19	8	13. ROCK AROUND THE CLOCK Bill Haley & His Comets
56	37	22	16	8	14. THE WAYWARD WIND Gogi Grant
55	22	19	16	8	15. SIXTEEN TONS Tennessee Ernie Ford
56	27	22	15	8	16. HEARTBREAK HOTEL Elvis Presley
83	22	20	13	8	17. EVERY BREATH YOU TAKE The Police
78	20	18	13	8	18. NIGHT FEVER Bee Gees
76	23	17	11	8	19. TONIGHT'S THE NIGHT (GONNA BE ALRIGHT) Rod Stewart
57	34	24	17	7	20. LOVE LETTERS IN THE SAND Pat Boone
57	27	19	15	7	21. JAILHOUSE ROCK Elvis Presley
57	25	18	14	7	22. (LET ME BE YOUR) TEDDY BEAR Elvis Presley
78	25	19	12	7	23. SHADOW DANCING Andy Gibb
58	21	18	12	7	24. AT THE HOP Danny & The Juniors
61	23	17	12	7	25. TOSSIN' AND TURNIN' Bobby Lewis
82	20	16	12	7	26. I LOVE ROCK 'N ROLL Joan Jett & The Blackhearts
82	19	15	12	7	27. EBONY AND IVORY Paul McCartney with Stevie Wonder
64	15	14	12	7	28. I WANT TO HOLD YOUR HAND The Beatles
66	15	13	12	7	29. I'M A BELIEVER The Monkees
83	24	17	11	7	30. BILLIE JEAN Michael Jackson
68	15	15	11	7	31. I HEARD IT THROUGH THE GRAPEVINE Marvin Gaye
55	21	21	17	6	32. LOVE IS A MANY-SPLENDORED THING Four Aces
56	25	20	16	6	33. ROCK AND ROLL WALTZ Kay Starr
55	19	19	16	6	34. THE YELLOW ROSE OF TEXAS Mitch Miller
56	24	20	15	6	35. THE POOR PEOPLE OF PARIS Les Baxter
78	25	19	15	6	36. LE FREAK Chic
56	24	19	15	6	37. MEMORIES ARE MADE OF THIS Dean Martin
82	25	18	15	6	38. EYE OF THE TIGER Survivor
83	25	20	14	6	39. FLASHDANCE...WHAT A FEELING Irene Cara
57	26	19	14	6	40. APRIL LOVE Pat Boone
80	25	19	13	6	41. LADY Kenny Rogers
83	22	18	13	6	42. SAY SAY SAY Paul McCartney & Michael Jackson
59	21	18	13	6	43. THE BATTLE OF NEW ORLEANS Johnny Horton
57	21	17	13	6	44. YOUNG LOVE Tab Hunter
82	25	20	12	6	45. CENTERFOLD The J. Geils Band

	WEEKS				THE TOP 100 RECORDS 1955-1988
YR	CHR	T40	T10	#1	TITLE/ARTIST
80	25	19	12	6	46. CALL ME Blondie
58	22	19	12	6	47. IT'S ALL IN THE GAME Tommy Edwards
79	22	16	12	6	48. MY SHARONA The Knack
69	17	16	11	6	49. AQUARIUS/LET THE SUNSHINE IN The 5th Dimension
72	18	15	11	6	50. THE FIRST TIME EVER I SAW YOUR FACE Roberta Flack
72	18	15	11	6	51. ALONE AGAIN (NATURALLY) Gilbert O'Sullivan
71	17	15	11	6	52. JOY TO THE WORLD Three Dog Night
60	16	14	11	6	53. ARE YOU LONESOME TO-NIGHT? Elvis Presley
58	14	14	10	6	54. THE PURPLE PEOPLE EATER Sheb Wooley
70	14	13	10	6	55. BRIDGE OVER TROUBLED WATER Simon & Garfunkel
84	19	14	9	6	56. LIKE A VIRGIN Madonna
69	13	12	9	6	57. IN THE YEAR 2525 (EXORDIUM & TERMINUS) Zager & Evans
57	31	23	16	5	58. TAMMY Debbie Reynolds
55	20	20	16	5	59. THE BALLAD OF DAVY CROCKETT Bill Hayes
56	23	19	15	5	60. LOVE ME TENDER Elvis Presley
56	23	20	14	5	61. MY PRAYER The Platters
80	22	19	14	5	62. (JUST LIKE) STARTING OVER John Lennon
77	23	17	12	5	63. BEST OF MY LOVE The Emotions
58	17	16	12	5	64. ALL I HAVE TO DO IS DREAM The Everly Brothers
84	21	16	11	5	65. WHEN DOVES CRY Prince
60	20	16	11	5	66. IT'S NOW OR NEVER Elvis Presley
58	19	16	11	5	67. TEQUILA The Champs
70	16	16	11	5	68. I'LL BE THERE The Jackson 5
76	19	15	11	5	69. SILLY LOVE SONGS Wings
71	17	15	11	5	70. MAGGIE MAY Rod Stewart
62	18	14	11	5	71. I CAN'T STOP LOVING YOU Ray Charles
58	20	16	10	5	72. DON'T Elvis Presley
84	21	15	10	5	73. JUMP Van Halen
79	20	15	10	5	74. BAD GIRLS Donna Summer
68	18	15	10	5	75. LOVE IS BLUE Paul Mauriat
71	17	15	10	5	76. IT'S TOO LATE Carole King
59	17	14	10	5	77. VENUS Frankie Avalon
62	16	14	10	5	78. BIG GIRLS DON'T CRY The 4 Seasons
58	16	13	10	5	79. NEL BLU DIPINTO DI BLU (VOLARE) Domenico Modugno
61	16	13	10	5	80. BIG BAD JOHN Jimmy Dean
63	15	13	10	5	81. SUGAR SHACK Jimmy Gilmer & The Fireballs
68	15	13	10	5	82. HONEY Bobby Goldsboro
67	17	15	9	5	83. TO SIR WITH LOVE Lulu
60	17	13	9	5	84. CATHY'S CLOWN The Everly Brothers
73	16	13	9	5	85. KILLING ME SOFTLY WITH HIS SONG Roberta Flack
68	14	13	9	5	86. PEOPLE GOT TO BE FREE The Rascals
71	15	12	9	5	87. ONE BAD APPLE The Osmonds
69	12	12	9	5	88. GET BACK The Beatles
66	13	11	9	5	89. THE BALLAD OF THE GREEN BERETS SSgt Barry Sadler
62	14	12	7	5	90. SHERRY The 4 Seasons

	WEEKS				THE TOP 100 RECORDS 1955-1988
YR	CHR	T40	T10	#1	TITLE/ARTIST
64	10	9	6	5	91. CAN'T BUY ME LOVE The Beatles
55	26	26	18	4	92. AUTUMN LEAVES Roger Williams
56	29	24	17	4	93. LISBON ANTIGUA Nelson Riddle
77	31	23	16	4	94. I JUST WANT TO BE YOUR EVERYTHING Andy Gibb
56	23	19	14	4	95. I ALMOST LOST MY MIND Pat Boone
80	29	17	14	4	96. UPSIDE DOWN Diana Ross
57	28	23	13	4	97. HONEYCOMB Jimmie Rodgers
78	27	22	13	4	98. STAYIN' ALIVE Bee Gees
70	22	19	13	4	99. RAINDROPS KEEP FALLIN' ON MY HEAD B.J. Thomas
83	24	17	13	4	100. ALL NIGHT LONG (ALL NIGHT) Lionel Richie

YR : Year record reached its peak position
CHR: Total weeks charted in the Top 100
T40 : Total weeks charted in the Top 40
T10 : Total weeks charted in the Top 10
#1 : Total weeks record held the #1 position

Records are ranked according to the number of weeks they held the #1 position. Ties are broken in the following order:

1. Total weeks in the Top 10
2. Total weeks in the Top 40
3. Total weeks charted in the Top 100

This ranking system is identical to the one used in compiling Record Research's *Top 3000 1955-1987* book. However, the above ranking takes into account all singles from 1955, whereas the *Top 3000* ranking begins on July 9, 1955, the date "Rock Around The Clock" peaked at position #1.

THE TOP 100 ARTISTS 1955-1988

	ARTIST	POINTS
	1. ELVIS PRESLEY	5132
	2. THE BEATLES	3038
	3. STEVIE WONDER	2568
	4. ELTON JOHN	2294
	5. THE ROLLING STONES	2180
	6. PAT BOONE	2042
	7. ARETHA FRANKLIN	2015
	8. MARVIN GAYE	2009
	9. PAUL MCCARTNEY (& WINGS)	1997
	10. RICKY NELSON	1924
	11. THE SUPREMES	1885
⌂	12. CHICAGO	1850
	13. NEIL DIAMOND	1803
	14. THE TEMPTATIONS	1776
	15. THE BEACH BOYS	1732
	16. CONNIE FRANCIS	1687
⌂	17. MICHAEL JACKSON	1665
	18. BEE GEES	1662
	19. DARYL HALL & JOHN OATES	1604
	20. FATS DOMINO	1587
	21. OLIVIA NEWTON-JOHN	1583
	22. THE 4 SEASONS	1558
	23. PAUL ANKA	1550
	24. JAMES BROWN	1489
	25. PERRY COMO	1444
*	26. KENNY ROGERS (& THE FIRST EDITION)	1423
	27. DIANA ROSS	1419
	28. BILLY JOEL	1406
	29. BRENDA LEE	1401
	30. DIONNE WARWICK	1394
	31. THE EVERLY BROTHERS	1382
	32. THE JACKSONS (JACKSON 5)	1290
	33. BOBBY VINTON	1267
	34. RAY CHARLES	1258
	35. FRANK SINATRA	1249
	36. SAM COOKE	1240
	37. BARRY MANILOW	1229
	38. CARPENTERS	1223
	39. THREE DOG NIGHT	1200
	40. NAT KING COLE	1196
	41. GLADYS KNIGHT & THE PIPS	1186
	42. THE MIRACLES	1178
⌂	43. ROD STEWART	1156
	44. FOUR TOPS	1144
	45. CHUBBY CHECKER	1142
	46. BROOK BENTON	1125
	47. THE PLATTERS	1125
⌂	48. KOOL & THE GANG	1120
⌂	49. MADONNA	1117
⌂	50. PRINCE	1114

⌂ - moved up 5 or more notches since last *Top 40 Hits* edition
* - higher ranking due to combining an artist's solo and group hits
NEW - new entry since last *Top 40 Hits* edition

The Top 100 artists are compiled from those records that peaked on the pop charts from 1955 through 1988. Points are awarded according to the following formula:

1. Each artist's charted singles are given points based on their highest charted position (#1 = 40; 2 = 39 points, etc.).
2. Bonus points are awarded to each single based on its highest charted position (#1-5 = 25; #6-10 = 20; #11-20 = 15; #21-30 = 10; #31-40 = 5).
3. Total weeks charted are added in.
4. Total weeks a single held the #1 position are also added in.

When two artists combine for a hit record, such as Aretha Franklin and George Michael, the full point value is given to both artists. A duo, such as Hall & Oates, is considered a regular recording team, and the points are not shared by either artist individually.

THE TOP 100 ARTISTS 1955-1988

	ARTIST	POINTS
	51. DONNA SUMMER	1108
	52. BOBBY DARIN	1079
	53. NEIL SEDAKA	1078
	54. ANDY WILLIAMS	1077
	55. BARBRA STREISAND	1062
*	56. DION (DION & THE BELMONTS)	1052
⌂	57. LIONEL RICHIE	1037
	58. BOB SEGER	1024
⌂	59. FLEETWOOD MAC	1018
	60. ROY ORBISON	995
⌂	61. FOREIGNER	995
	62. HERMAN'S HERMITS	992
	63. BOBBY RYDELL	980
	64. EAGLES	979
	65. LINDA RONSTADT	964
⌂	66. JOHN COUGAR MELLENCAMP	962
	67. COMMODORES	956
	68. THE 5TH DIMENSION	952
NEW	69. HUEY LEWIS & THE NEWS	951
	70. JACKIE WILSON	941
	71. JOHNNY MATHIS	941
	72. ELECTRIC LIGHT ORCHESTRA	939
	73. THE DAVE CLARK FIVE	917
	74. POINTER SISTERS	905
NEW	75. BRUCE SPRINGSTEEN	888
	76. JOHNNY RIVERS	882
	77. SIMON & GARFUNKEL	874
	78. SPINNERS	873
NEW	79. JEFFERSON STARSHIP (JEFFERSON AIRPLANE/STARSHIP)	870
	80. JOURNEY	849
*	81. TOMMY JAMES & THE SHONDELLS	848
	82. TOM JONES	832
	83. EARTH, WIND & FIRE	829
	84. CREEDENCE CLEARWATER REVIVAL	826
	85. RICK SPRINGFIELD	819
NEW	86. HEART	816
	87. JOHN LENNON (PLASTIC ONO BAND)	803
	88. JOHN DENVER	793
	89. PHIL COLLINS	793
NEW	90. DURAN DURAN	788
	91. PATTI PAGE	780
NEW	92. WHITNEY HOUSTON	778
NEW	93. CHER	772
	94. HELEN REDDY	767
	95. THE DRIFTERS	766
	96. THE IMPRESSIONS	765
	97. PAUL REVERE & THE RAIDERS	741
	98. GLEN CAMPBELL	737
	99. PETULA CLARK	737
NEW	100. HERB ALPERT (& THE TIJUANA BRASS)	731

TOP ARTISTS BY DECADE

FIFTIES ('55-'59)

ARTIST	POINTS
1. ELVIS PRESLEY	1997
2. PAT BOONE	1781
3. PERRY COMO	1232
4. RICKY NELSON	1081
5. FATS DOMINO	1071
6. THE PLATTERS	890
7. NAT KING COLE	876
8. FRANK SINATRA	765
9. THE EVERLY BROTHERS	695
10. THE FOUR LADS	682
11. JOHNNY MATHIS	671
12. PATTI PAGE	670
13. BILL HALEY & HIS COMETS	627
14. THE McGUIRE SISTERS	615
15. THE DIAMONDS	590
16. PAUL ANKA	582
17. TERESA BREWER	558
18. ANDY WILLIAMS	532
19. FRANKIE AVALON	530
20. JIMMIE RODGERS	522
21. CONNIE FRANCIS	504
22. THE FONTANE SISTERS	504
23. SARAH VAUGHAN	484
24. THE CREW-CUTS	469
25. THE AMES BROTHERS	457

SIXTIES ('60-'69)

ARTIST	POINTS
1. THE BEATLES	2729
2. ELVIS PRESLEY	2309
3. THE SUPREMES	1554
4. BRENDA LEE	1401
5. THE BEACH BOYS	1400
6. THE 4 SEASONS	1390
7. MARVIN GAYE	1271
8. THE TEMPTATIONS	1222
9. CONNIE FRANCIS	1183
10. RAY CHARLES	1146
11. BOBBY VINTON	1096
12. CHUBBY CHECKER	1084
13. THE ROLLING STONES	1059
14. ROY ORBISON	995
15. HERMAN'S HERMITS	992
16. THE DAVE CLARK FIVE	917
17. THE MIRACLES	901
18. ARETHA FRANKLIN	900
19. JAMES BROWN	892
20. SAM COOKE	888
21. DION (DION & THE BELMONTS)	887
22. BOBBY RYDELL	857
23. DIONNE WARWICK	813
24. BROOK BENTON	795
25. STEVIE WONDER	794

SEVENTIES ('70-'79)

ARTIST	POINTS
1. ELTON JOHN	1434
2. PAUL McCARTNEY (& WINGS)	1391
3. BEE GEES	1227
4. CHICAGO	1189
5. CARPENTERS	1175
6. THE JACKSON 5	1079
7. STEVIE WONDER	1076
8. THREE DOG NIGHT	964
9. OLIVIA NEWTON-JOHN	944
10. BARRY MANILOW	906
11. NEIL DIAMOND	878
12. EAGLES	812
13. ELVIS PRESLEY	798
14. GLADYS KNIGHT & THE PIPS	780
15. HELEN REDDY	767
16. JOHN DENVER	759
17. DIANA ROSS	730
18. DONNA SUMMER	723
19. ARETHA FRANKLIN	715
20. AL GREEN	706
21. DAWN	703
22. EARTH, WIND & FIRE	701
23. SPINNERS	675
24. BREAD	661
25. MARVIN GAYE	660

EIGHTIES ('80-'88)

ARTIST	POINTS
1. DARYL HALL & JOHN OATES	1294
2. MICHAEL JACKSON	1277
3. MADONNA	1117
4. PRINCE	1114
5. LIONEL RICHIE	1037
6. BILLY JOEL	993
7. HUEY LEWIS & THE NEWS	951
8. JOHN COUGAR MELLENCAMP	931
9. KOOL & THE GANG	923
10. ELTON JOHN	860
11. BRUCE SPRINGSTEEN	840
12. JOURNEY	797
13. PHIL COLLINS	793
14. DURAN DURAN	788
15. KENNY ROGERS	781
16. WHITNEY HOUSTON	778
17. RICK SPRINGFIELD	768
18. STEVIE WONDER	698
19. AIR SUPPLY	696
20. DIANA ROSS	689
21. BILLY OCEAN	670
22. BOB SEGER	661
23. CHICAGO	661
24. POINTER SISTERS	648
25. PAT BENATAR	647

TOP ARTIST ACHIEVEMENTS

MOST CHARTED RECORDS

ARTIST	POINTS
1. ELVIS PRESLEY	107
2. THE BEATLES	49
3. STEVIE WONDER	45
4. JAMES BROWN	44
5. ELTON JOHN	42
6. ARETHA FRANKLIN	40
7. MARVIN GAYE	40
8. THE ROLLING STONES	39
9. PAT BOONE	38
10. NEIL DIAMOND	37
11. THE TEMPTATIONS	37
12. FATS DOMINO	37
13. RICKY NELSON	35
14. CONNIE FRANCIS	35
15. PAUL McCARTNEY	34
16. THE SUPREMES	33
17. THE BEACH BOYS	33
18. PAUL ANKA	33
19. RAY CHARLES	32
20. CHICAGO	31
21. DIONNE WARWICK	31
22. THE 4 SEASONS	30
23. BOBBY VINTON	30
24. PERRY COMO	29
25. BRENDA LEE	29
26. SAM COOKE	29
27. THE MIRACLES	29

MOST #1 RECORDS

ARTIST	POINTS
1. THE BEATLES	20
2. ELVIS PRESLEY	18
3. THE SUPREMES	12
4. MICHAEL JACKSON	11
5. STEVIE WONDER	9
6. PAUL McCARTNEY	9
7. BEE GEES	9
8. THE ROLLING STONES	8
9. WHITNEY HOUSTON	7
10. ELTON JOHN	6
11. PAT BOONE	6
12. DARYL HALL & JOHN OATES	6
13. DIANA ROSS	6
14. MADONNA	6
15. OLIVIA NEWTON-JOHN	5
16. THE 4 SEASONS	5
17. LIONEL RICHIE	5
18. BARBRA STREISAND	5
19. EAGLES	5
20. KC & THE SUNSHINE BAND	5
21. THE TEMPTATIONS	4
22. THE EVERLY BROTHERS	4
23. THE JACKSON 5	4
24. BOBBY VINTON	4
25. DONNA SUMMER	4
26. THE PLATTERS	4
27. JOHN DENVER	4
28. PHIL COLLINS	4
29. GEORGE MICHAEL	4
30. BLONDIE	4

MOST TOP 10 RECORDS

ARTIST	POINTS
1. ELVIS PRESLEY	38
2. THE BEATLES	33
3. STEVIE WONDER	27
4. ELTON JOHN	22
5. THE ROLLING STONES	22
6. PAUL McCARTNEY	22
7. THE SUPREMES	20
8. MICHAEL JACKSON	20
9. RICKY NELSON	19
10. PAT BOONE	18
11. MARVIN GAYE	18
12. ARETHA FRANKLIN	17
13. CHICAGO	17
14. CONNIE FRANCIS	16
15. DARYL HALL & JOHN OATES	16
16. THE TEMPTATIONS	15
17. OLIVIA NEWTON-JOHN	15
18. THE 4 SEASONS	15
19. THE EVERLY BROTHERS	15
20. BEE GEES	14
21. THE BEACH BOYS	14
22. MADONNA	14
23. NEIL DIAMOND	13
24. PRINCE	13
25. DONNA SUMMER	13
26. LIONEL RICHIE	13

MOST WEEKS HELD #1 POSITION

ARTIST	POINTS
1. ELVIS PRESLEY	80
2. THE BEATLES	59
3. PAUL McCARTNEY	30
4. MICHAEL JACKSON	29
5. BEE GEES	27
6. THE SUPREMES	22
7. STEVIE WONDER	21
8. PAT BOONE	21
9. LIONEL RICHIE	21
10. DIANA ROSS	20
11. OLIVIA NEWTON-JOHN	18
12. THE 4 SEASONS	18
13. THE ROLLING STONES	17
14. ROD STEWART	17
15. ELTON JOHN	15
16. THE EVERLY BROTHERS	15
17. DARYL HALL & JOHN OATES	14
18. THE McGUIRE SISTERS	14
19. DONNA SUMMER	13
20. BARBRA STREISAND	13
21. WHITNEY HOUSTON	13
22. ANDY GIBB	13
23. BOBBY VINTON	12
24. MADONNA	12
25. THE MONKEES	12
26. ROBERTA FLACK	12
27. GUY MITCHELL	12

TOP RECORDS BY DECADE

YR	WEEKS CHR	T40	T10	#1	TITLE/ARTIST
					FIFTIES ('55-'59)
56	28	24	21	11	1. DON'T BE CRUEL/HOUND DOG Elvis Presley
55	26	26	20	10	2. CHERRY PINK AND APPLE BLOSSOM WHITE Perez Prado
55	21	21	18	10	3. SINCERELY The McGuire Sisters
56	26	22	17	10	4. SINGING THE BLUES Guy Mitchell
59	26	22	16	9	5. MACK THE KNIFE Bobby Darin
57	30	22	15	9	6. ALL SHOOK UP Elvis Presley
55	24	24	19	8	7. ROCK AROUND THE CLOCK Bill Haley & His Comets
56	28	22	16	8	8. THE WAYWARD WIND Gogi Grant
55	22	19	16	8	9. SIXTEEN TONS Tennessee Ernie Ford
56	27	22	15	8	10. HEARTBREAK HOTEL Elvis Presley
57	34	24	17	7	11. LOVE LETTERS IN THE SAND Pat Boone
57	27	19	15	7	12. JAILHOUSE ROCK Elvis Presley
57	25	18	14	7	13. (LET ME BE YOUR) TEDDY BEAR Elvis Presley
58	21	18	12	7	14. AT THE HOP Danny & The Juniors
55	21	21	17	6	15. LOVE IS A MANY-SPLENDORED THING Four Aces
56	25	20	16	6	16. ROCK AND ROLL WALTZ Kay Starr
55	19	19	16	6	17. THE YELLOW ROSE OF TEXAS Mitch Miller
56	24	20	15	6	18. THE POOR PEOPLE OF PARIS Les Baxter
56	24	19	15	6	19. MEMORIES ARE MADE OF THIS Dean Martin
57	26	19	14	6	20. APRIL LOVE Pat Boone
59	21	18	13	6	21. THE BATTLE OF NEW ORLEANS Johnny Horton
57	21	17	13	6	22. YOUNG LOVE Tab Hunter
58	22	19	12	6	23. IT'S ALL IN THE GAME Tommy Edwards
58	14	14	10	6	24. THE PURPLE PEOPLE EATER Sheb Wooley
57	31	23	16	5	25. TAMMY Debbie Reynolds
					SIXTIES ('60-'69)
68	19	19	14	9	1. HEY JUDE The Beatles
60	21	17	12	9	2. THE THEME FROM "A SUMMER PLACE" Percy Faith
61	23	17	12	7	3. TOSSIN' AND TURNIN' Bobby Lewis
64	15	14	12	7	4. I WANT TO HOLD YOUR HAND The Beatles
66	15	13	12	7	5. I'M A BELIEVER The Monkees
68	15	15	11	7	6. I HEARD IT THROUGH THE GRAPEVINE Marvin Gaye
69	17	16	11	6	7. AQUARIUS/LET THE SUNSHINE IN The 5th Dimension
60	16	14	11	6	8. ARE YOU LONESOME TO-NIGHT? Elvis Presley
69	13	12	9	6	9. IN THE YEAR 2525 (EXORDIUM & TERMINUS) Zager & Evans
60	20	16	11	5	10. IT'S NOW OR NEVER Elvis Presley
62	18	14	11	5	11. I CAN'T STOP LOVING YOU Ray Charles
68	18	15	10	5	12. LOVE IS BLUE Paul Mauriat
62	16	14	10	5	13. BIG GIRLS DON'T CRY The 4 Seasons
61	16	13	10	5	14. BIG BAD JOHN Jimmy Dean
63	15	13	10	5	15. SUGAR SHACK Jimmy Gilmer & The Fireballs
68	15	13	10	5	16. HONEY Bobby Goldsboro
67	17	15	9	5	17. TO SIR WITH LOVE Lulu
60	17	13	9	5	18. CATHY'S CLOWN The Everly Brothers
68	14	13	9	5	19. PEOPLE GOT TO BE FREE The Rascals
69	12	12	9	5	20. GET BACK The Beatles
66	13	11	9	5	21. THE BALLAD OF THE GREEN BERETS SSgt Barry Sadler
62	14	12	7	5	22. SHERRY The 4 Seasons
64	10	9	6	5	23. CAN'T BUY ME LOVE The Beatles
69	22	18	12	4	24. SUGAR, SUGAR The Archies
68	16	14	11	4	25. (SITTIN' ON) THE DOCK OF THE BAY Otis Redding

TOP RECORDS BY DECADE

YR	WEEKS CHR	T40	T10	#1	TITLE/ARTIST
					SEVENTIES ('70-'79)
77	25	21	14	10	1. YOU LIGHT UP MY LIFE Debby Boone
78	20	18	13	8	2. NIGHT FEVER Bee Gees
76	23	17	11	8	3. TONIGHT'S THE NIGHT (GONNA BE ALRIGHT) Rod Stewart
78	25	19	12	7	4. SHADOW DANCING Andy Gibb
78	25	19	15	6	5. LE FREAK Chic
79	22	16	12	6	6. MY SHARONA The Knack
72	18	15	11	6	7. THE FIRST TIME EVER I SAW YOUR FACE Roberta Flack
72	18	15	11	6	8. ALONE AGAIN (NATURALLY) Gilbert O'Sullivan
71	17	15	11	6	9. JOY TO THE WORLD Three Dog Night
70	14	13	10	6	10. BRIDGE OVER TROUBLED WATER Simon & Garfunkel
77	23	17	12	5	11. BEST OF MY LOVE The Emotions
70	16	16	11	5	12. I'LL BE THERE The Jackson 5
76	19	15	11	5	13. SILLY LOVE SONGS Wings
71	17	15	11	5	14. MAGGIE MAY Rod Stewart
79	20	15	10	5	15. BAD GIRLS Donna Summer
71	17	15	10	5	16. IT'S TOO LATE Carole King
73	16	13	9	5	17. KILLING ME SOFTLY WITH HIS SONG Roberta Flack
71	15	12	9	5	18. ONE BAD APPLE The Osmonds
77	31	23	16	4	19. I JUST WANT TO BE YOUR EVERYTHING Andy Gibb
78	27	22	13	4	20. STAYIN' ALIVE Bee Gees
70	22	19	13	4	21. RAINDROPS KEEP FALLIN' ON MY HEAD B.J. Thomas
79	21	18	12	4	22. DA YA THINK I'M SEXY? Rod Stewart
78	23	17	12	4	23. KISS YOU ALL OVER Exile
73	23	17	11	4	24. TIE A YELLOW RIBBON ROUND THE OLE OAK TREE Dawn featuring Tony Orlando
72	19	17	11	4	25. AMERICAN PIE - Parts I & II Don McLean
					EIGHTIES ('80-'88)
81	26	21	15	10	1. PHYSICAL Olivia Newton-John
81	26	20	14	9	2. BETTE DAVIS EYES Kim Carnes
81	27	19	13	9	3. ENDLESS LOVE Diana Ross & Lionel Richie
83	22	20	13	8	4. EVERY BREATH YOU TAKE The Police
82	20	16	12	7	5. I LOVE ROCK 'N ROLL Joan Jett & The Blackhearts
82	19	15	12	7	6. EBONY AND IVORY Paul McCartney with Stevie Wonder
83	24	17	11	7	7. BILLIE JEAN Michael Jackson
82	25	18	15	6	8. EYE OF THE TIGER Survivor
83	25	20	14	6	9. FLASHDANCE...WHAT A FEELING Irene Cara
80	25	19	13	6	10. LADY Kenny Rogers
83	22	18	13	6	11. SAY SAY SAY Paul McCartney & Michael Jackson
82	25	20	12	6	12. CENTERFOLD The J. Geils Band
80	25	19	12	6	13. CALL ME Blondie
84	19	14	9	6	14. LIKE A VIRGIN Madonna
80	22	19	14	5	15. (JUST LIKE) STARTING OVER John Lennon
84	21	16	11	5	16. WHEN DOVES CRY Prince
84	21	15	10	5	17. JUMP Van Halen
80	29	17	14	4	18. UPSIDE DOWN Diana Ross
83	24	17	13	4	19. ALL NIGHT LONG (ALL NIGHT) Lionel Richie
82	23	17	13	4	20. MANEATER Daryl Hall & John Oates
80	25	19	12	4	21. ANOTHER BRICK IN THE WALL (PART II) Pink Floyd
80	22	17	12	4	22. CRAZY LITTLE THING CALLED LOVE Queen
83	29	18	11	4	23. TOTAL ECLIPSE OF THE HEART Bonnie Tyler
83	25	19	10	4	24. DOWN UNDER Men At Work
86	23	17	10	4	25. THAT'S WHAT FRIENDS ARE FOR Dionne & Friends

#1 RECORDS LISTED CHRONOLOGICALLY 1955-1988

For the years 1955 through 1958 (when *Billboard* published more than one weekly pop chart) special columns are used to show the weeks each #1 record spent on each of the various pop charts.

The date shown is the earliest date that a record hit #1 on any of the pop charts. The weeks column (next to date) lists the total weeks at #1, from whichever chart it achieved its highest total. This total is not a combined total from the various pop charts.

Because of the multiple charts used in our research, some dates are duplicated, as certain #1 hits may have peaked on the same week on different charts. *Billboard* also showed ties at #1 on some of these charts, therefore the total weeks for each year may calculate out to more than 52.

Lines are drawn in on the charts column to show when any of the four pop charts were not published.

See the introduction of this book for more details about researching the four pop charts.

DATE : Date record first hit the #1 position
WKS : Total weeks record held the #1 position
* : Consensus #1 record—hit #1 on all pop charts published ('55-'58)
† : Indicates record hit #1, dropped down, then returned to the #1 spot

CHARTS COLUMN:
BS : Best Sellers
JY : Jockeys
JB : Juke Box
TP : Top 100
HT : Hot 100

744 records have hit the #1 position on *Billboard*'s pop charts from 1955 through 1988. "The Twist," even though it hit #1 in 1960 and again in 1962, is counted only once. There have been 678 #1 records since the Hot 100 chart began in 1958.

Billboard has not published an issue at the end of the year since 1976; therefore, the year's last regular chart is considered frozen and the #1 hit remains the same for the unpublished week. This frozen week is included when calculating total weeks at #1.

DATE	WKS	RECORD TITLE	ARTIST	BS	JY	JB	TP
		1955					
1/01	4	* 1. LET ME GO LOVER	Joan Weber	2	4†	4	—
2/05	3	2. HEARTS OF STONE	The Fontane Sisters	1	—	3	—
2/12	10	* 3. SINCERELY	The McGuire Sisters	6	10	7	—
3/26	5	* 4. THE BALLAD OF DAVY CROCKETT	Bill Hayes	5	3	3	—
4/30	10	* 5. CHERRY PINK AND APPLE BLOSSOM WHITE	Perez Prado	10	6†	8	—
5/14	3	6. DANCE WITH ME HENRY	Georgia Gibbs	—	—	3	—
5/14	2	7. UNCHAINED MELODY	Les Baxter	—	2†	—	—
7/09	8	* 8. ROCK AROUND THE CLOCK	Bill Haley & His Comets	8	6†	7	—
7/09	2	9. LEARNIN' THE BLUES	Frank Sinatra	—	2†	—	—
9/03	6	* 10. THE YELLOW ROSE OF TEXAS	Mitch Miller	6†	6	6	—
9/17	2	11. AIN'T THAT A SHAME	Pat Boone	—	—	2	—
10/08	6	* 12. LOVE IS A MANY-SPLENDORED THING (Top 100 chart debuted on 11/12/55)	Four Aces	2†	6	3	3
10/29	4	13. AUTUMN LEAVES	Roger Williams	4	—	—	—
11/26	8	* 14. SIXTEEN TONS	Tennessee Ernie Ford	7	6	8	6
		1956					
1/07	6	* 1. MEMORIES ARE MADE OF THIS	Dean Martin	5	6	4	5
2/18	6	* 2. ROCK AND ROLL WALTZ	Kay Starr	1	1	6	4
2/18	2	3. THE GREAT PRETENDER	The Platters	—	2	1	2
2/25	4	4. LISBON ANTIGUA	Nelson Riddle	4	2†	—	—
3/17	6	* 5. THE POOR PEOPLE OF PARIS	Les Baxter	4	6†	3	6
4/21	8	* 6. HEARTBREAK HOTEL	Elvis Presley	8	3	8	7
5/05	1	7. HOT DIGGITY	Perry Como	—	1	—	—

DATE	WKS	RECORD TITLE	ARTIST	CHARTS			
		1956 CONTINUED		BS	JY	JB	TP
6/02	3	8. MOONGLOW AND THEME FROM "PICNIC"	Morris Stoloff	—	3	—	—
6/16	8	* 9. THE WAYWARD WIND	Gogi Grant	6	8	4	7
7/28	4	10. I ALMOST LOST MY MIND	Pat Boone	—	—	4	2
7/28	1	11. I WANT YOU, I NEED YOU, I LOVE YOU	Elvis Presley	1	—	—	—
8/04	5	* 12. MY PRAYER	The Platters	2	3	1	5
8/18	11	* 13. DON'T BE CRUEL/ 14. HOUND DOG	Elvis Presley	11	8	11	7
11/03	5	* 15. LOVE ME TENDER	Elvis Presley	5	5	1	4†
11/03	3	16. THE GREEN DOOR	Jim Lowe	—	—	3	3
12/08	10	* 17. SINGING THE BLUES	Guy Mitchell	9	9	10	9
		1957					
2/09	3	1. TOO MUCH	Elvis Presley	3	—	1	—
2/09	1	2. DON'T FORBID ME	Pat Boone	—	—	1	1
2/09	1	3. YOUNG LOVE	Sonny James	—	1	—	—
2/16	6	* 4. YOUNG LOVE	Tab Hunter	4	6	5†	6
3/30	3	5. BUTTERFLY	Andy Williams	—	2	—	3
3/30	1	6. PARTY DOLL	Buddy Knox	1	—	—	—
4/06	2	7. ROUND AND ROUND	Perry Como	1	2	—	1
4/06	2	8. BUTTERFLY	Charlie Gracie	—	—	2	—
4/13	9	* 9. ALL SHOOK UP	Elvis Presley	8	7	9	8
		Juke Box chart terminated on 6/17/57					
6/03	7	* 10. LOVE LETTERS IN THE SAND	Pat Boone	5	7	—	5
7/08	7	* 11. (LET ME BE YOUR) TEDDY BEAR	Elvis Presley	7	3	—	7
8/19	5	* 12. TAMMY	Debbie Reynolds	3†	5	—	5
9/09	1	13. DIANA	Paul Anka	1	—	—	—
9/23	4	* 14. HONEYCOMB	Jimmie Rodgers	2	4	—	2
9/23	1	15. THAT'LL BE THE DAY	The Crickets	1	—	—	—
10/14	4	* 16. WAKE UP LITTLE SUSIE	The Everly Brothers	1	4	—	2
10/21	7	* 17. JAILHOUSE ROCK	Elvis Presley	7†	2	—	6
10/21	1	18. CHANCES ARE	Johnny Mathis	—	1	—	—
12/02	3	* 19. YOU SEND ME	Sam Cooke	2	1	—	3
12/16	6	* 20. APRIL LOVE	Pat Boone	2	6	—	1
		1958		BS	JY	JB	HT
1/06	7	* 1. AT THE HOP	Danny & The Juniors	5	3	7	—
2/10	5	* 2. DON'T	Elvis Presley	5	1	1	—
2/17	4	3. SUGARTIME	The McGuire Sisters	—	4	—	—
2/24	2	4. GET A JOB	The Silhouettes	—	—	2	—
3/17	5	* 5. TEQUILA	The Champs	5	2	5	—
3/24	1	6. CATCH A FALLING STAR	Perry Como	—	1	—	—
4/14	4	7. HE'S GOT THE WHOLE WORLD (IN HIS HANDS)	Laurie London	—	4	—	—
4/21	1	* 8. TWILIGHT TIME	The Platters	1	1	1	—
4/28	3	9. WITCH DOCTOR	David Seville	2	—	3	—
5/12	5	* 10. ALL I HAVE TO DO IS DREAM	The Everly Brothers	4	5	3	—
6/09	6	* 11. THE PURPLE PEOPLE EATER	Sheb Wooley	6	4	6	—
7/21	2	12. HARD HEADED WOMAN	Elvis Presley	2	1	—	—
7/21	1	13. YAKETY YAK	The Coasters	—	—	1	—

DATE	WKS	RECORD TITLE	ARTIST	BS	JY	JB	HT
		1958 CONTINUED					
7/28	1	14. PATRICIA Jockeys and Top 100 charts terminated on 7/28/58	Perez Prado	—	1	1	—
8/04	2	* 15. POOR LITTLE FOOL Hot 100 chart debuted on 8/4/58	Ricky Nelson	2	—	—	2
8/18	5	* 16. NEL BLU DIPINTO DI BLU (VOLARE)	Domenico Modugno	5†	—	—	5†
8/25	1	17. LITTLE STAR	The Elegants	—	—	—	1
8/25	1	18. BIRD DOG	The Everly Brothers	1	—	—	—
9/29	6	* 19. IT'S ALL IN THE GAME Best Sellers chart terminated on 10/13/58 Hot 100 chart used exclusively here on	Tommy Edwards	3	—	—	6
11/10	2	20. IT'S ONLY MAKE BELIEVE	Conway Twitty	—	—	—	2†
11/17	1	21. TOM DOOLEY	The Kingston Trio	—	—	—	1
12/01	3	22. TO KNOW HIM, IS TO LOVE HIM	The Teddy Bears	—	—	—	3
12/22	4	23. THE CHIPMUNK SONG	The Chipmunks	—	—	—	4

DATE	WKS	RECORD TITLE	ARTIST
		1959	
1/19	3	1. SMOKE GETS IN YOUR EYES	The Platters
2/09	4	2. STAGGER LEE	Lloyd Price
3/09	5	3. VENUS	Frankie Avalon
4/13	4	4. COME SOFTLY TO ME	The Fleetwoods
5/11	1	5. THE HAPPY ORGAN	Dave 'Baby' Cortez
5/18	2	6. KANSAS CITY	Wilbert Harrison
6/01	6	7. THE BATTLE OF NEW ORLEANS	Johnny Horton
7/13	4	8. LONELY BOY	Paul Anka
8/10	2	9. A BIG HUNK O' LOVE	Elvis Presley
8/24	4	10. THE THREE BELLS	The Browns
9/21	2	11. SLEEP WALK	Santo & Johnny
10/05	9	†12. MACK THE KNIFE	Bobby Darin
11/16	1	13. MR. BLUE	The Fleetwoods
12/14	2	14. HEARTACHES BY THE NUMBER	Guy Mitchell
12/28	1	15. WHY	Frankie Avalon
		1960	
1/04	2	1. EL PASO	Marty Robbins
1/18	3	2. RUNNING BEAR	Johnny Preston
2/08	2	3. TEEN ANGEL	Mark Dinning
2/22	9	4. THE THEME FROM "A SUMMER PLACE"	Percy Faith
4/25	4	5. STUCK ON YOU	Elvis Presley
5/23	5	6. CATHY'S CLOWN	The Everly Brothers
6/27	2	7. EVERYBODY'S SOMEBODY'S FOOL	Connie Francis
7/11	1	8. ALLEY-OOP	Hollywood Argyles
7/18	3	9. I'M SORRY	Brenda Lee
8/08	1	10. ITSY BITSY TEENIE WEENIE YELLOW POLKADOT BIKINI	Brian Hyland
8/15	5	11. IT'S NOW OR NEVER	Elvis Presley
9/19	1	12. THE TWIST re-entered #1 position in 1962 for 2 more weeks	Chubby Checker
9/26	2	13. MY HEART HAS A MIND OF ITS OWN	Connie Francis
10/10	1	14. MR. CUSTER	Larry Verne

DATE	WKS	RECORD TITLE	ARTIST
1960 CONTINUED			
10/17	3	†15. SAVE THE LAST DANCE FOR ME	The Drifters
10/24	1	16. I WANT TO BE WANTED	Brenda Lee
11/14	1	17. GEORGIA ON MY MIND	Ray Charles
11/21	1	18. STAY	Maurice Williams & The Zodiacs
11/28	6	19. ARE YOU LONESOME TO-NIGHT?	Elvis Presley
1961			
1/09	3	1. WONDERLAND BY NIGHT	Bert Kaempfert
1/30	2	2. WILL YOU LOVE ME TOMORROW	The Shirelles
2/13	2	3. CALCUTTA	Lawrence Welk
2/27	3	4. PONY TIME	Chubby Checker
3/20	2	5. SURRENDER	Elvis Presley
4/03	3	6. BLUE MOON	The Marcels
4/24	4	7. RUNAWAY	Del Shannon
5/22	1	8. MOTHER-IN-LAW	Ernie K-Doe
5/29	2	†9. TRAVELIN' MAN	Ricky Nelson
6/05	1	10. RUNNING SCARED	Roy Orbison
6/19	1	11. MOODY RIVER	Pat Boone
6/26	2	12. QUARTER TO THREE	U.S. Bonds
7/10	7	13. TOSSIN' AND TURNIN'	Bobby Lewis
8/28	1	14. WOODEN HEART	Joe Dowell
9/04	2	15. MICHAEL	The Highwaymen
9/18	3	16. TAKE GOOD CARE OF MY BABY	Bobby Vee
10/09	2	17. HIT THE ROAD JACK	Ray Charles
10/23	2	18. RUNAROUND SUE	Dion
11/06	5	19. BIG BAD JOHN	Jimmy Dean
12/11	1	20. PLEASE MR. POSTMAN	The Marvelettes
12/18	3	21. THE LION SLEEPS TONIGHT	The Tokens
1962			
1/13	2	1. THE TWIST first entered #1 position in 1960 for 1 week	Chubby Checker
1/27	3	2. PEPPERMINT TWIST	Joey Dee & The Starliters
2/17	3	3. DUKE OF EARL	Gene Chandler
3/10	3	4. HEY! BABY	Bruce Channel
3/31	1	5. DON'T BREAK THE HEART THAT LOVES YOU	Connie Francis
4/07	2	6. JOHNNY ANGEL	Shelley Fabares
4/21	2	7. GOOD LUCK CHARM	Elvis Presley
5/05	3	8. SOLDIER BOY	The Shirelles
5/26	1	9. STRANGER ON THE SHORE	Mr. Acker Bilk
6/02	5	10. I CAN'T STOP LOVING YOU	Ray Charles
7/07	1	11. THE STRIPPER	David Rose
7/14	4	12. ROSES ARE RED (MY LOVE)	Bobby Vinton
8/11	2	13. BREAKING UP IS HARD TO DO	Neil Sedaka
8/25	1	14. THE LOCO-MOTION	Little Eva
9/01	2	15. SHEILA	Tommy Roe
9/15	5	16. SHERRY	The 4 Seasons
10/20	2	17. MONSTER MASH	Bobby "Boris" Pickett
11/03	2	18. HE'S A REBEL	The Crystals
11/17	5	19. BIG GIRLS DON'T CRY	The 4 Seasons
12/22	3	20. TELSTAR	The Tornadoes

DATE	WKS	RECORD TITLE	ARTIST
1963			
1/12	2	1. GO AWAY LITTLE GIRL	Steve Lawrence
1/26	2	2. WALK RIGHT IN	The Rooftop Singers
2/09	3	3. HEY PAULA	Paul & Paula
3/02	3	4. WALK LIKE A MAN	The 4 Seasons
3/23	1	5. OUR DAY WILL COME	Ruby & The Romantics
3/30	4	6. HE'S SO FINE	The Chiffons
4/27	3	7. I WILL FOLLOW HIM	Little Peggy March
5/18	2	8. IF YOU WANNA BE HAPPY	Jimmy Soul
6/01	2	9. IT'S MY PARTY	Lesley Gore
6/15	3	10. SUKIYAKI	Kyu Sakamoto
7/06	2	11. EASIER SAID THAN DONE	The Essex
7/20	2	12. SURF CITY	Jan & Dean
8/03	1	13. SO MUCH IN LOVE	The Tymes
8/10	3	14. FINGERTIPS - PT 2	Little Stevie Wonder
8/31	3	15. MY BOYFRIEND'S BACK	The Angels
9/21	3	16. BLUE VELVET	Bobby Vinton
10/12	5	17. SUGAR SHACK	Jimmy Gilmer & The Fireballs
11/16	1	18. DEEP PURPLE	Nino Tempo & April Stevens
11/23	2	19. I'M LEAVING IT UP TO YOU	Dale & Grace
12/07	4	20. DOMINIQUE	The Singing Nun
1964			
1/04	4	1. THERE! I'VE SAID IT AGAIN	Bobby Vinton
2/01	7	2. I WANT TO HOLD YOUR HAND	The Beatles
3/21	2	3. SHE LOVES YOU	The Beatles
4/04	5	4. CAN'T BUY ME LOVE	The Beatles
5/09	1	5. HELLO, DOLLY!	Louis Armstrong
5/16	2	6. MY GUY	Mary Wells
5/30	1	7. LOVE ME DO	The Beatles
6/06	3	8. CHAPEL OF LOVE	The Dixie Cups
6/27	1	9. A WORLD WITHOUT LOVE	Peter & Gordon
7/04	2	10. I GET AROUND	The Beach Boys
7/18	2	11. RAG DOLL	The 4 Seasons
8/01	2	12. A HARD DAY'S NIGHT	The Beatles
8/15	1	13. EVERYBODY LOVES SOMEBODY	Dean Martin
8/22	2	14. WHERE DID OUR LOVE GO	The Supremes
9/05	3	15. THE HOUSE OF THE RISING SUN	The Animals
9/26	3	16. OH, PRETTY WOMAN	Roy Orbison
10/17	2	17. DO WAH DIDDY DIDDY	Manfred Mann
10/31	4	18. BABY LOVE	The Supremes
11/28	1	19. LEADER OF THE PACK	The Shangri-Las
12/05	1	20. RINGO	Lorne Greene
12/12	1	21. MR. LONELY	Bobby Vinton
12/19	2	†22. COME SEE ABOUT ME	The Supremes
12/26	3	23. I FEEL FINE	The Beatles

DATE	WKS	RECORD TITLE	ARTIST
1965			
1/23	2	1. DOWNTOWN	Petula Clark
2/06	2	2. YOU'VE LOST THAT LOVIN' FEELIN'	The Righteous Brothers
2/20	2	3. THIS DIAMOND RING	Gary Lewis & The Playboys
3/06	1	4. MY GIRL	The Temptations
3/13	2	5. EIGHT DAYS A WEEK	The Beatles
3/27	2	6. STOP! IN THE NAME OF LOVE	The Supremes
4/10	2	7. I'M TELLING YOU NOW	Freddie & The Dreamers
4/24	1	8. GAME OF LOVE	Wayne Fontana & The Mindbenders
5/01	3	9. MRS. BROWN YOU'VE GOT A LOVELY DAUGHTER	Herman's Hermits
5/22	1	10. TICKET TO RIDE	The Beatles
5/29	2	11. HELP ME, RHONDA	The Beach Boys
6/12	1	12. BACK IN MY ARMS AGAIN	The Supremes
6/19	2	†13. I CAN'T HELP MYSELF	Four Tops
6/26	1	14. MR. TAMBOURINE MAN	The Byrds
7/10	4	15. (I CAN'T GET NO) SATISFACTION	The Rolling Stones
8/07	1	16. I'M HENRY VIII, I AM	Herman's Hermits
8/14	3	17. I GOT YOU BABE	Sonny & Cher
9/04	3	18. HELP!	The Beatles
9/25	1	19. EVE OF DESTRUCTION	Barry McGuire
10/02	1	20. HANG ON SLOOPY	The McCoys
10/09	4	21. YESTERDAY	The Beatles
11/06	2	22. GET OFF OF MY CLOUD	The Rolling Stones
11/20	2	23. I HEAR A SYMPHONY	The Supremes
12/04	3	24. TURN! TURN! TURN!	The Byrds
12/25	1	25. OVER AND OVER	The Dave Clark Five
1966			
1/01	2	†1. THE SOUNDS OF SILENCE	Simon & Garfunkel
1/08	3	†2. WE CAN WORK IT OUT	The Beatles
2/05	2	3. MY LOVE	Petula Clark
2/19	1	4. LIGHTNIN' STRIKES	Lou Christie
2/26	1	5. THESE BOOTS ARE MADE FOR WALKIN'	Nancy Sinatra
3/05	5	6. THE BALLAD OF THE GREEN BERETS	SSgt Barry Sadler
4/09	3	7. (YOU'RE MY) SOUL AND INSPIRATION	The Righteous Brothers
4/30	1	8. GOOD LOVIN'	The Young Rascals
5/07	3	9. MONDAY, MONDAY	The Mamas & The Papas
5/28	2	10. WHEN A MAN LOVES A WOMAN	Percy Sledge
6/11	2	11. PAINT IT, BLACK	The Rolling Stones
6/25	2	†12. PAPERBACK WRITER	The Beatles
7/02	1	13. STRANGERS IN THE NIGHT	Frank Sinatra
7/16	2	14. HANKY PANKY	Tommy James & The Shondells
7/30	2	15. WILD THING	The Troggs
8/13	3	16. SUMMER IN THE CITY	The Lovin' Spoonful
9/03	1	17. SUNSHINE SUPERMAN	Donovan
9/10	2	18. YOU CAN'T HURRY LOVE	The Supremes
9/24	3	19. CHERISH	The Association
10/15	2	20. REACH OUT I'LL BE THERE	Four Tops

DATE	WKS	RECORD TITLE	ARTIST
1966 CONTINUED			
10/29	1	21. 96 TEARS	? & The Mysterians
11/05	1	22. LAST TRAIN TO CLARKSVILLE	The Monkees
11/12	1	23. POOR SIDE OF TOWN	Johnny Rivers
11/19	2	24. YOU KEEP ME HANGIN' ON	The Supremes
12/03	3	†25. WINCHESTER CATHEDRAL	The New Vaudeville Band
12/10	1	26. GOOD VIBRATIONS	The Beach Boys
12/31	7	27. I'M A BELIEVER	The Monkees
1967			
2/18	2	1. KIND OF A DRAG	The Buckinghams
3/04	1	2. RUBY TUESDAY	The Rolling Stones
3/11	1	3. LOVE IS HERE AND NOW YOU'RE GONE	The Supremes
3/18	1	4. PENNY LANE	The Beatles
3/25	3	5. HAPPY TOGETHER	The Turtles
4/15	4	6. SOMETHIN' STUPID	Nancy & Frank Sinatra
5/13	1	7. THE HAPPENING	The Supremes
5/20	4	†8. GROOVIN'	The Young Rascals
6/03	2	9. RESPECT	Aretha Franklin
7/01	4	10. WINDY	The Association
7/29	3	11. LIGHT MY FIRE	The Doors
8/19	1	12. ALL YOU NEED IS LOVE	The Beatles
8/26	4	13. ODE TO BILLIE JOE	Bobbie Gentry
9/23	4	14. THE LETTER	The Box Tops
10/21	5	15. TO SIR WITH LOVE	Lulu
11/25	1	16. INCENSE AND PEPPERMINTS	Strawberry Alarm Clock
12/02	4	17. DAYDREAM BELIEVER	The Monkees
12/30	3	18. HELLO GOODBYE	The Beatles
1968			
1/20	2	1. JUDY IN DISGUISE (WITH GLASSES)	John Fred & His Playboy Band
2/03	1	2. GREEN TAMBOURINE	The Lemon Pipers
2/10	5	3. LOVE IS BLUE	Paul Mauriat
3/16	4	4. (SITTIN' ON) THE DOCK OF THE BAY	Otis Redding
4/13	5	5. HONEY	Bobby Goldsboro
5/18	2	6. TIGHTEN UP	Archie Bell & The Drells
6/01	3	7. MRS. ROBINSON	Simon & Garfunkel
6/22	4	8. THIS GUY'S IN LOVE WITH YOU	Herb Alpert
7/20	2	9. GRAZING IN THE GRASS	Hugh Masekela
8/03	2	10. HELLO, I LOVE YOU	The Doors
8/17	5	11. PEOPLE GOT TO BE FREE	The Rascals
9/21	1	12. HARPER VALLEY P.T.A.	Jeannie C. Riley
9/28	9	13. HEY JUDE	The Beatles
11/30	2	14. LOVE CHILD	Diana Ross & The Supremes
12/14	7	15. I HEARD IT THROUGH THE GRAPEVINE	Marvin Gaye

DATE	WKS	RECORD TITLE	ARTIST
1969			
2/01	2	1. CRIMSON AND CLOVER	Tommy James & The Shondells
2/15	4	2. EVERYDAY PEOPLE	Sly & The Family Stone
3/15	4	3. DIZZY	Tommy Roe
4/12	6	4. AQUARIUS/LET THE SUNSHINE IN	The 5th Dimension
5/24	5	5. GET BACK	The Beatles
6/28	2	6. LOVE THEME FROM ROMEO & JULIET	Henry Mancini
7/12	6	7. IN THE YEAR 2525 (EXORDIUM & TERMINUS)	Zager & Evans
8/23	4	8. HONKY TONK WOMEN	The Rolling Stones
9/20	4	9. SUGAR, SUGAR	The Archies
10/18	2	10. I CAN'T GET NEXT TO YOU	The Temptations
11/01	1	11. SUSPICIOUS MINDS	Elvis Presley
11/08	3	12. WEDDING BELL BLUES	The 5th Dimension
11/29	1	13. COME TOGETHER	The Beatles
12/06	2	14. NA NA HEY HEY KISS HIM GOODBYE	Steam
12/20	1	15. LEAVING ON A JET PLANE	Peter, Paul & Mary
12/27	1	16. SOMEDAY WE'LL BE TOGETHER	Diana Ross & The Supremes
1970			
1/03	4	1. RAINDROPS KEEP FALLIN' ON MY HEAD	B.J. Thomas
1/31	1	2. I WANT YOU BACK	The Jackson 5
2/07	1	3. VENUS	The Shocking Blue
2/14	2	4. THANK YOU (FALETTINME BE MICE ELF AGIN)	Sly & The Family Stone
2/28	6	5. BRIDGE OVER TROUBLED WATER	Simon & Garfunkel
4/11	2	6. LET IT BE	The Beatles
4/25	2	7. ABC	The Jackson 5
5/09	3	8. AMERICAN WOMAN	The Guess Who
5/30	2	9. EVERYTHING IS BEAUTIFUL	Ray Stevens
6/13	2	10. THE LONG AND WINDING ROAD	The Beatles
6/27	2	11. THE LOVE YOU SAVE	The Jackson 5
7/11	2	12. MAMA TOLD ME (NOT TO COME)	Three Dog Night
7/25	4	13. (THEY LONG TO BE) CLOSE TO YOU	Carpenters
8/22	1	14. MAKE IT WITH YOU	Bread
8/29	3	15. WAR	Edwin Starr
9/19	3	16. AIN'T NO MOUNTAIN HIGH ENOUGH	Diana Ross
10/10	1	17. CRACKLIN' ROSIE	Neil Diamond
10/17	5	18. I'LL BE THERE	The Jackson 5
11/21	3	19. I THINK I LOVE YOU	The Partridge Family
12/12	2	20. THE TEARS OF A CLOWN	Smokey Robinson & The Miracles
12/26	4	21. MY SWEET LORD	George Harrison

DATE	WKS	RECORD TITLE	ARTIST
1971			
1/23	3	1. KNOCK THREE TIMES	Dawn
2/13	5	2. ONE BAD APPLE	The Osmonds
3/20	2	3. ME AND BOBBY MCGEE	Janis Joplin
4/03	2	4. JUST MY IMAGINATION (RUNNING AWAY WITH ME)	The Temptations
4/17	6	5. JOY TO THE WORLD	Three Dog Night
5/29	2	6. BROWN SUGAR	The Rolling Stones
6/12	1	7. WANT ADS	The Honey Cone
6/19	5	8. IT'S TOO LATE	Carole King
7/24	1	9. INDIAN RESERVATION	Raiders
7/31	1	10. YOU'VE GOT A FRIEND	James Taylor
8/07	4	11. HOW CAN YOU MEND A BROKEN HEART	The Bee Gees
9/04	1	12. UNCLE ALBERT/ADMIRAL HALSEY	Paul & Linda McCartney
9/11	3	13. GO AWAY LITTLE GIRL	Donny Osmond
10/02	5	14. MAGGIE MAY	Rod Stewart
11/06	2	15. GYPSYS, TRAMPS & THIEVES	Cher
11/20	2	16. THEME FROM SHAFT	Isaac Hayes
12/04	3	17. FAMILY AFFAIR	Sly & The Family Stone
12/25	3	18. BRAND NEW KEY	Melanie
1972			
1/15	4	1. AMERICAN PIE - PARTS I & II	Don McLean
2/12	1	2. LET'S STAY TOGETHER	Al Green
2/19	4	3. WITHOUT YOU	Nilsson
3/18	1	4. HEART OF GOLD	Neil Young
3/25	3	5. A HORSE WITH NO NAME	America
4/15	6	6. THE FIRST TIME EVER I SAW YOUR FACE	Roberta Flack
5/27	1	7. OH GIRL	Chi-Lites
6/03	1	8. I'LL TAKE YOU THERE	The Staple Singers
6/10	3	9. THE CANDY MAN	Sammy Davis, Jr.
7/01	1	10. SONG SUNG BLUE	Neil Diamond
7/08	3	11. LEAN ON ME	Bill Withers
7/29	6	†12. ALONE AGAIN (NATURALLY)	Gilbert O'Sullivan
8/26	1	13. BRANDY (YOU'RE A FINE GIRL)	Looking Glass
9/16	1	14. BLACK & WHITE	Three Dog Night
9/23	3	15. BABY DON'T GET HOOKED ON ME	Mac Davis
10/14	1	16. BEN	Michael Jackson
10/21	2	17. MY DING-A-LING	Chuck Berry
11/04	4	18. I CAN SEE CLEARLY NOW	Johnny Nash
12/02	1	19. PAPA WAS A ROLLIN' STONE	The Temptations
12/09	1	20. I AM WOMAN	Helen Reddy
12/16	3	21. ME AND MRS. JONES	Billy Paul

DATE	WKS	RECORD TITLE	ARTIST
		1973	
1/06	3	1. YOU'RE SO VAIN	Carly Simon
1/27	1	2. SUPERSTITION	Stevie Wonder
2/03	3	3. CROCODILE ROCK	Elton John
2/24	5	†4. KILLING ME SOFTLY WITH HIS SONG	Roberta Flack
3/24	1	5. LOVE TRAIN	O'Jays
4/07	2	6. THE NIGHT THE LIGHTS WENT OUT IN GEORGIA	Vicki Lawrence
4/21	4	7. TIE A YELLOW RIBBON ROUND THE OLE OAK TREE	Dawn featuring Tony Orlando
5/19	1	8. YOU ARE THE SUNSHINE OF MY LIFE	Stevie Wonder
5/26	1	9. FRANKENSTEIN	The Edgar Winter Group
6/02	4	10. MY LOVE	Paul McCartney & Wings
6/30	1	11. GIVE ME LOVE (GIVE ME PEACE ON EARTH)	George Harrison
7/07	2	12. WILL IT GO ROUND IN CIRCLES	Billy Preston
7/21	2	13. BAD, BAD LEROY BROWN	Jim Croce
8/04	2	14. THE MORNING AFTER	Maureen McGovern
8/18	1	15. TOUCH ME IN THE MORNING	Diana Ross
8/25	2	16. BROTHER LOUIE	Stories
9/08	2	†17. LET'S GET IT ON	Marvin Gaye
9/15	1	18. DELTA DAWN	Helen Reddy
9/29	1	19. WE'RE AN AMERICAN BAND	Grand Funk
10/06	2	20. HALF-BREED	Cher
10/20	1	21. ANGIE	The Rolling Stones
10/27	2	22. MIDNIGHT TRAIN TO GEORGIA	Gladys Knight & The Pips
11/10	2	23. KEEP ON TRUCKIN'	Eddie Kendricks
11/24	1	24. PHOTOGRAPH	Ringo Starr
12/01	2	25. TOP OF THE WORLD	Carpenters
12/15	2	26. THE MOST BEAUTIFUL GIRL	Charlie Rich
12/29	2	27. TIME IN A BOTTLE	Jim Croce

DATE	WKS	RECORD TITLE	ARTIST
1974			
1/12	1	1. THE JOKER	Steve Miller Band
1/19	1	2. SHOW AND TELL	Al Wilson
1/26	1	3. YOU'RE SIXTEEN	Ringo Starr
2/02	3	†4. THE WAY WE WERE	Barbra Streisand
2/09	1	5. LOVE'S THEME	Love Unlimited Orchestra
3/02	3	6. SEASONS IN THE SUN	Terry Jacks
3/23	1	7. DARK LADY	Cher
3/30	1	8. SUNSHINE ON MY SHOULDERS	John Denver
4/06	1	9. HOOKED ON A FEELING	Blue Swede
4/13	1	10. BENNIE AND THE JETS	Elton John
4/20	2	11. TSOP (THE SOUND OF PHILADELPHIA)	MFSB featuring The Three Degrees
5/04	2	12. THE LOCO-MOTION	Grand Funk
5/18	3	13. THE STREAK	Ray Stevens
6/08	1	14. BAND ON THE RUN	Paul McCartney & Wings
6/15	2	15. BILLY, DON'T BE A HERO	Bo Donaldson & The Heywoods
6/29	1	16. SUNDOWN	Gordon Lightfoot
7/06	1	17. ROCK THE BOAT	The Hues Corporation
7/13	2	18. ROCK YOUR BABY	George McCrae
7/27	2	19. ANNIE'S SONG	John Denver
8/10	1	20. FEEL LIKE MAKIN' LOVE	Roberta Flack
8/17	1	21. THE NIGHT CHICAGO DIED	Paper Lace
8/24	3	22. (YOU'RE) HAVING MY BABY	Paul Anka
9/14	1	23. I SHOT THE SHERIFF	Eric Clapton
9/21	1	24. CAN'T GET ENOUGH OF YOUR LOVE, BABE	Barry White
9/28	1	25. ROCK ME GENTLY	Andy Kim
10/05	2	26. I HONESTLY LOVE YOU	Olivia Newton-John
10/19	1	27. NOTHING FROM NOTHING	Billy Preston
10/26	1	28. THEN CAME YOU	Dionne Warwicke & Spinners
11/02	1	29. YOU HAVEN'T DONE NOTHIN	Stevie Wonder
11/09	1	30. YOU AIN'T SEEN NOTHING YET	Bachman-Turner Overdrive
11/16	1	31. WHATEVER GETS YOU THRU THE NIGHT	John Lennon with The Plastic Ono Nuclear Band
11/23	2	32. I CAN HELP	Billy Swan
12/07	2	33. KUNG FU FIGHTING	Carl Douglas
12/21	1	34. CAT'S IN THE CRADLE	Harry Chapin
12/28	1	35. ANGIE BABY	Helen Reddy

DATE	WKS	RECORD TITLE	ARTIST
1975			
1/04	2	1. LUCY IN THE SKY WITH DIAMONDS	Elton John
1/18	1	2. MANDY	Barry Manilow
1/25	1	3. PLEASE MR. POSTMAN	Carpenters
2/01	1	4. LAUGHTER IN THE RAIN	Neil Sedaka
2/08	1	5. FIRE	Ohio Players
2/15	1	6. YOU'RE NO GOOD	Linda Ronstadt
2/22	1	7. PICK UP THE PIECES	AWB
3/01	1	8. BEST OF MY LOVE	The Eagles
3/08	1	9. HAVE YOU NEVER BEEN MELLOW	Olivia Newton-John
3/15	1	10. BLACK WATER	The Doobie Brothers
3/22	1	11. MY EYES ADORED YOU	Frankie Valli
3/29	1	12. LADY MARMALADE	LaBelle
4/05	1	13. LOVIN' YOU	Minnie Riperton
4/12	2	14. PHILADELPHIA FREEDOM	The Elton John Band
4/26	1	15. (HEY WON'T YOU PLAY) ANOTHER SOMEBODY DONE SOMEBODY WRONG SONG	B.J. Thomas
5/03	3	16. HE DON'T LOVE YOU (LIKE I LOVE YOU)	Tony Orlando & Dawn
5/24	1	17. SHINING STAR	Earth, Wind & Fire
5/31	1	18. BEFORE THE NEXT TEARDROP FALLS	Freddy Fender
6/07	1	19. THANK GOD I'M A COUNTRY BOY	John Denver
6/14	1	20. SISTER GOLDEN HAIR	America
6/21	4	21. LOVE WILL KEEP US TOGETHER	The Captain & Tennille
7/19	1	22. LISTEN TO WHAT THE MAN SAID	Wings
7/26	1	23. THE HUSTLE	Van McCoy
8/02	1	24. ONE OF THESE NIGHTS	Eagles
8/09	2	25. JIVE TALKIN'	Bee Gees
8/23	1	26. FALLIN' IN LOVE	Hamilton, Joe Frank & Reynolds
8/30	1	27. GET DOWN TONIGHT	K.C. & The Sunshine Band
9/06	2	28. RHINESTONE COWBOY	Glen Campbell
9/20	2	†29. FAME	David Bowie
9/27	1	30. I'M SORRY	John Denver
10/11	3	31. BAD BLOOD	Neil Sedaka
11/01	3	32. ISLAND GIRL	Elton John
11/22	2	†33. THAT'S THE WAY (I LIKE IT)	KC & The Sunshine Band
11/29	3	34. FLY, ROBIN, FLY	Silver Convention
12/27	1	35. LET'S DO IT AGAIN	The Staple Singers

DATE	WKS	RECORD TITLE	ARTIST
		1976	
1/03	1	1. SATURDAY NIGHT	Bay City Rollers
1/10	1	2. CONVOY	C.W. McCall
1/17	1	3. I WRITE THE SONGS	Barry Manilow
1/24	1	4. THEME FROM MAHOGANY (DO YOU KNOW WHERE YOU'RE GOING TO)	Diana Ross
1/31	1	5. LOVE ROLLERCOASTER	Ohio Players
2/07	3	6. 50 WAYS TO LEAVE YOUR LOVER	Paul Simon
2/28	1	7. THEME FROM S.W.A.T	.Rhythm Heritage
3/06	1	8. LOVE MACHINE (PART 1)	The Miracles
3/13	3	9. DECEMBER, 1963 (OH, WHAT A NIGHT)	The Four Seasons
4/03	4	10. DISCO LADY	Johnnie Taylor
5/01	1	11. LET YOUR LOVE FLOW	Bellamy Brothers
5/08	1	12. WELCOME BACK	John Sebastian
5/15	1	13. BOOGIE FEVER	Sylvers
5/22	5	†14. SILLY LOVE SONGS	Wings
5/29	2	15. LOVE HANGOVER	Diana Ross
7/10	2	16. AFTERNOON DELIGHT	Starland Vocal Band
7/24	2	17. KISS AND SAY GOODBYE	Manhattans
8/07	4	18. DON'T GO BREAKING MY HEART	Elton John & Kiki Dee
9/04	1	19. YOU SHOULD BE DANCING	Bee Gees
9/11	1	20. (SHAKE, SHAKE, SHAKE) SHAKE YOUR BOOTY	KC & The Sunshine Band
9/18	3	21. PLAY THAT FUNKY MUSIC	Wild Cherry
10/09	1	22. A FIFTH OF BEETHOVEN	Walter Murphy & The Big Apple Band
10/16	1	23. DISCO DUCK (PART 1)	Rick Dees & His Cast Of Idiots
10/23	2	24. IF YOU LEAVE ME NOW	Chicago
11/06	1	25. ROCK'N ME	Steve Miller
11/13	8	26. TONIGHT'S THE NIGHT (GONNA BE ALRIGHT)	Rod Stewart
		1977	
1/08	1	1. YOU DON'T HAVE TO BE A STAR (TO BE IN MY SHOW)	Marilyn McCoo & Billy Davis, Jr.
1/15	1	2. YOU MAKE ME FEEL LIKE DANCING	Leo Sayer
1/22	1	3. I WISH	Stevie Wonder
1/29	1	4. CAR WASH	Rose Royce
2/05	2	5. TORN BETWEEN TWO LOVERS	Mary MacGregor
2/19	1	6. BLINDED BY THE LIGHT	Manfred Mann's Earth Band
2/26	1	7. NEW KID IN TOWN	Eagles
3/05	3	8. EVERGREEN	Barbra Streisand
3/26	2	9. RICH GIRL	Daryl Hall & John Oates

DATE	WKS	RECORD TITLE	ARTIST
1977 CONTINUED			
4/09	1	10. DANCING QUEEN	Abba
4/16	1	11. DON'T GIVE UP ON US	David Soul
4/23	1	12. DON'T LEAVE ME THIS WAY	Thelma Houston
4/30	1	13. SOUTHERN NIGHTS	Glen Campbell
5/07	1	14. HOTEL CALIFORNIA	Eagles
5/14	1	15. WHEN I NEED YOU	Leo Sayer
5/21	3	16. SIR DUKE	Stevie Wonder
6/11	1	17. I'M YOUR BOOGIE MAN	KC & The Sunshine Band
6/18	1	18. DREAMS	Fleetwood Mac
6/25	1	19. GOT TO GIVE IT UP (PT. I)	Marvin Gaye
7/02	1	20. GONNA FLY NOW	Bill Conti
7/09	1	21. UNDERCOVER ANGEL	Alan O'Day
7/16	1	22. DA DOO RON RON	Shaun Cassidy
7/23	1	23. LOOKS LIKE WE MADE IT	Barry Manilow
7/30	4	†24. I JUST WANT TO BE YOUR EVERYTHING	Andy Gibb
8/20	5	†25. BEST OF MY LOVE	The Emotions
10/01	2	26. STAR WARS THEME/CANTINA BAND	Meco
10/15	10	27. YOU LIGHT UP MY LIFE	Debby Boone
12/24	3	28. HOW DEEP IS YOUR LOVE	Bee Gees
1978			
1/14	3	1. BABY COME BACK	Player
2/04	4	2. STAYIN' ALIVE	Bee Gees
3/04	2	3. (LOVE IS) THICKER THAN WATER	Andy Gibb
3/18	8	4. NIGHT FEVER	Bee Gees
5/13	1	5. IF I CAN'T HAVE YOU	Yvonne Elliman
5/20	2	6. WITH A LITTLE LUCK	Wings
6/03	1	7. TOO MUCH, TOO LITTLE, TOO LATE	Johnny Mathis/ Deniece Williams
6/10	1	8. YOU'RE THE ONE THAT I WANT	John Travolta & Olivia Newton-John
6/17	7	9. SHADOW DANCING	Andy Gibb
8/05	1	10. MISS YOU	The Rolling Stones
8/12	2	11. THREE TIMES A LADY	Commodores
8/26	2	12. GREASE	Frankie Valli
9/09	3	13. BOOGIE OOGIE OOGIE	A Taste Of Honey
9/30	4	14. KISS YOU ALL OVER	Exile
10/28	1	15. HOT CHILD IN THE CITY	Nick Gilder
11/04	1	16. YOU NEEDED ME	Anne Murray
11/11	3	17. MACARTHUR PARK	Donna Summer
12/02	2	†18. YOU DON'T BRING ME FLOWERS	Barbra Streisand & Neil Diamond
12/09	6	†19. LE FREAK	Chic

DATE	WKS	RECORD TITLE	ARTIST
		1979	
1/06	2	1. TOO MUCH HEAVEN	Bee Gees
2/10	4	2. DA YA THINK I'M SEXY?	Rod Stewart
3/10	3	†3. I WILL SURVIVE	Gloria Gaynor
3/24	2	4. TRAGEDY	Bee Gees
4/14	1	5. WHAT A FOOL BELIEVES	The Doobie Brothers
4/21	1	6. KNOCK ON WOOD	Amii Stewart
4/28	1	7. HEART OF GLASS	Blondie
5/05	4	8. REUNITED	Peaches & Herb
6/02	3	†9. HOT STUFF	Donna Summer
6/09	1	10. LOVE YOU INSIDE OUT	Bee Gees
6/30	2	11. RING MY BELL	Anita Ward
7/14	5	12. BAD GIRLS	Donna Summer
8/18	1	13. GOOD TIMES	Chic
8/25	6	14. MY SHARONA	The Knack
10/06	1	15. SAD EYES	Robert John
10/13	1	16. DON'T STOP 'TIL YOU GET ENOUGH	Michael Jackson
10/20	2	17. RISE	Herb Alpert
11/03	1	18. POP MUZIK	M
11/10	1	19. HEARTACHE TONIGHT	Eagles
11/17	1	20. STILL	Commodores
11/24	2	21. NO MORE TEARS (ENOUGH IS ENOUGH)	Barbra Streisand/ Donna Summer
12/08	2	22. BABE	Styx
12/22	3	†23. ESCAPE (THE PINA COLADA SONG)	Rupert Holmes
		1980	
1/05	1	1. PLEASE DON'T GO	K.C. & The Sunshine Band
1/19	4	2. ROCK WITH YOU	Michael Jackson
2/16	1	3. DO THAT TO ME ONE MORE TIME	The Captain & Tennille
2/23	4	4. CRAZY LITTLE THING CALLED LOVE	Queen
3/22	4	5. ANOTHER BRICK IN THE WALL (PART II)	Pink Floyd
4/19	6	6. CALL ME	Blondie
5/31	4	7. FUNKYTOWN	Lipps, Inc.
6/28	3	8. COMING UP (LIVE AT GLASGOW)	Paul McCartney & Wings
7/19	2	9. IT'S STILL ROCK AND ROLL TO ME	Billy Joel
8/02	4	10. MAGIC	Olivia Newton-John
8/30	1	11. SAILING	Christopher Cross
9/06	4	12. UPSIDE DOWN	Diana Ross
10/04	3	13. ANOTHER ONE BITES THE DUST	Queen
10/25	3	14. WOMAN IN LOVE	Barbra Streisand
11/15	6	15. LADY	Kenny Rogers
12/27	5	16. (JUST LIKE) STARTING OVER	John Lennon

DATE	WKS	RECORD TITLE	ARTIST
		1981	
1/31	1	1. THE TIDE IS HIGH	Blondie
2/07	2	2. CELEBRATION	Kool & The Gang
2/21	2	†3. 9 TO 5	Dolly Parton
2/28	2	4. I LOVE A RAINY NIGHT	Eddie Rabbitt
3/21	1	5. KEEP ON LOVING YOU	REO Speedwagon
3/28	2	6. RAPTURE	Blondie
4/11	3	7. KISS ON MY LIST	Daryl Hall & John Oates
5/02	2	8. MORNING TRAIN (NINE TO FIVE)	Sheena Easton
5/16	9	†9. BETTE DAVIS EYES	Kim Carnes
6/20	1	10. STARS ON 45	Stars on 45
7/25	1	11. THE ONE THAT YOU LOVE	Air Supply
8/01	2	12. JESSIE'S GIRL	Rick Springfield
8/15	9	13. ENDLESS LOVE	Diana Ross & Lionel Richie
10/17	3	14. ARTHUR'S THEME (BEST THAT YOU CAN DO)	Christopher Cross
11/07	2	15. PRIVATE EYES	Daryl Hall & John Oates
11/21	10	16. PHYSICAL	Olivia Newton-John
		1982	
1/30	1	1. I CAN'T GO FOR THAT (NO CAN DO)	Daryl Hall & John Oates
2/06	6	2. CENTERFOLD	The J. Geils Band
3/20	7	3. I LOVE ROCK 'N ROLL	Joan Jett & The Blackhearts
5/08	1	4. CHARIOTS OF FIRE - TITLES	Vangelis
5/15	7	5. EBONY AND IVORY	Paul McCartney with Stevie Wonder
7/03	3	6. DON'T YOU WANT ME	The Human League
7/24	6	7. EYE OF THE TIGER	Survivor
9/04	2	†8. ABRACADABRA	The Steve Miller Band
9/11	2	9. HARD TO SAY I'M SORRY	Chicago
10/02	4	10. JACK & DIANE	John Cougar
10/30	1	11. WHO CAN IT BE NOW?	Men At Work
11/06	3	12. UP WHERE WE BELONG	Joe Cocker & Jennifer Warnes
11/27	2	13. TRULY	Lionel Richie
12/11	1	14. MICKEY	Toni Basil
12/18	4	15. MANEATER	Daryl Hall & John Oates

DATE	WKS	RECORD TITLE	ARTIST
1983			
1/15	4	†1. DOWN UNDER	Men At Work
2/05	1	2. AFRICA	Toto
2/19	2	3. BABY, COME TO ME	Patti Austin with James Ingram
3/05	7	4. BILLIE JEAN	Michael Jackson
4/23	1	5. COME ON EILEEN	Dexys Midnight Runners
4/30	3	6. BEAT IT	Michael Jackson
5/21	1	7. LET'S DANCE	David Bowie
5/28	6	8. FLASHDANCE . . . WHAT A FEELING	Irene Cara
7/09	8	9. EVERY BREATH YOU TAKE	The Police
9/03	1	10. SWEET DREAMS (ARE MADE OF THIS)	Eurythmics
9/10	2	11. MANIAC	Michael Sembello
9/24	1	12. TELL HER ABOUT IT	Billy Joel
10/01	4	13. TOTAL ECLIPSE OF THE HEART	Bonnie Tyler
10/29	2	14. ISLANDS IN THE STREAM	Kenny Rogers & Dolly Parton
11/12	4	15. ALL NIGHT LONG (ALL NIGHT)	Lionel Richie
12/10	6	16. SAY SAY SAY	Paul McCartney & Michael Jackson
1984			
1/21	2	1. OWNER OF A LONELY HEART	Yes
2/04	3	2. KARMA CHAMELEON	Culture Club
2/25	5	3. JUMP	Van Halen
3/31	3	4. FOOTLOOSE	Kenny Loggins
4/21	3	5. AGAINST ALL ODDS (TAKE A LOOK AT ME NOW)	Phil Collins
5/12	2	6. HELLO	Lionel Richie
5/26	2	7. LET'S HEAR IT FOR THE BOY	Deniece Williams
6/09	2	8. TIME AFTER TIME	Cyndi Lauper
6/23	2	9. THE REFLEX	Duran Duran
7/07	5	10. WHEN DOVES CRY	Prince
8/11	3	11. GHOSTBUSTERS	Ray Parker Jr.
9/01	3	12. WHAT'S LOVE GOT TO DO WITH IT	Tina Turner
9/22	1	13. MISSING YOU	John Waite
9/29	2	14. LET'S GO CRAZY	Prince & The Revolution
10/13	3	15. I JUST CALLED TO SAY I LOVE YOU	Stevie Wonder
11/03	2	16. CARIBBEAN QUEEN (NO MORE LOVE ON THE RUN)	Billy Ocean
11/17	3	17. WAKE ME UP BEFORE YOU GO-GO	Wham!
12/08	2	18. OUT OF TOUCH	Daryl Hall John Oates
12/22	6	19. LIKE A VIRGIN	Madonna

DATE	WKS	RECORD TITLE	ARTIST
1985			
2/02	2	1. I WANT TO KNOW WHAT LOVE IS	Foreigner
2/16	3	2. CARELESS WHISPER	Wham! featuring George Michael
3/09	3	3. CAN'T FIGHT THIS FEELING	REO Speedwagon
3/30	2	4. ONE MORE NIGHT	Phil Collins
4/13	4	5. WE ARE THE WORLD	USA for Africa
5/11	1	6. CRAZY FOR YOU	Madonna
5/18	1	7. DON'T YOU (FORGET ABOUT ME)	Simple Minds
5/25	2	8. EVERYTHING SHE WANTS	Wham!
6/08	2	9. EVERYBODY WANTS TO RULE THE WORLD	Tears For Fears
6/22	2	10. HEAVEN	Bryan Adams
7/06	1	11. SUSSUDIO	Phil Collins
7/13	2	12. A VIEW TO A KILL	Duran Duran
7/27	1	13. EVERYTIME YOU GO AWAY	Paul Young
8/03	3	14. SHOUT	Tears For Fears
8/24	2	15. THE POWER OF LOVE	Huey Lewis & The News
9/07	2	16. ST. ELMO'S FIRE (MAN IN MOTION)	John Parr
9/21	3	17. MONEY FOR NOTHING	Dire Straits
10/12	1	18. OH SHEILA	Ready For The World
10/19	1	19. TAKE ON ME	a-ha
10/26	1	20. SAVING ALL MY LOVE FOR YOU	Whitney Houston
11/02	1	21. PART-TIME LOVER	Stevie Wonder
11/09	1	22. MIAMI VICE THEME	Jan Hammer
11/16	2	23. WE BUILT THIS CITY	Starship
11/30	1	24. SEPARATE LIVES	Phil Collins & Marilyn Martin
12/07	2	25. BROKEN WINGS	Mr. Mister
12/21	4	26. SAY YOU, SAY ME	Lionel Richie

DATE	WKS	RECORD TITLE	ARTIST
1986			
1/18	4	1. THAT'S WHAT FRIENDS ARE FOR	Dionne & Friends
2/15	2	2. HOW WILL I KNOW	Whitney Houston
3/01	2	3. KYRIE	Mr. Mister
3/15	1	4. SARA	Starship
3/22	1	5. THESE DREAMS	Heart
3/29	3	6. ROCK ME AMADEUS	Falco
4/19	2	7. KISS	Prince & The Revolution
5/03	1	8. ADDICTED TO LOVE	Robert Palmer
5/10	1	9. WEST END GIRLS	Pet Shop Boys
5/17	3	10. GREATEST LOVE OF ALL	Whitney Houston
6/07	1	11. LIVE TO TELL	Madonna
6/14	3	12. ON MY OWN	Patti LaBelle & Michael McDonald
7/05	1	13. THERE'LL BE SAD SONGS (TO MAKE YOU CRY)	Billy Ocean
7/12	1	14. HOLDING BACK THE YEARS	Simply Red
7/19	1	15. INVISIBLE TOUCH	Genesis
7/26	1	16. SLEDGEHAMMER	Peter Gabriel
8/02	2	17. GLORY OF LOVE	Peter Cetera
8/16	2	18. PAPA DON'T PREACH	Madonna
8/30	1	19. HIGHER LOVE	Steve Winwood
9/06	1	20. VENUS	Bananarama
9/13	1	21. TAKE MY BREATH AWAY	Berlin
9/20	3	22. STUCK WITH YOU	Huey Lewis & The News
10/11	2	23. WHEN I THINK OF YOU	Janet Jackson
10/25	2	24. TRUE COLORS	Cyndi Lauper
11/08	2	25. AMANDA	Boston
11/22	1	26. HUMAN	Human League
11/29	1	27. YOU GIVE LOVE A BAD NAME	Bon Jovi
12/06	1	28. THE NEXT TIME I FALL	Peter Cetera with Amy Grant
12/13	1	29. THE WAY IT IS	Bruce Hornsby & The Range
12/20	4	30. WALK LIKE AN EGYPTIAN	Bangles

DATE	WKS	RECORD TITLE	ARTIST
1987			
1/17	1	1. SHAKE YOU DOWN	Gregory Abbott
1/24	2	2. AT THIS MOMENT	Billy Vera & The Beaters
2/07	1	3. OPEN YOUR HEART	Madonna
2/14	4	4. LIVIN' ON A PRAYER	Bon Jovi
3/14	1	5. JACOB'S LADDER	Huey Lewis & The News
3/21	2	6. LEAN ON ME	Club Nouveau
4/04	2	7. NOTHING'S GONNA STOP US NOW	Starship
4/18	2	8. I KNEW YOU WERE WAITING (FOR ME)	Aretha Franklin & George Michael
5/02	2	9. (I JUST) DIED IN YOUR ARMS	Cutting Crew
5/16	3	10. WITH OR WITHOUT YOU	U2
6/06	1	11. YOU KEEP ME HANGIN' ON	Kim Wilde
6/13	1	12. ALWAYS	Atlantic Starr
6/20	1	13. HEAD TO TOE	Lisa Lisa & Cult Jam
6/27	2	14. I WANNA DANCE WITH SOMEBODY (WHO LOVES ME)	Whitney Houston
7/11	3	15. ALONE	Heart
8/01	1	16. SHAKEDOWN	Bob Seger
8/08	2	17. I STILL HAVEN'T FOUND WHAT I'M LOOKING FOR	U2
8/22	1	18. WHO'S THAT GIRL	Madonna
8/29	3	19. LA BAMBA	Los Lobos
9/19	1	20. I JUST CAN'T STOP LOVING YOU	Michael Jackson
9/26	2	21. DIDN'T WE ALMOST HAVE IT ALL	Whitney Houston
10/10	1	22. HERE I GO AGAIN	Whitesnake
10/17	1	23. LOST IN EMOTION	Lisa Lisa & Cult Jam
10/24	2	24. BAD	Michael Jackson
11/07	2	25. I THINK WE'RE ALONE NOW	Tiffany
11/21	1	26. MONY MONY "LIVE"	Billy Idol
11/28	1	27. (I'VE HAD) THE TIME OF MY LIFE	Bill Medley & Jennifer Warnes
12/05	1	28. HEAVEN IS A PLACE ON EARTH	Belinda Carlisle
12/12	4	29. FAITH	George Michael

DATE	WKS	RECORD TITLE	ARTIST
		1988	
1/09	1	1. SO EMOTIONAL	Whitney Houston
1/16	1	2. GOT MY MIND SET ON YOU	George Harrison
1/23	1	3. THE WAY YOU MAKE ME FEEL	Michael Jackson
1/30	1	4. NEED YOU TONIGHT	INXS
2/06	2	5. COULD'VE BEEN	Tiffany
2/20	1	6. SEASONS CHANGE	Expose
2/27	2	7. FATHER FIGURE	George Michael
3/12	2	8. NEVER GONNA GIVE YOU UP	Rick Astley
3/26	2	9. MAN IN THE MIRROR	Michael Jackson
4/09	2	10. GET OUTTA MY DREAMS, GET INTO MY CAR	Billy Ocean
4/23	2	11. WHERE DO BROKEN HEARTS GO	Whitney Houston
5/07	1	12. WISHING WELL	Terence Trent D'Arby
5/14	2	13. ANYTHING FOR YOU	Gloria Estefan & Miami Sound Machine
5/28	3	14. ONE MORE TRY	George Michael
6/18	1	15. TOGETHER FOREVER	Rick Astley
6/25	1	16. FOOLISH BEAT	Debbie Gibson
7/02	1	17. DIRTY DIANA	Michael Jackson
7/09	2	18. THE FLAME	Cheap Trick
7/23	1	19. HOLD ON TO THE NIGHTS	Richard Marx
7/30	4	20. ROLL WITH IT	Steve Winwood
8/27	2	21. MONKEY	George Michael
9/10	2	22. SWEET CHILD O' MINE	Guns N' Roses
9/24	2	23. DON'T WORRY BE HAPPY	Bobby McFerrin
10/08	1	24. LOVE BITES	Def Leppard
10/15	1	25. RED RED WINE	UB40
10/22	2	26. GROOVY KIND OF LOVE	Phil Collins
11/05	1	27. KOKOMO	The Beach Boys
11/12	1	28. WILD, WILD WEST	The Escape Club
11/19	2	29. BAD MEDICINE	Bon Jovi
12/03	1	30. BABY, I LOVE YOUR WAY/FREEBIRD MEDLEY (FREE BABY)	Will To Power
12/10	2	31. LOOK AWAY	Chicago
12/24	3	32. EVERY ROSE HAS ITS THORN	Poison

CHART SMARTS

Only Joel Whitburn's Record Research Collection Tells You Everything You Need To Know About Billboard's *Charts.*

These Record Research books are the ones collectors, disc jockeys, programmers and artists the world over turn to for fast, accurate facts and data on every artist and record to ever appear on *Billboard*'s major charts.

Joel Whitburn's

TOP POP SINGLES

1955–1986

Our all-time bestseller—the only complete, artist-by-artist history of *Billboard*'s entire "Hot 100," listing nearly 18,000 charted Pop singles with peak position, date first charted, weeks charted, in-depth artist biographies and much more. 756 pages. $60.00 Hardcover. $50.00 Softcover.

Joel Whitburn's

POP SINGLES ANNUAL

1955–1986

A year-by-year ranking of the nearly 18,000 singles to appear on *Billboard's* "Hot 100" pop singles charts. Lists all charted titles for each year in rank order according to chart performance, with each record's peak position, peak date, peak weeks and much more. 684 pages. $60.00 Hardcover. $50.00 Softcover.

Joel Whitburn's

BUBBLING UNDER THE HOT 100

1959–1981

A fascinating, one-of-a-kind listing of over 4,000 of Pop's "near-hits"—semi-popular records by established superstars, one-shot efforts by obscure artists, and big regional records that never made it nationally, all with full chart data. 240 pages. $35.00 Softcover.

Joel Whitburn's

TOP COUNTRY SINGLES

1944–1988

Straight from the Chartland, here's the complete story of "America's most listened-to music"—45 years of charted Country singles, featuring detailed chart data and statistics plus comprehensive, fact-filled biographies on nearly every Country artist. Over 600 pages. $60.00 Hardcover. $50.00 Softcover.

Joel Whitburn's

TOP R & B SINGLES

1942–1988

Call it "Soul," call it "Black," call it "Urban Contemporary," call it "Rhythm & Blues"—call it the first complete history of *Billboard*'s R&B charts, with extensive data on every single ever charted and detailed biographies on most R&B artists. 624 pages. $60.00 Hardcover. $50.00 Softcover.

Billboard's

MUSIC & VIDEO YEARBOOKS 1988/1987

Compiled by Joel Whitburn

Each Yearbook is a comprehensive, fingertip guide to the year's charted music and videocassettes. Covers *Billboard*'s major singles and albums charts in depth, lists #1 hits from other *Billboard* charts, and updates all previous Record Research volumes. Includes full videocassette chart data. 1988 edition: over 200 pages/1987 edition: 240 pages. $35.00 each. Softcover.